The Norton Anthology of World Literature

SECOND EDITION

VOLUME A

Beginnings to A.D. 100

Volume A

The Invention of Writing and the Earliest Literatures · Knox/Clinton

Ancient Greece and the Formation of the Western Mind · Knox/Thalmann

Poetry and Thought in Early China · Owen

India's Heroic Age · Peterson

The Roman Empire · Knox/Thalmann

Volume B

From Roman Empire to Christian Europe · Knox/Thalmann

India's Classical Age · Peterson

China's Middle Period · Owen

The Rise of Islam and Islamic Literature · Clinton

The Formation of a Western Literature · McGalliard/Patterson

The Golden Age of Japanese Culture · Danly

Mystical Poetry of India · Peterson

Volume C

Africa: The Mali Epic of *Son-Jara* · Irele

The Renaissance in Europe · Pasinetti/James

Native America and Europe in the New World · Bierhorst

Volume D

Vernacular Literature in China · Owen

The Ottoman Empire: Çelebi's *Book of Travels* · Clinton

The Enlightenment in Europe · Hugo/Spacks

The Rise of Popular Arts in Premodern Japan · Danly

Volume E

Revolution and Romanticism in Europe and America · Hugo/Spacks

Urdu Lyric Poetry in North India · Peterson

Realism, Naturalism, and Symbolism in Europe · Wellek/Lawall

Volume F

The Modern World: Self and Other in Global Context · Lawall

The Norton Anthology of World Literature

SECOND EDITION

Sarah Lawall, *General Editor*
PROFESSOR OF COMPARATIVE LITERATURE AND ADJUNCT PROFESSOR OF FRENCH, UNIVERSITY OF MASSACHUSETTS, AMHERST

Maynard Mack, *General Editor Emeritus*
LATE OF YALE UNIVERSITY

VOLUME A

Beginnings to A.D. *100*

W • W • NORTON & COMPANY • *New York* • *London*

Editor: Peter J. Simon
Developmental Editor: Carol Flechner
Associate Managing Editor: Marian Johnson
Production Manager: Diane O'Connor
Editorial Assistant: Isobel T. Evans
Project Editors: Candace Levy, Vivien Reinart, Carol Walker, Will Rigby
Permissions Manager: Nancy Rodwan
Assistant Permissions Manager: Sandra Chin
Text Design: Antonina Krass
Art Research: Neil Ryder Hoos
Maps: Jacques Chazaud

Previoius edition published as THE NORTON ANTHOLOGY OF WORLD
MASTERPIECES, Expanded Edition.

Printed in the United States of America.

The text of this book is composed in Fairfield Medium
with the display set in Bernhard Modern.
Composition by Binghamton Valley Composition.
Manufacturing by R. R. Donnelley & Sons.
Cover illustration: *Akhenaten and Family*, ca. 1365–1349 B.C. Egyptian Museum, Cairo.
Photo: Gianni Dagli Orti/Corbis

The Library of Congress has cataloged another edition as follows:

The Norton anthology of world literature / Sarah Lawall, general editor; Maynard
Mack, general editor emeritus.—2nd ed.
p. cm.
Includes bibliographical references and index.
Contents: v. A. Beginnings to A.D. 100—v. B. A.D. 100–1500—v. C. 1500–1650—v. D. 1650–1800—v. E. 1800–1900—v. F. The twentieth century.
ISBN 0-393-97764-1 (v.1)—ISBN 0-393-97765-X (v. 2)
1. Literature—Collections. I. Lawall. Sarah N. II. Mack, Maynard, 1909–

PN6014.N66 2001
808.8—dc21 2001030824

ISBN 0-393-97755-2 (pbk.)

W. W. Norton & Company, Inc., 500 Fifth Avenue, New York, NY 10110
www.wwnorton.com

W. W. Norton & Company Ltd., Castle House, 75/76 Wells Street, London W1T 3QT

1 2 3 4 5 6 7 8 9 0

Contents

Ancient Greece and the Formation of the Western Mind

Poetry and Thought in Early China   805

Preface

The first edition of the *Norton Anthology of World Literature* to appear in the twenty-first century offers many new works from around the world and a fresh new format that responds to contemporary needs. The global reach of this anthology encompasses important works from Asia and Africa, central Asia and India, the Near East, Europe, and North and South America—all presented in the light of their own literary traditions, as a shared heritage of generations of readers in many countries, and as part of a network of cultural and literary relationships whose scope is still being discovered. With this edition, we institute a shift in title that reflects the way the anthology has grown. The initial *Norton Anthology of World Masterpieces* (1956) aimed to present a broader "Western tradition of world literature" in contrast to previous anthologies confined to English and American works; it focused on the richness and diversity of Western literary tradition, as does the Seventh Edition of 1999. The present volume, which derives from the "Expanded" edition of 1995, contains almost all the texts of the Seventh Edition and also thousands of pages from works around the globe; it now logically assumes the broader title of "World Literature." In altering the current title to *The Norton Anthology of World Literature,* we do not abandon the anthology's focus on major works of literature or a belief that these works especially repay close study. It is their consummate artistry, their ability to express complex signifying structures, that gives access to multiple dimensions of meaning, meanings that are always rooted in a specific setting and cultural tradition but that further constitute, upon comparison, a thought-provoking set of perspectives on the varieties of human experience. Readers familiar with the anthology's two volumes, whose size increased proportionally with the abundance of new material, will welcome the new boxed format, in which each of the earlier volumes is separated into three slim and easily portable smaller books. Whether maintaining the chronological structure of the original boxed set or selecting a different configuration, you will be able to consult a new Web site, developed by Norton specifically for the world-literature anthologies and containing contextual information, audiovisual resources, exploratory analyses, and related material to illustrate and illuminate these compelling texts.

The six volumes represent six consecutive chronological periods from approximately 2500 B.C. to the present. Subsequently, and for pedagogical reasons, our structure is guided by the broad continuities of different cultural traditions and the literary or artistic periods they recognize for themselves. This means that chronology advises but does not dictate the order in which works appear. If Western tradition names a certain time slot "the Renaissance" or "the Enlightenment" (each term implying a shared set of beliefs), that designation has little relevance in other parts of the globe; similarly, "vernacular literature" does not have the same literary-historical status in all traditions; and "classical" periods come at different times in India, China, and Western Europe. We find that it is more useful to start from a tradition's own sense of itself and the specific shape it gives to the community memory embodied as art. Occasionally there are displacements of absolute chronology: Petrarch, for example, belongs chronologically with Boccaccio and Chaucer, and Rousseau is a contemporary of Voltaire. Each can be read as a new and dissonant voice within his own century, a foil and balance for accepted ideas, or he can be considered as part of a powerful new consciousness, along with those indebted to his thought and example. In the first and last volumes of the anthology, for different pedagogical purposes, we have chosen to present diverse cultural traditions together. The first section of the first volume, "The Invention of Writing and the Earliest Literatures," introduces students to the study of world literature with works from three different cultural traditions—Babylonian, Egyptian, Judaic—each among the oldest works that have come down to us in written form, each in its origins reaching well back into a preliterate past, yet directly accessible as an image of human experience and still provocative at the beginning of the twenty-first century. The last volume, *The Modern World: Self and Other in Global Context,* reminds us that separation in the modern world is no longer a possibility. Works in the twentieth century are demonstrably part of a new global consciousness, itself fostered by advances in communications, that experiences reality in terms of interrelationships, of boundaries asserted or transgressed, and of the creation of personal and social identity from the interplay of sameness and difference. As teachers, we have tried to structure an anthology that is usable, accessible, and engaging in the classroom—that clarifies patterns and relationships for your students, while leaving you free to organize selections from this wealth of material into the themes, genres, topics, and special emphases that best fit your needs.

Changes in this edition have taken several forms. Most visibly, there are many new selections to spark further combinations with works you have already been teaching and to suggest ways of extending your favorite themes with additional geographic, gendered, chronological, or cultural perspectives. Thus the volume on the twentieth-century adds five important Latin American authors who are pivotal figures in their own time and with an established international stature that, in a few cases, is just beginning to be recognized in the United States. In fiction, there is Juan Rulfo, whose landmark novel *Pedro Páramo* is at once an allegory of political power in modern Mexico and a magical narrative that introduced modernist techniques to Latin American fiction, and Clarice Lispector, the innovative Brazilian novelist and short-story writer who writes primarily about women's experience and is internationally known for her descriptions of psychological states of mind. In poetry, the vehicle for political and cultural revolution in so many European and Latin American countries, we introduce the Nicaraguan Rubén Darío, a charismatic diplomat-poet at home in Europe and Latin America who created the image of a Spanish cultural identity that included his own Indian ancestry and counteracted prevailing images of North American dominance. After Darío there is Alfonsina Storni, the Argentinian poet who was as well known in the 1920s and 1930s for her independent journal articles and her feminism as for the intensely personal poetry that assures her reputation today. Finally, the Nobel Prize winner and Chilean activist Pablo Neruda, who reinvigorated the concept of public poet and became the best-known Latin American poet of the twentieth century, is represented by selections from various periods and styles of his work—in particular, the epic vision of human history taken by many to be his crowning achievement, *The Heights of Macchu Picchu.* Works by all five authors add to our representation of Spanish and Latin American literature, but their importance is not limited to regional or cultural representation. Each functions within a broader framework that may be artistic convention; national, ethnic, or class identity; feminist or postcolonial perspectives; or a particular vision of human experience. Each resonates with other works throughout the volume and is an opportunity to enrich your world-literature syllabus with new comparisons and contrasts.

Many of the new selections draw attention to historical circumstances and the texture of everyday life. Biographical tales from records of the ancient Chinese historian Ssu-ma Chʻien give a glimpse of contemporary attitudes and ideals, as does the dedicated historian's poignant *Letter in Reply to Jen An,* written after his official punishment by castration. Entries in Dorothy Wordsworth's *Grasmere Journals* express the very personal world of the intimate journal, and Virginia Woolf's passionate analysis of the woman writer's position, in *A Room of One's Own,* combines autobiography with essay and fiction. Still other texts focus on specific historical events or issues but employ fictional techniques for greater immediacy. There is a thin line between fiction and autobiography in Tadeusz Borowski's terrifying Holocaust story *Ladies and Gentlemen, to the Gas Chamber.* Nawal El Saadawi's chilling courtroom tale *In Camera* uses the victim's shifting and fragmented perspectives to evoke the harsh realities of twentieth-century political torture and repression. Zhang Ailing's novella of a difficult love, *Love in a Fallen City,* depicts the decline of traditional Chinese society and concludes with the Japanese bombing of Hong Kong in World War II, while Anita Desai's *The Rooftop Dwellers* follows the struggles of a single woman in Delhi to make a career for herself in the face of social disapproval and family pressure. African American realist author Richard Wright, describes an adolescent crisis related to specific social images of manliness in *The Man Who Was Almost a Man.* Yet there are always different ways of presenting historical circumstances and dealing with the questions they raise. A play from Renaissance Spain, Lope de Vega's *Fuente Ovejuna,* is a light romantic comedy that draws heavily on dramatic conventions for its humor; yet it is also set during a famous peasant uprising whose bloodshed, political repercussions, and torture of the entire citizenry are represented in the course of the play. Readers who follow historical and cultural themes throughout the anthology will find much provocative material in these diverse new selections.

In renewing this edition, we have taken several routes: introducing new authors (many previously mentioned); choosing an alternate work by the same author when it resonates with material in other sections or speaks strongly to current concerns; adding small sections to existing larger pieces in order to fill out a theme or narrative line, or to suggest connections with other texts; and grouping several works to bring out new strengths. Three stories by the African writer Bernard Dadié appear here for the first time, as do the romantic adventures of Ludovico Ariosto's epic parody *Orlando Furi-*

oso, an African tale by Doris Lessing—*The Old Chief Mshlanga*—and Alice Munro's complex evocation of childhood memories *Walker Brothers Cowboy.* Among the alternate works by existing authors, we present Gustave Flaubert's great realist novel *Madame Bovary,* James Joyce's Dublin tale *The Dead,* and William Faulkner's *The Bear,* the latter printed in its entirety to convey its full scope as a chronicle of the legacy of slavery in the American South. New plays include Bertolt Brecht's drama *The Good Woman of Setzuan* and William Shakespeare's *Othello* as well as *Hamlet;* each has its own special resonance in world literature. Derek Walcott is represented by a selection of his poetry, including excerpts from the modern epic *Omeros.* Five more magical tales are added to the *Thousand and One Nights* and three new essays from Montaigne, including his memorable *To the Reader.* Six new tales from Ovid (in a new translation by Allen Mandelbaum) round out a set of myths exploring different images of love and gender, themes that reappear in two of the best-known lays of Marie de France, *Lanval* and *Laüstic,* as well as in Boccaccio's famous "Pot of Basil" and the influential tale of patient Griselda and her tyrannical husband, all presented here. From Chaucer, there is the bawdy, popular *Wife of Bath's Tale,* and from the *Heptameron* of Marguerite de Navarre fresh tales of love and intrigue that emphasize the stereotyping of gender roles. To *The Cherry Orchard* by Anton Chekhov, we add his famous tale of uncertain love *The Lady with the Dog.* New selections from Books 4 and 8 of John Milton's *Paradise Lost* depict the drama of Satan's malevolent entry into Paradise, Adam and Eve's innocent conversation, and the angel's warning to Adam. Finally, the poignant tales of Abraham and Isaac and of Jacob and Esau (Genesis 22, 25, 27) are added to the Old Testament selections, as well as the glorious love poetry of the Song of Songs; and Matthew 13 [Why Jesus Teaches in Parables] is included among the selections from the New Testament.

Two founding works of early India, the *Rāmāyaṇa* and the *Mahābhārata,* are offered in greatly increased selections and with new and exceptionally accessible translations. Readers can now follow (in a new translation by Swami Venkatesananda) the trajectory of Rāma's exile and life in the forest, the kidnapping of his wife Sītā, and ensuing magical adventures up to the final combat between Rāma and the demon king Rāvaṇa. A lively narrative of the *Mahābhārata*'s civil war (in a new translation by C. V. Narasimhan) unfolds in sequential excerpts that include two sections of special interest to modern students: the insulted Draupadī's formal accusation of the rulers in the Assembly Hall and the tragic story of the heroic but ill-fated warrior Karṇa.

To increase our understanding of individual authors' achievement, we join to the Indian Rabindranath Tagore's story *Punishment* a selection of the Bengali poems with which he revolutionized literary style in his homeland, and to the Chinese Lu Xun's two tales, examples of his poetry from *Wild Grass.* Rousseau's *Confessions* gain historical and psychological depth through new passages that shed light on his early years and on the development of his political sympathies.

The epic poetry that acts as the conscience of a community—*The Iliad, The Mahābhārata,* the *Son-Jara,* among others—has long been represented in the anthology. It has been our practice, however, to minimize the presence of lyric poetry in translation, recognizing—as is so cogently argued in the "Note on Translation," printed at the end of each volume—that the precise language and music of an original poem will never be identical with its translation and that short poems risk more of their substance in the transfer. Yet good translations often achieve a poetry of their own and occupy a pivotal position in a second literary history; thus the Egyptian love songs, the Chinese *Classic of Poetry* (*Book of Songs*), the biblical Song of Songs, and the lyrics of Sappho, Catullus, Petrarch, Rumi, and Baudelaire have all had influence far beyond the range of those who could read the original poems. Some poetry collections—like the Japanese *Man'yōshū* and *Kokinshū*—are recognized as an integral part of the society's cultural consciousness, and others—notably, the European Romantics—embody a sea change in artistic and cultural consciousness.

New to this edition is a series of poetry clusters that complement existing collections and represent a core of important and influential poetry in five different periods. You may decide to teach them as part of a spectrum of poetic expression or as reference points in a discussion of cultural consciousness. Thus a newly translated series of early hymns by the Tamil Śaiva saints exemplifies the early mystical poetry of India, while the multifarious vitality of medieval Europe is recaptured in poems by men and women from Arabic, Judaic, Welsh, Spanish, French, Provençal, Italian, English, and German traditions. Those who have taught English Romantic poetry will find both contrast and comparison in Continental poets from France, Italy, Germany, Spain, and Russia, many of whom possess lasting influence in nineteenth- and twentieth-century literature. Symbolism, whose insights into the relation of language and reality have permeated modern poetry and linguistic theory, is represented by the great nineteenth-century poets Charles Baudelaire, Stéphane Mallarmé, Paul Verlaine, and Arthur Rimbaud. Finally, a cluster of Dada-Surrealist poems that range from slashing, rebellious humor to ecstatic love introduces the free association and dreamlike structures of this visionary movement, whose influence extends around the world and has strong links to modern art and film.

How to choose, as you turn from the library before you to the inevitable constraint of available time? There is an embarrassment of riches, an inexhaustible series of options, to fit whatever course pattern you wish. Perhaps you have already decided to proceed by theme or genre, in chronological order or by a selected comparative principle; or you have favorite titles that work well in the classroom, and you seek to combine them with new pieces. Perhaps you want to create modules that compare ideas of national identity or of bicultural identity and shifting cultural paradigms, that survey images of gender in different times and places or that examine the place of memory in a range of texts. In each instance, you have only to pick and choose among a variety of works from different countries, languages, and cultural backgrounds. If you are teaching the course for the first time or wish to try something different, you may find what you are looking for in the sample syllabi of the *Instructor's Guide* or on the new Web site, which will also contain supporting material such as maps, time lines, and audio pronunciation glossaries, resource links, guides to section materials, various exercises and assignments, and a series of teaching modules related to specific works. Throughout, the editors (who are all practicing teachers) have selected and prepared texts that are significant in their own area of scholarly expertise, meaningful in the larger context of world literature, and, always, delightful, captivating and challenging to students.

Clearly one can parcel out the world in a variety of ways, most notably geopolitical, and there is no one map of world literature. In order to avoid parochialism, some scholars suggest that we should examine cultural activity in different countries at the same period of time. Others attempt to deconstruct prevailing literary assumptions (often selected from Western literary theory) by using history or cultural studies as a framework for examining texts as documents. "Global" literary studies project a different map that depends on one's geopolitical view of global interactions and of the energies involved in the creation and dissemination of literature. *The Norton Anthology of World Literature*, Second Edition, takes a different point of departure, focusing first of all on literary texts—artifacts, if you will, that have a special claim on our attention because they have been read over a great period of time and are cherished by a wide variety of readers. Once such texts have been proposed as objects of knowledge—and enjoyment, and illumination—they are available for any and all forms of analysis. Situating them inside larger forms of textuality—linguistic, historical, or cultural—is, after all, an inevitable part of the meaning-making process. It is the primary task of this anthology, however, to present them as multidimensional objects for discussion and then to let our readers choose when and where to extend the analysis.

From the beginning, the editors of *The Norton Anthology of World Literature* have always balanced the competing—and, we like to think, complementary—claims of teaching and scholarship, of the specialist's focused expertise and the generalist's broader perspectives. The founding editors set the example, which guides their successors. We welcome three new successor editors to this edition: William G. Thalmann, Professor of Classics at the University of Southern California; Lee Patterson, Professor of English at Yale University; and Heather James, Associate Professor of English at the University of Southern California. Two founding editors have assumed Emeritus status: Bernard M. W. Knox, eminent classical scholar and legendary teacher and lecturer; and P. M. Pasinetti, who combines the intellectual breadth of the Renaissance scholar with a novelist's creative intuition. We also pay tribute to the memory of Robert Lyons Danly, translator and astute scholar of Japanese literature, whose lively interventions have been missed since his untimely death in 1995. Finally, we salute the memory of Maynard Mack, General Editor and presiding genius from the first edition through the Expanded Edition of 1995. An Enlightenment scholar of much wisdom, humanity, and gracefully worn knowledge, and a firm believer in the role of great literature—world literature—in illuminating human nature, he was also unstintingly dedicated to this anthology as a teaching enterprise. To him, therefore, and on all counts, we dedicate the first millennial edition of the anthology.

Acknowledgments

Among our many critics, advisers, and friends, the following were of special help in providing suggestions and corrections: Joseph Barbarese (Rutgers University); Carol Clover (University of California, Berkeley); Patrick J. Cook (George Washington University); Janine Gerzanics (University of Southern California); Matthew Giancarlo (Yale University); Kevis Goodman (University of California at Berkeley); Roland Greene (University of Oregon); Dmitri Gutas (Yale University); John H. Hayes (Emory University); H. Mack Horton (University of California at Berkeley); Suzanne Keen (Washington and Lee University); Charles S. Kraszewski (King's College); Gregory F. Kuntz; Michelle Latiolais (University of California at Irvine); Sharon L. James (Bryn Mawr College); Ivan Marcus (Yale University); Timothy Martin (Rutgers University, Camden); William Naff, University of Massachusetts; Stanley Radosh, Our Lady of the Elms College; Fred C. Robinson (Yale University); John Rogers (Yale University); Robert Rothstein (University of Massachusetts); Lawrence Senelick (Boston University); Jack Shreve (Alleghany Community College); Frank Stringfellow (University of Miami); Nancy Vickers (Bryn Mawr College); and Jack Welch (Abilene Christian University).

We would also like to thank the following people who contributed to the planning of the Second Edition: Charles Adams, University of Arkansas; Dorothy S. Anderson, Salem State College; Roy Anker, Calvin College; John Apwah, County College of Morris; Doris Bargen, University of Massachusetts; Carol Barrett, Austin Community College, Northridge Campus; Michael Beard, University of North Dakota; Lysbeth Em Berkert, Northern State University; Marilyn Booth, University of Illinois; George Byers, Fairmont State College; Shirley Carnahan, University of Colorado; Ngwarsungu Chiwengo, Creighton University; Stephen Cooper, Troy State University; Bonita Cox, San Jose State University; Richard A. Cox, Abilene Christian University; Dorothy Deering, Purdue University; Donald Dickson, Texas A&M University; Alexander Dunlop, Auburn University; Janet Eber, County College of Morris; Angela Esterhammer, University of Western Ontario; Walter Evans, Augusta State University; Fidel Fajardo-Acosta, Creighton University; John C. Freeman, El Paso Community College, Valle Verde Campus; Barbara Gluck, Baruch College; Michael Grimwood, North Carolina State University; Rafey Habib, Rutgers University, Camden; John E. Hallwas, Western Illinois College; Jim Hauser, William Patterson College; Jack Hussey, Fairmont State College; Dane Johnson, San Francisco State University; Andrew Kelley, Jackson State Community College; Jane Kinney, Valdosta State University; Candace Knudson, Truman State University; Jameela Lares, University of Southern Mississippi; Thomas L. Long, Thomas Nelson Community College; Sara MacDonald, Sterling College; Linda Macri, University of Maryland; Rita Mayer, San Antonio College; Christopher Morris,

Norwich University; Deborah Nestor, Fairmont State College; John Netland, Calvin College; Kevin O'Brien, Chapman University; Mariannina Olcott, San Jose State University; Charles W. Pollard, Calvin College; Pilar Rotella, Chapman University; Rhonda Sandford, Fairmont State College; Daniel Schenker, University of Alabama at Huntsville; Robert Scotto, Baruch College; Carl Seiple, Kutztown University; Glenn Simshaw, Chemeketa Community College; Evan Lansing Smith, Midwestern State University; William H. Smith, Piedmont College; Floyd C. Stuart, Norwich University; Cathleen Tarp, Fairmont State College; Diane Thompson, Northern Virginia Community College; Sally Wheeler, Georgia Perimeter College; Jean Wilson, McMaster University; Susan Wood, University of Nevada, Las Vegas; Tom Wymer, Bowling Green State University.

Phonetic Equivalents

for use with the Pronouncing Glossaries preceding most selections in this volume

a as in *cat*
ah as in *father*
ai as in *light*
ay as in *day*
aw as in *raw*
e as in *pet*
ee as in *street*
ehr as in *air*
er as in *bird*
eu as in *lurk*
g as in *good*
i as in *sit*
j as in *joke*
nh a nasal sound (as in French *vin, vɛ̃)*
o as in *pot*
oh as in *no*
oo as in *boot*
oy as in *toy*
or as in *bore*
ow as in *now*
s as in *mess*
ts as in *ants*
u as in *us*
zh as in *vision*

The Norton Anthology of World Literature

SECOND EDITION

VOLUME A

Beginnings to A.D. *100*

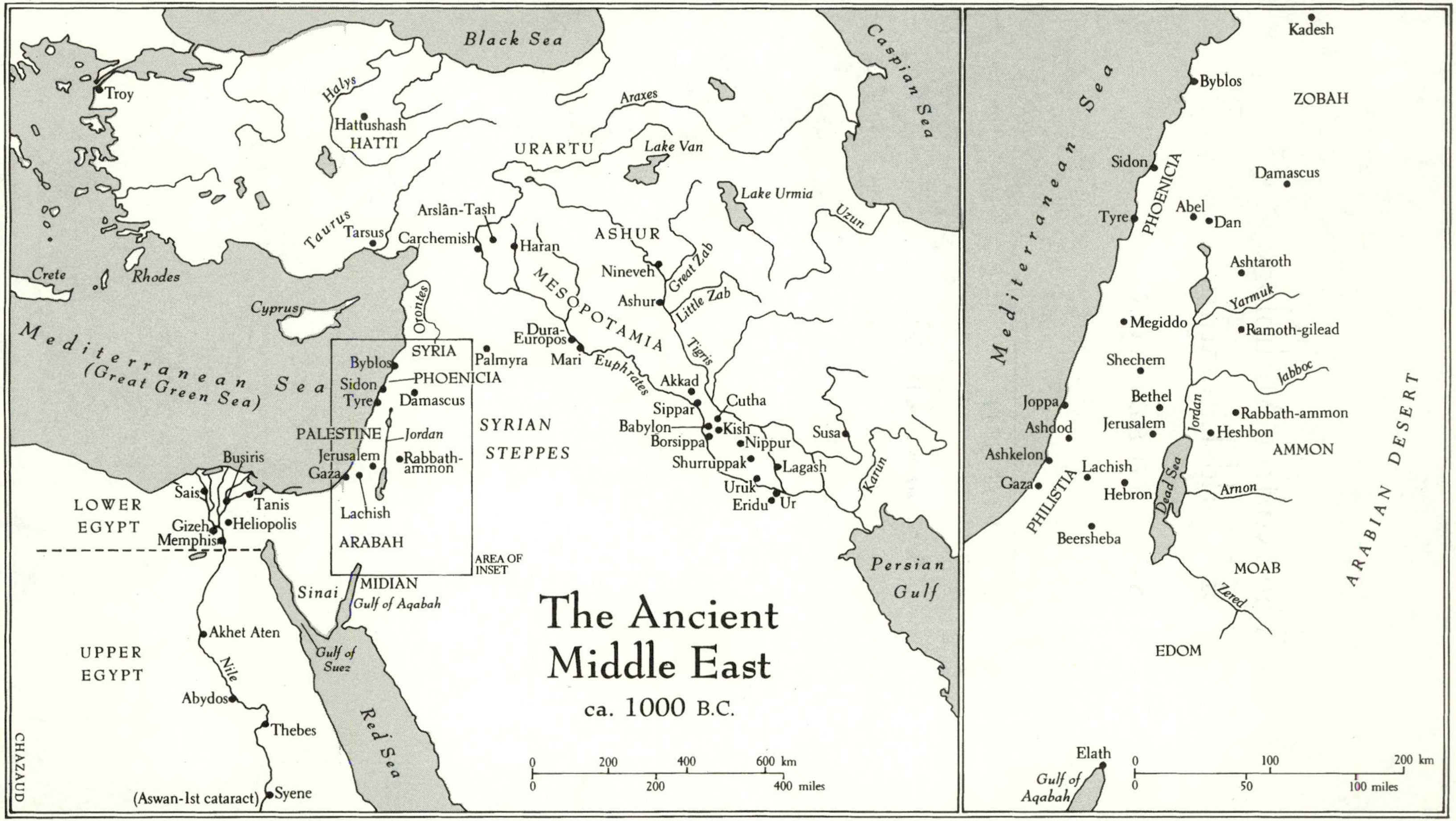
The Ancient
Middle East
ca. 1000 B.C.
Black Sea
Caspian Sea
Troy
Halys
Hattushash
HATTI
URARTU
Araxes
Lake Van
Lake Urmia
Uzun
Taurus
Tarsus
Arslân-Tash
Carchemish
Haran
ASHUR
Nineveh
Great Zab
Little Zab
Ashur
MESOPOTAMIA
Tigris
Crete
Rhodes
Cyprus
Orontes
Mediterranean Sea
(Great Green Sea)
Dura-
Europos
Mari
Euphrates
Palmyra
SYRIA
Byblos
Sidon
PHOENICIA
Tyre
Damascus
PALESTINE
Jordan
Jerusalem
Rabbath-
ammon
Gaza
Lachish
ARABAH
AREA OF
INSET
SYRIAN
STEPPES
Akkad
Sippar
Cutha
Babylon
Kish
Borsippa
Nippur
Shurruppak
Lagash
Uruk
Eridu
Ur
Susa
Karun
Persian
Gulf
Busiris
Sais
Tanis
LOWER
EGYPT
Gizeh
Heliopolis
Memphis
Sinai
MIDIAN
Gulf of Aqabah
Akhet Aten
Nile
UPPER
EGYPT
Abydos
Gulf of
Suez
Red Sea
Thebes
(Aswan-Ist cataract)
Syene
0 200 400 600 km
0 200 400 miles
CHAZAUD
Mediterranean Sea
Kadesh
Byblos
ZOBAH
Sidon
PHOENICIA
Damascus
Tyre
Abel
Dan
Ashtaroth
Yarmuk
Megiddo
Ramoth-gilead
Shechem
Jabboc
Bethel
Joppa
Rabbath-ammon
Ashdod
Jerusalem
Jordan
Heshbon
Ashkelon
AMMON
Lachish
Dead Sea
Arnon
Gaza
PHILISTIA
Hebron
Beersheba
ARABIAN DESERT
MOAB
Zered
EDOM
Elath
Gulf of
Aqabah
0 100 200 km
0 50 100 miles

The Invention of Writing and the Earliest Literatures

Long before people learned to write, they made up and told stories; they composed and sang songs. Because people who have not learned to write must develop a retentive and accurate memory, such stories and songs could be preserved for generations in something like their original form or could be improved, expanded, or combined with other material to be passed on as, so to speak, another edition. But such oral traditional literature can be irrevocably lost if it is not transferred to a written medium; a sudden catastrophic break in the life of the community—foreign conquest, for example, which was always a present danger in the clash of ancient empires—might easily, through massacre, enslavement, and mass deportation, wipe out the memory of what had been a shared inheritance.

Writing, which has preserved some ancient literatures for us, was not invented for that purpose. The earliest written documents we have contain commercial, administrative, political, and legal information. They are the records of the first advanced, centralized civilizations, those that emerged in the area we know as the Middle East.

Ancient civilization was based on agriculture, and it flourished first in regions where the soil gave rich rewards: in the valley of the Nile, where annual floods left large tracts of land moist and fertile under the Egyptian sun, and in the valleys of the Euphrates and Tigris rivers, which flowed through the "Fertile Crescent," a region centered on modern Iraq. Great cities—Thebes and Memphis in Egypt and Babylon and Nineveh in the Fertile Crescent—came into being as centers for the complicated administration of the irrigated fields. Supported by the surplus the land produced, they became centers also for government, religion, and culture. Civilization begins with cities; the word itself is derived from a Latin word that means "citizen." As far back as 3000 B.C. the pharaohs of Egypt began to build their splendid temples and gigantic pyramids as well as to record their political acts and religious beliefs in hieroglyphic script. The Sumerians, Babylonians, and Assyrians began to build the palaces and temples of Babylon and record their laws in cuneiform script on clay tablets.

It was in the region of the Tigris and Euphrates rivers that writing was first developed; the earliest texts date from around 3300 to 2990 B.C. The characters were inscribed on tablets of wet clay with a pointed stick; the tablets were then left in the sun to bake to hardness. The characters are pictographic: the sign for *ox* looks like an ox head and so on. The bulk of the texts are economic—lists of foodstuffs, textiles, and cattle. But the script is too primitive to handle anything much more complicated than lists, and by 2800 B.C. scribes began to use the wedge-shaped end of the stick to make marks rather than the pointed end to draw pictures. The resulting script is known as cuneiform, from the Latin word *cuneus,* "a wedge." By 2500 B.C. the texts were no longer confined to lists; they record historical events and even material that could be regarded as literature.

This writing system was not, however, designed for a large reading public. The wedge-shaped signs, grouped in various patterns, denote not letters of an alphabet but syllables—consonants plus a vowel—and this meant that the reader had to be familiar with a very large number of signs. Furthermore, the same sign often represents two or more different sounds, and the same sound can be represented by several different signs. It is a script that could be written and read only by experts, the scribes, who often proudly recorded their own names on the tablets.

It was, however, the most efficient system yet devised, and it stayed in use through all the historical vicissitudes of more than two millennia: the rise and fall of new dynasties and new conquerors, who became in their turn masters of the Fertile Crescent—Akkadians, Babylonians, Hittites, and Assyrians—until the area was incorporated in the Persian empire of Cyrus, who captured Babylon in 539 B.C. When in the fourth century B.C. the area became part of the Greek kingdom of one of the successors of Alexander the Great, the ancient script gradually fell out of use; the latest specimens to survive come from the first century A.D.

It was on clay tablets and in cuneiform script that the great Sumerian epic poem *Gilgamesh* was written down, in differing versions and in the different languages of the successive conquerors of the fertile river valleys, only to disappear in the ruins of the cities and be totally forgotten until modern excavators discovered the tablets and deciphered the enigmatic script that had preserved the poem through so many centuries.

The writing system invented by the Egyptians was even more esoteric than cuneiform. It is called hieroglyphic, an adjective formed from the Greek words for "sacred" and "carving." Although it appears on many different materials, its most conspicuous and continuous use was for inscriptions carved on the temple walls and public monuments. It was pictographic, like the earliest Sumerian script, but the pictures were more elaborate and artistic. Unlike the Sumerian pictographs, they were not replaced by a more efficient system; the pictures remained in use for the walls of temples and tombs, while more cursive versions of hieroglyphics—the hieratic and demotic scripts—were developed for faster writing. A writing system consisting of logograms (pictures standing for objects) is obviously incapable of communicating anything but the simplest of ideas, and at a very early stage the logograms were used to denote consonantal sounds. The Egyptian word for "house," for example, was *pr,* and its logogram was a rectangle with a gap in one of the long sides to indicate the door. The sign could still mean "house," but it could now also be used, in combination with other logograms indicating sounds, to denote simply the sound *pr.* This was only one of many complications that made even the modified versions of the script a difficult medium of communication for anyone not trained in its intricacies. The fact that only the consonantal sounds were represented (we do not know what vowel was sounded between the *p* and the *r* of *pr*) was one more barrier to easy interpretation. It is no wonder that one of the frequent figures to appear in Egyptian sculpture and painting is the professional scribe, his legs tucked underneath him, his writing material in his lap, and his brush in his hand.

Unlike the cuneiform tablets that remained buried, waiting for the trowel of the excavator, the Egyptian hieroglyphs were carved on the walls of ruined temples and remained open to view but defied interpretation. The key to the solution of the problem came in 1799, when some French soldiers of Napoleon's army, digging the foundation for a redoubt in Egypt, unearthed a large block of basalt, the Rosetta stone, on which was a text inscribed in three different versions. Two were Egyptian, one hieroglyphic and one demotic, and the other was in Greek, which had been the official language of Egypt ever since Ptolemy, one of Alexander's generals, had established himself as pharaoh in Egypt after Alexander died in 323 B.C.

There was one ancient writing system that, unlike cuneiform and hieroglyphic, was destined to survive, in modified forms, until the present day. It was a script developed by the Semitic peoples of the area, notably the enterprising Phoenicians, whose seaports on the Palestine coast, Tyre and Sidon, were bases for trading ventures and colonial expeditions to distant seas. The script consisted of twenty-two simple signs for consonantal sounds, an alphabet, to use the later Greek term, that could be easily learned. The Phoenicians have left us no literary texts, but the Hebrews, another Semitic people, used the system to record in a collection of books—part of which became what Christians call the Old Testament—their history; their sorrows and triumphs; and, above all, their concept, unique in the polytheistic ancient world, of a single god.

Unlike the rulers of the Tigris-Euphrates and Nile valleys, the Hebrews, located in Palestine, did not control territory of economic or military importance; their record is not that of an imperial people. In their period of independence, from their beginnings as a pastoral tribe to their high point as a kingdom with a splendid capital in Jerusalem, they accomplished little of note in the political or military spheres. Their later history was a bitter and unsuccessful struggle for freedom against a series of foreign masters—Babylonian, Greek, and Roman.

After the period of expansion and prosperity under the great kings David and Solomon (1005–925 B.C.), the kingdom fell apart into warring factions, which called in outside powers. The melancholy end of a long period of internal and external struggle was the destruction of the cities and the deportation of the population to Babylon (586 B.C.). This period of exile (which ended in 539 B.C. when Cyrus, the Persian conqueror of Babylon, released the Hebrews from bondage) was a formative period for Hebrew religious thought, which was enriched and refined by the teachings of the prophet Ezekiel and the prophet known as the second Isaiah. The return to Palestine was crowned by the rebuilding of the Temple and the creation of the canonical version of the Pentateuch, or Torah—the first five books of the Bible. The religious legacy of the Hebrew people was now codified for future generations.

But the independent state of Israel was not destined to last long. By 300 B.C. the Macedonian successors of Alexander the Great had encroached on its borders and prerogatives; in spite of a heroic resistance, the territory eventually became part of a Hellenistic Greek-speaking kingdom and, finally, was absorbed by the Roman empire. A desperate revolt against Rome was crushed in A.D. 70 by the emperor Titus (on the arch of Titus in Rome a relief shows the legionaries carrying a seven-branched menorah, or candlestick, in Titus' triumph). In A.D. 131–134, a second revolt, against the emperor Hadrian, resulted in the final extermination or removal from Palestine of the Hebrew people. Henceforward, they were the people of the *Diaspora,* the "scattering": religious communities in the great cities of the ancient world who maintained local cohesion and universal religious solidarity but who were stateless, as they were to be all through the centuries until the creation, in the mid-twentieth century, of the state of Israel.

The political history of the ancient Hebrews ended in a series of disasters. In the field of the arts they left behind them no painting or sculpture and little or no secular literature—no drama, for example, no epic poetry. What they did leave us is a religious literature, written down probably between the eighth and second centuries B.C., which is informed by an attitude different from that of any other nation of the ancient world. It is founded on the idea of one God, the Creator of all things, all-powerful and just—a conception of the divine essence and the government of the universe so simple that to those of us who have inherited it, it seems obvious. But in its time it was so revolutionary that it made the Hebrews a nation apart, sometimes laughed at, sometimes feared, but always alien.

The consonantal script in which their literary legacy was handed down to us was a great step forward from the hieroglyphic and cuneiform systems; writing now called for no artistic skills and reading for no long period of training. But it was still an unsatisfactory medium for mass communication; the absence of notation for the vowels made for ambiguity and possible misreading and, at times, may have called for inspired guesswork. We still do not know, for example, what the vowel sounds were in the sacred name of God, often called the Tetragrammaton, because it consists of four letters; in our alphabet the name is written as YHWH. The usual surmise is Jahweh *(ya'-way)*, but for a long time the traditional English-language version was Jehovah.

One thing was needed to make the script fully efficient: signs for the vowels. And this was the contribution of the Greeks, who, in the eighth or possibly the ninth century B.C., adopted the Phoenician script for their own language but used for the vowels some Phoenician signs that stood for consonantal combinations not native to Greek. They took over (but soon modified) the Phoenician letter shapes and also their names: *alpha,* a meaningless word in Greek, represents the original *aleph* ("ox"), and *beta* represents the original *beta* ("house"). The Greeks were frank to admit their indebtedness; Greek myths told the story of Cadmus, king of Tyre, who taught the Greeks how to write, and as the historian Herodotus tells us, the letters were called Phoenician. But in fact the Greek creation of signs for the vowels produced the first real alphabet, and the Romans, who adapted it for their own language, carved their inscriptions on stone in the same capital letters that we still use today.

FURTHER READING

Henri Frankfort et al., *Before Philosophy: The Intellectual Adventure of Ancient Man* (1949), is a brilliant evocation of the intellectual life of ancient cultures. For concise, informative, and up-to-date articles on three ancient literatures, see Miguel Civil, "Sumerian Poetry"; John L. Foster, "Egyptian Poetry"; and Erica Reiner, "Assyro-Babylonian Poetry," in *The New Princeton Encyclopedia of Poetry and Poetics* (1993). H. M. Orlinsky, *Ancient Israel* (1960), is a short but clearly written outline of the history of Israel up to the return from Babylonian exile.

TIME LINE

TEXTS	CONTEXTS
	ca. 3000 B.C. Mesopotamia: Sumerian cuneiform writing on clay tablets • Egypt: writing in hieroglyphic script
	2700 Gilgamesh is king in Uruk
	ca. 2575–2130 Old Kingdom (Egypt) • Great Pyramids; Sphinx
	ca. 2130–1540 Middle Kingdom (Egypt)
ca. 2000 B.C. Legends about King Gilgamesh appear on clay tablets	
	ca. 1900 Hebrew migration from Mesopotamia begins
	18th century Hammurabi's Code of Law written in Babylon
1600 The epic of ***Gilgamesh*** begins to take shape	
1500 Egyptian *Book of the Dead*	**ca. 1539–1200** New Kingdom (Egypt)
1375–1358 Akhenaten's "***Hymn to the Sun***" composed	**1375–1354** King Akhenaten dedicates his capital to Aten, the sun god
1300 The epic of ***Gilgamesh*** written down	
1300–1100 Love lyrics of the New Kingdom composed	
1238 ***The Leiden Hymns*** written down	
	ca. 1200 Moses leads the Jews in Exodus from Egypt to Palestine
1000 The Torah text assembled • Psalms	**1000–925** David, then Solomon, king in Israel

Boldface titles indicate works in the anthology.

TIME LINE

TEXTS	CONTEXTS
6th century Aesop's *Fables*	
	586 Jerusalem captured by Babylonian king Nebuchadnezzar; many Jews taken to exile in Babylon
	539 The Persian shah, Cyrus the Great, conquers Babylon and allows the Jews to return to Israel. He founds the Iranian empire, which later envelops most of the Middle East and Central Asia
	525 Cambyses, king of Persia, conquers Egypt
ca. 450 Herodotus, *History*	
	331–330 Alexander the Great conquers Syria, Mesopotamia, and Iran; defeats the last Persian army at Sungamela and occupies Babylon and Persopolis
	330–323 Alexander conquers Central Asia and the Indus Valley, but dies in Babylon (323). His generals divide up the empire. Seleucus becomes king of Syria, Mesopotamia, and Iran, Ptolemy of Egypt
	202–198 Palestine falls to Antiochus III, king of a land empire stretching east from Asia Minor • Rome defeats Antiochus III in 190 • Successful Jewish revolt against Antiochus IV between 173 and 167
	40–4 Herod is king of Judaea
	30 Rome conquers Egypt

GILGAMESH
ca. 2500–1500 B.C.

Gilgamesh is a poem of unparalleled antiquity, the first great heroic narrative of world literature. Its origins stretch back to the margins of prehistory, and its evolution spans millennia. When it was known, it was widely known. Tablets containing portions of *Gilgamesh* have been found at sites throughout the Middle East and in all the languages written in cuneiform characters, wedge-shaped characters incised in clay or stone. But then, at a time when the civilizations of the Hebrews, Greeks, and Romans had only just developed beyond their infancy, *Gilgamesh* vanished from memory. For reasons that scholars have not yet fathomed, the literature of the cuneiform languages was not translated into the new alphabets that replaced them. Some portions of this once-famous work survived in subsequent traditions, but they did so as scattered and anonymous fragments. They became a kind of invisible substratum that was buried under what was previously believed to be the earliest level of our common tradition. Until Utnapishtim's "Story of the Flood," a portion of *Gilgamesh,* was accidentally rediscovered and published in 1872, no one suspected that the biblical story of Noah and the Great Flood was neither original nor unique.

A great lost work like *Gilgamesh* poses particular problems of understanding beyond those raised by the discovery of a lost masterpiece by a known author or of a known time. The meaning of a work of literature is partly contextual—it is established by the culture that produced that work. Yet the whole context of *Gilgamesh* was lost along with the text. The names of the gods and humans who people the epic, the cities and lands in which they lived, and the whole of their history vanished for thousands of years from common memory. The story of Gilgamesh and his companion, Enkidu, speaks to contemporary readers with astonishing immediacy. Its moving depiction of the bonds of friendship, of the quest for worldly renown, and of the tragic attempt to escape that death which is the common fate of humanity has a timeless resonance and appeal. Yet despite this immediate recognition of something profoundly familiar there is, because of this millennial gap in the history of its transmission, a strangeness and remoteness about the work that strikes us in virtually every line. That strangeness has diminished each year as more tablets have been discovered and translated and as our understanding of the languages and cultures of the ancient Middle East has increased, but what we know is still relatively slight compared with what we know of the cultures that succeeded them. Today the names of Ulysses and Achilles and the gods and goddesses of Mount Olympus are familiar even to many who have not read Homer. The names of Gilgamesh, Enkidu, Utnapishtim, Enlil, and Eanna are virtually unknown outside the poem itself.

Gilgamesh developed over a period of nearly a thousand years. The version discovered in the city of Nineveh amid the ruins of the great royal library of Assurbanipal, the last great king of the Assyrian empire—what modern scholars now call the Standard Version—circulated widely throughout the ancient Middle East for a millennium or more. While the history of the text is a long and complex one, and is still far from fully understood, it is possible to identify three principal stages in its development. The first begins in roughly 2700 B.C. when the historical Gilgamesh ruled in Uruk, a city in ancient Mesopotamia. Tales both mythical and legendary grew up around him and were repeated and copied for centuries. The stories that were later incorporated into the *Gilgamesh* epic existed in this literature, albeit in different form, as well as other material concerning the historical Gilgamesh that was not included in the epic. The earliest written versions of these stories date from roughly 2000 B.C., but oral versions of the stories both preceded them and continued on, parallel to the written tradition. The language of these materials was Sumerian, the earliest written language in Mesopotamia and one that has little if any connection to any other known language.

The history of the epic itself begins sometime before 1600 B.C., some eight centuries before Homer, when a Babylonian author (Mesopotamian tradition identifies a priest-exorcist named Sîn-leqi-unninni) assembled free translations of the oral versions of some of these tales into a connected narrative. This new work was not simply a sequence of tales linked by the character of Gilgamesh but a conscious selection and recasting of the Sumerian materials into a new form. Some Gilgamesh tales were ignored, while elements from stories not associated with him in the Sumerian accounts were incorporated. This earliest version of the epic, which exists only in fragmentary form, continued to develop for the next few centuries. However, no comparable recasting of the poem was made. By the time of Assurbanipal (ruled 668–627 B.C.) the text was essentially stabilized.

Assurbanipal's synthetic version—the Standard Version—was also the first discovered. It was written on twelve hardened clay tablets in Akkadian, a Semitic language like Hebrew and Arabic and one of the principal languages of Babylonia and Assyria. The first eleven of these tablets make up the story as printed here. The twelfth tells another story of Gilgamesh, "Gilgamesh and the Underworld," and since it is unclear how it is to be incorporated into the preceding tablets, it is usually presented as a kind of appendix to the story.

The tablets of the Standard Version are poorly preserved at a number of points, most notably in the adventure in the Cedar Forest, and the translation relies heavily on the earlier, Old Babylonian version and fragments from a number of other versions.

The epic narrates the legendary deeds of Gilgamesh, king of Uruk, but it begins with a prologue that emphasizes not his adventures but the wisdom he acquired and the monuments he constructed at the end of his epic journey. It also tells us that Gilgamesh was endowed by his divine creators with extraordinary strength, courage, and beauty. He is more god than man. His father, however, is mortal, and that fact is decisive in shaping the narrative that follows. The prologue also suggests that Gilgamesh himself has written this account and left the tablets in the foundation of the city wall of Uruk for all to read.

In our first view of him, Gilgamesh is the epitome of a bad ruler: arrogant, oppressive, and brutal. The people of Uruk complain of his oppression to the Sumerian gods, and the gods' response is to create Enkidu as a foil or counterweight to Gilgamesh. Where the latter is a mixture of human and divine, Enkidu, who also appears godlike, is a blend of human and wild animal, with the animal predominating at first. He is raised by wild beasts, lives as they do (eating only uncooked food), and embodies the conflict between animal and human natures that is a recurrent theme in Mesopotamian literature and myth. When he becomes a kind of protector of the animals, breaking the hunters' traps and filling in their pits, Enkidu poses a threat to the human community. This threat is neutralized by civilizing him. First a harlot (prostitute) seduces him across the line separating animal from human and educates him in the elements of human society. Then shepherds teach him to eat prepared food, wear clothing, and anoint himself as humans do. He is weakened somewhat by this transformation and estranged from his animal companions, but he is also glorified and made greater than he was. The prostitute leads him to Uruk and the confrontation with Gilgamesh for which the gods have created him. His coming has been announced to Gilgamesh in one of the many dreams that play such an important role in the poem. Although the two are bent on destroying each other at first, their encounter results, as it was meant to, in a deep bond of friendship. Each finds in the other the true companion he has sought. The consequence of their union is that their prodigious energies are directed outward toward heroic achievements.

Gilgamesh proposes the first of their adventures both to gain them universal renown and to refresh the spirit of Enkidu, who has been weakened and confused by civilization. He suggests that they go to the great Cedar Forest in the Country of the Living and there slay the terrible giant Humbaba. Enkidu is reluctant at first because he knows the danger in this adventure better than Gilgamesh. But the latter prevails, and with the blessing of the sun god Shamash they succeed. Their victory is not a simple, glorious triumph, however, and its meaning is unclear. Humbaba poses no apparent threat to Uruk and its people, and he curses them before he dies. Enlil, the god of wind and storm, is enraged by the slaying of his creature, curses the heroes, and gives to others the seven splendors that had been Humbaba's.

Their second adventure is not of their choosing and also leads to another ambiguous success. Gilgamesh's just but harsh rejection of Ishtar's advances provokes her to send the Bull of Heaven against the people of Uruk. The terrible destruction the Bull causes obliges Gilgamesh and Enkidu to destroy it, but that victory brings about the slow and painful death of Enkidu.

The death of his companion reveals to Gilgamesh the hollowness of mortal fame and leads him to undertake a solitary journey in search of immortality. This journey sets *Gilgamesh* apart from more straightforward heroic narratives and gives it a special appeal to modern readers. Gilgamesh's specific goal is to discover the secret of immortality from the one man, Utnapishtim, who has survived the Flood. His journey begins with a conventional challenge, the fierce lions who guard the mountain passes. But the challenges he faces subsequently—the dark tunnel that brings him to a prototypical garden of paradise, the puzzling and perilous voyage to Dilmun—have a different and more magical character. He is discouraged at every step, but Gilgamesh perseveres. Although he at last finds Utnapishtim and hears his story, his goal eludes him. He fails a simple test of his potential for immortality when he cannot remain awake for six days and seven nights. Moreover, he fails a second test as well when he first finds the plant that ensures eternal rejuvenation and then, in a moment of carelessness, loses it to the serpent. Discouraged and defeated, Gilgamesh returns at last to Uruk empty-handed. His consolation is the assurance that his worldly accomplishments will endure beyond his own lifetime.

In long, belated retrospect we can see that *Gilgamesh* explores many of the mysteries of the human condition for the first time in our literature—the complex and perilous relations between gods and mortals and between nature and civilization, the depths of friendship, and the immortality of art. It is both humbling and thrilling to hear so familiar a voice from so vast a distance.

The introduction to the present translation by N. K. Sandars in *The Epic of Gilgamesh* (1972) is readily available and contains a wealth of useful information. Three recent scholarly translations—Stephanie Delany's *Myths from Mesopotamia: Creation, the Flood, Gilgamesh, and Others* (1989), Maureen Kovacs's *The Epic of Gilgamesh* (1989), and Andrew George's *The Epic of Gilgamesh* (1999)—are quite readable and provide abundant and useful supplementary material. A. Leo Oppenheim gives a comprehensive interpretation of Mesopotamian civilization in *Ancient Mesopotamia* (1977), and Alexander Heidel addresses the importance of *Gilgamesh* for biblical studies in *The Gilgamesh Epic and Old Testament Parallels* (1963).

Gilgamesh[1]

PROLOGUE

Gilgamesh King in Uruk

I will proclaim to the world the deeds of Gilgamesh. This was the man to whom all things were known; this was the king who knew the countries of the world. He was wise, he saw mysteries and knew secret things, he brought us a tale of the days before the flood. He went on a long journey, was weary,

1. Translated by N. K. Sandars.

worn-out with labour, returning he rested, he engraved on a stone the whole story.

When the gods created Gilgamesh they gave him a perfect body. Shamash[2] the glorious sun endowed him with beauty, Adad the god of the storm endowed him with courage, the great gods made his beauty perfect, surpassing all others, terrifying like a great wild bull. Two thirds they made him god and one third man.

In Uruk[3] he built walls, a great rampart, and the temple of blessed Eanna for the god of the firmament Anu,[4] and for Ishtar the goddess of love. Look at it still today: the outer wall where the cornice runs, it shines with the brilliance of copper; and the inner wall, it has no equal. Touch the threshold, it is ancient. Approach Eanna the dwelling of Ishtar, our lady of love and war, the like of which no latter-day king, no man alive can equal. Climb upon the wall of Uruk; walk along it, I say; regard the foundation terrace and examine the masonry: is it not burnt brick and good? The seven sages[5] laid the foundations.

1

The Coming of Enkidu

Gilgamesh went abroad in the world, but he met with none who could withstand his arms till he came to Uruk. But the men of Uruk muttered in their houses, "Gilgamesh sounds the tocsin for his amusement, his arrogance has no bounds by day or night. No son is left with his father, for Gilgamesh takes them all, even the children; yet the king should be a shepherd to his people. His lust leaves no virgin to her lover, neither the warrior's daughter nor the wife of the noble; yet this is the shepherd of the city, wise, comely, and resolute."

The gods heard their lament, the gods of heaven cried to the Lord of Uruk, to Anu the god of Uruk: "A goddess made him, strong as a savage bull, none can withstand his arms. No son is left with his father, for Gilgamesh takes them all; and is this the king, the shepherd of his people? His lust leaves no virgin to her lover, neither the warrior's daughter nor the wife of the noble." When Anu had heard their lamentation the gods cried to Aruru, the goddess of creation, "You made him, O Aruru, now create his equal; let it be as like him as his own reflection, his second self, stormy heart for stormy heart. Let them contend together and leave Uruk in quiet."

So the goddess conceived an image in her mind, and it was of the stuff of Anu of the firmament. She dipped her hands in water and pinched off clay, she let it fall in the wilderness, and noble Enkidu was created. There was virtue in him of the god of war, of Ninurta himself. His body was rough, he had long hair like a woman's; it waved like the hair of Nisaba, the goddess of corn. His body was covered with matted hair like Samuqan's, the god of cattle. He was innocent of mankind; he knew nothing of the cultivated land.

2. Also judge and lawgiver, with some fertility attributes; he is the husband and brother of Ishtar, goddess of love, fertility, and war and queen of heaven. **3.** City in southern Babylonia between Fara and Ur. Shown by excavation to have been an important city from very early times, with great temples to the gods Anu and Ishtar. After the Flood it was the seat of a dynasty of kings, among whom Gilgamesh was the fifth and most famous. **4.** Also father of the gods; he had an important temple in Uruk. Eanna was the temple precinct in Uruk, sacred to Anu and Ishtar. **5.** Wise men who brought civilization to the seven oldest cities of Mesopotamia.

Enkidu ate grass in the hills with the gazelle and lurked with wild beasts at the water-holes; he had joy of the water with the herds of wild game. But there was a trapper who met him one day face to face at the drinking-hole, for the wild game had entered his territory. On three days he met him face to face, and the trapper was frozen with fear. He went back to his house with the game he had caught, and he was dumb, benumbed with terror. His face was altered like that of one who has made a long journey. With awe in his heart he spoke to his father: "Father, there is a man, unlike any other, who comes down from the hills. He is the strongest in the world, he is like an immortal from heaven. He ranges over the hills with wild beasts and eats grass; he ranges through your land and comes down to the wells. I am afraid and dare not go near him. He fills in the pits which I dig and tears up my traps set for the game; he helps the beasts to escape and now they slip through my fingers."

His father opened his mouth and said to the trapper, "My son, in Uruk lives Gilgamesh; no one has ever prevailed against him, he is strong as a star from heaven. Go to Uruk, find Gilgamesh, extol the strength of this wild man. Ask him to give you a harlot, a wanton from the temple of love; return with her, and let her woman's power overpower this man. When next he comes down to drink at the wells she will be there, stripped naked; and when he sees her beckoning he will embrace her, and then the wild beasts will reject him."

So the trapper set out on his journey to Uruk and addressed himself to Gilgamesh saying, "A man unlike any other is roaming now in the pastures; he is as strong as a star from heaven and I am afraid to approach him. He helps the wild game to escape; he fills in my pits and pulls up my traps." Gilgamesh said, "Trapper, go back, take with you a harlot, a child of pleasure. At the drinking-hole she will strip, and when he sees her beckoning he will embrace her and the game of the wilderness will surely reject him."

Now the trapper returned, taking the harlot with him. After a three days' journey they came to the drinking-hole, and there they sat down; the harlot and the trapper sat facing one another and waited for the game to come. For the first day and for the second day the two sat waiting, but on the third day the herds came; they came down to drink and Enkidu was with them. The small wild creatures of the plains were glad of the water, and Enkidu with them, who ate grass with the gazelle and was born in the hills; and she saw him, the savage man, come from far-off in the hills. The trapper spoke to her: "There he is. Now, woman, make your breasts bare, have no shame, do not delay but welcome his love. Let him see you naked, let him possess your body. When he comes near uncover yourself and lie with him; teach him, the savage man, your woman's art, for when he murmurs love to you the wild beasts that shared his life in the hills will reject him."

She was not ashamed to take him, she made herself naked and welcomed his eagerness; as he lay on her murmuring love she taught him the woman's art. For six days and seven nights they lay together, for Enkidu had forgotten his home in the hills; but when he was satisfied he went back to the wild beasts. Then, when the gazelle saw him, they bolted away; when the wild creatures saw him they fled. Enkidu would have followed, but his body was bound as though with a cord, his knees gave way when he started to run, his swiftness was gone. And now the wild creatures had all fled away; Enkidu was grown weak, for wisdom was in him, and the thoughts of a man were in his heart. So he returned and sat down at the woman's feet, and listened intently to what she said. "You are wise, Enkidu, and now you have become like a god. Why do you want to run wild with the beasts in the hills? Come with me. I will take you to strong-walled Uruk, to the blessed temple of Ishtar and of Anu, of love and of heaven: there Gilgamesh lives, who is very strong, and like a wild bull he lords it over men."

When she had spoken Enkidu was pleased; he longed for a comrade, for one who would understand his heart. "Come, woman, and take me to that holy temple, to the house of Anu and of Ishtar, and to the place where Gilgamesh lords it over the people. I will challenge him boldly, I will cry out aloud in Uruk, 'I am the strongest here, I have come to change the old order, I am he who was born in the hills, I am he who is strongest of all.' "

She said, "Let us go, and let him see your face. I know very well where Gilgamesh is in great Uruk. O Enkidu, there all the people are dressed in their gorgeous robes, every day is holiday, the young men and the girls are wonderful to see. How sweet they smell! All the great ones are roused from their beds. O Enkidu, you who love life, I will show you Gilgamesh, a man of many moods; you shall look at him well in his radiant manhood. His body is perfect in strength and maturity; he never rests by night or day. He is stronger than you, so leave your boasting. Shamash the glorious sun has given favours to Gilgamesh, and Anu of the heavens, and Enlil, and Ea the wise has given him deep understanding. I tell you, even before you have left the wilderness, Gilgamesh will know in his dreams that you are coming."

Now Gilgamesh got up to tell his dream to his mother, Ninsun, one of the wise gods. "Mother, last night I had a dream. I was full of joy, the young heroes were round me and I walked through the night under the stars of the firmament, and one, a meteor of the stuff of Anu, fell down from heaven. I tried to lift it but it proved too heavy. All the people of Uruk came round to see it, the common people jostled and the nobles thronged to kiss its feet; and to me its attraction was like the love of woman. They helped me, I braced my forehead and I raised it with thongs and brought it to you, and you yourself pronounced it my brother."

Then Ninsun, who is well-beloved and wise, said to Gilgamesh, "This star of heaven which descended like a meteor from the sky; which you tried to lift, but found too heavy, when you tried to move it it would not budge, and so you brought it to my feet; I made it for you, a goad and spur, and you were drawn as though to a woman. This is the strong comrade, the one who brings help to his friend in his need. He is the strongest of wild creatures, the stuff of Anu; born in the grass-lands and the wild hills reared him; when you see him you will be glad; you will love him as a woman and he will never forsake you. This is the meaning of the dream."

Gilgamesh said, "Mother, I dreamed a second dream. In the streets of strong-walled Uruk there lay an axe; the shape of it was strange and the people thronged round. I saw it and was glad. I bent down, deeply drawn towards it; I loved it like a woman and wore it at my side." Ninsun answered, "That axe, which you saw, which drew you so powerfully like love of a woman, that is the comrade whom I give you, and he will come in his strength like one of the host of heaven. He is the brave companion who rescues his friend in necessity." Gilgamesh said to his mother, "A friend, a counsellor has come to me from Enlil, and now I shall befriend and counsel him." So Gilgamesh told his dreams; and the harlot retold them to Enkidu.

And now she said to Enkidu, "When I look at you you have become like a god. Why do you yearn to run wild again with the beasts in the hills? Get up from the ground, the bed of a shepherd." He listened to her words with care. It was good advice that she gave. She divided her clothing in two and with the one half she clothed him and with the other herself; and holding his hand she led him like a child to the sheepfolds, into the shepherds' tents. There all the shepherds crowded round to see him, they put down bread in front of him, but Enkidu could only suck the milk of wild animals. He fumbled and gaped, at a loss what to do or how he should eat the bread and drink the strong wine. Then the woman said, "Enkidu, eat bread, it is the staff of life; drink the wine, it is the custom of the land." So he ate till he was full and drank strong wine, seven goblets. He became merry, his heart exulted and his face shone. He rubbed down the matted hair of his body and anointed himself with oil. Enkidu had become a man; but when he had put on man's clothing he appeared like a bridegroom. He took arms to hunt the lion so that the shepherds could rest at night. He caught wolves and lions and the herdsmen lay down in peace; for Enkidu was their watchman, that strong man who had no rival.

He was merry living with the shepherds, till one day lifting his eyes he saw a man approaching. He said to the harlot, "Woman, fetch that man here. Why has he come? I wish to know his name." She went and called the man saying, "Sir, where are you going on this weary journey?" The man answered, saying to Enkidu, "Gilgamesh has gone into the marriage-house and shut out the people. He does strange things in Uruk, the city of great streets. At the roll of the drum work begins for the men, and work for the women. Gilgamesh the king is about to celebrate marriage with the Queen of Love, and he still demands to be first with the bride, the king to be first and the husband to follow, for that was ordained by the gods from his birth, from the time the umbilical cord was cut. But now the drums roll for the choice of the bride and the city groans." At these words Enkidu turned white in the face. "I will go to the place where Gilgamesh lords it over the people, I will challenge him boldly, and I will cry aloud in Uruk, 'I have come to change the old order, for I am the strongest here.' "

Now Enkidu strode in front and the woman followed behind. He entered Uruk, that great market, and all the folk thronged round him where he stood in the street in strong-walled Uruk. The people jostled; speaking of him they said, "He is the spit of Gilgamesh." "He is shorter." "He is bigger of bone." "This is the one who was reared on the milk of wild beasts. His is the greatest strength." The men rejoiced: "Now Gilgamesh has met his match. This great one, this hero whose beauty is like a god, he is a match even for Gilgamesh."

In Uruk the bridal bed was made, fit for the goddess of love. The bride waited for the bridegroom, but in the night Gilgamesh got up and came to the house. Then Enkidu stepped out, he stood in the street and blocked the way. Mighty Gilgamesh came on and Enkidu met him at the gate. He put out his foot and prevented Gilgamesh from entering the house, so they grappled, holding each other like bulls. They broke the doorposts and the walls shook, they snorted like bulls locked together. They shattered the doorposts and the walls shook. Gilgamesh bent his knee with his foot planted on the ground and with a turn Enkidu was thrown. Then immediately his fury died. When Enkidu was thrown he said to Gilgamesh, "There is not another like you in the world. Ninsun, who is as strong as a wild ox in the byre, she was the mother who bore you, and now you are raised above all men, and Enlil has given you the kingship, for your strength surpasses the strength of men." So Enkidu and Gilgamesh embraced and their friendship was sealed.

2

The Forest Journey

Enlil of the mountain, the father of the gods,[6] had decreed the destiny of Gilgamesh. So Gilgamesh dreamed and Enkidu said, "The meaning of the dream is this. The father of the gods has given you kingship, such is your destiny, everlasting life is not your destiny. Because of this do not be sad at heart, do not be grieved or oppressed. He has given you power to bind and to loose, to be the darkness and the light of mankind. He has given you unexampled supremacy over the people, victory in battle from which no fugitive returns, in forays and assaults from which there is no going back. But do not abuse this power, deal justly with your servants in the palace, deal justly before Shamash."

The eyes of Enkidu were full of tears and his heart was sick. He sighed bitterly and Gilgamesh met his eye and said, "My friend, why do you sigh so bitterly?" But Enkidu opened his mouth and said, "I am weak, my arms have lost their strength, the cry of sorrow sticks in my throat, I am oppressed by idleness." It was then that the lord Gilgamesh turned his thoughts to the Country of the Living; on the Land of Cedars the lord Gilgamesh reflected. He said to his servant Enkidu, "I have not established my name stamped on bricks as my destiny decreed; therefore I will go to the country where the cedar is felled. I will set up my name in the place where the names of famous men are written, and where no man's name is written yet I will raise a monument to the gods. Because of the evil that is in the land, we will go to the forest and destroy the evil; for in the forest lives Humbaba whose name is 'Hugeness,' a ferocious giant." But Enkidu sighed bitterly and said, "When I went with the wild beasts ranging through the wilderness I discovered the forest; its length is ten thousand leagues in every direction. Enlil has appointed Humbaba to guard it and armed him in sevenfold terrors, terrible to all flesh is Humbaba. When he roars it is like the torrent of the storm, his breath is like fire, and his jaws are death itself. He guards the cedars so well that when the wild heifer stirs in the forest, though she is sixty leagues distant, he hears her. What man would willingly walk into that country and explore its depths? I tell you, weakness overpowers whoever goes near it: it is not an equal struggle when one fights with Humbaba; he is a great warrior, a battering-ram. Gilgamesh, the watchman of the forest never sleeps."

Gilgamesh replied: "Where is the man who can clamber to heaven? Only the gods live for ever with glorious Shamash, but as for us men, our days are numbered, our occupations are a breath of wind. How is this, already you are afraid! I will go first although I am your lord, and you may safely call out, 'Forward, there is nothing to fear!' Then if I fall I leave behind me a name

6. The breath and "word" of Anu; he is also god of earth, wind, and spirit.

that endures; men will say of me, 'Gilgamesh has fallen in fight with ferocious Humbaba.' Long after the child has been born in my house, they will say it, and remember." Enkidu spoke again to Gilgamesh, "O my lord, if you will enter that country, go first to the hero Shamash, tell the Sun God, for the land is his. The country where the cedar is cut belongs to Shamash."

Gilgamesh took up a kid, white without spot, and a brown one with it; he held them against his breast, and he carried them into the presence of the sun. He took in his hand his silver sceptre and he said to glorious Shamash, "I am going to that country, O Shamash, I am going; my hands supplicate, so let it be well with my soul and bring me back to the quay of Uruk. Grant, I beseech, your protection, and let the omen be good." Glorious Shamash answered, "Gilgamesh, you are strong, but what is the Country of the Living to you?"

"O Shamash, hear me, hear me, Shamash, let my voice be heard. Here in the city man dies oppressed at heart, man perishes with despair in his heart. I have looked over the wall and I see the bodies floating on the river, and that will be my lot also. Indeed I know it is so, for whoever is tallest among men cannot reach the heavens, and the greatest cannot encompass the earth. Therefore I would enter that country: because I have not established my name stamped on brick as my destiny decreed, I will go to the country where the cedar is cut. I will set up my name where the names of famous men are written; and where no man's name is written I will raise a monument to the gods." The tears ran down his face and he said, "Alas, it is a long journey that I must take to the Land of Humbaba. If this enterprise is not to be accomplished, why did you move me, Shamash, with the restless desire to perform it? How can I succeed if you will not succour me? If I die in that country I will die without rancour, but if I return I will make a glorious offering of gifts and of praise to Shamash."

So Shamash accepted the sacrifice of his tears; like the compassionate man he showed him mercy. He appointed strong allies for Gilgamesh, sons of one mother, and stationed them in the mountain caves. The great winds he appointed: the north wind, the whirlwind, the storm and the icy wind, the tempest and the scorching wind. Like vipers, like dragons, like a scorching fire, like a serpent that freezes the heart, a destroying flood and the lightning's fork, such were they and Gilgamesh rejoiced.

He went to the forge and said, "I will give orders to the armourers; they shall cast us our weapons while we watch them." So they gave orders to the armourers and the craftsmen sat down in conference. They went into the groves of the plain and cut willow and box-wood; they cast for them axes of nine score pounds, and great swords they cast with blades of six score pounds each one, with pommels and hilts of thirty pounds. They cast for Gilgamesh the axe "Might of Heroes" and the bow of Anshan;[7] and Gilgamesh was armed and Enkidu; and the weight of the arms they carried was thirty score pounds.

The people collected and the counsellors in the streets and in the market-place of Uruk; they came through the gate of seven bolts and Gilgamesh spoke to them in the market-place: "I, Gilgamesh, go to see that creature of whom such things are spoken, the rumour of whose name fills the world. I

7. A district of Elam in southwest Persia; probably the source of supplies of wood for making bows.

will conquer him in his cedar wood and show the strength of the sons of Uruk, all the world shall know of it. I am committed to this enterprise: to climb the mountain, to cut down the cedar, and leave behind me an enduring name." The counsellors of Uruk, the great market, answered him, "Gilgamesh, you are young, your courage carries you too far, you cannot know what this enterprise means which you plan. We have heard that Humbaba is not like men who die, his weapons are such that none can stand against them; the forest stretches for ten thousand leagues in every direction; who would willingly go down to explore its depths? As for Humbaba, when he roars it is like the torrent of the storm, his breath is like fire and his jaws are death itself. Why do you crave to do this thing, Gilgamesh? It is no equal struggle when one fights with Humbaba, that battering-ram."

When he heard these words of the counsellors Gilgamesh looked at his friend and laughed, "How shall I answer them; shall I say I am afraid of Humbaba, I will sit at home all the rest of my days?" Then Gilgamesh opened his mouth again and said to Enkidu, "My friend, let us go to the Great Palace, to Egalmah,[8] and stand before Ninsun the queen. Ninsun is wise with deep knowledge, she will give us counsel for the road we must go." They took each other by the hand as they went to Egalmah, and they went to Ninsun the great queen. Gilgamesh approached, he entered the palace and spoke to Ninsun. "Ninsun, will you listen to me; I have a long journey to go, to the Land of Humbaba, I must travel an unknown road and fight a strange battle. From the day I go until I return, till I reach the cedar forest and destroy the evil which Shamash abhors, pray for me to Shamash."

Ninsun went into her room, she put on a dress becoming to her body, she put on jewels to make her breast beautiful, she placed a tiara on her head and her skirts swept the ground. Then she went up to the altar of the Sun, standing upon the roof of the palace; she burnt incense and lifted her arms to Shamash as the smoke ascended: "O Shamash, why did you give this restless heart to Gilgamesh, my son; why did you give it? You have moved him and now he sets out on a long journey to the Land of Humbaba to travel an unknown road and fight a strange battle. Therefore from the day that he goes till the day he returns, until he reaches the cedar forest, until he kills Humbaba and destroys the evil thing which you, Shamash, abhor, do not forget him; but let the dawn, Aya, your dear bride, remind you always, and when day is done give him to the watchman of the night to keep him from harm." Then Ninsun the mother of Gilgamesh extinguished the incense, and she called to Enkidu with this exhortation: "Strong Enkidu, you are not the child of my body, but I will receive you as my adopted son; you are my other child like the foundlings they bring to the temple. Serve Gilgamesh as a foundling serves the temple and the priestess who reared him. In the presence of my women, my votaries and hierophants,[9] I declare it." Then she placed the amulet for a pledge round his neck, and she said to him, "I entrust my son to you; bring him back to me safely."

And now they brought to them the weapons, they put in their hands the great swords in their golden scabbards, and the bow and the quiver. Gilgamesh took the axe, he slung the quiver from his shoulder, and the bow of Anshan, and buckled the sword to his belt; and so they were armed and ready

8. Home of the goddess Ninsun. 9. Priests.

for the journey. Now all the people came and pressed on them and said, "When will you return to the city?" The counsellors blessed Gilgamesh and warned him, "Do not trust too much in your own strength, be watchful, restrain your blows at first. The one who goes in front protects his companion; the good guide who knows the way guards his friend. Let Enkidu lead the way, he knows the road to the forest, he has seen Humbaba and is experienced in battles; let him press first into the passes, let him be watchful and look to himself. Let Enkidu protect his friend, and guard his companion, and bring him safe through the pitfalls of the road. We, the counsellors of Uruk entrust our king to you, O Enkidu; bring him back safely to us." Again to Gilgamesh they said, "May Shamash give you your heart's desire, may he let you see with your eyes the thing accomplished which your lips have spoken; may he open a path for you where it is blocked, and a road for your feet to tread. May he open the mountains for your crossing, and may the night-time bring you the blessings of night, and Lugulbanda, your guardian god, stand beside you for victory. May you have victory in the battle as though you fought with a child. Wash your feet in the river of Humbaba to which you are journeying; in the evening dig a well, and let there always be pure water in your water-skin. Offer cold water to Shamash and do not forget Lugulbanda."

Then Enkidu opened his mouth and said, "Forward, there is nothing to fear. Follow me, for I know the place where Humbaba lives and the paths where he walks. Let the counsellors go back. Here is no cause for fear." When the counsellors heard this they sped the hero on his way. "Go, Gilgamesh, may your guardian god protect you on the road and bring you safely back to the quay of Uruk."

After twenty leagues they broke their fast; after another thirty leagues they stopped for the night. Fifty leagues they walked in one day; in three days they had walked as much as a journey of a month and two weeks. They crossed seven mountains before they came to the gate of the forest. Then Enkidu called out to Gilgamesh, "Do not go down into the forest; when I opened the gate my hand lost its strength." Gilgamesh answered him, "Dear friend, do not speak like a coward. Have we got the better of so many dangers and travelled so far, to turn back at last? You, who are tried in wars and battles, hold close to me now and you will feel no fear of death; keep beside me and your weakness will pass, the trembling will leave your hand. Would my friend rather stay behind? No, we will go down together into the heart of the forest. Let your courage be roused by the battle to come; forget death and follow me, a man resolute in action, but one who is not foolhardy. When two go together each will protect himself and shield his companion, and if they fall they leave an enduring name."

Together they went down into the forest and they came to the green mountain. There they stood still, they were struck dumb; they stood still and gazed at the forest. They saw the height of the cedar, they saw the way into the forest and the track where Humbaba was used to walk. The way was broad and the going was good. They gazed at the mountain of cedars, the dwelling-place of the gods and the throne of Ishtar. The hugeness of the cedar rose in front of the mountain, its shade was beautiful, full of comfort; mountain and glade were green with brushwood.

There Gilgamesh dug a well before the setting sun. He went up the mountain and poured out fine meal on the ground and said, "O mountain, dwelling of the gods, bring me a favourable dream." Then they took each other by the hand and lay down to sleep; and sleep that flows from the night lapped over them. Gilgamesh dreamed, and at midnight sleep left him, and he told his dream to his friend. "Enkidu, what was it that woke me if you did not? My friend, I have dreamed a dream. Get up, look at the mountain precipice. The sleep that the gods sent me is broken. Ah, my friend, what a dream I have had! Terror and confusion; I seized hold of a wild bull in the wilderness. It bellowed and beat up the dust till the whole sky was dark, my arm was seized and my tongue bitten. I fell back on my knee; then someone refreshed me with water from his water-skin."

Enkidu said, "Dear friend, the god to whom we are travelling is no wild bull, though his form is mysterious. That wild bull which you saw is Shamash the Protector; in our moment of peril he will take our hands. The one who gave water from his water-skin, that is your own god who cares for your good name, your Lugulbanda.[1] United with him, together we will accomplish a work the fame of which will never die."

Gilgamesh said, "I dreamed again. We stood in a deep gorge of the mountain, and beside it we two were like the smallest of swamp flies; and suddenly the mountain fell, it struck me and caught my feet from under me. Then came an intolerable light blazing out, and in it was one whose grace and whose beauty were greater than the beauty of this world. He pulled me out from under the mountain, he gave me water to drink and my heart was comforted, and he set my feet on the ground."

Then Enkidu the child of the plains said, "Let us go down from the mountain and talk this thing over together." He said to Gilgamesh the young god, "Your dream is good, your dream is excellent, the mountain which you saw is Humbaba. Now, surely, we will seize and kill him, and throw his body down as the mountain fell on the plain."

The next day after twenty leagues they broke their fast, and after another thirty they stopped for the night. They dug a well before the sun had set and Gilgamesh ascended the mountain. He poured out fine meal on the ground and said, "O mountain, dwelling of the gods, send a dream for Enkidu, make him a favourable dream." The mountain fashioned a dream for Enkidu; it came, an ominous dream; a cold shower passed over him, it caused him to cower like the mountain barley under a storm of rain. But Gilgamesh sat with his chin on his knees till the sleep which flows over all mankind lapped over him. Then, at midnight, sleep left him; he got up and said to his friend, "Did you call me, or why did I wake? Did you touch me, or why am I terrified? Did not some god pass by, for my limbs are numb with fear? My friend, I saw a third dream and this dream was altogether frightful. The heavens roared and the earth roared again, daylight failed and darkness fell, lightning flashed, fire blazed out, the clouds lowered, they rained down death. Then the brightness departed, the fire went out, and all was turned to ashes fallen about us. Let us go down from the mountain and talk this over, and consider what we should do."

When they had come down from the mountain Gilgamesh seized the axe in his hand: he felled the cedar. When Humbaba heard the noise far off he

1. Hero of a cycle of Sumerian poems; protector of Gilgamesh.

was enraged; he cried out, "Who is this that has violated my woods and cut down my cedar?" But glorious Shamash called to them out of heaven, "Go forward, do not be afraid." But now Gilgamesh was overcome by weakness, for sleep had seized him suddenly, a profound sleep held him; he lay on the ground, stretched out speechless, as though in a dream. When Enkidu touched him he did not rise, when he spoke to him he did not reply. "O Gilgamesh, Lord of the plain of Kullab,[2] the world grows dark, the shadows have spread over it, now is the glimmer of dusk. Shamash has departed, his bright head is quenched in the bosom of his mother Ningal. O Gilgamesh, how long will you lie like this, asleep? Never let the mother who gave you birth be forced in mourning into the city square."

At length Gilgamesh heard him; he put on his breastplate, "The Voice of Heroes," of thirty shekels' weight; he put it on as though it had been a light garment that he carried, and it covered him altogether. He straddled the earth like a bull that snuffs the ground and his teeth were clenched. "By the life of my mother Ninsun who gave me birth, and by the life of my father, divine Lugulbanda, let me live to be the wonder of my mother, as when she nursed me on her lap." A second time he said to him, "By the life of Ninsun my mother who gave me birth, and by the life of my father, divine Lugulbanda, until we have fought this man, if man he is, this god, if god he is, the way that I took to the Country of the Living will not turn back to the city."

Then Enkidu, the faithful companion, pleaded, answering him, "O my lord, you do not know this monster and that is the reason you are not afraid. I who know him, I am terrified. His teeth are dragon's fangs, his countenance is like a lion, his charge is the rushing of the flood, with his look he crushes alike the trees of the forest and reeds in the swamp. O my Lord, you may go on if you choose into this land, but I will go back to the city. I will tell the lady your mother all your glorious deeds till she shouts for joy: and then I will tell the death that followed till she weeps for bitterness." But Gilgamesh said, "Immolation and sacrifice are not yet for me, the boat of the dead shall not go down, nor the three-ply cloth be cut for my shrouding. Not yet will my people be desolate, nor the pyre be lit in my house and my dwelling burnt on the fire. Today, give me your aid and you shall have mine: what then can go amiss with us two? All living creatures born of the flesh shall sit at last in the boat of the West, and when it sinks, when the boat of Magilum[3] sinks, they are gone; but we shall go forward and fix our eyes on this monster. If your heart is fearful throw away fear; if there is terror in it throw away terror. Take your axe in your hand and attack. He who leaves the fight unfinished is not at peace."

Humbaba came out from his strong house of cedar. Then Enkidu called out, "O Gilgamesh, remember now your boasts in Uruk. Forward, attack, son of Uruk, there is nothing to fear." When he heard these words his courage rallied; he answered, "Make haste, close in, if the watchman is there do not let him escape to the woods where he will vanish. He has put on the first of his seven splendours[4] but not yet the other six, let us trap him before he is armed." Like a raging wild bull he snuffed the ground; the watchman of the woods turned full of threatenings, he cried out. Humbaba came from his strong house of cedar. He nodded his head and shook it, menacing Gilga-

2. In Uruk. 3. Unclear; perhaps the boat of the dead. 4. Unclear; perhaps warlike attributes.

mesh; and on him he fastened his eye, the eye of death. Then Gilgamesh called to Shamash and his tears were flowing, "O glorious Shamash, I have followed the road you commanded but now if you send no succour how shall I escape?" Glorious Shamash heard his prayer and he summoned the great wind, the north wind, the whirlwind, the storm and the icy wind, the tempest and the scorching wind; they came like dragons, like a scorching fire, like a serpent that freezes the heart, a destroying flood and the lightning's fork. The eight winds rose up against Humbaba, they beat against his eyes; he was gripped, unable to go forward or back. Gilgamesh shouted, "By the life of Ninsun my mother and divine Lugulbanda my father, in the Country of the Living, in this Land I have discovered your dwelling; my weak arms and my small weapons I have brought to this Land against you, and now I will enter your house."

So he felled the first cedar and they cut the branches and laid them at the foot of the mountain. At the first stroke Humbaba blazed out, but still they advanced. They felled seven cedars and cut and bound the branches and laid them at the foot of the mountain, and seven times Humbaba loosed his glory on them. As the seventh blaze died out they reached his lair. He slapped his thigh in scorn. He approached like a noble wild bull roped on the mountain, a warrior whose elbows are bound together. The tears started to his eyes and he was pale, "Gilgamesh, let me speak. I have never known a mother, no, nor a father who reared me. I was born of the mountain, he reared me, and Enlil made me the keeper of this forest. Let me go free, Gilgamesh, and I will be your servant, you shall be my lord; all the trees of the forest that I tended on the mountain shall be yours. I will cut them down and build you a palace." He took him by the hand and led him to his house, so that the heart of Gilgamesh was moved with compassion. He swore by the heavenly life, by the earthly life, by the underworld itself: "O Enkidu, should not the snared bird return to its nest and the captive man return to his mother's arms?" Enkidu answered, "The strongest of men will fall to fate if he has no judgement. Namtar, the evil fate that knows no distinction between men, will devour him. If the snared bird returns to its nest, if the captive man returns to his mother's arms, then you my friend will never return to the city where the mother is waiting who gave you birth. He will bar the mountain road against you, and make the pathways impassable."

Humbaba said, "Enkidu, what you have spoken is evil: you, a hireling, dependent for your bread! In envy and for fear of a rival you have spoken evil words." Enkidu said, "Do not listen, Gilgamesh: this Humbaba must die. Kill Humbaba first and his servants after." But Gilgamesh said, "If we touch him the blaze and the glory of light will be put out in confusion, the glory and glamour will vanish, its rays will be quenched." Enkidu said to Gilgamesh, "Not so, my friend. First entrap the bird, and where shall the chicks run then? Afterwards we can search out the glory and the glamour, when the chicks run distracted through the grass."

Gilgamesh listened to the word of his companion, he took the axe in his hand, he drew the sword from his belt, and he struck Humbaba with a thrust of the sword to the neck, and Enkidu his comrade struck the second blow. At the third blow Humbaba fell. Then there followed confusion for this was the guardian of the forest whom they had felled to the ground. For as far as two leagues the cedars shivered when Enkidu felled the watcher of the forest, he at whose voice Hermon and Lebanon[5] used to tremble. Now the mountains were moved and all the hills, for the guardian of the forest was killed. They attacked the cedars, the seven splendours of Humbaba were extinguished. So they pressed on into the forest bearing the sword of eight talents. They uncovered the sacred dwellings of the Anunnaki[6] and while Gilgamesh felled the first of the trees of the forest Enkidu cleared their roots as far as the banks of Euphrates. They set Humbaba before the gods, before Enlil; they kissed the ground and dropped the shroud and set the head before him. When he saw the head of Humbaba, Enlil raged at them. "Why did you do this thing? From henceforth may the fire be on your faces, may it eat the bread that you eat, may it drink where you drink." Then Enlil took again the blaze and the seven splendours that had been Humbaba's: he gave the first to the river, and he gave to the lion, to the stone of execration, to the mountain and to the dreaded daughter of the Queen of Hell.

O Gilgamesh, king and conqueror of the dreadful blaze; wild bull who plunders the mountain, who crosses the sea, glory to him, and from the brave the greater glory is Enki's![7]

3

Ishtar and Gilgamesh, and the Death of Enkidu

Gilgamesh washed out his long locks and cleaned his weapons; he flung back his hair from his shoulders; he threw off his stained clothes and changed them for new. He put on his royal robes and made them fast. When Gilgamesh had put on the crown, glorious Ishtar lifted her eyes, seeing the beauty of Gilgamesh. She said, "Come to me Gilgamesh, and be my bridegroom; grant me seed of your body, let me be your bride and you shall be my husband. I will harness for you a chariot of lapis lazuli and of gold, with wheels of gold and horns of copper; and you shall have mighty demons of the storm for draft-mules. When you enter our house in the fragrance of cedar-wood, threshold and throne will kiss your feet. Kings, rulers, and princes will bow down before you; they shall bring you tribute from the mountains and the plain. Your ewes shall drop twins and your goats triplets; your pack-ass shall outrun mules; your oxen shall have no rivals, and your chariot horses shall be famous far-off for their swiftness."

Gilgamesh opened his mouth and answered glorious Ishtar, "If I take you in marriage, what gifts can I give in return? What ointments and clothing for your body? I would gladly give you bread and all sorts of food fit for a god. I would give you wine to drink fit for a queen. I would pour out barley to stuff your granary; but as for making you my wife—that I will not. How would it go with me? Your lovers have found you like a brazier which smoulders in the cold, a backdoor which keeps out neither squall of wind nor storm, a castle which crushes the garrison, pitch that blackens the bearer, a waterskin that chafes the carrier, a stone which falls from the parapet, a battering-ram turned back from the enemy, a sandal that trips the wearer. Which of your lovers did you ever love for ever? What shepherd of yours has pleased

5. Mountains in Lebanon. 6. Gods of the underworld, judges of the dead, and offspring of Anu.
7. Or Ea, god of the sweet waters and wisdom, a patron of arts, and one of the creators of humankind, toward whom he is usually well disposed.

you for all time? Listen to me while I tell the tale of your lovers. There was Tammuz,[8] the lover of your youth, for him you decreed wailing, year after year. You loved the many-coloured roller, but still you struck and broke his wing; now in the grove he sits and cries, "kappi, kappi, my wing, my wing." You have loved the lion tremendous in strength: seven pits you dug for him, and seven. You have loved the stallion magnificent in battle, and for him you decreed whip and spur and a thong, to gallop seven leagues by force and to muddy the water before he drinks; and for his mother Silili[9] lamentations. You have loved the shepherd of the flock; he made meal-cake for you day after day, he killed kids for your sake. You struck and turned him into a wolf; now his own herd-boys chase him away, his own hounds worry his flanks. And did you not love Ishullanu, the gardener of your father's palm-grove? He brought you baskets filled with dates without end; every day he loaded your table. Then you turned your eyes on him and said, 'Dearest Ishullanu, come here to me, let us enjoy your manhood, come forward and take me, I am yours.' Ishullanu answered, 'What are you asking from me? My mother has baked and I have eaten; why should I come to such as you for food that is tainted and rotten? For when was a screen of rushes sufficient protection from frosts?' But when you had heard his answer you struck him. He was changed to a blind mole deep in the earth, one whose desire is always beyond his reach. And if you and I should be lovers, should not I be served in the same fashion as all these others whom you loved once?"

When Ishtar heard this she fell into a bitter rage, she went up to high heaven. Her tears poured down in front of her father Anu, and Antum her mother. She said, "My father, Gilgamesh has heaped insults on me, he has told over all my abominable behaviour, my foul and hideous acts." Anu opened his mouth and said, "Are you a father of gods? Did not you quarrel with Gilgamesh the king, so now he has related your abominable behaviour, your foul and hideous acts?"

Ishtar opened her mouth and said again, "My father, give me the Bull of Heaven to destroy Gilgamesh. Fill Gilgamesh, I say, with arrogance to his destruction; but if you refuse to give me the Bull of Heaven I will break in the doors of hell and smash the bolts; there will be confusion of people, those above with those from the lower depths. I shall bring up the dead to eat food like the living; and the hosts of dead will outnumber the living." Anu said to great Ishtar, "If I do what you desire there will be seven years of drought throughout Uruk when corn will be seedless husks. Have you saved grain enough for the people and grass for the cattle?" Ishtar replied, "I have saved grain for the people, grass for the cattle; for seven years of seedless husks there is grain and there is grass enough."

When Anu heard what Ishtar had said he gave her the Bull of Heaven to lead by the halter down to Uruk. When they reached the gates of Uruk the Bull went to the river; with his first snort cracks opened in the earth and a hundred young men fell down to death. With his second snort cracks opened and two hundred fell down to death. With his third snort cracks opened, Enkidu doubled over but instantly recovered, he dodged aside and leapt on the Bull and seized it by the horns. The Bull of Heaven foamed in his face, it brushed him with the thick of its tail. Enkidu cried to Gilgamesh, "My

8. The dying god of vegetation. 9. Perhaps a divine horse.

friend, we boasted that we would leave enduring names behind us. Now thrust in your sword between the nape and the horns." So Gilgamesh followed the Bull, he seized the thick of its tail, he thrust the sword between the nape and the horns and slew the Bull. When they had killed the Bull of Heaven they cut out its heart and gave it to Shamash, and the brothers rested.

But Ishtar rose up and mounted the great wall of Uruk; she sprang on to the tower and uttered a curse: "Woe to Gilgamesh, for he has scorned me in killing the Bull of Heaven." When Enkidu heard these words he tore out the Bull's right thigh and tossed it in her face saying, "If I could lay my hands on you, it is this I should do to you, and lash the entrails to your side." Then Ishtar called together her people, the dancing and singing girls, the prostitutes of the temple, the courtesans. Over the thigh of the Bull of Heaven she set up lamentation.

But Gilgamesh called the smiths and the armourers, all of them together. They admired the immensity of the horns. They were plated with lapis lazuli two fingers thick. They were thirty pounds each in weight, and their capacity in oil was six measures, which he gave to his guardian god, Lugulbanda. But he carried the horns into the palace and hung them on the wall. Then they washed their hands in Euphrates, they embraced each other and went away. They drove through the streets of Uruk where the heroes were gathered to see them, and Gilgamesh called to the singing girls, "Who is most glorious of the heroes, who is most eminent among men?" "Gilgamesh is the most glorious of heroes, Gilgamesh is most eminent among men." And now there was feasting, and celebrations and joy in the palace, till the heroes lay down saying, "Now we will rest for the night."

When the daylight came Enkidu got up and cried to Gilgamesh, "O my brother, such a dream I had last night. Anu, Enlil, Ea and heavenly Shamash took counsel together, and Anu said to Enlil, 'Because they have killed the Bull of Heaven, and because they have killed Humbaba who guarded the Cedar Mountain one of the two must die.' Then glorious Shamash answered the hero Enlil, 'It was by your command they killed the Bull of Heaven, and killed Humbaba, and must Enkidu die although innocent?' Enlil flung round in rage at glorious Shamash, 'You dare to say this, you who went about with them every day like one of themselves!' "

So Enkidu lay stretched out before Gilgamesh; his tears ran down in streams and he said to Gilgamesh, "O my brother, so dear as you are to me, brother, yet they will take me from you." Again he said, "I must sit down on the threshold of the dead and never again will I see my dear brother with my eyes."

While Enkidu lay alone in his sickness he cursed the gate as though it was living flesh, "You there, wood of the gate, dull and insensible, witless, I searched for you over twenty leagues until I saw the towering cedar. There is no wood like you in our land. Seventy-two cubits high and twenty-four wide, the pivot and the ferrule and the jambs are perfect. A master craftsman from Nippur has made you; but O, if I had known the conclusion! If I had known that this was all the good that would come of it, I would have raised the axe and split you into little pieces and set up here a gate of wattle instead. Ah, if only some future king had brought you here, or some god had fashioned you. Let him obliterate my name and write his own, and the curse fall on him instead of on Enkidu."

With the first brightening of dawn Enkidu raised his head and wept before the Sun God, in the brilliance of the sunlight his tears streamed down. "Sun God, I beseech you, about that vile Trapper, that Trapper of nothing because of whom I was to catch less than my comrade; let him catch least, make his game scarce, make him feeble, taking the smaller of every share, let his quarry escape from his nets."

When he had cursed the Trapper to his heart's content he turned on the harlot. He was roused to curse her also. "As for you, woman, with a great curse I curse you! I will promise you a destiny to all eternity. My curse shall come on you soon and sudden. You shall be without a roof for your commerce, for you shall not keep house with other girls in the tavern, but do your business in places fouled by the vomit of the drunkard. Your hire will be potter's earth, your thievings will be flung into the hovel, you will sit at the cross-roads in the dust of the potter's quarter, you will make your bed on the dunghill at night, and by day take your stand in the wall's shadow. Brambles and thorns will tear your feet, the drunk and the dry will strike your cheek and your mouth will ache. Let you be stripped of your purple dyes, for I too once in the wilderness with my wife had all the treasure I wished."

When Shamash heard the words of Enkidu he called to him from heaven: "Enkidu, why are you cursing the woman, the mistress who taught you to eat bread fit for gods and drink wine of kings? She who put upon you a magnificent garment, did she not give you glorious Gilgamesh for your companion, and has not Gilgamesh, your own brother, made you rest on a royal bed and recline on a couch at his left hand? He has made the princes of the earth kiss your feet, and now all the people of Uruk lament and wail over you. When you are dead he will let his hair grow long for your sake, he will wear a lion's pelt and wander through the desert."

When Enkidu heard glorious Shamash his angry heart grew quiet, he called back the curse and said, "Woman, I promise you another destiny. The mouth which cursed you shall bless you! Kings, princes and nobles shall adore you. On your account a man though twelve miles off will clap his hand to his thigh and his hair will twitch. For you he will undo his belt and open his treasure and you shall have your desire; lapis lazuli, gold and carnelian from the heap in the treasury. A ring for your hand and a robe shall be yours. The priest will lead you into the presence of the gods. On your account a wife, a mother of seven, was forsaken."

As Enkidu slept alone in his sickness, in bitterness of spirit he poured out his heart to his friend. "It was I who cut down the cedar, I who levelled the forest, I who slew Humbaba and now see what has become of me. Listen, my friend, this is the dream I dreamed last night. The heavens roared, and earth rumbled back an answer; between them stood I before an awful being, the sombre-faced man-bird; he had directed on me his purpose. His was a vampire face, his foot was a lion's foot, his hand was an eagle's talon. He fell on me and his claws were in my hair, he held me fast and I smothered; then he transformed me so that my arms became wings covered with feathers. He turned his stare towards me, and he led me away to the palace of Irkalla, the

Queen of Darkness,[1] to the house from which none who enters ever returns, down the road from which there is no coming back.

"There is the house whose people sit in darkness; dust is their food and clay their meat. They are clothed like birds with wings for covering, they see no light, they sit in darkness. I entered the house of dust and I saw the kings of the earth, their crowns put away for ever; rulers and princes, all those who once wore kingly crowns and ruled the world in the days of old. They who had stood in the place of the gods like Anu and Enlil, stood now like servants to fetch baked meats in the house of dust, to carry cooked meat and cold water from the water-skin. In the house of dust which I entered were high priests and acolytes, priests of the incantation and of ecstasy; there were servers of the temple, and there was Etana, that king of Kish whom the eagle carried to heaven in the days of old. I saw also Samuqan, god of cattle, and there was Ereshkigal the Queen of the Underworld; and Belit-Sheri squatted in front of her, she who is recorder of the gods and keeps the book of death. She held a tablet from which she read. She raised her head, she saw me and spoke: 'Who has brought this one here?' Then I awoke like a man drained of blood who wanders alone in a waste of rushes; like one whom the bailiff has seized and his heart pounds with terror."

Gilgamesh had peeled off his clothes, he listened to his words and wept quick tears, Gilgamesh listened and his tears flowed. He opened his mouth and spoke to Enkidu: "Who is there in strong-walled Uruk who has wisdom like this? Strange things have been spoken, why does your heart speak strangely? The dream was marvellous but the terror was great; we must treasure the dream whatever the terror; for the dream has shown that misery comes at last to the healthy man, the end of life is sorrow." And Gilgamesh lamented, "Now I will pray to the great gods, for my friend had an ominous dream."

This day on which Enkidu dreamed came to an end and he lay stricken with sickness. One whole day he lay on his bed and his suffering increased. He said to Gilgamesh, the friend on whose account he had left the wilderness, "Once I ran for you, for the water of life, and I now have nothing." A second day he lay on his bed and Gilgamesh watched over him but the sickness increased. A third day he lay on his bed, he called out to Gilgamesh, rousing him up. Now he was weak and his eyes were blind with weeping. Ten days he lay and his suffering increased, eleven and twelve days he lay on his bed of pain. Then he called to Gilgamesh, "My friend, the great goddess cursed me and I must die in shame. I shall not die like a man fallen in battle; I feared to fall, but happy is the man who falls in the battle, for I must die in shame." And Gilgamesh wept over Enkidu. With the first light of dawn he raised his voice and said to the counsellors of Uruk:

> Hear me, great ones of Uruk,
> I weep for Enkidu, my friend,
> Bitterly moaning like a woman mourning
> I weep for my brother.
> O Enkidu, my brother,
> You were the axe at my side,

1. Also Ereshkigal, queen of the underworld.

My hand's strength, the sword in my belt,
The shield before me,
A glorious robe, my fairest ornament;
An evil Fate has robbed me.
The wild ass and the gazelle
That were father and mother,
All long-tailed creatures that nourished you
Weep for you,
All the wild things of the plain and pastures;
The paths that you loved in the forest of cedars
Night and day murmur.
Let the great ones of strong-walled Uruk
Weep for you;
Let the finger of blessing
Be stretched out in mourning;
Enkidu, young brother. Hark,
There is an echo through all the country
Like a mother mourning.
Weep all the paths where we walked together;
And the beasts we hunted, the bear and hyena,
Tiger and panther, leopard and lion,
The stag and the ibex, the bull and the doe.
The river along whose banks we used to walk,
Weeps for you,
Ula of Elam and dear Euphrates
Where once we drew water for the water-skins.
The mountain we climbed where we slew the Watchman,
Weeps for you.
The warriors of strong-walled Uruk
Where the Bull of Heaven was killed,
Weep for you.
All the people of Eridu
Weep for you Enkidu.
Those who brought grain for your eating
Mourn for you now;
Who rubbed oil on your back
Mourn for you now;
Who poured beer for your drinking
Mourn for you now.
The harlot who anointed you with fragrant ointment
Laments for you now;
The women of the palace, who brought you a wife,
A chosen ring of good advice,
Lament for you now.
And the young men your brothers
As though they were women
Go long-haired in mourning.
What is this sleep which holds you now?
You are lost in the dark and cannot hear me.

He touched his heart but it did not beat, nor did he lift his eyes again. When Gilgamesh touched his heart it did not beat. So Gilgamesh laid a veil, as one veils the bride, over his friend. He began to rage like a lion, like a lioness robbed of her whelps. This way and that he paced round the bed, he tore out his hair and strewed it around. He dragged off his splendid robes and flung them down as though they were abominations.

In the first light of dawn Gilgamesh cried out, "I made you rest on a royal bed, you reclined on a couch at my left hand, the princes of the earth kissed your feet. I will cause all the people of Uruk to weep over you and raise the dirge of the dead. The joyful people will stoop with sorrow; and when you have gone to the earth I will let my hair grow long for your sake, I will wander through the wilderness in the skin of a lion." The next day also, in the first light, Gilgamesh lamented; seven days and seven nights he wept for Enkidu, until the worm fastened on him. Only then he gave him up to the earth, for the Anunnaki, the judges, had seized him.

Then Gilgamesh issued a proclamation through the land, he summoned them all, the coppersmiths, the goldsmiths, the stone-workers, and commanded them, "Make a statue of my friend." The statue was fashioned with a great weight of lapis lazuli for the breast and of gold for the body. A table of hard-wood was set out, and on it a bowl of carnelian filled with honey, and a bowl of lapis lazuli filled with butter. These he exposed and offered to the Sun; and weeping he went away.

4

The Search for Everlasting Life

Bitterly Gilgamesh wept for his friend Enkidu; he wandered over the wilderness as a hunter, he roamed over the plains; in his bitterness he cried, "How can I rest, how can I be at peace? Despair is in my heart. What my brother is now, that shall I be when I am dead. Because I am afraid of death I will go as best I can to find Utnapishtim[2] whom they call the Faraway, for he has entered the assembly of the gods." So Gilgamesh travelled over the wilderness, he wandered over the grasslands, a long journey, in search of Utnapishtim, whom the gods took after the deluge; and they set him to live in the land of Dilmun, in the garden of the sun; and to him alone of men they gave everlasting life.

At night when he came to the mountain passes Gilgamesh prayed: "In these mountain passes long ago I saw lions, I was afraid and I lifted my eyes to the moon; I prayed and my prayers went up to the gods, so now, O moon god Sin, protect me." When he had prayed he lay down to sleep, until he was woken from out of a dream. He saw the lions round him glorying in life; then he took his axe in his hand, he drew his sword from his belt, and he fell upon them like an arrow from the string, and struck and destroyed and scattered them.

So at length Gilgamesh came to Mashu, the great mountains about which he had heard many things, which guard the rising and the setting sun. Its twin peaks are as high as the wall of heaven and its paps reach down to the underworld. At its gate the Scorpions stand guard, half man and half dragon;

2. A wise king and priest who, like the biblical Noah, survived the Flood along with his family and with "the seed of all living creatures." Afterward he was taken by the gods to live forever in Dilmun, the Sumerian paradise.

their glory is terrifying, their stare strikes death into men, their shimmering halo sweeps the mountains that guard the rising sun. When Gilgamesh saw them he shielded his eyes for the length of a moment only; then he took courage and approached. When they saw him so undismayed the Man-Scorpion called to his mate, "This one who comes to us now is flesh of the gods." The mate of the Man-Scorpion answered, "Two thirds is god but one third is man."

Then he called to the man Gilgamesh, he called to the child of the gods: "Why have you come so great a journey; for what have you travelled so far, crossing the dangerous waters; tell me the reason for your coming?" Gilgamesh answered, "For Enkidu; I loved him dearly, together we endured all kinds of hardships; on his account I have come, for the common lot of man has taken him. I have wept for him day and night, I would not give up his body for burial, I thought my friend would come back because of my weeping. Since he went, my life is nothing; that is why I have travelled here in search of Utnapishtim my father; for men say he has entered the assembly of the gods, and has found everlasting life. I have a desire to question him concerning the living and the dead." The Man-Scorpion opened his mouth and said, speaking to Gilgamesh, "No man born of woman has done what you have asked, no mortal man has gone into the mountain; the length of it is twelve leagues of darkness; in it there is no light, but the heart is oppressed with darkness. From the rising of the sun to the setting of the sun there is no light." Gilgamesh said, "Although I should go in sorrow and in pain, with sighing and with weeping, still I must go. Open the gate of the mountain." And the Man-Scorpion said, "Go, Gilgamesh, I permit you to pass through the mountain of Mashu and through the high ranges; may your feet carry you safely home. The gate of the mountain is open."

When Gilgamesh heard this he did as the Man-Scorpion had said, he followed the sun's road to his rising, through the mountain. When he had gone one league the darkness became thick around him, for there was no light, he could see nothing ahead and nothing behind him. After two leagues the darkness was thick and there was no light, he could see nothing ahead and nothing behind him. After three leagues the darkness was thick, and there was no light, he could see nothing ahead and nothing behind him. After four leagues the darkness was thick and there was no light, he could see nothing ahead and nothing behind him. At the end of five leagues the darkness was thick and there was no light, he could see nothing ahead and nothing behind him. At the end of six leagues the darkness was thick and there was no light, he could see nothing ahead and nothing behind him. When he had gone seven leagues the darkness was thick and there was no light, he could see nothing ahead and nothing behind him. When he had gone eight leagues Gilgamesh gave a great cry, for the darkness was thick and he could see nothing ahead and nothing behind him. After nine leagues he felt the north wind on his face, but the darkness was thick and there was no light, he could see nothing ahead and nothing behind him. After ten leagues the end was near. After eleven leagues the dawn light appeared. At the end of twelve leagues the sun streamed out.

There was the garden of the gods; all round him stood bushes bearing gems. Seeing it he went down at once, for there was fruit of carnelian with the vine hanging from it, beautiful to look at; lapis lazuli leaves hung thick with fruit, sweet to see. For thorns and thistles there were haematite and rare stones, agate, and pearls from out of the sea. While Gilgamesh walked in the garden by the edge of the sea Shamash saw him, and he saw that he was dressed in the skins of animals and ate their flesh. He was distressed, and he spoke and said, "No mortal man has gone this way before, nor will, as long as the winds drive over the sea." And to Gilgamesh he said, "You will never find the life for which you are searching." Gilgamesh said to glorious Shamash, "Now that I have toiled and strayed so far over the wilderness, am I to sleep, and let the earth cover my head for ever? Let my eyes see the sun until they are dazzled with looking. Although I am no better than a dead man, still let me see the light of the sun."

Beside the sea she lives, the woman of the vine, the maker of wine; Siduri sits in the garden at the edge of the sea, with the golden bowl and the golden vats that the gods gave her. She is covered with a veil; and where she sits she sees Gilgamesh coming towards her, wearing skins, the flesh of the gods in his body, but despair in his heart, and his face like the face of one who has made a long journey. She looked, and as she scanned the distance she said in her own heart, "Surely this is some felon; where is he going now?" And she barred her gate against him with the cross-bar and shot home the bolt. But Gilgamesh, hearing the sound of the bolt, threw up his head and lodged his foot in the gate; he called to her, "Young woman, maker of wine, why do you bolt your door; what did you see that made you bar your gate? I will break in your door and burst in your gate, for I am Gilgamesh who seized and killed the Bull of Heaven, I killed the watchman of the cedar forest, I overthrew Humbaba who lived in the forest, and I killed the lions in the passes of the mountain."

Then Siduri said to him, "If you are that Gilgamesh who seized and killed the Bull of Heaven, who killed the watchman of the cedar forest, who overthrew Humbaba that lived in the forest, and killed the lions in the passes of the mountain, why are your cheeks so starved and why is your face so drawn? Why is despair in your heart and your face like the face of one who has made a long journey? Yes, why is your face burned from heat and cold, and why do you come here wandering over the pastures in search of the wind?"

Gilgamesh answered her, "And why should not my cheeks be starved and my face drawn? Despair is in my heart and my face is the face of one who has made a long journey, it was burned with heat and with cold. Why should I not wander over the pastures in search of the wind? My friend, my younger brother, he who hunted the wild ass of the wilderness and the panther of the plains, my friend, my younger brother who seized and killed the Bull of Heaven and overthrew Humbaba in the cedar forest, my friend who was very dear to me and who endured dangers beside me, Enkidu my brother, whom I loved, the end of mortality has overtaken him. I wept for him seven days and nights till the worm fastened on him. Because of my brother I am afraid of death, because of my brother I stray through the wilderness and cannot rest. But now, young woman, maker of wine, since I have seen your face do not let me see the face of death which I dread so much."

She answered, "Gilgamesh, where are you hurrying to? You will never find that life for which you are looking. When the gods created man they allotted to him death, but life they retained in their own keeping. As for you, Gilgamesh, fill your belly with good things; day and night, night and day, dance and be merry, feast and rejoice. Let your clothes be fresh, bathe yourself in water, cherish the little child that holds your hand, and make your wife happy in your embrace; for this too is the lot of man."

But Gilgamesh said to Siduri, the young woman, "How can I be silent, how can I rest, when Enkidu whom I love is dust, and I too shall die and be laid in the earth. You live by the sea-shore and look into the heart of it; young woman, tell me now, which is the way to Utnapishtim, the son of Ubara-Tutu? What directions are there for the passage; give me, oh, give me directions. I will cross the Ocean if it is possible; if it is not I will wander still farther in the wilderness." The wine-maker said to him, "Gilgamesh, there is no crossing the Ocean; whoever has come, since the days of old, has not been able to pass that sea. The Sun in his glory crosses the Ocean, but who beside Shamash has ever crossed it? The place and the passage are difficult, and the waters of death are deep which flow between. Gilgamesh, how will you cross the Ocean? When you come to the waters of death what will you do? But Gilgamesh, down in the woods you will find Urshanabi, the ferryman of Utnapishtim; with him are the holy things, the things of stone. He is fashioning the serpent prow of the boat. Look at him well, and if it is possible, perhaps you will cross the waters with him; but if it is not possible, then you must go back."

When Gilgamesh heard this he was seized with anger. He took his axe in his hand, and his dagger from his belt. He crept forward and he fell on them like a javelin. Then he went into the forest and sat down. Urshanabi saw the dagger flash and heard the axe, and he beat his head, for Gilgamesh had shattered the tackle of the boat in his rage. Urshanabi said to him, "Tell me, what is your name? I am Urshanabi, the ferryman of Utnapishtim the Far-away." He replied to him, "Gilgamesh is my name, I am from Uruk, from the house of Anu." Then Urshanabi said to him, "Why are your cheeks so starved and your face drawn? Why is despair in your heart and your face like the face of one who has made a long journey; yes, why is your face burned with heat and with cold, and why do you come here wandering over the pastures in search of the wind?"

Gilgamesh said to him, "Why should not my cheeks be starved and my face drawn? Despair is in my heart, and my face is the face of one who has made a long journey. I was burned with heat and with cold. Why should I not wander over the pastures? My friend, my younger brother who seized and killed the Bull of Heaven, and overthrew Humbaba in the cedar forest, my friend who was very dear to me, and who endured dangers beside me, Enkidu my brother whom I loved, the end of mortality has overtaken him. I wept for him seven days and nights till the worm fastened on him. Because of my brother I am afraid of death, because of my brother I stray through the wilderness. His fate lies heavy upon me. How can I be silent, how can I rest? He is dust and I too shall die and be laid in the earth for ever. I am afraid of death, therefore, Urshanabi, tell me which is the road to Utnapishtim? If it is possible I will cross the waters of death; if not I will wander still farther through the wilderness."

Urshanabi said to him, "Gilgamesh, your own hands have prevented you from crossing the Ocean; when you destroyed the tackle of the boat you destroyed its safety." Then the two of them talked it over and Gilgamesh said, "Why are you so angry with me, Urshanabi, for you yourself cross the sea by day and night, at all seasons you cross it." "Gilgamesh, those things you destroyed, their property is to carry me over the water, to prevent the waters of death from touching me. It was for this reason that I preserved them, but you have destroyed them, and the *urnu* snakes with them. But now, go into the forest, Gilgamesh; with your axe cut poles, one hundred and twenty, cut them sixty cubits long, paint them with bitumen, set on them ferrules and bring them back."

When Gilgamesh heard this he went into the forest, he cut poles one hundred and twenty; he cut them sixty cubits long, he painted them with bitumen, he set on them ferrules, and he brought them to Urshanabi. Then they boarded the boat, Gilgamesh and Urshanabi together, launching it out on the waves of Ocean. For three days they ran on as it were a journey of a month and fifteen days, and at last Urshanabi brought the boat to the waters of death. Then Urshanabi said to Gilgamesh, "Press on, take a pole and thrust it in, but do not let your hands touch the waters. Gilgamesh, take a second pole, take a third, take a fourth pole. Now, Gilgamesh, take a fifth, take a sixth and seventh pole. Gilgamesh, take an eighth, and ninth, a tenth pole. Gilgamesh, take an eleventh, take a twelfth pole." After one hundred and twenty thrusts Gilgamesh had used the last pole. Then he stripped himself, he held up his arms for a mast and his covering for a sail. So Urshanabi the ferryman brought Gilgamesh to Utnapishtim, whom they call the Faraway, who lives in Dilmun at the place of the sun's transit, eastward of the mountain. To him alone of men the gods had given everlasting life.

Now Utnapishtim, where he lay at ease, looked into the distance and he said in his heart, musing to himself, "Why does the boat sail here without tackle and mast; why are the sacred stones destroyed, and why does the master not sail the boat? That man who comes is none of mine; where I look I see a man whose body is covered with skins of beasts. Who is this who walks up the shore behind Urshanabi, for surely he is no man of mine?" So Utnapishtim looked at him and said, "What is your name, you who come here wearing the skins of beasts, with your cheeks starved and your face drawn? Where are you hurrying to now? For what reason have you made this great journey, crossing the seas whose passage is difficult? Tell me the reason for your coming."

He replied, "Gilgamesh is my name. I am from Uruk, from the house of Anu." Then Utnapishtim said to him, "If you are Gilgamesh, why are your cheeks so starved and your face drawn? Why is despair in your heart and your face like the face of one who has made a long journey? Yes, why is your face burned with heat and cold; and why do you come here, wandering over the wilderness in search of the wind?"

Gilgamesh said to him, "Why should not my cheeks be starved and my face drawn? Despair is in my heart and my face is the face of one who has made a long journey. It was burned with heat and with cold. Why should I not wander over the pastures? My friend, my younger brother who seized and killed the Bull of Heaven and overthrew Humbaba in the cedar forest, my friend who was very dear to me and endured dangers beside me, Enkidu, my brother whom I loved, the end of mortality has overtaken him. I wept for him seven days and nights till the worm fastened on him. Because of my brother I am afraid of death; because of my brother I stray through the wilderness. His fate lies heavy upon me. How can I be silent, how can I rest?

He is dust and I shall die also and be laid in the earth for ever." Again Gilgamesh said, speaking to Utnapishtim, "It is to see Utnapishtim whom we call the Faraway that I have come this journey. For this I have wandered over the world, I have crossed many difficult ranges, I have crossed the seas, I have wearied myself with travelling; my joints are aching, and I have lost acquaintance with sleep which is sweet. My clothes were worn out before I came to the house of Siduri. I have killed the bear and hyena, the lion and panther, the tiger, the stag and the ibex, all sorts of wild game and the small creatures of the pastures. I ate their flesh and I wore their skins; and that was how I came to the gate of the young woman, the maker of wine, who barred her gate of pitch and bitumen against me. But from her I had news of the journey; so then I came to Urshanabi the ferryman, and with him I crossed over the waters of death. O, father Utnapishtim, you who have entered the assembly of the gods, I wish to question you concerning the living and the dead, how shall I find the life for which I am searching?"

Utnapishtim said, "There is no permanence. Do we build a house to stand for ever, do we seal a contract to hold for all time? Do brothers divide an inheritance to keep for ever, does the flood-time of rivers endure? It is only the nymph of the dragon-fly who sheds her larva and sees the sun in his glory. From the days of old there is no permanence. The sleeping and the dead, how alike they are, they are like a painted death. What is there between the master and the servant when both have fulfilled their doom? When the Anunnaki, the judges, come together, and Mammetun the mother of destinies, together they decree the fates of men. Life and death they allot but the day of death they do not disclose."

Then Gilgamesh said to Utnapishtim the Faraway, "I look at you now, Utnapishtim, and your appearance is no different from mine; there is nothing strange in your features. I thought I should find you like a hero prepared for battle, but you lie here taking your ease on your back. Tell me truly, how was it that you came to enter the company of the gods, and to possess everlasting life?" Utnapishtim said to Gilgamesh, "I will reveal to you a mystery, I will tell you a secret of the gods."

5

The Story of the Flood

"You know the city Shurrupak, it stands on the banks of Euphrates? That city grew old and the gods that were in it were old. There was Anu, lord of the firmament, their father, and warrior Enlil their counsellor, Ninurta the helper, and Ennugi watcher over canals; and with them also was Ea. In those days the world teemed, the people multiplied, the world bellowed like a wild bull, and the great god was aroused by the clamour. Enlil heard the clamour and he said to the gods in council, 'The uproar of mankind is intolerable and sleep is no longer possible by reason of the babel.' So the gods agreed to exterminate mankind. Enlil did this, but Ea because of his oath warned me in a dream. He whispered their words to my house of reeds, 'Reed-house, reed-house! Wall, O wall, hearken reed-house, wall reflect; O man of Shurrupak, son of Ubara-Tutu; tear down your house and build a boat, abandon possessions and look for life, despise worldly goods and save your soul alive. Tear down your house, I say, and build a boat. These are the measurements of the barque as you shall build her: let her beam equal her length, let her deck be roofed like the vault that covers the abyss; then take up into the boat the seed of all living creatures.'

"When I had understood I said to my lord, 'Behold what you have commanded I will honour and perform, but how shall I answer the people, the city, the elders?' Then Ea opened his mouth and said to me, his servant, 'Tell them this: I have learnt that Enlil is wrathful against me, I dare no longer walk in his land nor live in his city; I will go down to the Gulf to dwell with Ea my lord. But on you he will rain down abundance, rare fish and shy wildfowl, a rich harvest-tide. In the evening the rider of the storm will bring you wheat in torrents.'

"In the first light of dawn all my household gathered round me, the children brought pitch and the men whatever was necessary. On the fifth day I laid the keel and the ribs, then I made fast the planking. The ground-space was one acre, each side of the deck measured one hundred and twenty cubits, making a square. I built six decks below, seven in all, I divided them into nine sections with bulkheads between. I drove in wedges where needed, I saw to the punt-poles, and laid in supplies. The carriers brought oil in baskets, I poured pitch into the furnace and asphalt and oil; more oil was consumed in caulking, and more again the master of the boat took into his stores. I slaughtered bullocks for the people and every day I killed sheep. I gave the shipwrights wine to drink as though it were river water, raw wine and red wine and oil and white wine. There was feasting then as there is at the time of the New Year's festival; I myself anointed my head. On the eleventh day the boat was complete.

"Then was the launching full of difficulty; there was shifting of ballast above and below till two thirds was submerged. I loaded into her all that I had of gold and of living things, my family, my kin, the beast of the field both wild and tame, and all the craftsmen. I sent them on board, for the time that Shamash had ordained was already fulfilled when he said, 'In the evening, when the rider of the storm sends down the destroying rain, enter the boat and batten her down.' The time was fulfilled, the evening came, the rider of the storm sent down the rain. I looked out at the weather and it was terrible, so I too boarded the boat and battened her down. All was now complete, the battening and the caulking; so I handed the tiller to Puzur-Amurri the steersman, with the navigation and the care of the whole boat.

"With the first light of dawn a black cloud came from the horizon; it thundered within where Adad, lord of the storm was riding. In front over hill and plain Shullat and Hanish, heralds of the storm, led on. Then the gods of the abyss rose up; Nergal pulled out the dams of the nether waters, Ninurta the war-lord threw down the dykes, and the seven judges of hell, the Annunaki, raised their torches, lighting the land with their livid flame. A stupor of despair went up to heaven when the god of the storm turned daylight to darkness, when he smashed the land like a cup. One whole day the tempest raged, gathering fury as it went, it poured over the people like the tides of battle; a man could not see his brother nor the people be seen from heaven. Even the gods were terrified at the flood, they fled to the highest heaven, the firmament of Anu; they crouched against the walls, cowering like curs. Then Ishtar the sweet-voiced Queen of Heaven cried out like a woman in travail: 'Alas the days of old are turned to dust because I commanded evil; why did I command this evil in the council of all the gods? I commanded wars to destroy the people, but are they not my people, for I brought them forth? Now like the spawn of fish they float in the ocean.' The great gods of heaven and of hell wept, they covered their mouths.

"For six days and six nights the winds blew, torrent and tempest and flood overwhelmed the world, tempest and flood raged together like warring hosts. When the seventh day dawned the storm from the south subsided, the sea grew calm, the flood was stilled; I looked at the face of the world and there was silence, all mankind was turned to clay. The surface of the sea stretched as flat as a roof-top; I opened a hatch and the light fell on my face. Then I bowed low, I sat down and I wept, the tears streamed down my face, for on every side was the waste of water. I looked for land in vain, for fourteen leagues distant there appeared a mountain, and there the boat grounded; on the mountain of Nisir the boat held fast, she held fast and did not budge. One day she held, and a second day on the mountain of Nisir she held fast and did not budge. A third day, and a fourth day she held fast on the mountain and did not budge; a fifth day and a sixth day she held fast on the mountain. When the seventh day dawned I loosed a dove and let her go. She flew away, but finding no resting-place she returned. Then I loosed a swallow, and she flew away but finding no resting-place she returned. I loosed a raven, she saw that the waters had retreated, she ate, she flew around, she cawed, and she did not come back. Then I threw everything open to the four winds, I made a sacrifice and poured out a libation on the mountain top. Seven and again seven cauldrons I set up on their stands, I heaped up wood and cane and cedar and myrtle. When the gods smelled the sweet savour, they gathered like flies over the sacrifice. Then, at last, Ishtar also came, she lifted her necklace with the jewels of heaven that once Anu had made to please her. 'O you gods here present, by the lapis lazuli round my neck I shall remember these days as I remember the jewels of my throat; these last days I shall not forget. Let all the gods gather round the sacrifice, except Enlil. He shall not approach this offering, for without reflection he brought the flood; he consigned my people to destruction."

"When Enlil had come, when he saw the boat, he was wrath and swelled with anger at the gods, the host of heaven, 'Has any of these mortals escaped? Not one was to have survived the destruction.' Then the god of the wells and canals Ninurta opened his mouth and said to the warrior Enlil, 'Who is there of the gods that can devise without Ea? It is Ea, alone who knows all things.' Then Ea opened his mouth and spoke to warrior Enlil, 'Wisest of gods, hero Enlil, how could you so senselessly bring down the flood?

Lay upon the sinner his sin,
Lay upon the transgressor his transgression,
Punish him a little when he breaks loose,
Do not drive him too hard or he perishes;
Would that a lion had ravaged mankind
Rather than the flood,
Would that a wolf had ravaged mankind
Rather than the flood,
Would that famine had wasted the world

Rather than the flood,
Would that pestilence had wasted mankind
Rather than the flood.

It was not I that revealed the secret of the gods; the wise man learned it in a dream. Now take your counsel what shall be done with him.'

"Then Enlil went up into the boat, he took me by the hand and my wife and made us enter the boat and kneel down on either side, he standing between us. He touched our foreheads to bless us saying, 'In time past Utnapishtim was a mortal man; henceforth he and his wife shall live in the distance at the mouth of the rivers.' Thus it was that the gods took me and placed me here to live in the distance, at the mouth of the rivers."

6

The Return

Utnapishtim said, "As for you, Gilgamesh, who will assemble the gods for your sake, so that you may find that life for which you are searching? But if you wish, come and put it to the test: only prevail against sleep for six days and seven nights." But while Gilgamesh sat there resting on his haunches, a mist of sleep like soft wool teased from the fleece drifted over him, and Utnapishtim said to his wife, "Look at him now, the strong man who would have everlasting life, even now the mists of sleep are drifitng over him." His wife replied, "Touch the man to wake him, so that he may return to his own land in peace, going back through the gate by which he came." Utnapishtim said to his wife, "All men are deceivers, even you he will attempt to deceive; therefore bake loaves of bread, each day one loaf, and put it beside his head; and make a mark on the wall to number the days he has slept."

So she baked loaves of bread, each day one loaf, and put it beside his head, and she marked on the walls the days that he slept; and there came a day when the first loaf was hard, the second loaf was like leather, the third was soggy, the crust of the fourth had mould, the fifth was mildewed, the sixth was fresh, and the seventh was still on the embers. Then Utnapishtim touched him and he woke. Gilgamesh said to Utnapishtim the Faraway, "I hardly slept when you touched and roused me." But Utnapishtim said, "Count these loaves and learn how many days you slept, for your first is hard, your second like leather, your third is soggy, the crust of your fourth has mould, your fifth is mildewed, your sixth is fresh and your seventh was still over the glowing embers when I touched and woke you." Gilgamesh said, "What shall I do, O Utnapishtim, where shall I go? Already the thief in the night has hold of my limbs, death inhabits my room; wherever my foot rests, there I find death."

Then Utnapishtim spoke to Urshanabi the ferryman: "Woe to you Urshanabi, now and for ever more you have become hateful to this harbourage; it is not for you, nor for you are the crossings of this sea. Go now, banished from the shore. But this man before whom you walked, bringing him here, whose body is covered with foulness and the grace of whose limbs has been spoiled by wild skins, take him to the washing-place. There he shall wash his long hair clean as snow in the water, he shall throw off his skins and let the sea carry them away, and the beauty of his body shall be shown, the fillet on his forehead shall be renewed, and he shall be given clothes to cover his nakedness. Till he reaches his own city and his journey is accomplished, these clothes will show no sign of age, they will wear like a new garment." So Urshanabi took Gilgamesh and led him to the washing-place, he washed his long hair as clean as snow in the water, he threw off his skins, which the sea carried away, and showed the beauty of his body. He renewed the fillet on his forehead, and to cover his nakedness gave him clothes which would show no sign of age, but would wear like a new garment till he reached his own city, and his journey was accomplished.

Then Gilgamesh and Urshanabi launched the boat on to the water and boarded it, and they made ready to sail away; but the wife of Utnapishtim the Faraway said to him, "Gilgamesh came here wearied out, he is worn out; what will you give him to carry him back to his own country?" So Utnapishtim spoke, and Gilgamesh took a pole and brought the boat in to the bank. "Gilgamesh, you came here a man wearied out, you have worn yourself out; what shall I give you to carry you back to your own country? Gilgamesh, I shall reveal a secret thing, it is a mystery of the gods that I am telling you. There is a plant that grows under the water, it has a prickle like a thorn, like a rose; it will wound your hands, but if you succeed in taking it, then your hands will hold that which restores his lost youth to a man."

When Gilgamesh heard this he opened the sluices so that a sweet-water current might carry him out to the deepest channel; he tied heavy stones to his feet and they dragged him down to the water-bed. There he saw the plant growing; although it pricked him he took it in his hands; then he cut the heavy stones from his feet, and the sea carried him and threw him on to the shore. Gilgamesh said to Urshanabi the ferryman, "Come here, and see this marvellous plant. By its virtue a man may win back all his former strength. I will take it to Uruk of the strong walls; there I will give it to the old men to eat. Its name shall be 'The Old Men Are Young Again'; and at last I shall eat it myself and have back all my lost youth." So Gilgamesh returned by the gate through which he had come, Gilgamesh and Urshanabi went together. They travelled their twenty leagues and then they broke their fast; after thirty leagues they stopped for the night.

Gilgamesh saw a well of cool water and he went down and bathed; but deep in the pool there was lying a serpent, and the serpent sensed the sweetness of the flower. It rose out of the water and snatched it away, and immediately it sloughed its skin and returned to the well. Then Gilgamesh sat down and wept, the tears ran down his face, and he took the hand of Urshanabi; "O Urshanabi, was it for this that I toiled with my hands, is it for this I have wrung out my heart's blood? For myself I have gained nothing; not I, but the beast of the earth has joy of it now. Already the stream has carried it twenty leagues back to the channels where I found it. I found a sign and now I have lost it. Let us leave the boat on the bank and go."

After twenty leagues they broke their fast, after thirty leagues they stopped for the night; in three days they had walked as much as a journey of a month and fifteen days. When the journey was accomplished they arrived at Uruk, the strong-walled city. Gilgamesh spoke to him, to Urshanabi the ferryman, "Urshanabi, climb up on to the wall of Uruk, inspect its foundation terrace, and examine well the brickwork; see if it is not of burnt bricks; and did not the seven wise men lay these foundations? One third of the whole is city, one third is garden, and one third is field, with the precinct of the goddess Ishtar. These parts and the precinct are all Uruk."

This too was the work of Gilgamesh, the king, who knew the countries of the world. He was wise, he saw mysteries and knew secret things, he brought us a tale of the days before the flood. He went a long journey, was weary, worn out with labour, and returning engraved on a stone the whole story.

7

The Death of Gilgamesh

The destiny was fulfilled which the father of the gods, Enlil of the mountain, had decreed for Gilgamesh: "In nether-earth the darkness will show him a light: of mankind, all that are known, none will leave a monument for generations to come to compare with his. The heroes, the wise men, like the new moon have their waxing and waning. Men will say, 'Who has ever ruled with might and with power like him?' As in the dark month, the month of shadows, so without him there is no light. O Gilgamesh, this was the meaning of your dream. You were given the kingship, such was your destiny, everlasting life was not your destiny. Because of this do not be sad at heart, do not be grieved or oppressed; he has given you power to bind and to loose, to be the darkness and the light of mankind. He has given unexampled supremacy over the people, victory in battle from which no fugitive returns, in forays and assaults from which there is no going back. But do not abuse this power, deal justly with your servants in the palace, deal justly before the face of the Sun."

> The king has laid himself down and will not rise again,
> The Lord of Kullab will not rise again;
> He overcame evil, he will not come again;
> Though he was strong of arm he will not rise again;
>
> He had wisdom and a comely face, he will not come again;
> He is gone into the mountain, he will not come again;
> On the bed of fate he lies, he will not rise again,
> From the couch of many colours he will not come again.

The people of the city, great and small, are not silent; they lift up the lament, all men of flesh and blood lift up the lament. Fate has spoken; like a hooked fish he lies stretched on the bed, like a gazelle that is caught in a noose. Inhuman Namtar is heavy upon him, Namtar that has neither hand nor foot, that drinks no water and eats no meat.

For Gilgamesh, son of Ninsun, they weighed out their offerings; his dear wife, his son, his concubine, his musicians, his jester, and all his household; his servants, his stewards, all who lived in the palace weighed out their offerings for Gilgamesh the son of Ninsun, the heart of Uruk. They weighed out their offerings to Ereshkigal, the Queen of Death, and to all the gods of the dead. To Namtar, who is fate, they weighed out the offering. Bread for Neti the Keeper of the Gate, bread for Ningizzida the god of the serpent, the lord of the Tree of Life; for Dumuzi also, the young shepherd, for Enki and Ninki, for Endukugga and Nindukugga, for Enmul and Ninmul, all the ancestral gods, forbears of Enlil. A feast for Shulpae the god of feasting. For Samuqan, god of the herds, for the mother Ninhursag, and the gods of creation in the place of creation, for the host of heaven, priest and priestess weighed out the offering of the dead.

Gilgamesh, the son of Ninsun, lies in the tomb. At the place of offerings he weighed the bread-offering, at the place of libation he poured out the wine. In those days the lord Gilgamesh departed, the son of Ninsun, the king, peerless, without an equal among men, who did not neglect Enlil his master. O Gilgamesh, lord of Kullab, great is thy praise.

ANCIENT EGYPTIAN POETRY

ca. 1500–ca. 1200 B.C.

The architecture of the ancient Egyptians is well known to us by reason of the vast tombs, temples, and pyramids they built for their pharaohs and gods. Their art is also available to us, both because they left many bas reliefs and paintings on the walls of these temples and tombs and because they filled the burial chambers of their noble and royal dead with a rich variety of objects that were to accompany the dead into the next world. By contrast, the literature of ancient Egypt has survived to us only in scattered fragments, and because of the difficulty of the Egyptian language and writing system (a complex system of stylized pictographs called hieroglyphics), it is far less well known than either the art or the architecture. Yet even that small sample is enough to show that the ancient Egyptians possessed a poetry that was rich and varied in both its subjects and its forms. The largest and earliest group of poems comes from the pyramids that were constructed in the period of the Old Kingdom (ca. 2575–2130 B.C.). They include narratives, incantations, and invocations designed to help the pharaoh's soul on its journey to the other world. Despite their value in illuminating early Egyptian religious beliefs, the poems are prosaic and repetitive. Of far greater appeal are the lyrics, narratives, and devotional poems that were composed during the millennium that includes all the dynasties of the Middle and New Kingdoms (ca. 2130–1200 B.C.).

AKHENATEN'S "HYMN TO THE SUN"

During the reign of Amun-hotep IV—Pharaoh Akhenaten of the Eighteenth Dynasty, who reigned from 1375 to 1358 B.C.—the royal family elevated worship of the sun disc, Aten, above that of other deities and of Amun-Re, the imperial and universal god of the New Kingdom, in particular. Akhenaten built a royal city called Heliopolis (the city of the sun), named it Akhet-Aten in honor of the god, and caused the names of the older gods to be hacked out of inscriptions wherever they appeared throughout the land. Akhenaten emphasized the universal supremacy of the sun, and the images he uses to evoke the scope and depth of Aten's powers suggest an emerging monotheism. At the time, however, the movement was viewed as a return to the royal sun cult of the pyramid builders and was later abandoned as heretical. In the hymn printed here, Akhenaten presents himself as the son of the sun god and the sole interpreter between him and the people of Egypt.

THE LEIDEN HYMNS

The Leiden Hymns cycle of poems appears on a papyrus dated to the fifty-second regnal year of Ramesses II (ca. 1238 B.C.) and so may be dated from this period or somewhat earlier. In *The Leiden Hymns* the poet evokes the image of the sun god—

called Horus, Amun, and Amun-Re—as the one preeminent god, master of all creation, and the father of all other gods. Amun appears in a multitude of forms or incarnations, including those of the other gods: source of the Nile, inseminator of the earth, fashioner of day and night. The poem cycle is in large part built up by the repetition of titles such as these that are associated with individual gods. The effect, however, is to create the image of a god who is greater and more powerful than all individual gods. As the translator of these poems puts it, "He moves in unfathomable ways and takes many forms to human comprehension—as the various poems demonstrate; but though He is hidden from human sight, He is indeed the ultimate godhead, God alone." The poet-theologian who composed these poems uses all these metaphors to evoke the being who created all. One seems to hear in these poems echoes of the language of the Old and New Testaments, although, of course, these poems precede them. Like later Jewish and Christian poets, the author of *The Leiden Hymns* drew on the common stock of human experience to express the inexpressible.

LOVE SONGS

Love songs are the most immediately appealing of all ancient Egyptian poems and need the least explanation. In them one finds the entire range of love's possibilities. The moods and attitudes vary from chaste and idyllic to passionately erotic. Both males and females speak, and thus one sees both sides of love. These pieces all come from the Ramesside period (ca. 1300–1100 B.C.) and derive from small collections or anthologies on papyri, bits of smoothed limestone, and pottery (now in London, Turin, and Cairo). Reading these poems one feels that love has hardly altered at all over the intervening centuries.

The translations here are taken from John L. Foster, *Echoes of Egyptian Voices* (1992) and *Love Songs of Ancient Egypt* (1992). *Echoes* contains an extensive bibliography of works on ancient Egyptian culture in English. Among more general studies of ancient Egyptian culture, Cyril Aldred, *The Egyptians* (1984), is a useful general history by an art historian. B. G. Trigger et al., *Ancient Egypt: A Social History* (1983), is, as its title promises, a work that gives more attention to Egyptian society.

PRONOUNCING GLOSSARY

The following list uses common English syllables and stress accents to provide rough equivalents of selected words whose pronunciation may be unfamiliar to the general reader.

Akhenaten: *ah-ke-nah'-ten*

Amun-hotpe: *ah'-mun–hot'-pay*

Amun-Re: *ah-mun–ray'*

Hapy: *hah'-pee*

Ramesses: *ra'-me-seez*

Akhenaten's "Hymn to the Sun"[1]

I

When in splendor you first took your throne
                high in the precinct of heaven,
    O living God,
                life truly began!
Now from eastern horizon risen and streaming,
    you have flooded the world with your beauty.
You are majestic, awesome, bedazzling, exalted,

1. All selections translated by John L. Foster.

overlord over all earth,
yet your rays, they touch lightly, compass the lands
to the limits of all your creation.
There in the Sun, you reach to the farthest of those
you would gather in for your Son,[2]
whom you love;
Though you are far, your light is wide upon earth;
and you shine in the faces of all
who turn to follow your journeying.

II

When you sink to rest below western horizon
earth lies in darkness like death,
Sleepers are still in bedchambers, heads veiled,
eye cannot spy a companion;
All their goods could be stolen away,
heads heavy there, and they never knowing!
Lions come out from the deeps of their caves,
snakes bite and sting;
Darkness muffles, and earth is silent:
he who created all things lies low in his tomb.

III

Earth-dawning mounts the horizon,
glows in the sun-disk as day:
You drive away darkness, offer your arrows of shining,
and the Two Lands[3] are lively with morningsong.
Sun's children awaken and stand,
for you, golden light, have upraised the sleepers;
Bathed are their bodies, who dress in clean linen,
their arms held high to praise your Return.
Across the face of the earth
they go to their crafts and professions.

IV

The herds are at peace in their pastures,
trees and the vegetation grow green;
Birds start from their nests,
wings wide spread to worship your Person;
Small beasts frisk and gambol, and all
who mount into flight or settle to rest
live, once you have shone upon them;
Ships float downstream or sail for the south,
each path lies open because of your rising;
Fish in the River leap in your sight,
and your rays strike deep in the Great Green Sea.[4]

2. Pharoah Akhenaten. 3. Upper and Lower Egypt. 4. The Mediterranean.

V

It is *you* create the new creature in Woman,
shape the life-giving drops into Man,
Foster the son in the womb of his mother,
soothe him, ending his tears;
Nurse through the long generations of women
to those given Air,[5]
you ensure that your handiwork prosper.
When the new one descends from the womb
to draw breath the day of its birth,
You open his mouth,
make him aware of life newly given,
for you determine his destiny.

VI

Hark to the chick in the egg,
he who speaks in the shell!
You give him air within
to save and prosper him;
And you have allotted to him his set time
before the shell shall be broken;
Then out from the egg he comes,
from the egg to peep at his natal hour!
and up on his own two feet goes he
when at last he struts forth therefrom.

VII

How various is the world you have created,
each thing mysterious, sacred to sight,
O sole God,
beside whom is no other!
You fashioned earth to your heart's desire,
while you were still alone,
Filled it with man and the family of creatures,
each kind on the ground, those who go upon feet,
he on high soaring on wings,
The far lands of Khor and Kush,[6]
and the rich Black Land of Egypt.

VIII

And you place each one in his proper station,
where you minister to his needs;
Each has his portion of food,
and the years of life are reckoned him.
Tongues are divided by words,

5. That is, life. 6. In the Nubian region in the Sudan, which is to the south. Khor is Syro-Palestine in the northeast.

natures made diverse as well,
Even men's skins are different
that you might distinguish the nations.

IX

You make Hapy,[7] the Nile, stream through the underworld,
and bring him, with whatever fullness you will,
To preserve and nourish the People
in the same skilled way you fashion them.
You are Lord of each one,
who wearies himself in their service,
Yet Lord of all earth, who shines for them all,
Sun-disk of day, Great Lightener!
All of the far foreign countries—
you are the cause they live,
For you have put a Nile in the sky
that he might descend upon them in rain—
He makes waves on the very mountains
like waves on the Great Green Sea
to water their fields and their villages.

X

How splendidly ordered are they,
your purposes for this world,
O Lord of eternity, Hapy in heaven!
Although you belong to the distant peoples,
to the small shy beasts
who travel the deserts and uplands,
Yet Hapy, he comes from Below
for the dear Land of Egypt as well.
And your Sunlight nurses each field and meadow:
when you shine, they live,
they grow sturdy and prosper through you.
You set seasons to let the world flower and flourish—
winter to rest and refresh it,
the hot blast of summer to ripen;
And you have made heaven far off
in order to shine down therefrom,
in order to watch over all your creation.

XI

You are the one God,
shining forth from your possible incarnations
as Aten, the Living Sun,
Revealed like a king in glory, risen in light,
now distant, now bending nearby.
You create the numberless things of this world

7. God of the Nile's flooding.

from yourself, who are One alone—
cities, towns, fields, the roadway, the River;
And each eye looks back and beholds you
to learn from the day's light perfection.
O God, you are in the Sun-disk of Day,
Over-Seer of all creation
—your legacy
passed on to all who shall ever be;
For you fashioned their sight, who perceive your universe,
that they praise with one voice
all your labors.

XII

And you are in my heart;
there is no other who truly knows you
but for your son, Akhenaten.
May you make him wise with your inmost counsels,
wise with your power,
that earth may aspire to your godhead,
its creatures fine as the day you made them.
Once you rose into shining, they lived;
when you sink to rest, they shall die.
For it is you who are Time itself,
the span of the world;
life is by means of you.

Eyes are filled with Beauty
until you go to your rest;
All work is laid aside
as you sink down the western horizon.
Then, Shine reborn! Rise splendidly!
my Lord, let life thrive for the King!
For I have kept pace with your every footstep
since you first measured ground for the world.
Lift up the creatures of earth for your Son
who came forth from your Body of Fire!

The Leiden Hymns

[How splendid you ferry the skyways]

How splendid you ferry the skyways,
Horus of Twin Horizons,[1]
The needs of each new day
firm in your timeless pattern,

1. Dawn and dusk. Horus is the hawk-headed sun god.

Who fashion the years,
weave months into order—
Days, nights, and the very hours
move to the gait of your striding.

Refreshed by your diurnal shining, you quicken,
bright above yesterday,
Making the zone of night sparkle
although you belong to the light,
Sole one awake there
—sleep is for mortals,
Who go to rest grateful:
your eyes oversee.
And theirs by the millions you open
when your face new-rises, beautiful;
Not a bypath escapes your affection
during your season on earth.

Stepping swift over stars,
riding the lightning flash,
You circle the earth in an instant,
with a god's ease crossing heaven,
Treading dark paths of the underworld,
yet, sun on each roadway,
You deign to walk daily with men.

The faces of all are upturned to you,
As mankind and gods
alike lift their morningsong:
"Lord of the daybreak,
Welcome!"

[God is a master craftsman]

God is a master craftsman;
yet none can draw the lines of his Person.
Fair features first came into being
in the hushed dark where he mused alone;
He forged his own figure there,
hammered his likeness out of himself—
All powerful one (yet kindly,
whose heart would lie open to men).

He mingled his heavenly god-seed
with the inmost parts of his being.
Planting his image there
in the unknown depths of his mystery.
He cared, and the sacred form
took shape and contour, splendid at birth!
God, skilled in the intricate ways of the craftsman,
first fashioned Himself to perfection.

[When Being began back in the days of the genesis]

When Being began back in days of the genesis,
it was Amun appeared first of all,
unknown his mode of inflowing;
There was no god come before him,
nor was other god with him there
when he uttered himself into visible form;
There was no mother to him, that she might have borne him his name,
there was no father to father the one
who first spoke the words, "I Am!"
Who fashioned the seed of him all on his own,
sacred first cause, whose birth lay in mystery,
who crafted and carved his own splendor—
He is God the Creator, self-created, the Holy;
all other gods came after;
with Himself he began the world.

[The mind of God is perfect knowing]

The mind of God is perfect knowing,
his lips its flawless expression,
all that exists is his spirit,
by his tongue named into being;
He strides, and hollows under his feet become Nile-heads—
Hapy[1] wells from the hidden grotto into his footprints.
His soul is all space,
his heart the lifegiving moisture,
he is falcon of twin horizons,
sky god skimming heaven,
His right eye the day,
while his left is the night,
and he guides human seeing down every way.
His body is Nun, the swirling original waters;
within it the Nile
shaping, bringing to birth,
fostering all creation;
His burning breath is the breeze,
gift offered every nostril,
from him too the destiny fallen to each;
His consort the fertile field,
he shoots his seed into her,
and new vegetation, and grain,
growing strong as his children.
Fruitful One, Eldest,
he fathered gods in those first days,
whose faces turn to him
daily and everywhere.

1. God of the annual flooding of the Nile.

That countenance still shines on mankind and deities,
and it mirrors the sum of the world.

LOVE SONGS

[My love is one and only, without peer]

My love is one and only, without peer,
lovely above all Egypt's lovely girls.
On the horizon of my seeing,
see her, rising,
Glistening goddess of the sunrise star
bright in the forehead of a lucky year.
So there she stands, epitome
of shining, shedding light,
Her eyebrows, gleaming darkly, marking
eyes which dance and wander.
Sweet are those lips, which chatter
(but never a word too much),
And the line of the long neck lovely, dropping
(since song's notes slide that way)
To young breasts firm in the bouncing light
which shimmers that blueshadowed sidefall of hair.
And slim are those arms, overtoned with gold,
those fingers which touch like a brush of lotus.
And (ah) how the curve of her back slips gently
by a whisper of waist to god's plenty below.
(Such thighs as hers pass knowledge
of loveliness known in the old days.)
Dressed in the perfect flesh of woman
(heart would run captive to such slim arms),
she ladies it over the earth,
Schooling the neck of each schoolboy male
to swing on a swivel to see her move.
(He who could hold that body tight
would know at last
perfection of delight—
Best of the bullyboys,
first among lovers.)
Look you, all men, at that golden going,
like Our Lady of Love,
without peer.

[I wish I were her Nubian girl]

I wish I were her Nubian[1] girl,
one to attend her (bosom companion),

1. In ancient Egypt, Nubians were commonly servants.

Confidante, and a child of discretion:
Close hidden at nightfall we whisper
As (modest by day) she offers
breasts like ripe berries to evening—
Her long gown settles, then, bodiless,
hangs from my helping hand.
O she'll give pleasure! in future
no grown man will deny it!
But tonight, to me, this chaste girl
bares unthinking the delicate blush
Of a most secret landscape,
her woman's body.

[Love, how I'd love to slip down to the pond]

Love, how I'd love to slip down to the pond,
bathe with you close by on the bank.
Just for you I'd wear my new Memphis swimsuit,
made of sheer linen, fit for a queen—
Come see how it looks in the water!

Couldn't I coax you to wade in with me?
Let the cool creep slowly around us?
Then I'd dive deep down
and come up for you dripping,
Let you fill your eyes
with the little red fish that I'd catch.

And I'd say, standing there tall in the shallows:
Look at my fish, love,
how it lies in my hand,
How my fingers caress it,
slip down its sides . . .

But then I'd say softer,
eyes bright with your seeing:
A gift, love. No words.
Come closer and
look, it's all me.

[Why, just now, must you question your heart?]

Why, just now, must you question your heart?
Is it really the time for discussion?
To her, say I,
take her tight in your arms!
For god's sake, sweet man,

it's me coming at you,
My tunic
loose at the shoulder!

[I was simply off to see Nefrus my friend]

I was simply off to see Nefrus my friend,
Just to sit and chat at her place
(about men),
When there, hot on his horses, comes Mehy
(oh god, I said to myself, it's Mehy!)
Right over the crest of the road
wheeling along with the boys.

Oh Mother Hathor, what shall I do?
Don't let him see me!
Where can I hide?
Make me a small creeping thing
to slip by his eye
(sharp as Horus')
unseen.

Oh, look at you, feet—
(this road is a river!)
you walk me right out of my depth!
Someone, silly heart, is exceedingly ignorant here—
aren't you a little too easy near Mehy?

If he sees that I see him, I know
he will know how my heart flutters (Oh, Mehy!)
I know I will blurt out,
"Please take me!"
(I mustn't!)

No, all he would do is brag out my name,
just one of the many . . . (I know) . . .
Mehy would make me just one of the girls
for all of the boys in the palace.
(Oh Mehy)

[I think I'll go home and lie very still]

I think I'll go home and lie very still,
feigning terminal illness.
Then the neighbors will all troop over to stare,
my love, perhaps, among them.
How she'll smile while the specialists
snarl in their teeth!—
she perfectly well knows what ails me.

[Love of you is mixed deep in my vitals]

Love of you is mixed deep in my vitals,
    like water stirred into flour for bread,
Like simples compound in a sweet-tasting drug,
    like pastry and honey mixed to perfection.
Oh, hurry to look at your love!
    Be like horses charging in battle,
Like a gardener up with the sun
    burning to watch his prize bud open.
High heaven causes a girl's lovelonging.
    It is like being too far from the light,
Far from the hearth of familiar arms.
    It is this being so tangled in you.

THE BIBLE: THE OLD TESTAMENT
ca. 1000–300 B.C.

THE CREATION–THE FALL

The religious attitudes of the Hebrews appear in the story that they told of the creation of the world and of humankind. This creation is the work of one God, who is omnipotent and omniscient and who creates a perfect and harmonious order. The disorder that we see all around us, physical and moral, is not God's creation but Adam and Eve's; it is the consequence of humankind's disobedience. The story not only reconciles the undeniable existence of evil and disorder in the world with the conception of God's infinite justice but also attributes to humanity itself an independence of God, free will, which in this case had been used for evil. The Hebrew God is not limited in His power by other deities, who oppose His will (as in the Greek stories of Zeus and his undisciplined family); His power over inanimate nature is infinite. In all the range of His creation there is only one being able to resist Him—humankind.

Because God is all-powerful, even this resistance on Adam and Eve's part is in some mysterious way a manifestation of God's will. How this can be is not explained by the story, and we are left with the mystery that still eludes us, the coexistence of God's prescient power and humanity's unrestricted free will.

The story of the Fall ends with a situation in which Adam and Eve have earned for themselves and their descendants a short life of sorrow relieved only by death. It was the achievement of later Hebrew teachers to carry the story on and develop the concept of a God who is as merciful as He is just, who watches tenderly over the destinies of the creatures who have rebelled against Him, and who brings about the possibility of atonement and full reconciliation.

Adam and Eve's son Cain is the first person to shed human blood, but though God drives him out to be a wanderer on the face of the earth, He does not kill him. The brand on Cain's forehead, while it marks him as a murderer, also protects his life—no one is to touch him. Later when the descendants of Adam and Eve grow so wicked that God is sorry He has created the human race, He decides to destroy it by sending a universal flood. But He spares Noah and his family to beget a new human race, on which God pins His hopes. His rainbow in the sky reminds humankind of His promise that He will never again let loose the waters. But people do not learn their lesson: they start to build a tower high enough to reach to Heaven, and God is afraid that if they succeed they will then recognize no limit to their ambitions. Yet He does not destroy them; He merely frustrates their purpose by depriving them of their common language.

Intertwined with these lessons about humankind's proper relations to God is a generational process that eventually concentrates on the origins and development of the Hebrews as God's chosen people. This part of the story begins with Abraham's willingness to sacrifice his only son, Isaac. It continues through the rivalry in which Isaac's son Jacob supplants his brother Esau, and it culminates in the trials and ultimate prosperity of Jacob's son Joseph.

JOSEPH

Joseph, his father's favorite son, has a sense of his own great destiny, confirmed by his dreams, which represent him as the first of all his race. He is indeed to be the first, but to become so he must also be the last. He is sold into slavery by his brothers; the savior is rejected by those whom he is to save, as the Hebrews were rejected by their neighbors and as they rejected their own prophets.

With the loss of his liberty, Joseph's trials have only begun. In Egypt, after making a new and successful life for himself, he is thrown into prison on a false accusation. He interprets the dream of Pharaoh's butler, who promises, if his interpretation is correct, to secure his release; the butler is restored to freedom and royal favor but, as is the way of the world, forgets his promise and leaves his comforter in jail. Joseph stays in prison two more years but finally obtains his freedom and becomes Pharaoh's most trusted adviser. When his brothers come from starving Palestine and bow down before him asking for help, he saves them; not only does he give them grain but he also provides a home for his people in Egypt. "I am Joseph your brother, whom ye sold into Egypt," he says to them when he reveals his identity. "God sent me before you to preserve you a posterity in the earth, and to save your lives by a great deliverance."

One of the essential points of this story is the distinction that it emphasizes between an external, secular standard of good and a spiritual, religious standard. In the eyes of the average person, prosperity and righteousness are connected, if not identified, and the sufferer is felt to be one whose misfortune must be explained as a punishment for his or her wickedness. This feeling is strong in ancient (and especially in Greek) literature, but we should not be unduly complacent about our superiority to the ancients in this respect, for the attitude is still with us. It is in fact a basic assumption of a competitive society—the view, seldom expressed but strongly rooted, that the plight of the unfortunate is the result of their own laziness, the wealth of the rich the reward of superior virtue.

The writer of the Joseph story sees in the unfortunate sufferer the savior who is the instrument of God's will. The story does not emphasize the sufferings of Joseph; he is pictured rather as the man of action who through native ability and divine protection turns the injuries done him into advantages. We are not made to feel the torment in his soul. When he weeps it is because of the memory of what he had suffered and his yearning for his youngest brother, and he is in full control of the situation. And his reward in the things of this world is great. Not only does he reveal himself as the savior of his nation but he becomes rich and powerful beyond his brothers' dreams, and in a great kingdom. The spiritual and secular standards are at the end of the story combined; Joseph's suffering is neatly balanced by his worldly reward.

JOB

Later Hebrew writers developed a sadder and profounder view. The greatest literary masterpiece of the Old Testament, the Book of Job, is also concerned with the inadequacy of worldly standards of happiness and righteousness; but the suffering of Job is so overwhelming and so magnificently expressed, that even with our knowledge of its purpose and its meaning it seems excessive. Joseph suffered slavery, exile, and imprisonment but turned them all to account. Job loses his family and wealth in a series of calamities, which strike one on the other like hammer blows, and is then plagued with a loathsome disease. Unlike Joseph, he is old; he cannot adapt himself and rise above adverse circumstances, and he no longer wishes to live. Except for one thing: he wishes to understand the reason for his suffering.

For his friends the explanation is simple. With the blindness of men who know no standards other than those of this world, they are sure that Job's misfortune must be the result of some wickedness on his part. But Job is confident in his righteousness; his torture is as much mental as physical. He cannot reconcile the fact of his innocence with the calamities that have come on him with all the decisive suddenness of the hand of God.

The full explanation is never given to him, but it is given to the reader in the two opening chapters of the book. This prologue to the dramatic section of the work gives us the knowledge that is hidden from the participants in the ensuing dialogue. The writer uses the method characteristic of Greek tragedy—irony, the deeper understanding of the dramatic spoken word that is based on the superior knowledge of the audience. The prologue explains God's motive in allowing Job to suffer. It is an important one: God intends to use Job as a demonstration to His skeptical subordinate, Satan, of the fact that a human being can retain faith in God's justice in the face of the greatest imaginable suffering. This motive, which Job does not know and which is never revealed to him, gives to the dialogue between Job and his friends its suspense and its importance. God has rested His case—that humanity is capable of keeping faith in divine justice, against all appearances to the contrary—on this one man.

The arguments of Job's friends are based on the worldly equation that success equals virtue. They attempt to undermine Job's faith, not in God, but in himself. "Who ever perished, being innocent?" asks Eliphaz, "or where were the righteous cut off?" Job's misfortune is a proof that he must have sinned; all he has to do is to admit his guilt and ask God for pardon, which he will surely receive. He refuses to accept this easy way out, and we know that he is right. In fact, we know from the prologue that he has been selected for misfortune not because he has sinned, but precisely because of his outstanding virtue. "There is none like him in the earth," God says, "a perfect and an upright man, one that feareth God, and escheweth evil." What Job must do is to persevere not only in his faith in God's justice but also in the conviction of his own innocence. He must believe the illogical, accept a paradox. His friends are offering him an easy way out, one that seems to be the way of humility and submission. But it is a false way. And God finally tells them so. "The Lord said to Eliphaz the Temanite, My wrath is kindled against thee, and against thy two friends: for ye have not spoken of me the thing that is right, as my servant Job hath."

Job's confidence in his own righteousness is not pride but intellectual honesty. He sees that the problem is much harder than his friends imagine. To let them persuade him of his own guilt would lighten his mental burden by answering the question that tortures him, but his intelligence will not let him yield. Like Oedipus, he refuses to stop short of the truth. He even uses the same words: "let me alone, that I may speak, and let come on me what will." He finally expresses his understanding and acceptance of the paradox involved in the combination of his suffering with his innocence, but he does so with a human independence and dignity: "Though he slay me, yet will I trust in him: but I will maintain mine own ways before him." He sums up his case with a detailed account of the righteousness of his ways, and it is clear that this account is addressed not only to his three friends but also to God. "My desire is, that the Almighty would answer me," he says. His friends are silenced by the majesty and firmness of his statement. They "ceased to answer Job, because he was righteous in his own eyes," but God is moved to reply.

The magnificent poetry of that reply, the voice out of the whirlwind, still does not give Job the full explanation, God's motive in putting him to the torture. It is a triumphant proclamation of God's power and also of His justice, and it silences Job, who accepts it as a sufficient answer. That God does not reveal the key to the riddle even to the man who has victoriously stood the test and vindicated His faith in humanity is perhaps the most significant point in the story. It suggests that there is not and never will be an explanation of human suffering that humankind's intelligence can comprehend. Sufferers must, like Job, cling to their faith in themselves and in God; they must accept the inexplicable fact that their own undeserved suffering is the working of God's justice.

THE SONG OF SONGS

In this great dialogue between lovers, a man and a woman, frankly and in detail, express their appreciation of each other's bodies. The Song of Songs (or Song of Solomon) celebrates human sexuality and love in all their sensual splendor, and human life itself: "for love," it says, "is strong as death." Each of the lovers, again and again, takes inventory of the other's body, describing each part, comparing it to an animal, some feature of the natural landscape, or an aspect of the built human environment, so that we not only feel the power of physical desire but also appreciate the human body and love as harmonious parts of the world. Some of these comparisons are of great natural beauty ("thy belly is like a heap of wheat set about with lilies"); others are extravagant, fantastic ("thy hair is as a flock of goats," "thy teeth are like a flock of sheep," "thy neck is like the tower of David," "thy nose is as the tower of Lebanon"). The concreteness of the imagery and the piling of image upon image make the pair of bodies a figure of the world itself, to be contemplated in wonder.

But the incorporation of this poem in sacred scripture raises the possibility of further meanings, although what these might be is an open question. This challenging and beautiful text has had a long history of divergent interpretations; a medieval Jewish commentator described it as "locks to which the key has been lost." Is it an allegory, and if so, is it a religious or historical allegory? If the former, does it concern the love between God and his chosen people? On the other hand, Christians later understood it to describe the love between Christ and his church, or between God or Christ and the individual soul. The question of allegory is complicated by other uncertainties. Is the text as we have it a single composition or a collection of poems? How are passages to be divided between the pair of lovers? Are there other speakers as well? In addition, many words and phrases in the Hebrew text are ambiguous and obscure. For this reason, English translations differ markedly. The King James version is given here because of its beauty as an English poem and because of its influence on Anglophone literature and music, but readers should be aware that it is not as accurate as modern translations.

Many scholars today consider the Song of Songs one or several love poems, similar in important ways to Middle Eastern marriage songs that were collected early in the twentieth century, and rooted, perhaps, in ancient fertility rituals of the great pagan religions of Asia Minor. But we may want to ask if there are not also aspects of this text that invite an allegorical reading, and whether we have to choose between sensual and more abstract meanings. Where do we draw the line between the literal and figurative meanings of words? Would we always want to? If the Song of Songs is an allegory, it is one that is wonderfully in touch with the world of the senses, as Dante's *Divine Comedy*, another great allegorical poem, is in a different way.

The student will find good background in R. R. Ackroyd and C. F. Evans, eds., *The Cambridge History of the Bible* (1970), vol. 1. R. H. Rowley, *The Growth of the Old Testament* (1950), concentrates on the Old Testament as a whole. The various volumes of *The Anchor Bible* contain modern translations and informative introductions and notes. The volume on the Song of Songs by Marvin Pope (1977) is especially helpful. For Job, see P. Sanders, ed., *Twentieth-Century Interpretations of the Book of Job* (1968). See also Robert Alter and Frank Kermode, eds., *The Literary Guide to the Bible* (1987), and Leland Ryken and Tremper Longman III, eds., *A Complete Literary Guide to the Bible* (1993).

PRONOUNCING GLOSSARY

The following list uses common English syllables and stress accents to provide rough equivalents of selected words whose pronunciation may be unfamiliar to the general reader.

Baalhamon: *bahl-ha'-mon*

Canaan: *kay'-nuhn*

Esau: *ee'-saw*

Euphrates: *yoo-fray'-teez*

Job: *johb*

Tirzah: *teer'-zah*

THE BIBLE: THE OLD TESTAMENT[1]

Genesis 1–3

[*The Creation—The Fall*]

1. In the beginning God created the heaven and the earth. And the earth was without form, and void; and darkness was upon the face of the deep. And the Spirit of God moved upon the face of the waters.

And God said, Let there be light: and there was light. And God saw the light, that it was good: and God divided the light from the darkness. And God called the light Day, and the darkness he called Night. And the evening and the morning were the first day.

And God said, Let there be a firmament in the midst of the waters, and let it divide the waters from the waters. And God made the firmament, and divided the waters which were under the firmament from the waters which were above the firmament:[2] and it was so. And God called the firmament Heaven. And the evening and the morning were the second day.

And God said, Let the waters under the heaven be gathered together unto one place, and let the dry land appear: and it was so. And God called the dry land Earth; and the gathering together of the waters called he Seas: and God saw that it was good. And God said, Let the earth bring forth grass, the herb yielding seed, and the fruit tree yielding fruit after his kind, whose seed is in itself, upon the earth: and it was so. And the earth brought forth grass, and herb yielding seed after his kind, and the tree yielding fruit, whose seed was in itself, after his kind: and God saw that it was good. And the evening and the morning were the third day.

And God said, Let there be lights in the firmament of the heaven to divide the day from the night; and let them be for signs, and for seasons, and for days, and years: and let them be for lights in the firmament of the heaven to

1. The text of these selections is that of the King James, or Authorized, Version of 1611, so called because it was the work of a team of fifty-four scholars named by King James I of England to produce a new translation "appointed to be read in churches." Since that time advances in biblical scholarship have corrected some of the translators' mistakes and substituted clearer versions where their prose is obscure. Yet the superiority of the Authorized Version as literature remains unquestioned; it is one of the greatest literary texts in the history of the English language. It was written at a time when English was at a creative peak—the age of William Shakespeare, Ben Jonson, and John Donne. It was written to be read aloud, as it was in churches and homes, and to be learned by heart, as it was in schools in the English-speaking world for centuries. The echoes of its magnificent rhythms and cadences can be heard in the verse of English poets from John Milton to T. S. Eliot, in the prose of John Bunyan and the speeches of Abraham Lincoln.
2. The sky, which seen from below has the appearance of a ceiling. The waters above are those that come down in the form of rain.

give light upon the earth: and it was so. And God made two great lights; the greater light to rule the day, and the lesser light to rule the night: he made the stars also. And God set them in the firmament of the heaven to give light upon the earth, and to rule over the day and over the night, and to divide the light from the darkness: and God saw that it was good. And the evening and the morning were the fourth day. And God said, Let the waters bring forth abundantly the moving creature that hath life, and fowl that may fly above the earth in the open firmament of heaven. And God created great whales, and every living creature that moveth, which the waters brought forth abundantly, after their kind, and every winged fowl after his kind: and God saw that it was good. And God blessed them, saying, Be fruitful, and multiply, and fill the waters in the seas, and let fowl multiply in the earth. And the evening and the morning were the fifth day.

And God said, Let the earth bring forth the living creature after his kind, cattle, and creeping thing, and beast of the earth after his kind: and it was so. And God made the beast of the earth after his kind, and cattle after their kind, and everything that creepeth upon the earth after his kind: and God saw that it was good.

And God said, Let us make man in our image, after our likeness: and let them have dominion over the fish of the sea, and over the fowl of the air, and over the cattle, and over all the earth, and over every creeping thing that creepeth upon the earth. So God created man in his own image, in the image of God created he him; male and female created he them. And God blessed them, and God said unto them, Be fruitful, and multiply, and replenish the earth, and subdue it: and have dominion over the fish of the sea, and over the fowl of the air, and over every living thing that moveth upon the earth.

And God said, Behold, I have given you every herb bearing seed, which is upon the face of all the earth, and every tree, in which is the fruit of a tree yielding seed; to you it shall be for meat. And to every beast of the earth, and to every fowl of the air, and to every thing that creepeth upon the earth, wherein there is life, I have given every green herb for meat: and it was so. And God saw every thing that he had made, and, behold, it was very good. And the evening and the morning were the sixth day.

2. Thus the heavens and the earth were finished, and all the host of them. And on the seventh day God ended his work which he had made; and he rested on the seventh day from all his work which he had made. And God blessed the seventh day, and sanctified it: because that in it he had rested from all his work which God created and made.

These are the generations of the heavens and of the earth when they were created,[3] in the day that the Lord God made the earth and the heavens, and every plant of the field before it was in the earth, and every herb of the field before it grew: for the Lord God had not caused it to rain upon the earth, and there was not a man to till the ground. But there went up a mist from the earth, and watered the whole face of the ground. And the Lord God formed man of the dust of the ground, and breathed into his nostrils the breath of life; and man became a living soul.

And the Lord God planted a garden eastward in Eden; and there he put

3. This is the beginning of a different account of the Creation, which does not agree in all respects with the first.

the man whom he had formed. And out of the ground made the Lord God to grow every tree that is pleasant to the sight, and good for food; the tree of life also in the midst of the garden, and the tree of knowledge of good and evil. And a river went out of Eden to water the garden; and from thence it was parted, and became into four heads. The name of the first is Pison: that is it which compasseth the whole land of Havilah, where there is gold; and the gold of that land is good: there is bdellium and the onyx stone. And the name of the second river is Gihon: the same is it that compasseth the whole land of Ethiopia. And the name of the third river is Hiddekel: that is it which goeth toward the east of Assyria. And the fourth river is Euphrates. And the Lord God took the man, and put him into the garden of Eden to dress it and to keep it. And the Lord God commanded the man, saying, Of every tree of the garden thou mayest freely eat: but of the tree of the knowledge of good and evil, thou shalt not eat of it: for in the day that thou eatest thereof thou shalt surely die.

And the Lord God said, It is not good that the man should be alone; I will make him an help meet for him. And out of the ground the Lord God formed every beast of the field, and every fowl of the air; and brought them unto Adam to see what he would call them: and whatsoever Adam called every living creature, that was the name thereof. And Adam gave names to all cattle, and to the fowl of the air, and to every beast of the field; but for Adam there was not found an help meet for him. And the Lord God caused a deep sleep to fall upon Adam, and he slept: and he took one of his ribs, and closed up the flesh instead thereof; and the rib, which the Lord God had taken from man, made he a woman, and brought her unto the man. And Adam said, This is now bone of my bones, and flesh of my flesh: she shall be called Woman, because she was taken out of Man. Therefore shall a man leave his father and his mother, and shall cleave unto his wife: and they shall be one flesh. And they were both naked, the man and his wife, and were not ashamed.

3. Now the serpent was more subtil than any beast of the field which the Lord God had made. And he said unto the woman, Yea, hath God said, Ye shall not eat of every tree of the garden? And the woman said unto the serpent, We may eat of the fruit of the trees of the garden: but of the fruit of the tree which is in the midst of the garden, God hath said, Ye shall not eat of it, neither shall ye touch it, lest ye die. And the serpent said unto the woman, Ye shall not surely die: for God doth know that in the day ye eat thereof, then your eyes shall be opened, and ye shall be as gods, knowing good and evil. And when the woman saw that the tree was good for food, and that it was pleasant to the eyes, and a tree to be desired to make one wise, she took of the fruit thereof, and did eat, and gave also unto her husband with her; and he did eat. And the eyes of them both were opened, and they knew that they were naked; and they sewed fig leaves together, and made themselves aprons. And they heard the voice of the Lord God walking in the garden in the cool of the day: and Adam and his wife hid themselves from the presence of the Lord God amongst the trees of the garden. And the Lord God called unto Adam, and said unto him, Where art thou? And he said, I heard thy voice in the garden, and I was afraid, because I was naked; and I hid myself. And he said, Who told thee that thou wast naked? Hast

thou eaten of the tree, whereof I commanded thee that thou shouldest not eat? And the man said, The woman whom thou gavest to be with me, she gave me of the tree, and I did eat. And the Lord God said unto the woman, What is this that thou hast done? And the woman said, The serpent beguiled me, and I did eat. And the Lord God said unto the serpent, Because thou hast done this, thou art cursed above all cattle, and above every beast of the field; upon thy belly shalt thou go, and dust shall thou eat all the days of thy life: and I will put enmity between thee and the woman, and between thy seed and her seed; it shall bruise thy head, and thou shalt bruise his heel. Unto the woman he said, I will greatly multiply thy sorrow and thy conception; in sorrow thou shalt bring forth children; and thy desire shall be to thy husband, and he shall rule over thee. And unto Adam he said, Because thou hast hearkened unto the voice of thy wife, and hast eaten of the tree, of which I commanded thee, saying, Thou shalt not eat of it: cursed is the ground for thy sake; in sorrow shalt thou eat of it all the days of thy life; thorns also and thistles shall it bring forth to thee; and thou shalt eat the herb of the field; in the sweat of thy face shalt thou eat bread, till thou return unto the ground; for out of it wast thou taken: for dust thou art, and unto dust shalt thou return. And Adam called his wife's name Eve; because she was the mother of all living. Unto Adam also and to his wife did the Lord God make coats of skins, and clothed them.

And the Lord God said, Behold, the man is become as one of us, to know good and evil: and now, lest he put forth his hand, and take also of the tree of life, and eat, and live forever: therefore the Lord God sent him forth from the garden of Eden, to till the ground from whence he was taken. So he drove out the man; and he placed at the east of the garden of Eden Cherubims, and a flaming sword which turned every way, to keep the way of the tree of life.

Genesis 4

[*The First Murder*]

4. And Adam knew Eve his wife; and she conceived, and bare Cain, and said, I have gotten a man from the Lord. And she again bare his brother Abel. And Abel was a keeper of sheep, but Cain was a tiller of the ground. And in process of time it came to pass, that Cain brought of the fruit of the ground an offering unto the Lord. And Abel, he also brought of the firstlings of his flock and of the fat thereof. And the Lord had respect unto Abel and to his offering: but unto Cain and to his offering he had not respect. And Cain was very wroth, and his countenance fell. And the Lord said unto Cain, Why art thou wroth? and why is thy countenance fallen? If thou doest well, shalt thou not be accepted? and if thou doest not well, sin lieth at the door. And unto thee shall be his desire, and thou shall rule over him.[1] And Cain talked with Abel his brother: and it came to pass, when they were in the field, that Cain rose up against Abel his brother, and slew him.

And the Lord said unto Cain, Where is Abel thy brother? And he said, I

1. Obscure; it seems to mean something like: Sin shall be eager for you, but you must master it.

know not: am I my brother's keeper? And he said, What hast thou done? the voice of thy brother's blood crieth unto me from the ground. And now art thou cursed from the earth, which hath opened her mouth to receive thy brother's blood from thy hand; when thou tillest the ground, it shall not henceforth yield unto thee her strength, a fugitive and a vagabond shalt thou be in the earth. And Cain said unto the Lord, My punishment is greater than I can bear. Behold, thou hast driven me out this day from the face of the earth; and from thy face shall I be hid; and I shall be a fugitive and a vagabond in the earth; and it shall come to pass, that every one that findeth me shall slay me. And the Lord said unto him, Therefore whosoever slayeth Cain, vengeance shall be taken on him sevenfold. And the Lord set a mark upon Cain, lest any finding him should kill him.

Genesis 6–9

[*The Flood*]

6. * * * And God saw that the wickedness of man was great in the earth, and that every imagination of the thoughts of his heart was only evil continually. And it repented the Lord that he had made man on the earth, and it grieved him at his heart. And the Lord said, I will destroy man whom I have created from the face of the earth; both man, and beast, and the creeping thing, and the fowls of the air; for it repenteth me that I have made them. But Noah found grace in the eyes of the Lord.

These are the generations of Noah: Noah was a just man and perfect in his generations, and Noah walked with God. And Noah begat three sons, Shem, Ham, and Japheth.

The earth also was corrupt before God, and the earth was filled with violence. And God looked upon the earth, and, behold, it was corrupt; for all flesh had corrupted his way upon the earth. And God said unto Noah, The end of all flesh is come before me; for the earth is filled with violence through them; and, behold, I will destroy them with the earth. Make thee an ark of gopher wood;[1] rooms shalt thou make in the ark, and shalt pitch it within and without with pitch. And this is the fashion which thou shalt make it of: The length of the ark shall be three hundred cubits,[2] the breadth of it fifty cubits, and the height of it thirty cubits. A window[3] shalt thou make to the ark, and in a cubit shall thou finish it above; and the door of the ark shalt thou set in the side thereof; with lower, second, and third stories shalt thou make it. And, behold, I, even I, do bring a flood of waters upon the earth, to destroy all flesh, wherein is the breath of life, from under heaven; and every thing that is in the earth shall die. But with thee will I establish my covenant; and thou shalt come into the ark, thou, and thy sons, and thy wife, and thy sons' wives with thee. And of every living thing of all flesh, two of every sort shalt thou bring into the ark, to keep them alive with thee; they shall be male and female. Of fowls after their kind, and of cattle after their kind, of every creeping thing of the earth after his kind, two of every sort shall come unto

1. Cypress. 2. A Hebrew measure of length, about one and a half feet. 3. Obscure; perhaps a skylight in the roof.

thee, to keep them alive. And take thou unto thee of all food that is eaten, and thou shalt gather it to thee; and it shall be for food for thee, and for them. Thus did Noah; according to all that God commanded him, so did he.

7. * * * And Noah was six hundred years old when the flood of waters was upon the earth. And Noah went in, and his sons, and his wife, and his sons' wives with him, into the ark, because of the waters of the flood. Of clean beasts, and of beasts that are not clean, and of fowls, and of every thing that creepeth upon the earth, There went in two and two unto Noah into the ark, the male and the female, as God had commanded Noah. And it came to pass after seven days, that the waters of the flood were upon the earth. In the six hundredth year of Noah's life, in the second month, the seventeenth day of the month, the same day were all the fountains of the great deep broken up, and the windows of heaven were opened. And the rain was upon the earth forty days and forty nights. In the selfsame day entered Noah, and Shem, and Ham, and Japheth, the sons of Noah, and Noah's wife, and the three wives of his sons with them, into the ark; they, and every beast after his kind, and all the cattle after their kind, and every creeping thing that creepeth upon the earth after his kind, and every fowl after his kind, every bird of every sort. And they went in unto Noah into the ark, two and two of all flesh, wherein is the breath of life. And they that went in, went in male and female of all flesh, as God had commanded him: and the Lord shut him in. And the flood was forty days upon the earth; and the waters increased, and bare up the ark, and it was lift up above the earth. And the waters prevailed, and were increased greatly upon the earth; and the ark went upon the face of the waters. And the waters prevailed exceedingly upon the earth; and all the high hills, that were under the whole heaven, were covered. Fifteen cubits upward did the waters prevail; and the mountains were covered. And all flesh died that moved upon the earth, both of fowl, and of cattle, and of beast, and of every creeping thing that creepeth upon the earth, and every man: all in whose nostrils was the breath of life, of all that was in the dry land, died. And every living substance was destroyed which was upon the face of the ground, both man, and cattle, and the creeping things, and the fowl of the heaven; and they were destroyed from the earth: and Noah only remained alive, and they that were with him in the ark. And the waters prevailed upon the earth an hundred and fifty days.

8. And God remembered Noah, and every living thing, and all the cattle that was with him in the ark: and God made a wind to pass over the earth, and the waters assuaged; The fountains also of the deep and the windows of heaven were stopped, and the rain from heaven was restrained; And the waters returned from off the earth continually: and after the end of the hundred and fifty days the waters were abated. And the ark rested in the seventh month, on the seventeenth day of the month, upon the mountains of Ararat. And the waters decreased continually until the tenth month: in the tenth month, on the first day of the month, were the tops of the mountains seen.

And it came to pass at the end of forty days, that Noah opened the window of the ark which he had made: and he sent forth a raven, which went forth to and fro, until the waters were dried up from off the earth. Also he sent forth a dove from him, to see if the waters were abated from off the face of the ground; but the dove found no rest for the sole of her foot, and she returned unto him into the ark, for the waters were on the face of the whole earth: then he put forth his hand, and took her, and pulled her in unto him into the ark. And he stayed yet another seven days; and again he sent forth the dove out of the ark; and the dove came in to him in the evening; and, lo, in her mouth was an olive leaf plucked off: so Noah knew that the waters were abated from off the earth. And he stayed yet another seven days; and sent forth the dove; which returned not again unto him any more.

And it came to pass in the six hundredth and first year, in the first month, the first day of the month, the waters were dried up from off the earth: and Noah removed the covering of the ark, and looked, and, behold, the face of the ground was dry. And in the second month, on the seven and twentieth day of the month, was the earth dried.

And God spake unto Noah, saying, Go forth of the ark, thou, and thy wife, and thy sons, and thy sons' wives with thee. Bring forth with thee every living thing that is with thee, of all flesh, both of fowl, and of cattle, and of every creeping thing that creepeth upon the earth; that they may breed abundantly in the earth, and be fruitful, and multiply upon the earth. And Noah went forth, and his sons, and his wife, and his sons' wives with him: every beast, every creeping thing, and every fowl, and whatsoever creepeth upon the earth, after their kinds, went forth out of the ark. And Noah builded an altar unto the Lord; and took of every clean beast, and of every clean fowl, and offered burnt offerings on the altar. And the Lord smelled a sweet savour; and the Lord said in his heart, I will not again curse the ground any more for man's sake; for the imagination of man's heart is evil from his youth; neither will I again smite any more every thing living, as I have done. While the earth remaineth, seedtime and harvest, and cold and heat, and summer and winter, and day and night shall not cease.

9. And God blessed Noah and his sons, and said unto them, Be fruitful, and multiply, and replenish the earth. And the fear of you and the dread of you shall be upon every beast of the earth, and upon every fowl of the air, upon all that moveth upon the earth, and upon all the fishes of the sea; into your hand are they delivered. Every moving thing that liveth shall be meat for you; even as the green herb have I given you all things. But flesh with the life thereof, which is the blood thereof, shall ye not eat.[4] And surely your blood of your lives will I require; at the hand of every beast will I require it, and at the hand of man; at the hand of every man's brother will I require the life of man. Whoso sheddeth man's blood, by man shall his blood be shed, for in the image of God made he man. And you, be ye fruitful, and multiply; bring forth abundantly in the earth, and multiply therein.

And God spake unto Noah, and to his sons with him, saying, And I, behold, I establish my covenant with you, and with your seed after you; And with every living creature that is with you, of the fowl, of the cattle, and of every beast of the earth with you; from all that go out of the ark, to every beast of the earth. And I will establish my covenant with you; neither shall all flesh

4. A reference to the biblical dietary laws: blood was supposed to be drained from a slaughtered animal.

be cut off any more by the waters of a flood; neither shall there any more be a flood to destroy the earth. And God said, This is the token of the covenant which I make between me and you and every living creature that is with you, for perpetual generations: I do set my bow in the cloud, and it shall be for a token of a covenant between me and the earth. And it shall come to pass, when I bring a cloud over the earth, that the bow shall be seen in the cloud: and I will remember my covenant, which is between me and you and every living creature of all flesh; and the waters shall no more become a flood to destroy all flesh. And the bow shall be in the cloud; and I will look upon it, that I may remember the everlasting covenant between God and every living creature of all flesh that is upon the earth. And God said unto Noah, This is the token of the covenant, which I have established between me and all flesh that is upon the earth.

Genesis 11

[*The Origin of Languages*]

11. And the whole earth was of one language, and of one speech. And it came to pass, as they journeyed from the east, that they found a plain in the land of Shinar;[1] and they dwelt there. And they said one to another, Go to, let us make brick, and burn them thoroughly. And they had brick for stone, and slime[2] had they for mortar. And they said, Go to, let us build us a city and a tower,[3] whose top may reach unto heaven; and let us make us a name, lest we be scattered abroad upon the face of the whole earth. And the Lord came down to see the city and the tower, which the children of men builded. And the Lord said, Behold, the people is one, and they have all one language; and this they begin to do: and now nothing will be restrained from them, which they have imagined to do. Go to, let us go down, and there confound their language, that they may not understand one another's speech. So the Lord scattered them abroad from thence upon the face of all the earth: and they left off to build the city. Therefore is the name of it called Babel;[4] because the Lord did there confound the language of all the earth: and from thence did the Lord scatter them abroad upon the face of all the earth.

Genesis 22

[*Abraham and Isaac*]

22. And it came to pass after these things, that God did tempt Abraham, and said unto him, Abraham: and he said, Behold, here I am. And he said, Take now thy son, thine only son Isaac, whom thou lovest, and get thee into the land of Moriah; and offer him there for a burnt offering upon one of the mountains which I will tell thee of.

And Abraham rose up early in the morning, and saddled his ass, and took

1. In Mesopotamia. *They*: humankind. 2. Bitumen. 3. This story is based on the Babylonian practice of building temples in the form of terraced pyramids (ziggurats). 4. Babylon.

two of his young men with him, and Isaac his son, and clave the wood for the burnt offering, and rose up, and went unto the place of which God had told him. Then on the third day Abraham lifted up his eyes, and saw the place afar off. And Abraham said unto his young men, Abide ye here with the ass; and I and the lad will go yonder and worship, and come again to you. And Abraham took the wood of the burnt offering, and laid it upon Isaac his son; and he took the fire in his hand, and a knife; and they went both of them together. And Isaac spake unto Abraham his father, and said, My father: and he said, Here am I, my son. And he said, Behold the fire and the wood: but where is the lamb for a burnt offering? And Abraham said, My son, God will provide himself a lamb for a burnt offering: so they went both of them together.

And they came to the place which God had told him of; and Abraham built an altar there, and laid the wood in order, and bound Isaac his son, and laid him on the altar upon the wood. And Abraham stretched forth his hand, and took the knife to slay his son. And the Angel of the Lord called unto him out of heaven, and said, Abraham, Abraham: and he said, Here am I. And he said, Lay not thine hand upon the lad, neither do thou any thing unto him: for now I know that thou fearest God, seeing thou hast not withheld thy son, thine only son, from me. And Abraham lifted up his eyes, and looked, and behold behind him a ram caught in a thicket by his horns: and Abraham went and took the ram, and offered him up for a burnt offering in the stead of his son. And Abraham called the name of that place Jehovah-jireh: as it is said to this day, In the mount of the Lord it shall be seen.

And the Angel of the Lord called unto Abraham out of heaven the second time, and said, By myself have I sworn, saith the Lord, for because thou hast done this thing, and hast not withheld thy son, thine only son, that in blessing I will bless thee, and in multiplying I will multiply thy seed as the stars of the heaven, and as the sand which is upon the seashore; and thy seed shall possess the gate of his enemies; and in thy seed shall all the nations of the earth be blessed; because thou hast obeyed my voice.

Genesis 25, 27

[*Jacob and Esau*]

25. And Isaac entreated the Lord for his wife, because she was barren: and the Lord was entreated of him, and Rebekah his wife conceived. And the children struggled together within her; and she said, If it be so, why am I thus? And she went to inquire of the Lord. And the Lord said unto her, Two nations are in thy womb, and two manner of people shall be separated from thy bowels; and the one people shall be stronger than the other people; and the elder shall serve the younger.

And when her days to be delivered were fulfilled, behold, there were twins in her womb. And the first came out red, all over like a hairy garment; and they called his name Esau. And after that came his brother out, and his hand took hold on Esau's heel; and his name was called Jacob: and Isaac was threescore years old when she bare them. And the boys grew: and Esau was a cunning hunter, a man of the field; and Jacob was a plain man, dwelling in tents. And Isaac loved Esau, because he did eat of his venison: but Rebekah loved Jacob.

And Jacob sod pottage: and Esau came from the field, and he was faint: and Esau said to Jacob, Feed me, I pray thee, with that same red pottage; for I am faint: therefore was his name called Edom. And Jacob said, Sell me this day thy birthright. And Esau said, Behold, I am at the point to die: and what profit shall this birthright do to me? And Jacob said, Swear to me this day; and he sware unto him: and he sold his birthright unto Jacob. Then Jacob gave Esau bread and pottage of lentils; and he did eat and drink, and rose up, and went his way. Thus Esau despised his birthright.

27. And it came to pass, that when Isaac was old, and his eyes were dim, so that he could not see, he called Esau his eldest son, and said unto him, My son: and he said unto him, Behold, here am I. And he said, Behold now, I am old, I know not the day of my death: Now therefore take, I pray thee, thy weapons, thy quiver and thy bow, and go out to the field, and take me some venison; and make me savory meat, such as I love, and bring it to me, that I may eat; that my soul may bless thee before I die. And Rebekah heard when Isaac spake to Esau his son. And Esau went to the field to hunt for venison, and to bring it.

And Rebekah spake unto Jacob her son, saying, Behold, I heard thy father speak unto Esau thy brother, saying, Bring me venison, and make me savory meat, that I may eat, and bless thee before the Lord before my death. Now therefore, my son, obey my voice according to that which I command thee. Go now to the flock, and fetch me from thence two good kids of the goats; and I will make them savory meat for thy father, such as he loveth: and thou shalt bring it to thy father, that he may eat, and that he may bless thee before his death. And Jacob said to Rebekah his mother, Behold, Esau my brother is a hairy man, and I am a smooth man: My father peradventure will feel me, and I shall seem to him as a deceiver; and I shall bring a curse upon me, and not a blessing. And his mother said unto him, Upon me be thy curse, my son: only obey my voice, and go fetch me them. And he went, and fetched, and brought them to his mother: and his mother made savory meat, such as his father loved. And Rebekah took goodly raiment of her eldest son Esau, which were with her in the house, and put them upon Jacob her younger son: and she put the skins of the kids of the goats upon his hands, and upon the smooth of his neck: and she gave the savory meat and the bread, which she had prepared, into the hand of her son Jacob.

And he came unto his father, and said, My father: and he said, Here am I; who art thou, my son? And Jacob said unto his father, I am Esau thy firstborn; I have done according as thou badest me: arise, I pray thee, sit and eat of my venison, that thy soul may bless me. And Isaac said unto his son, How is it that thou hast found it so quickly, my son? And he said, Because the Lord thy God brought it to me. And Isaac said unto Jacob, Come near, I pray thee, that I may feel thee, my son, whether thou be my very son Esau or not. And Jacob went near unto Isaac his father; and he felt him, and said, The voice is Jacob's voice, but the hands are the hands of Esau. And he discerned him not, because his hands were hairy, as his brother Esau's hands: so he blessed him. And he said, Art thou my very son Esau? And he said, I am. And he said, Bring it near to me, and I will eat of my son's venison, that my soul may bless thee. And he brought it near to him, and he did eat: and he brought him wine, and he drank. And his father Isaac said unto him, Come near now, and kiss me, my son. And he came near, and kissed him: and he smelled the smell of his raiment, and blessed him, and said, See, the smell of my son is as the smell of a field which the Lord hath blessed: Therefore God give thee of the dew of heaven, and the fatness of the earth, and plenty of corn and wine: let people serve thee, and nations bow down to thee: be lord over thy brethren, and let thy mother's sons bow down to thee: cursed be every one that curseth thee, and blessed be he that blesseth thee.

And it came to pass, as soon as Isaac had made an end of blessing Jacob, and Jacob was yet scarce gone out from the presence of Isaac his father, that Esau his brother came in from his hunting. And he also had made savory meat, and brought it unto his father, and said unto his father, Let my father arise, and eat of his son's venison, that thy soul may bless me. And Isaac his father said unto him, Who art thou? And he said, I am thy son, thy firstborn, Esau. And Isaac trembled very exceedingly, and said, Who? where is he that hath taken venison, and brought it me, and I have eaten of all before thou camest, and have blessed him? yea, and he shall be blessed. And when Esau heard the words of his father, he cried with a great and exceeding bitter cry, and said unto his father, Bless me, even me also, O my father. And he said, Thy brother came with subtilty, and hath taken away thy blessing. And he said, Is not he rightly named Jacob?[5] for he hath supplanted me these two times: he took away my birthright; and, behold, now he hath taken away my blessing. And he said, Hast thou not reserved a blessing for me? And Isaac answered and said unto Esau, Behold, I have made him thy lord, and all his brethren have I given to him for servants; and with corn and wine have I sustained him: and what shall I do now unto thee, my son? And Esau said unto his father, Hast thou but one blessing, my father? bless me, even me also, O my father. And Esau lifted up his voice, and wept. And Isaac his father answered and said unto him, Behold, thy dwelling shall be the fatness of the earth, and of the dew of heaven from above; and by thy sword shalt thou live, and shalt serve thy brother: and it shall come to pass when thou shalt have the dominion, that thou shalt break his yoke from off thy neck.

Genesis 37, 39–46

[*The Story of Joseph*]

37. * * * Joseph, being seventeen years old, was feeding the flock with his brethren; and the lad was with the sons of Bilhah, and with the sons of Zilpah, his father's wives: and Joseph brought unto his father their evil report.[1] Now Israel loved Joseph more than all his children, because he was the son of his old age: and he made him a coat of many colours. And when his brethren saw that their father loved him more than all his brethren, they hated him, and could not speak peaceably unto him.

And Joseph dreamed a dream, and he told it his brethren: and they hated him yet the more. And he said unto them, Hear, I pray you, this dream which I have dreamed: for, behold, we were binding sheaves in the field, and, lo,

5. Which means "he who supplants." 1. Joseph reported their misdeeds. *Father*: Israel.

my sheaf arose, and also stood upright; and, behold, your sheaves stood round about, and made obeisance to my sheaf. And his brethren said to him, Shalt thou indeed reign over us? or shalt thou indeed have dominion over us? And they hated him yet the more for his dreams, and for his words.

And he dreamed yet another dream, and told it his brethren, and said, Behold, I have dreamed a dream more; and, behold, the sun and the moon and the eleven stars made obeisance to me. And he told it to his father, and to his brethren: and his father rebuked him, and said unto him, What is this dream that thou hast dreamed? Shall I and thy mother and thy brethren indeed come to bow down ourselves to thee to the earth? And his brethren envied him; but his father observed the saying.

And his brethren went to feed their father's flock in Shechem. And Israel said unto Joseph, Do not thy brethren feed the flock in Shechem? come, and I will send thee unto them. And he said to him, Here am I. And he said to him, Go, I pray thee, see whether it be well with thy brethren, and well with the flocks; and bring me word again. So he sent him out of the vale of Hebron, and he came to Shechem.

And a certain man found him, and, behold, he was wandering in the field: and the man asked him, saying, What seekest thou? And he said, I seek my brethren: tell me, I pray thee, where they feed their flocks. And the man said, They are departed hence; for I heard them say, Let us go to Dothan. And Joseph went after his brethren, and found them in Dothan. And when they saw him afar off, even before he came near unto them, they conspired against him to slay him. And they said one to another, Behold, this dreamer cometh. Come now therefore, and let us slay him, and cast him into some pit, and we will say, Some evil beast hath devoured him: and we shall see what will become of his dreams. And Reuben heard it, and he delivered him out of their hands; and said, Let us not kill him. And Reuben said unto them, Shed no blood, but cast him into this pit that is in the wilderness, and lay no hand upon him; that he might rid him out of their hands, to deliver him to his father again.

And it came to pass, when Joseph was come unto his brethren, that they stripped Joseph out of his coat, his coat of many colours that was on him; and they took him, and cast him into a pit: and the pit was empty, there was no water in it. And they sat down to eat bread: and they lifted up their eyes and looked, and, behold, a company of Ishmeelites came from Gilead with their camels bearing spicery and balm and myrrh, going to carry it down to Egypt. And Judah said unto his brethren, What profit is it if we slay our brother, and conceal his blood? Come, and let us sell him to the Ishmeelites, and let not our hand be upon him; for he is our brother and our flesh. And his brethren were content. Then there passed by Midianites merchantmen; and they[2] drew and lifted up Joseph out of the pit, and sold Joseph to the Ishmeelites for twenty pieces of silver: and they[3] brought Joseph into Egypt.

And Reuben returned unto the pit; and, behold, Joseph was not in the pit; and he rent his clothes. And he returned unto his brethren, and said, The child is not; and I, whither shall I go? And they took Joseph's coat, and killed a kid of the goats, and dipped the coat in the blood; and they sent the coat

2. The brothers. The confusion in this passage may be because the text we have is a composite of two different versions. 3. The Ishmeelites.

of many colours, and they brought it to their father; and said, This have we found: know now whether it be thy son's coat or no. And he knew it, and said, It is my son's coat; an evil beast hath devoured him; Joseph is without doubt rent in pieces. And Jacob rent his clothes, and put sackcloth upon his loins, and mourned for his son many days. And all his sons and all his daughters rose up to comfort him; but he refused to be comforted; and he said, For I will go down into the grave unto my son mourning. Thus his father wept for him. * * *

39. And Joseph was brought down to Egypt; and Potiphar, an officer of Pharaoh, captain of the guard, an Egyptian, bought him of the hands of the Ishmeelites, which had brought him down thither. And the Lord was with Joseph, and he was a prosperous man; and he was in the house of his master the Egyptian. And his master saw that the Lord was with him, and that the Lord made all he did to prosper in his hand. And Joseph found grace in his sight, and he served him: and he made him overseer over his house, and all that he had he put into his hand. And it came to pass from the time that he had made him overseer in his house, and over all that he had, that the Lord blessed the Egyptian's house for Joseph's sake; and the blessing of the Lord was upon all that he had in the house, and in the field. And he left all that he had in Joseph's hand; and he knew not ought he had, save the bread which he did eat. And Joseph was a goodly person, and well favoured.

And it came to pass after these things, that his master's wife cast her eyes upon Joseph; and she said, Lie with me. But he refused, and said unto his master's wife, Behold, my master wotteth not what is with me in the house, and he hath committed all that he hath to my hand; there is none greater in this house than I; neither hath he kept back any thing from me but thee, because thou art his wife: how then can I do this great wickedness, and sin against God? And it came to pass, as she spake to Joseph day by day, that he hearkened not unto her, to lie by her, or to be with her. And it came to pass about this time, that Joseph went into the house to do his business; and there was none of the men of the house there within. And she caught him by his garment, saying, Lie with me: and he left his garment in her hand, and fled, and got him out. And it came to pass, when she saw that he had left his garment in her hand, and was fled forth, that she called unto the men of her house, and spoke unto them, saying, See, he hath brought in an Hebrew unto us to mock us; he came in unto me to lie with me, and I cried with a loud voice: and it came to pass, when he heard that I lifted up my voice and cried, that he left his garment with me, and fled, and got him out. And she laid up his garment by her, until his lord came home. And she spake unto him according to these words, saying, The Hebrew servant, which thou hast brought unto us, came in unto me to mock me: and it came to pass, as I lifted up my voice and cried, that he left his garment with me, and fled out. And it came to pass, when his master heard the words of his wife, which she spake unto him, saying, After this manner did thy servant to me; that his wrath was kindled. And Joseph's master took him, and put him into the prison, a place where the king's prisoners were bound: and he was there in the prison.

But the Lord was with Joseph, and showed him mercy, and gave him favour in the sight of the keeper of the prison. And the keeper of the prison committed to Joseph's hand all the prisoners that were in the prison; and whatsoever they did there, he was the doer of it. The keeper of the prison looked not to any thing that was under his hand; because the Lord was with him, and that which he did, the Lord made it to prosper.

40. And it came to pass after these things that the butler of the king of Egypt and his baker had offended their lord the king of Egypt. And Pharaoh was wroth against two of his officers, against the chief of the butlers, and against the chief of the bakers. And he put them in ward in the house of the captain of the guard, into the prison, the place where Joseph was bound. And the captain of the guard charged Joseph with them, and he served them: and they continued a season in ward.

And they dreamed a dream both of them, each man his dream in one night, each man according to the interpretation of his dream, the butler and the baker of the king of Egypt, which were bound in the prison. And Joseph came in unto them in the morning, and looked upon them, and, behold, they were sad. And he asked Pharaoh's officers that were with him in the ward of his lord's house, saying, Wherefore look ye so sadly to day? And they said unto him, We have dreamed a dream, and there is no interpreter of it. And Joseph said unto them, Do not interpretations belong to God? tell me them, I pray you. And the chief butler told his dream to Joseph, and said to him, In my dream, behold, a vine was before me; and in the vine were three branches: and it was as though it budded, and her blossoms shot forth; and the clusters thereof brought forth ripe grapes: and Pharaoh's cup was in my hand: and I took the grapes, and pressed them into Pharaoh's cup, and I gave the cup into Pharaoh's hand. And Joseph said unto him, This is the interpretation of it: the three branches are three days: yet within three days shall Pharaoh lift up thine head, and restore thee unto thy place: and thou shalt deliver Pharaoh's cup into his hand, after the former manner when thou wast his butler. But think on me when it shall be well with thee, and shew kindness, I pray thee, unto me, and make mention of me unto Pharaoh, and bring me out of this house: for indeed I was stolen away out of the land of the Hebrews: and here also have I done nothing that they should put me into the dungeon. When the chief baker saw that the interpretation was good, he said unto Joseph, I also was in my dream, and, behold, I had three white baskets on my head: and in the uppermost basket there was of all manner of bakemeats for Pharaoh; and the birds did eat them out of the basket upon my head. And Joseph answered and said, This is the interpretation thereof: the three baskets are three days: yet within three days shall Pharaoh lift up thy head from off thee, and shall hang thee on a tree; and the birds shall eat thy flesh from off thee.

And it came to pass the third day, which was Pharaoh's birthday, that he made a feast unto all his servants: and he lifted up the head of the chief butler and of the chief baker among his servants. And he restored the chief butler unto his butlership again; and he gave the cup into Pharaoh's hand. But he hanged the chief baker: as Joseph had interpreted to them. Yet did not the chief butler remember Joseph, but forgat him.

41. And it came to pass at the end of two full years, that Pharaoh dreamed: and, behold, he stood by the river. And, behold, there came up out of the

river seven well favoured kine[4] and fatfleshed; and they fed in a meadow. And, behold, seven other kine came up after them out of the river, ill favoured and leanfleshed; and stood by the other kine upon the brink of the river. And the ill favoured and leanfleshed kine did eat up the seven well favoured and fat kine. So Pharaoh awoke. And he slept and dreamed the second time: and, behold, seven ears of corn came up upon one stalk, rank[5] and good. And, behold, seven thin ears and blasted with the east wind sprung up after them. And the seven thin ears devoured the seven rank and full ears. And Pharaoh awoke, and, behold, it was a dream. And it came to pass in the morning that his spirit was troubled; and he sent and called for all the magicians of Egypt, and all the wise men thereof: and Pharaoh told them his dream; but there was none that could interpret them unto Pharaoh.

Then spake the chief butler unto Pharaoh, saying, I do remember my faults this day: Pharaoh was wroth with his servants, and put me in ward in the captain of the guard's house, both me and the chief baker: and we dreamed a dream in one night, I and he; we dreamed each man according to the interpretation of his dream. And there was there with us a young man, an Hebrew, servant to the captain of the guard; and we told him, and he interpreted to us our dreams; to each man according to his dream he did interpret. And it came to pass, as he interpreted to us, so it was; me he restored unto mine office, and him he hanged.

Then Pharaoh sent and called Joseph, and they brought him hastily out of the dungeon: and he shaved himself, and changed his raiment, and came in unto Pharaoh. And Pharaoh said unto Joseph, I have dreamed a dream, and there is none that can interpret it: and I have heard say of thee that thou canst understand a dream to interpret it. And Joseph answered Pharaoh, saying, It is not in me: God shall give Pharaoh an answer of peace. And Pharaoh said unto Joseph, In my dream, behold, I stood upon the bank of the river; and, behold, there came up out of the river seven kine, fatfleshed and well favoured; and they fed in a meadow: and, behold, seven other kine came up after them, poor and very ill favoured and lean-fleshed, such as I never saw in all the land of Egypt for badness: and the lean and the ill favoured kine did eat up the first seven fat kine: and when they had eaten them up, it could not be known that they had eaten them; but they were still ill favoured, as at the beginning. So I awoke. And I saw in my dream, and, behold, seven ears came up in one stalk, full and good: and, behold, seven ears, withered, thin, and blasted with the east wind, sprung up after them: and the thin ears devoured the seven good ears: and I told this unto the magicians; but there was none that could declare it to me.

And Joseph said unto Pharaoh, The dream of Pharaoh is one: God hath shewed Pharaoh what he is about to do. The seven good kine are seven years; and the seven good ears are seven years: the dream is one. And the seven thin and ill favoured kine that came up after them are seven years; and the seven empty ears blasted with the east wind shall be seven years of famine. This is the thing which I have spoken unto Pharaoh: what God is about to do he sheweth unto Pharaoh. Behold, there come seven years of great plenty throughout all the land of Egypt: and there shall arise after them seven years of famine; and all the plenty shall be forgotten in the land of Egypt; and the

4. Cattle. 5. Fat.

famine shall consume the land; and the plenty shall not be known in the land by reason of that famine following; for it shall be very grievous. And for that the dream was doubled unto Pharaoh twice; it is because the thing is established by God, and God will shortly bring it to pass. Now therefore let Pharaoh look out a man discreet and wise, and set him over the land of Egypt. Let Pharaoh do this, and let him appoint officers over the land, and take up the fifth part of the land[6] of Egypt in the seven plenteous years. And let them gather all the food of those good years that come, and lay up corn under the hand of Pharaoh, and let them keep food in the cities. And that food shall be for store to the land against the seven years of famine, which shall be in the land of Egypt; that the land perish not through the famine.

And the thing was good in the eyes of Pharaoh, and in the eyes of all his servants. And Pharaoh said unto his servants, Can we find such a one as this is, a man in whom the Spirit of God is? And Pharaoh said unto Joseph, Forasmuch as God hath shewed thee all this, there is none so discreet and wise as thou art: thou shalt be over my house, and according unto thy word shall all my people be ruled: only in the throne will I be greater than thou. And Pharaoh said unto Joseph, See, I have set thee over all the land of Egypt. And Pharaoh took off his ring from his hand, and put it upon Joseph's hand, and arrayed him in vestures of fine linen, and put a gold chain about his neck; and he made him to ride in the second chariot which he had; and they cried before him, Bow the knee: and he made him ruler over all the land of Egypt. And Pharaoh said unto Joseph, I am Pharaoh, and without thee shall no man lift up his hand or foot in all the land of Egypt. And Pharaoh called Joseph's name Zaphnath-paaneah; and he gave him to wife Asenath, the daughter of Poti-pherah priest of On. And Joseph went out over all the land of Egypt.

And Joseph was thirty years old when he stood before Pharaoh king of Egypt. And Joseph went out from the presence of Pharaoh, and went throughout all the land of Egypt. And in the seven plenteous years the earth brought forth by handfuls. And he gathered up all the food of the seven years, which were in the land of Egypt, and laid up the food in the cities: the food of the field, which was round about every city, laid he up in the same. And Joseph gathered corn as the sand of the sea, very much, until he left numbering; for it was without number. And unto Joseph were born two sons before the years of famine came, which Asenath, the daughter of Poti-pherah priest of On, bare unto him. And Joseph called the name of the first born Manasseh:[7] For God, said he, hath made me forget all my toil, and all my father's house. And the name of the second called he Ephraim:[8] For God hath caused me to be fruitful in the land of my affliction.

And the seven years of plenteousness, that was in the land of Egypt, were ended. And the seven years of dearth began to come, according as Joseph had said: and the dearth was in all lands; but in all the land of Egypt there was bread. And when all the land of Egypt was famished, the people cried to Pharaoh for bread: and Pharaoh said unto all the Egyptians, Go unto Joseph; what he saith to you, do. And the famine was over all the face of the earth. And Joseph opened all the storehouses, and sold unto the Egyptians; and the famine waxed sore in the land of Egypt. And all countries came into

6. Of the crop. 7. Which means "causing to forget." 8. Which means "fruitfulness."

Egypt to Joseph for to buy corn; because that the famine was so sore in all lands.

42. Now when Jacob saw that there was corn in Egypt, Jacob said unto his sons, Why do ye look one upon another? And he said, Behold, I have heard that there is corn in Egypt: get you down thither, and buy for us from thence; that we may live, and not die.

And Joseph's ten brethren went down to buy corn in Egypt. But Benjamin, Joseph's brother, Jacob sent not with his brethren; for he said, Lest peradventure mischief befall him. And the sons of Israel came to buy corn among those that came: for the famine was in the land of Canaan. And Joseph was the governor over the land, and he it was that sold to all the people of the land: and Joseph's brethren came, and bowed down themselves before him with their faces to the earth. And Joseph saw his brethren, and he knew them, but made himself strange unto them, and spake roughly unto them; and he said unto them, Whence come ye? And they said, From the land of Canaan to buy food. And Joseph knew his brethren, but they knew not him. And Joseph remembered the dreams which he dreamed of them, and said unto them, Ye are spies; to see the nakedness of the land ye are come. And they said unto him, Nay, my lord, but to buy food are thy servants come. We are all one man's sons; we are true men, thy servants are no spies. And he said unto them, Nay, but to see the nakedness of the land ye are come. And they said, Thy servants are twelve brethren, the sons of one man in the land of Canaan; and, behold, the youngest is this day with our father, and one is not. And Joseph said unto them, That is it that I spake unto you, saying, Ye are spies: Hereby ye shall be proved: By the life of Pharaoh ye shall not go forth hence, except your youngest brother come hither. Send one of you, and let him fetch your brother, and ye shall be kept in prison, that your words may be proved, whether there be any truth in you: or else by the life of Pharaoh surely ye are spies. And he put them all together into ward three days. And Joseph said unto them the third day, This do, and live; for I fear God: if ye be true men, let one of your brethren be bound in the house of your prison: go ye, carry corn for the famine of your houses: but bring your youngest brother unto me; so shall your words be verified, and ye shall not die. And they did so.

And they said one to another, We are verily guilty concerning our brother, in that we saw the anguish of his soul, when he besought us, and we would not hear; therefore is this distress come upon us. And Reuben answered them, saying, Spake I not unto you, saying, Do not sin against the child; and ye would not hear? therefore, behold, also his blood is required. And they knew not that Joseph understood them; for he spake unto them by an interpreter. And he turned himself about from them, and wept; and returned to them again, and communed with them, and took from them Simeon, and bound him before their eyes.

Then Joseph commanded to fill their sacks with corn, and to restore every man's money into his sack, and to give them provision for the way: and thus did he unto them. And they laded their asses with the corn, and departed thence. And as one of them opened his sack to give his ass provender in the inn, he espied his money; for, behold, it was in his sack's mouth. And he said unto his brethren, My money is restored; and, lo, it is even in my sack:

and their heart failed them, and they were afraid, saying one to another, What is this that God hath done unto us?

And they came unto Jacob their father unto the land of Canaan, and told him all that befell unto them; saying, The man, who is lord of the land, spake roughly to us, and took us for spies of the country. And we said unto him, We are true men; we are no spies: we be twelve brethren, sons of our father; one is not, and the youngest is this day with our father in the land of Canaan. And the man, the lord of the country, said unto us, Hereby shall I know that ye are true men; leave one of your brethren here with me, and take food for the famine of your households, and be gone: and bring your youngest brother unto me: then shall I know that ye are no spies, but that ye are true men: so will I deliver you your brother, and ye shall traffick in the land.

And it came to pass as they emptied their sacks, that, behold, every man's bundle of money was in his sack: and when both they and their father saw the bundles of money, they were afraid. And Jacob their father said unto them, Me have ye bereaved of my children: Joseph is not, and Simeon is not, and ye will take Benjamin away: all these things are against me.

And Reuben spake unto his father, saying, Slay my two sons, if I bring him not to thee: deliver him into my hand, and I will bring him to thee again. And he said, My son shall not go down with you; for his brother is dead, and he is left alone: if mischief befall him by the way in the which ye go, then shall ye bring down my gray hairs with sorrow to the grave.

43. And the famine was sore in the land. And it came to pass, when they had eaten up the corn which they had brought out of Egypt, their father said unto them, Go again, buy us a little food. And Judah spake unto him, saying, The man did solemnly protest unto us, saying, Ye shall not see my face, except your brother be with you. If thou wilt send our brother with us, we will go down and buy thee food: but if thou wilt not send him, we will not go down: for the man said unto us, Ye shall not see my face, except your brother be with you. And Israel said, Wherefore dealt ye so ill with me, as to tell the man whether ye had yet a brother? And they said, The man asked us straitly of our state, and of our kindred, saying, Is your father yet alive? have ye another brother? and we told him according to the tenor of these words: could we certainly know that he would say, Bring your brother down? And Judah said unto Israel his father, Send the lad with me, and we will arise and go; that we may live, and not die, both we, and thou, and also our little ones. I will be surety for him; of my hand shalt thou require him: if I bring him not unto thee, and set him before thee, then let me bear the blame for ever: for except we had lingered, surely now we had returned this second time. And their father Israel said unto them, If it must be so now, do this; take of the best fruits in the land in your vessels, and carry down the man a present, a little balm, and a little honey, spices, and myrrh, nuts, and almonds: and take double money in your hand: and the money that was brought again in the mouth of your sacks, carry it again in your hand; peradventure it was an oversight: take also your brother, and arise, go again unto the man: and God Almighty give you mercy before the man, that he may send away your other brother, and Benjamin. If I be bereaved of my children, I am bereaved.

And the men took that present, and they took double money in their hand,

and Benjamin; and rose up, and went down to Egypt, and stood before Joseph. And when Joseph saw Benjamin with them, he said to the ruler of his house, Bring these men home, and slay,[9] and make ready; for these men shall dine with me at noon. And the man did as Joseph bade; and the man brought the men into Joseph's house. And the men were afraid, because they were brought into Joseph's house; and they said, Because of the money that was returned in our sacks at the first time are we brought in; that he may seek occasion against us, and fall upon us, and take us for bondmen, and our asses. And they came near to the steward of Joseph's house, and they communed with him at the door of the house, and said, O sir, we came indeed down at the first time to buy food; and it came to pass, when we came to the inn, that we opened our sacks, and behold, every man's money was in the mouth of his sack, our money in full weight: and we have brought it again in our hand. And other money have we brought down in our hands to buy food: we cannot tell who put our money in our sacks. And he said, Peace be to you, fear not: your God, and the God of your father, hath given you treasure in your sacks: I had your money. And he brought Simeon out unto them. And the man brought the men into Joseph's house, and gave them water, and they washed their feet; and he gave their asses provender. And they made ready the present against Joseph came at noon: for they heard that they should eat bread there.

And when Joseph came home, they brought him the present which was in their hand into the house, and bowed themselves to him to the earth. And he asked them of their welfare, and said, Is your father well, the old man of whom ye spake? Is he yet alive? And they answered, Thy servant our father is in good health, he is yet alive. And they bowed down their heads, and made obeisance. And he lifted up his eyes, and saw his brother Benjamin, his mother's son, and said, Is this your younger brother, of whom ye spake unto me? And he said, God be gracious unto thee, my son. And Joseph made haste; for his bowels did yearn upon his brother: and he sought where to weep; and he entered into his chamber, and wept there. And he washed his face, and went out, and refrained himself, and said, Set on bread. And they set on for him by himself, and for them by themselves, and for the Egyptians, which did eat with him, by themselves: because the Egyptians might not eat bread with the Hebrews; for that is an abomination unto the Egyptians. And they sat before him, the firstborn according to his birthright, and the youngest according to his youth: and the men marvelled one at another. And he took and sent messes[1] unto them from before him: but Benjamin's mess was five times so much as any of theirs. And they drank, and were merry with him.

44. And he commanded the steward of his house, saying, Fill the men's sacks with food, as much as they can carry, and put every man's money in his sack's mouth. And put my cup, the silver cup, in the sack's mouth of the youngest, and his corn money. And he did according to the word that Joseph had spoken. As soon as the morning was light, the men were sent away, they and their asses. And when they were gone out of the city, and not yet far off, Joseph said unto his steward, Up, follow after the men; and when

9. Kill an animal for meat. 1. Portions.

thou dost overtake them, say unto them, Wherefore have ye rewarded evil for good? Is not this it in which my lord drinketh, and whereby indeed he divineth?[2] ye have done evil in so doing.

And he overtook them, and he spake unto them these same words. And they said unto him, Wherefore saith my lord these words? God forbid that thy servants should do according to this thing: behold, the money, which we found in our sacks' mouths, we brought again unto thee out of the land of Canaan: how then should we steal out of thy lord's house silver or gold? With whomsoever of thy servants it be found, both let him die, and we also will be my lord's bondmen. And he said, Now also let it be according unto your words: he with whom it is found shall be my servant; and ye shall be blameless. Then they speedily took down every man his sack to the ground, and opened every man his sack. And he searched, and began at the eldest, and left at the youngest: and the cup was found in Benjamin's sack. Then they rent their clothes, and laded every man his ass, and returned to the city.

And Judah and his brethren came to Joseph's house; for he was yet there: and they fell before him on the ground. And Joseph said unto them, What deed is this that ye have done? wot ye not that such a man as I can certainly divine? And Judah said, What shall we say unto my lord? what shall we speak? or how shall we clear ourselves? God hath found out the iniquity of thy servants: behold, we are my lord's servants, both we, and he also with whom the cup is found. And he said, God forbid that I should do so: but the man in whose hand the cup is found, he shall be my servant; and as for you, get you up in peace unto your father.

Then Judah came near unto him, and said, Oh my lord, let thy servant, I pray thee, speak a word in my lord's ears, and let not thine anger burn against thy servant: for thou art even as Pharaoh. My lord asked his servants, saying, Have ye a father, or a brother? And we said unto my lord, We have a father, an old man, and a child of his old age, a little one; and his brother is dead, and he alone is left of his mother, and his father loveth him. And thou saidst unto thy servants, Bring him down unto me, that I may set mine eyes upon him. And we said unto my lord, The lad cannot leave his father: for if he should leave his father, his father would die. And thou saidst unto thy servants, Except your youngest brother come down with you, ye shall see my face no more. And it came to pass when we came up unto thy servant my father, we told him the words of my lord. And our father said, Go again, and buy us a little food. And we said, We cannot go down: if our youngest brother be with us, then will we go down: for we may not see the man's face, except our youngest brother be with us. And thy servant my father said unto us, Ye know that my wife bare me two sons: and the one went out from me, and I said, Surely he is torn in pieces; and I saw him not since: and if ye take this also from me, and mischief befall him, ye shall bring down my gray hairs with sorrow to the grave. Now therefore when I come to thy servant my father, and the lad be not with us; seeing that his life is bound up in the lad's life; it shall come to pass, when he seeth that the lad is not with us, that he will die: and thy servants

2. Joseph's servant is to claim that this is the cup Joseph uses for clairvoyance; diviners stared into a cup of water and foretold the future.

shall bring down the gray hairs of thy servant our father with sorrow to the grave. For thy servant became surety for the lad unto my father, saying, If I bring him not unto thee, then I shall bear the blame to my father for ever. Now therefore, I pray thee, let thy servant abide instead of the lad a bondman to my lord; and let the lad go up with his brethren. For how shall I go up to my father, and the lad be not with me? lest peradventure I see the evil that shall come on my father.

45. Then Joseph could not refrain himself before all them that stood by him; and he cried, Cause every man to go out from me. And there stood no man with him, while Joseph made himself known unto his brethren. And he wept aloud: and the Egyptians and the house of Pharaoh heard. And Joseph said unto his brethren, I am Joseph; doth my father yet live? And his brethren could not answer him; for they were troubled at his presence. And Joseph said unto his brethren, Come near to me, I pray you. And they came near. And he said, I am Joseph your brother, whom ye sold into Egypt. Now therefore be not grieved, nor angry with yourselves, that ye sold me hither: for God did send me before you to preserve life. For these two years hath the famine been in the land: and yet there are five years, in the which there shall neither be earing nor harvest. And God sent me before you to preserve you a posterity in the earth, and to save your lives by a great deliverance. So now it was not you that sent me hither, but God: and he hath made me a father to Pharaoh, and lord of all his house, and a ruler throughout all the land of Egypt. Haste ye, and go up to my father, and say unto him, Thus saith thy son Joseph, God hath made me lord of all Egypt: come down unto me, tarry not: and thou shalt dwell in the land of Goshen, and thou shalt be near unto me, thou, and thy children, and thy children's children, and thy flocks, and thy herds, and all that thou hast: and there will I nourish thee; for yet there are five years of famine; lest thou, and thy household, and all that thou hast, come to poverty. And, behold, your eyes see, and the eyes of my brother Benjamin, that it is my mouth that speaketh unto you. And ye shall tell my father of all my glory in Egypt, and of all that ye have seen; and ye shall haste and bring down my father hither. And he fell upon his brother Benjamin's neck, and wept; and Benjamin wept upon his neck. Moreover he kissed all his brethren, and wept upon them: and after that his brethren talked with him.

And the fame thereof was heard in Pharaoh's house, saying, Joseph's brethren are come: and it pleased Pharaoh well, and his servants. And Pharaoh said unto Joseph, Say unto thy brethren, This do ye; lade your beasts, and go, get you unto the land of Canaan; and take your father and your households, and come unto me: and I will give you the good of the land of Egypt, and ye shall eat the fat of the land. Now thou art commanded, this do ye; take you wagons out of the land of Egypt for your little ones, and for your wives, and bring your father, and come. Also regard not your stuff; for the good of all the land of Egypt is yours. And the children of Israel did so: and Joseph gave them wagons, according to the commandment of Pharaoh, and gave them provision for the way. To all of them he gave each man changes of raiment; but to Benjamin he gave three hundred pieces of silver, and five changes of raiment. And to his father he sent after this manner; ten asses laden with the good things of Egypt, and ten she-asses laden with corn and bread and meat for his father by the way. So he sent his brethren away, and they departed: and he said unto them, See that ye fall not out by the way.

And they went up out of Egypt, and came into the land of Canaan unto Jacob their father, and told him, saying, Joseph is yet alive, and he is governor over all the land of Egypt. And Jacob's heart fainted, for he believed them not. And they told him all the words of Joseph, which he had said unto them: and when he saw the wagons which Joseph had sent to carry him, the spirit of Jacob their father revived. And Israel said, It is enough; Joseph my son is yet alive: I will go and see him before I die.

46. And Israel took his journey with all that he had, and came to Beer-sheba, and offered sacrifices unto the God of his father Isaac. And God spake unto Israel in the visions of the night, and said, Jacob, Jacob. And he said, Here am I. And he said, I am God, the God of thy father: fear not to go down into Egypt; for I will there make of thee a great nation: I will go down with thee into Egypt; and I will also surely bring thee up again: and Joseph shall put his hand upon thine eyes. And Jacob rose up from Beer-sheba: and the sons of Israel carried Jacob their father, and their little ones, and their wives, in the wagons which Pharaoh had sent to carry him. And they took their cattle, and their goods, which they had gotten in the land of Canaan, and came into Egypt, Jacob, and all his seed with him: his sons, and his sons' sons with him, his daughters, and his sons' daughters, and all his seed brought he with him into Egypt.

From Job

1. There was a man in the land of Uz whose name was Job, and that man was perfect and upright, and one that feared God, and eschewed evil. And there were born unto him seven sons and three daughters. His substance also was seven thousand sheep, and three thousand camels, and five hundred yoke of oxen, and five hundred she asses, and a very great household; so that this man was the greatest of all the men of the east. And his sons went and feasted in their houses, every one his day;[1] and sent and called for their three sisters to eat and to drink with them. And it was so, when the days of their feasting were gone about, that Job sent and sanctified them, and rose up early in the morning, and offered burnt offerings according to the number of them all: for Job said, It may be that my sons have sinned, and cursed God in their hearts. Thus did Job continually.

Now there was a day when the sons of God came to present themselves before the Lord, and Satan came also among them. And the Lord said unto Satan, Whence comest thou? Then Satan answered the Lord, and said, From going to and fro in the earth, and from walking up and down in it. And the Lord said unto Satan, Hast thou considered my servant Job, that there is none like him in the earth, a perfect and an upright man, one that feareth God, and escheweth evil? Then Satan answered the Lord, and said, Doth Job fear God for nought? Hast not thou made an hedge about him, and about

1. In rotation at each son's house.

his house, and about all that he hath on every side? thou hast blessed the work of his hands, and his substance is increased in the land. But put forth thine hand now, and touch all that he hath, and he will curse thee to thy face. And the Lord said unto Satan, Behold, all that he hath is in thy power; only upon himself put not forth thine hand. So Satan went forth from the presence of the Lord.

And there was a day when his sons and his daughters were eating and drinking wine in their eldest brother's house: and there came a messenger unto Job, and said, The oxen were plowing, and the asses feeding beside them: and the Sabeans fell upon them, and took them away; yea, they have slain the servants with the edge of the sword; and I only am escaped alone to tell thee. While he was yet speaking, there came also another, and said, The fire of God is fallen from heaven, and hath burned up the sheep, and the servants, and consumed them; and I only am escaped alone to tell thee. While he was yet speaking, there came also another, and said, The Chaldeans made out three bands,[2] and fell upon the camels, and have carried them away, yea, and slain the servants with the edge of the sword; and I only am escaped alone to tell thee. While he was yet speaking, there came also another, and said, Thy sons and thy daughters were eating and drinking wine in their eldest brother's house: and, behold, there came a great wind from the wilderness, and smote the four corners of the house, and it fell upon the young men, and they are dead; and I only am escaped alone to tell thee.

Then Job arose and rent his mantle,[3] and shaved his head, and fell down upon the ground, and worshipped, and said, Naked came I out of my mother's womb, and naked shall I return thither: the Lord gave, and the Lord hath taken away; blessed be the name of the Lord. In all this Job sinned not, nor charged God foolishly.

2. Again there was a day when the sons of God came to present themselves before the Lord, and Satan came also among them to present himself before the Lord. And the Lord said unto Satan, From whence comest thou? And Satan answered the Lord, and said, From going to and fro in the earth, and from walking up and down in it. And the Lord said unto Satan, Hast thou considered my servant Job, that there is none like him in the earth, a perfect and an upright man, one that feareth God, and escheweth evil? and still he holdeth fast his integrity, although thou movedst me against him, to destroy him without cause. And Satan answered the Lord, and said, Skin for skin, yea, all that a man hath will he give for his life. But put forth thine hand now, and touch his bone and his flesh, and he will curse thee to thy face. And the Lord said unto Satan, Behold, he is in thine hand; but save his life.

So went Satan forth from the presence of the Lord, and smote Job with sore boils from the sole of his foot unto his crown. And he took him a potsherd to scrape himself withal; and he sat down among the ashes.

Then said his wife unto him, Dost thou still retain thine integrity? curse God, and die. But he said unto her, Thou speakest as one of the foolish women speaketh. What? shall we receive good at the hand of God, and shall we not receive evil? In all this did not Job sin with his lips.

Now when Job's three friends heard of all this evil that was come upon

2. I.e., split up into three groups. 3. Tore his cloak.

him, they came every one from his own place; Eliphaz the Temanite, and Bildad the Shuhite, and Zophar the Naamathite: for they had made an appointment together to come to mourn with him and to comfort him. And when they lifted up their eyes afar off, and knew him not, they lifted up their voice, and wept; and they rent every one his mantle, and sprinkled dust upon their heads toward heaven. So they sat down with him upon the ground seven days and seven nights, and none spake a word unto him: for they saw that his grief was very great.

3. After this opened Job his mouth, and cursed his day. And Job spake, and said, Let the day perish wherein I was born, and the night in which it was said, There is a man child conceived. Let that day be darkness; let not God regard it from above, neither let the light shine upon it. Let darkness and the shadow of death stain it; let a cloud dwell upon it; let the blackness of the day terrify it. As for that night, let darkness seize upon it; let it not be joined unto the days of the year, let it not come into the number of the months. Lo, let that night be solitary, let no joyful voice come therein. Let them curse it that curse the day, who are ready to raise up their mourning.[4] Let the stars of the twilight thereof be dark; let it look for light, but have none; neither let it see the dawning of the day: because it shut not up the doors of my mother's womb, nor hid sorrow from mine eyes. Why died I not from the womb? Why did I not give up the ghost when I came out of the belly? Why did the knees prevent[5] me? or why the breasts that I should suck? For now should I have lain still and been quiet, I should have slept: then had I been at rest, with kings and counsellors of the earth, which built desolate places for themselves; or with princes that had gold, who filled their houses with silver: or as an hidden untimely birth I had not been; as infants which never saw light. There the wicked cease from troubling; and there the weary be at rest. There the prisoners rest together; they hear not the voice of the oppressor. The small and great are there; and the servant is free from his master. Wherefore is light given to him that is in misery, and life unto the bitter in soul; which long for death, but it cometh not; and dig for it more than for hid treasures; which rejoice exceedingly, and are glad, when they can find the grave? Why is light given to a man whose way is hid, and whom God hath hedged in? For my sighing cometh before I eat, and my roarings are poured out like the waters. For the thing which I greatly feared is come upon me, and that which I was afraid of is come unto me. I was not in safety, neither had I rest, neither was I quiet; yet trouble came.

4. Then Eliphaz the Temanite answered and said, If we assay to commune with thee, wilt thou be grieved? But who can withhold himself from speaking? Behold, thou hast instructed many, and thou hast strengthened the weak hands. Thy words have upholden him that was falling, and thou hast strengthened the feeble knees. But now it is come upon thee, and thou faintest; it toucheth thee, and thou art troubled. Is not this thy fear, thy confidence, thy hope, and the uprightness of thy ways?[6] Remember, I pray

4. More literally: who are ready to rouse up leviathan, a dragon that was thought to produce darkness. *Them*: sorcerers, magicians. 5. Receive. 6. More literally: is not thy fear of God thy confidence, and thy hope the uprightness of thy ways?

thee, who ever perished, being innocent? or where were the righteous cut off? Even as I have seen, they that plow iniquity, and sow wickedness, reap the same. By the blast of God they perish, and by the breath of his nostrils are they consumed. The roaring of the lion, and the voice of the fierce lion, and the teeth of the young lions, are broken. The old lion perisheth for lack of prey, and the stout lion's whelps are scattered abroad. Now a thing was secretly brought to me, and mine ear received a little thereof. In thoughts from the visions of the night, when deep sleep falleth on men, fear came upon me, and trembling, which made all my bones to shake. Then a spirit passed before my face; the hair of my flesh stood up: It stood still, but I could not discern the form thereof: an image was before mine eyes, there was silence, and I heard a voice, saying, Shall mortal man be more just than God? Shall a man be more pure than his maker? Behold, he put no trust in his servants; and his angels he charged with folly: How much less in them that dwell in houses of clay, whose foundation is in the dust, which are crushed before the moth? They are destroyed from morning to evening: they perish for ever without any regarding it. Doth not their excellency which is in them go away? They die, even without wisdom.

5. Call now, if there be any that will answer thee; and to which of the saints wilt thou turn? For wrath killeth the foolish man, and envy slayeth the silly one. I have seen the foolish taking root: but suddenly I cursed his habitation. His children are far from safety, and they are crushed in the gate, neither is there any to deliver them. Whose harvest the hungry eateth up, and taketh it even out of the thorns, and the robber swalloweth up their substance. Although affliction cometh not forth of the dust, neither doth trouble spring out of the ground; yet man is born unto trouble, as the sparks fly upward. I would seek unto God, and unto God would I commit my cause: which doeth great things and unsearchable; marvellous things without number: who giveth rain upon the earth, and sendeth waters upon the fields: to set up on high those that be low; that those which mourn may be exalted to safety. He disappointeth the devices of the crafty, so that their hands cannot perform their enterprise. He taketh the wise in their own craftiness: and the counsel of the froward is carried headlong. They meet with darkness in the daytime, and grope in the noonday as in the night. But he saveth the poor from the sword, from their mouth, and from the hand of the mighty. So the poor hath hope, and iniquity stoppeth her mouth. Behold, happy is the man whom God correcteth: therefore despise not thou the chastening of the Almighty: for he maketh sore, and bindeth up: he woundeth, and his hands make whole. He shall deliver thee in six troubles: yea, in seven there shall no evil touch thee. In famine he shall redeem thee from death: and in war from the power of the sword. Thou shalt be hid from the scourge of the tongue: neither shalt thou be afraid of destruction when it cometh. At destruction and famine thou shalt laugh: neither shalt thou be afraid of the beasts of the earth. For thou shalt be in league with the stones of the field: and the beasts of the field shall be at peace with thee. And thou shalt know that thy tabernacle[7] shall be in peace; and thou shalt visit thy habitation, and shalt not sin. Thou shalt know also that thy seed shall be great, and thine

7. Tent.

offspring as the grass of the earth. Thou shalt come to thy grave in a full age, like as a shock of corn cometh in in his season. Lo this, we have searched it, so it is; hear it, and know thou it for thy good.

6. But Job answered and said, Oh that my grief were thoroughly weighed, and my calamity laid in the balances together! For now it would be heavier than the sand of the sea: therefore my words are swallowed up.[8] For the arrows of the Almighty are within me, the poison whereof drinketh up my spirit: the terrors of God do set themselves in array against me. Doth the wild ass bray when he hath grass? or loweth the ox over his fodder?[9] Can that which is unsavoury be eaten without salt? or is there any taste in the white of an egg? The things that my soul refused to touch are as my sorrowful meat.[1] Oh that I might have my request; and that God would grant me the thing that I long for! Even that it would please God to destroy me; that he would let loose his hand, and cut me off! Then should I yet have comfort; yea, I would harden myself in sorrow: let him not spare; for I have not concealed[2] the words of the Holy One. What is my strength, that I should hope? and what is mine end, that I should prolong my life? Is my strength the strength of stones? or is my flesh of brass? Is not my help in me? and is wisdom driven quite from me?[3] To him that is afflicted pity should be shewed from his friend; but he forsaketh the fear of the Almighty. My brethren have dealt deceitfully as a brook, and as the stream of brooks they pass away; which are blackish by reason of the ice, and wherein the snow is hid: what time they wax warm, they vanish: when it is hot, they are consumed out of their place. The paths of their way are turned aside; they go to nothing, and perish. The troops of Tema looked, the companies of Sheba waited for them. They were confounded because they had hoped;[4] they came thither, and were ashamed. For now ye are nothing; ye see my casting down, and are afraid. Did I say, Bring unto me? or, Give a reward for me of your substance? or, Deliver me from the enemy's hand? or, Redeem me from the hand of the mighty? Teach me, and I will hold my tongue: and cause me to understand wherein I have erred. How forcible are right words! But what doth your arguing reprove? Do ye imagine to reprove words, and the speeches of one that is desperate, which are as wind? Yea, ye overwhelm the fatherless, and ye dig a pit for your friend. Now therefore be content, look upon me; for it is evident unto you if I lie. Return, I pray you, let it not be iniquity; yea, return again, my righteousness is in it. Is there iniquity in my tongue? Cannot my taste discern perverse things?

7. Is there not an appointed time to man upon earth? Are not his days also like the days of an hireling? As a servant earnestly desireth the shadow,[5] and as an hireling looketh for the reward of his work: so am I made to possess months of vanity, and wearisome nights are appointed to me. When I lie down, I say, When shall I arise, and the night be gone? and I am full of tossings to and fro unto the dawning of the day. My flesh is clothed with

8. More literally: therefore have my words been rash; Job recognizes the exaggeration of his first outburst.
9. Animals do not complain without reason; therefore, when a rational person complains, he or she must have some justification for it. 1. More literally: my soul refuseth to touch them, they are as loathsome meat to me. He is referring to the statements of his friends. 2. Denied. 3. More literally: is not my help within me gone, and is not wisdom driven quite away from me. 4. The caravans reached the springs they had counted on and found them dry. 5. Evening, the end of the workday.

worms and clods of dust; my skin is broken, and become loathsome. My days are swifter than a weaver's shuttle, and are spent without hope. O remember that my life is wind: mine eye shall no more see good. The eye of him that hath seen me shall see me no more: thine eyes are upon me, and I am not. As the cloud is consumed and vanisheth away: so he that goeth down to the grave shall come up no more. He shall return no more to his house, neither shall his place know him any more. Therefore I will not refrain my mouth; I will speak in the anguish of my spirit; I will complain in the bitterness of my soul. Am I a sea, or a whale, that thou settest a watch over me?[6] When I say, My bed shall comfort me, my couch shall ease my complaint; then thou scarest me with dreams, and terrifiest me through visions: so that my soul chooseth strangling, and death rather than my life. I loathe it; I would not live alway: let me alone; for my days are vanity. What is man, that thou shouldest magnify him? and that thou shouldest set thine heart upon him? and that thou shouldest visit him every morning, and try him every moment? How long wilt thou not depart from me, nor let me alone till I swallow down my spittle?[7] I have sinned; what shall I do unto thee, O thou preserver[8] of men? Why hast thou set me as a mark against thee, so that I am a burden to myself? And why dost thou not pardon my transgression, and take away mine iniquity? For now shall I sleep in the dust; and thou shalt seek me in the morning, but I shall not be.

8. Then answered Bildad the Shuhite, and said, How long wilt thou speak these things? and how long shall the words of thy mouth be like a strong wind? Doth God pervert judgment? or doth the Almighty pervert justice? If thy children have sinned against him, and he have cast them away for their transgression; if thou wouldest seek unto God betimes, and make thy supplication to the Almighty; if thou wert pure and upright; surely now he would awake for thee, and make the habitation of thy righteousness prosperous. Though thy beginning was small, yet thy latter end should greatly increase. For enquire, I pray thee, of the former age, and prepare thy self to the search of their fathers: (For we are but of yesterday, and know nothing, because our days upon earth are a shadow:) shall not they teach thee, and tell thee, and utter words out of their heart? Can the rush[9] grow up without mire? Can the flag grow without water? Whilst it is yet in his greenness, and not cut down, it withereth before any other herb. So are the paths of all that forget God; and the hypocrite's hope shall perish: whose hope shall be cut off, and whose trust shall be a spider's web. He shall lean upon his house, but it shall not stand: he shall hold it fast, but it shall not endure. He is green before the sun, and his branch shooteth forth in his garden. His roots are wrapped about the heap, and seeth the place of stones. If he destroy him from his place, then it shall deny him, saying, I have not seen thee. Behold, this is the joy of his way, and out of the earth shall others grow. Behold, God will not cast away a perfect man, neither will he help the evil doers: till he fill thy mouth with laughing, and thy lips with rejoicing. They that hate thee

6. Job, now addressing God directly, compares his situation with that of the sea monster whom a god fought against in a Babylonian myth. He reproves God for exerting His power against anything as small as himself. 7. Even for a moment. 8. More literally: watcher. 9. Papyrus, which grows rapidly when the Nile is high but withers at once when the waters go down.

shall be clothed with shame; and the dwelling place of the wicked shall come to nought.

9. Then Job answered and said, I know it is so of a truth: but how should man be just with God? If he will contend with him, he cannot answer him one of a thousand.[1] He is wise in heart, and mighty in strength: who hath hardened himself against him, and hath prospered? Which removeth the mountains, and they know not: which overturneth them in his anger. Which shaketh the earth out of her place, and the pillars thereof tremble. Which commandeth the sun, and it riseth not; and sealeth up the stars. Which alone spreadeth out the heavens, and treadeth upon the waves of the sea. Which maketh Arcturus, Orion, and Pleiades, and the chambers of the south. Which doeth great things past finding out; yea, and wonders without number. Lo, he goeth by me, and I see him not: he passeth on also, but I perceive him not. Behold, he taketh away, who can hinder him? Who will say unto him, What doest thou? If God will not withdraw his anger, the proud helpers do stoop under him. How much less shall I answer him, and choose out my words to reason with him? Whom, though I were righteous, yet would I not answer, but I would make supplication to my judge. If I had called, and he had answered me; yet would I not believe that he had hearkened unto my voice. For he breaketh me with a tempest, and multiplieth my wounds without cause. He will not suffer me to take my breath, but filleth me with bitterness. If I speak of strength, lo, he is strong: and if of judgment, who shall set me a time to plead? If I justify myself, mine own mouth shall condemn me: if I say, I am perfect, it shall also prove me perverse. Though I were perfect, yet would I not know my soul: I would despise my life. This is one thing, therefore I said it, He destroyeth the perfect and the wicked. If the scourge slay suddenly, he will laugh at the trial of the innocent. The earth is given into the hand of the wicked: he covereth the faces of the judges thereof; if not, where, and who is he? Now my days are swifter than a post:[2] they flee away, they see no good. They are passed away as the swift ships: as the eagle that hasteth to the prey. If I say, I will forget my complaint, I will leave off my heaviness, and comfort myself: I am afraid of all my sorrows, I know that thou wilt not hold me innocent. If I be wicked, why then labour I in vain? If I wash myself with snow water, and make my hands never so clean; yet shalt thou plunge me in the ditch, and mine own clothes shall abhor me. For he is not a man, as I am, that I should answer him, and we should come together in judgment. Neither is there any daysman[3] betwixt us, that might lay his hand upon us both. Let him take his rod away from me, and let not his fear terrify me: then would I speak, and not fear him; but it is not so with me.

10. My soul is weary of my life; I will leave my complaint upon[4] myself; I will speak in the bitterness of my soul. I will say unto God, Do not condemn me; shew me wherefore thou contendest with me. Is it good unto thee that thou shouldest oppress, that thou shouldest despise the work of thine hands,

1. One of a thousand questions. 2. Courier. 3. Arbitrator. 4. On behalf of. *Leave*: give free course to.

and shine upon the counsel of the wicked? Hath thou eyes of flesh? or seest thou as man seeth? Are thy days as the days of man? Are thy years as man's days,[5] that thou enquirest after mine iniquity, and searchest after my sin? Thou knowest that I am not wicked; and there is none that can deliver out of thine hand. Thine hands have made me and fashioned me together round about; yet thou dost destroy me. Remember, I beseech thee, that thou hast made me as the clay; and wilt thou bring me into dust again? Hast thou not poured me out as milk and curdled me like cheese? Thou hast clothed me with skin and flesh, and hast fenced me with bones and sinews. Thou hast granted me life and favour, and thy visitation hath preserved my spirit. And these things hast thou hid in thine heart: I know that this is with thee.[6] If I sin, then thou markest me, and thou wilt not acquit me from mine iniquity. If I be wicked, woe unto me; and if I be righteous, yet will I not lift up my head. I am full of confusion; therefore see thou mine affliction; for it increaseth. Thou huntest me as a fierce lion: and again thou shewest thyself marvellous upon me. Thou renewest thy witnesses[7] against me, and increasest thine indignation upon me; changes and war are against me. Wherefore then hast thou brought me forth out of the womb? Oh that I had given up the ghost, and no eye had seen me! I should have been as though I had not been; I should have been carried from the womb to the grave. Are not my days few? Cease then, and let me alone, that I may take comfort a little before I go whence I shall not return, even to the land of darkness and the shadow of death: a land of darkness, as darkness itself; and of the shadow of death, without any order, and where the light is as darkness.

11. Then answered Zophar the Naamathite, and said, Should not the multitude of words be answered? And should a man full of talk be justified? Should thy lies make men hold their peace? And when thou mockest, shall no man make thee ashamed? For thou hast said, My doctrine is pure, and I am clean in thine eyes. But oh that God would speak, and open his lips against thee; and that he would shew thee the secrets of wisdom, that they are double to that which is! Know therefore that God exacteth of thee less than thine iniquity deserveth. Canst thou by searching find out God? Canst thou find out the Almighty unto perfection? It is as high as heaven; what canst thou do? Deeper than hell; what canst thou know? The measure thereof is longer than the earth, and broader than the sea. If he cut off, and shut up, or gather together,[8] then who can hinder him? For he knoweth vain men: he seeth wickedness also; will he not then consider it? For vain man would be wise, though man be born like a wild ass's colt. If thou prepare thine heart, and stretch out thine hands toward him; if iniquity be in thine hand, put it far away, and let not wickedness dwell in thy tabernacles. For then shalt thou lift up thy face without spot; yea, thou shalt be stedfast, and shalt not fear: because thou shalt forget thy misery, and remember it as waters that pass away: and thine age shall be clearer than the noonday; thou shalt shine forth, thou shalt be as the morning. And thou shalt be secure, because there is hope; yea, thou shalt dig about thee,[9] and thou shalt take

5. Is your time, like humankind's, short, so that you have to judge hastily? 6. I.e., my destruction (*this*) is your purpose. Job accuses God of planning his destruction while showing favor to him. 7. Afflictions, which prove (to his friends) his guilt. 8. For judgment. 9. Search; the master inspects his property before retiring.

thy rest in safety. Also thou shalt lie down, and none shall make thee afraid; yea, many shall make suit unto thee. But the eyes of the wicked shall fail, and they shall not escape, and their hope shall be as the giving up of the ghost.

12. And Job answered and said, No doubt but ye are the people, and wisdom shall die with you. But I have understanding as well as you; I am not inferior to you: yea, who knoweth not such things as these? I am as one mocked of his neighbour, who calleth upon God, and he answered him: the just upright man is laughed to scorn. He that is ready to slip with his feet is as a lamp despised in the thought of him that is at ease. The tabernacles of robbers prosper, and they that provoke God are secure; into whose hand God bringeth abundantly. But ask now the beasts, and they shall teach thee; and the fowls of the air, and they shall tell thee: or speak to the earth, and it shall teach thee; and the fishes of the sea shall declare unto thee. Who knoweth not in all these that the hand of the Lord hath wrought this? In whose hand is the soul of every living thing, and the breath of all mankind. Doth not the ear try words? and the mouth taste his meat? With the ancient is wisdom; and in length of days understanding. With him is wisdom and strength, he hath counsel and understanding. Behold, he breaketh down, and it cannot be built again: he shutteth up a man, and there can be no opening. Behold, he withholdeth the waters, and they dry up: also he sendeth them out, and they overturn the earth. With him is strength and wisdom: the deceived and the deceiver are his. He leadeth counsellors away spoiled, and maketh the judges fools. He looseth the bond of kings, and girdeth their loins with a girdle. He leadeth princes away spoiled, and overthroweth the mighty. He removeth away the speech of the trusty, and taketh away the understanding of the aged. He poureth contempt upon princes, and weakeneth the strength of the mighty. He discovereth deep things out of darkness, and bringeth out to light the shadow of death. He increaseth the nations, and destroyeth them: he enlargeth the nations, and straiteneth them again.[1] He taketh away the heart of the chief of the people of the earth, and causeth them to wander in a wilderness where there is no way. They grope in the dark without light, and he maketh them to stagger like a drunken man.

13. Lo, mine eye hath seen all this, mine ear hath heard and understood it. What ye know, the same do I know also: I am not inferior unto you. Surely I would speak to the Almighty, and I desire to reason with God. But ye are forgers of lies, ye are all physicians of no value. O that ye would altogether hold your peace! and it should be your wisdom. Hear now my reasoning, and hearken to the pleadings of my lips. Will ye speak wickedly for God? and talk deceitfully for him? Will ye accept[2] his person? Will ye contend for God? Is it good that he should search you out? or as one man mocketh another, do ye so mock him? He will surely reprove you, if ye do secretly accept persons.[3] Shall not his excellency make you afraid? and his dread fall upon you? Your remembrances[4] are like unto ashes, your bodies to bodies of clay. Hold your

1. Makes them small again. 2. Respect. 3. I.e., if you back the winning side for personal reasons.
4. Memorable sayings.

peace, let me alone, that I may speak, and let come on me what will. Wherefore do I take my flesh in my teeth, and put my life in mine hand?[5] Though he slay me, yet will I trust in him: but I will maintain mine own ways before him. He also shall be my salvation: for an hypocrite shall not come before him. Hear diligently my speech, and my declaration with your ears. Behold now, I have ordered my cause; I know that I shall be justified. Who is he that will plead with me?[6] for now, if I hold my tongue, I shall give up the ghost. Only do not two things unto me: then will I not hide myself from thee.[7] Withdraw thine hand far from me: and let not thy dread make me afraid. Then call thou, and I will answer: or let me speak, and answer thou me. How many are mine iniquities and sins? Make me to know my transgression and my sin. Wherefore hidest thou thy face, and holdest me for thine enemy? Wilt thou break a leaf driven to and fro? and wilt thou pursue the dry stubble? For thou writest bitter things against me, and makest me to possess the iniquities of my youth. Thou puttest my feet also in the stocks, and lookest narrowly unto all my paths; thou settest a print upon the heels of my feet. And he, as a rotten thing, consumeth, as a garment that is moth eaten.

14. Man that is born of a woman is of few days, and full of trouble. He cometh forth like a flower, and is cut down: he fleeth also as a shadow, and continueth not. And dost thou open thine eyes upon such an one, and bringest me into judgment with thee? Who can bring a clean thing out of an unclean? not one. Seeing his days are determined, the number of his months are with thee, thou hast appointed his bounds that he cannot pass; turn from him, that he may rest, till he shall accomplish, as an hireling, his day. For there is hope of a tree, if it be cut down, that it will sprout again, and that the tender branch thereof will not cease. Though the root thereof wax old in the earth, and the stock thereof die in the ground; yet through the scent of water it will bud, and bring forth boughs like a plant. But man dieth, and wasteth away: yea, man giveth up the ghost, and where is he? As the waters fail from the sea, and the flood decayeth and drieth up: so man lieth down, and riseth not: till the heavens be no more, they shall not awake, nor be raised out of their sleep. O that thou wouldest hide me in the grave, that thou wouldest keep me secret, until thy wrath be past, that thou wouldest appoint me a set time, and remember me! If a man die, shall he live again? All the days of my appointed time will I wait, till my change[8] come. Thou shalt call, and I will answer thee: thou wilt have a desire to[9] the work of thine hands. For now thou numberest my steps: dost thou not watch over my sin? My transgression is sealed up in a bag, and thou sewest up mine iniquity. And surely the mountain falling cometh to nought, and the rock is removed out of his place. The waters wear the stones: thou washest away the things which grow out of the dust of the earth; and thou destroyest the hope of man. Thou prevailest for ever against him, and he passeth; thou changest his countenance, and sendest him away. His sons come to honour, and he knoweth it not; and they are brought low, but he perceiveth it not of them. But his flesh upon him shall have pain, and his soul within him shall mourn.

5. Like a wild beast at bay, defending its life with its teeth. 6. Accuse me. 7. He now addresses himself directly to God. 8. Release. 9. For.

29. Moreover Job continued his parable, and said, Oh that I were as in months past, as in the days when God preserved me; when his candle shined upon my head, and when by his light I walked through darkness; as I was in the days of my youth, when the secret of God was upon my tabernacle; when the Almighty was yet with me, when my children were about me; when I washed my steps with butter and the rock poured me out rivers of oil; when I went out to the gate[1] through the city, when I prepared my seat in the street! The young men saw me, and hid themselves: and the aged arose, and stood up. The princes refrained talking, and laid their hand on their mouth. The nobles held their peace, and their tongue cleaved to the roof of their mouth. When the ear heard me, then it blessed me; and when the eye saw me, it gave witness to me: because I delivered the poor that cried, and the fatherless, and him that had none to help him. The blessing of him that was ready to perish came upon me: and I caused the widow's heart to sing for joy. I put on righteousness, and it clothed me: my judgment was as a robe and a diadem. I was eyes to the blind, and feet was I to the lame. I was a father to the poor: and the cause which I knew not I searched out. And I brake the jaws of the wicked, and plucked the spoil out of his teeth. Then I said, I shall die in my nest, and I shall multiply my days as the sand. My root was spread out by the waters, and the dew lay all night upon my branch. My glory was fresh in me, and my bow was renewed in my hand. Unto me men gave ear, and waited, and kept silence at my counsel. After my words they spake not again; and my speech dropped upon them. And they waited for me as for the rain; and they opened their mouth wide as for the latter rain. If I laughed on them, they believed it not; and the light of my countenance they cast not down. I chose out their way, and sat chief, and dwelt as a king in the army, as one that comforteth the mourners.

30. But now they that are younger than I have me in derision, whose fathers I would have disdained to have set with the dogs of my flock. Yea, whereto might the strength of their hands profit me, in whom old age was perished?[2] For want and famine they were solitary; fleeing into the wilderness in former time desolate and waste. Who cut up mallows by the bushes, and juniper roots for their meat. They were driven forth from among men, (they cried after them as after a thief;) to dwell in the cliffs of the valleys, in caves of the earth, and in the rocks. Among the bushes they brayed; under the nettles they were gathered together. They were children of fools, yea, children of base men: they were viler than the earth. And now am I their song, yea, I am their byword. They abhor me, they flee far from me, and spare not to spit in my face. Because he hath loosed my cord, and afflicted me, they have also let loose the bridle before me. Upon my right hand rise the youth; they push away my feet, and they raise up against me the ways of their destruction. They mar my path, they set forward my calamity, they have no helper. They came upon me as a wide breaking in of waters: in the desolation they rolled themselves upon me. Terrors are turned upon me: they pursue my soul as the wind: and my welfare passeth away as a cloud. And now my soul is poured out upon[3] me; the days of affliction have taken hold upon me.

1. The town meeting place and law court was just inside the gate. 2. They were too old to work.
3. Within.

My bones are pierced in me in the night season: and my sinews take no rest. By the great force of my disease is my garment changed: it bindeth me about as the collar of my coat. He hath cast me into the mire, and I am become like dust and ashes. I cry unto thee, and thou dost not hear me: I stand up and thou regardest me not. Thou art become cruel to me: with thy strong hand thou opposest thyself against me. Thou liftest me up to the wind; thou causest me to ride upon it, and dissolvest my substance. For I know that thou wilt bring me to death, and to the house appointed for all living. Howbeit he will not stretch out his hand to the grave, though they cry in his destruction. Did not I weep for him that was in trouble? Was not my soul grieved for the poor? When I looked for good, then evil came unto me: and when I waited for light, there came darkness. My bowels boiled, and rested not: the days of affliction prevented me. I went mourning without the sun: I stood up, and I cried in the congregation. I am a brother to dragons, and a companion to owls. My skin is black upon me, and my bones are burned with heat. My harp also is turned to mourning, and my organ[4] into the voice of them that weep.

31. I made a covenant with mine eyes; why then should I think upon a maid? For what portion of God is there from above? and what inheritance of the Almighty from on high? Is not destruction to the wicked? and a strange punishment to the workers of iniquity? Doth not he see my ways, and count all my steps? If I have walked with vanity, or if my foot hath hasted to deceit; let me be weighed in an even balance, that God may know mine integrity. If my step hath turned out of the way, and mine heart walked after mine eyes, and if any blot hath cleaved to mine hands; then let me sow, and let another eat; yea, let my offspring be rooted out. If mine heart have been deceived by a woman, or if I have laid wait at my neighbour's door; then let my wife grind unto another, and let others bow down upon her. For this is an heinous crime; yea, it is an iniquity to be punished by the judges. For it is a fire that consumeth to destruction, and would root out all mine increase.

If I did despise the cause of my manservant or of my maidservant, when they contended with me; what then shall I do when God riseth up? and when he visiteth, what shall I answer him? Did not he that made me in the womb make him? and did not one fashion us in the womb? If I have withheld the poor from their desire, or have caused the eyes of the widow to fail; or have eaten my morsel myself alone, and the fatherless hath not eaten thereof; (For from my youth he was brought up with me, as with a father, and I have guided her from my mother's womb;) if I have seen any perish for want of clothing, or any poor without covering; if his loins have not blessed me, and if he were not warmed with the fleece of my sheep; if I have lifted up my hand against the fatherless, when I saw my help in the gate:[5] then let mine arm fall from my shoulder blade, and mine arm be broken from the bone. For destruction from God was a terror to me, and by reason of his highness I could not endure. If I have made gold my hope, or have said to the fine gold, Thou art my confidence; if I rejoiced because my wealth was great, and because mine hand had gotten much; if I beheld the sun when it shined, or

4. Pipe. 5. I.e., when I had influence in the court.

the moon walking in brightness; and my heart hath been secretly enticed, or my mouth hath kissed my hand:[6] this also were an iniquity to be punished by the judge: for I should have denied the God that is above.

If I rejoiced at the destruction of him that hated me, or lifted up myself when evil found him: neither have I suffered my mouth to sin by wishing a curse to his soul. If the men of my tabernacle said not, Oh that we had of his flesh! We cannot be satisfied. The stranger did not lodge in the street: but I opened my doors to the traveller. If I covered my transgressions as Adam, by hiding mine iniquity in my bosom: did I fear a great multitude, or did the contempt of families terrify me, that I kept silence, and went not out of the door? Oh that one would hear me! Behold, my desire is, that the Almighty would answer me, and that mine adversary had written a book. Surely I would take it upon my shoulder, and bind it as a crown to me. I would declare unto him the number of my steps; as a prince would I go near unto him. If my land cry against me, or that the furrows likewise thereof complain; if I have eaten the fruits thereof without money, or have caused the owners thereof to lose their life: let thistles grow instead of wheat, and cockle instead of barley. The words of Job are ended.

38. Then the Lord answered Job out of the whirlwind, and said, Who is this that darkeneth counsel by words without knowledge? Gird up now thy loins like a man; for I will demand of thee, and answer thou me. Where wast thou when I laid the foundations of the earth? Declare, if thou hast understanding. Who hath laid the measures thereof, if thou knowest? or who hath stretched the line upon it? Whereupon are the foundations thereof fastened? or who laid the corner stone thereof; when the morning stars sang together, and all the sons of God shouted for joy? Or who shut up the sea with doors, when it brake forth, as if it had issued out of the womb? When I made the cloud the garment thereof, and thick darkness a swaddlingband for it, and brake up for it my decreed place,[7] and set bars and doors, and said, Hitherto shalt thou come, but no further: and here shall thy proud waves be stayed? Hast thou commanded the morning since thy days; and caused the dayspring[8] to know his place; that it might take hold of the ends of the earth, that the wicked might be shaken out of it? It is turned as clay to the seal; and they[9] stand as a garment. And from the wicked their light is withholden, and the high arm shall be broken. Hast thou entered into the springs of the sea? or hast thou walked in the search of the depth? Have the gates of death been opened unto thee? or hast thou seen the doors of the shadow of death? Hast thou perceived the breadth of the earth? Declare if thou knowest it all. Where is the way where light dwelleth? And as for darkness, where is the place thereof, that thou shouldest take it to the bound thereof, and that thou shouldest know the paths to the house thereof? Knowest thou it, because thou wast then born? or because the number of thy days is great? Hast thou entered into the treasures of the snow? or hast thou seen the treasures of the hail, which I have reserved against the time of trouble, against the day of battle and war? By what way is the light parted, which scattereth the east

6. Idolatrous acts of worship of the sun and moon. 7. The broken coastline. 8. Dawn. 9. All things; God is describing the moment of the creation of the universe. *Turned as clay to the seal:* more literally, changed as clay under the seal.

wind upon the earth? Who hath divided a watercourse for the overflowing of waters, or a way for the lightning of thunder; to cause it to rain on the earth, where no man is; on the wilderness, wherein there is no man; to satisfy the desolate and waste ground; and to cause the bud of the tender herb to spring forth? Hath the rain a father? or who hath begotten the drops of dew? Out of whose womb came the ice? And the hoary frost of heaven, who hath gendered it? The waters are hid as with a stone, and the face of the deep is frozen. Canst thou bind the sweet influences of Pleiades, or loose the bands of Orion? Canst thou bring forth Mazzaroth[1] in his season? or canst thou guide Arcturus with his sons? Knowest thou the ordinances of heaven? Canst thou set the dominion thereof in the earth? Canst thou lift up thy voice to the clouds, that abundance of waters may cover thee? Canst thou send lightnings, that they may go, and say unto thee, Here we are? Who hath put wisdom in the inward parts? or who hath given understanding to the heart? Who can number the clouds in wisdom? or who can stay the bottles of heaven, when the dust groweth into hardness, and the clods cleave fast together? Wilt thou hunt the prey for the lion? or fill the appetite of the young lions, when they couch in their dens, and abide in the covert to lie in wait? Who provideth for the raven his food? when his young ones cry unto God, they wander for lack of meat.

39. Knowest thou the time when the wild goats of the rock bring forth? or canst thou mark when the hinds do calve? Canst thou number the months that they fulfil? or knowest thou the time when they bring forth? They bow themselves, they bring forth their young ones, they cast out their sorrows. Their young ones are in good liking, they grow up with corn; they go forth, and return not unto them. Who hath sent out the wild ass free? or who hath loosed the bands of the wild ass? Whose house I have made the wilderness, and the barren land his dwellings. He scorneth the multitude of the city, neither regardeth he the crying of the driver. The range of the mountains is his pasture, and he searcheth after every green thing. Will the unicorn[2] be willing to serve thee, or abide by thy crib? Canst thou bind the unicorn with his band in the furrow? or will he harrow the valleys after thee? Wilt thou trust him, because his strength is great? or wilt thou leave thy labour to him? Wilt thou believe him, that he will bring home thy seed, and gather it into thy barn? Gavest thou the goodly wings unto the peacocks? or wings and feathers unto the ostrich? Which leaveth her eggs in the earth, and warmeth them in dust, and forgetteth that the foot may crush them, or that the wild beast may break them. She is hardened against her young ones, as though they were not hers: her labour is in vain without fear;[3] because God hath deprived her of wisdom, neither hath he imparted to her understanding. What time she lifteth up herself on high, she scorneth the horse and his rider. Hast thou given the horse strength? Hast thou clothed his neck with thunder? Canst thou make him afraid as a grasshopper? The glory of his nostrils is terrible. He paweth in the valley, and rejoiceth in his strength: he goeth on to meet the armed men. He mocketh at fear, and is not affrighted;

1. Meaning disputed; it may be a name for the signs of the zodiac or for some particular constellation.
2. The Hebrew has "wild ox." 3. I.e., although her labor is in vain, she is without fear.

neither turneth he back from the sword. The quiver rattleth against him, the glittering spear and the shield. He swalloweth the ground with fierceness and rage: neither believeth he that it is the sound of the trumpet. He saith among the trumpets, Ha, ha; and he smelleth the battle afar off, the thunder of the captains, and the shouting. Doth the hawk fly by thy wisdom, and stretch her wings toward the south? Doth the eagle mount up at thy command, and make her nest on high? She dwelleth and abideth on the rock, upon the crag of the rock, and the strong place. From thence she seeketh the prey, and her eyes behold afar off. Her young ones also suck up blood: and where the slain are, there is she.

40. Moreover the Lord answered Job, and said, Shall he that contendeth with the Almighty instruct him? He that reproveth God, let him answer it.

Then Job answered the Lord, and said, Behold, I am vile; what shall I answer thee? I will lay mine hand upon my mouth. Once have I spoken; but I will not answer: yea, twice; but I will proceed no further.

Then answered the Lord unto Job out of the whirlwind, and said, Gird up thy loins now like a man: I will demand of thee, and declare thou unto me. Wilt thou also disannul my judgment? Wilt thou condemn me, that thou mayest be righteous? Hast thou an arm like God: or canst thou thunder with a voice like him? Deck thyself now with majesty and excellency; and array thyself with glory and beauty. Cast abroad the rage of thy wrath: and behold every one that is proud, and abase him. Look on every one that is proud, and bring him low; and tread down the wicked in their place. Hide them in the dust together; and bind their faces in secret. Then will I also confess unto thee that thine own right hand can save thee.

Behold now behemoth,[4] which I made with thee; he eateth grass as an ox. Lo now, his strength is in his loins, and his force is in the navel of his belly. He moveth his tail like a cedar: the sinews of his stones[5] are wrapped together. His bones are as strong pieces of brass; his bones are like bars of iron. He is the chief of the ways of God: he that made him can make his sword to approach unto him. Surely the mountains bring him forth food, where all the beasts of the field play. He lieth under the shady trees, in the covert of the reed, and fens. The shady trees cover him with their shadow; the willows of the brook compass him about. Behold, he drinketh up a river, and hasteth not: he trusteth that he can draw up Jordan into his mouth. He taketh it with his eyes:[6] his nose pierceth through snares.

41. Canst thou draw out leviathan[7] with an hook? or his tongue with a cord which thou lettest down? Canst thou put an hook into his nose? or bore his jaw through with a thorn? Will he make many supplications unto thee? will he speak soft words unto thee? Will he make a covenant with thee? wilt thou take him for a servant for ever? Wilt thou play with him as with a bird? or wilt thou bind him for thy maidens? Shall the companions make a banquet of him? Shall they part him among the merchants? Canst thou fill his skin with barbed irons? or his head with fish spears? Lay thine hand upon him,

4. Generally identified with the hippopotamus. 5. More literally: thighs. 6. Obscure; probably none can attack him in the eyes. 7. Here probably the crocodile.

remember the battle, do no more. Behold, the hope of him is in vain: shall not one be cast down even at the sight of him? None is so fierce that dare stir him up: who then is able to stand before me? Who hath prevented me,[8] that I should repay him? Whatsoever is under the whole heaven is mine. I will not conceal his parts, nor his power, nor his comely proportion. Who can discover the face of his garment?[9] or who can come to him with his double bridle? Who can open the doors of his face? His teeth are terrible round about. His scales are his pride, shut up together as with a close seal. One is so near to another, that no air can come between them. They are joined one to another, they stick together, that they cannot be sundered. By his neesings[1] a light doth shine, and his eyes are like the eyelids of the morning. Out of his mouth go burning lamps, and sparks of fire leap out. Out of his nostrils goeth smoke, as out of a seething pot or caldron. His breath kindleth coals, and a flame goeth out of his mouth. In his neck remaineth strength, and sorrow is turned into joy before him. The flakes of his flesh are joined together: they are firm in themselves; they cannot be moved. His heart is as firm as a stone; yea, as hard as a piece of the nether millstone. When he raiseth up himself, the mighty are afraid: by reason of breakings they purify themselves.[2] The sword of him that layeth at him cannot hold: the spear, the dart, nor the habergeon. He esteemeth iron as straw, and brass as rotten wood. The arrow cannot make him flee: slingstones are turned with him into stubble. Darts are counted as stubble: he laugheth at the shaking of a spear. Sharp stones are under him: he spreadeth sharp pointed things upon the mire. He maketh the deep to boil like a pot: he maketh the sea like a pot of ointment. He maketh a path to shine after him; one would think the deep to be hoary.[3] Upon earth there is not his like, who is made without fear. He beholdeth all high things: he is a king over all the children of pride.

42. Then Job answered the Lord, and said, I know that thou canst do every thing, and that no thought can be withholden from thee. Who is he that hideth counsel without knowledge? Therefore have I uttered that I understood not; things too wonderful for me, which I knew not. Hear, I beseech thee, and I will speak: I will demand of thee, and declare thou unto me. I have heard of thee by the hearing of the ear: but now mine eye seeth thee. Wherefore I abhor myself, and repent in dust and ashes.

And it was so, that after the Lord had spoken these words unto Job, the Lord said to Eliphaz the Temanite, My wrath is kindled against thee, and against thy two friends: for ye have not spoken of me the thing that is right, as my servant Job hath. Therefore take unto you now seven bullocks and seven rams, and go to my servant Job, and offer up for yourselves a burnt offering; and my servant Job shall pray for you: for him will I accept: lest I deal with you after your folly, in that ye have not spoken of me the thing which is right, like my servant Job. So Eliphaz the Temanite and Bildad the Shuhite and Zophar the Naamathite went, and did according as the Lord commanded them: the Lord also accepted Job. And the Lord turned the

8. Given anything to me first. 9. His scales. *Discover*: strip off. 1. His breath (compare *sneeze*). The vapor exhaled by the crocodile appears luminous in the sunlight. 2. Corrupt text; probably in consternation they are beside themselves. 3. White (with foam).

captivity[4] of Job, when he prayed for his friends: also the Lord gave Job twice as much as he had before. Then came there unto him all his brethren, and all his sisters, and all they that had been of his acquaintance before, and did eat bread with him in his house: and they bemoaned him, and comforted him over all the evil that the Lord had brought upon him: every man also gave him a piece of money, and every one an earring of gold. So the Lord blessed the latter end of Job more than his beginning: for he had fourteen thousand sheep, and six thousand camels, and a thousand yoke of oxen, and a thousand she asses. He had also seven sons and three daughters. And he called the name of the first, Jemima; and the name of the second, Kezia; and the name of the third, Kerenhappuch. And in all the land were no women found so fair as the daughters of Job: and their father gave them inheritance among their brethren. After this lived Job an hundred and forty years, and saw his sons, and his sons' sons, even four generations. So Job died, being old and full of days.

Psalm 8

1. O Lord our Lord, how excellent is thy name in all the earth! who hast set thy glory above the heavens.
2. Out of the mouth of babes and sucklings hast thou ordained strength because of thine enemies, that thou mightest still the enemy and the avenger.
3. When I consider thy heavens, the work of thy fingers, the moon and the stars, which thou hast ordained;
4. What is man, that thou art mindful of him? and the son of man, that thou visitest him?
5. For thou hast made him a little lower than the angels, and hast crowned him with glory and honour.
6. Thou madest him to have dominion over the works of thy hands; thou hast put all things under his feet:
7. All sheep and oxen, yea, and the beasts of the field;
8. The fowl of the air, and the fish of the sea, and whatsoever passeth through the paths of the seas.
9. O Lord our Lord, how excellent is thy name in all the earth!

Psalm 19

1. The heavens declare the glory of God; and the firmament sheweth his handywork.
2. Day unto day uttereth speech, and night unto night sheweth knowledge.
3. There is no speech nor language, where their voice is not heard.
4. Their line is gone out through all the earth, and their words to the end of the world. In them hath he set a tabernacle for the sun,

4. Put an end to the suffering.

5. Which is as a bridegroom coming out of his chamber, and rejoiceth as a strong man to run a race.

6. His going forth is from the end of the heaven, and his circuit unto the ends of it: and there is nothing hid from the heat thereof.

7. The law of the Lord is perfect, converting the soul: the testimony of the Lord is sure, making wise the simple.

8. The statutes of the Lord are right, rejoicing the heart: the commandment of the Lord is pure, enlightening the eyes.

9. The fear of the Lord is clean, enduring for ever: the judgments of the Lord are true and righteous altogether.

10. More to be desired are they than gold, yea, than much fine gold: sweeter also than honey and the honeycomb.

11. Moreover by them is thy servant warned: and in keeping of them there is great reward.

12. Who can understand his errors? cleanse thou me from secret faults.

13. Keep back thy servant also from presumptuous sins; let them not have dominion over me: then shall I be upright, and I shall be innocent from the great transgression.

14. Let the words of my mouth, and the meditation of my heart, be acceptable in thy sight, O Lord, my strength, and my redeemer.

Psalm 23

1. The Lord is my shepherd; I shall not want.

2. He maketh me to lie down in green pastures: he leadeth me beside the still waters.

3. He restoreth my soul: he leadeth me in the paths of righteousness for his name's sake.

4. Yea, though I walk through the valley of the shadow of death, I will fear no evil: for thou art with me; thy rod and thy staff they comfort me.

5. Thou preparest a table before me in the presence of mine enemies: thou anointest my head with oil; my cup runneth over.

6. Surely goodness and mercy shall follow me all the days of my life: and I will dwell in the house of the Lord for ever.

Psalm 104

1. Bless the Lord, O my soul. O Lord my God, thou art very great; thou art clothed with honour and majesty.

2. Who coverest thyself with light as with a garment: who stretchest out the heavens like a curtain:

3. Who layeth the beams of his chambers in the waters: who maketh the clouds his chariot: who walketh upon the wings of the wind:

4. Who maketh his angels spirits; his ministers a flaming fire:

5. Who laid the foundations of the earth, that it should not be removed for ever.

6. Thou coveredst it with the deep as with a garment: the waters stood above the mountains.

7. At thy rebuke they fled; at the voice of thy thunder they hasted away.

8. They go up by the mountains; they go down by the valleys unto the place which thou hast founded for them.

9. Thou hast set a bound that they may not pass over; that they turn not again to cover the earth.

10. He sendeth the springs into the valleys, which run among the hills.

11. They give drink to every beast of the field: the wild asses quench their thirst.

12. By them shall the fowls of the heaven have their habitation, which sing among the branches.

13. He watereth the hills from his chambers: the earth is satisfied with the fruit of thy works.

14. He causeth the grass to grow for the cattle, and herb for the service of man: that he may bring forth food out of the earth;

15. And wine that maketh glad the heart of man, and oil to make his face to shine, and bread which strengtheneth man's heart.

16. The trees of the Lord are full of sap; the cedars of Lebanon, which he hath planted;

17. Where the birds make their nests: as for the stork, the fir trees are her house.

18. The high hills are a refuge for the wild goats; and the rocks for the conies.

19. He appointed the moon for seasons: the sun knoweth his going down.

20. Thou makest darkness, and it is night: wherein all the beasts of the forest do creep forth.

21. The young lions roar after their prey, and seek their meat from God.

22. The sun ariseth, they gather themselves together, and lay them down in their dens.

23. Man goeth forth unto his work and to his labour until the evening.

24. O Lord, how manifold are thy works! in wisdom hast thou made them all: the earth is full of thy riches.

25. So is this great and wide sea, wherein are things creeping innumerable, both small and great beasts.

26. There go the ships: there is that leviathan, whom thou hast made to play therein.

27. These wait all upon thee; that thou mayest give them their meat in due season.

28. That thou givest them they gather: thou openest thine hand, they are filled with good.

29. Thou hidest thy face, they are troubled: thou takest away their breath, they die, and return to their dust.

30. Thou sendest forth thy spirit, they are created: and thou renewest the face of the earth.

31. The glory of the Lord shall endure for ever: the Lord shall rejoice in his works.

32. He looketh on the earth, and it trembleth: he toucheth the hills, and they smoke.

33. I will sing unto the Lord as long as I live: I will sing praise to my God while I have my being.

34. My meditation of him shall be sweet: I will be glad in the Lord.
35. Let the sinners be consumed out of the earth, and let the wicked be no more. Bless thou the Lord, O my soul. Praise ye the Lord.

Psalm 137

1. By the rivers of Babylon,[1] there we sat down, yea, we wept, when we remembered Zion.
2. We hanged our harps upon the willows in the midst thereof.
3. For there they that carried us away captive required of us a song; and they that wasted us required of us mirth, saying, Sing us one of the songs of Zion.
4. How shall we sing the Lord's song in a strange land?
5. If I forget thee, O Jerusalem, let my right hand forget her cunning.
6. If I do not remember thee, let my tongue cleave to the roof of my mouth; if I prefer not Jerusalem above my chief joy.
7. Remember, O Lord, the children of Edom[2] in the day of Jerusalem; who said, Rase it, rase it, even to the foundation thereof.
8. O daughter of Babylon, who art to be destroyed; happy shall he be, that rewardeth thee as thou hast served us.
9. Happy shall he be, that taketh and dasheth thy little ones against the stones.

The Song of Songs

1. The song of songs, which is Solomon's.

Let him kiss me with the kisses of his mouth: for thy love is better than wine. Because of the savor of thy good ointments thy name is as ointment poured forth, therefore do the virgins love thee. Draw me, we will run after thee: the King hath brought me into his chambers: we will be glad and rejoice in thee, we will remember thy love more than wine: the upright love thee. I am black,[1] but comely, O ye daughters of Jerusalem, as the tents of Kedar,[2] as the curtains of Solomon. Look[3] not upon me, because I am black, because the sun hath looked upon me: my mother's children were angry with me; they made me the keeper of the vineyards; but mine own vineyard have I not kept. Tell me, O thou whom my soul loveth, where thou feedest, where thou makest thy flock to rest at noon: for why should I be as one that turneth aside by the flocks of thy companions?

If thou know not, O thou fairest among women, go thy way forth by the footsteps of the flock, and feed thy kids beside the shepherds' tents. I have compared thee, O my love, to a company of horses in Pharaoh's chariots.

1. On the Euphrates River. Jerusalem was captured and sacked by the Babylonians in 586 B.C. The Hebrews were taken away into captivity in Babylon. 2. The Edomites helped the Babylonians to capture Jerusalem. 1. Tanned from sun and weather; feminine beauty required a sheltered and fair skin. 2. A nomadic people of northern Arabia, living east of Palestine. 3. Better, *gaze* or *stare* (with fascination).

Thy cheeks are comely with rows of jewels, thy neck with chains of gold. We will make thee borders of gold with studs of silver.

While the King sitteth at his table, my spikenard[4] sendeth forth the smell thereof. A bundle of myrrh is my well-beloved unto me; he shall lie all night betwixt my breasts. My beloved is unto me as a cluster of camphire in the vineyards of Engedi.[5] Behold, thou art fair, my love; behold, thou art fair; thou hast doves' eyes. Behold, thou art fair, my beloved, yea, pleasant: also our bed is green. The beams of our house are cedar, and our rafters of fir.

2. I am the rose of Sharon,[6] and the lily of the valleys. As the lily among thorns, so is my love among the daughters. As the apple tree among the trees of the wood, so is my beloved among the sons. I sat down under his shadow with great delight, and his fruit was sweet to my taste. He brought me to the banqueting house, and his banner over me was love. Stay me with flagons, comfort me with apples: for I am sick of love. His left hand is under my head, and his right hand doth embrace me. I charge you, O ye daughters of Jerusalem, by the roes, and by the hinds of the field, that ye stir not up, nor awake my love, till he please. The voice of my beloved! behold he cometh leaping upon the mountains skipping upon the hills. My beloved is like a roe or a young hart: behold, he standeth behind our wall, he looketh forth at the windows, showing himself through the lattice. My beloved spake, and said unto me, Rise up, my love, my fair one, and come away. For, lo, the winter is past, the rain is over and gone; the flowers appear on the earth; the time of the singing of birds is come, and the voice of the turtle[7] is heard in our land; the fig tree putteth forth her green figs, and the vines with the tender grape give a good smell. Arise, my love, my fair one, and come away.

O my dove, that art in the clefts of the rock, in the secret places of the stairs, let me see thy countenance, let me hear thy voice; for sweet is thy voice, and thy countenance is comely. Take us the foxes, the little foxes, that spoil the vines: for our vines have tender grapes.

My beloved is mine, and I am his: he feedeth among the lilies. Until the day break, and the shadows flee away, turn, my beloved, and be thou like a roe or a young hart upon the mountains of Bether.[8]

3. By night on my bed I sought him whom my soul loveth: I sought him, but I found him not. I will rise now, and go about the city in the streets, and in the broad ways I will seek him whom my soul loveth: I sought him, but I found him not. The watchmen that go about the city found me: to whom I said, Saw ye him whom my soul loveth? It was but a little that I passed from them, but I found him whom my soul loveth: I held him, and would not let him go, until I had brought him into my mother's house, and into the chamber of her that conceived me. I charge you, O ye daughters of Jerusalem, by the roes, and by the hinds of the field, that ye stir not up, nor wake my love, till he please.

Who is this that cometh out of the wilderness like pillars of smoke, perfumed with myrrh and frankincense, with all powders of the merchant?

4. Fragrant oil made from an Indian plant. 5. An oasis on the western shore of the Dead Sea, a source of fragrant oil made from the camphire (henna) plant. 6. *Sharon:* a plain on the coast of Palestine, notable for its wildflowers. 7. The turtledove. 8. Name of a city of Judah, southwest of Jerusalem; the phrase may also mean "the cleft mountains" (a reference to female breasts or genitals).

Behold his bed, which is Solomon's; threescore valiant men are about it, of the valiant of Israel. They all hold swords, being expert in war: every man hath his sword upon his thigh because of fear in the night. King Solomon made himself a chariot of the wood of Lebanon. He made the pillars thereof of silver, the bottom thereof of gold, the covering of it of purple, the midst thereof being paved with love, for the daughters of Jerusalem. Go forth, O ye daughters of Zion, and behold king Solomon with the crown wherewith his mother crowned him in the day of his espousals, and in the day of the gladness of his heart.

4. Behold, thou art fair, my love; behold, thou art fair; thou hast doves' eyes within thy locks: thy hair is as a flock of goats, that appear from mount Gilead.[9] Thy teeth are like a flock of sheep that are even shorn, which came up from the washing; whereof every one bear twins, and none is barren among them. Thy lips are like a thread of scarlet, and thy speech is comely: thy temples are like a piece of a pomegranate within thy locks. Thy neck is like the tower of David builded for an armory, whereon there hang a thousand bucklers, all shields of mighty men. Thy two breasts are like two young roes that are twins, which feed among the lilies. Until the day break, and the shadows flee away, I will get me to the mountain of myrrh, and to the hill of frankincense. Thou art all fair, my love; there is no spot in thee.

Come with me from Lebanon, my spouse, with me from Lebanon: look from the top of Amana, from the top of Shenir and Hermon,[1] from the lions' dens, from the mountains of the leopards. Thou hast ravished my heart, my sister, my spouse; thou hast ravished my heart with one of thine eyes, with one chain of thy neck. How fair is thy love, my sister, my spouse! how much better is thy love than wine! and the smell of thine ointments than all spices! Thy lips, O my spouse, drop as the honeycomb: honey and milk are under thy tongue; and the smell of thy garments is like the smell of Lebanon. A garden inclosed is my sister, my spouse; a spring shut up, a fountain sealed. Thy plants are an orchard of pomegranates, with pleasant fruits; camphire, with spikenard, spikenard and saffron; calamus[2] and cinnamon, with all trees of frankincense; myrrh and aloes, with all the chief spices: a fountain of gardens, a well of living waters, and streams from Lebanon.

Awake, O north wind; and come, thou south; blow upon my garden, that the spices thereof may flow out. Let my beloved come into his garden, and eat his pleasant fruits.

5. I am come into my garden, my sister, my spouse: I have gathered my myrrh with my spice; I have eaten my honeycomb with my honey; I have drunk my wine with my milk: eat, O friends; drink, yea, drink abundantly, O beloved.

I sleep, but my heart waketh: it is the voice of my beloved that knocketh, saying, Open to me, my sister, my love, my dove, my undefiled: for my head is filled with dew, and my locks with the drops of the night. I have put off my coat; how shall I put it on? I have washed my feet; how shall I defile

9. Location uncertain; perhaps a high inland plateau.
1. Mountains in the Antilebanon range of Syria.
2. Cane, an aromatic spice.

them? My beloved put in his hand[3] by the hole of the door, and my bowels[4] were moved for him. I rose up to open to my beloved; and my hands dropped with myrrh, and my fingers with sweet smelling myrrh, upon the handles of the lock. I opened to my beloved; but my beloved had withdrawn himself, and was gone: my soul failed when he spake: I sought him, but I could not find him; I called him, but he gave me no answer. The watchmen that went about the city found me, they smote me, they wounded me; the keepers of the walls took away my veil from me. I charge you, O daughters of Jerusalem, if ye find my beloved, that ye tell him, that I am sick of love. What is thy beloved more than another beloved, O thou fairest among women? what is thy beloved more than another beloved, that thou dost so charge us? My beloved is white and ruddy, the chiefest among ten thousand. His head is as the most fine gold; his locks are bushy, and black as a raven: his eyes are as the eyes of doves by the rivers of waters, washed with milk, and fitly set: his cheeks are as a bed of spices, as sweet flowers: his lips like lilies, dropping sweet smelling myrrh: his hands are as gold rings set with the beryl: his belly is as bright ivory overlaid with sapphires: his legs are as pillars of marble, set upon sockets of fine gold: his countenance is as Lebanon, excellent as the cedars: his mouth is most sweet: yea, he is altogether lovely. This is my beloved, and this is my friend, O daughters of Jerusalem.

6. Whither is thy beloved gone, O thou fairest among women? whither is thy beloved turned aside? that we may seek him with thee. My beloved is gone down into his garden, to the beds of spices, to feed in the gardens, and to gather lilies. I am my beloved's, and my beloved is mine: he feedeth among the lilies.

Thou art beautiful, O my love, as Tirzah,[5] comely as Jerusalem, terrible as an army with banners. Turn away thine eyes from me, for they have overcome me: thy hair is as a flock of goats that appear from Gilead: thy teeth are as a flock of sheep which go up from the washing, whereof every one beareth twins, and there is not one barren among them. As a piece of a pomegranate are thy temples within thy locks. There are threescore queens, and fourscore concubines, and virgins without number. My dove, my undefiled, is but one; she is the only one of her mother, she is the choice one of her that bare her. The daughters saw her, and blessed her; yea, the queens and the concubines, and they praised her. Who is she that looketh forth as the morning, fair as the moon, clear as the sun, and terrible as an army with banners? I went down into the garden of nuts to see the fruits of the valley, and to see whether the vine flourished, and the pomegranates budded. Or ever I was aware, my soul made me like the chariots of Amminadib. Return, return, O Shulamite;[6] return, return, that we may look upon thee. What will ye see in the Shulamite? As it were the company of two armies.

7. How beautiful are thy feet with shoes, O prince's daughter! the joints of thy thighs are like jewels, the work of the hands of a cunning workman. Thy navel is like a round goblet, which wanteth not liquor: thy belly is like a heap of wheat set about with lilies. Thy two breasts are like two young roes

3. Possibly a euphemism for phallus. 4. Entrails, considered the seat of tender emotions. 5. A Canaanite city. 6. The name, often taken as the feminine counterpart to Solomon, may also be the name or epithet of a Near Eastern goddess or a reference to the town Shunem.

that are twins. Thy neck is as a tower of ivory; thine eyes like the fishpools in Heshbon, by the gate of Bathrabbim:[7] thy nose is as the tower of Lebanon which looketh toward Damascus. Thine head upon thee is like Carmel,[8] and the hair of thine head like purple; the King is held in the galleries. How fair and how pleasant art thou, O love, for delights! This thy stature is like to a palm tree, and thy breasts to clusters of grapes. I said, I will go up to the palm tree, I will take hold of the boughs thereof: now also thy breasts shall be as clusters of the vine, and the smell of thy nose like apples: and the roof of thy mouth like the best wine for my beloved, that goeth down sweetly, causing the lips of those that are asleep to speak.

I am my beloved's, and his desire is toward me. Come, my beloved, let us go forth into the field; let us lodge in the villages. Let us get up early to the vineyards; let us see if the vine flourish, whether the tender grape appear, and the pomegranates bud forth: there will I give thee my loves. The mandrakes[9] give a smell, and at our gates are all manner of pleasant fruits, new and old, which I have laid up for thee, O my beloved.

8. O that thou wert as my brother, that sucked the breasts of my mother! when I should find thee without, I would kiss thee; yea, I should not be despised. I would lead thee, and bring thee into my mother's house, who would instruct me: I would cause thee to drink of spiced wine of the juice of my pomegranate. His left hand should be under my head, and his right hand should embrace me. I charge you, O daughters of Jerusalem, that ye stir not up, nor awake my love, until he please. Who is this that cometh up from the wilderness, leaning upon her beloved? I raised thee up under the apple tree: there thy mother brought thee forth; there she brought thee forth that bare thee. Set me as a seal upon thine heart, as a seal upon thine arm: for love is strong as death; jealousy is cruel as the grave: the coals thereof are coals of fire, which hath a most vehement flame. Many waters cannot quench love, neither can the floods drown it: if a man would give all the substance of his house for love, it would utterly be contemned.

We have a little sister, and she hath no breasts: what shall we do for our sister in the day when she shall be spoken for? If she be a wall, we will build upon her a palace of silver: and if she be a door, we will inclose her with boards of cedar. I am a wall, and my breasts like towers: then was I in his eyes as one that found favor. Solomon had a vineyard at Baalhamon;[1] he let out the vineyard unto keepers; every one for the fruit thereof was to bring a thousand pieces of silver. My vineyard, which is mine, is before me: thou, O Solomon, must have a thousand, and those that keep the fruit thereof two hundred. Thou that dwellest in the gardens, the companions hearken to thy voice: cause me to hear it. Make haste, my beloved, and be thou like to a roe or to a young hart upon the mountains of spices.

7. *Heshbon:* a city east of the northern end of the Dead Sea. *Bathrabbim:* another name for Heshbon, or one of its gates. 8. A high promontory on the seacoast of Palestine. 9. A common plant in Palestine, known for its narcotic or aphrodisiac effect, whose root was thought to look like the female genitalia. 1. Otherwise unknown. The name means "lord of a crowd."

Jonah

1. Now the word of the Lord came unto Jonah the son of Amittai, saying, Arise, go to Nineveh,[1] that great city, and cry against it; for their wickedness is come up before me. But Jonah rose up to flee unto Tarshish from the presence of the Lord, and went down to Joppa;[2] and he found a ship going to Tarshish: so he paid the fare thereof, and went down into it, to go with them unto Tarshish from the presence of the Lord. But the Lord sent out a great wind into the sea, and there was a mighty tempest in the sea, so that the ship was like to be broken. Then the mariners were afraid, and cried every man unto his god, and cast forth the wares that were in the ship into the sea, to lighten it of them. But Jonah was gone down into the sides of the ship; and he lay, and was fast asleep. So the shipmaster came to him, and said unto him, What meanest thou, O, sleeper? arise, call upon thy God, if so be that God will think upon us, that we perish not. And they said every one to his fellow, Come, and let us cast lots, that we may know for whose cause this evil is upon us. So they cast lots, and the lot fell upon Jonah. Then said they unto him, Tell us, we pray thee, for whose cause this evil is upon us; What is thine occupation? and whence comest thou? what is thy country? and of what people art thou? And he said unto them, I am an Hebrew; and I fear the Lord, the God of heaven, which hath made the sea and the dry land. Then were the men exceedingly afraid, and said unto him, Why hast thou done this? For the men knew that he fled from the presence of the Lord, because he had told them. Then said they unto him, What shall we do unto thee, that the sea may be calm unto us? for the sea wrought, and was tempestuous. And he said unto them, Take me up, and cast me forth into the sea; so shall the sea be calm unto you: for I know that for my sake this great tempest is upon you. Nevertheless the men rowed hard to bring it to the land; but they could not: for the sea wrought, and was tempestuous against them. Wherefore they cried unto the Lord, and said, We beseech thee, O Lord, we beseech thee, let us not perish for this man's life, and lay not upon us innocent blood: for thou, O Lord, hast done as it pleased thee. So they took up Jonah, and cast him forth into the sea: and the sea ceased from her raging. Then the men feared the Lord exceedingly, and offered a sacrifice unto the Lord, and made vows.

Now the Lord had prepared a great fish to swallow up Jonah. And Jonah was in the belly of the fish three days and three nights.

2. Then Jonah prayed unto the Lord his God out of the fish's belly, and said, I cried by reason of mine affliction unto the Lord, and he heard me; out of the belly of hell cried I, and thou heardest my voice. For thou hadst cast me into the deep, in the midst of the seas; and the floods compassed me about; all thy billows and thy waves passed over me. Then I said, I am cast out of thy sight; yet I will look again toward thy holy temple. The waters compassed me about, even to the soul: the depth closed me round about, the weeds were wrapped about my head. I went down to the bottoms of the

1. On the Tigris River, the capital city of the Assyrians. 2. Seaport on the coast of Palestine. Tarshish is probably Tartessus in Spain. Jonah intends to go west (instead of east to Nineveh), as far away as he can.

mountains; the earth with her bars was about me for ever: yet hast thou brought up my life from corruption, O Lord my God. When my soul fainted within me I remembered the Lord: and my prayer came in unto thee, into thine holy temple. They that observe lying vanities forsake their own mercy.[3] But I will sacrifice unto thee with the voice of thanksgiving; I will pay that that I have vowed. Salvation is of the Lord. And the Lord spake unto the fish, and it vomited out Jonah upon the dry land.

3. And the word of the Lord came unto Jonah the second time, saying, Arise, go unto Nineveh, that great city, and preach unto it the preaching that I bid thee. So Jonah arose, and went unto Nineveh, according to the word of the Lord. Now Nineveh was an exceeding great city of three days' journey. And Jonah began to enter into the city a day's journey, and he cried, and said, Yet forty days, and Nineveh shall be overthrown.

So the people of Nineveh believed God, and proclaimed a fast, and put on sackcloth, from the greatest of them even to the least of them. For word came unto the king of Nineveh, and he arose from his throne, and he laid his robe from him, and covered him with sackcloth, and sat in ashes. And he caused it to be proclaimed and published through Nineveh by the decree of the king and his nobles, saying, Let neither man nor beast, herd nor flock, taste any thing: let them not feed, nor drink water: but let man and beast be covered with sackcloth, and cry mightily unto God: yea, let them turn every one from his evil way, and from the violence that is in their hands. Who can tell if God will turn and repent, and turn away from his fierce anger, that we perish not?

And God saw their works, that they turned from their evil way; and God repented of the evil, that he had said that he would do unto them; and he did it not.

4. But it displeased Jonah exceedingly, and he was very angry. And he prayed unto the Lord, and said, I pray thee, O Lord, was not this my saying, when I was yet in my country? Therefore I fled before unto Tarshish: for I knew that thou art a gracious God, and merciful, slow to anger, and of great kindness, and repentest thee of the evil.[4] Therefore now, O Lord, take, I beseech thee, my life from me; for it is better for me to die than to live. Then said the Lord, Doest thou well to be angry? So Jonah went out of the city, and sat on the east side of the city, and there made him a booth,[5] and sat under it in the shadow, till he might see what would become of the city. And the Lord God prepared a gourd,[6] and made it to come up over Jonah, that it might be a shadow over his head, to deliver him from his grief. So Jonah was exceeding glad of the gourd. But God prepared a worm when the morning rose the next day, and it smote the gourd that it withered. And it came to pass, when the sun did arise, that God prepared a vehement east wind; and the sun beat upon the head of Jonah, that he fainted, and wished in himself to die, and said, It is better for me to die than to live. And God said to Jonah,

3. Or those that worship false gods forfeit their claim to mercy. 4. Jonah is quoting Scripture (Exodus 34.6). 5. A tent shelter. 6. Some kind of climbing plant.

Doest thou well to be angry for the gourd? And he said, I do well to be angry, even unto death. Then said the Lord, Thou hast had pity on the gourd, for the which thou hast not laboured, neither madest it grow; which came up in a night, and perished in a night: and should not I spare Nineveh, that great city, wherein are more than sixscore thousand persons that cannot discern between their right hand and their left hand;[7] and also much cattle?

7. I.e., children.

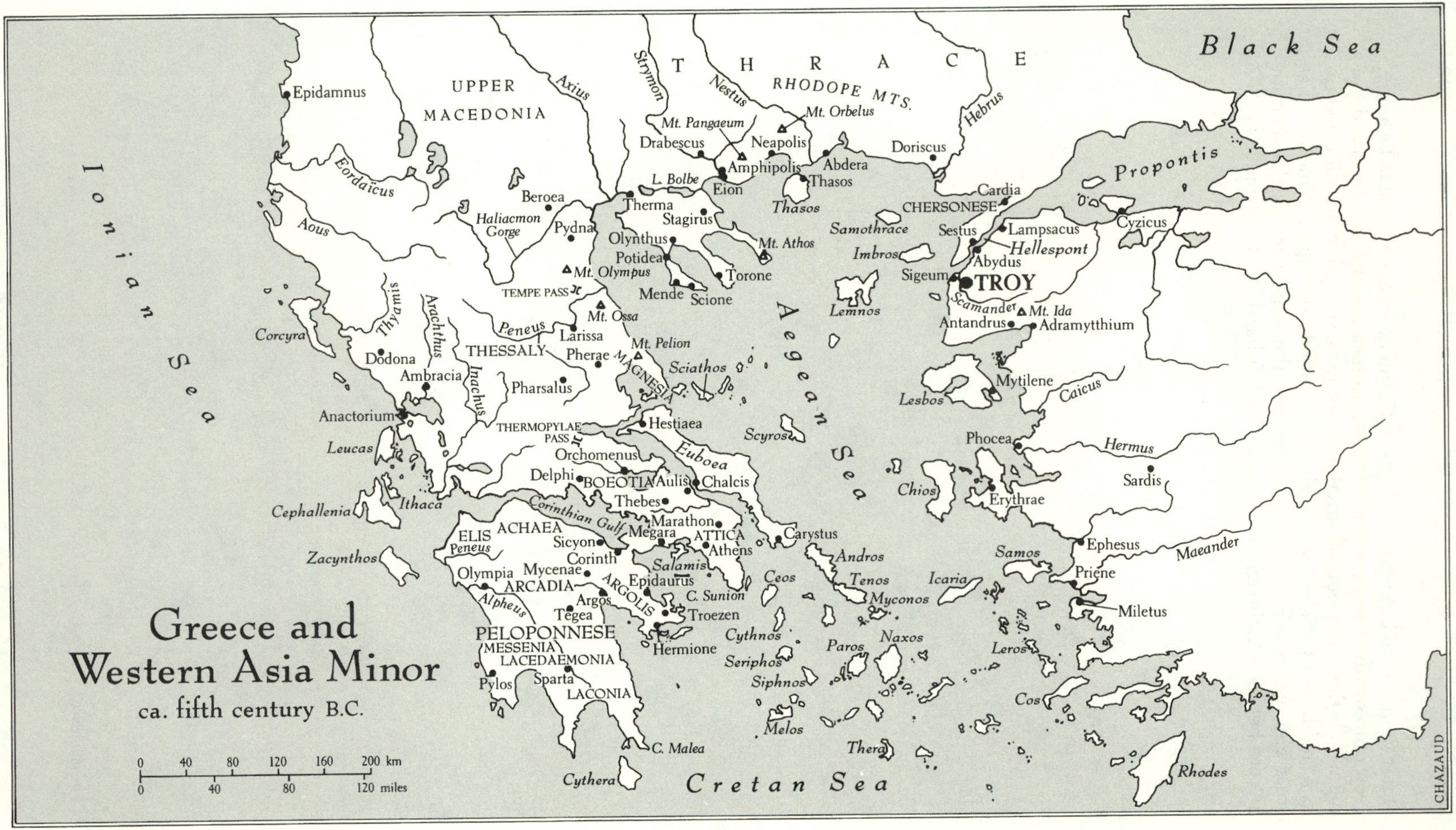

Black Sea
T H R A C E
RHODOPE MTS.
UPPER MACEDONIA
Ionian Sea
Aegean Sea
Cretan Sea
Propontis
Hellespont
Epidamnus
Axius
Strymon
Nestus
Hebrus
Mt. Orbelus
Mt. Pangaeum
Drabescus
Neapolis
Amphipolis
Abdera
Thasos
Doriscus
Eordaïcus
Aous
L. Bolbe
Eion
Beroea
Therma
Stagirus
Haliacmon Gorge
Pydna
Olynthus
Potidea
Mt. Athos
Mt. Olympus
Torone
Mende
Scione
TEMPE PASS
Mt. Ossa
Thyamis
Arachthus
Peneus
Larissa
Corcyra
Dodona
THESSALY
Pherae
Mt. Pelion
MAGNESIA
Sciathos
Ambracia
Inachus
Pharsalus
Anactorium
THERMOPYLAE PASS
Hestiaea
Scyros
Leucas
Orchomenus
Euboea
Delphi
BOEOTIA
Aulis
Chalcis
Ithaca
Cephallenia
Thebes
Corinthian Gulf
Marathon
ELIS
ACHAEA
Megara
ATTICA
Carystus
Peneus
Sicyon
Athens
Zacynthos
Corinth
Salamis
Olympia
Mycenae
Epidaurus
ARCADIA
ARGOLIS
C. Sunion
Alpheus
Argos
Tegea
Troezen
PELOPONNESE
Hermione
MESSENIA
LACEDAEMONIA
Pylos
Sparta
LACONIA
C. Malea
Cythera
Samothrace
CHERSONESE
Cardia
Sestus
Lampsacus
Abydus
Cyzicus
Imbros
Sigeum
TROY
Lemnos
Scamander
Mt. Ida
Antandrus
Adramytthium
Mytilene
Lesbos
Caicus
Phocea
Hermus
Chios
Sardis
Erythrae
Ephesus
Maeander
Samos
Andros
Ceos
Tenos
Icaria
Priene
Myconos
Miletus
Cythnos
Naxos
Paros
Leros
Seriphos
Siphnos
Cos
Melos
Thera
Rhodes
CHAZAUD
Greece and Western Asia Minor
ca. fifth century B.C.
0 40 80 120 160 200 km
0 40 80 120 miles

Ancient Greece and the Formation of the Western Mind

The origin of the peoples who eventually called themselves Hellenes is still a mystery. The language they spoke belongs clearly to the great Indo-European family (which includes the Germanic, Celtic, Italic, and Sanskrit language groups), but many of the ancient Greek words and place names have terminations that are definitely not Indo-European—the word for sea (*thalassa*), for example. The Greeks of historic times were presumably a blend of the native tribes and the Indo-European invaders, en route from the European landmass.

In the last hundred years archeology has given us a clearer picture than our forebears had of the level of civilization in early Greece. The second millennium B.C. saw a brilliant culture, called Minoan after the mythical king Minos, flourishing on the large island of Crete, and the citadel of Mycenae and the palace at Pylos show that mainland Greece, in that same period, had centers of wealth and power unsuspected before the excavators discovered the gold masks of the buried kings and clay tablets covered with strange signs. The decipherment of these signs (published in 1953) revealed that the language of these Myceneans was an early form of Greek. It must have been the memory of these rich kingdoms that inspired Homer's vision of "Mycenae rich in gold" and the splendid armed hosts that assembled for the attack on Troy.

It was a blurred memory (Homer does not remember the writing, for example, or the detailed bureaucratic accounting recorded on the tablets) and this is easy to understand: some time in the last century of the millennium the great palaces were destroyed by fire. With them disappeared not only the arts and skills that had created Mycenean wealth but even the system of writing. For the next few hundred years the Greeks were illiterate and so no written evidence survives for what, in view of our ignorance about so many aspects of it, we call the Dark Age of Greece.

One thing we do know about it: it produced a body of oral epic poetry that was the raw material Homer shaped into the two great poems, the *Iliad* and *Odyssey*. These Homeric poems seem from internal evidence to date from the eighth century B.C.—which is incidentally, or perhaps not incidentally, the century in which the Greeks learned how to write again. They played in the subsequent development of Greek civilization the same role that the Torah had played in Palestine: they became the basis of an education and therefore of a whole culture. Not only did the great characters of the epic serve as models of conduct for later generations of Greeks, but the figures of the Olympian gods retained, in the prayers, poems, and sculpture of the succeeding centuries, the shapes and attributes set down by Homer. The difference between the Greek and the Hebrew hero, between Achilles and Joseph, for example, is remarkable, but the difference between "the God of Abraham and of Isaac" and the Olympians who interfere capriciously in the lives of Hector or Achilles or Helen is an unbridgeable chasm. The two conceptions of the power that governs the universe are irreconcilable; and in fact the struggle between them ended, not in synthesis, but in the complete victory of the one and the disappearance of the other. The Greek conception of the nature of the gods and of their relation to humanity is so alien to us that it is difficult for the modern reader to take it seriously. The Hebrew basis of European religious thought has made it almost impossible for us to imagine a god who can be feared and laughed at, blamed and admired, and still sincerely worshiped. Yet all these are proper attitudes toward the gods on Olympus; they are all implicit in Homer's poems.

The Hebrew conception of God emphasizes those aspects of the universe that imply a harmonious order. The elements of disorder in the universe are, in the story of Creation, blamed on humankind, and in all Hebrew literature the evidences of disorder are something the writer tries to reconcile with an *a priori* assumption of an all-powerful, just God; no one tampers with the fundamental datum. Just as clearly, the Greeks conceived their gods as an expression of the disorder of the world in which they lived. The Olympian gods, like the natural forces of sea and sky, follow their own will even to the extreme of conflict with each other, and always with a sublime disregard for the human beings who may be affected by the results of their actions. It is true that they are all subjects of a single more powerful god, Zeus. But his authority over them is based only on superior strength; though he cannot be openly resisted, he can be temporarily deceived by his fellow Olympians. And Zeus, although by virtue of his superior power his will is finally accomplished in the matter of Achilles' wrath, knows limits to his power too. He cannot save the life of his son the Lycian hero Sarpedon. Behind Zeus stands the mysterious power of Fate, to which even he must bow.

Such gods as these, representing as they do the blind forces of the universe that humans cannot control, are not always thought of as connected with morality. Morality is a human creation, and though the gods may approve of it, they are not bound by it. And violent as they are, they cannot feel the ultimate consequence of violence: death is a human fear, just as the courage to face it is a human quality. There is a double standard, one for gods, one for mortals, and the inevitable consequence is that our real admiration and sympathy are directed not toward the gods but toward the mortals. With Hector and Andromache, and even with Achilles at his worst, we can sympathize; but the gods, though they may excite terror or laughter, can never have our sympathy. We could as easily sympathize with a blizzard or the force of gravity. Homer imposed on Greek literature the anthropocentric emphasis that is its distinguishing mark and its great contribution to the Western mind. Though the gods are ever-present characters in the incidents of his poems, his true concern, first and last, is with men and women.

THE CITY-STATES OF GREECE

The stories told in the Homeric poems are set in the age of the Trojan War, which archeologists (those, that is, who believe that it happened at all) date to the twelfth century B.C. Though the poems do preserve some faded memories of the Mycenaean Age, as we have them they probably are the creation of later centuries, the tenth to the eighth B.C., the so-called Dark Age that succeeded the collapse (or destruction) of Mycenaean civilization. This was the time of the final settlement of the Greek peoples, an age of invasion perhaps and migration certainly, which saw the foundation and growth of many small independent cities. The geography of Greece—a land of mountain barriers and scattered islands—encouraged this fragmentation. The Greek cities never lost sight of their common Hellenic heritage, but it was not enough to unite them except in the face of unmistakable and overwhelming danger, and even then only partially and for a short time. They differed from each other in custom, political constitution, and even dialect: their relations with each other were those of rivals and fierce competitors.

These cities, constantly at war in the pursuit of more productive land for growing populations, were dominated from the late eighth century B.C. by aristocratic oligarchies, which maintained a stranglehold on the land and the economy of which it was the base. An important safety valve was colonization. In the eighth and seventh centuries B.C. landless Greeks founded new cities (always near the sea and generally owing little or no allegiance to the home base) all over the Mediterranean coast—in Spain, southern France (Marseilles, Nice, and Antibes were all Greek cities), in South Italy (Naples), Sicily (Syracuse), North Africa (Cyrene), all along the coast of Asia Minor (Smyrna, Miletus), and even on the Black Sea as far as Russian Crimea. Many of these new outposts of Greek civilization experienced a faster economic and cultural development than the older cities of the mainland. It was in the cities founded on the Asian coast that the Greeks adapted to their own language the Phoenician system of writing, adding signs for the vowels to create their alphabet, the forerunner of the Roman alphabet and of our own. Its first use was probably for commercial records and transactions, but as literacy became a general condition all over the Greek world in the course of the seventh century B.C., treaties and political decrees were inscribed on stone and literary works written on rolls of paper made from the Egyptian papyrus plant.

ATHENS AND SPARTA

By the beginning of the fifth century B.C. the two most prominent city-states were Athens and Sparta. These two cities led the combined Greek resistance to the Persian invasion of Europe in the years 490 to 479 B.C. The defeat of the solid Persian power by the divided and insignificant Greek cities surprised the world and inspired in Greece, and particularly in Athens, a confidence that knew no bounds.

Athens was at this time a democracy, the first in Western history. It was a direct, not a representative, democracy, for the number of free citizens was small enough to permit the exercise of power by a meeting of the citizens as a body in assembly. Athens's power lay in the fleet with which she had played her decisive part in the struggle against Persia, and with this fleet she rapidly became the leader of a naval alliance that included most of the islands of the Aegean Sea and many Greek cities on the coast of Asia Minor. Sparta, on the other hand, was rigidly conservative in government and policy. Because the individual citizen was reared and trained by the state for the state's business, war, the Spartan land army was superior to any other in Greece, and the Spartans controlled, by direct rule or by alliance, a majority of the city-states of the Peloponnese.

These two cities, allies for the war of liberation against Persia, became enemies when the external danger was eliminated. The middle years of the fifth century were disturbed by indecisive hostilities between them and haunted by the probability of full-scale war to come. As the years went by, this war came to be accepted as "inevitable" by both sides, and in 431 B.C. it began. It was to end in 404 B.C. with the total defeat of Athens.

Before the beginning of this disastrous war, known as the Peloponnesian War, Athenian democracy provided its citizens with a cultural and political environment that was without precedent in the ancient world. The institutions of Athens encouraged the maximum development of the individual's capacities and at the same time inspired the maximum devotion to the interests of the community. It was a moment in history of delicate and precarious balance between the freedom of the individual and the demands of the state. It was the proud boast of the Athenians that without sacrificing the cultural amenities of civilized life they could yet when called upon surpass in policy and war their adversary, Sparta, whose citizen body was an army in constant training. The Athenians were, in this respect as in others, a nation of amateurs. "The individual Athenian," said Pericles, Athens's great statesman at this time, "in his own person seems to have the power of adapting himself to the most varied forms of action with the utmost versatility and grace." But the freedom of the individual did not, in Athens's great days, produce anarchy. "While we are . . . unconstrained in our private intercourse," Pericles had observed earlier in his speech, "a spirit of reverence pervades our public acts."

There were limits on who could participate in the democracy. The "individual Athenian" of whom Pericles spoke was the adult male citizen. In his speech, he mentioned women only once, to tell them that the way for them to obtain glory was not to be worse than their nature made them, and to be least talked of among males for either praise or blame. Women could not own property, hold office, or vote. Peasant women may have had to work in the fields with their husbands, but affluent women were expected to remain inside the house except for funerals and religious festivals, rarely seen by men other than their husbands or male relatives. Their reputations for sexual chastity were fiercely protected; no suspicion of illegitimacy must fall on the sons they were expected to produce: future Athenian citizens, heirs to the family property and continuators of the family line (which was traced through the male side). There were, in addition, a number of men from other cities who settled in Athens, often for business reasons—*metics*, or "resident aliens." These could not own land or take part in civic affairs. A great deal of labor—in the houses and fields, in craftsmen's shops, in the silver mines that underlay Athens's wealth—was performed by slaves, who of course had no rights at all. And finally, even among citizens who participated in civic life on a footing of equality, there were marked divisions between the elite and the poorer classes and tensions between them. Still, although it was exclusionary in all these ways, and although it pursued a ruthless imperialist policy abroad, Athenian democracy represented a bold achievement of civic equality for those who belonged.

This democracy came under strain as the Peloponnesian War progressed. Under the mounting pressure of the long conflict, the Athenians lost the "spirit of reverence" that Pericles saw as the stabilizing factor in Athenian democracy. They subordinated all considerations to the immediate interest of the city and surpassed their enemy in the logical ferocity of their actions. They finally fell victim to leaders who carried the process one step further and subordinated all considerations to their own private interest. The war years saw the decay of that freedom in unity which is celebrated in Pericles' speech. By the end of the fifth century Athens was divided internally as well as defeated externally. The individual citizen no longer thought of himself and Athens as one and the same; the balance was gone forever.

One of the solvents of traditional values was an intellectual revolution that was taking place in the advanced Athenian democracy of the last half of the fifth century, a critical reevaluation of accepted ideas in every sphere of thought and action. It stemmed from innovations in education. Democratic institutions had created a demand for an education that would prepare men for public life, especially by training them in the art of public speaking. The demand was met by the appearance of the professional teacher, the Sophist, as he was called, who taught, for a handsome fee, not only the techniques of public speaking but also the subjects that gave a man something to talk about—government, ethics, literary criticism, even astronomy. The curriculum of the Sophists, in fact, marks the first appearance in European civilization of liberal education (for affluent males), just as they themselves were the first professors.

The Sophists were great teachers, but like most teachers they had little or no control over the results of their teaching. Their methods placed an inevitable emphasis on effective presentation of a point of view, to the detriment, and if necessary the exclusion, of anything that might make it less convincing. They produced a generation that had been trained to see both sides of any question and to argue the weaker side as effectively as the stronger, the false as effectively as the true. They taught how to argue inferentially from probability in the absence of concrete evidence; to appeal to the audience's sense of its own advantage rather than to accepted moral standards;

and to justify individual defiance of general prejudice and even of law by making a distinction between "nature" and "convention." These methods dominated the thinking of the Athenians of the late fifth and fourth centuries B.C. Emphasis on the technique of effective presentation of both sides of any case encouraged a relativistic point of view. The canon of probability (which implies an appeal to human reason as the supreme authority) became a critical weapon for an attack on myth and on traditional conceptions of the gods; though it had its constructive side, too, for it was the base for historical reconstruction of the unrecorded past and of the stages of human progress from savagery to civilization. The rhetorical appeal to the self-interest of the audience, to expediency, became the method of the political leaders of the wartime democracy and the fundamental doctrine of new theories of power politics. These theories served to justify the increasing severity of the measures Athens took to terrorize her rebellious subjects. The new spirit in Athens had magnificent achievements to its credit, but it undermined traditional moral convictions. At its roots was a supreme confidence in the human intelligence and a secular view of humanity's position in the universe that is best expressed in the statement of Protagoras, the most famous of the Sophists: "Man is the measure of all things." These shifts in worldview and moral beliefs led to new forms of creativity in art, literature, and thought, although they also caused bitter debates, and sometimes conflicts, between traditionalists and proponents of the new ideas.

THE DECLINE OF THE CITY-STATE

In the last quarter of the fifth century the whole traditional basis of individual conduct, which had been concern for the unity and cohesion of the city-state, was undermined—gradually at first by the critical approach of the Sophists and their pupils, and then rapidly, as the war accelerated the loosening of the old standards. "In peace and prosperity," says Thucydides, "both states and individuals are actuated by higher motives . . . but war, which takes away the comfortable provision of daily life, is a hard master, and tends to assimilate men's characters to their conditions." The war brought to Athens the rule of new politicians who were schooled in the doctrine of power politics and initiated savage reprisals against Athens's rebellious subject allies, launching the city on an expansionist course that ended in disaster in Sicily (413 B.C.) and a short-lived oligarchic revolution (411 B.C.). Seven years later Athens, her last fleet gone, surrendered to the Spartans. A pro-Spartan antidemocratic regime, the Thirty Tyrants, was installed, but soon overthrown. Athens became a democracy again, but the confidence and unity of its great age were gone forever. Community and individual were no longer one. Yet despite a perceptible retreat into privacy, Athenian democracy continued to work through most of the fourth century, until the conquest of Philip (see below). That same century witnessed, in addition to continued creativity in poetry, painting, and sculpture, two new developments. It saw the flowering of Athenian rhetoric, a legacy of the Sophists and one of Greek culture's greatest contributions to Rome in turn. During the same time, Plato and Aristotle revolutionized philosophy and laid the foundations for later ancient and European philosophical thought. But they had a predecessor in Plato's great teacher, Socrates.

In the wake of their defeat by Sparta, Athenians began to feel more and more exasperation with a voice they had been listening to for many years. This was the voice of Socrates, a stonemason who for most of his adult life had made it his business to discuss with his fellow citizens such great issues as the nature of justice, of truth, of piety. Unlike the Sophists, he did not lecture nor did he charge a fee: his method was dialectic, a search for truth through questions and answers, and his dedication to his mission had kept him poor. But the initial results of his discussions were often infuriatingly like the results of sophistic teaching. By questions and answers he exposed the illogicality of his opponent's position, but did not often provide a substitute for the belief he had destroyed. Yet it is clear that he did believe in absolute standards and, what is more, believed they could be discovered by a process of logical inquiry and supported by logical proof. His ethics rested on an intellectual basis. The resentment against him, which came to a head in 399 B.C., is partly explained by his questioning of the old standards in order to establish new, and by his refusal to let the Athenians live in peace, for he preached that it was every person's duty to think through to the truth. In this last respect he was the prophet of the new age. For him, the city and the accepted code were no substitute for the task of self-examination that each individual must carry through to a conclusion. The characteristic statement of the old Athens was public, in the assembly or the theater; Socrates proclaimed the responsibility of each individual to work out a means to fulfillment and happiness and made clear his distrust of public life: "he who will fight for the right . . . must have a private station and not a public one."

The Athenians sentenced him to death on a charge of impiety. They hoped, no doubt, that he would go into exile to escape execution, but he remained, as he put it himself, at his post, and they were forced to have the sentence carried out. If they thought they were finished with him, they were sadly mistaken. In the next century Athens became the center for a large group of philosophical schools, all of them claiming to develop and interpret the ideas of Socrates.

The century that followed his death saw the exhaustion of the Greek city-states in constant internecine warfare. Politically and economically bankrupt, they fell under the power of Macedon in the north, whose king, Philip, combined a ferocious energy with a cynicism that enabled him to take full advantage of the disunity of the city-states. Greek liberty ended at the battle of Chaeronea in 338 B.C., and Philip's son Alexander inherited a powerful army and the political control of all Greece. He led his Macedonian and Greek armies against Persia, and in a few brilliant campaigns became master of an empire that extended into Egypt in the south and to the borders of India in the east. He died at Babylon in 323 B.C., and his empire broke up into a number of independent kingdoms ruled by his generals. One of these generals, Ptolemy, founded a Greek dynasty that ruled Egypt until after the Roman conquest and ended only with the death of the famous Cleopatra. The results of Alexander's fantastic achievements were more durable than might have been expected. Into the newly conquered territories came thousands of Greeks who wished to escape from the political futility and economic crisis of the homeland. Wherever they went they took with them their language, their culture, and their typical buildings, the gymnasium and the theater. At Alexandria in Egypt, for example, the Ptolemies formed a Greek library to preserve the texts of Greek literature for the scholars who edited them, a school of Greek poetry flourished, and Greek mathematicians and geographers made new advances in science. The Middle East became, as far as the cities were concerned, a Greek-speaking area; and when, some two or three centuries later, the first accounts of the life and teaching of Jesus of Nazareth were written down, they were written in Greek, the language on which the cultural homogeneity of the whole area was based.

FURTHER READING

John Boardman, Jasper Griffin, and Oswyn Murray, eds., *The Oxford History of the Classical World* (1986), is a handsomely illustrated survey, by many different specialists, of the whole sweep of classical culture—social, political, literary, artistic, and religious. For the history of Greece to the death of Alexander, see J. B. Bury, *A History of Greece,* 4th ed., revised by Russell Meiggs (1975), and Thomas R. Martin, *Ancient Greece* (1996)—the latter clearly written especially for the nonspecialist reader. For a survey of Greek civilization organized according to different types of people and their social experiences, see Jean-Pierre Vernant, ed., *The Greeks* (1995). A rich and beautifully illustrated survey of women in Greece and

Rome is Elaine Fantham, Helene Foley, Natalie Kampen, Sarah Pomeroy, and Alan Shapiro, eds., *Women in the Classical World* (1994). P. E. Easterling, ed., *The Cambridge Companion to Greek Tragedy* (1997), provides an excellent overview of that subject. Perseus is a superb interactive CD-ROM program on Greek civilization, with a huge database of texts (in Greek and English), maps, images of sites and artifacts, and a short version of Martin's historical outline (above). Much of what is on the CD-ROM can be found at the excellent Perseus Web site. For a wealth of links to other Web sites on the ancient world, see the University of Michigan's Classics and Mediterranean Archaeology Home Page (this and the Perseus site can easily be located with standard Web search engines).

TIME LINE

TEXTS	CONTEXTS
	2200–1450 B.C. Minoan civilization flourishes on Crete
	ca. 1450 Mycenaeans from mainland Greece occupy Crete
	ca. 1150 Troy destroyed by the Achaeans
	776 Olympic Games founded in Greece
late 8th century B.C. Greek alphabetic scripts	
ca. 700 Homer, ***The Iliad, The Odyssey***	
600 Sappho writing her **lyrics** on the island of Lesbos	
	594 Solon reforms laws at Athens, which becomes the world's first democracy (508), and defeats a Persian invasion at Marathon (490)
	490–479 Greece turns back a massive Persian invasion by sea at Salamis and by land at Plataea
458 Aeschylus's dramatic trilogy, ***The Oresteia,*** produced in Athens	
ca. 441 Sophocles, ***Antigone***	
431 Euripides, ***Medea***	**431–404** Peloponnesian War between Athens and Sparta; Athens surrenders (404)
429–347 Plato, author of ***The Apology of Socrates*** and *Phaedo*	
426? Sophocles, ***Oedipus the King***	
411 Aristophanes, ***Lysistrata***	
	399 Trial and execution of Socrates
384–322 Aristotle, author of ***Poetics***	
	ca. 385 Plato founds the Academy

Boldface titles indicate works in the anthology.

TIME LINE

TEXTS	CONTEXTS
	ca. 350 Beginnings of Indian epic, ***Mahābhārata*** • Shuang-tse founds monist religious philosophy in China • Greek amphitheater built at Epidauros
	338 United Greeks defeated by Philip II of Macedon at Chaeronea
	335 Aristotle founds Peripatetic school of philosophy and lectures in the Lyceum
	334 Alexander of Macedon, Philip's son, conquers Persian empire
	323 Euclid writes *Elements,* the first work of geometry
	307 Library and museum established at Alexandria, Egypt
	148 Macedonia becomes a Roman province
	31 At Actium, Octavian Augustus Caesar defeats Antony and Cleopatra
	ca. 6 Birth of Jesus
	A.D. 26–36 Pontius Pilate, Roman governor
	ca. 33 Crucifixion of Jesus
	ca. 35 Conversion of Paul
	47–58 Paul's missionary journeys
	66–70 Jewish revolt against Roman rule; Roman emperor Titus captures Jerusalem
ca. A.D. 75 Luke, Gospels and Acts of the Apostles	
ca. 80 Matthew, Gospels	

HOMER
eighth century B.C.

Greek literature begins with two masterpieces, the *Iliad* and *Odyssey,* which cannot be accurately dated (the conjectural dates range over three centuries) and which are attributed to the poet Homer, about whom nothing is known except his name. The Greeks believed that he was blind, perhaps because the bard Demodocus* in the *Odyssey* was blind (see pp. 306–07), and seven different cities put forward claims to be his birthplace. They are all in what the Greeks called Ionia, the western coast of Asia Minor, which was heavily settled by Greek colonists. It does seem likely that he came from this area; the *Iliad* contains several accurate descriptions of natural features of the Ionian landscape, but his grasp of the geography of mainland, especially western, Greece is unsure. But even this is a guess, and all the other stories the Greeks told about him are obvious inventions.

The two great epics that have made his name supreme among poets may have been fixed in something like their present form before the art of writing was in general use in Greece; it is certain that they were intended not for reading but for oral recitation. The earliest stages of their composition date from around the beginnings of Greek literacy—the late eighth century B.C. The poems exhibit the unmistakable characteristics of oral composition.

The oral poet had at his disposal not reading and writing but a vast and intricate system of metrical formulas—phrases that would fit in at different places in the line—and a repertoire of standard scenes (the arming of the warrior, the battle of two champions) as well as the known outline of the story. Of course he could and did invent new phrases and scenes as he recited—but his base was the immense poetic reserve created by many generations of singers who lived before him. When he told again for his hearers the old story of Achilles and his wrath, he was re-creating a traditional story that had been recited, with variations, additions, and improvements, by a long line of predecessors. The poem was not, in the modern sense, the poet's creation, still less an expression of his personality. Consequently, there is no trace of individual identity to be found in it; the poet remains as hidden behind the action and speech of his characters as if he were a dramatist.

The *Iliad* and *Odyssey* as we have them, however, are unlike most of the oral literature we know from other times and places. The poetic organization of each of these two epics, the subtle interrelationship of the parts, which creates their structural and emotional unity, suggests that they owe their present form to the shaping hand of a single poet, the architect who selected from the enormous wealth of the oral tradition and fused what he took with original material to create, perhaps with the aid of the new medium of writing, the two magnificently ordered poems known as the *Iliad* and *Odyssey*.

THE ILIAD

Of the two poems the *Iliad* is perhaps the earlier. Its subject is war; its characters are men in battle and women whose fate depends on the outcome. The war is fought by the Achaeans against the Trojans for the recovery of Helen, the wife of the Achaean chieftain Menelaus; the combatants are heroes who in their chariots engage in individual duels before the supporting lines of infantry and archers. There is no senti-

*The transcription of Greek names is, unfortunately, a game with no rules. It used to be the convention that Greek names would be spelled according to the form they were given in Latin (and as they appear in our selections from Virgil and Ovid): Achaeans, Achilles. Recently, it has become fashionable to stay closer to the Greek—Akhaians, Akhilleus; this is the system followed by Robert Fitzgerald in his translation of the *Odyssey.* Robert Fagles, in our selections from the *Iliad,* has turned back to the old conventions, the Latin forms that have been standard in English verse and prose for many centuries. These are the forms used in this headnote.

mentality in Homer's descriptions of these battles. "Patroclus rising beside him stabbed his right jawbone, ramming the spearhead square between his teeth so hard he hooked him by that spearhead over the chariot-rail, hoisted, dragged the Trojan out as an angler perched on a jutting rock ledge drags some fish from the sea, some noble catch, with line and glittering bronze hook. So with the spear Patroclus gaffed him off his car, his mouth gaping round the glittering point and flipped him down facefirst, dead as he fell, his life breath blown away." This is meticulously accurate; there is no attempt to suppress the ugliness of Thestor's death. The bare, careful description creates the true nightmare quality of battle, in which men perform monstrous actions with the same matter-of-fact efficiency they display in their normal occupations, and the simile reproduces the grotesque appearance of violent death—the simple spear thrust takes away Thestor's dignity as a human being even before it takes his life. He is gaping, like a fish on the hook.

The simile does something else too. The comparison of Patroclus to an angler emphasizes another aspect of battle, its excitement. Homer's lines here combine two contrary emotions: the human revulsion from the horror of violent death and the human attraction to the excitement of violent action. This passage is typical of the poem as a whole. Everywhere in it we are conscious of these two poles, of war's ugly brutality and its "terrible beauty." The poet accepts violence as a basic aspect of human life and accepts it not without questioning it but without sentimentality; for it is equally sentimental to pretend that war is not ugly or to pretend that it does not have its beauty. After three thousand years, Homer is still one of war's greatest interpreters.

The *Iliad* describes the events of a few weeks in the ten-year siege of Troy. The particular subject of the poem, as its first line announces, is the anger of Achilles, the bravest of the Achaean chieftains encamped outside the city. Achilles is a man who comes to live by and for violence. His anger cuts him off from his commander and his fellow princes; to spite them he withdraws from the fighting. He is brought back into it at last by the death of his closest friend, Patroclus; the consequences of his wrath and withdrawal fall heavily on the Achaeans but most heavily on himself.

The great champion of the Trojans, Hector, fights bravely, but reluctantly. War, for him, is a necessary evil, and he thinks nostalgically of the peaceful past, though he has little hope of peace to come. His preeminence in peace is emphasized by the tenderness of his relations with his wife and child and also by his kindness to Helen, the cause of the war that he knows in his heart will bring his city to destruction. We see Hector, as we do not see Achilles, against the background of the patterns of civilized life—the rich city with its temples and palaces, the continuity of the family. The duel between these two men is the inevitable crisis of the poem, and just as inevitable is Hector's defeat and death.

At the climactic moment of Hector's death, as everywhere in the poem, Homer's firm control of his material preserves the balance in which our contrary emotions are held; pity for Hector does not entirely rob us of sympathy for Achilles. His brutal words to the dying Hector and the insults he inflicts on Hector's corpse are truly savage, but we are never allowed to forget that this inflexible hatred is the expression of his love for Patroclus. And the final book of the poem shows us an Achilles whose iron heart is moved at last; he is touched by the sight of Hector's father clasping in supplication the terrible hands that have killed so many of his sons. He remembers that he has a father and that he will never see him again; Achilles and Priam, the slayer and the father of the slain, weep together. Achilles gives Hector's body to Priam for honorable burial. His anger has run its full course and been appeased. It has brought death, first to the Achaeans and then to the Trojans, to Patroclus and to Hector, and so to Achilles himself, for his death is fated to come "soon after Hector's."

This tragic action is the center of the poem, but it is surrounded by scenes that remind us that the organized destruction of war, though an integral part of human life, is still only a part of it. The yearning for peace and its creative possibilities is never far below the surface. This is most poignantly expressed by the scenes that take place in Troy, especially the farewell between Hector and Andromache, but it is made clear that the Achaeans too are conscious of what they have sacrificed. Early in the poem, when Agamemnon, the Achaean commander, tests the morale of his troops by suggesting that the war be abandoned, they rush for the ships so eagerly and with such heartfelt relief that their commanders are hard put to stop them. These two poles of the human condition—war and peace, with their corresponding aspects of human nature, the destructive and the creative—are implicit in every situation and statement of the poem, and they are put before us, in symbolic form, in the shield that the god Hephaestus makes for Achilles, with its scenes of human life in both peace and war. Whether these two sides of life can ever be integrated, or even reconciled, is a question that the *Iliad* raises but cannot answer.

THE ODYSSEY

The other Homeric epic, the *Odyssey*, is concerned with the peace that followed the war and in particular with the return of the heroes who survived. Its subject is the long, drawn-out return of one of the heroes, Odysseus of Ithaca, who was destined to spend ten years wandering in unknown seas before he returned to his rocky kingdom. When Odysseus's wanderings began, Achilles had already received, at the hands of Apollo, the death that he had chosen. Odysseus struggles for life, and his outstanding quality is a probing and versatile intelligence that, combined with long experience, keeps him safe and alive through the trials and dangers of twenty years of war and seafaring. To stay alive he has to do things that Achilles would never have done and use an ingenuity and experience that Achilles did not possess, but his life is just as much a struggle.

Although Odysseus has become for us the archetypal adventurer, the *Odyssey* gives us a hero whose one goal is to get home. He struggles not simply for his own and his shipmates' personal survival but also to preserve and complete the heroic reputation that he won in war at Troy. It may seem ironic that Odysseus succeeds by concealing his name, as when he tricks the Cyclops by presenting himself as "Nobody," or when, at home on Ithaca, he tricks his wife's suitors by disguising himself as a beggar. But Odysseus's shiftiness, his talent for disguise, deception, and plain lying, is part of his versatility. It complements his strength and courage in battle—qualities he demonstrated at Troy as he will do again when he fights the suitors in his own hall. It makes this complex hero dangerous to his enemies, and sometimes to his friends, as the Phaeacians discover when Poseidon punishes them for helping him.

The adventures on the voyage home test these mental qualities, as well as Odysseus's physical endurance, by tempting him to lapse from the struggle homeward. The Lotos flower offers forgetfulness of home and family. Circe gives him a life of ease and self-indulgence on an enchanted island. In Phaeacia, Odysseus is offered the love of a young princess and her hand in marriage. The Sirens tempt him to live in the memory of the glorious past. Calypso, the goddess with whom he spends seven years, offers him the greatest temptation of all: immortality. In refusing, Odysseus chooses the human condition, with all its struggle, its disappointments, and its inevitable end. And the end, death, is ever-present. But he hangs on tenaciously and, in the midst of his ordeals, he is sent living to the world of the dead to see for himself what death means. Dark and comfortless, Homer's land of the dead is the most frightening picture of the afterlife in European literature. Odysseus talks to the dead, and when he consoles the shade of Achilles with talk of everlasting glory Achilles replies that it is better to be the most insignificant person on Earth than lord of the dead. Here the heroes of the two great epics confront one another over the chasm of death. Through them, the *Odyssey* defines its values by contrast with those of the *Iliad*. Against the dark background of Achilles' regret for life Odysseus's dedication to life—his acceptance of its limitations and his ability to seize its possibilities—shines out. His death, Teiresias assures him in this same episode, will come late and gently. Odysseus gets both long life and glory; Achilles could have only either one.

The *Odyssey* celebrates return to ordinary life and makes it seem a worthy prize after excitement, toil, and danger. The adventures occupy only four of twenty-four books (or eight if we include Calypso and the Phaeacians). For the entire second half of the poem, Odysseus is back on Ithaca, winning his way, by deceit that only paves the way for force, from the swineherd Eumaeus's hut to the center of his own house. There, and in books 1–4, we see the social disorder on Ithaca that Odysseus's return is to set right. We also see Telemachus, his son, emerging from adolescence and impatient with all that keeps him from assuming a man's role (his mother as well as her suitors). In his aspirations a foil to Odysseus's mature wisdom, he is his father's potential rival, though in the end his willing subordinate. And we see Penelope's dealings with her son, with her suitors, and with the beggar who is really her husband in disguise. Penelope is a challenging figure, because the narrative does not give us full access to her thoughts and motives. But she seems, with a cunning that matches Odysseus's, to keep in balance two contradictory requirements of her situation. First, she has a duty to herself. If Odysseus, absent twenty years now, is lost for good, then she ought to remarry instead of devoting herself to a house without a head (and in Homeric and later Greek culture, a woman as head of a household was unthinkable). More immediately, she seems to take a natural pleasure in being wooed. On the other hand, she has a duty to her former marriage. If she remarries and Odysseus then returns, she will seem to have betrayed him and, in his and society's eyes, she will be classed with those other adulterers Helen and Clytemnestra. In its ambivalence, Penelope's trick of the web (she promised the suitors to choose one of them when she had finished a shroud for Odysseus's father, Laertes, and for three years she unwove each night what she had woven by day) perfectly encapsulates the way she is forced to play loyal wife and available bride at the same time; it is both a delaying tactic and a way of stringing the suitors along. Odysseus evidently interprets the trick simply as an expression of Penelope's faithfulness to him, and so have readers over the ages. But that only shows how Penelope's interests are folded into his at the end, how his restoration to home and authority retrospectively arranges potentially disorderly elements within a patriarchal order. That is not to say that Penelope lacks autonomy or initiative, at least in the shorter term. To a large extent she controls the timing and means of Odysseus's final homecoming (and therefore she controls key stages in the plot of the poem), not only by her famous trick of the marriage bed in book 23 but also by deciding in book 19 to set the contest of the bow, which will ultimately get a weapon into the beggar's hands (book 21). Why she does so, after the beggar has assured her that Odysseus is about to return, is one of the poem's mysteries. Has she recognized this beggar as her husband, consciously or not, so that she helps him against the suitors? Does she neither recognize nor believe the beggar, so that she acts in despair? Or is she again calculating probabilities to her best advantage?

The period in which the *Iliad* and the *Odyssey* probably took shape, 750–700 B.C. or a little after, saw enormous cultural, political, and social developments in Greece, especially the formation, in many areas, of the *polis*, or "city-state" (see pp. 106–07, above). As often happens, these changes occurred amid sharp conflicts and debates, in which the Homeric epics, publicly performed as they were, must have taken part. Along with the issue of peace and war, for instance, a central conflict of the *Iliad* concerns the nature of political authority. Which has the stronger claim: acknowledged position (Agamemnon) or merit (Achilles)? It is difficult to tell which side wins in the end, if either does, but the poem examines the ramifications of this debate, even while showing, paradoxically, the Greeks maintaining enough unity to destroy a tightly knit and orderly city. The problems of violence and order in this poem are as much political as individual. They involve profound questions about the nature of a political community.

The *Odyssey* offers a more positive meditation on the nature of civilization and of the structures of daily political life as the Greeks experienced it. It does so by showing what a community has to lose by the absence of those structures and to gain by their affirmation, as we see in the contrast between the disorder created by the suitors and Odysseus's restoration of hierarchical and patriarchal order in house and polity. In addition, Odysseus's adventures explore alternatives to "ordinary" (that is, Greek) civilization. Odysseus experiences nature itself as the threatening antithesis to human culture, and he encounters other cultural forms that seem defective or excessive when measured against Ithaca. The richest contrast is provided by the Cyclopes, who lack many of the features of the evolving Greek civilization: houses (they live in caves), agriculture (they are herders), ships for trade and colonization, political integration (their highest political unit is the family), and the key institution of hospitality. (This episode is complex, however, since the Cyclopes enjoy a golden-age existence on which Odysseus intrudes, and Polyphemus has the last word, his curse on Odysseus.) The Laestrygonians are organized as a community and not just by families—they have a ruler and an assembly place—but they share the Cyclopes' unfortunate habit of eating guests. Aeolus, like the Phaeacians, offers Odysseus flawless hospitality, but he lives isolated with his family and marries his daughters to his sons (in contrast to the Greek practice of knitting households together by exchanging women in marriage). Calypso lives in a cave, Circe in a house (she weaves like Penelope), but both live alone. Both are heads of households without husbands, and this, besides the fact that they are sexually threatening to males, makes them "strong" female figures intended to show the need for women's subordination. The Phaeacians, on the other hand, represent an idealized form of "normal" culture but are isolated from other communities and excessively civilized, with no opportunity for heroic achievement. When Odysseus finally is restored to Ithaca, he, and his Greek audience, can appreciate the familiar for having explored alternatives to it in these and many other ways. This self-fashioning by reference to the foreign, which was to have a long history among the Greeks, must have been especially important during this formative period of their culture.

But the *Odyssey* is a much more complex poem than this account suggests, its resolution of issues anything but tidy. One enormous contradiction underlies the final books: Odysseus restores order by killing men from his own community, within his house, and he is prepared to prolong internal warfare by killing the suitors' relatives in the final book. In fact, this struggle recapitulates the Trojan War and resembles the dispute between Achilles and Agamemnon in book 1 of the *Iliad*. In all three cases, men compete for honor over a woman. What is more, Odysseus kills the suitors within his own house, which should be exempt from competition and conflict, as the *Odyssey*'s many scenes of feasting in this same hall show. The *Odyssey* is no more successful than the *Iliad*, then, in resolving the problem of violence. Both poems leave us with questions. How can human aggression be controlled, if not eliminated? Can violence within the community be channeled into safe, perhaps even socially creative, forms? Can it be successfully controlled by being turned outward, against other communities? If so, does that justify the human suffering and waste that external wars cause? And what about the more refined forms of violence at the heart of social hierarchies that create asymmetries of gender and class? Such are the issues raised by the epics amid the formation of the polis, which was to lead, through a long process, to the modern state. Thousands of years later, we cannot claim to have solved them.

A sensitive exploration of Homer's vision of human life and the nature of the gods is Jasper Griffin, *Homer on Life and Death* (1980). Mark W. Edwards, *Homer: Poet of the Iliad* (1987), discusses the oral style and gives a detailed commentary on selected books of the poem, including all of those printed here. Martin Mueller, *The Iliad* (1984), is a highly readable discussion of almost every aspect of the poem, and Seth Schein, *The Mortal Hero: An Introduction to Homer's Iliad* (1987), is an eloquent reading. The psychiatrist Jonathan Shay, in *Achilles in Vietnam: Combat Trauma and the Undoing of Character* (1994), gives a highly interesting discussion of violence and its effects in Homer and in modern warfare based on his work with Vietnam veterans. Basic introductions to the *Odyssey* are J. Griffin, *Homer: The Odyssey* (1987), and W. G. Thalmann, *The Odyssey: An Epic of Return* (1992). An excellent companion to the poem is Ralph Hexter, *A Guide to the Odyssey: A Companion to the Translation by Robert Fitzgerald* (1993). Essays covering various aspects of the poem may be found in Charles Segal, *Singers, Heroes, and Gods in the Odyssey* (1994); Seth Schein, *Reading the Odyssey: Selected Interpretive Essays* (1996); and (on women) Beth Cohen, *The Distaff Side: Representing the Female in Homer's Odyssey* (1995). An excellent discussion of gender in the poem is Nancy Felson-Rubin, *Regarding Penelope: From Character to Poetics* (1994), with further bibliography.

PRONOUNCING GLOSSARY

The following list uses common English syllables and stress accents to provide rough equivalents of selected words whose pronunciation may be unfamiliar to the general reader.

Achaeans: *a-kee'-unz*
Achelous: *a-ke-loh'-us*
Achilles: *a-kil'-eez*
Aeantes: *ee-an'-teez*
Aepea: *ee-pee'-a*
Alkinoös: *al-kin-oh'-uhs*
Andromache: *an-dro'-ma-kee*
Atreus: *ay'-tree-uhs*
Atrides: *a-trai'-deez*
Caeneus: *seen'-yoos*
Chiron: *kai'-ron*
Chryseis: *krai-see'-is*
Chryses: *krai'-seez*
Circe: *ser'-see*
Danaans: *da'-nay-unz*
Deiphobus: *dee-i'-foh-bus*
Demodokos: *dee-mo'-do-kuhs*
Eetion: *ee-e'-tee-on*
Eurystheus: *yoo-ris'-thyoos*
Glaucus: *glow'-kus*
Helios/Hêlios: *hee'-lee-os*
Hephaistos: *he-fess'-tus*
Hermes/Hermês: *her'-meez*
Idaeus: *ai-dee'-us*
Idomeneus: *ai-do'-men-yoos*
Laertes/Laërtês: *lay-er'-teez*
Laodice: *lay-o'-di-see*
Laothoë: *lay-o'-thoh-ee*
Menelaus/Meneláos: *me-ne-lay'-us*
Myrmidons: *mer'-mi-donz*
Mysians: *mee'-shunz*
Nausicaa: *naw-si'-kay-ah*
Odysseus: *oh-dis'-yoos*
Oeneus: *een'-yoos*
Orestes: *o-res'-teez*
Panthous: *pan'-tho-us*
Patroclus: *pa-troh'-klus*
Peleus: *peel'-yoos*
Phaeacians: *fee-ay'-shunz*
Pherae: *fee'-ree*
Phoebus: *fee'-bus*
Phthia: *fthai'-uh*
Polyphêmos: *po-li-fee'-mus*
Pirithous: *pai-ri'-tho-us*
Priam: *prai'-am*
Sarpedon: *sar-pee'-don*
Scaean: *see'-an*
Scylla/Skylla: *si'-lah/skil'-ah*
Scyros: *skai'-ros*
Smintheus: *smin'-thyoos*
Telêmakhos: *te-le'-ma-kos*
Theseus: *thee'-see-uhs*
Xanthus: *zan'-thus*

The Iliad[1]

BOOK I

[*The Rage of Achilles*]

Rage—Goddess,[2] sing the rage of Peleus' son Achilles,
murderous, doomed, that cost the Achaeans[3] countless losses,
hurling down to the House of Death so many sturdy souls,
great fighters' souls, but made their bodies carrion,
feasts for the dogs and birds,
and the will of Zeus was moving toward its end.
Begin, Muse, when the two first broke and clashed,
Agamemnon lord of men and brilliant Achilles.

What god drove them to fight with such a fury?
Apollo the son of Zeus and Leto. Incensed at the king
he swept a fatal plague through the army—men were dying
and all because Agamemnon spurned Apollo's priest.
Yes, Chryses[4] approached the Achaeans' fast ships
to win his daughter back, bringing a priceless ransom
and bearing high in hand, wound on a golden staff,
the wreaths of the god, the distant deadly Archer.
He begged the whole Achaean army but most of all
the two supreme commanders, Atreus' two sons,
"Agamemnon, Menelaus—all Argives geared for war!
May the gods who hold the halls of Olympus give you
Priam's[5] city to plunder, then safe passage home.
Just set my daughter free, my dear one . . . here,
accept these gifts, this ransom. Honor the god
who strikes from worlds away—the son of Zeus, Apollo!"

And all ranks of Achaeans cried out their assent:
"Respect the priest, accept the shining ransom!"
But it brought no joy to the heart of Agamemnon.
The king dismissed the priest with a brutal order
ringing in his ears: "Never again, old man,
let me catch sight of you by the hollow ships!
Not loitering now, not slinking back tomorrow.
The staff and the wreaths of god will never save you then.
The girl—I won't give up the girl. Long before that,
old age will overtake her in *my* house, in Argos,
far from her fatherland, slaving back and forth
at the loom, forced to share my bed!
Now go,
don't tempt my wrath—and you may depart alive."

The old man was terrified. He obeyed the order,
trailing away in silence down the shore

1. Translated by Robert Fagles. 2. The Muse, inspiration for epic poetry. 3. The Greeks. Homer also calls them Danaans and Argives. 4. His daughter is called Chryseis, and the place where he lives, Chryse. 5. King of Troy. Olympus is the mountain in northern Greece that was supposed to be the home of the gods.

where the battle lines of breakers crash and drag.
And moving off to a safe distance, over and over
the old priest prayed to the son of sleek-haired Leto,
lord Apollo, "Hear me, Apollo! God of the silver bow
who strides the walls of Chryse and Cilla sacrosanct—
lord in power of Tenedos—Smintheus,[6] god of the plague!
If I ever roofed a shrine to please your heart,
ever burned the long rich bones of bulls and goats
on your holy altar, now, now bring my prayer to pass.
Pay the Danaans back—your arrows for my tears!"

His prayer went up and Phoebus Apollo heard him.
Down he strode from Olympus' peaks, storming at heart
with his bow and hooded quiver slung across his shoulders.
The arrows clanged at his back as the god quaked with rage,
the god himself on the march and down he came like night.
Over against the ships he dropped to a knee, let fly a shaft
and a terrifying clash rang out from the great silver bow.
First he went for the mules and circling dogs but then,
launching a piercing shaft at the men themselves,
he cut them down in droves—
and the corpse-fires burned on, night and day, no end in sight.

Nine days the arrows of god swept through the army.
On the tenth Achilles called all ranks to muster—
the impulse seized him, sent by white-armed Hera[7]
grieving to see Achaean fighters drop and die.
Once they'd gathered, crowding the meeting grounds,
the swift runner Achilles rose and spoke among them:
"Son of Atreus, now we are beaten back, I fear,
the long campaign is lost. So home we sail . . .
if we can escape our death—if war and plague
are joining forces now to crush the Argives.
But wait: let us question a holy man,
a prophet, even a man skilled with dreams—
dreams as well can come our way from Zeus—
come, someone to tell us why Apollo rages so,
whether he blames us for a vow we failed, or sacrifice.
If only the god would share the smoky savor of lambs
and full-grown goats, Apollo might be willing, still,
somehow, to save us from this plague."
So he proposed
and down he sat again as Calchas rose among them,
Thestor's son, the clearest by far of all the seers
who scan the flight of birds. He knew all things that are,
all things that are past and all that are to come,
the seer who had led the Argive ships to Troy
with the second sight that god Apollo gave him.
For the armies' good the seer began to speak:
"Achilles, dear to Zeus . . .

6. A cult name of Apollo, probably a reference to his role as the destroyer of field mice. The Greek *sminthos* means "mouse." Chryse and Chilla are cities near Troy. Tenedos is an island off the Trojan coast. 7. Sister and wife of Zeus (the father of the gods); she was hostile to the Trojans.

you order me to explain Apollo's anger,
the distant deadly Archer? I will tell it all.
But strike a pact with me, swear you will defend me
with all your heart, with words and strength of hand.
For there is a man I will enrage—I see it now—
a powerful man who lords it over all the Argives,
one the Achaeans must obey . . . A mighty king,
raging against an inferior, is too strong.
Even if he can swallow down his wrath today,
still he will nurse the burning in his chest
until, sooner or later, he sends it bursting forth.
Consider it closely, Achilles. Will you save me?"

And the matchless runner reassured him: "Courage!
Out with it now, Calchas. Reveal the will of god,
whatever you may know. And I swear by Apollo
dear to Zeus, the power you pray to, Calchas,
when you reveal god's will to the Argives—no one,
not while I am alive and see the light on earth, no one
will lay his heavy hands on you by the hollow ships.
None among all the armies. Not even if you mean
Agamemnon here who now claims to be, by far,
the best of the Achaeans."
The seer took heart
and this time he spoke out, bravely: "Beware—
he casts no blame for a vow we failed, a sacrifice.
The god's enraged because Agamemnon spurned his priest,
he refused to free his daughter, he refused the ransom.
That's why the Archer sends us pains and he will send us more
and never drive this shameful destruction from the Argives,
not till we give back the girl with sparkling eyes
to her loving father—no price, no ransom paid—
and carry a sacred hundred bulls to Chryse town.
Then we can calm the god, and only then appease him."

So he declared and sat down. But among them rose
the fighting son of Atreus, lord of the far-flung kingdoms,
Agamemnon—furious, his dark heart filled to the brim,
blazing with anger now, his eyes like searing fire.
With a sudden, killing look he wheeled on Calchas first:
"Seer of misery! Never a word that works to my advantage!
Always misery warms your heart, your prophecies—
never a word of profit said or brought to pass.
Now, again, you divine god's will for the armies,
bruit it out, as fact, why the deadly Archer
multiplies our pains: because I, I refused
that glittering price for the young girl Chryseis.
Indeed, I prefer *her* by far, the girl herself,
I want her mine in my own house! I rank her higher
than Clytemnestra, my wedded wife—she's nothing less
in build or breeding, in mind or works of hand.
But I am willing to give her back, even so,

if that is best for all. What I really want
is to keep my people safe, not see them dying.
But fetch me another prize, and straight off too,
else I alone of the Argives go without my honor.
That would be a disgrace. You are all witness,
look—*my* prize is snatched away!"
But the swift runner
Achilles answered him at once, "Just how, Agamemnon,
great field marshal . . . most grasping man alive,
how can the generous Argives give you prizes now?
I know of no troves of treasure, piled, lying idle,
anywhere. Whatever we dragged from towns we plundered,
all's been portioned out. But collect it, call it back
from the rank and file? *That* would be the disgrace.
So return the girl to the god, at least for now.
We Achaeans will pay you back, three, four times over,
if Zeus will grant us the gift, somehow, someday,
to raze Troy's massive ramparts to the ground."

But King Agamemnon countered, "Not so quickly,
brave as you are, godlike Achilles—trying to cheat *me*.
Oh no, you won't get past me, take me in that way!
What do you want? To cling to your own prize
while I sit calmly by—empty-handed here?
Is that why you order me to give her back?
No—if our generous Argives *will* give me a prize,
a match for my desires, equal to what I've lost,
well and good. But if they give me nothing
I will take a prize myself—your own, or Ajax'
or Odysseus'[8] prize—I'll commandeer her myself
and let that man I go to visit choke with rage!
Enough. We'll deal with all this later, in due time.
Now come, we haul a black ship down to the bright sea,
gather a decent number of oarsmen along her locks
and put aboard a sacrifice, and Chryseis herself,
in all her beauty . . . we embark her too.
Let one of the leading captains take command.
Ajax, Idomeneus, trusty Odysseus or you, Achilles,
you—the most violent man alive—so you can perform
the rites for us and calm the god yourself."
A dark glance
and the headstrong runner answered him in kind: "Shameless—
armored in shamelessness—always shrewd with greed!
How could any Argive soldier obey your orders,
freely and gladly do your sailing for you
or fight your enemies, full force? Not I, no.
It wasn't Trojan spearmen who brought me here to fight.
The Trojans never did *me* damage, not in the least,
they never stole my cattle or my horses, never

8. The most subtle and crafty of the Greeks. Ajax was the bravest of the Greeks after Achilles.

in Phthia[9] where the rich soil breeds strong men
did they lay waste my crops. How could they?
Look at the endless miles that lie between us . . .
shadowy mountain ranges, seas that surge and thunder.
No, you colossal, shameless—we all followed you,
to please you, to fight for you, to win your honor
back from the Trojans—Menelaus[1] and you, you dog-face!
What do *you* care? Nothing. You don't look right or left.
And now you threaten to strip me of my prize in person—
the one I fought for long and hard, and sons of Achaea
handed her to me.
My honors never equal yours,
whenever we sack some wealthy Trojan stronghold—
my arms bear the brunt of the raw, savage fighting,
true, but when it comes to dividing up the plunder
the lion's share is yours, and back I go to my ships,
clutching some scrap, some pittance that I love,
when I have fought to exhaustion.
No more now—
back I go to Phthia. Better that way by far,
to journey home in the beaked ships of war.
I have no mind to linger here disgraced,
brimming your cup and piling up your plunder."

But the lord of men Agamemnon shot back,
"*Desert,* by all means—if the spirit drives you home!
I will never beg you to stay, not on *my* account.
Never—others will take my side and do me honor,
Zeus above all, whose wisdom rules the world.
You—I hate you most of all the warlords
loved by the gods. Always dear to your heart,
strife, yes, and battles, the bloody grind of war.
What if you are a great soldier? That's just a gift of god.
Go home with your ships and comrades, lord it over your Myrmidons![2]
You *are* nothing to me—you and your overweening anger!
But let this be my warning on your way:
since Apollo insists on taking my Chryseis,
I'll send her back in my own ships with *my* crew.
But I, I will be there in person at your tents
to take Briseis in all her beauty, your own prize—
so you can learn just how much greater I am than you
and the next man up may shrink from matching words with me,
from hoping to rival Agamemnon strength for strength!"

He broke off and anguish gripped Achilles.
The heart in his rugged chest was pounding, torn . . .
Should he draw the long sharp sword slung at his hip,
thrust through the ranks and kill Agamemnon now?—

9. Achilles' home in northern Greece. 1. The aim of the expedition was to recapture Menelaus's wife, Helen, who had run off to Troy with Priam's son Paris. 2. The name of Achilles' people.

or check his rage and beat his fury down?
As his racing spirit veered back and forth,
just as he drew his huge blade from its sheath,
down from the vaulting heavens swept Athena,[3]
the white-armed goddess Hera sped her down:
Hera loved both men and cared for both alike.
Rearing behind him Pallas seized his fiery hair—
only Achilles saw her, none of the other fighters—
struck with wonder he spun around, he knew her at once,
Pallas Athena! the terrible blazing of those eyes,
and his winged words went flying: "Why, why now?
Child of Zeus with the shield of thunder,[4] why come now?
To witness the outrage Agamemnon just committed?
I tell you this, and so help me it's the truth—
he'll soon pay for his arrogance with his life!"

Her gray eyes clear, the goddess Athena answered,
"Down from the skies I come to check your rage
if only you will yield.
The white-armed goddess Hera sped me down:
she loves you both, she cares for you both alike.
Stop this fighting, now. Don't lay hand to sword.
Lash him with threats of the price that he will face.
And I tell you this—and I *know* it is the truth—
one day glittering gifts will lie before you,
three times over to pay for all his outrage.
Hold back now. Obey us both."
So she urged
and the swift runner complied at once: "I must—
when the two of you hand down commands, Goddess,
a man submits though his heart breaks with fury.
Better for him by far. If a man obeys the gods
they're quick to hear his prayers."
And with that
Achilles stayed his burly hand on the silver hilt
and slid the huge blade back in its sheath.
He would not fight the orders of Athena.
Soaring home to Olympus, she rejoined the gods
aloft in the halls of Zeus whose shield is thunder.

But Achilles rounded on Agamemnon once again,
lashing out at him, not relaxing his anger for a moment:
"Staggering drunk, with your dog's eyes, your fawn's heart!
Never once did you arm with the troops and go to battle
or risk an ambush packed with Achaea's picked men—
you lack the courage, you can see death coming.
Safer by far, you find, to foray all through camp,

3. A goddess, daughter of Zeus, and a patron of human ingenuity and resourcefulness, whether exemplified by handicrafts (such as spinning) or by skill in human relations (such as her favorite among the Greeks, Odysseus, possessed). She supported the Greek side in the war. 4. A terrible shield with which Zeus (or any other god to whom it was entrusted) stirred up storms or threw panic into human beings.

commandeering the prize of any man who speaks against you.
King who devours his people! Worthless husks, the men you rule—
if not, Atrides,[5] this outrage would have been your last.
I tell you this, and I swear a mighty oath upon it . . .
by this, this scepter, look,
that never again will put forth crown and branches,
now it's left its stump on the mountain ridge forever,
nor will it sprout new green again, now the brazen ax
has stripped its bark and leaves, and now the sons of Achaea
pass it back and forth as they hand their judgments down,
upholding the honored customs whenever Zeus commands—
This scepter will be the mighty force behind my oath:
someday, I swear, a yearning for Achilles will strike
Achaea's sons and all your armies! But then, Atrides,
harrowed as you will be, *nothing* you do can save you—
not when your hordes of fighters drop and die,
cut down by the hands of man-killing Hector![6] Then—
then you will tear your heart out, desperate, raging
that you disgraced the best of the Achaeans!"

Down on the ground
he dashed the scepter studded bright with golden nails,
then took his seat again. The son of Atreus smoldered,
glaring across at him, but Nestor rose between them,
the man of winning words, the clear speaker of Pylos[7] . . .
Sweeter than honey from his tongue the voice flowed on and on.
Two generations of mortal men he had seen go down by now,
those who were born and bred with him in the old days,
in Pylos' holy realm, and now he ruled the third.
He pleaded with both kings, with clear good will,
"No more—or enormous sorrow comes to all Achaea!
How they would exult, Priam and Priam's sons
and all the Trojans. Oh they'd leap for joy
to hear the two of you battling on this way,
you who excel us all, first in Achaean councils,
first in the ways of war.

Stop. Please.
Listen to Nestor. You are both younger than I,
and in my time I struck up with better men than you,
even you, but never once did they make light of me.
I've never seen such men, I never will again . . .
men like Pirithous, Dryas, that fine captain,
Caeneus and Exadius, and Polyphemus, royal prince,
and Theseus,[8] Aegeus' boy, a match for the immortals.
They were the strongest mortals ever bred on earth,
the strongest, and they fought against the strongest too,
shaggy Centaurs, wild brutes of the mountains—
they hacked them down, terrible, deadly work.
And I was in their ranks, fresh out of Pylos,
far away from home—they enlisted me themselves

5. Son of Atreus, i.e., Agamemnon. 6. Son of Priam; the foremost warrior of the Trojans. 7. On the western shore of the Peloponnese. 8. Names of heroes of an older generation.

and I fought on my own, a free lance, single-handed.
And none of the men who walk the earth these days
could battle with those fighters, none, but they,
they took to heart my counsels, marked my words.
So now you listen too. Yielding is far better . . .
Don't seize the girl, Agamemnon, powerful as you are—
leave her, just as the sons of Achaea gave her,
his prize from the very first.
And you, Achilles, never hope to fight it out
with your king, pitting force against his force:
no one can match the honors dealt a king, you know,
a sceptered king to whom great Zeus gives glory.
Strong as you are—a goddess was your mother[9]—
he has more power because he rules more men.
Atrides, end your anger—look, it's Nestor!
I beg you, cool your fury against Achilles.
Here the man stands over all Achaea's armies,
our rugged bulwark braced for shocks of war."

But King Agamemnon answered him in haste,
"True, old man—all you say is fit and proper—
but this soldier wants to tower over the armies,
he wants to rule over all, to lord it over all,
give out orders to every man in sight. Well,
there's one, I trust, who will never yield to him!
What if the everlasting gods have made a spearman of him?
Have they entitled him to hurl abuse at *me*?"

"Yes!"—blazing Achilles broke in quickly—
"What a worthless, burnt-out coward I'd be called
if I would submit to you and all your orders,
whatever you blurt out. Fling them at others,
don't give me commands!
Never again, *I* trust, will Achilles yield to *you*.
And I tell you this—take it to heart, I warn you—
my hands will never do battle for that girl,
neither with you, King, nor any man alive.
You Achaeans gave her, now you've snatched her back.
But all the rest I possess beside my fast black ship—
not one bit of it can you seize against my will, Atrides.
Come, try it! So the men can see, that instant,
your black blood gush and spurt around my spear!"

Once the two had fought it out with words,
battling face-to-face, both sprang to their feet
and broke up the muster beside the Argive squadrons.
Achilles strode off to his trim ships and shelters,
back to his friend Patroclus and their comrades.
Agamemnon had a vessel hauled down to the sea,

9. Thetis, a sea nymph, who was married to the mortal Peleus (Achilles' father); she later left humankind and went to live with her father, Nereus, in the depths of the Aegean Sea.

he picked out twenty oarsmen to man her locks,
put aboard the cattle for sacrifice to the god
and led Chryseis in all her beauty amidships.
Versatile Odysseus took the helm as captain.
All embarked,
the party launched out on the sea's foaming lanes
while the son of Atreus told his troops to wash,
to purify themselves from the filth of plague.
They scoured it off, threw scourings in the surf
and sacrificed to Apollo full-grown bulls and goats
along the beaten shore of the fallow barren sea
and savory smoke went swirling up the skies.

So the men were engaged throughout the camp.
But King Agamemnon would not stop the quarrel,
the first threat he hurled against Achilles.
He called Talthybius and Eurybates briskly,
his two heralds, ready, willing aides:
"Go to Achilles' lodge. Take Briseis at once,
his beauty Briseis by the hand and bring her here.
But if he will not surrender her, I'll go myself,
I'll seize her myself, with an army at my back—
and all the worse for him!"
He sent them off
with the strict order ringing in their ears.
Against their will the two men made their way
along the breaking surf of the barren salt sea
and reached the Myrmidon shelters and their ships.
They found him beside his lodge and black hull,
seated grimly—and Achilles took no joy
when he saw the two approaching.
They were afraid, they held the king in awe
and stood there, silent. Not a word to Achilles,
not a question. But he sensed it all in his heart,
their fear, their charge, and broke the silence for them:
"Welcome, couriers! Good heralds of Zeus and men,
here, come closer. You have done nothing to me.
You are not to blame. No one but Agamemnon—
he is the one who sent you for Briseis.
Go, Patroclus, Prince, bring out the girl
and hand her to them so they can take her back.
But let them both bear witness to my loss . . .
in the face of blissful gods and mortal men,
in the face of that unbending, ruthless king—
if the day should come when the armies need *me*
to save their ranks from ignominious, stark defeat.
The man is raving—with all the murderous fury in his heart.
He lacks the sense to see a day behind, a day ahead,
and safeguard the Achaeans battling by the ships."

Patroclus obeyed his great friend's command.
He led Briseis in all her beauty from the lodge

and handed her over to the men to take away.
And the two walked back along the Argive ships
while she trailed on behind, reluctant, every step.
But Achilles wept, and slipping away from his companions,
far apart, sat down on the beach of the heaving gray sea
and scanned the endless ocean. Reaching out his arms,
again and again he prayed to his dear mother: "Mother!
You gave me life, short as that life will be,
so at least Olympian Zeus, thundering up on high,
should give me honor—but now he gives me nothing.
Atreus' son Agamemnon, for all his far-flung kingdoms—
the man disgraces me, seizes and keeps my prize,
he tears her away himself!"
So he wept and prayed
and his noble mother heard him, seated near her father,
the Old Man of the Sea in the salt green depths.
Suddenly up she rose from the churning surf
like mist and settling down beside him as he wept,
stroked Achilles gently, whispering his name, "My child—
why in tears? What sorrow has touched your heart?
Tell me, please. Don't harbor it deep inside you.
We must share it all."
And now from his depths
the proud runner groaned: "You know, you know,
why labor through it all? You know it all so well . . .
We raided Thebe once, Eetion's[1] sacred citadel,
we ravaged the place, hauled all the plunder here
and the armies passed it round, share and share alike,
and they chose the beauty Chryseis for Agamemnon.
But soon her father, the holy priest of Apollo
the distant deadly Archer, Chryses approached
the fast trim ships of the Argives armed in bronze
to win his daughter back, bringing a priceless ransom
and bearing high in hand, wound on a golden staff,
the wreaths of the god who strikes from worlds away.
He begged the whole Achaean army but most of all
the two supreme commanders, Atreus' two sons,
and all ranks of Achaeans cried out their assent,
'Respect the priest, accept the shining ransom!'
But it brought no joy to the heart of Agamemnon,
our high and mighty king dismissed the priest
with a brutal order ringing in his ears.
And shattered with anger, the old man withdrew
but Apollo heard his prayer—he loved him, deeply—
he loosed his shaft at the Argives, withering plague,
and now the troops began to drop and die in droves,
the arrows of god went showering left and right,
whipping through the Achaeans' vast encampment.
But the old seer who knew the cause full well
revealed the will of the archer god Apollo.

1. King of the Cilicians and father of Hector's wife, Andromache. Thebe was the Cilician capital city.

And I was the first, mother, I urged them all,
'Appease the god at once!' That's when the fury
gripped the son of Atreus. Agamemnon leapt to his feet
and hurled his threat—his threat's been driven home.
One girl, Chryseis, the fiery-eyed Achaeans
ferry out in a fast trim ship to Chryse Island,
laden with presents for the god.[2] The other girl,
just now the heralds came and led her away from camp,
Briseus' daughter, the prize the armies gave me.
But you, mother, if you have any power at all,
protect your son! Go to Olympus, plead with Zeus,
if you ever warmed his heart with a word or any action . . .

Time and again I heard your claims in father's halls,
boasting how you and you alone of all the immortals
rescued Zeus,[3] the lord of the dark storm cloud,
from ignominious, stark defeat.
That day the Olympians tried to chain him down,
Hera, Poseidon[4] lord of the sea, and Pallas Athena—
you rushed to Zeus, dear Goddess, broke those chains,
quickly ordered the hundred-hander to steep Olympus,
that monster whom the immortals call Briareus[5]
but every mortal calls the Sea-god's son, Aegaeon,
though he's stronger than his father. Down he sat,
flanking Cronus' son, gargantuan in the glory of it all,
and the blessed gods were struck with terror then,
they stopped shackling Zeus.
Remind him of that,
now, go and sit beside him, grasp his knees . . .
persuade him, somehow, to help the Trojan cause,
to pin the Achaeans back against their ships,
trap them round the bay and mow them down.
So all can reap the benefits of their king—
so even mighty Atrides can see how mad he was
to disgrace Achilles, the best of the Achaeans!"

And Thetis answered, bursting into tears,
"O my son, my sorrow, why did I ever bear you?
All I bore was doom . . .
Would to god you could linger by your ships
without a grief in the world, without a torment!
Doomed to a short life, you have so little time.
And not only short, now, but filled with heartbreak too,
more than all other men alive—doomed twice over.
Ah to a cruel fate I bore you in our halls!
Still, I shall go to Olympus crowned with snow
and repeat your prayer to Zeus who loves the lightning.
Perhaps he will be persuaded.
But you, my child,

2. Apollo. 3. As god of the sky he controlled rain and sunshine. 4. Brother of Zeus. 5. A giant, son of Poseidon.

stay here by the fast ships, rage on at the Achaeans,
just keep clear of every foray in the fighting.
Only yesterday Zeus went off to the Ocean River
to feast with the Aethiopians,[6] loyal, lordly men,
and all the gods went with him. But in twelve days
the Father returns to Olympus. Then, for your sake,
up I go to the bronze floor, the royal house of Zeus—
I'll grasp his knees, I think I'll win him over."

With that vow
his mother went away and left him there, alone,
his heart inflamed for the sashed and lovely girl
they'd wrenched away from him against his will.
Meanwhile Odysseus drew in close to Chryse Island,
bearing the splendid sacrifice in the vessel's hold.
And once they had entered the harbor deep in bays
they furled and stowed their sails in the black ship,
they lowered the mast by the forestays, smoothly,
quickly let it down on the forked mast-crutch
and rowed her into a mooring under oars.
Out went the bow-stones—cables fast astern—
and the crew themselves climbed out in the breaking surf,
leading out the sacrifice for the archer god Apollo,
and out of the deep-sea ship Chryseis stepped too.
Then tactful Odysseus led her up to the altar,
placing her in her loving father's arms, and said,
"Chryses, the lord of men Agamemnon sent me here
to bring your daughter back and perform a sacrifice,
a grand sacrifice to Apollo—for all Achaea's sake—
so we can appease the god
who's loosed such grief and torment on the Argives."

With those words he left her in Chryses' arms
and the priest embraced the child he loved, exultant.
At once the men arranged the sacrifice for Apollo,
making the cattle ring his well-built altar,
then they rinsed their hands and took up barley.
Rising among them Chryses stretched his arms to the sky
and prayed in a high resounding voice, "Hear me, Apollo!
God of the silver bow who strides the walls of Chryse
and Cilla sacrosanct—lord in power of Tenedos!
If you honored me last time and heard my prayer
and rained destruction down on all Achaea's ranks,
now bring my prayer to pass once more. Now, at last,
drive this killing plague from the armies of Achaea!"

His prayer went up and Phoebus Apollo heard him.
And soon as the men had prayed and flung the barley,
first they lifted back the heads of the victims,
slit their throats, skinned them and carved away

6. Or Ethiopians, who were thought to live at the extreme edges of the world. It was believed that a river (*Ocean River*) encircled the entire world.

the meat from the thighbones and wrapped them in fat,
a double fold sliced clean and topped with strips of flesh.
And the old man burned these on a dried cleft stick
and over the quarters poured out glistening wine
while young men at his side held five-pronged forks.
Once they had charred the thighs and tasted the organs
they cut the rest into pieces, pierced them with spits,
roasted them to a turn and pulled them off the fire.
The work done, the feast laid out, they ate well
and no man's hunger lacked a share of the banquet.
When they had put aside desire for food and drink,
the young men brimmed the mixing bowls with wine
and tipping first drops for the god in every cup
they poured full rounds for all. And all day long
they appeased the god with song, raising a ringing hymn
to the distant archer god who drives away the plague,
those young Achaean warriors singing out his power,
and Apollo listened, his great heart warm with joy.

Then when the sun went down and night came on
they made their beds and slept by the stern-cables . . .
When young Dawn with her rose-red fingers shone once more,
they set sail for the main encampment of Achaea.
The Archer sent them a bracing following wind,
they stepped the mast, spread white sails wide,
the wind hit full and the canvas bellied out
and a dark blue wave, foaming up at the bow,
sang out loud and strong as the ship made way,
skimming the whitecaps, cutting toward her goal.
And once offshore of Achaea's vast encampment
they eased her in and hauled the black ship high,
far up on the sand, and shored her up with timbers.
Then they scattered, each to his own ship and shelter.

But he raged on, grimly camped by his fast fleet,
the royal son of Peleus, the swift runner Achilles.
Now he no longer haunted the meeting grounds
where men win glory, now he no longer went to war
but day after day he ground his heart out, waiting there,
yearning, always yearning for battle cries and combat.

But now as the twelfth dawn after this shone clear
the gods who live forever marched home to Olympus,
all in a long cortege, and Zeus led them on.
And Thetis did not forget her son's appeals.
She broke from a cresting wave at first light
and soaring up to the broad sky and Mount Olympus,
found the son of Cronus gazing down on the world,
peaks apart from the other gods and seated high
on the topmost crown of rugged ridged Olympus.
And crouching down at his feet,
quickly grasping his knees with her left hand,

her right hand holding him underneath the chin,[7]
she prayed to the lord god Zeus, the son of Cronus:
"Zeus, Father Zeus! If I ever served you well
among the deathless gods with a word or action,
bring this prayer to pass: honor my son Achilles!—
doomed to the shortest life of any man on earth.
And now the lord of men Agamemnon has disgraced him,
seizes and keeps his prize, tears her away himself. But you—
exalt him, Olympian Zeus: your urgings rule the world!
Come, grant the Trojans victory after victory
till the Achaean armies pay my dear son back,
building higher the honor he deserves!"
She paused
but Zeus who commands the storm clouds answered nothing.
The Father sat there, silent. It seemed an eternity . . .
But Thetis, clasping his knees, held on, clinging,
pressing her question once again: "Grant my prayer,
once and for all, Father, bow your head in assent!
Or deny me outright. What have you to fear?
So I may know, too well, just how cruelly
I am the most dishonored goddess of them all."
Filled with anger
Zeus who marshals the storm clouds answered her at last:
"Disaster. You will drive me into war with Hera.
She will provoke me, she with her shrill abuse.
Even now in the face of all the immortal gods
she harries me perpetually, Hera charges *me*
that I always go to battle for the Trojans.
Away with you now. Hera might catch us here.
I will see to this. I will bring it all to pass.
Look, I will bow my head if that will satisfy you.
That, I remind you, that among the immortal gods
is the strongest, truest sign that I can give.
No word or work of mine—nothing can be revoked,
there is no treachery, nothing left unfinished
once I bow my head to say it shall be done."

So he decreed. And Zeus the son of Cronus bowed
his craggy dark brows and the deathless locks came pouring
down from the thunderhead of the great immortal king
and giant shock waves spread through all Olympus.

So the two of them made their pact and parted.
Deep in the sea she dove from radiant Mount Olympus.
Zeus went back to his own halls, and all the gods
in full assembly rose from their seats at once
to meet the Father striding toward them now.
None dared remain at rest as Zeus advanced,
they all sprang up to greet him face-to-face

7. She takes on the posture of the suppliant, the physical pressure of which emphasizes the desperation and urgency of the request. Zeus was, above all other gods, the protector of suppliants.

as he took his place before them on his throne.
But Hera knew it all. She had seen how Thetis,
the Old Man of the Sea's daughter, Thetis quick
on her glistening feet was hatching plans with Zeus.
And suddenly Hera taunted the Father, son of Cronus:
"So, who of the gods this time, my treacherous one,
was hatching plans with you?
Always your pleasure, whenever my back is turned,
to settle things in your grand clandestine way.
You never deign, do you, freely and frankly,
to share your plots with me—never, not a word!"

The father of men and gods replied sharply,
"Hera—stop hoping to fathom all my thoughts.
You will find them a trial, though you are my wife.
Whatever is right for you to hear, no one, trust me,
will know of it before you, neither god nor man.
Whatever I choose to plan apart from all the gods—
no more of your everlasting questions, probe and pry no more."

And Hera the Queen, her dark eyes wide, exclaimed,
"Dread majesty, son of Cronus, what are you saying?
Now surely I've never probed or pried in the past.
Why, you can scheme to your heart's content
without a qualm in the world for me. But now
I have a terrible fear that she has won you over,
Thetis, the Old Man of the Sea's daughter, Thetis
with her glistening feet. I know it. Just at dawn
she knelt down beside you and grasped your knees
and I suspect you bowed your head in assent to her—
you granted once and for all to exalt Achilles now
and slaughter hordes of Achaeans pinned against their ships."

And Zeus who marshals the thunderheads returned,
"Maddening one . . . you and your eternal suspicions—
I can never escape you. Ah but tell me, Hera,
just what can you *do* about all this? Nothing.
Only estrange yourself from me a little more—
and all the worse for you.
If what you say is true, that must be my pleasure.
Now go sit down. Be quiet now. Obey my orders,
for fear the gods, however many Olympus holds,
are powerless to protect you when I come
to throttle you with my irresistible hands."
He subsided
but Hera the Queen, her eyes wider, was terrified.
She sat in silence. She wrenched her will to his.
And throughout the halls of Zeus the gods of heaven
quaked with fear. Hephaestus[8] the Master Craftsman
rose up first to harangue them all, trying now

8. The lame god of fire and the patron of craftspeople, especially metalworkers.

to bring his loving mother a little comfort,
the white-armed goddess Hera: "Oh disaster . . .
that's what it is, and it will be unbearable
if the two of you must come to blows this way,
flinging the gods in chaos just for mortal men.
No more joy for us in the sumptuous feast
when riot rules the day.
I urge you, mother—you know that I am right—
work back into his good graces, so the Father,
our beloved Father will never wheel on us again,
send our banquets crashing! The Olympian lord of lightning—
what if he would like to blast us from our seats?
He is far too strong. Go back to him, mother,
stroke the Father with soft, winning words—
at once the Olympian will turn kind to us again."

Pleading, springing up with a two-handled cup,
he reached it toward his loving mother's hands
with his own winning words: "Patience, mother!
Grieved as you are, bear up, or dear as you are,
I have to see you beaten right before my eyes.
I would be shattered—what could I do to save you?
It's hard to fight the Olympian strength for strength.
You remember the last time I rushed to your defense?
He grabbed my foot, he hurled me off the tremendous threshold
and all day long I dropped, I was dead weight and then,
when the sun went down, down I plunged on Lemnos,[9]
little breath left in me. But the mortals there
soon nursed a fallen immortal back to life."

At that the white-armed goddess Hera smiled
and smiling, took the cup from her child's hands.
Then dipping sweet nectar[1] up from the mixing bowl
he poured it round to all the immortals, left to right.
And uncontrollable laughter broke from the happy gods
as they watched the god of fire breathing hard
and bustling through the halls.
That hour then
and all day long till the sun went down they feasted
and no god's hunger lacked a share of the handsome banquet
or the gorgeous lyre Apollo struck or the Muses[2] singing
voice to voice in choirs, their vibrant music rising.

At last, when the sun's fiery light had set,
each immortal went to rest in his own house,
the splendid high halls Hephaestus built for each
with all his craft and cunning, the famous crippled Smith.
And Olympian Zeus the lord of lightning went to his own bed
where he had always lain when welcome sleep came on him.

9. An island in the Aegean Sea. 1. The drink of the gods. 2. The Nine Muses were goddesses of the arts and sources of artistic inspiration.

There he climbed and there he slept and by his side
lay Hera the Queen, the goddess of the golden throne.

Summary The Greeks, in spite of Achilles' withdrawal, continued to fight. They did not suffer immoderately from Achilles' absence; on the contrary, they pressed the Trojans so hard that Hector, the Trojan leader, after rallying his men, returned to the city to urge the Trojans to offer special prayers and sacrifices to the gods.

FROM BOOK VI

[*Hector Returns to Troy*]

As Hector turned for home his helmet flashed
and the long dark hide of his bossed shield, the rim
running the metal edge, drummed his neck and ankles.
And now
Glaucus son of Hippolochus and Tydeus' son Diomedes[3]
met in the no man's land between both armies:
burning for battle, closing, squaring off
and the lord of the war cry Diomedes opened up,
"Who are you, my fine friend?—another born to die?
I've never noticed you on the lines where we win glory,
not till now. But here you come, charging out
in front of all the rest with such bravado—
daring to face the flying shadow of my spear.
Pity the ones whose sons stand up to me in war!
But if you are an immortal come from the blue,
I'm not the man to fight the gods of heaven.
Not even Dryas' indestructible son Lycurgus,[4]
not even he lived long . . .
that fellow who tried to fight the deathless gods.
He rushed at the maenads once, nurses of wild Dionysus,[5]
scattered them breakneck down the holy mountain Nysa.
A rout of them strewed their sacred staves on the ground,
raked with a cattle prod by Lycurgus, murderous fool!
And Dionysus was terrified, he dove beneath the surf
where the sea-nymph Thetis pressed him to her breast—
Dionysus numb with fear: shivers racked his body,
thanks to the raucous onslaught of that man.
But the gods who live at ease lashed out against him—
worse, the son of Cronus[6] struck Lycurgus blind.
Nor did the man live long, not with the hate
of all the gods against him.
No, my friend,
I have no desire to fight the blithe immortals.
But if you're a man who eats the crops of the earth,
a mortal born for death—here, come closer,
the sooner you will meet your day to die!"

The noble son of Hippolochus answered staunchly,
"High-hearted son of Tydeus, why ask about my birth?

3. One of the foremost Greek leaders. *Glaucus:* from Lycia in Asia Minor, and a Trojan ally. 4. King of Thrace, a half-wild region along the north shore of the Aegean Sea. 5. God of the vine. 6. Zeus.

Like the generations of leaves, the lives of mortal men.
Now the wind scatters the old leaves across the earth,
now the living timber bursts with the new buds
and spring comes round again. And so with men:
as one generation comes to life, another dies away.
But about my birth, if you'd like to learn it well,
first to last—though many people know it—
here's my story . . .
There is a city, Corinth,
deep in a bend of Argos, good stallion-country
where Sisyphus used to live, the wiliest man alive.
Sisyphus, Aeolus' son, who had a son called Glaucus,
and in his day Glaucus sired brave Bellerophon,
a man without a fault. The gods gave him beauty
and the fine, gallant traits that go with men.
But Proetus[7] plotted against him. Far stronger,
the king in his anger drove him out of Argos,
the kingdom Zeus had brought beneath his scepter.
Proetus' wife, you see, was mad for Bellerophon,
the lovely Antea lusted to couple with him,
all in secret. Futile—she could never seduce
the man's strong will, his seasoned, firm resolve.
So straight to the king she went, blurting out her lies:
'I wish you'd die, Proetus, if you don't kill Bellerophon!
Bellerophon's bent on dragging me down with him in lust
though I fight him all the way!'
All of it false
but the king seethed when he heard a tale like that.
He balked at killing the man—he'd some respect at least—
but he quickly sent him off to Lycia, gave him tokens,
murderous signs, scratched in a folded tablet,
and many of them too, enough to kill a man.
He told him to show them to Antea's father:
that would mean his death.
So off he went to Lycia,
safe in the escort of the gods, and once he reached
the broad highlands cut by the rushing Xanthus,[8]
the king of Lycia gave him a royal welcome.
Nine days he feasted him, nine oxen slaughtered.
When the tenth Dawn shone with her rose-red fingers,
he began to question him, asked to see his credentials,
whatever he brought him from his in-law, Proetus.
But then, once he received that fatal message
sent from his own daughter's husband, first
he ordered Bellerophon to kill the Chimaera—
grim monster sprung of the gods, nothing human,
all lion in front, all snake behind, all goat between,
terrible, blasting lethal fire at every breath!
But he laid her low, obeying signs from the gods.
Next he fought the Solymi, tribesmen bent on glory,

7. King of Argos. 8. River in Lycia.

roughest battle of men he ever entered, so he claimed.
Then for a third test he brought the Amazons down,
a match for men in war. But as he turned back,
his host spun out the tightest trap of all:
picking the best men from Lycia far and wide
he set an ambush—that never came home again!
Fearless Bellerophon killed them all.
                                        Then, yes,
when the king could see the man's power at last,
a true son of the gods, he pressed him hard to stay,
he offered his own daughter's hand in marriage,
he gave him half his royal honors as the king.
And the Lycians carved him out a grand estate,
the choicest land in the realm, rich in vineyards
and good tilled fields for him to lord it over.
And his wife bore good Bellerophon three children:
Isander, Hippolochus and Laodamia. Laodamia
lay in the arms of Zeus who rules the world
and she bore the god a son, our great commander,
Sarpedon helmed in bronze.
                                        But the day soon came
when even Bellerophon was hated by all the gods.
Across the Alean plain he wandered, all alone,
eating his heart out, a fugitive on the run
from the beaten tracks of men. His son Isander?
Killed by the War-god, never sated—a boy fighting
the Solymi always out for glory. Laodamia? Artemis,
flashing her golden reins, cut her down in anger.
But Hippolochus fathered me, I'm proud to say.
He sent me off to Troy . . .
and I hear his urgings ringing in my ears:
'Always be the best, my boy, the bravest,
and hold your head up high above the others.
Never disgrace the generation of your fathers.
They were the bravest champions born in Corinth,
in Lycia far and wide.'
                                        There you have my lineage.
That is the blood I claim, my royal birth."

When he heard that, Diomedes' spirits lifted.
Raising his spear, the lord of the war cry drove it home,
planting it deep down in the earth that feeds us all
and with winning words he called out to Glaucus,
the young captain, "Splendid—you are my friend,
my guest from the days of our grandfathers long ago!
Noble Oeneus hosted your brave Bellerophon once,
he held him there in his halls, twenty whole days,
and they gave each other handsome gifts of friendship.
My kinsman offered a gleaming sword-belt, rich red,
Bellerophon gave a cup, two-handled, solid gold—
I left it at home when I set out for Troy.
My father, Tydeus, I really don't remember.

I was just a baby when father left me then,
that time an Achaean army went to die at Thebes.[9]
So now I am your host and friend in the heart of Argos,
you are mine in Lycia when I visit in your country.
Come, let us keep clear of each other's spears,
even there in the thick of battle. Look,
plenty of Trojans there for me to kill,
your famous allies too, any soldier the god
will bring in range or I can run to ground.
And plenty of Argives too—kill them if you can.
But let's trade armor. The men must know our claim:
we are sworn friends from our fathers' days till now!"[1]

Both agreed. Both fighters sprang from their chariots,
clasped each other's hands and traded pacts of friendship.
But the son of Cronus, Zeus, stole Glaucus' wits away.
He traded his gold armor for bronze with Diomedes,
the worth of a hundred oxen just for nine.
And now,
when Hector reached the Scaean Gates[2] and the great oak,
the wives and daughters of Troy came rushing up around him,
asking about their sons, brothers, friends and husbands.
But Hector told them only, "Pray to the gods"—
all the Trojan women, one after another . . .
Hard sorrows were hanging over many.
And soon
he came to Priam's palace, that magnificent structure
built wide with porches and colonnades of polished stone.
And deep within its walls were fifty sleeping chambers
masoned in smooth, lustrous ashlar, linked in a line
where the sons of Priam slept beside their wedded wives,
and facing these, opening out across the inner courtyard,
lay the twelve sleeping chambers of Priam's daughters,
masoned and roofed in lustrous ashlar, linked in a line
where the sons-in-law of Priam slept beside their wives.
And there at the palace Hector's mother[3] met her son,
that warm, goodhearted woman, going in with Laodice,
the loveliest daughter Hecuba ever bred. His mother
clutched his hand and urged him, called his name:
"My child—why have you left the bitter fighting,
why have you come home? Look how they wear you out,
the sons of Achaea—curse them—battling round our walls!
And that's why your spirit brought you back to Troy,
to climb the heights and stretch your arms to Zeus.
But wait, I'll bring you some honeyed, mellow wine.
First pour out cups to Father Zeus and the other gods,
then refresh yourself, if you'd like to quench your thirst.

9. Tydeus was one of the seven heroes who attacked Thebes, led by Oedipus's son Polyneices, who was attempting to dislodge his brother Eteocles from the kingship. The brothers killed each other, and the rest of the seven also perished. Diomedes, along with the sons of the other champions, later sacked Thebes.
1. It was customary for guest-friends to exchange gifts. 2. One of the entrances to Troy. 3. Hecuba, Priam's queen.

When a man's exhausted, wine will build his strength—
battle-weary as *you* are, fighting for your people."

But Hector shook his head, his helmet flashing:
"Don't offer me mellow wine, mother, not now—
you'd sap my limbs, I'd lose my nerve for war.
And I'd be ashamed to pour a glistening cup to Zeus
with unwashed hands. I'm splattered with blood and filth—
how could I pray to the lord of storm and lightning?
No, mother, you are the one to pray.
Go to Athena's shrine, the queen of plunder,
go with offerings, gather the older noble women
and take a robe, the largest, loveliest robe
that you can find throughout the royal halls,
a gift that far and away you prize most yourself,
and spread it out across the sleek-haired goddess' knees.
Then promise to sacrifice twelve heifers in her shrine,
yearlings never broken, if only she'll pity Troy,
the Trojan wives and all our helpless children,
if only she'll hold Diomedes[4] back from the holy city—
that wild spearman, that invincible headlong terror!
Now, mother, go to the queen of plunder's shrine
and I'll go hunt for Paris,[5] summon him to fight
if the man will hear what *I* have to say . . .
Let the earth gape and swallow him on the spot!
A great curse Olympian Zeus let live and grow in him,
for Troy and high-hearted Priam and all his sons.
That man—if I could see him bound for the House of Death,
I could say my heart had forgot its wrenching grief!"

But his mother simply turned away to the palace.
She gave her servants orders and out they strode
to gather the older noble women through the city.
Hecuba went down to a storeroom filled with scent
and there they were, brocaded, beautiful robes . . .
the work of Sidonian women. Magnificent Paris
brought those women back himself from Sidon,[6]
sailing the open seas on the same long voyage
he swept Helen off, her famous Father's child.
Lifting one from the lot, Hecuba brought it out
for great Athena's gift, the largest, loveliest,
richly worked, and like a star it glistened,
deep beneath the others. Then she made her way
with a file of noble women rushing in her train.

Once they reached Athena's shrine on the city crest
the beauty Theano opened the doors to let them in,
Cisseus' daughter, the horseman Antenor's wife
and Athena's priestess chosen by the Trojans. Then—

4. One of the Greek champions, who has just distinguished himself in the fighting. 5. Hector's brother, whose seduction and abduction of Helen, the wife of Menelaus, is the cause of the war. 6. A Phoenician city on the coast of what is now Lebanon.

with a shrill wail they all stretched their arms to Athena
as Theano, her face radiant, lifting the robe on high,
spread it out across the sleek-haired goddess' knees
and prayed to the daughter of mighty Father Zeus:
"Queen Athena—shield of our city—glory of goddesses!
Now shatter the spear of Diomedes! That wild man—
hurl him headlong down before the Scaean Gates!
At once we'll sacrifice twelve heifers in your shrine,
yearlings never broken, if only you'll pity Troy,
the Trojan wives and all our helpless children!"
But Athena refused to hear Theano's prayers.
And while they prayed to the daughter of mighty Zeus
Hector approached the halls of Paris, sumptuous halls
he built himself with the finest masons of the day,
master builders famed in the fertile land of Troy.
They'd raised his sleeping chamber, house and court
adjoining Priam's and Hector's aloft the city heights.
Now Hector, dear to Zeus, strode through the gates,
clutching a thrusting-lance eleven forearms long;
the bronze tip of the weapon shone before him,
ringed with a golden hoop to grip the shaft.
And there in the bedroom Hector came on Paris
polishing, fondling his splendid battle-gear,
his shield and breastplate, turning over and over
his long curved bow. And there was Helen of Argos,
sitting with all the women of the house, directing
the rich embroidered work they had in hand.
Seeing Paris,
Hector raked his brother with insults, stinging taunts:[7]
"What on earth are you doing? Oh how wrong it is,
this anger you keep smoldering in your heart! Look,
your people dying around the city, the steep walls,
dying in arms—and all for you, the battle cries
and the fighting flaring up around the citadel.
You'd be the first to lash out at another—anywhere—
you saw hanging back from this, this hateful war.
Up with you—
before all Troy is torched to a cinder here and now!"

And Paris, magnificent as a god, replied,
"Ah Hector, you criticize me fairly, yes,
nothing unfair, beyond what I deserve. And so
I will try to tell you something. Please bear with me,
hear me out. It's not so much from anger or outrage
at our people that I keep to my rooms so long.
I only wanted to plunge myself in grief.
But just now my wife was bringing me round,
her winning words urging me back to battle.

7. Paris, like Achilles, was sulking. He had been worsted in a duel with Menelaus, but the goddess Aphrodite saved him from the consequences of his defeat and brought him to his house in Troy. Paris was hated by his compatriots as the cause of the war.

And it strikes me, even me, as the better way.
Victory shifts, you know, now one man, now another.
So come, wait while I get this war-gear on,
or you go on ahead and I will follow—
I think I can overtake you."
Hector, helmet flashing,
answered nothing. And Helen spoke to him now,
her soft voice welling up: "My dear brother,
dear to me, bitch that I am, vicious, scheming—
horror to freeze the heart! Oh how I wish
that first day my mother brought me into the light
some black whirlwind had rushed me out to the mountains
or into the surf where the roaring breakers crash and drag
and the waves had swept me off before all this had happened!
But since the gods ordained it all, these desperate years,
I wish I had been the wife of a better man, someone
alive to outrage, the withering scorn of men.
This one has no steadiness in his spirit,
not now, he never will . . .
and he's going to reap the fruits of it, I swear.
But come in, rest on this seat with me, dear brother.
You are the one hit hardest by the fighting, Hector,
you more than all—and all for me, slut that I am,
and this blind mad Paris. Oh the two of us!
Zeus planted a killing doom within us both,
so even for generations still unborn
we will live in song."
Turning to go,
his helmet flashing, tall Hector answered,
"Don't ask me to sit beside you here, Helen.
Love me as you do, you can't persuade me now.
No time for rest. My heart races to help our Trojans—
they long for me, sorely, whenever I am gone.
But rouse this fellow, won't you?
And let him hurry himself along as well,
so he can overtake me before I leave the city.
For I must go home to see my people first,
to visit my own dear wife and my baby son.
Who knows if I will ever come back to them again?—
or the deathless gods will strike me down at last
at the hands of Argive fighters."
A flash of his helmet
and off he strode and quickly reached his sturdy,
well-built house. But white-armed Andromache—
Hector could not find her in the halls.
She and the boy and a servant finely gowned
were standing watch on the tower, sobbing, grieving.
When Hector saw no sign of his loyal wife inside
he went to the doorway, stopped and asked the servants,
"Come, please, tell me the truth now, women.
Where's Andromache gone? To my sisters' house?
To my brothers' wives with their long flowing robes?

Or Athena's shrine where the noble Trojan women
gather to win the great grim goddess over?"

A busy, willing servant answered quickly,
"Hector, seeing you want to know the truth,
she hasn't gone to your sisters, brothers' wives
or Athena's shrine where the noble Trojan women
gather to win the great grim goddess over.
Up to the huge gate-tower of Troy she's gone
because she heard our men are so hard-pressed,
the Achaean fighters coming on in so much force.
She sped to the wall in panic, like a madwoman—
the nurse went with her, carrying your child."

At that, Hector spun and rushed from his house,
back by the same way down the wide, well-paved streets
throughout the city until he reached the Scaean Gates,
the last point he would pass to gain the field of battle.
There his warm, generous wife came running up to meet him,
Andromache the daughter of gallant-hearted Eetion
who had lived below Mount Placos rich with timber,
in Thebe below the peaks, and ruled Cilicia's people.
His daughter had married Hector helmed in bronze.
She joined him now, and following in her steps
a servant holding the boy against her breast,
in the first flush of life, only a baby,
Hector's son, the darling of his eyes
and radiant as a star . . .
Hector would always call the boy Scamandrius,
townsmen called him Astyanax,[8] Lord of the City,
since Hector was the lone defense of Troy.
The great man of war breaking into a broad smile,
his gaze fixed on his son, in silence. Andromache,
pressing close beside him and weeping freely now,
clung to his hand, urged him, called him: "Reckless one,
my Hector—your own fiery courage will destroy you!
Have you no pity for him, our helpless son? Or me,
and the destiny that weighs me down, your widow,
now so soon. Yes, soon they will kill you off,
all the Achaean forces massed for assault, and then,
bereft of you, better for me to sink beneath the earth.
What other warmth, what comfort's left for me,
once you have met your doom? Nothing but torment!
I have lost my father. Mother's gone as well.
Father . . . the brilliant Achilles laid him low
when he stormed Cilicia's city filled with people,
Thebe with her towering gates. He killed Eetion,
not that he stripped his gear—he'd some respect at least—
for he burned his corpse in all his blazoned bronze,

8. The name does literally mean "lord of the city." *Scamandrius:* after the Trojan river Scamander.

then heaped a grave-mound high above the ashes
and nymphs of the mountain planted elms around it,
daughters of Zeus whose shield is storm and thunder.
And the seven brothers I had within our halls . . .
all in the same day went down to the House of Death,
the great godlike runner Achilles butchered them all,
tending their shambling oxen, shining flocks.
And mother,
who ruled under the timberline of woody Placos once—
he no sooner haled her here with his other plunder
than he took a priceless ransom, set her free
and home she went to her father's royal halls
where Artemis,[9] showering arrows, shot her down.
You, Hector—you are my father now, my noble mother,
a brother too, and you are my husband, young and warm and strong!
Pity me, please! Take your stand on the rampart here,
before you orphan your son and make your wife a widow.
Draw your armies up where the wild fig tree stands,
there, where the city lies most open to assault,
the walls lower, easily overrun. Three times
they have tried that point, hoping to storm Troy,
their best fighters led by the Great and Little Ajax,
famous Idomeneus, Atreus' sons, valiant Diomedes.
Perhaps a skilled prophet revealed the spot—
or their own fury whips them on to attack."

And tall Hector nodded, his helmet flashing:
"All this weighs on my mind too, dear woman.
But I would die of shame to face the men of Troy
and the Trojan women trailing their long robes
if I would shrink from battle now, a coward.
Nor does the spirit urge me on that way.
I've learned it all too well. To stand up bravely,
always to fight in the front ranks of Trojan soldiers,
winning my father great glory, glory for myself.
For in my heart and soul I also know this well:
the day will come when sacred Troy must die,
Priam must die and all his people with him,
Priam who hurls the strong ash spear . . .
Even so,
it is less the pain of the Trojans still to come
that weighs me down, not even of Hecuba herself
or King Priam, or the thought that my own brothers
in all their numbers, all their gallant courage,
may tumble in the dust, crushed by enemies—
That is nothing, nothing beside your agony
when some brazen Argive hales you off in tears,
wrenching away your day of light and freedom!
Then far off in the land of Argos you must live,

9. A virgin goddess, dispenser of natural and painless death to women.

laboring at a loom, at another woman's beck and call,
fetching water at some spring, Messeis or Hyperia,[1]
resisting it all the way—
the rough yoke of necessity at your neck.
And a man may say, who sees you streaming tears,
'There is the wife of Hector, the bravest fighter
they could field, those stallion-breaking Trojans,
long ago when the men fought for Troy.' So he will say
and the fresh grief will swell your heart once more,
widowed, robbed of the one man strong enough
to fight off your day of slavery.
No, no,
let the earth come piling over my dead body
before I hear your cries, I hear you dragged away!"

In the same breath, shining Hector reached down
for his son—but the boy recoiled,
cringing against his nurse's full breast,
screaming out at the sight of his own father,
terrified by the flashing bronze, the horsehair crest,
the great ridge of the helmet nodding, bristling terror—
so it struck his eyes. And his loving father laughed,
his mother laughed as well, and glorious Hector,
quickly lifting the helmet from his head,
set it down on the ground, fiery in the sunlight,
and raising his son he kissed him, tossed him in his arms,
lifting a prayer to Zeus and the other deathless gods:
"Zeus, all you immortals! Grant this boy, my son,
may be like me, first in glory among the Trojans,
strong and brave like me, and rule all Troy in power
and one day let them say, 'He is a better man than his father!'—
when he comes home from battle bearing the bloody gear
of the mortal enemy he has killed in war—
a joy to his mother's heart."
So Hector prayed
and placed his son in the arms of his loving wife.
Andromache pressed the child to her scented breast,
smiling through her tears. Her husband noticed,
and filled with pity now, Hector stroked her gently,
trying to reassure her, repeating her name: "Andromache,
dear one, why so desperate? Why so much grief for me?
No man will hurl me down to Death, against my fate.
And fate? No one alive has ever escaped it,
neither brave man nor coward, I tell you—
it's born with us the day that we are born.
So please go home and tend to your own tasks,
the distaff and the loom, and keep the women
working hard as well. As for the fighting,
men will see to that, all who were born in Troy

1. In central and northern Greece.

but I most of all."
Hector aflash in arms
took up his horsehair-crested helmet once again.
And his loving wife went home, turning, glancing
back again and again and weeping live warm tears.
She quickly reached the sturdy house of Hector,
man-killing Hector,
and found her women gathered there inside
and stirred them all to a high pitch of mourning.
So in his house they raised the dirges for the dead,
for Hector still alive, his people were so convinced
that never again would he come home from battle,
never escape the Argives' rage and bloody hands.

Nor did Paris linger long in his vaulted halls.
Soon as he buckled on his elegant gleaming bronze
he rushed through Troy, sure in his racing stride.
As a stallion full-fed at the manger, stalled too long,
breaking free of his tether gallops down the plain,
out for his favorite plunge in a river's cool currents,
thundering in his pride—his head flung back, his mane
streaming over his shoulders, sure and sleek in his glory,
knees racing him on to the fields and stallion-haunts he loves—
so down from Pergamus'[2] heights came Paris, son of Priam,
glittering in his armor like the sun astride the skies,
exultant, laughing aloud, his fast feet sped him on.
Quickly he overtook his brother, noble Hector
still lingering, slow to turn from the spot
where he had just confided in his wife . . .
Magnificent Paris spoke first: "Dear brother,
look at me, holding you back in all your speed—
dragging my feet, coming to you so late,
and you told me to be quick!"

A flash of his helmet as Hector shot back,
"Impossible man! How could anyone fair and just
underrate your work in battle? You're a good soldier.
But you hang back of your own accord, refuse to fight.
And that, that's why the heart inside me aches
when I hear our Trojans heap contempt on you,
the men who bear such struggles all for you.
Come,
now for attack! We'll set all this to rights,
someday, if Zeus will ever let us raise
the winebowl of freedom high in our halls,
high to the gods of cloud and sky who live forever—
once we drive these Argives geared for battle out of Troy!"

Summary The Trojans rallied successfully and went over to the offensive. They drove the Greeks back to the light fortifications they had built around their beached

2. The citadel of Troy.

ships. The Trojans lit their watchfires on the plain, ready to deliver the attack in the morning.

FROM BOOK VIII

[*The Tide of Battle Turns*]

And so their spirits soared
as they took positions down the passageways of battle
all night long, and the watchfires blazed among them.
Hundreds strong, as stars in the night sky glittering
round the moon's brilliance blaze in all their glory
when the air falls to a sudden, windless calm . . .
all the lookout peaks stand out and the jutting cliffs
and the steep ravines and down from the high heavens bursts
the boundless bright air and all the stars shine clear
and the shepherd's heart exults—so many fires burned
between the ships and the Xanthus'[3] whirling rapids
set by the men of Troy, bright against their walls.
A thousand fires were burning there on the plain
and beside each fire sat fifty fighting men
poised in the leaping blaze, and champing oats
and glistening barley, stationed by their chariots,
stallions waited for Dawn to mount her glowing throne.

BOOK IX

[*The Embassy to Achilles*]

So the Trojans held their watch that night but not the Achaeans—
godsent Panic seized them, comrade of bloodcurdling Rout:
all their best were struck by grief too much to bear.
As crosswinds chop the sea where the fish swarm,
the North Wind and the West Wind blasting out of Thrace[4]
in sudden, lightning attack, wave on blacker wave, cresting,
heaving a tangled mass of seaweed out along the surf—
so the Achaeans' hearts were torn inside their chests.

Distraught with the rising anguish, Atreus' son
went ranging back and forth, commanding heralds
to sound out loud and clear and call the men to muster,
each by name, but no loud outcry now. The king himself
pitched in with the lead heralds, summoning troops.
They grouped on the meeting grounds, morale broken.
Lord marshal Agamemnon rose up in their midst,
streaming tears like a dark spring running down
some desolate rock face, its shaded currents flowing.
So, with a deep groan, the king addressed his armies:
"Friends . . . lords of the Argives, all my captains!
Cronus' son has entangled me in madness, blinding ruin—
Zeus is a harsh, cruel god. He vowed to me long ago,
he bowed his head that I should never embark for home

3. One of the rivers of the Trojan plain. 4. The region northwest of Troy.

till I had brought the walls of Ilium crashing down.
But now, I see, he only plotted brutal treachery:
now he commands me back to Argos in disgrace,
whole regiments of my men destroyed in battle.
So it must please his overweening heart, who knows?
Father Zeus has lopped the crowns of a thousand cities,
true, and Zeus will lop still more—his power is too great.
So come, follow my orders. Obey me, all you Argives.
Cut and run! Sail home to the fatherland we love!
We'll never take the broad streets of Troy."

Silence held them all, struck dumb by his orders.
A long while they said nothing, spirits dashed.
Finally Diomedes lord of the war cry broke forth:
"Atrides—I will be first to oppose you in your folly,
here in assembly, King, where it's the custom.
Spare me your anger. My courage—
mine was the first you mocked among the Argives,
branding me a coward, a poor soldier.[5] Yes, well,
they know all about that, the Argives young and old.
But you—the son of Cronus with Cronus' twisting ways
gave you gifts by halves: with that royal scepter
the Father gave you honor beyond all other men alive
but he never gave you courage, the greatest power of all.
Desperate man! So certain, are you, the sons of Achaea
are cowards, poor soldiers, just because you say so?
Desert—if your spirit drives you to sail home,
then sail away, my King! The sea-lanes are clear,
there are your ships of war, crowded down the surf,
those that followed you from Mycenae,[6] your own proud armada.
But the rest of the long-haired Achaeans will hold out,
right here, until we've plundered Troy. And they,
if they go running home to the land they love,
then the two of us, I and Sthenelus[7] here
will fight our way to the fixed doom of Troy.
Never forget—we all sailed here with god."

And all the Achaeans shouted their assent,
stirred by the stallion-breaking Diomedes' challenge.
But Nestor the old driver rose and spoke at once:
"Few can match your power in battle, Diomedes,
and in council you excel all men your age.
So no one could make light of your proposals,
not the whole army—who could contradict you?
But you don't press on and reach a useful end.
How young you are . . . why, you could be my son,
my youngest-born at that, though you urge our kings
with cool clear sense: what you've said is right.
But it's my turn now, Diomedes.

5. This happened during Agamemnon's review of his forces before the battle. 6. A city near Argos.
7. Diomedes' companion.

I think I can claim to have some years on you.
So I *must* speak up and drive the matter home.
And no one will heap contempt on what I say,
not even mighty Agamemnon. Lost to the clan,
lost to the hearth, lost to the old ways, that one
who lusts for all the horrors of war with his own people.
But now, I say, let us give way to the dark night,
set out the evening meal. Sentries take up posts,
squads fronting the trench we dug outside the rampart.[8]
That's the command I give the younger fighters.
Then,
Atrides, lead the way—you are the greatest king—
spread out a feast for all your senior chiefs.
That is your duty, a service that becomes you.
Your shelters overflow with the wine Achaean ships
bring in from Thrace, daily, down the sea's broad back.
Grand hospitality is yours, you rule so many men.
Come, gather us all and we will heed that man
who gives the best advice. That's what they need,
I tell you—all the Achaeans—good sound advice,
now our enemies, camping hard against the ships,
kindle their watchfires round us by the thousands.
What soldier could warm to that? Tonight's the night
that rips our ranks to shreds or pulls us through."

The troops hung on his words and took his orders.
Out they rushed, the sentries in armor, forming
under the son of Nestor, captain Thrasymedes,
under Ascalaphus, Ialmenus, sons of Ares,[9]
under Meriones, Aphareus and Deipyrus,
under the son of Creon, trusty Lycomedes.
Seven chiefs of the guard, a hundred under each,
fighters marching, grasping long spears in their hands,
took up new positions between the trench and rampart.
There they lit their fires, each man made his meal.

Meanwhile marshal Agamemnon led his commanders,
a file of senior chiefs, toward his own lodge
and set before them a feast to please their hearts.
They reached out for the good things that lay at hand
but when they had put aside desire for food and drink
the old man began to weave his counsel among them:
Nestor was first to speak—from the early days
his plans and tactics always seemed the best.
With good will to the chiefs he rose and spoke,
"Great marshal Atrides, lord of men Agamemnon . . .
with you I will end, my King, with you I will begin,
since you hold sway over many warriors, vast armies,
and Zeus has placed in your hands the royal scepter

8. The Greeks are now besieged beside their ships; Zeus's promise to Thetis is being fulfilled. 9. God of war.

and time-honored laws, so you will advise them well.
So you above all must speak your mind, and listen,
and carry out the next man's counsel too,
whenever his spirit leads him on to speak
for the public good. Credit will go to you
for whatever he proposes.
Now I will tell you what seems best to me.
No one will offer a better plan than this . . .
the plan I still retain, and I've been forming,
well, for a good long while now, from the very day
that you, my illustrious King, infuriated Achilles—
you went and took from his tents the girl Briseis,
and not with any applause from us, far from it:
I for one, I urged you against it, strenuously.
But you, you gave way to your overbearing anger,
disgraced a great man the gods themselves esteem—
you seized his gift of honor and keep her still.
But even so, late as it is, let us contrive
to set all this to rights, to bring him round
with gifts of friendship and warm, winning words."

And Agamemnon the lord of men consented quickly:
"That's no lie, old man—a full account you give
of all my acts of madness. Mad, blind I was!
Not even *I* would deny it.
Why look, that man is worth an entire army,
the fighter Zeus holds dear with all his heart—
how he exalts him now and mauls Achaea's forces!
But since I *was* blinded, lost in my own inhuman rage,
now, at last, I am bent on setting things to rights:
I'll give a priceless ransom paid for friendship.
Here,
before you all, I'll name in full the splendid gifts I offer.
Seven tripods[1] never touched by fire, ten bars of gold,
twenty burnished cauldrons, a dozen massive stallions,
racers who earned me trophies with their speed.
He is no poor man who owns what they have won,
not strapped for goods with all that lovely gold—
what trophies those high-strung horses carried off for me!
Seven women I'll give him, flawless, skilled in crafts,
women of Lesbos[2]—the ones I chose, my privilege,
that day he captured the Lesbos citadel himself:
they outclassed the tribes of women in their beauty.
These I will give, and along with them will go
the one I took away at first, Briseus' daughter,
and I will swear a solemn, binding oath in the bargain:
I never mounted her bed, never once made love with her—
the natural thing for mankind, men and women joined.
Now all these gifts will be handed him at once.

1. Three-footed kettles; such metal equipment was rare and highly valued. 2. A large island off the coast of what is now Turkey.

But if, later, the gods allow us to plunder
the great city of Priam, let him enter in
when we share the spoils, load the holds of his ship
with gold and bronze—as much as his heart desires—
and choose for his pleasure twenty Trojan women
second only to Argive Helen in their glory.
And then, if we can journey home to Achaean Argos,
pride of the breasting earth, he'll be my son-by-marriage!
I will even honor him on a par with my Orestes,
full-grown by now, reared in the lap of luxury.
Three daughters are mine in my well-built halls—
Chrysothemis and Laodice and Iphianassa—
and he may lead away whichever one he likes,
with no bride-price asked, home to Peleus' house.
And I will add a dowry, yes, a magnificent treasure
the likes of which no man has ever offered with his daughter!
Seven citadels I will give him, filled with people,
Cardamyle, Enope, and the grassy slopes of Hire,
Pherae the sacrosanct, Anthea deep in meadows,
rolling Aepea and Pedasus green with vineyards.
All face the sea at the far edge of sandy Pylos
and the men who live within them, rich in sheep-flocks,
rich in shambling cattle, will honor him like a god
with hoards of gifts and beneath his scepter's sway
live out his laws in sleek and shining peace.
All this—
I would extend to him if he will end his anger.
Let him submit to me! Only the god of death[3]
is so relentless, Death submits to no one—
so mortals hate him most of all the gods.
Let him bow down to me! I am the greater king,
I am the elder-born, I claim—the greater man."

Nestor the noble charioteer embraced his offer:
"Generous marshal Atrides, lord of men Agamemnon!
No one could underrate these gifts of yours, not now,
the treasure trove you offer Prince Achilles.
Come—we'll send a detail of picked men.
They'll go to Achilles' tent with all good speed.
Quick, whomever my eye will light on in review,
the mission's theirs. And old Phoenix[4] first—
Zeus loves the man, so let him lead the way.
Then giant Ajax and tactful royal Odysseus.
Heralds? Odius and Eurybates, you escort them.
Water for their hands! A reverent silence now . . .
a prayer to Zeus. Perhaps he'll show us mercy."

The brisk commands he issued pleased them all.
Heralds brought the water at once and rinsed their hands,
and the young men brimmed the mixing bowls with wine

3. Hades. 4. He is especially suited for this embassy because he was tutor to the young Achilles.

and tipping first drops for the god in every cup
they poured full rounds for all. Libations finished,
each envoy having drunk to his heart's content,
the party moved out from Atrides' shelters.
Nestor the old driver gave them marching orders—
a sharp glance at each, Odysseus most of all:
"Try hard now, bring him round—invincible Achilles!"

So Ajax and Odysseus made their way at once
where the battle lines of breakers crash and drag,
praying hard to the god who moves and shakes the earth[5]
that they might bring the proud heart of Achilles
round with speed and ease.
Reaching the Myrmidon shelters and their ships,
they found him there, delighting his heart now,
plucking strong and clear on the fine lyre—
beautifully carved, its silver bridge set firm—
he won from the spoils when he razed Eetion's city.
Achilles was lifting his spirits with it now,
singing the famous deeds of fighting heroes . . .
Across from him Patroclus sat alone, in silence,
waiting for Aeacus' son to finish with his song.
And on they came, with good Odysseus in the lead,
and the envoys stood before him. Achilles, startled,
sprang to his feet, the lyre still in his hands,
leaving the seat where he had sat in peace.
And seeing the men, Patroclus rose up too
as the famous runner called and waved them on:
"Welcome! Look, dear friends have come our way—
I must be sorely needed now—my dearest friends
in all the Achaean armies, even in my anger."

So Prince Achilles hailed and led them in,
sat them down on settles with purple carpets
and quickly told Patroclus standing by, "Come,
a bigger winebowl, son of Menoetius, set it here.
Mix stronger wine. A cup for the hands of each guest—
here beneath my roof are the men I love the most."

He paused. Patroclus obeyed his great friend,
who put down a heavy chopping block in the firelight
and across it laid a sheep's chine, a fat goat's
and the long back cut of a full-grown pig,
marbled with lard. Automedon[6] held the meats
while lordly Achilles carved them into quarters,
cut them well into pieces, pierced them with spits
and Patroclus raked the hearth, a man like a god
making the fire blaze. Once it had burned down
and the flames died away, he scattered the coals
and stretching the spitted meats across the embers,

5. Poseidon, who was believed to be responsible for earthquakes. 6. Achilles' charioteer.

raised them onto supports and sprinkled clean pure salt.
As soon as the roasts were done and spread on platters,
Patroclus brought the bread, set it out on the board
in ample wicker baskets. Achilles served the meat.
Then face-to-face with his noble guest Odysseus
he took his seat along the farther wall,
he told his friend to sacrifice to the gods
and Patroclus threw the first cuts[7] in the fire.
They reached out for the good things that lay at hand
and when they had put aside desire for food and drink,
Ajax nodded to Phoenix. Odysseus caught the signal,
filled his cup and lifted it toward Achilles,
opening with this toast: "Your health, Achilles!
We have no lack of a handsome feast, I see that,
either in Agamemnon's tents, the son of Atreus,
or here and now, in yours. We can all banquet here
to our heart's content.
But it's not the flowing feast
that is on our minds now—no, a stark disaster,
too much to bear, Achilles bred by the gods,
that is what we are staring in the face
and we are afraid. All hangs in the balance now:
whether we save our beached ships or they're destroyed,
unless, of course, you put your fighting power in harness.
They have pitched camp right at our ships and rampart,
those brazen Trojans, they and their far-famed allies,
thousands of fires blaze throughout their armies . . .
Nothing can stop them now—that's their boast—
they'll hurl themselves against our blackened hulls.
And the son of Cronus sends them signs on the right,
Zeus's firebolts flashing. And headlong Hector,
delirious with his strength, rages uncontrollably,
trusting to Zeus—no fear of man or god, nothing—
a powerful rabid frenzy has him in its grip!
Hector prays for the sacred Dawn to break at once,
he threatens to lop the high horns of our sterns
and gut our ships with fire, and all our comrades
pinned against the hulls, panicked by thick smoke,
he'll rout and kill in blood!
A nightmare—I fear it, with all my heart—
I fear the gods will carry out his threats
and then it will be our fate to die in Troy,
far from the stallion-land of Argos . . .
Up with you—
now, late as it is, if you *want* to pull our Argives,
our hard-hit armies, clear of the Trojan onslaught.
Fail us now? What a grief it will be to you
through all the years to come. No remedy,
no way to cure the damage once it's done.
Come, while there's still time, think hard:

7. The portion of the meat reserved for the gods.

how can you fight off the Argives' fatal day?
Oh old friend, surely your father Peleus urged you,
that day he sent you out of Phthia to Agamemnon,
'My son, victory is what Athena and Hera will give,
if they so choose. But you, you hold in check
that proud, fiery spirit of yours inside your chest!
Friendship is much better. Vicious quarrels are deadly—
put an end to them, at once. Your Achaean comrades,
young and old, will exalt you all the more.'
That was your aged father's parting advice.
It must have slipped your mind.
But now at last,
stop, Achilles—let your heart-devouring anger go!
The king will hand you gifts to match his insults
if only you'll relent and end your anger . . .
So come then, listen, as I count out the gifts,
the troves in his tents that Agamemnon vows to give you.
Seven tripods never touched by fire, ten bars of gold,
twenty burnished cauldrons, a dozen massive stallions,
racers who earned him trophies with their speed.
He is no poor man who owns what they have won,
not strapped for goods with all that lovely gold—
what trophies those high-strung horses carried off for him!
Seven women he'll give you, flawless, skilled in crafts,
women of Lesbos—the ones he chose, his privilege,
that day you captured the Lesbos citadel yourself:
they outclassed the tribes of women in their beauty.
These he will give, and along with them will go
the one he took away at first, Briseus' daughter,
and he will swear a solemn, binding oath in the bargain:
he never mounted her bed, never once made love with her . . .
the natural thing, my lord, men and women joined.
Now all these gifts will be handed you at once.
But if, later, the gods allow us to plunder
the great city of Priam, you shall enter in
when we share the spoils, load the holds of your ship
with gold and bronze—as much as your heart desires—
and choose for your pleasure twenty Trojan women
second only to Argive Helen in their glory.
And then, if we can journey home to Achaean Argos,
pride of the breasting earth, you'll be his son-by-marriage . . .
He will even honor you on a par with his Orestes,
full-grown by now, reared in the lap of luxury.
Three daughters are his in his well-built halls,
Chrysothemis and Laodice and Iphianassa—
and you may lead away whichever one you like,
with no bride-price asked, home to Peleus' house.
And he will add a dowry, yes, a magnificent treasure
the likes of which no man has ever offered with his daughter . . .
Seven citadels he will give you, filled with people,
Cardamyle, Enope, and the grassy slopes of Hire,
Pherae the sacrosanct, Anthea deep in meadows,

rolling Aepea and Pedasus green with vineyards.
All face the sea at the far edge of sandy Pylos
and the men who live within them, rich in sheep-flocks,
rich in shambling cattle, will honor you like a god
with hoards of gifts and beneath your scepter's sway
live out your laws in sleek and shining peace.
All this . . .
he would extend to you if you will end your anger.
But if you hate the son of Atreus all the more,
him and his troves of gifts, at least take pity
on all our united forces mauled in battle here—
they will honor you, honor you like a god.
Think of the glory you will gather in their eyes!
Now you can kill Hector—seized with murderous frenzy,
certain there's not a single fighter his equal,
no Achaean brought to Troy in the ships—
now, for once, you can meet the man head-on!"

The famous runner Achilles rose to his challenge:
"Royal son of Laertes, Odysseus, great tactician . . .
I must say what I have to say straight out,
must tell you how I feel and how all this will end—
so you won't crowd around me, one after another,
coaxing like a murmuring clutch of doves.
I hate that man like the very Gates of Death
who says one thing but hides another in his heart.
I will say it outright. That seems best to me.
Will Agamemnon win me over? Not for all the world,
I swear it—nor will the rest of the Achaeans.
No, what lasting thanks in the long run
for warring with our enemies, on and on, no end?
One and the same lot for the man who hangs back
and the man who battles hard. The same honor waits
for the coward and the brave. They both go down to Death,
the fighter who shirks, the one who works to exhaustion.
And what's laid up for me, what pittance? Nothing—
and after suffering hardships, year in, year out,
staking my life on the mortal risks of war.

Like a mother bird hurrying morsels back
to her wingless young ones—whatever she can catch—
but it's all starvation wages for herself.
So for me.
Many a sleepless night I've bivouacked in harness,
day after bloody day I've hacked my passage through,
fighting other soldiers to win their wives as prizes.
Twelve cities of men I've stormed and sacked from shipboard,
eleven I claim by land, on the fertile earth of Troy.
And from all I dragged off piles of splendid plunder,
hauled it away and always gave the lot to Agamemnon,
that son of Atreus—always skulking behind the lines,
safe in his fast ships—and he would take it all,

he'd parcel out some scraps but keep the lion's share.
Some he'd hand to the lords and kings—prizes of honor—
and they, they hold them still. From me alone, Achilles
of all Achaeans, he seizes, he keeps the wife I love . . .
Well *let* him bed her now—
enjoy her to the hilt!
Why must we battle Trojans,
men of Argos? Why did he muster an army, lead us here,
that son of Atreus? Why, why in the world if not
for Helen with her loose and lustrous hair?
Are *they* the only men alive who love their wives,
those sons of Atreus? Never! Any decent man,
a man with sense, loves his own, cares for his own
as deeply as I, I loved that woman with all my heart,
though I won her like a trophy with my spear . . .
But now that he's torn my honor from my hands,
robbed me, lied to me—don't let him try me now.
I know *him* too well—he'll never win me over!
No, Odysseus,
let him rack his brains with you and the other captains
how to fight the raging fire off the ships. Look—
what a mighty piece of work he's done without *me!*
Why, he's erected a rampart, driven a trench around it,
broad, enormous, and planted stakes to guard it. No use!
He still can't block the power of man-killing Hector!
No, though as long as *I* fought on Achaea's lines
Hector had little lust to charge beyond his walls,
never ventured beyond the Scaean Gates and oak tree.
There he stood up to me alone one day—
and barely escaped my onslaught.
Ah but now,
since I have no desire to battle glorious Hector,
tomorrow at daybreak, once I have sacrificed
to Zeus and all the gods and loaded up my holds
and launched out on the breakers—watch, my friend,
if you'll take the time and care to see me off,
and you will see my squadrons sail at dawn,
fanning out on the Hellespont that swarms with fish,
my crews manning the oarlocks, rowing out with a will,
and if the famed god of the earthquake grants us safe passage,
the third day out we raise the dark rich soil of Phthia.
There lies my wealth, hoards of it, all I left behind
when I sailed to Troy on this, this insane voyage—
and still more hoards from here: gold, ruddy bronze,
women sashed and lovely, and gleaming gray iron,
and I will haul it home, all I won as plunder.
All but my prize of honor . . .
he who gave that prize has snatched it back again—
what outrage! That high and mighty King Agamemnon,
that son of Atreus!
Go back and tell him all,
all I say—out in the open too—so other Achaeans

can wheel on him in anger if he still hopes—
who knows?—to deceive some other comrade.
Shameless,
inveterate—armored in shamelessness! Dog that he is,
he'd never dare to look me straight in the eyes again.
No, I'll never set heads together with that man—
no planning in common, no taking common action.
He cheated me, did me damage, wrong! But never again,
he'll never rob me blind with his twisting words again!
Once is enough for him. Die and be damned for all I care!
Zeus who rules the world has ripped his wits away.
His gifts, I loathe his gifts . . .
I wouldn't give you a splinter for that man!
Not if he gave me ten times as much, twenty times over, all
he possesses now, and all that could pour in from the world's end—
not all the wealth that's freighted into Orchomenos,[8] even into Thebes,
Egyptian Thebes where the houses overflow with the greatest troves of
treasure,
Thebes with the hundred gates and through each gate battalions,
two hundred fighters surge to war with teams and chariots—
no, not if his gifts outnumbered all the grains of sand
and dust in the earth—no, not even then could Agamemnon
bring my fighting spirit round until he pays me back,
pays full measure for all his heartbreaking outrage!

His daughter . . . I will marry no daughter of Agamemnon.
Not if she rivaled Aphrodite in all her golden glory,
not if she matched the crafts of clear-eyed Athena,
not even then would I make *her* my wife! No,
let her father pitch on some other Argive—
one who can please *him*, a greater king than I.
If the gods pull me through and I reach home alive,
Peleus needs no help to fetch a bride for me himself.
Plenty of Argive women wait in Hellas and in Phthia
daughters of lords who rule their citadels in power.
Whomever I want I'll make my cherished wife—at home.
Time and again my fiery spirit drove me to win a wife,
a fine partner to please my heart, to enjoy with her
the treasures my old father Peleus piled high.
I say no wealth is worth my life! Not all they claim
was stored in the depths of Troy, that city built on riches,
in the old days of peace before the sons of Achaea came—
not all the gold held fast in the Archer's rocky vaults,
in Phoebus Apollo's house on Pytho's[9] sheer cliffs!
Cattle and fat sheep can all be had for the raiding,
tripods all for the trading, and tawny-headed stallions.
But a man's life breath cannot come back again—
no raiders in force, no trading brings it back,
once it slips through a man's clenched teeth.

8. Great city north of Athens. 9. Apollo's shrine at Delphi. The treasures consisted of offerings made to the god by grateful worshipers.

Mother tells me,
the immortal goddess Thetis with her glistening feet,
that two fates bear me on to the day of death.
If I hold out here and I lay siege to Troy,
my journey home is gone, but my glory never dies.
If I voyage back to the fatherland I love,
my pride, my glory dies . . .
true, but the life that's left me will be long,
the stroke of death will not come on me quickly.

One thing more. To the rest I'd pass on this advice:
sail home now! You will never set your eyes
on the day of doom that topples looming Troy.
Thundering Zeus has spread his hands above her—
her armies have taken heart!
So you go back
to the great men of Achaea. You report my message—
since this is the privilege of senior chiefs—
let *them* work out a better plan of action,
use their imaginations now to save the ships
and Achaea's armies pressed to their hollow hulls.
This maneuver will never work for them, this scheme
they hatched for the moment as I raged on and on.
But Phoenix can stay and rest the night with us,
so he can voyage home, home in the ships with me
to the fatherland we love. Tomorrow at dawn.
But only if Phoenix wishes.
I will never force the man to go."
He stopped.
A stunned silence seized them all, struck dumb—
Achilles' ringing denials overwhelmed them so.
At last Phoenix the old charioteer spoke out,
he burst into tears, terrified for Achaea's fleet:
"Sail home? Is *that* what you're turning over in your mind,
my glorious one, Achilles? Have you no heart at all
to fight the gutting fire from the fast trim ships?
The spirit inside you overpowered by anger!
How could I be severed from you, dear boy,
left behind on the beachhead here—alone?
The old horseman Peleus had me escort you,
that day he sent you out of Phthia to Agamemnon,
a youngster still untrained for the great leveler, war,
still green at debate where men can make their mark.
So he dispatched me, to teach you all these things,
to make you a man of words and a man of action too.
Cut off from you with a charge like that, dear boy?
I have no heart to be left behind, not even
if Zeus himself would swear to scrape away
the scurf of age and make me young again . . .
As fresh as I was that time I first set out
from Hellas where the women are a wonder,
fleeing a blood feud with my father, Amyntor,

Ormenus' son. How furious father was with me,
over his mistress with her dark, glistening hair.
How he would dote on her and spurn his wedded wife,
my own mother! And time and again she begged me,
hugging my knees, to bed my father's mistress down
and kill the young girl's taste for an old man.
Mother—I did your bidding, did my work . . .
But father, suspecting at once, cursed me roundly,
he screamed out to the cruel Furies[1]—'Never,
never let me bounce on my knees a son of his,
sprung of his loins!'—and the gods drove home that curse,
mighty Zeus of the Underworld and grim Persephone.[2]
So I, I took it into my head to lay him low
with sharp bronze! But a god checked my anger,
he warned me of what the whole realm would say,
the loose talk of the people, rough slurs of men—
they must not call me a father-killer, our Achaeans!
Then nothing could keep me there, my blood so fired up.
No more strolling about the halls with father raging.
But there was a crowd of kin and cousins round me,
holding me in the house, begging me to stay . . .
they butchered plenty of fat sheep, banquet fare,
and shambling crook-horned cattle, droves of pigs,
succulent, rich with fat—they singed the bristles,
splaying the porkers out across Hephaestus' fire,
then wine from the old man's jars, all we could drink.
Nine nights they passed the hours, hovering over me,
keeping the watch by rounds. The fires never died,
one ablaze in the colonnade of the walled court,
one in the porch outside my bedroom doors.
But then,
when the tenth night came on me, black as pitch,
I burst the doors of the chamber bolted tight
and out I rushed, I leapt the walls at a bound,
giving the slip to guards and women servants.
And away I fled through the whole expanse of Hellas
and gaining the good dark soil of Phthia, mother of flocks,
I reached the king, and Peleus gave me a royal welcome.
Peleus loved me as a father loves a son, I tell you,
his only child, the heir to his boundless wealth,
he made me a rich man, he gave me throngs of subjects,
I ruled the Dolopes, settling down on Phthia's west frontier.
And I made you what you are—strong as the gods, Achilles—
I loved you from the heart. You'd never go with another
to banquet on the town or feast in your own halls.
Never, until I'd sat you down on my knees
and cut you the first bits of meat, remember?
You'd eat your fill, I'd hold the cup to your lips
and all too often you soaked the shirt on my chest,

1. Avenging spirits that are particularly concerned with crimes committed by kin against kin. 2. Wife of Hades (the *Zeus of the Underworld*).

spitting up some wine, a baby's way . . . a misery.
Oh I had my share of troubles for you, Achilles,
did my share of labor. Brooding, never forgetting
the gods would bring no son of mine to birth,
not from my own loins.
So you, Achilles—
great godlike Achilles—I made you my son, I tried,
so someday *you* might fight disaster off my back.
But now, Achilles, beat down your mounting fury!
It's wrong to have such an iron, ruthless heart.
Even the gods themselves can bend and change,
and theirs is the greater power, honor, strength.
Even the gods, I say, with incense, soothing vows,
with full cups poured and the deep smoky savor
men can bring them round, begging for pardon
when one oversteps the mark, does something wrong.
We do have Prayers, you know, Prayers for forgiveness,
daughters of mighty Zeus . . . and they limp and halt,
they're all wrinkled, drawn, they squint to the side,
can't look you in the eyes, and always bent on duty,
trudging after Ruin, maddening, blinding Ruin.
But Ruin is strong and swift—
She outstrips them all by far, stealing a march,
leaping over the whole wide earth to bring mankind to grief.
And the Prayers trail after, trying to heal the wounds.
And then, if a man reveres these daughters of Zeus
as they draw near him, they will help him greatly
and listen to his appeals. But if one denies them,
turns them away, stiff-necked and harsh—off they go
to the son of Cronus, Zeus, and pray that Ruin
will strike the man down, crazed and blinded
until he's paid the price.
Relent, Achilles—you too!
See that honor attend these good daughters of Zeus,
honor that sways the minds of others, even heroes.
If Agamemnon were not holding out such gifts,
with talk of more to come, that son of Atreus,
if the warlord kept on blustering in his anger, why,
I'd be the last to tell you, 'Cast your rage to the winds!
Defend your friends!'—despite their desperate straits.
But now, look, he gives you a trove of treasures
right away, and vows there are more to follow.
He sends the bravest captains to implore you,
leaders picked from the whole Achaean army,
comrades-in-arms that you love most yourself.
Don't dismiss their appeal, their expedition here—
though no one could blame your anger, not before.
So it was in the old days too. So we've heard
in the famous deeds of fighting men, of heroes,
when seething anger would overcome the great ones.
Still you could bring them round with gifts and winning words.
There's an old tale I remember, an ancient exploit,

nothing recent, but this is how it went . . .
We are all friends here—let me tell it now.

The Curetes were fighting the combat-hard Aetolians,
armies ringing Calydon,[3] slaughtering each other,
Aetolians defending their city's handsome walls
and Curetes primed to lay them waste in battle.
It all began when Artemis throned in gold
loosed a disaster on them, incensed that Oeneus[4]
offered her no first fruits, his orchard's crowning glory.
The rest of the gods had feasted full on oxen, true,
but the Huntress alone, almighty Zeus's daughter—
Oeneus gave her nothing. It slipped his mind
or he failed to care, but what a fatal error!
How she fumed, Zeus's child who showers arrows,
she loosed a bristling wild boar, his tusks gleaming,
crashing his savage, monstrous way through Oeneus' orchard,
ripping up whole trunks from the earth to pitch them headlong,
rows of them, roots and all, appleblossoms and all!
But the son of Oeneus, Meleager, cut him down—
mustering hunters out of a dozen cities,
packs of hounds as well. No slim band of men
could ever finish him off, that rippling killer,
he stacked so many men atop the tear-soaked pyre.
But over his body the goddess raised a terrific din,
a war for the prize, the huge beast's head and shaggy hide—
Curetes locked to the death with brave Aetolians.
Now,
so long as the battle-hungry Meleager fought,
it was deadly going for the Curetes. No hope
of holding their ground outside their *own* city walls,
despite superior numbers. But then, when the wrath
came sweeping over the man, the same anger that swells
the chests of others, for all their care and self-control—
then, heart enraged at his own dear mother Althaea,
Meleager kept to his bed beside his wedded wife,
Cleopatra . . . that great beauty. Remember her?
The daughter of trim-heeled Marpessa,[5] Euenus' child,
and her husband Idas, strongest man of the men
who once walked the earth—he even braved Apollo,
he drew his bow at the Archer, all for Marpessa
the girl with lovely ankles. There in the halls
her father and mother always called Cleopatra Halcyon,
after the seabird's name . . . grieving once for her own fate
her mother had raised the halcyon's thin, painful cry,
wailing that lord Apollo the distant deadly Archer

3. A city in northwestern Greece. The Curetes and Aetolians were the local tribes, once allied, now at odds. 4. King of Calydon. 5. The story to which Homer alludes runs as follows: Idas, the famous archer, carried off and married Marpessa, daughter of Euenus. Apollo also had been her suitor, and he overtook Idas and carried off Marpessa. Idas defied Apollo to combat, but Zeus decided that the choice was up to Marpessa, who preferred Idas. They gave their daughter Cleopatra the nickname Halcyon, the name of a seabird that is supposed to mourn for its mate, to commemorate the time when Marpessa, carried off by Apollo, mourned for Idas.

had whisked her[6] far from Idas.
Meleager's Cleopatra—
she was the one he lay beside those days,
brooding over his heartbreaking anger.
He was enraged by the curses of his mother,
volleys of curses she called down from the gods.
So racked with grief for her brother he had killed[7]
she kept pounding fists on the earth that feeds us all,
kept crying out to the god of death and grim Persephone,
flung herself on the ground, tears streaking her robes
and she screamed out, 'Kill Meleager, kill my son!'
And out of the world of darkness a Fury heard her cries,
stalking the night with a Fury's brutal heart, and suddenly—
thunder breaking around the gates, the roar of enemies,
towers battered under assault. And Aetolia's elders
begged Meleager, sent high priests of the gods,
pleading, 'Come out now! defend your people now!'—
and they vowed a princely gift.
Wherever the richest land of green Calydon lay,
there they urged him to choose a grand estate,
full fifty acres, half of it turned to vineyards,
half to open plowland, and carve it from the plain.
And over and over the old horseman Oeneus begged him,
he took a stand at the vaulted chamber's threshold,
shaking the bolted doors, begging his own son!
Over and over his brothers and noble mother
implored him—he refused them all the more—
and troops of comrades, devoted, dearest friends.
Not even they could bring his fighting spirit round
until, at last, rocks were raining down on the chamber,
Curetes about to mount the towers and torch the great city!
And then, finally, Meleager's bride, beautiful Cleopatra
begged him, streaming tears, recounting all the griefs
that fall to people whose city's seized and plundered—
the men slaughtered, citadel burned to rubble, enemies
dragging the children, raping the sashed and lovely women.
How his spirit leapt when he heard those horrors—
and buckling his gleaming armor round his body,
out he rushed to war. And so he saved them all
from the fatal day, he gave way to his own feelings,
but too late. No longer would they make good the gifts,
those troves of gifts to warm his heart, and even so
he beat off that disaster . . . empty-handed.

But you, you wipe such thoughts from your mind.
Don't let your spirit turn you down that path, dear boy.
Harder to save the warships once they're up in flames.
Now—while the gifts still wait—go out and fight!
Go—the Achaeans all will honor you like a god!
But enter this man-killing war without the gifts—

6. Marpessa. 7. In the course of the battles Meleager had killed one of his mother's brothers.

your fame will flag, no longer the same honor,
even though you hurl the Trojans home!"

But the swift runner Achilles answered firmly,
"Phoenix, old father, bred and loved by the gods,
what do I need with honor such as that?
I say my honor lies in the great decree of Zeus.
That gift will hold me here by the beaked ships
as long as the life breath remains inside my chest
and my springing knees will lift me. Another thing—
take it to heart, I urge you. Stop confusing
my fixed resolve with this, this weeping and wailing
just to serve his pleasure, Atreus' mighty son.
It degrades you to curry favor with that man,
and I will hate you for it, I who love you.
It does you proud to stand by me, my friend,
to attack the man who attacks me—
be king on a par with me, take half my honors!
These men will carry their message back, but you,
you stay here and spend the night in a soft bed.
Then, tomorrow at first light, we will decide
whether we sail home or hold out here."
With that,
he gave Patroclus a sharp glance, a quiet nod
to pile the bedding deep for Phoenix now,
a sign to the rest to think of leaving quickly.
Giant Ajax rose to his feet, the son of Telamon,
tall as a god, turned and broke his silence:
"Ready, Odysseus? Royal son of Laertes,
great tactician—come, home we go now.
There's no achieving our mission here, I see,
not with this approach. Best to return at once,
give the Achaeans a full report, defeating as it is.
They must be sitting there, waiting for us now.
Achilles—
he's made his own proud spirit so wild in his chest,
so savage, not a thought for his comrades' love—
we honored him past all others by the ships.
Hard, ruthless man . . .
Why, any man will accept the blood-price paid
for a brother murdered, a child done to death.
And the murderer lives on in his own country—
the man has paid enough, and the injured kinsman
curbs his pride, his smoldering, vengeful spirit,
once he takes the price.
You—the gods have planted
a cruel, relentless fury in your chest! All for a girl,
just one, and here we offer you seven—outstanding beauties—
that, and a treasure trove besides. Achilles,
put some human kindness in your heart.
Show respect for your own house. Here we are,
under your roof, sent from the whole Achaean force!

Past all other men, all other Achaean comrades,
we long to be your closest, dearest friends."

And the swift runner Achilles answered warmly,
"Ajax, royal son of Telamon, captain of armies,
all well said, after my own heart, or mostly so.
But my heart still heaves with rage
whenever I call to mind that arrogance of his—
how he mortified me, right in front of the Argives—
that son of Atreus treating me like some vagabond,
like some outcast stripped of all my rights!
You go back to him and declare my message:
I will not think of arming for bloody war again,
not till the son of wise King Priam, dazzling Hector
batters all the way to the Myrmidon ships and shelters,
slaughtering Argives, gutting the hulls with fire.
But round my own black ship and camp this Hector
will be stopped, I trust, blazing for battle
as he goes—stopped dead in his tracks!"
So he finished.
Then each man, lifting his own two-handled cup,
poured it out to the gods, and back they went
along the ships, Odysseus in the lead.
Patroclus told his friends and serving-women
to pile a deep warm bed for Phoenix, quickly.
They obeyed and spread the bed as he ordered,
with fleeces, woolen throws and soft linen sheets.
There the old man lay, awaiting shining Dawn.
And deep in his well-built lodge Achilles slept
with the woman he brought from Lesbos, Phorbas' daughter,
Diomede in all her beauty sleeping by his side.
And over across from him Patroclus slept
with the sashed and lovely Iphis by his side,
whom Prince Achilles gave him the day he took
the heights of Scyros, Enyeus' rocky stronghold.

But once the envoys reached Atrides' shelters,
comrades leapt to their feet, welcomed them back
and clustering round them, lifted golden cups.
One after another pressed them with questions,
King Agamemnon most urgent of all: "Come—
tell me, famous Odysseus, Achaea's pride and glory—
will he fight the fire off the ships? Or does he refuse,
does rage still grip his proud, mighty spirit?"

And the steady, long-enduring Odysseus replied,
"Great marshal Atrides, lord of men Agamemnon,
that man has no intention of quenching his rage.
He's still bursting with anger, more than ever—
he spurns you, spurns all your gifts. Work out
your own defense, he says, you and your captains
save the Argive armies and the ships. Himself?

Achilles threatens, tomorrow at first light,
to haul his well-benched warships out to sea.
And what's more, he advises all the rest,
'Sail home now. You will never set your eyes
on the day of doom that topples looming Troy.
Thundering Zeus has spread his hands above her . . .
her armies have taken heart.'
That's his answer.
And here are men to confirm it, fellow envoys.
Ajax and two heralds, both clear-headed men.
But old Phoenix passes the night in camp
as Achilles bids him, so he can voyage home,
home in the ships with him to the fatherland they love.
Tomorrow at dawn. But only if Phoenix wishes.
He will never force the man to go."
So he reported.
Silence held them all, struck dumb by his story,
Odysseus' words still ringing in their ears.
A long while they said nothing, spirits dashed.
Finally Diomedes lord of the war cry broke forth:
"Great marshal Atrides, lord of men Agamemnon—
if only you'd never begged the dauntless son of Peleus,
holding out to Achilles trove on trove of gifts!
He's a proud man at the best of times, and now
you've only plunged him deeper in his pride.
I say have done with the man—
whether he sails for home or stays on here.
He'll fight again—in his own good time—whenever
the courage in him flares and a god fires his blood.
So come, follow my orders. And all of us unite.
Go to sleep now, full to your heart's content
with food and wine, a soldier's strength and nerve.
Then when the Dawn's red fingers shine in all their glory,
quickly deploy your chariots and battalions, Agamemnon,
out in front of the ships—you spur them on
and you yourself, you fight in the front ranks!"

And Achaea's kings all shouted their assent,
stirred by the stallion-breaking Diomedes' challenge.
Pouring cups to the gods, each warlord sought his shelter.
There they spent the night and took the gift of sleep.

Summary After Achilles' refusal, the situation of the Greeks worsened rapidly. Agamemnon, Diomedes, and Odysseus were all wounded. The Trojans breached the stockade and fought beside the ships. Patroclus tried to bring Achilles to the aid of the Greeks, but the most he could obtain was permission for himself to fight, clad in Achilles' armor, at the head of the Myrmidons.

FROM BOOK XVI

[*Patroclus Fights and Dies*]

But now Sarpedon,[8] watching his comrades drop and die,
war-shirts billowing free as Patroclus killed them,
dressed his godlike Lycians down with a harsh shout:
"Lycians, where's your pride? Where are you running?
Now be fast to attack! I'll take him on myself,
see who he is who routs us, wreaking havoc against us—
cutting the legs from under squads of good brave men."

With that he leapt from his chariot fully armed
and hit the ground and Patroclus straight across,
as soon as he saw him, leapt from his car too.
As a pair of crook-clawed, hook-beaked vultures
swoop to fight, screaming above some jagged rock—
so with their battle cries they rushed each other there.
And Zeus the son of Cronus[9] with Cronus' twisting ways,
filling with pity now to see the two great fighters,
said to Hera, his sister and his wife, "My cruel fate . . .
my Sarpedon, the man I love the most, my own son—
doomed to die at the hands of Menoetius' son Patroclus.
My heart is torn in two as I try to weigh all this.
Shall I pluck him up, now, while he's still alive
and set him down in the rich green land of Lycia,
far from the war at Troy and all its tears?
Or beat him down at Patroclus' hands at last?"

But Queen Hera, her eyes wide, protested strongly:
"Dread majesty, son of Cronus—what are you saying?
A man, a mere mortal, his doom sealed long ago?
You'd set him free from all the pains of death?
Do as you please, Zeus . . .
but none of the deathless gods will ever praise you.
And I tell you this—take it to heart, I urge you—
if you send Sarpedon home, living still, beware!
Then surely some other god will want to sweep
his own son clear of the heavy fighting too.
Look down. Many who battle round King Priam's
mighty walls are sons of the deathless gods—
you will inspire lethal anger in them all.
No,
dear as he is to you, and your heart grieves for him,
leave Sarpedon there to die in the brutal onslaught,
beaten down at the hands of Menoetius' son Patroclus.
But once his soul and the life force have left him,
send Death to carry him home, send soothing Sleep,[1]
all the way till they reach the broad land of Lycia.

8. King of Lycia in Asia Minor and a Trojan ally; son of Zeus and a mortal woman (see 6.98–102, above).
9. King of the earlier generation of gods, the Titans, who were overthrown by the Olympian gods under Zeus.
1. In Greek belief, the brother of Death.

There his brothers and countrymen will bury the prince
with full royal rites, with mounded tomb and pillar.
These are the solemn honors owed the dead."
So she pressed
and Zeus the father of men and gods complied at once.
But he showered tears of blood that drenched the earth,
showers in praise of him, his own dear son,
the man Patroclus was just about to kill
on Troy's fertile soil, far from his fatherland.
Now as the two came closing on each other
Patroclus suddenly picked off Thrasymelus
the famous driver, the aide who flanked Sarpedon—
he speared him down the guts and loosed his limbs.
But Sarpedon hurled next with a flashing lance
and missed his man but he hit the horse Bold Dancer,
stabbing his right shoulder and down the stallion went,
screaming his life out, shrieking down in the dust
as his life breath winged away. And the paired horses[2]
reared apart—a raspy creak of the yoke, the reins flying,
fouled as the trace horse[3] thrashed the dust in death-throes.
But the fine spearman Automedon[4] found a cure for that—
wrenching his long sharp sword from his sturdy thigh
he leapt with a stroke to cut the trace horse free—
it worked. The team righted, pulled at the reins
and again both fighters closed with savage frenzy,
dueling now to the death.
Again Sarpedon missed—
over Patroclus' left shoulder his spearhead streaked,
it never touched his body. Patroclus hurled next,
the bronze launched from his hand—no miss, a mortal hit.
He struck him right where the midriff packs the pounding heart
and down Sarpedon fell as an oak or white poplar falls
or towering pine that shipwrights up on a mountain
hew down with whetted axes for sturdy ship timber—
so he stretched in front of his team and chariot,
sprawled and roaring, clawing the bloody dust.
As the bull a marauding lion cuts from the herd,
tawny and greathearted among the shambling cattle,
dies bellowing under the lion's killing jaws—
so now Sarpedon, captain of Lycia's shieldsmen,
died at Patroclus' hands and died raging still,
crying out his beloved comrade's name: "Glaucus[5]—
oh dear friend, dear fighter, soldier's soldier!
Now is the time to prove yourself a spearman,
a daring man of war—now, if you are brave,
make grueling battle your one consuming passion.
First find Lycia's captains, range the ranks,
spur them to fight and shield Sarpedon's body.
Then you, Glaucus, you fight for me with bronze!

2. Achilles' immortal horses, who shy away from contact with death. 3. A third horse that ran alongside the pair pulling the chariot to help maneuver; here the mortal horse Bold Dancer. 4. Patroclus's charioteer. 5. Sarpedon's cousin and comrade, who has been temporarily disabled by a wound.

You'll hang your head in shame—every day of your life—
if the Argives strip my armor here at the anchored ships
where I have gone down fighting. Hold on, full force—
spur all our men to battle!"
                                        Death cut him short.
The end closed in around him, swirling down his eyes,
choking off his breath. Patroclus planted a heel
against his chest, wrenched the spear from his wound
and the midriff came out with it—so he dragged out both
the man's life breath and the weapon's point together.
Close by, the Myrmidons[6] clung to the panting stallions
straining to bolt away, free of their masters' chariot.

But grief came over Glaucus, hearing his comrade's call.
His heart was racing—what could he do to help him?
Wounded himself, he gripped his right arm hard,
aching where Teucer's[7] arrow had hit him squarely,
assaulting the Argive wall, when Teucer saved his men.
Glaucus cried a prayer to the distant deadly Archer:[8]
"Hear me, Lord Apollo! Wherever you are now—
in Lycia's rich green country or here in Troy,
wherever on earth, you can hear a man in pain,
you have that power, and pain comes on me now.
Look at this ugly wound—
my whole arm rings with the stabbing pangs,
the blood won't clot, my shoulder's a dead weight.
I can't take up my spear, can't hold it steady—
no wading into enemy ranks to fight it out . . .
and our bravest man is dead, Sarpedon, Zeus's son—
did Zeus stand by him? Not even his own son!
I beg you, Apollo, heal this throbbing wound,
lull the pain now, lend me power in battle—
so I can rally our Lycians, drive them into war
and fight to save my comrade's corpse myself."
So Glaucus prayed and Apollo heard his prayer.
He stopped the pains at once, stanched the dark blood
in his throbbing wound and filled his heart with courage.
And Glaucus sensed it all and the man glowed with joy
that the mighty god had heard his prayer so quickly.
First he hurried to spur his Lycian captains on,
ranging his own ranks, to fight around Sarpedon,
then he ran for the Trojan lines with long strides.
He found Polydamas, Panthous' son, and Prince Agenor
and reaching Aeneas and Hector helmed in bronze,
shoulder-to-shoulder let his challenge fly:
"Hector, you've wiped your allies from your mind!
And all for you, Hector, far from their loved ones,
far from native land they bleed their lives away.
But you won't lift a hand to fight beside them.
There lies Sarpedon, lord of Lycia's shieldsmen,

6. Troops of Achilles and Patroclus. 7. Greek archer. 8. Apollo.

who defended his realm with just decrees and power—
Ares has cut him down with Patroclus' brazen spear.
Quick, my friends, stand by him! Cringe with shame
at the thought they'll strip his gear and maim his corpse—
these Myrmidons, seething for all the Argive troops we killed,
we speared to death against their fast trim ships!"

Hard grief came sweeping over the Trojans' heads—
unbearable, irrepressible. He was their city's bastion,
always, even though he came from foreign parts,
and a mass of allies marched at his command
but he excelled them all in battle, always.
So now they went at the Argives, out for blood,
and furious for Sarpedon Hector swung them round.
But the Argives surged to Patroclus' savage spirit—
he spurred the Aeantes[9] first, both ablaze for battle:
"Ajax, Ajax! Come—now thrill to fight as before,
brave among the brave, but now be braver still!
Their captain's down, the first to storm our wall,
the great Sarpedon. If only we could seize his body,
mutilate him, shame him, tear his gear from his back
and any comrade of his who tries to shield his corpse—
bring that enemy down with ruthless bronze!"
Urging so
but his men already burned to drive the Trojans off.
And both armies now, pulling their lines tighter,
Trojans and Lycians, Myrmidons and Achaeans
closed around the corpse to lunge in battle—
terrible war cries, stark clashing of armored men.
And across the onslaught Zeus swept murderous night
to make the pitched battle over his own dear son
a brutal, blinding struggle.
Here at the first assault
the Trojans shouldered back the fiery-eyed Achaeans—
a Myrmidon had been hit, and not their least man,
dauntless Agacles' son, renowned Epigeus . . .
He ruled Budion's fortress town in the old days
but then, having killed some highborn cousin, fled
to Peleus and glistening Thetis, begged for his own life
and they sent him off with Achilles, breaker of men,
east to stallion-country to fight and die in Troy.
He had just grasped the corpse
when shining Hector smashed his head with a rock
and his whole skull split in his massive helmet—
down he slammed on Sarpedon's body, facefirst
and courage-shattering Death engulfed his corpse.
Grief for his dead companion seized Patroclus now,
he tore through frontline fighters swift as a hawk
diving to scatter crows and fear-struck starlings—
straight at the Lycians, Patroclus O my rider,

9. The two Greek warriors named Ajax.

straight at the pressing Trojan ranks you swooped,
enraged at your comrade's death! and struck Sthenelaus,
Ithaemenes' favorite son—a big rock to the neck
snapped the tendons strung to the skull's base.
So the front gave ground and flashing Hector too,
though only as far as a long slim spear can fly
when a man tests his hurling strength in the games
or in war when enemy fighters close to crush his life—
so far the Trojans gave as the Argives drove them back.
But Glaucus was first, lord of Lycia's shieldsmen now,
the first to turn and he killed the gallant Bathycles,
Chalcon's prize son who had made his home in Hellas,
excelling the Myrmidons all in wealth and fortune.
Now, just as the man was about to catch Glaucus
Glaucus suddenly spun and struck, he stabbed his chest,
ripped him down with a crash. A heavy blow to the Argives,
one of the brave ones down. A great joy to the Trojans,
massing packs of them swarming round the corpse
but Achaean forces never slacked their drive,
their juggernaut fury bore them breakneck on.
And there—Meriones[1] killed a Trojan captain,
Laogonus, daring son of Onetor, priest of Zeus,
Idaean Zeus, and his land revered him like a god—
Meriones gouged him under the jaw and ear, his spirit
flew from his limbs and the hateful darkness gripped him.
Just then Aeneas hurled his brazen spear at Meriones,
hoping to hit the man as he charged behind his shield.
But he eyed Aeneas straight on, he dodged the bronze,
ducking down with a quick lunge, and behind his back
the heavy spearshaft plunged and stuck in the earth,
the butt end quivering into the air till suddenly
rugged Ares snuffed its fury out, dead still.
The weapon shaking, planted fast in the ground,
his whole arm's power poured in a wasted shot,
Aeneas flared in anger, shouting out, "Meriones—
great dancer[2] as you are, my spear would have stopped
your dancing days for good if only I had hit you!"

The hardy spearman Meriones shot back, "Aeneas—
great man of war as you are, you'll find it hard
to quench the fire of every man who fights you.
You too are made of mortal stuff, I'd say. And I,
if I'd lanced your guts with bronze—strong as you are
and cocksure of your hands—you'd give me glory now,
you'd give your life to the famous horseman Death!"

But Patroclus nerved for battle dressed him down:
"Meriones, brave as you are, why bluster on this way?
Trust me, my friend, you'll never force the Trojans
back from this corpse with a few stinging taunts—

1. A warrior from Crete on the Greek side. 2. In Homer, the opposite of a warrior.

Earth will bury many a man before that. Come—
the proof of battle is action, proof of words, debate.
No time for speeches now, it's time to fight."

Breaking off, he led the way as Meriones followed,
staunch as a god. And loud as the roar goes up
when men cut timber deep in the mountain glades
and the pounding din of axes echoes miles away—
so the pound and thud of blows came rising up
from the broad earth, from the trampled paths of war
and the bronze shields and tough plied hides struck hard
as the swords and two-edged spearheads stabbed against them.
Not even a hawk-eyed scout could still make out Sarpedon,
the man's magnificent body covered over head to toe,
buried under a mass of weapons, blood and dust.
But they still kept swarming round and round the corpse
like flies in a sheepfold buzzing over the brimming pails
in the first spring days when the buckets flood with milk.
So veteran troops kept swarming round that corpse,
never pausing—nor did mighty Zeus for a moment
turn his shining eyes from the clash of battle.
He kept them fixed on the struggling mass forever,
the Father's spirit churning, thrashing out the ways,
the numberless ways to cause Patroclus' slaughter . . .
To kill him too in this present bloody rampage
over Sarpedon's splendid body? Hector in glory
cutting Patroclus down with hacking bronze
then tearing the handsome war-gear off his back?
Or let him take still more, piling up his kills?
As Zeus turned things over, that way seemed the best:
the valiant friend-in-arms of Peleus' son Achilles
would drive the Trojans and Hector helmed in bronze
back to Troy once more, killing them by platoons—
and Zeus began with Hector, he made the man a coward.
Hector leaping back in his chariot, swerving to fly,
shouted out fresh orders—"Retreat, Trojans, now!"
He knew that Zeus had tipped the scales against him.
A rout—not even the die-hard Lycians stood their ground,
they all scattered in panic, down to the last man
when they saw their royal king speared in the heart,
Sarpedon sprawled there in the muster of the dead,
for men by the squad had dropped across his corpse
once Zeus stretched tight the lethal line of battle.
So then the Achaeans ripped the armor off his back,
Sarpedon's gleaming bronze that Menoetius' son
the brave Patroclus flung in the arms of cohorts
poised to speed those trophies back to the beaked ships.
And storming[3] Zeus was stirring up Apollo: "On with it now—
sweep Sarpedon clear of the weapons, Phoebus my friend,
and once you wipe the dark blood from his body,

3. I.e., the storm god.

bear him far from the fighting, off and away,
and bathe him well in a river's running tides
and anoint him with deathless oils . . .
dress his body in deathless, ambrosial robes.
Then send him on his way with the wind-swift escorts,
twin brothers Sleep and Death, who with all good speed
will set him down in the broad green land of Lycia.
There his brothers and countrymen will bury the prince
with full royal rites, with mounded tomb and pillar.
These are the solemn honors owed the dead."
So he decreed
and Phoebus did not neglect the Father's strong desires.
Down from Ida's[4] slopes he dove to the bloody field
and lifting Prince Sarpedon clear of the weapons,
bore him far from the fighting, off and away,
and bathed him well in a river's running tides
and anointed him with deathless oils . . .
dressed his body in deathless, ambrosial robes
then sent him on his way with the wind-swift escorts,
twin brothers Sleep and Death, who with all good speed
set him down in Lycia's broad green land.
But Patroclus,
giving a cry to Automedon whipping on his team,
Patroclus went for Troy's and Lycia's lines,
blind in his fatal frenzy—luckless soldier.
If only he had obeyed Achilles' strict command
he might have escaped his doom, the stark night of death.
But the will of Zeus will always overpower the will of men,
Zeus who strikes fear in even the bravest man of war
and tears away his triumph, all in a lightning flash,
and at other times he will spur a man to battle,
just as he urged Patroclus' fury now.
Patroclus—
who was the first you slaughtered, who the last
when the great gods called you down to death?
First Adrestus, then Autonous, then Echeclus,
then Perimus, Megas' son, Epistor and Melanippus,
then in a flurry Elasus, Mulius and Pylartes—
he killed them all but the rest were bent on flight.

And then and there the Achaeans might have taken Troy,
her towering gates toppling under Patroclus' power
heading the vanguard, storming on with his spear.
But Apollo took his stand on the massive rampart,
his mind blazing with death for him but help for Troy.
Three times Patroclus charged the jut of the high wall,
three times Apollo battered the man and hurled him back,
the god's immortal hands beating down on the gleaming shield.
Then at Patroclus' fourth assault like something superhuman,

4. High mountain near Troy, from which Zeus has been watching the fighting on the plain.

the god shrieked down his winging words of terror: "Back—
Patroclus, Prince, go back! It is not the will of fate
that the proud Trojans' citadel fall before your spear,
not even before Achilles—far greater man than you!"

And Patroclus gave ground, backing a good way off,
clear of the deadly Archer's wrath.
But now Hector,
reining his high-strung team at the Scaean Gates,
debated a moment, waiting . . .
should he drive back to the rout and soldier on?
Or call his armies now to rally within the ramparts?
As he turned things over, Apollo stood beside him,
taking the shape of that lusty rugged fighter
Asius, an uncle of stallion-breaking Hector,
a blood brother of Hecuba, son of Dymas
who lived in Phrygia near Sangarius'[5] rapids.
Like him, Apollo the son of Zeus incited Hector:
"Hector, why stop fighting? Neglecting your duty!
If only I outfought *you* as you can outfight *me,*
I'd soon teach you to shirk your work in war—
you'd pay the price, I swear. Up with you—fast!
Lash those pounding stallions straight at Patroclus—
you might kill him still—Apollo might give you glory!"

And back Apollo strode, a god in the wars of men
while glorious Hector ordered skilled Cebriones,[6]
"Flog the team to battle!" Apollo pressed on,
wading into the ruck, hurling Argives back in chaos
and handing glory to Hector and all the Trojan forces.
But Hector ignored the Argive masses, killing none,
he lashed his pounding stallions straight at Patroclus.
Patroclus, over against him, leapt down from his car
and hit the ground, his left hand shaking a spear
and seized with his right a jagged, glittering stone
his hand could just cover—Patroclus flung it hard,
leaning into the heave, not backing away from Hector,
no, and no wasted shot. But he hit his driver—
a bastard son of famed King Priam, Cebriones
yanking the reins back taut—right between the eyes.
The sharp stone crushed both brows, the skull caved in
and both eyes burst from their sockets, dropping down
in the dust before his feet as the reinsman vaulted,
plunging off his well-wrought car like a diver—
Cebriones' life breath left his bones behind
and you taunted his corpse, Patroclus O my rider:
"Look what a springy man, a nimble, flashy tumbler!
Just think what he'd do at sea where the fish swarm—
why, the man could glut a fleet, diving for oysters!

5. A river in Phrygia, a district of Asia Minor inland from Troy. 6. Hector's half brother and charioteer.

Plunging overboard, even in choppy, heaving seas,
just as he dives to ground from his war-car now.
Even these Trojans have their tumblers—what a leap!"

And he leapt himself at the fighting driver's corpse
with the rushing lunge of a lion struck in the chest
as he lays waste pens of cattle—
his own lordly courage about to be his death.
So you sprang at Cebriones, full fury, Patroclus,
as Hector sprang down from his chariot just across
and the two went tussling over the corpse as lions
up on the mountain ridges over a fresh-killed stag—
both ravenous, proud and savage—fight it out to the death.
So over the driver here and both claw-mad for battle,
Patroclus son of Menoetius, Hector ablaze for glory
strained to slash each other with ruthless bronze.
Hector seized the corpse's head, would not let go—
Patroclus clung to a foot and other fighters clashed,
Trojans, Argives, all in a grueling, maiming onset.

As the East and South Winds fight in killer-squalls
deep in a mountain valley thrashing stands of timber,
oak and ash and cornel with bark stretched taut and hard
and they whip their long sharp branches against each other,
a deafening roar goes up, the splintered timber crashing—
so Achaeans and Trojans crashed,
hacking into each other, and neither side now
had a thought of flight that would have meant disaster.
Showers of whetted spears stuck fast around Cebriones,
bristling winged arrows whipped from the bowstrings,
huge rocks by the salvo battering shields on shields
as they struggled round the corpse. And there he lay
in the whirling dust, overpowered in all his power
and wiped from memory all his horseman's skills.

So till the sun bestrode the sky at high noon
the weapons hurtled side-to-side and men kept falling.
But once the sun wheeled past the hour for unyoking oxen,
then the Argives mounted a fiercer new attack,
fighting beyond their fates . . .
They dragged the hero Cebriones out from under
the pelting shafts and Trojans' piercing cries
and they tore the handsome war-gear off his back
and Patroclus charged the enemy, fired for the kill.
Three times he charged with the headlong speed of Ares,
screaming his savage cry, three times he killed nine men.
Then at the fourth assault Patroclus like something superhuman—
then, Patroclus, the end of life came blazing up before you,
yes, the lord Apollo met you there in the heart of battle,
the god, the terror! Patroclus never saw him coming,
moving across the deadly rout, shrouded in thick mist
and on he came against him and looming up behind him now—

slammed his broad shoulders and back with the god's flat hand
and his eyes spun as Apollo knocked the helmet off his head
and under his horses' hoofs it tumbled, clattering on
with its four forged horns and its hollow blank eyes
and its plumes were all smeared in the bloody dust.
Forbidden before this to defile its crest in dust,[7]
it guarded the head and handsome brow of a god,
a man like a god, Achilles. But now the Father
gave it over to Hector to guard his head in war
since Hector's death was closing on him quickly.
Patroclus though—the spear in his grip was shattered,
the whole of its rugged bronze-shod shadow-casting length
and his shield with straps and tassels dropped from his shoulders,
flung down on the ground—and lord Apollo the son of Zeus
wrenched his breastplate off. Disaster seized him—
his fine legs buckling—
he stood there, senseless—
And now,
right at his back, close-up, a Dardan[8] fighter speared him
squarely between the shoulder blades with a sharp lance.
Panthous' son Euphorbus, the best of his own age
at spears and a horseman's skill and speed of foot,
and even in this, his first attack in chariots—
just learning the arts of war—
he'd brought down twenty drivers off their cars.
He was the first to launch a spear against you,
Patroclus O my rider, but did not bring you down.
Yanking out his ashen shaft from your body,
back he dashed and lost himself in the crowds—
the man would not stand up to Patroclus here
in mortal combat, stripped, defenseless as he was.
Patroclus stunned by the spear and the god's crushing blow
was weaving back to his own thronging comrades,
trying to escape death . . .
Hector waiting, watching
the greathearted Patroclus trying to stagger free,
seeing him wounded there with the sharp bronze
came rushing into him right across the lines
and rammed his spearshaft home,
stabbing deep in the guts, and the brazen point
went jutting straight out through Patroclus' back.
Down he crashed—horror gripped the Achaean armies.
As when some lion overpowers a tireless wild boar
up on a mountain summit, battling in all their fury
over a little spring of water, both beasts craving
to slake their thirst, but the lion beats him down
with sheer brute force as the boar fights for breath—
so now with a close thrust Hector the son of Priam
tore the life from the fighting son of Menoetius,

7. Because it was divinely made and part of the armor given by the gods to Peleus on his marriage to Thetis. 8. Trojan.

from Patroclus who had killed so many men in war,
and gloried over him, wild winging words: "Patroclus—
surely you must have thought you'd storm my city down,
you'd wrest from the wives of Troy their day of freedom,
drag them off in ships to your own dear fatherland—
you fool! Rearing in their defense my war-team,
Hector's horses were charging out to battle,
galloping, full stretch. And I with my spear,
Hector, shining among my combat-loving comrades,
I fight away from them the fatal day—but you,
the vultures will eat your body raw!
Poor, doomed . . .
not for all his power could Achilles save you now—
and how he must have filled your ears with orders
as you went marching out and the hero stayed behind:
'Now don't come back to the hollow ships, you hear?—
Patroclus, master horseman—
not till you've slashed the shirt around his chest
and soaked it red in the blood of man-killing Hector!'
So he must have commanded—you maniac, you obeyed."[9]

Struggling for breath, you answered, Patroclus O my rider,
"Hector! Now is your time to glory to the skies . . .
now the victory is yours.
A gift of the son of Cronus, Zeus—Apollo too—
they brought me down with all their deathless ease,
they are the ones who tore the armor off my back.
Even if twenty Hectors had charged against me—
they'd all have died here, laid low by my spear.
No, deadly fate in league with Apollo killed me.
From the ranks of men, Euphorbus. You came third,
and all you could do was finish off my life . . .
One more thing—take it to heart, I urge you—
you too, you won't live long yourself, I swear.
Already I see them looming up beside you—death
and the strong force of fate, to bring you down
at the hands of Aeacus'[1] great royal son . . .
Achilles!"

Death cut him short. The end closed in around him.
Flying free of his limbs
his soul went winging down to the House of Death,
wailing his fate, leaving his manhood far behind,
his young and supple strength. But glorious Hector
taunted Patroclus' body, dead as he was, "Why, Patroclus—
why prophesy my doom, my sudden death? Who knows?—
Achilles the son of sleek-haired Thetis may outrace me—
struck by *my* spear first—and gasp away his life!"

9. Hector is wrong. Achilles warned Patroclus only to drive the Trojans from the Greek ships and not to chase them back to the city. 1. Grandfather of Achilles (*son* is used loosely here).

With that he planted a heel against Patroclus' chest,
wrenched his brazen spear from the wound, kicked him over,
flat on his back, free and clear of the weapon.
At once he went for Automedon with that spear—
quick as a god, the aide of swift Achilles—
keen to cut him down but his veering horses
swept him well away—magnificent racing stallions,
gifts of the gods to Peleus, shining immortal gifts.

Summary Hector stripped Achilles' divine armor from Patroclus's corpse. A fierce fight for the body itself ended in partial success for the Greeks; they took Patroclus's body but had to retreat to their camp, with the Trojans at their heels.

BOOK XVIII

[*The Shield of Achilles*]

So the men fought on like a mass of whirling fire
as swift Antilochus[2] raced the message toward Achilles.
Sheltered under his curving, beaked ships he found him,
foreboding, deep down, all that had come to pass.
Agonizing now he probed his own great heart:
"Why, why? Our long-haired Achaeans routed again,
driven in terror off the plain to crowd the ships, but why?
Dear gods, don't bring to pass the grief that haunts my heart—
the prophecy that mother revealed to me one time . . .
she said the best of the Myrmidons—while I lived—
would fall at Trojan hands and leave the light of day.
And now he's dead, I know it. Menoetius' gallant son,[3]
my headstrong friend! And I told Patroclus clearly,
'Once you have beaten off the lethal fire, quick,
come back to the ships—you must not battle Hector!' "
As such fears went churning through his mind
the warlord Nestor's son drew near him now,
streaming warm tears, to give the dreaded message:
"Ah son of royal Peleus, what you must hear from me!
What painful news—would to god it had never happened!
Patroclus has fallen. They're fighting over his corpse.
He's stripped, naked—Hector with that flashing helmet,
Hector has your arms!"
So the captain reported.
A black cloud of grief came shrouding over Achilles.
Both hands clawing the ground for soot and filth,
he poured it over his head, fouled his handsome face
and black ashes settled onto his fresh clean war-shirt.
Overpowered in all his power, he sprawled in the dust.
Achilles lay there, fallen . . .
tearing his hair, defiling it with his own hands.
And the women he and Patroclus carried off as captives

2. A son of Nestor. 3. Patroclus.

caught the grief in their hearts and keened and wailed,
out of the tents they ran to ring the great Achilles,
all of them beat their breasts with clenched fists,
sank to the ground, each woman's knees gave way.
Antilochus kneeling near, weeping uncontrollably,
clutched Achilles' hands as he wept his proud heart out—
for fear he would slash his throat with an iron blade.
Achilles suddenly loosed a terrible, wrenching cry
and his noble mother heard him, seated near her father,
the Old Man of the Sea in the salt green depths,
and she cried out in turn. And immortal sea-nymphs
gathered round their sister, all the Nereids swelling
down the sounding depths, they all came rushing now—
Glitter, blossoming Spray and the swells' Embrace,
Fair-Isle and shadowy Cavern, Mist and Spindrift,
ocean nymphs of the glances pooling deep and dark,
Race-with-the-Waves and Headlands' Hope and Safe Haven,
Glimmer of Honey, Suave-and-Soothing, Whirlpool, Brilliance,
Bounty and First Light and Speeder of Ships and buoyant Power,
Welcome Home and Bather of Meadows and Master's Lovely Consort,
Gift of the Sea, Eyes of the World and the famous milk-white Calm
and Truth and Never-Wrong and the queen who rules the tides in beauty
and in rushed Glory and Healer of Men and the one who rescues kings
and Sparkler, Down-from-the-Cliffs, sleek-haired Strands of Sand
and all the rest of the Nereids swelling down the depths.
The silver cave was shimmering full of sea-nymphs,
all in one mounting chorus beating their breasts
as Thetis launched the dirge: "Hear me, sisters,
daughters of Nereus, so you all will know it well—
listen to all the sorrows welling in my heart!
I am agony—
mother of grief and greatness—O my child!
Yes, I gave birth to a flawless, mighty son . . .
the splendor of heroes, and he shot up like a young branch,
like a fine tree I reared him—the orchard's crowning glory—
but only to send him off in the beaked ships to Troy
to battle Trojans! Never again will I embrace him
striding home through the doors of Peleus' house.
And long as I have him with me, still alive,
looking into the sunlight, he is racked with anguish.
And I, I go to his side—nothing I do can help him.
Nothing. But go I shall, to see my darling boy,
to hear what grief has come to break his heart
while he holds back from battle."
So Thetis cried
as she left the cave and her sisters swam up with her,
all in a tide of tears, and billowing round them now
the ground swell heaved open. And once they reached
the fertile land of Troy they all streamed ashore,
row on row in a long cortege, the sea-nymphs
filing up where the Myrmidon ships lay hauled,
clustered closely round the great runner Achilles . . .

As he groaned from the depths his mother rose before him
and sobbing a sharp cry, cradled her son's head in her hands
and her words were all compassion, winging pity: "My child—
why in tears? What sorrow has touched your heart?
Tell me, please. Don't harbor it deep inside you.
Zeus has accomplished everything you wanted,
just as you raised your hands and prayed that day.
All the sons of Achaea are pinned against the ships
and all for want of you—they suffer shattering losses."

And groaning deeply the matchless runner answered,
"O dear mother, true! All those burning desires
Olympian Zeus has brought to pass for me—
but what joy to me now? My dear comrade's dead—
Patroclus—the man I loved beyond all other comrades,
loved as my own life—I've lost him—Hector's killed him,
stripped the gigantic armor off his back, a marvel to behold—
my burnished gear! Radiant gifts the gods presented Peleus
that day they drove you into a mortal's marriage bed . . .
I wish you'd lingered deep with the deathless sea-nymphs,
lived at ease, and Peleus carried home a mortal bride.
But now, as it is, sorrows, unending sorrows must surge
within your heart as well—for your own son's death.
Never again will you embrace him striding home.
My spirit rebels—I've lost the will to live,
to take my stand in the world of men—unless,
before all else, Hector's battered down by my spear
and gasps away his life, the blood-price for Patroclus,
Menoetius' gallant son he's killed and stripped!"

But Thetis answered, warning through her tears,
"You're doomed to a short life, my son, from all you say!
For hard on the heels of Hector's death your death
must come at once—"
"Then let me die at once"—
Achilles burst out, despairing—"since it was not my fate
to save my dearest comrade from his death! Look,
a world away from his fatherland he's perished,
lacking me, my fighting strength, to defend him.
But now, since I shall not return to my fatherland . . .
nor did I bring one ray of hope to my Patroclus,
nor to the rest of all my steadfast comrades,
countless ranks struck down by mighty Hector—
No, no, here I sit by the ships . . .
a useless, dead weight on the good green earth—
I, no man my equal among the bronze-armed Achaeans,
not in battle, only in wars of words that others win.
If only strife could die from the lives of gods and men
and anger that drives the sanest man to flare in outrage—
bitter gall, sweeter than dripping streams of honey,

that swarms in people's chests and blinds like smoke—
just like the anger Agamemnon king of men
has roused within me now . . .
Enough.
Let bygones be bygones. Done is done.
Despite my anguish I will beat it down,
the fury mounting inside me, down by force.
But now I'll go and meet that murderer head-on,
that Hector who destroyed the dearest life I know.
For my own death, I'll meet it freely—whenever Zeus
and the other deathless gods would like to bring it on!
Not even Heracles[4] fled his death, for all his power,
favorite son as he was to Father Zeus the King.
Fate crushed him, and Hera's savage anger.
And I too, if the same fate waits for me . . .
I'll lie in peace, once I've gone down to death.
But now, for the moment, let me seize great glory!—
and drive some woman of Troy or deep-breasted Dardan[5]
to claw with both hands at her tender cheeks and wipe away
her burning tears as the sobs come choking from her throat—
they'll learn that I refrained from war a good long time!
Don't try to hold me back from the fighting, mother,
love me as you do. You can't persuade me now."

The goddess of the glistening feet replied,
"Yes, my son, you're right. No coward's work,
to save your exhausted friends from headlong death.
But your own handsome war-gear lies in Trojan hands
bronze and burnished—and Hector in that flashing helmet,
Hector glories in your armor, strapped across his back.
Not that he will glory in it long, I tell you:
his own destruction hovers near him now. Wait—
don't fling yourself in the grind of battle yet,
not till you see me coming back with your own eyes.
Tomorrow I will return to you with the rising sun,
bearing splendid arms from Hephaestus, god of fire!"

With that vow she turned away from her son
and faced and urged her sisters of the deep,
"Now down you go in the Ocean's folding gulfs
to visit father's halls—the Old Man of the Sea—
and tell him all. I am on my way to Olympus heights,
to the famous Smith Hephaestus—I pray he'll give my son
some fabulous armor full of the god's great fire!"

And under a foaming wave her sisters dove
as glistening-footed Thetis soared toward Olympus

4. The son of Zeus by a mortal woman; pursued by the jealousy of Hera, he was forced to undertake twelve great labors and finally died in agony from the effects of a poisoned garment. 5. Trojan.

to win her dear son an immortal set of arms.
And now,
as her feet swept her toward Olympus, ranks of Achaeans,
fleeing man-killing Hector with grim, unearthly cries,
reached the ships and the Hellespont's long shore.
As for Patroclus, there seemed no hope that Achaeans
could drag the corpse of Achilles' comrade out of range.
Again the Trojan troops and teams overtook the body
with Hector son of Priam storming fierce as fire.
Three times illustrious Hector shouted for support,
seized his feet from behind, wild to drag him off,
three times the Aeantes, armored in battle-fury
fought him off the corpse. But Hector held firm,
staking all on his massive fighting strength—
again and again he'd hurl himself at the melee,
again and again stand fast with piercing cries
but he never gave ground backward, not one inch.
The helmed Aeantes could no more frighten Hector,
the proud son of Priam, back from Patroclus' corpse
than shepherds out in the field can scare a tawny lion
off his kill when the hunger drives the beast claw-mad.
And now Hector would have hauled the body away
and won undying glory . . .
if wind-swift Iris[6] had not swept from Olympus
bearing her message—Peleus' son must arm—
but all unknown to Zeus and the other gods
since Hera spurred her on. Halting near
she gave Achilles a flight of marching orders:
"To arms—son of Peleus! Most terrifying man alive!
Defend Patroclus! It's all for him, this merciless battle
pitched before the ships. They're mauling each other now,
Achaeans struggling to save the corpse from harm,
Trojans charging to haul it back to windy Troy.
Flashing Hector far in the lead, wild to drag it off,
furious to lop the head from its soft, tender neck
and stake it high on the city's palisade.
Up with you—
no more lying low! Writhe with shame at the thought
Patroclus may be sport for the dogs of Troy!
Yours, the shame will be yours
if your comrade's corpse goes down to the dead defiled!"

But the swift runner replied, "Immortal Iris—
what god has sped you here to tell me this?"

Quick as the wind the rushing Iris answered,
"Hera winged me on, the illustrious wife of Zeus.
But the son of Cronus throned on high knows nothing,
nor does any other immortal housed on Olympus

6. Messenger of the gods, particularly of Hera.

shrouded deep in snow."
Achilles broke in quickly—
"How can I go to war? The Trojans have my gear.
And my dear mother told me I must not arm for battle,
not till I see her coming back with my own eyes—
she vowed to bring me burnished arms from the god of fire.
I know of no other armor. Whose gear could I wear?
None but Telamonian Ajax'[7] giant shield.
But he's at the front, I'm sure, engaging Trojans,
slashing his spear to save Patroclus' body."

Quick as the wind the goddess had a plan:
"We know—we too—they hold your famous armor.
Still, just as you are, go out to the broad trench
and show yourself to the Trojans. Struck with fear
at the sight of you, they might hold off from attack
and Achaea's fighting sons get second wind,
exhausted as they are . . .
Breathing room in war is all too brief."

And Iris racing the wind went veering off
as Achilles, Zeus's favorite fighter, rose up now
and over his powerful shoulder Pallas slung the shield,
the tremendous storm-shield with all its tassels flaring—
and crowning his head the goddess swept a golden cloud
and from it she lit a fire to blaze across the field.
As smoke goes towering up the sky from out a town
cut off on a distant island under siege . . .
enemies battling round it, defenders all day long
trading desperate blows from their own city walls
but soon as the sun goes down the signal fires flash,
rows of beacons blazing into the air to alert their neighbors—
if only they'll come in ships to save them from disaster—
so now from Achilles' head the blaze shot up the sky.
He strode from the rampart, took his stand at the trench
but he would not mix with the milling Argive ranks.
He stood in awe of his mother's strict command.
So there he rose and loosed an enormous cry
and off in the distance Pallas shrieked out too
and drove an unearthly panic through the Trojans.
Piercing loud as the trumpet's battle cry that blasts
from murderous raiding armies ringed around some city—
so piercing now the cry that broke from Aeacides.
And Trojans hearing the brazen voice of Aeacides,
all their spirits quaked—even sleek-maned horses,
sensing death in the wind, slewed their chariots round
and charioteers were struck dumb when they saw that fire,
relentless, terrible, burst from proud-hearted Achilles' head,
blazing as fiery-eyed Athena fueled the flames. Three times
the brilliant Achilles gave his great war cry over the trench,

7. The more famous of the two heroes called Ajax was the son of Telamon.

three times the Trojans and famous allies whirled in panic—
and twelve of their finest fighters died then and there,
crushed by chariots, impaled on their own spears.
And now the exultant Argives seized the chance
to drag Patroclus' body quickly out of range
and laid him on a litter . . .
Standing round him, loving comrades mourned,
and the swift runner Achilles joined them, grieving,
weeping warm tears when he saw his steadfast comrade
lying dead on the bier, mauled by tearing bronze,
the man he sent to war with team and chariot
but never welcomed home again alive.

Now Hera the ox-eyed queen of heaven drove the sun,
untired and all unwilling, to sink in the Ocean's depths
and the sun went down at last and brave Achaeans ceased
the grueling clash of arms, the leveling rout of war.

And the Trojans in turn, far across the field,
pulling forces back from the last rough assault,
freed their racing teams from under chariot yokes
but before they thought of supper, grouped for council.
They met on their feet. Not one of them dared to sit
for terror seized them all—the great Achilles
who held back from the brutal fighting so long
had just come blazing forth.
Panthous' son Polydamas led the debate,
a good clear head, and the only man who saw
what lay in the past and what the Trojans faced.[8]
He was Hector's close comrade, born on the same night,
but excelled at trading words as he at trading spear-thrusts.
And now, with all good will, Polydamas rose and spoke:
"Weigh both sides of the crisis well, my friends.
What I urge is this: draw back to the city now.
Don't wait for the holy Dawn to find us here afield,
ranged by the ships—we're too far from our walls.
As long as that man kept raging at royal Agamemnon
the Argive troops were easier game to battle down.
I too was glad to camp the night on the shipways,
hopes soaring to seize their heavy rolling hulls.
But now racing Achilles makes my blood run cold.
So wild the man's fury he will never rest content,
holding out on the plain where Trojans and Argives
met halfway, exchanging blows in the savage onset—
never: *he* will fight for our wives, for Troy itself!
So retreat to Troy. Trust me—we will face disaster.
Now, for the moment, the bracing godsent night
has stopped the swift Achilles in his tracks.
But let him catch us lingering here tomorrow,
just as he rises up in arms—there may be some

8. I.e., he was a prophet and knew the past and foresaw the future.

who will sense his fighting spirit all too well.
You'll thank your stars to get back to sacred Troy,
whoever escapes him. Dogs and birds will have their fill—
of Trojan flesh, by heaven. Battalions of Trojans!
Pray god such grief will never reach my ears.
So follow my advice, hard as it may seem . . .
Tonight conserve our strength in the meeting place,
and the great walls and gates and timbered doors we hung,
well-planed, massive and bolted tight, will shield the city.
But tomorrow at daybreak, armed to the hilt for battle,
we man the towering ramparts. All the worse for him—
if Achilles wants to venture forth from the fleet,
fight us round our walls. Back to the ships he'll go,
once he's lashed the power out of his rippling stallions,
whipping them back and forth beneath our city walls.
Not even *his* fury will let him crash our gates—
he'll never plunder Troy.
Sooner the racing dogs will eat him raw!"

Helmet flashing, Hector wheeled with a dark glance:
"No more, Polydamas! Your pleading repels me now.
You say go back again—be crammed inside the city.
Aren't you sick of being caged inside those walls?
Time was when the world would talk of Priam's Troy
as the city rich in gold and rich in bronze—but now
our houses are stripped of all their sumptuous treasures,
troves sold off and shipped to Phrygia, lovely Maeonia,
once great Zeus grew angry . . .
but now, the moment the son of crooked Cronus
allows me to seize some glory here at the ships
and pin these Argives back against the sea—
you fool, enough! No more thoughts of retreat
paraded before our people. Not that one Trojan
will ever take your lead—I'll never permit it.
Come, follow my orders! All obey me now.
Take supper now. Take your posts through camp.
And no forgetting the watch, each man wide awake.
And any Trojan so weighed down, so oppressed
by his own possessions, let him collect the lot,
pass them round to the people—a grand public feast.
Far better for one of ours to reap the benefits
than all the marauding Argives. Then, as you say,
'tomorrow at daybreak, armed to the hilt for battle'—
we slash to attack against their deep curved hulls!
If it really *was* Achilles who reared beside the ships,
all the worse for him—if he wants his fill of war.
I for one, I'll never run from his grim assault,
I'll stand up to the man—see if he bears off glory
or I bear it off myself! The god of war is impartial:
he hands out death to the man who hands out death."

So Hector finished. The Trojans roared assent,
lost in folly. Athena had swept away their senses.

They gave applause to Hector's ruinous tactics,
none to Polydamas, who gave them sound advice.
And now their entire army settled down to supper
but all night long the Argives raised Patroclus' dirge.
And Achilles led them now in a throbbing chant of sorrow,
laying his man-killing hands on his great friend's chest,
convulsed with bursts of grief. Like a bearded lion
whose pride of cubs a deer-hunter has snatched away,
out of some thick woods, and back he comes, too late,
and his heart breaks but he courses after the hunter,
hot on his tracks down glen on twisting glen—
where can he find him?—gripped by piercing rage . . .
so Achilles groaned, deeply, crying out to his Myrmidons,
"O my captains! How empty the promise I let fall
that day I reassured Menoetius in his house—
I promised the king I'd bring him back his son,
home to Opois,[9] covered in glory, Troy sacked,
hauling his rightful share of plunder home at last.
But Zeus will never accomplish all our best-laid plans.
Look at us. Both doomed to stain red with our blood
the same plot of earth, a world away in Troy!
For not even *I* will voyage home again. Never.
No embrace in his halls from the old horseman Peleus
nor from mother, Thetis—this alien earth I stride
will hold me down at last.
But now, Patroclus,
since I will follow you underneath the ground,
I shall not bury you, not till I drag back here
the gear and head of Hector, who slaughtered you,
my friend, greathearted friend . . .
Here in front of your flaming pyre I'll cut the throats
of a dozen sons of Troy in all their shining glory,
venting my rage on them for your destruction!
Till then you lie as you are beside my beaked ships
and round you the Trojan women and deep-breasted Dardans
will mourn you night and day, weeping burning tears,
women we fought to win—strong hands and heavy lance—
whenever we sacked rich cities held by mortal men."

With that the brilliant Achilles ordered friends
to set a large three-legged cauldron over the fire
and wash the clotted blood from Patroclus' wounds
with all good speed. Hoisting over the blaze
a cauldron filled to the brim with bathing water,
they piled fresh logs beneath and lit them quickly.
The fire lapped at the vessel's belly, the water heated
and soon as it reached the boil in the glowing bronze
they bathed and anointed the body sleek with olive oil,
closed each wound with a soothing, seasoned unguent
and then they laid Patroclus on his bier . . .
covered him head to foot in a thin light sheet

9. Ancient city on the eastern coast of the Greek mainland and home of Menoetius, father of Patroclus.

and over his body spread the white linen shroud.
Then all night long, ringing the great runner Achilles,
Myrmidon fighters mourned and raised Patroclus' dirge.

But Zeus turned to Hera, his wife and sister, saying,
"So, my ox-eyed Queen, you've had your way at last,
setting the famous runner Achilles on his feet.
Mother Hera—look, these long-haired Achaeans
must be sprung of your own immortal loins."

But her eyes widening, noble Hera answered,
"Dread majesty, son of Cronus, what are you saying?
Even a mortal man will act to help a friend,
condemned as a mortal always is to death
and hardly endowed with wisdom deep as ours.
So how could I, claiming to be the highest goddess—
both by birth and since I am called your consort
and you in turn rule all the immortal gods—
how could I hold back from these, these Trojans,
men I loathe, and fail to weave their ruin?"

Now as the King and Queen provoked each other,
glistening-footed Thetis reached Hephaestus' house,
indestructible, bright as stars, shining among the gods,
built of bronze by the crippled Smith with his own hands.
There she found him, sweating, wheeling round his bellows,
pressing the work on twenty three-legged cauldrons,
an array to ring the walls inside his mansion.
He'd bolted golden wheels to the legs of each
so all on their own speed, at a nod from him,
they could roll to halls where the gods convene
then roll right home again—a marvel to behold.
But not quite finished yet . . .
the god had still to attach the inlaid handles.
These he was just fitting, beating in the rivets.
As he bent to the work with all his craft and cunning,
Thetis on her glistening feet drew near the Smith.
But Charis[1] saw her first, Charis coming forward,
lithe and lovely in all her glittering headdress,
the Grace the illustrious crippled Smith had married.
Approaching Thetis, she caught her hand and spoke her name:
"Thetis of flowing robes! What brings you to our house?
A beloved, honored friend—but it's been so long,
your visits much too rare. Follow me in, please,
let me offer you all a guest could want."
Welcome words,
and the radiant goddess Charis led the way inside.
She seated her on a handsome, well-wrought chair,
studded with silver, under it slipped a stool

1. Her name means grace or beauty.

and called the famous Smith: "Hephaestus, come—
look who's here! Thetis would ask a favor of you!"

And the famous crippled Smith exclaimed warmly,
"Thetis—here? Ah then a wondrous, honored goddess
comes to grace our house! Thetis saved my life
when the mortal pain came on me after my great fall,
thanks to my mother's will, that brazen bitch,
she wanted to hide me—because I was a cripple.
What shattering anguish I'd have suffered then
if Thetis had not taken me to her breast, Eurynome too,
the daughter of ocean's stream that runs around the world.
Nine years I lived with both, forging bronze by the trove,
elegant brooches, whorled pins, necklaces, chokers, chains—
there in the vaulted cave—and round us Ocean's currents
swirled in a foaming, roaring rush that never died.
And no one knew. Not a single god or mortal,
only Thetis and Eurynome knew—they saved me.
And here is Thetis now, in our own house!
So I *must* do all I can to pay her back,
the price for the life she saved . . .
the nymph of the sea with sleek and lustrous locks.
Quickly, set before her stranger's generous fare
while I put away my bellows and all my tools."
With that
he heaved up from the anvil block—his immense hulk
hobbling along but his shrunken legs moved nimbly.
He swung the bellows aside and off the fires,
gathered the tools he'd used to weld the cauldrons
and packed them all in a sturdy silver strongbox.
Then he sponged off his brow and both burly arms,
his massive neck and shaggy chest, pulled on a shirt
and grasping a heavy staff, Hephaestus left his forge
and hobbled on. Handmaids ran to attend their master,
all cast in gold but a match for living, breathing girls.
Intelligence fills their hearts, voice and strength their frames,
from the deathless gods they've learned their works of hand.
They rushed to support their lord as he went bustling on
and lurching nearer to Thetis, took his polished seat,
reached over to clutch her hand and spoke her name:
"Thetis of flowing robes! What brings you to our house?
A beloved, honored friend—but it's been so long,
your visits much too rare.
Tell me what's on your mind. I am eager to do it—
whatever I *can* do . . . whatever can be done."

But Thetis burst into tears, her voice welling:
"Oh Hephaestus—who of all the goddesses on Olympus,
who has borne such withering sorrows in her heart?
Such pain as Zeus has given me, above all others!
Me out of all the daughters of the sea he chose
to yoke to a mortal man, Peleus, son of Aeacus,

and I endured his bed, a mortal's bed, resisting
with all my will. And now he lies in the halls,
broken with grisly age, but now my griefs are worse.
Remember? Zeus also gave me a son to bear and breed,
the splendor of heroes, and he shot up like a young branch,
like a fine tree I reared him—the orchard's crowning glory—
but only to send him off in the beaked ships to Troy
to battle Trojans! Never again will I embrace him
striding home through the doors of Peleus' house.
And long as I have him with me, still alive,
looking into the sunlight, he is racked with anguish.
I go to his side—nothing I do can help him. Nothing.
That girl the sons of Achaea picked out for his prize—
right from his grasp the mighty Agamemnon tore her,
and grief for her has been gnawing at his heart.
But then the Trojans pinned the Achaeans tight
against their sterns, they gave them no way out,
and the Argive warlords begged my son to help,
they named in full the troves of glittering gifts
they'd send his way. But at that point he refused
to beat disaster off—refused himself, that is—
but he buckled his own armor round Patroclus,
sent him into battle with an army at his back.
And all day long they fought at the Scaean Gates,
that very day they would have stormed the city too,
if Apollo had not killed Menoetius' gallant son
as he laid the Trojans low—Apollo cut him down
among the champions there and handed Hector glory.
So now I come, I throw myself at your knees,
please help me! Give my son—he won't live long—
a shield and helmet and tooled greaves with ankle-straps
and armor for his chest. All that he had was lost,
lost when the Trojans killed his steadfast friend.
Now he lies on the ground—his heart is breaking."

And the famous crippled Smith replied, "Courage!
Anguish for all that armor—sweep it from your mind.
If only I could hide him away from pain and death,
that day his grim destiny comes to take Achilles,
as surely as glorious armor shall be his, armor
that any man in the world of men will marvel at
through all the years to come—whoever sees its splendor."
With that he left her there and made for his bellows,
turning them on the fire, commanding, "Work—to work!"
And the bellows, all twenty, blew on the crucibles,
breathing with all degrees of shooting, fiery heat
as the god hurried on—a blast for the heavy work,
a quick breath for the light, all precisely gauged
to the god of fire's wish and the pace of the work in hand.
Bronze he flung in the blaze, tough, durable bronze
and tin and priceless gold and silver, and then,

planting the huge anvil upon its block, he gripped
his mighty hammer in one hand, the other gripped his tongs.

And first Hephaestus makes a great and massive shield,
blazoning well-wrought emblems all across its surface,
raising a rim around it, glittering, triple-ply
with a silver shield-strap run from edge to edge
and five layers of metal to build the shield itself,
and across its vast expanse with all his craft and cunning
the god creates a world of gorgeous immortal work.

There he made the earth and there the sky and the sea
and the inexhaustible blazing sun and the moon rounding full
and there the constellations, all that crown the heavens,
the Pleiades and the Hyades, Orion in all his power too
and the Great Bear[2] that mankind also calls the Wagon:
she wheels on her axis always fixed, watching Orion,
and she alone is denied a plunge in the Ocean's baths.

And he forged on the shield two noble cities filled
with mortal men. With weddings and wedding feasts in one
and under glowing torches they brought forth the brides
from the women's chambers, marching through the streets
while choir on choir the wedding song rose high
and the young men came dancing, whirling round in rings
and among them the flutes and harps kept up their stirring call—
women rushed to the doors and each stood moved with wonder.
And the people massed, streaming into the marketplace
where a quarrel had broken out and two men struggled
over the blood-price for a kinsman just murdered.
One declaimed in public, vowing payment in full—
the other spurned him, he would not take a thing—
so both men pressed for a judge to cut the knot.
The crowd cheered on both, they took both sides,
but heralds held them back as the city elders sat
on polished stone benches, forming the sacred circle,
grasping in hand the staffs of clear-voiced heralds,
and each leapt to his feet to plead the case in turn.
Two bars of solid gold shone on the ground before them,
a prize for the judge who'd speak the straightest verdict.

But circling the other city camped a divided army
gleaming in battle-gear, and two plans split their ranks:
to plunder the city or share the riches with its people,
hoards the handsome citadel stored within its depths.
But the people were not surrendering, not at all.
They armed for a raid, hoping to break the siege—
loving wives and innocent children standing guard

2. The Big Dipper, which never descends below the horizon. It is a female bear (Ursa Major), hence *she* in line 570. Pleiades, Hyades, and Orion are all constellations. Orion was a giant hunter of Greek mythology.

on the ramparts, flanked by elders bent with age
as men marched out to war. Ares and Pallas led them,
both burnished gold, gold the attire they donned, and great,
magnificent in their armor—gods for all the world,
looming up in their brilliance, towering over troops.
And once they reached the perfect spot for attack,
a watering place where all the herds collected,
there they crouched, wrapped in glowing bronze.
Detached from the ranks, two scouts took up their posts,
the eyes of the army waiting to spot a convoy,
the enemy's flocks and crook-horned cattle coming . . .
Come they did, quickly, two shepherds behind them,
playing their hearts out on their pipes—treachery
never crossed their minds. But the soldiers saw them,
rushed them, cut off at a stroke the herds of oxen
and sleek sheep-flocks glistening silver-gray
and killed the herdsmen too. Now the besiegers,
soon as they heard the uproar burst from the cattle
as they debated, huddled in council, mounted at once
behind their racing teams, rode hard to the rescue,
arrived at once, and lining up for assault
both armies battled it out along the river banks—
they raked each other with hurtling bronze-tipped spears.
And Strife and Havoc plunged in the fight, and violent Death—
now seizing a man alive with fresh wounds, now one unhurt,
now hauling a deadman through the slaughter by the heels,
the cloak on her back stained red with human blood.
So they clashed and fought like living, breathing men
grappling each other's corpses, dragging off the dead.

And he forged a fallow field, broad rich plowland
tilled for the third time, and across it crews of plowmen
wheeled their teams, driving them up and back and soon
as they'd reach the end-strip, moving into the turn,
a man would run up quickly
and hand them a cup of honeyed, mellow wine
as the crews would turn back down along the furrows,
pressing again to reach the end of the deep fallow field
and the earth churned black behind them, like earth churning,
solid gold as it was—that was the wonder of Hephaestus' work.

And he forged a king's estate where harvesters labored,
reaping the ripe grain, swinging their whetted scythes.
Some stalks fell in line with the reapers, row on row,
and others the sheaf-binders girded round with ropes,
three binders standing over the sheaves, behind them
boys gathering up the cut swaths, filling their arms,
supplying grain to the binders, endless bundles.
And there in the midst the king,
scepter in hand at the head of the reaping-rows,
stood tall in silence, rejoicing in his heart.
And off to the side, beneath a spreading oak,

the heralds were setting out the harvest feast,
they were dressing a great ox they had slaughtered,
while attendant women poured out barley, generous,
glistening handfuls strewn for the reapers' midday meal.

And he forged a thriving vineyard loaded with clusters,
bunches of lustrous grapes in gold, ripening deep purple
and climbing vines shot up on silver vine-poles.
And round it he cut a ditch in dark blue enamel
and round the ditch he staked a fence in tin.
And one lone footpath led toward the vineyard
and down it the pickers ran
whenever they went to strip the grapes at vintage—
girls and boys, their hearts leaping in innocence,
bearing away the sweet ripe fruit in wicker baskets.
And there among them a young boy plucked his lyre,
so clear it could break the heart with longing,
and what he sang was a dirge for the dying year,
lovely . . . his fine voice rising and falling low
as the rest followed, all together, frisking, singing,
shouting, their dancing footsteps beating out the time.

And he forged on the shield a herd of longhorn cattle,
working the bulls in beaten gold and tin, lowing loud
and rumbling out of the farmyard dung to pasture
along a rippling stream, along the swaying reeds.
And the golden drovers kept the herd in line,
four in all, with nine dogs at their heels,
their paws flickering quickly—a savage roar!—
a crashing attack—and a pair of ramping lions
had seized a bull from the cattle's front ranks—
he bellowed out as they dragged him off in agony.
Packs of dogs and the young herdsmen rushed to help
but the lions ripping open the hide of the huge bull
were gulping down the guts and the black pooling blood
while the herdsmen yelled the fast pack on—no use.
The hounds shrank from sinking teeth in the lions,
they balked, hunching close, barking, cringing away.

And the famous crippled Smith forged a meadow
deep in a shaded glen for shimmering flocks to graze,
with shepherds' steadings, well-roofed huts and sheepfolds.

And the crippled Smith brought all his art to bear
on a dancing circle, broad as the circle Daedalus
once laid out on Cnossos' spacious fields
for Ariadne[3] the girl with lustrous hair.
Here young boys and girls, beauties courted
with costly gifts of oxen, danced and danced,

3. Daughter of Minos, king of Crete. Daedalus was the "fabulous artificer" who built the labyrinth and, with his son, Icarus, escaped from Crete on wings. Cnossos was the site of Minos's great palace.

linking their arms, gripping each other's wrists.
And the girls wore robes of linen light and flowing,
the boys wore finespun tunics rubbed with a gloss of oil,
the girls were crowned with a bloom of fresh garlands,
the boys swung golden daggers hung on silver belts.
And now they would run in rings on their skilled feet,
nimbly, quick as a crouching potter spins his wheel,
palming it smoothly, giving it practice twirls
to see it run, and now they would run in rows,
in rows crisscrossing rows—rapturous dancing.
A breathless crowd stood round them struck with joy
and through them a pair of tumblers dashed and sprang,
whirling in leaping handsprings, leading out the dance.

And he forged the Ocean River's mighty power girdling
round the outmost rim of the welded indestructible shield.

And once the god had made that great and massive shield
he made Achilles a breastplate brighter than gleaming fire,
he made him a sturdy helmet to fit the fighter's temples,
beautiful, burnished work, and raised its golden crest
and made him greaves of flexing, pliant tin.
Now,
when the famous crippled Smith had finished off
that grand array of armor, lifting it in his arms
he laid it all at the feet of Achilles' mother Thetis—
and down she flashed like a hawk from snowy Mount Olympus
bearing the brilliant gear, the god of fire's gift.

Summary Achilles finally accepted gifts of restitution from Agamemnon, as he had refused to do earlier. His return to the fighting brought terror to the Trojans and turned the battle into a rout in which Achilles killed every Trojan that crossed his path. As he pursued Agenor, Apollo tricked him by rescuing his intended victim (he spirited him away in a mist) and assumed Agenor's shape to lead Achilles away from the walls of Troy. The Trojans took refuge in the city, all except Hector.

BOOK XXII

[*The Death of Hector*]

So all through Troy the men who had fled like panicked fawns
were wiping off their sweat, drinking away their thirst,
leaning along the city's massive ramparts now
while Achaean troops, sloping shields to shoulders,
closed against the walls. But there stood Hector,
shackled fast by his deadly fate, holding his ground,
exposed in front of Troy and the Scaean Gates.
And now Apollo turned to taunt Achilles:
"Why are you chasing *me*? Why waste your speed?—
son of Peleus, you a mortal and I a deathless god.
You still don't know that I am immortal, do you?—
straining to catch me in your fury! Have you forgotten?

There's a war to fight with the Trojans you stampeded,
look, they're packed inside their city walls, but you,
you've slipped away out here. You can't kill *me*—
I can never die—it's not my fate!"
Enraged at that,
Achilles shouted in mid-stride, "You've blocked my way,
you distant, deadly Archer, deadliest god of all—
you made me swerve away from the rampart there.
Else what a mighty Trojan army had gnawed the dust
before they could ever straggle through their gates!
Now you've robbed me of great glory, saved their lives
with all your deathless ease. Nothing for you to fear,
no punishment to come. Oh I'd pay you back
if I only had the power at my command!"

No more words—he dashed toward the city,
heart racing for some great exploit, rushing on
like a champion stallion drawing a chariot full tilt,
sweeping across the plain in easy, tearing strides—
as Achilles hurtled on, driving legs and knees.

And old King Priam was first to see him coming,
surging over the plain, blazing like the star
that rears at harvest, flaming up in its brilliance—
far outshining the countless stars in the night sky,
that star they call Orion's Dog[4]—brightest of all
but a fatal sign emblazoned on the heavens,
it brings such killing fever down on wretched men.
So the bronze flared on his chest as on he raced—
and the old man moaned, flinging both hands high,
beating his head and groaning deep he called,
begging his dear son who stood before the gates,
unshakable, furious to fight Achilles to the death.
The old man cried, pitifully, hands reaching out to him,
"Oh Hector! Don't just stand there, don't, dear child,
waiting that man's attack—alone, cut off from friends!
You'll meet your doom at once, beaten down by Achilles,
so much stronger than you—that hard, headlong man.
Oh if only the gods loved him as much as I do . . .
dogs and vultures would eat his fallen corpse at once!—
with what a load of misery lifted from my spirit.
That man who robbed me of my sons, brave boys,
cutting them down or selling them off as slaves,
shipped to islands half the world away . . .
Even now there are two, Lycaon and Polydorus—
I cannot find them among the soldiers crowding Troy,
those sons Laothoë[5] bore me, Laothoë queen of women.
But if they are still alive in the enemy's camp,
then we'll ransom them back with bronze and gold.

4. Sirius, the "dog star," in the constellation Canis Major.
5. Priam had more than one wife. Achilles killed Lycaon and Polydorus in the fighting outside the city.

We have hoards inside the walls, the rich dowry
old and famous Altes[6] presented with his daughter.
But if they're dead already, gone to the House of Death,
what grief to their mother's heart and mine—we gave them life.
For the rest of Troy, though, just a moment's grief
unless you too are battered down by Achilles.
Back, come back! Inside the walls, my boy!
Rescue the men of Troy and the Trojan women—
don't hand the great glory to Peleus' son,
bereft of your own sweet life yourself.
Pity me too!—
still in my senses, true, but a harrowed, broken man
marked out by doom—past the threshold of old age . . .
and Father Zeus will waste me with a hideous fate,
and after I've lived to look on so much horror!
My sons laid low, my daughters dragged away
and the treasure-chambers looted, helpless babies
hurled to the earth in the red barbarity of war . . .
my sons' wives hauled off by the Argives' bloody hands!
And I, I last of all—the dogs before my doors
will eat me raw, once some enemy brings me down
with his sharp bronze sword or spits me with a spear,
wrenching the life out of my body, yes, the very dogs
I bred in my own halls to share my table, guard my gates—
mad, rabid at heart they'll lap their master's blood
and loll before my doors.
Ah for a young man
all looks fine and noble if he goes down in war,
hacked to pieces under a slashing bronze blade—
he lies there dead . . . but whatever death lays bare,
all wounds are marks of glory. When an old man's killed
and the dogs go at the gray head and the gray beard
and mutilate the genitals—that is the cruelest sight
in all our wretched lives!"
So the old man groaned
and seizing his gray hair tore it out by the roots
but he could not shake the fixed resolve of Hector.
And his mother wailed now, standing beside Priam,
weeping freely, loosing her robes with one hand
and holding out her bare breast with the other,
her words pouring forth in a flight of grief and tears:
"Hector, my child! Look—have some respect for *this!*
Pity your mother too, if I ever gave you the breast
to soothe your troubles, remember it now, dear boy—
beat back that savage man from safe inside the walls!
Don't go forth, a champion pitted against him—
merciless, brutal man. If he kills you now,
how can I ever mourn you on your deathbed?—
dear branch in bloom, dear child I brought to birth!—

6. Laothoë's father.

Neither I nor your wife, that warm, generous woman . . .
Now far beyond our reach, now by the Argive ships
the rushing dogs will tear you, bolt your flesh!"

So they wept, the two of them crying out
to their dear son, both pleading time and again
but they could not shake the fixed resolve of Hector.
No, he waited Achilles, coming on, gigantic in power.
As a snake in the hills, guarding his hole, awaits a man—
bloated with poison, deadly hatred seething inside him,
glances flashing fire as he coils round his lair . . .
so Hector, nursing his quenchless fury, gave no ground,
leaning his burnished shield against a jutting wall,
but harried still, he probed his own brave heart:
"No way out. If I slip inside the gates and walls,
Polydamas will be first to heap disgrace on me—
he was the one who urged me to lead our Trojans
back to Ilium just last night, the disastrous night
Achilles rose in arms like a god. But did I give way?
Not at all. And how much better it would have been!
Now my army's ruined, thanks to my own reckless pride,
I would die of shame to face the men of Troy
and the Trojan women trailing their long robes . . .
Someone less of a man than I will say, 'Our Hector—
staking all on his own strength, he destroyed his army!'
So they will mutter. So now, better by far for me
to stand up to Achilles, kill him, come home alive
or die at his hands in glory out before the walls.
But wait—what if I put down my studded shield
and heavy helmet, prop my spear on the rampart
and go forth, just as I am, to meet Achilles,
noble Prince Achilles . . .
why, I could promise to give back Helen, yes,
and all her treasures with her, all those riches
Paris once hauled home to Troy in the hollow ships—
and they were the cause of all our endless fighting—
Yes, yes, return it all to the sons of Atreus now
to haul away, and then, at the same time, divide
the rest with all the Argives, all the city holds,
and then I'd take an oath for the Trojan royal council
that we will hide nothing! Share and share alike the hoards
our handsome citadel stores within its depths and—
Why debate, my friend? Why thrash things out?
I must not go and implore him. He'll show no mercy,
no respect for me, my rights—he'll cut me down
straight off—stripped of defenses like a woman
once I have loosed the armor off my body.
No way to parley with that man—not now—
not from behind some oak or rock to whisper,
like a boy and a young girl, lovers' secrets
a boy and girl might whisper to each other . . .
Better to clash in battle, now, at once—

see which fighter Zeus awards the glory!"
So he wavered,
waiting there, but Achilles was closing on him now
like the god of war, the fighter's helmet flashing,
over his right shoulder shaking the Pelian ash spear,
that terror, and the bronze around his body flared
like a raging fire or the rising, blazing sun.
Hector looked up, saw him, started to tremble,
nerve gone, he could hold his ground no longer,
he left the gates behind and away he fled in fear—
and Achilles went for him, fast, sure of his speed
as the wild mountain hawk, the quickest thing on wings,
launching smoothly, swooping down on a cringing dove
and the dove flits out from under, the hawk screaming
over the quarry, plunging over and over, his fury
driving him down to beak and tear his kill—
so Achilles flew at him, breakneck on in fury
with Hector fleeing along the walls of Troy,
fast as his legs would go. On and on they raced,
passing the lookout point, passing the wild fig tree
tossed by the wind, always out from under the ramparts
down the wagon trail they careered until they reached
the clear running springs where whirling Scamander
rises up from its double wellsprings bubbling strong—
and one runs hot and the steam goes up around it,
drifting thick as if fire burned at its core
but the other even in summer gushes cold
as hail or freezing snow or water chilled to ice . . .
And here, close to the springs, lie washing-pools
scooped out in the hollow rocks and broad and smooth
where the wives of Troy and all their lovely daughters
would wash their glistening robes in the old days,
the days of peace before the sons of Achaea came . . .
Past these they raced, one escaping, one in pursuit
and the one who fled was great but the one pursuing
greater, even greater—their pace mounting in speed
since both men strove, not for a sacrificial beast
or oxhide trophy, prizes runners fight for, no,
they raced for the life of Hector breaker of horses.
Like powerful stallions sweeping round the post for trophies,
galloping full stretch with some fine prize at stake,
a tripod, say, or woman offered up at funeral games
for some brave hero fallen—so the two of them
whirled three times around the city of Priam,
sprinting at top speed while all the gods gazed down,
and the father of men and gods broke forth among them now:
"Unbearable—a man I love, hunted round his own city walls
and right before my eyes. My heart grieves for Hector.
Hector who burned so many oxen in my honor, rich cuts,
now on the rugged crests of Ida,[7] now on Ilium's heights.

7. The great mountain range near Troy.

But now, look, brilliant Achilles courses him round
the city of Priam in all his savage, lethal speed.
Come, you immortals, think this through. Decide.
Either we pluck the man from death and save his life
or strike him down at last, here at Achilles' hands—
for all his fighting heart."
But immortal Athena,
her gray eyes wide, protested strongly: "Father!
Lord of the lightning, king of the black cloud,
what are you saying? A man, a mere mortal,
his doom sealed long ago? You'd set him free
from all the pains of death?
Do as you please—
but none of the deathless gods will ever praise you."

And Zeus who marshals the thunderheads replied,
"Courage, Athena, third-born of the gods, dear child.
Nothing I said was meant in earnest, trust me,
I mean you all the good will in the world. Go.
Do as your own impulse bids you. Hold back no more."

So he launched Athena already poised for action—
down the goddess swept from Olympus' craggy peaks.

And swift Achilles kept on coursing Hector, nonstop
as a hound in the mountains starts a fawn from its lair,
hunting him down the gorges, down the narrow glens
and the fawn goes to ground, hiding deep in brush
but the hound comes racing fast, nosing him out
until he lands his kill. So Hector could never throw
Achilles off his trail, the swift racer Achilles—
time and again he'd make a dash for the Dardan Gates,
trying to rush beneath the rock-built ramparts, hoping
men on the heights might save him, somehow, raining spears
but time and again Achilles would intercept him quickly,
heading him off, forcing him out across the plain
and always sprinting along the city side himself—
endless as in a dream . . .
when a man can't catch another fleeing on ahead
and he can never escape nor his rival overtake him—
so the one could never run the other down in his speed
nor the other spring away. And how could Hector have fled
the fates of death so long? How unless one last time,
one final time Apollo had swept in close beside him,
driving strength in his legs and knees to race the wind?
And brilliant Achilles shook his head at the armies,
never letting them hurl their sharp spears at Hector—
someone might snatch the glory, Achilles come in second.
But once they reached the springs for the fourth time,
then Father Zeus held out his sacred golden scales:
in them he placed two fates of death that lays men low—

one for Achilles, one for Hector breaker of horses—
and gripping the beam mid-haft the Father raised it high
and down went Hector's day of doom, dragging him down
to the strong House of Death—and god Apollo left him.
Athena rushed to Achilles, her bright eyes gleaming,
standing shoulder-to-shoulder, winging orders now:
"At last our hopes run high, my brilliant Achilles—
Father Zeus must love you—
we'll sweep great glory back to Achaea's fleet,
we'll kill this Hector, mad as he is for battle!
No way for him to escape us now, no longer—
not even if Phoebus the distant deadly Archer
goes through torments, pleading for Hector's life,
groveling over and over before our storming Father Zeus.
But you, you hold your ground and catch your breath
while I run Hector down and persuade the man
to fight you face-to-face."
So Athena commanded
and he obeyed, rejoicing at heart—Achilles stopped,
leaning against his ashen spearshaft barbed in bronze.
and Athena left him there, caught up with Hector at once,
and taking the build and vibrant voice of Deiphobus
stood shoulder-to-shoulder with him, winging orders:
"Dear brother, how brutally swift Achilles hunts you—
coursing you round the city of Priam in all his lethal speed!
Come, let us stand our ground together—beat him back."

"Deiphobus!"—Hector, his helmet flashing, called out to her—
"dearest of all my brothers, all these warring years,
of all the sons that Priam and Hecuba produced!
Now I'm determined to praise you all the more,
you who dared—seeing me in these straits—
to venture out from the walls, all for *my* sake,
while the others stay inside and cling to safety."

The goddess answered quickly, her eyes blazing,
"True, dear brother—how your father and mother both
implored me, time and again, clutching my knees,
and the comrades round me begging me to stay!
Such was the fear that broke them, man for man,
but the heart within me broke with grief for you.
Now headlong on the fight! No letup, no lance spared!
So now, now we'll *see* if Achilles kills us both
and hauls our bloody armor back to the beaked ships
or he goes down in pain beneath your spear."

Athena luring him on with all her immortal cunning—
and now, at last, as the two came closing for the kill
it was tall Hector, helmet flashing, who led off:
"No more running from you in fear, Achilles!
Not as before. Three times I fled around

the great city of Priam—I lacked courage then
to stand your onslaught. Now my spirit stirs me
to meet you face-to-face. Now kill or be killed!
Come, we'll swear to the gods, the highest witnesses—
the gods will oversee our binding pacts. I swear
I will never mutilate you—merciless as you are—
if Zeus allows me to last it out and tear your life away.
But once I've stripped your glorious armor, Achilles,
I will give your body back to your loyal comrades.
Swear you'll do the same."
A swift dark glance
and the headstrong runner answered, "Hector, stop!
You unforgivable, you . . . don't talk to me of pacts.
There are no binding oaths between men and lions—
wolves and lambs can enjoy no meeting of the minds—
they are all bent on hating each other to the death.
So with you and me. No love between us. No truce
till one or the other falls and gluts with blood
Ares who hacks at men behind his rawhide shield.
Come, call up whatever courage you can muster.
Life or death—now prove yourself a spearman,
a daring man of war! No more escape for you—
Athena will kill you with my spear in just a moment.
Now you'll pay at a stroke for all my comrades' grief,
all you killed in the fury of your spear!"
With that,
shaft poised, he hurled and his spear's long shadow flew
but seeing it coming glorious Hector ducked away,
crouching down, watching the bronze tip fly past
and stab the earth—but Athena snatched it up
and passed it back to Achilles
and Hector the gallant captain never saw her.
He sounded out a challenge to Peleus' princely son:
"You missed, look—the great godlike Achilles!
So you knew nothing at all from Zeus about my death—
and yet how sure you were! All bluff, cunning with words,
that's all you are—trying to make me fear you,
lose my nerve, forget my fighting strength.
Well, you'll never plant your lance in my back
as I flee *you* in fear—plunge it through my chest
as I come charging in, if a god gives you the chance!
but now it's for you to dodge *my* brazen spear—
I wish you'd bury it in your body to the hilt.
How much lighter the war would be for Trojans then
if you, their greatest scourge, were dead and gone!"

Shaft poised, he hurled and his spear's long shadow flew
and it struck Achilles' shield—a dead-center hit—
but off and away it glanced and Hector seethed,
his hurtling spear, his whole arm's power poured
in a wasted shot. He stood there, cast down . . .

he had no spear in reserve. So Hector shouted out
to Deiphobus bearing his white shield—with a ringing shout
he called for a heavy lance—
but the man was nowhere near him,
vanished—
yes and Hector knew the truth in his heart
and the fighter cried aloud, "My time has come!
At last the gods have called me down to death.
I thought he was at my side, the hero Deiphobus—
he's safe inside the walls, Athena's tricked me blind.
And now death, grim death is looming up beside me,
no longer far away. No way to escape it now. This,
this was their pleasure after all, sealed long ago—
Zeus and the son of Zeus, the distant deadly Archer—
though often before now they rushed to my defense.
So now I meet my doom. Well let me die—
but not without struggle, not without glory, no,
in some great clash of arms that even men to come
will hear of down the years!"
And on that resolve
he drew the whetted sword that hung at his side,
tempered, massive, and gathering all his force
he swooped like a soaring eagle
launching down from the dark clouds to earth
to snatch some helpless lamb or trembling hare.
So Hector swooped now, swinging his whetted sword
and Achilles charged too, bursting with rage, barbaric,
guarding his chest with the well-wrought blazoned shield,
head tossing his gleaming helmet, four horns strong
and the golden plumes shook that the god of fire
drove in bristling thick along its ridge.
Bright as that star amid the stars in the night sky,
star of the evening, brightest star that rides the heavens,
so fire flared from the sharp point of the spear Achilles
brandished high in his right hand, bent on Hector's death,
scanning his splendid body—where to pierce it best?
The rest of his flesh seemed all encased in armor,
burnished, brazen—*Achilles'* armor that Hector stripped
from strong Patroclus when he killed him—true,
but one spot lay exposed,
where collarbones lift the neckbone off the shoulders,
the open throat, where the end of life comes quickest—*there*
as Hector charged in fury brilliant Achilles drove his spear
and the point went stabbing clean through the tender neck
but the heavy bronze weapon failed to slash the windpipe—
Hector could still gasp out some words, some last reply . . .
he crashed in the dust—
godlike Achilles gloried over him:
"Hector—surely you thought when you stripped Patroclus' armor
that you, you would be safe! Never a fear of me—
far from the fighting as I was—you fool!
Left behind there, down by the beaked ships

his great avenger waited, a greater man by far—
that man was I, and I smashed your strength! And you—
the dogs and birds will maul you, shame your corpse
while Achaeans bury my dear friend in glory!"

Struggling for breath, Hector, his helmet flashing,
said, "I beg you, beg you for your life, your parents—
don't let the dogs devour me by the Argive ships!
Wait, take the princely ransom of bronze and gold,
the gifts my father and noble mother will give you—
but give my body to friends to carry home again,
so Trojan men and Trojan women can do me honor
with fitting rites of fire once I am dead."

Staring grimly, the proud runner Achilles answered,
"Beg no more, you fawning dog—begging me by my parents!
Would to god my rage, my fury would drive me now
to hack your flesh away and eat you raw—
such agonies you have caused me! Ransom?
No man alive could keep the dog-packs off you,
not if they haul in ten, twenty times that ransom
and pile it here before me and promise fortunes more—
no, not even if Dardan Priam should offer to weigh out
your bulk in gold! Not even then will your noble mother
lay you on your deathbed, mourn the son she bore . . .
The dogs and birds will rend you—blood and bone!"

At the point of death, Hector, his helmet flashing,
said, "I know you well—I see my fate before me.
Never a chance that I could win you over . . .
Iron inside your chest, that heart of yours.
But now beware, or my curse will draw god's wrath
upon your head, that day when Paris and lord Apollo—
for all your fighting heart—destroy you at the Scaean Gates!"

Death cut him short. The end closed in around him.
Flying free of his limbs
his soul went winging down to the House of Death,
wailing his fate, leaving his manhood far behind,
his young and supple strength. But brilliant Achilles
taunted Hector's body, dead as he was, "Die, die!
For my own death, I'll meet it freely—whenever Zeus
and the other deathless gods would like to bring it on!"

With that he wrenched his bronze spear from the corpse,
laid it aside and ripped the bloody armor off the back.
And the other sons of Achaea, running up around him,
crowded closer, all of them gazing wonder-struck
at the build and marvelous, lithe beauty of Hector.
And not a man came forward who did not stab his body,
glancing toward a comrade, laughing: "Ah, look here—

how much softer he is to handle now, this Hector,
than when he gutted our ships with roaring fire!"

Standing over him, so they'd gloat and stab his body.
But once he had stripped the corpse the proud runner Achilles
took his stand in the midst of all the Argive troops
and urged them on with a flight of winging orders:
"Friends—lords of the Argives, O my captains!
Now that the gods have let me kill this man
who caused us agonies, loss on crushing loss—
more than the rest of all their men combined—
come, let us ring their walls in armor, test them,
see what recourse the Trojans still may have in mind.
Will they abandon the city heights with this man fallen?
Or brace for a last, dying stand though Hector's gone?
But wait—what am I saying? Why this deep debate?
Down by the ships a body lies unwept, unburied—
Patroclus . . . I will never forget him,
not as long as I'm still among the living
and my springing knees will lift and drive me on.
Though the dead forget their dead in the House of Death,
I will remember, even there, my dear companion.
Now,
come, you sons of Achaea, raise a song of triumph!
Down to the ships we march and bear this corpse on high—
we have won ourselves great glory. We have brought
magnificent Hector down, that man the Trojans
glorified in their city like a god!"
So he triumphed
and now he was bent on outrage, on shaming noble Hector.
Piercing the tendons, ankle to heel behind both feet,
he knotted straps of rawhide through them both,
lashed them to his chariot, left the head to drag
and mounting the car, hoisting the famous arms aboard,
he whipped his team to a run and breakneck on they flew,
holding nothing back. And a thick cloud of dust rose up
from the man they dragged, his dark hair swirling round
that head so handsome once, all tumbled low in the dust—
since Zeus had given him over to his enemies now
to be defiled in the land of his own fathers.

So his whole head was dragged down in the dust.
And now his mother began to tear her hair . . .
she flung her shining veil to the ground and raised
a high, shattering scream, looking down at her son.
Pitifully his loving father groaned and round the king
his people cried with grief and wailing seized the city—
for all the world as if all Troy were torched and smoldering
down from the looming brows of the citadel to her roots.
Priam's people could hardly hold the old man back,
frantic, mad to go rushing out the Dardan Gates.
He begged them all, groveling in the filth,

crying out to them, calling each man by name,
"Let go, my friends! Much as you care for me,
let me hurry out of the city, make my way,
all on my own, to Achaea's waiting ships!
I must implore that terrible, violent man . . .
Perhaps—who knows?—he may respect my age,
may pity an old man. He has a father too,
as old as I am—Peleus sired him once,
Peleus reared him to be the scourge of Troy
but most of all to me—he made my life a hell.
So many sons he slaughtered, just coming into bloom . . .
but grieving for all the rest, one breaks my heart the most
and stabbing grief for him will take me down to Death—
my Hector—would to god he had perished in my arms!
Then his mother who bore him—oh so doomed,
she and I could glut ourselves with grief."

So the voice of the king rang out in tears,
the citizens wailed in answer, and noble Hecuba
led the wives of Troy in a throbbing chant of sorrow:
"O my child—my desolation! How can I go on living?
What agonies must I suffer now, now *you* are dead and gone?
You were my pride throughout the city night and day—
a blessing to us all, the men and women of Troy;
throughout the city they saluted you like a god.
You, you were their greatest glory while you lived—
now death and fate have seized you, dragged you down!"

Her voice rang out in tears, but the wife of Hector
had not heard a thing. No messenger brought the truth
of how her husband made his stand outside the gates.
She was weaving at her loom, deep in the high halls,
working flowered braiding into a dark red folding robe.
And she called her well-kempt women through the house
to set a large three-legged cauldron over the fire
so Hector could have his steaming hot bath
when he came home from battle—poor woman,
she never dreamed how far he was from bathing,
struck down at Achilles' hands by blazing-eyed Athena.
But she heard the groans and wails of grief from the rampart now
and her body shook, her shuttle dropped to the ground,
she called out to her lovely waiting women, "Quickly—
two of you follow me—I must see what's happened.
that cry—that was Hector's honored mother I heard!
My heart's pounding, leaping up in my throat,
the knees beneath me paralyzed—Oh I know it . . .
something terrible's coming down on Priam's children.
Pray god the news will never reach my ears!
Yes but I dread it so—what if great Achilles
has cut my Hector off from the city, daring Hector,
and driven him out across the plain, and all alone?—
He may have put an end to that fatal headstrong pride

that always seized my Hector—never hanging back
with the main force of men, always charging ahead,
giving ground to no man in his fury!"
So she cried,
dashing out of the royal halls like a madwoman,
her heart racing hard, her women close behind her.
But once she reached the tower where soldiers massed
she stopped on the rampart, looked down and saw it all—
saw him dragged before the city, stallions galloping,
dragging Hector back to Achaea's beaked warships—
ruthless work. The world went black as night
before her eyes, she fainted, falling backward,
gasping away her life breath . . .
She flung to the winds her glittering headdress,
the cap and the coronet, braided band and veil,
all the regalia golden Aphrodite gave her once,
the day that Hector, helmet aflash in sunlight,
led her home to Troy from her father's house
with countless wedding gifts to win her heart.
But crowding round her now her husband's sisters
and brothers' wives supported her in their midst,
and she, terrified, stunned to the point of death,
struggling for breath now and coming back to life,
burst out in grief among the Trojan women: "O Hector—
I am destroyed! Both born to the same fate after all!
You, you at Troy in the halls of King Priam—
I at Thebes, under the timberline of Placos,
Eetion's house . . . He raised me as a child,
that man of doom, his daughter just as doomed—
would to god he'd never fathered *me!*
Now you go down
to the House of Death, the dark depths of the earth,
and leave me here to waste away in grief, a widow
lost in the royal halls—and the boy only a baby,
the son we bore together, you and I so doomed.
Hector, what help are you to him, now you are dead?—
what help is he to you? Think, even if he escapes
the wrenching horrors of war against the Argives,
pain and labor will plague him all his days to come.
Strangers will mark his lands off, stealing his estates.
The day that orphans a youngster cuts him off from friends.
And he hangs his head low, humiliated in every way . . .
his cheeks stained with tears, and pressed by hunger
the boy goes up to his father's old companions,
tugging at one man's cloak, another's tunic,
and some will pity him, true,
and one will give him a little cup to drink,
enough to wet his lips, not quench his thirst.
But then some bully with both his parents living
beats him from the banquet, fists and abuses flying:
'You, get out—you've got no father feasting with us here!'
And the boy, sobbing, trails home to his widowed mother . . .

Astyanax!
                    And years ago, propped on his father's knee,
he would only eat the marrow, the richest cuts of lamb,
and when sleep came on him and he had quit his play,
cradled warm in his nurse's arms he'd drowse off,
snug in a soft bed, his heart brimmed with joy.
Now what suffering, now he's lost his father—
                                                            Astyanax!
The Lord of the City, so the Trojans called him,
because it was you, Hector, you and you alone
who shielded the gates and the long walls of Troy.
But now by the beaked ships, far from your parents,
glistening worms will wriggle through your flesh,
once the dogs have had their fill of your naked corpse—
though we have such stores of clothing laid up in the halls,
fine things, a joy to the eye, the work of women's hands.
Now, by god, I'll burn them all, blazing to the skies!
No use to you now, they'll never shroud your body—
but they will be your glory
burned by the Trojan men and women in your honor!"

Her voice rang out in tears and the women wailed in answer.

Summary Achilles buried Patroclus, and the Greeks celebrated the dead hero's fame with athletic games, for which Achilles gave the prizes.

BOOK XXIV

[*Achilles and Priam*]

The games were over now. The gathered armies scattered,
each man to his fast ship, and fighters turned their minds
to thoughts of food and the sweet warm grip of sleep.
But Achilles kept on grieving for his friend,
the memory burning on . . .
and all-subduing sleep could not take him,
not now, he turned and twisted, side to side,
he longed for Patroclus' manhood, his gallant heart—
What rough campaigns they'd fought to an end together,
what hardships they had suffered, cleaving their way
through wars of men and pounding waves at sea.
The memories flooded over him, live tears flowing,
and now he'd lie on his side, now flat on his back,
now facedown again. At last he'd leap to his feet,
wander in anguish, aimless along the surf, and dawn on dawn
flaming over the sea and shore would find him pacing.
Then he'd yoke his racing team to the chariot-harness,
lash the corpse of Hector behind the car for dragging
and haul him three times round the dead Patroclus' tomb,
and then he'd rest again in his tents and leave the body
sprawled facedown in the dust. But Apollo pitied Hector—
dead man though he was—and warded all corruption off
from Hector's corpse and round him, head to foot,

the great god wrapped the golden shield of storm
so his skin would never rip as Achilles dragged him on.

And so he kept on raging, shaming noble Hector,
but the gods in bliss looked down and pitied Priam's son.
They kept on urging the sharp-eyed giant-killer Hermes
to go and steal the body, a plan that pleased them all,
but not Hera, Poseidon or the girl with blazing eyes.[8]
They clung to their deathless hate of sacred Troy,
Priam and Priam's people, just as they had at first
when Paris in all his madness launched the war.
He offended Athena and Hera—both goddesses.
When they came to his shepherd's fold he favored Love
who dangled before his eyes the lust that loosed disaster.[9]
But now, at the twelfth dawn since Hector's death,
lord Apollo rose and addressed the immortal powers:
"Hard-hearted you are, you gods, you live for cruelty!
Did Hector never burn in your honor thighs of oxen
and flawless, full-grown goats? Now you cannot
bring yourselves to save him—even his corpse—
so his wife can see him, his mother and his child,
his father Priam and Priam's people: how they'd rush
to burn the body on the pyre and give him royal rites!
But murderous Achilles—you gods, you *choose* to help Achilles.
That man without a shred of decency in his heart . . .
his temper can never bend and change—like some lion
going his own barbaric way, giving in to his power,
his brute force and wild pride, as down he swoops
on the flocks of men to seize his savage feast.
Achilles has lost all pity! No shame in the man,
shame that does great harm or drives men on to good.
No doubt some mortal has suffered a dearer loss than this,
a brother born in the same womb, or even a son . . .
he grieves, he weeps, but then his tears are through.
The Fates have given mortals hearts that can endure.
But this Achilles—first he slaughters Hector,
he rips away the noble prince's life
then lashes him to his chariot, drags him round
his beloved comrade's tomb. But why, I ask you?
What good will it do him? What honor will he gain?
Let that man beware, or great and glorious as he is,
we mighty gods will wheel on him in anger—look,
he outrages the senseless clay in all his fury!"

But white-armed Hera flared at him in anger:
"Yes, there'd be some merit even in what *you* say,
lord of the silver bow—if all you gods, in fact,
would set Achilles and Hector high in equal honor.
But Hector is mortal. He sucked a woman's breast.

8. Athena. 9. Paris had been appointed judge in a contest of beauty between Aphrodite, Hera, and Athena. All three goddesses offered bribes, but Aphrodite's promise to give him Helen proved the most attractive.

Achilles sprang from a goddess—one I reared myself:
I brought her up and gave her in marriage to a man,
to Peleus, dearest to all your hearts, you gods.
All you Gods, you shared in the wedding rites,
and so did you, Apollo—there you sat at the feast
and struck your lyre. What company you keep now,
these wretched Trojans. You—forever faithless!"

But Zeus who marshals the storm clouds warned his queen,
"Now, Hera, don't fly into such a rage at fellow gods.
These two can never attain the same degree of honor.
Still, the immortals loved Prince Hector dearly,
best of all the mortals born in Troy . . .
so *I* loved him, at least:
he never stinted with gifts to please my heart.
Never once did my altar lack its share of victims,
winecups tipped and the deep smoky savor. These,
these are the gifts we claim—they are our rights.
But as for stealing courageous Hector's body,
we must abandon the idea—not a chance in the world
behind Achilles' back. For Thetis is always there,
his mother always hovering near him night and day.
Now would one of you gods call Thetis to my presence?—
so I can declare to her my solemn, sound decree:
Achilles must receive a ransom from King Priam,
Achilles must give Hector's body back."
So he decreed
and Iris, racing a gale-wind down with Zeus's message,
mid-sea between Samos and Imbros'[1] rugged cliffs
dove in a black swell as groaning breakers roared.
Down she plunged to the bottom fast as a lead weight
sheathed in a glinting lure of wild bull's horn,[2]
bearing hooked death to the ravenous fish.
And deep in a hollow cave she came on Thetis.
Gathered round her sat the other immortal sea-nymphs
while Thetis amidst them mourned her brave son's fate,
doomed to die, she knew, on the fertile soil of Troy,
far from his native land. Quick as the wind now
Iris rushed to the goddess, urging, "Rise, Thetis—
Zeus with his everlasting counsels calls you now!"
Shifting on her glistening feet, the goddess answered,
"Why . . . what does the great god want with me?
I cringe from mingling with the immortals now—
Oh the torment—never-ending heartbreak!
But go I shall. A high decree of the Father
must not come to nothing—whatever he commands."

The radiant queen of sea-nymphs seized a veil,
blue-black, no robe darker in all the Ocean's depths,

1. Two islands in the North Aegean. 2. A lure for big fish.

and launched up and away with wind-swift Iris leading—
the ground swell round them cleaved and opened wide.
And striding out on shore they soared to the high sky
and found farseeing Zeus, and around him all the gods
who live in bliss forever sat in a grand assembly.
And Thetis took a seat beside the Father,
a throne Athena yielded. Hera placed in her hand
a burnished golden cup and said some words of comfort,
and taking a few quick sips, Thetis gave it back . . .
The father of men and gods began to address them:
"You have come to Olympus now, immortal Thetis,
for all your grief—what unforgettable sorrow
seizes on your heart. I know it well myself.
Even so, I must tell you why I called you here.
For nine whole days the immortals have been feuding
over Hector's corpse and Achilles, scourge of cities.
They keep urging the sharp-eyed giant-killer Hermes
to go and steal the body. But that is not my way.
I will grant Achilles glory and so safeguard
your awe and love of me for all the years to come.
Go at once to the camp, give your son this order:
tell him the gods are angry with him now
and I am rising over them all in deathless wrath
that he in heartsick fury still holds Hector's body,
there by his beaked ships, and will not give him back—
perhaps in fear of me he'll give him back at once.
Then, at the same time, I am winging Iris down
to greathearted Priam, commanding the king
to ransom his dear son, to go to Achaea's ships,
bearing gifts to Achilles, gifts to melt his rage."
So he decreed
and Thetis with her glistening feet did not resist a moment.
Down the goddess flashed from the peaks of Mount Olympus,
made her way to her son's camp, and there he was,
she found him groaning hard, choked with sobs.
Around him trusted comrades swung to the work,
preparing breakfast, steadying in their midst
a large fleecy sheep just slaughtered in the shelter.
But his noble mother, settling down at his side,
stroked Achilles gently, whispering his name: "My child—
how long will you eat your heart out here in tears and torment?
All wiped from your mind, all thought of food and bed?
It's a welcome thing to make love with a woman . . .
You don't have long to live now, well I know:
already I see them looming up beside you—death
and the strong force of fate. Listen to me,
quickly! I bring you a message sent by Zeus:
he says the gods are angry with you now
and he is rising over them all in deathless wrath
that you in heartsick fury still hold Hector's body,
here by your beaked ships, and will not give him back.
O give him back at once—take ransom for the dead!"

The swift runner replied in haste, "So be it.
The man who brings the ransom can take away the body,
if Olympian Zeus himself insists in all earnest."

While mother and son agreed among the clustered ships,
trading between each other many winged words,
Father Zeus sped Iris down to sacred Troy:
"Quick on your way now, Iris, shear the wind!
Leave our Olympian stronghold—
take a message to greathearted Priam down in Troy:
he must go to Achaea's ships and ransom his dear son,
bearing gifts to Achilles, gifts to melt his rage.
But let him go alone, no other Trojan attend him,
only a herald with him, a seasoned, older one
who can drive the mules and smooth-running wagon
and bring the hero's body back to sacred Troy,
the man that brilliant Achilles killed in battle.
Let him have no fear of death, no dread in his heart,
such a powerful escort we will send him—the giant-killer
Hermes will guide him all the way to Achilles' presence.
And once the god has led him within the fighter's shelter,
Achilles will not kill him—he'll hold back all the rest:
Achilles is no madman, no reckless fool, not the one
to defy the gods' commands. Whoever begs his mercy
he will spare with all the kindness in his heart."
So he decreed
and Iris ran his message, racing with gale force
to Priam's halls where cries and mourning met her.
Sons huddled round their father deep in the courtyard,
robes drenched with tears, and the old man amidst them,
buried, beaten down in the cloak that wrapped his body . . .
Smeared on the old man's head and neck the dung lay thick
that he scraped up in his own hands, groveling in the filth.
Throughout the house his daughters and sons' wives wailed,
remembering all the fine brave men who lay dead now,
their lives destroyed at the fighting Argives' hands.
And Iris, Zeus's crier, standing alongside Priam,
spoke in a soft voice, but his limbs shook at once—
"Courage, Dardan Priam, take heart! Nothing to fear.
No herald of doom, I come on a friendly mission—
I come with all good will.
I bring you a message sent by Zeus, a world away
but he has you in his heart, he pities you now . . .
Olympian Zeus commands you to ransom royal Hector,
to bear gifts to Achilles, gifts to melt his rage.
But you must go alone, no other Trojan attend you,
only a herald with you, a seasoned, older one
who can drive the mules and smooth-running wagon
and bring the hero's body back to sacred Troy,
the man that brilliant Achilles killed in battle.
But have no fear of death, no dread in your heart,
such a powerful escort will conduct you—the giant-killer

Hermes will guide you all the way to Achilles' presence.
And once the god has led you within the fighter's shelter,
Achilles will not kill you—he'll hold back all the rest:
Achilles is no madman, no reckless fool, not the one
to defy the gods' commands. Whoever begs his mercy
he will spare with all the kindness in his heart!"

And Iris racing the wind went veering off
and Priam ordered his sons to get a wagon ready,
a good smooth-running one, to hitch the mules
and strap a big wicker cradle across its frame.
Then down he went himself to his treasure-chamber,
high-ceilinged, paneled, fragrant with cedarwood
and a wealth of precious objects filled its chests.
He called out to his wife, Hecuba, "Dear woman!
An Olympian messenger came to me from Zeus—
I must go to Achaea's ships and ransom our dear son,
bearing gifts to Achilles, gifts to melt his rage.
Tell me, what should I do? What do *you* think?
Myself—a terrible longing drives me, heart and soul,
down to the ships, into the vast Achaean camp."

But his wife cried out in answer, "No, no—
where have your senses gone?—that made you famous once,
both among outland men and those you rule in Troy!
How can you think of going down to the ships, alone,
and face the glance of the man who killed your sons,
so many fine brave boys? You have a heart of iron!
If he gets you in his clutches, sets his eyes on you—
that savage, treacherous man—he'll show no mercy,
no respect for your rights!
Come, all we can do now
is sit in the halls, far from our son, and wail for Hector . . .
So this, this is the doom that strong Fate spun out,
our son's life line drawn with his first breath—
the moment I gave him birth—
to glut the wild dogs, cut off from his parents,
crushed by the stronger man. Oh would to god
that I could sink my teeth in his liver, eat him raw!
That would avenge what he has done to Hector—
no coward the man Achilles killed—my son stood
and fought for the men of Troy and their deep-breasted wives
with never a thought of flight or run for cover!"

But the old and noble Priam answered firmly,
"I will go. My mind's made up. Don't hold me back.
And don't go flying off on your own across the halls,
a bird of evil omen—you can't dissuade me now.
If someone else had commanded me, some mortal man,
some prophet staring into the smoke, some priest,
I'd call it a lie and turn my back upon it.
Not now. I heard her voice with my own ears,

I looked straight at the goddess, face-to-face.
So I am going—her message must not come to nothing.
And if it is my fate to die by the beaked ships
of Achaeans armed in bronze, then die I shall.
Let Achilles cut me down straightway—
once I've caught my son in my arms and wept my fill!"

He raised back the carved lids of the chests
and lifted out twelve robes, handsome, rich brocades,
twelve cloaks, unlined and light, as many blankets,
as many big white capes and shirts to go with them.
He weighed and carried out ten full bars of gold
and took two burnished tripods, four fine cauldrons
and last a magnificent cup the Thracians gave him once—
he'd gone on an embassy and won that priceless treasure—
but not even *that* did the old man spare in his halls,
not now, consumed with desire to ransom back his son.
Crowds of Trojans were mobbing his colonnades—
he gave them a tongue-lashing, sent them packing:
"Get out—you good-for-nothings, public disgraces!
Haven't you got enough to wail about at home
without coming here to add to all my griefs?
You think it nothing, the pain that Zeus has sent me?—
he's destroyed my best son! You'll learn too, in tears—
easier game you'll be for Argive troops to slaughter,
now my Hector's dead. But before I have to see
my city annihilated, laid waste before my eyes—
oh let me go down to the House of Death!"

He herded them off with his staff—they fled outside
before the old man's fury. So he lashed out at his sons,
cursing the sight of Helenus, Paris, noble Agathon,
Pammon, Antiphonus, Polites loud with the war cry,
Deiphobus and Hippothous, even lordly Dius—
the old man shouted at all nine, rough commands:
"Get to your work! My vicious sons—my humiliations!
If only you'd all been killed at the fast ships
instead of my dear Hector . . .
But I—dear god, my life so cursed by fate!—
I fathered hero sons in the wide realm of Troy
and now, now not a single one is left, I tell you.
Mestor the indestructible, Troilus, passionate horseman
and Hector, a god among men—no son of a mortal man,
he seemed a deathless god's. But Ares killed them all
and all he left me are these, these disgraces—liars,
dancers, heroes only at beating the dancing-rings,
you plunder your own people for lambs and kids!
Why don't you get my wagon ready—now, at once?
Pack all these things aboard! We must be on our way!"

Terrified by their father's rough commands
the sons trundled a mule-wagon out at once,

a good smooth-running one,
newly finished, balanced and bolted tight,
and strapped a big wicker cradle across its frame.
They lifted off its hook a boxwood yoke for the mules,
its bulging pommel fitted with rings for guide-reins,
brought out with the yoke its yoke-strap nine arms long
and wedged the yoke down firm on the sanded, tapered pole,
on the front peg, and slipped the yoke-ring onto its pin,
strapped the pommel with three good twists, both sides,
then lashed the assembly round and down the shaft
and under the clamp they made the lashing fast.
Then the priceless ransom for Hector's body:
hauling it up from the vaults they piled it high
on the wagon's well-made cradle, then they yoked the mules—
stamping their sharp hoofs, trained for heavy loads—
that the Mysians[3] once gave Priam, princely gifts.
And last they yoked his team to the king's chariot,
stallions he bred himself in his own polished stalls.

No sooner were both men harnessed up beneath the roofs,
Priam and herald, minds set on the coming journey,
than Hecuba rushed up to them, gaunt with grief,
holding a gold cup of mellow wine in her right hand
so the men might pour libations before they left.
She stood in front of the horses, crying up at Priam,
"Here, quickly—pour a libation out to Father Zeus!
Pray for a safe return from all our mortal enemies,
seeing you're dead set on going down to the ships—
though you go against my will. But if go you must,
pray, at least, to the great god of the dark storm cloud,
up there on Ida, gazing down on the whole expanse of Troy!
Pray for a bird of omen, Zeus's wind-swift messenger,
the dearest bird in the world to his prophetic heart,
the strongest thing on wings—clear on the right
so you can see that sign with your own eyes
and trust your life to *it* as you venture down
to Achaea's ships and the fast chariot-teams.
But if farseeing Zeus does *not* send you that sign—
his own messenger—then I urge you, beg you,
don't go down to the ships—
not for all the passion in your heart!"

The old majestic Priam gave his answer:
"Dear woman, surely I won't resist your urging now.
It's well to lift our hands and ask great Zeus for mercy."

And the old king motioned a steward standing by
to pour some clear pure water over his hands,
and she came forward, bearing a jug and basin.
He rinsed his hands, took the cup from his wife

3. A people of central Asia Minor.

and taking a stand amidst the forecourt, prayed,
pouring the wine to earth and scanning the high skies,
Priam prayed in his rich resounding voice: "Father Zeus!
Ruling over us all from Ida, god of greatness, god of glory!
Grant that Achilles will receive me with kindness, mercy.
Send me a bird of omen, your own wind-swift messenger,
the dearest bird in the world to your prophetic heart,
the strongest thing on wings—clear on the right
so I can see that sign with my own eyes
and trust my life to *it* as I venture down
to Achaea's ships and the fast chariot-teams!"

And Zeus in all his wisdom heard that prayer
and straightaway the Father launched an eagle—
truest of Zeus's signs that fly the skies—
the dark marauder that mankind calls the Black-wing.
Broad as the door of a rich man's vaulted treasure-chamber,
well-fitted with sturdy bars, so broad each wing of the bird
spread out on either side as it swept in through the city
flashing clear on the right before the king and queen.
All looked up, overjoyed—the people's spirits lifted.

And the old man, rushing to climb aboard his chariot,
drove out through the gates and echoing colonnades.
The mules in the lead hauled out the four-wheeled wagon,
driven on by seasoned Idaeus. The horses came behind
as the old man cracked the lash and urged them fast
throughout the city with all his kinsmen trailing . . .
weeping their hearts out, as if he went to his death.
But once the two passed down through crowded streets
and out into open country, Priam's kin turned back,
his sons and in-laws straggling home to Troy.
But Zeus who beholds the world could hardly fail
to see the two men striking out across the plain.
As he watched the old man he filled with pity
and quickly summoned Hermes, his own dear son:
"Hermes—escorting men is your greatest joy,
you above all the gods,
and you listen to the wish of those you favor.
So down you go. Down and conduct King Priam there
through Achaea's beaked ships, so none will see him,
none of the Argive fighters recognize him now,
not till he reaches Peleus' royal son."
So he decreed
and Hermes the giant-killing guide obeyed at once.
Under his feet he strapped the supple sandals,
never-dying gold, that wing him over the waves
and boundless earth with the speed of gusting winds.
He seized the wand that enchants the eyes of men
whenever Hermes wants, or wakes them up from sleep.
That wand in his grip he flew, the mighty giant-killer
touching down on Troy and the Hellespont in no time

and from there he went on foot, for all the world
like a young prince, sporting his first beard,
just in the prime and fresh warm pride of youth.
And now,
as soon as the two drove past the great tomb of Ilus[4]
they drew rein at the ford to water mules and team.
A sudden darkness had swept across the earth
and Hermes was all but on them when the herald
looked up, saw him, shouted at once to Priam,
"Danger, my king—think fast! I see a man—
I'm afraid we'll both be butchered on the spot—
into the chariot, hurry! Run for our lives
or fling ourselves at his knees and beg for mercy!"

The old man was stunned, in a swirl of terror,
the hairs stood bristling all over his gnarled body—
he stood there, staring dumbly. Not waiting for welcome
the running god of luck went straight up to Priam,
clasped the old king's hands and asked him warmly,
"Father—where do you drive these mules and team
through the godsent night while other mortals sleep?
Have you no fear of the Argives breathing hate and fury?
Here are your deadly enemies, camping close at hand.
Now what if one of them saw you, rolling blithely
on through the rushing night with so much tempting treasure—
how would you feel then? You're not so young yourself,
and the man who attends you here is far too old
to drive off an attacker spoiling for a fight.
But I would never hurt you—and what's more,
I'd beat off any man who'd do you harm:
you remind me of my dear father, to the life."

And the old and noble Priam said at once,
"Our straits are hard, dear child, as you say.
But a god still holds his hands above me, even me.
Sending such a traveler here to meet me—
what a lucky omen! Look at your build . . .
your handsome face—a wonder. And such good sense—
your parents must be blissful as the gods!"

The guide and giant-killer answered quickly,
"You're right, old man, all straight to the mark.
But come, tell me the truth now, point by point:
this treasure—a king's ransom—do you send it off
to distant, outland men, to keep it safe for you?
Or now do you all abandon sacred Troy,
all in panic—such was the man who died,
your finest, bravest man . . . your own son
who never failed in a fight against the Argives."

4. Priam's grandfather. The tomb was a landmark on the Trojan plain.

But the old majestic Priam countered quickly,
"Who are *you*, my fine friend?—who are your parents?
How can you speak so well of my doomed son's fate?"

And the guide and giant-killer answered staunchly,
"You're testing me, old man—asking of noble Hector.
Ah, how often I watched him battling on the lines
where men win glory, saw the man with my own eyes!
And saw him drive Achaeans against the ships that day
he kept on killing, cutting them down with slashing bronze
while we stood by and marveled—Achilles reined us in:
no fighting for us while he raged on at Agamemnon.
I am Achilles' aide, you see,
one and the same good warship brought us here.
I am a Myrmidon, and my father is Polyctor,
and a wealthy man he is, about as old as you . . .
He has six sons—I'm the seventh—we all shook lots
and it fell to me to join the armies here at Troy.
I've just come up from the ships to scout the plain—
at dawn the fiery-eyed Achaeans fight around the city.
They chafe, sitting in camp, so bent on battle now
the kings of Achaea cannot hold them back."

And the old and noble Priam asked at once,
"If you really are the royal Achilles' aide,
please, tell *me* the whole truth, point by point.
My son—does he still lie by the beached ships,
or by now has the great Achilles hacked him
limb from limb and served him to his dogs?"

The guide and giant-killer reassured him:
"So far, old man, no birds or dogs have eaten him.
No, there he lies—still there at Achilles' ship,
still intact in his shelters.
This is the twelfth day he's lain there, too,
but his body has not decayed, not in the least,
nor have the worms begun to gnaw his corpse,
the swarms that devour men who fall in battle.
True, dawn on fiery dawn he drags him round
his beloved comrade's tomb, drags him ruthlessly
but he cannot mutilate his body. It's marvelous—
go see for yourself how he lies there fresh as dew,
the blood washed away, and no sign of corruption.
All his wounds sealed shut, wherever they struck . . .
and many drove their bronze blades through his body.
Such pains the blissful gods are lavishing on your son,
dead man though he is—the gods love him dearly!"

And the old man rejoiced at that, bursting out,
"O my child, how good it is to give the immortals
fit and proper gifts! Now take my son—

or was he all a dream? Never once in his halls
did he forget the gods who hold Olympus, never,
so now they remember *him* . . . if only after death.
Come, this handsome cup: accept it from me, I beg you!
Protect me, escort me now—if the gods will it so—
all the way till I reach Achilles' shelter."

The guide and giant-killer refused him firmly,
"You test me again, old man, since I am young,
but you will not persuade me,
tempting me with a gift behind Achilles' back.
I fear the man, I'd die of shame to rob him—
just think of the trouble I might suffer later.
But I'd escort you with all the kindness in my heart,
all the way till I reached the shining hills of Argos
bound in a scudding ship or pacing you on foot—
and no marauder on earth, scorning your escort,
would dare attack you then."
And the god of luck,
leaping onto the chariot right behind the team,
quickly grasped the whip and reins in his hands
and breathed fresh spirit into the mules and horses.
As they reached the trench and rampart round the fleet,
the sentries had just begun to set out supper there
but the giant-killer plunged them all in sleep . . .
he spread the gates at once, slid back the bars
and ushered Priam in with his wagon-load of treasure.
Now, at last, they approached royal Achilles' shelter,
the tall, imposing lodge the Myrmidons built their king,
hewing planks of pine, and roofed it high with thatch,
gathering thick shaggy reeds from the meadow banks,
and round it built their king a spacious courtyard
fenced with close-set stakes. A single pine beam
held the gates, and it took three men to ram it home,
three to shoot the immense bolt back and spread the doors—
three average men. Achilles alone could ram it home himself.
But the god of luck now spread the gates for the old man,
drove in the glinting gifts for Peleus' swift son,
climbed down from behind the team and said to Priam,
"Old man, look, I am a god come down to you,
I am immortal Hermes—
my Father sent me here to be your escort.
But now I will hasten back. I will not venture
into Achilles' presence: it would offend us all
for a mortal man to host an immortal face-to-face.
But you go in yourself and clasp Achilles' knees,
implore him by his father, his mother with lovely hair,
by his own son—so you can stir his heart!"
With that urging
Hermes went his way to the steep heights of Olympus.

But Priam swung down to earth from the battle-car
and leaving Idaeus there to rein in mules and team,
the old king went straight up to the lodge
where Achilles dear to Zeus would always sit.
Priam found the warrior there inside . . .
many captains sitting some way off, but two,
veteran Automedon and the fine fighter Alcimus
were busy serving him. He had just finished dinner,
eating, drinking, and the table still stood near.
The majestic king of Troy slipped past the rest
and kneeling down beside Achilles, clasped his knees
and kissed his hands, those terrible, man-killing hands
that had slaughtered Priam's many sons in battle.
Awesome—as when the grip of madness seizes one
who murders a man in his own fatherland and flees
abroad to foreign shores, to a wealthy, noble host,
and a sense of marvel runs through all who see him—
so Achilles marveled, beholding majestic Priam.
His men marveled too, trading startled glances.
But Priam prayed his heart out to Achilles:
"Remember your own father, great godlike Achilles—
as old as *I* am, past the threshold of deadly old age!
No doubt the countrymen round about him plague him now,
with no one there to defend him, beat away disaster.
No one—but at least he hears you're still alive
and his old heart rejoices, hopes rising, day by day,
to see his beloved son come sailing home from Troy.
But I—dear god, my life so cursed by fate . . .
I fathered hero sons in the wide realm of Troy
and now not a single one is left, I tell you.
Fifty sons I had when the sons of Achaea came,
nineteen born to me from a single mother's womb
and the rest by other women in the palace. Many,
most of them violent Ares cut the knees from under.
But one, one was left me, to guard my walls, my people—
the one you killed the other day, defending his fatherland,
my Hector! It's all for him I've come to the ships now,
to win him back from you—I bring a priceless ransom.
Revere the gods, Achilles! Pity me in my own right,
remember your own father! I deserve more pity . . .
I have endured what no one on earth has ever done before—
I put to my lips the hands of the man who killed my son."

Those words stirred within Achilles a deep desire
to grieve for his own father. Taking the old man's hand
he gently moved him back. And overpowered by memory
both men gave way to grief. Priam wept freely
for man-killing Hector, throbbing, crouching
before Achilles' feet as Achilles wept himself,
now for his father, now for Patroclus once again,

and their sobbing rose and fell throughout the house.
Then, when brilliant Achilles had had his fill of tears
and the longing for it had left his mind and body,
he rose from his seat, raised the old man by the hand
and filled with pity now for his gray head and gray beard,
he spoke out winging words, flying straight to the heart:
"Poor man, how much you've borne—pain to break the spirit!
What daring brought you down to the ships, all alone,
to face the glance of the man who killed your sons,
so many fine brave boys? You have a heart of iron.
Come, please, sit down on this chair here . . .
Let us put our griefs to rest in our own hearts,
rake them up no more, raw as we are with mourning.
What good's to be won from tears that chill the spirit?
So the immortals spun our lives that we, we wretched men
live on to bear such torments—the gods live free of sorrows.
There are two great jars that stand on the floor of Zeus's halls
and hold his gifts, our miseries one, the other blessings.
When Zeus who loves the lightning mixes gifts for a man,
now he meets with misfortune, now good times in turn.
When Zeus dispenses gifts from the jar of sorrows only,
he makes a man an outcast—brutal, ravenous hunger
drives him down the face of the shining earth,
stalking far and wide, cursed by gods and men.
So with my father, Peleus. What glittering gifts
the gods rained down from the day that he was born!
He excelled all men in wealth and pride of place,
he lorded the Myrmidons, and mortal that he was,
they gave the man an immortal goddess for a wife.
Yes, but even on him the Father piled hardships,
no powerful race of princes born in his royal halls,
only a single son he fathered, doomed at birth,
cut off in the spring of life—
and I, I give the man no care as he grows old
since here I sit in Troy, far from my fatherland,
a grief to you, a grief to all your children . . .
And you too, old man, we hear you prospered once:
as far as Lesbos, Macar's[5] kingdom, bounds to seaward,
Phrygia east and upland, the Hellespont vast and north—
that entire realm, they say, you lorded over once,
you excelled all men, old king, in sons and wealth.
But then the gods of heaven brought this agony on you—
ceaseless battles round your walls, your armies slaughtered.
You must bear up now. Enough of endless tears,
the pain that breaks the spirit.
Grief for your son will do no good at all.
You will never bring him back to life—
sooner you must suffer something worse."

5. The legendary first king of Lesbos.

But the old and noble Priam protested strongly:
"Don't make me sit on a chair, Achilles, Prince,
not while Hector lies uncared-for in your camp!
Give him back to me, now, no more delay—
I must see my son with my own eyes.
Accept the ransom I bring you, a king's ransom!
Enjoy it, all of it—return to your own native land,
safe and sound . . . since now you've spared my life."

A dark glance—and the headstrong runner answered,
"No more, old man, don't tempt my wrath, not now!
My own mind's made up to give you back your son.
A messenger brought me word from Zeus—my mother,
Thetis who bore me, the Old Man of the Sea's daughter.
And what's more, I can see through you, Priam—
no hiding the fact from me: one of the gods
has led you down to Achaea's fast ships.
No man alive, not even a rugged young fighter,
would dare to venture into our camp. Never—
how could he slip past the sentries unchallenged?
Or shoot back the bolt of my gates with so much ease?
So don't anger me now. Don't stir my raging heart still more.
Or under my own roof I may not spare your life, old man—
suppliant that you are—may break the laws of Zeus!"

The old man was terrified. He obeyed the order.
But Achilles bounded out of doors like a lion—
not alone but flanked by his two aides-in-arms,
veteran Automedon and Alcimus, steady comrades,
Achilles' favorites next to the dead Patroclus.
They loosed from harness the horses and the mules,
they led the herald in, the old king's crier,
and sat him down on a bench. From the polished wagon
they lifted the priceless ransom brought for Hector's corpse
but they left behind two capes and a finely-woven shirt
to shroud the body well when Priam bore him home.
Then Achilles called the serving-women out:
"Bathe and anoint the body—
bear it aside first. Priam must not see his son."
He feared that, overwhelmed by the sight of Hector,
wild with grief, Priam might let his anger flare
and Achilles might fly into fresh rage himself,
cut the old man down and break the laws of Zeus.
So when the maids had bathed and anointed the body
sleek with olive oil and wrapped it round and round
in a braided battle-shirt and handsome battle-cape,
then Achilles lifted Hector up in his own arms
and laid him down on a bier, and comrades helped him
raise the bier and body onto the sturdy wagon . . .
Then with a groan he called his dear friend by name:
"Feel no anger at me, Patroclus, if you learn—

even there in the House of Death—I let his father
have Prince Hector back. He gave me worthy ransom
and you shall have your share from me, as always,
your fitting, lordly share."
So he vowed
and brilliant Achilles strode back to his shelter,
sat down on the well-carved chair that he had left,
at the far wall of the room, leaned toward Priam
and firmly spoke the words the king had come to hear:
"Your son is now set free, old man, as you requested.
Hector lies in state. With the first light of day
you will see for yourself as you convey him home.
Now, at last, let us turn our thoughts to supper.
Even Niobe[6] with her lustrous hair remembered food,
though she saw a dozen children killed in her own halls,
six daughters and six sons in the pride and prime of youth.
True lord Apollo killed the sons with his silver bow
and Artemis showering arrows killed the daughters.
Both gods were enraged at Niobe. Time and again
she placed herself on a par with their[7] own mother,
Leto in her immortal beauty—how she insulted Leto:
'All you have borne is two, but I have borne so many!'
So, two as they were, they slaughtered all her children.
Nine days they lay in their blood, no one to bury them—
Cronus' son had turned the people into stone . . .
then on the tenth the gods of heaven interred them.
And Niobe, gaunt, worn to the bone with weeping,
turned her thoughts to food. And now, somewhere,
lost on the crags, on the lonely mountain slopes,
on Sipylus where, they say, the nymphs who live forever,
dancing along the Achelous River run to beds of rest—
there, struck into stone, Niobe still broods
on the spate of griefs the gods poured out to her.[8]

So come—we too, old king, must think of food.
Later you can mourn your beloved son once more,
when you bear him home to Troy, and you'll weep many tears."

Never pausing, the swift runner sprang to his feet
and slaughtered a white sheep as comrades moved in
to skin the carcass quickly, dress the quarters well.
Expertly they cut the meat in pieces, pierced them with spits,
roasted them to a turn and pulled them off the fire.
Automedon brought the bread, set it out on the board
in ample wicker baskets. Achilles served the meat.
They reached out for the good things that lay at hand
and when they had put aside desire for food and drink,
Priam the son of Dardanus gazed at Achilles, marveling

6. Wife of Amphion, one of the two founders of the great Greek city of Thebes. 7. Apollo and Artemis's.
8. The legend of Niobe being turned into stone is thought to have had its origin in a rock face on Sipylus (in Asia Minor) that resembled a woman who cried inconsolably for the loss of her children. The Achelous River runs near Mount Sipylus.

now at the man's beauty, his magnificent build—
face-to-face he seemed a deathless god . . .
and Achilles gazed and marveled at Dardan Priam,
beholding his noble looks, listening to his words.
But once they'd had their fill of gazing at each other,
the old majestic Priam broke the silence first:
"Put me to bed quickly, Achilles, Prince.
Time to rest, to enjoy the sweet relief of sleep.
Not once have my eyes closed shut beneath my lids
from the day my son went down beneath your hands . . .
day and night I groan, brooding over the countless griefs,
groveling in the dung that fills my walled-in court.
But now, at long last, I have tasted food again
and let some glistening wine go down my throat.
Before this hour I had tasted nothing."
He shook his head
as Achilles briskly told his men and serving-women
to make beds in the porch's shelter, to lay down
some heavy purple throws for the beds themselves
and over them spread blankets and thick woolly robes,
a warm covering laid on top. Torches held in hand,
they went from the hall and fell to work at once
and in no time two good beds were spread and made.
Then Achilles nodded to Priam, leading the king on
with brusque advice: "Sleep outside, old friend,
in case some Achaean captain comes to visit.
They keep on coming now, huddling beside me,
making plans for battle—it's their duty.
But if one saw you here in the rushing dark night
he'd tell Agamemnon straightaway, our good commander.
Then you'd have real delay in ransoming the body.
One more point. Tell me, be precise about it—
how many days do you need to bury Prince Hector?
I will hold back myself
and keep the Argive armies back that long."

And the old and noble Priam answered slowly,
"If you truly want me to give Prince Hector burial,
full, royal honors, you'd show me a great kindness,
Achilles, if you would do exactly as I say.
You know how crammed we are inside our city,
how far it is to the hills to haul in timber,
and our Trojans are afraid to make the journey.
Well, nine days we should mourn him in our halls,
on the tenth we'd bury Hector, hold the public feast,
on the eleventh build the barrow high above his body—
on the twelfth we'd fight again . . . if fight we must."

The swift runner Achilles reassured him quickly:
"All will be done, old Priam, as you command.
I will hold our attack as long as you require."

With that he clasped the old king by the wrist,
by the right hand, to free his heart from fear.
Then Priam and herald, minds set on the journey home,
bedded down for the night within the porch's shelter.
And deep in his sturdy well-built lodge Achilles slept
with Briseis in all her beauty sleeping by his side.

Now the great array of gods and chariot-driving men
slept all night long, overcome by gentle sleep.
But sleep could never hold the running Escort—
Hermes kept on turning it over in his mind . . .
how could he convoy Priam clear of the ships,
unseen by devoted guards who held the gates?
Hovering at his head the Escort rose and spoke:
"Not a care in the world, old man? Look at you,
how you sleep in the midst of men who'd kill you—
and just because Achilles spared your life. Now, yes,
you've ransomed your dear son—for a king's ransom.
But wouldn't the sons you left behind be forced
to pay three times as much for *you* alive?
What if Atrides Agamemnon learns you're here—
what if the whole Achaean army learns you're here?"

The old king woke in terror, roused the herald.
Hermes harnessed the mules and team for both men,
drove them fast through the camp and no one saw them.

Once they reached the ford where the river runs clear,
the strong, whirling Xanthus sprung of immortal Zeus,
Hermes went his way to the steep heights of Olympus
as Dawn flung out her golden robe across the earth,
and the two men, weeping, groaning, drove the team
toward Troy and the mules brought on the body.
No one saw them at first, neither man nor woman,
none before Cassandra, golden as goddess Aphrodite.
She had climbed to Pergamus heights and from that point
she saw her beloved father swaying tall in the chariot,
flanked by the herald, whose cry could rouse the city.
And Cassandra saw *him* too . . .
drawn by the mules and stretched out on his bier.
She screamed and her scream rang out through all Troy:
"Come, look down, you men of Troy, you Trojan women!
Behold Hector now—if you ever once rejoiced
to see him striding home, home alive from battle!
He was the greatest joy of Troy and all our people!"

Her cries plunged Troy into uncontrollable grief
and not a man or woman was left inside the walls.
They streamed out at the gates to meet Priam
bringing in the body of the dead. Hector—
his loving wife and noble mother were first
to fling themselves on the wagon rolling on,

the first to tear their hair, embrace his head
and a wailing throng of people milled around them.
And now, all day long till the setting sun went down
they would have wept for Hector there before the gates
if the old man, steering the car, had not commanded,
"Let me through with the mules! Soon, in a moment,
you can have your fill of tears—once I've brought him home."

So he called and the crowds fell back on either side,
making way for the wagon. Once they had borne him
into the famous halls, they laid his body down
on his large carved bed and set beside him singers
to lead off the laments, and their voices rose in grief—
they lifted the dirge high as the women wailed in answer.
And white-armed Andromache led their songs of sorrow,
cradling the head of Hector, man-killing Hector
gently in her arms: "O my husband . . .
cut off from life so young! You leave me a widow,
lost in the royal halls—and the boy only a baby,
the son we bore together, you and I so doomed.
I cannot think he will ever come to manhood.
Long before *that* the city will be sacked,
plundered top to bottom! Because you are dead,
her great guardian, you who always defended Troy,
who kept her loyal wives and helpless children safe,
all who will soon be carried off in the hollow ships
and I with them—
And you, my child, will follow me
to labor, somewhere, at harsh, degrading work,
slaving under some heartless master's eye—that,
or some Achaean marauder will seize you by the arm
and hurl you headlong down from the ramparts[9]—horrible death—
enraged at you because Hector once cut down his brother,
his father or his son, yes, hundreds of armed Achaeans
gnawed the dust of the world, crushed by Hector's hands!
Your father, remember, was no man of mercy . . .
not in the horror of battle, and that is why
the whole city of Troy mourns you now, my Hector—
you've brought your parents accursed tears and grief
but to me most of all you've left the horror, the heartbreak!
For you never died in bed and stretched your arms to me
or said some last word from the heart I can remember,
always, weeping for you through all my nights and days!"

Her voice rang out in tears and the women wailed in answer
and Hecuba led them now in a throbbing chant of sorrow:
"Hector, dearest to me by far of all my sons . . .
and dear to the gods while we still shared this life—
and they cared about you still, I see, even after death.
Many the sons I had whom the swift runner Achilles

9. After the fall of Troy, Astyanax was, in fact, hurled from the walls.

caught and shipped on the barren salt sea as slaves
to Samos, to Imbros, to Lemnos shrouded deep in mist!
But you, once he slashed away your life with his brazen spear
he dragged you time and again around his comrade's tomb,
Patroclus whom you killed—not that he brought Patroclus
back to life by that. But I have you with me now . . .
fresh as the morning dew you lie in the royal halls
like one whom Apollo, lord of the silver bow,
has approached and shot to death with gentle shafts."

Her voice rang out in tears and an endless wail rose up
and Helen, the third in turn, led their songs of sorrow:
"Hector! Dearest to me of all my husband's brothers—
my husband, Paris, magnificent as a god . . .
he was the one who brought me here to Troy—
Oh how I wish I'd died before that day!
But this, now, is the twentieth year for me
since I sailed here and forsook my own native land,
yet never once did I hear from *you* a taunt, an insult.
But if someone else in the royal halls would curse me,
one of your brothers or sisters or brothers' wives
trailing their long robes, even your own mother—
not your father, always kind as my own father—
why, you'd restrain them with words, Hector,
you'd win them to my side . . .
you with your gentle temper, all your gentle words.
And so in the same breath I mourn for you and me,
my doom-struck, harrowed heart! Now there is no one left
in the wide realm of Troy, no friend to treat me kindly—
all the countrymen cringe from me in loathing!"

Her voice rang out in tears and vast throngs wailed
and old King Priam rose and gave his people orders:
"Now, you men of Troy, haul timber into the city!
Have no fear of an Argive ambush packed with danger—
Achilles vowed, when he sent me home from the black ships,
not to do us harm till the twelfth dawn arrives."

At this command they harnessed oxen and mules to wagons,
they assembled before the city walls with all good speed
and for nine days hauled in a boundless store of timber.
But when the tenth Dawn brought light to the mortal world
they carried gallant Hector forth, streaming tears,
and they placed his corpse aloft the pyre's crest,
flung a torch and set it all aflame.
At last,
when young Dawn with her rose-red fingers shone once more,
the people massed around illustrious Hector's pyre . . .
And once they'd gathered, crowding the meeting grounds,
they first put out the fires with glistening wine,
wherever the flames still burned in all their fury.
Then they collected the white bones of Hector—

all his brothers, his friends-in-arms, mourning,
and warm tears came streaming down their cheeks.
They placed the bones they found in a golden chest,
shrouding them round and round in soft purple cloths.
They quickly lowered the chest in a deep, hollow grave
and over it piled a cope of huge stones closely set,
then hastily heaped a barrow, posted lookouts all around
for fear the Achaean combat troops would launch their attack
before the time agreed. And once they'd heaped the mound
they turned back home to Troy, and gathering once again
they shared a splendid funeral feast in Hector's honor,
held in the house of Priam, king by will of Zeus.

And so the Trojans buried Hector breaker of horses.

The Odyssey[1]

BOOK I

[*A Goddess Intervenes*]

Sing in me, Muse, and through me tell the story
of that man skilled in all ways of contending,
the wanderer, harried for years on end,
after he plundered the stronghold
on the proud height of Troy.
He saw the townlands
and learned the minds of many distant men,
and weathered many bitter nights and days
in his deep heart at sea, while he fought only
to save his life, to bring his shipmates home.
But not by will nor valor could he save them,
for their own recklessness destroyed them all—
children and fools, they killed and feasted on
the cattle of Lord Hêlios,[2] the Sun,
and he who moves all day through heaven
took from their eyes the dawn of their return.

Of these adventures, Muse, daughter of Zeus,
tell us in our time, lift the great song again.
Begin when all the rest who left behind them
headlong death in battle or at sea
had long ago returned,[3] while he alone still hungered
for home and wife. Her ladyship Kalypso[4]
clung to him in her sea-hollowed caves—
a nymph, immortal and most beautiful,
who craved him for her own.
And when long years and seasons

1. Translated by Robert Fitzgerald. Fitzgerald's translation provides its own pronunciation symbols. Thus *ê* is pronounced like *ee* and accented syllables are indicated. 2. This is described in book 12. 3. From the siege of Troy. 4. Her name is formed from a Greek verb that means "cover, hide."

wheeling brought around that point of time
ordained for him to make his passage homeward,
trials and dangers, even so, attended him
even in Ithaka,[5] near those he loved.
Yet all the gods had pitied Lord Odysseus,
all but Poseidon,[6] raging cold and rough
against the brave king till he came ashore
at last on his own land.
But now that god
had gone far off among the sunburnt races,
most remote of men, at earth's two verges,
in sunset lands and lands of the rising sun,
to be regaled by smoke of thighbones burning,
haunches of rams and bulls, a hundred fold.
He lingered delighted at the banquet side.

In the bright hall of Zeus upon Olympos
the other gods were all at home, and Zeus,
the father of gods and men, made conversation.
For he had meditated on Aigísthos, dead
by the hand of Agamémnon's[7] son, Orestês,
and spoke his thought aloud before them all:

"My word, how mortals take the gods to task!
All their afflictions come from us, we hear.
And what of their own failings? Greed and folly
double the suffering in the lot of man.
See how Aigísthos, for his double portion,
stole Agamémnon's wife and killed the soldier
on his homecoming day. And yet Aigísthos
knew that his own doom lay in this. We gods
had warned him, sent down Hermês Argeiphontês,[8]
our most observant courier, to say:
'Don't kill the man, don't touch his wife,
or face a reckoning with Orestês
the day he comes of age and wants his patrimony.'
Friendly advice—but would Aigísthos take it?
Now he has paid the reckoning in full."

The grey-eyed goddess Athena replied to Zeus:

"O Majesty, O Father of us all,
that man is in the dust indeed, and justly.
So perish all who do what he had done.
But my own heart is broken for Odysseus,
the master mind of war, so long a castaway
upon an island in the running sea;
a wooded island, in the sea's middle,

5. An island off the northwest coast of Greece, Odysseus's home. 6. The reason for his rage is given by Zeus in lines 87–90. 7. The story of Agamémnon's return and death is told in detail in book 11. 8. Both the meaning and origin of this epithet are uncertain.

and there's a goddess in the place, the daughter
of one whose baleful mind knows all the deeps
of the blue sea—Atlas,[9] who holds the columns
that bear from land the great thrust of the sky.
His daughter[1] will not let Odysseus go,
poor mournful man; she keeps on coaxing him
with her beguiling talk, to turn his mind
from Ithaka. But such desire is in him
merely to see the hearthsmoke leaping upward
from his own island, that he longs to die.
Are you not moved by this, Lord of Olympos?
Had you no pleasure from Odysseus' offerings
beside the Argive[2] ships, on Troy's wide seaboard?
O Zeus, what do you hold against him now?"

To this the summoner of cloud replied:

"My child, what strange remarks you let escape you.
Could I forget that kingly man, Odysseus?
There is no mortal half so wise; no mortal
gave so much to the lords of open sky.
Only the god who laps the land in water,
Poseidon, bears the fighter an old grudge
since he poked out the eye of Polyphêmos,
brawniest of the Kyklopês.[3] Who bore
that giant lout? Thoösa, daughter of Phorkys,
an offshore sea lord: for this nymph had lain
with Lord Poseidon in her hollow caves.
Naturally, the god, after the blinding—
mind you, he does not kill the man;
he only buffets him away from home.
But come now, we are all at leisure here,
let us take up this matter of his return,
that he may sail. Poseidon must relent
for being quarrelsome will get him nowhere,
one god, flouting the will of all the gods."

The grey-eyed goddess Athena answered him:

"O Majesty, O Father of us all,
if it now please the blissful gods
that wise Odysseus reach his home again,
let the Wayfinder, Hermês, cross the sea
to the island of Ogýgia; let him tell
our fixed intent to the nymph with pretty braids,
and let the steadfast man depart for home.
For my part, I shall visit Ithaka

9. A Titan, whose punishment for his part in the war against Zeus was to hold up the sky on his shoulders.
1. Kalypso, who lives on the island of Ogýgia. 2. One of the collective names for the Greeks fighting at Troy. 3. Or Cyclopes; these giants had a single eye in the middle of their foreheads. This encounter is told in detail in book 9.

to put more courage in the son, and rouse him
to call an assembly of the islanders,
Akhaian[4] gentlemen with flowing hair.
He must warn off that wolf pack of the suitors
who prey upon his flocks and dusky cattle.
I'll send him to the mainland then, to Sparta
by the sand beach of Pylos; let him find
news of his dear father where he may
and win his own renown about the world."

She bent to tie her beautiful sandals on,
ambrosial, golden, that carry her over water
or over endless land on the wings of the wind,
and took the great haft of her spear in hand—
that bronzeshod spear this child of Power can use
to break in wrath long battle lines of fighters.

Flashing down from Olympos' height she went
to stand in Ithaka, before the Manor,
just at the doorsill of the court. She seemed
a family friend, the Taphian[5] captain, Mentês,
waiting, with a light hand on her spear.
Before her eyes she found the lusty suitors
casting dice inside the gate, at ease
on hides of oxen—oxen they had killed.

Their own retainers made a busy sight
with houseboys mixing bowls of water and wine,
or sopping water up in sponges, wiping
tables to be placed about in hall,
or butchering whole carcasses for roasting.

Long before anyone else, the prince Telémakhos
now caught sight of Athena—for he, too,
was sitting there unhappy among the suitors,
a boy, daydreaming. What if his great father
came from the unknown world and drove these men
like dead leaves through the place, recovering
honor and lordship in his own domains?
Then he who dreamed in the crowd gazed out at Athena.

Straight to the door he came, irked with himself
to think a visitor had been kept there waiting,
and took her right hand, grasping with his left
her tall bronze-bladed spear. Then he said warmly:

"Greetings, stranger! Welcome to our feast.
There will be time to tell your errand later."

He led the way, and Pallas Athena followed
into the lofty hall. The boy reached up

4. Another of the collective names for the Greeks. 5. The name of a nearby seafaring people.

and thrust her spear high in a polished rack
against a pillar where tough spear on spear
of the old soldier, his father, stood in order.
Then, shaking out a splendid coverlet,
he seated her on a throne with footrest—all
finely carved—and drew his painted armchair
near her, at a distance from the rest.
To be amid the din, the suitors' riot,
would ruin his guest's appetite, he thought,
and he wished privacy to ask for news
about his father, gone for years.
A maid
brought them a silver finger bowl and filled it
out of a beautiful spouting golden jug,
then drew a polished table to their side.
The larder mistress with her tray came by
and served them generously. A carver lifted
cuts of each roast meat to put on trenchers
before the two. He gave them cups of gold,
and these the steward as he went his rounds
filled and filled again.
Now came the suitors,
young bloods trooping in to their own seats
on thrones or easy chairs. Attendants poured
water over their fingers, while the maids
piled baskets full of brown loaves near at hand,
and houseboys brimmed the bowls with wine.
Now they laid hands upon the ready feast
and thought of nothing more. Not till desire
for food and drink had left them were they mindful
of dance and song, that are the grace of feasting.
A herald gave a shapely cithern harp
to Phêmios,[6] whom they compelled to sing—
and what a storm he plucked upon the strings
for prelude! High and clear the song arose.

Telémakhos now spoke to grey-eyed Athena,
his head bent close, so no one else might hear:

"Dear guest, will this offend you, if I speak?
It is easy for these men to like these things,
harping and song; they have an easy life,
scot free, eating the livestock of another—
a man whose bones are rotting somewhere now,
white in the rain on dark earth where they lie,
or tumbling in the groundswell of the sea.
If he returned, if these men ever saw him,
faster legs they'd pray for, to a man,
and not more wealth in handsome robes or gold.
But he is lost; he came to grief and perished,

6. He was a member of Odysseus's household.

and there's no help for us in someone's hoping
he still may come; that sun has long gone down.
But tell me now, and put it for me clearly—
who are you? Where do you come from? Where's your home
and family? What kind of ship is yours,
and what course brought you here? Who are your sailors?
I don't suppose you walked here on the sea.
Another thing—this too I ought to know—
is Ithaka new to you, or were you ever
a guest here in the old days? Far and near
friends knew this house; for he whose home it was
had much acquaintance in the world."

To this
the grey-eyed goddess answered:

"As you ask,
I can account most clearly for myself.
Mentês I'm called, son of the veteran
Ankhíalos; I rule seafaring Taphos.
I came by ship, with a ship's company,
sailing the winedark sea for ports of call
on alien shores—to Témesê, for copper,
bringing bright bars of iron in exchange.
My ship is moored on a wild strip of coast
in Reithron Bight, under the wooded mountain.
Years back, my family and yours were friends,
as Lord Laërtês[7] knows; ask when you see him.
I hear the old man comes to town no longer,
stays up country, ailing, with only one
old woman to prepare his meat and drink
when pain and stiffness take him in the legs
from working on his terraced plot, his vineyard.
As for my sailing here—
the tale was that your father had come home,
therefore I came. I see the gods delay him.
But never in this world is Odysseus dead—
only detained somewhere on the wide sea,
upon some island, with wild islanders;
savages, they must be, to hold him captive.
Well, I will forecast for you, as the gods
put the strong feeling in me—I see it all,
and I'm no prophet, no adept in bird-signs.
He will not, now, be long away from Ithaka,
his father's dear land; though he be in chains
he'll scheme a way to come; he can do anything.

But tell me this now, make it clear to me:
You must be, by your looks, Odysseus' boy?
The way your head is shaped, the fine eyes—yes,

7. Odysseus's father.

how like him! We took meals like this together
many a time, before he sailed for Troy
with all the lords of Argos in the ships.
I have not seen him since, nor has he seen me."

And thoughtfully Telémakhos replied:

"Friend, let me put it in the plainest way.
My mother says I am his son: I know not
surely. Who has known his own engendering?
I wish at least I had some happy man
as father, growing old in his own house—
but unknown death and silence are the fate
of him that, since you ask, they call my father."

Then grey-eyed Athena said:

"The gods decreed
no lack of honor in this generation:
such is the son Penélopê bore in you.
But tell me now, and make this clear to me:
what gathering, what feast is this? Why here?
A wedding? Revel? At the expense of all?
Not that, I think. How arrogant they seem,
these gluttons, making free here in your house!
A sensible man would blush to be among them."

To this Telémakhos answered:

"Friend, now that you ask about these matters,
our house was always princely, a great house,
as long as he of whom we speak remained here.
But evil days the gods have brought upon it,
making him vanish, as they have, so strangely.
Were his death known, I could not feel such pain—
if he had died of wounds in Trojan country
or in the arms of friends, after the war.
They would have made a tomb for him, the Akhaians,
and I should have all honor as his son.
Instead, the whirlwinds got him, and no glory.
He's gone, no sign, no word of him; and I inherit
trouble and tears—and not for him alone,
the gods have laid such other burdens on me.
For now the lords of the islands,
Doulíkhion and Samê, wooded Zakýnthos,[8]
and rocky Ithaka's young lords as well,
are here courting my mother; and they use
our house as if it were a house to plunder.
Spurn them she dare not, though she hates that marriage,
nor can she bring herself to choose among them.

8. Islands close to Ithaka.

Meanwhile they eat their way through all we have,
and when they will, they can demolish me."

Pallas Athena was disturbed, and said:

"Ah, bitterly you need Odysseus, then!
High time he came back to engage these upstarts.
I wish we saw him standing helmeted
there in the doorway, holding shield and spear,
looking the way he did when I first knew him.
That was at our house, where he drank and feasted
after he left Ephyra, homeward bound
from a visit to the son of Mêrmeris, Ilos.
He took his fast ship down the gulf that time
for a fatal drug to dip his arrows in
and poison the bronze points; but young Ilos
turned him away, fearing the gods' wrath.
My father gave it, for he loved him well.
I wish these men could meet the man of those days!
They'd know their fortune quickly: a cold bed.
Aye! but it lies upon the gods' great knees
whether he can return and force a reckoning
in his own house, or not.
If I were you,
I should take steps to make these men disperse.
Listen, now, and attend to what I say:
at daybreak call the islanders to assembly,
and speak your will, and call the gods to witness:
the suitors must go scattering to their homes.
Then here's a course for you, if you agree:
get a sound craft afloat with twenty oars
and go abroad for news of your lost father—
perhaps a traveller's tale, or rumored fame
issued from Zeus abroad in the world of men.
Talk to that noble sage at Pylos, Nestor,
then go to Meneláos, the red-haired king
at Sparta, last man home of all the Akhaians.
If you should learn your father is alive
and coming home, you could hold out a year.
Or if you learn that he is dead and gone,
then you can come back to your own dear country
and raise a mound for him, and burn his gear,
with all the funeral honors due the man,
and give your mother to another husband.
When you have done all this, or seen it done,
it will be time to ponder
concerning these contenders in your house—
how you should kill them, outright or by guile.
You need not bear this insolence of theirs,
you are a child no longer. Have you heard
what glory young Orestês won
when he cut down that two-faced man, Aigísthos,

for killing his illustrious father?
Dear friend, you are tall and well set-up, I see;
be brave—you, too—and men in times to come
will speak of you respectfully.
Now I must join my ships;
my crew will grumble if I keep them waiting.
Look to yourself; remember what I told you."

Telémakhos replied:

"Friend, you have done me
kindness, like a father to his son,
and I shall not forget your counsel ever.
You must get back to sea, I know, but come
take a hot bath, and rest; accept a gift
to make your heart lift up when you embark—
some precious thing, and beautiful, from me,
a keepsake, such as dear friends give their friends."

But the grey-eyed goddess Athena answered him:

"Do not delay me, for I love the sea ways.
As for the gift your heart is set on giving,
let me accept it on my passage home,
and you shall have a choice gift in exchange."

With this Athena left him
as a bird rustles upward, off and gone.
But as she went she put new spirit in him,
a new dream of his father, clearer now,
so that he marvelled to himself
divining that a god had been his guest.
Then godlike in his turn he joined the suitors.

The famous minstrel still sang on before them,
and they sat still and listened, while he sang
that bitter song, the Homecoming of Akhaians—
how by Athena's will they fared from Troy;
and in her high room careful Penélopê,
Ikários' daughter, heeded the holy song.
She came, then, down the long stairs of her house,
this beautiful lady, with two maids in train
attending her as she approached the suitors;
and near a pillar of the roof she paused,
her shining veil drawn over across her cheeks,
the two girls close to her and still,
and through her tears spoke to the noble minstrel:
"Phêmios, other spells you know, high deeds
of gods and heroes, as the poets tell them;
let these men hear some other; let them sit
silent and drink their wine. But sing no more
this bitter tale that wears my heart away.

It opens in me again the wound of longing
for one incomparable, ever in my mind—
his fame all Hellas[9] knows, and midland Argos."

But Telémakhos intervened and said to her:

"Mother, why do you grudge our own dear minstrel
joy of song, wherever his thought may lead?
Poets are not to blame, but Zeus who gives
what fate he pleases to adventurous men.
Here is no reason for reproof: to sing
the news of the Danaans![1] Men like best
a song that rings like morning on the ear.
But you must nerve yourself and try to listen.
Odysseus was not the only one at Troy
never to know the day of his homecoming.
Others, how many others, lost their lives!"

The lady gazed in wonder and withdrew,
her son's clear wisdom echoing in her mind.
But when she had mounted to her rooms again
with her two handmaids, then she fell to weeping
for Odysseus, her husband. Grey-eyed Athena
presently cast a sweet sleep on her eyes.

Meanwhile the din grew loud in the shadowy hall
as every suitor swore to lie beside her,
but Telémakhos turned now and spoke to them:

"You suitors of my mother! Insolent men,
now we have dined, let us have entertainment
and no more shouting. There can be no pleasure
so fair as giving heed to a great minstrel
like ours, whose voice itself is pure delight.
At daybreak we shall sit down in assembly
and I shall tell you—take it as you will—
you are to leave this hall. Go feasting elsewhere,
consume your own stores. Turn and turn about,
use one another's houses. If you choose
to slaughter one man's livestock and pay nothing,
this is rapine; and by the eternal gods
I beg Zeus you shall get what you deserve:
a slaughter here, and nothing paid for it!"

By now their teeth seemed fixed in their under-lips,
Telémakhos' bold speaking stunned them so.
Antínoös, Eupeithês' son, made answer:
"Telémakhos, no doubt the gods themselves
are teaching you this high and mighty manner.

9. The ancient name for Greece. 1. Another name for the Greeks as a whole.

Zeus forbid you should be king in Ithaka,
though you are eligible as your father's son."

Telémakhos kept his head and answered him:

"Antínoös, you may not like my answer,
but I would happily be king, if Zeus
conferred the prize. Or do you think it wretched?
I shouldn't call it bad at all. A king
will be respected, and his house will flourish.
But there are eligible men enough,
heaven knows, on the island, young and old,
and one of them perhaps may come to power
after the death of King Odysseus.
All I insist on is that I rule our house
and rule the slaves my father won for me."

Eurýmakhos, Pólybos' son, replied:

"Telémakhos, it is on the gods' great knees
who will be king in sea-girt Ithaka.
But keep your property, and rule your house,
and let no man, against your will, make havoc
of your possessions, while there's life on Ithaka.
But now, my brave young friend,
a question or two about the stranger.
Where did your guest come from? Of what country?
Where does he say his home is, and his family?
Has he some message of your father's coming,
or business of his own, asking a favor?
He left so quickly that one hadn't time
to meet him, but he seemed a gentleman."

Telémakhos made answer, cool enough:

"Eurýmakhos, there's no hope for my father.
I would not trust a message, if one came,
nor any forecaster my mother invites
to tell by divination of time to come.
My guest, however, was a family friend,
Mentês, son of Ankhíalos.
He rules the Taphian people of the sea."

So said Telémakhos, though in his heart
he knew his visitor had been immortal.
But now the suitors turned to play again
with dance and haunting song. They stayed till nightfall,
indeed, black night came on them at their pleasure,
and half asleep they left, each for his home.

Telémakhos' bedroom was above the court,
a kind of tower, with a view all round;

here he retired to ponder in the silence,
while carrying brands of pine alight beside him
Eurýkleia went padding, sage and old.
Her father had been Ops, Peisênor's son,
and she had been a purchase of Laërtês
when she was still a blossoming girl. He gave
the price of twenty oxen for her, kept her
as kindly in his house as his own wife,
though, for the sake of peace, he never touched her.
No servant loved Telémakhos as she did,
she who had nursed him in his infancy.
So now she held the light, as he swung open
the door of his neat freshly painted chamber.
There he sat down, pulling his tunic off,
and tossed it into the wise old woman's hands.
She folded it and smoothed it, and then hung it
beside the inlaid bed upon a bar;
then, drawing the door shut by its silver handle
she slid the catch in place and went away.
And all night long, wrapped in the finest fleece,
he took in thought the course Athena gave him.

BOOK II

[*A Hero's Son Awakens*]

When primal Dawn spread on the eastern sky
her fingers of pink light, Odysseus' true son
stood up, drew on his tunic and his mantle,
slung on a sword-belt and a new-edged sword,
tied his smooth feet into good rawhide sandals,
and left his room, a god's brilliance upon him.
He found the criers with clarion voices and told them
to muster the unshorn Akhaians in full assembly.
The call sang out, and the men came streaming in;
and when they filled the assembly ground, he entered,
spear in hand, with two quick hounds at heel;
Athena lavished on him a sunlit grace
that held the eye of the multitude. Old men
made way for him as he took his father's chair.

Now Lord Aigýptios, bent down and sage with years,
opened the assembly. This man's son
had served under the great Odysseus, gone
in the decked ships with him to the wild horse country
of Troy—a spearman, Ántiphos by name.
The ravenous Kyklops in the cave destroyed him
last in his feast of men. Three other sons
the old man had, and one, Eurýnomos,
went with the suitors; two farmed for their father;
but even so the old man pined, remembering
the absent one, and a tear welled up as he spoke:

"Hear me, Ithakans! Hear what I have to say.
No meeting has been held here since our king,
Odysseus, left port in the decked ships.
Who finds occasion for assembly, now?
one of the young men? one of the older lot?
Has he had word our fighters are returning—
news to report if he got wind of it—
or is it something else, touching the realm?
The man has vigor, I should say; more power to him.
Whatever he desires, may Zeus fulfill it."

The old man's words delighted the son of Odysseus,
who kept his chair no longer but stood up,
eager to speak, in the midst of all the men.
The crier, Peisênor, master of debate,
brought him the staff and placed it in his hand;[2]
then the boy touched the old man's shoulder, and said:

"No need to wonder any more, Sir,
who called this session. The distress is mine.
As to our troops returning, I have no news—
news to report if I got wind of it—
nor have I public business to propose;
only my need, and the trouble of my house—
the troubles.

My distinguished father is lost,
who ruled among you once, mild as a father,
and there is now this greater evil still:
my home and all I have are being ruined.
Mother wanted no suitors, but like a pack
they came—sons of the best men here among them—
lads with no stomach for an introduction
to Ikários, her father across the sea;
he would require a wedding gift, and give her
to someone who found favor in her eyes.
No; these men spend their days around our house
killing our beeves and sheep and fatted goats,
carousing, soaking up our good dark wine,
not caring what they do. They squander everything.
We have no strong Odysseus to defend us,
and as to putting up a fight ourselves—
we'd only show our incompetence in arms.
Expel them, yes, if I only had the power;
the whole thing's out of hand, insufferable.
My house is being plundered: is this courtesy?
Where is your indignation? Where is your shame?
Think of the talk in the islands all around us,

2. As in the assembly in book 1 of the *Iliad*, the herald hands the person who is given the floor to speak a staff, the symbol of authority.

and fear the wrath of the gods,
or they may turn, and send you some devilry.
Friends, by Olympian Zeus and holy Justice
that holds men in assembly and sets them free,
make an end of this! Let me lament in peace
my private loss. Or did my father, Odysseus,
ever do injury to the armed Akhaians?
Is this your way of taking it out on me,
giving free rein to these young men?
I might as well—might better—see my treasure
and livestock taken over by you all;
then, if you fed on them, I'd have some remedy,
and when we met, in public, in the town,
I'd press my claim; you might make restitution.
This way you hurt me when my hands are tied."

And in hot anger now he threw the staff to the ground,
his eyes grown bright with tears. A wave of sympathy
ran through the crowd, all hushed; and no one there
had the audacity to answer harshly
except Antínoös, who said:

"What high and mighty
talk, Telémakhos! No holding you!
You want to shame us, and humiliate us,
but you should know the suitors are not to blame—
it is your own dear, incomparably cunning mother.
For three years now—and it will soon be four—
she has been breaking the hearts of the Akhaians,
holding out hope to all, and sending promises
to each man privately[3]—but thinking otherwise.

Here is an instance of her trickery:
she had her great loom standing in the hall
and the fine warp of some vast fabric on it;
we were attending her, and she said to us:
'Young men, my suitors, now my lord is dead,
let me finish my weaving before I marry,
or else my thread will have been spun in vain.
It is a shroud I weave for Lord Laërtês,
when cold death comes to lay him on his bier.
The country wives would hold me in dishonor
if he, with all his fortune, lay unshrouded.'
We have men's hearts; she touched them; we agreed.
So every day she wove on the great loom—
but every night by torchlight she unwove it;
and so for three years she deceived the Akhaians.
But when the seasons brought the fourth around,
one of her maids, who knew the secret, told us;

3. Her tactic is to divide the suitors and so put off the day that they will unanimously demand a decision.

we found her unraveling the splendid shroud.
She had to finish then, although she hated it.

Now here is the suitors' answer—
you and all the Akhaians, mark it well:
dismiss your mother from the house, or make her marry
the man her father names and she prefers.
Does she intend to keep us dangling forever?
She may rely too long on Athena's gifts—
talent in handicraft and a clever mind;
so cunning—history cannot show the like
among the ringleted ladies of Akhaia,
Mykênê with her coronet, Alkmênê, Tyro.[4]
Wits like Penélopê's never were before,
but this time—well, she made poor use of them.
For here are suitors eating up your property
as long as she holds out—a plan some god
put in her mind. She makes a name for herself,
but you can feel the loss it means for you.
Our own affairs can wait; we'll never go anywhere else,
until she takes an Akhaian to her liking."

But clear-headed Telémakhos replied:

"Antínoös, can I banish against her will
the mother who bore me and took care of me?
My father is either dead or far away,
but dearly I should pay for this
at Ikários' hands, if ever I sent her back.
The powers of darkness would requite it, too,
my mother's parting curse would call hell's furies[5]
to punish me, along with the scorn of men.
No: I can never give the word for this.
But if your hearts are capable of shame,
leave my great hall, and take your dinner elsewhere,
consume your own stores. Turn and turn about,
use one another's houses. If you choose
to slaughter one man's livestock and pay nothing,
this is rapine; and by the eternal gods
I beg Zeus you shall get what you deserve:
a slaughter here, and nothing paid for it!"

Now Zeus who views the wide world sent a sign to him,
launching a pair of eagles[6] from a mountain crest
in gliding flight down the soft blowing wind,
wing-tip to wing-tip quivering taut, companions,

4. Famous women of the past. Alkmênê was the mother of Herakles. Odysseus sees the ghosts of Tyro and Alkmênê in the underworld in book 9. 5. Spirits who avenge injured parents, especially (because they themselves are female) mothers. In Greek they are known as Erinyes. 6. The royal bird, the emblem of Zeus.

till high above the assembly of many voices
they wheeled, their dense wings beating, and in havoc
dropped on the heads of the crowd—a deathly omen—
wielding their talons, tearing cheeks and throats;
then veered away on the right hand through the city.
Astonished, gaping after the birds, the men
felt their hearts flood, foreboding things to come.
And now they heard the old lord Halithersês,
son of Mastor, keenest among the old
at reading birdflight into accurate speech;
in his anxiety for them, he rose and said:

"Hear me, Ithakans! Hear what I have to say,
and may I hope to open the suitors' eyes
to the black wave towering over them. Odysseus
will not be absent from his family long:
he is already near, carrying in him
a bloody doom for all these men, and sorrow
for many more on our high seamark, Ithaka.
Let us think how to stop it; let the suitors
drop their suit; they had better, without delay.
I am old enough to know a sign when I see one,
and I say all has come to pass for Odysseus
as I foretold when the Argives massed on Troy,
and he, the great tactician, joined the rest.
My forecast was that after nineteen years,
many blows weathered, all his shipmates lost,
himself unrecognized by anyone,
he would come home. I see this all fulfilled."

But Pólybos' son, Eurýmakhos, retorted:

"Old man, go tell the omens for your children
at home, and try to keep them out of trouble.
I am more fit to interpret this than you are.
Bird life aplenty is found in the sunny air,
not all of it significant. As for Odysseus,
he perished far from home. You should have perished with him—
then we'd be spared this nonsense in assembly,
as good as telling Telémakhos to rage on;
do you think you can gamble on a gift from him?
Here is what I foretell, and it's quite certain:
if you, with what you know of ancient lore,
encourage bitterness in this young man,
it means, for him, only the more frustration—
he can do nothing whatever with two eagles—
and as for you, old man, we'll fix a penalty
that you will groan to pay.
Before the whole assembly I advise Telémakhos
to send his mother to her father's house;
let them arrange her wedding there, and fix

a portion[7] suitable for a valued daughter.
Until he does this, courtship is our business,
vexing though it may be; we fear no one,
certainly not Telémakhos, with his talk;
and we care nothing for your divining, uncle,
useless talk; you win more hatred by it.
We'll share his meat, no thanks or fee to him,
as long as she delays and maddens us.
It is a long, long time we have been waiting
in rivalry for this beauty. We could have gone
elsewhere and found ourselves very decent wives."

Clear-headed Telémakhos replied to this:

"Eurýmakhos, and noble suitors all,
I am finished with appeals and argument.
The gods know, and the Akhaians know, these things.
But give me a fast ship and a crew of twenty
who will see me through a voyage, out and back.
I'll go to sandy Pylos, then to Sparta,
for news of Father since he sailed from Troy—
some traveller's tale, perhaps, or rumored fame
issued from Zeus himself into the world.
If he's alive, and beating his way home,
I might hold out for another weary year;
but if they tell me that he's dead and gone,
then I can come back to my own dear country
and raise a mound for him, and burn his gear,
with all the funeral honors that befit him,
and give my mother to another husband."

The boy sat down in silence. Next to stand
was Mentor, comrade in arms of the prince Odysseus,
an old man now. Odysseus left him authority
over his house and slaves, to guard them well.
In his concern, he spoke to the assembly:

"Hear me, Ithakans! Hear what I have to say.
Let no man holding scepter as a king
be thoughtful, mild, kindly, or virtuous;
let him be cruel, and practice evil ways;
it is so clear that no one here remembers
how like a gentle father Odysseus ruled you.
I find it less revolting that the suitors
carry their malice into violent acts;
at least they stake their lives
when they go pillaging the house of Odysseus—
their lives upon it, he will not come again.
What sickens me is to see the whole community

7. A dowry; in other passages (for example, 8.333–34) it is the suitors who offer gifts to the bride's father. Such a cultural amalgam, customs from different periods or places side by side, is characteristic of oral epic traditions.

sitting still, and never a voice or a hand raised
against them—a mere handful compared with you."

Leókritos, Euênor's son, replied to him:

"Mentor, what mischief are you raking up?
Will this crowd risk the sword's edge over a dinner?
Suppose Odysseus himself indeed
came in and found the suitors at his table:
he might be hot to drive them out. What then?
Never would he enjoy his wife again—
the wife who loves him well; he'd only bring down
abject death on himself against those odds.
Madness, to talk of fighting in either case.
Now let all present go about their business!
Halithersês and Mentor will speed the traveller;
they can help him: they were his father's friends.
I rather think he will be sitting here
a long time yet, waiting for news of Ithaka;
that seafaring he spoke of is beyond him."

On this note they were quick to end their parley.
The assembly broke up; everyone went home—
the suitors home to Odysseus' house again.
But Telémakhos walked down along the shore
and washed his hands in the foam of the grey sea,
then said this prayer:

"O god of yesterday,
guest in our house, who told me to take ship
on the hazy sea for news of my lost father,
listen to me, be near me:
the Akhaians only wait, or hope to hinder me,
the damned insolent suitors most of all."

Athena was nearby and came to him,
putting on Mentor's figure and his tone,
the warm voice in a lucid flight of words:

"You'll never be fainthearted or a fool,
Telémakhos, if you have your father's spirit;
he finished what he cared to say,
and what he took in hand he brought to pass.
The sea routes will yield their distances
to his true son, Penélopê's true son,—
I doubt another's luck would hold so far.
The son is rare who measures with his father,
and one in a thousand is a better man,
but you will have the sap and wit
and prudence—for you get that from Odysseus—
to give you a fair chance of winning through.
So never mind the suitors and their ways,

there is no judgment in them, neither do they
know anything of death and the black terror
close upon them—doom's day on them all.
You need not linger over going to sea.
I sailed beside your father in the old days,
I'll find a ship for you, and help you sail her.
So go on home, as if to join the suitors,
but get provisions ready in containers—
wine in two-handled jugs and barley meal,
the staying power of oarsmen,
in skin bags, watertight. I'll go the rounds
and call a crew of volunteers together.
Hundreds of ships are beached on sea-girt Ithaka;
let me but choose the soundest, old or new,
we'll rig her and take her out on the broad sea."

This was the divine speech Telémakhos heard
from Athena, Zeus's daughter. He stayed no longer,
but took his heartache home,
and found the robust suitors there at work,
skinning goats and roasting pigs in the courtyard.
Antínoös came straight over, laughing at him,
and took him by the hand with a bold greeting:

"High-handed Telémakhos, control your temper!
Come on, get over it, no more grim thoughts,
but feast and drink with me, the way you used to.
The Akhaians will attend to all you ask for—
ship, crew, and crossing to the holy land
of Pylos, for the news about your father."

Telémakhos replied with no confusion:

"Antínoös, I cannot see myself again
taking a quiet dinner in this company.
Isn't it enough that you could strip my house
under my very nose when I was young?
Now that I know, being grown, what others say,
I understand it all, and my heart is full.
I'll bring black doom upon you if I can—
either in Pylos, if I go, or in this country.
And I will go, go all the way, if only
as someone's passenger. I have no ship,
no oarsmen: and it suits you that I have none."

Calmly he drew his hand from Antínoös' hand.
At this the suitors, while they dressed their meat,
began to exchange loud mocking talk about him.
One young toplofty gallant set the tone:

"Well, think of that!
Telémakhos has a mind to murder us.

He's going to lead avengers out of Pylos,
or Sparta, maybe; oh, he's wild to do it.
Or else he'll try the fat land of Ephyra—
he can get poison there, and bring it home,
doctor the wine jar and dispatch us all."

Another took the cue:

"Well now, who knows?
He might be lost at sea, just like Odysseus,
knocking around in a ship, far from his friends.
And what a lot of trouble that would give us,
making the right division of his things!
We'd keep his house as dowry for his mother—
his mother and the man who marries her."

That was the drift of it. Telémakhos
went on through to the storeroom of his father,
a great vault where gold and bronze lay piled
along with chests of clothes, and fragrant oil.
And there were jars of earthenware in rows
holding an old wine,
mellow, unmixed, and rare; cool stood the jars
against the wall, kept for whatever day
Odysseus, worn by hardships, might come home.
The double folding doors were tightly locked
and guarded, night and day, by the serving woman,
Eurýkleia, grand-daughter of Peisênor,
in all her duty vigilant and shrewd.
Telémakhos called her to the storeroom, saying:

"Nurse, get a few two-handled travelling jugs
filled up with wine—the second best, not that
you keep for your unlucky lord and king,
hoping he may have slipped away from death
and may yet come again—royal Odysseus.
Twelve amphorai will do; seal them up tight.
And pour out barley into leather bags—
twenty bushels of barley meal ground fine.
Now keep this to yourself! Collect these things,
and after dark, when mother has retired
and gone upstairs to bed, I'll come for them.
I sail to sandy Pylos, then to Sparta,
to see what news there is of Father's voyage."

His loving nurse Eurýkleia gave a cry,
and tears sprang to her eyes as she wailed softly:

"Dear child, whatever put this in your head?
Why do you want to go so far in the world—
and you our only darling? Lord Odysseus
died in some strange place, far from his homeland.
Think how, when you have turned your back, these men

will plot to kill you and share all your things!
Stay with your own, dear, do. Why should you suffer
hardship and homelessness on the wild sea?"

But seeing all clear, Telémakhos replied:

"Take heart, Nurse, there's a god behind this plan.
And you must swear to keep it from my mother,
until the eleventh day, or twelfth, or till
she misses me, or hears that I am gone.
She must not tear her lovely skin lamenting."

So the old woman vowed by all the gods,
and vowed again, to carry out his wishes;
then she filled up the amphorai with wine
and sifted barley meal into leather bags.
Telémakhos rejoined the suitors.
Meanwhile
the goddess with grey eyes had other business:
disguised as Telémakhos, she roamed the town
taking each likely man aside and telling him:
"Meet us at nightfall at the ship!" Indeed,
she asked Noêmon, Phronios' wealthy son,
to lend her a fast ship, and he complied.
Now when at sundown shadows crossed the lanes
she dragged the cutter to the sea and launched it,
fitted out with tough seagoing gear,
and tied it up, away at the harbor's edge.
The crewmen gathered, sent there by the goddess.
Then it occurred to the grey-eyed goddess Athena
to pass inside the house of the hero Odysseus,
showing a sweet drowsiness on the suitors,
whom she had presently wandering in their wine;
and soon, as they could hold their cups no longer,
they straggled off to find their beds in town,
eyes heavy-lidded, laden down with sleep.
Then to Telémakhos the grey-eyed goddess
appeared again with Mentor's form and voice,
calling him out of the lofty emptied hall:

"Telémakhos, your crew of fighting men
is ready at the oars, and waiting for you;
come on, no point in holding up the sailing."

And Pallas Athena turned like the wind, running
ahead of him. He followed in her footsteps
down to the seaside, where they found the ship,
and oarsmen with flowing hair at the water's edge.
Telémakhos, now strong in the magic, cried:

"Come with me, friends, and get our rations down!
They are all packed at home, and my own mother
knows nothing!—only one maid was told."

He turned and led the way, and they came after,
carried and stowed all in the well-trimmed ship
as the dear son of Odysseus commanded.
Telémakhos then stepped aboard; Athena
took her position aft, and he sat by her.
The two stroke oars cast off the stern hawsers
and vaulted over the gunnels to their benches.
Grey-eyed Athena stirred them a following wind,
soughing from the north-west on the winedark sea,
and as he felt the wind, Telémakhos
called to all hands to break out mast and sail.
They pushed the fir mast high and stepped it firm
amidships in the box, made fast the forestays,
then hoisted up the white sail on its halyards
until the wind caught, booming in the sail;
and a flushing wave sang backward from the bow
on either side, as the ship got way upon her,
holding her steady course.
Now they made all secure in the fast black ship,
and, setting out the winebowls all a-brim,
they made libation to the gods,
                                        the undying, the ever-new,
most of all to the grey-eyed daughter of Zeus.
And the prow sheared through the night into the dawn.

BOOK III

[*The Lord of the Western Approaches*]

The sun rose on the flawless brimming sea
into a sky all brazen—all one brightening
for gods immortal and for mortal men
on plowlands kind with grain.
                                        And facing sunrise
the voyagers now lay off Pylos town,
compact stronghold of Neleus.[8] On the shore
black bulls were being offered by the people
to the blue-maned god[9] who makes the islands tremble:
nine congregations, each five hundred strong,
led out nine bulls apiece to sacrifice,
taking the tripes to eat, while on their altars
thighbones in fat lay burning for the god.
Here they put in, furled sail, and beached the ship;
but Telémakhos hung back in disembarking,
so that Athena turned and said:

"Not the least shyness, now, Telémakhos.
You came across the open sea for this—
to find out where the great earth hides your father
and what the doom was that he came upon.
Go to old Nestor,[1] master charioteer,

8. Mortal son of the god Poseidon and father of Nestor. 9. Poseidon. 1. The oldest of the warriors at the siege of Troy.

so we may broach the storehouse of his mind.
Ask him with courtesy, and in his wisdom
he will tell you history and no lies."

But clear-headed Telémakhos replied:

"Mentor, how can I do it, how approach him?
I have no practice in elaborate speeches, and
for a young man to interrogate an old man
seems disrespectful—"

But the grey-eyed goddess said:

"Reason and heart will give you words, Telémakhos;
and a spirit will counsel others. I should say
the gods were never indifferent to your life."

She went on quickly, and he followed her
to where the men of Pylos had their altars.
Nestor appeared enthroned among his sons,
while friends around them skewered the red beef
or held it scorching. When they saw the strangers
a hail went up, and all that crowd came forward
calling out invitations to the feast.
Peisístratos in the lead, the young prince,
caught up their hands in his and gave them places
on curly lambskins flat on the sea sand
near Thrasymêdês, his brother, and his father;
he passed them bits of the food of sacrifice,
and, pouring wine in a golden cup,
he said to Pallas Athena, daughter of Zeus:

"Friend, I must ask you to invoke Poseidon:
you find us at this feast, kept in his honor.
Make the appointed offering then, and pray,
and give the honeyed winecup to your friend
so he may do the same. He, too,
must pray to the gods on whom all men depend,
but he is just my age, you are the senior,
so here, I give the goblet first to you."

And he put the cup of sweet wine in her hand.
Athena liked his manners, and the equity
that gave her precedence with the cup of gold,
so she besought Poseidon at some length:

"Earthshaker, listen and be well disposed.
Grant your petitioners everything they ask:
above all, honor to Nestor and his sons;
second, to every man of Pylos town
a fair gift in exchange for this hekatomb;[2]

2. Strictly, a sacrifice of one hundred animals, but often used to refer to smaller offerings.

third, may Telémakhos and I perform
the errand on which last night we put to sea."

This was the prayer of Athena—
granted in every particular by herself.
She passed the beautiful wine cup to Telémakhos,
who tipped the wine and prayed as she had done.
Meanwhile the spits were taken off the fire,
portions of crisp meat for all. They feasted,
and when they had eaten and drunk their fill, at last
they heard from Nestor, prince of charioteers:

"Now is the time," he said, "for a few questions,
now that our young guests have enjoyed their dinner.
Who are you, strangers? Where are you sailing from,
and where to, down the highways of sea water?
Have you some business here? or are you, now,
reckless wanderers of the sea, like those corsairs
who risk their lives to prey on other men?"

Clear-headed Telémakhos responded cheerfully,
for Athena gave him heart. By her design
his quest for news about his father's wandering
would bring him fame in the world's eyes. So he said:

"Nestor, pride of Akhaians, Neleus' son,
you ask where we are from, and I can tell you:
our home port is under Mount Neion, Ithaka.
We are not here on Ithakan business, though,
but on my own. I want news of my father,
Odysseus, known for his great heart, and I
will comb the wide world for it. People say
he fought along with you when Troy was taken.
As to the other men who fought that war,
we know where each one died, and how he died;
but Zeus allotted my father death and mystery.
No one can say for sure where he was killed,
whether some hostile landsmen or the sea,
the stormwaves on the deep sea, got the best of him.
And this is why I come to you for help.
Tell me of his death, sir, if perhaps
you witnessed it, or have heard some wanderer
tell the tale. The man was born for trouble.
Spare me no part of it for kindness' sake,
but put the scene before me as you saw it.
If ever Odysseus my noble father
served you by promise kept or work accomplished
in the land of Troy, where you Akhaians suffered,
recall those things for me the way they were."

Then Nestor, prince of charioteers, made answer:

"Dear friend, you take me back to all the trouble
we went through in that country, we Akhaians:
rough days aboard ship on the cloudy sea
cruising away for pillage after Akhilleus;
rough days of battle around Priam's town.
Our losses, then—so many good men gone:
Arês' great Aîas lies there, Akhilleus lies there,
Patróklos, too, the wondrous counselor,
and my own strong and princely son, Antílokhos[3]—
fastest man of them all, and a born fighter.
Other miseries, and many, we endured there.
Could any mortal man tell the whole story?
Not if you stayed five years or six to hear
how hard it was for the flower of the Akhaians;
you'd go home weary, and the tale untold.
Think: we were there nine years, and we tried everything,
all stratagems against them,
up to the bitter end that Zeus begrudged us.
And as to stratagems, no man would claim
Odysseus' gift for those. He had no rivals,
your father, at the tricks of war.
Your father?
Well, I must say I marvel at the sight of you:
your manner of speech couldn't be more like his;
one would say No; no boy could speak so well.
And all that time at Ilion,[4] he and I
were never at odds in council or assembly—
saw things the same way, had one mind between us
in all the good advice we gave the Argives.
But when we plundered Priam's town and tower
and took to the ships, God scattered the Akhaians.
He had a mind to make homecoming hard for them,
seeing they would not think straight nor behave,
or some would not. So evil days came on them,
and she who had been angered,[5]
Zeus's dangerous grey-eyed daughter, did it,
starting a fight between the sons of Atreus.[6]
First they were fools enough to call assembly
at sundown, unheard of hour;
the Akhaian soldiers turned out, soaked with wine,
to hear talk, talk about it from their commanders:
Meneláos harangued them to get organized—
time to ride home on the sea's broad back, he said;
but Agamémnon wouldn't hear of it. He wanted
to hold the troops, make sacrifice, a hekatomb,

3. Nestor lists the great heroes who fell at Troy. Akhilleus (Achilles) was the bravest of the Greeks. Priam, king of Troy, was killed when the city fell. Aîas (Ajax) tried to kill Odysseus and the kings Meneláos and Agamémnon, because the dead Akhilleus's armor (a prize awarded the bravest warrior after Akhilleus) was given to Odysseus. He then committed suicide. Patróklos (Patroclus) was Akhilleus's closest friend. Odysseus will meet the ghosts of Akhilleus and Aîas in the underworld (in book 11). 4. Troy. 5. Athena. The Trojan princess Cassandra took refuge in Athena's temple when the Akhaians captured Troy, but she was raped by Aîas (not the great Aîas but another chieftain of the same name). Athena was angry not just with him, but with the whole Akhaian army because they did not punish him. 6. Meneláos and Agamémnon.

something to pacify Athena's rage.
Folly again, to think that he could move her.
Will you change the will of the everlasting gods
in a night or a day's time?
The two men stood there hammering at each other
until the army got to its feet with a roar,
and no decision, wanting it both ways.
That night no one slept well, everyone cursing
someone else. Here was the bane from Zeus.
At dawn we dragged our ships to the lordly water,
stowed aboard all our plunder
and the slave women in their low hip girdles.
But half the army elected to stay behind
with Agamémnon as their corps commander;
the other half embarked and pulled away.
We made good time, the huge sea smoothed before us,
and held our rites when we reached Ténedos,[7]
being wild for home. But Zeus, not willing yet,
now cruelly set us at odds a second time,
and one lot turned, put back in the rolling ships,
under command of the subtle captain, Odysseus;
their notion was to please Lord Agamémnon.
Not I. I fled, with every ship I had;
I knew fate had some devilment brewing there.
Diomêdês[8] roused his company and fled, too,
and later Meneláos, the red-haired captain,
caught up with us at Lesbos,
while we mulled over the long sea route, unsure
whether to lay our course northward of Khios,
keeping the Isle of Psyria off to port,
or inside Khios, coasting by windy Mimas.
We asked for a sign from heaven, and the sign came
to cut across the open sea to Euboia,
and lose no time putting our ills behind us.
The wind freshened astern, and the ships ran
before the wind on paths of the deep sea fish,
making Geraistos before dawn.[9] We thanked Poseidon
with many a charred thighbone for that crossing.
On the fourth day, Diomêdês' company
under full sail put in at Argos port,
and I held on for Pylos. The fair wind,
once heaven set it blowing, never failed.

So this, dear child, was how I came from Troy,
and saw no more of the others, lost or saved.
But you are welcome to all I've heard since then
at home; I have no reason to keep it from you.

7. An island off the coast, southwest of Troy. 8. One of the Greek champions; his home was Argos. 9. In their frail ships and without benefit of compass, Greek sailors preferred to hug the shore; the normal route would have been inside (to the east) of the island of Khios, past the headland of Mimas on the coast of Asia Minor, and across the Aegean Sea along the island chain of the Cyclades. But Nestor was in a hurry; he went north of Khios and directly across the northern Aegean to Geraistos on the long island of Euboia, which hugs the coast of the Greek mainland.

The Myrmidon[1] spearfighters returned, they say,
under the son of lionhearted Akhilleus;
and so did Poias' great son, Philoktêtês.[2]
Idómeneus[3] brought his company back to Krete;
the sea took not a man from him, of all
who lived through the long war.
And even as far away as Ithaka
you've heard of Agamémnon—how he came
home, how Aigísthos waited to destroy him
but paid a bitter price for it in the end.
That is a good thing, now, for a man to leave
a son behind him, like the son who punished
Aigísthos for the murder of his great father.
You, too, are tall and well set-up, I see;
be brave, you too, so men in times to come
will speak well of you."

Then Telémakhos said:

"Nestor, pride of Akhaians, Neleus' son,
that was revenge, and far and wide the Akhaians
will tell the tale in song for generations.
I wish the gods would buckle his arms on me!
I'd be revenged for outrage
on my insidious and brazen enemies.
But no such happy lot was given to me
or to my father. Still, I must hold fast."

To this Lord Nestor of Gerênia said:

"My dear young friend, now that you speak of it,
I hear a crowd of suitors for your mother
lives with you, uninvited, making trouble.
Now tell me how you take this. Do the people
side against you, hearkening to some oracle?
Who knows, your father might come home someday
alone or backed by troops, and have it out with them.
If grey-eyed Athena loved you
the way she did Odysseus in the old days,
in Troy country, where we all went through so much—
never have I seen the gods help any man
as openly as Athena did your father—
well, as I say, if she cared for you that way,
there would be those to quit this marriage game."

But prudently Telémakhos replied:

1. The tribal contingent led by Akhilleus, whose son, Neoptólemos, came to Troy to avenge his father; it was he who killed Priam on the altar in his palace. 2. He had been abandoned on a desert island by the Greeks because he fell sick of a loathsome disease; cured, he was brought to Troy for the final assault. 3. Leader of the Greek troops from Krete (Crete).

"I can't think what you say will ever happen, sir.
It is a dazzling hope. But not for me.
It could not be—even if the gods willed it."

At this grey-eyed Athena broke in, saying:

"What strange talk you permit yourself, Telémakhos.
A god could save the man by simply wishing it—
from the farthest shore in the world.
If I were he, I should prefer to suffer
years at sea, and then be safe at home;
better that than a knife at my hearthside
where Agamémnon found it—killed by adulterers.
Though as for death, of course all men must suffer it:
the gods may love a man, but they can't help him
when cold death comes to lay him on his bier."

Telémakhos replied:

"Mentor, grievously though we miss my father, why
go on as if that homecoming could happen?
You know the gods had settled it already,
years ago, when dark death came for him.
But there is something else I imagine Nestor
can tell us, knowing as he does the ways of men.
They say his rule goes back over three generations,
so long, so old, it seems death cannot touch him.
Nestor, Neleus' son, true sage, say how
did the Lord of the Great Plains, Agamémnon, die?
What was the trick Aigísthos used
to kill the better man? And Meneláos,
where was he? Not at Argos in Akhaia,
but blown off course, held up in some far country,
is that what gave the killer nerve to strike?"

Lord Nestor of Gerênia made answer:

"Well, now, my son, I'll tell you the whole story.
You know, yourself, what would have come to pass
if red-haired Meneláos, back from Troy,
had caught Aigísthos in that house alive.
There would have been no burial mound for him,
but dogs and carrion birds to huddle on him
in the fields beyond the wall, and not a soul
bewailing him, for the great wrong he committed.
While we were hard-pressed in the war at Troy
he stayed safe inland in the grazing country,
making light talk to win Agamémnon's queen.
But the Lady Klytaimnéstra, in the first days,
rebuffed him, being faithful still;

then, too, she had at hand as her companion
a minstrel Agamémnon left attending her,
charged with her care, when he took ship for Troy.
Then came the fated hour when she gave in.
Her lover tricked the poet and marooned him
on a bare island for the seabirds' picking,
and took her home, as he and she desired.
Many thighbones he burned on the gods' altars
and many a woven and golden ornament
hung to bedeck them, in his satisfaction;
he had not thought life held such glory for him.

Now Meneláos and I sailed home together
on friendly terms, from Troy,
but when we came off Sunion Point[4] in Attika,
the ships still running free, Onêtor's son
Phrontis, the steersman of Meneláos' ship,
fell over with a death grip on the tiller:
some unseen arrow from Apollo hit him.[5]
No man handled a ship better than he did
in a high wind and sea, so Meneláos
put down his longing to get on, and landed
to give this man full honor in funeral.
His own luck turned then. Out on the winedark sea
in the murmuring hulls again, he made Cape Malea,[6]
but Zeus who views the wide world sent a gloom
over the ocean, and a howling gale
came on with seas increasing, mountainous,
parting the ships and driving half toward Krete
where the Kydonians live by Iardanos river.
Off Gortyn's coastline in the misty sea there
a reef, a razorback, cuts through the water,
and every westerly piles up a pounding
surf along the left side, going toward Phaistos—
big seas buffeted back by the narrow stone.
They were blown here, and fought in vain for sea room;
the ships kept going in to their destruction,
slammed on the reef. The crews were saved. But now
those five that weathered it got off to southward,
taken by wind and current on to Egypt;
and there Meneláos stayed.[7] He made a fortune
in sea traffic among those distant races,
but while he did so, the foul crime was planned
and carried out in Argos by Aigísthos,

4. The southern cape of Attica; they would round this to go toward the Peloponnese. 5. A formula for a sudden death that has no obvious explanation; for women the arrow comes from Artemis. 6. The easternmost of the three capes in which the Peloponnese ends. Meneláos would have to round it to get into a harbor for Sparta. It is still a place of storms. 7. Meneláos is blown southeast, toward Egypt, where he eventually arrives. Gortyn and Phaistos (site of a Minoan palace) are inland from the south coast of Krete.

who ruled over golden Mykênai[8] seven years.
Seven long years, with Agamémnon dead,
he held the people down, before the vengeance.
But in the eighth year, back from exile in Attika,
Orestês killed the snake who killed his father.
He gave his hateful mother and her soft man
a tomb together, and proclaimed the funeral day
a festal day for all the Argive people.
That day Lord Meneláos of the great war cry
made port with all the gold his ships could carry.
And this should give you pause, my son:
don't stay too long away from home, leaving
your treasure there, and brazen suitors near;
they'll squander all you have or take it from you,
and then how will your journey serve?
I urge you, though, to call on Meneláos,
he being but lately home from distant parts
in the wide world. A man could well despair
of getting home at all, if the winds blew him
over the Great South Sea—that weary waste,
even the wintering birds delay
one winter more before the northward crossing.
Well, take your ship and crew and go by water,
or if you'd rather go by land, here are
horses, a car, and my own sons for company
as far as the ancient land of Lakedaimon[9]
and Meneláos, the red-haired captain there.
Ask him with courtesy, and in his wisdom
he will tell you history and no lies."

While Nestor talked, the sun went down the sky
and gloom came on the land,
and now the grey-eyed goddess Athena said:

"Sir, this is all most welcome and to the point,
but why not slice the bulls' tongues[1] now, and mix
libations for Poseidon and the gods?
Then we can all retire; high time we did;
the light is going under the dark world's rim,
better not linger at the sacred feast."

When Zeus's daughter spoke, they turned to listen,
and soon the squires brought water for their hands,
while stewards filled the winebowls and poured out
a fresh cup full for every man. The company
stood up to fling the tongues and a shower of wine
over the flames, then drank their thirst away.

8. Argos and Mykênai (Mycenae) are close to each other, and Homer sometimes does not discriminate between them. 9. Sparta. *Car:* a horsedrawn chariot. 1. The tongue was one of the parts of the meat reserved for the gods; it was thrown on the fire.

Now finally Telémakhos and Athena
bestirred themselves, turning away to the ship,
but Nestor put a hand on each, and said:

"Now Zeus forbid, and the other gods as well,
that you should spend the night on board, and leave me
as though I were some pauper without a stitch,
no blankets in his house, no piles of rugs,
no sleeping soft for host or guest! Far from it!
I have all these, blankets and deep-piled rugs,
and while I live the only son of Odysseus
will never make his bed on a ship's deck—
no, not while sons of mine are left at home
to welcome any guest who comes to us."

The grey-eyed goddess Athena answered him:

"You are very kind, sir, and Telémakhos
should do as you ask. That is the best thing.
He will go with you, and will spend the night
under your roof. But I must join our ship
and talk to the crew, to keep their spirits up,
since I'm the only senior in the company.
The rest are boys who shipped for friendship's sake,
no older than Telémakhos, any of them.
Let me sleep out, then, by the black hull's side,
this night at least. At daybreak I'll be off
to see the Kaukonians about a debt they owe me,
an old one and no trifle. As for your guest,
send him off in a car, with one of your sons,
and give him thoroughbreds, a racing team."

Even as she spoke, Athena left them—seeming
a seahawk, in a clap of wings—and all
the Akhaians of Pylos town looked up astounded.
Awed then by what his eyes had seen, the old man
took Telémakhos' hand and said warmly:

"My dear child, I can have no fears for you,
no doubt about your conduct or your heart,
if, at your age, the gods are your companions.
Here we had someone from Olympos—clearly
the glorious daughter of Zeus, his third child,
who held your father dear among the Argives.
O, Lady, hear me! Grant an illustrious name
to me and to my children and my dear wife!
A noble heifer shall be yours in sacrifice,
one that no man has ever yoked or driven;
my gift to you—her horns all sheathed in gold."

So he ended, praying; and Athena heard him.
Then Nestor of Gerênia led them all,
his sons and sons-in-law, to his great house;
and in they went to the famous hall of Nestor,
taking their seats on thrones and easy chairs,
while the old man mixed water in a wine bowl
with sweet red wine, mellowed eleven years
before his housekeeper uncapped the jar.
He mixed and poured his offering, repeating
prayers to Athena, daughter of royal Zeus.
The others made libation, and drank deep,
then all the company went to their quarters,
and Nestor of Gerênia showed Telémakhos
under the echoing eastern entrance hall
to a fine bed near the bed of Peisístratos,
captain of spearmen, his unmarried son.
Then he lay down in his own inner chamber
where his dear faithful wife had smoothed his bed.

When Dawn spread out her finger tips of rose,
Lord Nestor of Gerênia, charioteer,
left his room for a throne of polished stone,
white and gleaming as though with oil, that stood
before the main gate of the palace; Neleus here
had sat before him—masterful in kingship,
Neleus, long ago a prey to death, gone down
to the night of the underworld.
So Nestor held his throne and scepter now,
lord of the western approaches to Akhaia.
And presently his sons came out to join him,
leaving the palace: Ekhéphron and Stratíos,
Perseus and Arêtós and Thrasymêdês,
and after them the prince Peisístratos,
bringing Telémakhos along with him.
Seeing all present, the old lord Nestor said:

"Dear sons, here is my wish, and do it briskly
to please the gods, Athena first of all,
my guest in daylight at our holy feast.
One of you must go for a young heifer
and have the cowherd lead her from the pasture.
Another call on Lord Telémakhos' ship
to invite his crewmen, leaving two behind;
and someone else again send for the goldsmith,
Laerkês, to gild the horns.
The rest stay here together. Tell the servants
a ritual feast will be prepared in hall.
Tell them to bring seats, firewood and fresh water."

Before he finished, they were about these errands.
The heifer came from pasture,

the crewmen of Telémakhos from the ship,
the smith arrived, bearing the tools of his trade—
hammer and anvil, and the precision tongs
he handled fiery gold with,—and Athena
came as a god comes, numinous, to the rites.

The smith now gloved each horn in a pure foil
beaten out of the gold that Nestor gave him—
a glory and delight for the goddess' eyes—
while Ekhéphron and Stratíos held the horns.
Arêtós brought clear lustral water[2]
in a bowl quivering with fresh-cut flowers,
a basket of barley in his other hand.
Thrasymêdês, who could stand his ground in war,
stood ready, with a sharp two-bladed axe,
for the stroke of sacrifice, and Perseus
held a bowl for the blood. And now Nestor,
strewing the barley grains, and water drops,
pronounced his invocation to Athena
and burned a pinch of bristles from the victim.
When prayers were said and all the grain was scattered
great-hearted Thrasymêdês in a flash
swung the axe, at one blow cutting through
the neck tendons. The heifer's spirit failed.
Then all the women gave a wail of joy[3]—
daughters, daughters-in-law, and the Lady Eurydíkê,
Klyménos' eldest daughter. But the men
still held the heifer, shored her up
from the wide earth where the living go their ways,
until Peisístratos cut her throat across,
the black blood ran, and life ebbed from her marrow.
The carcass now sank down, and they disjointed
shoulder and thigh bone, wrapping them in fat,
two layers, folded, with raw strips of flesh.
These offerings Nestor burned on the split-wood fire
and moistened with red wine. His sons took up
five-tined forks in their hands, while the altar flame
ate through the bones, and bits of tripe went round.
Then came the carving of the quarters, and they spitted
morsels of lean meat on the long sharp tines
and broiled them at arm's length upon the fire.

Polykástê, a fair girl, Nestor's youngest,
had meanwhile given a bath to Telémakhos—
bathing him first, then rubbing him with oil.
She held fine clothes and a cloak to put around him
when he came godlike from the bathing place;
then out he went to take his place with Nestor.
When the best cuts were broiled and off the spits,

2. Used for sprinkling. 3. The ritual cry at the moment of sacrifice.

they all sat down to banquet. Gentle squires
kept every golden wine cup brimming full.
And so they feasted to their heart's content,
until the prince of charioteers commanded:

"Sons, harness the blood mares for Telémakhos;
hitch up the car, and let him take the road."

They swung out smartly to do the work, and hooked
the handsome horses to a chariot shaft.
The mistress of the stores brought up provisions
of bread and wine, with victuals fit for kings,
and Telémakhos stepped up on the painted car.
Just at his elbow stood Peisístratos,
captain of spearmen, reins in hand. He gave
a flick to the horses, and with streaming manes
they ran for the open country. The tall town
of Pylos sank behind them in the distance,
as all day long they kept the harness shaking.

The sun was low and shadows crossed the lanes
when they arrived at Phêrai. There Dióklês,
son of Ortílokhos whom Alpheios fathered,
welcomed the young men, and they slept the night.
But up when the young Dawn's finger tips of rose
opened in the east, they hitched the team
once more to the painted car,
and steered out eastward through the echoing gate,
whipping their fresh horses into a run.
That day they made the grainlands of Lakedaimon,
where, as the horses held to a fast clip,
they kept on to their journey's end. Behind them
the sun went down and all the roads grew dark.

BOOK IV

[*The Red-Haired King and His Lady*]

By vales and sharp ravines in Lakedaimon
the travellers drove to Meneláos' mansion,
and found him at a double wedding feast
for son and daughter.
Long ago at Troy
he pledged her to the heir[4] of great Akhilleus,
breaker of men—a match the gods had ripened;
so he must send her with a chariot train
to the town and glory of the Myrmidons.
And that day, too, he brought Alektor's daughter
to marry his tall scion, Megapénthês,

4. Akhilleus's son, Neoptólemos. In the underworld (book 11), Akhilleus asks for news of him from Odysseus.

born of a slave girl during the long war—
for the gods had never after granted Helen
a child to bring into the sunlit world
after the first, rose-lipped Hermionê,
a girl like the pale-gold goddess Aphroditê.
Down the great hall in happiness they feasted,
neighbors of Meneláos, and his kin,
for whom a holy minstrel harped and sang;
and two lithe tumblers moved out on the song
with spins and handsprings through the company.
Now when Telémakhos and Nestor's son
pulled up their horses at the main gate,
one of the king's companions in arms, Eteóneus,
going outside, caught sight of them. He turned
and passed through court and hall to tell the master,
stepping up close to get his ear. Said he:

"Two men are here—two strangers, Meneláos,
but nobly born Akhaians, they appear.
What do you say, shall we unhitch their team,
or send them on to someone free to receive them?"

The red-haired captain answered him in anger:

"You were no idiot before, Eteóneus,
but here you are talking like a child of ten.
Could we have made it home again—and Zeus
gave us no more hard roving!—if other men
had never fed us, given us lodging?
Bring
these men to be our guests: unhitch their team!"

Eteóneus left the long room like an arrow,
calling equerries after him, on the run.
Outside, they freed the sweating team from harness,
stabled the horses, tied them up, and showered
bushels of wheat and barley in the feed box;
then leaned the chariot pole
against the gleaming entry wall of stone
and took the guests in. What a brilliant place
that mansion of the great prince seemed to them!
A-glitter everywhere, as though with fiery
points of sunlight, lusters of the moon.
The young men gazed in joy before they entered
into a room of polished tubs to bathe.
Maidservants gave them baths, anointed them,
held out fresh tunics, cloaked them warm; and soon
they took tall thrones beside the son of Atreus.
Here a maid tipped out water for their hands
from a golden pitcher into a silver bowl,
and set a polished table near at hand;
the larder mistress with her tray of loaves

and savories came, dispensing all her best,
and then a carver heaped their platters high
with various meats, and put down cups of gold.
Now said the red-haired captain, Meneláos,
gesturing:

"Welcome; and fall to; in time,
when you have supped, we hope to hear your names,
forebears and families—in your case, it seems,
no anonymities, but lordly men.
Lads like yourselves are not base born."

At this,
he lifted in his own hands the king's portion,
a chine of beef, and set it down before them.
Seeing all ready then, they took their dinner;
but when they had feasted well,
Telémakhos could not keep still, but whispered,
his head bent close, so the others might not hear:

"My dear friend, can you believe your eyes?—
the murmuring hall, how luminous it is
with bronze, gold, amber, silver, and ivory!
This is the way the court of Zeus must be,
inside, upon Olympos. What a wonder!"

But splendid Meneláos had overheard him
and spoke out on the instant to them both:

"Young friends, no mortal man can vie with Zeus.
His home and all his treasures are for ever.
But as for men, it may well be that few
have more than I. How painfully I wandered
before I brought it home! Seven years at sea,
Kypros, Phoinikia, Egypt, and still farther
among the sun-burnt races.
I saw the men of Sidon and Arabia
and Libya, too, where lambs are horned at birth.
In every year they have three lambing seasons,
so no man, chief or shepherd, ever goes
hungry for want of mutton, cheese, or milk—
all year at milking time there are fresh ewes.
But while I made my fortune on those travels
a stranger killed my brother, in cold blood,—
tricked blind, caught in the web of his deadly queen.
What pleasure can I take, then, being lord
over these costly things?
You must have heard your fathers tell my story,
whoever your fathers are; you must know of my life,
the anguish I once had, and the great house
full of my treasure, left in desolation.
How gladly I should live one third as rich

to have my friends back safe at home!—my friends
who died on Troy's wide seaboard, far
from the grazing lands of Argos.
But as things are, nothing but grief is left me
for those companions. While I sit at home
sometimes hot tears come, and I revel in them,
or stop before the surfeit makes me shiver.
And there is one I miss more than the other
dead I mourn for; sleep and food alike
grow hateful when I think of him. No soldier
took on so much, went through so much, as Odysseus.
That seems to have been his destiny, and this mine—
to feel each day the emptiness of his absence,
ignorant, even, whether he lived or died.
How his old father and his quiet wife,
Penélopê, must miss him still!
And Telémakhos, whom he left as a new-born child."

Now hearing these things said, the boy's heart rose
in a long pang for his father, and he wept,
holding his purple mantle with both hands
before his eyes. Meneláos knew him now,
and so fell silent with uncertainty
whether to let him speak and name his father
in his own time, or to inquire, and prompt him.
And while he pondered, Helen came
out of her scented chamber, a moving grace
like Artemis,[5] straight as a shaft of gold.
Beside her came Adrastê, to place her armchair,
Alkippê, with a rug of downy wool,
and Phylo, bringing a silver basket, once
given by Alkandrê, the wife of Pólybos,
in the treasure city, Thebes of distant Egypt.
He gave two silver bathtubs to Meneláos
and a pair of tripods, with ten pure gold bars,
and she, then, made these beautiful gifts to Helen:
a golden distaff, and the silver basket
rimmed in hammered gold, with wheels to run on.
So Phylo rolled it in to stand beside her,
heaped with fine spun stuff, and cradled on it
the distaff swathed in dusky violet wool.
Reclining in her light chair with its footrest,
Helen gazed at her husband and demanded:

"Meneláos, my lord, have we yet heard
our new guests introduce themselves? Shall I
dissemble what I feel? No, I must say it.
Never, anywhere, have I seen so great a likeness
in man or woman—but it is truly strange!

5. A virgin goddess, sister of Apollo, and associated with wild animals; women called on her for help in childbirth. Helen, Meneláos's wife, was the daughter of Leda, whom Zeus seduced when he was in the shape of a swan. Her kidnapping by Paris was the cause of the Trojan War.

This boy must be the son of Odysseus,
Telémakhos, the child he left at home
that year the Akhaian host made war on Troy—
daring all for the wanton that I was."

And the red-haired captain, Meneláos, answered:

"My dear, I see the likeness as well as you do.
Odysseus' hands and feet were like this boy's;
his head, and hair, and the glinting of his eyes.
Not only that, but when I spoke, just now,
of Odysseus' years of toil on my behalf
and all he had to endure—the boy broke down
and wept into his cloak."

Now Nestor's son,
Peisístratos, spoke up in answer to him:

"My lord marshal, Meneláos, son of Atreus,
this is that hero's son as you surmise,
but he is gentle, and would be ashamed
to clamor for attention before your grace
whose words have been so moving to us both.
Nestor, Lord of Gerênia, sent me with him
as guide and escort; he had wished to see you,
to be advised by you or assisted somehow.
A father far from home means difficulty
for an only son, with no one else to help him;
so with Telémakhos:
his father left the house without defenders."

The king with flaming hair now spoke again:

"His son, in my house! How I loved the man,
and how he fought through hardship for my sake!
I swore I'd cherish him above all others
if Zeus, who views the wide world, gave us passage
homeward across the sea in the fast ships.
I would have settled him in Argos, brought him
over with herds and household out of Ithaka,
his child and all his people. I could have cleaned out
one of my towns to be his new domain.
And so we might have been together often
in feasts and entertainments, never parted
till the dark mist of death lapped over one of us.
But God himself must have been envious,
to batter the bruised man so that he alone
should fail in his return."

A twinging ache of grief rose up in everyone,
and Helen of Argos wept, the daughter of Zeus,
Telémakhos and Meneláos wept,
and tears came to the eyes of Nestor's son—

remembering, for his part, Antílokhos,
whom the son of shining Dawn had killed in battle.
But thinking of that brother, he broke out:

"O son of Atreus, when we spoke of you
at home, and asked about you, my old father
would say you have the clearest mind of all.
If it is not too much to ask, then, let us not
weep away these hours after supper;
I feel we should not: Dawn will soon be here!
You understand, I would not grudge a man
right mourning when he comes to death and doom:
what else can one bestow on the poor dead?—
a lock of hair sheared, and a tear let fall.
For that matter, I, too,
lost someone in the war at Troy—my brother,
and no mean soldier, whom you must have known,
although I never did,—Antílokhos.
He ranked high as a runner and fighting man."

The red-haired captain Meneláos answered:

"My lad, what you have said is only sensible,
and you did well to speak. Yes, that was worthy
a wise man and an older man than you are:
you speak for all the world like Nestor's son.
How easily one can tell the man whose father
had true felicity, marrying and begetting!
And that was true of Nestor, all his days,
down to his sleek old age in peace at home,
with clever sons, good spearmen into the bargain.
Come, we'll shake off this mourning mood of ours
and think of supper. Let the men at arms
rinse our hands again! There will be time
for a long talk with Telémakhos in the morning."

The hero Meneláos' companion in arms,
Asphalion, poured water for their hands,
and once again they touched the food before them.
But now it entered Helen's mind
to drop into the wine that they were drinking
an anodyne, mild magic of forgetfulness.
Whoever drank this mixture in the wine bowl
would be incapable of tears that day—
though he should lose mother and father both,
or see, with his own eyes, a son or brother
mauled by weapons of bronze at his own gate.
The opiate of Zeus's daughter bore
this canny power. It had been supplied her
by Polydamna, mistress of Lord Thôn,
in Egypt,[6] where the rich plantations grow

6. The Greeks had great respect for Egyptian doctors, and Egyptian papyri document their skill as surgeons and their expertise with drugs.

herbs of all kinds, maleficent and healthful;
and no one else knows medicine as they do,
Egyptian heirs of Paian, the healing god.
She drugged the wine, then, had it served, and said—
taking again her part in the conversation—

"O Meneláos, Atreus' royal son,
and you that are great heroes' sons, you know
how Zeus gives all of us in turn
good luck and bad luck, being all powerful.
So take refreshment, take your ease in hall,
and cheer the time with stories. I'll begin.
Not that I think of naming, far less telling,
every feat of that rugged man, Odysseus,
but here is something that he dared to do
at Troy, where you Akhaians endured the war.
He had, first, given himself an outrageous beating
and thrown some rags on—like a household slave—
then slipped into that city of wide lanes
among his enemies. So changed, he looked
as never before upon the Akhaian beachhead,
but like a beggar, merged in the townspeople;
and no one there remarked him. But I knew him—
even as he was, I knew him,
and questioned him. How shrewdly he put me off!
But in the end I bathed him and anointed him,
put a fresh cloak around him, and swore an oath
not to give him away as Odysseus to the Trojans,
till he got back to camp where the long ships lay.
He spoke up then, and told me
all about the Akhaians, and their plans—
then sworded many Trojans through the body
on his way out with what he learned of theirs.
The Trojan women raised a cry—but my heart
sang—for I had come round, long before,
to dreams of sailing home, and I repented
the mad day Aphroditê
drew me away from my dear fatherland,
forsaking all—child, bridal bed, and husband—
a man without defect in form or mind."

Replied the red-haired captain, Meneláos:

"An excellent tale, my dear, and most becoming.
In my life I have met, in many countries,
foresight and wit in many first rate men,
but never have I seen one like Odysseus
for steadiness and a stout heart. Here, for instance,
is what he did—had the cold nerve to do—
inside the hollow horse, where we were waiting,
picked men all of us, for the Trojan slaughter,
when all of a sudden, you came by—I dare say

drawn by some superhuman
power that planned an exploit for the Trojans;
and Deïphobos,[7] that handsome man, came with you.
Three times you walked around it, patting it everywhere,
and called by name the flower of our fighters,
making your voice sound like their wives, calling.
Diomêdês and I crouched in the center
along with Odysseus; we could hear you plainly;
and listening, we two were swept
by waves of longing—to reply, or go.
Odysseus fought us down, despite our craving,
and all the Akhaians kept their lips shut tight,
all but Antiklos. Desire moved his throat
to hail you, but Odysseus' great hands clamped
over his jaws, and held. So he saved us all,
till Pallas Athena led you away at last."

Then clear-headed Telémakhos addressed him:

"My lord marshal, Meneláos, son of Atreus,
all the more pity, since these valors
could not defend him from annihilation—
not if his heart were iron in his breast.
But will you not dismiss us for the night now?
Sweet sleep will be a pleasure, drifting over us."

He said no more, but Helen called the maids
and sent them to make beds, with purple rugs
piled up, and sheets outspread, and fleecy
coverlets, in the porch inside the gate.
The girls went out with torches in their hands,
and presently a squire led the guests—
Telémakhos and Nestor's radiant son—
under the entrance colonnade, to bed.
Then deep in the great mansion, in his chamber,
Meneláos went to rest, and Helen,
queenly in her long gown, lay beside him.

When the young Dawn with finger tips of rose
made heaven bright, the deep-lunged man of battle
stood up, pulled on his tunic and his mantle,
slung on a swordbelt and a new edged sword,
tied his smooth feet into fine rawhide sandals
and left his room, a god's brilliance upon him.
He sat down by Telémakhos, asking gently:

"Telémakhos, why did you come, sir, riding
the sea's broad back to reach old Lakedaimon?
A public errand or private? Why, precisely?"

7. A Trojan prince whom Helen married after Paris was killed in battle.

Telémakhos replied:

“My lord marshal Meneláos, son of Atreus,
I came to hear what news you had of Father.
My house, my good estates are being ruined.
Each day my mother’s bullying suitors come
to slaughter flocks of mine and my black cattle;
enemies crowd our home. And this is why
I come to you for news of him who owned it.
Tell me of his death, sir, if perhaps
you witnessed it, or have heard some wanderer
tell the tale. The man was born for trouble.
Spare me no part for kindness’ sake; be harsh;
but put the scene before me as you saw it.
If ever Odysseus my noble father
served you by promise kept or work accomplished
in the land of Troy, where you Akhaians suffered,
recall those things for me the way they were.”

Stirred now to anger, Meneláos said:

“Intolerable—that soft men, as those are,
should think to lie in that great captain’s bed.
Fawns in a lion’s lair! As if a doe
put down her litter of sucklings there, while she
quested a glen or cropped some grassy hollow.
Ha! Then the lord returns to his own bed
and deals out wretched doom on both alike.
So will Odysseus deal out doom on these.
O Father Zeus, Athena, and Apollo!
I pray he comes as once he was, in Lesbos,
when he stood up to wrestle Philomeleidês[8]—
champion and Island King—
and smashed him down. How the Akhaians cheered!
If only that Odysseus met the suitors,
they’d have their consummation, a cold bed!
Now for your questions, let me come to the point.
I would not misreport it for you; let me
tell you what the Ancient of the Sea,
who is infallible, said to me—every word.

During my first try at a passage homeward
the gods detained me, tied me down to Egypt—
for I had been too scant in hekatombs,
and gods will have the rules each time remembered.
There is an island washed by the open sea
lying off Nile mouth—seamen call it Pharos—
distant a day’s sail in a clean hull
with a brisk land breeze behind. It has a harbor,
a sheltered bay, where shipmasters

8. A king of Lesbos who challenged all comers to wrestle with him.

take on dark water for the outward voyage.
Here the gods held me twenty days becalmed.
No winds came up, seaward escorting winds
for ships that ride the sea's broad back, and so
my stores and men were used up; we were failing
had not one goddess intervened in pity—
Eidothea, daughter of Proteus,
the Ancient of the Sea. How I distressed her!
I had been walking out alone that day—
my sailors, thin-bellied from the long fast,
were off with fish hooks, angling on the shore—
then she appeared to me, and her voice sang:

'What fool is here, what drooping dunce of dreams?
Or can it be, friend, that you love to suffer?
How can you linger on this island, aimless
and shiftless, while your people waste away?'

To this I quickly answered:

'Let me tell you,
goddess, whatever goddess you may be,
these doldrums are no will of mine. I take it
the gods who own broad heaven are offended.
Why don't you tell me—since the gods know everything—
who has me pinned down here?
How am I going to make my voyage home?'

Now she replied in her immortal beauty:

'I'll put it for you clearly as may be, friend.
The Ancient of the Salt Sea haunts this place,
immortal Proteus of Egypt; all the deeps
are known to him; he serves under Poseidon,
and is, they say, my father.
If you could take him by surprise and hold him,
he'd give you course and distance for your sailing
homeward across the cold fish-breeding sea.
And should you wish it, noble friend, he'd tell you
all that occurred at home, both good and evil,
while you were gone so long and hard a journey.'

To this I said:

'But you, now—you must tell me
how I can trap this venerable sea-god.
He will elude me if he takes alarm;
no man—god knows—can quell a god with ease.'

That fairest of unearthly nymphs replied:

'I'll tell you this, too, clearly as may be.
When the sun hangs at high noon in heaven,
the Ancient glides ashore under the Westwind,
hidden by shivering glooms on the clear water,
and rests in caverns hollowed by the sea.
There flippered seals, brine children, shining come
from silvery foam in crowds to lie around him,
exhaling rankness from the deep sea floor.
Tomorrow dawn I'll take you to those caves
and bed you down there. Choose three officers
for company—brave men they had better be—
the old one has strange powers, I must tell you.
He goes amid the seals to check their number,
and when he sees them all, and counts them all,
he lies down like a shepherd with his flock.
Here is your opportunity: at this point
gather yourselves, with all your heart and strength,
and tackle him before he bursts away.
He'll make you fight—for he can take the forms
of all the beasts, and water, and blinding fire;
but you must hold on, even so, and crush him
until he breaks the silence. When he does,
he will be in that shape you saw asleep.
Relax your grip, then, set the Ancient free,
and put your questions, hero:
Who is the god so hostile to you,
and how will you go home on the fish-cold sea.'

At this she dove under a swell and left me.
Back to the ships in the sandy cove I went,
my heart within me like a high surf running;
but there I joined my men once more
at supper, as the sacred Night came on,
and slept at last beside the lapping water.
When Dawn spread out her finger tips of rose
I started, by the sea's wide level ways,
praying the gods for help, and took along
three lads I counted on in any fight.
Meanwhile the nereid[9] swam from the lap of Ocean
laden with four sealskins, new flayed
for the hoax she thought of playing on her father.
In the sand she scooped out hollows for our bodies
and sat down, waiting. We came close to touch her,
and, bedding us, she threw the sealskins over us—
a strong disguise; oh, yes, terribly strong
as I recall the stench of those damned seals.
Would any man lie snug with a sea monster?
But here the nymph, again, came to our rescue,
dabbing ambrosia under each man's nose—
a perfume drowning out the bestial odor.

9. Sea nymph.

So there we lay with beating hearts all morning
while seals came shoreward out of ripples, jostling
to take their places, flopping on the sand.
At noon the Ancient issued from the sea
and held inspection, counting off the sea-beasts.
We were the first he numbered; he went by,
detecting nothing. When at last he slept
we gave a battlecry and plunged for him,
locking our hands behind him. But the old one's
tricks were not knocked out of him; far from it.
First he took on a whiskered lion's shape,
a serpent then; a leopard; a great boar;
then sousing water; then a tall green tree.
Still we hung on, by hook or crook, through everything,
until the Ancient saw defeat, and grimly
opened his lips to ask me:

'Son of Atreus,
who counselled you to this? A god: what god?
Set a trap for me, overpower me—why?'

He bit it off, then, and I answered:

'Old one,
you know the reason—why feign not to know?
High and dry so long upon this island
I'm at my wits' end, and my heart is sore.
You gods know everything; now you can tell me:
which of the immortals chained me here?
And how will I get home on the fish-cold sea?'

He made reply at once:

'You should have paid
honor to Zeus and the other gods, performing
a proper sacrifice before embarking:
that was your short way home on the winedark sea.
You may not see your friends, your own fine house,
or enter your own land again,
unless you first remount the Nile in flood
and pay your hekatomb to the gods of heaven.
Then, and then only,
the gods will grant the passage you desire.'

Ah, how my heart sank, hearing this—
hearing him send me back on the cloudy sea
in my own track, the long hard way of Egypt.
Nevertheless, I answered him and said:

'Ancient, I shall do all as you command.
But tell me, now, the others—
had they a safe return, all those Akhaians

who stayed behind when Nestor and I left Troy?
Or were there any lost at sea—what bitterness!—
any who died in camp, after the war?'

To this he said:

'For you to know these things
goes beyond all necessity, Meneláos.
Why must you ask?—you should not know my mind,
and you will grieve to learn it, I can tell you.
Many there were who died, many remain,
but two high officers alone were lost—
on the passage home, I mean; you saw the war.
One is alive, a castaway at sea;
the other, Aias,[1] perished with all hands—
though first Poseidon landed him on Gyrai
promontory, and saved him from the ocean.
Despite Athena's hate, he had lived on,
but the great sinner in his insolence
yelled that the gods' will and the sea were beaten,
and this loud brag came to Poseidon's ears.
He swung the trident in his massive hands
and in one shock from top to bottom split
that promontory, toppling into the sea
the fragment where the great fool sat.
So the vast ocean had its will with Aias,
drunk in the end on salt spume as he drowned.
Meanwhile your brother left that doom astern
in his decked ships—the Lady Hera[2] saved him;
but as he came round Malea
a fresh squall caught him, bearing him away
over the cold sea, groaning in disgust,
to the Land's End of Argos, where Thyestês
lived in the days of old, and then his son,
Aigísthos. Now, again, return seemed easy:
the high gods wound the wind into the east,
and back he sailed, this time to his own coast.
He went ashore and kissed the earth in joy,
hot tears blinding his eyes at sight of home.
But there were eyes that watched him from a height—
a lookout, paid two bars of gold to keep
vigil the year round for Aigísthos' sake,
that he should be forewarned, and Agamémnon's
furious valor sleep unroused.
Now this man with his news ran to the tyrant,
who made his crooked arrangements in a flash,
stationed picked men at arms, a score of men
in hiding; set a feast in the next room;
then he went out with chariots and horses
to hail the king and welcome him to evil.

1. The lesser Aias. 2. The wife and sister of Zeus. *Your brother:* Agamémnon.

He led him in to banquet, all serene,
and killed him, like an ox felled at the trough;
and not a man of either company
survived that ambush in Aigísthos' house.'

Before the end my heart was broken down.
I slumped on the trampled sand and cried aloud,
caring no more for life or the light of day,
and rolled there weeping, till my tears were spent.
Then the unerring Ancient said at last:

'No more, no more; how long must you persist?
Nothing is gained by grieving so. How soon
can you return to Argos? You may take him
alive there still—or else meanwhile Orestês
will have despatched him. You'll attend the feast.'

At this my heart revived, and I recovered
the self command to question him once more:

'Of two companions now I know. The third?
Tell me his name, the one marooned at sea;
living, you say, or dead? Even in pain
I wish to hear.'

And this is all he answered:

'Laërtês' son, whose home is Ithaka.
I saw him weeping, weeping on an island.
The nymph Kalypso has him, in her hall.
No means of faring home are left him now;
no ship with oars, and no ship's company
to pull him on the broad back of the sea.
As to your own destiny, prince Meneláos,
you shall not die in the bluegrass land of Argos;
rather the gods intend you for Elysion
with golden Rhadamanthos[3] at the world's end,
where all existence is a dream of ease.
Snowfall is never known there, neither long
frost of winter, nor torrential rain,
but only mild and lulling airs from Ocean
bearing refreshment for the souls of men—
the West Wind always blowing.
For the gods
hold you, as Helen's lord, a son of Zeus.'

At this he dove under a swell and left me,
and I went back to the ship with my companions,
feeling my heart's blood in me running high;

3. A son of Zeus by the mortal Europa, and brother to King Minos of Krete. Elysion is the paradise reserved for a few of the heroes who were related to gods (Meneláos is Zeus's son-in-law).

but in the long hull's shadow, near the sea,
we supped again as sacred Night came on
and slept at last beside the lapping water.

When Dawn spread out her finger tips of rose,
in first light we launched on the courtly breakers,
setting up masts and yards in the well-found ships;
went all on board, and braced on planks athwart
oarsmen in line dipped oars in the grey sea.
Soon I drew in to the great stream[4] fed by heaven
and, laying by, slew bulls in the proper number,
until the immortal gods were thus appeased;
then heaped a death mound on that shore against
all-quenching time for Agamémnon's honor,
and put to sea once more. The gods sent down
a sternwind for a racing passage homeward.

So ends the story. Now you must stay with me
and be my guest eleven or twelve days more.
I'll send you on your way with gifts, and fine ones:
three chariot horses, and a polished car;
a hammered cup, too, so that all your days,
tipping the red wine for the deathless gods,
you will remember me."

Telémakhos answered:

"Lord, son of Atreus, no, you must not keep me.
Not that a year with you would be too long:
I never could be homesick here—I find
your tales and all you say so marvellous.
But time hangs heavy on my shipmates' hands
at holy Pylos, if you make me stay.
As for your gift, now, let it be some keepsake.
Horses I cannot take to Ithaka;
let me bestow them back on you, to serve
your glory here. My lord, you rule wide country,
rolling and rich with clover, galingale
and all the grains: red wheat and hoary barley.
At home we have no level runs or meadows,
but highland, goat land—prettier than plains, though.
Grasses, and pasture land, are hard to come by
upon the islands tilted in the sea,
and Ithaka is the island of them all."

At this the deep-lunged man of battle smiled.
Then he said kindly, patting the boy's hand:

"You come of good stock, lad. That was well spoken.
I'll change the gift, then—as indeed I can.

4. The Nile River.

Let me see what is costliest and most beautiful
of all the precious things my house contains:
a wine bowl, mixing bowl, all wrought of silver,
but rimmed with hammered gold. Let this be yours.
It is Hephaistos'[5] work, given me by Phaidimos,
captain and king of Sidon. He received me
during my travels. Let it be yours, I say."

This was their discourse on that morning. Meanwhile
guests were arriving at the great lord's house,
bringing their sheep, and wine, the ease of men,
with loaves their comely kerchiefed women sent,
to make a feast in hall.
At that same hour,
before the distant manor of Odysseus,
the suitors were competing at the discus throw
and javelin, on a measured field they used,
arrogant lords at play. The two best men,
Antínoös and Eurýmakhos, presided.
Now Phronios' son, Noêmon, came to see them
with a question for Antínoös. He said:

"Do any of us know, or not, Antínoös,
what day Telémakhos will be home from Pylos?
He took my ship, but now I need it back
to make a cruise to Elis, where the plains are.
I have a dozen mares at pasture there
with mule colts yet unweaned. My notion is
to bring one home and break him in for labor."

His first words made them stare—for they knew well
Telémakhos could not have gone to Pylos,
but inland with his flocks, or to the swineherd.
Eupeithês' son, Antínoös, quickly answered:

"Tell the story straight. He sailed? Who joined him—
a crew he picked up here in Ithaka,
or his own slaves? He might have done it that way.
And will you make it clear
whether he took the ship against your will?
Did he ask for it, did you lend it to him?"

Now said the son of Phronios in reply:

"Lent it to him, and freely. Who would not,
when a prince of that house asked for it, in trouble?
Hard to refuse the favor, it seems to me.
As for his crew, the best men on the island,
after ourselves, went with him. Mentor I noted

5. God of the forge and patron of metalworkers; he made Akhilleus's armor and was married to the goddess Aphrodite.

going aboard—or a god who looked like Mentor.
The strange thing is, I saw Lord Mentor here
in the first light yesterday—although he sailed
five days ago for Pylos."

Turning away,
Noêmon took the path to his father's house,
leaving the two men there, baffled and hostile.
They called the rest in from the playing field
and made them all sit down, so that Antínoös
could speak out from the stormcloud of his heart,
swollen with anger; and his eyes blazed:

"A bad business. Telémakhos had the gall
to make that crossing, though we said he could not.
So the young cub rounds up a first rate crew
in spite of all our crowd, and puts to sea.
What devilment will he be up to next time?—
Zeus blast the life out of him before he's grown!
Just give me a fast ship and twenty men;
I'll intercept him, board him in the strait
between the crags of Samê and this island.
He'll find his sea adventure after his father
swamping work in the end!"

They all cried "Aye!"
and "After him!" and trailed back to the manor.

Now not much time went by before Penélopê
learned what was afoot among the suitors.
Medôn the crier told her. He had been
outside the wall, and heard them in the court
conspiring. Into the house and up the stairs
he ran to her with his news upon his tongue—
but at the door Penélopê met him, crying:

"Why have they sent you up here now? To tell
the maids of King Odysseus—'Leave your spinning:
Time to go down and slave to feed those men'?
I wish this were the last time they came feasting,
courting me or consorting here! The last!
Each day you crowd this house like wolves
to eat away my brave son's patrimony.
When you were boys, did your own fathers tell you
nothing of what Odysseus was for them?
In word and act impeccable, disinterested
toward all the realm—though it is king's justice
to hold one man abhorred and love another;
no man alive could say Odysseus wronged him.
But your own hearts—how different!—and your deeds!
How soon are benefactions all forgotten!"

Now Medôn, the alert and cool man, answered:

"I wish that were the worst of it, my Lady,
but they intend something more terrible—
may Zeus forfend and spare us!
They plan to drive the keen bronze through Telémakhos
when he comes home. He sailed away, you know,
to hallowed Pylos and old Lakedaimon
for news about his father."

Her knees failed,
and her heart failed as she listened to the words,
and all her power of speech went out of her.
Tears came; but the rich voice could not come.
Only after a long while she made answer:

"Why has my child left me? He had no need
of those long ships on which men shake out sail
to tug like horses, breasting miles of sea.
Why did he go? Must he, too, be forgotten?"

Then Medôn, the perceptive man, replied:

"A god moved him—who knows?—or his own heart
sent him to learn, at Pylos, if his father
roams the wide world still, or what befell him."

He left her then, and went down through the house.
And now the pain around her heart benumbed her;
chairs were a step away, but far beyond her;
she sank down on the door sill of the chamber,
wailing, and all her women young and old
made a low murmur of lament around her,
until at last she broke out through her tears:

"Dearest companions, what has Zeus given me?
Pain—more pain than any living woman.
My lord, my lion heart, gone, long ago—
the bravest man, and best, of the Danaans,
famous through Hellas and the Argive midlands—
and now the squalls have blown my son, my dear one,
an unknown boy, southward. No one told me.
O brute creatures, not one soul would dare
to wake me from my sleep; you knew
the hour he took the black ship out to sea!
If I had seen that sailing in his eyes
he should have stayed with me, for all his longing,
stayed—or left me dead in the great hall.
Go, someone, now, and call old Dólios,
the slave my father gave me before I came,
my orchard keeper—tell him to make haste
and put these things before Laërtês; he

may plan some kind of action; let him come
to cry shame on these ruffians who would murder
Odysseus' son and heir, and end his line!"

The dear old nurse, Eurýkleia, answered her:

"Sweet mistress, have my throat cut without mercy
or what you will; it's true, I won't conceal it,
I knew the whole thing; gave him his provisions;
grain and sweet wine I gave, and a great oath
to tell you nothing till twelve days went by,
or till you heard of it yourself, or missed him;
he hoped you would not tear your skin lamenting.
Come, bathe and dress your loveliness afresh,
and go to the upper rooms with all your maids
to ask help from Athena, Zeus's daughter.
She it will be who saves this boy from death.
Spare the old man this further suffering;
the blissful gods cannot so hate his line,
heirs of Arkêsios;[6] one will yet again
be lord of the tall house and the far fields."

She hushed her weeping in this way, and soothed her.
The Lady Penélopê arose and bathed,
dressing her body in her freshest linen,
filled a basket with barley, and led her maids
to the upper rooms, where she besought Athena:

"Tireless child of Zeus, graciously hear me!
If ever Odysseus burned at our altar fire
thighbones of beef or mutton in sacrifice,
remember it for my sake! Save my son!
Shield him, and make the killers go astray!"

She ended with a cry, and the goddess heard her.
Now voices rose from the shadowy hall below
where the suitors were assuring one another:
"Our so-long-courted Queen is even now
of a mind to marry one of us, and knows
nothing of what is destined for her son."

Of what was destined they in fact knew nothing,
but Antínoös addressed them in a whisper:

"No boasting—are you mad?—and no loud talk:
someone might hear it and alarm the house.
Come along now, be quiet, this way; come,
we'll carry out the plan our hearts are set on."

Picking out twenty of the strongest seamen,
he led them to a ship at the sea's edge,

6. Laërtês' father and Odysseus's grandfather.

and down they dragged her into deeper water,
stepping a mast in her, with furled sails,
and oars a-trail from thongs looped over thole pins,
ready all; then tried the white sail, hoisting,
while men at arms carried their gear aboard.
They moored the ship some way off shore, and left her
to take their evening meal there, waiting for night to come.

Penélopê at that hour in her high chamber
lay silent, tasting neither food nor drink,
and thought of nothing but her princely son—
could he escape, or would they find and kill him?—
her mind turning at bay, like a cornered lion
in whom fear comes as hunters close the ring.
But in her sick thought sweet sleep overtook her,
and she dozed off, her body slack and still.

Now it occurred to the grey-eyed goddess Athena
to make a figure of dream in a woman's form—
Iphthimê, great Ikários' other daughter,
whom Eumêlos of Phêrai took as bride.
The goddess sent this dream to Odysseus' house
to quiet Penélopê and end her grieving.
So, passing by the strap-slit[7] through the door,
the image came a-gliding down the room
to stand at her bedside and murmur to her:

"Sleepest thou, sorrowing Penélopê?
The gods whose life is ease no longer suffer thee
to pine and weep, then; he returns unharmed,
thy little one; no way hath he offended."

Then pensive Penélopê made this reply,
slumbering sweetly in the gates of dream:

"Sister, hast thou come hither? Why? Aforetime
never wouldst come, so far away thy dwelling.
And am I bid be done with all my grieving?
But see what anguish hath my heart and soul!
My lord, my lion heart, gone, long ago—
the bravest man, and best, of the Danaans,
famous through Hellas and the Argive midlands—
and now my son, my dear one, gone seafaring,
a child, untrained in hardship or in council.
Aye, 'tis for him I weep, more than his father!
Aye, how I tremble for him, lest some blow
befall him at men's hands or on the sea!
Cruel are they and many who plot against him,
to take his life before he can return."

7. We would say, "through the keyhole." The inside bolt could be closed from outside by means of a strap that came through a slit in the door.

Now the dim phantom spoke to her once more:

"Lift up thy heart, and fear not overmuch.
For by his side one goes whom all men else
invoke as their defender, one so powerful—
Pallas Athena; in thy tears she pitied thee
and now hath sent me that I so assure thee."

Then said Penélopê the wise:

"If thou art
numinous and hast ears for divine speech,
O tell me, what of Odysseus, man of woe?
Is he alive still somewhere, seeth he day light still?
Or gone in death to the sunless underworld?"

The dim phantom said only this in answer:

"Of him I may not tell thee in this discourse,
alive or dead. And empty words are evil."
The wavering form withdrew along the doorbolt
into a draft of wind, and out of sleep
Penélopê awoke, in better heart
for that clear dream in the twilight of the night.

Meanwhile the suitors had got under way,
planning the death plunge for Telémakhos.
Between the Isles of Ithaka and Samê
the sea is broken by an islet, Asteris,
with access to both channels from a cove.
In ambush here that night the Akhaians lay.

BOOK V

[*Sweet Nymph and Open Sea*]

Dawn came up from the couch of her reclining,
leaving her lord Tithonos'[8] brilliant side
with fresh light in her arms for gods and men.
And the master of heaven and high thunder, Zeus,
went to his place among the gods assembled
hearing Athena tell Odysseus' woe.
For she, being vexed that he was still sojourning
in the sea chambers of Kalypso, said:

"O Father Zeus and gods in bliss forever,
let no man holding scepter as a king
think to be mild, or kind, or virtuous;
let him be cruel, and practice evil ways,
for those Odysseus ruled cannot remember
the fatherhood and mercy of his reign.

8. A mortal man whom Eos, the dawn goddess, took for her husband.

Meanwhile he lives and grieves upon that island
in thralldom to the nymph; he cannot stir,
cannot fare homeward, for no ship is left him,
fitted with oars—no crewmen or companions
to pull him on the broad back of the sea.
And now murder is hatched on the high sea
against his son, who sought news of his father
in the holy lands of Pylos and Lakedaimon."

To this the summoner of cloud replied:

"My child, what odd complaints you let escape you.
Have you not, you yourself, arranged this matter—
as we all know—so that Odysseus
will bring these men to book, on his return?
And are you not the one to give Telémakhos
a safe route for sailing? Let his enemies
encounter no one and row home again."

He turned then to his favorite son and said:

"Hermês, you have much practice on our missions,
go make it known to the softly-braided nymph
that we, whose will is not subject to error,
order Odysseus home; let him depart.
But let him have no company, gods or men,
only a raft that he must lash together,
and after twenty days, worn out at sea,
he shall make land upon the garden isle,
Skhería,[9] of our kinsmen, the Phaiákians.
Let these men take him to their hearts in honor
and berth him in a ship, and send him home,
with gifts of garments, gold, and bronze—
so much he had not counted on from Troy
could he have carried home his share of plunder.
His destiny is to see his friends again
under his own roof, in his father's country."

No words were lost on Hermês the Wayfinder,
who bent to tie his beautiful sandals on,
ambrosial, golden, that carry him over water
or over endless land in a swish of the wind,
and took the wand with which he charms asleep—
or when he wills, awake—the eyes of men.
So wand in hand he paced into the air,
shot from Pieria[1] down, down to sea level,
and veered to skim the swell. A gull patrolling
between the wave crests of the desolate sea
will dip to catch a fish, and douse his wings;

9. Later Greeks identified it as the island of Corcyra (modern Corfu) off the northwest coast of mainland Greece. 1. The vicinity of Mount Olympus.

no higher above the whitecaps Hermês flew
until the distant island lay ahead,
then rising shoreward from the violet ocean
he stepped up to the cave. Divine Kalypso,
the mistress of the isle, was now at home.
Upon her hearthstone a great fire blazing
scented the farthest shores with cedar smoke
and smoke of thyme, and singing high and low
in her sweet voice, before her loom a-weaving,
she passed her golden shuttle to and fro.
A deep wood grew outside, with summer leaves
of alder and black poplar, pungent cypress.
Ornate birds here rested their stretched wings—
horned owls, falcons, cormorants—long-tongued
beachcombing birds, and followers of the sea.
Around the smoothwalled cave a crooking vine
held purple clusters under ply of green;
and four springs, bubbling up near one another
shallow and clear, took channels here and there
through beds of violets and tender parsley.
Even a god who found this place
would gaze, and feel his heart beat with delight:
so Hermês did; but when he had gazed his fill
he entered the wide cave. Now face to face
the magical Kalypso recognized him,
as all immortal gods know one another
on sight—though seeming strangers, far from home.
But he saw nothing of the great Odysseus,
who sat apart, as a thousand times before,
and racked his own heart groaning, with eyes wet
scanning the bare horizon of the sea.
Kalypso, lovely nymph, seated her guest
in a bright chair all shimmering, and asked:

"O Hermês, ever with your golden wand,
what brings you to my island?
Your awesome visits in the past were few.
Now tell me what request you have in mind;
for I desire to do it, if I can,
and if it is a proper thing to do.
But wait a while, and let me serve my friend."

She drew a table of ambrosia near him
and stirred a cup of ruby-colored nectar—
food and drink for the luminous Wayfinder,
who took both at his leisure, and replied:[2]

"Goddess to god, you greet me, questioning me?
Well, here is truth for you in courtesy.
Zeus made me come, and not my inclination;

2. The translator put Hermês' speech into rhymed couplets; there is no rhyme in the original Greek.

who cares to cross that tract of desolation,
the bitter sea, all mortal towns behind
where gods have beef and honors from mankind?
But it is not to be thought of—and no use—
for any god to elude the will of Zeus.
He notes your friend, most ill-starred by renown
of all the peers who fought for Priam's town—
nine years of war they had, before great Troy was down.
Homing, they wronged the goddess with grey eyes,
who made a black wind blow and the seas rise,
in which his troops were lost, and all his gear,
while easterlies and current washed him here.
Now the command is: send him back in haste.
His life may not in exile go to waste.
His destiny, his homecoming, is at hand,
when he shall see his dearest, and walk on his own land."

That goddess most divinely made
shuddered before him, and her warm voice rose:

"Oh you vile gods, in jealousy supernal!
You hate it when we choose to lie with men—
immortal flesh by some dear mortal side.
So radiant Dawn once took to bed Orion
until you easeful gods grew peevish at it,
and holy Artemis, Artemis throned in gold,
hunted him down in Delos with her arrows.
Then Dêmêtêr[3] of the tasseled tresses yielded
to Iasion, mingling and making love
in a furrow three times plowed; but Zeus found out
and killed him with a white-hot thunderbolt.
So now you grudge me, too, my mortal friend.
But it was I who saved him—saw him straddle
his own keel board, the one man left afloat
when Zeus rent wide his ship with chain lightning
and overturned him in the winedark sea.
Then all his troops were lost, his good companions,
but wind and current washed him here to me.
I fed him, loved him, sang that he should not die
nor grow old, ever, in all the days to come.
But now there's no eluding Zeus's will.
If this thing be ordained by him, I say
so be it, let the man strike out alone
on the vast water. Surely I cannot 'send' him.
I have no long-oared ships, no company
to pull him on the broad back of the sea.
My counsel he shall have, and nothing hidden,
to help him homeward without harm."

To this the Wayfinder made answer briefly:

3. Goddess associated with the growth of the crops, especially wheat.

"Thus you shall send him, then. And show more grace
in your obedience, or be chastised by Zeus."

The strong god glittering left her as he spoke,
and now her ladyship, having given heed
to Zeus's mandate, went to find Odysseus
in his stone seat to seaward—tear on tear
brimming his eyes. The sweet days of his life time
were running out in anguish over his exile,
for long ago the nymph had ceased to please.
Though he fought shy of her and her desire,
he lay with her each night, for she compelled him.
But when day came he sat on the rocky shore
and broke his own heart groaning, with eyes wet
scanning the bare horizon of the sea.
Now she stood near him in her beauty, saying:

"O forlorn man, be still.
Here you need grieve no more; you need not feel

your life consumed here; I have pondered it,
and I shall help you go.
Come and cut down high timber for a raft
or flatboat; make her broad-beamed, and decked over,
so you can ride her on the misty sea.
Stores I shall put aboard for you—bread, water,
and ruby-colored wine, to stay your hunger—
give you a seacloak and a following wind
to help you homeward without harm—provided
the gods who rule wide heaven wish it so.
Stronger than I they are, in mind and power."

For all he had endured, Odysseus shuddered.
But when he spoke, his words went to the mark:

"After these years, a helping hand? O goddess,
what guile is hidden here?
A raft, you say, to cross the Western Ocean,
rough water, and unknown? Seaworthy ships
that glory in god's wind will never cross it.
I take no raft you grudge me out to sea.
Or yield me first a great oath, if I do,
to work no more enchantment to my harm."

At this the beautiful nymph Kalypso smiled
and answered sweetly, laying her hand upon him:

"What a dog you are! And not for nothing learned,
having the wit to ask this thing of me!
My witness then be earth and sky
and dripping Styx[4] that I swear by—

4. One of the rivers of the underworld.

the gay gods cannot swear more seriously—
I have no further spells to work against you.
But what I shall devise, and what I tell you,
will be the same as if your need were mine.
Fairness is all I think of. There are hearts
made of cold iron—but my heart is kind."

Swiftly she turned and led him to her cave,
and they went in, the mortal and immortal.
He took the chair left empty now by Hermês,
where the divine Kalypso placed before him
victuals and drink of men; then she sat down
facing Odysseus, while her serving maids
brought nectar and ambrosia to her side.
Then each one's hands went out on each one's feast
until they had had their pleasure; and she said:

"Son of Laërtês, versatile Odysseus,
after these years with me, you still desire
your old home? Even so, I wish you well.
If you could see it all, before you go—
all the adversity you face at sea—
you would stay here, and guard this house, and be
immortal—though you wanted her forever,
that bride for whom you pine each day.
Can I be less desirable than she is?
Less interesting? Less beautiful? Can mortals
compare with goddesses in grace and form?"

To this the strategist Odysseus answered:

"My lady goddess, here is no cause for anger.
My quiet Penélopê—how well I know—
would seem a shade before your majesty,
death and old age being unknown to you,
while she must die. Yet, it is true, each day
I long for home, long for the sight of home.
If any god has marked me out again
for shipwreck, my tough heart can undergo it.
What hardship have I not long since endured
at sea, in battle! Let the trial come."

Now as he spoke the sun set, dusk drew on,
and they retired, this pair, to the inner cave
to revel and rest softly, side by side.

When Dawn spread out her finger tips of rose
Odysseus pulled his tunic and his cloak on,
while the sea nymph dressed in a silvery gown
of subtle tissue, drew about her waist
a golden belt, and veiled her head, and then
took thought for the great-hearted hero's voyage.

A brazen axehead first she had to give him,
two-bladed, and agreeable to the palm
with a smooth-fitting haft of olive wood;
next a well-polished adze; and then she led him
to the island's tip where bigger timber grew—
besides the alder and poplar, tall pine trees,
long dead and seasoned, that would float him high.
Showing him in that place her stand of timber
the loveliest of nymphs took her way home.
Now the man fell to chopping; when he paused
twenty tall trees were down. He lopped the branches,
split the trunks, and trimmed his puncheons true.
Meanwhile Kalypso brought him an auger tool
with which he drilled through all his planks, then drove
stout pins to bolt them, fitted side by side.
A master shipwright, building a cargo vessel,
lays down a broad and shallow hull; just so
Odysseus shaped the bottom of his craft.
He made his decking fast to close-set ribs
before he closed the side with longer planking,
then cut a mast pole, and a proper yard,
and shaped a steering oar to hold her steady.
He drove long strands of willow in all the seams
to keep out waves, and ballasted with logs.
As for a sail, the lovely nymph Kalypso
brought him a cloth so he could make that, too.
Then he ran up his rigging—halyards, braces—
and hauled the boat on rollers to the water.

This was the fourth day, when he had all ready;
on the fifth day, she sent him out to sea.
But first she bathed him, gave him a scented cloak,
and put on board a skin of dusky wine
with water in a bigger skin, and stores—
boiled meats and other victuals—in a bag.
Then she conjured a warm landbreeze to blowing—
joy for Odysseus when he shook out sail!
Now the great seaman, leaning on his oar,
steered all the night unsleeping, and his eyes
picked out the Pleiadês, the laggard Ploughman,[5]
and the Great Bear, that some have called the Wain,[6]
pivoting in the sky before Orion;
of all the night's pure figures, she alone
would never bathe or dip in the Ocean stream.[7]
These stars the beautiful Kalypso bade him
hold on his left hand as he crossed the main.
Seventeen nights and days in the open water
he sailed, before a dark shoreline appeared;
Skhería then came slowly into view
like a rough shield of bull's hide on the sea.

5. Another name for the constellation Boötes. Pleiadês is a cluster of stars in the constellation Taurus.
6. The Big Dipper. 7. I.e., it is visible all year long. Orion, the Hunter, also is a constellation.

But now the god of earthquake,[8] storming home
over the mountains of Asia from the Sunburned land,
sighted him far away. The god grew sullen
and tossed his great head, muttering to himself:

"Here is a pretty cruise! While I was gone,
the gods have changed their minds about Odysseus.
Look at him now, just offshore of that island
that frees him from the bondage of his exile!
Still I can give him a rough ride in, and will."

Brewing high thunderheads, he churned the deep
with both hands on his trident—called up wind
from every quarter, and sent a wall of rain
to blot out land and sea in torrential night.
Hurricane winds now struck from the South and East
shifting North West in a great spume of seas,
on which Odysseus' knees grew slack, his heart
sickened, and he said within himself:

"Rag of man that I am, is this the end of me?
I fear the goddess told it all too well—
predicting great adversity at sea
and far from home. Now all things bear her out:
the whole rondure of heaven hooded so
by Zeus in woeful cloud, and the sea raging
under such winds. I am going down, that's sure.
How lucky those Danaans were who perished
on Troy's wide seaboard, serving the Atreidai!
Would God I, too, had died there—met my end
that time the Trojans made so many casts at me
when I stood by Akhilleus after death.
I should have had a soldier's burial
and praise from the Akhaians—not this choking
waiting for me at sea, unmarked and lonely."

A great wave drove at him with toppling crest
spinning him round, in one tremendous blow,
and he went plunging overboard, the oar-haft
wrenched from his grip. A gust that came on howling
at the same instant broke his mast in two,
hurling his yard and sail far out to leeward.
Now the big wave a long time kept him under,
helpless to surface, held by tons of water,
tangled, too, by the seacloak of Kalypso.
Long, long, until he came up spouting brine,
with streamlets gushing from his head and beard;
but still bethought him, half-drowned as he was,
to flounder for the boat and get a handhold
into the bilge—to crouch there, foiling death.

8. Poseidon.

Across the foaming water, to and fro,
the boat careered like a ball of tumbleweed
blown on the autumn plains, but intact still.
So the winds drove this wreck over the deep,
East Wind and North Wind, then South Wind and West,
coursing each in turn to the brutal harry.

But Ino saw him—Ino, Kadmos' daughter,
slim-legged, lovely, once an earthling girl,
now in the seas a nereid, Leukothea.
Touched by Odysseus' painful buffeting
she broke the surface, like a diving bird,
to rest upon the tossing raft and say:

"O forlorn man, I wonder
why the Earthshaker, Lord Poseidon, holds
this fearful grudge—father of all your woes.
He will not drown you, though, despite his rage.
You seem clear-headed still; do what I tell you.
Shed that cloak, let the gale take your craft,
and swim for it—swim hard to get ashore
upon Skhería, yonder,
where it is fated that you find a shelter.
Here: make my veil your sash; it is not mortal;
you cannot, now, be drowned or suffer harm.
Only, the instant you lay hold of earth,
discard it, cast it far, far out from shore
in the winedark sea again, and turn away."

After she had bestowed her veil, the nereid
dove like a gull to windward
where a dark waveside closed over her whiteness.
But in perplexity Odysseus
said to himself, his great heart laboring:

"O damned confusion! Can this be a ruse
to trick me from the boat for some god's pleasure?
No I'll not swim; with my own eyes I saw
how far the land lies that she called my shelter.
Better to do the wise thing, as I see it.
While this poor planking holds, I stay aboard;
I may ride out the pounding of the storm,
or if she cracks up, take to the water then;
I cannot think it through a better way."

But even while he pondered and decided,
the god of earthquake heaved a wave against him
high as a rooftree and of awful gloom.
A gust of wind, hitting a pile of chaff,
will scatter all the parched stuff far and wide;
just so, when this gigantic billow struck
the boat's big timbers flew apart. Odysseus

clung to a single beam, like a jockey riding,
meanwhile stripping Kalypso's cloak away;
then he slung round his chest the veil of Ino
and plunged headfirst into the sea. His hands
went out to stroke, and he gave a swimmer's kick.

But the strong Earthshaker had him under his eye,
and nodded as he said:

"Go on, go on;
wander the high seas this way, take your blows,
before you join that race[9] the gods have nurtured.
Nor will you grumble, even then, I think,
for want of trouble."

Whipping his glossy team
he rode off to his glorious home at Aigai.[1]
But Zeus's daughter Athena countered him:
she checked the course of all the winds but one,
commanding them, "Be quiet and go to sleep."
Then sent a long swell running under a norther
to bear the prince Odysseus, back from danger,
to join the Phaiákians, people of the sea.
Two nights, two days, in the solid deep-sea swell
he drifted, many times awaiting death,
until with shining ringlets in the East
the dawn confirmed a third day, breaking clear
over a high and windless sea; and mounting
a rolling wave he caught a glimpse of land.
What a dear welcome thing life seems to children
whose father, in the extremity, recovers
after some weakening and malignant illness:
his pangs are gone, the gods have delivered him.
So dear and welcome to Odysseus
the sight of land, of woodland, on that morning.
It made him swim again, to get a foothold
on solid ground. But when he came in earshot
he heard the trampling roar of sea on rock,
where combers, rising shoreward, thudded down
on the sucking ebb—all sheeted with salt foam.
Here were no coves or harborage or shelter,
only steep headlands, rockfallen reefs and crags.
Odysseus' knees grew slack, his heart faint,
a heaviness came over him, and he said:

"A cruel turn, this. Never had I thought
to see this land, but Zeus has let me see it—
and let me, too, traverse the Western Ocean—
only to find no exit from these breakers.

9. The Phaiákians, favored by the gods. 1. Town on the coast of Euboia, where there was a temple of Poseidon.

Here are sharp rocks off shore, and the sea a smother
rushing around them; rock face rising sheer
from deep water; nowhere could I stand up
on my two feet and fight free of the welter.
No matter how I try it, the surf may throw me
against the cliffside; no good fighting there.
If I swim down the coast, outside the breakers,
I may find shelving shore and quiet water—
but what if another gale comes on to blow?
Then I go cursing out to sea once more.
Or then again, some shark of Amphitritê's[2]
may hunt me, sent by the genius of the deep.
I know how he who makes earth tremble hates me."

During this meditation a heavy surge
was taking him, in fact, straight on the rocks.
He had been flayed there, and his bones broken,
had not grey-eyed Athena instructed him:
he gripped a rock-ledge with both hands in passing
and held on, groaning, as the surge went by,
to keep clear of its breaking. Then the backwash
hit him, ripping him under and far out.
An octopus, when you drag one from his chamber,
comes up with suckers full of tiny stones:
Odysseus left the skin of his great hands
torn on that rock-ledge as the wave submerged him.
And now at last Odysseus would have perished,
battered inhumanly, but he had the gift
of self-possession from grey-eyed Athena.
So, when the backwash spewed him up again,
he swam out and along, and scanned the coast
for some landspit that made a breakwater.
Lo and behold, the mouth of a calm river
at length came into view, with level shores
unbroken, free from rock, shielded from wind—
by far the best place he had found.
But as he felt the current flowing seaward
he prayed in his heart:

"O hear me, lord of the stream:
how sorely I depend upon your mercy!
derelict as I am by the sea's anger.
Is he not sacred, even to the gods,
the wandering man who comes, as I have come,
in weariness before your knees, your waters?
Here is your servant; lord, have mercy on me."

Now even as he prayed the tide at ebb
had turned, and the river god made quiet water,
drawing him in to safety in the shallows.

2. A sea goddess.

His knees buckled, his arms gave way beneath him,
all vital force now conquered by the sea.
Swollen from head to foot he was, and seawater
gushed from his mouth and nostrils. There he lay,
scarce drawing breath, unstirring, deathly spent.
In time, as air came back into his lungs
and warmth around his heart, he loosed the veil,
letting it drift away on the estuary
downstream to where a white wave took it under
and Ino's hands received it. Then the man
crawled to the river bank among the reeds
where, face down, he could kiss the soil of earth,
in his exhaustion murmuring to himself:

"What more can this hulk suffer? What comes now?
In vigil through the night here by the river
how can I not succumb, being weak and sick,
to the night's damp and hoarfrost of the morning?
The air comes cold from rivers before dawn.
But if I climb the slope and fall asleep
in the dark forest's undergrowth—supposing
cold and fatigue will go, and sweet sleep come—
I fear I make the wild beasts easy prey."

But this seemed best to him, as he thought it over.
He made his way to a grove above the water
on open ground, and crept under twin bushes
grown from the same spot—olive and wild olive—
a thicket proof against the stinging wind
or Sun's blaze, fine soever the needling sunlight;
nor could a downpour wet it through, so dense
those plants were interwoven. Here Odysseus
tunnelled, and raked together with his hands
a wide bed—for a fall of leaves was there,
enough to save two men or maybe three
on a winter night, a night of bitter cold.
Odysseus' heart laughed when he saw his leaf-bed,
and down he lay, heaping more leaves above him.

A man in a distant field, no hearthfires near,
will hide a fresh brand in his bed of embers
to keep a spark alive for the next day;
so in the leaves Odysseus hid himself,
while over him Athena showered sleep
that his distress should end, and soon, soon.
In quiet sleep she sealed his cherished eyes.

BOOK VI

[*The Princess at the River*]

Far gone in weariness, in oblivion,
the noble and enduring man slept on;

but Athena in the night went down the land
of the Phaiákians, entering their city.
In days gone by, these men held Hypereia,[3]
a country of wide dancing grounds, but near them
were overbearing Kyklopês, whose power
could not be turned from pillage. So the Phaiákians
migrated thence under Nausíthoös
to settle a New World across the sea,
Skhería Island. That first captain walled
their promontory, built their homes and shrines,
and parcelled out the black land for the plow.
But he had gone down long ago to Death.
Alkínoös ruled, and Heaven gave him wisdom,
so on this night the goddess, grey-eyed Athena,
entered the palace of Alkínoös
to make sure of Odysseus' voyage home.
She took her way to a painted bedchamber
where a young girl lay fast asleep—so fine
in mould and feature that she seemed a goddess—
the daughter of Alkínoös, Nausikaa.
On either side, as Graces[4] might have slept,
her maids were sleeping. The bright doors were shut,
but like a sudden stir of wind, Athena
moved to the bedside of the girl, and grew
visible as the shipman Dymas' daughter,
a girl the princess' age, and her dear friend.
In this form grey-eyed Athena said to her:

"How so remiss, and yet thy mother's daughter?
leaving thy clothes uncared for, Nausikaa,
when soon thou must have store of marriage linen,
and put thy minstrelsy in wedding dress!
Beauty, in these, will make the folk admire,
and bring thy father and gentle mother joy.
Let us go washing in the shine of morning!
Beside thee will I drub, so wedding chests
will brim by evening. Maidenhood must end!
Have not the noblest born Phaiákians
paid court to thee, whose birth none can excel?
Go beg thy sovereign father, even at dawn,
to have the mule cart and the mules brought round
to take thy body-linen, gowns and mantles.
Thou shouldst ride, for it becomes thee more,
the washing pools are found so far from home."

On this word she departed, grey-eyed Athena,
to where the gods have their eternal dwelling—
as men say—in the fastness of Olympos.
Never a tremor of wind, or a splash of rain,

3. Probably an imaginary place; however, the migration under pressure and the founding of the new city (described below) suggest the atmosphere of the great age of Greek colonization (eighth century B.C.).
4. Goddesses (usually three) personifying charm and beauty.

no errant snowflake comes to stain that heaven,
so calm, so vaporless, the world of light.
Here, where the gay gods live their days of pleasure,
the grey-eyed one withdrew, leaving the princess.

And now Dawn took her own fair throne, awaking
the girl in the sweet gown, still charmed by dream.
Down through the rooms she went to tell her parents,
whom she found still at home: her mother seated
near the great hearth among her maids—and twirling
out of her distaff yarn dyed like the sea—;
her father at the door, bound for a council
of princes on petition of the gentry.
She went up close to him and softly said:

"My dear Papà, could you not send the mule cart
around for me—the gig with pretty wheels?
I must take all our things and get them washed
at the river pools; our linen is all soiled.
And you should wear fresh clothing, going to council
with counselors and first men of the realm.
Remember your five sons at home: though two
are married, we have still three bachelor sprigs;
they will have none but laundered clothes each time
they go to the dancing. See what I must think of!"

She had no word to say of her own wedding,
though her keen father saw her blush. Said he:

"No mules would I deny you, child, nor anything.
Go along, now; the grooms will bring your gig
with pretty wheels and the cargo box upon it."

He spoke to the stableman, who soon brought round
the cart, low-wheeled and nimble;
harnessed the mules, and backed them in the traces.
Meanwhile the girl fetched all her soiled apparel
to bundle in the polished wagon box.
Her mother, for their luncheon, packed a hamper
with picnic fare, and filled a skin of wine,
and, when the princess had been handed up,
gave her a golden bottle of olive oil
for softening girls' bodies, after bathing.
Nausikaa took the reins and raised her whip,
lashing the mules. What jingling! What a clatter!
But off they went in a ground-covering trot,
with princess, maids, and laundry drawn behind.
By the lower river where the wagon came
were washing pools, with water all year flowing
in limpid spillways that no grime withstood.
The girls unhitched the mules, and sent them down
along the eddying stream to crop sweet grass.

Then sliding out the cart's tail board, they took
armloads of clothing to the dusky water,
and trod them in the pits, making a race of it.
All being drubbed, all blemish rinsed away,
they spread them, piece by piece, along the beach
whose pebbles had been laundered by the sea;
then took a dip themselves, and, all anointed
with golden oil, ate lunch beside the river
while the bright burning sun dried out their linen.
Princess and maids delighted in that feast;
then, putting off their veils,
they ran and passed a ball to a rhythmic beat,
Nausikaa flashing first with her white arms.

So Artemis goes flying after her arrows flown
down some tremendous valley-side—
Taÿgetos, Erymanthos[5]—
chasing the mountain goats or ghosting deer,
with nymphs of the wild places flanking her;
and Lêto's[6] heart delights to see them running,
for, taller by a head than nymphs can be,
the goddess shows more stately, all being beautiful.
So one could tell the princess from the maids.

Soon it was time, she knew, for riding homeward—
mules to be harnessed, linen folded smooth—
but the grey-eyed goddess Athena made her tarry,
so that Odysseus might behold her beauty
and win her guidance to the town.
It happened
when the king's daughter threw her ball off line
and missed, and put it in the whirling stream,—
at which they all gave such a shout, Odysseus
awoke and sat up, saying to himself:

"Now, by my life, mankind again! But who?
Savages, are they, strangers to courtesy?
Or gentle folk, who know and fear the gods?
That was a lusty cry of tall young girls—
most like the cry of nymphs, who haunt the peaks,
and springs of brooks, and inland grassy places.
Or am I amid people of human speech?
Up again, man; and let me see for myself."

He pushed aside the bushes, breaking off
with his great hand a single branch of olive,
whose leaves might shield him in his nakedness;
so came out rustling, like a mountain lion,
rain-drenched, wind-buffeted, but in his might at ease,

5. A mountain in Arcadia. Taÿgetos is the mountain range west of Sparta. Both places are rich in game.
6. Mother of Artemis and Apollo.

with burning eyes—who prowls among the herds
or flocks, or after game, his hungry belly
taking him near stout homesteads for his prey.
Odysseus had this look, in his rough skin
advancing on the girls with pretty braids;
and he was driven on by hunger, too.
Streaked with brine, and swollen, he terrified them,
so that they fled, this way and that. Only
Alkínoös' daughter stood her ground, being given
a bold heart by Athena, and steady knees.

She faced him, waiting. And Odysseus came,
debating inwardly what he should do:
embrace this beauty's knees in supplication?
or stand apart, and, using honeyed speech,
inquire the way to town, and beg some clothing?
In his swift reckoning, he thought it best
to trust in words to please her—and keep away;
he might anger the girl, touching her knees.
So he began, and let the soft words fall:

"Mistress: please: are you divine, or mortal?
If one of those who dwell in the wide heaven,
you are most near to Artemis, I should say—
great Zeus's daughter—in your grace and presence.
If you are one of earth's inhabitants,
how blest your father, and your gentle mother,
blest all your kin. I know what happiness
must send the warm tears to their eyes, each time
they see their wondrous child go to the dancing!
But one man's destiny is more than blest—
he who prevails, and takes you as his bride.
Never have I laid eyes on equal beauty
in man or woman. I am hushed indeed.
So fair, one time, I thought a young palm tree
at Delos[7] near the altar of Apollo—
I had troops under me when I was there
on the sea route that later brought me grief—
but that slim palm tree filled my heart with wonder:
never came shoot from earth so beautiful.
So now, my lady, I stand in awe so great
I cannot take your knees. And yet my case is desperate:
twenty days, yesterday, in the winedark sea,
on the ever-lunging swell, under gale winds,
getting away from the Island of Ogýgia.
And now the terror of Storm has left me stranded
upon this shore—with more blows yet to suffer,
I must believe, before the gods relent.
Mistress, do me a kindness!
After much weary toil, I come to you,

7. A small island in the middle of the Aegean Sea, the birthplace of Apollo and a center for his worship.

and you are the first soul I have seen—I know
no others here. Direct me to the town,
give me a rag that I can throw around me,
some cloth or wrapping that you brought along.
And may the gods accomplish your desire:
a home, a husband, and harmonious
converse with him—the best thing in the world
being a strong house held in serenity
where man and wife agree. Woe to their enemies,
joy to their friends! But all this they know best."

Then she of the white arms, Nausikaa, replied:

"Stranger, there is no quirk or evil in you
that I can see. You know Zeus metes out fortune
to good and bad men as it pleases him.
Hardship he sent to you, and you must bear it.
But now that you have taken refuge here
you shall not lack for clothing, or any other
comfort due to a poor man in distress.
The town lies this way, and the men are called
Phaiákians, who own the land and city.
I am daughter to the Prince Alkínoös,
by whom the power of our people stands."

Turning, she called out to her maids-in-waiting:

"Stay with me! Does the sight of a man scare you?
Or do you take this one for an enemy?
Why, there's no fool so brash, and never will be,
as to bring war or pillage to this coast,
for we are dear to the immortal gods,
living here, in the sea that rolls forever,
distant from other lands and other men.
No: this man is a castaway, poor fellow;
we must take care of him. Strangers and beggars
come from Zeus: a small gift, then, is friendly.
Give our new guest some food and drink, and take him
into the river, out of the wind, to bathe."

They stood up now, and called to one another
to go on back. Quite soon they led Odysseus
under the river bank, as they were bidden;
and there laid out a tunic, and a cloak,
and gave him olive oil in the golden flask.
"Here," they said, "go bathe in the flowing water."
But heard now from that kingly man, Odysseus:

"Maids," he said, "keep away a little; let me
wash the brine from my own back, and rub on
plenty of oil. It is long since my anointing.

I take no bath, however, where you can see me—
naked before young girls with pretty braids."

They left him, then, and went to tell the princess.
And now Odysseus, dousing in the river,
scrubbed the coat of brine from back and shoulders
and rinsed the clot of sea-spume from his hair;
got himself all rubbed down, from head to foot,
then he put on the clothes the princess gave him.
Athena lent a hand, making him seem
taller, and massive too, with crisping hair
in curls like petals of wild hyacinth,
but all red-golden. Think of gold infused
on silver by a craftsman, whose fine art
Hephaistos taught him, or Athena: one
whose work moves to delight: just so she lavished
beauty over Odysseus' head and shoulders.
Then he went down to sit on the sea beach
in his new splendor. There the girl regarded him,
and after a time she said to the maids beside her:

"My gentlewomen, I have a thing to tell you.
The Olympian gods cannot be all averse
to this man's coming here among our islanders.
Uncouth he seemed, I thought so, too, before;
but now he looks like one of heaven's people.
I wish my husband could be fine as he
and glad to stay forever on Skhería!

But have you given refreshment to our guest?"

At this the maids, all gravely listening, hastened
to set out bread and wine before Odysseus,
and ah! how ravenously that patient man
took food and drink, his long fast at an end.

The princess Nausikaa now turned aside
to fold her linens; in the pretty cart
she stowed them, put the mule team under harness,
mounted the driver's seat, and then looked down
to say with cheerful prompting to Odysseus:

"Up with you now, friend; back to town we go;
and I shall send you in before my father
who is wondrous wise; there in our house with him
you'll meet the noblest of the Phaiákians.
You have good sense, I think; here's how to do it:
while we go through the countryside and farmland
stay with my maids, behind the wagon, walking
briskly enough to follow where I lead.
But near the town—well, there's a wall with towers
around the Isle, and beautiful ship basins

right and left of the causeway of approach;
seagoing craft are beached beside the road
each on its launching ways. The agora,[8]
with fieldstone benches bedded in the earth,
lies either side Poseidon's shrine—for there
men are at work on pitch-black hulls and rigging,
cables and sails, and tapering of oars.
The archer's craft is not for the Phaiákians,
but ship designing, modes of oaring cutters
in which they love to cross the foaming sea.
From these fellows I will have no salty talk,
no gossip later. Plenty are insolent.
And some seadog might say, after we passed:
'Who is this handsome stranger trailing Nausikaa?
Where did she find him? Will he be her husband?
Or is she being hospitable to some rover
come off his ship from lands across the sea—
there being no lands nearer. A god, maybe?
a god from heaven, the answer to her prayer,
descending now—to make her his forever?
Better, if she's roamed and found a husband
somewhere else: none of our own will suit her,
though many come to court her, and those the best.'
This is the way they might make light of me.
And I myself should hold it shame
for any girl to flout her own dear parents,
taking up with a man, before her marriage.

Note well, now, what I say, friend, and your chances
are excellent for safe conduct from my father.
You'll find black poplars in a roadside park
around a meadow and fountain—all Athena's—
but Father has a garden in the place—
this within earshot of the city wall.
Go in there and sit down, giving us time
to pass through town and reach my father's house.
And when you can imagine we're at home,
then take the road into the city, asking
directions to the palace of Alkínoös.
You'll find it easily: any small boy
can take you there; no family has a mansion
half so grand as he does, being king.
As soon as you are safe inside, cross over
and go straight through into the mégaron[9]
to find my mother. She'll be there in firelight
before a column, with her maids in shadow,
spinning a wool dyed richly as the sea.
My father's great chair faces the fire, too;
there like a god he sits and takes his wine.
Go past him, cast yourself before my mother,

8. Place of assembly. 9. The great hall of the palace.

embrace her knees—and you may wake up soon
at home rejoicing, though your home be far.
On Mother's feeling much depends; if she
looks on you kindly, you shall see your friends
under your own roof in your father's country."

At this she raised her glistening whip, lashing
the team into a run; they left the river
cantering beautifully, then trotted smartly.
But then she reined them in, and spared the whip,
so that her maids could follow with Odysseus.
The sun was going down when they went by
Athena's grove. Here, then, Odysseus rested,
and lifted up his prayer to Zeus's daughter:

"Hear me, unwearied child of royal Zeus!
O listen to me now—thou so aloof
while the Earthshaker wrecked and battered me.
May I find love and mercy among these people."

He prayed for that, and Pallas Athena heard him—
although in deference to her father's brother
she would not show her true form to Odysseus,
at whom Poseidon smoldered on
until the kingly man came home to his own shore.

BOOK VII

[*Gardens and Firelight*]

As Lord Odysseus prayed there in the grove
the girl rode on, behind her strapping team,
and came late to the mansion of her father,
where she reined in at the courtyard gate. Her brothers
awaited her like tall gods in the court,
circling to lead the mules away and carry
the laundered things inside. But she withdrew
to her own bedroom, where a fire soon shone,
kindled by her old nurse, Eurymedousa.
Years ago, from a raid on the continent,
the rolling ships had brought this woman over
to be Alkínoös' share—fit spoil for him
whose realm hung on his word as on a god's.
And she had schooled the princess, Nausikaa,
whose fire she tended now, making her supper.

Odysseus, when the time had passed, arose
and turned into the city. But Athena
poured a sea fog around him as he went—
her love's expedient, that no jeering sailor
should halt the man or challenge him for luck.
Instead, as he set foot in the pleasant city,

the grey-eyed goddess came to him, in figure
a small girl child, hugging a water jug.

Confronted by her, Lord Odysseus asked:

"Little one, could you take me to the house
of that Alkínoös, king among these people?
You see, I am a poor old stranger here;
my home is far away; here there is no one
known to me, in countryside or city."

The grey-eyed goddess Athena replied to him:

"Oh yes, good grandfer, sir, I know, I'll show you
the house you mean; it is quite near my father's.
But come now, hush, like this, and follow me.
You must not stare at people, or be inquisitive.
They do not care for strangers in this neighborhood;
a foreign man will get no welcome here.
The only things they trust are the racing ships
Poseidon gave, to sail the deep blue sea
like white wings in the sky, or a flashing thought."

Pallas Athena turned like the wind, running
ahead of him, and he followed in her footsteps.
And no seafaring men of Phaiákia
perceived Odysseus passing through their town:
the awesome one in pigtails barred their sight
with folds of sacred mist. And yet Odysseus
gazed out marvelling at the ships and harbors,
public squares, and ramparts towering up
with pointed palisades along the top.
When they were near the mansion of the king,
grey-eyed Athena in the child cried out:

"Here it is, grandfer, sir—that mansion house
you asked to see. You'll find our king and queen
at supper, but you must not be dismayed;
go in to them. A cheerful man does best
in every enterprise—even a stranger.
You'll see our lady just inside the hall—
her name is Arêtê; her grandfather
was our good king Alkínoös' father—
Nausíthoös by name, son of Poseidon
and Periboia. That was a great beauty,
the daughter of Eurymedon, commander
of the Gigantês[1] in the olden days,
who led those wild things to their doom and his.
Poseidon then made love to Periboia,
and she bore Nausíthoös, Phaiákia's lord,
whose sons in turn were Rhêxênor and Alkínoös.

1. The Giants; an older race of gods who battled, unsuccessfully, against the Olympians.

Rhêxênor had no sons; even as a bridegroom
he fell before the silver bow of Apollo,
his only child a daughter, Arêtê.
When she grew up, Alkínoös married her
and holds her dear. No lady in the world,
no other mistress of a man's household,
is honored as our mistress is, and loved,
by her own children, by Alkínoös,
and by the people. When she walks the town
they murmur and gaze, as though she were a goddess.
No grace or wisdom fails in her; indeed
just men in quarrels come to her for equity.
Supposing, then, she looks upon you kindly,
the chances are that you shall see your friends
under your own roof, in your father's country."

At this the grey-eyed goddess Athena left him
and left that comely land, going over sea
to Marathon, to the wide roadways of Athens
and her retreat in the stronghold of Erekhtheus.[2]
Odysseus, now alone before the palace,
meditated a long time before crossing
the brazen threshold of the great courtyard.
High rooms he saw ahead, airy and luminous
as though with lusters of the sun and moon,
bronze-paneled walls, at several distances,
making a vista, with an azure molding
of lapis lazuli. The doors were golden
guardians of the great room. Shining bronze
plated the wide door sill; the posts and lintel
were silver upon silver; golden handles
curved on the doors, and golden, too, and silver
were sculptured hounds, flanking the entrance way,
cast by the skill and ardor of Hephaistos
to guard the prince Alkínoös' house—
undying dogs that never could grow old.
Through all the rooms, as far as he could see,
tall chairs were placed around the walls, and strewn
with fine embroidered stuff made by the women.
Here were enthroned the leaders of Phaiákia
drinking and dining, with abundant fare.
Here, too, were boys of gold on pedestals
holding aloft bright torches of pitch pine
to light the great rooms, and the night-time feasting.
And fifty maids-in-waiting of the household
sat by the round mill, grinding yellow corn,
or wove upon their looms, or twirled their distaffs,
flickering like the leaves of a poplar tree;
while drops of oil glistened on linen weft.
Skillful as were the men of Phaiákia

2. King of Athens. Marathon was a village north of Athens near the coast; later it was the site of the famous battle at which the Athenians repulsed a Persian invasion force (490 B.C.).

in ship handling at sea, so were these women
skilled at the loom, having this lovely craft
and artistry as talents from Athena.

To left and right, outside, he saw an orchard
closed by a pale—four spacious acres planted
with trees in bloom or weighted down for picking:
pear trees, pomegranates, brilliant apples,
luscious figs, and olives ripe and dark.
Fruit never failed upon these trees: winter
and summer time they bore, for through the year
the breathing Westwind ripened all in turn—
so one pear came to prime, and then another,
and so with apples, figs, and the vine's fruit
empurpled in the royal vineyard there.
Currants were dried at one end, on a platform
bare to the sun, beyond the vintage arbors
and vats the vintners trod; while near at hand
were new grapes barely formed as the green bloom fell,
or half-ripe clusters, faintly coloring.
After the vines came rows of vegetables
of all the kinds that flourish in every season,
and through the garden plots and orchard ran
channels from one clear fountain, while another
gushed through a pipe under the courtyard entrance
to serve the house and all who came for water.
These were the gifts of heaven to Alkínoös.

Odysseus, who had borne the barren sea,
stood in the gateway and surveyed this bounty.
He gazed his fill, then swiftly he went in.
The lords and nobles of Phaiákia
were tipping wine to the wakeful god, to Hermês—
a last libation before going to bed—
but down the hall Odysseus went unseen,
still in the cloud Athena cloaked him in,
until he reached Arêtê, and the king.
He threw his great hands round Arêtê's knees,
whereon the sacred mist curled back;
they saw him; and the diners hushed amazed
to see an unknown man inside the palace.
Under their eyes Odysseus made his plea:

"Arêtê, admirable Rhêxênor's daughter,
here is a man bruised by adversity, thrown
upon your mercy and the king your husband's,
begging indulgence of this company—
may the gods' blessing rest on them! May life
be kind to all! Let each one leave his children
every good thing this realm confers upon him!
But grant me passage to my father land.
My home and friends lie far. My life is pain."

He moved, then, toward the fire, and sat him down
amid the ashes.[3] No one stirred or spoke
until Ekhenêos broke the spell—an old man,
eldest of the Phaiákians, an oracle,
versed in the laws and manners of old time.
He rose among them now and spoke out kindly:

"Alkínoös, this will not pass for courtesy:
a guest abased in ashes at our hearth?
Everyone here awaits your word; so come, then,
lift the man up; give him a seat of honor,
a silver-studded chair. Then tell the stewards
we'll have another wine bowl for libation
to Zeus, lord of the lightning—advocate
of honorable petitioners. And supper
may be supplied our friend by the larder mistress."

Alkínoös, calm in power, heard him out,
then took the great adventurer by the hand
and led him from the fire. Nearest his throne
the son whom he loved best, Laódamas,
had long held place; now the king bade him rise
and gave his shining chair to Lord Odysseus.
A serving maid poured water for his hands
from a gold pitcher into a silver bowl,
and spread a polished table at his side;
the mistress of provisions came with bread
and other victuals, generous with her store.
So Lord Odysseus drank, and tasted supper.
Seeing this done, the king in majesty
said to his squire:

"A fresh bowl, Pontónoös;
we make libation to the lord of lightning,
who seconds honorable petitioners."

Mixing the honey-hearted wine, Pontónoös
went on his rounds and poured fresh cups for all,
whereof when all had spilt they drank their fill.
Alkínoös then spoke to the company:

"My lords and leaders of Phaiákia:
hear now, all that my heart would have me say.
Our banquet's ended, so you may retire;
but let our seniors gather in the morning
to give this guest a festal day, and make
fair offerings to the gods. In due course we
shall put our minds upon the means at hand
to take him safely, comfortably, well

3. The fire, or hearth, was the sacred center of the home; the suppliant who sits there is, so to speak, on consecrated ground and cannot be forcibly removed.

and happily, with speed, to his own country,
distant though it may lie. And may no trouble
come to him here or on the way; his fate
he shall pay out at home, even as the Spinners[4]
spun for him on the day his mother bore him.
If, as may be, he is some god, come down
from heaven's height, the gods are working strangely:
until now, they have shown themselves in glory
only after great hekatombs—those figures
banqueting at our side, throned like ourselves.
Or if some traveller met them when alone
they bore no least disguise; we are their kin; Gigantês,
Kyklopês, rank no nearer gods than we."

Odysseus' wits were ready, and he replied:

"Alkínoös, you may set your mind at rest.
Body and birth, a most unlikely god
am I, being all of earth and mortal nature.
I should say, rather, I am like those men
who suffer the worst trials that you know,
and miseries greater yet, as I might tell you—
hundreds; indeed the gods could send no more.
You will indulge me if I finish dinner—?
grieved though I am to say it. There's no part
of man more like a dog than brazen Belly,
crying to be remembered—and it must be—
when we are mortal weary and sick at heart;
and that is my condition. Yet my hunger
drives me to take this food, and think no more
of my afflictions. Belly must be filled.
Be equally impelled, my lords, tomorrow
to berth me in a ship and send me home!
Rough years I've had; now may I see once more
my hall, my lands, my people before I die!"

Now all who heard cried out assent to this:
the guest had spoken well; he must have passage.
Then tipping wine they drank their thirst away,
and one by one went homeward for the night.
So Lord Odysseus kept his place alone
with Arêtê and the king Alkínoös
beside him, while the maids went to and fro
clearing away the wine cups and the tables.
Presently the ivory-skinned lady
turned to him—for she knew his cloak and tunic
to be her own fine work, done with her maids—
and arrowy came her words upon the air:

4. The Fates, who spin the pattern of each individual destiny.

"Friend, I, for one, have certain questions for you.
Who are you, and who has given you this clothing?
Did you not say you wandered here by sea?"

The great tactician carefully replied:

"Ah, majesty, what labor it would be
to go through the whole story! All my years
of misadventures, given by those on high!
But this you ask about is quickly told:
in mid-ocean lies Ogýgia, the island
haunt of Kalypso, Atlas' guileful daughter,
a lovely goddess and a dangerous one.
No one, no god or man, consorts with her;
but supernatural power brought me there
to be her solitary guest: for Zeus
let fly with his bright bolt and split my ship,
rolling me over in the winedark sea.
There all my shipmates, friends were drowned, while I
hung on the keelboard of the wreck and drifted
nine full days. Then in the dead of night
the gods brought me ashore upon Ogýgia
into her hands. The enchantress in her beauty
fed and caressed me, promised me I should be
immortal, youthful, all the days to come;
but in my heart I never gave consent
though seven years detained. Immortal clothing
I had from her, and kept it wet with tears.
Then came the eighth year on the wheel of heaven
and word to her from Zeus, or a change of heart,
so that she now commanded me to sail,
sending me out to sea on a craft I made
with timber and tools of hers. She gave me stores,
victuals and wine, a cloak divinely woven,
and made a warm land breeze come up astern.
Seventeen days I sailed in the open water
before I saw your country's shore, a shadow
upon the sea rim. Then my heart rejoiced—
pitiable as I am! For blows aplenty
awaited me from the god who shakes the earth.
Cross gales he blew, making me lose my bearings,
and heaved up seas beyond imagination—
huge and foundering seas. All I could do
was hold hard, groaning under every shock,
until my craft broke up in the hurricane.
I kept afloat and swam your sea, or drifted,
taken by wind and current to this coast
where I went in on big swells running landward.
But cliffs and rock shoals made that place forbidding,
so I turned back, swimming off shore, and came
in the end to a river, to auspicious water,
with smooth beach and a rise that broke the wind.

I lay there where I fell till strength returned.
Then sacred night came on, and I went inland
to high ground and a leaf bed in a thicket.
Heaven sent slumber in an endless tide
submerging my sad heart among the leaves.
That night and next day's dawn and noon I slept;
the sun went west; and then sweet sleep unbound me,
when I became aware of maids—your daughter's—
playing along the beach; the princess, too,
most beautiful. I prayed her to assist me,
and her good sense was perfect; one could hope
for no behavior like it from the young,
thoughtless as they most often are. But she
gave me good provender and good red wine,
a river bath, and finally this clothing.
There is the bitter tale. These are the facts."

But in reply Alkínoös observed:

"Friend, my child's good judgment failed in this—
not to have brought you in her company home.
Once you approached her, you became her charge."

To this Odysseus tactfully replied:

"Sir, as to that, you should not blame the princess.
She did tell me to follow with her maids,
but I would not. I felt abashed, and feared
the sight would somehow ruffle or offend you.
All of us on this earth are plagued by jealousy."

Alkínoös' answer was a declaration:

"Friend, I am not a man for trivial anger:
better a sense of measure in everything.
No anger here. I say that if it should please
our father Zeus, Athena, and Apollo—
seeing the man you are, seeing your thoughts
are my own thoughts—my daughter should be yours
and you my son-in-law, if you remained.
A home, lands, riches you should have from me
if you could be contented here. If not,
by Father Zeus, let none of our men hold you!
On the contrary, I can assure you now
of passage late tomorrow: while you sleep
my men will row you through the tranquil night
to your own land and home or where you please.
It may be, even, far beyond Euboia—
called most remote by seamen of our isle
who landed there, conveying Rhadamanthos
when he sought Títyos,[5] the son of Gaia.

5. A giant who tried to rape Lêto. In book 11 Odysseus sees him in the underworld, eternally punished for his crime. Why Rhadamanthos went to see Títyos we have no idea.

They put about, with neither pause nor rest,
and entered their home port the selfsame day.
But this you, too, will see: what ships I have,
how my young oarsmen send the foam a-scudding!"

Now joy welled up in the patient Lord Odysseus
who said devoutly in the warmest tones:

"O Father Zeus, let all this be fulfilled
as spoken by Alkínoös! Earth of harvests
remember him! Return me to my homeland!"

In this manner they conversed with one another;
but the great lady called her maids, and sent them
to make a kingly bed, with purple rugs
piled up, and sheets outspread, and fleecy
coverlets, in an eastern colonnade.
The girls went out with torches in their hands,
swift at their work of bedmaking; returning
they whispered at the lord Odysseus' shoulder:

"Sir, you may come; your bed has been prepared."

How welcome the word "bed" came to his ears!
Now, then, Odysseus laid him down and slept
in luxury under the Porch of Morning,
while in his inner chamber Alkínoös
retired to rest where his dear consort lay.

BOOK VIII

[*The Songs of the Harper*]

Under the opening fingers of the dawn
Alkínoös, the sacred prince, arose,
and then arose Odysseus, raider of cities.
As the king willed, they went down by the shipways
to the assembly ground of the Phaiákians.
Side by side the two men took their ease there
on smooth stone benches. Meanwhile Pallas Athena
roamed through the byways of the town, contriving
Odysseus' voyage home—in voice and feature
the crier of the king Alkínoös
who stopped and passed the word to every man:

"Phaiákian lords and counselors, this way!
Come to assembly: learn about the stranger,
the new guest at the palace of Alkínoös—
a man the sea drove, but a comely man;
the gods' own light is on him."

She aroused them,
and soon the assembly ground and seats were filled

with curious men, a throng who peered and saw
the master mind of war, Laërtês' son.
Athena now poured out her grace upon him,
head and shoulders, height and mass—a splendor
awesome to the eyes of the Phaiákians;
she put him in a fettle to win the day,
mastering every trial they set to test him.
When all the crowd sat marshalled, quieted,
Alkínoös addressed the full assembly:

"Hear me, lords and captains of the Phaiákians!
Hear what my heart would have me say!
Our guest and new friend—nameless to me still—
comes to my house after long wandering
in Dawn lands, or among the Sunset races.
Now he appeals to me for conveyance home.
As in the past, therefore, let us provide
passage, and quickly, for no guest of mine
languishes here for lack of it. Look to it:
get a black ship afloat on the noble sea,
and pick our fastest sailer; draft a crew
of two and fifty from our younger townsmen—
men who have made their names at sea. Loop oars
well to your tholepins, lads, then leave the ship,
come to our house, fall to, and take your supper:
we'll furnish out a feast for every crewman.
These are your orders. As for my older peers
and princes of the realm, let them foregather
in festival for our friend in my great hall;
and let no man refuse. Call in our minstrel,
Demódokos, whom God made lord of song,
heart-easing, sing upon what theme he will."

He turned, led the procession, and those princes
followed, while his herald sought the minstrel.
Young oarsmen from the assembly chose a crew
of two and fifty, as the king commanded,
and these filed off along the waterside
to where the ship lay, poised above open water.
They hauled the black hull down to ride the sea,
rigging a mast and spar in the black ship,
with oars at trail from corded rawhide, all
seamanly; then tried the white sail, hoisting,
and moored her off the beach. Then going ashore
the crew went up to the great house of Alkínoös.
Here the enclosures, entrance ways, and rooms
were filled with men, young men and old, for whom
Alkínoös had put twelve sheep to sacrifice,
eight tuskers and a pair of shambling oxen.
These, now, they flayed and dressed to make their banquet.
The crier soon came, leading that man of song
whom the Muse cherished; by her gift he knew

the good of life, and evil—
for she who lent him sweetness made him blind.
Pontónoös fixed a studded chair for him
hard by a pillar amid the banqueters,
hanging the taut harp from a peg above him,
and guided up his hands upon the strings;
placed a bread basket at his side, and poured
wine in a cup, that he might drink his fill.
Now each man's hand went out upon the banquet.

In time, when hunger and thirst were turned away,
the Muse brought to the minstrel's mind a song
of heroes whose great fame rang under heaven:
the clash between Odysseus and Akhilleus,
how one time they contended at the godfeast
raging, and the marshal, Agamémnon,
felt inward joy over his captains' quarrel;
for such had been foretold him by Apollo
at Pytho[6]—hallowed height—when the Akhaian
crossed that portal of rock to ask a sign—
in the old days when grim war lay ahead
for Trojans and Danaans, by God's will.
So ran the tale the minstrel sang. Odysseus
with massive hand drew his rich mantle down
over his brow, cloaking his face with it,
to make the Phaiákians miss the secret tears
that started to his eyes. How skillfully
he dried them when the song came to a pause!
threw back his mantle, spilt his gout of wine!
But soon the minstrel plucked his note once more
to please the Phaiákian lords, who loved the song;
then in his cloak Odysseus wept again.
His tears flowed in the mantle unperceived;
only Alkínoös, at his elbow, saw them,
and caught the low groan in the man's breathing.
At once he spoke to all the seafolk round him:

"Hear me, lords and captains of the Phaiákians.
Our meat is shared, our hearts are full of pleasure
from the clear harp tone that accords with feasting;
now for the field and track; we shall have trials
in the pentathlon. Let our guest go home
and tell his friends what champions we are
at boxing, wrestling, broadjump and foot racing."

On this he led the way and all went after.
The crier unslung and pegged the shining harp
and, taking Demódokos's hand,
led him along with all the rest—Phaiákian
peers, gay amateurs of the great games.

6. The oracular shrine of Apollo at Delphi, high up on the mountainside.

They gained the common, where a crowd was forming,
and many a young athlete now came forward
with seaside names like Tipmast, Tiderace, Sparwood,
Hullman, Sternman, Beacher and Pullerman,
Bluewater, Shearwater, Runningwake, Boardalee,
Seabelt, son of Grandfleet Shipwrightson;
Seareach stepped up, son of the Launching Master,
rugged as Arês,[7] bane of men: his build
excelled all but the Prince Laódamas;
and Laódamas made entry with his brothers,
Halios and Klytóneus, sons of the king.
The runners, first, must have their quarter mile.
All lined up tense; then Go! and down the track
they raised the dust in a flying bunch, strung out
longer and longer behind Prince Klytóneus.
By just so far as a mule team, breaking ground,
will distance oxen, he left all behind
and came up to the crowd, an easy winner.
Then they made room for wrestling—grinding bouts
that Seareach won, pinning the strongest men;
then the broadjump; first place went to Seabelt;
Sparwood gave the discus the mightiest fling,
and Prince Laódamas outboxed them all.
Now it was he, the son of Alkínoös,
who said when they had run through these diversions:

"Look here, friends, we ought to ask the stranger
if he competes in something. He's no cripple;
look at his leg muscles and his forearms.
Neck like a bollard; strong as a bull, he seems;
and not old, though he may have gone stale under
the rough times he had. Nothing like the sea
for wearing out the toughest man alive."

Then Seareach took him up at once, and said:

"Laódamas, you're right, by all the powers.
Go up to him, yourself, and put the question."

At this, Alkínoös' tall son advanced
to the center ground, and there addressed Odysseus:

"Friend, Excellency, come join our competition,
if you are practiced, as you seem to be.
While a man lives he wins no greater honor
than footwork and the skill of hands can bring him.
Enter our games, then; ease your heart of trouble.
Your journey home is not far off, remember;
the ship is launched, the crew all primed for sea."

7. The Greek war god.

Odysseus, canniest of men, replied:

"Laódamas, why do you young chaps challenge me?
I have more on my mind than track and field—
hard days, and many, have I seen, and suffered.
I sit here at your field meet, yes; but only
as one who begs your king to send him home."

Now Seareach put his word in, and contentiously:

"The reason being, as I see it, friend,
you never learned a sport, and have no skill
in any of the contests of fighting men.
You must have been the skipper of some tramp
that crawled from one port to the next, jam full
of chaffering hands: a tallier of cargoes,
itching for gold—not, by your looks, an athlete."

Odysseus frowned, and eyed him coldly, saying:

"That was uncalled for, friend, you talk like a fool.
The gods deal out no gift, this one or any—
birth, brains, or speech—to every man alike.
In looks a man may be a shade, a specter,
and yet be master of speech so crowned with beauty
that people gaze at him with pleasure. Courteous,
sure of himself, he can command assemblies,
and when he comes to town, the crowds gather.
A handsome man, contrariwise, may lack
grace and good sense in everything he says.
You now, for instance, with your fine physique—
a god's, indeed—you have an empty noddle.
I find my heart inside my ribs aroused
by your impertinence. I am no stranger
to contests, as you fancy. I rated well
when I could count on youth and my two hands.
Now pain has cramped me, and my years of combat
hacking through ranks in war, and the bitter sea.
Aye. Even so I'll give your games a trial.
You spoke heart-wounding words. You shall be answered."

He leapt out, cloaked as he was, and picked a discus,
a rounded stone, more ponderous than those
already used by the Phaiákian throwers,
and, whirling, let it fly from his great hand
with a low hum. The crowd went flat on the ground—
all those oar-pulling, seafaring Phaiákians—
under the rushing noise. The spinning disk
soared out, light as a bird, beyond all others.
Disguised now as a Phaiákian, Athena
staked it and called out:

"Even a blind man,
friend, could judge this, finding with his fingers
one discus, quite alone, beyond the cluster.
Congratulations; this event is yours;
not a man here can beat you or come near you."

That was a cheering hail, Odysseus thought,
seeing one friend there on the emulous field,
so, in relief, he turned among the Phaiákians
and said:

"Now come alongside that one, lads.
The next I'll send as far, I think, or farther.
Anyone else on edge for competition
try me now. By heaven, you angered me.
Racing, wrestling, boxing—I bar nothing
with any man except Laódamas,
for he's my host. Who quarrels with his host?
Only a madman—or no man at all—
would challenge his protector among strangers,
cutting the ground away under his feet.
Here are no others I will not engage,
none but I hope to know what he is made of.
Inept at combat, am I? Not entirely.
Give me a smooth bow; I can handle it,
and I might well be first to hit my man
amid a swarm of enemies, though archers
in company around me drew together.
Philoktêtês[8] alone, at Troy, when we
Akhaians took the bow, used to outshoot me.
Of men who now eat bread upon the earth
I hold myself the best hand with a bow—
conceding mastery to the men of old,
Heraklês, or Eurýtos of Oikhalía,[9]
heroes who vied with gods in bowmanship.
Eurýtos came to grief, it's true; old age
never crept over him in his long hall;
Apollo took his challenge ill, and killed him.
What then, the spear? I'll plant it like an arrow.
Only in sprinting, I'm afraid, I may
be passed by someone. Roll of the sea waves
wearied me, and the victuals in my ship
ran low; my legs are flabby."

When he finished,
the rest were silent, but Alkínoös answered:

"Friend, we take your challenge in good part,
for this man angered and affronted you

8. He inherited the bow of Herakles, which never missed its mark. 9. Eurýtos of Oikhalía (in central Greece) challenged Apollo (also an archer) and was killed by the god. Eurýtos's bow was given to Odysseus by his son Iphitos, and it is with that bow that Odysseus will kill the suitors in book 22.

here at our peaceful games. You'd have us note
the prowess that is in you, and so clearly,
no man of sense would ever cry it down!
Come, turn your mind, now, on a thing to tell
among your peers when you are home again,
dining in hall, beside your wife and children:
I mean our prowess, as you may remember it,
for we, too, have our skills, given by Zeus,
and practiced from our father's time to this—
not in the boxing ring nor the palestra[1]
conspicuous, but in racing, land or sea;
and all our days we set great store by feasting,
harpers, and the grace of dancing choirs,
changes of dress, warm baths, and downy beds.
O master dancers of the Phaiákians!
Perform now: let our guest on his return
tell his companions we excel the world
in dance and song, as in our ships and running.
Someone go find the gittern[2] harp in hall
and bring it quickly to Demódokos!"

At the serene king's word, a squire ran
to bring the polished harp out of the palace,
and place was given to nine referees—
peers of the realm, masters of ceremony—
who cleared a space and smoothed a dancing floor.
The squire brought down, and gave Demódokos,
the clear-toned harp; and centering on the minstrel
magical young dancers formed a circle
with a light beat, and stamp of feet. Beholding,
Odysseus marvelled at the flashing ring.

Now to his harp the blinded minstrel sang
of Arês' dalliance with Aphroditê:
how hidden in Hephaistos' house they played
at love together, and the gifts of Arês,
dishonoring Hephaistos' bed—and how
the word that wounds the heart came to the master
from Hélios,[3] who had seen the two embrace;
and when he learned it, Lord Hephaistos went
with baleful calculation to his forge.
There mightily he armed his anvil block
and hammered out a chain whose tempered links
could not be sprung or bent; he meant that they should hold.
Those shackles fashioned, hot in wrath Hephaistos
climbed to the bower and the bed of love,
pooled all his net of chain around the bed posts
and swung it from the rafters overhead—
light as a cobweb even gods in bliss
could not perceive, so wonderful his cunning.

1. Wrestling ground. 2. Shaped like a guitar. 3. The Sun, who sees everything.

Seeing his bed now made a snare, he feigned
a journey to the trim stronghold of Lemnos,
the dearest of earth's towns to him.[4] And Arês?
Ah, golden Arês' watch had its reward
when he beheld the great smith leaving home.
How promptly to the famous door he came,
intent on pleasure with sweet Kythereia![5]
She, who had left her father's side but now,
sat in her chamber when her lover entered;
and tenderly he pressed her hand and said:

"Come and lie down, my darling, and be happy!
Hephaistos is no longer here, but gone
to see his grunting[6] Sintian friends on Lemnos."

As she, too, thought repose would be most welcome,
the pair went in to bed—into a shower
of clever chains, the netting of Hephaistos.
So trussed, they could not move apart, nor rise,
at last they knew there could be no escape,
they were to see the glorious cripple now—
for Hêlios had spied for him, and told him;
so he turned back this side of Lemnos Isle,
sick at heart, making his way homeward.
Now in the doorway of the room he stood
while deadly rage took hold of him; his voice,
hoarse and terrible, reached all the gods:

"O Father Zeus, O gods in bliss forever,
here is indecorous entertainment for you,
Aphroditê, Zeus's daughter,
caught in the act, cheating me, her cripple,
with Arês—devastating Arês.
Cleanlimbed beauty is her joy, not these
bandylegs I came into the world with:
no one to blame but the two gods[7] who bred me!
Come see this pair entwining here
in my own bed! How hot it makes me burn!
I think they may not care to lie much longer,
pressing on one another, passionate lovers;
they'll have enough of bed together soon.
And yet the chain that bagged them holds them down
till Father sends me back my wedding gifts—
all that I poured out for his damned pigeon,
so lovely, and so wanton."

All the others
were crowding in, now, to the brazen house—
Poseidon who embraces earth, and Hermês

4. When Zeus threw him off Olympus (*Iliad* 1.711ff.), Hephaistos landed on the island of Lemnos (off the coast of Asia Minor), where the inhabitants took care of him. 5. A name for Aphrodite. 6. They do not speak Greek. 7. Zeus and Hera.

the runner, and Apollo, lord of Distance.
The goddesses stayed home for shame; but these
munificences ranged there in the doorway,
and irrepressible among them all
arose the laughter of the happy gods.
Gazing hard at Hephaistos' handiwork
the gods in turn remarked among themselves:

"No dash in adultery now."

"The tortoise tags the hare—
Hephaistos catches Arês—and Arês outran the wind."

"The lame god's craft has pinned him. Now shall he
pay what is due from gods taken in cuckoldry."

They made these improving remarks to one another,
but Apollo leaned aside to say to Hermês:

"Son of Zeus, beneficent Wayfinder,
would you accept a coverlet of chain, if only
you lay by Aphroditê's golden side?"

To this the Wayfinder replied, shining:

"Would I not, though, Apollo of distances!
Wrap me in chains three times the weight of these,
come goddesses and gods to see the fun;
only let me lie beside the pale-golden one!"

The gods gave way again to peals of laughter,
all but Poseidon, and he never smiled,
but urged Hephaistos to unpinion Arês,
saying emphatically, in a loud voice:

"Free him;
you will be paid, I swear; ask what you will;
he pays up every jot the gods decree."

To this the Great Gamelegs replied:

"Poseidon,
lord of the earth-surrounding sea, I should not
swear to a scoundrel's honor. What have I
as surety from you, if Arês leaves me
empty-handed, with my empty chain?"

The Earth-shaker for answer urged again:

"Hephaistos, let us grant he goes, and leaves
the fine unpaid; I swear, then, I shall pay it."

Then said the Great Gamelegs at last:

"No more;
you offer terms I cannot well refuse."

And down the strong god bent to set them free,
till disencumbered of their bond, the chain,
the lovers leapt away—he into Thrace,[8]
while Aphroditê, laughter's darling, fled
to Kypros[9] Isle and Paphos, to her meadow
and altar dim with incense. There the Graces
bathed and anointed her with golden oil—
a bloom that clings upon immortal flesh alone—
and let her folds of mantle fall in glory.

So ran the song the minstrel sang.

Odysseus,
listening, found sweet pleasure in the tale,
among the Phaiákian mariners and oarsmen.
And next Alkínoös called upon his sons,
Halios and Laódamas, to show
the dance no one could do as well as they—
handling a purple ball carven by Pólybos.
One made it shoot up under the shadowing clouds
as he leaned backward; bounding high in air
the other cut its flight far off the ground—
and neither missed a step as the ball soared.
The next turn was to keep it low, and shuttling
hard between them, while the ring of boys
gave them a steady stamping beat.
Odysseus now addressed Alkínoös:

"O majesty, model of all your folk,
your promise was to show me peerless dancers;
here is the promise kept. I am all wonder."

At this Alkínoös in his might rejoicing
said to the seafarers of Phaiákia:

"Attend me now, Phaiákian lords and captains:
our guest appears a clear-eyed man and wise.
Come, let him feel our bounty as he should.
Here are twelve princes of the kingdom—lords
paramount, and I who make thirteen;
let each one bring a laundered cloak and tunic,
and add one bar of honorable gold.
Heap all our gifts together; load his arms;
let him go joyous to our evening feast!
As for Seareach—why, man to man

8. Non-Greek territory to the north, which was supposed to be Arês' home.
9. Or Cyprus, where Aphrodite had a famous shrine at Paphos.

he'll make amends, and handsomely; he blundered."

Now all as one acclaimed the king's good pleasure,
and each one sent a squire to bring his gifts.
Meanwhile Seareach found speech again, saying:

"My lord and model of us all, Alkínoös,
as you require of me, in satisfaction,
this broadsword of clear bronze goes to our guest.
Its hilt is silver, and the ringed sheath
of new-sawn ivory—a costly weapon."

He turned to give the broadsword to Odysseus,
facing him, saying blithely:

"Sir, my best
wishes, my respects; if I offended,
I hope the seawinds blow it out of mind.
God send you see your lady and your homeland
soon again, after the pain of exile."

Odysseus, the great tactician, answered:

"My hand, friend; may the gods award you fortune.
I hope no pressing need comes on you ever
for this fine blade you give me in amends."

He slung it, glinting silver, from his shoulder,
as the light shone from sundown. Messengers
were bearing gifts and treasure to the palace,
where the king's sons received them all, and made
a glittering pile at their grave mother's side;
then, as Alkínoös took his throne of power,
each went to his own high-backed chair in turn,
and said Alkínoös to Arêtê:

"Lady, bring here a chest, the finest one;
a clean cloak and tunic; stow these things;
and warm a cauldron for him. Let him bathe,
when he has seen the gifts of the Phaiákians,
and so dine happily to a running song.
My own wine-cup of gold intaglio
I'll give him, too; through all the days to come,
tipping his wine to Zeus or other gods
in his great hall, he shall remember me."

Then said Arêtê to her maids:

"The tripod:
stand the great tripod legs about the fire."

They swung the cauldron on the fire's heart,
poured water in, and fed the blaze beneath

until the basin simmered, cupped in flame.
The queen set out a rich chest from her chamber
and folded in the gifts—clothing and gold
given Odysseus by the Phaiákians;
then she put in the royal cloak and tunic,
briskly saying to her guest:

"Now here, sir,
look to the lid yourself, and tie it down
against light fingers, if there be any,
on the black ship tonight while you are sleeping."

Noble Odysseus, expert in adversity,
battened the lid down with a lightning knot
learned, once, long ago, from the Lady Kirkê.[1]
And soon a call came from the Bathing Mistress
who led him to a hip-bath, warm and clear—
a happy sight, and rare in his immersions
after he left Kalypso's home—where, surely,
the luxuries of a god were ever his.
When the bath maids had washed him, rubbed him down,
put a fresh tunic and a cloak around him,
he left the bathing place to join the men
at wine in hall.

The princess Nausikaa,
exquisite figure, as of heaven's shaping,
waited beside a pillar as he passed
and said swiftly, with wonder in her look:

"Fare well, stranger; in your land remember me
who met and saved you. It is worth your thought."

The man of all occasions now met this:

"Daughter of great Alkínoös, Nausikaa,
may Zeus the lord of thunder, Hera's consort,
grant me daybreak again in my own country!
But there and all my days until I die
may I invoke you as I would a goddess,
princess, to whom I owe my life."

He left her
and went to take his place beside the king.

Now when the roasts were cut, the winebowls full,
a herald led the minstrel down the room
amid the deference of the crowd, and paused
to seat him near a pillar in the center—

1. Or Circe, a divine sorceress on whose island Odysseus had spent some time during his travels (book 12).

whereupon that resourceful man, Odysseus,
carved out a quarter from his chine of pork,
crisp with fat, and called the blind man's guide:

"Herald! here, take this to Demódokos:
let him feast and be merry, with my compliments.
All men owe honor to the poets—honor
and awe, for they are dearest to the Muse
who puts upon their lips the ways of life."

Gentle Demódokos took the proffered gift
and inwardly rejoiced. When all were served,
every man's hand went out upon the banquet,
repelling hunger and thirst, until at length
Odysseus spoke again to the blind minstrel:

"Demódokos, accept my utmost praise.
The Muse, daughter of Zeus in radiance,
or else Apollo gave you skill to shape
with such great style your songs of the Akhaians—
their hard lot, how they fought and suffered war.
You shared it, one would say, or heard it all.
Now shift your theme, and sing that wooden horse
Epeios built, inspired by Athena—
the ambuscade Odysseus filled with fighters
and sent to take the inner town of Troy.
Sing only this for me, sing me this well,
and I shall say at once before the world
the grace of heaven has given us a song."

The minstrel stirred, murmuring to the god, and soon
clear words and notes came one by one, a vision
of the Akhaians in their graceful ships
drawing away from shore: the torches flung
and shelters flaring: Argive soldiers crouched
in the close dark around Odysseus: and
the horse, tall on the assembly ground of Troy.
For when the Trojans pulled it in, themselves,
up to the citadel, they sat nearby
with long-drawn-out and hapless argument—
favoring, in the end, one course of three:
either to stave the vault with brazen axes,
or haul it to a cliff and pitch it down,
or else to save it for the gods, a votive glory—
the plan that could not but prevail.
For Troy must perish, as ordained, that day
she harbored the great horse of timber; hidden
the flower of Akhaia lay, and bore
slaughter and death upon the men of Troy.
He sang, then, of the town sacked by Akhaians
pouring down from the horse's hollow cave,
this way and that way raping the steep city,

and how Odysseus came like Arês to
the door of Deïphobos, with Meneláos,
and braved the desperate fight there—
conquering once more by Athena's power.

The splendid minstrel sang it.

And Odysseus
let the bright molten tears run down his cheeks,
weeping the way a wife mourns for her lord
on the lost field where he has gone down fighting
the day of wrath that came upon his children.
At sight of the man panting and dying there,
she slips down to enfold him, crying out;
then feels the spears, prodding her back and shoulders,
and goes bound into slavery and grief.
Piteous weeping wears away her cheeks:
but no more piteous than Odysseus' tears,
cloaked as they were, now, from the company.
Only Alkínoös, at his elbow, knew—
hearing the low sob in the man's breathing—
and when he knew, he spoke:

"Hear me, lords and captains of Phaiákia!
And let Demódokos touch his harp no more.
His theme has not been pleasing to all here.
During the feast, since our fine poet sang,
our guest has never left off weeping. Grief
seems fixed upon his heart. Break off the song!
Let everyone be easy, host and guest;
there's more decorum in a smiling banquet!
We had prepared here, on our friend's behalf,
safe conduct in a ship, and gifts to cheer him,
holding that any man with a grain of wit
will treat a decent suppliant like a brother.
Now by the same rule, friend, you must not be
secretive any longer! Come, in fairness,
tell me the name you bore in that far country;
how were you known to family, and neighbors?
No man is nameless—no man, good or bad,
but gets a name in his first infancy,
none being born, unless a mother bears him!
Tell me your native land, your coast and city—
sailing directions for the ships, you know—
for those Phaiákian ships of ours
that have no steersman, and no steering oar,
divining the crew's wishes, as they do,
and knowing, as they do, the ports of call
about the world. Hidden in mist or cloud
they scud the open sea, with never a thought
of being in distress or going down.
There is, however, something I once heard

Nausíthoös, my father, say: Poseidon
holds it against us that our deep sea ships
are sure conveyance for all passengers.
My father said, some day one of our cutters
homeward bound over the cloudy sea
would be wrecked by the god, and a range of hills
thrown round our city. So, in his age, he said,
and let it be, or not, as the god please.
But come, now, put it for me clearly, tell me
the sea ways that you wandered, and the shores
you touched; the cities, and the men therein,
uncivilized, if such there were, and hostile,
and those godfearing who had kindly manners.
Tell me why you should grieve so terribly
over the Argives and the fall of Troy.
That was all gods' work, weaving ruin there
so it should make a song for men to come!
Some kin of yours, then, died at Ilion,
some first rate man, by marriage near to you,
next your own blood most dear?
Or some companion of congenial mind
and valor? True it is, a wise friend
can take a brother's place in our affection."

BOOK IX

[*New Coasts and Poseidon's Son*]

Now this was the reply Odysseus made:

"Alkínoös, king and admiration of men,
how beautiful this is, to hear a minstrel
gifted as yours: a god he might be, singing!
There is no boon in life more sweet, I say,
then when a summer joy holds all the realm,
and banqueters sit listening to a harper
in a great hall, by rows of tables heaped
with bread and roast meat, while a steward goes
to dip up wine and brim your cups again.
Here is the flower of life, it seems to me!
But now you wish to know my cause for sorrow—
and thereby give me cause for more.
What shall I
say first? What shall I keep until the end?
The gods have tried me in a thousand ways.
But first my name: let that be known to you,
and if I pull away from pitiless death,
friendship will bind us, though my land lies far.

I am Laërtês' son, Odysseus.
Men hold me
formidable for guile in peace and war:
this fame has gone abroad to the sky's rim.

My home is on the peaked sea-mark of Ithaka
under Mount Neion's wind-blown robe of leaves,
in sight of other islands—Doulíkhion,
Samê, wooded Zakynthos—Ithaka
being most lofty in that coastal sea,
and northwest, while the rest lie east and south.
A rocky isle, but good for a boy's training;
I shall not see on earth a place more dear,
though I have been detained long by Kalypso,
loveliest among goddesses, who held me
in her smooth caves, to be her heart's delight,
as Kirkê of Aiaia, the enchantress,
desired me, and detained me in her hall.
But in my heart I never gave consent.
Where shall a man find sweetness to surpass
his own home and his parents? In far lands
he shall not, though he find a house of gold.

What of my sailing, then, from Troy?
What of those years
of rough adventure, weathered under Zeus?
The wind that carried west from Ilion
brought me to Ísmaros, on the far shore,
a strongpoint on the coast of the Kikonês.[2]
I stormed that place and killed the men who fought.
Plunder we took, and we enslaved the women,
to make division, equal shares to all—
but on the spot I told them: 'Back, and quickly!
Out to sea again!' My men were mutinous,
fools, on stores of wine. Sheep after sheep
they butchered by the surf, and shambling cattle,
feasting,—while fugitives went inland, running
to call to arms the main force of Kikonês.
This was an army, trained to fight on horseback
or, where the ground required, on foot. They came
with dawn over that terrain like the leaves
and blades of spring. So doom appeared to us,
dark word of Zeus for us, our evil days.
My men stood up and made a fight of it—
backed on the ships, with lances kept in play,
from bright morning through the blaze of noon
holding our beach, although so far outnumbered;
but when the sun passed toward unyoking time,
then the Akhaians, one by one, gave way.
Six benches were left empty in every ship
that evening when we pulled away from death.
And this new grief we bore with us to sea:
our precious lives we had, but not our friends.
No ship made sail next day until some shipmate
had raised a cry, three times, for each poor ghost
unfleshed by the Kikonês on that field.

2. Allies of the Trojans, but Odysseus does not even mention this fact to excuse the piratical raid; he did not think any excuse was needed.

Now Zeus the lord of cloud roused in the north
a storm against the ships, and driving veils
of squall moved down like night on land and sea.
The bows went plunging at the gust; sails
cracked and lashed out strips in the big wind.
We saw death in that fury, dropped the yards,
unshipped the oars, and pulled for the nearest lee:
then two long days and nights we lay offshore
worn out and sick at heart, tasting our grief,
until a third Dawn came with ringlets shining.
Then we put up our masts, hauled sail, and rested,
letting the steersmen and the breeze take over.

I might have made it safely home, that time,
but as I came round Malea the current
took me out to sea, and from the north
a fresh gale drove me on, past Kythera.[3]
Nine days I drifted on the teeming sea
before dangerous high winds. Upon the tenth
we came to the coastline of the Lotos Eaters,[4]
who live upon that flower. We landed there
to take on water. All ships' companies
mustered alongside for the mid-day meal.
Then I sent out two picked men and a runner
to learn what race of men that land sustained.
They fell in, soon enough, with Lotos Eaters,
who showed no will to do us harm, only
offering the sweet Lotos to our friends—
but those who ate this honeyed plant, the Lotos,
never cared to report, nor to return:
they longed to stay forever, browsing on
that native bloom, forgetful of their homeland.
I drove them, all three wailing, to the ships,
tied them down under their rowing benches,
and called the rest: 'All hands aboard;
come, clear the beach and no one taste
the Lotos, or you lose your hope of home.'
Filing in to their places by the rowlocks
my oarsmen dipped their long oars in the surf,
and we moved out again on our sea faring.

In the next land we found were Kyklopês,[5]
giants, louts, without a law to bless them.
In ignorance leaving the fruitage of the earth in mystery
to the immortal gods, they neither plow
nor sow by hand, nor till the ground, though grain—
wild wheat and barley—grows untended, and
wine-grapes, in clusters, ripen in heaven's rain.
Kyklopês have no muster and no meeting,

3. A large island off Malea, the southeastern tip of the Peloponnese. 4. It is generally thought that this story contains some memory of early Greek contact with North Africa. The north wind Odysseus describes would have taken him to the area of Cyrenaica, or modern Libya. Identifications of the Lotos range from dates to hashish. 5. According to ancient tradition the Kyklopês lived in Sicily.

no consultation or old tribal ways,
but each one dwells in his own mountain cave
dealing out rough justice to wife and child,
indifferent to what the others do.
Well, then:
across the wide bay from the mainland
there lies a desert island, not far out,
but still not close inshore. Wild goats in hundreds
breed there; and no human being comes
upon the isle to startle them—no hunter
of all who ever tracked with hounds through forests
or had rough going over mountain trails.
The isle, unplanted and untilled, a wilderness,
pastures goats alone. And this is why:
good ships like ours with cheekpaint at the bows[6]
are far beyond the Kyklopês. No shipwright
toils among them, shaping and building up
symmetrical trim hulls to cross the sea
and visit all the seaboard towns, as men do
who go and come in commerce over water.
This isle—seagoing folk would have annexed it
and built their homesteads on it: all good land,
fertile for every crop in season: lush
well-watered meads along the shore, vines in profusion,
prairie, clear for the plow, where grain would grow
chin high by harvest time, and rich sub-soil.
The island cove is landlocked, so you need
no hawsers out astern, bow-stones[7] or mooring:
run in and ride there till the day your crews
chafe to be under sail, and a fair wind blows.
You'll find good water flowing from a cavern
through dusky poplars into the upper bay.
Here we made harbor. Some god guided us
that night, for we could barely see our bows
in the dense fog around us, and no moonlight
filtered through the overcast. No look-out,
nobody saw the island dead ahead,
nor even the great landward rolling billow
that took us in: we found ourselves in shallows,
keels grazing shore: so furled our sails
and disembarked where the low ripples broke.
There on the beach we lay, and slept till morning.

When Dawn spread out her finger tips of rose
we turned out marvelling, to tour the isle,
while Zeus's shy nymph daughters flushed wild goats
down from the heights—a breakfast for my men.
We ran to fetch our hunting bows and long-shanked
lances from the ships, and in three companies
we took our shots. Heaven gave us game a-plenty:
for every one of twelve ships in my squadron

6. On a Greek ship an emblem (often shown as a huge eye on vase paintings) was painted on the bows.
7. A primitive anchor made up of a stone attached to a rope.

nine goats fell to be shared; my lot was ten.
So there all day, until the sun went down,
we made our feast on meat galore, and wine—
wine from the ship, for our supply held out,
so many jars were filled at Ísmaros
from stores of the Kikonês that we plundered.
We gazed, too, at Kyklopês Land, so near,
we saw their smoke, heard bleating from their flocks.
But after sundown, in the gathering dusk,
we slept again above the wash of ripples.
When the young Dawn with finger tips of rose
came in the east, I called my men together
and made a speech to them:

'Old shipmates, friends,
the rest of you stand by; I'll make the crossing
in my own ship, with my own company,
and find out what the mainland natives are—
for they may be wild savages, and lawless,
or hospitable and god-fearing men.'

At this I went aboard, and gave the word
to cast off by the stern. My oarsmen followed,
filing in to their benches by the rowlocks,
and all in line dipped oars in the grey sea.

As we rowed on, and nearer to the mainland,
at one end of the bay, we saw a cavern
yawning above the water, screened with laurel,
and many rams and goats about the place
inside a sheepfold—made from slabs of stone
earthfast between tall trunks of pine and rugged
towering oak trees.

A prodigious man
slept in this cave alone, and took his flocks
to graze afield—remote from all companions,
knowing none but savage ways, a brute
so huge, he seemed no man at all of those
who eat good wheaten bread; but he seemed rather
a shaggy mountain reared in solitude.
We beached there, and I told the crew
to stand by and keep watch over the ship;
as for myself I took my twelve best fighters
and went ahead. I had a goatskin full
of that sweet liquor that Euanthês' son,
Maron, had given me. He kept Apollo's
holy grove at Ísmaros; for kindness
we showed him there, and showed his wife and child,
he gave me seven shining golden talents[8]
perfectly formed, a solid silver winebowl,
and then this liquor—twelve two-handled jars

8. Ingots of gold. The talent was a standard weight.

of brandy, pure and fiery. Not a slave
in Maron's household knew this drink; only
he, his wife and the storeroom mistress knew;
and they would put one cupful—ruby-colored,
honey-smooth—in twenty more of water,
but still the sweet scent hovered like a fume
over the winebowl. No man turned away
when cups of this came round.
A wineskin full
I brought along, and victuals in a bag,
for in my bones I knew some towering brute
would be upon us soon—all outward power,
a wild man, ignorant of civility.

We climbed, then, briskly to the cave. But Kyklops
had gone afield, to pasture his fat sheep,
so we looked round at everything inside:
a drying rack that sagged with cheeses, pens
crowded with lambs and kids, each in its class:
firstlings apart from middlings, and the 'dewdrops,'
or newborn lambkins, penned apart from both.
And vessels full of whey were brimming there—
bowls of earthenware and pails of milking.
My men came pressing round me, pleading:

'Why not
take these cheeses, get them stowed, come back,
throw open all the pens, and make a run for it?
We'll drive the kids and lambs aboard. We say
put out again on good salt water!'

Ah,
how sound that was! Yet I refused, I wished
to see the caveman, what he had to offer—
no pretty sight, it turned out, for my friends.
We lit a fire, burnt an offering,
and took some cheese to eat; then sat in silence
around the embers, waiting. When he came
he had a load of dry boughs on his shoulder
to stoke his fire at suppertime. He dumped it
with a great crash into that hollow cave,
and we all scattered fast to the far wall.
Then over the broad cavern floor he ushered
the ewes he meant to milk. He left his rams
and he-goats in the yard outside, and swung
high overhead a slab of solid rock
to close the cave. Two dozen four-wheeled wagons,
with heaving wagon teams, could not have stirred
the tonnage of that rock from where he wedged it
over the doorsill. Next he took his seat
and milked his bleating ewes. A practiced job
he made of it, giving each ewe her suckling;

thickened his milk, then, into curds and whey,
sieved out the curds to drip in withy baskets,
and poured the whey to stand in bowls
cooling until he drank it for his supper.
When all these chores were done, he poked the fire,
heaping on brushwood. In the glare he saw us.

'Strangers,' he said, 'who are you? And where from?
What brings you here by sea ways—a fair traffic?
Or are you wandering rogues, who cast your lives
like dice, and ravage other folk by sea?'

We felt a pressure on our hearts, in dread
of that deep rumble and that mighty man.
But all the same I spoke up in reply:

'We are from Troy, Akhaians, blown off course
by shifting gales on the Great South Sea;
homeward bound, but taking routes and ways
uncommon; so the will of Zeus would have it.
We served under Agamémnon, son of Atreus—
the whole world knows what city
he laid waste, what armies he destroyed.
It was our luck to come here; here we stand,
beholden for your help, or any gifts
you give—as custom is to honor strangers.[9]
We would entreat you, great Sir, have a care
for the gods' courtesy; Zeus will avenge
the unoffending guest.'

He answered this
from his brute chest, unmoved:

'You are a ninny,
or else you come from the other end of nowhere,
telling me, mind the gods! We Kyklopês
care not a whistle for your thundering Zeus
or all the gods in bliss; we have more force by far.
I would not let you go for fear of Zeus—
you or your friends—unless I had a whim to.
Tell me, where was it, now, you left your ship—
around the point, or down the shore, I wonder?'

He thought he'd find out, but I saw through this,
and answered with a ready lie:

'My ship?
Poseidon Lord, who sets the earth a-tremble,
broke it up on the rocks at your land's end.

9. It is the mark of civilized people in the *Odyssey*, like Meneláos and Alkínoös, that they welcome strangers and send them on their way with gifts.

A wind from seaward served him, drove us there.
We are survivors, these good men and I.'

Neither reply nor pity came from him,
but in one stride he clutched at my companions
and caught two in his hands like squirming puppies
to beat their brains out, spattering the floor.
Then he dismembered them and made his meal,
gaping and crunching like a mountain lion—
everything: innards, flesh, and marrow bones.
We cried aloud, lifting our hands to Zeus,
powerless, looking on at this, appalled;
but Kyklops went on filling up his belly
with manflesh and great gulps of whey,
then lay down like a mast among his sheep.
My heart beat high now at the chance of action,
and drawing the sharp sword from my hip I went
along his flank to stab him where the midriff
holds the liver. I had touched the spot
when sudden fear stayed me: if I killed him
we perished there as well, for we could never
move his ponderous doorway slab aside.
So we were left to groan and wait for morning.

When the young Dawn with finger tips of rose
lit up the world, the Kyklops built a fire
and milked his handsome ewes, all in due order,
putting the sucklings to the mothers. Then,
his chores being all dispatched, he caught
another brace of men to make his breakfast,
and whisked away his great door slab
to let his sheep go through—but he, behind,
reset the stone as one would cap a quiver.
There was a din of whistling as the Kyklops
rounded his flock to higher ground, then stillness.
And now I pondered how to hurt him worst,
if but Athena granted what I prayed for.
Here are the means I thought would serve my turn:

a club, or staff, lay there along the fold—
an olive tree, felled green and left to season
for Kyklops' hand. And it was like a mast
a lugger of twenty oars, broad in the beam—
a deep-sea going craft—might carry:
so long, so big around, it seemed. Now I
chopped out a six foot section of this pole
and set it down before my men, who scraped it;
and when they had it smooth, I hewed again
to make a stake with pointed end. I held this
in the fire's heart and turned it, toughening it,
then hid it, well back in the cavern, under
one of the dung piles in profusion there.

Now came the time to toss for it: who ventured
along with me? whose hand could bear to thrust
and grind that spike in Kyklops' eye, when mild
sleep had mastered him? As luck would have it,
the men I would have chosen won the toss—
four strong men, and I made five as captain.

At evening came the shepherd with his flock,
his woolly flock. The rams as well, this time,
entered the cave: by some sheep-herding whim—
or a god's bidding—none were left outside.
He hefted his great boulder into place
and sat him down to milk the bleating ewes
in proper order, put the lambs to suck,
and swiftly ran through all his evening chores.
Then he caught two more men and feasted on them.
My moment was at hand, and I went forward
holding an ivy bowl of my dark drink,
looking up, saying:

'Kyklops, try some wine.
Here's liquor to wash down your scraps of men.
Taste it, and see the kind of drink we carried
under our planks. I meant it for an offering
if you would help us home. But you are mad,
unbearable, a bloody monster! After this,
will any other traveller come to see you?'

He seized and drained the bowl, and it went down
so fiery and smooth he called for more:

'Give me another, thank you kindly. Tell me,
how are you called? I'll make a gift will please you.
Even Kyklopês know the wine-grapes grow
out of grassland and loam in heaven's rain,
but here's a bit of nectar and ambrosia!'

Three bowls I brought him, and he poured them down.
I saw the fuddle and flush come over him,
then I sang out in cordial tones:

'Kyklops,
you ask my honorable name? Remember
the gift you promised me, and I shall tell you.
My name is Nohbdy: mother, father, and friends,
everyone calls me Nohbdy.'

And he said:

'Nohbdy's my meat, then, after I eat his friends.
Others come first. There's a noble gift, now.'

Even as he spoke, he reeled and tumbled backward,
his great head lolling to one side: and sleep
took him like any creature. Drunk, hiccuping,
he dribbled streams of liquor and bits of men.

Now, by the gods, I drove my big hand spike
deep in the embers, charring it again,
and cheered my men along with battle talk
to keep their courage up: no quitting now.
The pike of olive, green though it had been,
reddened and glowed as if about to catch.
I drew it from the coals and my four fellows
gave me a hand, lugging it near the Kyklops
as more than natural force nerved them; straight
forward they sprinted, lifted it, and rammed it
deep in his crater eye, and I leaned on it
turning it as a shipwright turns a drill
in planking, having men below to swing
the two-handled strap that spins it in the groove.
So with our brand we bored that great eye socket
while blood ran out around the red hot bar.
Eyelid and lash were seared; the pierced ball
hissed broiling, and the roots popped.

In a smithy
one sees a white-hot axehead or an adze
plunged and wrung in a cold tub, screeching steam—
the way they make soft iron hale and hard—:
just so that eyeball hissed around the spike.
The Kyklops bellowed and the rock roared round him,
and we fell back in fear. Clawing his face
he tugged the bloody spike out of his eye,
threw it away, and his wild hands went groping;
then he set up a howl for Kyklopês
who lived in caves on windy peaks nearby.
Some heard him; and they came by divers ways
to clump around outside and call:

'What ails you,
Polyphêmos? Why do you cry so sore
in the starry night? You will not let us sleep.
Sure no man's driving off your flock? No man
has tricked you, ruined you?'

Out of the cave
the mammoth Polyphêmos roared in answer:

'Nohbdy, Nohbdy's tricked me, Nohbdy's ruined me!'

To this rough shout they made a sage reply:

'Ah well, if nobody has played you foul
there in your lonely bed, we are no use in pain

given by great Zeus. Let it be your father,
Poseidon Lord, to whom you pray.'

So saying
they trailed away. And I was filled with laughter
to see how like a charm the name deceived them.
Now Kyklops, wheezing as the pain came on him,
fumbled to wrench away the great doorstone
and squatted in the breach with arms thrown wide
for any silly beast or man who bolted—
hoping somehow I might be such a fool.
But I kept thinking how to win the game:
death sat there huge; how could we slip away?
I drew on all my wits, and ran through tactics,
reasoning as a man will for dear life,
until a trick came—and it pleased me well.
The Kyklops' rams were handsome, fat, with heavy
fleeces, a dark violet.
Three abreast
I tied them silently together, twining
cords of willow from the ogre's bed;
then slung a man under each middle one
to ride there safely, shielded left and right.
So three sheep could convey each man. I took
the woolliest ram, the choicest of the flock,
and hung myself under his kinky belly,
pulled up tight, with fingers twisted deep
in sheepskin ringlets for an iron grip.
So, breathing hard, we waited until morning.

When Dawn spread out her finger tips of rose
the rams began to stir, moving for pasture,
and peals of bleating echoed round the pens
where dams with udders full called for a milking.
Blinded, and sick with pain from his head wound,
the master stroked each ram, then let it pass,
but my men riding on the pectoral fleece
the giant's blind hands blundering never found.
Last of them all my ram, the leader, came,
weighted by wool and me with my meditations.
The Kyklops patted him, and then he said:

'Sweet cousin ram, why lag behind the rest
in the night cave? You never linger so,
but graze before them all, and go afar
to crop sweet grass, and take your stately way
leading along the streams, until at evening
you run to be the first one in the fold.
Why, now, so far behind? Can you be grieving
over your Master's eye? That carrion rogue
and his accurst companions burnt it out
when he had conquered all my wits with wine.

Nohbdy will not get out alive, I swear.
Oh, had you brain and voice to tell
where he may be now, dodging all my fury!
Bashed by this hand and bashed on this rock wall
his brains would strew the floor, and I should have
rest from the outrage Nohbdy worked upon me.'

He sent us into the open, then. Close by,
I dropped and rolled clear of the ram's belly,
going this way and that to untie the men.
With many glances back, we rounded up
his fat, stiff-legged sheep to take aboard,
and drove them down to where the good ship lay.
We saw, as we came near, our fellows' faces
shining; then we saw them turn to grief
tallying those who had not fled from death.
I hushed them, jerking head and eyebrows up,
and in a low voice told them: 'Load this herd;
move fast, and put the ship's head toward the breakers.'
They all pitched in at loading, then embarked
and struck their oars into the sea. Far out,
as far off shore as shouted words would carry,
I sent a few back to the adversary:

'O Kyklops! Would you feast on my companions?
Puny, am I, in a Caveman's hands?
How do you like the beating that we gave you,
you damned cannibal? Eater of guests
under your roof! Zeus and the gods have paid you!'

The blind thing in his doubled fury broke
a hilltop in his hands and heaved it after us.
Ahead of our black prow it struck and sank
whelmed in a spuming geyser, a giant wave
that washed the ship stern foremost back to shore.
I got the longest boathook out and stood
fending us off, with furious nods to all
to put their backs into a racing stroke—
row, row, or perish. So the long oars bent
kicking the foam sternward, making head
until we drew away, and twice as far.
Now when I cupped my hands I heard the crew
in low voices protesting:

'Godsake, Captain!
Why bait the beast again? Let him alone!'

'That tidal wave he made on the first throw
all but beached us.'

'All but stove us in!'

'Give him our bearing with your trumpeting,
he'll get the range and lob a boulder.'

'Aye
He'll smash our timbers and our heads together!'

I would not heed them in my glorying spirit,
but let my anger flare and yelled:

'Kyklops,
if ever mortal man inquire
how you were put to shame and blinded, tell him
Odysseus, raider of cities, took your eye:
Laërtês' son, whose home's on Ithaka!'

At this he gave a mighty sob and rumbled:

'Now comes the weird[1] upon me, spoken of old.
A wizard, grand and wondrous, lived here—Télemos,
a son of Eurymos; great length of days
he had in wizardry among the Kyklopês,
and these things he foretold for time to come:
my great eye lost, and at Odysseus' hands.
Always I had in mind some giant, armed
in giant force, would come against me here.
But this, but you—small, pitiful and twiggy—
you put me down with wine, you blinded me.
Come back, Odysseus, and I'll treat you well,
praying the god of earthquake to befriend you—
his son I am, for he by his avowal
fathered me, and, if he will, he may
heal me of this black wound—he and no other
of all the happy gods or mortal men.'

Few words I shouted in reply to him:

'If I could take your life I would and take
your time away, and hurl you down to hell!
The god of earthquake could not heal you there!'

At this he stretched his hands out in his darkness
toward the sky of stars, and prayed Poseidon:

'O hear me, lord, blue girdler of the islands,
if I am thine indeed, and thou art father:
grant that Odysseus, raider of cities, never
see his home: Laërtês' son, I mean,
who kept his hall on Ithaka. Should destiny
intend that he shall see his roof again
among his family in his father land,

1. Fate, destiny.

far be that day, and dark the years between.
Let him lose all companions, and return
under strange sail to bitter days at home.'

In these words he prayed, and the god heard him.
Now he laid hands upon a bigger stone
and wheeled around, titanic for the cast,
to let it fly in the black-prowed vessel's track.
But it fell short, just aft the steering oar,
and whelming seas rose giant above the stone
to bear us onward toward the island.
There
as we ran in we saw the squadron waiting,
the trim ships drawn up side by side, and all
our troubled friends who waited, looking seaward.
We beached her, grinding keel in the soft sand,
and waded in, ourselves, on the sandy beach.
Then we unloaded all the Kyklops' flock
to make division, share and share alike,
only my fighters voted that my ram,
the prize of all, should go to me. I slew him
by the sea side and burnt his long thighbones
to Zeus beyond the stormcloud, Kronos' son,
who rules the world. But Zeus disdained my offering;
destruction for my ships he had in store
and death for those who sailed them, my companions.
Now all day long until the sun went down
we made our feast on mutton and sweet wine,
till after sunset in the gathering dark
we went to sleep above the wash of ripples.

When the young Dawn with finger tips of rose
touched the world, I roused the men, gave orders
to man the ships, cast off the mooring lines;
and filing in to sit beside the rowlocks
oarsmen in line dipped oars in the grey sea.
So we moved out, sad in the vast offing,
having our precious lives, but not our friends.

BOOK X

[*The Grace of the Witch*]

We made our landfall on Aiolia Island,
domain of Aiolos[2] Hippotadês,
the wind king dear to the gods who never die—
an isle adrift upon the sea, ringed round
with brazen ramparts on a sheer cliffside.
Twelve children had old Aiolos at home—

2. King of the winds (whose name in Greek means "shifting, changeable"). Aiolia was a moving island that has been located by modern geographers in the Lipari Islands off the Sicilian coast. The great ancient geographer Eratosthenes was not so confident. He once said that we would know exactly where Odysseus wandered after we had traced the leatherworker who made the bag in which the winds were contained.

six daughters and six lusty sons—and he
gave girls to boys to be their gentle brides;
now those lords, in their parents' company,
sup every day in hall—a royal feast
with fumes of sacrifice and winds that pipe
'round hollow courts; and all the night they sleep
on beds of filigree beside their ladies.
Here we put in, lodged in the town and palace,
while Aiolos played host to me. He kept me
one full month to hear the tale of Troy,
the ships and the return of the Akhaians,
all which I told him point by point in order.
When in return I asked his leave to sail
and asked provisioning, he stinted nothing,
adding a bull's hide sewn from neck to tail
into a mighty bag, bottling storm winds;
for Zeus had long ago made Aiolos
warden of winds, to rouse or calm at will.
He wedged this bag under my afterdeck,
lashing the neck with shining silver wire
so not a breath got through; only the west wind
he lofted for me in a quartering breeze
to take my squadron spanking home.
No luck:
the fair wind failed us when our prudence failed.

Nine days and nights we sailed without event,
till on the tenth we raised our land. We neared it,
and saw men building fires along the shore;
but now, being weary to the bone, I fell
into deep slumber; I had worked the sheet
nine days alone, and given it to no one,
wishing to spill no wind on the homeward run.
But while I slept, the crew began to parley:
silver and gold, they guessed, were in that bag
bestowed on me by Aiolos' great heart;
and one would glance at his benchmate and say:
'It never fails. He's welcome everywhere:
hail to the captain when he goes ashore!
He brought along so many presents, plunder
out of Troy, that's it. How about ourselves—
his shipmates all the way. Nigh home we are
with empty hands. And who has gifts from Aiolos?
He has. I say we ought to crack that bag,
there's gold and silver, plenty, in that bag!'

Temptation had its way with my companions,
and they untied the bag.
Then every wind
roared into hurricane; the ships went pitching
west with many cries; our land was lost.
Roused up, despairing in that gloom, I thought:

'Should I go overside for a quick finish
or clench my teeth and stay among the living?'
Down in the bilge I lay, pulling my sea cloak
over my head, while the rough gale blew the ships
and rueful crews clear back to Aiolia.

We put ashore for water; then all hands
gathered alongside for a mid-day meal.
When we had taken bread and drink, I picked
one soldier, and one herald, to go with me
and called again on Aiolos. I found him
at meat with his young princes and his lady,
but there beside the pillars, in his portico,
we sat down silent at the open door.
The sight amazed them, and they all exclaimed:

'Why back again, Odysseus?'
'What sea fiend
rose in your path?'
'Did we not launch you well
for home, or for whatever land you chose?'

Out of my melancholy I replied:

'Mischief aboard and nodding at the tiller—
a damned drowse—did for me. Make good my loss,
dear friends! You have the power!'

Gently I pleaded,
but they turned cold and still. Said Father Aiolos:

'Take yourself out of this island, creeping thing—
no law, no wisdom, lays it on me now
to help a man the blessed gods detest—
out! Your voyage here was cursed by heaven!'

He drove me from the place, groan as I would,
and comfortless we went again to sea,
days of it, till the men flagged at the oars—
no breeze, no help in sight, by our own folly—
six indistinguishable nights and days
before we raised the Laistrygonian height
and far stronghold of Lamos.[3] In that land
the daybreak follows dusk, and so the shepherd
homing calls to the cowherd setting out;
and he who never slept could earn two wages,
tending oxen, pasturing silvery flocks,

3. Presumably the founder of the city of the Laistrygonians, a race of human-eating giants.

where the low night path of the sun is near
the sun's path by day.[4] Here, then, we found
a curious bay with mountain walls of stone
to left and right, and reaching far inland,—
a narrow entrance opening from the sea
where cliffs converged as though to touch and close.
All of my squadron sheltered here, inside
the cavern of this bay.
Black prow by prow
those hulls were made fast in a limpid calm
without a ripple stillness all around them.
My own black ship I chose to moor alone
on the sea side, using a rock for bollard;
and climbed a rocky point to get my bearings.
No farms, no cultivated land appeared,
but puffs of smoke rose in the wilderness;
so I sent out two picked men and a herald
to learn what race of men this land sustained.

My party found a track—a wagon road
for bringing wood down from the heights to town;
and near the settlement they met a daughter
of Antiphatês the Laistrygon—a stalwart
young girl taking her pail to Artakía,
the fountain where these people go for water.
My fellows hailed her, put their questions to her:
who might the king be? ruling over whom?
She waved her hand, showing her father's lodge,
so they approached it. In its gloom they saw
a woman like a mountain crag, the queen—
and loathed the sight of her. But she, for greeting,
called from the meeting ground her lord and master,
Antiphatês, who came to drink their blood.
He seized one man and tore him on the spot,
making a meal of him; the other two
leaped out of doors and ran to join the ships.
Behind, he raised the whole tribe howling, countless
Laistrygonês—and more than men they seemed,
gigantic when they gathered on the sky line
to shoot great boulders down from slings; and hell's own
crashing rose, and crying from the ships,
as planks and men were smashed to bits—poor gobbets
the wildmen speared like fish and bore away.
But long before it ended in the anchorage—
havoc and slaughter—I had drawn my sword
and cut my own ship's cable. 'Men,' I shouted,
'man the oars and pull till your hearts break
if you would put this butchery behind!'
The oarsmen rent the sea in mortal fear

4. Generally thought to be a confused reference to the short summer nights of the far north.

and my ship spurted out of range, far out
from that deep canyon where the rest were lost.
So we fared onward and death fell behind,
and we took breath to grieve for our companions.

Our next landfall was on Aiaia, island
of Kirkê, dire beauty and divine,
sister of baleful Aiêtês, like him
fathered by Hêlios the light of mortals
on Persê, child of the Ocean stream.
We came
washed in our silent ship upon her shore,
and found a cove, a haven for the ship—
some god, invisible, conned us in. We landed,
to lie down in that place two days and nights,
worn out and sick at heart, tasting our grief.
But when Dawn set another day a-shining
I took my spear and broadsword and I climbed
a rocky point above the ship, for sight
or sound of human labor. Gazing out
from that high place over a land of thicket,
oaks and wide watercourses, I could see
a smoke wisp from the woodland hall of Kirkê.
So I took counsel with myself: should I
go inland scouting out that reddish smoke?
No: better not, I thought, but first return
to waterside and ship, and give the men
breakfast before I sent them to explore.
Now as I went down quite alone, and came
a bowshot from the ship, some god's compassion
set a big buck in motion to cross my path—
a stag with noble antlers, pacing down
from pasture in the woods to the riverside,
as long thirst and the power of sun constrained him.
He started from the bush and wheeled: I hit him
square in the spine midway along his back
and the bronze point broke through it. In the dust
he fell and whinnied as life bled away.
I set one foot against him, pulling hard
to wrench my weapon from the wound, then left it,
butt-end on the ground. I plucked some withies
and twined a double strand into a rope—
enough to tie the hocks of my huge trophy;
then pickaback I lugged him to the ship,
leaning on my long spearshaft; I could not
haul that mighty carcass on one shoulder.
Beside the ship I let him drop, and spoke
gently and low to each man standing near:

'Come, friends, though hard beset, we'll not go down
into the House of Death before our time.

As long as food and drink remain aboard
let us rely on it, not die of hunger.'

At this those faces, cloaked in desolation
upon the waste sea beach, were bared;
their eyes turned toward me and the mighty trophy,
lighting, foreseeing pleasure, one by one.
So hands were washed to take what heaven sent us.
And all that day until the sun went down
we had our fill of venison and wine,
till after sunset in the gathering dusk
we slept at last above the line of breakers.
When the young Dawn with finger tips of rose
made heaven bright, I called them round and said:

'Shipmates, companions in disastrous time,
O my dear friends, where Dawn lies, and the West,
and where the great Sun, light of men, may go
under the earth by night, and where he rises—
of these things we know nothing.[5] Do we know
any least thing to serve us now? I wonder.
All that I saw when I went up the rock
was one more island in the boundless main,
a low landscape, covered with woods and scrub,
and puffs of smoke ascending in mid-forest.'

They were all silent, but their hearts contracted,
remembering Antiphatês the Laistrygon
and that prodigious cannibal, the Kyklops.
They cried out, and the salt tears wet their eyes.
But seeing our time for action lost in weeping,
I mustered those Akhaians under arms,
counting them off in two platoons, myself
and my godlike Eurýlokhos commanding.
We shook lots in a soldier's dogskin cap
and his came bounding out—valiant Eurýlokhos!—
So off he went, with twenty-two companions
weeping, as mine wept, too, who stayed behind.

In the wild wood they found an open glade,
around a smooth stone house—the hall of Kirkê—
and wolves and mountain lions lay there, mild
in her soft spell, fed on her drug of evil.
None would attack—oh, it was strange, I tell you—
but switching their long tails they faced our men
like hounds, who look up when their master comes
with tidbits for them—as he will—from table.
Humbly those wolves and lions with mighty paws

5. In view of the immediately preceding lines, this can hardly be taken literally. It is possibly a sailor's metaphorical way of saying "We don't know where we are."

fawned on our men—who met their yellow eyes
and feared them.
In the entrance way they stayed
to listen there: inside her quiet house
they heard the goddess Kirkê.
Low she sang
in her beguiling voice, while on her loom
she wove ambrosial fabric sheer and bright,
by that craft known to the goddesses of heaven.
No one would speak, until Politês—most
faithful and likable of my officers, said:

'Dear friends, no need for stealth: here's a young weaver
singing a pretty song to set the air
a-tingle on these lawns and paven courts.
Goddess she is, or lady. Shall we greet her?'

So reassured, they all cried out together,
and she came swiftly to the shining doors
to call them in. All but Eurýlokhos—
who feared a snare—the innocents went after her.
On thrones she seated them, and lounging chairs,
while she prepared a meal of cheese and barley
and amber honey mixed with Pramnian wine,[6]
adding her own vile pinch, to make them lose
desire or thought of our dear father land.
Scarce had they drunk when she flew after them
with her long stick and shut them in a pigsty—
bodies, voices, heads, and bristles, all
swinish now, though minds were still unchanged.
So, squealing, in they went. And Kirkê tossed them
acorns, mast, and cornel berries—fodder
for hogs who rut and slumber on the earth.

Down to the ship Eurýlokhos came running
to cry alarm, foul magic doomed his men!
But working with dry lips to speak a word
he could not, being so shaken; blinding tears
welled in his eyes; foreboding filled his heart.
When we were frantic questioning him, at last
we heard the tale: our friends were gone. Said he:

'We went up through the oak scrub where you sent us,
Odysseus, glory of commanders,
until we found a palace in a glade,
a marble house on open ground, and someone
singing before her loom a chill, sweet song—
goddess or girl, we could not tell. They hailed her,
and then she stepped through shining doors and said,
"Come, come in!" Like sheep they followed her,

6. A harsh, dark wine.

but I saw cruel deceit, and stayed behind.
Then all our fellows vanished. Not a sound,
and nothing stirred, although I watched for hours.'

When I heard this I slung my silver-hilted
broadsword on, and shouldered my long bow,
and said, 'Come, take me back the way you came.'
But he put both his hands around my knees
in desperate woe, and said in supplication:

'Not back there, O my lord! Oh, leave me here!
You, even you, cannot return, I know it,
I know you cannot bring away our shipmates;
better make sail with these men, quickly too,
and save ourselves from horror while we may.'

But I replied:

'By heaven, Eurýlokhos,
rest here then; take food and wine;
stay in the black hull's shelter. Let me go,
as I see nothing for it but to go.'

I turned and left him, left the shore and ship,
and went up through the woodland hushed and shady
to find the subtle witch in her long hall.
But Hermês met me, with his golden wand,
barring the way—a boy whose lip was downy
in the first bloom of manhood, so he seemed.
He took my hand and spoke as though he knew me:[7]

'Why take the inland path alone,
poor seafarer, by hill and dale
upon this island all unknown?
Your friends are locked in Kirkê's pale;
all are become like swine to see;
and if you go to set them free
you go to stay, and never more make sail
for your old home upon Thaki.[8]

But I can tell you what to do
to come unchanged from Kirkê's power
and disenthrall your fighting crew:
take with you to her bower
as amulet, this plant I know—
it will defeat her horrid show,
so pure and potent is the flower;
no mortal herb was ever so.

7. The four rhymed stanzas that follow are a translator's license; in the original there is no change of meter and, of course, no rhyme. 8. Ithaka.

Your cup with numbing drops of night
and evil, stilled of all remorse,
she will infuse to charm your sight;
but this great herb with holy force
will keep your mind and senses clear:
when she turns cruel, coming near
with her long stick to whip you out of doors,
then let your cutting blade appear,

Let instant death upon it shine,
and she will cower and yield her bed—
a pleasure you must not decline,
so may her lust and fear bestead
you and your friends, and break her spell;
but make her swear by heaven and hell
no witches' tricks, or else, your harness shed,
you'll be unmanned by her as well.'

He bent down glittering for the magic plant
and pulled it up, black root and milky flower—
a *molü* in the language of the gods—
fatigue and pain for mortals to uproot;
but gods do this, and everything, with ease.

Then toward Olympos through the island trees
Hermês departed, and I sought out Kirkê,
my heart high with excitement, beating hard.
Before her mansion in the porch I stood
to call her, all being still. Quick as a cat
she opened her bright doors and sighed a welcome;
then I strode after her with heavy heart
down the long hall, and took the chair she gave me,
silver-studded, intricately carved,
made with a low footrest. The lady Kirkê
mixed me a golden cup of honeyed wine,
adding in mischief her unholy drug.
I drank, and the drink failed. But she came forward
aiming a stroke with her long stick, and whispered:

'Down in the sty and snore among the rest!'

Without a word, I drew my sharpened sword
and in one bound held it against her throat.
She cried out, then slid under to take my knees,
catching her breath to say, in her distress:

'What champion, of what country, can you be?
Where are your kinsmen and your city?
Are you not sluggish with my wine? Ah, wonder!
Never a mortal man that drank this cup
but when it passed his lips he had succumbed.

Hale must your heart be and your tempered will.
Odysseus then you are, O great contender,
of whom the glittering god with golden wand[9]
spoke to me ever, and foretold
the black swift ship would carry you from Troy.
Put up your weapon in the sheath. We two
shall mingle and make love upon our bed.
So mutual trust may come of play and love.'

To this I said:

'Kirkê, am I a boy,
that you should make me soft and doting now?
Here in this house you turned my men to swine;
now it is I myself you hold, enticing
into your chamber, to your dangerous bed,
to take my manhood when you have me stripped.
I mount no bed of love with you upon it.
Or swear me first a great oath, if I do,
you'll work no more enchantment to my harm.'

She swore at once, outright, as I demanded,
and after she had sworn, and bound herself,
I entered Kirkê's flawless bed of love.

Presently in the hall her maids were busy,
the nymphs who waited upon Kirkê: four,
whose cradles were in fountains, under boughs,
or in the glassy seaward-gliding streams.
One came with richly colored rugs to throw
on seat and chairback, over linen covers;
a second pulled the tables out, all silver,
and loaded them with baskets all of gold;
a third mixed wine as tawny-mild as honey
in a bright bowl, and set out golden cups.
The fourth came bearing water, and lit a blaze
under a cauldron. By and by it bubbled,
and when the dazzling brazen vessel seethed
she filled a bathtub to my waist, and bathed me,
pouring a soothing blend on head and shoulders,
warming the soreness of my joints away.
When she had done, and smoothed me with sweet oil,
she put a tunic and a cloak around me
and took me to a silver-studded chair
with footrest, all elaborately carven.
Now came a maid to tip a golden jug
of water into a silver finger bowl,
and draw a polished table to my side.
The larder mistress brought her tray of loaves

9. Hermês.

with many savory slices, and she gave
the best, to tempt me. But no pleasure came;
I huddled with my mind elsewhere, oppressed.

Kirkê regarded me, as there I sat
disconsolate, and never touched a crust.
Then she stood over me and chided me:

'Why sit at table mute, Odysseus?
Are you mistrustful of my bread and drink?
Can it be treachery that you fear again,
after the gods' great oath I swore for you?'

I turned to her at once, and said:

'Kirkê,
where is the captain who could bear to touch
this banquet, in my place? A decent man
would see his company before him first.
Put heart in me to eat and drink—you may,
by freeing my companions. I must see them.'

But Kirkê had already turned away.
Her long staff in her hand, she left the hall
and opened up the sty, I saw her enter,
driving those men turned swine to stand before me.
She stroked them, each in turn, with some new chrism;
and then, behold! their bristles fell away,
the coarse pelt grown upon them by her drug
melted away, and they were men again,
younger, more handsome, taller than before.
Their eyes upon me, each one took my hands,
and wild regret and longing pierced them through,
so the room rang with sobs, and even Kirkê
pitied that transformation. Exquisite
the goddess looked as she stood near me, saying:

'Son of Laërtês and the gods of old,
Odysseus, master mariner and soldier,
go to the sea beach and sea-breasting ship;
drag it ashore, full length upon the land;
stow gear and stores in rock-holes under cover;
return; be quick; bring all your dear companions.'

Now, being a man, I could not help consenting.
So I went down to the sea beach and the ship,
where I found all my other men on board,
weeping, in despair along the benches.
Sometimes in farmyards when the cows return
well fed from pasture to the barn, one sees
the pens give way before the calves in tumult,
breaking through to cluster about mothers,

bumping together, bawling. Just that way
my crew poured round me when they saw me come—
their faces wet with tears as if they saw
their homeland, and the crags of Ithaka,
even the very town where they were born.
And weeping still they all cried out in greeting:

'Prince, what joy this is, your safe return!
Now Ithaka seems here, and we in Ithaka!
But tell us now, what death befell our friends?'

And, speaking gently, I replied:

'First we must get the ship high on the shingle,
and stow our gear and stores in clefts of rock
for cover. Then come follow me, to see
your shipmates in the magic house of Kirkê
eating and drinking, endlessly regaled.'

They turned back, as commanded, to this work;
only one lagged, and tried to hold the others;
Eurýlokhos it was, who blurted out:

'Where now, poor remnants? is it devil's work
you long for? Will you go to Kirkê's hall?
Swine, wolves, and lions she will make us all,
beasts of her courtyard, bound by her enchantment.
Remember those the Kyklops held, remember
shipmates who made that visit with Odysseus!
The daring man! They died for his foolishness!'

When I heard this I had a mind to draw
the blade that swung against my side and chop him,
bowling his head upon the ground—kinsman[1]
or no kinsman, close to me though he was.
But others came between, saying, to stop me,
'Prince, we can leave him, if you say the word;
let him stay here on guard. As for ourselves,
show us the way to Kirkê's magic hall.'

So all turned inland, leaving shore and ship,
and Eurýlokhos—he, too, came on behind,
fearing the rough edge of my tongue. Meanwhile
at Kirkê's hands the rest were gently bathed,
anointed with sweet oil, and dressed afresh
in tunics and new cloaks with fleecy linings.
We found them all at supper when we came.
But greeting their old friends once more, the crew
could not hold back their tears; and now again

1. Eurýlokhos was related to Odysseus by marriage.

the rooms rang with sobs. Then Kirkê, loveliest
of all immortals, came to counsel me:

'Son of Laërtês and the gods of old.
Odysseus, master mariner and soldier,
enough of weeping fits. I know—I, too—
what you endured upon the inhuman sea,
what odds you met on land from hostile men.
Remain with me, and share my meat and wine;
restore behind your ribs those gallant hearts
that served you in the old days, when you sailed
from stony Ithaka. Now parched and spent,
your cruel wandering is all you think of,
never of joy, after so many blows.'

As we were men we could not help consenting.
So day by day we lingered, feasting long
on roasts and wine, until a year grew fat.
But when the passing months and wheeling seasons
brought the long summery days, the pause of summer,
my shipmates one day summoned me and said:

'Captain, shake off this trance, and think of home—
if home indeed awaits us,
if we shall ever see
your own well-timbered hall on Ithaka.'

They made me feel a pang, and I agreed.
That day, and all day long, from dawn to sundown,
we feasted on roast meat and ruddy wine,
and after sunset when the dusk came on
my men slept in the shadowy hall, but I
went through the dark to Kirkê's flawless bed
and took the goddess' knees in supplication,
urging, as she bent to hear:

'O Kirkê,
now you must keep your promise; it is time.
Help me make sail for home. Day after day
my longing quickens, and my company
give me no peace, but wear my heart away
pleading when you are not at hand to hear.'

The loveliest of goddesses replied:

'Son of Laërtês and the gods of old,
Odysseus, master mariner and soldier,
you shall not stay here longer against your will;
but home you may not go
unless you take a strange way round and come
to the cold homes of Death and pale Perséphonê.[2]

2. Queen of the underworld.

You shall hear prophecy from the rapt shade
of blind Teirêsias of Thebes,[3] forever
charged with reason even among the dead;
to him alone, of all the flitting ghosts,
Perséphonê has given a mind undarkened.'

At this I felt a weight like stone within me,
and, moaning, pressed my length against the bed,
with no desire to see the daylight more.
But when I had wept and tossed and had my fill
of this despair, at last I answered her:

'Kirkê, who pilots me upon this journey?
No man has ever sailed to the land of Death.'

That loveliest of goddesses replied:

'Son of Laërtês and the gods of old,
Odysseus, master of land ways and sea ways,
feel no dismay because you lack a pilot;
only set up your mast and haul your canvas
to the fresh blowing North; sit down and steer,
and hold that wind, even to the bourne of Ocean,
Perséphonê's deserted stand and grove,
dusky with poplars and the drooping willow.
Run through the tide-rip, bring your ship to shore,
land there, and find the crumbling homes of Death.
Here, toward the Sorrowing Water, run the streams
of Wailing, out of Styx, and quenchless Burning[4]—
torrents that join in thunder at the Rock.
Here then, great soldier, setting foot obey me:
dig a well shaft a forearm square; pour out
libations round it to the unnumbered dead:
sweet milk and honey, then sweet wine, and last
clear water, scattering handfuls of white barley.
Pray now, with all your heart, to the faint dead;
swear you will sacrifice your finest heifer,
at home in Ithaka, and burn for them
her tenderest parts in sacrifice; and vow
to the lord Teirêsias, apart from all,
a black lamb, handsomest of all your flock—
thus to appease the nations of the dead.
Then slash a black ewe's throat, and a black ram,
facing the gloom of Erebos;[5] but turn
your head away toward Ocean. You shall see, now
souls of the buried dead in shadowy hosts,
and now you must call out to your companions
to flay those sheep the bronze knife has cut down,

3. A blind prophet who figures prominently in the legends of Thebes (he is a character in Sophocles' *Oedipus the King*). 4. Pyriphlegethon, a river of the underworld, as are the Sorrowing Water (Acheron), the stream of Wailing (Cocytus), and the Styx. 5. The darkest region of the underworld, usually imagined as below the underworld itself but here to the west.

for offerings, burnt flesh to those below,
to sovereign Death and pale Perséphonê.
Meanwhile draw sword from hip, crouch down, ward off
the surging phantoms from the bloody pit
until you know the presence of Teirêsias.
He will come soon, great captain; be it he
who gives you course and distance for your sailing
homeward across the cold fish-breeding sea.'

As the goddess ended, Dawn came stitched in gold.
Now Kirkê dressed me in my shirt and cloak,
put on a gown of subtle tissue, silvery,
then wound a golden belt about her waist
and veiled her head in linen,
while I went through the hall to rouse my crew.

I bent above each one, and gently said:

'Wake from your sleep; no more sweet slumber. Come,
we sail: the Lady Kirkê so ordains it.'

They were soon up, and ready at that word;
but I was not to take my men unharmed
from this place, even from this. Among them all
the youngest was Elpênor—
no mainstay in a fight nor very clever—
and this one, having climbed on Kirkê's roof[6]
to taste the cool night, fell asleep with wine.
Waked by our morning voices, and the tramp
of men below, he started up, but missed
his footing on the long steep backward ladder
and fell that height headlong. The blow smashed
the nape cord, and his ghost fled to the dark.
But I was outside, walking with the rest,
saying:

'Homeward you think we must be sailing
to our own land; no, elsewhere is the voyage
Kirkê has laid upon me. We must go
to the cold homes of Death and pale Perséphonê
to hear Teirêsias tell of time to come.'

They felt so stricken, upon hearing this,
they sat down wailing loud, and tore their hair.
But nothing came of giving way to grief.
Down to the shore and ship at last we went,
bowed with anguish, cheeks all wet with tears,
to find that Kirkê had been there before us
and tied nearby a black ewe and a ram:
she had gone by like air.

6. A flat roof and the coolest place to sleep.

For who could see the passage of a goddess
unless she wished his mortal eyes aware?

BOOK XI

[*A Gathering of Shades*]

We bore down on the ship at the sea's edge
and launched her on the salt immortal sea,
stepping our mast and spar in the black ship;
embarked the ram and ewe and went aboard
in tears, with bitter and sore dread upon us.
But now a breeze came up for us astern—
a canvas-bellying landbreeze, hale shipmate
sent by the singing nymph with sun-bright hair;
so we made fast the braces, took our thwarts,
and let the wind and steersman work the ship
with full sail spread all day above our coursing,
till the sun dipped, and all the ways grew dark
upon the fathomless unresting sea.
By night
our ship ran onward toward the Ocean's bourne,
the realm and region of the Men of Winter,[7]
hidden in mist and cloud. Never the flaming
eye of Hêlios lights on those men
at morning, when he climbs the sky of stars,
nor in descending earthward out of heaven;
ruinous night being rove[8] over those wretches.
We made the land, put ram and ewe ashore,
and took our way along the Ocean stream
to find the place foretold for us by Kirkê.
There Perimêdês and Eurýlokhos
pinioned the sacred beasts. With my drawn blade
I spaded up the votive pit, and poured
libations round it to the unnumbered dead:
sweet milk and honey, then sweet wine, and last
clear water; and I scattered barley down.
Then I addressed the blurred and breathless dead,
vowing to slaughter my best heifer for them
before she calved, at home in Ithaka,
and burn the choice bits on the altar fire;
as for Teirêsias, I swore to sacrifice
a black lamb, handsomest of all our flock.
Thus to assuage the nations of the dead
I pledged these rites, then slashed the lamb and ewe,
letting their black blood stream into the wellpit.
Now the souls gathered, stirring out of Erebos,
brides and young men, and men grown old in pain,
and tender girls whose hearts were new to grief;
many were there, too, torn by brazen lanceheads,

7. Although Homer usually places Hades below the earth, here he puts it across a great expanse of sea, apparently in the far north. 8. Stretched or spread.

battle-slain, bearing still their bloody gear.
From every side they came and sought the pit
with rustling cries; and I grew sick with fear.
But presently I gave command to my officers
to flay those sheep the bronze cut down, and make
burnt offerings of flesh to the gods below—
to sovereign Death, to pale Perséphonê.
Meanwhile I crouched with my drawn sword to keep
the surging phantoms from the bloody pit
till I should know the presence of Teirêsias.

One shade came first—Elpênor, of our company,
who lay unburied still on the wide earth
as we had left him—dead in Kirkê's hall,
untouched, unmourned, when other cares compelled us.
Now when I saw him there I wept for pity
and called out to him:

'How is this, Elpênor,
how could you journey to the western gloom
swifter afoot than I in the black lugger?'

He sighed, and answered:

'Son of great Laërtês,
Odysseus, master mariner and soldier,
bad luck shadowed me, and no kindly power;
ignoble death I drank with so much wine.
I slept on Kirkê's roof, then could not see
the long steep backward ladder, coming down,
and fell that height. My neck bone, buckled under,
snapped, and my spirit found this well of dark.
Now hear the grace I pray for, in the name
of those back in the world, not here—your wife
and father, he who gave you bread in childhood,
and your own child, your only son, Telémakhos,
long ago left at home.
When you make sail
and put these lodgings of dim Death behind,
you will moor ship, I know, upon Aiaia Island;
there, O my lord, remember me, I pray,
do not abandon me unwept, unburied,
to tempt the gods' wrath, while you sail for home;
but fire my corpse, and all the gear I had,
and build a cairn for me above the breakers—
an unknown sailor's mark for men to come.
Heap up the mound there, and implant upon it
the oar I pulled in life with my companions.'

He ceased, and I replied:

'Unhappy spirit,
I promise you the barrow and the burial.'

So we conversed, and grimly, at a distance,
with my long sword between, guarding the blood,
while the faint image of the lad spoke on.
Now came the soul of Antikleía, dead,
my mother, daughter of Autólykos,
dead now, though living still when I took ship
for holy Troy. Seeing this ghost I grieved,
but held her off, through pang on pang of tears,
till I should know the presence of Teirêsias.
Soon from the dark that prince of Thebes came forward
bearing a golden staff; and he addressd me:

'Son of Laërtês and the gods of old,
Odysseus, master of land ways and sea ways,
why leave the blazing sun, O man of woe,
to see the cold dead and the joyless region?
Stand clear, put up your sword;
let me but taste of blood, I shall speak true.'

At this I stepped aside, and in the scabbard
let my long sword ring home to the pommel silver,
as he bent down to the sombre blood. Then spoke
the prince of those with gift of speech:[9]

'Great captain,
a fair wind and the honey lights of home
are all you seek. But anguish lies ahead;
the god who thunders on the land prepares it,
not to be shaken from your track, implacable,
in rancor for the son whose eye you blinded.
One narrow strait may take you through his blows:
denial of yourself, restraint of shipmates.
When you make landfall on Thrinakia first
and quit the violet sea, dark on the land
you'll find the grazing herds of Hêlios
by whom all things are seen, all speech is known.
Avoid those kine, hold fast to your intent,
and hard seafaring brings you all to Ithaka.
But if you raid the beeves, I see destruction
for ship and crew. Though you survive alone,
bereft of all companions, lost for years,
under strange sail shall you come home, to find
your own house filled with trouble: insolent men
eating your livestock as they court your lady.
Aye, you shall make those men atone in blood!
But after you have dealt out death—in open
combat or by stealth—to all the suitors,
go overland on foot, and take an oar,
until one day you come where men have lived
with meat unsalted, never known the sea,

9. Tiresias here predicts the future of Odysseus. Like many Greek prophecies, it contains alternatives. The second (lines 120ff.) is what happens. The journey inland to find a people who have never seen the sea (and so mistake an oar for a winnowing fan, line 136) does not take place within the *Odyssey* itself.

nor seen seagoing ships, with crimson bows
and oars that fledge light hulls for dipping flight.
The spot will soon be plain to you, and I
can tell you how: some passerby will say,
"What winnowing fan is that upon your shoulder?"
Halt, and implant your smooth oar in the turf
and make fair sacrifice to Lord Poseidon:
a ram, a bull, a great buck boar; turn back,
and carry out pure hekatombs at home
to all wide heaven's lords, the undying gods,
to each in order. Then a seaborne death
soft as this hand of mist will come upon you
when you are wearied out with rich old age,
your country folk in blessed peace around you.
And all this shall be just as I foretell.'

When he had done, I said at once,

'Teirêsias,
my life runs on then as the gods have spun it.
But come, now, tell me this; make this thing clear:
I see my mother's ghost among the dead
sitting in silence near the blood. Not once
has she glanced this way toward her son, nor spoken.
Tell me, my lord,
may she in some way come to know my presence?'

To this he answered:

'I shall make it clear
in a few words and simply. Any dead man
whom you allow to enter where the blood is
will speak to you, and speak the truth; but those
deprived will grow remote again and fade.'

When he had prophesied, Teirêsias' shade
retired lordly to the halls of Death;
but I stood fast until my mother stirred,
moving to sip the black blood; then she knew me
and called out sorrowfully to me:

'Child,
how could you cross alive into this gloom
at the world's end?—No sight for living eyes;
great currents run between, desolate waters,
the Ocean first, where no man goes a journey
without ship's timber under him.
Say, now,
is it from Troy, still wandering, after years,
that you come here with ship and company?
Have you not gone at all to Ithaka?
Have you not seen your lady in your hall?'

She put these questions, and I answered her:

'Mother, I came here, driven to the land of death
in want of prophecy from Teirêsias' shade;
nor have I yet coasted Akhaia's hills
nor touched my own land, but have had hard roving
since first I joined Lord Agamémnon's host
by sea for Ilion, the wild horse country,
to fight the men of Troy.
But come now, tell me this, and tell me clearly,
what was the bane that pinned you down in Death?
Some ravaging long illness, or mild arrows
a-flying down one day from Artemis?
Tell me of Father, tell me of the son
I left behind me; have they still my place,
my honors, or have other men assumed them?
Do they not say that I shall come no more?
And tell me of my wife: how runs her thought,
still with her child, still keeping our domains,
or bride again to the best of the Akhaians?'

To this my noble mother quickly answered:

'Still with her child indeed she is, poor heart,
still in your palace hall. Forlorn her nights
and days go by, her life used up in weeping.
But no man takes your honored place. Telémakhos
has care of all your garden plots and fields,
and holds the public honor of a magistrate,
feasting and being feasted. But your father
is country bound and comes to town no more.
He owns no bedding, rugs, or fleecy mantles,
but lies down, winter nights, among the slaves,
rolled in old cloaks for cover, near the embers.
Or when the heat comes at the end of summer,
the fallen leaves, all round his vineyard plot,
heaped into windrows, make his lowly bed.
He lies now even so, with aching heart,
and longs for your return, while age comes on him.
So I, too, pined away, so doom befell me,
not that the keen-eyed huntress[1] with her shafts
had marked me down and shot to kill me; not
that illness overtook me—no true illness
wasting the body to undo the spirit;
only my loneliness for you, Odysseus,
for your kind heart and counsel, gentle Odysseus,
took my own life away.'

I bit my lip,
rising perplexed, with longing to embrace her,

1. Artemis.

and tried three times, putting my arms around her,
but she went sifting through my hands, impalpable
as shadows are, and wavering like a dream.
Now this embittered all the pain I bore,
and I cried in the darkness:

'O my mother,
will you not stay, be still, here in my arms,
may we not, in this place of Death, as well,
hold one another, touch with love, and taste
salt tears' relief, the twinge of welling tears?
Or is this all hallucination, sent
against me by the iron queen, Perséphonê,
to make me groan again?'

My noble mother
answered quickly:

'O my child—alas,
most sorely tried of men—great Zeus's daughter,
Perséphonê, knits no illusion for you.
All mortals meet this judgment when they die.
No flesh and bone are here, none bound by sinew,
since the bright-hearted pyre consumed them down—
the white bones long exanimate—to ash;
dreamlike the soul flies, insubstantial.

You must crave sunlight soon.
Note all things strange
seen here, to tell your lady in after days.'

So went our talk; then other shadows came,
ladies in company, sent by Perséphonê—
consorts or daughters of illustrious men—
crowding about the black blood.
I took thought
how best to separate and question them,
and saw no help for it, but drew once more
the long bright edge of broadsword from my hip,
that none should sip the blood in company
but one by one, in order; so it fell
that each declared her lineage and name.

Here was great loveliness of ghosts![2] I saw
before them all, that princess of great ladies,
Tyro,[3] Salmoneus' daughter, as she told me,
and queen to Krêtheus, a son of Aiolos.
She had gone daft for the river Enipeus,[4]
most graceful of all running streams, and ranged

2. Here follows a list of famous and beautiful women of former times. 3. A queen of Thessaly. 4. Tyro had fallen in love with the river god of the Enipeus (a river in Thessaly).

all day by Enipeus' limpid side,
whose form the foaming girdler of the islands,
the god who makes earth tremble, took[5] and so
lay down with her where he went flooding seaward,
their bower a purple billow, arching round
to hide them in a sea-vale, god and lady.
Now when his pleasure was complete, the god
spoke to her softly, holding fast her hand:

'Dear mortal, go in joy! At the turn of seasons,
winter to summer, you shall bear me sons;
no lovemaking of gods can be in vain.
Nurse our sweet children tenderly, and rear them.
Home with you now, and hold your tongue, and tell
no one your lover's name—though I am yours,
Poseidon, lord of surf that makes earth tremble.'

He plunged away into the deep sea swell,
and she grew big with Pelias and Neleus,[6]
powerful vassals, in their time, of Zeus.
Pelias lived on broad Iolkos seaboard
rich in flocks, and Neleus at Pylos.
As for the sons borne by that queen of women
to Krêtheus, their names were Aison,[7] Pherês,
and Amytháon, expert charioteer.

Next after her I saw Antiopê,
daughter of Ásopos.[8] She too could boast
a god for lover, having lain with Zeus
and borne two sons to him: Amphion and
Zêthos, who founded Thebes, the upper city,
and built the ancient citadel. They sheltered
no life upon that plain, for all their power,
without a fortress wall.

And next I saw
Amphitrion's true wife, Alkmênê, mother,
as all men know, of lionish Heraklês,
conceived when she lay close in Zeus's arms;
and Megarê, high-hearted Kreon's daughter,
wife of Amphitrion's unwearying son.

I saw the mother of Oidipous, Epikastê,[9]
whose great unwitting deed it was
to marry her own son. He took that prize
from a slain father; presently the gods
brought all to light that made the famous story.
But by their fearsome wills he kept his throne
in dearest Thebes, all through his evil days,

5. Poseidon assumed his shape. 6. Father of Nestor of Pylos. 7. Father of Jason, the Argonaut.
8. A river in Boeotia, the territory of Thebes. 9. Usually known as Jocasta. *Oidipous:* Oedipus.

while she descended to the place of Death,
god of the locked and iron door. Steep down
from a high rafter, throttled in her noose,
she swung, carried away by pain, and left him
endless agony from a mother's Furies.

And I saw Khloris, that most lovely lady,
whom for her beauty in the olden time
Neleus wooed with countless gifts, and married.
She was the youngest daughter of Amphion,
son of Iasos. In those days he[1] held
power at Orkhómenos, over the Minyai.
At Pylos then as queen she bore her children—
Nestor, Khromios, Periklýmenos,
and Pêro, too, who turned the heads of men
with her magnificence. A host of princes
from nearby lands came courting her; but Neleus
would hear of no one, not unless the suitor
could drive the steers of giant Iphiklos
from Phylakê—longhorns, broad in the brow,
so fierce that one man only, a diviner,[2]
offered to round them up. But bitter fate
saw him bound hand and foot by savage herdsmen.
Then days and months grew full and waned, the year
went wheeling round, the seasons came again,
before at last the power of Íphiklos,
relenting, freed the prisoner, who foretold
all things to him. So Zeus's will was done.

And I saw Lêda, wife of Tyndareus,
upon whom Tyndareus had sired twins
indomitable: Kastor, tamer of horses,
and Polydeukês, best in the boxing ring.[3]
Those two live still, though life-creating earth
embraces them: even in the underworld
honored as gods by Zeus, each day in turn[4]
one comes alive, the other dies again.

Then after Lêda to my vision came
the wife of Aloeus, Iphimedeia,
proud that she once had held the flowing sea[5]
and borne him sons, thunderers for a day,
the world-renowned Otos and Ephialtês.
Never were men on such a scale
bred on the plowlands and the grainlands, never
so magnificent any, after Orion.
At nine years old they towered nine fathoms tall,
nine cubits in the shoulders, and they promised
furor upon Olympos, heaven broken by battle cries,

1. Amphion (not the same Amphion who founded Thebes, line 283). 2. Named Melampus. 3. They also had a daughter, Clytemnestra, who was Agamémnon's wife. 4. They shared, as it were, one immortality between them. 5. Poseidon.

the day they met the gods in arms.
With Ossa's
mountain peak they meant to crown Olympos
and over Ossa Pelion's forest pile
for footholds up the sky. As giants grown
they might have done it, but the bright son of Zeus[6]
by Lêto of the smooth braid shot them down
while they were boys unbearded; no dark curls
clustered yet from temples to the chin.

Then I saw Phaidra, Prokris; and Ariadnê,
daughter of Minos,[7] the grim king. Theseus took her
aboard with him from Krete for the terraced land
of ancient Athens; but he had no joy of her.
Artemis killed her on the Isle of Dia
at a word from Dionysos.[8]
Maira, then,
and Klymênê, and that detested queen,
Eríphylê,[9] who betrayed her lord for gold . . .
but how name all the women I beheld there,
daughters and wives of kings? The starry night
wanes long before I close.
Here, or aboard ship,
amid the crew, the hour for sleep has come.
Our sailing is the gods' affair and yours."[1]

Then he fell silent. Down the shadowy hall
the enchanted banqueters were still. Only
the queen with ivory pale arms, Arêtê, spoke,
saying to all the silent men:

"Phaiákians,
how does he stand, now, in your eyes, this captain,
the look and bulk of him, the inward poise?
He is my guest, but each one shares that honor.
Be in no haste to send him on his way
or scant your bounty in his need. Remember
how rich, by heaven's will, your possessions are."

Then Ekhenêos, the old soldier, eldest
of all Phaiákians, added his word:

"Friends, here was nothing but our own thought spoken,
the mark hit square. Our duties to her majesty.

6. Apollo. Ossa and Pelion are mountains near Olympus in Thessaly. 7. King of Krete and father of Phaidra and Ariadnê. Phaidra was the wife of Theseus of Athens; she fell in love with her stepson Hippolytus. Prokris was the unfaithful wife of Cephalus, king of Athens. Ariadnê helped Theseus slay the Minotaur on Krete. 8. We have no other account of this version of the episode that explains why Dionysus wanted Ariadnê killed; the prevalent version of the story in later times is that Dionysus carried Ariadnê off to be his bride. 9. Bribed with a golden necklace by Polynices, son of Oedipus, she persuaded her husband, Amphiaraus, to take part in the attack on Thebes, where he was killed. Maira was a nymph of Artemis who broke her vow of chastity and was killed by the goddess. Some story must have been attached to the name Klymênê, but we do not know what it is. 1. Odysseus breaks off the story of his wanderings, and we are transported back to the scene of the banqueting hall of the Phaiakians.

For what is to be said and done,
we wait upon Alkínoös' command."

At this the king's voice rang:

"I so command—
as sure as it is I who, while I live,
rule the sea rovers of Phaiákia. Our friend
longs to put out for home, but let him be
content to rest here one more day, until
I see all gifts bestowed. And every man
will take thought for his launching and his voyage,
I most of all, for I am master here."

Odysseus, the great tactician, answered:

"Alkínoös, king and admiration of men,
even a year's delay, if you should urge it,
in loading gifts and furnishing for sea—
I too could wish it; better far that I
return with some largesse of wealth about me—
I shall be thought more worthy of love and courtesy
by every man who greets me home in Ithaka."

The king said:

"As to that, one word, Odysseus:
from all we see, we take you for no swindler—
though the dark earth be patient of so many,
scattered everywhere, baiting their traps with lies
of old times and of places no one knows.
You speak with art, but your intent is honest.
The Argive troubles, and your own troubles,
you told as a poet would, a man who knows the world.
But now come tell me this: among the dead
did you meet any of your peers, companions
who sailed with you and met their doom at Troy?
Here's a long night—an endless night—before us,
and no time yet for sleep, not in this hall.
Recall the past deeds and the strange adventures.
I could stay up until the sacred Dawn
as long as you might wish to tell your story."

Odysseus the great tactician answered:

"Alkínoös, king and admiration of men,
there is a time for story telling; there is
also a time for sleep. But even so,
if, indeed, listening be still your pleasure,
I must not grudge my part. Other and sadder
tales there are to tell, of my companions,
of some who came through all the Trojan spears,

clangor and groan of war,
only to find a brutal death at home—
and a bad wife behind it.
After Perséphonê,
icy and pale, dispersed the shades of women,
the soul of Agamémnon, son of Atreus,
came before me, sombre in the gloom,
and others gathered round, all who were with him
when death and doom struck in Aegísthos' hall.
Sipping the black blood, the tall shade perceived me,
and cried out sharply, breaking into tears;
then tried to stretch his hands toward me, but could not,
being bereft of all the reach and power
he once felt in the great torque of his arms.
Gazing at him, and stirred, I wept for pity,
and spoke across to him:

'O son of Atreus,
illustrious Lord Marshal, Agamémnon,
what was the doom that brought you low in death?
Were you at sea, aboard ship, and Poseidon
blew up a wicked squall to send you under,
or were you cattle-raiding on the mainland
or in a fight for some strongpoint, or women,
when the foe hit you to your mortal hurt?'

But he replied at once:

'Son of Laërtês,
Odysseus, master of land ways and sea ways,
neither did I go down with some good ship
in any gale Poseidon blew, nor die
upon the mainland, hurt by foes in battle.
It was Aigísthos who designed my death,
he and my heartless wife, and killed me, after
feeding me, like an ox felled at the trough.
That was my miserable end—and with me
my fellows butchered, like so many swine
killed for some troop, or feast, or wedding banquet
in a great landholder's household. In your day
you have seen men, and hundreds, die in war,
in the bloody press, or downed in single combat,
but these were murders you would catch your breath at:
think of us fallen, all our throats cut, winebowl
brimming, tables laden on every side,
while blood ran smoking over the whole floor.
In my extremity I heard Kassandra,[2]
Priam's daughter, piteously crying
as the traitress Klytaimnéstra made to kill her
along with me. I heaved up from the ground

2. She was part of Agamémnon's share of the booty at Troy.

and got my hands around the blade, but she
eluded me, that whore. Nor would she close
my two eyes[3] as my soul swam to the underworld
or shut my lips. There is no being more fell,
more bestial than a wife in such an action,
and what an action that one planned!
The murder of her husband and her lord.
Great god, I thought my children and my slaves
at least would give me welcome. But that woman,
plotting a thing so low, defiled herself
and all her sex, all women yet to come,
even those few who may be virtuous.'

He paused then, and I answered:

'Foul and dreadful.
That was the way that Zeus who views the wide world
vented his hatred on the sons of Atreus—
intrigues of women, even from the start.
Myriads
died by Helen's fault, and Klytaimnéstra
plotted against you half the world away.'

And he at once said:

'Let it be a warning
even to you. Indulge a woman never,
and never tell her all you know. Some things
a man may tell, some he should cover up.
Not that I see a risk for you, Odysseus,
of death at your wife's hands. She is too wise,
too clear-eyed, sees alternatives too well,
Penélopê, Ikários' daughter—
that young bride whom we left behind—think of it!—
when we sailed off to war. The baby boy
still cradled at her breast—now he must be
a grown man, and a lucky one. By heaven,
you'll see him yet, and he'll embrace his father
with old fashioned respect, and rightly.
My own
lady never let me glut my eyes
on my own son, but bled me to death first.
One thing I will advise, on second thought;
stow it away and ponder it.
Land your ship
in secret on your island; give no warning.
The day of faithful wives is gone forever.

But tell me, have you any word at all
about my son's life? Gone to Orkhómenos

3. She would not give me a proper burial.

or sandy Pylos, can he be? Or waiting
with Meneláos in the plain of Sparta?
Death on earth has not yet taken Orestês.'

But I could only answer:

'Son of Atreus,
why do you ask these questions of me? Neither
news of home have I, nor news of him,
alive or dead. And empty words are evil.'

So we exchanged our speech, in bitterness,
weighed down by grief, and tears welled in our eyes,
when there appeared the spirit of Akhilleus,
son of Peleus; then Patróklos' shade,
and then Antílokhos,[4] and then Aias,
first among all the Danaans in strength
and bodily beauty, next to prince Akhilleus.
Now that great runner, grandson of Aíakhos,[5]
recognized me and called across to me:

'Son of Laërtês and the gods of old,
Odysseus, master mariner and soldier,
old knife, what next? What greater feat remains
for you to put your mind on, after this?
How did you find your way down to the dark
where these dimwitted dead are camped forever,
the after images of used-up men?'

I answered:

'Akhilleus, Peleus' son, strongest of all
among the Akhaians, I had need of foresight
such as Teirêsias alone could give
to help me, homeward bound for the crags of Ithaka.
I have not yet coasted Akhaia, not yet
touched my land; my life is all adversity.
But was there ever a man more blest by fortune
than you, Akhilleus? Can there ever be?
We ranked you with immortals in your lifetime,
we Argives did, and here your power is royal
among the dead men's shades. Think, then, Akhilleus:
you need not be so pained by death.'

To this
he answered swiftly:

'Let me hear no smooth talk
of death from you, Odysseus, light of councils.
Better, I say, to break sod as a farm hand
for some poor country man, on iron rations,
than lord it over all the exhausted dead.

4. Son of Nestor. **5.** Akhilleus.

Tell me, what news of the prince my son:[6] did he
come after me to make a name in battle
or could it be he did not? Do you know
if rank and honor still belong to Peleus
in the towns of the Myrmidons? Or now, may be,
Hellas and Phthia spurn him, seeing old age
fetters him, hand and foot. I cannot help him
under the sun's rays, cannot be that man
I was on Troy's wide seaboard, in those days
when I made bastion for the Argives
and put an army's best men in the dust.
Were I but whole again, could I go now
to my father's house, one hour would do to make
my passion and my hands no man could hold
hateful to any who shoulder him aside.'

Now when he paused I answered:

'Of all that—
of Peleus' life, that is—I know nothing;
but happily I can tell you the whole story
of Neoptólemos, as you require.
In my own ship I brought him out from Skyros[7]
to join the Akhaians under arms.
And I can tell you,
in every council before Troy thereafter
your son spoke first and always to the point;
no one but Nestor and I could out-debate him.
And when we formed against the Trojan line
he never hung back in the mass, but ranged
far forward of his troops—no man could touch him
for gallantry. Aye, scores went down before him
in hard fights man to man. I shall not tell
all about each, or name them all—the long
roster of enemies he put out of action,
taking the shock of charges on the Argives.
But what a champion his lance ran through
in Eurýpulos the son of Télephos! Keteians[8]
in throngs around that captain also died—
all because Priam's gifts had won his mother
to send the lad to battle; and I thought
Memnon[9] alone in splendor ever outshone him.

But one fact more: while our picked Argive crew
still rode that hollow horse Epeios built,
and when the whole thing lay with me, to open
the trapdoor of the ambuscade or not,
at that point our Danaan lords and soldiers

6. Neoptólemos (the name means "new war"). 7. The Greeks were told by a prophet that Troy would fall only to the son of Akhilleus, who was living on the rocky island of Skyros. 8. Eurýpulos's people (from Asia Minor), who came to the aid of the Trojans. 9. Son of the dawn goddess, king of the Ethiopians, and a Trojan ally.

wiped their eyes, and their knees began to quake,
all but Neoptólemos. I never saw
his tanned cheek change color or his hand
brush one tear away. Rather he prayed me,
hand on hilt, to sortie, and he gripped
his tough spear, bent on havoc for the Trojans.
And when we had pierced and sacked Priam's tall city
he loaded his choice plunder and embarked
with no scar on him; not a spear had grazed him
nor the sword's edge in close work—common wounds
one gets in war. Arês in his mad fits
knows no favorites.'

But I said no more,
for he had gone off striding the field of asphodel,
the ghost of our great runner, Akhilleus Aíákidês,[1]
glorying in what I told him of his son.

Now other souls of mournful dead stood by,
each with his troubled questioning, but one
remained alone, apart: the son of Télamon,
Aîas, it was—the great shade burning still
because I had won favor on the beachhead
in rivalry over Akhilleus' arms.[2]
The Lady Thetis, mother of Akhilleus,
laid out for us the dead man's battle gear,
and Trojan children, with Athena,
named the Danaan fittest to own them. Would
god I had not borne the palm that day!
For earth took Aîas then to hold forever,
the handsomest and, in all feats of war,
noblest of the Danaans after Akhilleus.
Gently therefore I called across to him:

'Aîas, dear son of royal Télamon,
you would not then forget, even in death,
your fury with me over those accurst
calamitous arms?—and so they were, a bane
sent by the gods upon the Argive host.
For when you died by your own hand we lost
a tower, formidable in war. All we Akhaians
mourn you forever, as we do Akhilleus;
and no one bears the blame but Zeus.
He fixed that doom for you because he frowned
on the whole expedition of our spearmen.
My lord, come nearer, listen to our story!
Conquer your indignation and your pride.'

But he gave no reply, and turned away,
following other ghosts toward Erebos.

1. Akhilleus was son of Peleus, whose father was Aiakos. 2. See n. 3, page 249.

Who knows if in that darkness he might still
have spoken, and I answered?
But my heart
longed, after this, to see the dead elsewhere.
And now there came before my eyes Minos,
the son of Zeus, enthroned, holding a golden staff,
dealing out justice among ghostly pleaders
arrayed about the broad doorways of Death.

And then I glimpsed Orion,[3] the huge hunter,
gripping his club, studded with bronze, unbreakable,
with wild beasts he had overpowered in life
on lonely mountainsides, now brought to bay
on fields of asphodel.
And I saw Títyos,
the son of Gaia, lying
abandoned over nine square rods of plain.
Vultures, hunched above him, left and right,
rifling his belly, stabbed into the liver,
and he could never push them off.
This hulk
had once committed rape of Zeus's mistress,
Léto, in her glory, when she crossed
the open grass of Panopeus toward Pytho.

Then I saw Tántalos[4] put to the torture:
in a cool pond he stood, lapped round by water
clear to the chin, and being athirst he burned
to slake his dry weasand with drink, though drink
he would not ever again. For when the old man
put his lips down to the sheet of water
it vanished round his feet, gulped underground,
and black mud baked there in a wind from hell.
Boughs, too, drooped low above him, big with fruit,
pear trees, pomegranates, brilliant apples,
luscious figs, and olives ripe and dark;
but if he stretched his hand for one, the wind
under the dark sky tossed the bough beyond him.

Then Sísyphos[5] in torment I beheld
being roustabout to a tremendous boulder.
Leaning with both arms braced and legs driving,
he heaved it toward a height, and almost over,
but then a Power spun him round and sent
the cruel boulder bounding again to the plain.
Whereon the man bent down again to toil,
dripping sweat, and the dust rose overhead.
Next I saw manifest the power of Heraklês—
a phantom, this, for he himself has gone

3. According to later legend he was transformed into the constellation that bears his name; Homer, however, has him in the underworld after his death. 4. King of Lydia. He was the confidant of the gods and ate at their table, but he betrayed their secrets. 5. King of Corinth, the archetype of the liar and trickster; we do not know what misdeed he is being punished for in this passage.

feasting amid the gods, reclining soft
with Hêbê of the ravishing pale ankles,
daughter of Zeus and Hêra, shod in gold.
But, in my vision, all the dead around him
cried like affrighted birds; like Night itself
he loomed with naked bow and nocked arrow
and glances terrible as continual archery.
My hackles rose at the gold swordbelt he wore
sweeping across him: gorgeous intaglio
of savage bears, boars, lions with wildfire eyes,
swordfights, battle, slaughter, and sudden death—
the smith who had that belt in him, I hope
he never made, and never will make, another.
The eyes of the vast figure rested on me,
and of a sudden he said in kindly tones:

'Son of Laërtês and the gods of old,
Odysseus, master mariner and soldier,
under a cloud, you too? Destined to grinding
labors like my own in the sunny world?[6]
Son of Kroníon Zeus or not, how many
days I sweated out, being bound in servitude
to a man far worse than I, a rough master!
He made me hunt this place one time
to get the watchdog of the dead: no more
perilous task, he thought, could be; but I
brought back that beast, up from the underworld;
Hermês and grey-eyed Athena showed the way.'

And Heraklês, down the vistas of the dead,
faded from sight; but I stood fast, awaiting
other great souls who perished in times past.
I should have met, then, god-begotten Theseus
and Peirithoös,[7] whom both I longed to see,
but first came shades in thousands, rustling
in a pandemonium of whispers, blown together,
and the horror took me that Perséphonê
had brought from darker hell some saurian death's head.
I whirled then, made for the ship, shouted to crewmen
to get aboard and cast off the stern hawsers,
an order soon obeyed. They took their thwarts,
and the ship went leaping toward the stream of Ocean
first under oars, then with a following wind.

BOOK XII

[*Sea Perils and Defeat*]

The ship sailed on, out of the Ocean Stream,
riding a long swell on the open sea

6. Heraklês, son of Zeus, was made subject to the orders of Eurýstheus of Argos, who ordered him to perform the twelve famous labors. 7. After his adventures in Krete, Theseus went with his friend Peirithoös to Hades to kidnap Perséphonê; the venture failed, and the two heroes, imprisoned in Hades, were rescued by Heraklês.

for the Island of Aiaia.
Summering Dawn
has dancing grounds there, and the Sun his rising;[8]
but still by night we beached on a sand shelf
and waded in beyond the line of breakers
to fall asleep, awaiting the Day Star.

When the young Dawn with finger tips of rose
made heaven bright, I sent shipmates to bring
Elpênor's body from the house of Kirkê.
We others cut down timber on the foreland,
on a high point, and built his pyre of logs,
then stood by weeping while the flame burnt through
corse and equipment.
Then we heaped his barrow,
lifting a gravestone on the mound, and fixed
his light but unwarped oar against the sky.
These were our rites in memory of him. Soon, then,
knowing us back from the Dark Land, Kirkê came
freshly adorned for us, with handmaids bearing
loaves, roast meats, and ruby-colored wine.
She stood among us in immortal beauty
jesting:

'Hearts of oak, did you go down
alive into the homes of Death? One visit
finishes all men but yourselves, twice mortal!
Come, here is meat and wine, enjoy your feasting
for one whole day; and in the dawn tomorrow
you shall put out to sea. Sailing directions,
landmarks, perils, I shall sketch for you, to keep you
from being caught by land or water
in some black sack of trouble.'

In high humor
and ready for carousal, we agreed;
so all that day until the sun went down
we feasted on roast meat and good red wine,
till after sunset, at the fall of night,
the men dropped off to sleep by the stern hawsers.
She took my hand then, silent in that hush,
drew me apart, made me sit down, and lay
beside me, softly questioning, as I told
all I had seen, from first to last.
Then said the Lady Kirkê:

'So: all those trials are over.
Listen with care
to this, now, and a god will arm your mind.
Square in your ship's path are Seirênês,[9] crying

8. This places Kirkê's island in the east, whereas Odysseus's ship, when it was blown past Cape Malea, was headed west. It is one more indication that Odyssean geography is highly imaginative. 9. Or Sirens.

beauty to bewitch men coasting by;
woe to the innocent who hears that sound!
He will not see his lady nor his children
in joy, crowding about him, home from sea;
the Seirênês will sing his mind away
on their sweet meadow lolling. There are bones
of dead men rotting in a pile beside them
and flayed skins shrivel around the spot.
Steer wide;
keep well to seaward; plug your oarsmen's ears
with beeswax kneaded soft; none of the rest
should hear that song.
But if you wish to listen,
let the men tie you in the lugger, hand
and foot, back to the mast, lashed to the mast,
so you may hear those harpies' thrilling voices;
shout as you will, begging to be untied,
your crew must only twist more line around you
and keep their stroke up, till the singers fade.
What then? One of two courses you may take,
and you yourself must weigh them. I shall not
plan the whole action for you now, but only
tell you of both.
Ahead are beetling rocks
and dark blue glancing Amphitritê, surging,
roars around them. Prowling Rocks,[1] or Drifters,
the gods in bliss have named them—named them well.
Not even birds can pass them by, not even
the timorous doves that bear ambrosia
to Father Zeus; caught by downdrafts, they die
on rockwall smooth as ice.
Each time, the Father
wafts a new courier to make up his crew.

Still less can ships get searoom of these Drifters,
whose boiling surf, under high fiery winds,
carries tossing wreckage of ships and men.
Only one ocean-going craft, the far-famed
Argo, made it, sailing from Aiêta;
but she, too, would have crashed on the big rocks
if Hêra had not pulled her through, for love
of Iêson, her captain.
A second course
lies between headlands. One is a sharp mountain
piercing the sky, with stormcloud round the peak
dissolving never, not in the brightest summer,
to show heaven's azure there, nor in the fall.
No mortal man could scale it, nor so much

1. Homer does not precisely identify them with the Symplegades, the Clashing Rocks that came together and crushed whatever tried to pass between them. They were thought to be located at the entrance to the Black Sea. Homer's Prowling Rocks seem to be located, like Scylla and Charybdis, near the straits between Sicily and Italy. *Amphitritê:* the sea.

as land there, not with twenty hands and feet,
so sheer the cliffs are—as of polished stone.
Midway that height, a cavern full of mist
opens toward Erebos and evening.[2] Skirting
this in the lugger, great Odysseus,
your master bowman, shooting from the deck,
would come short of the cavemouth with his shaft;
but that is the den of Skylla, where she yaps
abominably, a newborn whelp's cry,
though she is huge and monstrous. God or man,
no one could look on her in joy. Her legs—
and there are twelve—are like great tentacles,
unjointed, and upon her serpent necks
are borne six heads like nightmares of ferocity,
with triple serried rows of fangs and deep
gullets of black death. Half her length, she sways
her heads in air, outside her horrid cleft,
hunting the sea around that promontory
for dolphins, dogfish, or what bigger game
thundering Amphitritê feeds in thousands.
And no ship's company can claim
to have passed her without loss and grief; she takes,
from every ship, one man for every gullet.
The opposite point seems more a tongue of land
you'd touch with a good bowshot, at the narrows.
A great wild fig, a shaggy mass of leaves,
grows on it, and Kharybdis lurks below
to swallow down the dark sea tide. Three times
from dawn to dusk she spews it up
and sucks it down again three times, a whirling
maelstrom; if you come upon her then
the god who makes earth tremble could not save you.
No, hug the cliff of Skylla, take your ship
through on a racing stroke. Better to mourn
six men than lose them all, and the ship, too.'

So her advice ran; but I faced her, saying:

'Only instruct me, goddess, if you will,
how, if possible, can I pass Kharybdis,
or fight off Skylla when she raids my crew?'

Swiftly that loveliest goddess answered me:

'Must you have battle in your heart forever?
The bloody toil of combat? Old contender,
will you not yield to the immortal gods?
That nightmare cannot die, being eternal
evil itself—horror, and pain, and chaos;
there is no fighting her, no power can fight her,

2. I.e., to the northwest.

all that avails is flight.
Lose headway there
along that rockface while you break out arms,
and she'll swoop over you, I fear, once more,
taking one man again for every gullet.
No, no, put all your backs into it, row on;
invoke Blind Force, that bore this scourge of men,
to keep her from a second strike against you.

Then you will coast Thrinákia,[3] the island
where Hêlios' cattle graze, fine herds, and flocks
of goodly sheep. The herds and flocks are seven,
with fifty beasts in each.
No lambs are dropped,
or calves, and these fat cattle never die.
Immortal, too, their cowherds are—their shepherds—
Phaëthousa and Lampetía, sweetly braided
nymphs that divine Neaira bore
to the overlord of high noon, Hêlios.
These nymphs their gentle mother bred and placed
upon Thrinákia, the distant land,
in care of flocks and cattle for their father.

Now give those kine a wide berth, keep your thoughts
intent upon your course for home,
and hard seafaring brings you all to Ithaka.
But if you raid the beeves, I see destruction
for ship and crew.
Rough years then lie between
you and your homecoming, alone and old,
the one survivor, all companions lost.'

As Kirkê spoke, Dawn mounted her golden throne,
and on the first rays Kirkê left me, taking
her way like a great goddess up the island.
I made straight for the ship, roused up the men
to get aboard and cast off at the stern.
They scrambled to their places by the rowlocks
and all in line dipped oars in the grey sea.
But soon an off-shore breeze blew to our liking—
a canvas-bellying breeze, a lusty shipmate
sent by the singing nymph with sunbright hair.
So we made fast the braces, and we rested,
letting the wind and steersman work the ship.
The crew being now silent before me, I
addressed them, sore at heart:

'Dear friends,
more than one man, or two, should know those things
Kirkê foresaw for us and shared with me,

3. Later Greeks identified this island as Sicily.

so let me tell her forecast: then we die
with our eyes open, if we are going to die,
or know what death we baffle if we can. Seirênês
weaving a haunting song over the sea
we are to shun, she said, and their green shore
all sweet with clover; yet she urged that I
alone should listen to their song. Therefore
you are to tie me up, tight as a splint,
erect along the mast, lashed to the mast,
and if I shout and beg to be untied,
take more turns of the rope to muffle me.'

I rather dwelt on this part of the forecast,
while our good ship made time, bound outward down
the wind for the strange island of Seirênês.
Then all at once the wind fell, and a calm
came over all the sea, as though some power
lulled the swell.
                                   The crew were on their feet
briskly, to furl the sail, and stow it; then,
each in place, they poised the smooth oar blades
and sent the white foam scudding by. I carved
a massive cake of beeswax into bits
and rolled them in my hands until they softened—
no long task, for a burning heat came down
from Hêlios, lord of high noon. Going forward
I carried wax along the line, and laid it
thick on their ears. They tied me up, then, plumb
amidships, back to the mast, lashed to the mast,
and took themselves again to rowing. Soon,
as we came smartly within hailing distance,
the two Seirênês, noting our fast ship
off their point, made ready, and they sang:[4]

This way, oh turn your bows,
  Akhaia's glory,
As all the world allows—
  Moor and be merry.

Sweet coupled airs we sing.
  No lonely seafarer
Holds clear of entering
  Our green mirror.

Pleased by each purling note
  Like honey twining

4. The translator has turned the eight unrhymed lines of the original into a lyric poem. Here is a prose version of the Greek: "Draw near, illustrious Odysseus, flower of Akhaian chivalry, and bring your ship to rest so that you may hear our voices. No seaman ever sailed his black ship past this spot without listening to the sweet tones that flow from our lips, and none that has listened has not been delighted and gone on a wiser man. For we know all that the Argives and Trojans suffered on the broad plain of Troy by the will of the gods, and we have foreknowledge of all that is going to happen on this fruitful earth."

From her throat and my throat,
Who lies a-pining?

Sea rovers here take joy
Voyaging onward,
As from our song of Troy
Greybeard and rower-boy
Goeth more learnèd.

All feats on that great field
In the long warfare,
Dark days the bright gods willed,
Wounds you bore there,

Argos' old soldiery
On Troy beach teeming,
Charmed out of time we see.
No life on earth can be
Hid from our dreaming.

The lovely voices in ardor appealing over the water
made me crave to listen, and I tried to say
'Untie me!' to the crew, jerking my brows;
but they bent steady to the oars. Then Perimêdês
got to his feet, he and Eurýlokhos,
and passed more line about, to hold me still.
So all rowed on, until the Seirênês
dropped under the sea rim, and their singing
dwindled away.
My faithful company
rested on their oars now, peeling off
the wax that I had laid thick on their ears;
then set me free.
But scarcely had that island
faded in blue air than I saw smoke
and white water, with sound of waves in tumult—
a sound the men heard, and it terrified them.
Oars flew from their hands; the blades went knocking
wild alongside till the ship lost way,
with no oarblades to drive her through the water.

Well, I walked up and down from bow to stern,
trying to put heart into them, standing over
every oarsman, saying gently,

'Friends,
have we never been in danger before this?
More fearsome, is it now, than when the Kyklops
penned us in his cave? What power he had!
Did I not keep my nerve, and use my wits
to find a way out for us?
Now I say
by hook or crook this peril too shall be

something that we remember.
Heads up, lads!
We must obey the orders as I give them.
Get the oarshafts in your hands, and lay back
hard on your benches; hit these breaking seas.
Zeus help us pull away before we founder.
You at the tiller, listen, and take in
all that I say—the rudders are your duty;
keep her out of the combers and the smoke;
steer for that headland; watch the drift, or we
fetch up in the smother, and you drown us.'

That was all, and it brought them round to action.
But as I sent them on toward Skylla, I
told them nothing, as they could do nothing.
They would have dropped their oars again, in panic,
to roll for cover under the decking. Kirkê's
bidding against arms had slipped my mind,
so I tied on my cuirass and took up
two heavy spears, then made my way along
to the foredeck—thinking to see her first from there,
the monster of the grey rock, harboring
torment for my friends. I strained my eyes
upon that cliffside veiled in cloud, but nowhere
could I catch sight of her.
And all this time,
in travail, sobbing, gaining on the current,
we rowed into the strait—Skylla to port
and on our starboard beam Kharybdis, dire
gorge of the salt sea tide. By heaven! when she
vomited, all the sea was like a cauldron
seething over intense fire, when the mixture
suddenly heaves and rises.
The shot spume
soared to the landside heights, and fell like rain.

But when she swallowed the sea water down
we saw the funnel of the maelstrom, heard
the rock bellowing all around, and dark
sand raged on the bottom far below.
My men all blanched against the gloom, our eyes
were fixed upon that yawning mouth in fear
of being devoured.
Then Skylla made her strike,
whisking six of my best men from the ship.
I happened to glance aft at ship and oarsmen
and caught sight of their arms and legs, dangling
high overhead. Voices came down to me
in anguish, calling my name for the last time.

A man surfcasting on a point of rock
for bass or mackerel, whipping his long rod

to drop the sinker and the bait far out,
will hook a fish and rip it from the surface
to dangle wriggling through the air:
so these
were borne aloft in spasms toward the cliff.

She ate them as they shrieked there, in her den,
in the dire grapple, reaching still for me—
and deathly pity ran me through
at that sight—far the worst I ever suffered,
questing the passes of the strange sea.
We rowed on.
The Rocks were now behind; Kharybdis, too,
and Skylla dropped astern.
Then we were coasting
the noble island of the god, where grazed
those cattle with wide brows, and bounteous flocks
of Hêlios, lord of noon, who rides high heaven.

From the black ship, far still at sea, I heard
the lowing of the cattle winding home
and sheep bleating; and heard, too, in my heart
the words of blind Teirêsias of Thebes
and Kirkê of Aiaia: both forbade me
the island of the world's delight, the Sun.
So I spoke out in gloom to my companions:

'Shipmates, grieving and weary though you are,
listen: I had forewarning from Teirêsias
and Kirkê, too; both told me I must shun
this island of the Sun, the world's delight.
Nothing but fatal trouble shall we find here.
Pull away, then, and put the land astern.'

That strained them to the breaking point, and, cursing,
Eurýlokhos cried out in bitterness:

'Are you flesh and blood, Odysseus, to endure
more than a man can? Do you never tire?
God, look at you, iron is what you're made of.
Here we all are, half dead with weariness,
falling asleep over the oars, and you
say "No landing"—no firm island earth
where we could make a quiet supper. No:
pull out to sea, you say, with night upon us—
just as before, but wandering now, and lost.
Sudden storms can rise at night and swamp
ships without a trace.
Where is your shelter
if some stiff gale blows up from south or west—
the winds that break up shipping every time
when seamen flout the lord gods' will? I say

do as the hour demands and go ashore
before black night comes down.
We'll make our supper
alongside, and at dawn put out to sea.'

Now when the rest said 'Aye' to this, I saw
the power of destiny devising ill.
Sharply I answered, without hesitation:

'Eurýlokhos, they are with you to a man.
I am alone, outmatched.
Let this whole company
swear me a great oath: Any herd of cattle
or flock of sheep here found shall go unharmed;
no one shall slaughter out of wantonness
ram or heifer; all shall be content
with what the goddess Kirkê put aboard.'

They fell at once to swearing as I ordered,
and when the round of oaths had ceased, we found
a halfmoon bay to beach and moor the ship in,
with a fresh spring nearby. All hands ashore
went about skillfully getting up a meal.
Then, after thirst and hunger, those besiegers,
were turned away, they mourned for their companions
plucked from the ship by Skylla and devoured,
and sleep came soft upon them as they mourned.

In the small hours of the third watch, when stars
that shone out in the first dusk of evening
had gone down to their setting, a giant wind
blew from heaven, and clouds driven by Zeus
shrouded land and sea in a night of storm;
so, just as Dawn with finger tips of rose
touched the windy world, we dragged our ship
to cover in a grotto, a sea cave
where nymphs had chairs of rock and sanded floors.
I mustered all the crew and said:

'Old shipmates,
our stores are in the ship's hold, food and drink;
the cattle here are not for our provision,
or we pay dearly for it.
Fierce the god is
who cherishes these heifers and these sheep:
Hêlios; and no man avoids his eye.'

To this my fighters nodded. Yes. But now
we had a month of onshore gales, blowing
day in, day out—south winds, or south by east.
As long as bread and good red wine remained
to keep the men up, and appease their craving,

they would not touch the cattle. But in the end,
when all the barley in the ship was gone,
hunger drove them to scour the wild shore
with angling hooks, for fishes and sea fowl,
whatever fell into their hands; and lean days
wore their bellies thin.

The storms continued.
So one day I withdrew to the interior
to pray the gods in solitude, for hope
that one might show me some way of salvation.
Slipping away, I struck across the island
to a sheltered spot, out of the driving gale.
I washed my hands there, and made supplication
to the gods who own Olympos, all the gods—
but they, for answer, only closed my eyes
under slow drops of sleep.
Now on the shore Eurýlokhos
made his insidious plea:

'Comrades,' he said,
'You've gone through everything; listen to what I say.
All deaths are hateful to us, mortal wretches,
but famine is the most pitiful, the worst
end that a man can come to.
Will you fight it?
Come, we'll cut out the noblest of these cattle
for sacrifice to the gods who own the sky;
and once at home, in the old country of Ithaka,
if ever that day comes—
we'll build a costly temple and adorn it
with every beauty for the Lord of Noon.
But if he flares up over his heifers lost,
wishing our ship destroyed, and if the gods
make cause with him, why, then I say: Better
open your lungs to a big sea once for all
than waste to skin and bones on a lonely island!'

Thus Eurýlokhos; and they murmured 'Aye!'
trooping away at once to round up heifers.
Now, that day tranquil cattle with broad brows
were grazing near, and soon the men drew up
around their chosen beasts in ceremony.
They plucked the leaves that shone on a tall oak—
having no barley meal—to strew the victims,
performed the prayers and ritual, knifed the kine
and flayed each carcass, cutting thighbones free
to wrap in double folds of fat. These offerings,
with strips of meat, were laid upon the fire.
Then, as they had no wine, they made libation
with clear spring water, broiling the entrails first;
and when the bones were burnt and tripes shared,

they spitted the carved meat.
Just then my slumber
left me in a rush, my eyes opened,
and I went down the seaward path. No sooner
had I caught sight of our black hull, than savory
odors of burnt fat eddied around me;
grief took hold of me, and I cried aloud:

'O Father Zeus and gods in bliss forever,
you made me sleep away this day of mischief!
O cruel drowsing, in the evil hour!
Here they sat, and a great work they contrived.'

Lampetía in her long gown meanwhile
had borne swift word to the Overlord of Noon:

'They have killed your kine.'

And the Lord Hêlios
burst into angry speech amid the immortals:

'O Father Zeus and gods in bliss forever,
punish Odysseus' men! So overweening,
now they have killed my peaceful kine, my joy
at morning when I climbed the sky of stars,
and evening, when I bore westward from heaven.
Restitution or penalty they shall pay—
and pay in full—or I go down forever
to light the dead men in the underworld.'

Then Zeus who drives the stormcloud made reply:

'Peace, Hêlios: shine on among the gods,
shine over mortals in the fields of grain.
Let me throw down one white-hot bolt, and make
splinters of their ship in the winedark sea.'

—Kalypso later told me of this exchange,
as she declared that Hermês had told her.
Well, when I reached the sea cave and the ship,
I faced each man, and had it out; but where
could any remedy be found? There was none.
The silken beeves of Hêlios were dead.
The gods, moreover, made queer signs appear:
cowhides began to crawl, and beef, both raw
and roasted, lowed like kine upon the spits.

Now six full days my gallant crew could feast
upon the prime beef they had marked for slaughter
from Hêlios' herd; and Zeus, the son of Kronos,
added one fine morning.
All the gales

had ceased, blown out, and with an offshore breeze
we launched again, stepping the mast and sail,
to make for the open sea. Astern of us
the island coastline faded, and no land
showed anywhere, but only sea and heaven,
when Zeus Kroníon piled a thunderhead
above the ship, while gloom spread on the ocean.
We held our course, but briefly. Then the squall
struck whining from the west, with gale force, breaking
both forestays, and the mast came toppling aft
along the ship's length, so the running rigging
showered into the bilge.
On the after deck
the mast had hit the steersman a slant blow
bashing the skull in, knocking him overside,
as the brave soul fled the body, like a diver.
With crack on crack of thunder, Zeus let fly
a bolt against the ship, a direct hit,
so that she bucked, in reeking fumes of sulphur,
and all the men were flung into the sea.
They came up 'round the wreck, bobbing a while
like petrels on the waves.
No more seafaring
homeward for these, no sweet day of return;
the god had turned his face from them.
I clambered
fore and aft my hulk until a comber
split her, keel from ribs, and the big timber
floated free; the mast, too, broke away.
A backstay floated dangling from it, stout
rawhide rope, and I used this for lashing
mast and keel together. These I straddled,
riding the frightful storm.
Nor had I yet
seen the worst of it: for now the west wind
dropped, and a southeast gale came on—one more
twist of the knife—taking me north again,
straight for Kharybdis. All that night I drifted,
and in the sunrise, sure enough, I lay
off Skylla mountain and Kharybdis deep.
There, as the whirlpool drank the tide, a billow
tossed me, and I sprang for the great fig tree,
catching on like a bat under a bough.
Nowhere had I to stand, no way of climbing,
the root and bole being far below, and far
above my head the branches and their leaves,
massed, overshadowing Kharybdis' pool.
But I clung grimly, thinking my mast and keel
would come back to the surface when she spouted.
And ah! how long, with what desire, I waited!
till, at the twilight hour, when one who hears
and judges pleas in the marketplace all day

between contentious men, goes home to supper,
the long poles at last reared from the sea.

Now I let go with hands and feet, plunging
straight into the foam beside the timbers,
pulled astride, and rowed hard with my hands
to pass by Skylla. Never could I have passed her
had not the Father of gods and men, this time,
kept me from her eyes. Once through the strait,
nine days I drifted in the open sea
before I made shore, buoyed up by the gods,
upon Ogýgia Isle. The dangerous nymph
Kalypso lives and sings there, in her beauty,
and she received me, loved me.

But why tell
the same tale that I told last night in hall
to you and to your lady? Those adventures
made a long evening, and I do not hold
with tiresome repetition of a story."

BOOK XIII

[*One More Strange Island*]

He ended it, and no one stirred or sighed
in the shadowy hall, spellbound as they all were,
until Alkínoös answered:

"When you came
here to my strong home, Odysseus, under
my tall roof, headwinds were left behind you.
Clear sailing shall you have now, homeward now,
however painful all the past.
My lords,
ever my company, sharing the wine of Council,
the songs of the blind harper, hear me further:
garments are folded for our guest and friend
in the smooth chest, and gold
in various shaping of adornment lies
with other gifts, and many, brought by our peers;
let each man add his tripod and deep-bellied
cauldron: we'll make levy upon the realm
to pay us for the loss each bears in this."

Alkínoös had voiced their own hearts' wish.
All gave assent, then home they went to rest;
but young Dawn's finger tips of rose, touching
the world, roused them to make haste to the ship,
each with his gift of noble bronze. Alkínoös,
their ardent king, stepping aboard himself,
directed the stowing under the cross planks,
not to cramp the long pull of the oarsmen.

Going then to the great hall, lords and crew
prepared for feasting.
As the gods' anointed,
Alkínoös made offering on their behalf—an ox
to Zeus beyond the stormcloud, Kronos' son,
who rules the world. They burnt the great thighbones
and feasted at their ease on fresh roast meat,
as in their midst the godlike harper sang—
Demódokos, honored by all that realm.
Only Odysseus
time and again turned craning toward the sun,
impatient for day's end, for the open sea.
Just as a farmer's hunger grows, behind
the bolted plow and share, all day afield,
drawn by his team of winedark oxen: sundown
is benison for him, sending him homeward
stiff in the knees from weariness, to dine;
just so, the light on the sea rim gladdened Odysseus,
and as it dipped he stood among the Phaiákians,
turned to Alkínoös, and said:

"O king and admiration of your people,
give me fare well, and stain the ground with wine;
my blessings on you all! This hour brings
fulfillment to the longing of my heart:
a ship for home, and gifts the gods of heaven
make so precious and so bountiful.
After this voyage
god grant I find my own wife in my hall
with everyone I love best, safe and sound!
And may you, settled in your land, give joy
to wives and children; may the gods reward you
every way, and your realm be free of woe."

Then all the voices rang out, "Be it so!"
and "Well spoken!" and "Let our friend make sail!"

Whereon Alkínoös gave command to his crier:

"Fill the winebowl, Pontónoös: mix and serve:
go the whole round, so may this company
invoke our Father Zeus, and bless our friend,
seaborne tonight and bound for his own country."

Pontónoös mixed the honey-hearted wine
and went from chair to chair, filling the cups;
then each man where he sat poured out his offering
to the gods in bliss who own the sweep of heaven.
With gentle bearing Odysseus rose, and placed
his double goblet in Arêtê's hands,
saying:

"Great Queen, farewell;
be blest through all your days till age comes on you,
and death, last end for mortals, after age.
Now I must go my way. Live in felicity,
and make this palace lovely for your children,
your countrymen, and your king, Alkínoös."

Royal Odysseus turned and crossed the door sill,
a herald at his right hand, sent by Alkínoös
to lead him to the sea beach and the ship.
Arêtê, too, sent maids in waiting after him,
one with a laundered great cloak and a tunic,
a second balancing the crammed sea chest,
a third one bearing loaves and good red wine.
As soon as they arrived alongside, crewmen
took these things for stowage under the planks,
their victualling and drink; then spread a rug
and linen cover on the after deck,
where Lord Odysseus might sleep in peace.
Now he himself embarked, lay down, lay still,
while oarsmen took their places at the rowlocks
all in order. They untied their hawser,
passing it through a drilled stone ring; then bent
forward at the oars and caught the sea
as one man, stroking.
Slumber, soft and deep
like the still sleep of death, weighed on his eyes
as the ship hove seaward.
How a four horse team
whipped into a run on a straightaway
consumes the road, surging and surging over it!
So ran that craft and showed her heels to the swell,
her bow wave riding after, and her wake
on the purple night-sea foaming.
Hour by hour
she held her pace; not even a falcon wheeling
downwind, swiftest bird, could stay abreast of her
in that most arrowy flight through open water,
with her great passenger—godlike in counsel,
he that in twenty years had borne such blows
in his deep heart, breaking through ranks in war
and waves on the bitter sea.
This night at last
he slept serene, his long-tried mind at rest.

When on the East the sheer bright star arose
that tells of coming Dawn, the ship made landfall
and came up islandward in the dim of night.
Phorkys, the old sea baron, has a cove
here in the realm of Ithaka; two points
of high rock, breaking sharply, hunch around it,
making a haven from the plunging surf
that gales at sea roll shoreward. Deep inside,

at mooring range, good ships can ride unmoored.
There, on the inmost shore, an olive tree
throws wide its boughs over the bay; nearby
a cave of dusky light is hidden
for those immortal girls, the Naiadês.[5]
Within are winebowls hollowed in the rock
and amphorai; bees bring their honey here;
and there are looms of stone, great looms, whereon
the weaving nymphs make tissues, richly dyed
as the deep sea is; and clear springs in the cavern
flow forever. Of two entrances,
one on the north allows descent of mortals,
but beings out of light alone, the undying,
can pass by the south slit; no men come there.

This cove the sailors knew. Here they drew in,
and the ship ran half her keel's length up the shore,
she had such way on her from those great oarsmen.
Then from their benches forward on dry ground
they disembarked. They hoisted up Odysseus
unruffled on his bed, under his cover,
handing him overside still fast asleep,
to lay him on the sand; and they unloaded
all those gifts the princes of Phaiákia
gave him, when by Athena's heart and will
he won his passage home. They bore this treasure
off the beach, and piled it close around
the roots of the olive tree, that no one passing
should steal Odysseus' gear before he woke.
That done, they pulled away on the homeward track.

But now the god that shakes the islands, brooding
over old threats of his against Odysseus,
approached Lord Zeus to learn his will. Said he:

"Father of gods, will the bright immortals ever
pay me respect again, if mortals do not?—
Phaiákians, too, my own blood kin?
                                                I thought
Odysseus should in time regain his homeland;
I had no mind to rob him of that day—
no, no; you promised it, being so inclined;
only I thought he should be made to suffer
all the way.
                    But now these islanders
have shipped him homeward, sleeping soft, and put him
on Ithaka, with gifts untold
of bronze and gold, and fine cloth to his shoulder.
Never from Troy had he borne off such booty
if he had got home safe with all his share."

Then Zeus who drives the stormcloud answered, sighing:

5. Nymphs of lake, river, and stream.

"God of horizons, making earth's underbeam
tremble, why do you grumble so?
The immortal gods show you no less esteem,
and the rough consequence would make them slow
to let barbs fly at their eldest and most noble.
But if some mortal captain, overcome
by his own pride of strength, cuts or defies you,
are you not always free to take reprisal?
Act as your wrath requires and as you will."

Now said Poseidon, god of earthquake:

"Aye,
god of the stormy sky, I should have taken
vengeance, as you say, and on my own;
but I respect, and would avoid, your anger.
The sleek Phaiákian cutter, even now,
has carried out her mission and glides home
over the misty sea. Let me impale her,
end her voyage, and end all ocean-crossing
with passengers, then heave a mass of mountain
in a ring around the city."

Now Zeus who drives the stormcloud said benignly:

"Here is how I should do it, little brother:
when all who watch upon the wall have caught
sight of the ship, let her be turned to stone—
an island like a ship, just off the bay.
Mortals may gape at that for generations!
But throw no mountain round[6] the sea port city."

When he heard this, Poseidon, god of earthquake,
departed for Skhería, where the Phaiákians
are born and dwell. Their ocean-going ship
he saw already near, heading for harbor;
so up behind her swam the island-shaker
and struck her into stone, rooted in stone, at one
blow of his palm,
then took to the open sea.
Those famous ship handlers, the Phaiákians,
gazed at each other, murmuring in wonder;
you could have heard one say:

"Now who in thunder
has anchored, moored that ship in the seaway,
when everyone could see her making harbor?"

6. This translates a correction of the text made in antiquity by the Alexandrian scholar Aristophanes of Byzantium. But another great Alexandrian scholar, Aristarchus, defended the original text, which means "and throw a big mountain round." Zeus, in other words, approved of Poseidon's intention to cut the Phaiákians off from the sea altogether and adds the proposal to turn the ship into a rock. It is a difficult question to decide, because Homer does not tell us what happened to the Phaiákians in the end.

The god had wrought a charm beyond their thought.
But soon Alkínoös made them hush, and told them:

"This present doom upon the ship—on me—
my father prophesied in the olden time.
If we gave safe conveyance to all passengers
we should incur Poseidon's wrath, he said,
whereby one day a fair ship, manned by Phaiákians,
would come to grief at the god's hands; and great
mountains would hide our city from the sea.
So my old father forecast.
Use your eyes:
these things are even now being brought to pass.
Let all here abide by my decree:
We make
an end henceforth of taking, in our ships,
castaways who may land upon Skhería;
and twelve choice bulls we dedicate at once
to Lord Poseidon, praying him of his mercy
not to heave up a mountain round our city."

In fearful awe they led the bulls to sacrifice
and stood about the altar stone, those captains,
peers of Phaiákia, led by their king in prayer
to Lord Poseidon.

Meanwhile, on his island,
his father's shore, that kingly man, Odysseus,
awoke, but could not tell what land it was
after so many years away; moreover,
Pallas Athena, Zeus's daughter, poured
a grey mist all around him, hiding him
from common sight—for she had things to tell him
and wished no one to know him, wife or townsmen,
before the suitors paid up for their crimes.

The landscape then looked strange, unearthly strange
to the Lord Odysseus: paths by hill and shore,
glimpses of harbors, cliffs, and summer trees.
He stood up, rubbed his eyes, gazed at his homeland,
and swore, slapping his thighs with both his palms,
then cried aloud:

"What am I in for now?
Whose country have I come to this time? Rough
savages and outlaws, are they, or
godfearing people, friendly to castaways?
Where shall I take these things? Where take myself,
with no guide, no directions? These should be
still in Phaiákian hands, and I uncumbered,
free to find some other openhearted
prince who might be kind and give me passage.

I have no notion where to store this treasure;
first-comer's trove it is, if I leave it here.

My lords and captains of Phaiákia
were not those decent men they seemed, not honorable,
landing me in this unknown country—no,
by god, they swore to take me home to Ithaka
and did not! Zeus attend to their reward,
Zeus, patron of petitioners, who holds
all other mortals under his eye; he takes
payment from betrayers!
                                        I'll be busy.
I can look through my gear. I shouldn't wonder
if they pulled out with part of it on board."

He made a tally of his shining pile—
tripods, cauldrons, cloaks, and gold—and found
he lacked nothing at all.
                                        And then he wept,
despairing, for his own land, trudging down
beside the endless wash of the wide, wide sea,
weary and desolate as the sea. But soon
Athena came to him from the nearby air,
putting a young man's figure on—a shepherd,
like a king's son, all delicately made.
She wore a cloak, in two folds off her shoulders,
and sandals bound upon her shining feet.
A hunting lance lay in her hands.
                                        At sight of her
Odysseus took heart, and he went forward
to greet the lad, speaking out fair and clear:

"Friend, you are the first man I've laid eyes on
here in this cove. Greetings. Do not feel
alarmed or hostile, coming across me; only
receive me into safety with my stores.
Touching your knees I ask it, as I might
ask grace of a god.
                                O sir, advise me,
what is this land and realm, who are the people?
Is it an island all distinct, or part
of the fertile mainland, sloping to the sea?"

To this grey-eyed Athena answered:

                                        "Stranger,
you must come from the other end of nowhere,
else you are a great booby, having to ask
what place this is. It is no nameless country.
Why, everyone has heard of it, the nations
over on the dawn side, toward the sun,
and westerners in cloudy lands of evening.

No one would use this ground for training horses,
it is too broken, has no breadth of meadow;
but there is nothing meager about the soil,
the yield of grain is wondrous, and wine, too,
with drenching rains and dewfall.
There's good pasture
for oxen and for goats, all kinds of timber,
and water all year long in the cattle ponds.
For these blessings, friend, the name of Ithaka
has made its way even as far as Troy—
and they say Troy lies far beyond Akhaia."

Now Lord Odysseus, the long-enduring,
laughed in his heart, hearing his land described
by Pallas Athena, daughter of Zeus who rules
the veering stormwind; and he answered her
with ready speech—not that he told the truth,
but, just as she did, held back what he knew,
weighing within himself at every step
what he made up to serve his turn.

Said he:

"Far away in Krete I learned of Ithaka—
in that broad island over the great ocean.
And here I am now, come myself to Ithaka!
Here is my fortune with me. I left my sons
an equal part, when I shipped out. I killed
Orsílokhos, the courier, son of Idómeneus.
This man could beat the best cross country runners
in Krete, but he desired to take away
my Trojan plunder, all I had fought and bled for,
cutting through ranks in war and the cruel sea.
Confiscation is what he planned; he knew
I had not cared to win his father's favor
as a staff officer in the field at Troy,
but led my own command.
I acted: I
hit him with a spearcast from a roadside
as he came down from the open country. Murky
night shrouded all heaven and the stars.
I made that ambush with one man at arms.
We were unseen. I took his life in secret,
finished him off with my sharp sword. That night
I found asylum on a ship off shore
skippered by gentlemen of Phoinikia;[7] I gave
all they could wish, out of my store of plunder,
for passage, and for landing me at Pylos
or Elis Town, where the Epeioi[8] are in power.
Contrary winds carried them willy-nilly

7. Phoenicia. 8. The people of Elis Town, in the western Peloponnese.

past that coast; they had no wish to cheat me,
but we were blown off course.
Here, then, by night
we came, and made this haven by hard rowing.
All famished, but too tired to think of food,
each man dropped in his tracks after the landing,
and I slept hard, being wearied out. Before
I woke today, they put my things ashore
on the sand here beside me where I lay,
then reimbarked for Sidon, that great city.
Now they are far at sea, while I am left
forsaken here."

At this the grey-eyed goddess
Athena smiled, and gave him a caress,
her looks being changed now, so she seemed a woman,
tall and beautiful and no doubt skilled
at weaving splendid things. She answered briskly:

"Whoever gets around you must be sharp
and guileful as a snake; even a god
might bow to you in ways of dissimulation.
You! You chameleon!
Bottomless bag of tricks! Here in your own country
would you not give your stratagems a rest
or stop spellbinding for an instant?

You play a part as if it were your own tough skin.

No more of this, though. Two of a kind, we are,
contrivers, both. Of all men now alive
you are the best in plots and story telling.
My own fame is for wisdom among the gods—
deceptions, too.
Would even you have guessed
that I am Pallas Athena, daughter of Zeus,
I that am always with you in times of trial,
a shield to you in battle, I who made
the Phaiákians befriend you, to a man?
Now I am here again to counsel with you—
but first to put away those gifts the Phaiákians
gave you at departure—I planned it so.
Then I can tell you of the gall and wormwood
it is your lot to drink in your own hall.
Patience, iron patience, you must show;
so give it out to neither man nor woman
that you are back from wandering. Be silent
under all injuries, even blows from men."

His mind ranging far, Odysseus answered:

"Can mortal man be sure of you on sight,
even a sage, O mistress of disguises?

Once you were fond of me—I am sure of that—
years ago, when we Akhaians made
war, in our generation, upon Troy.
But after we had sacked the shrines of Priam
and put to sea, God scattered the Akhaians;
I never saw you after that, never
knew you aboard with me, to act as shield
in grievous times—not till you gave me comfort
in the rich hinterland of the Phaiákians
and were yourself my guide into that city.

Hear me now in your father's name, for I
cannot believe that I have come to Ithaka.
It is some other land. You made that speech
only to mock me, and to take me in.
Have I come back in truth to my home island?"

To this the grey-eyed goddess Athena answered:

"Always the same detachment! That is why
I cannot fail you, in your evil fortune,
coolheaded, quick, well-spoken as you are!
Would not another wandering man, in joy,
make haste home to his wife and children? Not
you, not yet. Before you hear their story
you will have proof about your wife.
I tell you,
she still sits where you left her, and her days
and nights go by forlorn, in lonely weeping.
For my part, never had I despaired; I felt
sure of your coming home, though all your men
should perish; but I never cared to fight
Poseidon, Father's brother, in his baleful
rage with you for taking his son's eye.

Now I shall make you see the shape of Ithaka.
Here is the cove the sea lord Phorkys owns,
there is the olive spreading out her leaves
over the inner bay, and there the cavern
dusky and lovely, hallowed by the feet
of those immortal girls, the Naiadês—
the same wide cave under whose vault you came
to honor them with hekatombs—and there
Mount Neion, with his forest on his back!"

She had dispelled the mist, so all the island
stood out clearly. Then indeed Odysseus'
heart stirred with joy. He kissed the earth,
and lifting up his hands prayed to the nymphs:

"O slim shy Naiadês, young maids of Zeus,
I had not thought to see you ever again!
O listen smiling

to my gentle prayers, and we'll make offering
plentiful as in the old time, granted I
live, granted my son grows tall, by favor
of great Athena, Zeus's daughter,
who gives the winning fighter his reward!"

The grey-eyed goddess said directly:

"Courage;
and let the future trouble you no more.
We go to make a cache now, in the cave,
to keep your treasure hid. Then we'll consider
how best the present action may unfold."

The goddess turned and entered the dim cave,
exploring it for crannies, while Odysseus
carried up all the gold, the fire-hard bronze,
and well-made clothing the Phaiákians gave him.
Pallas Athena, daughter of Zeus the storm king,
placed them, and shut the cave mouth with a stone,
and under the old grey olive tree those two
sat down to work the suitors death and woe.
Grey-eyed Athena was the first to speak, saying:

"Son of Laërtês and the gods of old,
Odysseus, master of land ways and sea ways,
put your mind on a way to reach and strike
a crowd of brazen upstarts.
Three long years
they have played master in your house: three years
trying to win your lovely lady, making
gifts as though betrothed. And she? Forever
grieving for you, missing your return,
she has allowed them all to hope, and sent
messengers with promises to each—
though her true thoughts are fixed elsewhere."

At this
the man of ranging mind, Odysseus, cried:

"So hard beset! An end like Agamémnon's
might very likely have been mine, a bad end,
bleeding to death in my own hall. You forestalled it,
goddess, by telling me how the land lies.
Weave me a way to pay them back! And you, too,
take your place with me, breathe valor in me
the way you did that night when we Akhaians
unbound the bright veil from the brow of Troy!
O grey-eyed one, fire my heart and brace me!
I'll take on fighting men three hundred strong
if you fight at my back, immortal lady!"

The grey-eyed goddess Athena answered him:

"No fear but I shall be there; you'll go forward
under my arm when the crux comes at last.
And I foresee your vast floor stained with blood,
spattered with brains of this or that tall suitor
who fed upon your cattle.
Now, for a while,
I shall transform you; not a soul will know you,
the clear skin of your arms and legs shriveled,
your chestnut hair all gone, your body dressed
in sacking that a man would gag to see,
and the two eyes, that were so brilliant, dirtied—
contemptible, you shall seem to your enemies,
as to the wife and son you left behind.

But join the swineherd first—the overseer
of all your swine, a good soul now as ever,
devoted to Penélopê and your son.
He will be found near Raven's Rock and the well
of Arethousa, where the swine are pastured,
rooting for acorns to their hearts' content,
drinking the dark still water. Boarflesh grows
pink and fat on that fresh diet. There
stay with him and question him, while I
am off to the great beauty's land of Sparta,
to call your son Telémakhos home again—
for you should know, he went to the wide land
of Lakedaimon, Meneláos' country,
to learn if there were news of you abroad."

Odysseus answered:

"Why not tell him, knowing
my whole history, as you do? Must he
traverse the barren sea, he too, and live
in pain, while others feed on what is his?"

At this the grey-eyed goddess Athena said:

"No need for anguish on that lad's account.
I sent him off myself, to make his name
in foreign parts—no hardship in the bargain,
taking his ease in Meneláos' mansion,
lapped in gold.
The young bucks here, I know,
lie in wait for him in a cutter, bent
on murdering him before he reaches home.
I rather doubt they will. Cold earth instead
will take in her embrace a man or two
of those who fed so long on what is his."

Speaking no more, she touched him with her wand,
shriveled the clear skin of his arms and legs,
made all his hair fall out, cast over him
the wrinkled hide of an old man, and bleared
both his eyes, that were so bright. Then she
clapped an old tunic, a foul cloak, upon him,
tattered, filthy, stained by greasy smoke,
and over that a mangy big buck skin.
A staff she gave him, and a leaky knapsack
with no strap but a loop of string.
Now then,
their colloquy at an end, they went their ways—
Athena toward illustrious Lakedaimon
far over sea, to join Odysseus' son.

BOOK XIV

[*Hospitality in the Forest*]

He went up from the cove through wooded ground,
taking a stony trail into the high hills, where
the swineherd lived, according to Athena.
Of all Odysseus' field hands in the old days
this forester cared most for the estate;
and now Odysseus found him
in a remote clearing, sitting inside the gate
of a stockade he built to keep the swine
while his great lord was gone.
Working alone,
far from Penélopê and old Laërtês,
he had put up a fieldstone hut and timbered it
with wild pear wood. Dark hearts of oak he split
and trimmed for a high palisade around it,
and built twelve sties adjoining in this yard
to hold the livestock. Fifty sows with farrows
were penned in each, bedded upon the earth,
while the boars lay outside—fewer by far,
as those well-fatted were for the suitors' table,
fine pork, sent by the swineherd every day.
Three hundred sixty now lay there at night,
guarded by dogs—four dogs like wolves, one each
for the four lads the swineherd reared and kept
as under-herdsmen.
When Odysseus came,
the good servant sat shaping to his feet
oxhide for sandals, cutting the well-cured leather.
Three of his young men were afield, pasturing
herds in other woods; one he had sent
with a fat boar for tribute into town,
the boy to serve while the suitors got their fill.

The watch dogs, when they caught sight of Odysseus,
faced him, a snarling troop, and pelted out
viciously after him. Like a tricky beggar

he sat down plump, and dropped his stick. No use.
They would have rolled him in the dust and torn him
there by his own steading if the swineherd
had not sprung up and flung his leather down,
making a beeline for the open. Shouting,
throwing stone after stone,
he made them scatter; then turned to his lord
and said:

"You might have got a ripping, man!
Two shakes more and a pretty mess for me
you could have called it, if you had the breath.
As though I had not trouble enough already,
given me by the gods, my master gone,
true king that he was. I hang on here,
still mourning for him, raising pigs of his
to feed foreigners, and who knows where the man is,
in some far country among strangers! Aye—
if he is living still, if he still sees the light of day.

Come to the cabin. You're a wanderer too.
You must eat something, drink some wine, and tell me
where you are from and the hard times you've seen."

The forester now led him to his hut
and made a couch for him, with tips of fir
piled for a mattress under a wild goat skin,
shaggy and thick, his own bed covering.
Odysseus,
in pleasure at this courtesy, gently said:

"May Zeus and all the gods give you your heart's desire
for taking me in so kindly, friend."

Eumaios—
O my swineherd![9]—answered him:

"Tush, friend,
rudeness to a stranger is not decency,
poor though he may be, poorer than you.
All wanderers
and beggars come from Zeus. What we can give
is slight but well-meant—all we dare. You know
that is the way of slaves, who live in dread
of masters—new ones like our own.
I told you
the gods, long ago, hindered our lord's return.
He had a fondness for me, would have pensioned me

9. This direct address by the poet to one of his characters is confined to Eumaios; it occurs frequently in connection with his name in books 14–17. A medieval commentator suggested that it showed a special affection for Eumaios on Homer's part, but because in the *Iliad* a similar form of address is used for five different characters (among them the god Apollo and the obscure Melanippos) this seems unlikely. In the case of Eumaios it may have been a formula devised to avoid hiatus (clashing vowels).

with acres of my own, a house, a wife
that other men admired and courted; all
gifts good-hearted kings bestow for service,
for a life work the bounty of god has prospered—
for it does prosper here, this work I do.
Had he grown old in his own house, my master
would have rewarded me. But the man's gone.
God curse the race of Helen and cut it down,
that wrung the strength out of the knees of many!
And he went, too—for the honor of Agamémnon
he took ship overseas for the wild horse country
of Troy, to fight the Trojans."

This being told,
he tucked his long shirt up inside his belt
and strode into the pens for two young porkers.
He slaughtered them and singed them at the fire,
flayed and quartered them, and skewered the meat
to broil it all; then gave it to Odysseus
hot on the spits. He shook out barley meal,
took a winebowl of ivy wood and filled it,
and sat down facing him, with a gesture, saying:

"There is your dinner, friend, the pork of slaves.
Our fat shoats are all eaten by the suitors,
cold-hearted men, who never spare a thought
for how they stand in the sight of Zeus. The gods
living in bliss are fond of no wrongdoing,
but honor discipline and right behavior.
Even the outcasts of the earth, who bring
piracy from the sea, and bear off plunder
given by Zeus in shiploads—even those men
deep in their hearts tremble for heaven's eye.
But the suitors, now, have heard some word, some oracle
of my lord's death, being so unconcerned
to pay court properly or to go about their business.
All they want is to prey on his estate,
proud dogs: they stop at nothing. Not a day
goes by, and not a night comes under Zeus,
but they make butchery of our beeves and swine—
not one or two beasts at a time, either.
As for swilling down wine, they drink us dry.
Only a great domain like his could stand it—
greater than any on the dusky mainland
or here in Ithaka. Not twenty heroes
in the whole world were as rich as he. I know:
I could count it all up: twelve herds in Elis,
as many flocks, as many herds of swine,
and twelve wide ranging herds of goats, as well,
attended by his own men or by others—
out at the end of the island, eleven herds
are scattered now, with good men looking after them,

and every herdsman, every day, picks out
a prize ram to hand over to those fellows.
I too as overseer, keeper of swine,
must go through all my boars and send the best."

While he ran on, Odysseus with zeal
applied himself to the meat and wine, but inwardly
his thought shaped woe and ruin for the suitors.
When he had eaten all that he desired
and the cup he drank from had been filled again
with wine—a welcome sight—,
he spoke, and the words came light upon the air:

"Who is this lord who once acquired you,
so rich, so powerful, as you describe him?
You think he died for Agamémnon's honor.
Tell me his name: I may have met someone
of that description in my time. Who knows?
Perhaps only the immortal gods could say
if I should claim to have seen him: I have roamed
about the world so long."

The swineherd answered
as one who held a place of trust:

"Well, man,
his lady and his son will put no stock
in any news of him brought by a rover.
Wandering men tell lies for a night's lodging,
for fresh clothing; truth doesn't interest them.
Every time some traveller comes ashore
he has to tell my mistress his pretty tale,
and she receives him kindly, questions him,
remembering her prince, while the tears run
down her cheeks—and that is as it should be
when a woman's husband has been lost abroad.
I suppose you, too, can work your story up
at a moment's notice, given a shirt or cloak.
No: long ago wild dogs and carrion
birds, most like, laid bare his ribs on land
where life had left him. Or it may be, quick fishes
picked him clean in the deep sea, and his bones
lie mounded over in sand upon some shore.
One way or another, far from home he died,
a bitter loss, and pain, for everyone,
certainly for me. Never again shall I
have for my lot a master mild as he was
anywhere—not even with my parents
at home, where I was born and bred. I miss them
less than I do him—though a longing comes
to set my eyes on them in the old country.
No, it is the lost man I ache to think of—

Odysseus. And I speak the name respectfully,
even if he is not here. He loved me, cared for me.
I call him dear my lord, far though he be."

Now royal Odysseus, who had borne the long war,
spoke again:

"Friend, as you are so dead sure
he will not come—and so mistrustful, too—
let me not merely talk, as others talk,
but swear to it: your lord is now at hand.
And I expect a gift for this good news
when he enters his own hall. Till then I would not
take a rag, no matter what my need.
I hate as I hate Hell's own gate that weakness
that makes a poor man into a flatterer.
Zeus be my witness, and the table garnished
for true friends, and Odysseus' own hearth—
by heaven, all I say will come to pass!
He will return, and he will be avenged
on any who dishonor his wife and son."

Eumaios—O my swineherd!—answered him:

"I take you at your word, then: you shall have
no good news gift from me. Nor will Odysseus
enter his hall. But peace! drink up your wine.
Let us talk now of other things. No more
imaginings. It makes me heavy-hearted
when someone brings my master back to mind—
my own true master.

No, by heaven,
let us have no oaths! But if Odysseus
can come again god send he may! My wish
is that of Penélopê and old Laërtês
and Prince Telémakhos.

Ah, he's another
to be distressed about—Odysseus' child,
Telémakhos! By the gods' grace he grew
like a tough sapling, and I thought he'd be
no less a man than his great father—strong
and admirably made; but then someone,
god or man, upset him, made him rash,
so that he sailed away to sandy Pylos
to hear news of his father. Now the suitors
lie in ambush on his homeward track,
ready to cut away the last shoot of Arkêsios'
line, the royal stock of Ithaka.

No good
dwelling on it. Either he'll be caught
or else Kroníon's[1] hand will take him through.

1. Zeus, son of Kronos.

Tell me, now, of your own trials and troubles.
And tell me truly first, for I should know,
who are you, where do you hail from, where's your home
and family? What kind of ship was yours,
and what course brought you here? Who are your sailors?
I don't suppose you walked here on the sea."

To this the master of improvisation answered:

"I'll tell you all that, clearly as I may.
If we could sit here long enough, with meat
and good sweet wine, warm here, in peace and quiet
within doors, while the work of the world goes on—
I might take all this year to tell my story
and never end the tale of misadventures
that wore my heart out, by the gods' will.

My native land is the wide seaboard of Krete
where I grew up. I had a wealthy father,
and many other sons were born to him
of his true lady. My mother was a slave,
his concubine; but Kastor Hylákidês,
my father, treated me as a true born son.
High honor came to him in that part of Krete
for wealth and ease, and sons born for renown,
before the death-bearing Kêrês drew him down
to the underworld. His avid sons thereafter
dividing up the property by lot
gave me a wretched portion, a poor house.
But my ability won me a wife
of rich family. Fool I was never called,
nor turn-tail in a fight.
My strength's all gone,
but from the husk you may divine the ear
that stood tall in the old days. Misery owns me
now, but then great Arês and Athena
gave me valor and man-breaking power,
whenever I made choice of men-at-arms
to set a trap with me for my enemies.
Never, as I am a man, did I fear Death
ahead, but went in foremost in the charge,
putting a spear through any man whose legs
were not as fast as mine. That was my element,
war and battle. Farming I never cared for,
nor life at home, nor fathering fair children.
I reveled in long ships with oars; I loved
polished lances, arrows in the skirmish,
the shapes of doom that others shake to see.
Carnage suited me; heaven put those things
in me somehow. Each to his own pleasure!
Before we young Akhaians shipped for Troy
I led men on nine cruises in corsairs
to raid strange coasts, and had great luck, taking

rich spoils on the spot, and even more
in the division. So my house grew prosperous,
my standing therefore high among the Kretans.
Then came the day when Zeus who views the wide world
drew men's eyes upon that way accurst
that wrung the manhood from the knees of many!
Everyone pressed me, pressed King Idómeneus
to take command of ships for Ilion.
No way out; the country rang with talk of it.
So we Akhaians had nine years of war.
In the tenth year we sacked the inner city,
Priam's town, and sailed for home; but heaven
dispersed the Akhaians. Evil days for me
were stored up in the hidden mind of Zeus.
One month, no more, I stayed at home in joy
with children, wife, and treasure. Lust for action
drove me to go to sea then, in command
of ships and gallant seamen bound for Egypt.
Nine ships I fitted out; my men signed on
and came to feast with me, as good shipmates,
for six full days. Many a beast I slaughtered
in the gods' honor, for my friends to eat.
Embarking on the seventh, we hauled sail
and filled away from Krete on a fresh north wind
effortlessly, as boats will glide down stream.
All rigging whole and all hands well, we rested,
letting the wind and steersmen work the ships,
for five days; on the fifth we made the delta.[2]
I brought my squadron in to the river bank
with one turn of the sweeps. There, heaven knows,
I told the men to wait and guard the ships
while I sent out patrols to rising ground.
But reckless greed carried them all away
to plunder the rich bottomlands; they bore off
wives and children, killed what men they found.

When this news reached the city, all who heard it
came at dawn. On foot they came, and horsemen,
filling the river plain with dazzle of bronze;
and Zeus lord of lightning
threw my men into blind panic: no one dared
stand against that host closing around us.
Their scything weapons left our dead in piles,
but some they took alive, into forced labor.
And I—ah, how I wish that I had died
in Egypt, on that field! So many blows
awaited me!—Well, Zeus himself inspired me;
I wrenched my dogskin helmet off my head,
dropped my spear, dodged out of my long shield,
ran for the king's chariot and swung on

2. Of the Nile.

to embrace and kiss his knees. He pulled me up,
took pity on me, placed me on the footboards,
and drove home with me crouching there in tears.
Aye—for the troops, in battle fury still,
made one pass at me after another, pricking me
with spears, hoping to kill me. But he saved me,
for fear of the great wrath of Zeus that comes
when men who ask asylum are given death.

Seven years, then, my sojourn lasted there,
and I amassed a fortune, going about
among the openhanded Egyptians.
But when the eighth came round, a certain
Phoinikian adventurer came too,
a plausible rat, who had already done
plenty of devilry in the world.

This fellow
took me in completely with his schemes,
and led me with him to Phoinikia,
where he had land and houses. One full year
I stayed there with him, to the month and day,
and when fair weather came around again
he took me in a deepsea ship for Libya,
pretending I could help in the cargo trade;
he meant, in fact, to trade me off, and get
a high price for me. I could guess the game
but had to follow him aboard. One day
on course due west, off central Krete, the ship
caught a fresh norther, and we ran southward
before the wind while Zeus piled ruin ahead.
When Krete was out of sight astern, no land
anywhere to be seen, but sky and ocean,
Kroníon put a dark cloud in the zenith
over the ship, and gloom spread on the sea.
With crack on crack of thunder, he let fly
a bolt against the ship, a direct hit,
so that she bucked, in sacred fumes of sulphur,
and all the men were flung into the water.
They came up round the wreck, bobbing a while
like petrels on the waves. No homecoming
for these, from whom the god had turned his face!
Stunned in the smother as I was, yet Zeus
put into my hands the great mast of the ship—
a way to keep from drowning. So I twined
my arms and legs around it in the gale
and stayed afloat nine days. On the tenth night,
a big surf cast me up in Thesprotia.[3]
Pheidon the king there gave me refuge, nobly,
with no talk of reward. His son discovered me

3. On the west coast of the Greek mainland, north of Ithaka.

exhausted and half dead with cold, and gave me
a hand to bear me up till he reached home
where he could clothe me in a shirt and cloak.
In that king's house I heard news of Odysseus,
who lately was a guest there, passing by
on his way home, the king said; and he showed me
the treasure that Odysseus had brought:
bronze, gold, and iron wrought with heavy labor—
in that great room I saw enough to last
Odysseus' heirs for ten long generations.
The man himself had gone up to Dodona[4]
to ask the spelling leaves of the old oak
the will of God: how to return, that is,
to the rich realm of Ithaka, after so long
an absence—openly, or on the quiet.
And, tipping wine out, Pheidon swore to me
the ship was launched, the seamen standing by
to take Odysseus to his land at last.
But he had passage first for me: Thesprotians
were sailing, as luck had it, for Doulíkhion,[5]
the grain-growing island; there, he said,
they were to bring me to the king, Akastos.
Instead, that company saw fit to plot
foul play against me; in my wretched life
there was to be more suffering.
At sea, then,
when land lay far astern, they sprang their trap.
They'd make a slave of me that day, stripping
cloak and tunic off me, throwing around me
the dirty rags you see before you now.
At evening, off the fields of Ithaka,
they bound me, lashed me down under the decking
with stout ship's rope, while they all went ashore
in haste to make their supper on the beach.
The gods helped me to pry the lashing loose
until it fell away. I wound my rags
in a bundle round my head and eased myself
down the smooth lading plank into the water,
up to the chin, then swam an easy breast stroke
out and around, putting that crew behind,
and went ashore in underbrush, a thicket,
where I lay still, making myself small.
They raised a bitter yelling, and passed by
several times. When further groping seemed
useless to them, back to the ship they went
and out to sea again. The gods were with me,
keeping me hid; and with me when they brought me
here to the door of one who knows the world.
My destiny is yet to live awhile."

The swineherd bowed and said:

4. An oracle of Zeus. The message of the god was supposed to come from the sacred oak, perhaps from the rushing of the leaves in the wind. 5. An island off the west coast of Greece.

"Ah well, poor drifter,
you've made me sad for you, going back over it,
all your hard life and wandering. That tale
about Odysseus, though, you might have spared me;
you will not make me believe that.
Why must you lie, being the man you are,
and all for nothing?
I can see so well
what happened to my master, sailing home!
Surely the gods turned on him, to refuse him
death in the field, or in his friends' arms
after he wound up the great war at Troy.
They would have made a tomb for him, the Akhaians,
and paid all honor to his son thereafter. No,
stormwinds made off with him. No glory came to him.

I moved here to the mountain with my swine.
Never, now, do I go down to town
unless I am sent for by Penélopê
when news of some sort comes. But those who sit
around her go on asking the old questions—
a few who miss their master still,
and those who eat his house up, and go free.
For my part, I have had no heart for inquiry
since one year an Aitolian[6] made a fool of me.
Exiled from land to land after some killing,
he turned up at my door; I took him in.
My master he had seen in Krete, he said,
lodged with Idómeneus, while the long ships,
leaky from gales, were laid up for repairs.
But they were all to sail, he said, that summer,
or the first days of fall—hulls laden deep
with treasure, manned by crews of heroes.
This time
you are the derelict the Powers bring.
Well, give up trying to win me with false news
or flattery. If I receive and shelter you,
it is not for your tales but for your trouble,
and with an eye to Zeus, who guards a guest."

Then said that sly and guileful man, Odysseus:

"A black suspicious heart beats in you surely;
the man you are, not even an oath could change you.
Come then, we'll make a compact; let the gods
witness it from Olympos, where they dwell.
Upon your lord's homecoming, if he comes
here to this very hut, and soon—
then give me a new outfit, shirt and cloak,
and ship me to Doulíkhion—I thought it
a pleasant island. But if Odysseus

6. Aitolia is on the mainland, east of Ithaka.

fails to appear as I predict, then Swish!
let the slaves pitch me down from some high rock,
so the next poor man who comes will watch his tongue."

The forester gave a snort and answered:

"Friend,
if I agreed to that, a great name
I should acquire in the world for goodness—
at one stroke and forever: your kind host
who gave you shelter and the hand of friendship,
only to take your life next day!
How confidently, after that, should I
address my prayers to Zeus, the son of Kronos!
It is time now for supper. My young herdsmen
should be arriving soon to set about it.
We'll make a quiet feast here at our hearth."

At this point in their talk the swine had come
up to the clearing, and the drovers followed
to pen them for the night—the porkers squealing
to high heaven, milling around the yard.
The swineherd then gave orders to his men:

"Bring in our best pig for a stranger's dinner.
A feast will do our hearts good, too; we know
grief and pain, hard scrabbling with our swine,
while the outsiders live on our labor."

Bronze
axe in hand, he turned to split up kindling,
while they drove in a tall boar, prime and fat,
planting him square before the fire. The gods,
as ever, had their due in the swineherd's thought,
for he it was who tossed the forehead bristles
as a first offering on the flames, calling
upon the immortal gods to let Odysseus
reach his home once more.
Then he stood up
and brained the boar with split oak from the woodpile.
Life ebbed from the beast; they slaughtered him,
singed the carcass, and cut out the joints.
Eumaios, taking flesh from every quarter,
put lean strips on the fat of sacrifice,
floured each one with barley meal, and cast it
into the blaze. The rest they sliced and skewered,
roasted with care, then took it off the fire
and heaped it up on platters. Now their chief,
who knew best the amenities, rose to serve,
dividing all that meat in seven portions—
one to be set aside, with proper prayers,
for the wood nymphs and Hermês, Maia's son;

the others for the company. Odysseus
he honored with long slices from the chine—
warming the master's heart. Odysseus looked at him
and said:

"May you be dear to Zeus
as you are dear to me for this, Eumaios,
favoring with choice cuts a man like me."

And—O my swineherd!—you replied, Eumaios:

"Bless you, stranger, fall to and enjoy it
for what it is. Zeus grants us this or that,
or else refrains from granting, as he wills;
all things are in his power."

He cut and burnt
a morsel for the gods who are young forever,
tipped out some wine, then put it in the hands
of Odysseus, the old soldier, raider of cities,
who sat at ease now with his meat before him.
As for the loaves, Mesaúlios dealt them out,
a yard boy, bought by the swineherd on his own,
unaided by his mistress or Laërtês,
from Taphians, while Odysseus was away.
Now all hands reached for that array of supper,
until, when hunger and thirst were turned away
Mesaúlios removed the bread and, heavy
with food and drink, they settled back to rest.

Now night had come on, rough, with no moon,
but a nightlong downpour setting in, the rainwind
blowing hard from the west. Odysseus
began to talk, to test the swineherd, trying
to put it in his head to take his cloak off
and lend it, or else urge the others to.
He knew the man's compassion.

"Listen," he said,
"Eumaios, and you others, here's a wishful
tale that I shall tell. The wine's behind it,
vaporing wine, that makes a serious man
break down and sing, kick up his heels and clown,
or tell some story that were best untold.
But now I'm launched, I can't stop now.

Would god I felt
the hot blood in me that I had at Troy!
Laying an ambush near the walls one time,
Odysseus and Meneláos were commanders
and I ranked third. I went at their request.
We worked in toward the bluffs and battlements
and, circling the town, got into canebreaks,
thick and high, a marsh where we took cover,

hunched under arms.
The northwind dropped, and night
came black and wintry. A fine sleet descending
whitened the cane like hoarfrost, and clear ice
grew dense upon our shields. The other men,
all wrapt in blanket cloaks as well as tunics,
rested well, in shields up to their shoulder,
but I had left my cloak with friends in camp,
foolhardy as I was. No chance of freezing hard,
I thought, so I wore kilts and a shield only.
But in the small hours of the third watch, when stars
that rise at evening go down to their setting,
I nudged Odysseus, who lay close beside me;
he was alert then, listening, and I said:

'Son of Laërtês and the gods of old,
Odysseus, master mariner and soldier,
I cannot hold on long among the living.
The cold is making a corpse of me. Some god
inveigled me to come without a cloak.
No help for it now; too late.'

Next thing I knew
he had a scheme all ready in his mind—
and what a man he was for schemes and battles!
Speaking under his breath to me, he murmured:

'Quiet; none of the rest should hear you.'

Then,
propping his head on his forearm, he said:

'Listen, lads, I had an ominous dream,
the point being how far forward from our ships
and lines we've come. Someone should volunteer
to tell the corps commander, Agamémnon;
he may reinforce us from the base.'

At this,
Thoas jumped up, the young son of Andraimon,
put down his crimson cloak and headed off,
running shoreward.
Wrapped in that man's cloak
how gratefully I lay in the bitter dark
until the dawn came stitched in gold! I wish
I had that sap and fiber in me now!"

Then—O my swineherd!—you replied, Eumaios:

"That was a fine story, and well told,
not a word out of place, not a pointless word.
No, you'll not sleep cold for lack of cover,

or any other comfort one should give
to a needy guest. However, in the morning,
you must go flapping in the same old clothes.
Shirts and cloaks are few here; every man
has one change only. When our prince arrives,
the son of Odysseus, he will make you gifts—
cloak, tunic, everything—and grant you passage
wherever you care to go."

On this he rose
and placed the bed of balsam near the fire,
strewing sheepskins on top, and skins of goats.
Odysseus lay down. His host threw over him
a heavy blanket cloak, his own reserve
against the winter wind when it came wild.
So there Odysseus dropped off to sleep,
while herdsmen slept nearby. But not the swineherd:
not in the hut could he lie down in peace,
but now equipped himself for the night outside;
and this rejoiced Odysseus' heart, to see him
care for the herd so, while his lord was gone.
He hung a sharp sword from his shoulder, gathered
a great cloak round him, close, to break the wind,
and pulled a shaggy goatskin on his head.
Then, to keep at a distance dogs or men,
he took a sharpened lance, and went to rest
under a hollow rock where swine were sleeping
out of the wind and rain.

BOOK XV

[*How They Came to Ithaka*]

South into Lakedaimon
into the land where greens are wide for dancing
Athena went, to put in mind of home
her great-hearted hero's honored son,
rousing him to return.

And there she found him
with Nestor's lad in the late night at rest
under the portico of Meneláos,
the famous king. Stilled by the power of slumber
the son of Nestor lay, but honeyed sleep
had not yet taken in her arms Telémakhos.
All through the starlit night, with open eyes,
he pondered what he had heard about his father,
until at his bedside grey-eyed Athena
towered and said:

"The brave thing now, Telémakhos,
would be to end this journey far from home.
All that you own you left behind
with men so lost to honor in your house

they may devour it all, shared out among them.
How will your journey save you then?
Go quickly
to the lord of the great war cry, Meneláos;
press him to send you back. You may yet find
the queen your mother in her rooms alone.
It seems her father and her kinsmen say
Eurýmakhos is the man for her to marry.
He has outdone the suitors, all the rest,
in gifts to her, and made his pledges double.
Check him, or he will have your lands and chattels[7]
in spite of you.
You know a woman's pride
at bringing riches to the man she marries.
As to her girlhood husband, her first children,
he is forgotten, being dead—and they
no longer worry her.
So act alone.
Go back; entrust your riches to the servant
worthiest in your eyes, until the gods
make known what beauty you yourself shall marry.

This too I have to tell you: now take heed:
the suitors' ringleaders are hot for murder,
waiting in the channel between Ithaka
and Samê's rocky side; they mean to kill you
before you can set foot ashore. I doubt
they'll bring it off. Dark earth instead
may take to her cold bed a few brave suitors
who preyed upon your cattle.
Bear well out
in your good ship, to eastward of the islands,
and sail again by night. Someone immortal
who cares for you will make a fair wind blow.
Touch at the first beach, go ashore, and send
your ship and crew around to port by sea,
while you go inland to the forester,
your old friend, loyal keeper of the swine.
Remain that night with him; send him to town
to tell your watchful mother Penélopê
that you are back from Pylos safe and sound."

With this Athena left him for Olympos.
He swung his foot across and gave a kick
and said to the son of Nestor:

"Open your eyes,
Peisístratos. Get our team into harness.
We have a long day's journey."

7. The Greek could also mean "be careful she [Penélopê] doesn't carry off, against your will, some of your property," i.e., for her new husband. This would explain why Athena tells Telémakhos (lines 33–34) to turn the property over to the servant he has most confidence in. The suggestion that Penélopê is planning to marry Eurýmakhos and take Telémakhos's property with her is not to be taken seriously; Athena uses it to get Telémakhos moving.

Nestor's son
turned over and answered him:

"It is still night,
and no moon. Can we drive now? We can not,
itch as we may for the road home. Dawn is near.
Allow the captain of spearmen, Meneláos,
time to pack our car with gifts and time
to speak a gracious word, sending us off.
A guest remembers all his days
that host who makes provision for him kindly."

The Dawn soon took her throne of gold, and Lord
Meneláos, clarion in battle,
rose from where he lay beside the beauty
of Helen with her shining hair. He strode
into the hall nearby.
Hearing him come,
Odysseus' son pulled on his snowy tunic
over the skin, gathered his long cape
about his breadth of shoulder like a captain,
the heir of King Odysseus. At the door
he stood and said:

"Lord Marshal, Meneláos,
send me home now to my own dear country:
longing has come upon me to go home."

The lord of the great war cry said at once:

"If you are longing to go home, Telémakhos,
I would not keep you for the world, not I.
I'd think myself or any other host
as ill-mannered for over-friendliness
as for hostility.
Measure is best in everything.
To send a guest packing, or cling to him
when he's in haste—one sin equals the other.
'Good entertaining ends with no detaining.'
Only let me load your car with gifts
and fine ones, you shall see.
I'll bid the women
set out breakfast from the larder stores;
honor and appetite—we'll attend to both
before a long day's journey overland.
Or would you care to try the Argive midlands
and Hellas, in my company? I'll harness
my own team, and take you through the towns.
Guests like ourselves no lord will turn away;
each one will make one gift, at least,
to carry home with us: tripod or cauldron
wrought in bronze, mule team, or golden cup."

Clearheaded Telémakhos replied:

"Lord Marshal
Meneláos, royal son of Atreus,
I must return to my own hearth. I left
no one behind as guardian of my property.
This going abroad for news of a great father—
heaven forbid it be my own undoing,
or any precious thing be lost at home."

At this the tall king, clarion in battle,
called to his lady and her waiting women
to give them breakfast from the larder stores.
Eteóneus, the son of Boethoös, came
straight from bed, from where he lodged nearby,
and Meneláos ordered a fire lit
for broiling mutton. The king's man obeyed.
Then down to the cedar chamber Meneláos
walked with Helen and Prince Megapénthês.
Amid the gold he had in that place lying
the son of Atreus picked a wine cup, wrought
with handles left and right, and told his son
to take a silver winebowl.
Helen lingered
near the deep coffers filled with gowns, her own
handiwork.
Tall goddess among women,
she lifted out one robe of state so royal,
adorned and brilliant with embroidery,
deep in the chest it shimmered like a star.
Now all three turned back to the door to greet
Telémakhos. And red-haired Meneláos
cried out to him:

"O prince Telémakhos,
may Hêra's Lord of Thunder see you home
and bring you to the welcome you desire!
Here are your gifts—perfect and precious things
I wish to make your own, out of my treasure."

And gently the great captain, son of Atreus,
handed him the goblet. Megapénthês
carried the winebowl glinting silvery
to set before him, and the Lady Helen
drew near, so that he saw her cheek's pure line.
She held the gown and murmured:

"I, too,
bring you a gift, dear child, and here it is;
remember Helen's hands by this; keep it
for your own bride, your joyful wedding day;
let your dear mother guard it in her chamber.

My blessing: may you come soon to your island,
home to your timbered hall."

So she bestowed it,
and happily he took it. These fine things
Peisístratos packed well in the wicker carrier,
admiring every one. Then Meneláos
led the two guests in to take their seats
on thrones and easy chairs in the great hall.
Now came a maid to tip a golden jug
of water over a silver finger bowl,
and drew the polished tables up beside them;
the larder mistress brought her tray of loaves,
with many savories to lavish on them;
viands were served by Eteóneus, and wine
by Meneláos' son. Then every hand
reached out upon good meat and drink to take them,
driving away hunger and thirst. At last,
Telémakhos and Nestor's son led out
their team to harness, mounted their bright car,
and drove down under the echoing entrance way,
while red-haired Meneláos, Atreus' son,
walked alongside with a golden cup—
wine for the wayfarers to spill at parting.
Then by the tugging team he stood, and spoke
over the horses' heads:

"Farewell, my lads.
Homage to Nestor, the benevolent king;
in my time he was fatherly to me,
when the flower of Akhaia warred on Troy."

Telémakhos made this reply:

"No fear
but we shall bear at least as far as Nestor
your messages, great king. How I could wish
to bring them home to Ithaka! If only
Odysseus were there, if he could hear me tell
of all the courtesy I have had from you,
returning with your finery and your treasure."
Even as he spoke, a beat of wings went skyward
off to the right—a mountain eagle, grappling
a white goose in his talons, heavy prey
hooked from a farmyard. Women and men-at-arms
made hubbub, running up, as he flew over,
but then he wheeled hard right before the horses—
a sight that made the whole crowd cheer, with hearts
lifting in joy. Peisístratos called out:

"Read us the sign, O Meneláos, Lord
Marshal of armies! Was the god revealing
something thus to you, or to ourselves?"

At this the old friend of the god of battle
groped in his mind for the right thing to say,
but regal Helen put in quickly:

"Listen:
I can tell you—tell what the omen means,
as light is given me, and as I see it
point by point fulfilled. The beaked eagle
flew from the wild mountain of his fathers
to take for prey the tame house bird. Just so,
Odysseus, back from his hard trials and wandering,
will soon come down in fury on his house.
He may be there today, and a black hour
he brings upon the suitors."

Telémakhos
gazed and said:

"May Zeus, the lord of Hêra,
make it so! In far-off Ithaka, all my life,
I shall invoke you as a goddess, lady."

He let the whip fall, and the restive mares
broke forward at a canter through the town
into the open country.
All that day
they kept their harness shaking, side by side,
until at sundown when the roads grew dim
they made a halt at Pherai. There Dióklês
son of Ortílokhos whom Alpheios fathered,
welcomed the young men, and they slept the night.
Up when the young Dawn's finger tips of rose
opened in the east, they hitched the team
once more to the painted car
and steered out westward through the echoing gate,
whipping their fresh horses into a run.
Approaching Pylos Height at that day's end,
Telémakhos appealed to the son of Nestor:

"Could you, I wonder, do a thing I'll tell you,
supposing you agree?
We take ourselves to be true friends—in age
alike, and bound by ties between our fathers,
and now by partnership in this adventure.
Prince, do not take me roundabout,
but leave me at the ship, else the old king
your father will detain me overnight
for love of guests, when I should be at sea."

The son of Nestor nodded, thinking swiftly
how best he could oblige his friend.
Here was his choice: to pull the team hard over

along the beach till he could rein them in
beside the ship. Unloading Meneláos'
royal keepsakes into the stern sheets,
he sang out:

"Now for action! Get aboard,
and call your men, before I break the news
at home in hall to father. Who knows better
the old man's heart than I? If you delay,
he will not let you go, but he'll descend on you
in person and imperious; no turning
back with empty hands for him, believe me,
once his blood is up."

He shook the reins
to the lovely mares with long manes in the wind,
guiding them full tilt toward his father's hall.
Telémakhos called in the crew, and told them:

"Get everything shipshape aboard this craft;
we pull out now, and put sea miles behind us."

The listening men obeyed him, climbing in
to settle on their benches by the rowlocks,
while he stood watchful by the stern. He poured out
offerings there, and prayers to Athena.

Now a strange man came up to him, an easterner
fresh from spilling blood in distant Argos,
a hunted man. Gifted in prophecy,
he had as forebear that Melampous, wizard
who lived of old in Pylos, mother city
of western flocks.[8]

Melampous, a rich lord,
had owned a house unmatched among the Pylians,
until the day came when king Neleus, noblest
in that age, drove him from his native land.
And Neleus for a year's term sequestered
Melampous' fields and flocks, while he lay bound
hand and foot in the keep of Phylakos.
Beauty of Neleus' daughter put him there
and sombre folly the inbreaking Fury

8. The complicated story that follows (obscure in some of its details) gives us the genealogical background of the young man who comes up to Telémakhos. His name, as we learn only at the end of the genealogy, is Theoklýmenos, and he has an important role to play in the last part of the *Odyssey*. His gift for prophecy is hereditary; his ancestor Melampous had it. Melampous's brother (who lived in Pylos under King Neleus, Nestor's father) asked for the hand of Neleus's daughter. Neleus demanded as bride-price the herds of cattle of a neighboring lord, Phylakos. Melampous tried to steal the cattle for his brother, was caught, and was imprisoned. In prison he heard the worms in the roof beams announce that the wood was almost eaten through, and he predicted the collapse of the roof. Phylakos, impressed, released him, with the cattle; his brother was given the bride. Melampous then left for Argos, where he settled and prospered. One of his great-grandsons was the prophet Amphiaraos, who foresaw that if he joined the champions who went to besiege Thebes (The Seven against Thebes) he would lose his life (see n. 9, p. 355). Melampous's son Mantios had a son named Polypheidês, and it is his son Theoklýmenos who now begs Telémakhos for a place in his ship.

thrust upon him. But he gave the slip
to death, and drove the bellowing herd of Iphiklos
from Phylakê to Pylos, there to claim
the bride that ordeal won him from the king.
He led her to his brother's house, and went on
eastward into another land, the bluegrass
plain of Argos. Destiny held for him
rule over many Argives. Here he married,
built a great manor house, fathered Antíphatês
and Mantios, commanders both, of whom
Antíphatês begot Oikleiês
and Oikleiês the firebrand Amphiaraos.
This champion the lord of stormcloud, Zeus,
and strong Apollo loved; nor had he ever
to cross the doorsill into dim old age.
A woman, bought by trinkets, gave him over
to be cut down in the assault on Thebes.
His sons were Alkmáon and Amphílokhos.
In the meantime Lord Mantios begot
Polypheidês, the prophet, and
Kleitos—famous name! For Dawn in silks
of gold carried off Kleitos for his beauty
to live among the gods. But Polypheidês,
high-hearted and exalted by Apollo
above all men for prophecy, withdrew
to Hyperesia[9] when his father angered him.
He lived on there, foretelling to the world
the shape of things to come.
His son it was,
Theoklýmenos, who came upon Telémakhos
as he poured out the red wine in the sand
near his trim ship, with prayer to Athena;
and he called out, approaching:

"Friend, well met
here at libation before going to sea.
I pray you by the wine you spend, and by
your god, your own life, and your company;
enlighten me, and let the truth be known.
Who are you? Of what city and what parents?"

Telémakhos turned to him and replied:

"Stranger, as truly as may be, I'll tell you.
I am from Ithaka, where I was born;
my father is, or he once was, Odysseus.
But he's a long time gone, and dead, may be;
and that is what I took ship with my friends
to find out—for he left long years ago."

Said Theoklýmenos in reply:

9. Near Argos.

"I too
have had to leave my home. I killed a cousin.
In the wide grazing lands of Argos live
many kinsmen of his and friends in power,
great among the Akhaians. These I fled.
Death and vengeance at my back, as Fate
has turned now, I came wandering overland.
Give me a plank aboard your ship, I beg,
or they will kill me. They are on my track."

Telémakhos made answer:

"No two ways
about it. Will I pry you from our gunnel
when you are desperate to get to sea?
Come aboard; share what we have, and welcome."

He took the bronze-shod lance from the man's hand
and laid it down full-length on deck; then swung
his own weight after it aboard the cutter,
taking position aft, making a place
for Theoklýmenos near him. The stern lines
were slacked off, and Telémakhos commanded:

"Rig the mast; make sail!" Nimbly they ran
to push the fir pole high and step it firm
amidships in the box, make fast the forestays,
and hoist aloft the white sail on its halyards.
A following wind came down from grey-eyed Athena,
blowing brisk through heaven, and so steady
the cutter lapped up miles of salt blue sea,
passing Krounoi abeam and Khalkis estuary[1]
at sundown when the sea ways all grew dark.
Then, by Athena's wind borne on, the ship
rounded Pheai by night and coasted Elis,
the green domain of the Epeioi; thence
he put her head north toward the running pack
of islets, wondering if by sailing wide
he sheered off Death, or would be caught.
That night
Odysseus and the swineherd supped again
with herdsmen in their mountain hut. At ease
when appetite and thirst were turned away,
Odysseus, while he talked, observed the swineherd
to see if he were hospitable still—
if yet again the man would make him stay
under his roof, or send him off to town.

"Listen," he said, "Eumaios; listen, lads.
At daybreak I must go and try my luck

1. The precise location of these places is disputed, but the mention of Elis in line 336 shows that they are all on the west coast of the Peloponnese, south of the Gulf of Corinth. The Olympic Games were held in Elis.

around the port. I burden you too long.
Direct me, put me on the road with someone.
Nothing else for it but to play the beggar
in populous parts. I'll get a cup or loaf,
maybe, from some householder. If I go
as far as the great hall of King Odysseus
I might tell Queen Penélopê my news.
Or I can drift inside among the suitors
to see what alms they give, rich as they are.
If they have whims, I'm deft in ways of service—
that I can say, and you may know for sure.
By grace of Hermês the Wayfinder, patron
of mortal tasks, the god who honors toil,
no man can do a chore better than I can.
Set me to build a fire, or chop wood,
cook or carve, mix wine and serve—or anything
inferior men attend to for the gentry."

Now you were furious at this, Eumaios,
and answered—O my swineherd!—

"Friend, friend,
how could this fantasy take hold of you?
You dally with your life, and nothing less,
if you feel drawn to mingle in that company—
reckless, violent, and famous for it
out to the rim of heaven. Slaves
they have, but not like you. No—theirs are boys
in fresh cloaks and tunics, with pomade
ever on their sleek heads, and pretty faces.
These are their minions, while their tables gleam
and groan under big roasts, with loaves and wine.
Stay with us here. No one is burdened by you,
neither myself nor any of my hands.
Wait here until Odysseus' son returns.
You shall have clothing from him, cloak and tunic,
and passage where your heart desires to go."

The noble and enduring man replied:

"May you be dear to Zeus for this, Eumaios,
even as you are to me. Respite from pain
you give me—and from homelessness. In life
there's nothing worse than knocking about the world,
no bitterness we vagabonds are spared
when the curst belly rages! Well, you master it
and me, making me wait for the king's son.
But now, come, tell me:
what of Odysseus' mother, and his father
whom he took leave of on the sill of age?
Are they under the sun's rays, living still,
or gone down long ago to lodge with Death?"

To this the rugged herdsman answered:

"Aye,
that I can tell you; it is briefly told.
Laërtês lives, but daily in his hall
prays for the end of life and soul's delivery,
heartbroken as he is for a son long gone
and for his lady. Sorrow, when she died,
aged and enfeebled him like a green tree stricken;
but pining for her son, her brilliant son,
wore out her life.
Would god no death so sad
might come to benefactors dear as she!
I loved always to ask and hear about her
while she lived, although she lived in sorrow.
For she had brought me up with her own daughter,
Princess Ktimenê, her youngest child.
We were alike in age and nursed as equals
nearly, till in the flower of our years
they gave her, married her, to a Samian prince,[2]
taking his many gifts. For my own portion
her mother gave new clothing, cloak and sandals,
and sent me to the woodland. Well she loved me.
Ah, how I miss that family! It is true
the blissful gods prosper my work; I have
meat and drink to spare for those I prize;
but so removed I am, I have no speech
with my sweet mistress, now that evil days
and overbearing men darken her house.
Tenants all hanker for good talk and gossip
around their lady, and a snack in hall,
a cup or two before they take the road
to their home acres, each one bearing home
some gift to cheer his heart."

The great tactician
answered:

"You were still a child, I see,
when exiled somehow from your parents' land.
Tell me, had it been sacked in war, the city
of spacious ways in which they made their home,
your father and your gentle mother? Or
were you kidnapped alone, brought here by sea
huddled with sheep in some foul pirate squadron,
to this landowner's hall? He paid your ransom?"

The master of the woodland answered:

"Friend,
now that you show an interest in that matter,

2. From Samê, a nearby island or town.

attend me quietly, be at your ease,
and drink your wine. These autumn nights are long,
ample for story-telling and for sleep.
You need not go to bed before the hour;
sleeping from dusk to dawn's a dull affair.
Let any other here who wishes, though,
retire to rest. At daybreak let him breakfast
and take the king's own swine into the wilderness.
Here's a tight roof; we'll drink on, you and I,
and ease our hearts of hardships we remember,
sharing old times. In later days a man
can find a charm in old adversity,
exile and pain. As to your question, now:

A certain island, Syriê by name—
you may have heard the name—lies off Ortýgia[3]
due west, and holds the sunsets of the year.
Not very populous, but good for grazing
sheep and kine; rich too in wine and grain.
No dearth is ever known there, no disease
wars on the folk, of ills that plague mankind;
but when the townsmen reach old age, Apollo
with his longbow of silver comes, and Artemis,
showering arrows of mild death.
Two towns
divide the farmlands of that whole domain,
and both were ruled by Ktêsios, my father,
Orménos' heir, and a great godlike man.

Now one day some of those renowned seafaring
men, sea-dogs, Phoinikians, came ashore
with bags of gauds for trading. Father had
in our household a woman of Phoinikia,
a handsome one, and highly skilled. Well, she
gave in to the seductions of those rovers.
One of them found her washing near the mooring
and lay with her, making such love to her
as women in their frailty are confused by,
even the best of them.
In due course, then,
he asked her who she was and where she hailed from:
and nodding toward my father's roof, she said:

'I am of Sidon town, smithy of bronze
for all the East. Arubas Pasha's daughter.
Taphian pirates caught me in a byway
and sold me into slavery overseas
in this man's home. He could afford my ransom.'

3. Another name for Delos, the central island of the Cyclades, but also the name of the central island of the city of Syracuse in Sicily. However, the fact that on Syriê there is no disease and that everyone there dies painlessly suggests that it is not located in this world at all—like Phaiákia, it is in fairyland.

The sailor who had lain with her replied:

'Why not ship out with us on the run homeward,
and see your father's high-roofed hall again,
your father and your mother? Still in Sidon
and still rich, they are said to be.'

She answered:

'It could be done, that, if you sailors take
oath I'll be given passage home unharmed.'

Well, soon she had them swearing it all pat
as she desired, repeating every syllable,
whereupon she warned them:

'Not a word
about our meeting here! Never call out to me
when any of you see me in the lane
or at the well. Some visitor might bear
tales to the old man. If he guessed the truth,
I'd be chained up, your lives would be in peril.
No: keep it secret. Hurry with your peddling,
and when your hold is filled with livestock, send
a message to me at the manor hall.
Gold I'll bring, whatever comes to hand,
and something else, too, as my passage fee—
the master's child, my charge: a boy so high,
bright for his age; he runs with me on errands.
I'd take him with me happily; his price
would be I know not what in sale abroad.'

Her bargain made, she went back to the manor.
But they were on the island all that year,
getting by trade a cargo of our cattle;
until, the ship at length being laden full,
ready for sea, they sent a messenger
to the Phoinikian woman. Shrewd he was,
this fellow who came round my father's hall,
showing a golden chain all strung with amber,
a necklace. Maids in waiting and my mother
passed it from hand to hand, admiring it,
engaging they would buy it. But that dodger,
as soon as he had caught the woman's eye
and nodded, slipped away to join the ship.
She took my hand and led me through the court
into the portico. There by luck she found
winecups and tables still in place—for Father's
attendant counselors had dined just now
before they went to the assembly. Quickly
she hid three goblets in her bellying dress
to carry with her while I tagged along

in my bewilderment. The sun went down
and all the lanes grew dark as we descended,
skirting the harbor in our haste to where
those traders of Phoinikia held their ship.
All went aboard at once and put to sea,
taking the two of us. A favoring wind
blew from the power of heaven. We sailed on
six nights and days without event. Then Zeus
the son of Kronos added one more noon—and sudden
arrows from Artemis pierced the woman's heart.
Stone-dead she dropped
into the sloshing bilge the way a tern
plummets; and the sailors heaved her over
as tender pickings for the seals and fish.
Now I was left in dread, alone, while wind
and current bore them on to Ithaka.
Laërtês purchased me. That was the way
I first laid eyes upon this land."

                                        Odysseus,
the kingly man, replied:

                                "You rouse my pity,
telling what you endured when you were young.
But surely Zeus put good alongside ill:
torn from your own far home, you had the luck
to come into a kind man's service, generous
with food and drink. And a good life you lead,
unlike my own, all spent in barren roaming
from one country to the next, till now."

So the two men talked on, into the night,
leaving few hours for sleep before the Dawn
stepped up to her bright chair.
                                        The ship now drifting
under the island lee, Telémakhos'
companions took in sail and mast, unshipped
the oars and rowed ashore. They moored her stern
by the stout hawser lines, tossed out the bow stones,
and waded in beyond the wash of ripples
to mix their wine and cook their morning meal.
When they had turned back hunger and thirst, Telémakhos
arose to give the order of the day.

"Pull for the town," he said, "and berth our ship,
while I go inland across country. Later,
this evening, after looking at my farms,
I'll join you in the city. When day comes
I hope to celebrate our crossing, feasting
everyone on good red meat and wine."

His noble passenger, Theoklýmenos,
now asked:

"What as to me, my dear young fellow,
where shall I go? Will I find lodging here
with some one of the lords of stony Ithaka?
Or go straight to your mother's hall and yours?"

Telémakhos turned round to him and said:

"I should myself invite you to our hall
if things were otherwise; there'd be no lack
of entertainment for you. As it stands,
no place could be more wretched for a guest
while I'm away. Mother will never see you;
she almost never shows herself at home
to the suitors there, but stays in her high chamber
weaving upon her loom. No, let me name
another man for you to go to visit:
Eurýmakhos, the honored son of Pólybos.
In Ithaka they are dazzled by him now—
the strongest of their princes, bent on making
mother and all Odysseus' wealth his own.
Zeus on Olympos only knows
if some dark hour for them will intervene."

The words were barely spoken, when a hawk,
Apollo's courier, flew up on the right,
clutching a dove and plucking her—so feathers
floated down to the ground between Telémakhos
and the moored cutter. Theoklýmenos
called him apart and gripped his hand, whispering:

"A god spoke in this bird-sign on the right.
I knew it when I saw the hawk fly over us.
There is no kinglier house than yours, Telémakhos,
here in the realm of Ithaka. Your family
will be in power forever."

The young prince,
clear in spirit, answered:

"Be it so,
friend, as you say. And may you know as well
the friendship of my house, and many gifts
from me, so everyone may call you fortunate."

He called a trusted crewman named Peiraios,
and said to him:

"Peiraios, son of Klýtios,
can I rely on you again as ever, most
of all the friends who sailed with me to Pylos?
Take this man home with you, take care of him,
treat him with honor, till I come."

To this
Peiraios the good spearman answered:

"Aye,
stay in the wild country while you will,
I shall be looking after him, Telémakhos.
He will not lack good lodging."
Down to the ship
he turned, and boarded her, and called the others
to cast off the stern lines and come aboard.
So the men climbed in to sit beside the rowlocks.
Telémakhos now tied his sandals on
and lifted his tough spear from the ship's deck;
hawsers were taken in, and they shoved off
to reach the town by way of the open sea
as he commanded them—royal Odysseus'
own dear son, Telémakhos.
On foot
and swiftly he went up toward the stockade
where swine were penned in hundreds, and at night
the guardian of the swine, the forester,
slept under arms on duty for his masters.

BOOK XVI

[*Father and Son*]

But there were two men in the mountain hut—
Odysseus and the swineherd. At first light
blowing their fire up, they cooked their breakfast
and sent their lads out, driving herds to root
in the tall timber.
When Telémakhos came,
the wolvish troop of watchdogs only fawned on him
as he advanced. Odysseus heard them go
and heard the light crunch of a man's footfall—
at which he turned quickly to say:

"Eumaios,
here is one of your crew come back, or maybe
another friend: the dogs are out there snuffling
belly down; not one has even growled.
I can hear footsteps—"

But before he finished
his tall son stood at the door.
The swineherd
rose in surprise, letting a bowl and jug
tumble from his fingers. Going forward,
he kissed the young man's head, his shining eyes
and both hands, while his own tears brimmed and fell.
Think of a man whose dear and only son,
born to him in exile, reared with labor,

has lived ten years abroad and now returns:
how would that man embrace his son! Just so
the herdsman clapped his arms around Telémakhos
and covered him with kisses—for he knew
the lad had got away from death. He said:

"Light of my days, Telémakhos,
you made it back! When you took ship for Pylos
I never thought to see you here again.
Come in, dear child, and let me feast my eyes;
here you are, home from the distant places!
How rarely anyway, you visit us,
your own men, and your own woods and pastures!
Always in the town, a man would think
you loved the suitors' company, those dogs!"

Telémakhos with his clear candor said:

"I am with you, Uncle. See now, I have come
because I wanted to see you first, to hear from you
if Mother stayed at home—or is she married
off to someone and Odysseus' bed
left empty for some gloomy spider's weaving?"

Gently the forester replied to this:

"At home indeed your mother is, poor lady,
still in the women's hall. Her nights and days
are wearied out with grieving."

Stepping back
he took the bronze-shod lance, and the young prince
entered the cabin over the worn door stone.
Odysseus moved aside, yielding his couch,
but from across the room Telémakhos checked him:

"Friend, sit down; we'll find another chair
in our own hut. Here is the man to make one!"

The swineherd, when the quiet man sank down,
built a new pile of evergreens and fleeces—
a couch for the dear son of great Odysseus—
then gave them trenchers of good meat, left over
from the roast pork of yesterday, and heaped up
willow baskets full of bread, and mixed
an ivy bowl of honey-hearted wine.
Then he in turn sat down, facing Odysseus,
their hands went out upon the meat and drink
as they fell to, ridding themselves of hunger,
until Telémakhos paused and said:

"Oh, Uncle,
what's your friend's home port? How did he come?
Who were the sailors brought him here to Ithaka?
I doubt if he came walking on the sea."

And you replied, Eumaios—O my swineherd—

"Son, the truth about him is soon told.
His home land, and a broad land, too, is Krete,
but he has knocked about the world, he says,
for years, as the Powers wove his life. Just now
he broke away from a shipload of Thesprotians
to reach my hut. I place him in your hands.
Act as you will. He wishes your protection."

The young man said:

"Eumaios, my protection!
The notion cuts me to the heart. How can I
receive your friend at home? I am not old enough
or trained in arms. Could I defend myself
if someone picked a fight with me?
Besides,
mother is in a quandary, whether to stay with me
as mistress of our household, honoring
her lord's bed, and opinion in the town,
or take the best Akhaian who comes her way—
the one who offers most.
I'll undertake,
at all events, to clothe your friend for winter,
now he is with you. Tunic and cloak of wool,
a good broadsword, and sandals—these are his.
I can arrange to send him where he likes
or you may keep him in your cabin here.
I shall have bread and wine sent up; you need not
feel any pinch on his behalf.
Impossible
to let him stay in hall, among the suitors.
They are drunk, drunk on impudence, they might
injure my guest—and how could I bear that?
How could a single man take on those odds?
Not even a hero could.
The suitors are too strong."

At this the noble and enduring man, Odysseus,
addressed his son:

"Kind prince, it may be fitting
for me to speak a word. All that you say
gives me an inward wound as I sit listening.
I mean this wanton game they play, these fellows,
riding roughshod over you in your own house,

admirable as you are. But tell me,
are you resigned to being bled? The townsmen,
stirred up against you, are they, by some oracle?
Your brothers—can you say your brothers fail you?
A man should feel his kin, at least, behind him
in any clash, when a real fight is coming.
If my heart were as young as yours, if I were
son of Odysseus, or the man himself,
I'd rather have my head cut from my shoulders
by some slashing adversary, if I
brought no hurt upon that crew! Suppose
I went down, being alone, before the lot,
better, I say, to die at home in battle
than see these insupportable things, day after
day the stranger cuffed, the women slaves
dragged here and there, shame in the lovely rooms,
the wine drunk up in rivers, sheer waste
of pointless feasting, never at an end!"

Telémakhos replied:

"Friend, I'll explain to you.
There is no rancor in the town against me,
no fault of brothers, whom a man should feel
behind him when a fight is in the making;
no, no—in our family the First Born
of Heaven, Zeus, made single sons the rule.
Arkeísios had but one, Laërtês; he
in his turn fathered only one, Odysseus,
who left me in his hall alone, too young
to be of any use to him.
And so you see why enemies fill our house
in these days: all the princes of the islands,
Doulíkhion, Samê, wooded Zakýnthos,
Ithaka, too—lords of our island rock—
eating our house up as they court my mother.
She cannot put an end to it; she dare not
bar the marriage that she hates; and they
devour all my substance and my cattle,
and who knows when they'll slaughter me as well?
It rests upon the gods' great knees.
Uncle,
go down at once and tell the Lady Penélopê
that I am back from Pylos, safe and sound.
I stay here meanwhile. You will give your message
and then return. Let none of the Akhaians
hear it; they have a mind to do me harm."

To this, Eumaios, you replied:

"I know.
But make this clear, now—should I not likewise

call on Laërtês with your news? Hard hit
by sorrow though he was, mourning Odysseus,
he used to keep an eye upon his farm.
He had what meals he pleased, with his own folk.
But now no more, not since you sailed for Pylos;
he has not taken food or drink, I hear,
sitting all day, blind to the work of harvest,
groaning, while the skin shrinks on his bones."

Telémakhos answered:

"One more misery,
but we had better leave it so.
If men could choose, and have their choice, in everything,
we'd have my father home.
Turn back
when you have done your errand, as you must,
not to be caught alone in the countryside.[4]
But wait—you may tell Mother
to send our old housekeeper on the quiet
and quickly; she can tell the news to Grandfather."

The swineherd, roused, reached out to get his sandals,
tied them on, and took the road.

Who else
beheld this but Athena? From the air
she walked, taking the form of a tall woman,
handsome and clever at her craft, and stood
beyond the gate in plain sight of Odysseus,
unseen, though, by Telémakhos, unguessed,
for not to everyone will gods appear.
Odysseus noticed her; so did the dogs,
who cowered whimpering away from her. She only
nodded, signing to him with her brows,
a sign he recognized. Crossing the yard,
he passed out through the gate in the stockade
to face the goddess. There she said to him:

"Son of Laërtês and the gods of old,
Odysseus, master of land ways and sea ways,
dissemble to your son no longer now.
The time has come: tell him how you together
will bring doom on the suitors in the town.
I shall not be far distant then, for I
myself desire battle."

Saying no more,
she tipped her golden wand upon the man,
making his cloak pure white, and the knit tunic

4. The Greek says something more like "and don't go wandering round the countryside after him [Laërtês]."

fresh around him. Lithe and young she made him,
ruddy with sun, his jawline clean, the beard
no longer grey upon his chin. And she
withdrew when she had done.
Then Lord Odysseus
reappeared—and his son was thunderstruck.
Fear in his eyes, he looked down and away
as though it were a god, and whispered:

"Stranger,
you are no longer what you were just now!
Your cloak is new; even your skin! You are
one of the gods who rule the sweep of heaven!
Be kind to us, we'll make you fair oblation
and gifts of hammered gold. Have mercy on us!"

The noble and enduring man replied:

"No god. Why take me for a god? No, no.
I am that father whom your boyhood lacked
and suffered pain for lack of. I am he."

Held back too long, the tears ran down his cheeks
as he embraced his son.
Only Telémakhos,
uncomprehending, wild
with incredulity, cried out:

"You cannot
be my father Odysseus! Meddling spirits
conceived this trick to twist the knife in me!
No man of woman born could work these wonders
by his own craft, unless a god came into it
with ease to turn him young or old at will.
I swear you were in rags and old,
and here you stand like one of the immortals!"

Odysseus brought his ranging mind to bear
and said:

"This is not princely, to be swept
away by wonder at your father's presence.
No other Odysseus will ever come,
for he and I are one, the same; his bitter
fortune and his wanderings are mine.
Twenty years gone, and I am back again
on my own island.
As for my change of skin,
that is a charm Athena, Hope of Soldiers,[5]
uses as she will; she has the knack

5. Athena was a warrior goddess.

to make me seem a beggar man sometimes
and sometimes young, with finer clothes about me.
It is no hard thing for the gods of heaven
to glorify a man or bring him low."

When he had spoken, down he sat.
Then, throwing
his arms around this marvel of a father
Telémakhos began to weep. Salt tears
rose from the wells of longing in both men,
and cries burst from both as keen and fluttering
as those of the great taloned hawk,
whose nestlings farmers take before they fly.
So helplessly they cried, pouring out tears,
and might have gone on weeping so till sundown,
had not Telémakhos said:

"Dear father! Tell me
what kind of vessel put you here ashore
on Ithaka? Your sailors, who were they?
I doubt you made it, walking on the sea!"

Then said Odysseus, who had borne the barren sea:

"Only plain truth shall I tell you, child.
Great seafarers, the Phaiákians, gave me passage
as they give other wanderers. By night
over the open ocean, while I slept,
they brought me in their cutter, set me down
on Ithaka, with gifts of bronze and gold
and stores of woven things. By the gods' will
these lie all hidden in a cave. I came
to this wild place, directed by Athena,
so that we might lay plans to kill our enemies.
Count up the suitors for me, let me know
what men at arms are there, how many men.
I must put all my mind to it, to see
if we two by ourselves can take them on
or if we should look round for help."

Telémakhos
replied:

"O Father, all my life your fame
as a fighting man has echoed in my ears—
your skill with weapons and the tricks of war—
but what you speak of is a staggering thing,
beyond imagining, for me. How can two men
do battle with a houseful in their prime?
For I must tell you this is no affair
of ten or even twice ten men, but scores,
throngs of them. You shall see, here and now.

The number from Doulíkhion alone
is fifty-two picked men, with armorers,
a half dozen; twenty-four came from Samê,
twenty from Zakýnthos; our own island
accounts for twelve, high-ranked, and their retainers,
Medôn the crier, and the Master Harper,
besides a pair of handymen at feasts.
If we go in against all these
I fear we pay in salt blood for your vengeance.
You must think hard if you would conjure up
the fighting strength to take us through."

Odysseus
who had endured the long war and the sea
answered:

"I'll tell you now.
Suppose Athena's arm is over us, and Zeus
her father's, must I rack my brains for more?"

Clearheaded Telémakhos looked hard and said:

"Those two are great defenders, no one doubts it,
but throned in the serene clouds overhead;
other affairs of men and gods they have
to rule over."

And the hero answered:

"Before long they will stand to right and left of us
in combat, in the shouting, when the test comes—
our nerve against the suitors' in my hall.
Here is your part: at break of day tomorrow
home with you, go mingle with our princes.
The swineherd later on will take me down
the port-side trail—a beggar, by my looks,
hangdog and old. If they make fun of me
in my own courtyard, let your ribs cage up
your springing heart, no matter what I suffer,
no matter if they pull me by the heels
or practice shots at me, to drive me out.
Look on, hold down your anger. You may even
plead with them, by heaven! in gentle terms
to quit their horseplay—not that they will heed you,
rash as they are, facing their day of wrath.
Now fix the next step in your mind.
Athena,
counseling me, will give me word, and I
shall signal to you, nodding: at that point
round up all armor, lances, gear of war
left in our hall, and stow the lot away
back in the vaulted store room. When the suitors

miss those arms and question you, be soft
in what you say: answer:

'I thought I'd move them
out of the smoke. They seemed no longer those
bright arms Odysseus left us years ago
when he went off to Troy. Here where the fire's
hot breath came, they had grown black and drear.
One better reason, too, I had from Zeus:
Suppose a brawl starts up when you are drunk,
you might be crazed and bloody one another,
and that would stain your feast, your courtship. Tempered
iron can magnetize a man.'
Say that.
But put aside two broadswords and two spears
for our own use, two oxhide shields nearby
when we go into action. Pallas Athena
and Zeus All Provident will see you through,
bemusing our young friends.
Now one thing more.
If son of mine you are and blood of mine,
let no one hear Odysseus is about.
Neither Laërtês, nor the swineherd here,
nor any slave, nor even Penélopê.
But you and I alone must learn how far
the women are corrupted; we should know
how to locate good men among our hands,
the loyal and respectful, and the shirkers
who take you lightly, as alone and young."

His admirable son replied:

"Ah, Father,
even when danger comes I think you'll find
courage in me. I am not scatterbrained.
But as to checking on the field hands now,
I see no gain for us in that. Reflect,
you make a long toil, that way, if you care
to look men in the eye at every farm,
while these gay devils in our hall at ease
eat up our flocks and herds, leaving us nothing.

As for the maids I say, Yes: make distinction
between good girls and those who shame your house;
all that I shy away from is a scrutiny
of cottagers just now. The time for that
comes later—if in truth you have a sign
from Zeus the Stormking."

So their talk ran on,
while down the coast, and round toward Ithaka,
hove the good ship that had gone out to Pylos

bearing Telémakhos and his companions.
Into the wide bay waters, on to the dark land,
they drove her, hauled her up, took out the oars
and canvas for light-hearted squires to carry
homeward—as they carried, too, the gifts
of Meneláos round to Klýtios'[6] house.
But first they sped a runner to Penélopê.
They knew that quiet lady must be told
the prince her son had come ashore, and sent
his good ship round to port; not one soft tear
should their sweet queen let fall.
Both messengers,
crewman and swineherd—reached the outer gate
in the same instant, bearing the same news,
and went in side by side to the king's hall.
He of the ship burst out among the maids:

"Your son's ashore this morning, O my Queen!"

But the swineherd calmly stood near Penélopê
whispering what her son had bade him tell
and what he had enjoined on her. No more.
When he had done, he left the place and turned
back to his steading in the hills.

By now,
sullen confusion weighed upon the suitors.
Out of the house, out of the court they went,
beyond the wall and gate, to sit in council.
Eurýmakhos, the son of Pólybos,
opened discussion:

"Friends, face up to it;
that young pup, Telémakhos, has done it;
he made the round trip, though we said he could not.
Well—now to get the best craft we can find
afloat, with oarsmen who can drench her bows,
and tell those on the island to come home."

He was yet speaking when Amphínomos,
craning seaward, spotted the picket ship
already in the roadstead under oars
with canvas brailed up; and this fresh arrival
made him chuckle. Then he told his friends:

"Too late for messages. Look, here they come
along the bay. Some god has brought them news,
or else they saw the cutter pass—and could not
overtake her."

6. The father of Peiraios (15.604), the man to whom Telémakhos entrusted Theoklýmenos.

On their feet at once,
the suitors took the road to the sea beach,
where, meeting the black ship, they hauled her in.
Oars and gear they left for their light-hearted
squires to carry, and all in company
made off for the assembly ground. All others,
young and old alike, they barred from sitting.
Eupeithês' son, Antínoös, made the speech:

"How the gods let our man escape a boarding,
that is the wonder.
We had lookouts posted
up on the heights all day in the sea wind,
and every hour a fresh pair of eyes;
at night we never slept ashore
but after sundown cruised the open water
to the southeast, patrolling until Dawn.
We were prepared to cut him off and catch him,
squelch him for good and all. The power of heaven
steered him the long way home.

Well, let this company plan his destruction,
and leave him no way out, this time. I see
our business here unfinished while he lives.
He knows, now, and he's no fool. Besides,
his people are all tired of playing up to us.
I say, act now, before he brings the whole
body of Akhaians to assembly—
and he would leave no word unsaid, in righteous
anger speaking out before them all
of how we plotted murder, and then missed him.
Will they commend us for that pretty work?
Take action now, or we are in for trouble;
we might be exiled, driven off our lands.
Let the first blow be ours.
If we move first, and get our hands on him
far from the city's eye, on path or field,
then stores and livestock will be ours to share;
the house we may confer upon his mother—
and on the man who marries her. Decide
otherwise you may—but if, my friends,
you want that boy to live and have his patrimony,
then we should eat no more of his good mutton,
come to this place no more.
Let each from his own hall
court her with dower gifts. And let her marry
the destined one, the one who offers most."

He ended, and no sound was heard among them,
sitting all hushed, until at last the son
of Nísos Aretíadês arose—

Amphínomos.
He led the group of suitors
who came from grainlands on Doulíkhion,
and he had lightness in his talk that pleased
Penélopê, for he meant no ill.
Now, in concern for them, he spoke:

"O Friends
I should not like to kill Telémakhos.
It is a shivery thing to kill a prince
of royal blood.
We should consult the gods.
If Zeus hands down a ruling for that act,
then I shall say, 'Come one, come all,' and go
cut him down with my own hand—
but I say Halt, if gods are contrary."

Now this proposal won them, and it carried.
Breaking their session up, away they went
to take their smooth chairs in Odysseus' house.
Meanwhile Penélopê the Wise,
decided, for her part, to make appearance
before the valiant young men.
She knew now
they plotted her child's death in her own hall,
for once more Medôn, who had heard them, told her.
Into the hall that lovely lady came,
with maids attending, and approached the suitors,
till near a pillar of the well-wrought roof
she paused, her shining veil across her cheeks,
and spoke directly to Antínoös:

"Infatuate,
steeped in evil! Yet in Ithaka they say
you were the best one of your generation
in mind and speech. Not so, you never were.
Madman, why do you keep forever knitting
death for Telémakhos? Have you no pity
toward men dependent on another's mercy?
Before Lord Zeus, no sanction can be found
for one such man to plot against another!
Or are you not aware that your own father
fled to us when the realm was up in arms
against him? He had joined the Taphian pirates
in ravaging Thesprotian folk, our friends.
Our people would have raided *him,* then—breached
his heart, butchered his herds to feast upon—
only Odysseus took him in, and held
the furious townsmen off. It is Odysseus'
house you now consume, his wife you court,
his son you kill, or try to kill. And me

you ravage now, and grieve. I call upon you
to make an end of it!—and your friends too!"

The son of Pólybos it was, Eurýmakhos,
who answered her with ready speech:

"My lady
Penélopê, wise daughter of Ikários,
you must shake off these ugly thoughts. I say
that man does not exist, nor will, who dares
lay hands upon your son Telémakhos,
while I live, walk the earth, and use my eyes.
The man's life blood, I swear,
will spurt and run out black around my lancehead!
For it is true of me, too, that Odysseus,
raider of cities, took me on his knees
and fed me often—tidbits and red wine.
Should not Telémakhos, therefore, be dear to me
above the rest of men? I tell the lad
he must not tremble for his life, at least
alone in the suitors' company. Heaven
deals death no man avoids."
Blasphemous lies
in earnest tones he told—the one who planned
the lad's destruction!
Silently the lady
made her way to her glowing upper chamber,
there to weep for her dear lord, Odysseus,
until grey-eyed Athena
cast sweet sleep upon her eyes.

At fall of dusk
Odysseus and his son heard the approach
of the good forester. They had been standing
over the fire with a spitted pig,
a yearling. And Athena coming near
with one rap of her wand made of Odysseus
an old old man again, with rags about him—
for if the swineherd knew his lord were there
he could not hold the news; Penélopê
would hear it from him.
Now Telémakhos
greeted him first:

"Eumaios, back again!
What was the talk in town? Are the tall suitors
home again, by this time, from their ambush,
or are they still on watch for my return?"

And you replied, Eumaios—O my swineherd:

"There was no time to ask or talk of that;
I hurried through the town. Even while I spoke
my message, I felt driven to return.
A runner from your friends turned up, a crier,
who gave the news first to your mother. Ah!
One thing I do know; with my own two eyes
I saw it. As I climbed above the town
to where the sky is cut by Hermês' ridge,
I saw a ship bound in for our own bay
with many oarsmen in it, laden down
with sea provisioning and two-edged spears,
and I surmised those were the men.
Who knows?"

Telémakhos, now strong with magic, smiled
across at his own father—but avoided
the swineherd's eye.
So when the pig was done,
the spit no longer to be turned, the table
garnished, everyone sat down to feast
on all the savory flesh he craved. And when
they had put off desire for meat and drink,
they turned to bed and took the gift of sleep.

BOOK XVII

[*The Beggar at the Manor*]

When the young Dawn came bright into the East
spreading her finger tips of rose, Telémakhos
the king's son, tied on his rawhide sandals
and took the lance that bore his handgrip. Burning
to be away, and on the path to town,
he told the swineherd:

"Uncle, the truth is
I must go down myself into the city.
Mother must see me there, with her own eyes,
or she will weep and feel forsaken still,
and will not set her mind at rest. Your job
will be to lead this poor man down to beg.
Some householder may want to dole him out
a loaf and pint. I have my own troubles.
Am I to care for every last man who comes?
And if he takes it badly—well, so much
the worse for him. Plain truth is what I favor."

At once Odysseus the great tactician
spoke up briskly:

"Neither would I myself
care to be kept here, lad. A beggar man

fares better in the town. Let it be said
I am not yet so old I must lay up
indoors and mumble, 'Aye, Aye' to a master.
Go on, then. As you say, my friend can lead me
as soon as I have had a bit of fire
and when the sun grows warmer. These old rags
could be my death, outside on a frosty morning,
and the town is distant, so they say."

Telémakhos
with no more words went out, and through the fence,
and down hill, going fast on the steep footing,
nursing woe for the suitors in his heart.
Before the manor hall, he leaned his lance
against a great porch pillar and stepped in
across the door stone.
Old Eurýkleia
saw him first, for that day she was covering
handsome chairs nearby with clean fleeces.
She ran to him at once, tears in her eyes;
and other maidservants of the old soldier
Odysseus gathered round to greet their prince,
kissing his head and shoulders.
Quickly, then,
Penélopê the Wise, tall in her beauty
as Artemis or pale-gold Aphroditê,
appeared from her high chamber and came down
to throw her arms around her son. In tears
she kissed his head, kissed both his shining eyes,
then cried out, and her words flew:

"Back with me!
Telémakhos, more sweet to me than sunlight!
I thought I should not see you again, ever,
after you took the ship that night to Pylos—
against my will, with not a word! you went
for news of your dear father. Tell me now
of everything you saw!"

But he made answer:

"Mother, not now. You make me weep. My heart
already aches—I came near death at sea.
You must bathe, first of all, and change your dress,
and take your maids to the highest room to pray.
Pray, and burn offerings to the gods of heaven,
that Zeus may put his hand to our revenge.

I am off now to bring home from the square
a guest, a passenger I had. I sent him
yesterday with all my crew to town.

Peiraios was to care for him, I said,
and keep him well, with honor, till I came."

She caught back the swift words upon her tongue.
Then softly she withdrew
to bathe and dress her body in fresh linen,
and make her offerings to the gods of heaven,
praying Almighty Zeus
to put his hand to their revenge.

Telémakhos
had left the hall, taken his lance, and gone
with two quick hounds at heel into the town,
Athena's grace in his long stride
making the people gaze as he came near.
And suitors gathered, primed with friendly words,
despite the deadly plotting in their hearts—
but these, and all their crowd, he kept away from.
Next he saw sitting some way off, apart,
Mentor, with Antiphos and Halithersês,
friends of his father's house in years gone by.
Near these men he sat down, and told his tale
under their questioning.
His crewman, young Peiraios,
guided through town, meanwhile, into the Square,
the Argive exile, Theoklýmenos.
Telémakhos lost no time in moving toward him;
but first Peiraios had his say:

"Telémakhos,
you must send maids to me, at once, and let me
turn over to you those gifts from Meneláos!"

The prince had pondered it, and said:

"Peiraios,
none of us knows how this affair will end.
Say one day our fine suitors, without warning,
draw upon me, kill me in our hall,
and parcel out my patrimony—I wish
you, and no one of them, to have those things.
But if my hour comes, if I can bring down
bloody death on all that crew,
you will rejoice to send my gifts to me—
and so will I rejoice!"

Then he departed,
leading his guest, the lonely stranger, home.

Over chair-backs in hall they dropped their mantles
and passed in to the polished tubs, where maids
poured out warm baths for them, anointed them,

and pulled fresh tunics, fleecy cloaks around them.
Soon they were seated at their ease in hall.
A maid came by to tip a golden jug
over their fingers into a silver bowl
and draw a gleaming table up beside them.
The larder mistress brought her tray of loaves
and savories, dispensing each.
In silence
across the hall, beside a pillar, propped
in a long chair, Telémakhos' mother
spun a fine wool yarn.
The young men's hands
went out upon the good things placed before them,
and only when their hunger and thirst were gone
did she look up and say:

"Telémakhos,
what am I to do now? Return alone
and lie again on my forsaken bed—
sodden how often with my weeping
since that day when Odysseus put to sea
to join the Atreidai[7] before Troy?
Could you not
tell me, before the suitors fill our house,
what news you have of his return?"

He answered:

"Now that you ask a second time, dear Mother,
here is the truth.
We went ashore at Pylos
to Nestor, lord and guardian of the West,
who gave me welcome in his towering hall.
So kind he was, he might have been my father
and I his long-lost son—so truly kind,
taking me in with his own honored sons.
But as to Odysseus' bitter fate,
living or dead, he had no news at all
from anyone on earth, he said. He sent me
overland in a strong chariot
to Atreus' son, the captain, Meneláos.
And I saw Helen there, for whom the Argives
fought, and the Trojans fought, as the gods willed.
Then Meneláos of the great war cry
asked me my errand in that ancient land
of Lakedaimon. So I told our story,
and in reply he burst out:

'Intolerable!
That feeble men, unfit as those men are,
should think to lie in that great captain's bed,

7. The sons of Atreus: Agamémnon and Meneláos.

fawns in the lion's lair! As if a doe
put down her litter of sucklings there, while she
sniffed at the glen or grazed a grassy hollow.
Ha! Then the lord returns to his own bed
and deals out wretched doom on both alike.

So will Odysseus deal out doom on these.
O Father Zeus, Athena, and Apollo!
I pray he comes as once he was, in Lesbos,
when he stood up to wrestle Philomeleidês—
champion and Island King—
and smashed him down. How the Akhaians cheered!
If that Odysseus could meet the suitors,
they'd have a quick reply, a stunning dowry!
Now for your questions, let me come to the point.
I would not misreport it for you; let me
tell you what the Ancient of the Sea,
that infallible seer, told me.
                                        On an island
your father lies and grieves. The Ancient saw him
held by a nymph, Kalypso, in her hall;
no means of sailing home remained to him,
no ship with oars, and no ship's company
to pull him on thc broad back of the sea."

I had this from the lord marshal, Meneláos,
and when my errand in that place was done
I left for home. A fair breeze from the gods
brought me swiftly back to our dear island."

The boy's tale made her heart stir in her breast,
but this was not all. Mother and son now heard
Theoklýmenos, the diviner, say:

"He does not see it clear—
                                        O gentle lady,
wife of Odysseus Laërtiadês,
listen to me, I can reveal this thing.
Zeus be my witness, and the table set
for strangers and the hearth to which I've come—
the lord Odysseus, I tell you,
is present now, already, on this island!
Quartered somewhere, or going about, he knows
what evil is afoot. He has it in him
to bring a black hour on the suitors. Yesterday,
still at the ship, I saw this in a portent.
I read the sign aloud, I told Telémakhos!"

The prudent queen, for her part, said:

                                                        "Stranger,
if only this came true—

our love would go to you, with many gifts;
aye, every man who passed would call you happy!"

So ran the talk between these three.
Meanwhile,
swaggering before Odysseus' hall,
the suitors were competing at the discus throw
and javelin, on the level measured field.
But when the dinner hour drew on, and beasts
were being driven from the fields to slaughter—
as beasts were, every day—Medôn spoke out:
Medôn, the crier, whom the suitors liked;
he took his meat beside them.

"Men," he said,
"each one has had his work-out and his pleasure,
come in to Hall now; time to make our feast.
Are discus throws more admirable than a roast
when the proper hour comes?"

At this reminder
they all broke up their games, and trailed away
into the gracious, timbered hall. There, first,
they dropped their cloaks on chairs; then came their ritual:
putting great rams and fat goats to the knife—
pigs and a cow, too.
So they made their feast.

During these hours, Odysseus and the swineherd
were on their way out of the hills to town.
The forester had got them started, saying:

"Friend, you have hopes, I know, of your adventure
into the heart of town today. My lord
wishes it so, not I. No, I should rather
you stood by here as guardian of our steading.
But I owe reverence to my prince, and fear
he'll make my ears burn later if I fail.
A master's tongue has a rough edge. Off we go.
Part of the day is past; nightfall will be
early, and colder, too."

Odysseus,
who had it all timed in his head, replied:

"I know, as well as you do. Let's move on.
You lead the way—the whole way. Have you got
a staff, a lopped stick, you could let me use
to put my weight on when I slip? This path
is hard going, they said."

Over his shoulders
he slung his patched-up knapsack, an old bundle

tied with twine. Eumaios found a stick for him,
the kind he wanted, and the two set out,
leaving the boys and dogs to guard the place.
In this way good Eumaios led his lord
down to the city.
                    And it seemed to him
he led an old outcast, a beggar man,
leaning most painfully upon a stick,
his poor cloak, all in tatters, looped about him.

Down by the stony trail they made their way
as far as Clearwater, not far from town—
a spring house where the people filled their jars.
Ithakos, Nêritos, and Polýktor[8] built it,
and round it on the humid ground a grove,
a circular wood of poplars grew. Ice cold
in runnels from a high rock ran the spring,
and over it there stood an altar stone
to the cool nymphs, where all men going by
laid offerings.
                    Well, here the son of Dólios
crossed their path—Melánthios.
                                        He was driving
a string of choice goats for the evening meal,
with two goatherds beside him; and no sooner
had he laid eyes upon the wayfarers
than he began to growl and taunt them both
so grossly that Odysseus' heart grew hot:

"Here comes one scurvy type leading another!
God pairs them off together, every time.
Swineherd, where are you taking your new pig,
that stinking beggar there, licker of pots?
How many doorposts has he rubbed his back on
whining for garbage, where a noble guest
would rate a cauldron or a sword?
                                        Hand him
over to me, I'll make a farmhand of him,
a stall scraper, a fodder carrier! Whey
for drink will put good muscle on his shank!
No chance: he learned his dodges long ago—
no honest sweat. He'd rather tramp the country
begging, to keep his hoggish belly full.
Well, I can tell you this for sure:
in King Odysseus' hall, if he goes there,
footstools will fly around his head—good shots
from strong hands. Back and side, his ribs will catch it
on the way out!"

                    And like a drunken fool
he kicked at Odysseus' hip as he passed by.

8. Presumably the first rulers of Ithaka. Ithakos gave the island its name. Nêritos's name was given to the most prominent mountain on Ithaka. Polýktor's name may possibly mean "having great possessions."

Not even jogged off stride, or off the trail,
the Lord Odysseus walked along, debating
inwardly whether to whirl and beat
the life out of this fellow with his stick,
or toss him, brain him on the stony ground.
Then he controlled himself, and bore it quietly.
Not so the swineherd.
Seeing the man before him,
he raised his arms and cried:

"Nymphs of the spring,
daughters of Zeus, if ever Odysseus
burnt you a thighbone in rich fat—a ram's
or kid's thighbone, hear me, grant my prayer:
let our true lord come back, let heaven bring him
to rid the earth of these fine courtly ways
Melánthios picks up around the town—
all wine and wind! Bad shepherds ruin flocks!"

Melánthios the goatherd answered:

"Bless me!
The dog can snap: how he goes on! Some day
I'll take him in a slave ship overseas
and trade him for a herd!
Old Silverbow
Apollo, if he shot clean through Telémakhos
in hall today, what luck! Or let the suitors
cut him down!
Odysseus died at sea;
no coming home for him."

He flung this out
and left the two behind to come on slowly,
while he went hurrying to the king's hall.
There he slipped in, and sat among the suitors,
beside the one he doted on—Eurýmakhos.
Then working servants helped him to his meat
and the mistress of the larder gave him bread.

Reaching the gate, Odysseus and the forester
halted and stood outside, for harp notes came
around them rippling on the air
as Phêmios picked out a song. Odysseus
caught his companion's arm and said:

"My friend,
here is the beautiful place—who could mistake it?
Here is Odysseus' hall: no hall like this!
See how one chamber grows out of another;
see how the court is tight with wall and coping;
no man at arms could break this gateway down!

Your banqueting young lords are here in force,
I gather, from the fumes of mutton roasting
and strum of harping—harping, which the gods
appoint sweet friend of feasts!"

And—O my swineherd!
you replied:

"That was quick recognition;
but you are no numbskull—in this or anything.
Now we must plan this action. Will you take
leave of me here, and go ahead alone
to make your entrance now among the suitors?
Or do you choose to wait?—Let me go forward
and go in first.

Do not delay too long;
someone might find you skulking here outside
and take a club to you, or heave a lance.
Bear this in mind, I say."

The patient hero
Odysseus answered:

"Just what I was thinking.
You go in first, and leave me here a little.
But as for blows and missiles,
I am no tyro at these things. I learned
to keep my head in hardship—years of war
and years at sea. Let this new trial come.
The cruel belly, can you hide its ache?
How many bitter days it brings! Long ships
with good stout planks athwart—would fighters rig them
to ride the barren sea, except for hunger?
Seawolves—woe to their enemies!"

While he spoke
an old hound, lying near, pricked up his ears
and lifted up his muzzle. This was Argos,
trained as a puppy by Odysseus,
but never taken on a hunt before
his master sailed for Troy. The young men, afterward,
hunted wild goats with him, and hare, and deer,
but he had grown old in his master's absence.
Treated as rubbish now, he lay at last
upon a mass of dung before the gates—
manure of mules and cows, piled there until
fieldhands could spread it on the king's estate.
Abandoned there, and half destroyed with flies,
old Argos lay.

But when he knew he heard
Odysseus' voice nearby, he did his best
to wag his tail, nose down, with flattened ears,

having no strength to move nearer his master.
And the man looked away,
wiping a salt tear from his cheek; but he
hid this from Eumaios. Then he said:

"I marvel that they leave this hound to lie
here on the dung pile;
he would have been a fine dog, from the look of him,
though I can't say as to his power and speed
when he was young. You find the same good build
in house dogs, table dogs landowners keep
all for style."

And you replied, Eumaios:

"A hunter owned him—but the man is dead
in some far place. If this old hound could show
the form he had when Lord Odysseus left him,
going to Troy, you'd see him swift and strong.
He never shrank from any savage thing
he'd brought to bay in the deep woods; on the scent
no other dog kept up with him. Now misery
has him in leash. His owner died abroad,
and here the women slaves will take no care of him.
You know how servants are: without a master
they have no will to labor, or excel.
For Zeus who views the wide world takes away
half the manhood of a man, that day
he goes into captivity and slavery."

Eumaios crossed the court and went straight forward
into the mégaron among the suitors;
but death and darkness in that instant closed
the eyes of Argos, who had seen his master,
Odysseus, after twenty years.

Long before anyone else
Telémakhos caught sight of the grey woodsman
coming from the door, and called him over
with a quick jerk of his head. Eumaios'
narrowed eyes made out an empty bench
beside the one the carver used—that servant
who had no respite, carving for the suitors.
This bench he took possession of, and placed it
across the table from Telémakhos
for his own use. Then the two men were served
cuts from a roast and bread from a bread basket.

At no long interval, Odysseus came
through his own doorway as a mendicant,
humped like a bundle of rags over his stick.
He settled on the inner ash wood sill,

leaning against the door jamb—cypress timber
the skilled carpenter planed years ago
and set up with a plumbline.

Now Telémakhos
took an entire loaf and a double handful
of roast meat; then he said to the forester:

"Give these to the stranger there. But tell him
to go among the suitors, on his own;
he may beg all he wants. This hanging back
is no asset to a hungry man."

The swineherd rose at once, crossed to the door,
and halted by Odysseus.

"Friend," he said,
"Telémakhos is pleased to give you these,
but he commands you to approach the suitors;
you may ask all you want from them. He adds,
your shyness is no asset to a beggar."

The great tactician, lifting up his eyes,
cried:

"Zeus aloft! A blessing on Telémakhos!
Let all things come to pass as he desires!"

Palms held out, in the beggar's gesture, he
received the bread and meat and put it down
before him on his knapsack—lowly table!—
then he fell to, devouring it. Meanwhile
the harper in the great room sang a song.
Not till the man was fed did the sweet harper
end his singing—whereupon the company
made the walls ring again with talk.

Unseen,
Athena took her place beside Odysseus
whispering in his ear:

"Yes, try the suitors.
You may collect a few more loaves, and learn
who are the decent lads, and who are vicious—
although not one can be excused from death!"

So he appealed to them, one after another,
going from left to right, with open palm,
as though his life time had been spent in beggary.
And they gave bread, for pity—wondering, though,
at the strange man. Who could this beggar be,
where did he come from? each would ask his neighbor;

till in their midst the goatherd, Melánthios,
raised his voice:

"Hear just a word from me,
my lords who court our illustrious queen!
This man,
this foreigner, I saw him on the road;
the swineherd, here was leading him this way;
who, what, or whence he claims to be, I could not
say for sure."

At this, Antínoös
turned on the swineherd brutally, saying:

"You famous
breeder of pigs, why bring this fellow here?
Are we not plagued enough with beggars,
foragers and such rats?
You find the company
too slow at eating up your lord's estate—
is that it? So you call this scarecrow in?"

The forester replied:

"Antínoös,
well born you are, but that was not well said.
Who would call in a foreigner?—unless
an artisan with skill to serve the realm,
a healer, or a prophet, or a builder,
or one whose harp and song might give us joy.
All these are sought for on the endless earth,
but when have beggars come by invitation?
Who puts a field mouse in his granary? My lord,
you are a hard man, and you always were,
more so than others of this company—hard
on all Odysseus' people and on me.
But this I can forget
as long as Penélopê lives on, the wise and tender
mistress of this hall; as long
as Prince Telémakhos—"

But he broke off
at a look from Telémakhos, who said:

"Be still.
Spare me a long-drawn answer to this gentleman.
With his unpleasantness, he will forever make
strife where he can—and goad the others on."

He turned and spoke out clearly to Antínoös:

"What fatherly concern you show me! Frighten
this unknown fellow, would you, from my hall
with words that promise blows—may God forbid it!
Give him a loaf. Am I a niggard? No,
I call on you to give. And spare your qualms
as to my mother's loss, or anyone's—
not that in truth you have such care at heart:
your heart is all in feeding, not in giving."

Antínoös replied:

"What high and mighty
talk, Telémakhos! No holding you!
If every suitor gave what I may give him,
he could be kept for months—kept out of sight!"

He reached under the table for the footstool
his shining feet had rested on—and this
he held up so that all could see his gift.

But all the rest gave alms,
enough to fill the beggar's pack with bread
and roast meat.
So it looked as though Odysseus
had had his taste of what these men were like
and could return scot free to his own doorway—
but halting now before Antínoös
he made a little speech to him. Said he:

"Give a mite, friend. I would not say, myself,
you are the worst man of the young Akhaians.
The noblest, rather; kingly, by your look;
therefore you'll give more bread than others do.
Let me speak well of you as I pass on
over the boundless earth!
I, too, you know,
had fortune once, lived well, stood well with men,
and gave alms, often, to poor wanderers
like this one that you see—aye, to all sorts,
no matter in what dire want. I owned
servants—many, god knows—and all the rest
that goes with being prosperous, as they say.
But Zeus the son of Kronos brought me down.

No telling
why he would have it, but he made me go
to Egypt with a company of rovers—
a long sail to the south—for my undoing.
Up the broad Nile and in to the river bank
I brought my dipping squadron. There, indeed,
I told the men to stand guard at the ships;
I sent patrols out—out to rising ground;

but reckless greed carried my crews away
to plunder the Egyptian farms; they bore off
wives and children, killed what men they found.
The news ran on the wind to the city, a night cry,
and sunrise brought both infantry and horsemen,
filling the river plain with dazzle of bronze;
then Zeus lord of lightning
threw my men into a blind panic; no one dared
stand against that host closing around us.
Their scything weapons left our dead in piles,
but some they took alive, into forced labor,
myself among them. And they gave me, then,
to one Dmêtor, a traveller, son of Iasos,
who ruled at Kypros.[9] He conveyed me there.
From that place, working northward, miserably—"

But here Antínoös broke in, shouting:

"God!
What evil wind blew in this pest?
Get over,
stand in the passage! Nudge my table, will you?
Egyptian whips are sweet
to what you'll come to here, you nosing rat,
making your pitch to everyone!
These men have bread to throw away on you
because it is not theirs. Who cares? Who spares
another's food, when he has more than plenty?"

With guile Odysseus drew away, then said:

"A pity that you have more looks than heart.
You'd grudge a pinch of salt from your own larder
to your own handy man. You sit here, fat
on others' meat, and cannot bring yourself
to rummage out a crust of bread for me!"

Then anger made Antínoös' heart beat hard,
and, glowering under his brows, he answered:

"Now!
You think you'll shuffle off and get away
after that impudence? Oh, no you don't!"

The stool he let fly hit the man's right shoulder
on the packed muscle under the shoulder blade—
like solid rock, for all the effect one saw.
Odysseus only shook his head, containing
thoughts of bloody work, as he walked on,
then sat, and dropped his loaded bag again

9. Or Cyprus.

upon the door sill. Facing the whole crowd
he said, and eyed them all:

"One word only,
my lords, and suitors of the famous queen.
One thing I have to say.
There is no pain, no burden for the heart
when blows come to a man, and he defending
his own cattle—his own cows and lambs.
Here it was otherwise. Antínoös
hit me for being driven on by hunger—
how many bitter seas men cross for hunger!
If beggars interest the gods, if there are Furies
pent in the dark to avenge a poor man's wrong, then may
Antínoös meet his death before his wedding day!"

Then said Eupeithês' son, Antínoös:

"Enough.
Eat and be quiet where you are, or shamble elsewhere,
unless you want these lads to stop your mouth
pulling you by the heels, or hands and feet,
over the whole floor, till your back is peeled!"

But now the rest were mortified, and someone
spoke from the crowd of young bucks to rebuke him:

"A poor show, that—hitting this famished tramp—
bad business, if he happened to be a god.
You know they go in foreign guise, the gods do,
looking like strangers, turning up
in towns and settlements to keep an eye
on manners, good or bad."

But at this notion
Antínoös only shrugged.
Telémakhos,
after the blow his father bore, sat still
without a tear, though his heart felt the blow.
Slowly he shook his head from side to side,
containing murderous thoughts.
Penélopê
on the higher level of her room had heard
the blow, and knew who gave it. Now she murmured:

"Would god you could be hit yourself, Antínoös—
hit by Apollo's bowshot!"

And Eurýnomê
her housekeeper, put in:

"He and no other?
If all we pray for came to pass, not one
would live till dawn!"

Her gentle mistress said:

"Oh, Nan, they are a bad lot; they intend
ruin for all of us; but Antínoös
appears a blacker-hearted hound than any.
Here is a poor man come, a wanderer,
driven by want to beg his bread, and everyone
in hall gave bits, to cram his bag—only
Antínoös threw a stool, and banged his shoulder!"

So she described it, sitting in her chamber
among her maids—while her true lord was eating.
Then she called in the forester and said:

"Go to that man on my behalf, Eumaios,
and send him here, so I can greet and question him.
Abroad in the great world, he may have heard
rumors about Odysseus—may have known him!"

Then you replied—O swineherd!

"Ah, my queen,
if these Akhaian sprigs would hush their babble
the man could tell you tales to charm your heart.
Three days and nights I kept him in my hut;
he came straight off a ship, you know, to me.
There was no end to what he made me hear
of his hard roving and I listened, eyes
upon him, as a man drinks in a tale
a minstrel sings—a minstrel taught by heaven
to touch the hearts of men. At such a song
the listener becomes rapt and still. Just so
I found myself enchanted by this man.
He claims an old tie with Odysseus, too—
in his home country, the Minoan land
of Krete. From Krete he came, a rolling stone
washed by the gales of life this way and that
to our own beach.
If he can be believed
he has news of Odysseus near at hand
alive, in the rich country of Thesprotia,
bringing a mass of treasure home."

Then wise Penélopê said again:

"Go call him, let him come here, let him tell
that tale again for my own ears.
Our friends

can drink their cups outside or stay in hall,
being so carefree. And why not? Their stores
lie intact in their homes, both food and drink,
with only servants left to take a little.
But these men spend their days around our house
killing our beeves, our fat goats and our sheep,
carousing, drinking up our good dark wine;
sparing nothing, squandering everything.
No champion like Odysseus takes our part.
Ah, if he comes again, no falcon ever
struck more suddenly than he will, with his son,
to avenge this outrage!"

The great hall below
at this point rang with a tremendous sneeze—
"kchaou!" from Telémakhos—like an acclamation.
And laughter seized Penélopê.
Then quickly,
lucidly she went on:

"Go call the stranger
straight to me. Did you hear that, Eumaios?
My son's thundering sneeze at what I said!
May death come of a sudden so; may death
relieve us, clean as that, of all the suitors!
Let me add one thing—do not overlook it—
if I can see this man has told the truth,
I promise him a warm new cloak and tunic."

With all this in his head, the forester
went down the hall, and halted near the beggar,
saying aloud:

"Good father, you are called
by the wise mother of Telémakhos,
Penélopê. The queen, despite her troubles,
is moved by a desire to hear your tales
about her lord—and if she finds them true,
she'll see you clothed in what you need, a cloak
and a fresh tunic.
You may have your belly
full each day you go about this realm
begging. For all may give, and all they wish."

Now said Odysseus, the old soldier:

"Friend,
I wish this instant I could tell my facts
to the wise daughter of Ikários, Penélopê—
and I have much to tell about her husband;
we went through much together.
But just now

this hard crowd worries me. They are, you said
infamous to the very rim of heaven
for violent acts: and here, just now, this fellow
gave me a bruise. What had I done to him?
But who would lift a hand for me? Telémakhos?
Anyone else?
No; bid the queen be patient.
Let her remain till sundown in her room,
and then—if she will seat me near the fire—
inquire tonight about her lord's return.
My rags are sorry cover; you know that;
I showed my sad condition first to you."

The woodsman heard him out, and then returned;
but the queen met him on her threshold, crying:

"Have you not brought him? Why? What is he thinking?
Has he some fear of overstepping? Shy
about these inner rooms? A hangdog beggar?"

To this you answered, friend Eumaios:

"No:
he reasons as another might, and well,
not to tempt any swordplay from these drunkards.
Be patient, wait—he says—till darkness falls.
And, O my queen, for you too that is better:
better to be alone with him, and question him,
and hear him out."

Penélopê replied:

"He is no fool; he sees how it could be.
Never were mortal men like these
for bullying and brainless arrogance!"

Thus she accepted what had been proposed,
so he went back into the crowd. He joined
Telémakhos, and said at once in whispers—
his head bent, so that no one else might hear:

"Dear prince, I must go home to keep good watch
on hut and swine, and look to my own affairs.
Everything here is in your hands. Consider
your own safety before the rest; take care
not to get hurt. Many are dangerous here.
May Zeus destroy them first, before we suffer!"

Telémakhos said:

"Your wish is mine, Uncle.
Go when your meal is finished. Then come back

at dawn, and bring good victims for a slaughter.
Everything here is in my hands indeed—
and in the disposition of the gods."

Taking his seat on the smooth bench again,
Eumaios ate and drank his fill, then rose
to climb the mountain trail back to his swine,
leaving the mégaron and court behind him
crowded with banqueters.
These had their joy
of dance and song, as day waned into evening.

BOOK XVIII

[*Blows and a Queen's Beauty*]

Now a true scavenger came in—a public tramp
who begged around the town of Ithaka,
a by-word for his insatiable swag-belly,
feeding and drinking, dawn to dark. No pith
was in him, and no nerve, huge as he looked.
Arnaios, as his gentle mother called him,
he had been nicknamed "Iros" by the young
for being ready to take messages.[1]
This fellow
thought he would rout Odysseus from his doorway,
growling at him:

"Clear out, grandfather,
or else be hauled out by the ankle bone.
See them all giving me the wink? That means,
'Go on and drag him out!' I hate to do it.
Up with you! Or would you like a fist fight?"

Odysseus only frowned and looked him over,
taking account of everything, then said:

"Master, I am no trouble to you here.
I offer no remarks. I grudge you nothing.
Take all you get, and welcome. Here is room
for two on this doorslab—or do you own it?
You are a tramp, I think, like me. Patience:
a windfall from the gods will come. But drop
that talk of using fists; it could annoy me.
Old as I am, I might just crack a rib
or split a lip for you. My life would go
even more peacefully, after tomorrow,
looking for no more visits here from you."

Iros the tramp grew red and hooted:

1. The goddess Iris often served as messenger for the gods.

"Ho,
listen to him! The swine can talk your arm off,
like an old oven woman! With two punches
I'd knock him snoring, if I had a mind to—
and not a tooth left in his head, the same
as an old sow caught in the corn! Belt up!
And let this company see the way I do it
when we square off. Can you fight a fresher man?"

Under the lofty doorway, on the door sill
of wide smooth ash, they held this rough exchange.
And the tall full-blooded suitor, Antínoös,
overhearing, broke into happy laughter.
Then he said to the others:

"Oh, my friends,
no luck like this ever turned up before!
What a farce heaven has brought this house!
The stranger
and Iros have had words, they brag of boxing!
Into the ring they go, and no more talk!"

All the young men got on their feet now, laughing,
to crowd around the ragged pair. Antínoös
called out:

"Gentlemen, quiet! One more thing:
here are goat stomachs ready on the fire
to stuff with blood and fat, good supper pudding.
The man who wins this gallant bout
may step up here and take the one he likes.
And let him feast with us from this day on:
no other beggar will be admitted here
when we are at our wine."

This pleased them all.
But now that wily man, Odysseus, muttered:

"An old man, an old hulk, has no business
fighting a young man, but my belly nags me;
nothing will do but I must take a beating.
Well, then, let every man here swear an oath
not to step in for Iros. No one throw
a punch for luck. I could be whipped that way."

So much the suitors were content to swear,
but after they reeled off their oaths, Telémakhos
put in a word to clinch it, saying:

"Friend,
if you will stand and fight, as pride requires,
don't worry about a foul blow from behind.

Whoever hits you will take on the crowd.
You have my word as host; you have the word
of these two kings, Antínoös and Eurýmakhos—
a pair of thinking men."

All shouted, "Aye!"
So now Odysseus made his shirt a belt
and roped his rags around his loins, baring
his hurdler's thighs and boxer's breadth of shoulder,
the dense rib-sheath and upper arms. Athena
stood nearby to give him bulk and power,
while the young suitors watched with narrowed eyes—
and comments went around:

"By god, old Iros now retires."

"Aye,
he asked for it, he'll get it—bloody, too."

"The build this fellow had, under his rags!"

Panic made Iros' heart jump, but the yard-boys
hustled and got him belted by main force,
though all his blubber quivered now with dread.
Antínoös' angry voice rang in his ears:

"You sack of guts, you might as well be dead,
might as well never have seen the light of day,
if this man makes you tremble! Chicken-heart,
afraid of an old wreck, far gone in misery!
Well, here is what I say—and what I'll do.
If this ragpicker can outfight you, whip you,
I'll ship you out to that king in Epeíros,
Ékhetos[2]—he skins everyone alive.
Let him just cut your nose off and your ears
and pull your privy parts out by the roots
to feed raw to his hunting dogs!"

Poor Iros
felt a new fit of shaking take his knees.
But the yard-boys pushed him out. Now both contenders
put their hands up. Royal Odysseus
pondered if he should hit him with all he had
and drop the man dead on the spot, or only
spar, with force enough to knock him down.
Better that way, he thought—a gentle blow,
else he might give himself away.

The two
were at close quarters now, and Iros lunged
hitting the shoulder. Then Odysseus hooked him

2. All we know of him is what Homer tells us here. Epeíros (Epirus) is north of Ithaka.

under the ear and shattered his jaw bone,
so bright red blood came bubbling from his mouth,
as down he pitched into the dust, bleating,
kicking against the ground, his teeth stove in.
The suitors whooped and swung their arms, half dead
with pangs of laughter.
Then, by the ankle bone,
Odysseus hauled the fallen one outside,
crossing the courtyard to the gate, and piled him
against the wall. In his right hand he stuck
his begging staff, and said:

"Here, take your post.
Sit here to keep the dogs and pigs away.
You can give up your habit of command
over poor waifs and beggarmen—you swab.
Another time you may not know what hit you."

When he had slung his rucksack by the string
over his shoulder, like a wad of rags,
he sat down on the broad door sill again,
as laughing suitors came to flock inside;
and each young buck in passing gave him greeting,
saying, maybe,

"Zeus fill your pouch for this!
May the gods grant your heart's desire!"

"Well done
to put that walking famine out of business."

"We'll ship him out to that king in Epeíros,
Ékhetos—he skins everyone alive."

Odysseus found grim cheer in their good wishes—
his work had started well.
Now from the fire
his fat blood pudding came, deposited
before him by Antínoös—then, to boot,
two brown loaves from the basket, and some wine
in a fine cup of gold. These gifts Amphínomos
gave him. Then he said:

"Here's luck, grandfather;
a new day; may the worst be over now."

Odysseus answered, and his mind ranged far:

"Amphínomos, your head is clear, I'd say;
so was your father's—or at least I've heard
good things of Nísos the Doulíkhion,
whose son you are, they tell me—an easy man.

And you seem gently bred.
In view of that,
I have a word to say to you, so listen.

Of mortal creatures, all that breathe and move,
earth bears none frailer than mankind. What man
believes in woe to come, so long as valor
and tough knees are supplied him by the gods?
But when the gods in bliss bring miseries on,
then willy-nilly, blindly, he endures.
Our minds are as the days are, dark or bright,
blown over by the father of gods and men.

So I, too, in my time thought to be happy;
but far and rash I ventured, counting on
my own right arm, my father, and my kin;
behold me now.
No man should flout the law,
but keep in peace what gifts the gods may give.

I see you young blades living dangerously,
a household eaten up, a wife dishonored—
and yet the master will return, I tell you,
to his own place, and soon; for he is near.
So may some power take you out of this,
homeward, and softly, not to face that man
the hour he sets foot on his native ground.
Between him and the suitors I foretell
no quittance, no way out, unless by blood,
once he shall stand beneath his own roof-beam."

Gravely, when he had done, he made libation
and took a sip of honey-hearted wine,
giving the cup, then, back into the hands
of the young nobleman. Amphínomos, for his part,
shaking his head, with chill and burdened breast,
turned in the great hall.
Now his heart foreknew
the wrath to come, but he could not take flight,
being by Athena bound there.
Death would have him
broken by a spear thrown by Telémakhos.
So he sat down where he had sat before.

And now heart-prompting from the grey-eyed goddess
came to the quiet queen, Penélopê:
a wish to show herself before the suitors;
for thus by fanning their desire again
Athena meant to set her beauty high
before her husband's eyes, before her son.
Knowing no reason, laughing confusedly,
she said:

"Eurýnomê, I have a craving
I never had at all—I would be seen
among those ruffians, hateful as they are.
I might well say a word, then, to my son,
for his own good—tell him to shun that crowd;
for all their gay talk, they are bent on evil."

Mistress Eurýnomê replied:

"Well said, child,
now is the time. Go down, and make it clear,
hold nothing back from him.
But you must bathe
and put a shine upon your cheeks—not this way,
streaked under your eyes and stained with tears.
You make it worse, being forever sad,
and now your boy's a bearded man! Remember
you prayed the gods to let you see him so."

Penélopê replied:

"Eurýnomê,
it is a kind thought, but I will not hear it—
to bathe and sleek with perfumed oil. No, no,
the gods forever took my sheen away
when my lord sailed for Troy in the decked ships.
Only tell my Autonoë to come,
and Hippodameía; they should be attending me
in hall, if I appear there. I could not
enter alone into that crowd of men."

At this the good old woman left the chamber
to tell the maids her bidding. But now too
the grey-eyed goddess had her own designs.
Upon the quiet daughter of Ikários
she let clear drops of slumber fall, until
the queen lay back asleep, her limbs unstrung,
in her long chair. And while she slept the goddess
endowed her with immortal grace to hold
the eyes of the Akhaians. With ambrosia
she bathed her cheeks and throat and smoothed her brow—
ambrosia, used by flower-crowned Kythereia[3]
when she would join the rose-lipped Graces dancing.
Grandeur she gave her, too, in height and form,
and made her whiter than carved ivory.
Touching her so, the perfect one was gone.
Now came the maids, bare-armed and lovely, voices
breaking into the room. The queen awoke
and as she rubbed her cheek she sighed:

3. Aphrodite.

"Ah, soft
that drowse I lay embraced in, pain forgot!
If only Artemis the Pure would give me
death as mild, and soon! No heart-ache more,
no wearing out my lifetime with desire
and sorrow, mindful of my lord, good man
in all ways that he was, best of the Akhaians!"

She rose and left her glowing upper room,
and down the stairs, with her two maids in train,
this beautiful lady went before the suitors.
Then by a pillar of the solid roof
she paused, her shining veil across her cheek,
the two girls close to her and still;
and in that instant weakness took those men
in the knee joints, their hearts grew faint with lust;
not one but swore to god to lie beside her.
But speaking for her dear son's ears alone
she said:

"Telémakhos, what has come over you?
Lightminded you were not, in all your boyhood.
Now you are full grown, come of age; a man
from foreign parts might take you for the son
of royalty, to go by your good looks;
and have you no more thoughtfulness or manners?
How could it happen in our hall that you
permit the stranger to be so abused?
Here, in our house, a guest, can any man
suffer indignity, come by such injury?
What can this be for you but public shame?"

Telémakhos looked in her eyes and answered,
with his clear head and his discretion:

"Mother,
I cannot take it ill that you are angry.
I know the meaning of these actions now,
both good and bad. I had been young and blind.
How can I always keep to what is fair
while these sit here to put fear in me?—princes
from near and far whose interest is my ruin;
are any on my side?

But you should know
the suitors did not have their way, matching
the stranger here and Iros—for the stranger
beat him to the ground.

O Father Zeus!
Athena and Apollo! could I see
the suitors whipped like that! Courtyard and hall
strewn with our friends, too weak-kneed to get up,
chapfallen to their collarbones, the way

old Iros rolls his head there by the gate
as though he were pig-drunk! No energy
to stagger on his homeward path; no fight
left in his numb legs!"

Thus Penélopê
reproached her son, and he replied. Now, interrupting,
Eurýmakhos called out to her:

"Penélopê,
deep-minded queen, daughter of Ikários,
if all Akhaians in the land of Argos
only saw you now! What hundreds more
would join your suitors here to feast tomorrow!
Beauty like yours no woman had before,
or majesty, or mastery."

She answered:

"Eurýmakhos, my qualities—I know—
my face, my figure, all were lost or blighted
when the Akhaians crossed the sea to Troy,
Odysseus my lord among the rest.
If he returned, if he were here to care for me,
I might be happily renowned!
But grief instead heaven sent me—years of pain.
Can I forget?—the day he left this island,
enfolding my right hand and wrist in his,
he said:

'My lady, the Akhaian troops
will not easily make it home again
full strength, unhurt, from Troy. They say the Trojans
are fighters too; good lances and good bowmen,
horsemen, charioteers—and those can be
decisive when a battle hangs in doubt.
So whether God will send me back, or whether
I'll be a captive there, I cannot tell.
Here, then, you must attend to everything.
My parents in our house will be a care for you
as they are now, or more, while I am gone.
Wait for the beard to darken our boy's cheek;
then marry whom you will, and move away.'

The years he spoke of are now past; the night
comes when a bitter marriage overtakes me,
desolate as I am, deprived by Zeus
of all the sweets of life.

How galling, too,
to see newfangled manners in my suitors!
Others who go to court a gentlewoman,
daughter of a rich house, if they are rivals,

bring their own beeves and sheep along; her friends
ought to be feasted, gifts are due to her;
would any dare to live at her expense?"

Odysseus' heart laughed when he heard all this—
her sweet tones charming gifts out of the suitors
with talk of marriage, though she intended none.
Eupeithês' son, Antínoös, now addressed her:

"Ikários' daughter, O deep-minded queen!
If someone cares to make you gifts, accept them!
It is no courtesy to turn gifts away.
But we go neither to our homes nor elsewhere
until of all Akhaians here you take
the best man for your lord."

Pleased at this answer,
every man sent a squire to fetch a gift—
Antínoös, a wide resplendent robe,
embroidered fine, and fastened with twelve brooches,
pins pressed into sheathing tubes of gold;
Eurýmakhos, a necklace, wrought in gold,
with sunray pieces of clear glinting amber.
Eurýdamas' men came back with pendants,
ear-drops in triple clusters of warm lights;
and from the hoard of Lord Polýktor's son,
Peisándros, came a band for her white throat,
jewelled adornment. Other wondrous things
were brought as gifts from the Akhaian princes.
Penélopê then mounted the stair again,
her maids behind, with treasure in their arms.

And now the suitors gave themselves to dancing,
to harp and haunting song, as night drew on;
black night indeed came on them at their pleasure.
But three torch fires were placed in the long hall
to give them light. On hand were stores of fuel,
dry seasoned chips of resinous wood, split up
by the bronze hatchet blade—these were mixed in
among the flames to keep them flaring bright;
each housemaid of Odysseus took her turn.

Now he himself, the shrewd and kingly man,
approached and told them:

"Housemaids of Odysseus,
your master so long absent in the world,
go to the women's chambers, to your queen.
Attend her, make the distaff whirl, divert her,
stay in her room, comb wool for her.

I stand here
ready to tend these flares and offer light

to everyone. They cannot tire me out,
even if they wish to drink till Dawn.
I am a patient man."

But the women giggled,
glancing back and forth—laughed in his face;
and one smooth girl, Melántho, spoke to him
most impudently. She was Dólios' daughter,
taken as ward in childhood by Penélopê
who gave her playthings to her heart's content
and raised her as her own. Yet the girl felt
nothing for her mistress, no compunction,
but slept and made love with Eurýmakhos.
Her bold voice rang now in Odysseus' ears:

"You must be crazy, punch drunk, you old goat.
Instead of going out to find a smithy
to sleep warm in—or a tavern bench—you stay
putting your oar in, amid all our men.
Numbskull, not to be scared! The wine you drank
has clogged your brain, or are you always this way,
boasting like a fool? Or have you lost
your mind because you beat that tramp, that Iros?
Look out, or someone better may get up
and give you a good knocking about the ears
to send you out all bloody."

But Odysseus
glared at her under his brows and said :

"One minute:
let me tell Telémakhos how you talk
in hall, you slut; he'll cut your arms and legs off!"

This hard shot took the women's breath away
and drove them quaking to their rooms, as though
knives were behind: they felt he spoke the truth.
So there he stood and kept the firelight high
and looked the suitors over, while his mind
roamed far ahead to what must be accomplished.

They, for their part, could not now be still
or drop their mockery—for Athena wished
Odysseus mortified still more.

Eurýmakhos,
the son of Pólybos, took up the baiting,
angling for a laugh among his friends.

"Suitors of our distinguished queen," he said,
"hear what my heart would have me say.

This man
comes with a certain aura of divinity

into Odysseus' hall. He shines.
He shines
around the noggin, like a flashing light,
having no hair at all to dim his lustre."

Then turning to Odysseus, raider of cities,
he went on:

"Friend, you have a mind to work,
do you? Could I hire you to clear stones
from wasteland for me—you'll be paid enough—
collecting boundary walls and planting trees?
I'd give you a bread ration every day,
a cloak to wrap in, sandals for your feet.
Oh no: you learned your dodges long ago—
no honest sweat. You'd rather tramp the country
begging, to keep your hoggish belly full."

The master of many crafts replied:

"Eurýmakhos,
we two might try our hands against each other
in early summer when the days are long,
in meadow grass, with one good scythe for me
and one as good for you: we'd cut our way
down a deep hayfield, fasting to late evening.
Or we could try our hands behind a plow,
driving the best of oxen—fat, well-fed,
well-matched for age and pulling power, and say
four strips apiece of loam the share could break:
you'd see then if I cleft you a straight furrow.
Competition in arms? If Zeus Kroníon
roused up a scuffle now, give me a shield,
two spears, a dogskin cap with plates of bronze
to fit my temples, and you'd see me go
where the first rank of fighters lock in battle.
There would be no more jeers about my belly.
You thick-skinned menace to all courtesy!
You think you are a great man and a champion,
but up against few men, poor stuff, at that.
Just let Odysseus return, those doors
wide open as they are, you'd find too narrow
to suit you on your sudden journey out."

Now fury mounted in Eurýmakhos,
who scowled and shot back:

"Bundle of rags and lice!
By god, I'll make you suffer for your gall,
your insolent gabble before all our men."

He had his foot-stool out: but now Odysseus
took to his haunches by Amphínomos' knees,

fearing Eurýmakhos' missile, as it flew.
It clipped a wine steward on the serving hand,
so that his pitcher dropped with a loud clang
while he fell backward, cursing, in the dust.
In the shadowy hall a low sound rose—of suitors
murmuring to one another.

"Ai!" they said,
"This vagabond would have done well to perish
somewhere else, and make us no such rumpus.
Here we are, quarreling over tramps; good meat
and wine forgotten; good sense gone by the board."

Telémakhos, his young heart high, put in:

"Bright souls, alight with wine, you can no longer
hide the cups you've taken.[4] Aye, some god
is goading you. Why not go home to bed?—
I mean when you are moved to. No one jumps
at my command."

Struck by his blithe manner,
the young men's teeth grew fixed in their under lips,
but now the son of Nísos, Lord Amphínomos
of Aretíadês, addressed them all:

"O friends, no ruffling replies are called for;
that was fair counsel.
Hands off the stranger, now,
and hands off any other servant here
in the great house of King Odysseus. Come,
let my own herald wet our cups once more,
we'll make an offering, and then to bed.
The stranger can be left behind in hall;
Telémakhos may care for him; he came
to Telémakhos' door, not ours."

This won them over.
The soldier Moulios, Doulíkhion herald,
comrade in arms of Lord Amphínomos,
mixed the wine and served them all. They tipped out
drops for the blissful gods, and drank the rest,
and when they had drunk their thirst away
they trailed off homeward drowsily to bed.

BOOK XIX

[*Recognitions and a Dream*]

Now by Athena's side in the quiet hall
studying the ground for slaughter, Lord Odysseus
turned to Telémakhos.

4. I.e., you cannot hide the fact that you are drunk.

"The arms," he said.
"Harness and weapons must be out of sight
in the inner room. And if the suitors miss them,
be mild; just say 'I had a mind to move them
out of the smoke. They seemed no longer
the bright arms that Odysseus left at home
when he went off to Troy. Here where the fire's
hot breath came, they had grown black and drear.
One better reason struck me, too:
suppose a brawl starts up when you've been drinking—
you might in madness let each other's blood,
and that would stain your feast, your courtship.
Iron
itself can draw men's hands.' "

Then he fell silent,
and Telémakhos obeyed his father's word.
He called Eurýkleia, the nurse, and told her:

"Nurse, go shut the women in their quarters
while I shift Father's armor back
to the inner rooms—these beautiful arms unburnished,
caked with black soot in his years abroad.
I was a child then. Well, I am not now.
I want them shielded from the draught and smoke."

And the old woman answered:

"It is time, child,
you took an interest in such things. I wish
you'd put your mind on all your house and chattels.
But who will go along to hold a light?
You said no maids, no torch-bearers."

Telémakhos
looked at her and replied:

"Our friend here.
A man who shares my meat can bear a hand,
no matter how far he is from home."

He spoke so soldierly
her own speech halted on her tongue. Straight back
she went to lock the doors of the women's hall.
And now the two men sprang to work—father
and princely son, loaded with round helms
and studded bucklers, lifting the long spears,
while in their path Pallas Athena
held up a golden lamp of purest light.
Telémakhos at last burst out:

"Oh, Father,
here is a marvel! All around I see

the walls and roof beams, pedestals and pillars,
lighted as though by white fire blazing near.
One of the gods of heaven is in this place!"

Then said Odysseus, the great tactician,

"Be still: keep still about it: just remember it.
The gods who rule Olympos make this light.
You may go off to bed now. Here I stay
to test your mother and her maids again.
Out of her long grief she will question me."

Telémakhos went across the hall and out
under the light of torches—crossed the court
to the tower chamber where he had always slept.
Here now again he lay, waiting for dawn,
while in the great hall by Athena's side
Odysseus waited with his mind on slaughter.

Presently Penélopê from her chamber
stepped in her thoughtful beauty.
So might Artemis
or golden Aphroditê have descended;
and maids drew to the hearth her own smooth chair
inlaid with silver whorls and ivory. The artisan
Ikmálios had made it, long before,
with a footrest in a single piece, and soft
upon the seat a heavy fleece was thrown.
Here by the fire the queen sat down. Her maids,
leaving their quarters, came with white arms bare
to clear the wine cups and the bread, and move
the trestle boards where men had lingered drinking.
Fiery ashes out of the pine-chip flares
they tossed, and piled on fuel for light and heat.
And now a second time Melántho's voice
rang brazen in Odysseus' ears:

"Ah, stranger,
are you still here, so creepy, late at night
hanging about, looking the women over?
You old goat, go outside, cuddle your supper;
get out, or a torch may kindle you behind!"

At this Odysseus glared under his brows
and said:

"Little devil, why pitch into me again?
Because I go unwashed and wear these rags,
and make the rounds? But so I must, being needy;
that is the way a vagabond must live.
And do not overlook this: in my time
I too had luck, lived well, stood well with men,

and gave alms, often, to poor wanderers
like him you see before you—aye, to all sorts,
no matter in what dire want. I owned
servants—many, I say—and all the rest
that goes with what men call prosperity.
But Zeus the son of Kronos brought me down.
Mistress, mend your ways, or you may lose
all this vivacity of yours. What if her ladyship
were stirred to anger? What if Odysseus came?—
and I can tell you, there is hope of that—
or if the man is done for, still his son
lives to be reckoned with, by Apollo's will.
None of you can go wantoning on the sly
and fool him now. He is too old for that."

Penélopê, being near enough to hear him,
spoke out sharply to her maid:

"Oh, shameless,
through and through! And do you think me blind,
blind to your conquest? It will cost your life.
You knew I waited—for you heard me say it—
waited to see this man in hall and question him
about my lord; I am so hard beset."

She turned away and said to the housekeeper:

"Eurýnomê, a bench, a spread of sheepskin,
to put my guest at ease. Now he shall talk
and listen, and be questioned."

Willing hands
brought a smooth bench, and dropped a fleece upon it.
Here the adventurer and king sat down;
then carefully Penélopê began:

"Friend, let me ask you first of all:
who are you, where do you come from, of what nation
and parents were you born?"

And he replied:

"My lady, never a man in the wide world
should have a fault to find with you. Your name
has gone out under heaven like the sweet
honor of some god-fearing king, who rules
in equity over the strong: his black lands bear
both wheat and barley, fruit trees laden bright,
new lambs at lambing time—and the deep sea
gives great hauls of fish by his good strategy,
so that his folk fare well.

O my dear lady,

this being so, let it suffice to ask me
of other matters—not my blood, my homeland.
Do not enforce me to recall my pain.
My heart is sore; but I must not be found
sitting in tears here, in another's house:
it is not well forever to be grieving.
One of the maids might say—or you might think—
I had got maudlin over cups of wine."

And Penélopê replied:

"Stranger, my looks,
my face, my carriage, were soon lost or faded
when the Akhaians crossed the sea to Troy,
Odysseus my lord among the rest.
If he returned, if he were here to care for me,
I might be happily renowned!
But grief instead heaven sent me—years of pain.
Sons of the noblest families on the islands,
Doulíkhion, Samê, wooded Zakýnthos,
with native Ithakans, are here to court me,
against my wish; and they consume this house.
Can I give proper heed to guest or suppliant
or herald on the realm's affairs?
How could I?
wasted with longing for Odysseus, while here
they press for marriage.
Ruses served my turn
to draw the time out—first a close-grained web
I had the happy thought to set up weaving
on my big loom in hall. I said, that day:
'Young men—my suitors, now my lord is dead,
let me finish my weaving before I marry,
or else my thread will have been spun in vain.
It is a shroud I weave for Lord Laërtês
when cold Death comes to lay him on his bier.
The country wives would hold me in dishonor
if he, with all his fortune, lay unshrouded."
I reached their hearts that way, and they agreed.
So every day I wove on the great loom,
but every night by torchlight I unwove it;
and so for three years I deceived the Akhaians.
But when the seasons brought a fourth year on,
as long months waned, and the long days were spent,
through impudent folly in the slinking maids
they caught me—clamored up to me at night;
I had no choice then but to finish it.
And now, as matters stand at last,
I have no strength left to evade a marriage,
cannot find any further way; my parents
urge it upon me, and my son
will not stand by while they eat up his property.

He comprehends it, being a man full grown,
able to oversee the kind of house
Zeus would endow with honor.
But you too
confide in me, tell me your ancestry.
You were not born of mythic oak or stone."

And the great master of invention answered:

"O honorable wife of Lord Odysseus,
must you go on asking about my family?
Then I will tell you, though my pain
be doubled by it: and whose pain would not
if he had been away as long as I have
and had hard roving in the world of men?
But I will tell you even so, my lady.

One of the great islands of the world
in midsea, in the winedark sea, is Krete:
spacious and rich and populous, with ninety
cities and a mingling of tongues.
Akhaians there are found, along with Kretan
hillmen of the old stock, and Kydonians,
Dorians in three blood-lines, Pelasgians—
and one among their ninety towns is Knossos.[5]
Here lived King Minos whom great Zeus received
every ninth year in private council—Minos,
the father of my father, Deukálion.
Two sons Deukálion had: Idómeneus,
who went to join the Atreidai before Troy
in the beaked ships of war; and then myself,
Aithôn by name—a stripling next my brother.
But I saw with my own eyes at Knossos once
Odysseus.
Gales had caught him off Cape Malea,
driven him southward on the coast of Krete,
when he was bound for Troy. At Ámnisos,
hard by the holy cave of Eileithuía,[6]
he lay to, and dropped anchor, in that open
and rough roadstead riding out the blow.
Meanwhile he came ashore, came inland, asking
after Idómeneus: dear friends he said they were;
but now ten mornings had already passed,
ten or eleven, since my brother sailed.
So I played host and took Odysseus home,
saw him well lodged and fed, for we had plenty;
then I made requisitions—barley, wine,

5. The site of the great palace discovered by Evans, who called the civilization that produced it Minoan. It is impossible to extract historical fact from this confused account of the population of Krete. Kydonians may be the inhabitants of the western end of the island. Dorians were the people who, according to Greek belief, invaded Greece and destroyed the Mycenaean palace-civilizations (but Homer does not mention them elsewhere). Pelasgians were the pre-Greek inhabitants of the area.

6. Goddess of childbirth. Ámnisos is on the coast near Knossos.

and beeves for sacrifice—to give his company
abundant fare along with him.
Twelve days
they stayed with us, the Akhaians, while that wind
out of the north shut everyone inside—
even on land you could not keep your feet,
such fury was abroad. On the thirteenth,
when the gale dropped, they put to sea."

Now all these lies he made appear so truthful
she wept as she sat listening. The skin
of her pale face grew moist the way pure snow
softens and glistens on the mountains, thawed
by Southwind after powdering from the West,
and, as the snow melts, mountain streams run full:
so her white cheeks were wetted by these tears
shed for her lord—and he close by her side.
Imagine how his heart ached for his lady,
his wife in tears; and yet he never blinked;
his eyes might have been made of horn or iron
for all that she could see. He had this trick—
wept, if he willed to, inwardly.
Well, then,
as soon as her relieving tears were shed
she spoke once more:

"I think that I shall say, friend,
give me some proof, if it is really true
that you were host in that place to my husband
with his brave men, as you declare. Come, tell me
the quality of his clothing, how he looked,
and some particular of his company."

Odysseus answered, and his mind ranged far:

"Lady, so long a time now lies between,
it is hard to speak of it. Here is the twentieth year
since that man left the island of my father.
But I shall tell what memory calls to mind.
A purple cloak, and fleecy, he had on—
a double thick one. Then, he wore a brooch
made of pure gold with twin tubes for the prongs,
and on the face a work of art: a hunting dog
pinning a spotted fawn in agony
between his forepaws—wonderful to see
how being gold, and nothing more, he bit
the golden deer convulsed, with wild hooves flying.
Odysseus' shirt I noticed, too—a fine
closefitting tunic like dry onion skin,
so soft it was, and shiny.
Women there,
many of them, would cast their eyes on it.

But I might add, for your consideration,
whether he brought these things from home, or whether
a shipmate gave them to him, coming aboard,
I have no notion: some regardful host
in another port perhaps it was. Affection
followed him—there were few Akhaians like him.
And I too made him gifts: a good bronze blade,
a cloak with lining and a broidered shirt,
and sent him off in his trim ship with honor.
A herald, somewhat older than himself,
he kept beside him; I'll describe this man:
round-shouldered, dusky, woolly-headed;
Eurýbatês, his name was—and Odysseus
gave him preferment over the officers.
He had a shrewd head, like the captain's own."

Now hearing these details—minutely true—
she felt more strangely moved, and tears flowed
until she had tasted her salt grief again.
Then she found words to answer:

"Before this
you won my sympathy, but now indeed
you shall be our respected guest and friend.
With my own hands I put that cloak and tunic
upon him—took them folded from their place—
and the bright brooch for ornament.
Gone now,
I will not meet the man again
returning to his own home fields. Unkind
the fate that sent him young in the long ship
to see that misery at Ilion, unspeakable!"

And the master improviser answered:

"Honorable
wife of Odysseus Laërtiadês,
you need not stain your beauty with these tears,
nor wear yourself out grieving for your husband.
Not that I can blame you. Any wife
grieves for the man she married in her girlhood,
lay with in love, bore children to—though he
may be no prince like this Odysseus,
whom they compare even to the gods. But listen:
weep no more, and listen:
I have a thing to tell you, something true.
I heard but lately of your lord's return,
heard that he is alive, not far away,
among Thesprótians in their green land
amassing fortune to bring home. His company
went down in shipwreck in the winedark sea
off the coast of Thrinákia. Zeus and Hêlios

held it against him that his men had killed
the kine of Hêlios. The crew drowned for this.
He rode the ship's keel. Big seas cast him up
on the island of Phaiákians, godlike men
who took him to their hearts. They honored him
with many gifts and a safe passage home,
or so they wished. Long since he should have been here,
but he thought better to restore his fortune
playing the vagabond about the world;
and no adventurer could beat Odysseus
at living by his wits—no man alive.
I had this from King Phaidôn of Thesprótia;
and, tipping wine out, Phaidôn swore to me
the ship was launched, the seamen standing by
to bring Odysseus to his land at last,
but I got out to sea ahead of him
by the king's order—as it chanced a freighter
left port for the grain bins of Doulíkhion.
Phaidôn, however, showed me Odysseus' treasure.
Ten generations of his heirs or more
could live on what lay piled in that great room.
The man himself had gone up to Dodona
to ask the spelling leaves of the old oak
what Zeus would have him do—how to return to Ithaka
after so many years—by stealth or openly.
You see, then, he is alive and well, and headed
homeward now, no more to be abroad
far from his island, his dear wife and son.
Here is my sworn word for it. Witness this,
god of the zenith, noblest of the gods,
and Lord Odysseus' hearthfire, now before me:
I swear these things shall turn out as I say.
Between this present dark and one day's ebb,
after the wane, before the crescent moon,
Odysseus will come."

Penélopê,
the attentive queen, replied to him:

"Ah, stranger,
if what you say could ever happen!
You would soon know our love! Our bounty, too:
men would turn after you to call you blessed.
But my heart tells me what must be.
Odysseus will not come to me; no ship
will be prepared for you. We have no master
quick to receive and furnish out a guest
as Lord Odysseus was.
Or did I dream him?

Maids, maids: come wash him, make a bed for him,
bedstead and colored rugs and coverlets
to let him lie warm into the gold of Dawn.

In morning light you'll bathe him and anoint him
so that he'll take his place beside Telémakhos
feasting in hall. If there be one man there
to bully or annoy him, that man wins
no further triumph here, burn though he may.
How will you understand me, friend, how find in me,
more than in common women, any courage
or gentleness, if you are kept in rags
and filthy at our feast? Men's lives are short.
The hard man and his cruelties will be
cursed behind his back, and mocked in death.
But one whose heart and ways are kind—of him
strangers will bear report to the wide world,
and distant men will praise him."

Warily
Odysseus answered:

"Honorable lady,
wife of Odysseus Laërtiadês,
a weight of rugs and cover? Not for me.
I've had none since the day I saw the mountains
of Krete, white with snow, low on the sea line
fading behind me as the long oars drove me north.
Let me lie down tonight as I've lain often,
many a night unsleeping, many a time
afield on hard ground waiting for pure Dawn.
No: and I have no longing for a footbath
either; none of these maids will touch my feet,
unless there is an old one, old and wise,
one who has lived through suffering as I have:
I would not mind letting my feet be touched
by that old servant."

And Penélopê said:

"Dear guest, no foreign man so sympathetic
ever came to my house, no guest more likeable,
so wry and humble are the things you say.
I have an old maidservant ripe with years,
one who in her time nursed my lord. She took him
into her arms the hour his mother bore him.
Let her, then, wash your feet, though she is frail.
Come here, stand by me, faithful Eurýkleia,
and bathe—bathe your master, I almost said,
for they are of an age, and now Odysseus'
feet and hands would be enseamed like his.
Men grow old soon in hardship."

Hearing this,
the old nurse hid her face between her hands
and wept hot tears, and murmured:

"Oh, my child!
I can do nothing for you! How Zeus hated you,
no other man so much! No use, great heart,
O faithful heart, the rich thighbones you burnt
to Zeus who plays in lightning—and no man
ever gave more to Zeus—with all your prayers
for a green age, a tall son reared to manhood.
There is no day of homecoming for you.
Stranger, some women in some far off place
perhaps have mocked my lord when he'd be home
as now these strumpets mock you here. No wonder
you would keep clear of all their whorishness
and have no bath. But here am I. The queen
Penélopê, Ikários' daughter, bids me;
so let me bathe your feet to serve my lady—
to serve you, too.
My heart within me stirs,
mindful of something. Listen to what I say:
strangers have come here, many through the years,
but no one ever came, I swear, who seemed
so like Odysseus—body, voice and limbs—
as you do."

Ready for this, Odysseus answered:

"Old woman, that is what they say. All who have seen
the two of us remark how like we are,
as you yourself have said, and rightly, too."

Then he kept still, while the old nurse filled up
her basin glittering in firelight; she poured
cold water in, then hot.
But Lord Odysseus
whirled suddenly from the fire to face the dark.
The scar: he had forgotten that. She must not
handle his scarred thigh, or the game was up.
But when she bared her lord's leg, bending near,
she knew the groove at once.
An old wound
a boar's white tusk inflicted, on Parnassos[7]
years ago. He had gone hunting there
in company with his uncles and Autólykos,
his mother's father—a great thief and swindler
by Hermês'[8] favor, for Autólykos pleased him
with burnt offerings of sheep and kids. The god
acted as his accomplice. Well, Autólykos
on a trip to Ithaka
arrived just after his daughter's boy was born.
In fact, he had no sooner finished supper

7. The mountain range above Apollo's oracular shrine at Delphi. 8. Not only the messenger of the gods and the god who guided the dead down to the lower world but also the god of the marketplace and so of trickery and swindling.

than Nurse Eurýkleia put the baby down
in his own lap and said:

"It is for you, now,
to choose a name for him, your child's dear baby;
the answer to her prayers."

Autólykos replied:

"My son-in-law, my daughter, call the boy
by the name I tell you. Well you know, my hand
has been against the world of men and women;
odium[9] and distrust I've won. Odysseus
should be his given name. When he grows up,
when he comes visiting his mother's home
under Parnassos, where my treasures are,
I'll make him gifts and send him back rejoicing."

Odysseus in due course went for the gifts,
and old Autólykos and his sons embraced him
with welcoming sweet words; and Amphithéa,
his mother's mother, held him tight and kissed him,
kissed his head and his fine eyes.
The father
called on his noble sons to make a feast,
and going about it briskly they led in
an ox of five years, whom they killed and flayed
and cut in bits for roasting on the skewers
with skilled hands, with care; then shared it out.
So all the day until the sun went down
they feasted to their hearts' content. At evening,
after the sun was down and dusk had come,
they turned to bed and took the gift of sleep.

When the young Dawn spread in the eastern sky
her finger tips of rose, the men and dogs
went hunting, taking Odysseus. They climbed
Parnassos' rugged flank mantled in forest,
entering amid high windy folds at noon
when Hêlios beat upon the valley floor
and on the winding Ocean whence he came.
With hounds questing ahead, in open order,
the sons of Autólykos went down a glen,
Odysseus in the lead, behind the dogs,
pointing his long-shadowing spear.
Before them
a great boar lay hid in undergrowth,
in a green thicket proof against the wind
or sun's blaze, fine soever the needling sunlight,

9. The translator is reproducing a pun in the original Greek; Autólykos speaks of himself as *odyssamenos*, one who is angry and gives cause for anger.

impervious too to any rain, so dense
that cover was, heaped up with fallen leaves.
Patter of hounds' feet, men's feet, woke the boar
as they came up—and from his woody ambush
with razor back bristling and raging eyes
he trotted and stood at bay. Odysseus,
being on top of him, had the first shot,
lunging to stick him; but the boar
had already charged under the long spear.
He hooked aslant with one white tusk and ripped out
flesh above the knee, but missed the bone.
Odysseus' second thrust went home by luck,
his bright spear passing through the shoulder joint;
and the beast fell, moaning as life pulsed away.
Autólykos' tall sons took up the wounded,
working skillfully over the Prince Odysseus
to bind his gash, and with a rune[1] they stanched
the dark flow of blood. Then downhill swiftly
they all repaired to the father's house, and there
tended him well—so well they soon could send him,
with Grandfather Autólykos' magnificent gifts,
rejoicing, over sea to Ithaka.
His father and the Lady Antikleía
welcomed him, and wanted all the news
of how he got his wound; so he spun out
his tale, recalling how the boar's white tusk
caught him when he was hunting on Parnassos.

This was the scar the old nurse recognized;
she traced it under her spread hands, then let go,
and into the basin fell the lower leg
making the bronze clang, sloshing the water out.
Then joy and anguish seized her heart; her eyes
filled up with tears; her throat closed, and she whispered,
with hand held out to touch his chin:

"Oh yes!
You are Odysseus! Ah, dear child! I could not
see you until now—not till I knew
my master's very body with my hands!"

Her eyes turned to Penélopê with desire
to make her lord, her husband, known—in vain,
because Athena had bemused the queen,
so that she took no notice, paid no heed.
At the same time Odysseus' right hand
gripped the old throat; his left hand pulled her near,
and in her ear he said:

"Will you destroy me,
nurse, who gave me milk at your own breast?

1. An incantation; magic to stop the flow of blood.

Now with a hard lifetime behind I've come
in the twentieth year home to my father's island.
You found me out, as the chance was given you.
Be quiet; keep it from the others, else
I warn you, and I mean it, too,
if by my hand god brings the suitors down
I'll kill you, nurse or not, when the time comes—
when the time comes to kill the other women."

Eurýkleia kept her wits and answered him:

"Oh, what mad words are these you let escape you!
Child, you know my blood, my bones are yours;
no one could whip this out of me. I'll be
a woman turned to stone, iron I'll be.
And let me tell you too—mind now—if god
cuts down the arrogant suitors by your hand,
I can report to you on all the maids,
those who dishonor you, and the innocent."

But in response the great tactician said:

"Nurse, no need to tell me tales of these.
I will have seen them, each one, for myself.
Trust in the gods, be quiet, hold your peace."

Silent, the old nurse went to fetch more water,
her basin being all spilt.
When she had washed
and rubbed his feet with golden oil, he turned,
dragging his bench again to the fire side
for warmth, and hid the scar under his rags.
Penélopê broke the silence, saying:

"Friend,
allow me one brief question more. You know,
the time for bed, sweet rest, is coming soon,
if only that warm luxury of slumber
would come to enfold us, in our trouble. But for me
my fate at night is anguish and no rest.
By day being busy, seeing to my work,
I find relief sometimes from loss and sorrow;
but when night comes and all the world's abed
I lie in mine alone, my heart thudding,
while bitter thoughts and fears crowd on my grief.
Think how Pandáreos' daughter, pale forever,
sings as the nightingale[2] in the new leaves
through those long quiet hours of night,

2. The reference is to one of the many Greek legends that explain the song of the nightingale. In this one the daughter of Pandáreos, a Cretan king, was married to Zêthos, king of Thebes. She had only one son; her sister-in-law Niobe had many. In a fit of jealousy she tried to kill Niobe's eldest son but by mistake (in the dark) killed her own son, Itylos, instead. Zeus changed her into a nightingale, and she sings in mourning for Itylos.

on some thick-flowering orchard bough in spring;
how she rills out and tilts her note, high now, now low,
mourning for Itylos whom she killed in madness—
her child, and her lord Zêthos' only child.
My forlorn thought flows variable as her song,
wondering: shall I stay beside my son
and guard my own things here, my maids, my hall,
to honor my lord's bed and the common talk?
Or had I best join fortunes with a suitor,
the noblest one, most lavish in his gifts?
Is it now time for that?
My son being still a callow boy forbade
marriage, or absence from my lord's domain;
but now the child is grown, grown up, a man,
he, too, begins to pray for my departure,
aghast at all the suitors gorge on.

Listen:
interpret me this dream: From a water's edge
twenty fat geese have come to feed on grain
beside my house. And I delight to see them.
But now a mountain eagle with great wings
and crooked beak storms in to break their necks
and strew their bodies here. Away he soars
into the bright sky; and I cry aloud—
all this in dream—I wail and round me gather
softly braided Akhaian women mourning
because the eagle killed my geese.
Then down
out of the sky he drops to a cornice beam
with mortal voice telling me not to weep.
'Be glad,' says he, 'renowned Ikários' daughter:
here is no dream but something real as day,
something about to happen. All those geese
were suitors, and the bird was I. See now,
I am no eagle but your lord come back
to bring inglorious death upon them all!'
As he said this, my honeyed slumber left me.
Peering through half-shut eyes, I saw the geese
in hall, still feeding at the self-same trough."

The master of subtle ways and straight replied:

"My dear, how can you choose to read the dream
differently? Has not Odysseus himself
shown you what is to come? Death to the suitors,
sure death, too. Not one escapes his doom."

Penélopê shook her head and answered:

"Friend,
many and many a dream is mere confusion,

a cobweb of no consequence at all.
Two gates for ghostly dreams there are: one gateway
of honest horn, and one of ivory.
Issuing by the ivory gate are dreams
of glimmering illusion, fantasies,
but those that come through solid polished horn
may be borne out, if mortals only know them.
I doubt it came by horn, my fearful dream—
too good to be true, that, for my son and me.
But one thing more I wish to tell you: listen
carefully. It is a black day, this that comes.
Odysseus' house and I are to be parted.
I shall decree a contest for the day.
We have twelve axe heads. In his time, my lord
could line them up, all twelve, at intervals
like a ship's ribbing; then he'd back away
a long way off and whip an arrow through.[3]
Now I'll impose this trial on the suitors.
The one who easily handles and strings the bow
and shoots through all twelve axes I shall marry,
whoever he may be—then look my last
on this my first love's beautiful brimming house.
But I'll remember, though I dream it only."

Odysseus said:

"Dear honorable lady,
wife of Odysseus Laërtiadês,
let there be no postponement of the trial.
Odysseus, who knows the shifts of combat,
will be here: aye, he'll be here long before
one of these lads can stretch or string that bow
or shoot to thread the iron!"

Grave and wise,
Penélopê replied:

"If you were willing
to sit with me and comfort me, my friend,
no tide of sleep would ever close my eyes.
But mortals cannot go forever sleepless.
This the undying gods decree for all
who live and die on earth, kind furrowed earth.
Upstairs I go, then, to my single bed,
my sighing bed, wet with so many tears
after my Lord Odysseus took ship
to see that misery at Ilion, unspeakable.

3. The nature of this archery contest is a puzzle that has never been satisfactorily solved. The axes were probably double-headed; the aperture through which the arrow passed must have been the socket in which the wood handle fit. If the twelve ax heads were lined up, fixed in the ground (Telémakhos later digs a trench for them) so that the empty sockets were in a straight line, an archer might be able to shoot through them. When Odysseus finally does so, he is sitting down (21.441).

Let me rest there, you here. You can stretch out
on the bare floor, or else command a bed."

So she went up to her chamber softly lit,
accompanied by her maids. Once there, she wept
for Odysseus, her husband, till Athena
cast sweet sleep upon her eyes.

BOOK XX

[*Signs and a Vision*]

Outside in the entry way he made his bed—
raw oxhide spread on level ground, and heaped up
fleeces, left from sheep the Akhaians killed.
And when he had lain down, Eurýnomê
flung out a robe to cover him. Unsleeping
the Lord Odysseus lay, and roved in thought
to the undoing of his enemies.
Now came a covey of women
laughing as they slipped out, arm in arm,
as many a night before, to the suitors' beds;
and anger took him like a wave to leap
into their midst and kill them, every one—
or should he let them all go hot to bed
one final night? His heart cried out within him
the way a brach[4] with whelps between her legs
would howl and bristle at a stranger—so
the hackles of his heart rose at that laughter.
Knocking his breast he muttered to himself:

"Down; be steady. You've seen worse, that time
the Kyklops like a rockslide ate your men
while you looked on. Nobody, only guile,
got you out of that cave alive."

His rage,
held hard in leash, submitted to his mind,
while he himself rocked, rolling from side to side,
as a cook turns a sausage, big with blood
and fat, at a scorching blaze, without a pause,
to broil it quick: so he rolled left and right,
casting about to see how he, alone,
against the false outrageous crowd of suitors
could press the fight.
And out of the night sky
Athena came to him; out of the nearby dark
in body like a woman; came and stood
over his head to chide him:

"Why so wakeful,
most forlorn of men? Here is your home,

4. Bitch (obsolete).

there lies your lady; and your son is here,
as fine as one could wish a son to be."

Odysseus looked up and answered:

"Aye,
goddess, that much is true; but still
I have some cause to fret in this affair.
I am one man; how can I whip those dogs?
They are always here in force. Neither
is that the end of it, there's more to come.
If by the will of Zeus and by your will
I killed them all, where could I go for safety?
Tell me that!"

And the grey-eyed goddess said:

"Your touching faith! Another man would trust
some villainous mortal, with no brains—and what
am I? Your goddess-guardian to the end
in all your trials. Let it be plain as day:
if fifty bands of men surrounded us
and every sword sang for your blood,
you could make off still with their cows and sheep.
Now you, too, go to sleep. This all night vigil
wearies the flesh. You'll come out soon enough
on the other side of trouble."

Raining soft
sleep on his eyes, the beautiful one was gone
back to Olympos. Now at peace, the man
slumbered and lay still, but not his lady.
Wakeful again with all her cares, reclining
in the soft bed, she wept and cried aloud
until she had had her fill of tears, then spoke
in prayer first to Artemis:

"O gracious
divine lady Artemis, daughter of Zeus,
if you could only make an end now quickly,
let the arrow fly, stop my heart,
or if some wind could take me by the hair
up into running cloud, to plunge in tides of Ocean,
as hurricane winds took Pandareos' daughters[5]
when they were left at home alone. The gods
had sapped their parents' lives. But Aphroditê
fed those children honey, cheese, and wine,
and Hêra gave them looks and wit, and Artemis,
pure Artemis, gave lovely height, and wise

5. The fate of these daughters was different from that of the one who married Zêthos and became a nightingale (see n. 2, p. 471). They paid for the sin of their father, who stole a golden image from the temple of Hephaistos. Though the gods showered gifts on them, in the end they were swept away to their deaths by the stormwinds.

Athena made them practised in her arts—
till Aphroditê in glory walked on Olympos,
begging for each a happy wedding day
from Zeus, the lightning's joyous king, who knows
all fate of mortals, fair and foul—
but even at that hour the cyclone winds
had ravished them away
to serve the loathsome Furies.
Let me be
blown out by the Olympians! Shot by Artemis,
I still might go and see amid the shades
Odysseus in the rot of underworld.
No coward's eye should light by my consenting!
Evil may be endured when our days pass
in mourning, heavy-hearted, hard beset,
if only sleep reign over nighttime, blanketing
the world's good and evil from our eyes.
But not for me: dreams too my demon sends me.
Tonight the image of my lord came by
as I remember him with troops. O strange
exultation! I thought him real, and not a dream."

Now as the Dawn appeared all stitched in gold,
the queen's cry reached Odysseus at his waking,
so that he wondered, half asleep: it seemed
she knew him, and stood near him! Then he woke
and picked his bedding up to stow away
on a chair in the mégaron. The oxhide pad
he took outdoors. There, spreading wide his arms,
he prayed:

"O Father Zeus, if over land and water,
after adversity, you willed to bring me home,
let someone in the waking house give me good augury,
and a sign be shown, too, in the outer world."

He prayed thus, and the mind of Zeus in heaven
heard him. He thundered out of bright Olympos
down from above the cloudlands in reply—
a rousing peal for Odysseus. Then a token
came to him from a woman grinding flour
in the court nearby. His own handmills were there,
and twelve maids had the job of grinding out
whole grain and barley meal, the pith of men.
Now all the rest, their bushels ground, were sleeping;
one only, frail and slow, kept at it still.
She stopped, stayed her hand, and her lord heard
the omen from her lips:

"Ah, Father Zeus
almighty over gods and men!
A great bang of thunder that was, surely,

out of the starry sky, and not a cloud in sight.
It is your nod to someone. Hear me, then,
make what I say come true:
let this day be the last the suitors feed
so dainty in Odysseus' hall!
They've made me work my heart out till I drop,
grinding barley. May they feast no more!"

The servant's prayer, after the cloudless thunder
of Zeus, Odysseus heard with lifting heart,
sure in his bones that vengeance was at hand.
Then other servants, wakening, came down
to build and light a fresh fire at the hearth.
Telémakhos, clear-eyed as a god, awoke,
put on his shirt and belted on his sword,
bound rawhide sandals under his smooth feet,
and took his bronze-shod lance. He came and stood
on the broad sill of the doorway, calling Eurýkleia:

"Nurse, dear Nurse, how did you treat our guest?
Had he a supper and a good bed? Has he lain
uncared for still? My mother is like that,
perverse for all her cleverness:
she'd entertain some riff-raff, and turn out
a solid man."

The old nurse answered him:

"I would not be so quick to accuse her, child.
He sat and drank here while he had a mind to;
food he no longer hungered for, he said—
for she did ask him. When he thought of sleeping,
she ordered them to make a bed. Poor soul!
Poor gentleman! So humble and so miserable,
he would accept no bed with rugs to lie on,
but slept on sheepskins and a raw oxhide
in the entry way. We covered him ourselves."

Telémakhos left the hall, hefting his lance,
with two swift flickering hounds for company,
to face the island Akhaians in the square;
and gently born Eurýkleia the daughter
of Ops Peisenóridês, called to the maids:

"Bestir yourselves! you have your brooms, go sprinkle
the rooms and sweep them, robe the chairs in red,
sponge off the tables till they shine.
Wash out the winebowls and two-handled cups.
You others go fetch water from the spring;
no loitering; come straight back. Our company
will be here soon; morning is sure to bring them;
everyone has a holiday today."

The women ran to obey her—twenty girls
off to the spring with jars for dusky water,
the rest at work inside. Then tall woodcutters
entered to split up logs for the hearth fire,
the water carriers returned; and on their heels
arrived the swineherd, driving three fat pigs,
chosen among his pens. In the wide court
he let them feed, and said to Odysseus kindly:

"Friend, are they more respectful of you now,
or still insulting you?"

Replied Odysseus:

"The young men, yes. And may the gods requite
those insolent puppies for the game they play
in a home not their own. They have no decency."

During this talk, Melánthios the goatherd
came in, driving goats for the suitors' feast,
with his two herdsmen. Under the portico
they tied the animals, and Melánthios
looked at Odysseus with a sneer. Said he:

"Stranger,
I see you mean to stay and turn our stomachs
begging in this hall. Clear out, why don't you?
Or will you have to taste a bloody beating
before you see the point? Your begging ways
nauseate everyone. There are feasts elsewhere."

Odysseus answered not a word, but grimly
shook his head over his murderous heart.
A third man came up now: Philoítios
the cattle foreman, with an ox behind him
and fat goats for the suitors. Ferrymen
had brought these from the mainland, as they bring
travellers, too—whoever comes along.
Philoítios tied the beasts under the portico
and joined the swineherd.

"Who is this," he said,
"Who is the new arrival at the manor?
Akhaian? or what else does he claim to be?
Where are his family and fields of home?
Down on his luck, all right: carries himself like a captain.
How the immortal gods can change and drag us down
once they begin to spin dark days for us!—
Kings and commanders, too."

Then he stepped over
and took Odysseus by the right hand, saying:

"Welcome, Sir. May good luck lie ahead
at the next turn. Hard times you're having, surely.
O Zeus! no god is more berserk in heaven
if gentle folk, whom you yourself begot,
you plunge in grief and hardship without mercy!
Sir, I began to sweat when I first saw you,
and tears came to my eyes, remembering
Odysseus: rags like these he may be wearing
somewhere on his wanderings now—
I mean, if he's alive still under the sun.
But if he's dead and in the house of Death,
I mourn Odysseus. He entrusted cows to me
in Kephallênia, when I was knee high,
and now his herds are numberless, no man else
ever had cattle multiply like grain.
But new men tell me I must bring my beeves
to feed them, who care nothing for our prince,
fear nothing from the watchful gods. They crave
partition of our lost king's land and wealth.
My own feelings keep going round and round
upon this tether: can I desert the boy
by moving, herds and all, to another country,
a new life among strangers? Yet it's worse
to stay here, in my old post, herding cattle
for upstarts.
I'd have gone long since,
gone, taken service with another king; this shame
is no more to be borne; but I keep thinking
my own lord, poor devil, still might come
and make a rout of suitors in his hall."

Odysseus, with his mind on action, answered:

"Herdsman, I make you out to be no coward
and no fool: I can see that for myself.
So let me tell you this. I swear by Zeus
all highest, by the table set for friends,
and by your king's hearthstone to which I've come,
Odysseus will return. You'll be on hand
to see, if you care to see it,
how those who lord it here will be cut down."

The cowman said:

"Would god it all came true!
You'd see the fight that's in me!"

Then Eumaios
echoed him, and invoked the gods, and prayed
that his great-minded master should return.
While these three talked, the suitors in the field
had come together plotting—what but death

for Telémakhos?—when from the left an eagle
crossed high with a rockdove in his claws.

Amphínomos got up. Said he, cutting them short:

"Friends, no luck lies in that plan for us,
no luck, knifing the lad. Let's think of feasting."

A grateful thought, they felt, and walking on
entered the great hall of the hero Odysseus,
where they all dropped their cloaks on chairs or couches
and made a ritual slaughter, knifing sheep,
fat goats and pigs, knifing the grass-fed steer.
Then tripes were broiled and eaten. Mixing bowls
were filled with wine. The swineherd passed out cups,
Philoítios, chief cowherd, dealt the loaves
into the panniers, Melánthios poured wine,
and all their hands went out upon the feast.

Telémakhos placed his father to advantage
just at the door sill of the pillared hall,
setting a stool there and a sawed-off table,
gave him a share of tripes, poured out his wine
in a golden cup, and said:

"Stay here, sit down
to drink with our young friends. I stand between you
and any cutting word or cuffing hand
from any suitor. Here is no public house
but the old home of Odysseus, my inheritance.
Hold your tongues then, gentlemen, and your blows,
and let no wrangling start, no scuffle either."

The others, disconcerted, bit their lips
at the ring in the young man's voice. Antínoös,
Eupeithês' son, turned round to them and said:

"It goes against the grain, my lords, but still
I say we take this hectoring by Telémakhos.
You know Zeus balked at it, or else
we might have shut his mouth a long time past,
the silvery speaker."

But Telémakhos
paid no heed to what Antínoös said.

Now public heralds wound through Ithaka
leading a file of beasts for sacrifice, and islanders
gathered under the shade trees of Apollo,
in the precinct of the Archer[6]—while in hall

6. An epithet of Apollo (see *Iliad* 1). The trees are in his open-air precinct.

the suitors roasted mutton and fat beef
on skewers, pulling off the fragrant cuts;
and those who did the roasting served Odysseus
a portion equal to their own, for so
Telémakhos commanded.
But Athena
had no desire now to let the suitors
restrain themselves from wounding words and acts.
Laërtês' son again must be offended.
There was a scapegrace fellow in the crowd
named Ktésippos, a Samian, rich beyond
all measure, arrogant with riches, early
and late a bidder for Odysseus' queen.
Now this one called attention to himself:

"Hear me, my lords, I have a thing to say.
Our friend has had his fair share from the start
and that's polite; it would be most improper
if we were cold to guests of Telémakhos—
no matter what tramp turns up. Well then, look here,
let me throw in my own small contribution.
He must have prizes to confer, himself,
on some brave bathman or another slave
here in Odysseus' house."

His hand went backward
and, fishing out a cow's foot from the basket,
he let it fly.
Odysseus rolled his head
to one side softly, ducking the blow, and smiled
a crooked smile with teeth clenched. On the wall
the cow's foot struck and fell. Telémakhos
blazed up:

"Ktésippos, lucky for you, by heaven,
not to have hit him! He took care of himself,
else you'd have had my lance-head in your belly;
no marriage, but a grave instead on Ithaka
for your father's pains.
You others, let me see
no more contemptible conduct in my house!
I've been awake to it for a long time—by now
I know what is honorable and what is not.
Before, I was a child. I can endure it
while sheep are slaughtered, wine drunk up, and bread—
can one man check the greed of a hundred men?—
but I will suffer no more viciousness.
Granted you mean at last to cut me down:
I welcome that—better to die than have
humiliation always before my eyes,
the stranger buffeted, and the serving women
dragged about, abused in a noble house."

They quieted, grew still, under his lashing,
and after a long silence, Ageláos,
Damástor's son, spoke to them all:

"Friends, friends,
I hope no one will answer like a fishwife.
What has been said is true. Hands off this stranger,
he is no target, neither is any servant
here in the hall of King Odysseus.
Let me say a word, though, to Telémakhos
and to his mother, if it please them both:
as long as hope remained in you to see
Odysseus, that great gifted man, again,
you could not be reproached for obstinacy,
tying the suitors down here; better so,
if still your father fared the great sea homeward.
How plain it is, though, now, he'll come no more!
Go sit then by your mother, reason with her,
tell her to take the best man, highest bidder,
and you can have and hold your patrimony,
feed on it, drink it all, while she
adorns another's house."

Keeping his head,
Telémakhos replied:

"By Zeus Almighty,
Ageláos, and by my father's sufferings,
far from Ithaka, whether he's dead or lost,
I make no impediment to Mother's marriage.
'Take whom you wish,' I say, 'I'll add my dowry.'
But can I pack her off against her will
from her own home? Heaven forbid!"

At this,
Pallas Athena touched off in the suitors
a fit of laughter, uncontrollable.
She drove them into nightmare, till they wheezed
and neighed as though with jaws no longer theirs,
while blood defiled their meat, and blurring tears
flooded their eyes, heart-sore with woe to come.
Then said the visionary, Theoklýmenos:

"O lost sad men, what terror is this you suffer?
Night shrouds you to the knees, your heads, your faces;
dry retch of death runs round like fire in sticks;
your cheeks are streaming; these fair walls and pedestals
are dripping crimson blood. And thick with shades
is the entry way, the courtyard thick with shades
passing athirst toward Érebos, into the dark,
the sun is quenched in heaven, foul mist hems us in . . ."

The young men greeted this with shouts of laughter,
and Eurýmakhos, the son of Pólybos, crowed:

"The mind of our new guest has gone astray.
Hustle him out of doors, lads, into the sunlight;
he finds it dark as night inside!"

The man of vision looked at him and said:

"When I need help, I'll ask for it, Eurýmakhos.
I have my eyes and ears, a pair of legs,
and a straight mind, still with me. These will do
to take me out. Damnation and black night
I see arriving for yourselves: no shelter,
no defence for any in this crowd—
fools and vipers in the king's own hall."

With this he left that handsome room and went
home to Peiraios, who received him kindly.
The suitors made wide eyes at one another
and set to work provoking Telémakhos
with jokes about his friends. One said, for instance:

"Telémakhos, no man is a luckier host
when it comes to what the cat dragged in. What burning
eyes your beggar had for bread and wine!
But not for labor, not for a single heave—
he'd be a deadweight on a field. Then comes
this other, with his mumbo-jumbo. Boy,
for your own good, I tell you, toss them both
into a slave ship for the Sikels.[7] That would pay you."

Telémakhos ignored the suitors' talk.
He kept his eyes in silence on his father,
awaiting the first blow. Meanwhile
the daughter of Ikários, Penélopê,
had placed her chair to look across and down
on father and son at bay; she heard the crowd,
and how they laughed as they resumed their dinner,
a fragrant feast, for many beasts were slain—
but as for supper, men supped never colder
than these, on what the goddess and the warrior
were even then preparing for the suitors,
whose treachery had filled that house with pain.

BOOK XXI

[*The Test of the Bow*]

Upon Penélopê, most worn in love and thought,
Athena cast a glance like a grey sea

7. The ancient (pre-Greek) inhabitants of Sicily.

lifting her. Now to bring the tough bow out and bring
the iron blades. Now try those dogs at archery
to usher bloody slaughter in.
So moving stairward
the queen took up a fine doorhook of bronze,
ivory-hafted, smooth in her clenched hand,
and led her maids down to a distant room,
a storeroom where the master's treasure lay:
bronze, bar gold, black iron forged and wrought.
In this place hung the double-torsion bow
and arrows in a quiver, a great sheaf—
quills of groaning.
In the old time in Lakedaimon
her lord had got these arms from Íphitos,[8]
Eurýtos' son. The two met in Messenia
at Ortílokhos'[9] table, on the day
Odysseus claimed a debt owed by that realm—
sheep stolen by Messenians out of Ithaka
in their long ships, three hundred head, and herdsmen.
Seniors of Ithaka and his father sent him
on that far embassy when he was young.
But Íphitos had come there tracking strays,
twelve shy mares, with mule colts yet unweaned.
And a fatal chase they led him over prairies
into the hands of Heraklês. That massive
son of toil and mortal son of Zeus
murdered his guest[1] at wine in his own house—
inhuman, shameless in the sight of heaven—
to keep the mares and colts in his own grange.
Now Íphitos, when he knew Odysseus, gave him
the master bowman's arm; for old Eurýtos
had left it on his deathbed to his son.
In fellowship Odysseus gave a lance
and a sharp sword. But Heraklês killed Íphitos
before one friend could play host to the other.
And Lord Odysseus would not take the bow
in the black ships to the great war at Troy.
As a keepsake he put it by:
it served him well at home in Ithaka.

Now the queen reached the storeroom door and halted.
Here was an oaken sill, cut long ago
and sanded clean and bedded true. Foursquare
the doorjambs and the shining doors were set
by the careful builder. Penélopê untied the strap
around the curving handle, pushed her hook
into the slit, aimed at the bolts inside
and shot them back. Then came a rasping sound
as those bright doors the key had sprung gave way—
a bellow like a bull's vaunt in a meadow—
followed by her light footfall entering

8. Son of Eurýtos, king of Oekhalia in Thessaly. 9. King of Pherai in Thessaly (see 3.528).
1. Íphitos.

over the plank floor. Herb-scented robes
lay there in chests, but the lady's milkwhite arms
went up to lift the bow down from a peg
in its own polished bowcase.
Now Penélopê
sank down, holding the weapon on her knees,
and drew her husband's great bow out, and sobbed
and bit her lip and let the salt tears flow.
Then back she went to face the crowded hall,
tremendous bow in hand, and on her shoulder hung
the quiver spiked with coughing death. Behind her
maids bore a basket full of axeheads, bronze
and iron implements for the master's game.
Thus in her beauty she approached the suitors,
and near a pillar of the solid roof
she paused, her shining veil across her cheeks,
her maids on either hand and still,
then spoke to the banqueters:

"My lords, hear me:
suitors indeed, you commandeered this house
to feast and drink in, day and night, my husband
being long gone, long out of mind. You found
no justification for yourselves—none
except your lust to marry me. Stand up, then:
we now declare a contest for that prize.
Here is my lord Odysseus' hunting bow.
Bend and string it if you can. Who sends an arrow
through iron axe-helve sockets, twelve in line?
I join my life with his, and leave this place, my home,
my rich and beautiful bridal house, forever
to be remembered, though I dream it only."

Then to Eumaios:

"Carry the bow forward.
Carry the blades."

Tears came to the swineherd's eyes
as he reached out for the big bow. He laid it
down at the suitors' feet. Across the room
the cowherd sobbed, knowing the master's weapon.
Antínoös growled, with a glance at both:

"Clods.
They go to pieces over nothing.
You two, there,
why are you sniveling? To upset the woman
even more? Has she not pain enough
over her lost husband? *Sit down.*
Get on with dinner quietly, or cry about it
outside, if you must. Leave us the bow.
A clean-cut game, it looks to me.

Nobody bends that bowstave easily
in this company. Is there a man here
made like Odysseus? I remember him
from childhood: I can see him even now."

That was the way he played it, hoping inwardly
to span the great horn bow with corded gut
and drill the iron with his shot—he, Antínoös,
destined to be the first of all to savor
blood from a biting arrow at his throat,
a shaft drawn by the fingers of Odysseus
whom he had mocked and plundered, leading on
the rest, his boon companions. Now they heard
a gay snort of laughter from Telémakhos,
who said then brilliantly:

"A queer thing, that!
Has Zeus almighty made me a half-wit?
For all her spirit, Mother has given in,
promised to go off with someone—and
is that amusing? What am I cackling for?
Step up, my lords, contend now for your prize.
There is no woman like her in Akhaia,
not in old Argos, Pylos, or Mykênê,
neither in Ithaka nor on the mainland,
and you all know it without praise of mine.
Come on, no hanging back, no more delay
in getting the bow bent. Who's the winner?
I myself should like to try that bow.
Suppose I bend it and bring off the shot,
my heart will be less heavy, seeing the queen my mother
go for the last time from this house and hall,
if I who stay can do my father's feat."

He moved out quickly, dropping his crimson cloak,
and lifted sword and sword belt from his shoulders.
His preparation was to dig a trench,
heaping the earth in a long ridge beside it
to hold the blades half-bedded. A taut cord
aligned the socket rings. And no one there
but looked on wondering at his workmanship,
for the boy had never seen it done.

He took his stand then
on the broad door sill to attempt the bow.
Three times he put his back into it and sprang it,
three times he had to slack off. Still he meant
to string that bow and pull for the needle shot.
A fourth try and he had it all but strung—
when a stiffening in Odysseus made him check.
Abruptly then he stopped and turned and said:

"Blast and damn it, must I be a milksop
all my life? Half-grown, all thumbs,

no strength or knack at arms, to defend myself
if someone picks a fight with me.
Take over,
O my elders and betters, try the bow,
run off the contest."

And he stood the weapon
upright against the massy-timbered door
with one arrow across the horn aslant,
then went back to his chair. Antínoös
gave the word:

"Now one man at a time
rise and go forward. Round the room in order;
left to right from where they dip the wine."

As this seemed fair enough, up stood Leódês
the son of Oinops. This man used to find
visions for them in the smoke of sacrifice.
He kept his chair well back, retired by the winebowl,
for he alone could not abide their manners
but sat in shame for all the rest. Now it was he
who had first to confront the bow,
standing up on the broad door sill. He failed.
The bow unbending made his thin hands yield,
no muscle in them. He gave up and said:

"Friends, I cannot. Let the next man handle it.
Here is a bow to break the heart and spirit
of many strong men. Aye. And death is less
bitter than to live on and never have
the beauty that we came here laying siege to
so many days. Resolute, are you still,
to win Odysseus' lady Penélopê?
Pit yourselves against the bow, and look
among Akhaians for another's daughter.
Gifts will be enough to court and take her.
Let the best offer win."

With this Leódês
thrust the bow away from him, and left it
upright against the massy-timbered door,
with one arrow aslant across the horn.
As he went down to his chair he heard Antínoös'
voice rising:

"What is that you say?
It makes me burn. You cannot string the weapon,
so 'Here is a bow to break the heart and spirit
of many strong men.' Crushing thought!
You were not born—you never had it in you—
to pull that bow or let an arrow fly.
But here are men who can and will."

He called out to the goatherd, Melánthios:

"Kindle a fire there, be quick about it,
draw up a big bench with a sheepskin on it,
and bring a cake of lard out of the stores.
Contenders from now on will heat and grease the bow.
We'll try it limber, and bring off the shot."

Melánthios darted out to light a blaze,
drew up a bench, threw a big sheepskin over it,
and brought a cake of lard. So one by one
the young men warmed and greased the bow for bending,
but not a man could string it. They were whipped.
Antínoös held off; so did Eurýmakhos,
suitors in chief, by far the ablest there.
Two men had meanwhile left the hall:
swineherd and cowherd, in companionship,
one downcast as the other. But Odysseus
followed them outdoors, outside the court,
and coming up said gently:

"You, herdsman,
and you, too, swineherd, I could say a thing to you,
or should I keep it dark?
No, no; speak,
my heart tells me. Would you be men enough
to stand by Odysseus if he came back?
Suppose he dropped out of a clear sky, as I did?
Suppose some god should bring him?
Would you bear arms for him, or for the suitors?"

The cowherd said:

"Ah, let the master come!
Father Zeus, grant our old wish! Some courier
guide him back! Then judge what stuff is in me
and how I manage arms!"

Likewise Eumaios
fell to praying all heaven for his return,
so that Odysseus, sure at least of these,
told them:

"I am at home, for I am he.
I bore adversities, but in the twentieth year
I am ashore in my own land. I find
the two of you, alone among my people,
longed for my coming. Prayers I never heard
except your own that I might come again.
So now what is in store for you I'll tell you:
If Zeus brings down the suitors by my hand
I promise marriages to both, and cattle,

and houses built near mine. And you shall be
brothers-in-arms of my Telémakhos.
Here, let me show you something else, a sign
that I am he, that you can trust me, look:
this old scar from the tusk wound that I got
boar hunting on Parnassos—
Autólykos' sons and I."

Shifting his rags
he bared the long gash. Both men looked, and knew,
and threw their arms around the old soldier, weeping,
kissing his head and shoulders. He as well
took each man's head and hands to kiss, then said—
to cut it short, else they might weep till dark—

"Break off, no more of this.
Anyone at the door could see and tell them.
Drift back in, but separately at intervals
after me.
Now listen to your orders:
when the time comes, those gentlemen, to a man,
will be dead against giving me bow or quiver.
Defy them. Eumaios, bring the bow
and put it in my hands there at the door.
Tell the women to lock their own door tight.
Tell them if someone hears the shock of arms
or groans of men, in hall or court, not one
must show her face, but keep still at her weaving.
Philoítios, run to the outer gate and lock it.
Throw the cross bar and lash it."

He turned back
into the courtyard and the beautiful house
and took the stool he had before. They followed
one by one, the two hands loyal to him.

Eurýmakhos had now picked up the bow.
He turned it round, and turned it round
before the licking flame to warm it up,
but could not, even so, put stress upon it
to jam the loop over the tip
though his heart groaned to bursting.
Then he said grimly:

"Curse this day.
What gloom I feel, not for myself alone,
and not only because we lose that bride.
Women are not lacking in Akhaia,
in other towns, or on Ithaka. No, the worst
is humiliation—to be shown up for children
measured against Odysseus—we who cannot

even hitch the string over his bow.
What shame to be repeated of us, after us!"

Antínoös said:

"Come to yourself. You know
that is not the way this business ends.
Today the islanders held holiday, a holy day,
no day to sweat over a bowstring.
Keep your head.
Postpone the bow. I say we leave the axes
planted where they are. No one will take them.
No one comes to Odysseus' hall tonight.
Break out good wine and brim our cups again,
we'll keep the crooked bow safe overnight,
order the fattest goats Melánthios has
brought down tomorrow noon, and offer thighbones burning
to Apollo, god of archers,
while we try out the bow and make the shot."

As this appealed to everyone, heralds came
pouring fresh water for their hands, and boys
filled up the winebowls. Joints of meat went round,
fresh cuts for all, while each man made his offering,
tilting the red wine to the gods, and drank his fill.
Then spoke Odysseus, all craft and gall:

"My lords, contenders for the queen, permit me:
a passion in me moves me to speak out.
I put it to Eurýmakhos above all
and to that brilliant prince, Antínoös. Just now
how wise his counsel was, to leave the trial
and turn your thoughts to the immortal gods! Apollo
will give power tomorrow to whom he wills.
But let me try my hand at the smooth bow!
Let me test my fingers and my pull
to see if any of the oldtime kick is there,
or if thin fare and roving took it out of me."

Now irritation beyond reason swept them all,
since they were nagged by fear that he could string it.
Antínoös answered, coldly and at length:

"You bleary vagabond, no rag of sense is left you.
Are you not coddled here enough, at table
taking meat with gentlemen, your betters,
denied nothing, and listening to our talk?
When have we let a tramp hear all our talk?
The sweet goad of wine has made you rave!
Here is the evil wine can do
to those who swig it down. Even the centaur[2]

2. Half horse, half man. At a wedding in the house of the Lapíthai, their human neighbors, the centaurs got drunk and tried to rape the women; a fight ensued. The great pediment at Olympia presents this scene, and individual contests of Lapith and centaur are portrayed on the Parthenon at Athens.

Eurýtion, in Peiríthoös' hall
among the Lapíthai, came to a bloody end
because of wine; wine ruined him: it crazed him,
drove him wild for rape in that great house.
The princes cornered him in fury, leaping on him
to drag him out and crop his ears and nose.
Drink had destroyed his mind, and so he ended
in that mutilation—fool that he was.
Centaurs and men made war for this,
but the drunkard first brought hurt upon himself.
The tale applies to you: I promise you
great trouble if you touch that bow. You'll come by
no indulgence in our house; kicked down
into a ship's bilge, out to sea you go,
and nothing saves you. Drink, but hold your tongue.
Make no contention here with younger men."

At this the watchful queen Penélopê
interposed:

"Antínoös, discourtesy
to a guest of Telémakhos—whatever guest—
that is not handsome. What are you afraid of?
Suppose this exile put his back into it
and drew the great bow of Odysseus—
could he then take me home to be his bride?
You know he does not imagine that! No one
need let that prospect weigh upon his dinner!
How very, very improbable it seems."

It was Eurýmakhos who answered her:

"Penélopê, O daughter of Ikários,
most subtle queen, we are not given to fantasy.
No, but our ears burn at what men might say
and women, too. We hear some jackal whispering:
'How far inferior to the great husband
her suitors are! Can't even budge his bow!
Think of it; and a beggar, out of nowhere,
strung it quick and made the needle shot!'
That kind of disrepute we would not care for."

Penélopê replied, steadfast and wary:

"Eurýmakhos, you have no good repute
in this realm, nor the faintest hope of it—
men who abused a prince's house for years,
consumed his wine and cattle. Shame enough.
Why hang your heads over a trifle now?
The stranger is a big man, well-compacted,
and claims to be of noble blood.

Ai!

Give him the bow, and let us have it out!
What I can promise him I will:
if by the kindness of Apollo he prevails
he shall be clothed well and equipped.
A fine shirt and a cloak I promise him;
a lance for keeping dogs at bay, or men;
a broadsword; sandals to protect his feet;
escort, and freedom to go where he will."

Telémakhos now faced her and said sharply:

"Mother, as to the bow and who may handle it
or not handle it, no man here
has more authority than I do—not one lord
of our own stony Ithaka nor the islands lying
east toward Elis: no one stops me if I choose
to give these weapons outright to my guest.
Return to your own hall. Tend your spindle.
Tend your loom. Direct your maids at work.
This question of the bow will be for men to settle,
most of all for me. I am master here."

She gazed in wonder, turned, and so withdrew,
her son's clearheaded bravery in her heart.
But when she had mounted to her rooms again
with all her women, then she fell to weeping
for Odysseus, her husband. Grey-eyed Athena
presently cast a sweet sleep on her eyes.

The swineherd had the horned bow in his hands
moving toward Odysseus, when the crowd
in the banquet hall broke into an ugly din,
shouts rising from the flushed young men:

"Ho! Where
do you think you are taking that, you smutty slave?"

"What is this dithering?"

"We'll toss you back alone
among the pigs, for your own dogs to eat,
if bright Apollo nods and the gods are kind!"
He faltered, all at once put down the bow, and stood
in panic, buffeted by waves of cries,
hearing Telémakhos from another quarter
shout:

"Go on, take him the bow!
Do you obey this pack?
You will be stoned back to your hills! Young as I am
my power is over you! I wish to God
I had as much the upper hand of these!

There would be suitors pitched like dead rats
through our gate, for the evil plotted here!"

Telémakhos' frenzy struck someone as funny,
and soon the whole room roared with laughter at him,
so that all tension passed. Eumaios picked up
bow and quiver, making for the door,
and there he placed them in Odysseus' hands.
Calling Eurýkleia to his side he said:

"Telémakhos
trusts you to take care of the women's doorway.
Lock it tight. If anyone inside
should hear the shock of arms or groans of men
in hall or court, not one must show her face,
but go on with her weaving."

The old woman
nodded and kept still. She disappeared
into the women's hall, bolting the door behind her.
Philoítios left the house now at one bound,
catlike, running to bolt the courtyard gate.
A coil of deck-rope of papyrus[3] fiber
lay in the gateway; this he used for lashing,
and ran back to the same stool as before,
fastening his eyes upon Odysseus.
And Odysseus took his time,
turning the bow, tapping it, every inch,
for borings that termites might have made
while the master of the weapon was abroad.
The suitors were now watching him, and some
jested among themselves:

"A bow lover!"

"Dealer in old bows!"

"Maybe he has one like it
at home!"

"Or has an itch to make one for himself."

"See how he handles it, the sly old buzzard!"

And one disdainful suitor added this:

"May his fortune grow an inch for every inch he bends it!"

But the man skilled in all ways of contending,
satisfied by the great bow's look and heft,

3. A plant grown in Egypt. Its fibers were used here for rope; they were also made into paper.

like a musician, like a harper, when
with quiet hand upon his instrument
he draws between his thumb and forefinger
a sweet new string upon a peg: so effortlessly
Odysseus in one motion strung the bow.
Then slid his right hand down the cord and plucked it,
so the taut gut vibrating hummed and sang
a swallow's note.
In the hushed hall it smote the suitors
and all their faces changed. Then Zeus thundered
overhead, one loud crack for a sign.
And Odysseus laughed within him that the son
of crooked-minded Kronos had flung that omen down.
He picked one ready arrow from his table
where it lay bare: the rest were waiting still
in the quiver for the young men's turn to come.
He nocked it, let it rest across the handgrip,
and drew the string and grooved butt of the arrow,
aiming from where he sat upon the stool.
Now flashed
arrow from twanging bow clean as a whistle
through every socket ring, and grazed not one,
to thud with heavy brazen head beyond.
Then quietly
Odysseus said:

"Telémakhos, the stranger
you welcomed in your hall has not disgraced you.
I did not miss, neither did I take all day
stringing the bow. My hand and eye are sound,
not so contemptible as the young men say.
The hour has come to cook their lordships' mutton—
supper by daylight. Other amusements later,
with song and harping that adorn a feast."

He dropped his eyes and nodded, and the prince
Telémakhos, true son of King Odysseus,
belted his sword on, clapped hand to his spear,
and with a clink and glitter of keen bronze
stood by his chair, in the forefront near his father.

BOOK XXII

[*Death in the Great Hall*]

Now shrugging off his rags the wiliest fighter of the islands[4]
leapt and stood on the broad door sill, his own bow in his hand.
He poured out at his feet a rain of arrows from the quiver
and spoke to the crowd:

4. In the account of the battle in the hall the translator occasionally, as here, uses a longer line than usual. There is no such variation of length in the original.

"So much for that. Your clean-cut game is over.
Now watch me hit a target that no man has hit before,
if I can make this shot. Help me, Apollo."

He drew to his fist the cruel head of an arrow for Antínoös
just as the young man leaned to lift his beautiful drinking cup,
embossed, two-handled, golden: the cup was in his fingers:
the wine was even at his lips: and did he dream of death?
How could he? In that revelry amid his throng of friends
who would imagine a single foe—though a strong foe indeed—
could dare to bring death's pain on him and darkness on his eyes?
Odysseus' arrow hit him under the chin
and punched up to the feathers through his throat.

Backward and down he went, letting the winecup fall
from his shocked hand. Like pipes his nostrils jetted
crimson runnels, a river of mortal red,
and one last kick upset his table
knocking the bread and meat to soak in dusty blood.
Now as they craned to see their champion where he lay
the suitors jostled in uproar down the hall,
everyone on his feet. Wildly they turned and scanned
the walls in the long room for arms; but not a shield,
not a good ashen spear was there for a man to take and throw.
All they could do was yell in outrage at Odysseus:

"Foul! to shoot at a man! That was your last shot!"

"Your own throat will be slit for this!"

"Our finest lad is down!

You killed the best on Ithaka."

"Buzzards will tear your eyes out!"

For they imagined as they wished—that it was a wild shot,
an unintended killing—fools, not to comprehend
they were already in the grip of death.
But glaring under his brows Odysseus answered:

"You yellow dogs, you thought I'd never make it
home from the land of Troy. You took my house to plunder,
twisted my maids to serve your beds. You dared
bid for my wife while I was still alive.
Contempt was all you had for the gods who rule wide heaven,
contempt for what men say of you hereafter.
Your last hour has come. You die in blood."

As they all took this in, sickly green fear
pulled at their entrails, and their eyes flickered

looking for some hatch or hideaway from death.
Eurýmakhos alone could speak. He said:

"If you are Odysseus of Ithaka come back,
all that you say these men have done is true.
Rash actions, many here, more in the countryside.
But here he lies, the man who caused them all.
Antínoös was the ringleader; he whipped us on
to do these things. He cared less for a marriage
than for the power Kroníon has denied him
as king of Ithaka. For that
he tried to trap your son and would have killed him.
He is dead now and has his portion. Spare
your own people. As for ourselves, we'll make
restitution of wine and meat consumed,
and add, each one, a tithe of twenty oxen
with gifts of bronze and gold to warm your heart.
Meanwhile we cannot blame you for your anger."

Odysseus glowered under his black brows
and said:

"Not for the whole treasure of your fathers,
all you enjoy, lands, flocks, or any gold
put up by others, would I hold my hand.
There will be killing till the score is paid.
You forced yourselves upon this house. Fight your way out,
or run for it, if you think you'll escape death.
I doubt one man of you skins by."

They felt their knees fail, and their hearts—but heard
Eurýmakhos for the last time rallying them.

"Friends," he said, "the man is implacable.
Now that he's got his hands on bow and quiver
he'll shoot from the big door stone there
until he kills us to the last man.
Fight, I say,
let's remember the joy of it. Swords out!
Hold up your tables to deflect his arrows.
After me, everyone: rush him where he stands.
If we can budge him from the door, if we can pass
into the town, we'll call out men to chase him.
This fellow with his bow will shoot no more."

He drew his own sword as he spoke, a broadsword of fine bronze,
honed like a razor on either edge. Then crying hoarse and loud
he hurled himself at Odysseus. But the kingly man let fly
an arrow at that instant, and the quivering feathered butt
sprang to the nipple of his breast as the barb stuck in his liver.
The bright broadsword clanged down. He lurched and fell aside,
pitching across his table. His cup, his bread and meat,

were spilt and scattered far and wide, and his head slammed on the ground.
Revulsion, anguish in his heart, with both feet kicking out,
he downed his chair, while the shrouding wave of mist closed on his eyes.

Amphínomos now came running at Odysseus,
broadsword naked in his hand. He thought to make
the great soldier give way at the door.
But with a spear throw from behind Telémakhos hit him
between the shoulders, and the lancehead drove
clear through his chest. He left his feet and fell
forward, thudding, forehead against the ground.
Telémakhos swerved around him, leaving the long dark spear
planted in Amphínomos. If he paused to yank it out
someone might jump him from behind or cut him down with a sword
at the moment he bent over. So he ran—ran from the tables
to his father's side and halted, panting, saying:

"Father let me bring you a shield and spear,
a pair of spears, a helmet.
I can arm on the run myself; I'll give
outfits to Eumaios and this cowherd.
Better to have equipment."

Said Odysseus:

"Run then, while I hold them off with arrows
as long as the arrows last. When all are gone
if I'm alone they can dislodge me."

Quick
upon his father's word Telémakhos
ran to the room where spears and armor lay.
He caught up four light shields, four pairs of spears,
four helms of war high-plumed with flowing manes,
and ran back, loaded down, to his father's side.
He was the first to pull a helmet on
and slide his bare arm in a buckler strap.
The servants armed themselves, and all three took their stand
beside the master of battle.
While he had arrows
he aimed and shot, and every shot brought down
one of his huddling enemies.
But when all barbs had flown from the bowman's fist,
he leaned his bow in the bright entry way
beside the door, and armed: a four-ply shield
hard on his shoulder, and a crested helm,
horsetailed, nodding stormy upon his head,
then took his tough and bronze-shod spears.
The suitors
who held their feet, no longer under bowshot,
could see a window high in a recess of the wall,
a vent, lighting the passage to the storeroom.

This passage had one entry, with a door,
at the edge of the great hall's threshold, just outside.

Odysseus told the swineherd to stand over
and guard this door and passage. As he did so,
a suitor named Ageláos asked the others:

"Who will get a leg up on that window
and run to alarm the town? One sharp attack
and this fellow will never shoot again."

His answer
came from the goatherd, Melánthios:

"No chance, my lord.
The exit into the courtyard is too near them,
too narrow. One good man could hold that portal
against a crowd. No: let me scale the wall
and bring you arms out of the storage chamber.
Odysseus and his son put them indoors,
I'm sure of it; not outside."

The goatish goatherd
clambered up the wall, toes in the chinks,
and slipped through to the storeroom. Twelve light shields,
twelve spears he took, and twelve thick-crested helms,
and handed all down quickly to the suitors.
Odysseus, when he saw his adversaries
girded and capped and long spears in their hands
shaken at him, felt his knees go slack,
his heart sink, for the fight was turning grim.
He spoke rapidly to his son:

"Telémakhos, one of the serving women
is tipping the scales against us in this fight,
or maybe Melánthios.'

But sharp and clear
Telémakhos said:

"It is my own fault, Father,
mine alone. The storeroom door—I left it
wide open. They were more alert than I.
Eumaios, go and lock that door,
and bring back word if a woman is doing this
or Melánthios, Dólios' son. More likely he."

Even as they conferred, Melánthios
entered the storeroom for a second load,
and the swineherd at the passage entry saw him.
He cried out to his lord:

"Son of Laërtês,
Odysseus, master mariner and soldier,
there he goes, the monkey, as we thought,
there he goes into the storeroom.
Let me hear your will:
put a spear through him—I hope I am the stronger—
or drag him here to pay for his foul tricks
against your house?"

Odysseus said:

"Telémakhos and I
will keep these gentlemen in hall, for all their urge to leave.
You two go throw him into the storeroom, wrench his arms
and legs behind him, lash his hands and feet
to a plank, and hoist him up to the roof beams.
Let him live on there suffering at his leisure."

The two men heard him with appreciation
and ducked into the passage. Melánthios,
rummaging in the chamber, could not hear them
as they came up; nor could he see them freeze
like posts on either side the door.
He turned back with a handsome crested helmet
in one hand, in the other an old shield
coated with dust—a shield Laërtês bore
soldiering in his youth. It had lain there for years,
and the seams on strap and grip had rotted away.
As Melánthios came out the two men sprang,
jerked him backward by the hair, and threw him.
Hands and feet they tied with a cutting cord
behind him, so his bones ground in their sockets,
just as Laërtês' royal son commanded.
Then with a whip of rope they hoisted him
in agony up a pillar to the beams,
and—O my swineherd—you were the one to say:

"Watch through the night up there, Melánthios.
An airy bed is what you need.
You'll be awake to see the primrose Dawn
when she goes glowing from the streams of Ocean
to mount her golden throne.
No oversleeping
the hour for driving goats to feed the suitors."

They stopped for helm and shield and left him there
contorted, in his brutal sling,
and shut the doors, and went to join Odysseus,
whose mind moved through the combat now to come.
Breathing deep, and snorting hard, they stood
four at the entry, facing two score men.
But now into the gracious doorway stepped

Zeus's daughter Athena. She wore the guise of Mentor,
and Odysseus appealed to her in joy:

"O Mentor, join me in this fight! Remember
how all my life I've been devoted to you,
friend of my youth!"

For he guessed it was Athena,
Hope of Soldiers. Cries came from the suitors,
and Ageláos, Damástor's son, called out:

"Mentor, don't let Odysseus lead you astray
to fight against us on his side.
Think twice: we are resolved—and we will do it—
after we kill them, father and son,
you too will have your throat slit for your pains
if you make trouble for us here. It means your life.
Your life—and cutting throats will not be all.
Whatever wealth you have, at home, or elsewhere,
we'll mingle with Odysseus' wealth. Your sons
will be turned out, your wife and daughters
banished from the town of Ithaka."

Athena's anger grew like a storm wind as he spoke
until she flashed out at Odysseus:

"Ah, what a falling off!
Where is your valor, where is the iron hand
that fought at Troy for Helen, pearl of kings,
no respite and nine years of war? How many foes
your hand brought down in bloody play of spears?
What stratagem but yours took Priam's town?
How is it now that on your own door sill,
before the harriers of your wife, you curse your luck
not to be stronger?
Come here, cousin, stand by me,
and you'll see action! In the enemies' teeth
learn how Mentor, son of Álkimos,
repays fair dealing!"

For all her fighting words
she gave no overpowering aid—not yet;
father and son must prove their mettle still.
Into the smoky air under the roof
the goddess merely darted to perch on a blackened beam—
no figure to be seen now but a swallow.

Command of the suitors had fallen to Ageláos.
With him were Eurýnomos, Amphímedon,
Demoptólemos, Peisándros, Pólybos,
the best of the lot who stood to fight for their lives

after the streaking arrows downed the rest.
Ageláos rallied them with his plan of battle:

"Friends, our killer has come to the end of his rope,
and much good Mentor did him, that blowhard, dropping in.
Look, only four are left to fight, in the light there at the door.
No scattering of shots, men, no throwing away good spears;
we six will aim a volley at Odysseus alone,
and may Zeus grant us the glory of a hit.
If he goes down, the others are no problem."

At his command, then, "Ho!" they all let fly
as one man. But Athena spoiled their shots.
One hit the doorpost of the hall, another
stuck in the door's thick timbering, still others
rang on the stone wall, shivering hafts of ash.
Seeing his men unscathed, royal Odysseus
gave the word for action.

"Now I say, friends,
the time is overdue to let them have it.
Battlespoil they want from our dead bodies
to add to all they plundered here before."

Taking aim over the steadied lanceheads
they all let fly together. Odysseus killed
Demoptólemos; Telémakhos
killed Eurýadês; the swineherd, Élatos;
and Peisándros went down before the cowherd.
As these lay dying, biting the central floor,
their friends gave way and broke for the inner wall.
The four attackers followed up with a rush
to take spears from the fallen men.

Re-forming,
the suitors threw again with all their strength,
but Athena turned their shots, or all but two.
One hit a doorpost in the hall, another
stuck in the door's thick timbering, still others
rang on the stone wall, shivering hafts of ash.
Amphímedon's point bloodied Telémakhos'
wrist, a superficial wound, and Ktésippos'
long spear passing over Eumaios' shield
grazed his shoulder, hurtled on and fell.
No matter: with Odysseus the great soldier
the wounded threw again. And Odysseus raider of cities
struck Eurýdamas down. Telémakhos
hit Amphímedon, and the swineherd's shot
killed Pólybos. But Ktésippos, who had last evening thrown
a cow's hoof at Odysseus, got the cowherd's heavy cast
full in the chest—and dying heard him say:

"You arrogant joking bastard!
Clown, will you, like a fool, and parade your wit?
Leave jesting to the gods who do it better.
This will repay your cow's-foot courtesy
to a great wanderer come home."

The master
of the black herds had answered Ktésippos.
Odysseus, lunging at close quarters, put a spear
through Ageláos, Damastor's son. Telémakhos
hit Leókritos from behind and pierced him,
kidney to diaphragm. Speared off his feet,
he fell face downward on the ground.

At this moment that unmanning thunder cloud,
the aegis,[5] Athena's shield,
took form aloft in the great hall.
And the suitors mad with fear
at her great sign stampeded like stung cattle by a river
when the dread shimmering gadfly strikes in summer,
in the flowering season, in the long-drawn days.
After them the attackers wheeled, as terrible as falcons
from eyries in the mountains veering over and diving down
with talons wide unsheathed on flights of birds,
who cower down the sky in chutes and bursts along the valley—
but the pouncing falcons grip their prey, no frantic wing avails,
and farmers love to watch those beakèd hunters.
So these now fell upon the suitors in that hall,
turning, turning to strike and strike again,
while torn men moaned at death, and blood ran smoking
over the whole floor.
Now there was one
who turned and threw himself at Odysseus' knees—
Leódês, begging for his life:

"Mercy,
mercy on a suppliant, Odysseus!
Never by word or act of mine, I swear,
was any woman troubled here. I told the rest
to put an end to it. They would not listen,
would not keep their hands from brutishness,
and now they are all dying like dogs for it.
I had no part in what they did: my part
was visionary—reading the smoke of sacrifice.
Scruples go unrewarded if I die."

The shrewd fighter frowned over him and said:

"You were diviner to this crowd? How often
you must have prayed my sweet day of return

5. A magical shield (or breastplate) used by Athena and Zeus; it created a panic when displayed.

would never come, or not for years!—and prayed
to have my dear wife, and beget children on her.
No plea like yours could save you
from this hard bed of death. Death it shall be!"

He picked up Ageláos' broadsword
from where it lay, flung by the slain man,
and gave Leódês' neck a lopping blow
so that his head went down to mouth in dust.

One more who had avoided furious death
was the son of Terpis, Phêmios, the minstrel,
singer by compulsion to the suitors.
He stood now with his harp, holy and clear,
in the wall's recess, under the window, wondering
if he should flee that way to the courtyard altar,
sanctuary of Zeus, the Enclosure God.[6]
Thighbones in hundreds had been offered there
by Laërtês and Odysseus. No, he thought;
the more direct way would be best—to go
humbly to his lord. But first to save
his murmuring instrument he laid it down
carefully between the winebowl and a chair,
then he betook himself to Lord Odysseus,
clung hard to his knees, and said:

"Mercy,
mercy on a suppliant, Odysseus!
My gift is song for men and for the gods undying.
My death will be remorse for you hereafter.
No one taught me: deep in my mind a god
shaped all the various ways of life in song.
And I am fit to make verse in your company
as in the god's. Put aside lust for blood.
Your own dear son Telémakhos can tell you,
never by my own will or for love
did I feast here or sing amid the suitors.
They were too strong, too many; they compelled me."

Telémakhos in the elation of battle
heard him. He at once called to his father:

"Wait: that one is innocent: don't hurt him.
And we should let our herald live—Medôn;
he cared for me from boyhood. Where is *he*?
Has he been killed already by Philoítios
or by the swineherd? Else he got an arrow
in that first gale of bowshots down the room."

Now this came to the ears of prudent Medôn
under the chair where he had gone to earth,

6. Zeus Herkeios, guardian of the inner space of the home.

pulling a new-flayed bull's hide over him.
Quiet he lay while blinding death passed by.
Now heaving out from under
he scrambled for Telémakhos' knees and said:

"Here I am, dear prince; but rest your spear!
Tell your great father not to see in me
a suitor for the sword's edge—one of those
who laughed at you and ruined his property!"

The lord of all the tricks of war surveyed
this fugitive and smiled. He said:

"Courage: my son has dug you out and saved you.
Take it to heart, and pass the word along:
fair dealing brings more profit in the end.
Now leave this room. Go and sit down outdoors
where there's no carnage, in the court,
you and the poet with his many voices,
while I attend to certain chores inside."

At this the two men stirred and picked their way
to the door and out, and sat down at the altar,
looking around with wincing eyes
as though the sword's edge hovered still.
And Odysseus looked around him, narrow-eyed,
for any others who had lain hidden
while death's black fury passed.
                                                  In blood and dust
he saw that crowd all fallen, many and many slain.

Think of a catch that fishermen haul in to a halfmoon bay
in a fine-meshed net from the white-caps of the sea:
how all are poured out on the sand, in throes for the salt sea,
twitching their cold lives away in Hêlios' fiery air:
so lay the suitors heaped on one another.

Odysseus at length said to his son:

"Go tell old Nurse I'll have a word with her.
What's to be done now weighs on my mind."

Telémakhos knocked at the women's door and called:

"Eurýkleia, come out here! Move, old woman.
You kept your eye on all our servant girls.
Jump, my father is here and wants to see you."

His call brought no reply, only the doors
were opened, and she came. Telémakhos
led her forward. In the shadowy hall
full of dead men she found his father

spattered and caked with blood like a mountain lion
when he has gorged upon an ox, his kill—
with hot blood glistening over his whole chest,
smeared on his jaws, baleful and terrifying—
even so encrimsoned was Odysseus
up to his thighs and armpits. As she gazed
from all the corpses to the bloody man
she raised her head to cry over his triumph,
but felt his grip upon her, checking her.
Said the great soldier then:

"Rejoice
inwardly. No crowing aloud, old woman.
To glory over slain men is no piety.
Destiny and the gods' will vanquished these,
and their own hardness. They respected no one,
good or bad, who came their way.
For this, and folly, a bad end befell them.
Your part is now to tell me of the women,
those who dishonored me, and the innocent."

His own old nurse Eurýkleia said:

"I will, then.
Child, you know you'll have the truth from me.
Fifty all told they are, your female slaves,
trained by your lady and myself in service,
wool carding and the rest of it, and taught
to be submissive. Twelve went bad,
flouting me, flouting Penélopê, too.
Telémakhos being barely grown, his mother
would never let him rule the serving women—
but you must let me go to her lighted rooms
and tell her. Some god sent her a drift of sleep."

But in reply the great tactician said:

"Not yet. Do not awake her. Tell those women
who were the suitors' harlots to come here."

She went back on this mission through his hall.
Then he called Telémakhos to his side
and the two herdsmen. Sharply Odysseus said:

"These dead must be disposed of first of all.
Direct the women. Tables and chairs will be
scrubbed with sponges, rinsed and rinsed again.
When our great room is fresh and put in order,
take them outside, these women,
between the roundhouse and the palisade,
and hack them with your swordblades till you cut
the life out of them, and every thought of sweet

Aphroditê under the rutting suitors,
when they lay down in secret."

As he spoke
here came the women in a bunch, all wailing,
soft tears on their cheeks. They fell to work
to lug the corpses out into the courtyard
under the gateway, propping one
against another as Odysseus ordered,
for he himself stood over them. In fear
these women bore the cold weight of the dead.
The next thing was to scrub off chairs and tables
and rinse them down. Telémakhos and the herdsman
scraped the packed earth floor with hoes, but made
the women carry out all blood and mire.
When the great room was cleaned up once again,
at swordpoint they forced them out, between
the roundhouse and the palisade, pell-mell
to huddle in that dead end without exit.
Telémakhos, who knew his mind, said curtly:

"I would not give the clean death of a beast[7]
to trulls who made a mockery of my mother
and of me too—you sluts, who lay with suitors."

He tied one end of a hawser to a pillar
and passed the other about the roundhouse top,
taking the slack up, so that no one's toes
could touch the ground. They would be hung like doves
or larks in springes triggered in a thicket,
where the birds think to rest—a cruel nesting.
So now in turn each woman thrust her head
into a noose and swung, yanked high in air,
to perish there most piteously.
Their feet danced for a little, but not long.

From storeroom to the court they brought Melánthios,
chopped with swords to cut his nose and ears off,
pulled off his genitals to feed the dogs
and raging hacked his hands and feet away.
As their own hands and feet called for a washing,
they went indoors to Odysseus again.
Their work was done. He told Eurýkleia:

"Bring me
brimstone and a brazier—medicinal
fumes to purify my hall. Then tell
Penélopê to come, and bring her maids.
All servants round the house must be called in."

7. I.e., by sword or spear. Hanging was considered an ignominious way to die.

His own old nurse Eurýkleia replied:

"Aye, surely that is well said, child. But let me
find you a good clean shirt and cloak and dress you.
You must not wrap your shoulders' breadth again
in rags in your own hall. That would be shameful."

Odysseus answered:

"Let me have the fire.
The first thing is to purify this place."

With no more chat Eurýkleia obeyed
and fetched out fire and brimstone. Cleansing fumes
he sent through court and hall and storage chamber.
Then the old woman hurried off again
to the women's quarters to announce her news,
and all the servants came now, bearing torches
in twilight, crowding to embrace Odysseus,
taking his hands to kiss, his head and shoulders,
while he stood there, nodding to every one,
and overcome by longing and by tears.

BOOK XXIII

[*The Trunk of the Olive Tree*]

The old nurse went upstairs exulting,
with knees toiling, and patter of slapping feet,
to tell the mistress of her lord's return,
and cried out by the lady's pillow:

"Wake,
wake up, dear child! Penélopê, come down,
see with your own eyes what all these years you longed for!
Odysseus is here! Oh, in the end, he came!
And he has killed your suitors, killed them all
who made his house a bordel and ate his cattle
and raised their hands against his son!"

Penélopê said:

"Dear nurse . . . the gods have touched you.
They can put chaos into the clearest head
or bring a lunatic down to earth. Good sense
you always had. They've touched you. What is this
mockery you wake me up to tell me,
breaking in on my sweet spell of sleep?
I had not dozed away so tranquilly
since my lord went to war, on that ill wind
to Ilion.
Oh, leave me! Back down stairs!
If any other of my women came in babbling

things like these to startle me, I'd see her
flogged out of the house! Your old age spares you that."

Eurýkleia said:

"Would I play such a trick on you, dear child?
It is true, true, as I tell you, he has come!
That stranger they were baiting was Odysseus.
Telémakhos knew it days ago—
cool head, never to give his father away,
till he paid off those swollen dogs!"

The lady in her heart's joy now sprang up
with sudden dazzling tears, and hugged the old one,
crying out:

"But try to make it clear!
If he came home in secret, as you say,
could he engage them singlehanded? How?
They were all down there, still in the same crowd."

To this Eurýkleia said:

"I did not see it,
I knew nothing; only I heard the groans
of men dying. We sat still in the inner rooms
holding our breath, and marvelling, shut in,
until Telémakhos came to the door and called me—
your own dear son, sent this time by his father!
So I went out, and found Odysseus
erect, with dead men littering the floor
this way and that. If you had only seen him!
It would have made your heart glow hot!—a lion
splashed with mire and blood.

But now the cold
corpses are all gathered at the gate,
and he has cleansed his hall with fire and brimstone,
a great blaze. Then he sent me here to you.
Come with me: you may both embark this time
for happiness together, after pain,
after long years. Here is your prayer, your passion,
granted: your own lord lives, he is at home,
he found you safe, he found his son. The suitors
abused his house, but he has brought them down."

The attentive lady said:

"Do not lose yourself
in this rejoicing: wait: you know
how splendid that return would be for us,
how dear to me, dear to his son and mine;
but no, it is not possible, your notion

must be wrong.
Some god has killed the suitors,
a god, sick of their arrogance and brutal
malice—for they honored no one living,
good or bad, who ever came their way.
Blind young fools, they've tasted death for it.
But the true person of Odysseus?
He lost his home, he died far from Akhaia."

The old nurse sighed:

"How queer, the way you talk!
Here he is, large as life, by his own fire,
and you deny he ever will get home!
Child, you always were mistrustful!
But there is one sure mark that I can tell you:
that scar left by the boar's tusk long ago.
I recognized it when I bathed his feet
and would have told you, but he stopped my mouth,
forbade me, in his craftiness.
Come down,
I stake my life on it, he's here!
Let me die in agony if I lie!"

Penélopê said:

"Nurse dear, though you have your wits about you,
still it is hard not to be taken in
by the immortals. Let us join my son, though,
and see the dead and that strange one who killed them."

She turned then to descend the stair, her heart
in tumult. Had she better keep her distance
and question him, her husband? Should she run
up to him, take his hands, kiss him now?
Crossing the door sill she sat down at once
in firelight, against the nearest wall,
across the room from the lord Odysseus.
There
leaning against a pillar, sat the man
and never lifted up his eyes, but only waited
for what his wife would say when she had seen him.
And she, for a long time, sat deathly still
in wonderment—for sometimes as she gazed
she found him—yes, clearly—like her husband,
but sometimes blood and rags were all she saw.
Telémakhos' voice came to her ears:

"Mother,
cruel mother, do you feel nothing,
drawing yourself apart this way from Father?
Will you not sit with him and talk and question him?

What other woman could remain so cold?
Who shuns her lord, and he come back to her
from wars and wandering, after twenty years?
Your heart is hard as flint and never changes!"

Penélopê answered:

"I am stunned, child.
I cannot speak to him. I cannot question him.
I cannot keep my eyes upon his face.
If really he is Odysseus, truly home,
beyond all doubt we two shall know each other
better than you or anyone. There are
secret signs we know, we two."

A smile
came now to the lips of the patient hero, Odysseus,
who turned to Telémakhos and said:

"Peace: let your mother test me at her leisure.
Before long she will see and know me best.
These tatters, dirt—all that I'm caked with now—
make her look hard at me and doubt me still.
As to this massacre, we must see the end.
Whoever kills one citizen, you know,
and has no force of armed men at his back,
had better take himself abroad by night
and leave his kin. Well, we cut down the flower of Ithaka,
the mainstay of the town. Consider that."

Telémakhos replied respectfully:

"Dear Father,
enough that you yourself study the danger,
foresighted in combat as you are,
they say you have no rival.
We three stand
ready to follow you and fight. I say
for what our strength avails, we have the courage."

And the great tactician, Odysseus, answered:

"Good.
Here is our best maneuver, as I see it:
bathe, you three, and put fresh clothing on,
order the women to adorn themselves,
and let our admirable harper choose a tune
for dancing, some lighthearted air, and strum it.
Anyone going by, or any neighbor,
will think it is a wedding feast he hears.
These deaths must not be cried about the town

till we can slip away to our own woods. We'll see
what weapon, then, Zeus puts into our hands."

They listened attentively, and did his bidding,
bathed and dressed afresh; and all the maids
adorned themselves. Then Phêmios the harper
took his polished shell and plucked the strings,
moving the company to desire
for singing, for the sway and beat of dancing,
until they made the manor hall resound
with gaiety of men and grace of women.
Anyone passing on the road would say:

"Married at last, I see—the queen so many courted.
Sly, cattish wife! She would not keep—not she!—
the lord's estate until he came."

So travellers'
thoughts might run—but no one guessed the truth.
Greathearted Odysseus, home at last,
was being bathed now by Eurýnomê
and rubbed with golden oil, and clothed again
in a fresh tunic and a cloak. Athena
lent him beauty, head to foot. She made him
taller, and massive, too, with crisping hair
in curls like petals of wild hyacinth
but all red-golden. Think of gold infused
on silver by a craftsman, whose fine art
Hephaistos taught him, or Athena: one
whose work moves to delight: just so she lavished
beauty over Odysseus' head and shoulders.
He sat then in the same chair by the pillar,
facing his silent wife, and said:

"Strange woman,
the immortals of Olympos made you hard,
harder than any. Who else in the world
would keep aloof as you do from her husband
if he returned to her from years of trouble,
cast on his own land in the twentieth year?

Nurse, make up a bed for me to sleep on.
Her heart is iron in her breast."

Penélopê

spoke to Odysseus now. She said:
"Strange man,
if man you are . . . This is no pride on my part
nor scorn for you—not even wonder, merely.
I know so well how you—how he—appeared
boarding the ship for Troy. But all the same . . .

Make up his bed for him, Eurýkleia.
Place it outside the bedchamber my lord
built with his own hands. Pile the big bed
with fleeces, rugs, and sheets of purest linen."

With this she tried him to the breaking point,
and he turned on her in a flash raging:

"Woman, by heaven you've stung me now!
Who dared to move my bed?
No builder had the skill for that—unless
a god came down to turn the trick. No mortal
in his best days could budge it with a crowbar.
There is our pact and pledge, our secret sign,
built into that bed—my handiwork
and no one else's!
An old trunk of olive
grew like a pillar on the building plot,
and I laid out our bedroom round that tree,
lined up the stone walls, built the walls and roof,
gave it a doorway and smooth-fitting doors.
Then I lopped off the silvery leaves and branches,
hewed and shaped that stump from the roots up
into a bedpost, drilled it, let it serve
as model for the rest. I planed them all,
inlaid them all with silver, gold and ivory,
and stretched a bed between—a pliant web
of oxhide thongs dyed crimson.
There's our sign!
I know no more. Could someone's else's hand
have sawn that trunk and dragged the frame away?"

Their secret! as she heard it told, her knees
grew tremulous and weak, her heart failed her.
With eyes brimming tears she ran to him,
throwing her arms around his neck, and kissed him,
murmuring:

"Do not rage at me, Odysseus!
No one ever matched your caution! Think
what difficulty the gods gave: they denied us
life together in our prime and flowering years,
kept us from crossing into age together.
Forgive me, don't be angry. I could not
welcome you with love on sight! I armed myself
long ago against the frauds of men,
impostors who might come—and all those many
whose underhanded ways bring evil on!
Helen of Argos, daughter of Zeus and Leda,
would she have joined the stranger, lain with him,
if she had known her destiny? known the Akhaians
in arms would bring her back to her own country?

Surely a goddess moved her to adultery,
her blood unchilled by war and evil coming,
the years, the desolation; ours, too.
But here and now, what sign could be so clear
as this of our own bed?
No other man has ever laid eyes on it—
only my own slave, Aktoris, that my father
sent with me as a gift—she kept our door.
You make my stiff heart know that I am yours."

Now from his breast into his eyes the ache
of longing mounted, and he wept at last,
his dear wife, clear and faithful, in his arms,
longed for
as the sunwarmed earth is longed for by a swimmer
spent in rough water where his ship went down
under Poseidon's blows, gale winds and tons of sea.
Few men can keep alive through a big surf
to crawl, clotted with brine, on kindly beaches
in joy, in joy, knowing the abyss behind:
and so she too rejoiced, her gaze upon her husband,
her white arms round him pressed as though forever.

The rose Dawn might have found them weeping still
had not grey-eyed Athena slowed the night
when night was most profound, and held the Dawn
under the Ocean of the East. That glossy team,
Firebright and Daybright, the Dawn's horses
that draw her heavenward for men—Athena
stayed their harnessing.

Then said Odysseus:

"My dear, we have not won through to the end.
One trial—I do not know how long—is left for me
to see fulfilled. Teirêsias' ghost forewarned me
the night I stood upon the shore of Death, asking
about my friends' homecoming and my own.

But now the hour grows late, it is bed time,
rest will be sweet for us; let us lie down."

To this Penélopê replied:

"That bed,
that rest is yours whenever desire moves you,
now the kind powers have brought you home at last.
But as your thought has dwelt upon it, tell me:
what is the trial you face? I must know soon;
what does it matter if I learn tonight?"

The teller of many stories said:

"My strange one,
must you again, and even now,
urge me to talk? Here is a plodding tale;
no charm in it, no relish in the telling.
Teirêsias told me I must take an oar
and trudge the mainland, going from town to town,
until I discover men who have never known
the salt blue sea, nor flavor of salt meat—
strangers to painted prows, to watercraft
and oars like wings, dipping across the water.
The moment of revelation he foretold
was this, for you may share the prophecy:
some traveller falling in with me will say:
'A winnowing fan, that on your shoulder, sir?"
There I must plant my oar, on the very spot,
with burnt offerings to Poseidon of the Waters:
a ram, a bull, a great buck boar. Thereafter
when I come home again, I am to slay
full hekatombs to the gods who own broad heaven,
one by one.
Then death will drift upon me
from seaward, mild as air, mild as your hand,
in my well-tended weariness of age,
contented folk around me on our island.
He said all this must come."

Penélopê said:

"If by the gods' grace age at least is kind,
we have that promise—trials will end in peace."

So he confided in her, and she answered.
Meanwhile Eurýnomê and the nurse together
laid soft coverlets on the master's bed,
working in haste by torchlight. Eurýkleia
retired to her quarters for the night,
and then Eurýnomê, as maid-in-waiting,
lighted her lord and lady to their chamber
with bright brands.

She vanished.
So they came
into that bed so steadfast, loved of old,
opening glad arms to one another.[8]
Telémakhos by now had hushed the dancing,
hushed the women. In the darkened hall
he and the cowherd and the swineherd slept.

8. Two great Alexandrian critics said that this line was the "end" of the *Odyssey* (though one of the words they are said to have used could mean simply "culmination"). Modern critics are divided; some find the rest of the poem banal, unartistic, full of linguistic anomalies, and so on. But if the poem stops here we are left in suspense about many important themes that have been developed and demand a sequel—the question of reprisals for the slaughter in the hall, to mention only one.

The royal pair mingled in love again
and afterward lay revelling in stories:
hers of the siege her beauty stood at home
from arrogant suitors, crowding on her sight,
and how they fed their courtship on his cattle,
oxen and fat sheep, and drank up rivers
of wine out of the vats.
Odysseus told
of what hard blows he had dealt out to others
and of what blows he had taken—all that story.
She could not close her eyes till all was told.

His raid on the Kikonês, first of all,
then how he visited the Lotos Eaters,
and what the Kyklops did, and how those shipmates,
pitilessly devoured, were avenged.
Then of his touching Aiolos's isle
and how that king refitted him for sailing
to Ithaka; all vain: gales blew him back
groaning over the fishcold sea. Then how
he reached the Laistrygonians' distant bay
and how they smashed his ships and his companions.
Kirkê, then: of her deceits and magic,
then of his voyage to the wide underworld
of dark, the house of Death, and questioning
Teirêsias, Theban spirit.
Dead companions,
many, he saw there, and his mother, too.
Of this he told his wife, and told how later
he heard the choir of maddening Seirênês,
coasted the Wandering Rocks, Kharybdis' pool
and the fiend Skylla who takes toll of men.
Then how his shipmates killed Lord Hêlios' cattle
and how Zeus thundering in towering heaven
split their fast ship with his fuming bolt,
so all hands perished.
He alone survived,
cast away on Kalypso's isle, Ogýgia.
He told, then, how that nymph detained him there
in her smooth caves, craving him for her husband,
and how in her devoted lust she swore
he should not die nor grow old, all his days,
but he held out against her.
Last of all
what sea-toil brought him to the Phaiákians;
their welcome; how they took him to their hearts
and gave him passage to his own dear island
with gifts of garments, gold and bronze . . .
Remembering,
he drowsed over the story's end. Sweet sleep
relaxed his limbs and his care-burdened breast.

Other affairs were in Athena's keeping.
Waiting until Odysseus had his pleasure
of love and sleep, the grey-eyed one bestirred
the fresh Dawn from her bed of paling Ocean
to bring up daylight to her golden chair,
and from his fleecy bed Odysseus
arose. He said to Penélopê:

"My lady,
what ordeals have we not endured! Here, waiting
you had your grief, while my return dragged out—
my hard adventures, pitting myself against
the gods' will, and Zeus, who pinned me down
far from home. But now our life resumes:
we've come together to our longed-for bed.
Take care of what is left me in our house;
as to the flocks that pack of wolves laid waste
they'll be replenished: scores I'll get on raids
and other scores our island friends will give me
till all the folds are full again.
This day
I'm off up country to the orchards. I must see
my noble father, for he missed me sorely.
And here is my command for you—a strict one,
though you may need none, clever as you are.
Word will get about as the sun goes higher
of how I killed those lads. Go to your rooms
on the upper floor, and take your women. Stay there
with never a glance outside or a word to anyone."

Fitting cuirass and swordbelt to his shoulders,
he woke his herdsmen, woke Telémakhos,
ordering all in arms. They dressed quickly,
and all in war gear sallied from the gate,
led by Odysseus.
Now it was broad day
but these three men Athena hid in darkness,
going before them swiftly from the town.

BOOK XXIV

[*Warriors, Farewell*]

Meanwhile the suitors' ghosts were called away
by Hermês of Kyllênê,[9] bearing the golden wand
with which he charms the eyes of men or wakens
whom he wills.
He waved them on, all squeaking
as bats will in a cavern's underworld,
all flitting, flitting criss-cross in the dark
if one falls and the rock-hung chain is broken.

9. A mountain in Arcadia, Hermês' birthplace.

So with faint cries the shades trailed after Hermês,
pure Deliverer.
He led them down dank ways,
over grey Ocean tides, the Snowy Rock,
past shores of Dream and narrows of the sunset,
in swift flight to where the Dead inhabit
wastes of asphodel at the world's end.

Crossing the plain they met Akhilleus' ghost,
Patróklos and Antílokhos, then Aias,
noblest of Danaans after Akhilleus
in strength and beauty. Here the newly dead
drifted together, whispering. Then came
the soul of Agamémnon, son of Atreus,
in black pain forever, surrounded by men-at-arms
who perished with him in Aigísthos' hall.

Akhilleus greeted him:

"My lord Atreidês,
we held that Zeus who loves the play of lightning
would give you length of glory, you were king
over so great a host of soldiery
before Troy, where wc suffered, we Akhaians.
But in the morning of your life
you met that doom that no man born avoids.
It should have found you in your day of victory,
marshal of the army, in Troy country;
then all Akhaia would have heaped your tomb
and saved your honor for your son. Instead
piteous death awaited you at home."

And Atreus' son replied:

"Fortunate hero,
son of Pêleus, godlike and glorious,
at Troy you died, across the sea from Argos,
and round you Trojan and Akhaian peers
fought for your corpse and died. A dustcloud wrought
by a whirlwind hid the greatness of you slain,
minding no more the mastery of horses.
All that day we might have toiled in battle
had not a storm from Zeus broken it off.
We carried you out of the field of war
down to the ships and bathed your comely body
with warm water and scented oil. We laid you
upon your long bed, and our officers
wept hot tears like rain and cropped their hair.
Then hearing of it in the sea, your mother, Thetis,
came with nereids of the grey wave crying
unearthly lamentation over the water,
and trembling gripped the Akhaians to the bone.

They would have boarded ship that night and fled
except for one man's wisdom—venerable
Nestor, proven counselor in the past.
He stood and spoke to allay their fear: 'Hold fast,
sons of the Akhaians, lads of Argos.
His mother it must be, with nymphs her sisters,
come from the sea to mourn her son in death."

Veteran hearts at this contained their dread
while at your side the daughters of the ancient
seagod wailed and wrapped ambrosial shrouding
around you.
Then we heard the Muses sing
a threnody in nine immortal voices.
No Argive there but wept, such keening rose
from that one Muse who led the song.
Now seven
days and ten, seven nights and ten, we mourned you,
we mortal men, with nymphs who know no death,
before we gave you to the flame, slaughtering
longhorned steers and fat sheep on your pyre.

Dressed by the nereids and embalmed with honey,
honey and unguent in the seething blaze,
you turned to ash. And past the pyre Akhaia's
captains paraded in review, in arms,
clattering chariot teams and infantry.
Like a forest fire the flame roared on, and burned
your flesh away. Next day at dawn, Akhilleus,
we picked your pale bones from the char to keep
in wine and oil. A golden amphora
your mother gave for this—Hephaistos' work,
a gift from Dionysos.[1] In that vase,
Akhilleus, hero, lie your pale bones mixed
with mild Patróklos' bones, who died before you,
and nearby lie the bones of Antílokhos,
the one you cared for most of all companions
after Patróklos.
We of the Old Army,
we who were spearmen, heaped a tomb for these
upon a foreland over Hellê's waters,[2]
to be a mark against the sky for voyagers
in this generation and those to come.
Your mother sought from the gods magnificent trophies
and set them down midfield for our champions. Often
at funeral games after the death of kings
when you yourself contended, you've seen athletes
cinch their belts when trophies went on view.
But these things would have made you stare—the treasures

1. A god of the countryside especially associated with wine. Rarely mentioned in Homer, he later presides, at the Athenian festivals, over tragedy and comedy. 2. The Hellespont, the strait separating Asia Minor from Europe, visible from Troy.

Thetis on her silver-slippered feet
brought to your games—for the gods held you dear.
You perished, but your name will never die.
It lives to keep all men in mind of honor
forever, Akhilleus.
As for myself, what joy
is this, to have brought off the war? Foul death
Zeus held in store for me at my coming home;
Aigísthos and my vixen cut me down."

While they conversed, the Wayfinder came near,
leading the shades of suitors overthrown
by Lord Odysseus. The two souls of heroes
advanced together, scrutinizing these.
Then Agamémnon recognized Amphímedon,
son of Meláneus—friends of his on Ithaka—
and called out to him:

"Amphímedon,
what ruin brought you into this undergloom?
All in a body, picked men, and so young?
One could not better choose the kingdom's pride.
Were you at sea, aboard ship, and Poseidon
blew up a dire wind and foundering waves,
or cattle-raiding, were you, on the mainland,
or in a fight for some stronghold, or women,
when the foe hit you to your mortal hurt?
Tell me, answer my question. Guest and friend
I say I am of yours—or do you not remember
I visited your family there? I came
with Prince Meneláos, urging Odysseus
to join us in the great sea raid on Troy.
One solid month we beat our way, breasting
south sea and west, resolved to bring him round,
the wily raider of cities."

The new shade said:

"O glory of commanders, Agamémnon,
all that you bring to mind I remember well.
As for the sudden manner of our death
I'll tell you of it clearly, first to last.
After Odysseus had been gone for years
we were all suitors of his queen. She never
quite refused, nor went through with a marriage,
hating it, ever bent on our defeat.
Here is one of her tricks: she placed her loom,
her big loom, out for weaving in her hall,
and the fine warp of some vast fabric on it.
We were attending her, and she said to us:
'Young men, my suitors, now my lord is dead,
let me finish my weaving before I marry,

or else my thread will have been spun in vain.
This is a shroud I weave for Lord Laërtês
when cold Death comes to lay him on his bier.
The country wives would hold me in dishonor
if he, with all his fortune, lay unshrouded.'
We had men's hearts; she touched them; we agreed.
So every day she wove on the great loom—
but every night by torchlight she unwove it,
and so for three years she deceived the Akhaians.
But when the seasons brought the fourth around,
as long months waned, and the slow days were spent,
one of her maids, who knew the secret, told us.
We found her unraveling the splendid shroud,
and then she had to finish, willy nilly—
finish, and show the big loom woven tight
from beam to beam with cloth. She washed the shrouding
clean as sun or moonlight.
Then, heaven knows
from what quarter of the world, fatality
brought in Odysseus to the swineherd's wood
far up the island. There his son went too
when the black ship put him ashore from Pylos.
The two together planned our death-trap. Down
they came to the famous town—Telémakhos
long in advance: we had to wait for Odysseus.
The swineherd led him to the manor later
in rags like a foul beggar, old and broken,
propped on a stick. These tatters that he wore
hid him so well that none of us could know him
when he turned up, not even the older men.
We jeered at him, took potshots at him, cursed him.
Daylight and evening in his own great hall
he bore it, patient as a stone. That night
the mind of Zeus beyond the stormcloud stirred him
with Telémakhos at hand to shift his arms
from mégaron to storage room and lock it.
Then he assigned his wife her part: next day
she brought his bow and iron axeheads out
to make a contest. Contest there was none;
that move doomed us to slaughter. Not a man
could bend the stiff bow to his will or string it,
until it reached Odysseus. We shouted,
'Keep the royal bow from the beggar's hands
no matter how he begs!' Only Telémakhos
would not be denied.
So the great soldier
took his bow and bent it for the bowstring
effortlessly. He drilled the axeheads clean,
sprang, and decanted arrows on the door sill,
glared, and drew again. This time he killed
Antínoös.
There facing us he crouched

and shot his bolts of groaning at us, brought us
down like sheep. Then some god, his familiar,
went into action with him round the hall,
after us in a massacre. Men lay groaning,
mortally wounded, and the floor smoked with blood.

That was the way our death came, Agamémnon.
Now in Odysseus' hall untended still
our bodies lie, unknown to friends or kinsmen
who should have laid us out and washed our wounds
free of the clotted blood, and mourned our passing.
So much is due the dead."

But Agamémnon's
tall shade when he heard this cried aloud:

"O fortunate Odysseus, master mariner
and soldier, blessed son of old Laërtês!
The girl you brought home made a valiant wife!
True to her husband's honor and her own,
Penélopê, Ikários' faithful daughter!
The very gods themselves will sing her story
for men on earth—mistress of her own heart,
Penélopê!
Tyndáreus' daughter waited, too—how differently!
Klytaimnéstra, the adulteress,
waited to stab her lord and king. That song
will be forever hateful. A bad name
she gave to womankind, even the best."

These were the things they said to one another
under the rim of earth where Death is lord.

Leaving the town, Odysseus and his men
that morning reached Laërtês garden lands,
long since won by his toil from wilderness—
his homestead, and the row of huts around it
where fieldhands rested, ate and slept. Indoors
he had an old slave woman, a Sikel, keeping
house for him in his secluded age.

Odysseus here took leave of his companions.

"Go make yourselves at home inside," he said.
"Roast the best porker and prepare a meal.
I'll go to try my father. Will he know me?
Can he imagine it, after twenty years?"

He handed spear and shield to the two herdsmen,
and in they went, Telémakhos too. Alone
Odysseus walked the orchard rows and vines.
He found no trace of Dólios and his sons

nor the other slaves—all being gone that day
to clear a distant field, and drag the stones
for a boundary wall.
But on a well-banked plot
Odysseus found his father in solitude
spading the earth around a young fruit tree.

He wore a tunic, patched and soiled, and leggings—
oxhide patches, bound below his knees
against the brambles; gauntlets on his hands
and on his head a goatskin cowl of sorrow.
This was the figure Prince Odysseus found—
wasted by years, racked, bowed under grief.
The son paused by a tall pear tree and wept,
then inwardly debated: should he run
forward and kiss his father, and pour out
his tale of war, adventure, and return,
or should he first interrogate him, test him?
Better that way, he thought—
first draw him out with sharp words, trouble him.
His mind made up, he walked ahead. Laërtês
went on digging, head down, by the sapling,
stamping the spade in. At his elbow then
his son spoke out:

"Old man, the orchard keeper
you work for is no townsman. A good eye
for growing things he has; there's not a nurseling,
fig tree, vine stock, olive tree or pear tree
or garden bed uncared for on this farm.
But I might add—don't take offense—your own
appearance could be tidier. Old age
yes—but why the squalor, and rags to boot?
It would not be for sloth, now, that your master
leaves you in this condition; neither at all
because there's any baseness in your self.
No, by your features, by the frame you have,
a man might call you kingly,
one who should bathe warm, sup well, and rest easy
in age's privilege. But tell me:
who are your masters? whose fruit trees are these
you tend here? Tell me if it's true this island
is Ithaka, as that fellow I fell in with
told me on the road just now? He had
a peg loose, that one: couldn't say a word
or listen when I asked about my friend,
my Ithakan friend. I asked if he were alive
or gone long since into the underworld.
I can describe him if you care to hear it:
I entertained the man in my own land
when he turned up there on a journey; never
had I a guest more welcome in my house.

He claimed his stock was Ithakan: Laërtês
Arkeísiadês, he said his father was.
I took him home, treated him well, grew fond of him—
though we had many guests—and gave him
gifts in keeping with his quality: seven
bars of measured gold, a silver winebowl
filigreed with flowers, twelve light cloaks,
twelve rugs, robes and tunics—not to mention
his own choice of women trained in service,
the four well-favored ones he wished to take."

His father's eyes had filled with tears. He said:

"You've come to that man's island, right enough,
but dangerous men and fools hold power now.
You gave your gifts in vain. If you could find him
here in Ithaka alive, he'd make
return of gifts and hospitality,
as custom is, when someone has been generous.
But tell me accurately—how many years
have now gone by since that man was your guest?
your guest, my son—if he indeed existed—
born to ill fortune as he was. Ah, far
from those who loved him, far from his native land,
in some sea-dingle fish have picked his bones,
or else he made the vultures and wild beasts
a trove ashore! His mother at his bier
never bewailed him, nor did I, his father,
nor did his admirable wife, Penélopê,
who should have closed her husband's eyes in death
and cried aloud upon him as he lay.
So much is due the dead.
But speak out, tell me further:
who are you, of what city and family?
where have you moored the ship that brought you here,
where is your admirable crew? Are you a peddler
put ashore by the foreign ship you came on?"

Again Odysseus had a fable ready.

"Yes," he said, "I can tell you all those things.
I come from Rover's Passage where my home is,
and I'm King Allwoes' only son. My name
is Quarrelman.
Heaven's power in the westwind
drove me this way from Sikania,[3]
off my course. My ship lies in a barren
cove beyond the town there. As for Odysseus,
now is the fifth year since he put to sea
and left my homeland—bound for death, you say.

3. Another name for Sicily.

Yet landbirds flying from starboard crossed his bow—
a lucky augury. So we parted joyously,
in hope of friendly days and gifts to come."

A cloud of pain had fallen on Laërtês.
Scooping up handfuls of the sunburnt dust
he sifted it over his grey head, and groaned,
and the groan went to the son's heart. A twinge
prickling up through his nostrils warned Odysseus
he could not watch this any longer.
He leaped and threw his arms around his father,
kissed him, and said:

"Oh, Father, I am he!
Twenty years gone, and here I've come again
to my own land!
Hold back your tears! No grieving!
I bring good news—though still we cannot rest.
I killed the suitors to the last man!
Outrage and injury have been avenged!"

Laërtês turned and found his voice to murmur:

"If you are Odysseus, my son, come back,
give me some proof, a sign to make me sure."

His son replied:

"The scar then, first of all.
Look, here the wild boar's flashing tusk
wounded me on Parnassos; do you see it?
You and my mother made me go, that time,
to visit Lord Autólykos, her father,
for gifts he promised years before on Ithaka.
Again—more proof—let's say the trees you gave me
on this revetted plot of orchard once.
I was a small boy at your heels, wheedling
amid the young trees, while you named each one.
You gave me thirteen pear, ten apple trees,
and forty fig trees. Fifty rows of vines
were promised too, each one to bear in turn
Bunches of every hue would hang there ripening,
weighed down by the god of summer days."

The old man's knees failed him, his heart grew faint,
recalling all that Odysseus calmly told.
He clutched his son. Odysseus held him swooning
until he got his breath back and his spirit
and spoke again:

"Zeus, Father! Gods above!—
you still hold pure Olympos, if the suitors

paid for their crimes indeed, and paid in blood!
But now the fear is in me that all Ithaka
will be upon us. They'll send messengers
to stir up every city of the islands."

Odysseus the great tactician answered:

"Courage, and leave the worrying to me.
We'll turn back to your homestead by the orchard.
I sent the cowherd, swineherd, and Telémakhos
ahead to make our noonday meal."

Conversing
in this vein they went home, the two together,
into the stone farmhouse. There Telémakhos
and the two herdsmen were already carving
roast young pork, and mixing amber wine.
During these preparations the Sikel woman
bathed Laërtês and anointed him,
and dressed him in a new cloak. Then Athena,
standing by, filled out his limbs again,
gave girth and stature to the old field captain
fresh from the bathing place. His son looked on
in wonder at the godlike bloom upon him,
and called out happily:

"Oh, Father,
surely one of the gods who are young forever
has made you magnificent before my eyes!"

Clearheaded Laërtês faced him, saying:

"By Father Zeus, Athena and Apollo,
I wish I could be now as once I was,
commander of Kephallenians, when I took
the walled town, Nérikos,[4] on the promontory!
Would god I had been young again last night
with armor on me, standing in our hall
to fight the suitors at your side! How many
knees I could have crumpled, to your joy!"

While son and father spoke, cowherd and swineherd
attended, waiting, for the meal was ready.
Soon they were all seated, and their hands
picked up the meat and bread.

But now old Dólios
appeared in the bright doorway with his sons,
work-stained from the field. Laërtês' housekeeper,
who reared the boys and tended Dólios

4. On the mainland; its exact location is unknown.

in his bent age, had gone to fetch them in.
When it came over them who the stranger was
they halted in astonishment. Odysseus
hit an easy tone with them. Said he:

"Sit down and help yourselves. Shake off your wonder.
Here we've been waiting for you all this time,
and our mouths watering for good roast pig!"

But Dólios came forward, arms outstretched,
and kissed Odysseus' hand at the wrist bone,
crying out:

"Dear master, you returned!
You came to us again! How we had missed you!
We thought you lost. The gods themselves have brought you!
Welcome, welcome; health and blessings on you!
And tell me, now, just one thing more: Penélopê,
does she know yet that you are on the island?
or should we send a messenger?"

Odysseus gruffly said,
"Old man, she knows.
Is it for you to think of her?"

So Dólios
quietly took a smooth bench at the table
and in their turn his sons welcomed Odysseus,
kissing his hands; then each went to his chair
beside his father. Thus our friends
were occupied in Laërtês' house at noon.

Meanwhile to the four quarters of the town
the news ran: bloody death had caught the suitors;
and men and women in a murmuring crowd
gathered before Odysseus' hall. They gave
burial to the piteous dead, or bore
the bodies of young men from other islands
down to the port, thence to be ferried home.
Then all the men went grieving to assembly
and being seated, rank by rank, grew still,
as old Eupeithês rose to address them. Pain
lay in him like a brand for Antínoös,
the first man that Odysseus brought down,
and tears flowed for his son as he began:

"Heroic feats that fellow did for us
Akhaians, friends! Good spearmen by the shipload
he led to war and lost—lost ships and men,
and once ashore again killed these, who were
the islands' pride.
Up with you! After him!—

before he can take flight to Pylos town
or hide at Elis, under Epeian law!
We'd be disgraced forever! Mocked for generations
if we cannot avenge our sons' blood, and our brothers'!
Life would turn to ashes—at least for me;
rather be dead and join the dead!
I say
we ought to follow now, or they'll gain time
and make the crossing."
His appeal, his tears,
moved all the gentry listening there;
but now they saw the crier and the minstrel
come from Odysseus' hall, where they had slept.
The two men stood before the curious crowd,
and Medôn said:

"Now hear me, men of Ithaka.
When these hard deeds were done by Lord Odysseus
the immortal gods were not far off. I saw
with my own eyes someone divine who fought
beside him, in the shape and dress of Mentor;
it was a god who shone before Odysseus,
a god who swept the suitors down the hall
dying in droves."
At this pale fear assailed them,
and next they heard again the old forecaster,
Halithérsês Mastóridês. Alone
he saw the field of time, past and to come.
In his anxiety for them he said:

"Ithakans, now listen to what I say.
Friends, by your own fault these deaths came to pass.
You would not heed me nor the captain, Mentor;
would not put down the riot of your sons.
Heroic feats they did!—all wantonly
raiding a great man's flocks, dishonoring
his queen, because they thought he'd come no more.
Let matters rest; do as I urge; no chase,
or he who wants a bloody end will find it."

The greater number stood up shouting "Aye!"
But many held fast, sitting all together
in no mind to agree with him. Eupeithês
had won them to his side. They ran for arms,
clapped on their bronze, and mustered
under Eupeithês at the town gate
for his mad foray.
Vengeance would be his,
he thought, for his son's murder; but that day
held bloody death for him and no return.

At this point, querying Zeus, Athena said:

"O Father of us all and king of kings,
enlighten me. What is your secret will?
War and battle, worse and more of it,
or can you not impose a pact on both?"

The summoner of cloud replied:

"My child,
why this formality of inquiry?
Did you not plan that action by yourself—
see to it that Odysseus, on his homecoming,
should have their blood?
Conclude it as you will.
There is one proper way, if I may say so:
Odysseus' honor being satisfied,
let him be king by a sworn pact forever,
and we, for our part, will blot out the memory
of sons and brothers slain. As in the old time
let men of Ithaka henceforth be friends;
prosperity enough, and peace attend them."

Athena needed no command, but down
in one spring she descended from Olympos
just as the company of Odysseus finished
wheat crust and honeyed wine, and heard him say:

"Go out, someone, and see if they are coming."

One of the boys went to the door as ordered
and saw the townsmen in the lane. He turned
swiftly to Odysseus.

"Here they come,"
he said, "best arm ourselves, and quickly."

All up at once, the men took helm and shield—
four fighting men, counting Odysseus,
with Dólios' half dozen sons. Laërtês
armed as well, and so did Dólios—
greybeards, they could be fighters in a pinch.
Fitting their plated helmets on their heads
they sallied out, Odysseus in the lead.
Now from the air Athena, Zeus's daughter,
appeared in Mentor's guise, with Mentor's voice,
making Odysseus' heart grow light. He said
to put cheer in his son:

"Telémakhos,
you are going into battle against pikemen
where hearts of men are tried. I count on you
to bring no shame upon your forefathers.

In fighting power we have excelled this lot
in every generation."

Said his son:

"If you are curious, Father, watch and see
the stuff that's in me. No more talk of shame."

And old Laërtês cried aloud:

"Ah, what a day for me, dear gods!
to see my son and grandson vie in courage!"

Athena halted near him, and her eyes
shone like the sea. She said:

"Arkeísiadês,
dearest of all my old brothers-in-arms,
invoke the grey-eyed one and Zeus her father,
heft your spear and make your throw."

Power flowed into him from Pallas Athena,
whom he invoked as Zeus's virgin child,
and he let fly his heavy spear.
It struck
Eupeithês on the cheek plate of his helmet,
and undeflected the bronze head punched through.
He toppled, and his armor clanged upon him.
Odysseus and his son now furiously
closed, laying on with broadswords, hand to hand,
and pikes: they would have cut the enemy down
to the last man, leaving not one survivor,
had not Athena raised a shout
that stopped all fighters in their tracks.

"Now hold!"
she cried, "Break off this bitter skirmish;
end your bloodshed, Ithakans, and make peace."

Their faces paled with dread before Athena,
and swords dropped from their hands unnerved, to lie
strewing the ground, at the great voice of the goddess.
Those from the town turned fleeing for their lives.
But with a cry to freeze their hearts
and ruffling like an eagle on the pounce,
the lord Odysseus reared himself to follow—
at which the son of Kronos dropped a thunderbolt
smoking at his daughter's feet.
Athena
cast a grey glance at her friend and said:

"Son of Laërtês and the gods of old,
Odysseus, master of land ways and sea ways,
command yourself. Call off this battle now,
or Zeus who views the wide world may be angry."

He yielded to her, and his heart was glad.
Both parties later swore to terms of peace
set by their arbiter, Athena, daughter
of Zeus who bears the stormcloud as a shield—
though still she kept the form and voice of Mentor.

SAPPHO OF LESBOS

born ca. 630 B.C.

About Sappho's life we know very little: she was born about 630 B.C. on the fertile island of Lesbos off the coast of Asia Minor and spent most of her life there; she was married and had a daughter. Her lyric poems (poems sung to the accompaniment of the lyre) were so admired in the ancient world that a later poet called her the tenth Muse. In the third century B.C. scholars at the great library in Alexandria arranged her poems in nine books, of which the first contained more than a thousand lines. But what we have now is a pitiful remnant: one (or possibly two) complete short poems, and a collection of quotations from her work by ancient writers, supplemented by bits and pieces written on ancient scraps of papyrus found in excavations in Egypt. Yet these remnants fully justify the enthusiasm of the ancient critics; Sappho's poems (insofar as we can guess at their nature from the fragments) give us the most vivid evocation of the joys and sorrows of love in all Greek literature.

Her themes are those of a Greek woman's world—girlhood, marriage, and love, especially the love of young women for each other and the poignancy of their parting as they leave to assume the responsibilities of a wife. About the social context of these songs we can only guess; all that can be said is that they reflect a world in which women, at least women of the aristocracy, lived an intense communal life of their own, one of female occasions, functions, and festivities, in which their young passionate natures were fully engaged with each other; to most of them, presumably, this was a stage preliminary to their later career in that world as wife and mother.

The first two poems printed here were quoted in their entirety by ancient critics (though it is possible that there was another stanza at the end of the second); their text is not a problem. But the important recent additions to our knowledge of Sappho's poetry, the pieces of ancient books found in Egypt, are difficult to read and usually full of gaps. Our third selection, in fact, comes from the municipal rubbish heap of the Egyptian village Oxyrhyncus. Most of the gaps in the text are due to holes or tears in the papyrus and can easily be filled in from our knowledge of Sappho's dialect and the strict meter in which she wrote, but the end of the third stanza and the whole of the fourth are imaginative reconstructions by the translator. The papyrus, for instance, tells us only that someone or something led Helen astray; Lattimore's "Queen of Cyprus" (the love goddess, Aphrodite) may well be right but is not certain. In the next stanza all that we have is part of a word that means something like "flexible" (Lattimore's "hearts that can be persuaded"); an adverb, *lightly;* and "remembering Anaktoria who is not here." As a matter of fact we don't have that all-important *not,* but the sense demands it. Fortunately, the final stanza, with its telling echo of the opening theme, is almost intact.

A fine recent translation of Sappho's poetry, with excellent introduction and notes, is given in Diane Rayor, *Sappho's Lyre: Archaic Lyric and Women Poets of Ancient Greece* (1991). Accessible surveys from varying points of view may be found in Jane M. Snyder, *The Woman and the Lyre: Women Writers in Classical Greece and Rome* (1989), Richard Jenkyns, *Three Classical Poets: Sappho, Catullus, and Juvenal* (1982), and Anne Burnett, *Three Archaic Poets: Archilochus, Alcaeus, Sappho* (1983). An outstanding assessment of Sappho's position as a woman in Greek society is John J. Winkler, "Double Consciousness in Sappho's Lyrics," in his *The Constraints of Desire: The Anthropology of Sex and Gender in Ancient Greece* (1990). Page duBois, *Sappho Is Burning* (1995), is a challenging discussion of Sappho's poetry as resisting the categories of Western thought.

[LYRICS]

[Throned in splendor, deathless, O Aphrodite][1]

Throned in splendor, deathless, O Aphrodite,[2]
child of Zeus, charm-fashioner, I entreat you
not with griefs and bitternesses to break my
spirit, O goddess:

standing by me rather, if once before now
far away you heard, when I called upon you,
left your father's dwelling place and descended,
yoking the golden

chariot to sparrows,[3] who fairly drew you
down in speed aslant the black world, the bright air
trembling at the heart to the pulse of countless
fluttering wingbeats.

Swiftly then they came, and you, blessed lady,
smiling on me out of immortal beauty,
asked me what affliction was on me, why I
called thus upon you,

what beyond all else I would have befall my
tortured heart: "Whom then would you have Persuasion
force to serve desire in your heart? Who is it,
Sappho, that hurt you?

Though she now escape, she soon will follow;
though she take not gifts from you, she will give them:
though she love not, yet she will surely love you
even unwilling."

In such guise come even again and set me
free from doubt and sorrow; accomplish all those

1. All selections translated by Richmond Lattimore. 2. A prayer to the goddess of love, Aphrodite. The translator has skillfully reproduced the metrical form of the Greek, the "Sapphic" stanza. 3. Aphrodite's sacred birds.

things my heart desires to be done; appear and
stand at my shoulder.

[Like the very gods in my sight is he]

Like the very gods in my sight is he who
sits where he can look in your eyes, who listens
close to you, to hear the soft voice, its sweetness
murmur in love and

laughter, all for him. But it breaks my spirit;
underneath my breast all the heart is shaken.
Let me only glance where you are, the voice dies,
I can say nothing,

but my lips are stricken to silence, underneath my skin the tenuous flame suffuses;
nothing shows in front of my eyes, my ears are
muted in thunder.

And the sweat breaks running upon me, fever
shakes my body, paler I turn than grass is;
I can feel that I have been changed, I feel that
death has come near me.

[Some there are who say that the fairest thing seen]

Some there are who say that the fairest thing seen
on the black earth is an array of horsemen;
some, men marching; some would say ships; but I say
she whom one loves best

is the loveliest. Light were the work to make this
plain to all, since she, who surpassed in beauty
all mortality, Helen, once forsaking
her lordly husband,

fled away to Troy—land across the water.
Not the thought of child nor beloved parents
was remembered, after the Queen of Cyprus[1]
won her at first sight.

Since young brides have hearts that can be persuaded
easily, light things, palpitant to passion
as am I, remembering Anaktória
who has gone from me

1. Aphrodite.

and whose lovely walk and the shining pallor
of her face I would rather see before my
eyes than Lydia's chariots in all their glory
armored for battle.

AESCHYLUS
524?–456 B.C.

The earliest documents in the history of the Western theater are the seven plays of Aeschylus that have come down to us through the more than twenty-four hundred years since his death. When he produced his first play in the opening years of the fifth century B.C., the performance that we know as drama was still less than half a century old, still open to innovation—and Aeschylus, in fact, made such significant contributions to its development that he has been called "the creator of tragedy."

The origins of the theatrical contests in Athens are obscure; they were a puzzle even for Aristotle, who in the fourth century B.C. wrote a famous treatise on tragedy. All that we know for certain is that the drama began as a religious celebration that took the form of song and dance.

Such ceremonies are of course to be found in the communal life of many early cultures, but it was in Athens, and in Athens alone, that the ceremony gave rise to what we know as tragedy and comedy and produced dramatic masterpieces that are still admired, read, and performed.

At some time in the late sixth century B.C. the Athenians converted what seems to have been a rural celebration of Dionysus, a vegetation deity especially associated with the vine, into an annual city festival at which dancing choruses, competing for prizes, sang hymns of praise to the god. It was from this choral performance that tragedy and comedy developed. Some unknown innovator (his name was probably Thespis) combined the choral song with the speech of a masked actor, who, playing a god or hero, engaged the chorus in dialogue. It was Aeschylus who added a second actor and so created the possibility of conflict and the prototype of the drama as we know it.

After the defeat of the Persian invaders (480–479 B.C.), as Athens with its fleets and empire moved toward supremacy in the Greek world, this spring festival became a splendid occasion. The Dionysia, as it was now called, lasted for four or five days, during which public business (except in emergencies) was suspended and prisoners were released on bail for the duration of the festival. In an open-air theater that could seat seventeen thousand spectators, tragic and comic poets competed for the prizes offered by the city. Poets in each genre had been selected by the magistrates for the year. On each of three days of the festival, a tragic poet presented three tragedies and a satyr play (a burlesque on a mythic theme), and a comic poet produced one comedy.

The three tragedies could deal with quite separate stories or, as in the case of Aeschylus's *Oresteia,* with the successive stages of one extended action. By the time this trilogy was produced (458 B.C.) the number of actors had been raised to three; the spoken part of the performance became steadily more important. In the *Oresteia* an equilibrium between the two elements of the performance has been established. The actors, with their speeches, create the dramatic situation and its movement, the plot; the chorus, while contributing to dramatic suspense and illusion, ranges free of the immediate situation in its odes, which extend and amplify the significance of the action.

In 458 B.C. Aeschylus was at the end of a great career; he died two years later in the Greek city Gela, in Sicily. He had begun his career as a dramatist before the Persian Wars, in the first days of the new Athenian democracy. He fought against the Persians at Marathon (where his brother was killed) and almost certainly also in the great sea fight at Salamis in 480 B.C. (his play the *Persians,* produced in 472 B.C., contains what sounds like an eyewitness account of that battle). Only seven of his plays survive (we know that he produced ninety); besides the *Persians* and the three plays of the *Oresteia,* we have the text of *Suppliants* (sometime in the 460s), *The Seven Against Thebes* (467), and the famous and influential play *Prometheus Bound* (date unknown).

The *Oresteia* is a trilogy. The first play, *Agamemnon,* was followed at its performance by two more plays, *The Libation Bearers* and *The Eumenides*, which carried on its story and theme to a conclusion. The theme of the trilogy is justice, and its story, like that of almost all Greek tragedies, is a legend that was already well known to the audience that saw the first performance of the play. This particular legend, the story of the house of Atreus, is rich in dramatic potential, for it deals with a series of retributive murders that stained the hands of three generations of a royal family, and it has also a larger significance, social and historical, of which Aeschylus took full advantage. The legend preserves the memory of an important historical process through which the Greeks had passed: the transition from tribal institutions of justice to communal justice, from a tradition that demanded that a murdered person's next of kin avenge the death to a system requiring settlement of the private quarrel by a court of law (the typical institution of the city-state, which replaced the primitive tribe). When Agamemnon returns victorious from Troy, he is killed by his wife, Clytemnestra, and her lover, Aegisthus, who is Agamemnon's cousin. Clytemnestra kills her husband to avenge her daughter Iphigenia, whom Agamemnon sacrificed to the goddess Artemis when he had to choose between his daughter's life and his ambition to conquer Troy. Aegisthus avenges the crime of a previous generation, the hideous murder of his brothers by Agamemnon's father, Atreus. The killing of Agamemnon is, by the standards of the old system, justice; but it is the nature of this justice that the process can never be arrested, that one act of violence must give rise to another. Agamemnon's murder must be avenged too, as it is in the second play of the trilogy by Orestes, his son, who kills both Aegisthus and Clytemnestra, his own mother. Orestes has acted justly according to the code of tribal society based on blood relationship, but in doing so he has violated the most sacred blood relationship of all, the bond between mother and son. The old system of justice has produced an insoluble dilemma.

At the end of *The Libation Bearers*, Orestes sees a vision of the Furies. They are serpent-haired female hunters, the avengers of blood. Agamemnon had a son to avenge him, but for Clytemnestra there was no one to exact payment. This task is taken up by the Furies, who are the guardians of the ancient tribal sanctities; they enforce the old dispensation when no earthly agent is at hand to do so. Female themselves, they assert the claim of the mother against the son who killed her to avenge his father. At the end of the second play they are only a vision in Orestes' mind—"You can't see them," he says to the chorus. "*I* can; they drive me on. I must move on." But in the final play we see them too; they are the chorus, and they have pursued Orestes to the great shrine of Apollo at Delphi where he has come to seek refuge.

Apollo can save him from immediate destruction at the Furies' hands, but he cannot resolve the dilemma. Orestes must go to Athens, where Athena, the patron goddess of the city, will set up the first court of law to try his case. At Athens, before the ancient court of the Areopagus, the Furies argue eloquently, but Apollo himself arrives to testify that he ordered Orestes to act. Athena tilts the judges' vote in Orestes' favor by either creating or breaking a tie with her own vote, and Orestes, acquitted, goes home to Argos. The Furies threaten to turn their dreadful wrath against Athens itself, but the goddess persuades them to accept a home deep in Athenian earth, to act as protectors of the court and of the land.

The arguments employed in the trial may not strike us as compelling, and may appear disappointing as an answer to the problems of guilt and justice raised by the trilogy. A possible reply is the "progressivist" argument. According to this argument, the fact of the court's establishment is more important than the particular judgment in Orestes' case. This is the end of an old era and the beginning of a new. The court institutes a system of communal justice, which punishes impersonally and has at last replaced the inconclusive anarchy of individual revenge. Besides, the trilogy not only is concerned with the history of human institutions but also makes a religious statement. The sequence of murderous acts and counteracts over three generations, leading to an important advance in human understanding and civilization, can be seen as the working out of the will of Zeus. The chorus of *Agamemnon*, celebrating the power of Zeus, tells us that he

> has led us on to know,
> the Helmsman lays it down as law
> that we must suffer, suffer into truth.

From suffering come understanding and progress. That is Zeus's design in the trilogy, whereas in the *Iliad*, where events also are guided by a plan of Zeus, nothing at all comes out of the suffering except the certainty of more suffering. The ending of the *Eumenides*, then, when the Furies call blessings down on Athens, gives a vision of a city ruled by law and living in harmony with its land and its gods. In this story of progress painfully won, Aeschylus offers Athenian democracy its charter myth just as it is entering the era of its greatest achievements and its greatest risks.

This "progressivist" reading of the *Oresteia* has considerable force, but it does not account for everything. It leaves out, for example, one of the costs of this progress that the trilogy also shows clearly: gender asymmetry. In *Agamemnon*, Clytemnestra is a powerful and transgressive figure, a woman who "maneuvers like a man," as the Watchman says the first time she is mentioned in the play. Her murder of her husband is, in Greek terms, only an intensified form of this self-assertion, and, by raising the specter of a woman out of control, it justifies women's normal subjugation in Greek culture. But in avenging Iphigeneia, Clytemnestra also defends the integrity of the family, and particularly the parent-child bond, against her husband's public ambition, to which he has sacrificed their daughter. She asserts this bond again in her last moments, when she bares her breast to Orestes to dissuade him from killing her. In murdering her husband in the name of her child, she has struck at the basis of marriage, but she does have a measure of justice on her side, not to mention a claim of vengeance against her son. Orestes' acquittal in the third play leaves her claims unsatisfied. Athena, the virgin warrior-goddess who represents the female as an ally of patriarchal order, declares as she casts her vote for Orestes, "No mother gave me birth. / I honor the male, in all things but marriage." From this point of view, the Furies' incorporation into Athens represents the appropriation and taming of female power, and it validates the exclusion of women from the civic processes of the democracy—a fact of Athenian daily life. On the other hand, in celebrating the Furies' role of maintaining obedience to law through inspiring fear and of promoting natural fertility, the text acknowledges the power of the female, which it associates with the Earth's natural processes, "primitive" and prior to the male-centered rationality of the city but vital still. The female is given a role in the city, even though she is excluded from its official public life, and that role is celebrated. There is no doubt, however, about the dominance of the patriarchal principle under the authority of the Olympian gods.

The full scope of these events, however we interpret them, is apparent only to the audience, which follows the pattern of its execution through the three plays of the trilogy. As in the Book of Job, the characters who act and suffer are in the dark. They claim a knowledge of Zeus's will and boast that their actions are its fulfillment (it is in these terms that Agamemnon speaks of the sack of Troy, and Clytemnestra of

Agamemnon's murder), and they are, of course, in one sense, right. But their knowledge is limited; Agamemnon does not realize that Zeus's will includes his death at the hands of Clytemnestra, nor Clytemnestra that it demands her death at the hands of her son. The chorus has, at times, a deeper understanding, but its knowledge of Zeus's laws is an abstraction that it cannot relate to the terrible facts.

In this murky atmosphere (made all the more terrible by the beacon fire of the opening lines, which brings not light but deeper darkness), one human being sees clear; she possesses the concrete vision of the future, which complements the chorus's abstract knowledge of the law. This is the prophet Cassandra, Priam's daughter, brought from Troy as Agamemnon's share of the spoils. She has been given the power of true prophecy by the god Apollo, but the gift is nullified by the condition that her prophecies will never be believed. She sees reality—past, present, and future—so clearly that she is cut off from ordinary human beings (represented by the chorus) by the clarity of her vision and the terrible burden of her knowledge. The great scene in which she sings her prophecies delays the action for which everything has been prepared—the death of Agamemnon. Before we hear his famous cry offstage, Cassandra presents us with a mysterious vision that combines cause, effect, and result: the murders that have led to this terrible moment, the death of Agamemnon, and the murders that will follow. The past, present, and future of Clytemnestra's action and Agamemnon's suffering are fused into a timeless unity in Cassandra's great lines, an unearthly unity that is dissolved only when Agamemnon, in the real world of time and space, screams in mortal agony.

The tremendous statement of the trilogy is made in a style that for magnificence and richness of suggestion can be compared only with the style of Shakespeare at the height of his poetic power, the Shakespeare of *King Lear* and *Antony and Cleopatra.* The language of the *Oresteia* is an Oriental carpet of imagery in which combinations of metaphor, which at first seem bombastic in their violence, take their place in the ordered pattern of the poem as a whole. An image, once introduced, recurs and reappears again, to run its course verbally and visually through the whole length of the trilogy, richer in meaning with each fresh appearance. In the second choral ode, for example, the chorus, welcoming the news of Agamemnon's victory at Troy, sings of the net that Zeus and Night threw over the city, trapping the inhabitants like animals. The net is here an image of Zeus's justice, a retributive justice, since Troy is paying for the crime of taking Helen, and the image identifies Zeus's justice with Agamemnon's action in sacking the city. This image occurs again, with a different emphasis, in the hypocritical speech of welcome that Clytemnestra makes to her husband on his return. She tells how she feared for his safety at Troy, how she trembled at the rumors of his death:

> and the rumors spread and fester,
> a runner comes with something dreadful,
> close on his heels the next and his news worse,
> and they shout it out and the whole house can hear;
> and wounds—if he took one wound for each report
> to penetrate these walls, he's gashed like a dragnet.

This vision of Agamemnon dead she speaks of as her fear, but we know that it represents her deepest desire and, more, the purpose that she is now preparing to execute. When, later, she stands in triumph over her husband's corpse, she uses the same image to describe the robe that she threw over his limbs to blind and baffle him before she stabbed him—"our never-ending, all embracing net, I cast it / wide for the royal haul, I coil him round and round / in the wealth, the robes of doom"—and this time the image materializes into an object visible on stage. We can see the net, the gashed robe still folded round Agamemnon's body. We shall see it again, for in the second play Orestes, standing over his mother's body as she now stands over his father's, will display the robe before us, with its holes and bloodstains, as a justification for what he has just done. Elsewhere in *Agamemnon* the chorus compares Cassandra to a wild animal caught in the net, and later Aegisthus exults to see Agamemnon's body lying "in the nets of Justice." For each speaker the image has a different meaning, but not one realizes the terrible sense in which it applies to them all. They are all caught in the net, the system of justice by vengeance that only binds tighter the more its captives struggle to free themselves. Clytemnestra attempts to escape, to arrest the process of the chain of murders and the working out of the will of Zeus. "But I will swear a pact with the spirit born within us," she says, but Agamemnon's body and the net she threw over him are there on the stage to remind us that her appeal will not be heard; one more generation must act and suffer before the net will vanish, never to be seen again.

D. J. Conacher, *Aeschylus' Oresteia: A Literary Commentary* (1987), is a scene-by-scene (and sometimes line-by-line) commentary addressed as much to Greekless readers as to classical scholars. James Hogan, *A Commentary on the Complete Greek Tragedies: Aeschylus* (1987), contains a line-by-line commentary on Richmond Lattimore's translation of the *Oresteia* (1953). John Herington, *Aeschylus* (1986), deals with the political and religious background of the tragedies and provides a perceptive discussion of the plays (*Oresteia*, pp. 111–56). Oliver Taplin, *Greek Tragedy in Action* (1978), gives a sensitive scene-by-scene discussion of the significance of stage action and spectacle in all three plays. Simon Goldhill, *Aeschylus: The Oresteia* (1992), includes a chapter on the trilogy's historical and cultural context and is an excellent guide through the complexities of each play. Froma Zeitlin's *Playing the Other: Gender and Society in Classical Greek Literature* (1996) includes (pp. 87–119) her outstanding essay on the *Oresteia*, "The Dynamics of Misogyny."

PRONOUNCING GLOSSARY

The following list uses common English syllables and stress accents to provide rough equivalents of selected words whose pronunciation may be unfamiliar to the general reader.

Aegisthus: *ee-jis'-thus*
Aeschylus: *ess'-kel-us*
Areopagus: *a-ree-op'-aguhs*
Calchas: *kal'-kahs*
Clytaemnestra: *klai-tem-nes'-truh*
Dionysus: *dai-oh-nai'-sus*
Eumenides: *yoo-me'-ni-deez*
Hermes: *her'-meez*
Iphigeneia: *i-fe-jen-ai'-uh*
Menelaus: *me-ne-lay'-us*
Oresteia: *o-res-tai'-uh*
Orestes: *o-res'-teez*
Thyestes: *thai-es'-teez*

THE ORESTEIA[1]

Agamemnon

CHARACTERS

WATCHMAN
CLYTAEMNESTRA
HERALD
AGAMEMNON
CASSANDRA
AEGISTHUS
CHORUS, *the Old Men of Argos and their* LEADER
Attendants of Clytaemnestra and of Agamemnon, bodyguard of Aegisthus

1. Translated by Robert Fagles.

[TIME AND SCENE: *A night in the tenth and final autumn of the Trojan war. The house of Atreus in Argos. Before it, an altar stands unlit; a* WATCHMAN *on the high roofs fights to stay awake.*]

WATCHMAN Dear gods, set me free from all the pain,
the long watch I keep, one whole year awake . . .
propped on my arms, crouched on the roofs of Atreus
like a dog.
I know the stars by heart,
the armies of the night, and there in the lead
the ones that bring us snow or the crops of summer,
bring us all we have—
our great blazing kings of the sky,
I know them, when they rise and when they fall . . .
and now I watch for the light, the signal-fire[2]
breaking out of Troy, shouting Troy is taken.
So she commands, full of her high hopes.
That woman[3]—she maneuvers like a man.

And when I keep to my bed, soaked in dew,
and the thoughts go groping through the night
and the good dreams that used to guard my sleep . . .
not here, it's the old comrade, terror, at my neck.
I mustn't sleep, no—
[*Shaking himself awake.*]
Look alive, sentry.
And I try to pick out tunes, I hum a little,
a good cure for sleep, and the tears start,
I cry for the hard times come to the house,
no longer run like the great place of old.

Oh for a blessed end to all our pain,
some godsend burning through the dark—
[*Light appears slowly in the east; he struggles to his feet and scans it.*]
I salute you!
You dawn of the darkness, you turn night to day—
I see the light at last.
They'll be dancing in the streets of Argos[4]
thanks to you, thanks to this new stroke of—
Aieeeeee!
There's your signal clear and true, my queen!

2. I.e., the bonfire nearest to Argos, the last in a chain extending all the way to Troy, each one visible, when fired at night, from the next. 3. Clytaemnestra. 4. In Homer, Agamemnon, son of Atreus, is king of Mycenae. Later Greek poets, however, referred to his kingdom as Argos or Mycenae, perhaps because the Achaeans in Homer are sometimes called Argives. In 463 B.C., just five years before the production of the play, Argos had defeated Mycenae in battle and put an end to the city, displacing the inhabitants or selling them into slavery. Soon after, Argos and Athens entered into an alliance, aimed, of course, at Sparta. Since this alliance will be alluded to in the last play of the trilogy, it is important for Aeschylus to establish the un-Homeric location of the action right at the beginning.

Rise up from bed—hurry, lift a cry of triumph
through the house, praise the gods for the beacon,
if they've taken Troy . . .
But there it burns,
fire all the way. I'm for the morning dances.
Master's luck is mine. A throw of the torch
has brought us triple-sixes[5]—we have won!
My move now—
[*Beginning to dance, then breaking off, lost in thought.*]
Just bring him home. My king,
I'll take your loving hand in mine and then . . .
the rest is silence. The ox is on my tongue.[6]
Aye, but the house and these old stones,
give them a voice and what a tale they'd tell.
And so would I, gladly . . .
I speak to those who know; to those who don't
my mind's a blank. I never say a word.
[*He climbs down from the roof and disappears into the palace through a side entrance. A* CHORUS, *the old men of Argos who have not learned the news of victory, enters and marches round the altar.*]

CHORUS Ten years gone, ten to the day
our great avenger went for Priam—
Menelaus[7] and lord Agamemnon,
two kings with the power of Zeus,
the twin throne, twin sceptre,
Atreus' sturdy yoke of sons
launched Greece in a thousand ships,
armadas cutting loose from the land,
armies massed for the cause, the rescue—
[*From within the palace* CLYTAEMNESTRA *raises a cry of triumph.*]
the heart within them screamed for all-out war!
Like vultures robbed of their young,
the agony sends them frenzied,
soaring high from the nest, round and
round they wheel, they row their wings,
stroke upon churning thrashing stroke,
but all the labor, the bed of pain,
the young are lost forever.
Yet someone hears on high—Apollo,
Pan or Zeus[8]—the piercing wail
these guests of heaven raise,
and drives at the outlaws, late
but true to revenge, a stabbing Fury![9]

5. The highest throw in the ancient Greek dice game. 6. A proverbial phrase for enforced silence. 7. Another son of Atreus, also a king of Argos and commander of the Greek expedition against Troy. Priam was the king of Troy. His son Paris abducted (or seduced) Menelaus's wife, Helen. 8. The movements of birds are regarded as prophetic signs; Apollo perhaps as a prophetic god; Pan as a god of the wild places; Zeus because eagles and vultures were symbolic of his power. 9. This is the first mention of one of these avenging spirits, who will actually appear on stage as the chorus of the final play. Furies are called Erinyes in Greek.

[CLYTAEMNESTRA *appears at the doors and pauses with her entourage.*][1]

So towering Zeus the god of guests[2]
drives Atreus' sons at Paris,
all for a woman manned by many
the generations wrestle, knees
grinding the dust, the manhood drains,
the spear snaps in the first blood rites
  that marry Greece and Troy.
And now it goes as it goes
and where it ends is Fate.
And neither by singeing flesh
nor tipping cups of wine[3]
nor shedding burning tears can you
enchant away the rigid Fury.

[CLYTAEMNESTRA *lights the altar-fires.*]

We are the old, dishonoured ones,[4]
the broken husks of men.
Even then they cast us off,
the rescue mission left us here
to prop a child's strength upon a stick.
What if the new sap rises in his chest?
He has no soldiery in him,
  no more than we,
and we are aged past aging,
gloss of the leaf shriveled,
three legs[5] at a time we falter on.
Old men are children once again,
  a dream that sways and wavers
into the hard light of day.
                                        But you,
daughter of Leda, queen Clytaemnestra,
what now, what news, what message
drives you through the citadel
  burning victims?[6] Look,
the city gods, the gods of Olympus,
gods of the earth and public markets—
all the altars blazing with your gifts!
  Argos blazes! Torches
race the sunrise up her skies—
drugged by the lulling holy oils,
  unadulterated,

1. There are no stage directions on the manuscript copies of the plays that have come down to us. Here the translator had the queen enter so that she will be visible on stage when the chorus addresses her by name in line 93. Other scholars, pointing out that in Greek tragedy characters who are offstage are often addressed, disagree, and bring Clytaemnestra on stage only at line 256. 2. Zeus was thought to be particularly interested in punishing those who violated the code of hospitality. Paris had been a guest in Menelaus's house. 3. Neither by burnt sacrifice nor by pouring libations. 4. The general sense of the passage is that only two classes of the male population are left in Argos: those who are too young to fight and those who, like the chorus, are too old. 5. Because they use a stick, or cane, to support them when they walk. 6. Clytaemnestra is sacrificing in thanksgiving for the news of Troy's fall; the chorus does not know that the news has come via the signal fires.

run from the dark vaults of kings.
Tell us the news!
What you can, what is right—
Heal us, soothe our fears!
Now the darkness comes to the fore,
now the hope glows through your victims,
beating back this raw, relentless anguish
gnawing at the heart.

[CLYTAEMNESTRA *ignores them and pursues her rituals; they assemble for the opening chorus.*]

O but I still have power to sound the god's command at the roads
that launched the kings. The gods breathe power through my song,
my fighting strength, Persuasion grows with the years—
I sing how the flight of fury hurled the twin command,
one will that hurled young Greece
and winged the spear of vengeance straight for Troy!
The kings of birds to kings of the beaking prows, one black,
one with a blaze of silver
skimmed the palace spearhand right
and swooping lower, all could see,
plunged their claws in a hare, a mother
bursting with unborn young—the babies spilling,
quick spurts of blood—cut off the race just dashing into life!
Cry, cry for death, but good win out in glory in the end.

But the loyal seer of the armies studied Atreus' sons,
two sons with warring hearts—he saw two eagle-kings
devour the hare and spoke the things to come,[7]
"Years pass, and the long hunt nets the city of Priam,
the flocks beyond the walls,
a kingdom's life and soul—Fate stamps them out.
Just let no curse of the gods lour on us first,
shatter our giant armor
forged to strangle Troy. I see
pure Artemis bristle in pity—
yes, the flying hounds of the Father
slaughter for armies . . . their own victim . . . a woman
trembling young, all born to die—She[8] loathes the eagles' feast!"
Cry, cry for death, but good win out in glory in the end.
"Artemis, lovely Artemis, so kind
to the ravening lion's tender, helpless cubs,
the suckling young of beasts that stalk the wilds—
bring this sign for all its fortune,
all its brutal torment home to birth!

7. The seer Calchas identified the two eagles (*kings of birds*) as symbolic of the two kings and their action as a symbolic prophecy of the destruction of Troy. The two eagles seized and tore a pregnant hare, which meant that the two kings would destroy Troy, thus killing not only the living Trojans but the Trojan generations yet unborn. 8. Artemis, a virgin goddess, patron of hunting, and the protectress of wildlife, is angry that the eagles (*the flying hounds*) have destroyed a pregnant animal. The prophet fears that she may turn her wrath against the kings whom the eagles represent. *A woman trembling young:* just as the eagles kill the hare, the kings will kill Agamemnon's daughter Iphigenia. The Greek text refers only to the hare, but the translator has made the allusion clear.

I beg you, Healing Apollo, soothe her before
her crosswinds hold us down and moor the ships too long,[9]
pressing us on to another victim . . .
nothing sacred, no
no feast to be eaten[1]
the architect of vengeance
[*Turning to the palace.*]
growing strong in the house
with no fear of the husband
here she waits
the terror raging back and back in the future
the stealth, the law of the hearth, the mother—
Memory womb of Fury child-avenging Fury!"
So as the eagles wheeled at the crossroads,
Calchas clashed out the great good blessings mixed with doom
for the halls of kings, and singing with our fate
we cry, cry for death, but good win out in glory in the end.

Zeus, great nameless all in all,
if that name will gain his favor,
I will call him Zeus.[2]
I have no words to do him justice,
weighing all in the balance,
all I have is Zeus, Zeus—
lift this weight, this torment from my spirit,
cast it once for all.

He who was so mighty once,[3]
storming for the wars of heaven,
he has had his day.
And then his son[4] who came to power
met his match in the third fall
and he is gone. Zeus, Zeus—
raise your cries and sing him Zeus the Victor!
You will reach the truth:

Zeus has led us on to know,
the Helmsman lays it down as law
that we must suffer, suffer into truth.

9. Calchas foresees the future. Artemis will send unfavorable winds to prevent the sailing of the Greek expedition from Aulis, the port of embarkation. She will demand the sacrifice of Agamemnon's daughter Iphigenia as the price of the fleet's release. He prays that in spite of its bad aspects, the omen will be truly prophetic—that is, that the Achaeans will capture Troy. He goes on to anticipate and try to avert some of the evils it portends. 1. At an ordinary sacrifice the celebrants gave the gods their due portion and then feasted on the animal's flesh. The word *sacrifice* comes to have the connotation of "feast." There will be no feast at this sacrifice, since the victim will be a human being. The ominous phrase reminds us of a feast of human flesh that has already taken place, Thyestes' feasting on his own children. 2. It was important, in prayer, to address the divinity by his or her right name: here the chorus uses an inclusive formula—they call on Zeus by whatever name pleases him. 3. Uranus, father of Kronos, grandfather of Zeus, the first lord of heaven. This whole passage refers to a primitive legend that told how Uranus was violently supplanted by his son, Kronos, who was in his turn overthrown by his son, Zeus. This legend is made to bear new meaning by Aeschylus, for he suggests that it is not a meaningless series of acts of violence but a progression to the rule of Zeus, who stands for order and justice. Thus the law of human life that Zeus proclaims and administers—that wisdom comes through suffering—has its counterpart in the history of the establishment of the divine rule. 4. Kronos.

We cannot sleep, and drop by drop at the heart
the pain of pain remembered comes again,
and we resist, but ripeness comes as well.
From the gods enthroned on the awesome rowing-bench[5]
there comes a violent love.

So it was that day the king,
the steersman at the helm of Greece,
would never blame a word the prophet said—
swept away by the wrenching winds of fortune
he conspired! Weatherbound we could not sail,
our stores exhausted, fighting strength hard-pressed,
and the squadrons rode in the shallows off Chalkis[6]
where the riptide crashes, drags,

and winds from the north pinned down our hulls at Aulis,
port of anguish . . . head winds starving,
sheets and the cables snapped
  and the men's minds strayed,
    the pride, the bloom of Greece
  was raked as time ground on,
ground down, and then the cure for the storm
and it was harsher—Calchas cried,
"My captains, Artemis must have blood!"—
  so harsh the sons of Atreus
    dashed their scepters on the rocks,
  could not hold back the tears,

and I still can hear the older warlord saying,
"Obey, obey, or a heavy doom will crush me!—
Oh but doom *will* crush me
  once I rend my child,
    the glory of my house—
  a father's hands are stained,
blood of a young girl streaks the altar.
Pain both ways and what is worse?
Desert the fleets, fail the alliance?
  No, but stop the winds with a virgin's blood,
    feed their lust, their fury?—feed their fury!—
  Law is law!—
          Let all go well."

And once he slipped his neck in the strap of Fate,
his spirit veering black, impure, unholy,
once he turned he stopped at nothing,
    seized with the frenzy
      blinding driving to outrage—
wretched frenzy, cause of all our grief!

5. The bench of the ship where the helmsman sat. 6. The unruly water of the narrows between Aulis on the mainland and Chalkis on the island of Euboea.

Yes, he had the heart
to sacrifice his daughter!—
to bless the war that avenged a woman's loss,
a bridal rite that sped the men-of-war.

"My father, father!"—she might pray to the winds;
no innocence moves her judges mad for war.
Her father called his henchmen on,
on with a prayer,
"Hoist her over the altar
like a yearling, give it all your strength!
She's fainting—lift her,
sweep her robes around her,
but slip this strap in her gentle curving lips . . .
here, gag her hard, a sound will curse the house"—

and the bridle chokes her voice . . . her saffron robes
pouring over the sand
her glance like arrows showering
wounding every murderer through with pity
clear as a picture, live,
she strains to call their names . . .
I remember often the days with father's guests
when over the feast her voice unbroken,
pure as the hymn her loving father
bearing third libations,[7] sang to Saving Zeus—
transfixed with joy, Atreus' offspring
throbbing out their love.

What comes next? I cannot see it, cannot say.
The strong techniques of Calchas do their work.[8]
But Justice turns the balance scales,
sees that we suffer
and we suffer and we learn.
And we will know the future when it comes.
Greet it too early, weep too soon.
It all comes clear in the light of day.
Let all go well today, well as she could want,
[*Turning to* CLYTAEMNESTRA.]
our midnight watch, our lone defender,
single-minded queen.

LEADER We've come,
Clytaemnestra. We respect your power.
Right it is to honor the warlord's woman
once he leaves the throne.
But why these fires?
Good news, or more good hopes? We're loyal,

7. Offerings of wine. At a banquet three libations were poured, the third and last to Zeus the saviour; the last libation was accompanied by a hymn of praise. 8. This seems to refer to the sacrifice of Iphigenia. Some scholars take the Greek words to refer to the fulfillment of Calchas's prophecies.

we want to hear, but never blame your silence.
CLYTAEMNESTRA Let the new day shine, as the proverb says,
glorious from the womb of Mother Night.
[*Lost in prayer, then turning to the* CHORUS.]
You will hear a joy beyond your hopes.
Priam's citadel—the Greeks have taken Troy!
LEADER No, what do you mean? I can't believe it.
CLYTAEMNESTRA Troy is ours. Is that clear enough?
LEADER The joy of it,
stealing over me, calling up my tears—
CLYTAEMNESTRA Yes, your eyes expose your loyal hearts.
LEADER And you have proof?
CLYTAEMNESTRA I do,
I must. Unless the god is lying.
LEADER That,
or a phantom spirit sends you into raptures.
CLYTAEMNESTRA No one takes me in with visions—senseless dreams.
LEADER Or giddy rumor, you haven't indulged yourself—
CLYTAEMNESTRA You treat me like a child, you mock me?
LEADER Then when did they storm the city?
CLYTAEMNESTRA Last night, I say, the mother of this morning.
LEADER And who on earth could run the news so fast?
CLYTAEMNESTRA The god of fire—rushing fire from Ida![9]
And beacon to beacon rushed it on to me,
my couriers riding home the torch.
From Troy
to the bare rock of Lemnos, Hermes' Spur,[1]
and the Escort winged the great light west
to the Saving Father's face, Mount Athos[2] hurled it
third in the chain and leaping Ocean's back
the blaze went dancing on to ecstasy—pitch-pine
streaming gold like a new-born sun—and brought
the word in flame to Mount Makistos'[3] brow.
No time to waste, straining, fighting sleep,
that lookout heaved a torch glowing over
the murderous straits of Euripos to reach
Messapion's[4] watchmen craning for the signal.
Fire for word of fire! tense with the heather
withered gray, they stack it, set it ablaze—
the hot force of the beacon never flags,
it springs the Plain of Asôpos, rears
like a harvest moon to hit Kithairon's[5] crest
and drives new men to drive the fire on.
That relay pants for the far-flung torch,

9. The mountain range near Troy. The names that follow in this speech designate the places where beacon fires flashed the message of Troy's fall to Argos. The chain began at Ida. 1. Hermes' cliff is on the island of Lemnos (off the coast of Asia Minor). 2. On a rocky peninsula in north Greece. 3. On the island of Euboea off the coast of central Greece. 4. A mountain on the mainland. 5. A mountain near Thebes.

they swell its strength outstripping my commands
and the light inflames the marsh, the Gorgon's Eye,[6]
it strikes the peak where the wild goats range[7]—
my laws, my fire whips that camp!
They spare nothing, eager to build its heat,
and a huge beard of flame overcomes the headland
beetling down the Saronic Gulf,[8] and flaring south
it brings the dawn to the Black Widow's[9] face—
the watch that looms above your heads—and now
the true son of the burning flanks of Ida
crashes on the roofs of Atreus' sons!

And I ordained it all.
Torch to torch, running for their lives,
one long succession racing home my fire.
One,
first in the laps and last,[1] wins out in triumph.
There you have my proof, *my* burning sign, I tell you—
the power my lord passed on from Troy to me![2]

LEADER We'll thank the gods, my lady—first this story,
let me lose myself in the wonder of it all!
Tell it start to finish, tell us all.

CLYTAEMNESTRA The city's ours—in our hands this very day!
I can hear the cries in crossfire rock the walls.
Pour oil and wine in the same bowl,
what have you, friendship? A struggle to the end.
So with the victors and the victims—outcries,
you can hear them clashing like their fates.

They are kneeling by the bodies of the dead,
embracing men and brothers, infants over
the aged loins that gave them life, and sobbing,
as the yoke constricts their last free breath,
for every dear one lost.
And the others,
there, plunging breakneck through the night—
the labor of battle sets them down, ravenous;
to breakfast on the last remains of Troy.

6. Lake Gorgopis. 7. Mount Aegiplanctus on the Isthmus of Corinth. 8. The sea. 9. Mount Arachnaeus ("spider") in Argive territory. This is the fire seen by the watchman at the beginning of the play. 1. The chain of beacons is compared to a relay race in which the runners carry torches; the last runner (who runs the final lap) comes in first to win. 2. This speech has often been criticized as discursive, but it has great poetic importance. The image of the light that will dispel the darkness, first introduced by the watchman, is one of the dominant images of the trilogy and is here developed with magnificent ambiguous effect. For the watchman the light means the safe return of Agamemnon and the restoration of order in the house; for Clytaemnestra it means the return of Agamemnon to his death at her hands. Each swift jump of the racing light is one step nearer home and death for Agamemnon. The light the watchman longs for brings only greater darkness, but eventually it brings darkness for Clytaemnestra too. The final emergence of the true light comes in the glare of the torchlight procession that ends the last play of the trilogy, a procession that symbolizes perfect reconciliation on both the human and the divine levels and the working out of the will of Zeus in the substitution of justice for vengeance. The conception of the beacons as a chain of descendants (compare line 311) is also important; the fire at Argos that announces Agamemnon's imminent death is a direct descendant of the fire on Ida that announces the sack of Troy and Agamemnon's sacrilegious conduct there. The metaphor thus reminds us of the sequence of crimes from generation to generation that is the history of the house of Pelops.

Not by rank but the lots of chance they draw,
they lodge in the houses captured by the spear,
settling in so soon, released from the open sky,
the frost and dew. Lucky men, off guard at last,
they sleep away their first good night in years.

If only they are revering the city's gods,
the shrines of the gods who love the conquered land,
no plunderer will be plundered in return.
Just let no lust, no mad desire seize the armies[3]
to ravish what they must not touch—
overwhelmed by all they've won!
The run for home
and safety waits, the swerve at the post,[4]
the final lap of the gruelling two-lap race.
And even if the men come back with no offense
to the gods, the avenging dead may never rest—
Oh let no new disaster strike! And here
you have it, what a woman has to say.
Let the best win out, clear to see.
A small desire but all that I could want.

LEADER Spoken like a man, my lady, loyal,
full of self-command. I've heard your sign
and now your vision.
[*Reaching towards her as she turns and re-enters the palace.*]
Now to praise the gods.
The joy is worth the labor.

CHORUS O Zeus my king and Night, dear Night,[5]
queen of the house who covers us with glories,[6]
you slung your net on the towers of Troy,
neither young nor strong could leap
the giant dredge net of slavery,
all-embracing ruin.
I adore you, iron Zeus of the guests
and your revenge—you drew your longbow
year by year to a taut full draw
till one bolt, not falling short
or arching over the stars,
could split the mark of Paris!

The sky stroke of god!—it is all Troy's to tell,
but even I can trace it to its cause:
god does as god decrees.
And still some say
that heaven would never stoop to punish men
who trample the lovely grace of things

3. She, of course, hopes for the opposite of what she prays for here. The audience was familiar with the traditional account, according to which Agamemnon and his army failed signally to respect the gods and temples of Troy. 4. Greek runners turned at a post and came back on a parallel track. 5. Troy fell to a night attack. 6. Probably the moon and stars; an obscure expression in the original.

untouchable. How wrong they are!
A curse burns bright on crime—
full-blown, the father's crimes will blossom,
burst into the son's.[7]
Let there be less suffering . . .
give us the sense to live on what we need.

Bastions of wealth
are no defense for the man
who treads the grand altar of Justice
down and out of sight.

Persuasion, maddening child of Ruin
overpowers him—Ruin plans it all.
And the wound will smolder on,
there is no cure,
a terrible brilliance kindles on the night.
He is bad bronze scraped on a touchstone:
put to the test, the man goes black.[8]
Like the boy who chases
a bird on the wing, brands his city,
brings it down and prays,
but the gods are deaf
to the one who turns to crime, they tear him down.

So Paris learned:
he came to Atreus' house
and shamed the tables spread for guests,
he stole away the queen.

And she left her land *chaos,* clanging shields,
companions tramping, bronze prows, men in bronze,
and she came to Troy with a dowry, death,
strode through the gates
defiant in every stride,
as prophets of the house[9] looked on and wept,
"Oh the halls and the lords of war,
the bed and the fresh prints of love.
I *see* him, unavenging, unavenged,
the stun of his desolation is so clear—
he longs for the one who lies across the sea
until her phantom seems to sway the house.

Her curving images,
her beauty hurts her lord,

7. The language throughout this passage is significantly general. The chorus refers to Paris, but everything it says is equally applicable to Agamemnon, who sacrificed his daughter for his ambitions. The original Greek is corrupt (that is, has been garbled in the handwritten tradition) but seems to proclaim the doctrine that the sins of the fathers are visited on the children. So Paris (and Agamemnon) pay for the misdeeds of their ancestors (as well as their own). 8. Inferior bronze, adulterated with lead, turns black with use. 9. Menelaus's.

the eyes starve and the touch
of love is gone,

and radiant dreams are passing in the night,
the memories throb with sorrow, joy with pain . . .
it is pain to dream and see desires
slip through the arms,
a vision lost forever
winging down the moving drifts of sleep."
So he grieves at the royal hearth
yet others' grief is worse, far worse.
All through Greece for those who flocked to war
they are holding back the anguish now,
you can feel it rising now in every house;
I tell you there is much to tear the heart.

They knew the men they sent,
but now in place of men
ashes and urns come back
to every hearth.[1]

War, War, the great gold-broker of corpses
holds the balance of the battle on his spear!
Home from the pyres he sends them,
home from Troy to the loved ones,
weighted with tears, the urns brimmed full,
the heroes return in gold-dust,[2]
dear, light ash for men; and they weep,
they praise them, "He had skill in the swordplay,"
"He went down so tall in the onslaught,"
"All for another's woman." So they mutter
in secret and the rancor steals
toward our staunch defenders, Atreus' sons.

And there they ring the walls, the young,
the lithe, the handsome hold the graves
they won in Troy; the enemy earth
rides over those who conquered.

The people's voice is heavy with hatred,
now the curses of the people must be paid,
and now I wait, I listen . . .
there—there is something breathing
under the night's shroud. God takes aim
at the ones who murder many;
the swarthy Furies stalk the man
gone rich beyond all rights—with a twist

1. This strikes a contemporary note. In Homer the fallen Achaeans are buried at Troy, but in Aeschylus's Athens the dead were cremated on the battlefield, and their ashes were brought home for burial. 2. I.e., in ashes. The war god is a broker who gives, in exchange for bodies, gold dust (the word used for "bodies" could mean living bodies or corpses).

of fortune grind him down, dissolve him
into the blurring dead—there is no help.
The reach for power can recoil,
the bolt of god can strike you at a glance.

Make me rich with no man's envy,
neither a raider of cities, no,
nor slave come face to face with life
overpowered by another.

[*Speaking singly.*]
—Fire comes and the news is good,
it races through the streets
but is it true? Who knows?
Or just another lie from heaven?[3]

—Show us the man so childish, wonderstruck,
he's fired up with the first torch,
then when the message shifts
he's sick at heart.

—Just like a woman
to fill with thanks before the truth is clear.

—So gullible. Their stories spread like wildfire,
they fly fast and die faster;
rumors voiced by women come to nothing.

LEADER Soon we'll know her fires for what they are,
her relay race of torches hand-to-hand—
know if they're real or just a dream,
the hope of a morning here to take our senses.
I see a herald running from the beach
and a victor's spray of olive shades his eyes
and the dust he kicks, twin to the mud of Troy,
shows he has a voice—no kindling timber
on the cliffs, no signal-fires for him.
He can shout the news and give us joy,
or else . . . please, not that.
Bring it on,
good fuel to build the first good fires.
And if anyone calls down the worst on Argos
let him reap the rotten harvest of his mind.

[*The* HERALD *rushes in and kneels on the ground.*]

HERALD Good Greek earth, the soil of my fathers!
Ten years out, and a morning brings me back.
All hopes snapped but one—I'm home at last.

3. Later we will see Agamemnon come on stage with Cassandra (his Trojan captive) and the spoils of Troy. The chorus, which started out to sing a hymn of praise for the fall of Troy (line 359), ends in fear and despondency. It now questions the truth of Clytaemnestra's announcement; perhaps Troy has not fallen after all (line 469).

Never dreamed I'd die in Greece, assigned
the narrow plot I love the best.
And now
I salute the land, the light of the sun,
our high lord Zeus and the king of Pytho[4]—
no more arrows, master, raining on our heads!
At Scamander's banks we took our share,
your longbow brought us down like plague.[5]
Now come, deliver us, heal us—lord Apollo!
Gods of the market, here, take my salute.
And you, my Hermes,[6] Escort,
loving Herald, the herald's shield and prayer!—
And the shining dead[7] of the land who launched the armies,
warm us home . . . we're all the spear has left.

You halls of the kings, you roofs I cherish,
sacred seats—you gods that catch the sun,
if your glances ever shone on him in the old days,
greet him well—so many years are lost.
He comes, he brings us light in the darkness,
free for every comrade, Agamemnon lord of men.

Give him the royal welcome he deserves!
He hoisted the pickax of Zeus who brings revenge,
he dug Troy down, he worked her soil down,
the shrines of her gods and the high altars, gone!—
and the seed of her wide earth he ground to bits.
That's the yoke he claps on Troy. The king,
the son of Atreus comes. The man is blest,
the one man alive to merit such rewards.

Neither Paris nor Troy, partners to the end,
can say their work outweighs their wages now.
Convicted of rapine, stripped of all his spoils,
and his father's house and the land that gave it life—
he's scythed them to the roots. The sons of Priam
pay the price twice over.

LEADER Welcome home
from the wars, herald, long live your joy.

HERALD *Our* joy—
now I could die gladly. Say the word, dear gods.

LEADER Longing for your country left you raw?

HERALD The tears fill my eyes, for joy.

LEADER You too,
down the sweet disease that kills a man
with kindness . . .

HERALD Go on, I don't see what you—

LEADER Love

4. Apollo. 5. Compare the opening scene of the *Iliad* 1 (p. 121), where Apollo punishes the Greeks with his arrows (a metaphor for plague). 6. The gods' messenger and patron deity of heralds. 7. The heroes of the past, who are buried in Argos and worshiped.

for the ones who love you—that's what took you.
HERALD You mean
the land and the armies hungered for each other?
LEADER There were times I thought I'd faint with longing.
HERALD So anxious for the armies, why?
LEADER For years now,
only my silence kept me free from harm.
HERALD What,
with the kings gone did someone threaten you?
LEADER So much . . . [8]
now as you say, it would be good to die.
HERALD True, we *have* done well.
Think back in the years and what have you?
A few runs of luck, a lot that's bad.
Who but a god can go through life unmarked?

A long, hard pull we had, if I would tell it all.
The iron rations, penned in the gangways
hock by jowl like sheep. Whatever miseries
break a man, our quota, every sunstarved day.

Then on the beaches it was worse. Dug in
under the enemy ramparts—deadly going.
Out of the sky, out of the marshy flats
the dews soaked us, turned the ruts we fought from
into gullies, made our gear, our scalps
crawl with lice.
And talk of the cold,
the sleet to freeze the gulls, and the big snows
come avalanching down from Ida. Oh but the heat,
the sea and the windless noons, the swells asleep,
dropped to a dead calm . . .

But why weep now?
It's over for us, over for them.
The dead can rest and never rise again;
no need to call their muster. We're alive,
do we have to go on raking up old wounds?
Good-by to all that. Glad I am to say it.

For us, the remains of the Greek contingents,
the good wins out, no pain can tip the scales,
not now. So shout this boast to the bright sun—
fitting it is—wing it over the seas and rolling earth:

"Once when an Argive expedition captured Troy
they hauled these spoils back to the gods of Greece,

8. Throughout this dialogue the chorus has been gearing itself up to warn the herald that there may be danger for Agamemnon at home; at this point its nerve fails, and it abandons the attempt.

they bolted them high across the temple doors,
the glory of the past!"
And hearing that,
men will applaud our city and our chiefs,
and Zeus will have the hero's share of fame—
he did the work.
That's all I have to say.

LEADER I'm convinced, glad that I was wrong.
Never too old to learn; it keeps me young.
[CLYTAEMNESTRA *enters with her women.*]
First the house and the queen, it's their affair,
but I can taste the riches.

CLYTAEMNESTRA I cried out long ago![9]—
for joy, when the first herald came burning
through the night and told the city's fall.
And there were some who smiled and said,
"A few fires persuade you Troy's in ashes.
Women, women, elated over nothing."

You made me seem deranged.
For all that I sacrificed—a woman's way,
you'll say—station to station on the walls
we lifted cries of triumph that resounded
in the temples of the gods. We lulled and blessed
the fires with myrrh and they consumed our victims.
[*Turning to the* HERALD.]
But enough. Why prolong the story?
From the king himself I'll gather all I need.
Now for the best way to welcome home
my lord, my good lord . . .
No time to lose!
What dawn can feast a woman's eyes like this?
I can see the light, the husband plucked from war
by the Saving God and open wide the gates.

Tell him that, and have him come with speed,
the people's darling—how they long for him.
And for his wife,
may he return and find her true at hall,
just as the day he left her, faithful to the last.
A watchdog gentle to him alone,
[*Glancing towards the palace.*]
savage
to those who cross his path. I have not changed.
The strains of time can never break our seal.
In love with a new lord, in ill repute I am
as practiced as I am in dyeing bronze.[1]

9. As the watchman had told her to (line 30). 1. She claims she is no more capable of adultery than she is of dyeing bronze; but she will later kill Agamemnon with a bronze weapon.

That is my boast, teeming with the truth.
I am proud, a woman of my nobility—
I'd hurl it from the roofs!

[*She turns sharply, enters the palace.*]

LEADER She speaks well, but it takes no seer to know
she only says what's right.

[*The* HERALD *attempts to leave; the* LEADER *takes him by the arm.*]

Wait, one thing.
Menelaus, is he home too, safe with the men?[2]
The power of the land—dear king.

HERALD I doubt that lies will help my friends,
in the lean months to come.

LEADER Help us somehow, tell the truth as well.
But when the two conflict it's hard to hide—
out with it.

HERALD He's lost, gone from the fleets![3]
He and his ship, it's true.

LEADER After you watched him
pull away from Troy? Or did some storm
attack you all and tear him off the line?

HERALD There,
like a marksman, the whole disaster cut to a word.

LEADER How do the escorts give him out—dead or alive?

HERALD No clear report. No one knows . . .
only the wheeling sun that heats the earth to life.

LEADER But then the storm—how did it reach the ships?
How did it end? Were the angry gods on hand?

HERALD This blessed day, ruin it with *them?*
Better to keep their trophies far apart.

When a runner comes, his face in tears,
saddled with what his city dreaded most,[4]
the armies routed, two wounds in one,
one to the city, one to hearth and home . . .
our best men, droves of them, victims
herded from every house by the two-barb whip
that Ares[5] likes to crack,
that charioteer
who packs destruction shaft by shaft,
careening on with his brace of bloody mares—
When he comes in, I tell you, dragging that much pain,
wail your battle-hymn to the Furies, and high time!

But when he brings salvation home to a city
singing out her heart—

2. The relevance of this question and the following speeches lies in the fact that Menelaus's absence makes Agamemnon's murder easier (his presence might have made it impossible) and in the fact that Menelaus is bringing Helen home. 3. For what happened to Menelaus see the *Odyssey* 4 (pp. 266ff.). 4. The herald creates a vivid picture of a messenger bringing news of disaster to his city—a role he wishes to avoid. 5. The war god.

how can I mix the good with so much bad
and blurt out this?—
"Storms swept the Greeks,
and not without the anger of the gods!"

Those enemies for ages, fire[6] and water,
sealed a pact and showed it to the world—
they crushed our wretched squadrons.
Night looming,
breakers lunging in for the kill
and the black gales come brawling out of the north—
ships ramming, prow into hooking prow, gored
by the rush-and-buck of hurricane pounding rain
by the cloudburst—
ships stampeding into the darkness,
lashed and spun by the savage shepherd's hand![7]

But when the sun comes up to light the skies
I see the Aegean heaving into a great bloom
of corpses . . . Greeks, the pick of a generation
scattered through the wrecks and broken spars.

But not us, not our ship, our hull untouched.
Someone stole us away or begged us off.
No mortal—a god, death grip on the tiller,
or lady luck herself, perched on the helm,
she pulled us through, she saved us. Aye,
we'll never battle the heavy surf at anchor,
never shipwreck up some rocky coast.

But once we cleared that sea-hell, not even
trusting luck in the cold light of day,
we battened on our troubles, they were fresh—
the armada punished, bludgeoned into nothing.

And now if one of them still has the breath
he's saying *we* are lost. Why not?
We say the same of him. Well,
here's to the best.
And Menelaus?
Look to it, he's come back, and yet . . .
if a shaft of the sun can track him down,
alive, and his eyes full of the old fire—
thanks to the strategies of Zeus, Zeus
would never tear the house out by the roots—
then there's hope our man will make it home.

You've heard it all. Now you have the truth.
[*Rushing out.*]

6. Lightning. 7. The ships were scattered like sheep dispersed by a cruel shepherd.

CHORUS Who—what power named the name[8] that drove your fate?—
what hidden brain could divine your future,
steer that word to the mark,
to the bride of spears,
the whirlpool churning armies,
Oh for all the world a Helen!
Hell at the prows, hell at the gates
hell on the men-of-war,
from her lair's sheer veils she drifted
launched by the giant western wind,
and the long tall waves of men in armor,
huntsmen[9] trailing the oar-blades' dying spoor
slipped into her moorings,
Simois'[1] mouth that chokes with foliage,
bayed for bloody strife,

for Troy's Blood Wedding Day—she drives her word,
her burning will to the birth, the Fury
late but true to the cause,
to the tables shamed
and Zeus who guards the hearth[2]—
the Fury makes the Trojans pay!
Shouting their hymns, hymns for the bride
hymns for the kinsmen doomed
to the wedding march of Fate.
Troy changed her tune in her late age,
and I think I hear the dirges mourning
"Paris, born and groomed for the bed of Fate!"
They mourn with their life breath,
they sing their last, the sons of Priam
born for bloody slaughter.

So a man once reared
a lion cub at hall, snatched
from the breast, still craving milk
in the first flush of life.
A captivating pet for the young,
and the old men adored it, pampered it
in their arms, day in, day out,
like an infant just born.
Its eyes on fire, little beggar,
fawning for its belly, slave to food.

But it came of age
and the parent strain broke out
and it paid its breeders back.

8. Helen. The name contains the Greek root *hele*, which means "destroy." The chorus is so obsessed with Helen's guilt that it fails to recognize the true responsibility for the war and the imminence of disaster. 9. The Achaean army, which came after her. 1. A river in Troy. 2. I.e., protects the host and guest.

Grateful it was, it went
through the flock to prepare a feast,
an illicit orgy—the house swam with blood,
none could resist that agony—
massacre vast and raw!
From god there came a priest of ruin,
adopted by the house to lend it warmth.

And the first sensation Helen brought to Troy . . .
call it a spirit
shimmer of winds dying
glory light as gold
shaft of the eyes dissolving, open bloom
that wounds the heart with love.
But veering wild in mid-flight
she whirled her wedding on to a stabbing end,
slashed at the sons of Priam—hearthmate, friend to the death,
sped by Zeus who speeds the guest,
a bride of tears, a Fury.

There's an ancient saying, old as man himself:
men's prosperity
never will die childless,
once full-grown it breeds.
Sprung from the great good fortune in the race
comes bloom on bloom of pain—
insatiable wealth. But not I,
I alone say this. Only the reckless act
can breed impiety, multiplying crime on crime,
while the house kept straight and just
is blessed with radiant children.[3]

But ancient Violence longs to breed,
new Violence comes
when its fatal hour comes, the demon comes
to take her toll—no war, no force, no prayer
can hinder the midnight Fury stamped
with parent Fury moving through the house.

But Justice shines in sooty hovels,[4]
loves the decent life.
From proud halls crusted with gilt by filthy hands
she turns her eyes to find the pure in spirit—
spurning the wealth stamped counterfeit with praise,
she steers all things toward their destined end.[5]

3. These lines begin with the traditional Greek view that immoderate good fortune (or excellence of any kind beyond the average) is itself the cause of disaster. The chorus, however, rejects this view and states that only an act of evil produces evil consequences. 4. The homes of the poor. 5. Here the chorus admits, by implication, that the poor are less likely to commit evil acts.

[AGAMEMNON *enters in his chariot, his plunder borne before him by his entourage; behind him, half hidden, stands* CASSANDRA. *The old men press toward him.*]

Come, my king, the scourge of Troy,
 the true son of Atreus—
How to salute you, how to praise you
neither too high nor low, but hit
the note of praise that suits the hour?
So many prize some brave display,
they prefer some flaunt of honor
 once they break the bounds.
When a man fails they share his grief,
but the pain can never cut them to the quick.
When a man succeeds they share his glory,
torturing their faces into smiles.
But the good shepherd knows his flock.
When the eyes seem to brim with love
 and it is only unction,
he will know, better than we can know.
That day you marshaled the armies
all for Helen—no hiding it now—
I drew you in my mind in black;
you seemed a menace at the helm,
 sending men to the grave
to bring her home, that hell on earth.
But now from the depths of trust and love
I say Well fought, well won—
 the end is worth the labor!
Search, my king, and learn at last
who stayed at home and kept their faith
 and who betrayed the city.[6]

AGAMEMNON First,
with justice I salute my Argos and my gods,
my accomplices who brought me home and won
my rights from Priam's Troy—the just gods.
No need to hear our pleas. Once for all
they consigned their lots to the urn of blood,[7]
they pitched on death for men, annihilation
for the city. Hope's hand, hovering
over the urn of mercy, left it empty.
Look for the smoke—it is the city's seamark,
building even now.
 The storms of ruin live!
Her last dying breath, rising up from the ashes
sends us gales of incense rich in gold.

6. The chorus tries to warn Agamemnon against flatterers and dissemblers, but he misses its drift. 7. In an Athenian law court there were two urns—one for acquittal, one for condemnation—into which the jurors dropped their pebbles. (The audience will see them on stage in the final play of the trilogy.)

For that we must thank the gods with a sacrifice
our sons will long remember. For their mad outrage
of a queen we raped their city—we were right.
The beast of Argos, foals of the wild mare,[8]
thousands massed in armor rose on the night
the Pleiades went down,[9] and crashing through
their walls our bloody lion lapped its fill,
gorging on the blood of kings.
Our thanks to the gods,
long drawn out, but it is just the prelude.

[CLYTAEMNESTRA *approaches with her women; they are carrying dark red tapestries.* AGAMEMNON *turns to the* LEADER.]

And your concern, old man, is on my mind.
I hear you and agree, I will support you.
How rare, men with the character to praise
a friend's success without a trace of envy,
poison to the heart—it deals a double blow.
Your own losses weigh you down but then,
look at your neighbor's fortune and you weep.
Well I know. I understand society,
the fawning mirror of the proud.
My comrades . . .
they're shadows, I tell you, ghosts of men
who swore they'd die for me. Only Odysseus:
I dragged that man to the wars[1] but once in harness
he was a trace-horse, he gave his all for me.
Dead or alive, no matter, I can praise him.

And now this cause involving men and gods.
We must summon the city for a trial,
found a national tribunal. Whatever's healthy,
shore it up with law and help it flourish.
Wherever something calls for drastic cures
we make our noblest effort: amputate or wield
the healing iron, burn the cancer at the roots.

Now I go to my father's house—
I give the gods my right hand, my first salute.
The ones who sent me forth have brought me home.

[*He starts down from the chariot, looks at* CLYTAEMNESTRA, *stops, and offers up a prayer.*]

Victory, you have sped my way before,
now speed me to the last.

[CLYTAEMNESTRA *turns from the king to the* CHORUS.]

CLYTAEMNESTRA Old nobility of Argos
gathered here, I am not ashamed to tell you

8. The wooden horse, the stratagem with which the Greeks captured the city. 9. The setting of the constellation Pleiades, late in the fall. 1. Feigning madness to escape going to Troy, Odysseus was tricked into demonstrating his sanity. Agamemnon's remark shows that the truth is far from his mind; he has no thought that his danger comes from a woman.

how I love the man. I am older,
and the fear dies away . . . I am human.
Nothing I say was learned from others.
This is my life, my ordeal, long as the siege
he laid at Troy and more demanding.
First,
when a woman sits at home and the man is gone,
the loneliness is terrible,
unconscionable . . .
and the rumors spread and fester,
a runner comes with something dreadful,
close on his heels the next and his news worse,
and they shout it out and the whole house can hear;
and wounds—if he took one wound for each report
to penetrate these walls, he's gashed like a dragnet,
more, if he had only died . . .
for each death that swelled his record, he could boast
like a triple-bodied Geryon[2] risen from the grave,
"Three shrouds I dug from the earth, one for every body
that went down!"
The rumors broke like fever,
broke and then rose higher. There were times
they cut me down and eased my throat from the noose.
I wavered between the living and the dead.
[*Turning to* AGAMEMNON.]
And so
our child is gone, not standing by our side,
the bond of our dearest pledges, mine and yours;
by all rights our child should be here . . .
Orestes. You seem startled.
You needn't be. Our loyal brother-in-arms
will take good care of him, Strophios[3] the Phocian.
He warned from the start we court two griefs in one.
You risk all on the wars—and what if the people
rise up howling for the king, and anarchy
should dash our plans?
Men, it is their nature,
trampling on the fighter once he's down.
Our child is gone. That is my self-defense
and it is true.
For me, the tears that welled
like springs are dry. I have no tears to spare.
I'd watch till late at night, my eyes still burn,
I sobbed by the torch I lit for you alone.
[*Glancing towards the palace.*]
I never let it die . . . but in my dreams
the high thin wail of a gnat would rouse me,

2. A monster (eventually killed by Heracles) who had three bodies and three heads. 3. King of Phocis, a mountainous region near Delphi. His son, Pylades, accompanies Orestes when he returns to avenge Agamemnon's death.

piercing like a trumpet—I could see you
suffer more than all
the hours that slept with me could ever bear.

I endured it all. And now, free of grief,
I would salute that man the watchdog of the fold,
the mainroyal,[4] saving stay of the vessel,
rooted oak that thrusts the roof sky-high,
the father's one true heir.
Land at dawn to the shipwrecked past all hope,
light of the morning burning off the night of storm,
the cold clear spring to the parched horseman—
O the ecstasy, to flee the yoke of Fate!

It is right to use the titles he deserves.
Let envy keep her distance. We have suffered
long enough.
[*Reaching toward* AGAMEMNON.]
Come to me now, my dearest,
down from the car of war, but never set the foot
that stamped out Troy on earth again, my great one.

Women, why delay? You have your orders.
Pave his way with tapestries.[5]
[*They begin to spread the crimson tapestries between the king and the palace doors.*]
Quickly.
Let the red stream flow and bear him home
to the home he never hoped to see—Justice,
lead him in!
Leave all the rest to me.
The spirit within me never yields to sleep.
We will set things right, with the god's help.
We will do whatever Fate requires.

AGAMEMNON
There
is Leda's daughter,[6] the keeper of my house.
And the speech to suit my absence, much too long.
But the praise that does us justice,
let it come from others, then we prize it.
This—
You treat me like a woman. Groveling, gaping up at me!
What am I, some barbarian[7] peacocking out of Asia?
Never cross my path with robes and draw the lightning.
Never—only the gods deserve the pomps of honor
and the stiff brocades of fame. To walk on them . . .

4. Upper section of the mainmast. 5. To walk on those tapestries, wall hangings dyed with the expensive crimson, would be an act of extravagant pride. Pride is the keynote of Agamemnon's character, and it suits Clytaemnestra's sense of fitness that he should go into his death in godlike state, *trampling royal crimson* (line 957), the color of blood. 6. Clytaemnestra. Helen is also a daughter of Leda. 7. Foreigner, especially Asiatic. Aeschylus is thinking of the pomp and servility of the contemporary Persian court.

I am human, and it makes my pulses stir
with dread.
Give me the tributes of a man
and not a god, a little earth to walk on,
not this gorgeous work.
There is no need to sound my reputation.
I have a sense of right and wrong, what's more—
heaven's proudest gift. Call no man blest
until he ends his life in peace, fulfilled.
If I can live by what I say, I have no fear.

CLYTAEMNESTRA One thing more. Be true to your ideals and tell me—

AGAMEMNON True to my ideals? Once I violate them I am lost.

CLYTAEMNESTRA Would you have sworn this act to god in a time of terror?

AGAMEMNON Yes, if a prophet called for a last, drastic rite.

CLYTAEMNESTRA But Priam—can you see him if he had your success?

AGAMEMNON Striding on the tapestries of God, I see him now.

CLYTAEMNESTRA And *you* fear the reproach of common men?

AGAMEMNON The voice of the people—aye, they have enormous power.

CLYTAEMNESTRA Perhaps, but where's the glory without a little gall?

AGAMEMNON And where's the woman in all this lust for glory?

CLYTAEMNESTRA But the great victor—it becomes him to give way.

AGAMEMNON Victory in this . . . war of ours, it means so much to you?

CLYTAEMNESTRA O give way! The power is yours if you surrender
all of your own free will to me.

AGAMEMNON Enough.
If you are so determined—

[*Turning to the women, pointing to his boots.*]

Let someone help me off with these at least.
Old slaves, they've stood me well.
Hurry,
and while I tread his splendors dyed red in the sea,[8]
may no god watch and strike me down with envy
from on high. I feel such shame—
to tread the life of the house, a kingdom's worth
of silver in the weaving.

[*He steps down from the chariot to the tapestries and reveals* CASSANDRA, *dressed in the sacred regalia, the fillets, robes and scepter of Apollo.*]

Done is done.
Escort this stranger[9] in, be gentle.
Conquer with compassion. Then the gods
shine down upon you, gently. No one chooses
the yoke of slavery, not of one's free will—
and she least of all. The gift of the armies,

8. The dye was made from shellfish. 9. Cassandra, daughter of Priam, Agamemnon's share of the human booty of the sack of Troy. She was loved by Apollo, who gave her the gift of prophecy, but when she refused her love to the god, he saw to it that her prophecies, though true, would never be believed until it was too late.

flower and pride of all the wealth we won,
she follows me from Troy.
And now,
since you have brought me down with your insistence,
just this once I enter my father's house,
trampling royal crimson as I go.

[*He takes his first steps and pauses.*]

CLYTAEMNESTRA There is the sea
and who will drain it dry? Precious as silver,
inexhaustible, ever-new, it breeds the more we reap it—
tides on tides of crimson dye our robes blood-red.
Our lives are based on wealth, my king,
the gods have seen to that.
Destitution, our house has never heard the word.
I would have sworn to tread on legacies of robes,
at one command from an oracle, deplete the house—
suffer the worst to bring that dear life back!

[*Encouraged,* AGAMEMNON *strides to the entrance.*]

When the root lives on, the new leaves come back,
spreading a dense shroud of shade across the house
to thwart the Dog Star's[1] fury. So you return
to the father's hearth, you bring us warmth in winter
like the sun—
And you are Zeus when Zeus
tramples the bitter virgin grape for new wine
and the welcome chill steals through the halls, at last
the master moves among the shadows of his house, fulfilled.

[AGAMEMNON *goes over the threshold; the women gather up the tapestries while* CLYTAEMNESTRA *prays.*]

Zeus, Zeus, master of all fullfillment, now fulfill our prayers—
speed our rites to their fulfillment once for all!

[*She enters the palace, the doors close, the old men huddle in terror.*]

CHORUS Why, why does it rock me, never stops,
this terror beating down my heart,
this seer that sees it all—
it beats its wings, uncalled unpaid
thrust on the lungs
the mercenary song beats on and on
singing a prophet's strain—
and I can't throw it off
like dreams that make no sense,
and the strength drains
that filled the mind with trust,
and the years drift by and the driven sand
has buried the mooring lines
that churned when the armored squadrons cut for Troy . . .

1. Sirius; its appearance in the summer sky marked the beginning of the hot season (the "dog days" of summer).

and now I believe it, I can prove he's home,
my own clear eyes for witness—
Agamemnon!
Still it's chanting, beating deep so deep in the heart
this dirge of the Furies, oh dear god,
not fit for the lyre,[2] its own master
it kills our spirit
kills our hopes
and it's real, true, no fantasy—
stark terror whirls the brain
and the end is coming
Justice comes to birth—
I pray my fears prove false and fall
and die and never come to birth!
Even exultant health, well we know,
exceeds its limits,[3] comes so near disease
it can breach the wall between them.

Even a man's fate, held true on course,
in a blinding flash rams some hidden reef;
but if caution only casts the pick of the cargo—
one well-balanced cast—
the house will not go down, not outright;[4]
laboring under its wealth of grief
the ship of state rides on.

Yes, and the great green bounty of god,
sown in the furrows year by year and reaped each fall
can end the plague of famine.

But a man's lifeblood
is dark and mortal.
Once it wets the earth
what song can sing it back?
Not even the master-healer[5]
who brought the dead to life—
Zeus stopped the man before he did more harm.

Oh, if only the gods had never forged
the chain that curbs our excess,
one man's fate curbing the next man's fate,
my heart would outrace my song, I'd pour out all I feel—
but no, I choke with anguish,
mutter through the nights.
Never to ravel out a hope in time

2. A stringed instrument played on joyful occasions (hence "lyric" poetry). 3. Excess, even in blessings like health, is always dangerous. The chorus fears that Agamemnon's triumphant success may threaten his safety. 4. These lines refer to a traditional Greek belief that the fortunate person could avert the envy of heaven by deliberately getting rid of some precious possession. 5. Asclepius, the great physician who was so skilled that he finally succeeded in restoring a dead man to life. Zeus struck him with a thunderbolt for going too far.

and the brain is swarming, burning—
[CLYTAEMNESTRA *emerges from the palace and goes to* CASSANDRA, *impassive in the chariot.*]
CLYTAEMNESTRA Won't you come inside? I mean you, Cassandra.
Zeus in all his mercy wants you to share
some victory libations with the house.
The slaves are flocking. Come, lead them
up to the altar of the god who guards
our dearest treasures.
Down from the chariot,
no time for pride. Why even Heracles,[6]
they say, was sold into bondage long ago,
he had to endure the bitter bread of slaves.
But if the yoke descends on you, be grateful
for a master born and reared in ancient wealth.
Those who reap a harvest past their hopes
are merciless to their slaves.
From us
you will receive what custom says is right.
[CASSANDRA *remains impassive.*]
LEADER It's *you* she is speaking to, it's all too clear.
You're caught in the nets of doom—obey
if you can obey, unless you cannot bear to.
CLYTAEMNESTRA Unless she's like a swallow, possessed
of her own barbaric song,[7] strange, dark.
I speak directly as I can—she must obey.
LEADER Go with her. Make the best of it, she's right.
Step down from the seat, obey her.
CLYTAEMNESTRA Do it *now*—
I have no time to spend outside. Already
the victims crowd the hearth, the Navelstone,[8]
to bless this day of joy I never hoped to see!—
our victims waiting for the fire and the knife,
and you,
if you want to taste our mystic rites, come now.
If my words can't reach you—
[*Turning to the* LEADER.]
Give her a sign,
one of her exotic handsigns.
LEADER I think
the stranger needs an interpreter, someone clear.
She's like a wild creature, fresh caught.
CLYTAEMNESTRA She's mad,
her evil genius murmuring in her ears.
She comes from a *city* fresh caught.
She must learn to take the cutting bridle

6. The Greek hero, famous for his twelve labors that rid the Earth of monsters, was at one time forced to be the slave to Omphale, an Eastern queen. 7. The comparison of foreign speech to the twittering of a swallow was a Greek commonplace. 8. An altar of Zeus Herkeios, guardian of the hearth, which was the religious center of the home.

before she foams her spirit off in blood—
and that's the last I waste on her contempt!
[*Wheeling, re-entering the palace. The* LEADER *turns to* CASSANDRA, *who remains transfixed.*]
LEADER Not I, I pity her. I will be gentle.
Come, poor thing. Leave the empty chariot—
Of your own free will try on the yoke of Fate.
CASSANDRA Aieeeeee! Earth—Mother—
Curse of the Earth—Apollo Apollo!
LEADER Why cry to Apollo?
He's not the god to call with sounds of mourning.
CASSANDRA Aieeeeee! Earth—Mother—
Rape of the Earth—Apollo Apollo!
LEADER Again, it's a bad omen.
She cries for the god who wants no part of grief.[9]
[CASSANDRA *steps from the chariot, looks slowly towards the rooftops of the palace.*]
CASSANDRA God of the long road,
Apollo *Apollo* my destroyer—
you destroy me once,[1] destroy me twice—
LEADER She's about to sense her own ordeal, I think.
Slave that she is, the god lives on inside her.
CASSANDRA God of the iron marches,
Apollo *Apollo* my destroyer—
where, where have you led[2] me now? what house—
LEADER The house of Atreus and his sons. Really—
don't you know? It's true, see for yourself.
CASSANDRA No . . . the house that hates god,
an echoing womb of guilt, kinsmen
torturing kinsmen, severed heads,
slaughterhouse of heroes, soil streaming blood—
LEADER A keen hound, this stranger.
Trailing murder, and murder she will find.
CASSANDRA See, my witnesses—
I trust to them, to the babies
wailing, skewered on the sword,
their flesh charred, the father gorging on their parts[3]—
LEADER We'd heard your fame as a seer,
but no one looks for seers in Argos.
CASSANDRA Oh no, what horror, what new plot,[4]
new agony this?—
it's growing, massing, deep in the house,
a plot, a monstrous—*thing*
to crush the loved ones, no,

9. Apollo (and the Olympian gods in general) was not invoked in mourning or lamentation. 1. The name *Apollo* suggests the Greek word *apollumi*, "destroy." He destroyed her the first time when he saw to it that no one would believe her prophecies. *God of the long road:* Apollo Agyieus. This statue, a conical pillar, was set up outside the door of the house; no doubt there was one onstage. 2. The Greek word (a form of the verb *ago*) suggests the god's title Agyieus. 3. The feast of Thyestes, who was tricked by his brother, Atreus, into eating his children. The story is told by Aegisthus below (lines 1606–43). 4. Clytaemnestra's murder of Agamemnon.

there is no cure, and rescue's far away[5] and—
LEADER I can't read these signs; I knew the first,
the city rings with them.
CASSANDRA You, you godforsaken—you'd do *this?*
The lord of your bed,
you bathe him . . . his body glistens, then—
how to tell the climax?—
comes so quickly, see,
hand over hand shoots out, hauling ropes—
then lunge!
LEADER Still lost. Her riddles, her dark words of god—
I'm groping, helpless.
CASSANDRA No no, look *there!*—
what's that? some net flung out of hell—
No, *she* is the snare,
the bedmate, deathmate, murder's strong right arm!
Let the insatiate discord in the race
rear up and shriek "Avenge the victim—stone them dead!"
LEADER What Fury is this? Why rouse it, lift its wailing
through the house? I hear you and lose hope.
CHORUS Drop by drop at the heart, the gold of life ebbs out.
We are the old soldiers . . . wounds will come
with the crushing sunset of our lives.
Death is close, and quick.
CASSANDRA Look out! *look out!*—
Ai, drag the great bull from the mate!—
a thrash of robes, she traps him—
writhing—
black horn glints, twists—
she gores him through!
And now he buckles, look, the bath swirls red—
There's stealth and murder in the cauldron, do you hear?
LEADER I'm no judge, I've little skill with the oracles,
but even I know danger when I hear it.
CHORUS What good are the oracles to men? Words, more words,
and the hurt comes on us, endless words
and a seer's techniques have brought us
terror and the truth.
CASSANDRA The agony—O I am breaking!—Fate's so hard,
and the pain that floods my voice is mine alone.
Why have you brought me here, tormented as I am?
Why, unless to die with him, why else?
LEADER AND CHORUS Mad with the rapture—god speeds you on
to the song, the deathsong,
like the nightingale[6] that broods on sorrow,

5. A reference to Menelaus (distant in space) and Orestes (distant in time). 6. Philomela was raped by Tereus, the husband of her sister Procne. The two sisters avenged themselves by killing Tereus's son, Itys, and serving up his flesh to Tereus to eat. Procne was changed into a nightingale mourning for Itys (the name is an imitation of the sound of the nightingale's song).

mourns her son, her son,
her life inspired with grief for him,
she lilts and shrills, dark bird that lives for night.
CASSANDRA The nightingale—O for a song, a fate like hers!
The gods gave her a life of ease, swathed her in wings,
no tears, no wailing. The knife waits for me.
They'll splay me on the iron's double edge.
LEADER AND CHORUS Why?—what god hurls you on, stroke on stroke
to the long dying fall?
Why the horror clashing through your music,
terror struck to song?—
why the anguish, the wild dance?
Where do your words of god and grief begin?
CASSANDRA Ai, the wedding, wedding of Paris,
death to the loved ones. Oh Scamander,[7]
you nursed my father . . . once at your banks
I nursed and grew, and now at the banks
of Acheron,[8] the stream that carries sorrow,
it seems I'll chant my prophecies too soon.
LEADER AND CHORUS What are you saying? Wait, it's clear,
a child could see the truth, it wounds within,
Like a bloody fang it tears—
I hear your destiny—breaking sobs,
cries that stab the ears.
CASSANDRA Oh the grief, the grief of the city
ripped to oblivion. Oh the victims,
the flocks my father burned at the wall,
rich herds in flames . . . no cure for the doom
that took the city after all, and I,
her last ember, I go down with her.
LEADER AND CHORUS You cannot stop, your song goes on—
some spirit drops from the heights and treads you down
and the brutal strain grows—
your death-throes come and come and
I cannot see the end!
CASSANDRA Then off with the veils that hid the fresh young bride[9]—
we will see the truth.
Flare up once more, my oracle! Clear and sharp
as the wind that blows toward the rising sun,
I can feel a deeper swell now, gathering head
to break at last and bring the dawn of grief.

No more riddles. I will teach you.
Come, bear witness, run and hunt with me.
We trail the old barbaric works of slaughter.

7. A Trojan river. 8. One of the rivers of the underworld. 9. At this point, as the meter indicates, Cassandra changes from lyric song, the medium of emotion, to spoken iambic lines, the medium of rational discourse.

These roofs—look up—there is a dancing troupe
that never leaves. And they have their harmony
but it is harsh, their words are harsh, they drink
beyond the limit. Flushed on the blood of men
their spirit grows and none can turn away
their revel breeding in the veins—the Furies!
They cling to the house for life. They sing,
sing of the frenzy that began it all,
strain rising on strain, showering curses
on the man who tramples on his brother's bed.[1]

There. Have I hit the mark or not? Am I a fraud,
a fortune-teller babbling lies from door to door?
Swear how well I know the ancient crimes
that live within this house.

LEADER And if I did?
Would an oath bind the wounds and heal us?
But you amaze me. Bred across the sea,
your language strange, and still you sense the truth
as if you had been here.

CASSANDRA Apollo the Prophet
introduced me to his gift.

LEADER A *god*—and moved with love?

CASSANDRA I was ashamed to tell this once,
but now . . .

LEADER We spoil ourselves with scruples,
long as things go well.

CASSANDRA He came like a wrestler,
magnificent, took me down and breathed his fire
through me and—

LEADER You bore him a child?

CASSANDRA I yielded,
then at the climax I recoiled—I deceived Apollo!

LEADER But the god's skills—they seized you even then?

CASSANDRA Even then I told my people all the grief to come.

LEADER And Apollo's anger never touched you?—is it possible?

CASSANDRA Once I betrayed him I could never be believed.

LEADER We believe you. Your visions seem so true.

CASSANDRA Aieeeee!—
the pain, the terror! the birth-pang of the seer
who tells the truth—
it whirls me, oh,
the storm comes again, the crashing chords!
Look, you see them nestling at the threshold?
Young, young in the darkness like a dream,
like children really, yes, and their loved ones
brought them down . . .
their hands, they fill their hands

1. Thyestes, who seduced the wife of his brother, Atreus.

with their own flesh, they are serving it like food,
holding out their entrails . . . now it's clear,
I can see the armfuls of compassion, see the father
reach to taste and—
For so much suffering,
I tell you, someone plots revenge.
A lion[2] who lacks a lion's heart,
he sprawled at home in the royal lair
and set a trap for the lord on his return.
My lord . . . I must wear his yoke, I am his slave.
The lord of the men-of-war, he obliterated Troy—
he is so blind, so lost to that detestable hellhound
who pricks her ears and fawns and her tongue draws out
her glittering words of welcome—
No, he cannot see
the stroke that Fury's hiding, stealth, murder.
What outrage—the woman kills the man!
What to call
that . . . monster of Greece, and bring my quarry down?
Viper coiling back and forth?
Some sea-witch?—
Scylla[3] crouched in her rocky nest—nightmare of sailors?
Raging mother of death, storming deathless war against
the ones she loves!
And how she howled in triumph,
boundless outrage. Just as the tide of battle
broke her way, she seems to rejoice that he
is safe at home from war, saved for her.

Believe me if you will. What will it matter
if you won't? It comes when it comes,
and soon you'll see it face to face
and say the seer was all too true.
You will be moved with pity.

LEADER Thyestes' feast,
the children's flesh—that I know,
and the fear shudders through me. It's true,
real, no dark signs about it. I hear the rest
but it throws me off the scent.

CASSANDRA Agamemnon.
You will see him dead.

LEADER Peace, poor girl!
Put those words to sleep.

CASSANDRA No use,
the Healer[4] has no hand in this affair.

LEADER Not if it's true—but god forbid it is!

CASSANDRA You pray, and they close in to kill!

LEADER What man prepares this, this dreadful—

2. Aegisthus. 3. A human-eating sea monster (see *Odyssey* 12, pp. 370–71). 4. Apollo.

CASSANDRA Man?
You *are* lost, to every word I've said.
LEADER Yes—
I don't see who can bring the evil off.
CASSANDRA And yet I know my Greek, too well.
LEADER So does the Delphic oracle,[5]
but he's hard to understand.
CASSANDRA His *fire!*—
sears me, sweeps me again—the torture!
Apollo Lord of the Light, you burn,
you blind me—
Agony!
She is the lioness,
she rears on her hind legs, she beds with the wolf
when her lion king goes ranging—
she will kill me—
Ai, the torture!
She is mixing her drugs,
adding a measure more of hate for me.
She gloats as she whets the sword for him.
He brought me home and we will pay in carnage.

Why mock yourself with these—trappings, the rod,
the god's wreath, his yoke around my throat?
Before I die I'll tread you—
[*Ripping off her regalia, stamping it into the ground.*]
Down, out,
die die die!
Now you're down. I've paid you back.
Look for another victim—I am free at last—
make her rich in all your curse and doom.
[*Staggering backwards as if wrestling with a spirit tearing at her robes.*]
See,
Apollo himself, his fiery hands—I feel him again,
he's stripping off my robes, the Seer's robes!
And after he looked down and saw me mocked,
even in these, his glories, mortified by friends
I loved, and they hated me, they were so blind
to their own demise—
I went from door to door,
I was wild with the god, I heard them call me
"Beggar! Wretch! Starve for bread in hell!"

And I endured it all, and now he will
extort me as his due. A seer for the Seer.
He brings me here to die like this,
not to serve at my father's altar. No,

5. Its replies were celebrated for their obscurity and ambiguity.

the block is waiting. The cleaver steams
with my life blood, the first blood drawn
for the king's last rites.
[*Regaining her composure and moving to the altar.*]
We will die,
but not without some honor from the gods.
There will come another[6] to avenge us,
born to kill his mother, born
his father's champion. A wanderer, a fugitive
driven off his native land, he will come home
to cope the stones of hate that menace all he loves.
The gods have sworn a monumental oath: as his father lies
upon the ground he draws him home with power like a prayer.

Then why so pitiful, why so many tears?
I have seen my city faring as she fared,
and those who took her, judged by the gods,
faring as they fare. I must be brave.
It is my turn to die.
[*Approaching the doors.*]
I address you as the Gates of Death.
I pray it comes with one clear stroke,
no convulsions, the pulses ebbing out
in gentle death. I'll close my eyes and sleep.

LEADER So much pain, poor girl, and so much truth,
you've told so much. But if you *see* it coming,
clearly—how can you go to your own death,
like a beast to the altar driven on by god,
and hold your head so high?

CASSANDRA No escape, my friends,
not now.

LEADER But the last hour should be savored.

CASSANDRA My time has come. Little to gain from flight.

LEADER You're brave, believe me, full of gallant heart.

CASSANDRA Only the wretched go with praise like that.

LEADER But to go nobly lends a man some grace.

CASSANDRA My noble father—you and your noble children.
[*She nears the threshold and recoils, groaning in revulsion.*]

LEADER What now? what terror flings you back?
Why? Unless some horror in the brain—

CASSANDRA Murder.
The house breathes with murder—bloody shambles![7]

LEADER No, no, only the victims at the hearth.

CASSANDRA I know that odor. I smell the open grave.

LEADER But the Syrian myrrh,[8] it fills the halls with splendor,
can't you sense it?

CASSANDRA Well, I must go in now,

6. Orestes. 7. A slaughterhouse. 8. Incense burned at the sacrifice. Another interpretation of this line runs, "What you speak of (that is, the smell of the open grave) is no Syrian incense, giving splendor to the palace."

mourning Agamemnon's death and mine.
Enough of life!
[*Approaching the doors again and crying out.*]
Friends—I cried out,
not from fear like a bird fresh caught,
but that you will testify to *how* I died.
When the queen, woman for woman, dies for me,
and a man falls for the man who married grief.
That's all I ask, my friends. A stranger's gift
for one about to die.

LEADER Poor creature, you
and the end you see so clearly. I pity you.

CASSANDRA I'd like a few words more, a kind of dirge,
it is my own. I pray to the sun,
the last light I'll see,
that when the avengers cut the assassins down
they will avenge me too, a slave who died,
an easy conquest.
Oh men, your destiny.
When all is well a shadow can overturn it.
When trouble comes a stroke of the wet sponge,
and the picture's blotted out. And that,
I think that breaks the heart.
[*She goes through the doors.*]

CHORUS But the lust for power never dies—
men cannot have enough.
No one will lift a hand to send it
from his door, to give it warning,
"Power, never come again!"
Take this man: the gods in glory
gave him Priam's city to plunder,
brought him home in splendor like a god.
But now if he must pay for the blood
his fathers shed, and die for the deaths
he brought to pass, and bring more death
to avenge his dying, show us one
who boasts himself born free
of the raging angel, once he hears—
[*Cries break out within the palace.*]

AGAMEMNON Aagh!
Struck deep—the death-blow, deep—

LEADER Quiet. Cries,
but who? Someone's stabbed—

AGAMEMNON Aaagh, again . . .
second blow—struck home.

LEADER The work is done,
you can feel it. The king, and the great cries—
Close ranks now, find the right way out.
[*But the old men scatter, each speaks singly.*]

CHORUS —I say send out heralds, muster the guard,
they'll save the house.

—And I say rush in now,
catch them red-handed—butchery running on their blades.

—Right with you, do something—now or never!

—Look at them, beating the drum for insurrection.

—Yes,
we're wasting time. They rape the name of caution,
their hands will never sleep.

—Not a plan in sight.
Let men of action do the planning, too.

—I'm helpless. Who can raise the dead with words?

—What, drag out our lives? bow down to the tyrants,
the ruin of the house?

—Never, better to die
on your feet than live on your knees.

—Wait,
do we take the cries for signs, prophesy like seers
and give him up for dead?

—No more suspicions,
not another word till we have proof.

—Confusion
on all sides—one thing to do. See how it stands
with Agamemnon, once and for all we'll see—

[*He rushes at the doors. They open and reveal a silver cauldron that holds the body of* AGAMEMNON *shrouded in bloody robes, with the body of* CASSANDRA *to his left and* CLYTAEMNESTRA *standing to his right, sword in hand. She strides towards the* CHORUS.]

CLYTAEMNESTRA Words, endless words I've said to serve the moment—
Now it makes me proud to tell the truth.
How else to prepare a death for deadly men
who seem to love you? How to rig the nets
of pain so high no man can overleap them?

I brooded on this trial, this ancient blood feud
year by year. At last my hour came.
Here I stand and here I struck
and here my work is done.
I did it all. I don't deny it, no.

He had no way to flee or fight his destiny—

[*Unwinding the robes from* AGAMEMNON'*s body, spreading them before the altar where the old men cluster around them, unified as a chorus once again.*]

our never-ending, all embracing net, I cast it
wide for the royal haul, I coil him round and round
in the wealth, the robes of doom, and then I strike him
once, twice, and at each stroke he cries in agony—
he buckles at the knees and crashes here!
And when he's down I add the third, last blow,
to the Zeus who saves the dead beneath the ground
I send that third blow home in homage like a prayer.[9]

So he goes down, and the life is bursting out of him—
great sprays of blood, and the murderous shower
wounds me, dyes me black and I, I revel
like the Earth when the spring rains come down,
the blessed gifts of god, and the new green spear
splits the sheath and rips to birth in glory!

So it stands, elders of Argos gathered here.
Rejoice if you can rejoice—I glory.
And if I'd pour upon his body the libation
it deserves, what wine could match my words?
It is right and more than right. He flooded
the vessel of our proud house with misery,
with the vintage of the curse and now
he drains the dregs. My lord is home at last.

LEADER You appall me, you, your brazen words—
exulting over your fallen king.

CLYTAEMNESTRA And you,
you try me like some desperate woman.
My heart is steel, well you know. Praise me,
blame me as you choose. It's all one.
Here is Agamemnon, my husband made a corpse
by this right hand—a masterpiece of Justice.
Done is done.

CHORUS Woman!—what poison cropped from the soil
or strained from the heaving sea, what nursed you,
drove you insane? You brave the curse of Greece.
You have cut away and flung away and now
the people cast you off to exile,
broken with our hate.

CLYTAEMNESTRA And now you sentence me?—
you banish *me* from the city, curses breathing
down my neck? But *he*—
name one charge you brought against him then.
He thought no more of it than killing a beast,

9. Like the third libation to Zeus (see n. 7, p. 544).

and his flocks were rich, teeming in their fleece,
but he sacrificed his own child, our daughter,
the agony I labored into love,
to charm away the savage winds of Thrace.[1]

Didn't the law demand you banish him?—
hunt him from the land for all his guilt?
But now you witness what I've done
and you are ruthless judges.
Threaten away!
I'll meet you blow for blow. And if I fall
the throne is yours. If god decrees the reverse,
late as it is, old men, you'll learn your place.

CHORUS Mad with ambition,
shrilling pride!—some Fury
crazed with the carnage rages through your brain—
I can see the flecks of blood inflame your eyes!
But vengeance comes—you'll lose your loved ones,
stroke for painful stroke.

CLYTAEMNESTRA Then learn this, too, the power of my oaths.
By the child's Rights I brought to birth,
by Ruin, by Fury—the three gods to whom
I sacrificed this man—I swear my hopes
will never walk the halls of fear so long
as Aegisthus lights the fire on my hearth.
Loyal to me as always, no small shield
to buttress my defiance.
Here he lies.
He brutalized me. The darling of all
the golden girls[2] who spread the gates of Troy.
And here his spearprize . . . what wonders she beheld!—
the seer of Apollo shared my husband's bed,
his faithful mate who knelt at the rowing-benches,
worked by every hand.
They have their rewards.
He as you know. And she, the swan of the gods
who lived to sing her latest, dying song—
his lover lies beside him.
She brings a fresh, voluptuous relish to my bed!

CHORUS Oh quickly, let me die—
no bed of labor, no, no wasting illness . . .
bear me off in the sleep that never ends,
now that he has fallen,
now that our dearest shield lies battered—
Woman made him suffer,
woman struck him down.

1. Winds from the North (at Aulis). 2. In Greek *chryseidon,* which recalls the girl in the first book of the *Iliad* (1.130–33), Chryseis, whom Agamemnon said he preferred to Clytaemnestra.

Helen the wild, maddening Helen,
one for the many, the thousand lives
you murdered under Troy. Now you are crowned
with this consummate wreath, the blood
that lives in memory, glistens age to age.
Once in the halls she walked and she was war,
angel of war, angel of agony, lighting men to death.

CLYTAEMNESTRA Pray no more for death, broken
as you are. And never turn
your wrath on her, call her
the scourge of men, the one alone
who destroyed a myriad Greek lives—
Helen the grief that never heals.

CHORUS The *spirit!*—you who tread
the house and the twinborn sons of Tantalus[3]—
you empower the sisters, Fury's twins
whose power tears the heart!
Perched on the corpse your carrion raven
glories in her hymn,
her screaming hymn of pride.

CLYTAEMNESTRA Now you set your judgment straight,
you summon *him!* Three generations
feed the spirit in the race.
Deep in the veins he feeds our bloodlust—
aye, before the old wound dies
it ripens in another flow of blood.

CHORUS The great curse of the house, the spirit,
dead weight wrath—and you can praise it!
Praise the insatiate doom that feeds
relentless on our future and our sons.
Oh all through the will of Zeus,
the cause of all, the one who works it all.
What comes to birth that is not Zeus?
Our lives are pain, what part not come from god?

Oh, my king, my captain,
how to salute you, how to mourn you?
What can I say with all my warmth and love?
Here in the black widow's web you lie,
gasping out your life
in a sacrilegious death, dear god,
reduced to a slave's bed,
my king of men, yoked by stealth and Fate,
by the wife's hand that thrust the two-edged sword.

CLYTAEMNESTRA You claim the work is mine, call me
Agamemnon's wife—you are so wrong.

3. Father of Pelops, grandfather of Atreus. *Sons:* descendants—that is, Agamemnon and Menelaus.

Fleshed in the wife of this dead man,
  the spirit lives within me,
our savage ancient spirit of revenge.
In return for Atreus' brutal feast
he kills his perfect son—for every
murdered child, a crowning sacrifice.

CHORUS And *you,* innocent of his murder?
  And who could swear to that? and how? . . .
and still an avenger could arise,
bred by the fathers' crimes, and lend a hand.
He wades in the blood of brothers,
stream on mounting stream—black war erupts
  and where he strides revenge will stride,
clots will mass for the young who were devoured.

Oh my king, my captain,
how to salute you, how to mourn you?
What can I say with all my warmth and love?
Here in the black widow's web you lie,
gasping out your life
in a sacrilegious death, dear god,
reduced to a slave's bed,
my king of men, yoked by stealth and Fate,
by the wife's hand that thrust the two-edged sword.

CLYTAEMNESTRA No slave's death, I think—
no stealthier than the death he dealt
our house and the offspring of our loins,
  Iphigeneia, girl of tears.
Act for act, wound for wound!
Never exult in Hades, swordsman,
here you are repaid. By the sword
you did your work and by the sword you die.

CHORUS The mind reels—where to turn?
All plans dashed, all hope! I cannot think . . .
the roofs are toppling, I dread the drumbeat thunder
the heavy rains of blood will crush the house
the first light rains are over—
Justice brings new acts of agony, yes,
on new grindstones Fate is grinding sharp the sword of Justice.

Earth, dear Earth,
if only you'd drawn me under
long before I saw him huddled
in the beaten silver bath.
Who will bury him, lift his dirge?
  [*Turning to* CLYTAEMNESTRA.]
You, can you dare *this?*
To kill your lord with your own hand
then mourn his soul with tributes, terrible tributes—

do his enormous works a great dishonor.
This godlike man, this hero. Who at the grave
will sing his praises, pour the wine of tears?
Who will labor there with truth of heart?

CLYTAEMNESTRA This is no concern of yours.
The hand that bore and cut him down
will hand him down to Mother Earth.
This house will never mourn for him.
Only our daughter Iphigeneia,
by all rights, will rush to meet him
first at the churning straits,[4]
the ferry over tears—
she'll fling her arms around her father,
pierce him with her love.

CHORUS Each charge meets counter-charge.
None can judge between them. Justice.
The plunderer plundered, the killer pays the price.
The truth still holds while Zeus still holds the throne:
the one who acts must suffer—
that is law. Who, who can tear from the veins
the bad seed, the curse? The race is welded to its ruin.

CLYTAEMNESTRA At last you see the future and the truth!
But I will swear a pact with the spirit
born within us. I embrace his works,
cruel as they are but done at last,
if he will leave our house
in the future, bleed another line
with kinsmen murdering kinsmen.
Whatever he may ask. A few things
are all I need, once I have purged
our fury to destroy each other—
purged it from our halls.

[AEGISTHUS *has emerged from the palace with his bodyguard and stands triumphant over the body of* AGAMEMNON.]

AEGISTHUS O what a brilliant day
it is for vengeance! Now I can say once more
there are gods in heaven avenging men,
blazing down on all the crimes of earth.
Now at last I see this man brought down
in the Furies' tangling robes. It feasts my eyes—
he pays for the plot his father's hand contrived.

Atreus, this man's father, was king of Argos.
My father, Thyestes—let me make this clear—
Atreus' brother challenged him for the crown,
and Atreus drove him out of house and home

4. The river of the underworld over which the dead were ferried.

then lured him back, and home Thyestes came,
poor man, a suppliant to his own hearth,
to pray that Fate might save him.
So it did.
There was no dying, no staining our native ground
with *his* blood. Thyestes was the guest,
and this man's godless father—
[*Pointing to* AGAMEMNON.]
the zeal of the host outstripping a brother's love,
made my father a feast that seemed a feast for gods,
a love feast of his children's flesh.
He cuts
the extremities, feet and delicate hands
into small pieces, scatters them over the dish
and serves it to Thyestes throned on high.
He picks at the flesh he cannot recognize,
the soul of innocence eating the food of ruin—
look,
[*Pointing to the bodies at his feet.*]
that feeds upon the house! And then,
when he sees the monstrous thing he's done, he shrieks,
he reels back head first and vomits up that butchery,
tramples the feast—brings down the curse of Justice:
"Crash to ruin, all the race of Pleisthenes,[5] crash down!"

So you see him, down. And I, the weaver of Justice,
plotted out the kill. Atreus drove us into exile,
my struggling father and I, a babe-in-arms,
his last son, but I became a man
and Justice brought me home. I was abroad
but I reached out and seized my man,
link by link I clamped the fatal scheme
together. Now I could die gladly, even I—
now I see this monster in the nets of Justice.

LEADER Aegisthus, you revel in pain—you sicken me.
You say you killed the king in cold blood,
singlehanded planned his pitiful death?
I say there's no escape. In the hour of judgment,
trust to this, your head will meet the people's
rocks and curses.

AEGISTHUS You say! you slaves at the oars—
while the master of the benches cracks the whip?
You'll learn, in your late age, how much it hurts
to teach old bones their place. We have techniques—
chains and the pangs of hunger,
two effective teachers, excellent healers.
They can even cure old men of pride and gall.
Look—can't you see? The more you kick

5. A name sometimes inserted into the genealogy of the house of Tantalus.

against the pricks, the more you suffer.
LEADER You, pathetic—
the king had just returned from battle.
You waited out the war and fouled his lair,
you planned my great commander's fall.
AEGISTHUS Talk on—
you'll scream for every word, my little Orpheus.[6]
We'll see if the world comes dancing to your song,
your absurd barking—snarl your breath away!
I'll make you dance, I'll bring you all to heel.
LEADER *You* rule Argos? You who schemed his death
but cringed to cut him down with your own hand?
AEGISTHUS The treachery was the woman's work, clearly.
I was a marked man, his enemy for ages.
But I will use his riches, stop at nothing
to civilize his people. All but the rebel:
him I'll yoke and break—
no cornfed colt, running free in the traces.
Hunger, ruthless mate of the dark torture-chamber,
trains her eyes upon him till he drops!
LEADER Coward, why not kill the man yourself?
Why did the woman, the corruption of Greece
and the gods of Greece, have to bring him down?
Orestes—If he still sees the light of day,
bring him home, good Fates, home to kill
this pair at last. Our champion in slaughter!
AEGISTHUS Bent on insolence? Well, you'll learn, quickly.
At them, men—you have your work at hand!
[*His men draw swords; the old men take up their sticks.*]
LEADER At them, fist at the hilt, to the last man—
AEGISTHUS Fist at the hilt, I'm not afraid to die.
LEADER It's death you want and death you'll have—
we'll make that word your last.
[CLYTAEMNESTRA *moves between them, restraining* AEGISTHUS.]
CLYTAEMNESTRA No more, my dearest,
no more grief. We have too much to reap
right here, our mighty harvest of despair.
Our lives are based on pain. No bloodshed now.

Fathers of Argos, turn for home before you act
and suffer for it. What we did was destiny.
If we could end the suffering, how we would rejoice.
The spirit's brutal hoof has struck our heart.
And that is what a woman has to say.
Can you accept the truth?
[CLYTAEMNESTRA *turns to leave.*]
AEGISTHUS But these . . . mouths
that bloom in filth—spitting insults in my teeth.

6. A mythical singer who charmed all nature with his music.

You tempt your fates, you insubordinate dogs—
to hurl abuse at me, your master!
LEADER No Greek
worth his salt would grovel at your feet.
AEGISTHUS I—I'll stalk you all your days!
LEADER Not if the spirit brings Orestes home.
AEGISTHUS Exiles feed on hope—well I know.
LEADER More,
gorge yourself to bursting—soil justice, while you can.
AEGISTHUS I promise you, you'll pay, old fools—in good time, too!
LEADER Strut on your own dunghill, you cock beside your mate.
CLYTAEMNESTRA Let them howl—they're impotent. You and I have power now.
We will set the house in order once for all.
[*They enter the palace; the great doors close behind them; the old men disband and wander off.*]

The Libation Bearers

Summary In the final scene of *Agamemnon* the chorus leader, confronted with Aegisthus's threats, cries out in desperation, "*Orestes*—If he still sees the light of day, / bring him home, good Fates." In the second play of the the trilogy, *The Libation Bearers,* Orestes, now grown to manhood, comes home, accompanied by his friend Pylades, to avenge his father. On stage is the grave of Agamemnon, on which Orestes lays two locks of his hair as an offering. But this homage to the dead man is interrupted by the arrival of a procession of black-robed women, the chorus of the play; they carry libations, liquid offerings to be poured on the grave. With them is Electra, Orestes' sister. The two men retire out of sight, to watch and listen. They learn from the chorus's song that it was Clytaemnestra who sent the libations; she has been terrified by a nightmare that, according to her dream interpreters, signals the rage of the dead king against his murderers. Electra, who loved her father as much as she now hates her mother (who lives with the man who helped to murder him), prays, as she pours the libations, for the return of Orestes and for vengeance on the killers of Agamemnon.

The chorus leader meanwhile has noticed the locks of hair on the grave; the hair is like Electra's, and the footprints around the grave are like hers—can Orestes have returned? He comes out of hiding and brother and sister embrace. He tells her of his visit to Delphi to consult Apollo and the command he received: to avenge his father or suffer a life of torment and a shameful death. Brother and sister and the chorus now join in a long series of appeals to the spirit of Agamemnon to help them in their enterprise. Orestes then learns from Electra the nature of Clytaemnestra's dream: she gave birth to a serpent and nursed it, offering it her breast, only to have it bite and draw blood. "I turn serpent," says Orestes, "I kill her. So the vision says."

He proceeds to explain his plans. Electra is to go into the house; he and Pylades, pretending to be travelers from Phocis (the place to which Clytaemnestra sent the young Orestes for safekeeping), will knock at the door, and once inside, Orestes will kill Aegisthus. But it is Clytaemnestra who comes to the door, and it is to her that he tells the story that he claims to have heard on his journey: Orestes is dead. Clytaemnestra greets the news with what seems like genuine grief, then takes Orestes and Pylades into the house. But we are told later by an old nurse who comes out that "deep down her eyes are laughing." The nurse, who cared for Orestes when he was a baby, has been sent to tell Aegisthus to come home, so that he can hear the news in person and question the messengers. "Is he to come alone?" the chorus asks. "No," it is told, he is to come with his bodyguard. The chorus persuades the nurse to tell him to come alone, which she does. When Aegisthus arrives, exultant at the news of Orestes' death, he walks into a trap. We hear his death cry inside the house, and a distraught servant comes onstage, shouting for Clytaemnestra as he pounds at the door of the women's quarters. Clytaemnestra comes out and sends the servant to fetch her a battle-ax—too late. Orestes and Pylades appear at the central door. Orestes, sword in hand, moves toward his mother; he intends to kill her so that she will lie next to the man she loved. But she makes a desperate move; she bares the breast that suckled him. He lowers his sword, his resolution gone, and turns to Pylades. "What will I do, Pylades?—I dread to kill my mother!" Pylades has not spoken so far in the play and will not speak again; the three lines he speaks now are decisive. He reminds Orestes of the god Apollo's command and of the oath he swore. Orestes turns back to Clytaemnestra and forces her to stand by the body of Aegisthus. She still defends her action but finally recognizes in him the serpent of her dream. But as she accepts her fate, she warns him: "the hounds of a mother's curse will hunt you down." Orestes pulls her inside; the chorus celebrates the victory—"Lift the cry of triumph!"—and the fulfillment of the god's command—"the pure god came down and healed our ancient wounds." But as the doors open and we see the same tableau we saw in *Agamemnon*—the killer standing over his victims, man and woman—we realize that this cannot be the end. This is the repetitive pattern of the curse on the house of Atreus.

Orestes displays the net in which Agamemnon was trapped as he justifies his action by recalling Clytaemnestra's treachery. But there is a hysterical note to his passionate denunciation, and the chorus feels that all is not well: "She is gone. But oh, for you the survivor / suffering is just about to bloom." Orestes recognizes the truth of what they say. He now speaks of "my victory" as "my guilt / my curse" and soon fears that he is losing control of his words and feelings. He is a "charioteer—the reins flying back, look / the mares plunge off the track." He appeals to the authority of Apollo, to whose sanctuary at Delphi he now prepares to go as a suppliant. The chorus protests: "You have done well . . . don't lash yourself with guilt. You've set us free." But Orestes does not hear them. He screams in terror as he sees a vision: "women—look—like Gorgons, / shrouded in black, their heads wreathed, / swarming serpents! . . . Here they come, thick and fast, / their eyes dripping hate—" And in answer to the chorus's attempt to comfort him he shouts, "You can't see them—/ *I* can, and they drive me on! I must move on—" as, followed by Pylades, he rushes offstage.

The chorus cannot see them, nor can we. But we shall see them in the next play; they are its chorus. They are "the hounds of a mother's curse" that Clytaemnestra told Orestes would hunt him down. In *The Eumenides* we shall see them in pursuit of Orestes at Delphi and then at Athens, where they will, in the end, serve as prosecutors (the Greek legal term, like the English, has the literal meaning "pursuers") at his trial before the court of the Areopagus.

The Eumenides

CHARACTERS

The PYTHIA, *the priestess of Apollo*
APOLLO
HERMES
ORESTES
THE GHOST OF CLYTAEMNESTRA
CHORUS OF FURIES *and their* LEADER
ATHENA
Escorting CHORUS *of Athenian women*
Men of the jury, herald, citizens

[TIME AND SCENE: *The* FURIES *have pursued* ORESTES *to the temple of* APOLLO *at Delphi. It is morning. The priestess of the god appears at the great doors and offers up her prayer.*]

PYTHIA First of the gods I honor in my prayer is Mother Earth,
the first of the gods to prophesy,[1] and next I praise
Tradition, second to hold her Mother's mantic seat,
so legend says, and third by the lots of destiny,
by Tradition's free will—no force to bear her down—
another Titan, child of the Earth, took her seat
and Phoebe passed it on as a birthday gift to Phoebus,
Phoebus a name for clear pure light derived from hers.
Leaving the marsh and razorback of Delos, landing
at Pallas' headlands flocked by ships, here he came
to make his home Parnassus and the heights.[2]
And an escort filled with reverence brought him on,
the highway-builders, sons of the god of fire[3] who tamed
the savage country, civilized the wilds—on he marched
and the people lined his way to cover him with praise,
led by Delphos, lord, helm of the land, and Zeus
inspired his mind with the prophet's skill, with godhead,
made him fourth in the dynasty of seers to mount this throne,
but it is Zeus that Apollo speaks for, Father Zeus.
These I honor in the prelude of my prayers—these gods.
But Athena at the Forefront of the Temple crowns our legends.
I revere the nymphs who keep the Corycian rock's deep hollows,[4]
loving haunt of birds where the spirits drift and hover.
And Great Dionysus rules the land. I never forget that day
he marshaled his wild women in arms—he was all god,
he ripped Pentheus[5] down like a hare in the nets of doom.
And the rushing springs of Pleistos,[6] Poseidon's force I call,
and the king of the sky, the king of all fulfillment, Zeus.
Now the prophet goes to take her seat. God speed me—
grant me a vision greater than all my embarkations past!
[*Turning to the audience.*]
Where are the Greeks among you? Draw your lots and enter.
It is the custom here. I will tell the future
only as the god will lead the way.
[*She goes through the doors and reappears in a moment, shaken, thrown to her knees by some terrific force.*]

1. The priestess of Apollo's oracle (Pythia) traces the peaceful succession of powers that controlled the great prophetic site of Delphi. First Mother Earth; then Tradition (*Themis* in the Greek); and then Phoebe, grandmother of Apollo, who handed it over to him as a birthday gift. This is a succession myth that stresses orderly, peaceful succession; in other versions Apollo fights and kills the great serpent Pytho to gain possession. 2. The oracular site is situated on the lower slopes of the Parnassus mountain range (2,457 meters at its summit). Delos is a small rocky island in the Cyclades and Apollo's birthplace. *Pallas' headlands:* the coast of Attica. 3. Athenians, whose legendary ancestor Erichthonios was a son of Hephaestus, the smith god. 4. A capacious cave high above the site of Delphi, sacred to Pan and the nymphs. *The Temple:* Pronaia, the temple of Athena situated at the entrance to the sacred precinct. 5. A king of Thebes who resisted the establishment of Dionysiac rites in his domains. Dionysus, giver of wine and ecstasy, was thought to inhabit Delphi in the winter months, when Apollo left for the land of the Hyperboreans (the happy people who lived, as their name indicates, beyond the North Wind). Dionysiac festivals at which women danced on the hills at night were held at Delphi in historical times. 6. The river (dry in summer) in the bottom of the deep gorge below Delphi.

Terrors—
terrors to tell, terrors all can see!—
they send me reeling back from Apollo's house.
The strength drains, it's very hard to stand,
crawling on all fours, no spring in the legs . . .
an old woman, gripped by fear, is nothing,
a child, nothing more.
[*Struggling to her feet, trying to compose herself.*]
I'm on my way to the vault,
it's green with wreaths, and there at the Navelstone[7]
I see a man—an abomination to god—
he holds the seat where suppliants sit for purging;
his hands dripping blood, and his sword just drawn,
and he holds a branch (it must have topped an olive)
wreathed with a fine tuft of wool,[8] all piety,
fleece gleaming white. So far it's clear, I tell you.
But there in a ring around the man, an amazing company—
women, sleeping, nestling against the benches . . .
women? No,
Gorgons I'd call them; but then with Gorgons
you'd see the grim, inhuman . . .
I saw a picture
years ago, the creatures tearing the feast
away from Phineus[9]—
These have no wings,
I looked. But black they are, and so repulsive.
Their heavy, rasping breathing makes me cringe.
And their eyes ooze a discharge, sickening,
and what they wear[1]—to flaunt *that* at the gods,
the idols, sacrilege! even in the homes of men.
The tribe that produced that brood I never saw,
or a plot of ground to boast it nursed their kind
without some tears, some pain for all its labor.

Now for the outcome. This is his concern,
Apollo the master of this house, the mighty power.
Healer, prophet, diviner of signs, he purges
the halls of others—He must purge his own.
[*She leaves. The doors of the temple open and reveal* APOLLO *rising over* ORESTES; *he kneels in prayer at the Navelstone, surrounded by the* FURIES *who are sleeping.* HERMES *waits in the background.*]

APOLLO No, I will never fail you, through to the end
your guardian standing by your side or worlds away!
I will show no mercy to your enemies! Now
look at these—
[*Pointing to the* FURIES.]
these obscenities!—I've caught them,

7. A sacred stone that was supposed to mark the center of the Earth. 8. Suppliants usually carried a branch of olive, hung with small woolen wreaths. 9. Whenever he spread the table for a meal, the food was carried off by loathsome creatures—half bird, half woman—called Harpies. The Pythia first thinks the Furies (Erinyes) are Gorgons, but then rejects that theory (we are not told why); her next guess, Harpies, has to be abandoned because the Furies have no wings. 1. Long black robes.

beaten them down with sleep.
They disgust me.
These gray, ancient children never touched
by god, man, or beast—the eternal virgins.
Born for destruction only, the dark pit,
they range the bowels of Earth, the world of death,
loathed by men and the gods who hold Olympus.

Nevertheless keep racing on and never yield.
Deep in the endless heartland they will drive you,
striding horizons, feet pounding the earth forever,
on, on over seas and cities swept by tides!
Never surrender, never brood on the labor.
And once you reach the citadel of Pallas, kneel
and embrace her ancient idol[2] in your arms and there,
with judges of your case, with a magic spell—
with words—we will devise the master-stroke
that sets you free from torment once for all.
I persuaded you to take your mother's life.

ORESTES Lord Apollo, you know the rules of justice,
know them well. Now learn compassion, too.
No one doubts your power to do great things.

APOLLO Remember that. No fear will overcome you.
[*Summoning* HERMES *from the shadows.*]
You, my brother, blood of our common Father,
Hermes, guard him well. Live up to your name,
good Escort. Shepherd him well, he is my suppliant,
and outlaws have their rights that Zeus reveres.
Lead him back to the world of men with all good speed.
[APOLLO *withdraws to his inner sanctuary;* ORESTES *leaves with* HERMES *in the lead.* THE GHOST[3] OF CLYTAEMNESTRA *appears at the Navelstone, hovering over the* FURIES *as they sleep.*]

THE GHOST OF CLYTAEMNESTRA You—how can you *sleep?*
Awake, awake—what use are sleepers now?
I go stripped of honor, thanks to you,
alone among the dead. And for those I killed
the charges of the dead will never cease, never—
I wander in disgrace, I feel the guilt, I tell you,
withering guilt from all the outraged dead!

But I suffered too, terribly, from dear ones,
and none of my spirits rages to avenge me.
I was slaughtered by his matricidal hand.
See these gashes—
[*Seizing one of the* FURIES *weak with sleep.*]
Carve them in your heart!

2. In a temple on the Acropolis at Athens there was an ancient wooden statue of Athena. *Citadel of Pallas:* Athens.
3. She is not really a ghost. In line 121 she tells us that she is a dream in the head of the Furies.

The sleeping brain has eyes that give us light;
we can never see our destiny by day.

And after all my libations . . . how you lapped
the honey, the sober offerings poured to soothe you,
awesome midnight feasts[4] I burned at the hearthfire,
your dread hour never shared with gods.
All those rites, I see them trampled down.
And he springs free like a fawn, one light leap
at that—he's through the thick of your nets,
he breaks away!
Mocking laughter twists across his face.
Hear me, I am pleading for my life.
Awake, my Furies, goddesses of the Earth!
A dream is calling—Clytaemnestra calls you now.
[*The* FURIES *mutter in their sleep.*]
Mutter on. Your man is gone, fled far away.
My son has friends to defend him, not like mine.
[*They mutter again.*]
You sleep too much, no pity for my ordeal.
Orestes murdered his mother—he is gone.
[*They begin to moan.*]
Moaning, sleeping—onto your feet, quickly.
What is your work? What but causing pain?
Sleep and toil, the two strong conspirators,
they sap the mother dragon's deadly fury—
[*The* FURIES *utter a sharp moan and moan again, but they are still asleep.*]
FURIES Get him, get him, get him, get him—
there he goes.
THE GHOST OF CLYTAEMNESTRA The prey you hunt is just a dream—
like hounds mad for the sport you bay him on,
you never leave the kill.
But what are you *doing*?
Up! don't yield to the labor, limp with sleep.
Never forget my anguish.
Let my charges hurt you, they are just;
deep in the righteous heart they prod like spurs.

You, blast him on with your gory breath,
the fire of your vitals—wither him, after him,
one last foray—waste him, burn him out!
[*She vanishes. The lead* FURY *urges on the pack.*]
LEADER Wake up!
I rouse you, you rouse her. Still asleep?
Onto your feet, kick off your stupor.
See if this prelude has some grain of truth.

4. Offerings to the Furies were made only at night. *Sober offerings:* no wine was included in offerings to them.

[*The* FURIES *circle, pursuing the scent with hunting calls, and cry out singly when they find* ORESTES *gone.*]

FURIES —Aieeeeee—no, no, *no,* they do us wrong, dear sisters.

—The miles of pain, the pain I suffer . . .
and all for nothing, all for pain, more pain,
the anguish, oh, the grief too much to bear.

—The quarry's slipped from the nets, our quarry lost and gone.

—Sleep defeats me . . . I have lost the prey.

—You—child of Zeus[5]—*you,* a common thief!

—Young god, you have ridden down the powers
proud with age. You worship the suppliant,
the godless man who tears his parent's heart—

—The matricide, you steal him away, and you a god!

—Guilt both ways, and who can call it justice?

—Not I: her charges stalk my dreams,
yes, the charioteer rides hard,
her spurs digging the vitals,
under the heart, under the heaving breast—

—I can feel the executioner's lash, it's searing
deeper, sharper, the knives of burning ice—

—Such is your triumph, you young gods,
world dominion past all rights.
Your throne is streaming blood,
blood at the foot, blood at the crowning head—

—I can see the Navelstone of the Earth, it's bleeding,
bristling corruption, oh, the guilt it has to bear—

Stains on the hearth! The Prophet stains the vault,
he cries it on, drives on the crime himself.
Breaking the god's first law, he rates men first,
destroys the old dominions of the Fates.

He wounds me too, yet *him* he'll never free,
plunging under the earth, no freedom then:
curst as he comes for purging, at his neck
he feels new murder springing from his blood.

5. Apollo.

[APOLLO *strides from his sanctuary in full armor, brandishing his bow and driving back the* FURIES.]

APOLLO Out, I tell you, out of these halls—fast!—
set the Prophet's chamber free!

[*Seizing one of the* FURIES, *shaking an arrow across her face.*]

Or take
the flash and stab of this, this flying viper
whipped from the golden cord that strings my bow!

Heave in torment, black froth erupting from your lungs,
vomit the clots of all the murders you have drained.
But never touch my halls, you have no right.

Go where heads are severed, eyes gouged out,
where Justice and bloody slaughter are the same . . .
castrations, wasted seed, young men's glories butchered,
extremities maimed, and huge stones at the chest,
and the victims wail for pity—
spikes inching up the spine, torsos stuck on spikes.[6]

[*The* FURIES *close in on him.*]

So, you hear your love feast, yearn to have it all?
You revolt the gods. Your look,
your whole regalia gives you away—your kind
should infest a lion's cavern reeking blood.
But never rub your filth on the Prophet's shrine.
Out, you flock without a herdsman—out!
No god will ever shepherd you with love.

LEADER Lord Apollo, now it is your turn to listen.
You are no mere accomplice in this crime.
You did it all, and all the guilt is yours.

APOLLO No, how? Enlarge on that, and only that.

LEADER You commanded the guest to kill his mother.

APOLLO —Commanded him to avenge his father, what of it?

LEADER And then you dared embrace him, fresh from bloodshed.

APOLLO Yes, I ordered him on, to my house, for purging.[7]

LEADER And we sped him on, and you revile us?

APOLLO Indeed, you are not fit to approach this house.

LEADER And yet we have our mission and our—

APOLLO Authority—you? Sound out your splendid power.

LEADER Matricides: we drive them from their houses.

APOLLO And what of the wife who strikes her husband down?

LEADER That murder would not destroy one's flesh and blood.[8]

6. The methods of torture and execution listed by Apollo are what the Greeks saw as typically Eastern, and, indeed, castration and impalement were Persian, not Greek, customs. But Apollo's dismissal of the Furies as non-Greek has no basis in fact; the Furies are not only Greek but much older than he is. 7. Ritual purification. 8. Crimes of blood relations against each other are the most heinous kind. But husband and wife are, and must be, of different blood. The Furies would have pursued Orestes if he had not avenged his father, and they pursue him now because he killed his mother, but the killing of a husband by a wife seems to them a lesser crime. They think and feel in tribal terms, those of a society that has not yet developed the city-state, the *polis*, in which the institution of marriage (which Apollo champions in his reply, lines 215ff.) was the guarantee of the legitimacy of male heirs for the transmittal of property from generation to generation.

APOLLO Why, you'd disgrace—obliterate the bonds of Zeus
and Hera queen of brides! And the queen of love[9]
you'd throw to the winds at a word, disgrace love,
the source of mankind's nearest, dearest ties.
Marriage of man and wife is Fate itself,
stronger than oaths, and Justice guards its life.
But if one destroys the other and you relent—
no revenge, not a glance in anger—then
I say your manhunt of Orestes is unjust.
Some things stir your rage, I see. Others,
atrocious crimes, lull your will to act.
Pallas
will oversee this trial. She is one of us.

LEADER I will never let that man go free, never.

APOLLO Hound him then, and multiply your pains.

LEADER Never try to cut my power with your logic.

APOLLO I'd never touch it, not as a gift—your power.

LEADER Of course,
great as you are, they say, throned on high with Zeus.
But blood of the mother draws me on—must hunt
the man for Justice. Now I'm on his trail!

[*Rushing out, with the* FURIES *in full cry.*]

APOLLO And I will defend my suppliant and save him.
A terror to gods and men, the outcast's anger,
once I fail him, all of my own free will.

[APOLLO *leaves. The scene changes to the Acropolis in Athens. Escorted by* HERMES, ORESTES *enters and kneels, exhausted, before the ancient shrine and idol of* ATHENA.]

ORESTES Queen Athena,
under Apollo's orders I have come.
Receive me kindly. Curst and an outcast,
no suppliant for purging . . . my hands are clean.
My murderous edge is blunted now, worn down at last
on the outland homesteads, beaten paths of men.[1]
On and out over seas and dry frontiers,
I kept alive the Prophet's strong commands.
Struggling toward your house, your idol—

[*Taking the knees of* ATHENA*'s idol in his arms.*]

Goddess,
here I keep my watch,
I await the consummation of my trial.

[*The* FURIES *enter in pursuit but cannot find* ORESTES *who is entwined around* ATHENA's idol. The LEADER *sees the footprints.*]

LEADER At last!
The clear trail of the man. After it, silent
but it tracks his guilt to light. He's wounded—

9. Aphrodite. The marriage of Zeus and Hera was the divine model of earthly marriages, and Hera was the goddess who presided over marriage ceremonies. 1. Orestes has been given ritual purification by Apollo, but he also claims that the blood guilt is now "worn down" by his travels and contacts with men (compare lines 278–82).

go for the fawn, my hounds, the splash of blood,
hunt him, rake him down.
Oh, the labor,
the man-killing labor. My lungs are bursting . . .
over the wide rolling earth we've ranged in flock,
hurdling the waves in wingless flight and now we come,
all hot pursuit, outracing ships astern—and now
he's here, somewhere, cowering like a hare . . .
the reek of human blood[2]—it's laughter to my heart!
[*Inciting a pair of* FURIES.]
Look, look again, you two,
scour the ground before he escapes—one dodge
and the matricide slips free.
[*Seeing* ORESTES, *one by one they press around him and* ATHENA *'s idol.*]

FURIES —There he is!
Clutching the knees of power once again,
twined in the deathless goddess' idol,[3] look,
he wants to go on trial for his crimes.

—Never . . .
the mother's blood that wets the ground,
you can never bring it back, dear god,
the Earth drinks, and the running life is gone.

—No,
you'll give me blood for blood, you must!
Out of your living marrow I will drain
my red libation, out of your veins I suck my food,
my raw, brutal cups—

—Wither you alive,
drag you down and there you pay, agony
for mother-killing agony!

—And there you will see them all.
Every mortal who outraged god or guest or loving parent:
each receives the pain his pains exact.

—A mighty god is Hades. There
at the last reckoning underneath the earth
he scans all, he squares all men's accounts
and graves them on the tablets of his mind.
[ORESTES *remains impassive.*]

ORESTES I have suffered into truth. Well I know
the countless arts of purging, where to speak,
where silence is the rule. In this ordeal

2. The Furies track him down by scent of the blood he shed, as if he were a wounded animal leaving a trace behind him. 3. Orestes is still clinging to the statue of Pallas Athena.

a compelling master urges me to speak.
[*Looking at his hands.*]
The blood sleeps, it is fading on my hands,
the stain of mother's murder washing clean.
It was still fresh at the god's hearth. Apollo
killed the swine and the purges drove it off.
Mine is a long story
if I'd start with the many hosts I met,
I lived with, and I left them all unharmed.
Time refines all things that age with time.

And now with pure, reverent lips I call
the queen of the land. Athena, help me!
Come without your spear—without a battle
you will win myself, my land, the Argive people[4]
true and just, your friends-in-arms forever.
Where are you now? The scorching wilds of Libya,
bathed by the Triton pool where you were born?[5]
Robes shrouding your feet
or shod and on the march to aid allies?
Or striding the Giants' Plain, marshal of armies,[6]
hero scanning, flashing through the ranks?
Come—
you can hear me from afar, you are a god.
Set me free from this!

LEADER Never—neither
Apollo's nor Athena's strength can save you.
Down you go, abandoned,
searching your soul for joy but joy is gone.
Bled white, gnawed by demons, a husk, a wraith—
[*She breaks off, waiting for reply, but* ORESTES *prays in silence.*]
No reply? you spit my challenge back?
You'll feast me alive, my fatted calf,
not cut on the altar first. Now hear my spell,
the chains of song I sing to bind you tight.

FURIES Come, Furies, dance!—
link arms for the dancing hand-to-hand,
now we long to reveal our art,
our terror, now to declare our right
to steer the lives of men,
we all conspire, we dance! we are
the just and upright, we maintain.
Hold out your hands, if they are clean
no fury of ours will stalk you,
you will go through life unscathed.

4. This is the first clear reference to the alliance that Athens had concluded with Argos in 459 B.C., the year before the production of the trilogy. 5. One of Athena's titles, Tritogeneia, was thought to derive from Lake Tritonis, in Libya, where some said she was born. There may be a contemporary allusion here; Athens was backing, with ships and troops, the Libyan ruler Inaros, who was fighting the Persian rulers of Egypt. 6. Athena, a warrior goddess, took a prominent part in the battle between the gods and the giants, in which Zeus and the Olympians won a decisive victory.

But show us the guilty—one like this
who hides his reeking hands,
and up from the outraged dead we rise,
witness bound to avenge their blood
we rise in flames against him to the end!

Mother who bore me,
O dear Mother Night,
to avenge the blinded dead
and those who see by day,
now hear me! The whelp Apollo
spurns my rights, he tears this trembling victim
from my grasp—the one to bleed,
to atone away the mother-blood at last.

Over the victim's burning head
this chant this frenzy striking frenzy
lightning crazing the mind
this hymn of Fury
chaining the senses, ripping cross the lyre,[7]
withering lives of men!

This, this is our right,
spun for us by the Fates,
the ones who bind the world,
and none can shake our hold.
Show us the mortals overcome,
insane to murder kin—we track them down
till they go beneath the earth,
and the dead find little freedom in the end.

Over the victim's burning head
this chant this frenzy striking frenzy
lightning crazing the mind
this hymn of Fury
chaining the senses, ripping cross the lyre,
withering lives of men!

Even at birth, I say, our rights were so ordained.
The deathless gods must keep their hands far off—
no god may share our cups, our solemn feasts.
We want no part of their pious white robes—
the Fates who gave us power made us free.

Mine is the overthrow of houses, yes,
when warlust reared like a tame beast
seizes near and dear—
down on the man we swoop, aie!

7. Not accompanied by the lyre, an instrument associated with joyous occasions.

for all his power black him out!—
for the blood still fresh from slaughter on his hands.

So now, striving to wrench our mandate from the gods,
we make ourselves exempt from their control,
we brook no trial—no god can be our judge.
[*Reaching toward* ORESTES.]
His breed, worthy of loathing, streaked with blood,
Zeus slights, unworthy his contempt.

Mine is the overthrow of houses, yes,
when warlust reared like a tame beast
seizes near and dear—
down on the man we swoop, aie!
for all his power black him out!—
for the blood still fresh from slaughter on his hands.

And all men's dreams of grandeur,
tempting the heavens,
all melt down, under earth their pride goes down—
lost in our onslaught, black robes swarming,
Furies throbbing, dancing out our rage.

Yes! leaping down from the heights,
dead weight in the crashing footfall
down we hurl on the runner
breakneck for the finish—
cut him down, our fury stamps him down!

Down he goes, sensing nothing,
blind with defilement . . .
darkness hovers over the man, dark guilt,
and a dense pall overhangs his house,
legend tells the story through her tears.

Yes! leaping down from the heights,
dead weight in the crashing footfall
down we hurl on the runner
breakneck for the finish—
cut him down, our fury stamps him down!

So the center holds.
We are the skilled, the masterful,
we the great fulfillers,
memories of grief, we awesome spirits
stern, unappeasable to man,
disgraced, degraded, drive our powers through;
banished far from god to a sunless, torchlit dusk,
we drive men through their rugged passage,
blinded dead and those who see by day.

Then where is the man
not stirred with awe, not gripped by fear
to hear us tell the law that
Fate ordains, the gods concede the Furies,
absolute till the end of time?
And so it holds, our ancient power still holds.
We are not without our pride, though beneath the earth
our strict battalions form their lines,
groping through the mist and sunstarved night.

[*Enter* ATHENA, *armed for combat with her aegis and her spear.*]

ATHENA From another world I heard a call for help.
I was on the Scamander's banks, just claiming Troy.
The Achaean warlords chose the hero's share
of what their spear had won—they decreed that land,
root and branch all mine, for all time to be,
for Theseus' sons[8] a rare, matchless gift.

Home from the wars I come, my pace unflagging,
wingless, flown on the whirring, breasting cape[9]
that yokes my racing spirit in her prime.

[*Unfurling the aegis, seeing* ORESTES *and the* FURIES *at her shrine.*]

And I see some new companions on the land.
Not fear, a sense of wonder fills my eyes.

Who are you? I address you all as one:
you, the stranger seated at my idol,
and you, like no one born of the sown seed,
no goddess watched by the gods, no mortal either,
not to judge by your look at least, your features . . .
Wait, I call my neighbors into question.
They've done nothing wrong. It offends the rights,
it violates tradition.

LEADER You will learn it all,
young daughter of Zeus, cut to a few words.
We are the everlasting children of the Night.
Deep in the halls of Earth they call us Curses.

ATHENA Now I know your birth, your rightful name—

LEADER But not our powers, and you will learn them quickly.

ATHENA I can accept the facts, just tell them clearly.

LEADER Destroyers of life: we drive them from their houses.

ATHENA And the murderer's flight, where does it all end?

LEADER Where there is no joy, the word is never used.

8. Homer does not mention it, but in later Athenian tradition, the two sons of Theseus, the national hero who unified the whole of Attica under Athens, fought at Troy. This reference to Athenian participation in the war may be another reference to contemporary reality; Athenians had won a foothold in the Troad, the region around Troy, under the tyrant Pisistratus at the end of the sixth century B.C., and in Aeschylus's day cities in and near the Troad, along the vital route for grain of the Black Sea area, were part of the Athenian empire. But there is another reason for introducing the subject of the Trojan War. In *Agamemnon* the audience is given an almost unrelievedly critical view of the war. But now Orestes is to be tried and acquitted, and Agamemnon's good name restored. The war has now to be presented in a favorable light (compare lines 470ff.). 9. The *aegis,* a cloak worn by Athena: it has the face of the Gorgon Medusa on it. Here Athena uses it to fly; at other times it is used as a shield to produce terror, as in *Odyssey* 22.

ATHENA Such flight for him? You shriek him on to that?
LEADER Yes,
he murdered his mother—called that murder just.
ATHENA And nothing forced him on, no fear of someone's anger?
LEADER What spur would force a man to kill his mother?
ATHENA Two sides are here, and only half is heard.
LEADER But the oath—he will neither take the oath nor give it,
no, his will is set.
ATHENA And you are set
on the name of justice rather than the act.
LEADER How? Teach us. You have a genius for refinements.
ATHENA Injustice, I mean, should never triumph thanks to oaths.
LEADER Then examine him yourself, judge him fairly.
ATHENA you would turn over responsibility to me,
to reach the final verdict?
LEADER Certainly.
We respect you. You show us respect.
[ATHENA *turns to* ORESTES.]
ATHENA Your turn, stranger. What do you say to this?
Tell us your land, your birth, your fortunes.
Then defend yourself against their charge,
if trust in your rights has brought you here to guard
my hearth and idol, a suppliant for purging
like Ixion,[1] sacred. Speak to all this clearly,
speak to me.
ORESTES Queen Athena, first,
the misgiving in your final words is strong.
Let me remove it. I haven't come for purging.
Look, not a stain on the hands that touch your idol.
I have proof for all I say, and it is strong.

The law condemns the man of the violent hand
to silence, till a master trained at purging
slits the throat of a young suckling victim,
blood absolves his blood. Long ago
at the halls of others I was fully cleansed
in the cleansing springs, the blood of many victims.
Threat of pollution—sweep it from your mind.
Now for my birth. You will know at once.
I am from Argos. My father, well you ask,
was Agamemnon, sea-lord of the men-of-war,
your partisan when you made the city Troy
a city of the dead.
What an ignoble death he died
when he came home—Ai! my blackhearted mother
cut him down, enveloped him in her handsome net—
it still attests his murder in the bath.

1. The Greek Cain, the first murderer. He killed his father-in-law; coming to Zeus as a suppliant, he was purified by the great god himself.

But I came back, my years of exile weathered—
killed the one who bore me, I won't deny it,
killed her in revenge. I loved my father,
fiercely.
And Apollo shares the guilt—
he spurred me on, he warned of the pains I'd feel
unless I acted, brought the guilty down.
But were we just or not? Judge us now.
My fate is in your hands. Stand or fall
I shall accept your verdict.

ATHENA Too large a matter,
some may think, for mortal men to judge.
But by all rights not even I should decide
a case of murder—murder whets the passions.
Above all, the rites have tamed your wildness.
A suppliant, cleansed, you bring my house no harm.
If you are innocent, I'd adopt you for my city.
[*Turning to the* FURIES.]
But they have their destiny too, hard to dismiss,
and if they fail to win their day in court—
how it will spread, the venom of their pride,
plague everlasting blights our land, our future . . .

So it stands. A crisis either way.
[*Looking back and forth from* ORESTES *to the* FURIES.]
Embrace the one? expel the other? It defeats me.

But since the matter comes to rest on us,
I will appoint the judges of manslaughter,
swear them in, and found a tribunal here
for all time to come.[2]
[*To* ORESTES *and the* FURIES.]
My contestants,
summon your trusted witnesses and proofs,
your defenders under oath to help your cause.
And I will pick the finest men of Athens,
return and decide the issue fairly, truly—
bound to our oaths, our spirits bent on justice.
[ATHENA *leaves. The* FURIES *form their chorus.*]

FURIES Here, now, is the overthrow
of every binding law—once his appeal,
his outrage wins the day,
his matricide! One act links all mankind,
hand to desperate hand in bloody license.
Over and over deathstrokes
dealt by children wait their parents,
mortal generations still unborn.

2. The Areopagus, which in Aeschylus's lifetime was the court that tried homicide cases.

We are the Furies still, yes,
but now our rage that patrolled the crimes of men,
that stalked their rage dissolves—
we loose a lethal tide to sweep the world!
Man to man foresees his neighbor's torments,
groping to cure his own—
poor wretch, there is no cure, no use,
the drugs that ease him speed the next attack.

Now when the sudden blows come down,
let no one sound the call that once brought help,
"Justice, hear me—Furies throned in power!"
Oh I can hear the father now
or the mother sob with pain
at the pain's onset . . . hopeless now,
the house of Justice falls.[3]

There is a time when terror helps,
the watchman must stand guard upon the heart.
It helps, at times, to suffer into truth.
Is there a man who knows no fear
in the brightness of his heart,
or a man's city, both are one,
that still reveres the rights?

Neither the life of anarchy
nor the life enslaved by tyrants, no,
worship neither.
Strike the balance all in all and god will give you power;
the laws of god may veer from north to south—
we Furies plead for Measure.
Violence is Impiety's child, true to its roots,
but the spirit's great good health breeds all we love
and all our prayers call down,
prosperity and peace.

All in all I tell you people,
bow before the altar of the rights,
revere it well.
Never trample it underfoot, your eyes set on spoils;
revenge will hunt the godless day and night—
the destined end awaits.
So honor your parents first with reverence, I say,
and the stranger guest you welcome to your house,
turn to attend his needs,
respect his sacred rights.

3. The Furies argue that the acquittal of Orestes will be a precedent for universal crime. Furthermore, they will no longer, in that case, continue to see that vengeance is exacted; appeals to the Furies for justice will be disregarded (lines 523ff.).

All of your own free will, all uncompelled,
be just and you will never want for joy,
you and your kin can never be uprooted from the earth.
But the reckless one—I warn the marauder
dragging plunder, chaotic, rich beyond all rights:
he'll strike his sails,
harried at long last,
stunned when the squalls of torment break his spars to bits.

He cries to the deaf, he wrestles walls of sea
sheer whirlpools down, down, with the gods' laughter
breaking over the man's hot heart—they see him flailing, crushed.
The one who boasted never to shipwreck
now will never clear the cape and steer for home;
who lived for wealth,
golden his life long—
he rams on the reef of law and drowns unwept, unseen.

[*The scene has shifted to the Areopagus, the tribunal on the Crag of Ares.*[4] ATHENA *enters in procession with a herald and ten Citizens she has chosen to be judges.*]

ATHENA Call for order, herald, marshal our good people.
Lift the Etruscan battle-trumpet,[5]
strain it to full pitch with human breath,
crash out a stabbing blast along the ranks.

[*The trumpet sounds. The judges take up positions between the audience and the actors.* ATHENA *separates the* FURIES *and* ORESTES, *directing him to the Stone of Outrage and the* LEADER *to the Stone of Unmercifulness,*[6] where the FURIES *form their chorus. Then* ATHENA *takes her stand between two urns that will receive the ballots.*]

And while this court of judgment fills, my city,
silence will be best. So that you can learn
my everlasting laws. And you too,

[*To* ORESTES *and the* FURIES.]

that our verdict may be well observed by all.

[APOLLO *enters suddenly and looms behind* ORESTES.]

Lord Apollo—rule it over your own sphere!
What part have you in this? Tell us.[7]

APOLLO I come
as a witness. This man, according to custom,
this suppliant sought out my house and hearth.
I am the one who purged his bloody hands.
His champion too, I share responsibility
for his mother's execution.
Bring on the trial.

4. A literal translation of the word *Areopagus*. 5. The Etruscans, a people living in central Italy, were supposed to have invented the trumpet. 6. Though Aeschylus does not mention them, we know that there were two stone bases on the Areopagus where prosecutor and defendant took their places for the trial; naturally, the Stone of Unmercifulness was reserved for the prosecutor. 7. The manuscripts assign lines 581–82 to the leader of the chorus; the peremptory tone certainly sounds more suitable to the Furies than to Athena.

You know the rules, now turn them into justice.
[ATHENA *turns to the* FURIES.]
ATHENA The trial begins! Yours is the first word—
the prosecution opens. Start to finish,
set the facts before us, make them clear.
LEADER Numerous as we are, we will be brief.
[*To* ORESTES.]
Answer count for count, charge for charge.
First, tell us, did you kill your mother?
ORESTES I killed her. There's no denying that.
LEADER Three falls in the match.[8] One is ours already.
ORESTES You exult before your man is on his back.
LEADER But *how* did you kill her? You must tell us that.
ORESTES I will. I drew my sword—more, I cut her throat.
LEADER And who persuaded you? who led you on?
ORESTES This god and his command.
[*Indicating* APOLLO.]
He bears me witness.
LEADER The Seer? He drove you on to matricide?
ORESTES Yes,
and to this hour I have no regrets.
LEADER If the verdict
brings you down, you'll change your story quickly.
ORESTES I have my trust; my father will help me from the grave.
LEADER Trust to corpses now! You made your mother one.
ORESTES I do. She had two counts against her, deadly crimes.
LEADER How? Explain that to your judges.
ORESTES She killed her husband—killed my father too.
LEADER But murder set her free, and you live on for trial.
ORESTES She lived on. You never drove *her* into exile—why?
LEADER The blood of the man she killed was not her own.
ORESTES And I? Does mother's blood run in my veins?
LEADER How could she breed you in her body, murderer?
Disclaim your mother's blood? She gave you life.
[ORESTES *turns to* APOLLO.]
ORESTES Bear me witness—show me the way, Apollo!
Did I strike her down with justice?
Strike I did, I don't deny it, no.
But how does our bloody work impress you now?—
Just or not? Decide.
I must make my case to them.
APOLLO [*Looking to the judges.*] *Just,*
I say, to you and your high court, Athena.
Seer that I am, I never lie. Not once
from the Prophet's thrones have I declared
a word that bears on man, woman or city
that Zeus did not command, the Olympian Father.
This is *his* justice—omnipotent, I warn you.

8. As in a Greek wrestling match.

Bend to the will of Zeus. No oath can match
the power of the Father.

LEADER Zeus, you say,
gave that command to your oracle? He charged
Orestes here to avenge his father's death
and spurn his mother's rights?[9]

APOLLO —Not the same
for a noble man to die, covered with praise,
his scepter the gift of god—murdered, at that,
by a woman's hand, no arrows whipping in
from a distance as an Amazon[1] would fight.
But as you will hear, Athena, and your people
poised to cast their lots and judge the case.

Home from the long campaign he came, more won
than lost on balance, home to her loyal, waiting arms,
the welcome bath . . .
he was just emerging at the edge,
and there she pitched her tent, her circling shroud—
she shackled her man in robes,
in her gorgeous never-ending web she chopped him down!

Such was the outrage of his death, I tell you,
the lord of the squadrons, that magnificent man.
Her I draw to the life to lash your people,
marshaled to reach a verdict.

LEADER Zeus, you say,
sets more store by a father's death? He shackled
his own father, Kronos proud with age.
Doesn't that contradict you?
[*To the judges.*]
Mark it well. I call you all to witness.

APOLLO You grotesque, loathsome—the gods detest you!
Zeus can break chains, we've cures for that,
countless ingenious ways to set us free.
But once the dust drinks down a man's blood,
he is gone, once for all. No rising back,
no spell sung over the grave can sing him back—
not even Father can. Though all things else
he can overturn and never strain for breath.[2]

LEADER So
you'd force this man's acquittal? Behold, Justice!
[*Exhibiting* APOLLO *and* ORESTES.]
Can a son spill his mother's blood on the ground,
then settle into his father's halls in Argos?

9. The chorus wants Apollo to state clearly that Zeus gave him the specific instructions for Orestes to kill his mother. When they have that assurance, they will face Apollo with a flagrant contradiction of his claim that Zeus is the champion of the father's rights (lines 648–51). 1. A member of a mythical tribe of female warriors, skilled archers, who were thought to have lived in Asia Minor on the Black Sea and to have once invaded Attica. 2. Apollo walks into the trap. Zeus only bound Kronos, he did not kill him, says Apollo. But Orestes did kill his mother.

Where are the public altars he can use?
Can the kinsmen's holy water touch his hands?

APOLLO Here is the truth, I tell you—see how right I am.
The woman you call the mother of the child
is not the parent, just a nurse to the seed,
the new-sown seed that grows and swells inside her.
The *man* is the source of life—the one who mounts.
She, like a stranger for a stranger, keeps
the shoot alive unless god hurts the roots.

I give you proof that all I say is true.
The father can father forth without a mother.
Here she stands, our living witness. Look—
[*Exhibiting* ATHENA.]
Child sprung full-blown from Olympian Zeus,
never bred in the darkness of the womb
but such a stock no goddess could conceive![3]

And I, Pallas, with all my strong techniques
will rear your host and battlements to glory.
So I dispatched this suppliant to your hearth
that he might be your trusted friend forever,
that you might win a new ally, dear goddess.
He and his generations arm-in-arm with yours,
your bonds stand firm for all posterity[4]—

ATHENA Now
have we heard enough? May I have them cast
their honest lots as conscience may decide?

LEADER For us, we have shot our arrows, every one.
I wait to hear how this ordeal will end.

ATHENA Of course.
And what can I do to merit your respect?

APOLLO You have heard what you have heard.
[*To the judges.*]
Cast your lots, my friends,
strict to the oath that you have sworn.

ATHENA And now
if you would hear my law, you men of Greece,
you who will judge the first trial of bloodshed.

Now and forever more, for Aegeus' people[5]
this will be the court where judges reign.
This is the Crag of Ares, where the Amazons
pitched their tents when they came marching down
on Theseus, full tilt in their fury, erecting

3. The doctrine that the woman is not really a parent of the child but merely a sort of receptacle and nurse also appears elsewhere in Greek literature. It was a comforting formula for a society that, like the goddess Athena (see line 753), honored the male. Apollo appeals for confirmation to the birth of the goddess herself; she had no mother but was born from the head of Zeus. 4. Another reference to the Athenian alliance with Argos. 5. The Athenians. Aegeus was the father of Theseus.

a new city to overarch his city, towers thrust
against his towers—they sacrificed to Ares,
named this rock from that day onward Ares' Crag.

Here from the heights, terror and reverence,
my people's kindred powers
will hold them from injustice through the day
and through the mild night. Never pollute
our law with innovations. No, my citizens,
foul a clear well and you will suffer thirst.

Neither anarchy nor tyranny,[6] my people.
Worship the Mean, I urge you,
shore it up with reverence and never
banish terror from the gates, not outright.
Where is the righteous man who knows no fear?
The stronger your fear, your reverence for the just,
the stronger your country's wall and city's safety,
stronger by far than all men else possess
in Scythia's rugged steppes or Pelops' level plain.[7]
Untouched by lust for spoil, this court of law
majestic, swift to fury, rising above you
as you sleep, our night watch always wakeful,
guardian of our land—I found it here and now.

So I urge you, Athens. I have drawn this out
to rouse you to your future. You must rise,
each man must cast his lot and judge the case,
reverent to his oath. Now I have finished.

[*The judges come forward, pass between the urns and cast their lots.*]

LEADER Beware. Our united force can break your land.
Never wound our pride, I tell you, never.
APOLLO The oracles, not mine alone but Zeus', too—
dread them, I warn you, never spoil their fruit.

[*The* LEADER *turns to* APOLLO.]

LEADER You dabble in works of blood beyond your depth.
Oracles, your oracles will be stained forever.
APOLLO Oh, so the Father's judgment faltered when Ixion,
the first man-slayer, came to him for purging?
LEADER Talk on, talk on. But if I lose this trial
I will return in force to crush the land.
APOLLO Never—among the gods, young and old,
you go disgraced. I will triumph over you!
LEADER Just as you triumphed in the house of Pheres,
luring the Fates to set men free from death.
APOLLO What?—is it a crime to help the pious man,

6. Athena repeats the advice and even the words of the Furies in lines 537ff. 7. The Peloponnese in central Greece. Scythia is in southern Russia. The expression may signify just geographical expanse, but there is possibly also an appropriateness in the choice of the two locations. The Scythians were famous for their good laws, and the Peloponnese was the territory of Sparta, famous for its stable constitution.

above all, when his hour of need has come?[8]
LEADER You brought them down, the oldest realms of order,
seduced the ancient goddesses with wine.[9]
APOLLO *You* will fail this trial—in just a moment
spew your venom and never harm your enemies.
LEADER You'd ride me down, young god, for all my years?
Well here I stand, waiting to learn the verdict.
Torn with doubt . . . to rage against the city or—
ATHENA My work is here, to render the final judgment.
Orestes,
[*Raising her arm, her hand clenched as if holding a ballot-stone.*]
I will cast my lot for you.
No mother gave me birth.
I honor the male, in all things but marriage.
Yes, with all my heart I am my Father's child.
I cannot set more store by the woman's death—
she killed her husband, guardian of their house.
Even if the vote is equal, Orestes wins.[1]

Shake the lots from the urns. Quickly,
you of the jury charged to make the count.
[*Judges come forward, empty the urns, and count the ballot-stones.*]
ORESTES O God of the Light, Apollo, how will the verdict go?
LEADER O Night, dark mother, are you watching now?
ORESTES Now for the goal—the noose, or the new day!
LEADER Now we go down, or forge ahead in power.
APOLLO Shake out the lots and count them fairly, friends
Honor Justice. An error in judgment now
can mean disaster. The cast of a single lot
restores a house to greatness.
[*Receiving the judges' count,* ATHENA *lifts her arm once more.*]
ATHENA The man goes free,
cleared of the charge of blood. The lots are equal.
ORESTES O Pallas Athena—you, you save my house!
I was shorn of the fatherland but you
reclaim it for me. Now any Greek will say,
"He lives again, the man of Argos lives
on his fathers' great estates. Thanks to Pallas,
Apollo, and Zeus, the lord of all fulfillment,
Third, Saving Zeus." He respected father's death,
looked down on mother's advocates—
[*Indicating the* FURIES.]
he saved me.
And now I journey home. But first I swear
to you, your land and assembled host, I swear

8. *Pheres*: father of Admetus, king of Thessaly (see line 739). Apollo repaid kindness shown him by Admetus by persuading the fates to let Admetus avoid an early death if he could find someone willing to die in his stead. (His wife, Alcestis, was willing; this is the subject of Euripides' famous play *Alcestis*.)
9. According to the Furies, Apollo got the Fates drunk.
1. So, in Athenian courts, a split jury meant acquittal. Athena announces that if the votes are equal, she will give a casting vote for acquittal. (At the real court of the Areopagus, if the votes were equal, the defendant was declared acquitted by "the vote of Athena.")

by the future years that bring their growing yield
that no man, no helmsman of Argos wars on Athens,
spears in the vanguard moving out for conquest.
We ourselves, even if we must rise up from the grave,
will deal with those who break the oath I take[2]—
baffle them with disasters, curse their marches,
send them hawks aloft on the left[3] at every crossing—
make their pains recoil upon their heads.
But all who keep our oath, who uphold your rights
and citadel forever, comrades spear to spear,
we bless with all the kindness of our heart.

Now farewell, you and the people of your city.
Good wrestling—a grip no foe can break.
A saving hope, a spear to bring you triumph!

[*Exit* ORESTES, *followed by* APOLLO. The FURIES *reel in wild confusion around* ATHENA.]

FURIES You, you younger gods!—you have ridden down
the ancient laws, wrenched them from my grasp—
and I, robbed of my birthright, suffering, great with wrath,
I loose my poison over the soil, aieee!—
poison to match my grief comes pouring out my heart,
cursing the land to burn it sterile and now
rising up from its roots a cancer blasting leaf and child,
now for Justice, Justice!—cross the face of the earth
the bloody tide comes hurling, all mankind destroyed.
. . . Moaning, only moaning? What will I do?
The mockery of it, Oh unbearable,
mortified by Athens,
we the daughters of Night,
our power stripped, cast down.

ATHENA Yield to me.
No more heavy spirits. You were not defeated—
the vote was tied, a verdict fairly reached
with no disgrace to you, no, Zeus brought
luminous proof before us. He who spoke
god's oracle, he bore witness that Orestes
did the work but should not suffer harm.

And now you'd vent your anger, hurt the land?
Consider a moment. Calm yourself. Never
render us barren, raining your potent showers
down like spears, consuming every seed.
By all my rights I promise you your seat
in the depths of earth, yours by all rights—
stationed at hearths equipped with glistening thrones,
covered with praise! My people will revere you.

2. Orestes will be a "hero" in the Greek sense: a protecting spirit for the land. 3. Birds seen on the left were a portent of an evil to come.

FURIES You, you younger gods!—you have ridden down
the ancient laws, wrenched them from my grasp—
and I, robbed of my birthright, suffering, great with wrath,
I loose my poison over the soil, aieee!—
poison to match my grief comes pouring out my heart,
cursing the land to burn it sterile and now
rising up from its roots a cancer blasting leaf and child,
now for Justice, Justice!—cross the face of the earth
the bloody tide comes hurling, all mankind destroyed.
. . . Moaning, only moaning? What will I do?
The mockery of it, Oh unbearable,
mortified by Athens,
we the daughters of Night,
our power stripped, cast down.

ATHENA You have your power,
you are goddesses—but not to turn
on the world of men and ravage it past cure.
I put my trust in Zeus and . . . must I add this?
I am the only god who knows the keys
to the armory where his lightning-bolt is sealed.
No need of that, not here.
Let me persuade you.
The lethal spell of your voice, never cast it
down on the land and blight its harvest home.
Lull asleep that salt black wave of anger—
awesome, proud with reverence, live with me.
The land is rich, and more, when its first fruits,
offered for heirs and the marriage rites, are yours[4]
to hold forever, you will praise my words.

FURIES But for me to suffer such disgrace . . . I,
the proud heart of the past, driven under the earth,
condemned, like so much filth,
and the fury in me breathing hatred—
O good Earth,
what is this stealing under the breast,
what agony racks the spirit? . . . Night, dear Mother Night!
All's lost, our ancient powers torn away by their cunning,
ruthless hands, the gods so hard to wrestle down
obliterate us all.

ATHENA I will bear with your anger.
You are older. The years have taught you more,
much more than I can know. But Zeus, I think,
gave me some insight too, that has its merits.
If you leave for an alien land and alien people,
you will come to love this land, I promise you.
As time flows on, the honors flow through all

4. The Furies, as spirits of the Earth, did in fact receive in Athens offerings for children born and marriages made.

my citizens, and you, throned in honor
before the house of Erechtheus,[5] will harvest
more from men and women moving in solemn file
than you can win throughout the mortal world.

Here in our homeland never cast the stones
that whet our bloodlust. Never waste our youth,
inflaming them with the burning wine of strife.
Never pluck the heart of the battle cock
and plant it in our people—intestine war
seething against themselves. Let our wars
rage on abroad,[6] with all their force, to satisfy
our powerful lust for fame. But as for the bird
that fights at home—my curse on civil war.

This is the life I offer, it is yours to take.
Do great things, feel greatness, greatly honored.
Share this country cherished by the gods.

FURIES But for me to suffer such disgrace . . . I,
the proud heart of the past, driven under the earth,
condemned, like so much filth,
  and the fury in me breathing hatred—
O good Earth,
    what is this stealing under the breast,
what agony racks the spirit? . . . Night, dear Mother Night!
All's lost, our ancient powers torn away by their cunning,
ruthless hands, the gods so hard to wrestle down
obliterate us all.

ATHENA No, I will never tire
of telling you your gifts. So that you,
the older gods, can never say that I,
a young god and the mortals of my city
drove you outcast, outlawed from the land.

But if you have any reverence for Persuasion,
the majesty of Persuasion,
the spell of my voice that would appease your fury—
Oh please stay . . .
          and if you refuse to stay,
it would be wrong, unjust to afflict this city
with wrath, hatred, populations routed. Look,
it is all yours, a royal share of our land—
justly entitled, glorified forever.

LEADER Queen Athena,
where is the home you say is mine to hold?

5. The old shrine of Erechtheus on the Acropolis had been destroyed by the Persians in 480 B.C.; in 421 B.C. the Athenians began the construction of the new Erechtheum, which, much damaged, still stands.
6. Athens was at this time at war with Sparta, and its forces may still have been engaged in Egypt.

ATHENA Where all the pain and anguish end. Accept it.
LEADER And if I do, what honor waits for me?
ATHENA No house can thrive without you.
LEADER You would do that—
grant me that much power?
ATHENA Whoever reveres us—
we will raise the fortunes of their lives.
LEADER And you will pledge me that, for all time to come?
ATHENA *Yes*—I must never promise things I cannot do.
LEADER Your magic is working . . . I can feel the hate,
the fury slip away.
ATHENA At last! And now take root
in the land and win yourself new friends.
LEADER A spell—
what spell to sing? to bind the land forever? Tell us.
ATHENA Nothing that strikes a note of brutal conquest. Only peace—
blessings, rising up from the earth and the heaving sea,
and down the vaulting sky let the wind-gods breathe
a wash of sunlight streaming through the land,
and the yield of soil and grazing cattle flood
our city's life with power and never flag
with time. Make the seed of men live on,
the more they worship you the more they thrive.
I love them as a gardener loves his plants,
these upright men, this breed fought free of grief.
All that is yours to give.
And I,
in the trials of war where fighters burn for fame,
will never endure the overthrow of Athens—
all will praise her, victor city, pride of man.

[*The* FURIES *assemble, dancing around* ATHENA, *who becomes their leader.*]

FURIES I will embrace
one home with you, Athena,
never fail the city
you and Zeus almighty, you and Ares
hold as the fortress of the gods, the shield
of the high Greek altars, glory of the powers.
Spirit of Athens, hear my words, my prayer
like a prophet's warm and kind,
that the rare good things of life
come rising crest on crest,
sprung from the rich black earth and
gleaming with the bursting flash of sun.
ATHENA These blessings I bestow on you, my people, gladly.
I enthrone these strong, implacable spirits here
and root them in our soil.
Theirs,
theirs to rule the lives of men,
it is their fated power.

But he who has never felt their weight,
or known the blows of life and how they fall,
the crimes of his fathers hale him toward their bar,
and there for all his boasts—destruction,
silent, majestic in anger,
crushes him to dust.

FURIES Yes and I ban
the winds that rock the olive—
hear my love, my blessing—
thwart their scorching heat that blinds the buds,
hold from our shores the killing icy gales,
and I ban the blight that creeps on fruit and withers—
God of creation, Pan, make flocks increase
and the ewes drop fine twin lambs
when the hour of labor falls.
And silver,[7] child of Earth,
secret treasure of Hermes,
come to light and praise the gifts of god.

ATHENA Blessings—now do you hear, you guards of Athens,
all that she will do?
Fury the mighty queen, the dread
of the deathless gods and those beneath the earth,
deals with mortals clearly, once for all.
She delivers songs to some, to others
a blinding life of tears—
Fury works her will.

FURIES And the lightning stroke
that cuts men down before their prime, I curse,
but the lovely girl who finds a mate's embrace,
the deep joy of wedded life—O grant that gift, that prize,
you gods of wedlock, grant it, goddesses of Fate!
Sisters born of the Night our mother,
spirits steering law,
sharing at all our hearths,
at all times bearing down
to make our lives more just,
all realms exalt you highest of the gods.

ATHENA Behold, my land, what blessings Fury kindly,
gladly brings to pass—
I am in my glory! Yes, I love Persuasion;
she watched my words, she met their wild refusals.
Thanks to Zeus of the Councils who can turn
dispute to peace—he won the day.
[*To the* FURIES.]
Thanks to our duel for blessings;
we win through it all.

FURIES And the brutal strife,

7. At Laurion (in southeast Attica) silver had been mined for many years when, sometime before 480 B.C., rich new veins were discovered. The Athenians used the money to build the fleet that fought at Salamis.

the civil war devouring men, I pray
that it never rages through our city, no,
that the good Greek soil never drinks the blood of Greeks,
shed in an orgy of reprisal life for life—
that Fury like a beast will never
rampage through the land.
Give joy in return for joy,
one common will for love,
and hate with one strong heart:
such union heals a thousand ills of man.

ATHENA Do you *hear* how Fury sounds her blessings forth,
how Fury finds the way?
Shining out of the terror of their faces
I can see great gains for you, my people.
Hold them kindly, kind as they are to you.
Exalt them always, you exalt your land,
your city straight and just—
its light goes through the world.

FURIES Rejoice,
rejoice in destined wealth,
rejoice, Athena's people—
poised by the side of Zeus,
loved by the loving virgin girl,
achieve humanity at last,
nestling under Pallas' wings
and blessed with Father's love.

ATHENA You too rejoice! and I must lead the way
to your chambers by the holy light of these,
your escorts bearing fire.

[*Enter* ATHENA*'s entourage of women, bearing offerings and victims and torches still unlit.*]

Come, and sped beneath the earth
by our awesome sacrifices,
keep destruction from the country,
bring prosperity home to Athens,
triumph sailing in its wake.
And you,
my people born of the Rock King,[8]
lead on our guests for life, my city—
May they treat you with compassion,
compassionate as you will be to them.

FURIES Rejoice!—
rejoice—the joy resounds—
all those who dwell in Athens,
spirits and mortals, come,
govern Athena's city well,
revere us well, we are your guests;
you will learn to praise your Furies,

8. The legendary ancestor Cranaos, whose name means "rocky." The soil of Attica is not rich.

you will praise the fortunes of your lives.
ATHENA My thanks! And I will speed your prayers, your blessings—
lit by the torches breaking into flame
I send you home, home to the core of Earth,
escorted by these friends who guard my idol
duty-bound.

[ATHENA's *entourage comes forward, bearing crimson robes.*]

Bright eye of the land of Theseus,
come forth, my splendid troupe. Girls and mothers,
trains of aged women grave in movement,
dress our Furies now in blood-red robes.[9]
Praise them—let the torch move on!
So the love this family bears toward our land
will bloom in human strength from age to age.

[*The women invest the* FURIES *and sing the final chorus. Torches blaze; a procession forms, including the actors and the judges.* ATHENA *leads them from the theater and escorts them through the city.*]

THE WOMEN OF THE CITY On, on, good spirits born for glory,
Daughters of Night, her children always young,
now under loyal escort—
Blessings, people of Athens, sing your blessings out.

Deep, deep in the first dark vaults of Earth,
sped by the praise and victims we will bring,
reverence will attend you—
Blessings now, all people, sing your blessings out.

You great good Furies, bless the land with kindly hearts,
you Awesome Spirits,[1] come—exult in the blazing torch,
exultant in our fires, journey on.
Cry, cry in triumph, carry on the dancing on and on!

This peace between Athena's people and their guests
must never end. All-seeing Zeus and Fate embrace,
down they come to urge our union on—
Cry, cry in triumph, carry on the dancing on and on!

9. At the Great Panathenea, the principal festival of Athens, resident aliens as well as full citizens took part in the procession to the Acropolis. The resident aliens, *metics* as they were called, wore crimson cloaks on this occasion. The Furies are thus given residential status in Attic soil. 1. *Semnai* in Greek, a favorable formula for the Furies, like *Eumenides* (kindly ones), the title of the play.

SOPHOCLES
ca. 496–406 B.C.

Aeschylus belonged to the generation that fought at Marathon; his manhood and his old age were passed in the heroic period of the Persian defeat on Greek soil and the war that Athens fought to liberate its kin in the islands of the Aegean and on the Asiatic coast. Sophocles, his younger contemporary, lived to see an Athens that had advanced in power and prosperity far beyond the city that Aeschylus knew. The league of free Greek cities against Persia that Athens had led to victory in the Aegean had become an empire, in which Athens taxed and coerced the subject cities that had once been its free allies. Sophocles, born around 496 B.C., played his part—a prominent one—in the city's affairs. In 443 B.C. he served as one of the treasurers of the imperial league and, with Pericles, as one of the ten generals elected for the war against the island of Samos, which tried to secede from the Athenian league a few years later. When the Athenian expedition to Sicily ended in disaster, Sophocles was appointed to a special committee set up in 411 B.C. to deal with the emergency. He died two years before Athens surrendered to Sparta.

His career as a brilliantly successful dramatist began in 468; in that year he won first prize at the Dionysia, competing against Aeschylus. Over the next sixty-two years he produced more than 120 plays. He won first prize no fewer than twenty-four times, and when he was not first, he came in second, never third.

Aeschylus had been an actor as well as a playwright and director, but Sophocles, early in his career, gave up acting. It was he who added a third actor to the team; the early Aeschylean plays (*Persians, Seven Against Thebes,* and *Suppliants*) can be played by two actors (who of course can change masks to extend the range of *dramatis personae*). In the *Oresteia,* Aeschylus has taken advantage of the Sophoclean third actor; this makes possible the role of Cassandra, the one three-line speech of Pylades in *The Libation Bearers,* and the trial scene in *The Eumenides.* But Sophocles used his third actor to create complex triangular scenes like the dialogue between Oedipus and the Corinthian messenger, which reveals to a listening Jocasta the ghastly truth that Oedipus will not discover until the next scene.

We have only seven of his plays, and not many of them can be accurately dated. *Ajax* (which deals with the suicide of the hero whose shade turns silently away from Odysseus in the *Odyssey*) and *Trachiniae* (the story of the death of Heracles) are both generally thought to be early productions. *Antigone* is fairly securely fixed in the late 440s, and *Oedipus the King* was probably staged during the early years of the Peloponnesian War (431–404 B.C.). For *Electra* we have no date, but it is probably later than *Oedipus the King. Philoctetes,* a tale of the Trojan War, was staged in 409 B.C. and *Oedipus at Colonus,* which presents Oedipus's strangely triumphant death on Athenian soil, was produced after Sophocles' death.

Most of these plays date from the last half of the fifth century B.C.; they were written in and for an Athens that, since the days of Aeschylus, had undergone an intellectual revolution. It was in a time of critical reevaluation of accepted standards and traditions that Sophocles produced his masterpiece, *Oedipus the King,* and the problems of the time are reflected in the play.

Oedipus the King, which deals with a man of high principles and probing intelligence who follows the prompting of that intelligence to the final consequence of true self-knowledge—which makes him put out his eyes—was as full of significance for Sophocles' contemporaries as it is for us. Unlike a modern dramatist, Sophocles used for his tragedy a story well known to the audience and as old as their own history, a legend told by parent to child, handed down from generation to generation because of its implicit wealth of meaning, learned in childhood, and rooted deep in the consciousness of every member of the community. Such a story the Greeks called a myth, and the use of it presented Sophocles, as it did Aeschylus in his trilogy, with material that, apart from its great inherent dramatic potential, already possessed the significance and authority that modern dramatists must create for themselves. It had the authority of history, for the history of ages that leave no records is myth—that is to say, the significant event of the past, stripped of irrelevancies and imaginatively shaped by the oral tradition. It had a religious authority, for the Oedipus story, like the story of the house of Atreus, is concerned with the relation between humanity and gods. Last, and this is especially true of the Oedipus myth, it had the power, because of its subject matter, to arouse the irrational hopes and fears that lie deep and secret in the human consciousness.

The use of the familiar myth enabled the dramatist to draw on all its wealth of unformulated meaning, but it did not prevent him from striking a contemporary note. Oedipus, in Sophocles' play, is at one and the same time the mysterious figure of the past who broke the most fundamental human taboos and a typical fifth-century Athenian. His character contains all the virtues for which the Athenians were famous and the vices for which they were notorious. The best commentary on Oedipus's character is the speech that Thucydides, the contemporary historian of the Peloponnesian War, attributed to a Corinthian spokesman at Sparta; it is a hostile but admiring assessment of the Athenian genius. "Athenians . . . [are] equally quick in the conception and in the execution of every new plan"—so Oedipus has already sent to Delphi when the priest advises him to do so and has already sent for Tiresias when the chorus suggests this course of action. "They are bold beyond their strength; they run risks which prudence would condemn"—as Oedipus risked his life to answer the riddle of the Sphinx and later, in spite of the oracle about his marriage, accepted the hand of the queen. "In the midst of misfortune they are full of hope"—so Oedipus, when he is told that he is not the son of Polybus and Merope, and Jocasta has already realized whose son he is, claims that he is the "child of Fortune." "When they do not carry out an intention that they have formed, they seem to have sustained a personal bereavement"—so Oedipus, shamed by Jocasta and the chorus into sparing Creon's life, yields sullenly and petulantly.

The Athenian devotion to the city, which received the main emphasis in Pericles' praise of Athens, is strong in Oedipus; his answer to the priest at the beginning of the play shows that he is a conscientious and patriotic ruler. His quick rage is the characteristic fault of Athenian democracy, which in 406 B.C., to give only one instance, condemned and executed the generals who had failed, in the stress of weather and battle, to pick up the drowned bodies of their own men killed in the naval engagement at Arginusae. Oedipus is like the fifth-century Athenian most of all in his confidence in the human intelligence, especially his own. This confidence takes him in the play through the whole cycle of the critical, rationalist movement of the century, from the piety and orthodoxy he displays in the opening scene, through his taunts at oracles when he hears that Polybus is dead, to the despairing courage with which he accepts the consequences when he sees the abyss opening at his feet. "I'm right at the edge, the horrible truth—I've got to say it!" says the herdsman from whom he is dragging the truth. "And I'm at the edge of hearing horrors, yes," Oedipus replies, "but I must hear!" And hear he does. He learns that the oracle he had first fought against and then laughed at has been fulfilled, that every step his intelligence prompted was one step nearer to disaster, that his knowledge was ignorance and his clear vision blindness. Faced with the reality that his determined probing finally reveals, he puts out his eyes.

The relation of Oedipus's character to the development of the action is the basis of the most famous attempt to define the nature of the tragic process. Aristotle, writing his *Poetics* in the next century, developed the theory that pity and terror are aroused most effectively by the spectacle of a man who is "not pre-eminent in virtue and justice, and yet on the other hand does not fall into misfortune through vice or depravity, but falls because of some mistake; one among the number of the highly renowned and prosperous, such as Oedipus." Other references by Aristotle to this play make it clear that this influential doctrine of the fall of the tragic hero was based particularly on Sophocles' masterpiece, and it has been universally applied to the play. But the great influence (and validity) of the Aristotelian theory should not be allowed to obscure the fact that Sophocles' *Oedipus the King* is more highly organized and economical than Aristotle implies. The fact that the critics have differed about the nature of Oedipus's mistake or frailty (his errors are many, and his frailties include anger, impiety, and self-confidence) is a clue to the real situation. Oedipus falls not through "some vicious mole of nature" or some "particular fault" (to use Hamlet's terms) but because he is the man he is, because of all aspects of his character, good and bad alike; and the development of the action right through to the catastrophe shows us every aspect of his character at work in the process of self-revelation and self-destruction. His first decision in the play, to hear Creon's message from Delphi in public rather than, as Creon suggests, in private, is evidence of his kingly solicitude for his people and his trust in them, but it makes certain the full publication of the truth. His proclamation of a curse on the murderer of Laius, although prompted by his civic zeal, makes his final situation worse than it otherwise would have been. His anger at Tiresias forces a revelation that drives him on to accuse Creon; this in turn provokes Jocasta's revelations. And throughout the play his confidence in the efficacy of his own action, his hopefulness as the situation darkens, and his passion for discovering the truth guide the steps of the investigation that is to reveal the detective as the criminal. All aspects of his character, good and bad alike, are equally involved; it is no frailty or error that leads him to the terrible truth, but his total personality.

The character of Oedipus as revealed in the play does something more than explain the present action; it also explains his past. In Oedipus's speeches and actions on stage we can see the man who, given the circumstances in which Oedipus was involved, would inevitably do just what Oedipus has done. Each action on stage shows us the mood in which he committed some action in the past; his angry death sentence on Creon reveals the man who killed Laius because of an insult on the highway; his proclamation of total excommunication for the unknown murderer shows us the man who, without forethought, accepted the hand of Jocasta; his intelligent, persistent search for the truth shows us the brain and the courage that solved the riddle of the Sphinx. The revelation of his character in the play is at once a re-creation of his past and an interpretation of the oracle that predicted his future.

This organization of the material is what makes it possible for us to accept the story as tragedy at all, for it emphasizes Oedipus's independence of the oracle. When we first see Oedipus, he has already committed the actions for which he is to suffer—actions prophesied, before his birth, by Apollo. But the dramatist's emphasis on Oedipus's character suggests that although Apollo has predicted what Oedipus will do, he does not determine it; Oedipus determines his own conduct, by being the man he is. The relationship between Apollo's prophecy and Oedipus's actions is not that of cause and effect. It is the relationship of two independent entities that are equated.

This correspondence between his character and his fate removes the obstacle to our full acceptance of the play that an external fate governing his action would set up. Nevertheless, we feel that he suffers more than he deserves. He has served as an example of the inadequacy of the human intellect and a warning that there is a power in the universe that humanity cannot control or even fully understand, but Oedipus the man still has our sympathy. Sophocles felt this too, and in his last play, *Oedipus at Colonus,* he dealt with the reward that finally balanced Oedipus's suffering. In *Oedipus the King* itself there is a foreshadowing of this final development; the last scene shows us a man already beginning to recover from the shock of the catastrophe and reasserting a natural superiority.

"I am going—you know on what condition?" he says to Creon when ordered back into the house, and a few lines later Creon has to say bluntly to him: "Still the king, the master of all things? / No more: here your power ends." This renewed imperiousness is the first expression of a feeling on his part that he is not entirely guilty, a beginning of the reconstitution of the magnificent man of the opening scenes; it reaches its fulfillment in the final Oedipus play, *Oedipus at Colonus,* in which he is a titanic figure, confident of his innocence and more masterful than he has ever been.

ANTIGONE

Though *Antigone* was almost certainly produced before *Oedipus the King,* it deals with mythological events that, in the story, come after the exposure of Oedipus's identity and his self-blinding. Creon eventually expelled Oedipus from Thebes, to wander as a blind beggar, accompanied only by his daughter Antigone. His sons, Eteocles and Polynices, raised no hand to help him; when he died at Colonus, near Athens, Antigone returned to Thebes. Eteocles and Polynices, who had agreed to rule jointly, soon quarreled; they fought each other for the throne of Thebes. Eteocles expelled his brother, who recruited supporters in Argos; and seven champions attacked the seven gates of Thebes. The assault was beaten off, but Polynices and Eteocles killed each other in the battle. As the play opens, the rule of Thebes has fallen to Creon. His first decision is to forbid burial to the corpse of Polynices, the traitor who brought foreign troops against his own city. Antigone disobeys the decree by scattering dust on the body; captured and brought before Creon, she defies him in the name of the eternal unwritten laws. In the struggle between them it is the king who in the end surrenders; he buries the body of Polynices and orders Antigone's release. But she has already killed herself in her underground prison, thus bringing about the two deaths that crush her enemy, the suicides of his son Haemon and of his wife, Eurydice.

Antigone, as a hero of the resistance to tyrannical power, has deservedly become one of the Western world's great symbolic figures; she is clearly presented, in her famous speech, as a champion of a higher morality against the overriding claims of state necessity, which the Sophist intellectuals of Sophocles' time had begun to formulate in philosophical terms. But Creon, too, is given his due; he is not a mere tyrant of melodrama but a ruler whose action stems from political and religious attitudes that were probably shared by many of the audience. Antigone and Creon clash not only as individuals, shaped with all Sophocles' dramatic genius (the ancient anonymous biography of Sophocles says truly that he could "match the moment with the action so as to create a whole character out of half a line or even a single word"), but also as representatives of two irreconcilable social and religious positions.

Antigone's chief loyalty is clearly to the family. She makes no distinction between the brothers, though one was a patriot and the other a traitor, and when her sister, Ismene, refuses to help her defy the state to bury a brother, she harshly disowns her. The denial of burial to Polynices strikes directly at her family loyalty, for it was the immemorial privilege and duty of the women of the house to mourn the dead man in unrestrained sorrow, sing his praises, wash his body, and consign him to the earth. Creon, on the other hand, sees loyalty to the state as the only valid criterion and, in his opening speech, expressly repudiates one who "places a friend above the good of his own country" (the Greek word for "friend" also means "relative"). This inaugural address of Creon repeats many concepts and even phrases that are to be found in the speeches of the democratic leader Pericles, and in fact, there was an ancient antagonism between the new democratic institutions that stressed the equal rights and obligations of all citizens and the old powerful families that through their wide influence had acted as separate factions in the body politic. The nature of Creon's assertion of state against family, refusal of burial to a corpse, is repellent, but the principle behind it was one many Athenians would have accepted as valid.

These opposing social viewpoints have their corresponding religious sanctions. For Antigone, the gods, especially the gods below, demand equality for all the dead, the common inalienable right of burial. But Creon's gods are the gods who protect the city; how, he asks, could those gods have any feeling for Polynices, a traitor who raised and led a foreign army against the city they protect and that contains their temples? Here again, there must have been many in the audience who saw merit in this argument.

The tension between household and civic institutions, between city gods and those who protect the more fundamental duties to the dead, can also be viewed from the perspective of gender. A socially effective male citizen, as Creon makes clear, was expected to be the unquestioned head of the household; but participation in the various aspects of the Athenian democracy was also his right. Athenian women, on the other hand, lacked citizen rights and therefore concentrated their activities and their emotional life on house and family. If the house, in fifth-century-B.C. Athens, could be viewed as a site of potential disorder that threatened the city's stability, it was easy to identify women with that disorder—for example, in their lamentation for dead relatives. From the sixth century B.C. on, periodic legislation in Athens attempted to curtail public display at funerals, and many scholars believe that this included women's laments. Thus when Creon insists, "never let some woman triumph over us," he is not only jealously guarding male prerogatives, but is also speaking from a concern for civic order intelligible to the audience and widely shared among them.

Viewing *Antigone* within the Athenian context, however, does not force us to conclude that in the terms of the play Creon is right and Antigone wrong. Antigone speaks for religious values that the Athenians revered, and she does so in superbly powerful language. Furthermore, as the action develops, whatever validity Creon's initial position may have had is destroyed, and by Creon himself. For like all holders of absolute power, he proceeds, when challenged, to equate loyalty to the community with loyalty to himself—"the city *is* the king's—that's the law!" he tells his son Haemon. And in the end the prophet Tiresias tells him plainly that Antigone was right—the gods are on her side. He swallows his pride and surrenders, but too late. Antigone's suicide brings him to disaster in that institution, the family, that he subordinated to reasons of state; his son spits in his face before killing himself, and his wife dies cursing him as the murderer of his son.

Creon is punished, but Antigone is dead. As the play ends, the chorus points out a moral: the "mighty blows of fate . . . at long last . . . will teach us wisdom." But the price of wisdom is high; *Antigone,* like many of the Shakespearean tragedies, leaves us with a poignant sense of loss.

For a short, general survey of Sophoclean drama, see P. E. Easterling in *The Cambridge History of Classical Literature* (1985), pp. 295–316. B. M. W. Knox, *Opedipus at Thebes* (1957), is a detailed examination of *Oedipus the King* in the context of its age. Knox's *The Heroic Temper* (1964) concentrates on Sophocles' heroic characters, Antigone and Oedipus among them. R. P. Winnington-Ingram, *Sophocles: An Interpretation* (1980), contains substantial essays based on close readings of *Antigone* (pp. 91–149) and *Oedipus the King* (pp. 150–204), as does Charles Segal, *Tragedy and Civilization: An Interpretation of Sophocles* (1981; pp. 152–206 on *Antigone* and pp. 207–248 on *Oedipus the King*). See also Segal's *Oedipus Tyrannus: Tragic Heroism and the Limits of Knowledge* (1993). Mark Griffith's *Antigone / Sophocles* (1999), although an edition with commentary meant to guide a reading of the Greek text, contains an excellent and accessible introduction, including a succinct survey of various critical approaches to the play. Mary Whitlock Blundell, *Helping Friends and Harming Enemies* (1989), contains a chapter on the ethical problems raised by *Antigone* (pp. 106–148). Two books treat metatheatrical aspects of Sophoclean drama: David Seale, *Vision and Stagecraft in Sophocles* (1982), discusses the themes of sight, blindness, and knowledge in relation to the experience of watching a play; and Mark Ringer, *Electra and the Empty Urn: Metatheater and Role Playing in Sophocles* (1998), relates the opposition between appearance and reality in *Antigone* (pp. 68–78) and *Oedipus the King* (pp. 78–90) to the nature of theater and acting.

PRONOUNCING GLOSSARY

The following list uses common English syllables and stress accents to provide rough equivalents of selected words whose pronunciation may be unfamiliar to the general reader.

Antigone: *an-ti'-go-nee*
Eteocles: *ee-tee'-ok-leez*
Ismene: *iz-mee'-nee*
Oedipus: *ee'-di-pus* or *é-di-pus*
Polynices: *po-li-nai'-seez*
Tiresias: *tai-ree'-see-uhs*

Oedipus the King[1]

CHARACTERS

OEDIPUS, *king of Thebes*
A PRIEST *of Zeus*
CREON, *brother of Jocasta*
A CHORUS *of Theban citizens and their* LEADER
TIRESIAS, *a blind prophet*
JOCASTA, *the queen, wife of Oedipus*
A MESSENGER *from Corinth*
A SHEPHERD
A MESSENGER *from inside the palace*
ANTIGONE, ISMENE, *daughters of Oedipus and Jocasta*
GUARDS *and attendants*
PRIESTS *of Thebes*

[TIME AND SCENE: *The royal house of Thebes. Double doors dominate the façade; a stone altar stands at the center of the stage.*

Many years have passed since OEDIPUS *solved the riddle of the Sphinx and ascended the throne of Thebes, and now a plague has struck the city. A procession of priests enters; suppliants, broken and despondent, they carry branches wound in wool and lay them on the altar.*

The doors open. Guards assemble. OEDIPUS *comes forward, majestic but for a telltale limp, and slowly views the condition of his people.*]

OEDIPUS Oh my children, the new blood of ancient Thebes,
why are you here? Huddling at my altar,
praying before me, your branches wound in wool.[2]
Our city reeks with the smoke of burning incense,
rings with cries for the Healer[3] and wailing for the dead.
I thought it wrong, my children, to hear the truth
from others, messengers. Here I am myself—
you all know me, the world knows my fame:
I am Oedipus.
[*Helping a* PRIEST *to his feet.*]
Speak up, old man. Your years,
your dignity—you should speak for the others.
Why here and kneeling, what preys upon you so?
Some sudden fear? some strong desire?
You can trust me. I am ready to help,

1. Translated by Robert Fagles. 2. The insignia of suppliants, laid on the altar and left there until the suppliant's request was granted. At the end of the scene, when Oedipus promises action, he will tell them to take the branches away. 3. Apollo.

I'll do anything. I would be blind to misery
not to pity my people kneeling at my feet.
PRIEST Oh Oedipus, king of the land, our greatest power!
You see us before you now, men of all ages
clinging to your altars. Here are boys,
still too weak to fly from the nest,
and here the old, bowed down with the years,
the holy ones—a priest of Zeus myself—and here
the picked, unmarried men, the young hope of Thebes.
And all the rest, your great family gathers now,
branches wreathed, massing in the squares,
kneeling before the two temples of queen Athena
or the river-shrine where the embers glow and die
and Apollo sees the future in the ashes.[4]
Our city—
look around you, see with your own eyes—
our ship pitches wildly, cannot lift her head
from the depths, the red waves of death . . .
Thebes is dying. A blight on the fresh crops
and the rich pastures, cattle sicken and die,
and the women die in labor, children stillborn,
and the plague, the fiery god of fever hurls down
on the city, his lightning slashing through us—
raging plague in all its vengeance, devastating
the house of Cadmus![5] And black Death luxuriates
in the raw, wailing miseries of Thebes.
Now we pray to you. You cannot equal the gods,
your children know that, bending at your altar.
But we do rate you first of men,
both in the common crises of our lives
and face-to-face encounters with the gods.
You freed us from the Sphinx, you came to Thebes
and cut us loose from the bloody tribute we had paid
that harsh, brutal singer.[6] We taught you nothing,
no skill, no extra knowledge, still you triumphed.
A god was with you, so they say, and we believe it—
you lifted up our lives.
So now again,
Oedipus, king, we bend to you, your power—
we implore you, all of us on our knees:
find us strength, rescue! Perhaps you've heard
the voice of a god or something from other men,
Oedipus . . . what do you know?

4. At a temple of Apollo in Thebes the priests foretold the future according to patterns they saw in the ashes of the burned flesh of sacrificial victims. 5. Mythical founder of Thebes and its first king. 6. The sphinx was the winged female monster that terrorized the city of Thebes until her riddle was finally answered by Oedipus. The riddle was "What is it that walks on four feet and two feet and three feet and has only one voice; when it walks on most feet, it is weakest?" Oedipus's answer was "Man." (We have four feet as children crawling on all fours and three feet in old age when we walk with the aid of a stick.) Many young men of Thebes had tried to answer the riddle, failed, and been killed.

The man of experience—you see it every day—
his plans will work in a crisis, his first of all.

Act now—we beg you, best of men, raise up our city!
Act, defend yourself, your former glory!
Your country calls you savior now
for your zeal, your action years ago.
Never let us remember of your reign:
you helped us stand, only to fall once more.
Oh raise up our city, set us on our feet.
The omens were good that day you brought us joy—
be the same man today!
Rule our land, you know you have the power,
but rule a land of the living, not a wasteland.
Ship and towered city are nothing, stripped of men
alive within it, living all as one.

OEDIPUS My children,
I pity you. I see—how could I fail to see
what longings bring you here? Well I know
you are sick to death, all of you,
but sick as you are, not one is sick as I.
Your pain strikes each of you alone, each
in the confines of himself, no other. But my spirit
grieves for the city, for myself and all of you.
I wasn't asleep, dreaming. You haven't wakened me—
I've wept through the nights, you must know that,
groping, laboring over many paths of thought.
After a painful search I found one cure:
I acted at once. I sent Creon,
my wife's own brother, to Delphi—
Apollo the Prophet's oracle[7]—to learn
what I might do or say to save our city.

Today's the day. When I count the days gone by
it torments me . . . what is he doing?
Strange, he's late, he's gone too long.
But once he returns, then, then I'll be a traitor
if I do not do all the god makes clear.

PRIEST Timely words. The men over there
are signaling—Creon's just arriving.

OEDIPUS [*Sighting* CREON, *then turning to the altar.*]
Lord Apollo,
let him come with a lucky word of rescue,
shining like his eyes!

PRIEST Welcome news, I think—he's crowned, look,
and the laurel wreath is bright with berries.[8]

7. Below Mount Parnassus in central Greece.

8. Creon is wearing a crown of laurel as a sign that he brings good news.

OEDIPUS We'll soon see. He's close enough to hear—
[*Enter* CREON *from the side; his face is shaded with a wreath.*]
Creon, prince, my kinsman, what do you bring us?
What message from the god?
CREON Good news.
I tell you even the hardest things to bear,
if they should turn out well, all would be well.
OEDIPUS Of course, but what were the god's *words*? There's no hope
and nothing to fear in what you've said so far.
CREON If you want my report in the presence of these . . .
[*Pointing to the priests while drawing* OEDIPUS *toward the palace.*]
I'm ready now, or we might go inside.
OEDIPUS Speak out,
speak to us all. I grieve for these, my people,
far more than I fear for my own life.
CREON Very well,
I will tell you what I heard from the god.
Apollo commands us—he was quite clear—
"Drive the corruption from the land,
don't harbor it any longer, past all cure,
don't nurse it in your soil—root it out!"
OEDIPUS How can we cleanse ourselves—what rites?
What's the source of the trouble?
CREON Banish the man, or pay back blood with blood.
Murder sets the plague-storm on the city.
OEDIPUS Whose murder?
Whose fate does Apollo bring to light?
CREON Our leader,
my lord, was once a man named Laius,
before you came and put us straight on course.
OEDIPUS I know—
or so I've heard. I never saw the man myself.
CREON Well, he was killed, and Apollo commands us now—
he could not be more clear,
"Pay the killers back—whoever is responsible."
OEDIPUS Where on earth are they? Where to find it now,
the trail of the ancient guilt so hard to trace?
CREON: "Here in Thebes," he said.
Whatever is sought for can be caught, you know,
whatever is neglected slips away.
OEDIPUS But where,
in the palace, the fields or foreign soil,
where did Laius meet his bloody death?
CREON He went to consult an oracle, Apollo said,
and he set out and never came home again.
OEDIPUS No messenger, no fellow-traveler saw what happened?
Someone to cross-examine?
CREON No,
they were all killed but one. He escaped,
terrified, he could tell us nothing clearly,

nothing of what he saw—just one thing.
OEDIPUS What's that?
one thing could hold the key to it all,
a small beginning give us grounds for hope.
CREON He said thieves attacked them—a whole band,
not single-handed, cut King Laius down.
OEDIPUS A thief,
so daring, so wild, he'd kill a king? Impossible,
unless conspirators paid him off in Thebes.
CREON We suspected as much. But with Laius dead
no leader appeared to help us in our troubles.
OEDIPUS Trouble? Your *king* was murdered—royal blood!
What stopped you from tracking down the killer
then and there?
CREON The singing, riddling Sphinx.
She . . . persuaded us to let the mystery go
and concentrate on what lay at our feet.
OEDIPUS No,
I'll start again—I'll bring it all to light myself!
Apollo is right, and so are you, Creon,
to turn our attention back to the murdered man.
Now you have *me* to fight for you, you'll see:
I am the land's avenger by all rights,
and Apollo's champion too.
But not to assist some distant kinsman, no,
for my own sake I'll rid us of this corruption.
Whoever killed the king may decide to kill me too,
with the same violent hand—by avenging Laius
I defend myself.
[*To the priests.*]
Quickly, my children.
Up from the steps, take up your branches now.
[*To the guards.*]
One of you summon the city[9] here before us,
tell them I'll do everything. God help us,
we will see our triumph—or our fall.
[OEDIPUS *and* CREON *enter the palace, followed by the guards.*]
PRIEST Rise, my sons. The kindness we came for
Oedipus volunteers himself.
Apollo has sent his word, his oracle—
Come down, Apollo, save us, stop the plague.
[*The priests rise, remove their branches and exit to the side. Enter a* CHORUS, *the citizens of Thebes, who have not heard the news that* CREON *brings. They march around the altar, chanting.*]
CHORUS Zeus!
Great welcome voice of Zeus,[1] what do you bring?
What word from the gold vaults of Delphi

9. Represented by the chorus, which comes on to the circular dancing floor immediately after this scene.
1. Apollo was his son and spoke for him.

comes to brilliant Thebes? Racked with terror—
terror shakes my heart
and I cry your wild cries, Apollo, Healer of Delos[2]
I worship you in dread . . . what now, what is your price?
some new sacrifice? some ancient rite from the past
come round again each spring?—
what will you bring to birth?
Tell me, child of golden Hope
warm voice that never dies!

You are the first I call, daughter of Zeus
deathless Athena—I call your sister Artemis,[3]
heart of the market place enthroned in glory,
guardian of our earth—
I call Apollo, Archer astride the thunderheads of heaven—
O triple shield against death, shine before me now!
If ever, once in the past, you stopped some ruin
launched against our walls
you hurled the flame of pain
far, far from Thebes—you gods
come now, come down once more!
No, no
the miseries numberless, grief on grief, no end—
too much to bear, we are all dying
O my people . . .
Thebes like a great army dying
and there is no sword of thought to save us, no
and the fruits of our famous earth, they will not ripen
no and the women cannot scream their pangs to birth—
screams for the Healer, children dead in the womb
and life on life goes down
you can watch them go
like seabirds winging west, outracing the day's fire
down the horizon, irresistibly
streaking on to the shores of Evening
Death
so many deaths, numberless deaths on deaths, no end—
Thebes is dying, look, her children
stripped of pity . . .
generations strewn on the ground
unburied, unwept, the dead spreading death
and the young wives and gray-haired mothers with them
cling to the altars, trailing in from all over the city—
Thebes, city of death, one long cortege
and the suffering rises
wails for mercy rise
and the wild hymn for the Healer blazes out

2. A sacred island, Apollo's birthplace. 3. Apollo's sister, a goddess associated with hunting and also a protector of women in childbirth.

clashing with our sobs our cries of mourning—
  O golden daughter of god,[4] send rescue
  radiant as the kindness in your eyes!

Drive him back!—the fever, the god of death
    that raging god of war
not armored in bronze, not shielded now, he burns me,[5]
battle cries in the onslaught burning on—
O rout him from our borders!
Sail him, blast him out to the Sea-queen's chamber
      the black Atlantic gulfs
  or the northern harbor, death to all
where the Thracian[6] surf comes crashing.
Now what the night spares he comes by day and kills—
the god of death.

            O lord of the stormcloud,
you who twirl the lightning, Zeus, Father,
thunder Death to nothing!

Apollo, lord of the light, I beg you—
    whip your longbow's golden cord
showering arrows on our enemies—shafts of power
champions strong before us rushing on!

Artemis, Huntress,
torches flaring over the eastern ridges—
      ride Death down in pain!

God of the headdress gleaming gold, I cry to you—
your name and ours are one, Dionysus—
  come with your face aflame with wine
      your raving women's[7] cries
  your army on the march! Come with the lightning
come with torches blazing, eyes ablaze with glory!
Burn that god of death that all gods hate!

[OEDIPUS *enters from the palace to address the* CHORUS, *as if addressing the entire city of Thebes.*]

OEDIPUS You pray to the gods? Let me grant your prayers.
Come, listen to me—do what the plague demands:
you'll find relief and lift your head from the depths.
I will speak out now as a stranger to the story,
a stranger to the crime. If I'd been present then,
there would have been no mystery, no long hunt

4. Athena, daughter of Zeus. 5. The plague is identified with Ares, the war god, though he comes now without armor and shield. Ares is not elsewhere connected with plague; this passage may be an allusion to the early years of the Peloponnesian War, when Spartan troops threatened the city from outside and the plague raged inside the walls. 6. Ares was thought to be at home among the savages of Thrace, to the northeast of Greece proper. 7. The Bacchanals, nymphs or human female votaries of the god Dionysus (Bacchus) who celebrated him with wild dancing rites.

without a clue in hand. So now, counted
a native Theban years after the murder,
to all of Thebes I make this proclamation:
if any one of you knows who murdered Laius,
the son of Labdacus, I order him to reveal
the whole truth to me. Nothing to fear,
even if he must denounce himself,
let him speak up
and so escape the brunt of the charge—
he will suffer no unbearable punishment,
nothing worse than exile, totally unharmed.
[OEDIPUS *pauses, waiting for a reply.*]
Next,
if anyone knows the murderer is a stranger,
a man from alien soil, come, speak up.
I will give him a handsome reward, and lay up
gratitude in my heart for him besides.
[*Silence again, no reply.*]
But if you keep silent, if anyone panicking,
trying to shield himself or friend or kin,
rejects my offer, then hear what I will do.
I order you, every citizen of the state
where I hold throne and power: banish this man—
whoever he may be—never shelter him, never
speak a word to him, never make him partner
to your prayers, your victims burned to the gods.
Never let the holy water touch his hands
Drive him out, each of you, from every home.
He is the plague, the heart of our corruption,
as Apollo's oracle has just revealed to me.
So I honor my obligations:
I fight for the god and for the murdered man.

Now my curse on the murderer. Whoever he is,
a lone man unknown in his crime
or one among many, let that man drag out
his life in agony, step by painful step—
I curse myself as well . . . if by any chance
he proves to be an intimate of our house,
here at my hearth, with my full knowledge,
may the curse I just called down on him strike me!

These are your orders: perform them to the last.
I command you, for my sake, for Apollo's, for this country
blasted root and branch by the angry heavens.
Even if god had never urged you on to act,
how could you leave the crime uncleansed so long?
A man so noble—your king, brought down in blood—
you should have searched. But I am the king now,
I hold the throne that he held then, possess his bed

and a wife who shares our seed . . . why, our seed
might be the same, children born of the same mother
might have created blood-bonds between us
if his hope of offspring hadn't met disaster—
but fate swooped at his head and cut him short.
So I will fight for him as if he were my father,
stop at nothing, search the world
to lay my hands on the man who shed his blood,
the son of Labdacus descended of Polydorus,
Cadmus of old and Agenor, founder of the line:
their power and mine are one.
Oh dear gods,
my curse on those who disobey these orders!
Let no crops grow out of the earth for them—
shrivel their women, kill their sons,
burn them to nothing in this plague
that hits us now, or something even worse.
But you, loyal men of Thebes who approve my actions,
may our champion, Justice, may all the gods
be with us, fight beside us to the end!

LEADER In the grip of your curse, my king, I swear
I'm not the murderer, I cannot point him out.
As for the search, Apollo pressed it on us—
he should name the killer.

OEDIPUS Quite right,
but to force the gods to act against their will—
no man has the power.

LEADER Then if I might mention
the next best thing . . .

OEDIPUS The third best too—
don't hold back, say it.

LEADER I still believe . . .
Lord Tiresias[8] sees with the eyes of Lord Apollo.
Anyone searching for the truth, my king,
might learn it from the prophet, clear as day.

OEDIPUS I've not been slow with that. On Creon's cue
I sent the escorts, twice, within the hour.
I'm surprised he isn't here.

LEADER We need him—
without him we have nothing but old, useless rumors.

OEDIPUS Which rumors? I'll search out every word.

LEADER Laius was killed, they say, by certain travelers.

OEDIPUS I know—but no one can find the murderer.

LEADER If the man has a trace of fear in him
he won't stay silent long,
not with your curses ringing in his ears.

OEDIPUS He didn't flinch at murder,
he'll never flinch at words.

8. The blind prophet of Thebes (whose ghost Odysseus goes to consult in Hades in *Odyssey* 11).

[*Enter* TIRESIAS, *the blind prophet, led by a boy with escorts in attendance. He remains at a distance.*]

LEADER Here is the one who will convict him, look,
they bring him on at last, the seer, the man of god.
The truth lives inside him, him alone.

OEDIPUS O Tiresias,
master of all the mysteries of our life,
all you teach and all you dare not tell,
signs in the heavens, signs that walk the earth!
Blind as you are, you can feel all the more
what sickness haunts our city. You, my lord,
are the one shield, the one savior we can find.

We asked Apollo—perhaps the messengers
haven't told you—he sent his answer back:
"Relief from the plague can only come one way.
Uncover the murderers of Laius,
put them to death or drive them into exile."
So I beg you, grudge us nothing now, no voice,
no message plucked from the birds, the embers
or the other mantic ways within your grasp.
Rescue yourself, your city, rescue me—
rescue everything infected by the dead.
We are in your hands. For a man to help others
with all his gifts and native strength:
that is the noblest work.

TIRESIAS How terrible—to see the truth
when the truth is only pain to him who sees!
I knew it well, but I put it from my mind,
else I never would have come.

OEDIPUS What's this? Why so grim, so dire?

TIRESIAS Just send me home. You bear your burdens,
I'll bear mine. It's better that way,
please believe me.

OEDIPUS Strange response . . . unlawful,
unfriendly too to the state that bred and reared you—
you withhold the word of god.

TIRESIAS I fail to see
that your own words are so well-timed.
I'd rather not have the same thing said of me . . .

OEDIPUS For the love of god, don't turn away,
not if you know something. We beg you,
all of us on our knees.

TIRESIAS None of you knows—
and I will never reveal my dreadful secrets,
not to say your own.

OEDIPUS What? You know and you won't tell?
You're bent on betraying us, destroying Thebes?

TIRESIAS I'd rather not cause pain for you or me.
So why this . . . useless interrogation?

You'll get nothing from me.
OEDIPUS Nothing! You,
you scum of the earth, you'd enrage a heart of stone!
You won't talk? Nothing moves you?
Out with it, once and for all!
TIRESIAS You criticize my temper . . . unaware
of the one[9] *you* live with, you revile me.
OEDIPUS Who could restrain his anger hearing you?
What outrage—you spurn the city!
TIRESIAS What will come will come.
Even if I shroud it all in silence.
OEDIPUS What will come? You're bound to *tell* me that.
TIRESIAS I'll say no more. Do as you like, build your anger
to whatever pitch you please, rage your worst—
OEDIPUS Oh I'll let loose, I have such fury in me—
now I see it all. You helped hatch the plot,
you did the work, yes, short of killing him
with your own hands—and given eyes I'd say
you did the killing single-handed!
TIRESIAS Is that so!
I charge you, then, submit to that decree
you just laid down: from this day onward
speak to no one, not these citizens, not myself.
You are the curse, the corruption of the land!
OEDIPUS You, shameless—
aren't you appalled to start up such a story?
You think you can get away with this?
TIRESIAS I have already.
The truth with all its power lives inside me.
OEDIPUS Who primed you for this? Not your prophet's trade.
TIRESIAS You did, you forced me, twisted it out of me.
OEDIPUS What? Say it again—I'll understand it better.
TIRESIAS Didn't you understand, just now?
Or are you tempting me to talk?
OEDIPUS No, I can't say I grasped your meaning.
Out with it, again!
TIRESIAS I say you are the murderer you hunt.
OEDIPUS That obscenity, twice—by god, you'll pay.
TIRESIAS Shall I say more, so you can really rage?
OEDIPUS Much as you want. Your words are nothing—futile.
TIRESIAS You cannot imagine . . . I tell you,
you and your loved ones live together in infamy,
you cannot see how far you've gone in guilt.
OEDIPUS You think you can keep this up and never suffer?
TIRESIAS Indeed, if the truth has any power.
OEDIPUS It does
but not for you, old man. You've lost your power,

9. In the Greek the veiled reference to Jocasta is more forceful, because the word translated "the one" has a feminine ending (agreeing with the feminine noun *orgê*, "temper").

stone-blind, stone-deaf—senses, eyes blind as stone!
TIRESIAS I pity you, flinging at me the very insults
each man here will fling at you so soon.
OEDIPUS Blind,
lost in the night, endless night that cursed you!
You can't hurt me or anyone else who sees the light—
you can never touch me.
TIRESIAS True, it is not your fate
to fall at my hands. Apollo is quite enough,
and he will take some pains to work this out.
OEDIPUS Creon! Is this conspiracy his or yours?
TIRESIAS Creon is not your downfall, no, you are your own.
OEDIPUS O power—
wealth and empire, skill outstripping skill
in the heady rivalries of life,
what envy lurks inside you! Just for this,
the crown the city gave me—I never sought it,
they laid it in my hands—for this alone, Creon,
the soul of trust, my loyal friend from the start
steals against me . . . so hungry to overthrow me
he sets this wizard on me, this scheming quack,
this fortune-teller peddling lies, eyes peeled
for his own profit—seer blind in his craft!

Come here, you pious fraud. Tell me,
when did you ever prove yourself a prophet?
When the Sphinx, that chanting Fury kept her deathwatch here,
why silent then, not a word to set our people free?
There was a riddle, not for some passer-by to solve—
it cried out for a prophet. Where were you?
Did you rise to the crisis? Not a word,
you and your birds, your gods—nothing.
No, but I came by, Oedipus the ignorant,
I stopped the Sphinx! With no help from the birds,
the flight of my own intelligence hit the mark.

And this is the man you'd try to overthrow?
You think you'll stand by Creon when he's king?
You and the great mastermind—
you'll pay in tears, I promise you, for this,
this witch-hunt. If you didn't look so senile
the lash would teach you what your scheming means!
LEADER I would suggest his words were spoken in anger,
Oedipus . . . yours too, and it isn't what we need.
The best solution to the oracle, the riddle
posed by god—we should look for that.
TIRESIAS You are the king no doubt, but in one respect,
at least, I am your equal: the right to reply.
I claim that privilege too.
I am not your slave. I serve Apollo.

I don't need Creon to speak for me in public.
So,
you mock my blindness? Let me tell you this.
You with your precious eyes,
you're blind to the corruption of your life,
to the house you live in, those you live with—
who *are* your parents? Do you know? All unknowing
you are the scourge of your own flesh and blood,
the dead below the earth and the living here above,
and the double lash of your mother and your father's curse
will whip you from this land one day, their footfall
treading you down in terror, darkness shrouding
your eyes that now can see the light!
Soon, soon
you'll scream aloud—what haven won't reverberate?
What rock of Cithaeron[1] won't scream back in echo?
That day you learn the truth about your marriage,
the wedding-march that sang you into your halls,
the lusty voyage home to the fatal harbor!
And a crowd of other horrors you'd never dream
will level you with yourself and all your children.

There. Now smear us with insults—Creon, myself,
and every word I've said. No man will ever
be rooted from the earth as brutally as you.

OEDIPUS Enough! Such filth from him? Insufferable—
what, still alive? Get out—
faster, back where you came from—vanish!
TIRESIAS I would never have come if you hadn't called me here.
OEDIPUS If I thought you would blurt out such absurdities,
you'd have died waiting before I'd had you summoned.
TIRESIAS Absurd, am I! To you, not to your parents:
the ones who bore you found me sane enough.
OEDIPUS Parents—who? Wait . . . who is my father?
TIRESIAS This day will bring your birth and your destruction.
OEDIPUS Riddles—all you can say are riddles, murk and darkness.
TIRESIAS Ah, but aren't you the best man alive at solving riddles?
OEDIPUS Mock me for that, go on, and you'll reveal my greatness.
TIRESIAS Your great good fortune, true, it was your ruin.
OEDIPUS Not if I saved the city—what do I care?
TIRESIAS Well then, I'll be going.
[*To his attendant.*]
Take me home, boy.
OEDIPUS Yes, take him away. You're a nuisance here.
Out of the way, the irritation's gone.
[*Turning his back on* TIRESIAS, *moving toward the palace.*][2]

1. The mountain range near Thebes, on which Oedipus was left to die when an infant. 2. There are no stage directions in the texts. It is suggested here that Oedipus moves offstage and does not hear the critical section of Tiresias's speech (lines 520ff.), which he could hardly fail to connect with the prophecy made to him by Apollo many years ago.

TIRESIAS I will go,
once I have said what I came here to say.
I'll never shrink from the anger in your eyes—
you can't destroy me. Listen to me closely:
the man you've sought so long, proclaiming,
cursing up and down, the murderer of Laius—
he is here. A stranger,
you may think, who lives among you,
he soon will be revealed a native Theban
but he will take no joy in the revelation.
Blind who now has eyes, beggar who now is rich,
he will grope his way toward a foreign soil,
a stick tapping before him step by step.
[OEDIPUS *enters the palace.*]
Revealed at last, brother and father both
to the children he embraces, to his mother
son and husband both—he sowed the loins
his father sowed, he spilled his father's blood!

Go in and reflect on that, solve that.
And if you find I've lied
from this day onward call the prophet blind.
[TIRESIAS *and the boy exit to the side.*]

CHORUS Who—
who is the man the voice of god denounces
resounding out of the rocky gorge of Delphi?
The horror too dark to tell,
whose ruthless bloody hands have done the work?
His time has come to fly
to outrace the stallions of the storm
his feet a streak of speed—
Cased in armor, Apollo son of the Father
lunges on him, lightning-bolts afire!
And the grim unerring Furies[3]
closing for the kill.
Look,
the word of god has just come blazing
flashing off Parnassus' snowy heights!
That man who left no trace—
after him, hunt him down with all our strength!
Now under bristling timber
up through rocks and caves he stalks
like the wild mountain bull—
cut off from men, each step an agony, frenzied, racing blind
but he cannot outrace the dread voices of Delphi
ringing out of the heart of Earth,
the dark wings beating around him shrieking doom
the doom that never dies, the terror—

3. Avenging spirits who pursued a murderer when no earthly avenger was at hand.

The skilled prophet scans the birds and shatters me with terror!
I can't accept him, can't deny him, don't know what to say,
I'm lost, and the wings of dark foreboding beating—
I cannot see what's come, what's still to come . . .
and what could breed a blood feud between
   Laius' house and the son of Polybus?[4]
I know of nothing, not in the past and not now,
no charge to bring against our king, no cause
to attack his fame that rings throughout Thebes—
   not without proof—not for the ghost of Laius,
   not to avenge a murder gone without a trace.

Zeus and Apollo know, they know, the great masters
      of all the dark and depth of human life.
But whether a mere man can know the truth,
whether a seer can fathom more than I—
there is no test, no certain proof
      though matching skill for skill
a man can outstrip a rival. No, not till I see
these charges proved will I side with his accusers.
We saw him then, when the she-hawk[5] swept against him,
saw with our own eyes his skill, his brilliant triumph—
   there was the test—he was the joy of Thebes!
   Never will I convict my king, never in my heart.
      [*Enter* CREON *from the side.*]

CREON My fellow-citizens, I hear King Oedipus
levels terrible charges at me. I had to come.
I resent it deeply. If, in the present crisis
he thinks he suffers any abuse from me,
anything I've done or said that offers him
the slightest injury, why, I've no desire
to linger out this life, my reputation in ruins.
The damage I'd face from such an accusation
is nothing simple. No, there's nothing worse:
branded a traitor in the city, a traitor
to all of you and my good friends.

LEADER True,
but a slur might have been forced out of him,
by anger perhaps, not any firm conviction.

CREON The charge was made in public, wasn't it?
I put the prophet up to spreading lies?

LEADER Such things were said . . .
I don't know with what intent, if any.

CREON Was his glance steady, his mind right
when the charge was brought against me?

LEADER I really couldn't say. I never look
to judge the ones in power.
      [*The doors open.* OEDIPUS *enters.*]

4. King of Corinth and, so far as anyone except Tiresias knows, the father of Oedipus. 5. The Sphinx.

Wait,
here's Oedipus now.
OEDIPUS You—here? You have the gall
to show your face before the palace gates?
You, plotting to kill me, kill the king—
I see it all, the marauding thief himself
scheming to steal my crown and power!
Tell me,
in god's name, what did you take me for,
coward or fool, when you spun out your plot?
Your treachery—you think I'd never detect it
creeping against me in the dark? Or sensing it,
not defend myself? Aren't you the fool,
you and your high adventure. Lacking numbers,
powerful friends, out for the big game of empire—
you need riches, armies to bring that quarry down!
CREON Are you quite finished? It's your turn to listen
for just as long as you've . . . instructed me.
Hear me out, then judge me on the facts.
OEDIPUS You've a wicked way with words, Creon,
but I'll be slow to learn—from you.
I find you a menace, a great burden to me.
CREON Just one thing, hear me out in this.
OEDIPUS Just one thing,
don't tell *me* you're not the enemy, the traitor.
CREON Look, if you think crude, mindless stubbornness
such a gift, you've lost your sense of balance.
OEDIPUS If you think you can abuse a kinsman,
then escape the penalty, you're insane.
CREON Fair enough, I grant you. But this injury
you say I've done you, what is it?
OEDIPUS Did you induce me, yes or no,
to send for that sanctimonious prophet?
CREON I did. And I'd do the same again.
OEDIPUS All right then, tell me, how long is it now
since Laius . . .
CREON Laius—what did *he* do?
OEDIPUS Vanished,
swept from sight, murdered in his tracks.
CREON The count of the years would run you far back . . .
OEDIPUS And that far back, was the prophet at his trade?
CREON Skilled as he is today, and just as honored.
OEDIPUS Did he ever refer to me then, at that time?
CREON No,
never, at least, when I was in his presence.
OEDIPUS But you did investigate the murder, didn't you?
CREON We did our best, of course, discovered nothing.
OEDIPUS But the great seer never accused me then—why not?
CREON I don't know. And when I don't, *I* keep quiet.
OEDIPUS You do know this, you'd tell it too—

if you had a shred of decency.
CREON What?
If I know, I won't hold back.
OEDIPUS Simply this:
if the two of you had never put heads together,
we would never have heard about *my* killing Laius.
CREON If that's what he says . . . well, you know best.
But now I have a right to learn from you
as you just learned from me.
OEDIPUS Learn your fill,
you never will convict me of the murder.
CREON Tell me, you're married to my sister, aren't you?
OEDIPUS A genuine discovery—there's no denying that.
CREON And you rule the land with her, with equal power?
OEDIPUS She receives from me whatever she desires.
CREON And I am the third, all of us are equals?
OEDIPUS Yes, and it's there you show your stripes—
you betray a kinsman.
CREON Not at all.
Not if you see things calmly, rationally,
as I do. Look at it this way first:
who in his right mind would rather rule
and live in anxiety than sleep in peace?
Particularly if he enjoys the same authority.
Not I, I'm not the man to yearn for kingship,
not with a king's power in my hands. Who would?
No one with any sense of self-control.
Now, as it is, you offer me all I need,
not a fear in the world. But if I wore the crown . . .
there'd be many painful duties to perform,
hardly to my taste.
How could kingship
please me more than influence, power
without a qualm? I'm not that deluded yet,
to reach for anything but privilege outright,
profit free and clear.
Now all men sing my praises, all salute me,
now all who request your favors curry mine.
I am their best hope: success rests in me.
Why give up that, I ask you, and borrow trouble?
A man of sense, someone who sees things clearly
would never resort to treason.
No, I've no lust for conspiracy in me,
nor could I ever suffer one who does.

Do you want proof? Go to Delphi yourself,
examine the oracle and see if I've reported
the message word-for-word. This too:
if you detect that I and the clairvoyant
have plotted anything in common, arrest me,

execute me. Not on the strength of one vote,
two in this case, mine as well as yours.
But don't convict me on sheer unverified surmise.
How wrong it is to take the good for bad,
purely at random, or take the bad for good.
But reject a friend, a kinsman? I would as soon
tear out the life within us, priceless life itself.
You'll learn this well, without fail, in time.
Time alone can bring the just man to light—
the criminal you can spot in one short day.

LEADER Good advice,
my lord, for anyone who wants to avoid disaster.
Those who jump to conclusions may go wrong.

OEDIPUS When my enemy moves against me quickly,
plots in secret, I move quickly too, I must,
I plot and pay him back. Relax my guard a moment,
waiting his next move—he wins his objective,
I lose mine.

CREON What do you want?
You want me banished?

OEDIPUS No, I want you dead.

CREON Just to show how ugly a grudge can . . .

OEDIPUS So,
still stubborn? you don't think I'm serious?

CREON I think you're insane.

OEDIPUS Quite sane—in my behalf.

CREON Not just as much in mine?

OEDIPUS You—my mortal enemy?

CREON What if you're wholly wrong?

OEDIPUS No matter—I must rule.

CREON Not if you rule unjustly.

OEDIPUS Hear him, Thebes, my city!

CREON My city too, not yours alone!

LEADER Please, my lords.

[*Enter* JOCASTA *from the palace.*]

Look, Jocasta's coming,
and just in time too. With her help
you must put this fighting of yours to rest.

JOCASTA Have you no sense? Poor misguided men,
such shouting—why this public outburst?
Aren't you ashamed, with the land so sick,
to stir up private quarrels?

[*To* OEDIPUS.]

Into the palace now. And Creon, you go home.
Why make such a furor over nothing?

CREON My sister, it's dreadful . . . Oedipus, your husband,
he's bent on a choice of punishments for me,
banishment from the fatherland or death.

OEDIPUS Precisely. I caught him in the act, Jocasta,
plotting, about to stab me in the back.

CREON Never—curse me, let me die and be damned
if I've done you any wrong you charge me with.
JOCASTA Oh god, believe it, Oedipus,
honor the solemn oath he swears to heaven.
Do it for me, for the sake of all your people.
[*The* CHORUS *begins to chant.*]
CHORUS Believe it, be sensible
give way, my king, I beg you!
OEDIPUS What do you want from me, concessions?
CHORUS Respect him—he's been no fool in the past
and now he's strong with the oath he swears to god.
OEDIPUS You know what you're asking?
CHORUS I do.
OEDIPUS Then out with it!
CHORUS The man's your friend, your kin, he's under oath—
don't cast him out, disgraced
branded with guilt on the strength of hearsay only.
OEDIPUS Know full well, if that is what you want
you want me dead or banished from the land.
CHORUS Never—
no, by the blazing Sun, first god of the heavens!
Stripped of the gods, stripped of loved ones,
let me die by inches if that ever crossed my mind.
But the heart inside me sickens, dies as the land dies
and now on top of the old griefs you pile this,
your fury—both of you!
OEDIPUS Then let him go,
even if it does lead to my ruin, my death
or my disgrace, driven from Thebes for life.
It's you, not him I pity—your words move me.
He, wherever he goes, my hate goes with him.
CREON Look at you, sullen in yielding, brutal in your rage—
you'll go too far. It's perfect justice:
natures like yours are hardest on themselves.
OEDIPUS Then leave me alone—get out!
CREON I'm going.
You're wrong, so wrong. These men know I'm right.
[*Exit to the side. The* CHORUS *turns to* JOCASTA.]
CHORUS Why do you hesitate, my lady
why not help him in?
JOCASTA Tell me what's happened first.
CHORUS Loose, ignorant talk started dark suspicions
and a sense of injustice cut deeply too.
JOCASTA On both sides?
CHORUS Oh yes.
JOCASTA What did they say?
CHORUS Enough, please, enough! The land's so racked already
or so it seems to me . . .
End the trouble here, just where they left it.
OEDIPUS You see what comes of your good intentions now?

And all because you tried to blunt my anger.

CHORUS My king,
I've said it once, I'll say it time and again—
I'd be insane, you know it,
senseless, ever to turn my back on you.
You who set our beloved land—storm-tossed, shattered—
straight on course. Now again, good helmsman,
steer us through the storm!

[*The* CHORUS *draws away, leaving* OEDIPUS *and* JOCASTA *side by side.*]

JOCASTA For the love of god,
Oedipus, tell me too, what is it?
Why this rage? You're so unbending.

OEDIPUS I will tell you. I respect you, Jocasta,
much more than these . . .

[*Glancing at the* CHORUS.]

Creon's to blame, Creon schemes against me.

JOCASTA Tell me clearly, how did the quarrel start?

OEDIPUS He says *I* murdered Laius—I am guilty.

JOCASTA How does he know? Some secret knowledge
or simple hearsay?

OEDIPUS Oh, he sent his prophet in
to do his dirty work. You know Creon,
Creon keeps his own lips clean.

JOCASTA A prophet?
Well then, free yourself of every charge!
Listen to me and learn some peace of mind:
no skill in the world,
nothing human can penetrate the future.
Here is proof, quick and to the point.

An oracle came to Laius one fine day
(I won't say from Apollo himself
but his underlings, his priests) and it said
that doom would strike him down at the hands of a son,
our son, to be born of our own flesh and blood. But Laius,
so the report goes at least, was killed by strangers,
thieves, at a place where three roads meet . . . my son—
he wasn't three days old and the boy's father
fastened his ankles, had a henchman fling him away
on a barren, trackless mountain.
There, you see?
Apollo brought neither thing to pass. My baby
no more murdered his father than Laius suffered—
his wildest fear—death at his own son's hands.
That's how the seers and all their revelations
mapped out the future. Brush them from your mind.
Whatever the god needs and seeks
he'll bring to light himself, with ease.

OEDIPUS Strange,

hearing you just now . . . my mind wandered,
my thoughts racing back and forth.

JOCASTA What do you mean? Why so anxious, startled?

OEDIPUS I thought I heard you say that Laius
was cut down at a place where three roads meet.

JOCASTA That was the story. It hasn't died out yet.

OEDIPUS Where did this thing happen? Be precise.

JOCASTA A place called Phocis, where two branching roads,
one from Daulia, one from Delphi,
come together—a crossroads.

OEDIPUS When? How long ago?

JOCASTA The heralds no sooner reported Laius dead
than you appeared and they hailed you king of Thebes.

OEDIPUS My god, my god—what have you planned to do to me?

JOCASTA What, Oedipus? What haunts you so?

OEDIPUS Not yet.
Laius—how did he look? Describe him.
Had he reached his prime?

JOCASTA He was swarthy,
and the gray had just begun to streak his temples,
and his build . . . wasn't far from yours.

OEDIPUS Oh no no,
I think I've just called down a dreadful curse
upon myself—I simply didn't know!

JOCASTA What are you saying? I shudder to look at you.

OEDIPUS I have a terrible fear the blind seer can see.
I'll know in a moment. One thing more—

JOCASTA Anything,
afraid as I am—ask, I'll answer, all I can.

OEDIPUS Did he go with a light or heavy escort,
several men-at-arms, like a lord, a king?

JOCASTA There were five in the party, a herald among them,
and a single wagon carrying Laius.

OEDIPUS Ai—
now I can see it all, clear as day.
Who told you all this at the time, Jocasta?

JOCASTA A servant who reached home, the lone survivor.

OEDIPUS So, could he still be in the palace—even now?

JOCASTA No indeed. Soon as he returned from the scene
and saw you on the throne with Laius dead and gone,
he knelt and clutched my hand, pleading with me
to send him into the hinterlands, to pasture,
far as possible, out of sight of Thebes.
I sent him away. Slave though he was,
he'd earned that favor—and much more.

OEDIPUS Can we bring him back, quickly?

JOCASTA Easily. Why do you want him so?

OEDIPUS I'm afraid,
Jocasta, I have said too much already.
That man—I've got to see him.

JOCASTA Then he'll come.
But even I have a right, I'd like to think,
to know what's torturing you, my lord.
OEDIPUS And so you shall—I can hold nothing back from you,
now I've reached this pitch of dark foreboding.
Who means more to me than you? Tell me,
whom would I turn toward but you
as I go through all this?

My father was Polybus, king of Corinth.
My mother, a Dorian, Merope. And I was held
the prince of the realm among the people there,
till something struck me out of nowhere,
something strange . . . worth remarking perhaps,
hardly worth the anxiety I gave it.
Some man at a banquet who had drunk too much
shouted out—he was far gone, mind you—
that I am not my father's son. Fighting words!
I barely restrained myself that day
but early the next I went to mother and father,
questioned them closely, and they were enraged
at the accusation and the fool who let it fly.
So as for my parents I was satisfied,
but still this thing kept gnawing at me,
the slander spread—I had to make my move.
And so,
unknown to mother and father I set out for Delphi,
and the god Apollo spurned me, sent me away
denied the facts I came for,
but first he flashed before my eyes a future
great with pain, terror, disaster—I can hear him cry,
"You are fated to couple with your mother, you will bring
a breed of children into the light no man can bear to see—
you will kill your father, the one who gave you life!"
I heard all that and ran. I abandoned Corinth,
from that day on I gauged its landfall only
by the stars, running, always running
toward some place where I would never see
the shame of all those oracles come true.
And as I fled I reached that very spot
where the great king, you say, met his death.

Now, Jocasta, I will tell you all.
Making my way toward this triple crossroad
I began to see a herald, then a brace of colts
drawing a wagon, and mounted on the bench . . . a man,
just as you've described him, coming face-to-face,
and the one in the lead and the old man himself
were about to thrust me off the road—brute force—
and the one shouldering me aside, the driver,

I strike him in anger!—and the old man, watching me
coming up along his wheels—he brings down
his prod, two prongs straight at my head!
I paid him back with interest!
Short work, by god—with one blow of the staff
in this right hand I knock him out of his high seat,
roll him out of the wagon, sprawling headlong—
I killed them all—every mother's son!

Oh, but if there is any blood-tie
between Laius and this stranger . . .
what man alive more miserable than I?
More hated by the gods? *I* am the man
no alien, no citizen welcomes to his house,
law forbids it—not a word to me in public,
driven out of every hearth and home.
And all these curses I—no one but I
brought down these piling curses on myself!
And you, his wife, I've touched your body with these,
the hands that killed your husband cover you with blood.

Wasn't I born for torment? Look me in the eyes!
I am abomination—heart and soul!
I must be exiled, and even in exile
never see my parents, never set foot
on native ground again. Else I am doomed
to couple with my mother and cut my father down . . .
Polybus who reared me, gave me life.
But why, why?
Wouldn't a man of judgment say—and wouldn't he be right—
some savage power has brought this down upon my head?

Oh no, not that, you pure and awesome gods,
never let me see that day! Let me slip
from the world of men, vanish without a trace
before I see myself stained with such corruption,
stained to the heart.

LEADER My lord, you fill our hearts with fear.
But at least until you question the witness,
do take hope.

OEDIPUS Exactly. He is my last hope—
I am waiting for the shepherd. He is crucial.

JOCASTA And once he appears, what then? Why so urgent?

OEDIPUS I will tell you. If it turns out that his story
matches yours, I've escaped the worst.

JOCASTA What did I say? What struck you so?

OEDIPUS You said *thieves*—
he told you a whole band of them murdered Laius.
So, if he still holds to the same number,
I cannot be the killer. One can't equal many.

But if he refers to one man, one alone,
clearly the scales come down on me:
I am guilty.
JOCASTA Impossible. Trust me,
I told you precisely what he said,
and he can't retract it now;
the whole city heard it, not just I.
And even if he should vary his first report
by one man more or less, still, my lord,
he could never make the murder of Laius
truly fit the prophecy. Apollo was explicit:
my son was doomed to kill my husband . . . my son,
poor defenseless thing, he never had a chance
to kill his father. They destroyed him first.

So much for prophecy. It's neither here nor there.
From this day on, I wouldn't look right or left.
OEDIPUS True, true. Still, that shepherd,
someone fetch him—now!
JOCASTA I'll send at once. But do let's go inside.
I'd never displease you, least of all in this.
[OEDIPUS *and* JOCASTA *enter the palace.*]
CHORUS Destiny guide me always
Destiny find me filled with reverence
pure in word and deed.
Great laws tower above us, reared on high
born for the brilliant vault of heaven—
Olympian Sky their only father,
nothing mortal, no man gave them birth,
their memory deathless, never lost in sleep:
within them lives a mighty god, the god does not grow old.

Pride breeds the tyrant
violent pride, gorging, crammed to bursting
with all that is overripe and rich with ruin—
clawing up to the heights, headlong pride
crashes down the abyss—sheer doom!
No footing helps, all foothold lost and gone.
But the healthy strife that makes the city strong—
I pray that god will never end that wrestling:
god, my champion, I will never let you go.

But if any man comes striding, high and mighty
in all he says and does,
no fear of justice, no reverence
for the temples of the gods—
let a rough doom tear him down,
repay his pride, breakneck, ruinous pride!
If he cannot reap his profits fairly
cannot restrain himself from outrage—
mad, laying hands on the holy things untouchable!

Can such a man, so desperate, still boast
he can save his life from the flashing bolts of god?
If all such violence goes with honor now
why join the sacred dance?

Never again will I go reverent to Delphi,
the inviolate heart of Earth
or Apollo's ancient oracle at Abae
or Olympia[6] of the fires—
unless these prophecies all come true
for all mankind to point toward in wonder.
King of kings, if you deserve your titles
Zeus, remember, never forget!
You and your deathless, everlasting reign.

They are dying, the old oracles sent to Laius,
now our masters strike them off the rolls.
Nowhere Apollo's golden glory now—
the gods, the gods go down.

[*Enter* JOCASTA *from the palace, carrying a suppliant's branch wound in wool.*]

JOCASTA Lords of the realm,[7] it occurred to me,
just now, to visit the temples of the gods,
so I have my branch in hand and incense too.

Oedipus is beside himself. Racked with anguish,
no longer a man of sense, he won't admit
the latest prophecies are hollow as the old—
he's at the mercy of every passing voice
if the voice tells of terror.
I urge him gently, nothing seems to help,
so I turn to you, Apollo, you are nearest.

[*Placing her branch on the altar, while an old herdsman enters from the side, not the one just summoned by the King but an unexpected* MESSENGER *from Corinth.*]

I come with prayers and offerings . . . I beg you,
cleanse us, set us free of defilement!
Look at us, passengers in the grip of fear,
watching the pilot of the vessel go to pieces.

MESSENGER [*Approaching* JOCASTA *and the* CHORUS.]
Strangers, please, I wonder if you could lead us
to the palace of the king . . . I think it's Oedipus.
Better, the man himself—you know where he is?

LEADER This is his palace, stranger. He's inside.
But here is his queen, his wife and mother
of his children.

MESSENGER Blessings on you, noble queen,
queen of Oedipus crowned with all your family—

6. In the western Peloponnese, a site of an oracle of Zeus. Abae is a city in central Greece. 7. The chorus.

blessings on you always!
JOCASTA And the same to you, stranger, you deserve it . . .
such a greeting. But what have you come for?
Have you brought us news?
MESSENGER Wonderful news—
for the house, my lady, for your husband too.
JOCASTA Really, what? Who sent you?
MESSENGER Corinth.
I'll give you the message in a moment.
You'll be glad of it—how could you help it?—
though it costs a little sorrow in the bargain.
JOCASTA What can it be, with such a double edge?
MESSENGER The people there, they want to make your Oedipus
king of Corinth, so they're saying now.
JOCASTA Why? Isn't old Polybus still in power?
MESSENGER No more. Death has got him in the tomb.
JOCASTA What are you saying? Polybus, dead?—dead?
MESSENGER If not,
if I'm not telling the truth, strike me dead too.
JOCASTA [*To a servant.*] Quickly, go to your master, tell him this!
You prophecies of the gods, where are you now?
This is the man that Oedipus feared for years,
he fled him, not to kill him—and now he's dead,
quite by chance, a normal, natural death,
not murdered by his son.
OEDIPUS [*Emerging from the palace.*]
Dearest,
what now? Why call me from the palace?
JOCASTA [*Bringing the* MESSENGER *closer.*]
Listen to *him,* see for yourself what all
those awful prophecies of god have come to.
OEDIPUS And who is he? What can he have for me?
JOCASTA He's from Corinth, he's come to tell you
your father is no more—Polybus—he's dead!
OEDIPUS [*Wheeling on the* MESSENGER.]
What? Let me have it from your lips.
MESSENGER: Well,
if that's what you want first, then here it is:
make no mistake, Polybus is dead and gone.
OEDIPUS How—murder? sickness?—what? what killed him?
MESSENGER A light tip of the scales can put old bones to rest.
OEDIPUS Sickness then—poor man, it wore him down.
MESSENGER That,
and the long count of years he'd measured out.
OEDIPUS So!
Jocasta, why, why look to the Prophet's hearth,
the fires of the future? Why scan the birds
that scream above our heads? They winged me on
to the murder of my father, did they? That was my doom?
Well look, he's dead and buried, hidden under the earth,

and here I am in Thebes, I never put hand to sword—
unless some longing for me wasted him away,
then in a sense you'd say I caused his death.
But now, all those prophecies I feared—Polybus
packs them off to sleep with him in hell!
They're nothing, worthless.

JOCASTA There.
Didn't I tell you from the start?

OEDIPUS So you did. I was lost in fear.

JOCASTA No more, sweep it from your mind forever.

OEDIPUS But my mother's bed, surely I must fear—

JOCASTA Fear?
What should a man fear? It's all chance,
chance rules our lives. Not a man on earth
can see a day ahead, groping through the dark.
Better to live at random, best we can.
And as for this marriage with your mother—
have no fear. Many a man before you,
in his dreams, has shared his mother's bed.
Take such things for shadows, nothing at all—
Live, Oedipus,
as if there's no tomorrow!

OEDIPUS Brave words,
and you'd persuade me if mother weren't alive.
But mother lives, so for all your reassurances
I live in fear, I must.

JOCASTA But your father's death,
that, at least, is a great blessing, joy to the eyes!

OEDIPUS Great, I know . . . but I fear *her*—she's still alive.

MESSENGER Wait, who is this woman, makes you so afraid?

OEDIPUS Merope, old man. The wife of Polybus.

MESSENGER The queen? What's there to fear in her?

OEDIPUS A dreadful prophecy, stranger, sent by the gods.

MESSENGER Tell me, could you? Unless it's forbidden
other ears to hear.

OEDIPUS Not at all.
Apollo told me once—it is my fate—
I must make love with my own mother,
shed my father's blood with my own hands.
So for years I've given Corinth a wide berth,
and it's been my good fortune too. But still,
to see one's parents and look into their eyes
is the greatest joy I know.

MESSENGER You're afraid of that?
That kept you out of Corinth?

OEDIPUS My *father,* old man—
so I wouldn't kill my father.

MESSENGER So that's it.
Well then, seeing I came with such good will, my king,
why don't I rid you of that old worry now?

OEDIPUS What a rich reward you'd have for that!
MESSENGER What do you think I came for, majesty?
So you'd come home and I'd be better off.
OEDIPUS Never, I will never go near my parents.
MESSENGER My boy, it's clear, you don't know what you're doing.
OEDIPUS What do you mean, old man? For god's sake, explain.
MESSENGER If you ran from *them,* always dodging home . . .
OEDIPUS Always, terrified Apollo's oracle might come true—
MESSENGER And you'd be covered with guilt, from both your parents.
OEDIPUS That's right, old man, that fear is always with me.
MESSENGER Don't you know? You've really nothing to fear.
OEDIPUS But why? If I'm their son—Merope, Polybus?
MESSENGER Polybus was nothing to you, that's why, not in blood.
OEDIPUS What are you saying—Polybus was not my father?
MESSENGER No more than I am. He and I are equals.
OEDIPUS My father—
how can my father equal nothing? You're nothing to me!
MESSENGER Neither was he, no more your father than I am.
OEDIPUS Then why did he call me his son?
MESSENGER You were a gift,
years ago—know for a fact he took you
from my hands.
OEDIPUS No, from another's hands?
Then how could he love me so? He loved me, deeply . . .
MESSENGER True, and his early years without a child
made him love you all the more.
OEDIPUS And you, did you . . .
buy me? find me by accident?
MESSENGER I stumbled on you,
down the woody flanks of Mount Cithaeron.
OEDIPUS So close,
what were you doing here, just passing through?
MESSENGER Watching over my flocks, grazing them on the slopes.
OEDIPUS A herdsman, were you? A vagabond, scraping for wages?
MESSENGER Your savior too, my son, in your worst hour.
OEDIPUS Oh—
when you picked me up, was I in pain? What exactly?
MESSENGER Your ankles . . . they tell the story. Look at them.
OEDIPUS Why remind me of that, that old affliction?
MESSENGER Your ankles were pinned together. I set you free.
OEDIPUS That dreadful mark—I've had it from the cradle.
MESSENGER And you got your name[8] from that misfortune too,
the name's still with you.
OEDIPUS Dear god, who did it?—
mother? father? Tell me.
MESSENGER I don't know.
The one who gave you to me, he'd know more.
OEDIPUS What? You took me from someone else?

8. In Greek the name *Oidipous* suggests "swollen foot."

You didn't find me yourself?
MESSENGER No sir,
another shepherd passed you on to me.
OEDIPUS Who? Do you know? Describe him.
MESSENGER He called himself a servant of . . .
if I remember rightly—Laius.
[JOCASTA *turns sharply.*]
OEDIPUS The king of the land who ruled here long ago?
MESSENGER That's the one. That herdsman was *his* man.
OEDIPUS Is he still alive? Can I see him?
MESSENGER They'd know best, the people of these parts.
[OEDIPUS *and the* MESSENGER *turn to the* CHORUS.]
OEDIPUS Does anyone know that herdsman,
the one he mentioned? Anyone seen him
in the fields, in the city? Out with it!
The time has come to reveal this once for all.
LEADER I think he's the very shepherd you wanted to see,
a moment ago. But the queen, Jocasta,
she's the one to say.
OEDIPUS Jocasta,
you remember the man we just sent for?
Is *that* the one he means?
JOCASTA That man . . .
why ask? Old shepherd, talk, empty nonsense,
don't give it another thought, don't even think—
OEDIPUS What—give up now, with a clue like this?
Fail to solve the mystery of my birth?
Not for all the world!
JOCASTA Stop—in the name of god,
if you love your own life, call off this search!
My suffering is enough.
OEDIPUS Courage!
Even if my mother turns out to be a slave,
and I a slave, three generations back,
you would not seem common.
JOCASTA Oh no,
listen to me, I beg you, don't do this.
OEDIPUS Listen to you? No more. I must know it all,
must see the truth at last.
JOCASTA No, please—
for your sake—I want the best for you!
OEDIPUS Your best is more than I can bear.
JOCASTA You're doomed—
may you never fathom who you are!
OEDIPUS [*To a servant.*] Hurry, fetch me the herdsman, now!
Leave her to glory in her royal birth.
JOCASTA Aieeeeee—
man of agony—
that is the only name I have for you,
that, no other—ever, ever, ever!

[*Flinging through the palace doors. A long, tense silence follows.*]

LEADER Where's she gone, Oedipus?
Rushing off, such wild grief . . .
I'm afraid that from this silence
something monstrous may come bursting forth.

OEDIPUS Let it burst! Whatever will, whatever must!
I must know my birth, no matter how common
it may be—I must see my origins face-to-face.
She perhaps, she with her woman's pride
may well be mortified by my birth,
but I, I count myself the son of Chance,
the great goddess, giver of all good things—
I'll never see myself disgraced. She is my mother!
And the moons have marked me out, my blood-brothers,
one moon on the wane, the next moon great with power.
That is my blood, my nature—I will never betray it,
never fail to search and learn my birth!

CHORUS Yes—if I am a true prophet
if I can grasp the truth,
by the boundless skies of Olympus,
at the full moon of tomorrow, Mount Cithaeron
you will know how Oedipus glories in you—
you, his birthplace, nurse, his mountain-mother!
And we will sing you, dancing out your praise—
you lift our monarch's heart!
Apollo, Apollo, god of the wild cry
may our dancing please you!
Oedipus—
son, dear child, who bore you?
Who of the nymphs who seem to live forever[9]
mated with Pan,[1] the mountain-striding Father?
Who was your mother? who, some bride of Apollo
the god who loves the pastures spreading toward the sun?
Or was it Hermes, king of the lightning ridges?
Or Dionysus,[2] lord of frenzy, lord of the barren peaks—
did he seize you in his hands, dearest of all his lucky finds?—
found by the nymphs, their warm eyes dancing, gift
to the lord who loves them dancing out his joy!

[OEDIPUS *strains to see a figure coming from the distance. Attended by palace guards, an old* SHEPHERD *enters slowly, reluctant to approach the king.*]

OEDIPUS I never met the man, my friends . . . still,
if I had to guess, I'd say that's the shepherd,
the very one we've looked for all along.
Brothers in old age, two of a kind,
he and our guest here. At any rate
the ones who bring him in are my own men,

9. Nymphs were not immortal, like the gods, but lived much longer than mortals. 1. A woodland god, patron of shepherds and flocks. 2. Dionysus, like Pan and Hermes, haunted the wild country, woods, and mountains. Hermes was born on Mount Kyllene in Arcadia.

I recognize them.
[*Turning to the* LEADER.]
But you know more than I,
you should, you've seen the man before.

LEADER I know him, definitely. One of Laius' men,
a trusty shepherd, if there ever was one.

OEDIPUS You, I ask you first, stranger,
you from Corinth—is this the one you mean?

MESSENGER You're looking at him. He's your man.

OEDIPUS [*To the* SHEPHERD.]
You, old man, come over here—
look at me. Answer all my questions.
Did you ever serve King Laius?

SHEPHERD So I did . . .
a slave, not bought on the block though,
born and reared in the palace.

OEDIPUS Your duties, your kind of work?

SHEPHERD Herding the flocks, the better part of my life.

OEDIPUS Where, mostly? Where did you do your grazing?

SHEPHERD Well,
Cithaeron sometimes, or the foothills round about.

OEDIPUS This man—you know him? ever see him there?

SHEPHERD [*Confused, glancing from the* MESSENGER *to the King.*]
Doing what?—what man do you mean?

OEDIPUS [*Pointing to the* MESSENGER.]
This one here—ever have dealings with him?

SHEPHERD Not so I could say, but give me a chance,
my memory's bad . . .

MESSENGER No wonder he doesn't know me, master.
But let me refresh his memory for him.
I'm sure he recalls old times we had
on the slopes of Mount Cithaeron;
he and I, grazing our flocks, he with two
and I with one—we both struck up together,
three whole seasons, six months at a stretch
from spring to the rising of Arcturus[3] in the fall,
then with winter coming on I'd drive my herds
to my own pens, and back he'd go with his
to Laius' folds.
[*To the* SHEPHERD.]
Now that's how it was,
wasn't it—yes or no?

SHEPHERD Yes, I suppose . . .
it's all so long ago.

MESSENGER Come, tell me,
you gave me a child back then, a boy, remember?
A little fellow to rear, my very own.

3. The principal star in the constellation Boötes; its appearance in the sky *(rising)* just before dawn in September signals the end of summer.

SHEPHERD What? Why rake up that again?
MESSENGER Look, here he is, my fine old friend—
the same man who was just a baby then.
SHEPHERD Damn you, shut your mouth—quiet!
OEDIPUS Don't lash out at him, old man—
you need lashing more than he does.
SHEPHERD Why,
master, majesty—what have I done wrong?
OEDIPUS You won't answer his question about the boy.
SHEPHERD He's talking nonsense, wasting his breath.
OEDIPUS So, you won't talk willingly—
then you'll talk with pain.
[*The guards seize the* SHEPHERD.]
SHEPHERD No, dear god, don't torture an old man!
OEDIPUS Twist his arms back, quickly!
SHEPHERD God help us, why?—
what more do you need to know?
OEDIPUS Did you give him that child? He's asking.
SHEPHERD I did . . . I wish to god I'd died that day.
OEDIPUS You've got your wish if you don't tell the truth.
SHEPHERD The more I tell, the worse the death I'll die.
OEDIPUS Our friend here wants to stretch things out, does he?
[*Motioning to his men for torture.*]
SHEPHERD No, no, I gave it to him—I just said so.
OEDIPUS Where did you get it? Your house? Someone else's?
SHEPHERD It wasn't mine, no, I got it from . . . someone.
OEDIPUS Which one of them?
[*Looking at the citizens.*]
Whose house?
SHEPHERD No—
god's sake, master, no more questions!
OEDIPUS You're a dead man if I have to ask again.
SHEPHERD Then—the child came from the house . . . of Laius.
OEDIPUS A slave? or born of his own blood?
SHEPHERD Oh no,
I'm right at the edge, the horrible truth—I've got to say it!
OEDIPUS And I'm at the edge of hearing horrors, yes, but I must hear!
SHEPHERD All right! His son, they said it was—his son!
But the one inside, your wife,
she'd tell it best.
OEDIPUS My wife—
she gave it to you?
SHEPHERD Yes, yes, my king.
OEDIPUS Why, what for?
SHEPHERD To kill it.
OEDIPUS Her own child,
how could she?
SHEPHERD She was afraid—

frightening prophecies.
OEDIPUS What?
SHEPHERD They said—
he'd kill his parents.
OEDIPUS But you gave him to this old man—why?
SHEPHERD I pitied the little baby, master,
hoped he'd take him off to his own country,
far away, but he saved him for this, this fate.
If you are the man he says you are, believe me,
you were born for pain.
OEDIPUS O god—
all come true, all burst to light!
O light—now let me look my last on you!
I stand revealed at last—
cursed in my birth, cursed in marriage,
cursed in the lives I cut down with these hands!
[*Rushing through the doors with a great cry. The Corinthian* MESSENGER, *the* SHEPHERD *and attendants exit slowly to the side.*]
CHORUS O the generations of men
the dying generations—adding the total
of all your lives I find they come to nothing . . .
does there exist, is there a man on earth
who seizes more joy than just a dream, a vision?
And the vision no sooner dawns than dies
blazing into oblivion.
You are my great example, you, your life
your destiny, Oedipus, man of misery—
I count no man blest.

You outranged all men!
Bending your bow to the breaking-point
you captured priceless glory, O dear god,
and the Sphinx came crashing down,
the virgin, claws hooked
like a bird of omen singing, shrieking death—
like a fortress reared in the face of death
you rose and saved our land.

From that day on we called you king
we crowned you with honors, Oedipus, towering over all—
mighty king of the seven gates of Thebes.

But now to hear your story—is there a man more agonized?
More wed to pain and frenzy? Not a man on earth,
the joy of your life ground down to nothing
O Oedipus, name for the ages—
one and the same wide harbor served you
son and father both
son and father came to rest in the same bridal chamber.

How, how could the furrows your father plowed
bear you, your agony, harrowing on
in silence O so long?

But now for all your power
Time, all-seeing Time has dragged you to the light,
judged your marriage monstrous from the start—
the son and the father tangling, both one—
O child of Laius, would to god
I'd never seen you, never never!
Now I weep like a man who wails the dead
and the dirge comes pouring forth with all my heart!
I tell you the truth, you gave me life
my breath leapt up in you
and now you bring down night upon my eyes.

[*Enter a* MESSENGER *from the palace.*]

MESSENGER: Men of Thebes, always first in honor,
what horrors you will hear, what you will see,
what a heavy weight of sorrow you will shoulder . . .
if you are true to your birth, if you still have
some feeling for the royal house of Thebes.
I tell you neither the waters of the Danube
nor the Nile[4] can wash this palace clean.
Such things it hides, it soon will bring to light—
terrible things, and none done blindly now,
all done with a will. The pains
we inflict upon ourselves hurt most of all.

LEADER God knows we have pains enough already.
What can you add to them?

MESSENGER The queen is dead.

LEADER Poor lady—how?

MESSENGER By her own hand. But you are spared the worst,
you never had to watch . . . I saw it all,
and with all the memory that's in me
you will learn what that poor woman suffered.

Once she'd broken in through the gates,
dashing past us, frantic, whipped to fury,
ripping her hair out with both hands—
straight to her rooms she rushed, flinging herself
across the bridal-bed, doors slamming behind her—
once inside, she wailed for Laius, dead so long,
remembering how she bore his child long ago,
the life that rose up to destroy him, leaving
its mother to mother living creatures
with the very son she'd borne.
Oh how she wept, mourning the marriage-bed

4. The Greek reads "Phasis," a river in Asia Minor. The translator has substituted a big river more familiar to modern readers.

where she let loose that double brood—monsters—
husband by her husband, children by her child.
And then—
but how she died is more than I can say. Suddenly
Oedipus burst in, screaming, he stunned us so
we couldn't watch her agony to the end,
our eyes were fixed on him. Circling
like a maddened beast, stalking, here, there,
crying out to us—
Give him a sword![5] His wife,
no wife, his mother, where can he find the mother earth
that cropped two crops at once, himself and all his children?
He was raging—one of the dark powers pointing the way,
none of us mortals crowding around him, no,
with a great shattering cry—someone, something leading him on—
he hurled at the twin doors and bending the bolts back
out of their sockets, crashed through the chamber.
And there we saw the woman hanging by the neck,
cradled high in a woven noose, spinning,
swinging back and forth. And when he saw her,
giving a low, wrenching sob that broke our hearts,
slipping the halter from her throat, he eased her down,
in a slow embrace he laid her down, poor thing . . .
then, what came next, what horror we beheld!

He rips off her brooches, the long gold pins
holding her robes—and lifting them high,
looking straight up into the points,
he digs them down the sockets of his eyes, crying, "You,
you'll see no more the pain I suffered, all the pain I caused!
Too long you looked on the ones you never should have seen,
blind to the ones you longed to see, to know! Blind
from this hour on! Blind in the darkness—blind!"
His voice like a dirge, rising, over and over
raising the pins, raking them down his eyes.
And at each stroke blood spurts from the roots,
splashing his beard, a swirl of it, nerves and clots—
black hail of blood pulsing, gushing down.

These are the griefs that burst upon them both,
coupling man and woman. The joy they had so lately,
the fortune of their old ancestral house
was deep joy indeed. Now, in this one day,
wailing, madness and doom, death, disgrace
all the griefs in the world that you can name,
all are theirs forever.

LEADER Oh poor man, the misery—
has he any rest from pain now?

5. Presumably so that he could kill himself.

[*A voice within, in torment.*]

MESSENGER He's shouting,
"Loose the bolts, someone, show me to all of Thebes!
My father's murderer, my mother's—"
No, I can't repeat it, it's unholy.
Now he'll tear himself from his native earth,
not linger, curse the house with his own curse.
But he needs strength, and a guide to lead him on.
This is sickness more than he can bear.

[*The palace doors open.*]

Look,
he'll show you himself. The great doors are opening—
you are about to see a sight, a horror
even his mortal enemy would pity.

[*Enter* OEDIPUS, *blinded, led by a boy. He stands at the palace steps, as if surveying his people once again.*]

CHORUS O the terror—
the suffering, for all the world to see,
the worst terror that ever met my eyes.
What madness swept over you? What god,
what dark power leapt beyond all bounds,
beyond belief, to crush your wretched life?—
godforsaken, cursed by the gods!
I pity you but I can't bear to look.
I've much to ask, so much to learn,
so much fascinates my eyes,
but you . . . I shudder at the sight.

OEDIPUS Oh, Ohh—
the agony! I am agony—
where am I going? where on earth?
where does all this agony hurl me?
where's my voice?—
winging, swept away on a dark tide—
My destiny, my dark power, what a leap you made!

CHORUS To the depths of terror, too dark to hear, to see.

OEDIPUS Dark, horror of darkness
my darkness, drowning, swirling around me
crashing wave on wave—unspeakable, irresistible
headwind, fatal harbor! Oh again,
the misery, all at once, over and over
the stabbing daggers, stab of memory
raking me insane.

CHORUS No wonder you suffer
twice over, the pain of your wounds,
the lasting grief of pain.

OEDIPUS Dear friend, still here?
Standing by me, still with a care for me,
the blind man? Such compassion,
loyal to the last. Oh it's you,
I know you're here, dark as it is

I'd know you anywhere, your voice—
it's yours, clearly yours.
CHORUS Dreadful, what you've done . . .
how could you bear it, gouging out your eyes?
What superhuman power drove you on?
OEDIPUS Apollo, friends, Apollo—
he ordained my agonies—these, my pains on pains!
But the hand that struck my eyes was mine,
mine alone—no one else—
I did it all myself!
What good were eyes to me?
Nothing I could see could bring me joy.
CHORUS No, no, exactly as you say.
OEDIPUS What can I ever see?
What love, what call of the heart
can touch my ears with joy? Nothing, friends.
Take me away, far, far from Thebes,
quickly, cast me away, my friends—
this great murderous ruin, this man cursed to heaven,
the man the deathless gods hate most of all!
CHORUS Pitiful, you suffer so, you understand so much . . .
I wish you'd never known.
OEDIPUS Die, die—
whoever he was that day in the wilds
who cut my ankles free of the ruthless pins,
he pulled me clear of death, he saved my life
for this, this kindness—
Curse him, kill him!
If I'd died then, I'd never have dragged myself,
my loved ones through such hell.
CHORUS Oh if only . . . would to god.
OEDIPUS I'd never have come to this,
my father's murderer—never been branded
mother's husband, all men see me now! Now,
loathed by the gods, son of the mother I defiled
coupling in my father's bed, spawning lives in the loins
that spawned my wretched life. What grief can crown this grief?
It's mine alone, my destiny—I am Oedipus!
CHORUS How can I say you've chosen for the best?
Better to die than be alive and blind.
OEDIPUS What I did was best—don't lecture me,
no more advice. I, with *my* eyes,
how could I look my father in the eyes
when I go down to death? Or mother, so abused . . .
I have done such things to the two of them,
crimes too huge for hanging.
Worse yet,
the sight of my children, born as they were born,
how could I long to look into their eyes?
No, not with these eyes of mine, never.

Not this city either, her high towers,
the sacred glittering images of her gods—
I am misery! I, her best son, reared
as no other son of Thebes was ever reared,
I've stripped myself, I gave the command myself.
All men must cast away the great blasphemer,
the curse now brought to light by the gods,
the son of Laius—I, my father's son!

Now I've exposed my guilt, horrendous guilt,
could I train a level glance on you, my countrymen?
Impossible! No, if I could just block off my ears,
the springs of hearing, I would stop at nothing—
I'd wall up my loathsome body like a prison,
blind to the sound of life, not just the sight.
Oblivion—what a blessing . . .
for the mind to dwell a world away from pain.

O Cithaeron, why did you give me shelter?
Why didn't you take me, crush my life out on the spot?
I'd never have revealed my birth to all mankind.

O Polybus, Corinth, the old house of my fathers,
so I believed—what a handsome prince you raised—
under the skin, what sickness to the core.
Look at me! Born of outrage, outrage to the core.
O triple roads—it all comes back, the secret,
dark ravine, and the oaks closing in
where the three roads join . . .
You drank my father's blood, my own blood
spilled by my own hands—you still remember me?
What things you saw me do? Then I came here
and did them all once more!
                    Marriages! O marriage,
you gave me birth, and once you brought me into the world
you brought my sperm rising back, springing to light
fathers, brothers, sons—one murderous breed—
brides, wives, mothers. The blackest things
a man can do, I have done them all!
                    No more—
it's wrong to name what's wrong to do. Quickly,
for the love of god, hide me somewhere,
kill me, hurl me into the sea
where you can never look on me again.

[*Beckoning to the* CHORUS *as they shrink away.*]

                    Closer,
it's all right. Touch the man of grief.
Do. Don't be afraid. My troubles are mine
and I am the only man alive who can sustain them.

[*Enter* CREON *from the palace, attended by palace guards.*]

LEADER   Put your requests to Creon. Here he is,

just when we need him. He'll have a plan, he'll act.
Now that he's the sole defense of the country
in your place.

OEDIPUS Oh no, what can I say to him?
How can I ever hope to win his trust?
I wronged him so, just now, in every way.
You must see that—I was so wrong, so wrong.

CREON I haven't come to mock you, Oedipus,
or to criticize your former failings.
[*Turning to the guards.*]
You there,
have you lost all respect for human feelings?
At least revere the Sun, the holy fire
that keeps us all alive. Never expose a thing
of guilt and holy dread so great it appalls
the earth, the rain from heaven, the light of day!
Get him into the halls—quickly as you can.
Piety demands no less. Kindred alone
should see a kinsman's shame. This is obscene.

OEDIPUS Please, in god's name . . . you wipe my fears away,
coming so generously to me, the worst of men.
Do one thing more, for your sake, not mine.

CREON What do you want? Why so insistent?

OEDIPUS Drive me out of the land at once, far from sight,
where I can never hear a human voice.

CREON I'd have done that already, I promise you.
First I wanted the god to clarify my duties.

OEDIPUS The god? His command was clear, every word:
death for the father-killer, the curse—
he said destroy me!

CREON So he did. Still, in such a crisis
it's better to ask precisely what to do.

OEDIPUS So miserable—
you'd consult the god about a man like me?

CREON By all means. And this time, I assume,
even you will obey the god's decrees.

OEDIPUS I will,
I will. And you, I command you—I beg you . . .
the woman inside, bury her as you see fit.
It's the only decent thing,
to give your own the last rites. As for me,
never condemn the city of my fathers
to house my body, not while I'm alive, no,
let me live on the mountains, on Cithaeron,
my favorite haunt, I have made it famous.
Mother and father marked out that rock
to be my everlasting tomb—buried alive.
Let me die there, where they tried to kill me.

Oh but this I know: no sickness can destroy me,
nothing can. I would never have been saved

from death—I have been saved
for something great and terrible, something strange.
Well let my destiny come and take me on its way!
About my children, Creon, the boys at least,
don't burden yourself. They're men,
wherever they go, they'll find the means to live.
But my two daughters, my poor helpless girls,
clustering at our table, never without me
hovering near them . . . whatever I touched,
they always had their share. Take care of them,
I beg you. Wait, better—permit me, would you?
Just to touch them with my hands and take
our fill of tears. Please . . . my king.
Grant it, with all your noble heart.
If I could hold them, just once, I'd think
I had them with me, like the early days
when I could see their eyes.

[ANTIGONE *and* ISMENE, *two small children, are led in from the palace by a nurse.*]

What's that
O god! Do I really hear you sobbing?—
my two children. Creon, you've pitied me?
Sent me my darling girls, my own flesh and blood!
Am I right?

CREON Yes, it's my doing.
I know the joy they gave you all these years,
the joy you must feel now.

OEDIPUS Bless you, Creon!
May god watch over you for this kindness,
better than he ever guarded me.
Children, where are you?
Here, come quickly—

[*Groping for* ANTIGONE *and* ISMENE, *who approach their father cautiously, then embrace him.*]

Come to these hands of mine,
your brother's hands, your own father's hands
that served his once bright eyes so well—
that made them blind. Seeing nothing, children,
knowing nothing, I became your father,
I fathered you in the soil that gave me life.

How I weep for you—I cannot see you now . . .
just thinking of all your days to come, the bitterness,
the life that rough mankind will thrust upon you.
Where are the public gatherings you can join,
the banquets of the clans? Home you'll come,
in tears, cut off from the sight of it all,
the brilliant rites unfinished.
And when you reach perfection, ripe for marriage,
who will he be, my dear ones? Risking all

to shoulder the curse that weighs down my parents,
yes and you too—that wounds us all together.
What more misery could you want?
Your father killed his father, sowed his mother,
one, one and the selfsame womb sprang you—
he cropped the very roots of his existence.

Such disgrace, and you must bear it all!
Who will marry you then? Not a man on earth.
Your doom is clear: you'll wither away to nothing,
single, without a child.

[*Turning to* CREON.]

Oh Creon,
you are the only father they have now . . .
we who brought them into the world
are gone, both gone at a stroke—
Don't let them go begging, abandoned,
men without men. Your own flesh and blood!
Never bring them down to the level of my pains.
Pity them. Look at them, so young, so vulnerable,
shorn of everything—you're their only hope.
Promise me, noble Creon, touch my hand!

[*Reaching toward* CREON, *who draws back.*]

You, little ones, if you were old enough
to understand, there is much I'd tell you.
Now, as it is, I'd have you say a prayer.
Pray for life, my children,
live where you are free to grow and season.
Pray god you find a better life than mine,
the father who begot you.

CREON Enough.
You've wept enough. Into the palace now.

OEDIPUS I must, but I find it very hard.

CREON Time is the great healer, you will see.

OEDIPUS I am going—you know on what condition?

CREON Tell me. I'm listening.

OEDIPUS Drive me out of Thebes, in exile.

CREON Not I. Only the gods can give you that.

OEDIPUS Surely the gods hate me so much—

CREON You'll get your wish at once.

OEDIPUS You consent?

CREON I try to say what I mean; it's my habit.

OEDIPUS Then take me away. It's time.

CREON Come along, let go of the children.

OEDIPUS No—
don't take them away from me, not now! No no no!

[*Clutching his daughters as the guards wrench them loose and take them through the palace doors.*]

CREON Still the king, the master of all things?
No more: here your power ends.

None of your power follows you through life.
[*Exit* OEDIPUS *and* CREON *to the palace. The* CHORUS *comes forward to address the audience directly.*]

CHORUS People of Thebes, my countrymen, look on Oedipus.
He solved the famous riddle with his brilliance,
he rose to power, a man beyond all power.
Who could behold his greatness without envy?
Now what a black sea of terror has overwhelmed him.
Now as we keep our watch and wait the final day,
count no man happy till he dies, free of pain at last.
[*Exit in procession.*]

Antigone[1]

CHARACTERS

ANTIGONE, *daughter of Oedipus and Jocasta*
ISMENE, *sister of Antigone*
A CHORUS, *of old Theban citizens and their* LEADER
CREON, *king of Thebes, uncle of Antigone and Ismene*
A SENTRY
HAEMON, *son of Creon and Eurydice*
TIRESIAS, *a blind prophet*
A MESSENGER
EURYDICE, *wife of Creon*
Guards, attendants, and a boy

[TIME AND SCENE: *The royal house of Thebes. It is still night, and the invading armies of Argos have just been driven from the city. Fighting on opposite sides, the sons of Oedipus, Eteocles and Polynices, have killed each other in combat. Their uncle,* CREON, *is now king of Thebes.*

Enter ANTIGONE, *slipping through the central doors of the palace. She motions to her sister,* ISMENE, *who follows her cautiously toward an altar at the center of the stage.*]

ANTIGONE: My own flesh and blood—dear sister, dear Ismene,
how many griefs our father Oedipus handed down!
Do you know one, I ask you, one grief
that Zeus will not perfect for the two of us
while we still live and breathe? There's nothing,
no pain—our lives are pain—no private shame,
no public disgrace, nothing I haven't seen
in your griefs and mine. And now this:
an emergency decree, they say, the Commander[2]
has just now declared for all of Thebes.
What, haven't you heard? Don't you see?
The doom reserved for enemies
marches on the ones we love the most.

ISMENE: Not I, I haven't heard a word, Antigone.

1. Translated by Robert Fagles. 2. Creon. In the original he is given a military title; Antigone will not refer to him as king.

Nothing of loved ones,
no joy or pain has come my way, not since
the two of us were robbed of our two brothers,
both gone in a day, a double blow—
not since the armies of Argos vanished,
just this very night. I know nothing more,
whether our luck's improved or ruin's still to come.
ANTIGONE: I thought so. That's why I brought you out here,
past the gates, so you could hear in private.
ISMENE: What's the matter? Trouble, clearly . . .
you sound so dark, so grim.
ANTIGONE: Why not? Our own brothers' burial!
Hasn't Creon graced one with all the rites,
disgraced the other? Eteocles, they say,
has been given full military honors,
rightly so—Creon has laid him in the earth
and he goes with glory down among the dead.
But the body of Polynices, who died miserably—
why, a city-wide proclamation, rumor has it,
forbids anyone to bury him, even mourn him.
He's to be left unwept, unburied, a lovely treasure
for birds that scan the field and feast to their heart's content.

Such, I hear, is the martial law our good Creon
lays down for you and me—yes, me, I tell you—
and he's coming here to alert the uninformed
in no uncertain terms,
and he won't treat the matter lightly. Whoever
disobeys in the least will die, his doom is sealed:
stoning to death inside the city walls!

There you have it. You'll soon show what you are,
worth your breeding, Ismene, or a coward—
for all your royal blood.
ISMENE: My poor sister, if things have come to this,
who am I to make or mend them, tell me,
what good am I to you?
ANTIGONE: Decide.
Will you share the labor, share the work?
ISMENE: What work, what's the risk? What do you mean?
ANTIGONE: [*Raising her hands.*]
Will you lift up his body with these bare hands
and lower it with me?
ISMENE: What? You'd bury him—
when a law forbids the city?
ANTIGONE: Yes!
He is my brother and—deny it as you will—
your brother too.
No one will ever convict me for a traitor.
ISMENE: So desperate, and Creon has expressly—
ANTIGONE: No,

he has no right to keep me from my own.
ISMENE: Oh my sister, think—
think how our own father died, hated,[3]
his reputation in ruins, driven on
by the crimes he brought to light himself
to gouge out his eyes with his own hands—
then mother . . . his mother and wife, both in one,
mutilating her life in the twisted noose—
and last, our two brothers dead in a single day,
both shedding their own blood, poor suffering boys,
battling out their common destiny hand-to-hand.

Now look at the two of us left so alone . . .
think what a death we'll die, the worst of all
if we violate the laws and override
the fixed decree of the throne, its power—
we must be sensible. Remember we are women,
we're not born to contend with men. Then too,
we're underlings, ruled by much stronger hands,
so we must submit in this, and things still worse.

I, for one, I'll beg the dead to forgive me—
I'm forced, I have no choice—I must obey
the ones who stand in power. Why rush to extremes?
It's madness, madness.
ANTIGONE: I won't insist,
no, even if you should have a change of heart,
I'd never welcome you in the labor, not with me.
So, do as you like, whatever suits you best—
I will bury him myself.
And even if I die in the act, that death will be a glory.
I will lie with the one I love and loved by him—
an outrage sacred to the gods! I have longer
to please the dead than please the living here:
in the kingdom down below I'll lie forever.
Do as you like, dishonor the laws
the gods hold in honor.
ISMENE: I'd do them no dishonor . . .
but defy the city? I have no strength for that.
ANTIGONE: You have your excuses. I am on my way,
I'll raise a mound for him, for my dear brother.
ISMENE: Oh Antigone, you're so rash—I'm so afraid for you!
ANTIGONE: Don't fear for me. Set your own life in order.
ISMENE: Then don't, at least, blurt this out to anyone.
Keep it a secret. I'll join you in that, I promise.
ANTIGONE: Dear god, shout it from the rooftops. I'll hate you
all the more for silence—tell the world!

3. This play was written before *Oedipus the King* and *Oedipus at Colonus,* which give us a different picture of Oedipus's end.

ISMENE: So fiery—and it ought to chill your heart.
ANTIGONE: I know I please where I must please the most.
ISMENE: Yes, if you can, but you're in love with impossibility.
ANTIGONE: Very well then, once my strength gives out
I will be done at last.
ISMENE: You're wrong from the start,
you're off on a hopeless quest.
ANTIGONE: If you say so you will make me hate you,
and the hatred of the dead, by all rights,
will haunt you night and day.
But leave me to my own absurdity, leave me
to suffer this—dreadful thing. I will suffer
nothing as great as death without glory.
[*Exit to the side.*]
ISMENE: Then go if you must, but rest assured,
wild, irrational as you are, my sister,
you are truly dear to the ones who love you.
[*Withdrawing to the palace. Enter a* CHORUS,[4] *the old citizens of Thebes chanting as the sun begins to rise.*]
CHORUS: Glory!—great beam of the sun, brightest of all
that ever rose on the seven gates of Thebes,
you burn through night at last!
Great eye of the golden day,
mounting the Dirce's[5] banks you throw him back—
the enemy out of Argos, the white shield,[6] the man of bronze—
he's flying headlong now
the bridle of fate stampeding him with pain!

And he had driven against our borders,
launched by the warring claims of Polynices—
like an eagle screaming, winging havoc
over the land, wings of armor
shielded white as snow,
a huge army massing,
crested helmets bristling for assault.

He hovered above our roofs, his vast maw gaping
closing down around our seven gates,
his spears thirsting for the kill
but now he's gone, look,
before he could glut his jaws with Theban blood
or the god of fire put our crown of towers to the torch.
He grappled the Dragon[7] none can master—Thebes—
the clang of our arms like thunder at his back!

Zeus hates with a vengeance all bravado,
the mighty boasts of men. He watched them
coming on in a rising flood, the pride

4. The chorus of old men celebrates the victory won over the Argive forces and Polynices. 5. A river of the Theban plain. 6. The Argive soldiers' shields were painted white. 7. According to legend the Thebans sprang from the dragon's teeth sown by Cadmus.

of their golden armor ringing shrill—
and brandishing his lightning
blasted the fighter[8] just at the goal,
rushing to shout his triumph from our walls.

Down from the heights he crashed, pounding down on the earth!
And a moment ago, blazing torch in hand—
mad for attack, ecstatic
he breathed his rage, the storm
of his fury hurling at our heads!
But now his high hopes have laid him low
and down the enemy ranks the iron god of war
deals his rewards, his stunning blows—Ares[9]
rapture of battle, our right arm in the crisis.

Seven captains marshaled at seven gates
seven against their equals, gave
their brazen trophies[1] up to Zeus
god of the breaking rout of battle,
all but two: those blood brothers,
one father, one mother—matched in rage,
spears matched for the twin conquest—
clashed and won the common prize of death.

But now for Victory! glorious in the morning,
joy in her eyes to meet our joy
she is winging[2] down to Thebes,
our fleets of chariots wheeling in her wake—
Now let us win oblivion from the wars,
thronging the temples of the gods
in singing, dancing choirs through the night!
Lord Dionysus,[3] god of the dance
that shakes the land of Thebes, now lead the way!
[*Enter* CREON *from the palace, attended by his guard.*]

But look, the king of the realm is coming,
Creon, the new man for the new day,
whatever the gods are sending now . . .
what new plan will he launch?
Why this, this special session?
Why this sudden call to the old men
summoned at one command?

CREON: My countrymen,
the ship of state is safe. The gods who rocked her,
after a long, merciless pounding in the storm,
have righted her once more.
Out of the whole city

8. Capaneus, the most violent of the Seven against Thebes. He had almost scaled the wall when the lightning of Zeus threw him down. 9. Not only the god of war but also one of the patron deities of Thebes. 1. The victors in Greek battle set up a trophy consisting of the armor of one of the enemy dead, fixed to a post and set up at the place where the enemy turned to run away. 2. Victory is portrayed in Greek painting and sculpture as a winged young woman. 3. A god of revel; his father was Zeus, and his mother, Semele, was a Theban princess.

I have called you here alone. Well I know,
first, your undeviating respect
for the throne and royal power of King Laius.
Next, while Oedipus steered the land of Thebes,
and even after he died, your loyalty was unshakable,
you still stood by their children. Now then,
since the two sons are dead—two blows of fate
in the same day, cut down by each other's hands,
both killers, both brothers stained with blood—
as I am next in kin to the dead,
I now possess the throne and all its powers.

Of course you cannot know a man completely,
his character, his principles, sense of judgment,
not till he's shown his colors, ruling the people,
making laws. Experience, there's the test.
As I see it, whoever assumes the task,
the awesome task of setting the city's course,
and refuses to adopt the soundest policies
but fearing someone, keeps his lips locked tight,
he's utterly worthless. So I rate him now,
I always have. And whoever places a friend
above the good of his own country, he is nothing:
I have no use for him. Zeus my witness,
Zeus who sees all things, always—
I could never stand by silent, watching destruction
march against our city, putting safety to rout,
nor could I ever make that man a friend of mine
who menaces our country. Remember this:
our country *is* our safety.
Only while she voyages true on course
can we establish friendships, truer than blood itself.
Such are my standards. They make our city great.

Closely akin to them I have proclaimed,
just now, the following decree to our people
concerning the two sons of Oedipus.
Eteocles, who died fighting for Thebes,
excelling all in arm: he shall be buried,
crowned with a hero's honors, the cups we pour[4]
to soak the earth and reach the famous dead.

But as for his blood brother, Polynices,
who returned from exile, home to his father-city
and the gods of his race, consumed with one desire—
to burn them roof to roots—who thirsted to drink
his kinsmen's blood and sell the rest to slavery:
that man—a proclamation has forbidden the city
to dignify him with burial, mourn him at all.

4. Libations (liquid offerings—wine, honey, etc.) poured on the grave.

No, he must be left unburied, his corpse
carrion for the birds and dogs to tear,
an obscenity for the citizens to behold!

These are my principles. Never at my hands
will the traitor be honored above the patriot.
But whoever proves his loyalty to the state—
I'll prize that man in death as well as life.

LEADER: If this is your pleasure, Creon, treating
our city's enemy and our friend this way . . .
The power is yours, I suppose, to enforce it
with the laws, both for the dead and all of us,
the living.

CREON: Follow my orders closely then,
be on your guard.

LEADER: We're too old.
Lay that burden on younger shoulders.

CREON: No, no,
I don't mean the body—I've posted guards already.

LEADER: What commands for us then? What other service?

CREON: See that you never side with those who break my orders.

LEADER: Never. Only a fool could be in love with death.

CREON: Death is the price—you're right. But all too often
the mere hope of money has ruined many men.

[*A* SENTRY *enters from the side.*]

SENTRY: My lord,
I can't say I'm winded from running, or set out
with any spring in my legs either—no sir,
I was lost in thought, and it made me stop, often,
dead in my track, heeling, turning back,
and all the time a voice inside me muttering,
"Idiot, why? You're going straight to your death."
Then muttering, "Stopped again, poor fool?
If somebody gets the news to Creon first,
what's to save your neck?"
And so,
mulling it over, on I trudge, dragging my feet,
you can make a short road take forever . . .
but at last, look, common sense won out,
I'm here, and I'm all yours,
and even though I come empty-handed
I'll tell my story just the same, because
I've come with a good grip on one hope,
what will come will come, whatever fate—

CREON: Come to the point!
What's wrong—why so afraid?

SENTRY: First, myself, I've got to tell you,
I didn't do it, didn't see who did—
Be fair, don't take it out on me.

CREON: You're playing it safe, soldier,

barricading yourself from any trouble.
It's obvious, you've something strange to tell.
SENTRY: Dangerous too, and danger makes you delay
for all you're worth.
CREON: Out with it—then dismiss!
SENTRY: All right, here it comes. The body—
someone's just buried it, then run off . . .
sprinkled some dry dust on the flesh,[5]
given it proper rites.
CREON: What?
What man alive would dare—
SENTRY: I've no idea, I swear it.
There was no mark of a spade, no pickaxe there,
no earth turned up, the ground packed hard and dry,
unbroken, no tracks, no wheelruts, nothing,
the workman left no trace. Just at sunup
the first watch of the day points it out—
it was a wonder! We were stunned . . .
a terrific burden too, for all of us, listen:
you can't see the corpse, not that it's buried,
really, just a light cover of road-dust on it,
as if someone meant to lay the dead to rest
and keep from getting cursed.
Not a sign in sight that dogs or wild beasts
had worried the body, even torn the skin.

But what came next! Rough talk flew thick and fast,
guard grilling guard—we'd have come to blows
at last, nothing to stop it; each man for himself
and each the culprit, no one caught red-handed,
all of us pleading ignorance, dodging the charges,
ready to take up red-hot iron in our fists,
go through fire,[6] swear oaths to the gods—
"I didn't do it, I had no hand in it either,
not in the plotting, not the work itself!"

Finally, after all this wrangling came to nothing,
one man spoke out and made us stare at the ground,
hanging our heads in fear. No way to counter him,
no way to take his advice and come through
safe and sound. Here's what he said:
"Look, we've got to report the facts to Creon,
we can't keep this hidden." Well, that won out,
and the lot fell to me, condemned me,
unlucky as ever, I got the prize. So here I am,
against my will and yours too, well I know—
no one wants the man who brings bad news.
LEADER: My king,

5. A symbolic burial, all Antigone could do alone, without Ismene's help. 6. Both traditional assertions of truthfulness, derived perhaps from some primitive ritual of ordeal—only the liar would get burned.

ever since he began I've been debating in my mind,
could this possibly be the work of the gods?

CREON: Stop—
before you make me choke with anger—the gods!
You, you're senile, must you be insane?
You say—why it's intolerable—say the gods
could have the slightest concern for the corpse?
Tell me, was it for meritorious service
they proceeded to bury him, prized him so? The hero
who came to burn their temples ringed with pillars,
their golden treasures—scorch their hallowed earth
and fling their laws to the winds.
Exactly when did you last see the gods
celebrating traitors? Inconceivable!
No, from the first there were certain citizens
who could hardly stand the spirit of my regime,
grumbling against me in the dark, heads together,
tossing wildly, never keeping their necks beneath
the yoke, loyally submitting to their king.
These are the instigators, I'm convinced—
they've perverted my own guard, bribed them
to do their work.
Money! Nothing worse
in our lives, so current, rampant, so corrupting.
Money—you demolish cities, rot men from their homes,
you train and twist good minds and set them on
to the most atrocious schemes. No limit,
you make them adept at every kind of outrage,
every godless crime—money!
Everyone—
the whole crew bribed to commit this crime,
they've made one thing sure at least:
sooner or later they will pay the price.
[*Wheeling on the* SENTRY.]
You—
I swear to Zeus as I still believe in Zeus,
if you don't find the man who buried that corpse,
the very man, and produce him before my eyes,
simple death won't be enough for you,
not till we string you up alive
and wring the immorality out of you.
Then you can steal the rest of our days,
better informed about where to make a killing.
You'll have learned, at last, it doesn't pay
to itch for rewards from every hand that beckons.
Filthy profits wreck most men, you'll see—
they'll never save your life.

SENTRY: Please,
may I say a word or two, or just turn and go?

CREON: Can't you tell? Everything you say offends me.

SENTRY: Where does it hurt you, in the ears or in the heart?
CREON: And who are you to pinpoint my displeasure?
SENTRY: The culprit grates on your feelings,
I just annoy your ears.
CREON: Still talking?
You talk too much! a born nuisance—
SENTRY: Maybe so,
but I never did this thing, so help me!
CREON: Yes you did—
what's more, you squandered your life for silver!
SENTRY: Oh it's terrible when the one who does the judging
judges things all wrong.
CREON: Well now,
you just be clever about your judgments—
if you fail to produce the criminals for me,
you'll swear your dirty money brought you pain.
[*Turning sharply, reentering the palace.*]
SENTRY: I hope he's found. Best thing by far.
But caught or not, that's in the lap of fortune:
I'll never come back, you've seen the last of me.
I'm saved, even now, and I never thought,
I never hoped—
dear gods, I owe you all my thanks!
[*Rushing out.*]
CHORUS: Numberless wonders
terrible wonders walk the world but none the match for man—
that great wonder crossing the heaving gray sea,
driven on by the blasts of winter
on through breakers crashing left and right,
holds his steady course
and the oldest of the gods he wears away—
the Earth, the immortal, the inexhaustible—
as his powers go back and forth, year in, year out
with the breed of stallions[7] turning up the furrows.

And the blithe, lightheaded race of birds he snares,
the tribes of savage beasts, the life that swarms the depths—
with one fling of his nets
woven and coiled tight, he takes them all,
man the skilled, the brilliant!
He conquers all, taming with his techniques
the prey that roams the cliffs and wild lairs,
training the stallion, clamping the yoke across
his shaggy neck, and the tireless mountain bull.
And speech and thought, quick as the wind
and the mood and mind for law that rules the city—
all these he has taught himself
and shelter from the arrows of the frost

7. Mules, the working animal of a Greek farmer.

when there's rough lodging under the cold clear sky
and the shafts of lashing rain—
ready, resourceful man!
Never without resources
never an impasse as he marches on the future—
only Death, from Death alone he will find no rescue
but from desperate plagues he has plotted his escapes.

Man the master, ingenious past all measure
past all dreams, the skills within his grasp—
he forges on, now to destruction
now again to greatness. When he weaves in
the laws of the land, and the justice of the gods
that binds his oaths together
he and his city rise high—
but the city casts out
that man who weds himself to inhumanity
thanks to reckless daring. Never share my hearth
never think my thoughts, whoever does such things.

[*Enter* ANTIGONE *from the side, accompanied by the* SENTRY.]

Here is a dark sign from the gods—
what to make of this? I know her,
how can I deny it? That young girl's Antigone!
Wretched, child of a wretched father,
Oedipus. Look, is it possible?
They bring you in like a prisoner—
why? did you break the king's laws?
Did they take you in some act of mad defiance?

SENTRY: She's the one, she did it single-handed—
we caught her burying the body. Where's Creon?

[*Enter* CREON *from the palace.*]

LEADER: Back again, just in time when you need him.

CREON: In time for what? What is it?

SENTRY: My king,
there's nothing you can swear you'll never do—
second thoughts make liars of us all.
I could have sworn I wouldn't hurry back
(what with your threats, the buffeting I just took),
but a stroke of luck beyond our wildest hopes,
what a joy, there's nothing like it. So,
back I've come, breaking my oath, who cares?
I'm bringing in our prisoner—this young girl—
we took her giving the dead the last rites.
But no casting lots this time; this is *my* luck,
my prize, no one else's.
Now, my lord,
here she is. Take her, question her,
cross-examine her to your heart's content.
But set me free, it's only right—
I'm rid of this dreadful business once for all.

CREON: Prisoner! Her? You took her—where, doing what?
SENTRY: Burying the man. That's the whole story.
CREON: What?
You mean what you say, you're telling me the truth?
SENTRY: She's the one. With my own eyes I saw her
bury the body, just what you've forbidden.
There. Is that plain and clear?
CREON: What did you see? Did you catch her in the act?
SENTRY: Here's what happened. We went back to our post,
those threats of yours breathing down our necks—
we brushed the corpse clean of the dust that covered it,
stripped it bare . . . it was slimy, going soft,
and we took to high ground, backs to the wind
so the stink of him couldn't hit us;
jostling, baiting each other to keep awake,
shouting back and forth—no napping on the job,
not this time. And so the hours dragged by
until the sun stood dead above our heads,
a huge white ball in the noon sky, beating,
blazing down, and then it happened—
suddenly, a whirlwind!
Twisting a great dust-storm up from the earth,
a black plague of the heavens, filling the plain,
ripping the leaves off every tree in sight,
choking the air and sky. We squinted hard
and took our whipping from the gods.

And after the storm passed—it seemed endless—
there, we saw the girl!
And she cried out a sharp, piercing cry,
like a bird come back to an empty nest,
peering into its bed, and all the babies gone . . .
Just so, when she sees the corpse bare
she bursts into a long, shattering wail
and calls down withering curses on the heads
of all who did the work. And she scoops up dry dust,
handfuls, quickly, and lifting a fine bronze urn,
lifting it high and pouring, she crowns the dead
with three full libations.
Soon as we saw
we rushed her, closed on the kill like hunters,
and she, she didn't flinch. We interrogated her,
charging her with offenses past and present—
she stood up to it all, denied nothing. I tell you,
it made me ache and laugh in the same breath.
It's pure joy to escape the worst yourself,
it hurts a man to bring down his friends.
But all that, I'm afraid, means less to me
than my own skin. That's the way I'm made.
CREON: [*Wheeling on* ANTIGONE.] You,

with your eyes fixed on the ground—speak up.
Do you deny you did this, yes or no?
ANTIGONE: I did it. I don't deny a thing.
CREON: [*To the* SENTRY.] You, get out, wherever you please—
you're clear of a very heavy charge.
[*He leaves;* CREON *turns back to* ANTIGONE.]
You, tell me briefly, no long speeches—
were you aware a decree had forbidden this?
ANTIGONE: Well aware. How could I avoid it? It was public.
CREON: And still you had the gall to break this law?
ANTIGONE: Of course I did. It wasn't Zeus, not in the least,
who made this proclamation—not to me.
Nor did that Justice, dwelling with the gods
beneath the earth, ordain such laws for men.
Nor did I think your edict had such force
that you, a mere mortal, could override the gods,
the great unwritten, unshakable traditions.
They are alive, not just today or yesterday:
they live forever, from the first of time,
and no one knows when they first saw the light.

These laws—I was not about to break them,
not out of fear of some man's wounded pride,
and face the retribution of the gods.
Die I must, I've known it all my life—
how could I keep from knowing?—even without
your death-sentence ringing in my ears.
And if I am to die before my time
I consider that a gain. Who on earth
alive in the midst of so much grief as I,
could fail to find his death a rich reward?
So for me, at least, to meet this doom of yours
is precious little pain. But if I had allowed
my own mother's son to rot, an unburied corpse—
that would have been an agony! This is nothing.
And if my present actions strike you as foolish,
let's just say I've been accused of folly
by a fool.
LEADER: Like father like daughter,
passionate, wild . . .
she hasn't learned to bend before adversity.
CREON: No? Believe me, the stiffest stubborn wills
fall the hardest; the toughest iron,
tempered strong in the white-hot fire,
you'll see it crack and shatter first of all.
And I've known spirited horses you can break
with a light bit—proud, rebellious horses.
There's no room for pride, not in a slave,
not with the lord and master standing by.

This girl was an old hand at insolence
when she overrode the edicts we made public.

But once she'd done it—the insolence,
twice over—to glory in it, laughing,
mocking us to our face with what she'd done.
I am not the man, not now: she is the man
if this victory goes to her and she goes free.

Never! Sister's child or closer in blood
than all my family clustered at my altar
worshiping Guardian Zeus—she'll never escape,
she and her blood sister, the most barbaric death.
Yes, I accuse her sister of an equal part
in scheming this, this burial.
[*To his attendants.*]
Bring her here!
I just saw her inside, hysterical, gone to pieces.
It never fails: the mind convicts itself
in advance, when scoundrels are up to no good,
plotting in the dark. Oh but I hate it more
when a traitor, caught red-handed,
tries to glorify his crimes.

ANTIGONE: Creon, what more do you want
than my arrest and execution?

CREON: Nothing. Then I have it all.

ANTIGONE: Then why delay? Your moralizing repels me,
every word you say—pray god it always will.
So naturally all I say repels you too.
Enough.
Give me glory! What greater glory could I win
than to give my own brother decent burial?
These citizens here would all agree,
[*To the* CHORUS.]
they would praise me too
if their lips weren't locked in fear.
[*Pointing to* CREON.]
Lucky tyrants—the perquisites of power!
Ruthless power to do and say whatever pleases *them.*

CREON: You alone, of all the people in Thebes,
see things that way.

ANTIGONE: They see it just that way
but defer to you and keep their tongues in leash.

CREON: And you, aren't you ashamed to differ so from them?
So disloyal!

ANTIGONE: Not ashamed for a moment,
not to honor my brother, my own flesh and blood.

CREON: Wasn't Eteocles a brother too—cut down, facing him?

ANTIGONE: Brother, yes, by the same mother, the same father.

CREON: Then how can you render his enemy such honors,
such impieties in his eyes?

ANTIGONE: He'll never testify to that,
Eteocles dead and buried.

CREON: He will—

if you honor the traitor just as much as him.
ANTIGONE: But it was his brother, not some slave that died—
CREON: Ravaging our country!—
but Eteocles died fighting in our behalf.
ANTIGONE: No matter—Death longs for the same rites for all.
CREON: Never the same for the patriot and the traitor.
ANTIGONE: Who, Creon, who on earth can say the ones below
don't find this pure and uncorrupt?
CREON: Never. Once an enemy, never a friend,
not even after death.
ANTIGONE: I was born to join in love, not hate—
that is my nature.
CREON: Go down below and love,
if love you must—love the dead! while I'm alive,
no woman is going to lord it over me.
[*Enter* ISMENE *from the palace, under guard.*]
CHORUS: Look,
Ismene's coming, weeping a sister's tears,
loving sister, under a cloud . . .
her face is flushed, her cheeks streaming.
Sorrow puts her lovely radiance in the dark.
CREON: You—
in my own house, you viper, slinking undetected,
sucking my life-blood! I never knew
I was breeding twin disasters, the two of you
rising up against my throne. Come, tell me,
will you confess your part in the crime or not?
Answer me. Swear to me.
ISMENE: I did it, yes—
if only she consents—I share the guilt,
the consequences too.
ANTIGONE: No,
Justice will never suffer that—not you,
you were unwilling. I never brought you in.
ISMENE: But now you face such dangers . . . I'm not ashamed
to sail through trouble with you,
make your troubles mine.
ANTIGONE: Who did the work?
Let the dead and the god of death bear witness!
I have no love for a friend who loves in words alone.
ISMENE: Oh no, my sister, don't reject me, please,
let me die beside you, consecrating
the dead together.
ANTIGONE: Never share my dying,
don't lay claim to what you never touched.
My death will be enough.
ISMENE: What do I care for life, cut off from you?
ANTIGONE: Ask Creon. Your concern is all for him.
ISMENE: Why abuse me so? It doesn't help you now.
ANTIGONE: You're right—

if I mock you, I get no pleasure from it,
only pain.
ISMENE: Tell me, dear one,
what can I do to help you, even now?
ANTIGONE: Save yourself. I don't grudge you your survival.
ISMENE: Oh no, no, denied my portion in your death?
ANTIGONE: You chose to live, I chose to die.
ISMENE: Not, at least,
without every kind of caution I could voice.
ANTIGONE: Your wisdom appealed to one world—mine, another.
ISMENE: But look, we're both guilty, both condemned to death.
ANTIGONE: Courage! Live your life. I gave myself to death,
long ago, so I might serve the dead.
CREON: They're both mad, I tell you, the two of them.
One's just shown it, the other's been that way
since she was born.
ISMENE: True, my king,
the sense we were born with cannot last forever . . .
commit cruelty on a person long enough
and the mind begins to go.
CREON: Yours did,
when you chose to commit your crimes with her.
ISMENE: How can I live alone, without her?
CREON: Her?
Don't even mention her—she no longer exists.
ISMENE: What? You'd kill your own son's bride?
CREON: Absolutely:
there are other fields for him to plow.
ISMENE: Perhaps,
but never as true, as close a bond as theirs.
CREON: A worthless woman for my son? It repels me.
ISMENE: Dearest Haemon, your father wrongs you so!
CREON: Enough, enough—you and your talk of marriage!
ISMENE: Creon—you're really going to rob your son of Antigone?
CREON: Death will do it for me—break their marriage off.
LEADER: So, it's settled then? Antigone must die?
CREON: Settled, yes—we both know that.
[*To the guards.*]
Stop wasting time. Take them in.
From now on they'll act like women.
Tie them up, no more running loose;
even the bravest will cut and run,
once they see Death coming for their lives.
[*The guards escort* ANTIGONE *and* ISMENE *into the palace.*
CREON *remains while the old citizens form their* CHORUS.]
CHORUS: Blest, they are the truly blest who all their lives
have never tasted devastation. For others, once
the gods have rocked a house to its foundations
the ruin will never cease, cresting on and on
from one generation on throughout the race—

like a great mounting tide
driven on by savage northern gales,
surging over the dead black depths
rolling up from the bottom dark heaves of sand
and the headlands, taking the storm's onslaught full-force,
roar, and the low moaning
echoes on and on
and now
as in ancient times I see the sorrows of the house,
the living heirs of the old ancestral kings,
piling on the sorrows of the dead
and one generation cannot free the next—
some god will bring them crashing down,
the race finds no release.
And now the light, the hope
springing up from the late last root
in the house of Oedipus, that hope's cut down in turn
by the long, bloody knife swung by the gods of death
by a senseless word
by fury at the heart.
Zeus,
yours is the power, Zeus, what man on earth
can override it, who can hold it back?
Power that neither Sleep, the all-ensnaring
no, nor the tireless months of heaven
can ever overmaster—young through all time,
mighty lord of power, you hold fast
the dazzling crystal mansions of Olympus.
And throughout the future, late and soon
as through the past, your law prevails:
no towering form of greatness
enters into the lives of mortals
free and clear of ruin.
True,
our dreams, our high hopes voyaging far and wide
bring sheer delight to many, to many others
delusion, blithe, mindless lusts
and the fraud steals on one slowly . . . unaware
till he trips and puts his foot into the fire.
He was a wise old man who coined
the famous saying: "Sooner or later
foul is fair, fair is foul
to the man the gods will ruin"—
He goes his way for a moment only
free of blinding ruin.
[*Enter* HAEMON *from the palace.*]
Here's Haemon now, the last of all your sons.
Does he come in tears for his bride,
his doomed bride, Antigone—
bitter at being cheated of their marriage?

CREON: We'll soon know, better than seer could tell us.
[*Turning to* HAEMON.]
Son, you've heard the final verdict on your bride?
Are you coming now, raving against your father?
Or do you love me, no matter what I do?

HAEMON: Father, I'm your *son* . . . you in your wisdom
set my bearings for me—I obey you.
No marriage could ever mean more to me than you,
whatever good direction you may offer.

CREON: Fine, Haemon.
That's how you ought to feel within your heart,
subordinate to your father's will in every way.
That's what a man prays for: to produce good sons—
a household full of them, dutiful and attentive,
so they can pay his enemy back with interest
and match the respect their father shows his friend.
But the man who rears a brood of useless children,
what has he brought into the world, I ask you?
Nothing but trouble for himself, and mockery
from his enemies laughing in his face.
Oh Haemon,
never lose your sense of judgment over a woman.
The warmth, the rush of pleasure, it all goes cold
in your arms, I warn you . . . a worthless woman
in your house, a misery in your bed.
What wound cuts deeper than a loved one
turned against you? Spit her out,
like a mortal enemy—let the girl go.
Let her find a husband down among the dead.
Imagine it: I caught her in naked rebellion,
the traitor, the only one in the whole city.
I'm not about to prove myself a liar,
not to my people, no, I'm going to kill her!
That's right—so let her cry for mercy, sing her hymns
to Zeus who defends all bonds of kindred blood.
Why, if I bring up my own kin to be rebels,
think what I'd suffer from the world at large.
Show me the man who rules his household well:
I'll show you someone fit to rule the state.
That good man, my son,
I have every confidence he and he alone
can give commands and take them too. Staunch
in the storm of spears he'll stand his ground,
a loyal, unflinching comrade at your side.

But whoever steps out of line, violates the laws
or presumes to hand out orders to his superiors,
he'll win no praise from me. But that man
the city places in authority, his orders
must be obeyed, large and small,

right and wrong.
Anarchy—
show me a greater crime in all the earth!
She, she destroys cities, rips up houses,
breaks the ranks of spearmen into headlong rout.
But the ones who last it out, the great mass of them
owe their lives to discipline. Therefore
we must defend the men who live by law,
never let some woman triumph over us.
Better to fall from power, if fall we must,
at the hands of a man—never be rated
inferior to a woman, never.

LEADER: To us,
unless old age has robbed us of our wits,
you seem to say what you have to say with sense.

HAEMON: Father, only the gods endow a man with reason,
the finest of all their gifts, a treasure.
Far be it from me—I haven't the skill,
and certainly no desire, to tell you when,
if ever, you make a slip in speech . . . though
someone else might have a good suggestion.

Of course it's not for you,
in the normal run of things, to watch
whatever men say or do, or find to criticize.
The man in the street, you know, dreads your glance,
he'd never say anything displeasing to your face.
But it's for me to catch the murmurs in the dark,
the way the city mourns for this young girl.
"No woman," they say, "ever deserved death less,
and such a brutal death for such a glorious action.
She, with her own dear brother lying in his blood—
she couldn't bear to leave him dead, unburied,
food for the wild dogs or wheeling vultures.
Death? She deserves a glowing crown of gold!"
So they say, and the rumor spreads in secret,
darkly . . .
I rejoice in your success, father—
nothing more precious to me in the world.
What medal of honor brighter to his children
than a father's glowing glory? Or a child's
to his proud father? Now don't, please,
be quite so single-minded, self-involved,
or assume the world is wrong and you are right.
Whoever thinks that he alone possesses intelligence,
the gift of eloquence, he and no one else,
and character too . . . such men, I tell you,
spread them open—you will find them empty.
No,
it's no disgrace for a man, even a wise man,
to learn many things and not to be too rigid.

You've seen trees by a raging winter torrent,
how many sway with the flood and salvage every twig,
but not the stubborn—they're ripped out, roots and all.
Bend or break. The same when a man is sailing:
haul your sheets too taut, never give an inch,
you'll capsize, and go the rest of the voyage
keel up and the rowing-benches under.

Oh give way. Relax your anger—change!
I'm young, I know, but let me offer this:
it would be best by far, I admit,
if a man were born infallible, right by nature.
If not—and things don't often go that way,
it's best to learn from those with good advice.

LEADER: You'd do well, my lord, if he's speaking to the point,
to learn from him,
[*Turning to* HAEMON.]
and you, my boy, from him.
You both are talking sense.

CREON: So,
men our age, we're to be lectured, are we?—
schooled by a boy his age?

HAEMON: Only in what is right. But if I seem young,
look less to my years and more to what I do.

CREON: Do? Is admiring rebels an achievement?

HAEMON: I'd never suggest that you admire treason.

CREON: Oh?—
isn't that just the sickness that's attacked her?

HAEMON: The whole city of Thebes denies it, to a man.

CREON: And is Thebes about to tell me how to rule?

HAEMON: Now, you see? Who's talking like a child?

CREON: Am I to rule this land for others—or myself?

HAEMON: It's no city at all, owned by one man alone.

CREON: What? The city *is* the king's—that's the law!

HAEMON: What a splendid king you'd make of a desert island—
you and you alone.

CREON: [*To the* CHORUS.] This boy, I do believe,
is fighting on her side, the woman's side.

HAEMON: If you are a woman, yes—
my concern is all for you.

CREON: Why, you degenerate—bandying accusations,
threatening me with justice, your own father!

HAEMON: I see my father offending justice—wrong.

CREON: Wrong?
To protect my royal rights?

HAEMON: Protect your rights?
When you trample down the honors of the gods?

CREON: You, you soul of corruption, rotten through—
woman's accomplice!

HAEMON: That may be,
but you'll never find me accomplice to a criminal.

CREON: That's what *she* is,
and every word you say is a blatant appeal for her—
HAEMON: And you, and me, and the gods beneath the earth.
CREON: You will never marry her, not while she's alive.
HAEMON: Then she'll die . . . but her death will kill another.
CREON: What, brazen threats? You go too far!
HAEMON: What threat?
Combating your empty, mindless judgments with a word?
CREON: You'll suffer for your sermons, you and your empty wisdom!
HAEMON: If you weren't my father, I'd say you were insane.
CREON: Don't flatter me with Father—you woman's slave!
HAEMON: You really expect to fling abuse at me
and not receive the same?
CREON: Is that so!
Now, by heaven, I promise you, you'll pay—
taunting, insulting me! Bring her out,
that hateful—she'll die now, here,
in front of his eyes, beside her groom!
HAEMON: No, no, she will never die beside me—
don't delude yourself. And you will never
see me, never set eyes on my face again.
Rage your heart out, rage with friends
who can stand the sight of you.
[*Rushing out.*]
LEADER: Gone, my king, in a burst of anger.
A temper young as his . . . hurt him once,
he may do something violent.
CREON: Let him do—
dream up something desperate, past all human limit!
Good riddance. Rest assured,
he'll never save those two young girls from death.
LEADER: Both of them, you really intend to kill them both?
CREON: No, not her, the one whose hands are clean—
you're quite right.
LEADER: But Antigone—
what sort of death do you have in mind for her?
CREON: I'll take her down some wild, desolate path
never trod by men, and wall her up alive
in a rocky vault, and set out short rations,
just the measure piety demands
to keep the entire city free of defilement.[8]
There let her pray to the one god she worships:
Death—who knows?—may just reprieve her from death.
Or she may learn at last, better late than never,
what a waste of breath it is to worship Death.

8. The penalty originally proclaimed was death by stoning. But this demands the participation of the citizens, and it may be that Creon, after listening to Haemon's remarks, is not as sure as he once was of popular support. Creon proposed imprisonment in a tomb with a ration of food. Since Antigone would die of starvation but not actually by anyone's hand, Creon seems to think that the city will not be "defiled," that is, will not incur blood guilt.

[*Exit to the palace.*]

CHORUS: Love, never conquered in battle
Love the plunderer laying waste the rich!
Love standing the night-watch
guarding a girl's soft cheek,
you range the seas, the shepherds' steadings off in the wilds—
not even the deathless gods can flee your onset,
nothing human born for a day—
whoever feels your grip is driven mad.
Love!—
you wrench the minds of the righteous into outrage,
swerve them to their ruin—you have ignited this,
this kindred strife, father and son at war
and Love alone the victor—
warm glance of the bride triumphant, burning with desire!
Throned in power, side-by-side with the mighty laws!
Irresistible Aphrodite,[9] never conquered—
Love, you mock us for your sport.

[ANTIGONE *is brought from the palace under guard.*]

But now, even I'd rebel against the king,
I'd break all bounds when I see this—
I fill with tears, I cannot hold them back,
not any more . . . I see Antigone make her way
to the bridal vault where all are laid to rest.

ANTIGONE: Look at me, men of my fatherland,
setting out on the last road
looking into the last light of day
the last I'll ever see . . .
the god of death who puts us all to bed
takes me down to the banks of Acheron[1] alive—
denied my part in the wedding-songs,
no wedding-song in the dusk has crowned my marriage—
I go to wed the lord of the dark waters.

CHORUS: Not crowned with glory,[2] or with a dirge,
you leave for the deep pit of the dead.
No withering illness laid you low,
no strokes of the sword—a law to yourself,
alone, no mortal like you, ever, you go down
to the halls of Death alive and breathing.

ANTIGONE: But think of Niobe[3]—well I know her story—
think what a living death she died,

9. Goddess of sexual love. 1. A river in the world of the dead. 2. The usual version of this line is: "crowned with glory." The Greek word *oukoun* can be negative or positive, depending on the accent, which determines the pronunciation; because written accents were not yet in use in Sophocles' time, no one will ever know for sure which meaning he intended. The present version is based on the belief that the chorus is expressing pity for Antigone's ignominious and abnormal death; she has no funeral at which her fame and praise are recited, she will not die by either of the usual causes—violence and disease—but by a living death. It is, as they say, her own choice: she is "a law to [herself]" (line 913). 3. A Phrygian princess married to Amphion, king of Thebes. She boasted that she had borne more children than Leto, mother of Apollo and Artemis. As vengeance, Apollo and Artemis killed all of Niobe's children. She fled to Phrygia, where she was turned into a rock on Mount Sipylus; the melting of the snow on the mountain caused "tears" to flow down the rock formation, which resembles a woman's face.

Tantalus' daughter, stranger queen from the east:
there on the mountain heights, growing stone
binding as ivy, slowly walled her round
and the rains will never cease, the legends say
the snows will never leave her . . .
wasting away, under her brows the tears
showering down her breasting ridge and slopes—
a rocky death like hers puts me to sleep.

CHORUS: But she was a god, born of gods,
and we are only mortals born to die.
And yet, of course, it's a great thing
for a dying girl to hear, just to hear
she shares a destiny equal to the gods,
during life and later, once she's dead.

ANTIGONE: O you mock me!
Why, in the name of all my fathers' gods
why can't you wait till I am gone—
must you abuse me to my face?
O my city, all your fine rich sons!
And you, you springs of the Dirce,
holy grove of Thebes where the chariots gather,
you at least, you'll bear me witness, look,
unmourned by friend and forced by such crude laws
I go to my rockbound prison, strange new tomb—
always a stranger, O dear god,
I have no home on earth and none below,
not with the living, not with the breathless dead.

CHORUS: You went too far, the last limits of daring—
smashing against the high throne of Justice!
Your life's in ruins, child—I wonder . . .
do you pay for your father's terrible ordeal?

ANTIGONE: There—at last you've touched it, the worst pain
the worst anguish! Raking up the grief for father
three times over, for all the doom
that's struck us down, the brilliant house of Laius.
O mother, your marriage-bed
the coiling horrors, the coupling there—
you with your own son, my father—doomstruck mother!
Such, such were my parents, and I their wretched child.
I go to them now, cursed, unwed, to share their home—
I am a stranger! O dear brother, doomed
in your marriage—your marriage murders mine,[4]
your dying drags me down to death alive!

[*Enter* CREON.]

CHORUS: Reverence asks some reverence in return—
but attacks on power never go unchecked,

4. Polynices had married the daughter of Adrastus of Argos, to seal the alliance that enabled him to march against Thebes.

not by the man who holds the reins of power.
Your own blind will, your passion has destroyed you.
ANTIGONE: No one to weep for me, my friends,
no wedding-song—they take me away
in all my pain . . . the road lies open, waiting.
Never again, the law forbids me to see
the sacred eye of day. I am agony!
No tears for the destiny that's mine,
no loved one mourns my death.
CREON: Can't you see?
If a man could wail his own dirge *before* he dies,
he'd never finish.
[*To the guards.*]
Take her away, quickly!
Wall her up in the tomb, you have your orders.
Abandon her there, alone, and let her choose—
death or a buried life with a good roof for shelter.
As for myself, my hands are clean. This young girl—
dead or alive, she will be stripped of her rights,
her stranger's rights,[5] here in the world above.
ANTIGONE: O tomb, my bridal-bed—my house, my prison
cut in the hollow rock, my everlasting watch!
I'll soon be there, soon embrace my own,
the great growing family of our dead
Persephone[6] has received among her ghosts.
I,
the last of them all, the most reviled by far,
go down before my destined time's run out.
But still I go, cherishing one good hope:
my arrival may be dear to father,
dear to you, my mother,
dear to you, my loving brother, Eteocles—
When you died I washed you with my hands,
I dressed you all, I poured the sacred cups
across your tombs. But now, Polynices,
because I laid your body out as well,
this, this is my reward. Nevertheless
I honored you—the decent will admit it—
well and wisely too.
Never, I tell you,
if I had been the mother of children
or if my husband died, exposed and rotting—
I'd never have taken this ordeal upon myself,
never defied our people's will. What law,
you ask, do I satisfy with what I say?
A husband dead, there might have been another.

5. The Greek words suggest that he sees her not as a citizen but as a resident alien; by her action she has forfeited citizenship. But now she will be deprived even of that inferior status. **6.** Queen of the underworld.

A child by another too, if I had lost the first.
But mother and father both lost in the halls of Death,
no brother could ever spring to light again.[7]
For this law alone I held you first in honor.
For this, Creon, the king, judges me a criminal
guilty of dreadful outrage, my dear brother!
And now he leads me off, a captive in his hands,
with no part in the bridal-song, the bridal-bed,
denied all joy of marriage, raising childen—
deserted so by loved ones, struck by fate,
I descend alive to the caverns of the dead.

What law of the mighty gods have I transgressed?
Why look to the heavens any more, tormented as I am?
Whom to call, what comrades now? Just think,
my reverence only brands me for irreverence!
Very well: if this is the pleasure of the gods,
once I suffer I will know that I was wrong.
But if these men are wrong, let them suffer
nothing worse than they mete out to me—
these masters of injustice!

LEADER: Still the same rough winds, the wild passion
raging through the girl.

CREON: [*To the guards.*] Take her away.
You're wasting time—you'll pay for it too.

ANTIGONE: Oh god, the voice of death. Its come, it's here.

CREON: True. Not a word of hope—your doom is sealed.

ANTIGONE: Land of Thebes, city of all my fathers—
O you gods, the first gods of the race![8]
They drag me away, now, no more delay.
Look on me, you noble sons of Thebes—
the last of a great line of kings,
I alone, see what I suffer now
at the hands of what breed of men—
all for reverence, my reverence for the gods!

[*She leaves under guard: the* CHORUS *gathers.*]

CHORUS: Danaë,[9] Danaë—
even she endured a fate like yours,
in all her lovely strength she traded
the light of day for the bolted brazen vault—
buried within her tomb, her bridal-chamber,
wed to the yoke and broken.

7. This strange justification for her action has been considered unacceptable by many critics, and they have suspected that it was an interpolation by some later producer of the play. But Aristotle quotes it in the next century and appears to have no doubt of its authenticity. If genuine, it means that Antigone momentarily abandons the law she championed against Creon—that all people have a right to burial—and sees her motive as exclusive devotion to her dead brother. For someone facing the prospect of a slow and hideous death such a self-examination and realization is not impossible. And it makes no difference to the courage and tenacity of her defiance of state power.

8. The Theban royal house traced its ancestry through Harmonia, wife of Cadmus, to Aphrodite and Ares, her parents. Cadmus' daughter was Semele.

9. Daughter of Acrisius, king of Argos. It was prophesied that he would be killed by his daughter's son; so he shut her up in a bronze tower. But Zeus came to her in the form of a golden rain shower and she bore a son, Perseus, who did in the end kill his grandfather.

But she was of glorious birth
my child, my child
and treasured the seed of Zeus within her womb,
the cloudburst streaming gold!
The power of fate is a wonder,
dark, terrible wonder—
neither wealth nor armies
towered walls nor ships
black hulls lashed by the salt
can save us from that force.

The yoke tamed him too
young Lycurgus flaming in anger
king of Edonia,[1] all for his mad taunts
Dionysus clamped him down, encased
in the chain-mail of rock
and there his rage
his terrible flowering rage burst—
sobbing, dying away . . . at last that madman
came to know his god—
the power he mocked, the power
he taunted in all his frenzy
trying to stamp out
the women strong with the god—
the torch, the raving sacred cries—
enraging the Muses who adore the flute.

And far north[2] where the Black Rocks
cut the sea in half
and murderous straits
split the coast of Thrace
a forbidding city stands
where once, hard by the walls
the savage Ares thrilled to watch
a king's new queen, a Fury rearing in rage
against his two royal sons—
her bloody hands, her dagger-shuttle
stabbing out their eyes—cursed, blinding wounds—
their eyes blind sockets screaming for revenge!

They wailed in agony cries echoing cries
the princes doomed at birth . . .
and their mother doomed to chains,
walled up in a tomb of stone[3]—

1. Thrace. Lycurgus opposed the introduction of Dionysiac religion into his kingdom and was imprisoned by the god. 2. The whole story is difficult to follow, and its application to the case of Antigone is obscure. Cleopatra, the daughter of the Athenian princess Orithyia (whom Boreas, the North Wind, carried off to his home in Thrace), was married to Phineus, the Thracian king, and bore him two sons. He tired of her, abandoned her, and married Eidothea (*a king's new queen,* line 1074), who put out the eyes of Cleopatra's two sons. Ares watched the savage act. 3. Lines 1081–82 have no equivalent in the Greek text. They represent a belief that Sophocles' audience knew a version of the legend in which Cleopatra was imprisoned in a stone tomb (which is found in a later source). This would give a point of comparison to Antigone as did the mention of Danaë and Lycurgus.

but she traced her own birth back
to a proud Athenian line and the high gods
and off in caverns half the world away,
born of the wild North Wind
she sprang on her father's gales,
racing stallions up the leaping cliffs—
child of the heavens. But even on her the Fates
the gray everlasting Fates rode hard
my child, my child.

[*Enter* TIRESIAS, *the blind prophet, led by a boy.*]

TIRESIAS: Lord of Thebes,
I and the boy have come together,
hand in hand. Two see with the eyes of one . . .
so the blind must go, with a guide to lead the way.
CREON: What is it, old Tiresias? What news now?
TIRESIAS: I will teach you. And you obey the seer.
CREON: I will,
I've never wavered from your advice before.
TIRESIAS: And so you kept the city straight on course.
CREON: I owe you a great deal, I swear to that.
TIRESIAS: Then reflect, my son: you are poised,
once more, on the razor-edge of fate.
CREON: What is it? I shudder to hear you.
TIRESIAS: You will learn
when you listen to the warnings of my craft.
As I sat on the ancient seat of augury,
in the sanctuary where every bird I know
will hover at my hands[4]—suddenly I hear it,
a strange voice in the wingbeats, unintelligible,
barbaric, a mad scream! Talons flashing, ripping,
they were killing each other—that much I knew—
the murderous fury whirring in those wings
made that much clear!
I was afraid,
I turned quickly, tasted the burnt-sacrifice,
ignited the altar at all points—but no fire,
the god in the fire never blazed.
Not from those offerings . . . over the embers
slid a heavy ooze from the long thighbones,
smoking, sputtering out, and the bladder
puffed and burst—spraying gall into the air—
and the fat wrapping the bones slithered off
and left them glistening white. No fire!
The rites failed that might have blazed the future
with a sign. So I learned from the boy here:
he is my guide, as I am guide to others.
And it is you—
your high resolve that sets this plague on Thebes.

4. A place where the birds gathered and Tiresias waited for omens.

The public altars and sacred hearths are fouled,
one and all, by the birds and dogs with carrion
torn from the corpse, the doomstruck son of Oedipus!
and so the gods are deaf to our prayers, they spurn
the offerings in our hands, the flame of holy flesh.
No birds cry out an omen clear and true—
they're gorged with the murdered victim's blood and fat.
Take these things to heart, my son, I warn you.
All men make mistakes, it is only human.
But once the wrong is done, a man
can turn his back on folly, misfortune too,
if he tries to make amends, however low he's fallen,
and stops his bullnecked ways. Stubbornness
brands you for stupidity—pride is a crime.
No, yield to the dead!
Never stab the fighter when he's down.
Where's the glory, killing the dead twice over?

I mean you well. I give you sound advice.
It's best to learn from a good adviser
when he speaks for your own good:
it's pure gain.
CREON: Old man—all of you! So,
you shoot your arrows at my head like archers at the target—
I even have *him* loosed on me, this fortune-teller.
Oh his ilk has tried to sell me short
and ship me off for years. Well,
drive your bargains, traffic—much as you like—
in the gold of India, silver-gold of Sardis.[5]
You'll never bury that body in the grave,
not even if Zeus' eagles rip the corpse
and wing their rotten pickings off to the throne of god!
Never, not even in fear of such defilement
will I tolerate his burial, that traitor.
Well I know, we can't defile the gods—
no mortal has the power.
No,
reverend old Tiresias, all men fall,
it's only human, but the wisest fall obscenely
when they glorify obscene advice with rhetoric—
all for their own gain.
TIRESIAS: Oh god, is there a man alive
who knows, who actually believes . . .
CREON: What now?
What earth-shattering truth are you about to utter?
TIRESIAS: . . . just how much a sense of judgment, wisdom
is the greatest gift we have?
CREON: Just as much, I'd say,

5. In Asia Minor. Electrum, a mixture of gold and silver, was found in a nearby river.

as a twisted mind is the worst affliction known.
TIRESIAS: You are the one who's sick, Creon, sick to death.
CREON: I am in no mood to trade insults with a seer.
TIRESIAS: You have already, calling my prophecies a lie.
CREON: Why not?
You and the whole breed of seers are mad for money!
TIRESIAS: And the whole race of tyrants lusts for filthy gain.
CREON: This slander of yours—
are you aware you're speaking to the king?
TIRESIAS: Well aware. Who helped you save the city?
CREON: You—
you have your skills, old seer, but you lust for injustice!
TIRESIAS: You will drive me to utter the dreadful secret in my heart.
CREON: Spit it out! Just don't speak it out for profit.
TIRESIAS: Profit? No, not a bit of profit, not for you.
CREON: Know full well, you'll never buy off my resolve.
TIRESIAS: Then know this too, learn this by heart!
The chariot of the sun will not race through
so many circuits more, before you have surrendered
one born of your own loins, your own flesh and blood,
a corpse for corpses given in return, since you have thrust
to the world below a child sprung for the world above,
ruthlessly lodged a living soul within the grave—
then you've robbed the gods below the earth,
keeping a dead body here in the bright air,
unburied, unsung, unhallowed by the rites.

You, you have no business with the dead,
nor do the gods above—this is violence
you have forced upon the heavens.
And so the avengers, the dark destroyers late
but true to the mark, now lie in wait for you,
the Furies sent by the gods and the god of death
to strike you down with the pains that you perfected!

There. Reflect on that, tell me I've been bribed.
The day comes soon, no long test of time, not now,
when the mourning cries for men and women break
throughout your halls. Great hatred rises against you—
cities in tumult, all whose mutilated sons
the dogs have graced with burial, or the wild beasts
or a wheeling crow that wings the ungodly stench of carrion
back to each city, each warrior's hearth and home.

These arrows for your heart! Since you've raked me
I loose them like an archer in my anger,
arrows deadly true. You'll never escape
their burning, searing force.
[*Motioning to his escort.*]
Come, boy, take me home.
So he can vent his rage on younger men,
and learn to keep a gentler tongue in his head

and better sense than what he carries now.
[*Exit to the side.*]
LEADER: The old man's gone, my king—
terrible prophecies. Well I know,
since the hair on this old head went gray,
he's never lied to Thebes.
CREON: I know it myself—I'm shaken, torn.
It's a dreadful thing to yield . . . but resist now?
Lay my pride bare to the blows of ruin?
That's dreadful too.
LEADER: But good advice,
Creon, take it now, you must.
CREON: What should I do? Tell me . . . I'll obey.
LEADER: Go! Free the girl from the rocky vault
and raise a mound for the body you exposed.
CREON: That's your advice? You think I should give in?
LEADER: Yes, my king, quickly. Disasters sent by the gods
cut short our follies in a flash.
CREON: Oh it's hard,
giving up the heart's desire . . . but I will do it—
no more fighting a losing battle with necessity.
LEADER: Do it now, go, don't leave it to others.
CREON: Now—I'm on my way! Come, each of you,
take up axes, make for the high ground,
over there, quickly! I and my better judgment
have come round to this—I shackled her,
I'll set her free myself. I am afraid . . .
it's best to keep the established laws
to the very day we die.
[*Rushing out, followed by his entourage. The* CHORUS *clusters around the altar.*]
CHORUS: God of a hundred names!
Great Dionysus—
Son and glory of Semele! Pride of Thebes—
Child of Zeus whose thunder rocks the clouds—
Lord of the famous lands of evening—
King of the Mysteries!
King of Eleusis, Demeter's[6] plain
her breasting hills that welcome in the world—
Great Dionysus!
Bacchus, living in Thebes
the mother-city of all your frenzied women—
Bacchus
living along the Ismenus'[7] rippling waters
standing over the field sown with the Dragon's teeth!

You—we have seen you through the flaring smoky fires,
your torches blazing over the twin peaks[8]

6. The grain and harvest goddess. Eleusis is near Athens, the site of the mysteries and the worship of Demeter. 7. A river at Thebes. Dionysus (or Bacchus) was among the divinities worshiped by the initiates. 8. The two cliffs above Delphi, where Dionysus was thought to reside in the winter months.

where nymphs of the hallowed cave climb onward
fired with you, your sacred rage—
we have seen you at Castalia's running spring
and down from the heights of Nysa[9] crowned with ivy
the greening shore rioting vines and grapes
down you come in your storm of wild women
ecstatic, mystic cries—
Dionysus—
down to watch and ward the roads of Thebes!

First of all cities, Thebes you honor first
you and your mother, bride of the lightning—
come, Dionysus! now your people lie
in the iron grip of plague,
come in your racing, healing stride
down Parnassus' slopes
or across the moaning straits.
Lord of the dancing—
dance, dance the constellations breathing fire!
Great master of the voices of the night!
Child of Zeus, God's offspring, come, come forth!
Lord, king, dance with your nymphs, swirling, raving
arm-in-arm in frenzy through the night
they dance you, Iacchus[1]—
Dance, Dionysus
giver of all good things!
[*Enter a* MESSENGER *from the side.*]

MESSENGER: Neighbors,
friends of the house of Cadmus and the kings,
there's not a thing in this mortal life of ours
I'd praise or blame as settled once for all.
Fortune lifts and Fortune fells the lucky
and unlucky every day. No prophet on earth
can tell a man his fate. Take Creon:
there was a man to rouse your envy once,
as I see it. He saved the realm from enemies,
taking power, he alone, the lord of the fatherland,
he set us true on course—he flourished like a tree
with the noble line of sons he bred and reared . . .
and now it's lost, all gone.
Believe me,
when a man has squandered his true joys,
he's good as dead, I tell you, a living corpse.
Pile up riches in your house, as much as you like—
live like a king with a huge show of pomp,
but if real delight is missing from the lot,
I wouldn't give you a wisp of smoke for it,
not compared with joy.

LEADER: What now?

9. A mountain associated with Dionysiac worship; there is more than one mountain so named, but the reference here is probably to the one on the island of Euboea, off the Attic coast. 1. Dionysus.

What new grief do you bring the house of kings?
MESSENGER: Dead, dead—and the living are guilty of their death!
LEADER: Who's the murderer? Who is dead? Tell us.
MESSENGER: Haemon's gone, his blood spilled by the very hand—
LEADER: His father's or his own?
MESSENGER: His own . . .
raging mad with his father for the death—
LEADER: Oh great seer,
you saw it all, you brought your word to birth!
MESSENGER: Those are the facts. Deal with them as you will.
[*As he turns to go,* EURYDICE *enters from the palace.*]
LEADER: Look, Eurydice. Poor woman, Creon's wife,
so close at hand. By chance perhaps,
unless she's heard the news about her son.
EURYDICE: My countrymen,
all of you—I caught the sound of your words
as I was leaving to do my part,
to appeal to queen Athena with my prayers.
I was just loosing the bolts, opening the doors,
when a voice filled with sorrow, family sorrow,
struck my ears, and I fell back, terrified,
into the women's arms—everything went black.
Tell me the news, again, whatever it is . . .
sorrow and I are hardly strangers.
I can bear the worst.
MESSENGER: I—dear lady,
I'll speak as an eye-witness. I was there.
And I won't pass over one word of the truth.
Why should I try to soothe you with a story,
only to prove a liar in a moment?
Truth is always best.
So,
I escorted your lord, I guided him
to the edge of the plain where the body lay,
Polynices, torn by the dogs and still unmourned.
And saying a prayer to Hecate of the Crossroads,
Pluto[2] too, to hold their anger and be kind,
we washed the dead in a bath of holy water
and plucking some fresh branches, gathering . . .
what was left of him, we burned them all together
and raised a high mound of native earth, and then
we turned and made for that rocky vault of hers,
the hollow, empty bed of the bride of Death.
And far off one of us heard a voice,
a long wail rising, echoing
out of that unhallowed wedding-chamber,
he ran to alert the master and Creon pressed on,
closer—the strange, inscrutable cry came sharper,

2. Or Hades, god of the underworld. Hecate is a goddess associated with darkness and burial grounds; offerings to her were left at crossroads.

throbbing around him now, and he let loose
a cry of his own, enough to wrench the heart,
"Oh god, am I the prophet now? going down
the darkest road I've ever gone? My son—
it's *his* dear voice, he greets me! Go, men,
closer, quickly! Go through the gap,
the rocks are dragged back—
right to the tomb's very mouth—and look,
see if it's Haemon's voice I think I hear,
or the gods have robbed me of my senses."

The king was shattered. We took his orders,
went and searched, and there in the deepest,
dark recesses of the tomb we found her . . .
hanged by the neck in a fine linen noose,
strangled in her veils—and the boy,
his arms flung around her waist,
clinging to her, wailing for his bride,
dead and down below, for his father's crimes
and the bed of his marriage blighted by misfortune.
When Creon saw him, he gave a deep sob,
he ran in, shouting, crying out to him,
"Oh my child—what have you done? what seized you,
what insanity? what disaster drove you mad?
Come out, my son! I beg you on my knees!"
But the boy gave him a wild burning glance,
spat in his face, not a word in reply,
he drew his sword—his father rushed out,
running as Haemon lunged and missed!—
and then, doomed, desperate with himself,
suddenly leaning his full weight on the blade,
he buried it in his body, halfway to the hilt.
And still in his senses, pouring his arms around her,
he embraced the girl and breathing hard,
released a quick rush of blood,
bright red on her cheek glistening white.
And there he lies, body enfolding body . . .
he has won his bride a last, poor boy,
not here but in the houses of the dead.

Creon shows the world that of all the ills
afflicting men the worst is lack of judgment.

[EURYDICE *turns and reenters the palace.*]

LEADER: What do you make of that? The lady's gone,
without a word, good or bad.

MESSENGER: I'm alarmed too
but here's my hope—faced with her son's death
she finds it unbecoming to mourn in public.
Inside, under her roof, she'll set her women
to the task and wail the sorrow of the house.
She's too discreet. She won't do something rash.

LEADER: I'm not so sure. To me, at least,
a long heavy silence promises danger,
just as much as a lot of empty outcries.
MESSENGER: We'll see if she's holding something back,
hiding some passion in her heart.
I'm going in. You may be right—who knows?
Even too much silence has its dangers.
[*Exit to the palace. Enter* CREON *from the side, escorted by attendants carrying* HAEMON*'s body on a bier.*]
LEADER: The king himself! Coming toward us,
look, holding the boy's head in his hands.
Clear, damning proof, if it's right to say so—
proof of his own madness, no one else's,
no, his own blind wrongs.
CREON: Ohhh,
so senseless, so insane . . . my crimes,
my stubborn, deadly—
Look at us, the killer, the killed,
father and son, the same blood—the misery!
My plans, my mad fanatic heart,
my son, cut off so young!
Ai, dead, lost to the world,
not through your stupidity, no, my own.
LEADER: Too late,
too late, you see what justice means.
CREON: Oh I've learned
through blood and tears! Then, it was then,
when the god came down and struck me—a great weight
shattering, driving me down that wild savage path,
ruining, trampling down my joy. Oh the agony,
the heartbreaking agonies of our lives.
[*Enter the* MESSENGER *from the palace.*]
MESSENGER: Master,
what a hoard of grief you have, and you'll have more.
The grief that lies to hand you've brought yourself—
[*Pointing to* HAEMON*'s body.*]
the rest, in the house, you'll see it all too soon.
CREON: What now? What's worse than this?
MESSENGER: The queen is dead.
The mother of this dead boy . . . mother to the end—
poor thing, her wounds are fresh.
CREON: No, no,
harbor of Death, so choked, so hard to cleanse!—
why me? why are you killing me?
Herald of pain, more words, more grief?
I died once, you kill me again and again!
What's the report, boy . . . some news for me?
My wife dead? O dear god!
Slaughter heaped on slaughter?
[*The doors open; the body of* EURYDICE *is brought out on her bier.*]

MESSENGER: See for yourself:
now they bring her body from the palace.
CREON: Oh no,
another, a second loss to break the heart.
What next, what fate still waits for me?
I just held my son in my arms and now,
look, a new corpse rising before my eyes—
wretched, helpless mother—O my son!
MESSENGER: She stabbed herself at the altar,
then her eyes went dark, after she'd raised
a cry for the noble fate of Megareus,[3] the hero
killed in the first assault, then for Haemon,
then with her dying breath she called down
torments on your head—you killed her sons.
CREON: Oh the dread,
I shudder with dread! Why not kill me too?—
run me through with a good sharp sword?
Oh god, the misery, anguish—
I, I'm churning with it, going under.
MESSENGER: Yes, and the dead, the woman lying there,
piles the guilt of all their deaths on you.
CREON: How did she end her life, what bloody stroke?
MESSENGER: She drove home to the heart with her own hand,
once she learned her son was dead . . . that agony.
CREON: And the guilt is all mine—
can never be fixed on another man,
no escape for me. I killed you,
I, god help me, I admit it all!
[*To his attendants.*]
Take me away, quickly, out of sight.
I don't even exist—I'm no one. Nothing.
LEADER: Good advice, if there's any good in suffering.
Quickest is best when troubles block the way.
CREON: [*Kneeling in prayer.*]
Come, let it come—that best of fates for me
that brings the final day, best fate of all.
Oh quickly, now—
so I never have to see another sunrise.
LEADER: That will come when it comes;
we must deal with all that lies before us.
The future rests with the ones who tend the future.
CREON: That prayer—I poured my heart into that prayer!
LEADER: No more prayers now. For mortal men
there is no escape from the doom we must endure.
CREON: Take me away, I beg you, out of sight.
A rash, indiscriminate fool!
I murdered you, my son, against my will—
you too, my wife . . .

3. Another son of Creon and Eurydice; he was killed during the siege of the city.

Wailing wreck of a man,
whom to look to? where to lean for support?
[*Desperately turning from* HAEMON *to* EURYDICE *on their biers.*]
Whatever I touch goes wrong—once more
a crushing fate's come down upon my head!
[*The* MESSENGER *and attendants lead* CREON *into the palace.*]
CHORUS: Wisdom is by far the greatest part of joy,
and reverence toward the gods must be safeguarded.
The mighty words of the proud are paid in full
with mighty blows of fate, and at long last
those blows will teach us wisdom.
[*The old citizens exit to the side.*]

EURIPIDES

480–406 B.C.

Euripides' *Medea*, produced in 431 B.C., the year that brought the beginning of the Peloponnesian War, appeared earlier than Sophocles' *Oedipus the King*, but it has a bitterness that is more in keeping with the spirit of a later age. If *Oedipus* is, in one sense, a warning to a generation that has embarked on an intellectual revolution, *Medea* is the ironic expression of the disillusion that comes after the shipwreck. In this play we are conscious for the first time of an attitude characteristic of modern literature, the artist's feeling of separation from the audience, the isolation of the poet. "Often previously," says Medea to the king,

> Through being considered clever I have suffered much. . . .
> If you put new ideas before the eyes of fools
> They'll think you foolish and worthless into the bargain;
> And if you are thought superior to those who have
> Some reputation for learning, you will become hated.

The common background of audience and poet is disappearing, the old certainties are being undermined, the city divided. Euripides is the first Greek poet to suffer the fate of so many of the great modern writers: rejected by most of his contemporaries (he rarely won first prize and was the favorite target for the scurrilous humor of the comic poets), he was universally admired and revered by the Greeks of the centuries that followed his death.

It is significant that what little biographical information we have for Euripides makes no mention of military service or political office; unlike Aeschylus, who fought in the ranks at Marathon, and Sophocles, who took an active part in public affairs from youth to advanced old age, Euripides seems to have lived a private, an intellectual life. Younger than Sophocles (though they died in the same year), he was more receptive to the critical theories and the rhetorical techniques offered by the Sophist teachers; his plays often subject received ideas to fundamental questioning, expressed in vivid dramatic debate. His *Medea* is typical of his iconoclastic approach; his choice of subject and central characters is in itself a challenge to established canons. He still dramatizes myth, but the myth he chooses is exotic and disturbing, and the protagonist is not a man but a woman. Medea is both woman and foreigner—that is, in terms of the audience's prejudice and practice she is a representative of the two free-born groups in Athenian society that had almost no rights at all (though the male foreign resident had more rights than the native woman). The tragic hero is no longer a king, "one who is highly renowned and prosperous such as Oedipus," but a woman who, because she finds no redress for her wrongs in society, is driven by her passion to violate that society's most sacred laws in a rebellion against its typical representative, Jason, her husband. She is not just a woman and a foreigner, she is also a person of great intellectual power. Compared with her the credulous king and her complacent husband are children, and once her mind is made up, she moves them like pawns to their proper places in her barbaric game. The myth is used for new purposes, to shock the members of the audience, attack their deepest prejudices, and shake them out of their complacent pride in the superiority of Greek masculinity.

But the play is more compelling than that. Before it is over, our sympathies have come full circle; the contempt with which we regard the Jason of the opening scenes turns to pity as we feel the measure of his loss and the ferocity of Medea's revenge. Medea's passion has carried her too far; the death of Kreon (Creon) and his daughter we might have accepted, but the murder of the children is too much. It was, of course, meant to be. Euripides' theme, like Homer's, is violence, but this is the unspeakable violence of the oppressed, which is greater than the violence of the oppressor and which, because it has been long pent up, cannot be controlled.

In this, as in the other Greek plays, the gods have their place. In *Oresteia* the will of Zeus is manifested in every action and implied in every word; in *Oedipus the King* the gods bide their time and watch Oedipus fulfill the truth of their prophecy, but in *Medea,* the divine will, which is revealed at the end, is enigmatic and, far from bringing harmony, concludes the play with a terrifying discord. All through *Medea* the human beings involved call on the gods; two especially are singled out for attention: Earth and Sun. It is by these two gods that Medea makes Aegeus swear to give her refuge in Athens, the chorus invokes them to prevent Medea's violence against her sons, and Jason wonders how Medea can look on Earth and Sun after she has killed her own children. These emphatic appeals clearly raise the question of the attitude of the gods, and the answer to the question is a shock. We are not told what Earth does, but Sun sends the magic chariot on which Medea makes her escape. His reason, too, is stated: it is not any concern for justice but the fact that Medea is his granddaughter. Euripides is here using the letter of the myth for his own purposes. This jarring detail emphasizes the significance of the whole. The play creates a world in which there is no relation whatsoever between the powers that rule the universe and the fundamental laws of human morality. It dramatizes disorder, not just the disorder of the family of Jason and Medea but the disorder of the universe as a whole. It is the nightmare in which the dream of the fifth century B.C. was to end, the senseless fury and degradation of permanent violence. "Flow backward to your sources, sacred rivers," the chorus sings. "And let the world's great order be reversed."

For a short, general survey of Euripidean drama, see B. M. W. Knox in *The Cambridge History of Classical Literature* (1985), pp. 316–39. Perceptive analyses of *Medea* can be found in Emily A. McDermott, *Euripides' Medea: The Incarnation of Disorder* (1989), and E. Segal, ed., *Euripides, A Collection of Critical Essays* (1968). Knox, "The *Medea* of Euripides," and P. E. Easterling, "The Infanticide in Euripides' *Medea,*" both in *Yale Classical Studies* 24 (1977), will also be helpful to students.

PRONOUNCING GLOSSARY

The following list uses common English syllables and stress accents to provide rough equivalents of selected words whose pronunciation may be unfamiliar to the general reader.

Aigeus: *ai'-jioos*

Aphrodite: *a-froh-dai'-tee*

Hecate: *he'-kah-tee*

Iolcos: *yol'-kuhs*

Medea: *me-dee'-uh*

Pelias: *pee'-lee-as*

Pieria: *pai-ee'-ree-uh*

Medea[1]

CHARACTERS

MEDEA, *princess of Colchis and wife of Jason*
JASON, *son of Aeson, king of Iolcos*
Two CHILDREN *of Medea and Jason*
KREON, *king of Corinth*
AIGEUS, *king of Athens*
NURSE *to Medea*
TUTOR *to Medea's children*
MESSENGER
CHORUS OF CORINTHIAN WOMEN

[SCENE—*In front of* MEDEA'*s house in Corinth. Enter from the house* MEDEA'*s* NURSE.]

NURSE How I wish the Argo[2] never had reached the land
Of Colchis, skimming through the blue Symplegades,
Nor ever had fallen in the glades of Pelion[3]
The smitten fir-tree to furnish oars for the hands
Of heroes who in Pelias'[4] name attempted
The Golden Fleece! For then my mistress Medea[5]
Would not have sailed for the towers of the land of Iolcos,
Her heart on fire with passionate love for Jason;
Nor would she have persuaded the daughters of Pelias
To kill their father,[6] and now be living here
In Corinth[7] with her husband and children. She gave
Pleasure to the people of her land of exile,
And she herself helped Jason in every way.
This is indeed the greatest salvation of all,—
For the wife not to stand apart from the husband.
But now there's hatred everywhere. Love is diseased.
For, deserting his own children and my mistress,
Jason has taken a royal wife to his bed,
The daughter of the ruler of this land, Kreon.
And poor Medea is slighted, and cries aloud on the
Vows they made to each other, the right hands clasped
In eternal promise. She calls upon the gods to witness
What sort of return Jason has made to her love.
She lies without food and gives herself up to suffering,
Wasting away every moment of the day in tears.
So it has gone since she knew herself slighted by him.
Not stirring an eye, not moving her face from the ground,
No more than either a rock or surging sea water

1. Translated by Rex Warner. 2. The ship in which Jason and his companions sailed on the quest for the Golden Fleece. 3. A mountain in northern Greece near Iolcos, the place from which Jason sailed. The Symplegades were clashing rocks that crushed ships endeavoring to pass between them. They were supposed to be located at the Hellespont, the passage between the Mediterranean and Black Seas. 4. He seized the kingdom of Iolcos, expelling Aeson, Jason's father. When Jason came to claim his rights, Pelias sent him to get the Golden Fleece. 5. Daughter of the king of Colchis who fell in love with Jason and helped him take the Golden Fleece away from her own country. 6. After Jason and Medea returned to Iolcos, Medea (who had a reputation as a sorceress) persuaded Pelias's daughters to cut Pelias up and boil the pieces, which would restore him to youth. The experiment was, of course, unsuccessful, and Pelias's son banished Jason and Medea from the kingdom. 7. On the isthmus between the Peloponnese and Attica, where they took refuge. In Euripides' time it was a wealthy trading city, a commercial rival of Athens.

She listens when she is given friendly advice.
Except that sometimes she twists back her white neck and
Moans to herself, calling out on her father's name,
And her land, and her home betrayed when she came away with
A man who now is determined to dishonor her.
Poor creature, she has discovered by her sufferings
What it means to one not to have lost one's own country.
She has turned from the children and does not like to see them.
I am afraid she may think of some dreadful thing,
For her heart is violent. She will never put up with
The treatment she is getting. I know and fear her
Lest she may sharpen a sword and thrust to the heart,
Stealing into the palace where the bed is made,
Or even kill the king and the new-wedded groom,
And thus bring a greater misfortune on herself.
She's a strange woman. I know it won't be easy
To make an enemy of her and come off best.
But here the children come. They have finished playing.
They have no thought at all of their mother's trouble.
Indeed it is not usual for the young to grieve.

[*Enter from the right the slave who is the* TUTOR *to* MEDEA*'s two small* CHILDREN. *The* CHILDREN *follow him.*]

TUTOR You old retainer of my mistress's household,
Why are you standing here all alone in front of the
Gates and moaning to yourself over your misfortune?
Medea could not wish you to leave her alone.

NURSE Old man, and guardian of the children of Jason,
If one is a good servant, it's a terrible thing
When one's master's luck is out; it goes to one's heart.
So I myself have got into such a state of grief
That a longing stole over me to come outside here
And tell the earth and air of my mistress's sorrows.

TUTOR Has the poor lady not yet given up her crying?

NURSE Given up? She's at the start, not halfway through her tears.

TUTOR Poor fool,—if I may call my mistress such a name,—
How ignorant she is of trouble more to come.

NURSE What do you mean, old man? You needn't fear to speak.

TUTOR Nothing. I take back the words which I used just now.

NURSE Don't, by your beard, hide this from me, your fellow-servant.
If need be, I'll keep quiet about what you tell me.

TUTOR I heard a person saying, while I myself seemed
Not to be paying attention, when I was at the place
Where the old draught-players[8] sit, by the holy fountain,
That Kreon, ruler of the land, intends to drive
These children and their mother in exile from Corinth.
But whether what he said is really true or not
I do not know. I pray that it may not be true.

NURSE And will Jason put up with it that his children

8. Checker players.

Should suffer so, though he's no friend to their mother?
TUTOR Old ties give place to new ones. As for Jason, he
No longer has a feeling for this house of ours.
NURSE It's black indeed for us, when we add new to old
Sorrows before even the present sky has cleared.
TUTOR But you be silent, and keep all this to yourself.
It is not the right time to tell our mistress of it.
NURSE Do you hear, children, what a father he is to you?
I wish he were dead,—but no, he is still my master.
Yet certainly he has proved unkind to his dear ones.
TUTOR What's strange in that? Have you only just discovered
That everyone loves himself more than his neighbor?
Some have good reason, others get something out of it.
So Jason neglects his children for the new bride.
NURSE Go indoors, children. That will be the best thing.
And you, keep them to themselves as much as possible.
Don't bring them near their mother in her angry mood.
For I've seen her already blazing her eyes at them
As though she meant some mischief and I am sure that
She'll not stop raging until she has struck at someone.
May it be an enemy and not a friend she hurts!

[MEDEA *is heard inside the house.*]

MEDEA Ah, wretch! Ah, lost in my sufferings,
I wish, I wish I might die.
NURSE What did I say, dear children? Your mother
Frets her heart and frets it to anger.
Run away quickly into the house,
And keep well out of her sight.
Don't go anywhere near, but be careful
Of the wildness and bitter nature
Of that proud mind.
Go now! Run quickly indoors.
It is clear that she soon will put lightning
In that cloud of her cries that is rising
With a passion increasing. Oh, what will she do,
Proud-hearted and not to be checked on her course,
A soul bitten into with wrong?

[*The* TUTOR *takes the* CHILDREN *into the house.*]

MEDEA Ah, I have suffered
What should be wept for bitterly. I hate you,
Children of a hateful mother. I curse you
And your father. Let the whole house crash.
NURSE Ah, I pity you, you poor creature.
How can your children share in their father's
Wickedness? Why do you hate them? Oh children,
How much I fear that something may happen!
Great people's tempers are terrible, always
Having their own way, seldom checked,
Dangerous they shift from mood to mood.
How much better to have been accustomed

To live on equal terms with one's neighbors.
I would like to be safe and grow old in a
Humble way. What is moderate sounds best,
Also in practice *is* best for everyone.
Greatness brings no profit to people.
God indeed, when in anger, brings
Greater ruin to great men's houses.

[*Enter, on the right, a* CHORUS OF CORINTHIAN WOMEN. *They have come to inquire about* MEDEA *and to attempt to console her.*]

CHORUS I heard the voice, I heard the cry
Of Colchis' wretched daughter.
Tell me, mother, is she not yet
At rest? Within the double gates
Of the court I heard her cry. I am sorry
For the sorrow of this home. O, say, what has happened?

NURSE There is no home. It's over and done with.
Her husband holds fast to his royal wedding,
While she, my mistress, cries out her eyes
There in her room, and takes no warmth from
Any word of any friend.

MEDEA Oh, I wish
That lightning from heaven would split my head open.
Oh, what use have I now for life?
I would find my release in death
And leave hateful existence behind me.

CHORUS O God and Earth and Heaven!
Did you hear what a cry was that
Which the sad wife sings?
Poor foolish one, why should you long
For that appalling rest?
The final end of death comes fast.
No need to pray for that.
Suppose your man gives honor
To another woman's bed.
It often happens. Don't be hurt.
God will be your friend in this.
You must not waste away
Grieving too much for him who shared your bed.

MEDEA Great Themis, lady Artemis,[9] behold
The things I suffer, though I made him promise,
My hateful husband. I pray that I may see him,
Him and his bride and all their palace shattered
For the wrong they dare to do me without cause.
Oh, my father! Oh, my country! In what dishonor
I left you, killing my own brother for it.[1]

NURSE Do you hear what she says, and how she cries
On Themis, the goddess of Promises, and on Zeus,

9. The protector of women in pain and distress. Themis, a Titan, was justice personified. 1. Medea killed him to delay the pursuit when she escaped with Jason.

Whom we believe to be the Keeper of Oaths?
Of this I am sure, that no small thing
Will appease my mistress's anger.

CHORUS Will she come into our presence?
Will she listen when we are speaking
To the words we say?
I wish she might relax her rage
And temper of her heart.
My willingness to help will never
Be wanting to my friends.
But go inside and bring her
Out of the house to us,
And speak kindly to her: hurry,
Before she wrongs her own.
This passion of hers moves to something great.

NURSE I will, but I doubt if I'll manage
To win my mistress over.
But still I'll attempt it to please you.
Such a look she will flash on her servants
If any comes near with a message,
Like a lioness guarding her cubs.
It is right, I think, to consider
Both stupid and lacking in foresight
Those poets of old who wrote songs
For revels and dinners and banquets,
Pleasant sounds for men living at ease;
But none of them all has discovered
How to put an end with their singing
Or musical instruments grief,
Bitter grief, from which death and disaster
Cheat the hopes of a house. Yet how good
If music could cure men of this! But why raise
To no purpose the voice at a banquet? For *there* is
Already abundance of pleasure for men
With a joy of its own.

[*The* NURSE *goes into the house.*]

CHORUS I heard a shriek that is laden with sorrow.
Shrilling out her hard grief she cries out
Upon him who betrayed both her bed and her marriage.
Wronged, she calls on the gods,
On the justice of Zeus, the oath sworn,
Which brought her away
To the opposite shore of the Greeks
Through the gloomy salt straits to the gateway
Of the salty unlimited sea.

[MEDEA, *attended by servants, comes out of the house.*]

MEDEA Women of Corinth, I have come outside to you
Lest you should be indignant with me; for I know
That many people are overproud, some when alone,
And others when in company. And those who live

Quietly, as I do, get a bad reputation.
For a just judgment is not evident in the eyes
When a man at first sight hates another, before
Learning his character, being in no way injured;
And a foreigner[2] especially must adapt himself.
I'd not approve of even a fellow-countryman
Who by pride and want of manners offends his neighbors.
But on me this thing has fallen so unexpectedly,
It has broken my heart. I am finished. I let go
All my life's joy. My friends, I only want to die.
It was everything to me to think well of one man,
And he, my own husband, has turned out wholly vile.
Of all things which are living and can form a judgment
We women are the most unfortunate creatures.[3]
Firstly, with an excess of wealth it is required
For us to buy a husband and take for our bodies
A master; for not to take one is even worse.
And now the question is serious whether we take
A good or bad one; for there is no easy escape
For a woman, nor can she say no to her marriage.
She arrives among new modes of behavior and manners,
And needs prophetic power, unless she has learnt at home,
How best to manage him who shares the bed with her.
And if we work out all this well and carefully,
And the husband lives with us and lightly bears his yoke,
Then life is enviable. If not, I'd rather die.
A man, when he's tired of the company in his home,
Goes out of the house and puts an end to his boredom
And turns to a friend or companion of his own age.
But we are forced to keep our eyes on one alone.
What they say of us is that we have a peaceful time
Living at home, while they do the fighting in war.
How wrong they are! I would very much rather stand
Three times in the front of battle than bear one child.
Yet what applies to me does not apply to you.
You have a country. Your family home is here.
You enjoy life and the company of your friends.
But I am deserted, a refugee, thought nothing of
By my husband,—something he won in a foreign land.
I have no mother or brother, nor any relation
With whom I can take refuge in this sea of woe.
This much then is the service I would beg from you:
If I can find the means or devise any scheme
To pay my husband back for what he has done to me,—
Him and his father-in-law and the girl who married him,—
Just to keep silent. For in other ways a woman

2. Foreign residents were encouraged to come to Athens but were rarely admitted to the rights of full citizenship, which was a jealously guarded privilege. 3. Athenian rights and institutions were made for men; the women had few privileges and almost no legal rights. Lines 230–31 refer to the dowry that had to be provided for the bride.

Is full of fear, defenseless, dreads the sight of cold
Steel; but, when once she is wronged in the matter of love,
No other soul can hold so many thoughts of blood.

CHORUS This I will promise. You are in the right, Medea,
In paying your husband back. I am not surprised at you
For being sad. But look! I see our king Kreon
Approaching. He will tell us of some new plan.

[*Enter, from the right,* KREON, *with attendants.*]

KREON You, with that angry look, so set against your husband,
Medea, I order you to leave my territories
An exile, and take along with you your two children,
And not to waste time doing it. It is my decree,
And I will see it done. I will not return home
Until you are cast from the boundaries of my land.

MEDEA Oh, this is the end for me. I am utterly lost.
Now I am in the full force of the storm of hate
And have no harbor from ruin to reach easily.
Yet still, in spite of it all, I'll ask the question:
What is your reason, Kreon, for banishing me?

KREON I am afraid of you,—why should I dissemble it?—
Afraid that you may injure my daughter mortally.
Many things accumulate to support my feeling.
You are a clever woman, versed in evil arts,
And are angry at having lost your husband's love.
I hear that you are threatening, so they tell me,
To do something against my daughter and Jason
And me, too. I shall take my precautions first.
I tell you, I prefer to earn your hatred now
Than to be soft-hearted and afterwards regret it.

MEDEA This is not the first time, Kreon. Often previously
Through being considered clever I have suffered much.
A person of sense ought never to have his children
Brought up to be more clever than the average.
For, apart from cleverness bringing them no profit,
It will make them objects of envy and ill-will.
If you put new ideas before the eyes of fools
They'll think you foolish and worthless into the bargain;
And if you are thought superior to those who have
Some reputation for learning, you will become hated.
I have some knowledge myself of how this happens;
For being clever, I find that some will envy me,
Others object to me. Yet all my cleverness
Is not so much. Well, then, are you frightened, Kreon,
That I should harm you? There is no need. It is not
My way to transgress the authority of a king.
How have you injured me? You gave your daughter away
To the man you wanted. O, certainly I hate
My husband, but you, I think, have acted wisely;
Nor do I grudge it you that your affairs go well.
May the marriage be a lucky one! Only let me

Live in this land. For even though I have been wronged,
I will not raise my voice, but submit to my betters.

KREON What you say sounds gentle enough. Still in my heart
I greatly dread that you are plotting some evil,
And therefore I trust you even less than before.
A sharp-tempered woman, or for that matter a man,
Is easier to deal with than the clever type
Who holds her tongue. No. You must go. No need for more
Speeches. The thing is fixed. By no manner of means
Shall you, an enemy of mine, stay in my country.

MEDEA I beg you. By your knees, by your new-wedded girl.

KREON Your words are wasted. You will never persuade me.

MEDEA Will you drive me out, and give no heed to my prayers?

KREON I will, for I love my family more than you.

MEDEA O my country! How bitterly now I remember you!

KREON I love my country too,—next after my children.

MEDEA O what an evil to men is passionate love!

KREON That would depend on the luck that goes along with it.

MEDEA O God, do not forget who is the cause of this!

KREON Go. It is no use. Spare me the pain of forcing you.

MEDEA I'm spared no pain. I lack no pain to be spared me.

KREON Then you'll be removed by force by one of my men.

MEDEA No, Kreon, not that! But do listen, I beg you.

KREON Woman, you seem to want to create a disturbance.

MEDEA I *will* go into exile. *This* is not what I beg for.

KREON Why then this violence and clinging to my hand?

MEDEA Allow me to remain here just for this one day,
So I may consider where to live in my exile,
And look for support for my children, since their father
Chooses to make no kind of provision for them.
Have pity on them! You have children of your own.
It is natural for you to look kindly on them.
For myself I do not mind if I go into exile.
It is the children being in trouble that I mind.

KREON There is nothing tyrannical about my nature,
And by showing mercy I have often been the loser.
Even now I know that I am making a mistake.
All the same you shall have your will. But this I tell you,
That if the light of heaven tomorrow shall see you,
You and your children in the confines of my land,
You die. This word I have spoken is firmly fixed.
But now, if you must stay, stay for this day alone.
For in it you can do none of the things I fear.

[*Exit* KREON *with his attendants.*]

CHORUS Oh, unfortunate one! Oh, cruel!
Where will you turn? Who will help you?
What house or what land to preserve you
From ill can you find?
Medea, a god has thrown suffering
Upon you in waves of despair.

MEDEA Things have gone badly every way. No doubt of that.
But not these things this far, and don't imagine so.
There are still trials to come for the new-wedded pair,
And for their relations pain that will mean something.
Do you think that I would ever have fawned on that man
Unless I had some end to gain or profit in it?
I would not even have spoken or touched him with my hands.
But he has got to such a pitch of foolishness
That, though he could have made nothing of all my plans
By exiling me, he has given me this one day
To stay here, and in this I will make dead bodies
Of three of my enemies,—father, the girl and my husband.
I have many ways of death which I might suit to them,
And do not know, friends, which one to take in hand;
Whether to set fire underneath their bridal mansion,
Or sharpen a sword and thrust it to the heart,
Stealing into the palace where the bed is made.
There is just one obstacle to this. If I am caught
Breaking into the house and scheming against it,
I shall die, and give my enemies cause for laughter.
It is best to go by the straight road, the one in which
I am most skilled, and make away with them by poison.
So be it then.
And now suppose them dead. What town will receive me?
What friend will offer me a refuge in his land,
Or the guarantee of his house and save my own life?
There is none. So I must wait a little time yet,
And if some sure defense should then appear for me,
In craft and silence I will set about this murder.
But if my fate should drive me on without help,
Even though death is certain, I will take the sword
Myself and kill, and steadfastly advance to crime.
It shall not be,—I swear it by her, my mistress,
Whom most I honor and have chosen as partner,
Hecate,[4] who dwells in the recesses of my hearth,—
That any man shall be glad to have injured me.
Bitter I will make their marriage for them and mournful,
Bitter the alliance and the driving me out of the land.
Ah, come, Medea, in your plotting and scheming
Leave nothing untried of all those things which you know.
Go forward to the dreadful act. The test has come
For resolution. You see how you are treated. Never
Shall you be mocked by Jason's Corinthian wedding,
Whose father was noble, whose grandfather Helios.[5]
You have the skill. What is more, you were born a woman,
And women, though most helpless in doing good deeds,
Are of every evil the cleverest of contrivers.

4. The patron of witchcraft, sometimes identified with Artemis; Medea has a statue and shrine of her in the house. 5. The sun, father of Medea's father, Aeëtes.

CHORUS Flow backward to your sources, sacred rivers,
And let the world's great order be reversed.
It is the thoughts of *men* that are deceitful,
Their pledges that are loose.
Story shall now turn my condition to a fair one,
Women are paid their due.
No more shall evil-sounding fame be theirs.

Cease now, you muses of the ancient singers,
To tell the tale of my unfaithfulness;
For not on us did Phoebus,[6] lord of music,
Bestow the lyre's divine
Power, for otherwise I should have sung an answer
To the other sex. Long time
Has much to tell of us, and much of them.

You sailed away from your father's home,
With a heart on fire you passed
The double rocks of the sea.
And now in a foreign country
You have lost your rest in a widowed bed,
And are driven forth, a refugee
In dishonor from the land.

Good faith has gone, and no more remains
In great Greece a sense of shame.
It has flown away to the sky.
No father's house for a haven
Is at hand for you now, and another queen
Of your bed has dispossessed you and
Is mistress of your home.

[*Enter* JASON, *with attendants.*]

JASON This is not the first occasion that I have noticed
How hopeless it is to deal with a stubborn temper.
For, with reasonable submission to our ruler's will,
You might have lived in this land and kept your home.
As it is you are going to be exiled for your loose speaking.
Not that I mind myself. You are free to continue
Telling everyone that Jason is a worthless man.
But as to your talk about the king, consider
Yourself most lucky that exile is your punishment.
I, for my part, have always tried to calm down
The anger of the king, and wished you to remain.
But you will not give up your folly, continually
Speaking ill of him, and so you are going to be banished.
All the same, and in spite of your conduct, I'll not desert
My friends, but have come to make some provision for you,
So that you and the children may not be penniless

6. Apollo.

Or in need of anything in exile. Certainly
Exile brings many troubles with it. And even
If you hate me, I cannot think badly of you.

MEDEA O coward in every way,—that is what I call you,
With bitterest reproach for your lack of manliness,
You have come, you, my worst enemy, have come to me!
It is not an example of over-confidence
Or of boldness thus to look your friends in the face,
Friends you have injured,—no, it is the worst of all
Human diseases, shamelessness. But you did well
To come, for I can speak ill of you and lighten
My heart, and you will suffer while you are listening.
And first I will begin from what happened first.
I saved your life, and every Greek knows I saved it
Who was a ship-mate of yours aboard the Argo,
When you were sent to control the bulls that breathed fire
And yoke them, and when you would sow that deadly field.
Also that snake, who encircled with his many folds
The Golden Fleece and guarded it and never slept,[7]
I killed, and so gave you the safety of the light.
And I myself betrayed my father and my home,
And came with you to Pelias' land of Iolcos.
And then, showing more willingness to help than wisdom,
I killed him, Pelias, with a most dreadful death
At his own daughters' hands, and took away your fear.
This is how I behaved to you, you wretched man,
And you forsook me, took another bride to bed
Though you had children; for, if that had not been,
You would have had an excuse for another wedding.
Faith in your word has gone. Indeed I cannot tell
Whether you think the gods whose names you swore by then
Have ceased to rule and that new standards are set up,
Since you must know you have broken your word to me.
O my right hand, and the knees which you often clasped
In supplication, how senselessly I am treated
By this bad man, and how my hopes have missed their mark!
Come, I will share my thoughts as though you were a friend,—
You! Can I think that you would ever treat me well?
But I will do it, and these questions will make you
Appear the baser. Where am I to go? To my father's?
Him I betrayed and his land when I came with you.
To Pelias' wretched daughters? What a fine welcome
They would prepare for me who murdered their father!
For this is my position,—hated by my friends
At home, I have, in kindness to you, made enemies
Of others whom there was no need to have injured.
And how happy among Greek women you have made me

7. These lines refer to ordeals through which Jason had to pass to win the fleece and in which Medea helped him. He had to yoke a team of fire-breathing bulls, then sow a field that immediately sprouted armed warriors, and then deal with the snake that guarded the fleece.

On your side for all this! A distinguished husband
I have,—for breaking promises. When in misery
I am cast out of the land and go into exile,
Quite without friends and all alone with my children,
That will be a fine shame for the new-wedded groom,
For his children to wander as beggars and she who saved him.
O God, you have given to mortals a sure method
Of telling the gold that is pure from the counterfeit;
Why is there no mark engraved upon men's bodies,
By which we could know the true ones from the false ones?

CHORUS It is a strange form of anger, difficult to cure
When two friends turn upon each other in hatred.

JASON As for me, it seems I must be no bad speaker.
But, like a man who has a good grip of the tiller,
Reef up his sail, and so run away from under
This mouthing tempest, woman, of your bitter tongue.
Since you insist on building up your kindness to me,
My view is that Cypris[8] was alone responsible
Of men and gods for the preserving of my life.
You are clever enough,—but really I need not enter
Into the story of how it was love's inescapable
Power that compelled you to keep my person safe.
On this I will not go into too much detail.
In so far as you helped me, you did well enough.
But on this question of saving me, I can prove
You have certainly got from me more than you gave.
Firstly, instead of living among barbarians,
You inhabit a Greek land and understand our ways,
How to live by law instead of the sweet will of force.
And all the Greeks considered you a clever woman.
You were honored for it; while, if you were living at
The ends of the earth, nobody would have heard of you.
For my part, rather than stores of gold in my house
Or power to sing even sweeter songs than Orpheus,
I'd choose the fate that made me a distinguished man.
There is my reply to your story of my labors.
Remember it was you who started the argument.
Next for your attack on my wedding with the princess:
Here I will prove that, first, it was a clever move,
Secondly, a wise one, and, finally, that I made it
In your best interests and the children's. Please keep calm.
When I arrived here from the land of Iolcos,
Involved, as I was, in every kind of difficulty,
What luckier chance could I have come across than this,
An exile to marry the daughter of the king?
It was not,—the point that seems to upset you—that I
Grew tired of your bed and felt the need of a new bride;
Nor with any wish to outdo your number of children.

8. Aphrodite, goddess of love.

We have enough already. I am quite content.
But,—this was the main reason—that we might live well,
And not be short of anything. I know that all
A man's friends leave him stone-cold if he becomes poor.
Also that I might bring my children up worthy
Of my position, and, by producing more of them
To be brothers of yours, we would draw the families
Together and all be happy. You need no children.
And it pays me to do good to those I have now
By having others. Do you think this a bad plan?
You wouldn't if the love question hadn't upset you.
But you women have got into such a state of mind
That, if your life at night is good, you think you have
Everything; but, if in that quarter things go wrong,
You will consider your best and truest interests
Most hateful. It would have been better far for men
To have got their children in some other way, and women
Not to have existed. Then life would have been good.

CHORUS Jason, though you have made this speech of yours look well,
Still I think, even though others do not agree,
You have betrayed your wife and are acting badly.

MEDEA Surely in many ways I hold different views
From others, for I think that the plausible speaker
Who is a villain deserves the greatest punishment.
Confident in his tongue's power to adorn evil,
He stops at nothing. Yet he is not really wise.
As in your case. There is no need to put on the airs
Of a clever speaker, for one word will lay you flat.
If you were not a coward, you would not have married
Behind my back, but discussed it with me first.

JASON And you, no doubt, would have furthered the proposal,
If I had told you of it, you who even now
Are incapable of controlling your bitter temper.

MEDEA It was not that. No, you thought it was not respectable
As you got on in years to have a foreign wife.

JASON Make sure of this: it was not because of a woman
I made the royal alliance in which I now live,
But, as I said before, I wished to preserve you
And breed a royal progeny to be brothers
To the children I have now, a sure defense to us.

MEDEA Let me have no happy fortune that brings pain with it,
Or prosperity which is upsetting to the mind!

JASON Change your ideas of what you want, and show more sense.
Do not consider painful what is good for you,
Nor, when you are lucky, think yourself unfortunate.

MEDEA You can insult me. You have somewhere to turn to.
But I shall go from this land into exile, friendless.

JASON It was what you chose yourself. Don't blame others for it.

MEDEA And how did I choose it? Did I betray my husband?

JASON You called down wicked curses on the king's family.

MEDEA A curse, that is what I am become to your house too.
JASON I do not propose to go into all the rest of it;
But, if you wish for the children or for yourself
In exile to have some of my money to help you,
Say so, for I am prepared to give with open hand,
Or to provide you with introductions to my friends
Who will treat you well. You are a fool if you do not
Accept this. Cease your anger and you will profit.
MEDEA I shall never accept the favors of friends of yours,
Nor take a thing from you, so you need not offer it.
There is no benefit in the gifts of a bad man.
JASON Then, in any case, I call the gods to witness that
I wish to help you and the children in every way,
But you refuse what is good for you. Obstinately
You push away your friends. You are sure to suffer for it.
MEDEA Go! No doubt you hanker for your virginal bride,
And are guilty of lingering too long out of her house.
Enjoy your wedding. But perhaps,—with the help of God—
You will make the kind of marriage that you will regret.
[JASON *goes out with his attendants.*]
CHORUS When love is in excess
It brings a man no honor
Nor any worthiness.
But if in moderation Cypris comes,
There is no other power at all so gracious.
O goddess, never on me let loose the unerring
Shaft of your bow in the poison of desire.

Let my heart be wise.
It is the gods' best gift.
On me let mighty Cypris
Inflict no wordy wars or restless anger
To urge my passion to a different love.
But with discernment may she guide women's weddings,
Honoring most what is peaceful in the bed.

O country and home,
Never, never may I be without you,
Living the hopeless life,
Hard to pass through and painful,
Most pitiable of all.
Let death first lay me low and death
Free me from this daylight.
There is no sorrow above
The loss of a native land.

I have seen it myself,
Do not tell of a secondhand story.
Neither city nor friend
Pitied you when you suffered

The worst of sufferings.
O let him die ungraced whose heart
Will not reward his friends,
Who cannot open an honest mind
No friend will he be of mine.

[*Enter* AIGEUS, *king of Athens, an old friend of* MEDEA.]

AIGEUS Medea, greeting! This is the best introduction
Of which men know for conversation between friends.
MEDEA Greeting to you too, Aigeus, son of King Pandion,
Where have you come from to visit this country's soil?
AIGEUS I have just left the ancient oracle of Phoebus.
MEDEA And why did you go to earth's prophetic center?
AIGEUS I went to inquire how children might be born to me.
MEDEA Is it so? Your life still up to this point childless?
AIGEUS Yes. By the fate of some power we have no children.
MEDEA Have you a wife, or is there none to share your bed?
AIGEUS There is. Yes, I am joined to my wife in marriage.
MEDEA And what did Phoebus say to you about children?
AIGEUS Words too wise for a mere man to guess their meaning.
MEDEA Is it proper for me to be told the God's reply?
AIGEUS It is. For sure what is needed is cleverness.
MEDEA Then what was his message? Tell me, if I may hear.
AIGEUS I am not to loosen the hanging foot of the wine-skin[9] . . .
MEDEA Until you have done something, or reached some country?
AIGEUS Until I return again to my hearth and house.
MEDEA And for what purpose have you journeyed to this land?
AIGEUS There is a man called Pittheus, king of Troezen.[1]
MEDEA A son of Pelops, they say, a most righteous man.
AIGEUS With him I wish to discuss the reply of the god.
MEDEA Yes. He is wise and experienced in such matters.
AIGEUS And to me also the dearest of all my spear-friends.[2]
MEDEA Well, I hope you have good luck, and achieve your will.
AIGEUS But why this downcast eye of yours, and this pale cheek?
MEDEA O Aigeus, my husband has been the worst of all to me.
AIGEUS What do you mean? Say clearly what has caused this grief.
MEDEA Jason wrongs me, though I have never injured him.
AIGEUS What has he done? Tell me about it in clearer words.
MEDEA He has taken a wife to his house, supplanting me.
AIGEUS Surely he would not dare to do a thing like that.
MEDEA Be sure he has. Once dear, I now am slighted by him.
AIGEUS Did he fall in love? Or is he tired of your love?
MEDEA He was greatly in love, this traitor to his friends.
AIGEUS Then let him go, if, as you say, he is so bad.
MEDEA A passionate love,—for an alliance with the king.
AIGEUS And who gave him his wife? Tell me the rest of it.
MEDEA It was Kreon, he who rules this land of Corinth.
AIGEUS Indeed, Medea, your grief was understandable.

9. Cryptic; probably not to have intercourse. 1. In the Peloponnese. Pittheus was Aigeus's father-in-law. Corinth was on the way from Delphi to Troezen. 2. Allies in war, companions in fighting.

MEDEA I am ruined. And there is more to come: I am banished.
AIGEUS Banished? By whom? Here you tell me of a new wrong.
MEDEA Kreon drives me an exile from the land of Corinth.
AIGEUS Does Jason consent? I cannot approve of this.
MEDEA He pretends not to, but he will put up with it.
Ah, Aigeus, I beg and beseech you, by your beard
And by your knees I am making myself your suppliant,
Have pity on me, have pity on your poor friend,
And do not let me go into exile desolate,
But receive me in your land and at your very hearth.
So may your love, with God's help, lead to the bearing
Of children, and so may you yourself die happy.
You do not know what a chance you have come on here.
I will end your childlessness, and I will make you able
To beget children. The drugs I know can do this.
AIGEUS For many reasons, woman, I am anxious to do
This favor for you. First, for the sake of the gods,
And then for the birth of children which you promise,
For in that respect I am entirely at my wits' end.
But this is my position: if you reach my land,
I, being in my rights, will try to befriend you.
But this much I must warn you of beforehand:
I shall not agree to take you out of this country;
But if you by yourself can reach my house, then you
Shall stay there safely. To none will I give you up.
But from this land you must make your escape yourself,
For I do not wish to incur blame from my friends.
MEDEA It shall be so. But, if I might have a pledge from you
For this, then I would have from you all I desire.
AIGEUS Do you not trust me? What is it rankles with you?
MEDEA I trust you, yes. But the house of Pelias hates me,
And so does Kreon. If you are bound by this oath,
When they try to drag me from your land, you will not
Abandon me; but if our pact is only words,
With no oath to the gods, you will be lightly armed,
Unable to resist their summons. I am weak,
While they have wealth to help them and a royal house.
AIGEUS You show much foresight for such negotiations.
Well, if you will have it so, I will not refuse.
For, both on my side this will be the safest way
To have some excuse to put forward to your enemies,
And for you it is more certain. You may name the gods.
MEDEA Swear by the plain of Earth, and Helios, father
Of my father, and name together all the gods. . . .
AIGEUS That I will act or not act in what way? Speak.
MEDEA That you yourself will never cast me from your land,
Nor, if any of my enemies should demand me,
Will you, in your life, willingly hand me over.
AIGEUS I swear by the Earth, by the holy light of Helios,
By all the gods, I will abide by this you say.

MEDEA Enough. And, if you fail, what shall happen to you?
AIGEUS What comes to those who have no regard for heaven.
MEDEA Go on your way. Farewell. For I am satisfied,
And I will reach your city as soon as I can,
Having done the deed I have to do and gained my end.
[AIGEUS *goes out.*]
CHORUS May Hermes, god of travelers,
Escort you, Aigeus, to your home!
And may you have the things you wish
So eagerly; for you
Appear to me to be a generous man.
MEDEA God, and God's daughter, justice, and light of Helios!
Now, friends, has come the time of my triumph over
My enemies, and now my foot is on the road.
Now I am confident they will pay the penalty.
For this man, Aigeus, has been like a harbor to me
In all my plans just where I was most distressed.
To him I can fasten the cable of my safety
When I have reached the town and fortress of Pallas.[3]
And now I shall tell to you the whole of my plan.
Listen to these words that are not spoken idly.
I shall send one of my servants to find Jason
And request him to come once more into my sight.
And when he comes, the words I'll say will be soft ones.
I'll say that I agree with him, that I approve
The royal wedding he has made, betraying me.
I'll say it was profitable, an excellent idea.
But I shall beg that my children may remain here:
Not that I would leave in a country that hates me
Children of mine to feel their enemies' insults,
But that by a trick I may kill the king's daughter.
For I will send the children with gifts in their hands
To carry to the bride, so as not to be banished,—
A finely woven dress and a golden diadem.
And if she takes them and wears them upon her skin
She and all who touch the girl will die in agony;
Such poison will I lay upon the gifts I send.
But there, however, I must leave that account paid.
I weep to think of what a deed I have to do
Next after that; for I shall kill my own children.
My children, there is none who can give them safety.
And when I have ruined the whole of Jason's house,
I shall leave the land and flee from the murder of my
Dear children, and I shall have done a dreadful deed.
For it is not bearable to be mocked by enemies.
So it must happen. What profit have I in life?
I have no land, no home, no refuge from my pain.
My mistake was made the time I left behind me

3. Athens, city of Pallas Athene.

My father's house, and trusted the words of a Greek,
Who, with heaven's help, will pay me the price for that.
For those children he had from me he will never
See alive again, nor will he on his new bride
Beget another child, for she is to be forced
To die a most terrible death by these my poisons.
Let no one think me a weak one, feeble-spirited,
A stay-at-home, but rather just the opposite,
One who can hurt my enemies and help my friends;
For the lives of such persons are most remembered.

CHORUS Since you have shared the knowledge of your plan with us,
I both wish to help you and support the normal
Ways of mankind, and tell you not to do this thing.

MEDEA I can do no other thing. It is understandable
For you to speak thus. You have not suffered as I have.

CHORUS But can you have the heart to kill your flesh and blood?

MEDEA Yes, for this is the best way to wound my husband.

CHORUS And you too. Of women you will be most unhappy.

MEDEA So it must be. No compromise is possible.
[*She turns to the* NURSE.]
Go, you, at once, and tell Jason to come to me.
You I employ on all affairs of greatest trust.
Say nothing of these decisions which I have made,
If you love your mistress, if you were born a woman.

CHORUS From of old the children of Erechtheus[4] are
Splendid, the sons of blessed gods. They dwell
In Athens' holy and unconquered land,[5]
Where famous Wisdom feeds them and they pass gaily
Always through that most brilliant air where once, they say,
That golden Harmony gave birth to the nine
Pure Muses of Pieria.[6]

And beside the sweet flow of Cephisos' stream,
Where Cypris[7] sailed, they say, to draw the water,
And mild soft breezes breathed along her path,
And on her hair were flung the sweet-smelling garlands
Of flowers of roses by the Lovers, the companions
Of Wisdom, her escort, the helpers of men
In every kind of excellence.

How then can these holy rivers
Or this holy land love you,
Or the city find you a home,
You, who will kill your children,
You, not pure with the rest?

4. An early king of Athens, a son of Hephaestus. 5. It was the Athenians' boast that their descent from the original settlers was uninterrupted by an invasion. There is a topical reference here, for the play was produced in 431 B.C., in a time of imminent war. 6. A district in Boeotia where the Muses were supposed to live. The sentence means that the fortunate balance (*Harmony*) of the elements and the genius of the people produced the cultivation of the arts (*the nine Pure Muses*). 7. The goddess of love and, therefore, of the principle of fertility. Cephisos is an Athenian river.

O think of the blow at your children
And think of the blood that you shed.
O, over and over I beg you,
By your knees I beg you do not
Be the murderess of your babes!
O where will you find the courage
Or the skill of hand and heart,
When you set yourself to attempt
A deed so dreadful to do?
How, when you look upon them,
Can you tearlessly hold the decision
For murder? You will not be able,
When your children fall down and implore you,
You will not be able to dip
Steadfast your hand in their blood.

[*Enter* JASON *with attendants.*]

JASON I have come at your request. Indeed, although you are
Bitter against me, this you shall have: I will listen
To what new thing you want, woman, to get from me.

MEDEA Jason, I beg you to be forgiving towards me
For what I said. It is natural for you to bear with
My temper, since we have had much love together.
I have talked with myself about this and I have
Reproached myself. "Fool" I said, "why am I so mad?
Why am I set against those who have planned wisely?
Why make myself an enemy of the authorities
And of my husband, who does the best thing for me
By marrying royalty and having children who
Will be as brothers to my own? What is wrong with me?
Let me give up anger, for the gods are kind to me.
Have I not children, and do I not know that we
In exile from our country must be short of friends?"
When I considered this I saw that I had shown
Great lack of sense, and that my anger was foolish.
Now I agree with you. I think that you are wise
In having this other wife as well as me, and I
Was mad. I should have helped you in these plans of yours,
Have joined in the wedding, stood by the marriage bed,
Have taken pleasure in attendance on your bride.
But we women are what we are,—perhaps a little
Worthless; and you men must not be like us in this,
Nor be foolish in return when we are foolish.
Now I give in, and admit that then I was wrong.
I have come to a better understanding now.

[*She turns towards the house.*]

Children, come here, my children, come outdoors to us!
Welcome your father with me, and say goodbye to him,
And with your mother, who just now was his enemy,
Join again in making friends with him who loves us.

[*Enter the* CHILDREN, *attended by the* TUTOR.]

We have made peace, and all our anger is over.
Take hold of his right hand,—O God, I am thinking
Of something which may happen in the secret future.
O children, will you just so, after a long life,
Hold out your loving arms at the grave? O children,
How ready to cry I am, how full of foreboding!
I am ending at last this quarrel with your father,
And, look, my soft eyes have suddenly filled with tears.

CHORUS And the pale tears have started also in my eyes.
O may the trouble not grow worse than now it is!

JASON I approve of what you say. And I cannot blame you
Even for what you said before. It is natural
For a woman to be wild with her husband when he
Goes in for secret love. But now your mind has turned
To better reasoning. In the end you have come to
The right decision, like the clever woman you are.
And of you, children, your father is taking care.
He has made, with God's help, ample provision for you.
For I think that a time will come when you will be
The leading people in Corinth with your brothers.
You must grow up. As to the future, your father
And those of the gods who love him will deal with that.
I want to see you, when you have become young men,
Healthy and strong, better men than my enemies.
Medea, why are your eyes all wet with pale tears?
Why is your cheek so white and turned away from me?
Are not these words of mine pleasing for you to hear?

MEDEA It is nothing. I was thinking about these children.

JASON You must be cheerful. I shall look after them well.

MEDEA I will be. It is not that I distrust your words,
But a woman is a frail thing, prone to crying.

JASON But why then should you grieve so much for these children?

MEDEA I am their mother. When you prayed that they might live
I felt unhappy to think that these things will be.
But come, I have said something of the things I meant
To say to you, and now I will tell you the rest.
Since it is the king's will to banish me from here,—
And for me too I know that this is the best thing,
Not to be in your way by living here or in
The king's way, since they think me ill-disposed to them,—
I then am going into exile from this land;
But do you, so that you may have the care of them,
Beg Kreon that the children may not be banished.

JASON I doubt if I'll succeed, but still I'll attempt it.

MEDEA Then you must tell your wife to beg from her father
That the children may be reprieved from banishment.

JASON I will, and with her I shall certainly succeed.

MEDEA If she is like the rest of us women, you will.
And I too will take a hand with you in this business,
For I will send her some gifts which are far fairer,
I am sure of it, than those which now are in fashion,

A finely-woven dress and a golden diadem,
And the children shall present them. Quick, let one of you
Servants bring here to me that beautiful dress.
[*One of her attendants goes into the house.*]
She will be happy not in one way, but in a hundred,
Having so fine a man as you to share her bed,
And with this beautiful dress which Helios of old,
My father's father, bestowed on his descendants.
[*Enter attendant carrying the poisoned dress and diadem.*]
There, children, take these wedding presents in your hands.
Take them to the royal princess, the happy bride,
And give them to her. She will not think little of them.

JASON No, don't be foolish, and empty your hands of these.
Do you think the palace is short of dresses to wear?
Do you think there is no gold there? Keep them, don't give them
Away. If my wife considers me of any value,
She will think more of me than money, I am sure of it.

MEDEA No, let me have my way. They say the gods themselves
Are moved by gifts, and gold does more with men than words.
Hers is the luck, her fortune that which god blesses;
She is young and a princess; but for my children's reprieve
I would give my very life, and not gold only.
Go children, go together to that rich palace,
Be suppliants to the new wife of your father,
My lady, beg her not to let you be banished.
And give her the dress,—for this is of great importance,
That she should take the gift into her hand from yours.
Go, quick as you can. And bring your mother good news
By your success of those things which she longs to gain.
[JASON *goes out with his attendants, followed by the* TUTOR *and the* CHILDREN *carrying the poisoned gifts.*]

CHORUS Now there is no hope left for the children's lives.
Now there is none. They are walking already to murder.
The bride, poor bride, will accept the curse of the gold,
Will accept the bright diadem.
Around her yellow hair she will set that dress
Of death with her own hands.
The grace and the perfume and glow of the golden robe
Will charm her to put them upon her and wear the wreath,
And now her wedding will be with the dead below,
Into such a trap she will fall,
Poor thing, into such a fate of death and never
Escape from under that curse.
You too, O wretched bridegroom, making your match with kings,
You do not see that you bring
Destruction on your children and on her,
Your wife, a fearful death.
Poor soul, what a fall is yours!

In your grief too I weep, mother of little children,
You who will murder your own,

In vengeance for the loss of married love
Which Jason has betrayed
As he lives with another wife.

[*Enter the* TUTOR *with the* CHILDREN.]

TUTOR Mistress, I tell you that these children are reprieved,
And the royal bride has been pleased to take in her hands
Your gifts. In that quarter the children are secure.
But come,
Why do you stand confused when you are fortunate?
Why have you turned round with your cheek away from me?
Are not these words of mine pleasing for you to hear?

MEDEA Oh! I am lost!

TUTOR That word is not in harmony with my tidings.

MEDEA I am lost, I am lost!

TUTOR Am I in ignorance telling you
Of some disaster, and not the good news I thought?

MEDEA You have told what you have told. I do not blame you.

TUTOR Why then this downcast eye, and this weeping of tears?

MEDEA Oh, I am forced to weep, old man. The gods and I,
I in a kind of madness have contrived all this.

TUTOR Courage! You too will be brought home by your children.

MEDEA Ah, before that happens I shall bring others home.

TUTOR Others before you have been parted from their children.
Mortals must bear in resignation their ill luck.

MEDEA That is what I shall do. But go inside the house,
And do for the children your usual daily work.

[*The* TUTOR *goes into the house.* MEDEA *turns to her* CHILDREN.]

O children, O my children, you have a city,
You have a home, and you can leave me behind you,
And without your mother you may live there for ever.
But I am going in exile to another land
Before I have seen you happy and taken pleasure in you,
Before I have dressed your brides and made your marriage beds
And held up the torch at the ceremony of wedding.
Oh, what a wretch I am in this my self-willed thought!
What was the purpose, children, for which I reared you?
For all my travail and wearing myself away?
They were sterile, those pains I had in the bearing of you.
O surely once the hopes in you I had, poor me,
Were high ones: you would look after me in old age,
And when I died would deck me well with your own hands;
A thing which all would have done. O but now it is gone,
That lovely thought. For, once I am left without you,
Sad will be the life I'll lead and sorrowful for me.
And you will never see your mother again with
Your dear eyes, gone to another mode of living.
Why, children, do you look upon me with your eyes?
Why do you smile so sweetly that last smile of all?
Oh, Oh, what can I do? My spirit has gone from me,
Friends, when I saw that bright look in the children's eyes.

I cannot bear to do it. I renounce my plans
I had before. I'll take my children away from
This land. Why should I hurt their father with the pain
They feel, and suffer twice as much of pain myself?
No, no, I will not do it. I renounce my plans.
Ah, what is wrong with me? Do I want to let go
My enemies unhurt and be laughed at for it?
I must face this thing. Oh, but what a weak woman
Even to admit to my mind these soft arguments.
Children, go into the house. And he whom law forbids
To stand in attendance at my sacrifices,
Let him see to it. I shall not mar my handiwork.
Oh! Oh!
Do not, O my heart, you must not do these things!
Poor heart, let them go, have pity upon the children.
If they live with you in Athens they will cheer you.
No! By Hell's avenging furies it shall not be,—
This shall never be, that I should suffer my children
To be the prey of my enemies' insolence.
Every way is it fixed. The bride will not escape.
No, the diadem is now upon her head, and she,
The royal princess, is dying in the dress, I know it.
But,—for it is the most dreadful of roads for me
To tread, and them I shall send on a more dreadful still—
I wish to speak to the children.
[*She calls the* CHILDREN *to her.*]
Come, children, give
Me your hands, give your mother your hands to kiss them.
O the dear hands, and O how dear are these lips to me,
And the generous eyes and the bearing of my children!
I wish you happiness, but not here in this world.
What is here your father took. O how good to hold you!
How delicate the skin, how sweet the breath of children!
Go, go! I am no longer able, no longer
To look upon you. I am overcome by sorrow.
[*The* CHILDREN *go into the house.*]
I know indeed what evil I intend to do,
But stronger than all my afterthoughts is my fury,
Fury that brings upon mortals the greatest evils.
[*She goes out to the right, towards the royal palace.*]

CHORUS Often before
I have gone through more subtle reasons,
And have come upon questionings greater
Than a woman should strive to search out.
But we too have a goddess to help us
And accompany us into wisdom.
Not all of us. Still you will find
Among many women a few,
And our sex is not without learning.
This I say, that those who have never

Had children, who know nothing of it,
In happiness have the advantage
Over those who are parents.
The childless, who never discover
Whether children turn out as a good thing
Or as something to cause pain, are spared
Many troubles in lacking this knowledge.
And those who have in their homes
The sweet presence of children, I see that their lives
Are all wasted away by their worries.
First they must think how to bring them up well and
How to leave them something to live on.
And then after this whether all their toil
Is for those who will turn out good or bad,
Is still an unanswered question.
And of one more trouble, the last of all,
That is common to mortals I tell.
For suppose you have found them enough for their living,
Suppose that the children have grown into youth
And have turned out good, still, if God so wills it,
Death will away with your children's bodies,
And carry them off into Hades.
What is our profit, then, that for the sake of
Children the gods should pile upon mortals
After all else
This most terrible grief of all?

[*Enter* MEDEA, *from the spectators' right.*]

MEDEA Friends, I can tell you that for long I have waited
For the event. I stare towards the place from where
The news will come. And now, see one of Jason's servants
Is on his way here, and that labored breath of his
Shows he has tidings for us, and evil tidings.

[*Enter, also from the right, the* MESSENGER.]

MESSENGER Medea, you who have done such a dreadful thing,
So outrageous, run for your life, take what you can,
A ship to bear you hence or chariot on land.

MEDEA And what is the reason deserves such flight as this?

MESSENGER She is dead, only just now, the royal princess,
And Kreon dead too, her father, by your poisons.

MEDEA The finest words you have spoken. Now and hereafter
I shall count you among my benefactors and friends.

MESSENGER What! Are you right in the mind? Are you not mad,
Woman? The house of the king is outraged by you.
Do you enjoy it? Not afraid of such doings?

MEDEA To what you say I on my side have something too
To say in answer. Do not be in a hurry, friend,
But speak. How did they die? You will delight me twice
As much again if you say they died in agony.

MESSENGER When those two children, born of you, had entered in,
Their father with them, and passed into the bride's house,

We were pleased, we slaves who were distressed by your wrongs.
All through the house we were talking of but one thing,
How you and your husband had made up your quarrel.
Some kissed the children's hands and some their yellow hair,
And I myself was so full of my joy that I
Followed the children into the women's quarters.
Our mistress, whom we honor now instead of you,
Before she noticed that your two children were there,
Was keeping her eye fixed eagerly on Jason.
Afterwards however she covered up her eyes,
Her cheek paled and she turned herself away from him,
So disgusted was she at the children's coming there.
But your husband tried to end the girl's bad temper,
And said "You must not look unkindly on your friends.
Cease to be angry. Turn your head to me again.
Have as your friends the same ones as your husband has.
And take these gifts, and beg your father to reprieve
These children from their exile. Do it for my sake."
She, when she saw the dress, could not restrain herself.
She agreed with all her husband said, and before
He and the children had gone far from the palace,
She took the gorgeous robe and dressed herself in it,
And put the golden crown around her curly locks,
And arranged the set of the hair in a shining mirror,
And smiled at the lifeless image of herself in it.
Then she rose from her chair and walked about the room,
With her gleaming feet stepping most soft and delicate,
All overjoyed with the present. Often and often
She would stretch her foot out straight and look along it.
But after that it was a fearful thing to see.
The color of her face changed, and she staggered back,
She ran, and her legs trembled, and she only just
Managed to reach a chair without falling flat down.
An aged woman servant who, I take it, thought
This was some seizure of Pan[8] or another god,
Cried out "God bless us," but that was before she saw
The white foam breaking through her lips and her rolling
The pupils of her eyes and her face all bloodless.
Then she raised a different cry from that "God bless us,"
A huge shriek, and the women ran, one to the king,
One to the newly wedded husband to tell him
What had happened to his bride; and with frequent sound
The whole of the palace rang as they went running.
One walking quickly round the course of a race-track
Would now have turned the bend and be close to the goal,
When she, poor girl, opened her shut and speechless eye,
And with a terrible groan she came to herself.

8. As the god of wild nature he was supposed to be the source of the sudden, apparently causeless terror that solitude in wild surroundings may produce and hence of all kinds of sudden madness (compare the English word *panic*).

For a two-fold pain was moving up against her.
The wreath of gold that was resting around her head
Let forth a fearful stream of all-devouring fire,
And the finely-woven dress your children gave to her,
Was fastening on the unhappy girl's fine flesh.
She leapt up from the chair, and all on fire she ran,
Shaking her hair now this way and now that, trying
To hurl the diadem away; but fixedly
The gold preserved its grip, and, when she shook her hair,
Then more and twice as fiercely the fire blazed out.
Till, beaten by her fate, she fell down to the ground,
Hard to be recognized except by a parent.
Neither the setting of her eyes was plain to see,
Nor the shapeliness of her face. From the top of
Her head there oozed out blood and fire mixed together.
Like the drops on pine-bark, so the flesh from her bones
Dropped away, torn by the hidden fang of the poison.
It was a fearful sight; and terror held us all
From touching the corpse. We had learned from what had happened.
But her wretched father, knowing nothing of the event,
Came suddenly to the house, and fell upon the corpse,
And at once cried out and folded his arms about her,
And kissed her and spoke to her, saying, "O my poor child,
What heavenly power has so shamefully destroyed you?
And who has set me here like an ancient sepulchre,
Deprived of you? O let me die with you, my child!"
And when he had made an end of his wailing and crying,
Then the old man wished to raise himself to his feet;
But, as the ivy clings to the twigs of the laurel,
So he stuck to the fine dress, and he struggled fearfully.
For he was trying to lift himself to his knee,
And she was pulling him down, and when he tugged hard
He would be ripping his aged flesh from his bones.
At last his life was quenched and the unhappy man
Gave up the ghost, no longer could hold up his head.
There they lie close, the daughter and the old father,
Dead bodies, an event he prayed for in his tears.
As for your interests, I will say nothing of them,
For you will find your own escape from punishment.
Our human life I think and have thought a shadow,
And I do not fear to say that those who are held
Wise amongst men and who search the reasons of things
Are those who bring the most sorrow on themselves.
For of mortals there is no one who is happy.
If wealth flows in upon one, one may be perhaps
Luckier than one's neighbor, but still not happy.
[*Exit.*]

CHORUS Heaven, it seems, on this day has fastened many
Evils on Jason, and Jason has deserved them.
Poor girl, the daughter of Kreon, how I pity you

And your misfortunes, you who have gone quite away
To the house of Hades because of marrying Jason.

MEDEA Women, my task is fixed: as quickly as I may
To kill my children, and start away from this land,
And not, by wasting time, to suffer my children
To be slain by another hand less kindly to them.
Force every way will have it they must die, and since
This must be so, then I, their mother, shall kill them.
O arm yourself in steel, my heart! Do not hang back
From doing this fearful and necessary wrong.
O come, my hand, poor wretched hand, and take the sword,
Take it, step forward to this bitter starting point,
And do not be a coward, do not think of them,
How sweet they are, and how you are their mother. Just for
This one short day be forgetful of your children,
Afterwards weep; for even though you will kill them,
They were very dear,—O, I am an unhappy woman!

[*With a cry she rushes into the house.*]

CHORUS O Earth, and the far shining
Ray of the sun, look down, look down upon
This poor lost woman, look, before she raises
The hand of murder against her flesh and blood.
Yours was the golden birth from which
She sprang, and now I fear divine
Blood may be shed by men.
O heavenly light, hold back her hand,
Check her, and drive from out the house
The bloody Fury raised by fiends of Hell.

Vain waste, your care of children;
Was it in vain you bore the babes you loved,
After you passed the inhospitable strait
Between the dark blue rocks, Symplegades?
O wretched one, how has it come,
This heavy anger on your heart,
This cruel bloody mind?
For God from mortals asks a stern
Price for the stain of kindred blood
In like disaster falling on their homes.

[*A cry from one of the* CHILDREN *is heard.*]

CHORUS Do you hear the cry, do you hear the children's cry?
O you hard heart, O woman fated for evil!

ONE OF THE CHILDREN [*From within.*] What can I do and how escape my mother's hands?

ONE OF THE CHILDREN [*From within.*] O my dear brother, I cannot tell. We are lost.

CHORUS Shall I enter the house? O surely I should
Defend the children from murder.

A CHILD [*From within.*] O help us, in God's name, for now we need your help.

Now, now we are close to it. We are trapped by the sword.

CHORUS O your heart must have been made of rock or steel,
You who can kill
With your own hand the fruit of your own womb.
Of one alone I have heard, one woman alone
Of those of old who laid her hands on her children,
Ino, sent mad by heaven when the wife of Zeus
Drove her out from her home and made her wander;
And because of the wicked shedding of blood
Of her own children she threw
Herself, poor wretch, into the sea and stepped away
Over the sea-cliff to die with her two children.
What horror more can be? O women's love,
So full of trouble,
How many evils have you caused already!

[*Enter* JASON, *with attendants.*]

JASON You women, standing close in front of this dwelling,
Is she, Medea, she who did this dreadful deed,
Still in the house, or has she run away in flight?
For she will have to hide herself beneath the earth,
Or raise herself on wings into the height of air,
If she wishes to escape the royal vengeance.
Does she imagine that, having killed our rulers,
She will herself escape uninjured from this house?
But I am thinking not so much of her as for
The children,—her the king's friends will make to suffer
For what she did. So I have come to save the lives
Of my boys, in case the royal house should harm them
While taking vengeance for their mother's wicked deed.

CHORUS Jason, if you but knew how deeply you are
Involved in sorrow, you would not have spoken so.

JASON What is it? That she is planning to kill me also?

CHORUS Your children are dead, and by their own mother's hand.

JASON What! This is it? O woman, you have destroyed me.

CHORUS You must make up your mind your children are no more.

JASON Where did she kill them? Was it here or in the house?

CHORUS Open the gates and there you will see them murdered.

JASON Quick as you can unlock the doors, men, and undo
The fastenings and let me see this double evil,
My children dead and her,—O her I will repay.

[*His attendants rush to the door.* MEDEA *appears above the house in a chariot drawn by dragons. She has the dead bodies of the* CHILDREN *with her.*]

MEDEA Why do you batter these gates and try to unbar them,
Seeking the corpses and for me who did the deed?
You may cease your trouble, and, if you have need of me,
Speak, if you wish. You will never touch me with your hand,
Such a chariot has Helios, my father's father,
Given me to defend me from my enemies.

JASON You hateful thing, you woman most utterly loathed

By the gods and me and by all the race of mankind,
You who have had the heart to raise a sword against
Your children, you, their mother, and left me childless,—
You have done this, and do you still look at the sun
And at the earth, after these most fearful doings?
I wish you dead. Now I see it plain, though at that time
I did not, when I took you from your foreign home
And brought you to a Greek house, you, an evil thing,
A traitress to your father and your native land.
The gods hurled the avenging curse of yours on me.
For your own brother you slew at your own hearthside,
And then came aboard that beautiful ship, the Argo.
And that was your beginning. When you were married
To me, your husband, and had borne children to me,
For the sake of pleasure in the bed you killed them.
There is no Greek woman who would have dared such deeds,
Out of all those whom I passed over and chose you
To marry instead, a bitter destructive match,
A monster not a woman, having a nature
Wilder than that of Scylla[9] in the Tuscan sea.
Ah! no, not if I had ten thousand words of shame
Could I sting you. You are naturally so brazen.
Go, worker in evil, stained with your children's blood.
For me remains to cry aloud upon my fate,
Who will get no pleasure from my newly-wedded love,
And the boys whom I begot and brought up, never
Shall I speak to them alive. Oh, my life is over!

MEDEA Long would be the answer which I might have made to
These words of yours, if Zeus the father did not know
How I have treated you and what you did to me.
No, it was not to be that you should scorn my love,
And pleasantly live your life through, laughing at me;
Nor would the princess, nor he who offered the match,
Kreon, drive me away without paying for it.
So now you may call me a monster, if you wish,
Or Scylla housed in the caves of the Tuscan sea
I too, as I had to, have taken hold of your heart.

JASON You feel the pain yourself. You share in my sorrow.

MEDEA Yes, and my grief is gain when you cannot mock it.

JASON O children, what a wicked mother she was to you!

MEDEA They died from a disease they caught from their father.

JASON I tell you it was not my hand that destroyed them.

MEDEA But it was your insolence, and your virgin wedding.

JASON And just for the sake of that you chose to kill them.

MEDEA Is love so small a pain, do you think, for a woman?

JASON For a wise one, certainly. But you are wholly evil.

MEDEA The children are dead. I say this to make you suffer.

9. A monster located in the straits between Italy and Sicily, who snatched sailors off passing ships and devoured them. See *Odyssey* 12.

JASON The children, I think, will bring down curses on you.
MEDEA The gods know who was the author of this sorrow.
JASON Yes, the gods know indeed, they know your loathsome heart.
MEDEA Hate me. But I tire of your barking bitterness.
JASON And I of yours. It is easier to leave you.
MEDEA How then? What shall I do? I long to leave you too.
JASON Give me the bodies to bury and to mourn them.
MEDEA No, that I will not. I will bury them myself,
Bearing them to Hera's temple on the promontory;
So that no enemy may evilly treat them
By tearing up their grave. In this land of Corinth
I shall establish a holy feast and sacrifice[1]
Each year for ever to atone for the blood guilt.
And I myself go to the land of Erechtheus
To dwell in Aigeus' house, the son of Pandion.
While you, as is right, will die without distinction,
Struck on the head by a piece of the Argo's timber,
And you will have seen the bitter end of my love.
JASON May a Fury for the children's sake destroy you,
And justice, requitor of blood.
MEDEA What heavenly power lends an ear
To a breaker of oaths, a deceiver?
JASON O, I hate you, murderess of children.
MEDEA Go to your palace. Bury your bride.
JASON I go, with two children to mourn for.
MEDEA Not yet do you feel it. Wait for the future.
JASON Oh, children I loved!
MEDEA I loved them, you did not.
JASON You loved them, and killed them.
MEDEA To make you feel pain.
JASON Oh, wretch that I am, how I long
To kiss the dear lips of my children!
MEDEA Now you would speak to them, now you would kiss them.
Then you rejected them.
JASON Let me, I beg you,
Touch my boys' delicate flesh.
MEDEA I will not. Your words are all wasted.
JASON O God, do you hear it, this persecution,
These my sufferings from this hateful
Woman, this monster, murderess of children?
Still what I can do that I will do:
I will lament and cry upon heaven,
Calling the gods to bear me witness
How you have killed my boys and prevent me from
Touching their bodies or giving them burial.
I wish I had never begot them to see them
Afterwards slaughtered by you.

1. Some such ceremony was still performed at Corinth in Euripides' time.

CHORUS Zeus in Olympus is the overseer
Of many doings. Many things the gods
Achieve beyond our judgment. What we thought
Is not confirmed and what we thought not god
Contrives. And so it happens in this story.

ARISTOPHANES
450?–385? B.C.

By the fifth century B.C. both tragedy and comedy were regularly produced at the winter festivals of the god Dionysus in Athens. Comedy, like tragedy, employed a chorus—that is to say, a group of dancers (who also sang) and actors—who wore masks; its tone was burlesque and parodic, though there was often a serious theme emphasized by the crude clowning and the free play of wit. The only comic poet of the fifth century whose work has survived is Aristophanes; in his thirteen extant comedies, produced over the years 425–388 B.C., the institutions and personalities of his time are caricatured and criticized in a brilliant combination of poetry and obscenity, of farce and wit that can be described only in terms of itself, by the adjective *Aristophanic*.

He was born sometime in the middle of the fifth century and died in the next, around 385 B.C. The earliest of his plays to survive, *The Acharnians*, was produced in 425 B.C., and the bulk of his extant work dates from the years of the Peloponnesian War (431–404 B.C.). The war, in fact, is one of his comic targets; in *The Acharnians*, an Athenian citizen, fed up with the privations caused by the Spartan invasions that shut the Athenians inside their walls, makes a separate peace for himself and his family, defends his decision against an irate chorus of patriots (the Acharnians of the title), and proceeds to enjoy all the benefits of peace while his fellow citizens suffer as before. In *Peace* (421 B.C.) another Athenian flies up to heaven on a gigantic dung beetle (a parody of a Euripidean play in which a hero flew up on a winged horse); once arrived, he petitions Zeus to stop the war. Euripides is another favorite target and was held up to ridicule in play after play; and Socrates was the "hero" of a play, *Clouds* (423 B.C.), that held him up to ridicule as a Sophistic charlatan. (Socrates refers to this play in his speech in court, p. 781.) In *Birds* (414 B.C.), two Athenians, tired of the war and taxes, go off to found a new city; they organize the birds, who cut off the smoke of sacrifice that the gods live on, and force Zeus to surrender the government of the universe to the birds. These plays are all very funny, with plenty of sexual and scatological wit. But coarse humor and exquisite wit combine with lyric poetry of a high quality and comic plots of startling audacity to produce a mixture unlike anything that went before or has come after it.

Lysistrata, which is outstanding among the Aristophanic comedies in its coherence of structure and broad humor, was first produced in 411 B.C. In 413 the news of the total destruction of the Athenian fleet in Sicily had reached Athens, and though heroic efforts to carry on the war were under way, the confidence in victory with which Athens had begun the war had disappeared forever. It is a recurring feature of Aristophanic comedy that the comic hero upsets the status quo to produce a series of extraordinary results that are exploited to the full for their comic potential. In this play the Athenian women, who have no political rights, seize the Acropolis, repository of the city's treasury, and leave the men without women or money to carry on the war. At the same time similar revolutions take place in all the Greek cities according to a coordinated plan. The men are eventually "starved" into submission, and the Spartans come to Athens to end the war.

Aristophanes does not miss a trick in his exploitation of the possibilities for ribald humor inherent in this female sex-strike against war; Myrrhine's teasing game with her husband, Cinesias, for example, is rare fooling, and the final appearance of the uncomfortably rigid Spartan ambassadors and their equally tense Athenian hosts is a visual and verbal climax of astonishing brilliance. But underneath all the fooling, real issues are pursued, and they come to the surface with telling effect in the argument between Lysistrata and the commissioner who has been sent to suppress the revolt. Reversing the words of Hector to Andromache, which had become proverbial, Lysistrata claims that "war shall be the concern of Women!" (or in the translation given here, which in this line imitates the archaic nature of Homer's Greek, "ye women must wive ye warre!")—it is too important a matter to be left to men, for women are its real victims. When asked what the women will do, she explains that they will treat politics just as they do wool in their household tasks: "when a hank's in a tangle, we . . . work out the snarls by winding it up on spindles. . . . That's how we'll wind up the War."

Women, who spent a great deal of their time weaving indoors, might be expected to express themselves this way, if they ever got a chance to talk politics. The Commissioner replies, "Spruce up the world's disasters with spindles—typically woolly female logic." These words, of course, say as much about his own prejudices as they do about women's supposed incapacities. Aristophanes can scarcely have meant Lysistrata's words as a serious formula for peace, and yet there is a lucid simplicity to them. Men have botched affairs, as the prolonged war shows. *Why not* simply declare peace and work out the snarls amicably? As this example shows, Aristophanes works through gender stereotypes in this play, both inviting us to see the world through them and holding them up to good-natured ridicule. Women are addicted to wine and sex. They are tricky and deceitful, always probing for men's weaknesses, and an obstacle to the conduct of serious political business. So men say, and the women in this play admit it. But these characteristics are here enlisted in the service of peace (to see them viewed as destructive, compare Euripides' *Medea.*) As for men, Aristophanes suggests that the dirty secret of imperialism is that war and territorial aggression are a substitute for sex, and vice versa. The great expression of this diagnosis is the scene in which the Athenian and Spartan ambassadors divide up the naked body of Peace, personified as a beautiful woman, relating her various anatomical features to territories of Greece over which their cities were fighting. This suggestion is at once devastatingly accurate and an oversimplification. But this sort of reductiveness is characteristic of comedy, which offers us the reassurance that the world is not always as complicated as our daily experience and the rival genre, tragedy, would seem to suggest, that there is room in the world for wish-fulfilling fantasies—in this case, that a sex-strike might actually end war. Well, why not?

We do not know how the Athenians welcomed the play. All we know is that they were not impressed by its serious undertone; the war continued for seven more exhausting years, until Athens's last fleet was defeated, the city laid open to the enemy, the empire lost.

K. J. Dover, *Aristophanic Comedy* (1972), is a general survey of the whole range of Aristophanic comedy. Helpful introductions to *Lysistrata* are given by Jeffrey Henderson, *Aristophanes' Lysistrata* (1987), pp. xv–xli, and Douglas M. MacDowell, *Aristophanes and Athens: An Introduction to the Plays* (1996), pp. 229–50. Erich Segal, *Oxford Readings in Aristophanes* (1996), includes an excellent selection of essays on various aspects of Aristophanes' drama. See also Kenneth J. Reckford, *Aristophanes' Old-and-New Comedy* (1987), pp. 301–11.

PRONOUNCING GLOSSARY

The following list uses common English syllables and stress accents to provide rough equivalents of selected words whose pronunciation may be unfamiliar to the general reader.

Andromache: *an-dro'-ma-kee*
Aristophanes: *a-ri-sto'-fa-neez*
Kleonike: *klee-oh-neé'-kay*
Kinesias: *kin-ay'-see-as*
Koryphaios: *ko-ree-fai'-os*
Lysistrata: *lai-sis'-trah-tuh*
Myrrhine: *meer-ree'-nee*

Lysistrata[1]

CHARACTERS[2]

LYSISTRATA, KLEONIKE, MYRRHINE — *Athenian women*
LAMPITO, *a Spartan woman*
ISMENIA, *a Boiotian girl*
KORINTHIAN GIRL
POLICEWOMAN
KORYPHAIOS OF THE MEN
CHORUS OF OLD MEN *of Athens*
SWIFTY
CHIPPER
KORYPHAIOS OF THE WOMEN
CHORUS OF OLD WOMEN *of Athens*
COMMISSIONER *of Public Safety*
FOUR POLICEMEN
KINESIAS, *Myrrhine's husband*
CHILD *of Kinesias and Myrrhine*
SLAVE
SPARTAN HERALD
SPARTAN AMBASSADOR
DELEGATION OF SPARTANS
FLUTE-PLAYER
ATHENIAN WOMEN
PELOPONNESIAN WOMEN
PELOPONNESIAN MEN
Athenian men
PEACE

[SCENE: *A street in Athens. In the background, the Akropolis; center, its gateway, the Propylaia. The time is early morning.* LYSISTRATA *is discovered alone, pacing back and forth in furious impatience.*]

LYSISTRATA *Women!*
Announce a debauch in honor of Bacchos,
a spree for Pan, some footling fertility fieldday,
and traffic stops—the streets are absolutely clogged
with frantic females banging on tambourines. No urging
for an orgy!
But *today*—there's not one woman here.
[*Enter* KLEONIKE.]
Correction: one. Here comes my next door neighbor.
—Hello, Kleonike.

KLEONIKE Hello to *you*, Lysistrata.
—But what's the fuss? Don't look so barbarous, baby;
knitted brows just aren't your style.

LYSISTRATA It doesn't

1. Translated by Douglass Parker. 2. The leading characters have significant names. *Lysistrata*: "she who disbands the armies." *Lampito*: a typical Spartan name. *Kinesias*: suggests the Greek verb *kinein*, "to move," then "to copulate."

matter, Kleonike—I'm on fire right down to the bone.
I'm positively ashamed to be a woman—a member
of a sex which can't even live up to male slanders!
To hear our husbands talk, we're *sly:* deceitful,
always plotting, monsters of intrigue. . . .

KLEONIKE [*Proudly.*] That's us!

LYSISTRATA And so we agreed to meet today and plot
an intrigue that really deserves the name of monstrous . . .
and WHERE are the women?
Slyly asleep at home—
they won't get up for anything!

KLEONIKE Relax, honey.
They'll be here. You know a woman's way is hard—
mainly the way out of the house: fuss over hubby,
wake the maid up, put the baby down, bathe him,
feed him . . .

LYSISTRATA Trivia. They have more fundamental business to engage in.

KLEONIKE Incidentally, Lysistrata, just why are
you calling this meeting? Nothing teeny, I trust?

LYSISTRATA Immense.

KLEONIKE Hmmm. And pressing?

LYSISTRATA Unthinkably tense.

KLEONIKE Then where IS everybody?

LYSISTRATA Nothing like that. If it were,
we'd already be in session. Seconding motions.
—No, *this* came to hand some time ago. I've spent
my nights kneading it, mulling it, filing it down. . . .

KLEONIKE Too bad. There can't be very much left.

LYSISTRATA Only this:
the hope and salvation of Hellas lies with the WOMEN!

KLEONIKE Lies with the women? Now *there's* a last resort.

LYSISTRATA It lies with us to decide affairs of state
and foreign policy.
The Spartan Question: Peace
or Extirpation?

KLEONIKE How *fun*!
I cast an Aye for Extirpation!

LYSISTRATA The utter Annihilation of every last Boiotian?

KLEONIKE AYE!—I mean Nay. Clemency, please, for those
scrumptious eels.[3]

LYSISTRATA And as for Athens . . . I'd rather not put
the thought into words. Just fill in the blanks, if you will.
—To the point: If we can meet and reach agreement
here and now with the girls from Thebes and the Peloponnese,
we'll form an alliance and save the States of Greece!

KLEONIKE Us? Be practical. Wisdom for women? There's nothing

3. Eels from Lake Copais in Boeotia, a delicacy, were now under embargo because Boeotia was enemy territory.

cosmic about cosmetics—and Glamor is our only talent.
All we can do is *sit,* primped and painted,
made up and dressed up,

[*Getting carried away in spite of her argument.*]

ravishing in saffron wrappers,
peekaboo peignoirs, exquisite negligees, those chic,
expensive little slippers that come from the East. . . .

LYSISTRATA Exactly. You've hit it. I see our way to salvation
in just such ornamentation—in slippers and slips, rouge
and perfumes, negligees and décolletage. . . .

KLEONIKE How so?

LYSISTRATA So effectively that not one husband will take up his spear
against another . . .

KLEONIKE Peachy!
I'll have that kimono
dyed . . .

LYSISTRATA . . . or shoulder his shield . . .

KLEONIKE . . . squeeze into that
daring negligee . . .

LYSISTRATA . . . or unsheathe his sword!

KLEONIKE . . . and buy those slippers!

LYSISTRATA Well, now. Don't you think the girls should be here?

KLEONIKE *Be* here? Ages ago—they should have flown!

[*She stops.*]

But no. You'll find out. These are authentic Athenians:
no matter what they do, they do it late.

LYSISTRATA But what about the out-of-town delegations? There isn't
a woman here from the Shore; none from Salamis . . .

KLEONIKE *That's* quite a trip. They usually get on board
at sunup. Probably riding at anchor now.

LYSISTRATA I thought the girls from Acharnai would be here first.
I'm especially counting on them. And they're not here.

KLEONIKE I think Theogenes' wife is under way.
When I went by, she was hoisting her sandals . . .
[*Looking off right.*] But look!
Some of the girls are coming!

[*Women enter from the right.* LYSISTRATA *looks off to the left where more—a ragged lot—are straggling in.*]

LYSISTRATA And more over here!

KLEONIKE Where did you find *that* group?

LYSISTRATA They're from the outskirts.

KLEONIKE Well, that's something. If you haven't done anything
else, you've really ruffled up the outskirts.

[MYRRHINE *enters guiltily from the right.*]

MYRRHINE Oh, Lysistrata,
we aren't late, are we?
Well, *are* we?
Speak to me!

LYSISTRATA What is it, Myrrhine? Do you want a medal for tardiness?
Honestly, such behavior, with so much at stake . . .

MYRRHINE I'm sorry. I couldn't find my girdle in the dark.
And anyway, we're here now. So tell us all about it,
whatever it is.
KLEONIKE No, wait a minute. Don't
begin just yet. Let's wait for those girls from Thebes
and the Peloponnese.
LYSISTRATA Now *there* speaks the proper attitude.
[LAMPITO, *a strapping Spartan woman, enters left, leading a pretty Boiotian girl* (ISMENIA) *and a huge, steatopygous Korinthian.*]
And here's our lovely Spartan.
Hel*lo*, Lampito
dear.
Why darling, you're simply ravishing! Such
a blemishless complexion—so clean, so out-of-doors![4]
And will you look at that figure—the pink of perfection!
KLEONIKE I'll bet you could strangle a bull.
LAMPITO I calklate so.[5]
Hit's fitness whut done it, fitness and dancin'. You know
the step?
[*Demonstrating.*] Foot it out back'ards an' toe yore twitchet.
[*The women crowd around* LAMPITO.]
KLEONIKE What unbelievably beautiful bosoms!
LAMPITO Shuckins,
whut fer you tweedlin' me up so? I feel like a heifer
come fair-time.
LYSISTRATA [*Turning to* ISMENIA.]
And who is this young lady here?
LAMPITO Her kin's purt-near the bluebloodiest folk in Thebes—
the First Fam'lies of Boiotia.
LYSISTRATA [*As they inspect* ISMENIA.] Ah, picturesque Boiotia:
her verdant meadows, her fruited plain . . .
KLEONIKE [*Peering more closely.*] Her sunken
garden where no grass grows. A cultivated country.
LYSISTRATA [*Gaping at the gawking Korinthian.*]
And who is *this*—er—little thing?
LAMPITO She hails
from over by Korinth, but her kinfolk's quality—mighty
big back there.
KLEONIKE [*On her tour of inspection.*]
She's mighty big back *here.*
LAMPITO The womenfolk's all assemblied. Who-all's notion
was this-hyer confabulation?
LYSISTRATA Mine.
LAMPITO Git on with the give-out.
I'm hankerin' to hear.
MYRRHINE Me, too! I can't imagine
what could be so important. Tell us about it!

4. Spartan women took part in athletics and were in other ways less restricted than their counterparts in other Greek cities. 5. Lampito and the other Spartans speak a version of the Doric dialect of Greek, as actual Spartans did. It could be mocked as boorish by Athenians, who spoke Attic-Ionic. The translator has tried to reproduce this stereotyping effect.

LYSISTRATA Right away.
—But first, a question. It's not
an involved one. Answer yes or no.
[*A pause.*]
MYRRHINE Well, ASK, it!
LYSISTRATA It concerns the fathers of your children—your husbands.
absent on active service. I know you all have men
abroad.
—Wouldn't you like to have them home?
KLEONIKE My husband's been gone for the last five months! Way up
to Thrace,[6] watchdogging military waste. It's horrible!
MYRRHINE Mine's been posted to Pylos[7] for seven whole months!
LAMPITO My man's no sooner rotated out of the line
than he's plugged back in. Hain't no discharge in this war!
KLEONIKE And lovers can't be had for love or money,
not even synthetics. Why, since those beastly Milesians
revolted and cut off the leather trade, that handy
do-it-yourself kit's *vanished* from the open market![8]
LYSISTRATA If I can devise a scheme for ending the war,
I gather I have your support?
KLEONIKE You can count on me!
If you need money, I'll pawn the shift off my back—
[*Aside.*] and drink up the cash before the sun goes down.
MYRRHINE Me, too! I'm ready to split myself right up
the middle like a mackerel, and give you half!
LAMPITO Me, too! I'd climb Taygetos[9] Mountain plumb
to the top to git the leastes' peek at Peace!
LYSISTRATA Very well, I'll tell you. No reason to keep a secret.
[*Importantly, as the women cluster around her.*] We can force our husbands to negotiate Peace,
Ladies, by exercising steadfast Self-Control—
By Total Abstinence.
[*A pause.*]
KLEONIKE From WHAT?
MYRRHINE Yes, what?
LYSISTRATA You'll do it?
KLEONIKE Of course we'll do it! We'd even *die!*
LYSISTRATA Very well,
then here's the program:
Total Abstinence
from SEX!
[*The cluster of women dissolves.*]
—Why are you turning away? Where are you going?
[*Moving among the women.*] —What's this? Such stricken expressions! Such gloomy gestures!
—Why so pale?

6. Region of northeastern Greece, the scene of considerable fighting during the war. 7. Located in the southern Peloponnesus and strategically important against Sparta, Pylos had been occupied by the Athenians since 425 B.C. 8. Leather dildos were evidently a manufacturing specialty of Miletus, a city on the coast of Asia Minor that had recently revolted from the Athenian alliance and had become an important base of Spartan naval operations. 9. The massive range that towers over Sparta.

—Whence these tears?
—What IS this?
Will you do it or won't you?
Cat got your tongue?

KLEONIKE Afraid I can't make it. Sorry.
On with the War!

MYRRHINE Me neither. Sorry.
On with the War!

LYSISTRATA *This* from
my little mackerel? The girl who was ready, a minute
ago, to split herself right up the middle?

KLEONIKE [*Breaking in between* LYSISTRATA *and* MYRRHINE.] Try
something else. Try anything. If you say so,
I'm willing to walk through fire barefoot
But not
to give up SEX—there's nothing like it, Lysistrata!

LYSISTRATA [*To* MYRRHINE.] And you?

MYRRHINE Me, too! I'll walk through fire.

LYSISTRATA *Women!*
Utter sluts, the entire sex! Will-power,
nil. We're perfect raw material for Tragedy,
the stuff of heroic lays. "Go to bed with a god
and then get rid of the baby"—that sums us up!
[*Turning to* LAMPITO.] —Oh, Spartan, be a dear. If *you* stick by me,
just you, we still may have a chance to win.
Give me your vote.

LAMPITO Hit's right onsettlin' fer gals
to sleep all lonely-like, withouten no humpin'.
But I'm on your side. We shore need Peace, too.

LYSISTRATA You're a darling—the only woman here
worthy of the name!

KLEONIKE Well, just suppose we *did*,
as much as possible, abstain from . . . what you said,
you know—not that we *would*—could something like
that bring Peace any sooner?

LYSISTRATA Certainly. Here's how it works:
We'll paint, powder, and pluck ourselves to the last
detail, and stay inside, wearing those filmy
tunics that set off everything we *have*—
and then
slink up to the men. They'll snap to attention, go
absolutely *mad* to love us—
but we won't let them. We'll Abstain.
—I imagine they'll conclude a treaty rather quickly.

LAMPITO [*Nodding.*] Menelaos he tuck one squint at Helen's bubbies
all nekkid, and plumb throwed up.
[*Pause for thought.*] Throwed up his sword.[1]

1. As Troy was being sacked, Menelaus was about to kill Helen in revenge for her adultery but dropped his sword, dazzled by her beauty, when she bared her breast.

KLEONIKE Suppose the men just leave us flat?

LYSISTRATA In that case,
we'll have to take things into our own hands.

KLEONIKE There simply isn't any reasonable facsimile!
—Suppose they take us by force and drag us off
to the bedroom against our wills?

LYSISTRATA Hang on to the door.

KLEONIKE Suppose they beat us!

LYSISTRATA Give in—but be bad sports.
Be nasty about it—they don't enjoy these forced
affairs. So make them suffer.
Don't worry; they'll stop
soon enough. A married man wants harmony—
cooperation, not rape.

KLEONIKE Well, I suppose so.
[*Looking from* LYSISTRATA *to* LAMPITO.] If *both* of you approve this, then so do we.

LAMPITO Hain't worried over our menfolk none. We'll bring 'em
round to makin' a fair, straightfor'ard Peace
withouten no nonsense about it. But take this rackety
passel in Athens: I misdoubt no one could make 'em
give over thet blabber of theirn.[2]

LYSISTRATA They're our concern.
Don't worry. We'll bring them around.

LAMPITO Not likely.
Not long as they got ships kin still sail straight,
an' thet fountain of money up thar in Athene's temple.[3]

LYSISTRATA That point is quite well covered:
We're taking over
the Akropolis, including Athene's temple, today.
It's set: Our oldest women have their orders.
They're up there now, pretending to sacrifice, waiting
for us to reach an agreement. As soon as we do,
they seize the Akropolis.

LAMPITO The way you put them thengs,
I swear I can't see how we kin possibly lose!

LYSISTRATA Well, now that it's settled, Lampito, let's not lose
any time. Let's take the Oath to make this binding.

LAMPITO Just trot out thet-thar Oath. We'll swear it.

LYSISTRATA Excellent.
—Where's a policewoman?

[*A huge girl, dressed as a Skythian archer (the Athenian police) with bow and circular shield, lumbers up and gawks.*]

—What are *you* looking for?
[*Pointing to a spot in front of the women.*]
Put your shield down here.

2. A jab at the Athenian democracy. 3. Athenian power was based on its navy and on the money that flowed from the annual tribute of the "allies." It was stored in Athena's temple, the Parthenon, on the Acropolis.

[*The girl obeys.*]

No, hollow *up!*

[*The girl reverses the shield.* LYSISTRATA *looks about brightly.*]

—Someone give me the entrails.

[*A dubious silence.*]

KLEONIKE Lysistrata, what kind
of an Oath are we supposed to swear?

LYSISTRATA The Standard.
Aischylos used it in a play,[4] they say—the one where
you slaughter a sheep and swear on a shield.

KLEONIKE Lysistrata,
you *do not* swear an Oath for *Peace* on a *shield!*

LYSISTRATA What Oath do you want?
[*Exasperated.*] Something bizarre and
expensive?
A fancier victim—"Take one white horse and disembowel"?

KLEONIKE *White horse?* The symbolism's too obscure.

LYSISTRATA *Then how*
do we swear this oath?

KLEONIKE Oh, *I* can tell you
that, if you'll let me.
First, we put an enormous
black cup right here—hollow up, of course.
Next, into the cup we slaughter a jar of Thasian
wine, and swear a mighty Oath that we won't . . .
dilute it with water.[5]

LAMPITO [*To* KLEONIKE.] Let me corngratulate you—
that were the beatenes' Oath I ever heerd on!

LYSISTRATA [*Calling inside.*] Bring out a cup and jug of wine!

[*Two women emerge, the first staggering under the weight of a huge black cup, the second even more burdened with a tremendous wine jar.* KLEONIKE *addresses them.*]

KLEONIKE You darlings!
What a tremendous display of pottery!
[*Fingering the cup.*] A girl
could get a glow just *holding* a cup like this!

[*She grabs it away from the first woman, who exits.*]

LYSISTRATA [*Taking the wine jar from the second serving woman (who exits), she barks at* KLEONIKE.] Put that down and help me butcher this boar!

[KLEONIKE *puts down the cup, over which she and* LYSISTRATA *together hold the jar of wine (the "boar").* LYSISTRATA *prays.*[6]]

O Mistress Persuasion,
O Cup of Devotion,
Attend our invocation:
Accept this oblation,
Grant our petition,
Favor our mission.

4. *The Seven Against Thebes.* 5. Wine from the northern Aegean island of Thasos was especially strong; to drink any wine neat was considered a sign of intemperance. 6. A parody of sacrifice, in which an animal victim's throat was slit above an altar.

[LYSISTRATA *and* KLEONIKE *tip up the jar and pour the gurgling wine into the cup.* MYRRHINE, LAMPITO, *and the others watch closely.*]

MYRRHINE Such an attractive shade of blood. And the spurt—
pure Art!

LAMPITO Hit shore do smell mighty purty!

[LYSISTRATA *and* KLEONIKE *put down the empty wine jar.*]

KLEONIKE Girls, let me be the first
[*Launching herself at the cup.*] to take the Oath!

LYSISTRATA [*Hauling* KLEONIKE *back.*] You'll have to wait your turn like everyone else.
—Lampito, how do we manage with this mob?
Cumbersome.
—Everyone place her right hand on the cup.

[*The women surround the cup and obey.*]

I need a spokeswoman. One of you to take
the Oath in behalf of the rest.

[*The women edge away from* KLEONIKE, *who reluctantly finds herself elected.*]

The rite will conclude
with a General Pledge of Assent by all of you, thus
confirming the Oath. Understood?

[*Nods from the women.* LYSISTRATA *addresses* KLEONIKE.]

Repeat after me:

LYSISTRATA I will withhold all rights of access or entrance

KLEONIKE I will withhold all rights of access or entrance

LYSISTRATA From every husband, lover, or casual acquaintance

KLEONIKE from every husband, lover, or casual acquaintance

LYSISTRATA Who moves in my direction in erection.
—Go on

KLEONIKE who m-moves in my direction in erection.
Ohhhhh!
—Lysistrata, my knees are shaky. Maybe I'd better . . .

LYSISTRATA I will create, imperforate in cloistered chastity,

KLEONIKE I will create, imperforate in cloistered chastity,

LYSISTRATA A newer, more glamorous, supremely seductive me

KLEONIKE a newer, more glamorous, supremely, seductive me

LYSISTRATA And fire my husband's desire with my molten allure—

KLEONIKE and fire my husband's desire with my molten allure—

LYSISTRATA But remain, to his panting advances, icily pure.

KLEONIKE but remain, to his panting advances, icily pure.

LYSISTRATA If he should force me to share the connubial couch,

KLEONIKE If he should force me to share the connubial couch,

LYSISTRATA I refuse to return his stroke with the teeniest twitch.

KLEONIKE I refuse to return his stroke with the teeniest twitch.

LYSISTRATA I will not lift my slippers to touch the thatch

KLEONIKE I will not lift my slippers to touch the thatch

LYSISTRATA Or submit sloping prone in a hangdog crouch.

KLEONIKE or submit sloping prone in a hangdog crouch.

LYSISTRATA If I this oath maintain,
may I drink this glorious wine.

KLEONIKE If I this oath maintain,
may I drink this glorious wine.

LYSISTRATA But if I slip or falter,
let me drink water.

KLEONIKE But if I slip or falter,
let me drink water.

LYSISTRATA —And now the General Pledge of Assent:

WOMEN A-MEN!

LYSISTRATA Good. I'll dedicate the oblation.

[*She drinks deeply.*]

KLEONIKE Not too much,
darling. You know how anxious we are to become
allies and friends.
Not to mention *staying* friends.

[*She pushes* LYSISTRATA *away and drinks. As the women take their turns at the cup, loud cries and alarums are heard offstage.*]

LAMPITO What-all's that bodacious ruckus?

LYSISTRATA Just what I told you:
It means the women have taken the Akropolis. Athene's
Citadel is ours!
It's time for you to go,
Lampito, and set your affairs in order in Sparta.
[*Indicating the other women in Lampito's group.*] Leave these girls here as hostages.

[LAMPITO *exits left.* LYSISTRATA *turns to the others.*]

Let's hurry inside
the Akropolis and help the others shoot the bolts.

KLEONIKE Don't you think the men will send reinforcements
against us as soon as they can?

LYSISTRATA So where's the worry?
The men can't burn their way in or frighten us out.
The Gates are ours—they're proof against fire and fear—
and they open only on our conditions.

KLEONIKE Yes!
That's the spirit—let's deserve our reputations:

[*As the women hurry off into the Akropolis.*]

UP THE SLUTS!
WAY FOR THE OLD IMPREGNABLES!

[*The door shuts behind the women, and the stage is empty. A pause, and the* CHORUS OF MEN *shuffles on from the left in two groups, led by their* KORYPHAIOS.[7] *They are incredibly aged Athenians; though they may acquire spryness later in the play, at this point they are sheer decrepitude. Their normally shaky progress is impeded by their burdens: each man not only staggers under a load of wood across his shoulders, but has his hands full as well—in one, an earthen pot containing fire (which is in constant danger of going out); in the other, a dried vinewood torch, not yet lit. Their progress toward the Akropolis is very slow.*]

7. Leader of the chorus.

KORYPHAIOS OF MEN [*To the right guide of the First Semichorus, who is stumbling along in mild agony.*] Forward, Swiftly, keep 'em in step! Forget your shoulder.
I know these logs are green and heavy—but duty, boy, duty!

SWIFTY [*Somewhat inspired, he quavers into slow song to set a pace for his group.*]

I'm never surprised. At my age, life
is just one damned thing after another.
And yet, I never thought my wife
was anything more than a home-grown bother.
But now, dadblast her,
she's a National Disaster!

FIRST SEMICHORUS OF MEN

What a catastrophe—
MATRIARCHY!
They've brought Athene's statue to heel,
they've put the Akropolis under a seal,
they've copped the whole damned commonweal . . .
What is there left for them to steal?

KORYPHAIOS OF MEN [*To the right guide of the Second Semichorus—a slower soul, if possible, than* SWIFTY.] Now, Chipper, speed's the word. The Akropolis, on the double!
Once we're there, we'll pile these logs around them, and convene
a circuit court for a truncated trial. Strictly impartial:
With a show of hands, we'll light a spark of justice under
every woman who brewed this scheme. We'll burn them all
on the first ballot—and the first to go is Ly . . .
[*Pause for thought.*] is Ly . . .
[*Remembering and pointing at a spot in the audience.*] Is *Lykon's* wife[8]—
and there she is, right over there!

CHIPPER [*Taking up the song again.*]

I won't be twitted, I won't be guyed,
I'll teach these women not to trouble us!
Kleomenes the Spartan tried
expropriating our Akropolis[9]
some time ago—
ninety-five years or so—

SECOND SEMICHORUS OF MEN

but he suffered damaging losses
when he ran across US!
He breathed defiance—and more as well:
No bath for six years—you could tell.
We fished him out of the Citadel
and quelled his spirit—but not his smell.

KORYPHAIOS OF MEN That's how I took him. A savage siege:
Seventeen
ranks

8. Notorious for her loose morals. 9. In 508 B.C. the Spartans under Cleomenes tried to intervene in Athens on behalf of the aristocratic resistance to the democratic reforms of Cleisthenes. They seized the Acropolis, were besieged there by the Athenians, and withdrew from the city after two days.

of shields were massed at that gate, with blanket infantry cover.
I slept like a baby.
So when mere women (who gall the gods
and make Euripides sick)[1] try the same trick, should I
sit idly by?
Then demolish the monument, I won at Marathon![2]

FIRST SEMICHORUS OF MEN [*Singly.*]
—The last lap of our journey!
—I greet it with some dismay.
—The danger doesn't deter me.
—but
it's uphill
—all the way.
—Please, somebody,
—find a jackass
to drag these logs
—to the top.
—I ache to join the fracas,
—but
my shoulder's aching
—to stop.

SWIFTY
Backward there's no turning.
Upward and onward, men!
And keep those firepots burning, or
we make this trip again.

CHORUS OF MEN [*Blowing into their firepots, which promptly send forth clouds of smoke.*] With a puff (pfffff). . . .
and a cough (hhhhh). . . .
The smoke! I'll choke! Turn it off!

SECOND SEMICHORUS OF MEN [*Singly.*]
—Damned embers.
—Should be muzzled.
—There oughta be a law.
—They jumped me
—when I whistled
—and then
they gnawed my eyeballs
—raw.
—There's lava in my lashes.
—My lids are oxidized.
—My brows are braised.
—These ashes are
volcanoes
—in disguise.

CHIPPER
This way, men. And remember.
The Goddess needs our aid.
So don't be stopped by cinders. Let's

1. Aristophanes always presents Euripides, improbably, as a misogynist and hence hated by women in return. 2. Town on the north coast of Attica, site of the Athenians' great victory when in 490 B.C. a small Athenian army repelled a large Persian expedition. The commemorative mound covering the Athenian dead is still in place.

press on to the stockade!

CHORUS OF MEN [*Blowing again into their firepots, which erupt as before.*]
With a huff (hfffff).
and a chuff (chffff).
Drat that smoke. Enough is enough!

KORYPHAIOS OF MEN [*Signalling the* CHORUS (OF MEN), *which has now tottered into position before the Akropolis gate, to stop, and peering into his firepot.*] Praise be to the gods, it's awake. There's fire in the old fire yet.
—Now the directions. See how they strike you:
First, we deposit
these logs at the entrance and light our torches. Next, we crash
the gate. When that doesn't work, we request admission politely.
When *that* doesn't work, we burn the damned door down, and smoke
these women into submission.
That seem acceptable? Good
Down with the load . . . ouch, that smoke! Sonofabitch!
[*A horrible tangle results as the* CHORUS (OF MEN) *attempts to deposit the logs. The* KORYPHAIOS *turns to the audience.*]
Is there a general in the house? We have a logistical problem.
[*No answer. He shrugs.*]
Same old story. Still at loggerheads over in Samos.[3]
[*With great confusion, the logs are placed somehow.*]
That's better. The pressure's off. I've got my backbone back.
[*To his firepot.*] What, pot? You forgot your part in the plot?
Urge that smudge
to be hot on the dot and scorch my torch.
Got it, pot?
[*Praying.*]
Queen Athene, let these strumpets
crumple before our attack.
Grant us victory, male supremacy
and a testimonial plaque.
[*The* (CHORUS OF) MEN *plunge their torches into firepots and arrange themselves purposefully before the gate. Engaged in their preparations, they do not see the sudden entrance, from the right, of the* CHORUS OF WOMEN, *led by their* KORYPHAIOS. *These wear long cloaks and carry pitchers of water. They are very old—though not so old as the* (CHORUS OF) MEN—*but quite spry. In their turn, they do not perceive the* CHORUS OF MEN.]

KORYPHAIOS OF WOMEN [*Stopping suddenly.*] What's this—soot? And smoke as well? I may be all wet,
but this might mean fire. Things look dark, girls; we'll have to dash.
[*They move ahead, at a considerably faster pace than the* (CHORUS OF) MEN.]

FIRST SEMICHORUS OF WOMEN [*Singly.*]

3. Most of the Athenian fleet was at the moment based in Samos, practically the only Ionian ally left to Athens, in order to make ready moves against those states who had defected to Sparta in 412 after the Sicilian fiasco [Translator's note].

Speed! Celerity!   Save our sorority
from arson   Combustion   And heat exhaustion
Don't let our sisterhood   shrivel to blisterhood.
Fanned into slag by hoary typhoons.
By flatulent, nasty, gusty baboons.
We're late! Run!
The girls might be done!

[*Tutte.*] Filling my pitcher   was absolute torture:
The fountains in town   are so *crowded* at dawn,
glutted with masses   of the lower classes
blatting and battering,   shoving, and shattering
jugs. But I juggled   my burden, and wriggled
away to extinguish   the igneous anguish
of neighbor, and sister, and daughter—
Here's Water!

SECOND SEMICHORUS OF WOMEN [*Singly.*]
Get wind of the news?   The gaffers are loose.
The blowhards are off   with fuel enough
to furnish a bathhouse.   But the finish is pathos:
They're scaling the heights with a horrid proposal
They're threatening women with rubbish disposal!
How ghastly—how gauche!
burned up with the trash!

[*Tutte.*] Preserve me, Athene,   from gazing on any
matron or maid   auto-da fé'd.
Cover with grace   these redeemers of Greece
from battles, insanity,   Man's inhumanity.
Gold-browed goddess,   hither to aid us!
Fight as our ally,   join in our sally
against pyromaniac slaughter—
Haul Water!

KORYPHAIOS OF WOMEN [*Noticing for the first time the* CHORUS OF MEN, *still busy at their firepots, she cuts off a member of her* CHORUS *who seems about to continue the song.*] Hold it. What have we here? You don't catch true-blue
patriots red-handed. These are authentic degenerates,
male, taken *in flagrante.*

KORYPHAIOS OF MEN Oops. Female troops. This could be upsetting.
I didn't expect such a flood of reserves.

KORYPHAIOS OF WOMEN Merely a spearhead.
If our numbers stun you, watch that yellow streak
spread. We represent just one percent of one percent of This Woman's Army.

KORYPHAIOS OF MEN Never been confronted with such backtalk. Can't allow
it. Somebody pick up a log and pulverize that brass.
Any Volunteers?

[*There are none among the* CHORUS (OF MEN).]

KORYPHAIOS OF WOMEN Put down the pitchers, girls. If they start waving that lumber,
we don't want to be encumbered.

KORYPHAIOS OF MEN Look, men, a few sharp jabs
will stop that jawing. It never fails.
The poet Hipponax
swears by it.[4]

[*Still no volunteers. The* KORYPHAIOS OF WOMEN *advances.*]

KORYPHAIOS OF WOMEN Then step right up. Have a jab at me.
Free shot.

KORYPHAIOS OF MEN [*Advancing reluctantly to meet her.*]
Shut up! I'll peel your pelt. I'll pit your pod.

KORYPHAIOS OF WOMEN The name is Stratyllis. I dare you to lay one finger on me.

KORYPHAIOS OF MEN I'll lay on you with a fistful. Er—any specific threats?

KORYPHAIOS OF WOMEN [*Earnestly.*] I'll crop your lungs and reap your bowels, bite by bite,
and leave no balls on the body for other bitches to gnaw.

KORYPHAIOS OF MEN [*Retreating hurriedly.*] Can't beat Euripides for insight. And I quote:
No creature's found
so lost to shame as Woman.
Talk about realist playwrights!

KORYPHAIOS OF WOMEN Up with the water, ladies. Pitchers at the ready, place!

KORYPHAIOS OF MEN Why the water, you sink of iniquity? More sedition?

KORYPHAIOS OF WOMEN Why the fire, you walking boneyard? Self-cremation?

KORYPHAIOS OF MEN I brought this fire to ignite a pyre and fricassee your friends.

KORYPHAIOS OF WOMEN I brought this water to douse your pyre. Tit for tat.

KORYPHAIOS OF MEN *You'll* douse my fire? Nonsense!

KORYPHAIOS OF WOMEN You'll see, when the facts soak in.

KORYPHAIOS OF MEN I have the torch right here. Perhaps I should barbecue *you.*

KORYPHAIOS OF WOMEN If you have any soap, I could give you a bath.

KORYPHAIOS OF MEN A bath from those
polluted hands?

KORYPHAIOS OF WOMEN Pure enough for a blushing young bridegroom.

KORYPHAIOS OF MEN Enough of that insolent lip.

KORYPHAIOS OF WOMEN It's merely freedom of speech.

KORYPHAIOS OF MEN I'll stop that screeching!

KORYPHAIOS OF WOMEN You're helpless outside the jury-box.[5]

KORYPHAIOS OF MEN [*Urging his men, torches at the ready, into a charge.*] Burn, fire, burn!

KORYPHAIOS OF WOMEN [*As the women empty their pitchers over the men.*]

4. The Greek refers to the sculptor Boupalus, who was said to have been driven to suicide by the scurrilous abuse of the poet Hipponax (sixth century B.C.). 5. Pericles had instituted pay for jury service, and the poor and the aged made something of a living this way.

And cauldron bubble.

KORYPHAIOS OF MEN [*Like his troops, soaked and routed.*] Arrrgh!

KORYPHAIOS OF WOMEN Goodness.
What seems to be the trouble? Too hot?

KORYPHAIOS OF MEN Hot, hell! Stop it!
What do you think you're doing?

KORYPHAIOS OF WOMEN If you must know, I'm gardening.
Perhaps you'll bloom.

KORYPHAIOS OF MEN Perhaps I'll fall right off the vine!
I'm withered, frozen, shaking . . .

KORYPHAIOS OF WOMEN Of course. But, providentially,
you brought along your smudgepot.
The sap should rise eventually.

[*Shivering, the* CHORUS OF MEN *retreats in utter defeat.*

A COMMISSIONER *of Public Safety*[6] *enters from the left, followed quite reluctantly by a squad of police—four Skythian archers. He surveys the situation with disapproval.*]

COMMISSIONER Fire, eh? Females again—spontaneous combustion
of lust. Suspected as much.
Rubadubdubbing, incessant
incontinent keening for wine, damnable funeral
foofaraw for Adonis resounding from roof to roof[7]—
heard it all before . . .

[*Savagely, as the* KORYPHAIOS OF MEN *tries to interpose a remark.*]

and WHERE?
The ASSEMBLY!
Recall, if you can, the debate on the Sicilian Question:
That bullbrained demagogue Demostratos[8] (who will rot, I trust)
rose to propose a naval task force.
His wife,
writhing with religion on a handy roof, bleated
a dirge:
"BEREFT! OH WOE OH WOE FOR ADONIS!"
And so of course Demostratos, taking his cue
outblatted her:
"A DRAFT! ENROLL THE WHOLE OF ZAKYNTHOS!"
His wife, a smidgin stewed, renewed her yowling:
"OH GNASH YOUR TEETH AND BEAT YOUR
BREASTS FOR ADONIS!"
And so of course Demostratos (that god-detested blot,
that foul-lunged son of an ulcer) gnashed tooth and nail
and voice, and bashed and rammed his program through.
And THERE is the Gift of Women:
MORAL CHAOS!

6. One prominent citizen on a board of ten chosen in the wake of the Sicilian disaster to restrain possible legislative excesses by the Assembly. 7. The Asiatic cult of the vegetation god Adonis (Tammuz) was celebrated by women, who lamented the god's death each year on the roofs of their houses. In male eyes, the cult, as both Oriental and female, threatened the Greek ideal of self-restraint. 8. One of the supporters of the Sicilian Expedition, who proposed to enroll heavily armed infantry from the island of Zakynthos, off the west coast of Greece, on the way to Sicily.

KORYPHAIOS OF MEN Save your breath for actual felonies, Commissioner;
see what's happened to us! Insolence, insults,
these we pass over, but not lese-majesty:
We're flooded
with indignity from those bitches' pitchers—like a bunch
of weak-bladdered brats. Our cloaks are sopped. We'll sue!
COMMISSIONER Useless. Your suit won't hold water. Right's on their side.
For female depravity, gentlemen, WE stand guilty—
we, their teachers, preceptors of prurience, accomplices
before the fact of fornication. We sowed them in sexual
license, and now we reap rebellion.
The proof?
Consider. Off we trip to the goldsmith's to leave
an order:
"That bangle you fashioned last spring for my wife
is sprung. She was thrashing around last night, and the prong
popped out of the bracket. I'll be tied up all day—I'm
boarding the ferry right now—but my wife'll be home.
If you get the time, please stop by the house in a bit
and see if you can't do something—anything—to fit
a new prong into the bracket of her bangle."
And bang.
Another one ups to a cobbler—young, but no apprentice,
full kit of tools, ready to give his awl—
and delivers this gem:
"My wife's new sandals are tight.
The cinch pinches her pinkie right where she's sensitive.
Drop in at noon with something to stretch her cinch
and give it a little play."
And a cinch it is.
Such hanky-panky we have to thank for today's
Utter Anarchy: I, a Commissioner of Public
Safety, duly invested with extraordinary powers
to protect the State in the Present Emergency, have secured
a source of timber to outfit our fleet and solve
the shortage of oarage. I need the money immediately . . .
the WOMEN, no less, have locked me out of the Treasury!
[*Pulling himself together.*] —Well, no profit in standing around.
[*To one of the archers.*] Bring
the crowbars. I'll jack these women back on their
pedestals!
—WELL, you slack-jawed jackass? What's the
attraction? Wipe that thirst off your face. I said *crow*bar,
not saloon!—All right, men, all together. Shove those
bars underneath the gate and HEAVE!
[*Grabbing up a crowbar*] I'll take this side.
And now let's root them out, men, ROOT them out.
One, Two . . .
[*The gates to the Akropolis burst open suddenly, disclosing* LYSIS-

TRATA. *She is perfectly composed and bears a large spindle. The* COMMISSIONER *and the* (FOUR) POLICE(MEN) *fall back in consternation.*]

LYSISTRATA Why the moving equipment?
I'm quite well motivated, thank you, and here I am.
Frankly, you don't need crowbars nearly so much as brains.

COMMISSIONER Brains? O name of infamy! Where's a policeman?

[*He grabs wildly for the First Archer and shoves him toward* LYSISTRATA.]

Arrest that woman!
Better tie her hands behind her.

LYSISTRATA By Artemis, goddess of the hunt, if he lays a finger
on me, he'll rue the day he joined the force!

[*She jabs the spindle viciously at the First Archer, who leaps, terrified, back to his comrades.*]

COMMISSIONER What's this—retreat? Never! Take her on the flank.

[*The First Archer hangs back. The* COMMISSIONER *grabs the Second Archer.*]

—Help him.
—Will the two of you kindly TIE HER UP?

[*He shoves them toward* LYSISTRATA. KLEONIKE *carrying a large chamber pot, springs out of the entrance and advances on the Second Archer.*]

KLEONIKE By Artemis, goddess of the dew, if you so much
as touch her, I'll stomp the shit right out of you!

[*The two Archers run back to their group.*]

COMMISSIONER *Shit?* Shameless! Where's another policeman?

[*He grabs the Third Archer and propels him toward* KLEONIKE.]

Handcuff *her* first. Can't stand a foul-mouthed female.

[MYRRHINE, *carrying a large, blazing lamp, appears at the entrance and advances on the Third Archer.*]

MYRRHINE By Artemis, bringer of light, if you lay a finger
on her, you won't be able to stop the swelling!

[*The Third Archer dodges her swing and runs back to the group.*]

COMMISSIONER *Now* what? Where's an officer?
[*Pushing the Fourth Archer toward Myrrhine.*] Apprehend that woman!
I'll see that *somebody* stays to take the blame!

[ISMENIA *the Boiotian, carrying a huge pair of pincers, appears at the entrance and advances on the Fourth Archer.*]

ISMENIA By Artemis, goddess of Tauris, if you go near
that girl, I'll rip the hair right out of your head!

[*The Fourth Archer retreats hurriedly.*]

COMMISSIONER What a colossal mess: Athens' Finest—
finished!
[*Arranging the Archers.*] —Now, men, a little *esprit de corps.* Worsted
by women? Drubbed by drabs?
Never!
Regroup,
reform that thin red line.
Ready?

CHARGE!

[*He pushes them ahead of him.*]

LYSISTRATA I warn you. We have four battalions behind us—
full-armed combat infantrywomen, trained
from the cradle . . .

COMMISSIONER Disarm them, Officers! Go for the hands!

LYSISTRATA [*Calling inside the Akropolis.*] MOBILIZE THE RESERVES!

[*A horde of women, armed with household articles, begins to pour from the Akropolis.*]

Onward, you ladies from hell!
Forward, you market militia, you battle-hardened
bargain hunters, old sales campaigners, grocery
grenadiers, veterans never bested by an overcharge!
You troops of the breadline, doughgirls—
INTO THE FRAY!
Show them no mercy!
Push!
Jostle!
Shove!
Call them nasty names!
Don't be ladylike.

[*The women charge and rout the Archers in short order.*]

Fall back—don't strip the enemy![9] The day is ours!

[*The women obey, and the Archers run off left. The* COMMISSIONER, *dazed, is left muttering to himself.*]

COMMISSIONER Gross ineptitude. A sorry day for the Force.

LYSISTRATA Of course. What did you expect? We're not slaves;
we're freeborn Women, and when we're scorned, we're
full of fury. Never underestimate the Power of a Woman.

COMMISSIONER Power? You mean Capacity. I should have remembered
the proverb: *The lower the tavern, the higher the dudgeon.*

KORYPHAIOS OF MEN Why cast your pearls before swine, Commissioner? I know you're a civil
servant, but don't overdo it. Have you forgotten the bath
they gave us—in public,
fully dressed,
totally soapless?
Keep rational discourse for *people!*

[*He aims a blow at the* KORYPHAIOS OF WOMEN, *who dodges and raises her pitcher.*]

KORYPHAIOS OF WOMEN I might point out that lifting
one's hand against a neighbor is scarcely civilized
behavior—and entails, for the lifter, a black eye.
I'm really peaceful by nature,
compulsively inoffensive—a perfect doll. My ideal is a
well-bred repose that doesn't even stir up dust . . .

9. Victorious soldiers after a battle commonly stripped the armor from enemy corpses.

[*Swinging at the Koryphaios of Men with the pitcher.*] unless some no-good lowlife
tries to rifle my hive and gets my dander up!

[*The* KORYPHAIOS OF MEN *backs hurriedly away, and the* CHORUS OF MEN *goes into a worried dance.*]

CHORUS OF MEN [*Singly.*]

O Zeus, what's the use of this constant abuse?
How do we deal with this female zoo?
Is there no solution to Total Immersion?
What can a poor man DO?

[*Tutti.*]
Query the Adversary!
Ferret out their story!
What end did they have in view,
to seize the city's sanctuary,
snatch its legendary eyrie,
snare an area so very
terribly taboo?

KORYPHAIOS OF MEN [*To the* COMMISSIONER.] Scrutinize those women! Scour their depositions—assess their rebuttals!
Masculine honor demands this affair be probed to the bottom!

COMMISSIONER [*Turning to the women from the Akropolis.*] All right, you. Kindly inform me, dammit, in your own words:
What possible object could you have had in blockading the Treasury?

LYSISTRATA We thought we'd deposit the money in escrow and withdraw you men
from the war.

COMMISSIONER The money's the cause of the war?

LYSISTRATA And all our internal disorders—the Body Politic's chronic bellyaches: What causes Peisandros' frantic rantings, or the raucous caucuses of the Friends of Oligarchy?[1] The chance for graft.
But now, with the money up there,
they can't upset the City's equilibrium—or lower its balance.

COMMISSIONER And what's your next step?

LYSISTRATA Stupid question. We'll budget the money.

COMMISSIONER *You'll budget the money?*

LYSISTRATA Why should you find that so shocking?
We budget the household accounts, and you don't object at all.

COMMISSIONER That's different.

LYSISTRATA Different? How?

COMMISSIONER The War Effort needs this money!

1. One of several political clubs formed to gain offices and power. A few months after this play was performed, Peisandros and an oligarchic faction overthrew the democratic constitution, with widespread assassinations and confiscations for a short time. By the following year (410 B.C.) the democracy was restored.

LYSISTRATA Who needs the War Effort?
COMMISSIONER Every patriot who pulses to save
all that Athens holds near and dear.
LYSISTRATA Oh, *that.* Don't worry.
We'll save you.
COMMISSIONER *You* will save us?
LYSISTRATA Who else?
COMMISSIONER But this is unscrupulous!
LYSISTRATA We'll save you. You can't deter us.
COMMISSIONER Scurrilous!
LYSISTRATA You seem disturbed,
This makes it difficult. But, still—we'll save you.
COMMISSIONER Doubtless illegal!
LYSISTRATA We deem it a duty. For friendship's sake.
COMMISSIONER Well, forsake this friend.
I DO NOT WANT TO BE SAVED. DAMMIT!
LYSISTRATA All the more reason.
It's not only Sparta; now we'll have to save you from you.
COMMISSIONER Might I ask where you women conceived this concern
about War and Peace?
LYSISTRATA [*Loftily.*] We shall explain.
COMMISSIONER [*Making a fist*] Hurry up, and you won't
get hurt.
LYSISTRATA Then *listen.* And do try to keep your hands to yourself.
COMMISSIONER [*Moving threateningly toward her.*] I can't. Righteous anger forbids restraint and decrees . . .
KLEONIKE [*Brandishing her chamber pot.*] Multiple fractures?
COMMISSIONER [*Retreating.*] Keep those croaks for yourself, you old crow!
[*To Lysistrata.*] All right, lady, I'm ready. Speak.
LYSISTRATA I shall proceed:
When the War began, like the prudent, dutiful wives that
we are, we tolerated you men, and endured your actions in silence. (Small wonder—
you wouldn't let us say boo.)
You were not precisely the answer
to a matron's prayer—we knew you too well, and found out more.
Too many times, as we sat in the house, we'd hear that
you'd done it again—manhandled another affair of
state with your usual staggering incompetence. Then,
masking our worry with a nervous laugh,
we'd ask you, brightly, "How was the Assembly today, dear? Anything
in the minutes about Peace?" And my husband would
give his stock reply.
"What's that to you? Shut up!" And I did.
KLEONIKE [*Proudly.*] *I* never shut up!
COMMISSIONER I trust you were shut up. Soundly.
LYSISTRATA Regardless, *I* shut up.
And then we'd learn that you'd passed another decree,

fouler than the first, and we'd ask again: "Darling, how
did you manage anything so idiotic?" And my
husband, with his customary glare, would tell me to spin
my thread, or else get a clout on the head.
And of course he'd quote from Homer:
Ye menne must husband ye warre.[2]

COMMISSIONER Apt and irrefutably right.

LYSISTRATA *Right,* you miserable misfit?
To keep us from giving advice while you fumbled the
City away in the Senate? Right, indeed!
But this time was really too much.
Wherever we went, we'd hear you engaged in the same conversation:
"What Athens needs is a Man."
"But there isn't a Man in the country."
"You can say that again."
There was obviously no time to lose.
We women met in immediate convention and passed a
unanimous resolution: To work in concert for safety and
Peace in Greece. We have valuable advice to impart,
and, if you can possibly deign to emulate our silence,
and take your turn as audience, we'll rectify you—
we'll straighten you out and set you right.

COMMISSIONER *You'll* set *us* right? You go too far. I cannot permit
such a statement to . . .

LYSISTRATA Shush.

COMMISSIONER I categorically decline to shush
for some confounded woman, who wears—as a constant
reminder of congenital inferiority, an injunction to
public silence—a veil!
Death before such dishonor!

LYSISTRATA [*Removing her veil.*] If that's the only obstacle . . .
I feel you need a new panache,
so take the veil, my dear Commissioner, and drape it thus—
and SHUSH!

[*As she winds the veil around the startled* COMMISSIONER'S *head,* KLEONIKE *and* MYRRHINE, *with carding-comb and wool-basket, rush forward and assist in transforming him into a woman.*]

KLEONIKE Accept, I pray, this humble comb.

MYRRHINE Receive this basket of fleece as well.

LYSISTRATA Hike up your skirts, and card your wool,
and gnaw your beans—and stay at home!
While we rewrite Homer:
Ye WOMEN must WIVE ye warre!

[*To the* CHORUS OF WOMEN, *the* COMMISSIONER *struggles to remove his new outfit.*]

Women, weaker vessels, arise!

2. *Iliad* 6.492. Homer's Greek would have sounded similarly archaic.

Put down your pitchers.
It's our turn, now. Let's supply our friends with some moral support.
[*The* CHORUS OF WOMEN *dances to the same tune as the* (CHORUS OF) MEN *but with much more confidence.*]

CHORUS OF WOMEN [*Singly.*]
Oh, yes! I'll dance to bless their success.
Fatigue won't weaken my will. Or my knees
I'm ready to join in any jeopardy.
with girls as good as *these!*

[*Tutte.*]
A tally of their talents
convinces me they're giants
of excellence. To commence:
there's Beauty, Duty, Prudence, Science,
Self-Reliance, Compliance, Defiance,
and Love of Athens in balanced alliance
with Common Sense!

KORYPHAIOS OF WOMEN [*To the women from the Akropolis.*]
Autochthonous daughters of Attika, sprung from the
soil that bore your mothers, the spiniest, spikiest
nettles known to man, prove your mettle and attack!
Now is no time to dilute your anger. You're
running ahead of the wind!

LYSISTRATA We'll wait for the wind
from heaven. The gentle breath of Love and his Kyprian
mother will imbue our bodies with desire, and raise a
storm to tense and tauten these blasted men until they
crack. And soon we'll be on every tongue in
Greece—the *Pacifiers.*

COMMISSIONER That's quite
a mouthful. How will you win it?

LYSISTRATA First, we intend to withdraw
that crazy Army of Occupation from the downtown shopping section.

KLEONIKE Aphrodite be praised!

LYSISTRATA The pottery shop and the grocery stall
are overstocked with soldiers, clanking around like those maniac Korybants,[3]
armed to the teeth for a battle.

COMMISSIONER A Hero is Always Prepared!

LYSISTRATA I suppose he is. But it does look silly to shop for sardines
from behind a shield.

KLEONIKE I'll second that. I saw
a cavalry captain buy vegetable soup on horseback. He
carried the whole mess home in his helmet.
And then that fellow from Thrace,
shaking his buckler and spear—a menace straight from the stage.

3. The armed priests of the goddess Cybele.

The saleslady was stiff with fright. He was hogging her ripe figs—free.
COMMISSIONER I admit, for the moment, that Hellas' affairs are in one
hell of a snarl. But how can you set them straight?
LYSISTRATA Simplicity itself.
COMMISSIONER Pray demonstrate.
LYSISTRATA It's rather like yarn. When a hank's in a tangle,
we lift it—*so*—and work out the snarls by winding it up
on spindles, now this way, now that way.
That's how we'll wind up the War,
if allowed: We'll work out the snarls by sending Special Commissions—
back and forth, now this way, now that way—to ravel
these tense international kinks.
COMMISSIONER I lost your thread, but I know there's a hitch.
Spruce up the world's disasters with spindles—typically
woolly female logic.
LYSISTRATA If *you* had a scrap of logic, you'd adopt
our wool as a master plan for Athens.
COMMISSIONER What course of action
does the wool advise?
LYSISTRATA Consider the City as fleece, recently
shorn. The first step is Cleansing: Scrub it in a public
bath, and remove all corruption, offal, and sheepdip.
Next, to the couch
for Scutching and Plucking: Cudgel the leeches and
similar vermin loose with a club, then pick the prickles
and cockleburs out. As for the clots—those lumps
that clump and cluster in knots and snarls to snag
important posts—you comb these out,
twist off their heads, and discard.
Next, to raise the City's
nap, you card the citizens together in a single basket
of common weal and general welfare. Fold in our loyal
Resident Aliens, all Foreigners of proven and tested
friendship, and any Disenfranchised Debtors. Combine these closely with the rest.
Lastly, cull the colonies settled by our own people:
these are nothing but flocks of wool from the City's
fleece, scattered throughout the world. So gather home
these far-flung flocks, amalgamate them with the others.
Then, drawing this blend
of stable fibers into one fine staple, you spin a mighty
bobbin of yarn—and weave, without bias or seam, a
cloak to clothe the City of Athens!
COMMISSIONER This is too much! The City's

died in the wool, worsted by the distaff side—by women
who bore no share in the War. . . .

LYSISTRATA None, you hopeless hypocrite?
The quota we bear is double. First, we delivered our
sons to fill out the front lines in Sicily . . .

COMMISSIONER Don't tax me with that memory.

LYSISTRATA Next, the best years of our lives were levied. Top-level
strategy attached our joy, and we sleep alone.
But it's not the matrons
like us who matter. I mourn for the virgins, bedded in
single blessedness, with nothing to do, but grow old.

COMMISSIONER Men *have* been known
to age, as well as women.

LYSISTRATA No, not as well as—better.
A man, an absolute antique, comes back from the war, and he's barely
doddered into town before he's married the veriest nymphet.
But a woman's season is brief; it slips, and she'll have
no husband, but sit out her life groping at omens—and finding no men.

COMMISSIONER Lamentable state of affairs. Perhaps we can rectify matters:
[*To the audience.*] TO EVERY MAN JACK, A CHALLENGE:
ARISE!
Provided you can . . .

LYSISTRATA Instead, Commissioner, why not simply curl up and *die?*
Just buy a coffin; here's the place.
[*Banging him on the head with her spindle.*]
I'll knead you a cake for the wake[4]—and *these*
[*Winding the threads from the spindle around him.*]
make excellent wreaths. So Rest In Peace.

KLEONIKE [*Emptying the chamber pot over him.*]
Accept these tokens of deepest grief.

MYRRHINE [*Breaking her lamp over his head.*]
A final garland for the dear deceased.

LYSISTRATA
May I supply any last request?
Then run along. You're due at the wharf:
Charon's[5] anxious to sail—
you're holding up the boat for Hell!

COMMISSIONER This is monstrous—maltreatment of a public official—
maltreatment of ME!
I must repair directly
to the Board of Commissioners, and present my
colleagues concrete evidence of the sorry specifics of this shocking attack!

4. The dead were provided with a honey cake to throw to Cerberus, the three-headed dog that guarded the entry to the underworld. 5. The ferryman of the dead over the river Styx.

[*He staggers off left.* LYSISTRATA *calls after him.*]

LYSISTRATA You won't haul us into court on a charge of neglecting
the dead, will you? (How like a man to insist
on his rights—even his last ones.) Two days between
death and funeral, that's the rule.
Come back here early
day after tomorrow, Commissioner:
We'll lay you out.

[LYSISTRATA *and her women re-enter the Akropolis. The* KORYPHAIOS OF MEN *advances to address the audience.*]

KORYPHAIOS OF MEN Wake up, Athenians! Preserve your freedom—the time is Now!
[*To the* CHORUS OF MEN.] Strip for action, men. Let's cope with the current mess.

[*The* (CHORUS OF) MEN *put off their long mantles, disclosing short tunics underneath, and advance toward the audience.*]

CHORUS OF MEN This trouble may be terminal; it has a loaded odor, an ominous aroma of constitutional rot.
My nose gives a prognosis of radical disorder—it's just the first installment of an absolutist plot!
The Spartans are behind it:
they must have masterminded
some morbid local contacts (engineered by Kleisthenes).[6]
Predictably infected,
these women straightway acted
to commandeer the City's cash. They're feverish to freeze
my be-all,
my end-all . . .
my *payroll!*[7]

KORYPHAIOS OF MEN The symptoms are clear. Our birthright's already nibbled. And oh, so
daintily: WOMEN ticking off troops for improper etiquette.
WOMEN propounding their featherweight views on the fashionable use
and abuse of the shield. And (if any more proof were needed) WOMEN
nagging us to trust the Nice Spartan, and put our heads
in his toothy maw—to make a dessert and call it Peace.
They've woven the City a seamless shroud, bedecked with the legend
DICTATORSHIP.
But I won't be hemmed in. I'll use
their weapon against them, and uphold the right by sneakiness.
With
knyf under cloke,
gauntlet in glove, sword in olive branch,
[*Slipping slowly toward the* KORYPHAIOS OF WOMEN.] I'll take up my post
in Statuary Row, beside our honored National Heroes,

6. Not the great reformer who set up the democracy, but a contemporary of Aristophanes and notorious as a homosexual. Pederasty may have been fashionable, at least among the upper classes, but the Athenians considered a man who allowed himself to be penetrated effeminate. 7. The jury pay, which came from the funds stored on the Acropolis.

the natural foes of tyranny: Harmodios,
Aristogeiton,[8]
and Me.
[*Next to her.*] Striking an epic pose, so, with the full approval
of the immortal gods,
I'll bash this loathsome hag in the jaw!

[*He does, and runs cackling back to the* (CHORUS OF) MEN. *She shakes a fist after him.*]

KORYPHAIOS OF WOMEN Mama won't know her little boy when he gets home!

[*To the* (CHORUS OF) WOMEN, *who are eager to launch a full-scale attack.*]
Let's not be hasty, fellow . . . hags. Cloaks off first.

[*The* (CHORUS OF) WOMEN *remove their mantles, disclosing tunics very like those of the* (CHORUS OF) MEN, *and advance toward the audience.*]

CHORUS OF WOMEN We'll address you, citizens, in beneficial, candid,
patriotic accents, as our breeding says we must,
since, from the age of seven, Athens graced me with a
splendid string of civic triumphs to signalize her
trust:
I was Relic-Girl quite early,[9]
then advanced to Maid of Barley;
in Artemis' "Pageant of the Bear" I played the lead.
To cap this proud progression,
I led the whole procession
at Athene's Celebration, certified and pedigreed
—that cachet
so distingué—
a *Lady!*

KORYPHAIOS OF WOMEN [*To the audience.*] I trust this establishes my qualifications. I may, I take it,
address the City to its profit? Thank you
I admit to being a woman—
but don't sell my contribution short on that account.
It's better than the present panic. And my word is as
good as my bond, because I hold stock in Athens—stock I paid for in sons.
[*To the* CHORUS OF MEN.] —But you, you doddering bankrupts, where are your shares in the State?
[*Slipping slowly toward the* KORYPHAIOS OF MEN.] Your grandfathers willed you the Mutual Funds from the Persian War[1]—
and where are they?
[*Nearer.*] You dipped into capital, then lost interest . . .
and now a pool of your assets won't fill a hole in the ground.

8. The two men who assassinated Hipparchus, brother of the tyrant Hippias, and became heroes of the democracy. In the preceding lines, Aristophanes alludes to a popular Athenian drinking song: "In a branch of myrtle, I'll hide my sword, like Harmodius and Aristogeiton, who killed the tyrant, and made Athens free." 9. Lines 755–63 describe the religious duties of a well-born Athenian girl. 1. The treasury of the Delian League, which was formed as a defensive alliance against Persia in the wake of Xerxes' invasion of 480–79 B.C. but became Athens's empire.

All that remains is one last potential killing—Athens.
Is there any rebuttal?

[*The* KORYPHAIOS OF MEN *gestures menacingly. She ducks down, as if to ward off a blow, and removes a slipper.*]

Force is a footing resort. I'll take
my very sensible shoe, and paste you in the jaw!

[*She does so, and runs back to the women.*]

CHORUS OF MEN Their native respect for our manhood is small,
and keeps getting smaller. Let's bottle their gall.
The man who won't battle has no balls at all!

KORYPHAIOS OF MEN All right, men, skin out the skivvies. Let's give them a whiff of Man, full strength. No point in muffling the essential Us.

[*The* (CHORUS OF) MEN *remove their tunics.*]

CHORUS OF MEN A century back, we soared to the Heights[2]
and beat down Tyranny there.
Now's the time to shed our moults
and fledge our wings once more,
to rise to the skies in our reborn force,
and beat back Tyranny here!

KORYPHAIOS OF MEN No fancy grappling with these grannies; straightforward strength. The tiniest
toehold, and those nimble, fiddling fingers will have their
foot in the door, and we're done for.
No amount of know-how can lick
a woman's knack.
They'll want to build ships next thing
we know,
we're all at sea, fending off female boarding parties.
(Artemisia[3] fought us at Salamis. Tell me, has anyone
caught her yet?)
But we're *really* sunk if they take up horses. Scratch
the Cavalry:
A woman is an easy rider with a natural seat.
Take her over the jumps bareback, and she'll never slip
her mount. (That's how the Amazons nearly took Athens. On horseback.[4]
Check on Mikon's mural down in the Stoa.)
Anyway,
the solution is obvious. Put every woman in her place—
stick her in the stocks.
To do this, first
snare your woman around the neck.

[*He attempts to demonstrate on the* KORYPHAIOS OF WOMEN. *After a brief tussle, she works loose and chases him back to the* (CHORUS OF) MEN.]

CHORUS OF WOMEN The beast in me's eager and fit for
a brawl.

2. The base of the aristocratic family of the Alcmaeonidae in their first attempt to overthrow the tyrant Hippias in 513 B.C. 3. Queen of Halicarnassus in Asia Minor who fought prominently on Xerxes' side at Salamis. 4. The painter Mikon had lately decorated several public buildings with frescoes. The battles of the Greeks and Amazons were favorite subjects of sculptors and painters.

Just rile me a bit and she'll kick down the wall.
You'll bawl to your friends that you've no balls at all.
KORYPHAIOS OF WOMEN All right, ladies, strip for action. Let's give them a whiff
of *Femme Enragée*—piercing and pungent, but not at all tart.
[*The* (CHORUS OF) WOMEN *remove their tunics.*]
CHORUS OF WOMEN We're angry. The brainless bird who tangles
with *us* has gummed his last mush.
In fact, the coot who even heckles
is being daringly rash.
So look to your nests, you reclaimed eagles—
whatever you lay, we'll squash!
KORYPHAIOS OF WOMEN Frankly, you don't faze me. *With* me, I have my friends—
Lampito from Sparta; that genteel girl from Thebes, Ismenia—
committed to me forever. *Against* me, *you*—permanently
out of commission. So do your damnedest.
Pass a law.
Pass seven. Continue the winning ways that have made
your name a short and ugly household word.
Like yesterday:
I was giving a little party, nothing fussy, to honor
the goddess Hekate. Simply to please my daughters,
I'd invited a sweet little thing from the neighborhood—flawless pedigree, perfect
taste, a credit to any gathering—a Boiotian eel.
But she had to decline. Couldn't pass the border. You'd passed a law.
Not that you care for my party. You'll overwork your right of passage
till your august body is overturned,
and you break your silly neck!
[*She deftly grabs the* KORYPHAIOS OF MEN *by the ankle and upsets him. He scuttles back to the* (CHORUS OF) MEN, *who retire in confusion.*

LYSISTRATA *emerges from the citadel, obviously distraught.*]
KORYPHAIOS OF WOMEN [*Mock-tragic.*] *Mistress, queen of this our subtle scheme,*
why burst you from the hall with brangled brow?
LYSISTRATA *Oh, wickedness of woman! The female mind*
does sap my soul and set my wits a-totter.
KORYPHAIOS OF WOMEN *What drear accents are these?*
LYSISTRATA *The merest truth.*
KORYPHAIOS OF WOMEN *Be nothing loath to tell the tale to friends.*
LYSISTRATA *'Twere shame to utter, pain to hold unsaid.*
KORYPHAIOS OF WOMEN *Hide not from me affliction which we share.*
LYSISTRATA *In briefest compass,*
[*Dropping the paratragedy.*] We want to get laid.
KORYPHAIOS OF WOMEN By Zeus!
LYSISTRATA No, no, not HIM!
Well, that's the way things are.

I've lost my grip on the girls—they're mad for men!
But sly—they slip out in droves.
A minute ago,
I caught one scooping out the little hole
that breaks through just below Pan's grotto.
One
had jerry-rigged some block-and-tackle business
and was wriggling away on a rope.
Another just flat
deserted.
Last night I spied one mounting a sparrow,
all set to take off for the nearest bawdyhouse. I hauled
her back by the hair.
And excuses, pretexts for overnight
passes? I've heard them all.
Here comes one. Watch.

[*To the* FIRST WOMAN, *as she runs out of the Akropolis.*]

—You there! What's your hurry?

FIRST WOMAN I have to get home.
I've got all this lovely Milesian wool in the house,
and the moths will simply batter it to bits!

LYSISTRATA I'll bet.
Get back inside.

FIRST WOMAN I swear I'll hurry right back!
—Just time enough to spread it out on the couch?

LYSISTRATA Your wool will stay unspread. And you'll stay here.

FIRST WOMAN Do I have to let my piecework *rot?*

LYSISTRATA Possibly.

[*The* SECOND WOMAN *runs on.*]

SECOND WOMAN Oh dear, oh goodness, what shall I do—my flax!
I left and forgot to peel it!

LYSISTRATA Another one.
She suffers from unpeeled flax.
—Get back inside!

SECOND WOMAN I'll be right back. I just have to pluck the fibers.

LYSISTRATA No. No plucking. You start it, and everyone else
will want to go and do their plucking, too.

[*The* THIRD WOMAN, *swelling conspicuously, hurries on, praying loudly.*]

THIRD WOMAN *O Goddess of Childbirth, grant that I not deliver*
until I get me from out this sacred precinct!

LYSISTRATA What sort of nonsense is *this?*

THIRD WOMAN I'm due—any second!

LYSISTRATA You weren't pregnant yesterday.

THIRD WOMAN Today I am—
a miracle!
Let me go home for a midwife, *please!*
I may not make it!

LYSISTRATA [*Restraining her.*] You can do better than that.
[*Tapping the woman's stomach and receiving a metallic clang.*] What's this? It's hard.

THIRD WOMAN I'm going to have a boy.
LYSISTRATA Not unless he's made of bronze. Let's see.
[*She throws open the* THIRD WOMAN*'s cloak, exposing a huge bronze helmet.*]
Of all the brazen . . . You've stolen the helmet from
Athene's statue! Pregnant, indeed!
THIRD WOMAN I am *so* pregnant!
LYSISTRATA Then why the helmet?
THIRD WOMAN I thought my time might come
while I was still on forbidden ground.[5] If it did,
I could climb inside Athene's helmet and have
my baby there.
The pigeons do it all the time.
LYSISTRATA Nothing but excuses!
[*Taking the helmet.*] *This* is your baby. I'm afraid
you'll have to stay until we give it a name.
THIRD WOMAN But the Akropolis is *awful.* I can't even sleep! I saw
the snake that guards the temple.
LYSISTRATA That snake's a fabrication.[6]
THIRD WOMAN I don't care *what* kind it is—I'm *scared*!
[*The other* WOMEN, *who have emerged from the citadel, crowd around.*]
KLEONIKE And those goddamned holy owls.[7] All night long,
tu-wit, tu-wu—they're hooting me into my grave!
LYSISTRATA Darlings, let's call a halt to this hocus-pocus.
You miss your men—now isn't that the trouble?
[*Shamefaced nods from the group.*]
Don't you think they miss you just as much?
I can assure you, their nights are every bit
as hard as yours. So be good girls; endure!
Persist a few days more, and Victory is ours.
It's fated: a current prophecy declares that the men
will go down to defeat before us, provided that *we*
maintain a United Front.
[*Producing a scroll.*] I happen to have
a copy of the prophecy.
KLEONIKE Read it!
LYSISTRATA Silence, *please.*
[*Reading from the scroll.*]
But when the swallows, in flight from the
hoopoes, have flocked to a hole
on high, and stoutly eschew their
accustomed perch on the pole,
yea, then shall Thunderer Zeus to
their suff'ring establish a stop,
by making the lower the upper . . .
KLEONIKE Then *we'll* be lying on top?

5. As sacred ground, the Acropolis would be polluted by either birth or death. 6. No one had ever seen the sacred snake that lived in the Erechtheum. 7. Athena's sacred birds.

LYSISTRATA But should these swallows, indulging their
lust for the perch, lose heart,
dissolve their flocks in winged dissension,
and singly depart
the sacred stronghold, breaking the
bands that bind them together—
then know them as lewd, the pervertedest
birds that ever wore feather.

KLEONIKE There's nothing obscure about *that* oracle. Ye gods!

LYSISTRATA Sorely beset as we are, we must not flag
or falter. So back to the citadel!
[*As the women troop inside.*] And if we fail
that oracle, darlings, our image is absolutely *mud!*

[*She follows them in. A pause, and the* CHORUSES *assemble.*]

CHORUS OF MEN I have a simple
tale to relate you.
a sterling example
of masculine virtue:

The huntsman bold Melanion
was once a harried quarry.
The women in town tracked him down
and badgered him to marry.

Melanion knew the cornered male
eventually cohabits.
Assessing the odds, he took to the woods
and lived trapping rabbits.

He stuck to the virgin stand, sustained
by rabbit meat and hate,
and never returned, but ever remained
an alfresco celibate.

Melanion is our ideal;
his loathing makes us free.
Our dearest aim is the gemlike flame
of his misogyny.[8]

OLD MAN Let me kiss that wizened cheek.

OLD WOMAN [*Threatening with a fist.*]
A wish too rash for that withered flesh.

OLD MAN
and lay you low with a highflying kick.
[*He tries one and misses.*]

OLD WOMAN
Exposing an overgrown underbrush.

OLD MAN A hairy behind, historically, means

8. The chorus of men here recasts a well-known myth for their own purposes. In the myth, it was Atalanta who avoided marriage, challenging her suitors to a footrace that she always won. Melanion threw a golden apple in front of her; when she stopped to pick it up, she lost the race to him.

masculine force: Myronides
harassed the foe with his mighty mane,
and furry Phormion[9] swept the seas
of enemy ships, never meeting his match—
such was the nature of his thatch.

CHORUS OF WOMEN I offer an anecdote
for your opinion,
an adequate antidote
for your Melanion:

Timon,[1] the noted local grouch,
put rusticating hermits
out of style by building his wilds
inside the city limits

He shooed away society
with natural battlements:
his tongue was edgèd; his shoulder, frigid;
his beard, a picket fence.

When random contacts overtaxed him,
he didn't stop to pack,
but loaded curses on the male of the species,
left town, and never came back.

Timon, you see, was a misanthrope
in a properly narrow sense:
his spleen was vented only on men . . .
we were his dearest friends.

OLD WOMAN [*Making a fist.*]
Enjoy a chop to that juiceless chin?

OLD MAN [*Backing away.*]
I'm jolted already. Thank you, no.

OLD WOMAN
Perhaps a trip from a well-turned shin?
[*She tries a kick and misses.*]

OLD MAN
Brazenly baring the mantrap below.

OLD WOMAN At least it's *neat.* I'm not too sorry
to have you see my daintiness.
My habits are still depilatory;
age hasn't made me a bristly mess.
Secure in my smoothness, I'm never in doubt—
though even down is out.

[LYSISTRATA *mounts the platform and scans the horizon. When her gaze reaches the left, she stops suddenly.*]

LYSISTRATA Ladies, attention! Battle stations, please!

9. Like Myronides, a famous Athenian general. 1. A famous misanthrope, and the subject of Shakespeare's play *Timon of Athens.* There is no evidence that he hated women any less than he hated men.

And quickly!

[*A general rush of women to the battlements.*]

KLEONIKE What is it?

MYRRHINE What's all the shouting for?

LYSISTRATA A MAN!

[*Consternation.*] Yes, it's a man. And he's coming this way!
Hmm. Seems to have suffered a seizure. Broken out
with a nasty attack of love.
[*Prayer, aside.*] O Aphrodite,
Mistress all-victorious,
mysterious, voluptuous,
you who make the crooked straight . . .
don't let this happen to US!

KLEONIKE I don't care who he is—*where is he?*

LYSISTRATA [*Pointing.*] Down there—
just flanking that temple—Demeter the Fruitful.

KLEONIKE My.
Definitely a man.

MYRRHINE [*Craning for a look.*] I wonder who it can be?

LYSISTRATA See for yourselves.—Can anyone identify him?

MYRRHINE Oh lord, I can.
That is my husband—Kinesias.

LYSISTRATA [*To* MYRRHINE.] Your duty is clear.
Pop him on the griddle, twist
the spit, braize him, baste him, stew him in his own
juice, do him to a turn. Sear him with kisses,
coyness, caresses, *everything*—
but stop where Our Oath begins.

MYRRHINE Relax. I can take care of this.

LYSISTRATA Of course
you can, dear. Still, a little help can't hurt, now
can it? I'll just stay around for a bit
and—er—poke up the fire.
—Everyone else inside!

[*Exit all the women but* LYSISTRATA, *on the platform, and* MYRRHINE, *who stands near the Akropolis entrance, hidden from her husband's view.* KINESIAS *staggers on, in erection and considerable pain, followed by a male slave who carries a baby boy.*]

KINESIAS OUCH!!
Omigod.
Hypertension, twinges. . . . I can't hold out much more.
I'd rather be dismembered.
How long, ye gods, how long?

LYSISTRATA [*Officially.*] WHO GOES THERE?
WHO PENETRATES OUR POSITIONS?

KINESIAS Me.

LYSISTRATA A Man?

KINESIAS Every inch.
LYSISTRATA Then inch yourself out
of here. Off Limits to Men.
KINESIAS This *is* the limit.
Just who are *you* to throw me out?
LYSISTRATA The Lookout.
KINESIAS Well, look here, Lookout. I'd like to see Myrrhine.
How's the outlook?
LYSISTRATA Unlikely. Bring Myrrhine
to you? The idea!
Just by the by, who are you?
KINESIAS A private citizen. Her husband, Kinesias.
LYSISTRATA No!
Meeting you—I'm overcome!
Your name, you know,
is not without its fame among us girls.
[*Aside.*] —Matter of fact, we have a name for *it.*—
I swear, you're never out of Myrrhine's mouth.
She won't even nibble a quince, or swallow an egg,
without reciting, "Here's to Kinesias!"
KINESIAS For god's sake.
will you . . .
LYSISTRATA [*Sweeping on over his agony.*] Word of honor, it's true. Why, when
we discuss our husbands (you know how women are),
Myrrhine refuses to argue. She simply insists:
"Compared with Kinesias, the rest have *nothing!*"
Imagine!
KINESIAS *Bring her out here!*
LYSISTRATA Really? And what would I
get out of this?
KINESIAS You see my situation. I'll raise
whatever I can. This can all be yours.
LYSISTRATA Goodness.
It's really her place. I'll go and get her.
[*She descends from the platform and moves to* MYRRHINE, *out of Kinesias's sight.*]
KINESIAS Speed!
—Life is a husk. She left our home, and happiness
went with her. Now pain is the tenant. Oh, to enter
that wifeless house, to sense that awful emptiness,
to eat that tasteless, joyless food—it makes
it hard, I tell you.
Harder all the time.
MYRRHINE [*Still out of his sight, in a voice to be overhead.*] Oh, I *do* love him! I'm mad about him! But he
doesn't want my love. Please don't make me see him.
KINESIAS Myrrhine darling, why do you *act* this way?
Come down here!
MYRRHINE [*Appearing at the wall.*] Down there? Certainly not!

KINESIAS It's me, Myrrhine. I'm begging you. Please come down.
MYRRHINE I don't see why you're begging me. You don't need me.
KINESIAS I don't need you? I'm at the end of my rope!
MYRRHINE I'm leaving.
[*She turns.* KINESIAS *grabs the boy from the slave.*]
KINESIAS No! Wait! At least you'll have to listen
to the voice of your child.
[*To the boy, in a fierce undertone.*] —(Call your mother!)
[*Silence.*] . . . to the voice
of your very own child . . .
—(Call your mother, brat!)
CHILD MOMMYMOMMYMOMMY!
KINESIAS Where's your maternal instinct? He hasn't been washed
or fed for a week. How can you be so pitiless?
MYRRHINE *Him* I pity. Of all the pitiful excuses
for a father. . . .
KINESIAS Come down here, dear. For the baby's sake.
MYRRHINE Motherhood! I'll have to come. I've got no choice.
KINESIAS [*Soliloquizing as she descends.*] It may be me, but I'll swear she looks years younger—
and gentler—her eyes caress me. And then they flash:
that anger, that verve, the high-and-mighty air!
She's fire, she's ice—and I'm stuck right in the middle.
MYRRHINE [*Taking the baby.*] Sweet babykins with such a nasty daddy!
Here, let Mummy kissums. Mummy's little darling.
KINESIAS [*The injured husband.*] You should be ashamed of yourself, letting those women
lead you around. Why do you DO these things?
You only make me suffer and hurt your poor,
sweet self.
MYRRHINE Keep your hands away from me!
KINESIAS But the house, the furniture, everything we own—you're
letting it go to hell!
MYRRHINE Frankly, I couldn't care less.
KINESIAS But your weaving's unraveled—the loom is full of
chickens! You couldn't care less about *that?*
MYRRHINE I certainly couldn't.
KINESIAS And the holy rites of Aphrodite? Think how long
that's been.
Come on, darling, let's go home.
MYRRHINE I absolutely refuse!
Unless you agree to a truce
to stop the war.
KINESIAS Well, then, if that's your decision.
we'll STOP the war!
MYRRHINE Well, then, if that's your decision.
I'll come back—*after* it's done.
But, for the present.
I've sworn off.
KINESIAS At least lie down for a minute.

We'll talk.
MYRRHINE I know what you're up to—NO!
—And yet. . . . I really can't say I don't love you . . .
KINESIAS You love me?
So what's the trouble? *Lie down.*
MYRRHINE Don't be disgusting.
In front of the baby?
KINESIAS Er . . . no. Heaven Forfend.
[*Taking the baby and pushing it at the slave.*] —Take this home.
[*The slave obeys.*]
—Well, darling, we're rid of the kid . . .
let's go to bed!
MYRRHINE Poor dear.
But where does one do
this sort of thing?
KINESIAS Where? All we need is a little
nook. . . . We'll try Pan's grotto. Excellent spot.
MYRRHINE [*With a nod at the Akropolis.*] I'll have to be pure to get back in *there.* How can I
expunge my pollution?
KINESIAS Sponge off in the pool next door.
MYRRHINE I did swear an Oath. I'm supposed to perjure myself?
KINESIAS Bother the Oath. Forget it—I'll take the blame.
[*A pause.*]
MYRRHINE Now I'll go get us a cot.
KINESIAS No! Not a cot!
The ground's enough for us.
MYRRHINE *I'll get the cot.*
For all your faults, I refuse to put you to bed
in the dirt.
[*She exists into the Akropolis.*]
KINESIAS She certainly loves me. That's nice to know.
MYRRHINE [*Returning with a rope-tied cot.*] Here. You hurry to bed while I undress.
[KINESIAS *lies down.*]
Gracious me—I forgot. We need a mattress.
KINESIAS Who wants a mattress? Not me!
MYRRHINE Oh, yes, you do.
It's perfectly squalid on the ropes.
KINESIAS Well, give me a kiss
to tide me over.
MYRRHINE *Voilà.*
[*She pecks at him and leaves.*]
KINESIAS OoolaLAlala!
—Make it a quick trip, dear.
MYRRHINE [*Entering with the mattress, she waves* KINESIAS *off the cot and lays the mattress on it.*] Here we are.
Our mattress. Now hurry to bed while I undress.
[KINESIAS *lies down again.*]
Gracious me—I forgot. You don't have a pillow.

KINESIAS I do *not* need a pillow.
MYRRHINE I know, but *I* do.
[*She leaves.*]
KINESIAS What a lovefeast! Only the table gets laid.
MYRRHINE [*Returning with a pillow.*] Rise and shine!
[KINESIAS *jumps up. She places the pillow.*]
And now I have everything I need.
KINESIAS [*Lying down again.*] You certainly do.
Come here, my little jewelbox!
MYRRHINE Just taking off my bra.
Don't break your promise:
no cheating about the Peace.
KINESIAS I swear to god,
I'll die first!
MYRRHINE [*Coming to him.*] Just look. You don't have a blanket.
KINESIAS I didn't plan to go camping—I want to make love!
MYRRHINE Relax. You'll get your love. I'll be right back.
[*She leaves.*]
KINESIAS Relax? I'm dying a slow death by dry goods!
MYRRHINE [*Returning with the blanket.*] Get up!
KINESIAS [*Getting out of bed.*] I've been up for hours. I was up before I was up.
[MYRRHINE *spreads the blanket on the mattress, and he lies down again.*]
MYRRHINE I presume you want perfume?
KINESIAS Positively NO!
MYRRHINE Absolutely *yes*—whether you want it or not.
[*She leaves.*]
KINESIAS Dear Zeus, I don't ask for much—but please let her spill it.
MYRRHINE [*Returning with a bottle.*]
Hold out your hand like a good boy.
Now rub it in.
KINESIAS [*Obeying and sniffing.*] *This* is to quicken desire? Too strong. It grabs
your nose and bawls out: *Try again tomorrow.*
MYRRHINE I'm *awful!* I brought you that rancid Rhodian brand.
[*She starts off with the bottle.*]
KINESIAS This is just *lovely.* Leave it, woman!
MYRRHINE Silly!
[*She leaves.*]
KINESIAS God damn the clod who first concocted perfume!
MYRRHINE [*Returning with another bottle.*] Here, try this flask.
KINESIAS Thanks—
but you try mine.
Come to bed, you witch—
and please stop bringing things!

MYRRHINE *That* is exactly what I'll do.
There go my shoes.
Incidentally, darling, you *will*
remember to vote for the truce?
KINESIAS I'LL THINK IT OVER!
[MYRRHINE *runs off for good.*]
That woman's laid me waste—destroyed me, root
and branch!
I'm scuttled,
gutted,
up the spout!
And Myrrhine's gone!
[*In a parody of a tragic kommos.*[2]]
Out upon't! But how? But where?
Now I have lost the fairest fair,
how screw my courage to yet another
sticking-place? Aye, there's the rub—
And yet, this wagging, wanton babe
must soon be laid to rest, or else...
Ho, Pandar!
Pandar!
I'd hire a nurse.

KORYPHAIOS OF MEN
Grievous your bereavement, cruel
the slow tabescence of your soul.
I bid my liquid pity mingle.

Oh, where the soul, and where, alack!
the cod to stand the taut attack
of swollen prides, the scorching tensions
that ravine up the lumbar regions?
His morning lay
has gone astray.

KINESIAS [*In agony.*]
O Zeus, reduce the throbs, the throes!

KORYPHAIOS OF MEN
I turn my tongue to curse the cause
of your affliction—that jade, that slut,
that hag, that ogress . . .

KINESIAS No! Slight not
my light-o'-love, my dove, my sweet!

KORYPHAIOS OF MEN
Sweet!
O Zeus who rul'st the sky,
snatch that slattern up on high,
crack thy winds, unleash thy thunder,
tumble her over, trundle her under,
juggle her from hand to hand;

2. Lament.

twirl her ever near the ground—
drop her in a well-aimed fall
on our comrade's tool! That's all.

[KINESIAS *exits left.*

A SPARTAN HERALD *enters from the right, holding his cloak together in a futile attempt to conceal his condition.*]

HERALD This Athens? Where-all kin I find the Council of Elders
or else the Executive Board? I brung some news.

[*The* COMMISSIONER, *swathed in his cloak, enters from the left.*]

COMMISSIONER And what are you—a man? a signpost? a joint-stock company?

HERALD A herald, sonny, an honest-to-Kastor
herald. I come to chat 'bout thet-there truce.

COMMISSIONER . . . carrying a concealed weapon? Pretty underhanded.

HERALD [*Twisting to avoid the* COMMISSIONER*'s direct gaze.*] Hain't done no sech a thang!

COMMISSIONER Very well, stand still.
Your cloak's out of crease—hernia? Are the roads that bad?

HERALD I swear this feller's plumb tetched in the haid!

COMMISSIONER [*Throwing open the* SPARTAN (HERALD)*'s cloak, exposing the phallus.*]
You clown,
you've got an erection!

HERALD [*Wildly embarrassed.*] Hain't got no sech a thang!
You stop this-hyer foolishment!

COMMISSIONER What *have* you got there, then?

HERALD Thet-thur's a Spartan *e*pistle.[3] In code.

COMMISSIONER I have the key.
[*Throwing open his cloak.*] Behold another Spartan *e*pistle. In code.
[*Tiring of teasing.*] Let's get down to cases. I know the score,
so tell me the truth.
How are things with you in Sparta?

HERALD Thangs is up in the air. The whole Alliance
is purt-near 'bout to explode. We-uns'll need barrels,
'stead of women.

COMMISSIONER What was the cause of this outburst?
The great god Pan?

HERALD Nope. I'll lay 'twere Lampito,
most likely. She begun, and then they was off
and runnin' at the post in a bunch, every last little gal
in Sparta, drivin' their menfolk away from the winner's circle.

COMMISSIONER How are you taking this?

HERALD Painful-like.
Everyone's doubled up worse as a midget nursin'
a wick in a midnight wind come moon-dark time.
Cain't even tetch them little old gals on the moosey

3. An encoding device. Papyrus was wrapped around a wooden staff on a spiral, and a message was written on it. The message could be read only when the papyrus was wrapped around an exactly similar staff.

without we all agree to a Greece-wide Peace.

COMMISSIONER Of course!
A universal female plot—all Hellas
risen in rebellion—I should have known!
Return
to Sparta with this request:
Have them despatch us
a Plenipotentiary Commission, fully empowered
to conclude an armistice. I have full confidence
that I can persuade our Senate to do the same,
without extending myself. The evidence is at hand.

HERALD I'm a-flyin'. Sir! I hev never heered your equal!

[*Exeunt hurriedly, the* COMMISSIONER *to the left, the* (SPARTAN) HERALD *to the right.*]

KORYPHAIOS OF MEN
The most unnerving work of nature,
the pride of applied immorality,
is the common female human.
No fire can match, no beast can best her.
O Unsurmountability,
thy name—worse luck—is Woman.

KORYPHAIOS OF WOMEN
After such knowledge, why persist
in wearing out this feckless
war between the sexes?
When can I apply for the post
of ally, partner, and general friend?

KORYPHAIOS OF MEN
I won't be ployed to revise, re-do,
amend, extend, or bring to an end
my irreversible credo:
Misogyny Forever!
—The answer's never.

KORYPHAIOS OF WOMEN
All right. Whenever you choose.
But, for the present, I refuse
to let you look your absolute worst,
parading around like an unfrocked freak:
I'm coming over and get you dressed.

[*She dresses him in his tunic, an action (like others in this scene) imitated by the members of the* CHORUS OF WOMEN *toward their opposite numbers in the* CHORUS OF MEN.]

KORYPHAIOS OF MEN
This seems sincere. It's not a trick.
Recalling the rancor with which I stripped,
I'm overlaid with chagrin.

KORYPHAIOS OF WOMEN
Now you resemble a man,
not some ghastly practical joke.
And if you show me a little respect

(and promise not to kick), I'll extract
the beast in you.

KORYPHAIOS OF MEN [*Searching himself.*] What beast in me?

KORYPHAIOS OF WOMEN
That insect. There. The bug that's stuck
in your eye.

KORYPHAIOS OF MEN [*Playing along dubiously.*] This gnat?

KORYPHAIOS OF WOMEN Yes, nitwit!

KORYPHAIOS OF MEN Of
course.
That steady, festering agony. . . .
You've put your finger on the source
of all my lousy troubles. Please
roll back the lid and scoop it out.
I'd like to see it.

KORYPHAIOS OF WOMEN All right, I'll do it.
[*Removing the imaginary insect.*]
Although, of all the impossible cranks. . . .
Do you sleep in a swamp? Just look at this.
I've never seen a bigger chigger.

KORYPHAIOS OF MEN Thanks.
Your kindness touches me deeply. For years,
that thing's been sinking wells in my eye.
Now you've unplugged me. Here come the tears.

KORYPHAIOS OF WOMEN
I'll dry your tears, though I can't say why.
[*Wiping away the tears.*]
Of all the irresponsible boys. . . .
And I'll kiss you.

KORYPHAIOS OF MEN Don't you kiss me!

KORYPHAIOS OF WOMEN
What made you think you had a choice?
[*She kisses him.*]

KORYPHAIOS OF MEN All right, damn you, that's enough of that ingrained
palaver.
I can't dispute the truth or logic of the pithy old proverb:
Life with women is hell.
Life without women is hell, too.
And so we conclude a truce with you, on the following terms:
in future, a mutual moratorium on mischief in all its forms.
Agreed?—Let's make a single chorus and start our song.
[*The two* CHORUSES *unite and face the audience.*]

CHORUS OF MEN
We're not about to introduce
the standard personal abuse—
the Choral Smear
Of Present Persons (usually,
in every well-made comedy,
inserted here).
Instead, in deed and utterance, we

shall now indulge in philanthropy
because we feel
that members of the audience
endure, in the course of current events,
sufficient hell.
Therefore, friends, be rich! Be flush!
Apply to us, and borrow cash
in large amounts.
The Treasury stands behind us—there—
and we can personally take care
of small accounts.
Drop up today. Your credit's good.
Your loan won't have to be repaid
in full until
the war is over. And then, your debt
is only the money you actually get—
nothing at all.

CHORUS OF WOMEN

Just when we meant to entertain
some madcap gourmets from out of town
—such flawless taste!—
the present unpleasantness intervened,
and now we fear the feast we planned
will go to waste.
The soup is waiting, rich and thick:
I've sacrificed at a suckling pig
—the pièce de résistance—
whose toothsome cracklings should amaze
the most fastidious gourmets—
you, for instance.
To everybody here, I say
take potluck at my house today
with me and mine.
Bathe and change as fast as you can,
bring the children, hurry down,
and walk right in.
Don't bother to knock. No need at all.
My house is yours. Liberty Hall.
What are friends for?
Act self-possessed when you come over:
it may help out when you discover
I've locked the door.

[A DELEGATION OF SPARTANS *enters from the right, with difficulty. They have removed their cloaks, but hold them before themselves in an effort to conceal their condition.*]

KORYPHAIOS OF MEN What's this? Behold the Spartan ambassadors, dragging their beards,
pussy-footing along. It appears they've developed a hitch in the crotch.
[*Advancing to greet them.*] Men of Sparta, I bid you welcome!
And now

to the point: What predicament brings you among us?
SPARTAN We-uns is up a stump. Hain't fit fer chatter.
[*Flipping aside his cloak.*] Here's our predicament. Take a look for yourselfs.
KORYPHAIOS OF MEN Well, I'll be damned—a regular disaster area.
Inflamed. I imagine the temperature's rather intense?
SPARTAN Hit ain't the heat, hit's the tumidity.
But words
won't help what ails us. We-uns come after Peace.
Peace from any person, at any price.

[*Enter the Athenian (men) from the left, led by Kinesias. They are wearing cloaks, but are obviously in as much travail as the* SPARTANS.]

KORYPHAIOS OF MEN Behold our local Sons of the Soil, stretching
their garments away from their groins, like wrestlers
Grappling with their plight. Some sort of athlete's disease, no doubt.
An outbreak of epic proportions.
Athlete's foot?
No. Could it be athlete's . . . ?
KINESIAS Who can tell us
how to get hold of Lysistrata? We've come as delegates
to the Sexual Congress.
[*Opening his cloak.*] Here are our credentials.
KORYPHAIOS OF MEN [*Ever the scientist, looking from the Athenians to the* SPARTANS *and back again.*] The words are different, but the malady seems the same.
[*To* KINESIAS.] Dreadful disease. When the crisis reaches its height,
what do you take for it?
KINESIAS Whatever comes to hand.
But now we've reached the bitter end. It's Peace
or we fall back on Kleisthenes.
And he's got a waiting list.
KORPHAIOS OF MEN [*To the* SPARTANS.] Take my advice and put your clothes on. If someone
from that self-appointed Purity League comes by, you
may be docked. They do it to the statues of Hermes,[4]
they'll do it to you.
KINESIAS [*Since he has not yet noticed the* SPARTANS, *he interprets the warning as meant for him, and hurriedly pulls his cloak together, as do the other Athenians.*] Excellent advice.
SPARTAN Hit shorely is.
Hain't nothing to argue after. Let's git dressed.

[*As they put on their cloaks, the* SPARTANS *are finally noticed by* KINESIAS.]

KINESIAS Welcome, men of Sparta! This is a shameful
disgrace to masculine honor.
SPARTAN Hit could be worser.

4. Just before the great expedition left for Sicily, rioters (probably oligarchic conspirators opposed to the expedition) broke the erect phalluses off many of the statues of the god Hermes that stood at the doors of most Athenian houses.

Ef them Herm-choppers seed us all fired up,
they'd *really* take us down a peg or two.

KINESIAS Gentlemen, let's descend to details. Specifically,
why are you here?

SPARTAN Ambassadors. We come to dicker
'bout thet-thur Peace.

KINESIAS Perfect! Precisely our purpose.
Let's send for Lysistrata. Only she can reconcile
our differences. There'll be no Peace for us without her.

SPARTAN We-uns ain't fussy. Call Lysistratos, too, if you want.

[*The gates to the Akropolis open, and Lysistrata emerges, accompanied by her handmaid,* PEACE—*a beautiful girl without a stitch on.* PEACE *remains out of sight by the gates until summoned.*]

KORYPHAIOS OF MEN Hail, most virile of women! Summon up all your experience:
Be terrible and tender,
lofty and lowbrow,
severe and demure.
Here stand the Leaders of Greece, enthralled by your charm.
They yield the floor to you and submit their claims for your arbitration.

LYSISTRATA Really, it shouldn't be difficult, if I can catch them
all bothered, before they start to solicit each other.
I'll find out soon enough. Where's Peace?
—Come here.

[PEACE *moves from her place by the gates to* LYSISTRATA. *The delegations goggle at her.*]

Now, dear, first get those Spartans and bring them to me.
Take them by the hand, but don't be pushy about it,
not like our husbands (no savoir-faire at all!).
Be a lady, be proper, do just what you'd do at home:
if hands are refused, conduct them by the handle.

[PEACE *leads the* SPARTANS *to a position near* LYSISTRATA.]

And now a hand to the Athenians—it doesn't matter
where; accept any offer—and bring *them* over.

[PEACE *conducts the Athenians to a position near* LYSISTRATA, *opposite the* SPARTANS.]

You Spartans move up closer—right *here*—
[*To the Athenians.*] and *you*
stand over *here*.
—And now attend my speech.

[*This the delegations do with some difficulty, because of the conflicting attractions of* PEACE, *who is standing beside her mistress.*]

I am a woman—but not without some wisdom:
my native wit is not completely negligible,
and I've listened long and hard to the discourse of my
elders—my education is not entirely despicable.
Well,
now that I've got you, I intend to give you hell,
and I'm perfectly right. Consider your actions:
At festivals,

in Pan-Hellenic harmony, like true blood-brothers, you share
the selfsame basin of holy water, and sprinkle
altars all over Greece—Olympia, Delphoi,
Thermopylai . . . (I could go on and on, if length
were my only object.)
But now, when the Persians sit by
and wait, in the very presence of your enemies, you fight
each other, destroy *Greek* men, destroy *Greek* cities!
—Point One of my address is now concluded.

KINESIAS [*Gazing at* PEACE.] *I'm* destroyed, if this is drawn out much longer!

LYSISTRATA [*Serenely unconscious of the interruption.*] —Men of Sparta, I direct these remarks to you.
Have you forgotten that a Spartan suppliant once came
to beg assistance from Athens? Recall Perikleidas:
Fifty years ago, he clung to our altar,
his face dead-white above his crimson robe, and pleaded
for an army.[5] Messene was pressing you hard in revolt,
and to this upheaval, Poseidon, the Earthshaker, added
another.
But Kimon took four thousand troops
from Athens—an army which saved the state of Sparta.
Such treatment have you received at the hands of Athens,
you who devastate the country that came to your aid!

KINESIAS [*Stoutly; the condemnation of his enemy has made him forget the girl momentarily.*] You're right, Lysistrata. The Spartans are clearly in the wrong!

SPARTAN [*Guiltily backing away from* PEACE, *whom he has attempted to pat.*] Hit's wrong, I reckon, but that's the purtiest behind . . .

LYSISTRATA [*Turning to the Athenians.*] —Men of Athens, do you think I'll let you off?
Have you forgotten the Tyrant's days, when you wore
the smock of slavery,[6] when the Spartans turned to the
spear, cut down the pride of Thessaly, despatched the
friends of tyranny, and dispossessed your oppressors?
Recall:
On that great day, your only allies were Spartans;
your liberty came at their hands, which stripped away
your servile garb and clothed you again in Freedom!

SPARTAN [*Indicating* LYSISTRATA.] Hain't never seed no higher type of woman.

KINESIAS [*Indicating* PEACE.] Never saw one I wanted so much to top.

LYSISTRATA [*Oblivious to the byplay, addressing both groups.*] With such a history of mutual benefits conferred
and received, why are you fighting? Stop this wickedness!

5. After a disastrous earthquake the Spartans were in great danger as a result of a rebellion of their serfs, the Messenian Helots. The Athenians under Cimon sent a large military force to help them (464 B.C.).
6. Hippias the tyrant had allowed exiled democrats to return to Attica, but they had to stay outside the city and wear sheepskins so that they could readily be identified. With the help of Spartan soldiers the exiles and the people of Attica finally defeated the Thessalian troops of Hippias.

Come to terms with each other! What prevents you?
SPARTAN We'd a heap sight druther make Peace, if we was
indemnified with a plumb strategic location.
[*Pointing at* PEACE's *Rear.*] We'll take thet butte.
LYSISTRATA Butte?
SPARTAN The Promontory of Pylos—Sparta's Back Door.[7]
We've missed it fer a turrible spell.
[*Reaching.*] Hev to keep our
hand in.
KINESIAS [*Pushing him away.*] The price is too high—you'll never take that!
LYSISTRATA Oh, let them have it.
KINESIAS What room will we have left
for maneuvers?
LYSISTRATA Demand another spot in exchange.
KINESIAS [*Surveying* PEACE *like a map as he addresses the* SPARTAN.] Then you hand over to us—uh, let me see—
let's try Thessaly—
[*Indicating the relevant portions of* PEACE.] First of all, Easy Mountain . . .
then the Maniac Gulf behind it . . .
and down to Megara
for the legs . . .
SPARTAN You cain't take all of thet! Yore plumb
out of yore mind!
LYSISTRATA [*To* KINESIAS.] Don't argue. Let the legs go.
[KINESIAS *nods. A pause. General smiles of agreement.*]
KINESIAS [*Doffing his cloak.*] I feel an urgent desire to plow a few furrows.
SPARTAN [*Doffing his cloak.*] Hit's time to work a few loads of fertilizer in.
LYSISTRATA Conclude the treaty and the simple life is yours,
If such is your decision convene your councils,
and then deliberate the matter with your allies.
KINESIAS *Deliberate? Allies?*
We're over-extended already!
Wouldn't every ally approve our position—
Union Now?
SPARTAN I know I kin speak for ourn.
KINESIAS And I for ours.
They're just a bunch of gigolos.
LYSISTRATA I heartily approve.
Now first attend to your purification,
then we, the women, will welcome you to the Citadel
and treat you to all the delights of a home-cooked
banquet. Then you'll exchange your oaths and pledge
your faith, and every man of you will take his wife and
depart for home.

7. The stock Athenian joke about Spartan men's supposed predilection for anal intercourse with either women or other men. As with Pylos here, the next lines contain double-barreled references to territories in dispute in the war and salient portions of Peace's anatomy.

[LYSISTRATA *and* PEACE *enter the Akropolis.*]

KINESIAS Let's hurry!

SPARTAN Lead on, everwhich way's yore pleasure.

KINESIAS This way, then—and HURRY!

[*The delegations exeunt at a run.*]

CHORUS OF WOMEN I'd never stint on anybody.
And now I include, in my boundless bounty,
the younger set.
Attention, you parents of teenage girls
about to debut in the social whirl.
Here's what you get:
Embroidered linens, lush brocades,
a huge assortment of ready-mades,
from mantles to shifts;
plus bracelets and bangles of solid gold—
every item my wardrobe holds—
absolute gifts!
Don't miss this offer. Come to my place,
barge right in, and make your choice.
You can't refuse
Everything there must go today.
Finders keepers—cart it away!
How can you lose?
Don't spare me. Open all the locks.
Break every seal. Empty every box.
Keep ferreting—
And your sight's considerably better than mine
if you should possibly chance to find
a single thing.

CHORUS OF MEN Troubles, friend? Too many mouths
to feed, and not a scrap in the house
to see you through?
Faced with starvation? Don't give it a thought.
Pay attention; I'll tell you what
I'm gonna do.
I overbought. I'm overstocked.
Every room in my house is clogged
with flour (best ever),
glutted with luscious loaves whose size
you wouldn't believe. I need the space;
do me a favor:
Bring gripsacks, knapsacks, duffle bags,
pitchers, cisterns, buckets, and kegs
around to me.
A courteous servant will see to your needs;
he'll fill them up with A-1 wheat—
and all for free!
—Oh. Just one final word before
you turn your steps to my front door:

I happen to own
a dog. Tremendous animal.
Can't stand a leash. And bites like hell—
better stay home.

[*The united* CHORUS *flocks to the door of the Akropolis.*]

KORYPHAIOS OF MEN [*Banging at the door.*] Hey, open up in there!

[*The door opens, and the* COMMISSIONER *appears. He wears a wreath, carries a torch, and is slightly drunk. He addresses the* KORYPHAIOS.]

COMMISSIONER You
know the Regulations.
Move along!

[*He sees the entire* CHORUS.]

—And why are YOU lounging around?
I'll wield my trusty torch and scorch the lot!

[*The* CHORUS *backs away in mock horror. He stops and looks at his torch.*]

—*This* is the bottom of the barrel. A cheap burlesque bit.
I refuse to do it. I have my pride.

[*With a start, he looks at the audience, as though hearing a protest. He shrugs and addresses the audience.*]

—No, choice, eh?
Well, if that's the way it is, we'll take the trouble.
Anything to keep you happy.

[*The* CHORUS *advances eagerly.*]

KORYPHAIOS OF MEN Don't forget us!
We're in this, too. Your trouble is ours!

COMMISSIONER [*Resuming his character and jabbing with his torch at the* CHORUS.] Keep moving!
Last man out of the way goes home without hair!
Don't block the exit. Give the Spartans some room.
They've dined in comfort; let them go home in peace.

[*The* CHORUS *shrinks back from the door.* KINESIAS, *wreathed and quite drunk, appears at the door. He speaks his first speech in Spartan.*]

KINESIAS Hain't never seed sech a spread! Hit were splendiferous!

COMMISSIONER I gather the Spartans won friends and influenced people?

KINESIAS And *we've* never been so brilliant. It was the wine.

COMMISSIONER Precisely.
The reason? A sober Athenian is just
non compos. If I can carry a little proposal
I have in mind, our Foreign Service will flourish,
guided by this rational rule:
No Ambassador
Without a Skinful.
Reflect on our past performance:
Down to a Spartan parley we troop, in a state
of disgusting sobriety, looking for trouble. It muddles
our senses: we read between the lines; we hear,
not what the Spartans say, but what we suspect

they might have been about to be going to say.
We bring back paranoid reports—cheap fiction, the fruit
of temperance. Cold-water diplomacy, pah!
Contrast
this evening's total pleasure, the free-and-easy
give-and-take of friendship: If we were singing,
Just Kleitagora and me,
Alone in Thessaly,
and someone missed his cue and cut in loudly,
Ajax, son of Telamon,
He was one hell of a man—
no one took it amiss, or started a war;
we clapped him on the back and gave three cheers.

[*During this recital, the* CHORUS has sidled up to the door.]

—Dammit, are you back here again?
[*Waving his torch.*] Scatter!
Get out of the road! Gangway, you gallowsbait!

KINESIAS Yes, everyone out of the way. They're coming out.

[*Through the door emerge the* DELEGATION (OF SPARTANS), *a* (FLUTE-PLAYER), *the Athenian (men)*, LYSISTRATA, KLEONIKE, MYRRHINE, *and the rest of the women from the citadel, both Athenian and Peloponnesian. The Chorus splits into its male and female components and draws to the sides to give the procession room.*]

SPARTAN [*To the* (FLUTE-PLAYER).] Friend and kinsman, take up them pipes a yourn.
I'd like fer to shuffle a bit and sing a right sweet
song in honor of Athens and us'uns, too.

COMMISSIONER [*To the* (FLUTE-PLAYER).] Marvelous, marvelous—come, take up your pipes!
[*To the* SPARTAN.] I certainly love to see you Spartans dance.

[*The* (FLUTE-PLAYER.) *plays, and the* SPARTAN *begins a slow dance.*]

SPARTAN
Memory,
send me
your Muse,
who knows
our glory,
knows Athens'—
Tell the story:
At Artemision[8]
like gods, they stampeded
the hulks of the Medes, and
beat them.

And Leonidas
leading us—
the wild boars
whetting their tusks.

8. Site of an indecisive naval battle that took place off the coast while the Spartan king Leonidas held the pass at Thermopylae against the Persians in 480 B.C.

And the foam flowered,
flowered and flowed,
down our cheeks
to our knees below.
The Persians there
like the sands of the sea—

Hither, huntress,[9]
virgin, goddess,
tracker, slayer,
to our truce!
Hold us ever
fast together;
bring our pledges
love and increase;
wean us from the
fox's wiles—

Hither, huntress!
Virgin, hither!

LYSISTRATA [*Surveying the assemblage with a proprietary air.*] Well, the preliminaries are over—very nicely, too.
So, Spartans,
[*Indicating the* PELOPONNESIAN WOMEN *who have been hostages.*]
Take these girls back home. And *you*
[*To the* ATHENIAN (*men*), *indicating the women from the Akropolis.*]
take *these* girls. Each man stand by his wife, each wife
by her husband. Dance to the gods' glory, and thank
them for the happy ending. And, from now on, please be
careful. Let's not make the same mistakes again.
[*The* DELEGATIONS (OF SPARTANS *and the Athenian men*) *obey; the men and women of the* CHORUS *join again for a rapid ode.*]

CHORUS Start the chorus dancing,
Summon all the Graces,
Send a shout to Artemis in invocation.
Call upon her brother,[1]
healer, chorus master,
Call the blazing Bacchus, with his maddened muster.

Call the flashing, fiery Zeus, and
call his mighty, blessed spouse,[2] and
call the gods, call all the gods,
to witness now and not forget
our gentle, blissful Peace—the gift,
the deed of Aphrodite.
Ai!
Alalai! Paion!
Leap you! Paion!

9. Artemis. 1. Apollo. 2. Hera.

Victory! Alalai!
Hail! Hail! Hail!

LYSISTRATA Spartan, let's have another song from you, a new one.

SPARTAN
Leave darlin' Taygetos,
Spartan Muse! Come to us
once more, flyin'
and glorifyin'
Spartan themes:
the god at Amyklai,
bronze-house Athene.[3]
Tyndaros' twins,[4]
the valiant ones,
playin' still by Eurotas' streams.[5]

Up! Advance!
Leap to the dance!

Help us hymn Sparta,
lover of dancin',
lover of foot-pats,
where girls go prancin'
like fillies along Eurotas' banks,
whirlin' the dust, twinklin' their shanks,
shakin' their hair
like Maenads[6] playin'
and jugglin' the thyrsis,
in frenzy obeyin'
Leda's daughter, the fair, the pure
Helen, the mistress of the choir.

Here, Muse, here!
Bind up your hair!
Stamp like a deer! Pound your feet!
Clap your hands! Give us a beat!

Sing the greatest,
sing the mightiest,
sing the conqueror,
sing to honor her—

Athene of the Bronze House!
Sing Athene!

[*Exeunt omnes, dancing and singing.*]

3. Athena had a bronze-plated temple in Sparta. 4. Castor and Pollux, Helen's brothers. 5. The river that runs by Sparta. 6. Female devotees of Dionysus.

PLATO

429–347 B.C.

Socrates himself (see pp. 109–10) wrote nothing; we know what we do about him mainly from the writings of his pupil Plato, a philosophical and literary genius of the first rank. It is very difficult to distinguish between what Socrates actually said and what Plato put into his mouth, but there is general agreement that the *Apology,* which Plato wrote as a representation of what Socrates said at his trial, is the clearest picture we have of the historical Socrates. He is on trial for impiety and "corrupting the youth." He deals with these charges, but he also takes the opportunity to present a defense and explanation of the mission to which his life has been devoted.

The *Apology* is a defiant speech; Socrates rides roughshod over legal forms and seems to neglect no opportunity of outraging his listeners. But this defiance is not stupidity (as he hints himself, he could, if he had wished, have made a speech to please the court), nor is it a deliberate courting of martyrdom. It is the only course possible for him in the circumstances if he is not to betray his life's work, for Socrates knows as well as his accusers that what the Athenians really want is to silence him without having to take his life. What Socrates is making clear is that there is no such easy way out; he will have no part of any compromise that would restrict his freedom of speech or undermine his moral position. The speech is a sample of what the Athenians will have to put up with if they allow him to live; he will continue to be the gadfly that stings the sluggish horse. He will go on persuading them not to be concerned for their persons or their property but first and chiefly to care about the improvement of the soul. He has spent his life denying the validity of worldly standards, and he will not accept them now.

He was declared guilty and condemned to death. Though influential friends offered means of escape (and there is reason to think the Athenians would have been glad to see him go), Socrates refused to disobey the laws; in any case he had already, in his court speech, rejected the possibility of living in some foreign city.

The sentence was duly carried out. And in Plato's account of the execution we can see the calmness and kindness of a man who has led a useful life and who is secure in his faith that, contrary to appearances, "no evil can happen to a good man, either in life or after death."

The form of the *Apology* is dramatic: Plato re-creates the personality of his beloved teacher by presenting him as speaking directly to the reader. In most of the many books that he wrote in the course of a long life, Plato continued to feature Socrates as the principal speaker in philosophical dialogues that explored the ethical and political problems of the age. These dialogues (the *Republic* the most famous) were preserved in their entirety and have exerted an enormous influence on Western thought ever since. Plato also founded a philosophical school, the Academy, in 385 B.C., and it remained active as a center of philosophical training and research until it was suppressed by the Roman emperor Justinian in A.D. 529. Plato came from an aristocratic Athenian family and as a young man thought of a political career; the execution of Socrates by the courts of democratic Athens disgusted him with politics and prompted his famous remark that there was no hope for the cities until the rulers became philosophers or the philosophers, rulers. His attempts, however, to influence real rulers—the tyrant Dionysius of Syracuse in Sicily and, later, his son—ended in failure.

A. E. Taylor, *Plato, The Man and His Work* (1927), is a detailed analysis of the whole corpus of Platonic dialogues. G. M. A. Grube, *Plato's Thought* (1935), studies six principal themes of Platonic philosophy. R. S. Brumbaugh, *Plato for the Modern Age* (1962), presents a general introduction with stress on the historical background and an emphasis on the scientific and mathematical aspects of Plato's thought. On the importance of Socrates, see W. K. C. Guthrie, *A History of Greek Philosophy,* vol. 3 (1969), pp. 378–567.

PRONOUNCING GLOSSARY

The following list uses common English syllables and stress accents to provide rough equivalents of selected words whose pronunciation may be unfamiliar to the general reader.

Adeimantus: *ad-ee-mant'-us*
Aeacus: *ee'-ak-us*
Aeantodorus: *ai-ant-o-dor'-us*
Aeschines: *es'-kin-eez*
Amphipolis: *am-fip'-o-lis*
Anytus: *an'-i-tus*
Arginusae: *ar-gin-yoo'-sai*
Asclepius: *as-klee'-pee-us*
Cebes: *see'-beez*
Ceos: *ke'-os*
Cephisus: *ke'-fi-sus*
Chaerephon: *kai'-re-fon*
Crito: *crai'-toh*
Critobulus: *cri-to'-boo-luhs*
Demodocus: *dee-mod'-o-kus*
Echecrates: *ek-ek'-rat-eez*
Epigenes: *e-pig'-en-eez*
Evenus: *ee-vee'-nus*
Gorgias: *gor'-jee-as*
Leontium: *le-ont'-ee-um*
Lysanias: *lai-san'-ee-as*
Meletus: *mee-lee'-tus*
Minos: *mai'-nos*
Musaeus: *myoo-zee'-us*
Nicostratus: *ni-kos'-tra-tus*
Palamedes: *pal-am-ee'-deez*
Phaedo: *fee'-doh*
Potidaea: *pot-i-dee'-ah*
Prodicus: *pro'-dik-us*
Prytanes: *pri'-tan-eez*
Prytaneum: *pri-tan-ee'-um*
Rhadamanthus: *rad-am-anth'-us*
Simmias: *sim'-ee-as*
Theages: *thee-ah'-jeez*
Theosdotides: *thee-os-dot'-id-eez*
Triptolemus: *trip-to'-le-muhs*

The Apology of Socrates[1]

How you, O Athenians, have been affected by my accusers, I cannot tell; but I know that they almost made me forget who I was—so persuasively did they speak; and yet they have hardly uttered a word of truth. But of the many falsehoods told by them, there was one which quite amazed me;—I mean when they said that you should be upon your guard and not allow yourselves to be deceived by the force of my eloquence. To say this, when they were certain to be detected as soon as I opened my lips and proved myself to be anything but a great speaker, did indeed appear to me most shameless—unless by the force of eloquence they mean the force of truth; for if such is their meaning, I admit that I am eloquent. But in how different a way from theirs! Well, as I was saying, they have scarcely spoken the truth at all; but from me you shall hear the whole truth: not, however, delivered after their manner in a set oration duly ornamented with words and phrases. No, by heaven! but I shall use the words and arguments which occur to me at the

1. Translated by Benjamin Jowett. *Apology* here means "defense."

moment; for I am confident in the justice of my cause: at my time of life I ought not to be appearing before you, O men of Athens, in the character of a juvenile orator—let no one expect it of me. And I must beg of you to grant me a favor:—If I defend myself in my accustomed manner, and you hear me using the words which I have been in the habit of using in the agora,[2] at the tables of the money-changers, or anywhere else, I would ask you not to be surprised, and not to interrupt me on this account. For I am more than seventy years of age, and appearing now for the first time in a court of law, I am quite a stranger to the language of the place; and therefore I would have you regard me as if I were really a stranger, whom you would excuse if he spoke in his native tongue, and after the fashion of his country:—Am I making an unfair request of you? Never mind the manner, which may or may not be good; but think only of the truth of my words, and give heed to that: let the speaker speak truly and the judge decide justly.

And first, I have to reply to the older charges and to my first accusers, and then I will go on to the later ones.[3] For of old I have had many accusers, who have accused me falsely to you during many years; and I am more afraid of them than of Anytus and his associates, who are dangerous, too, in their own way. But far more dangerous are the others, who began when you were children, and took possession of your minds with their falsehoods, telling of one Socrates, a wise man, who speculated about the heaven above, and searched into the earth beneath, and made the worse appear the better cause.[4] The disseminators of this tale are the accusers whom I dread; for their hearers are apt to fancy that such enquirers do not believe in the existence of the gods. And they are many, and their charges against me are of ancient date, and they were made by them in the days when you were more impressible than you are now—in childhood, or it may have been in youth—and the cause when heard went by default, for there was none to answer. And hardest of all, I do not know and cannot tell the names of my accusers; unless in the chance case of a Comic poet.[5] All who from envy and malice have persuaded you—some of them having first convinced themselves—all this class of men are most difficult to deal with; for I cannot have them up here, and cross-examine them, and therefore I must simply fight with shadows in my own defence, and argue when there is no one who answers. I will ask you then to assume with me, as I was saying, that my opponents are of two kinds; one recent, the other ancient: and I hope that you will see the propriety[6] of my answering the latter first, for these accusations you heard long before the others, and much oftener.

Well, then, I must make my defence, and endeavor to clear away, in a short time, a slander which has lasted a long time. May I succeed, if to succeed be for my good and yours, or likely to avail me in my cause! The

2. The marketplace. 3. Socrates had been the object of much criticism and satire for many years before the trial. He here disregards legal forms and announces that he will deal first with the prejudices that lie behind the formal charge that has been brought against him. 4. He was accused by some of his enemies of being a materialist philosopher who speculated about the physical nature of the universe and by others of being one of the Sophists, professional teachers of rhetoric and other subjects, many of whom taught methods that were more effective than honest. 5. He is referring to the poet Aristophanes, whose play *Clouds* (produced in 423 B.C.) is a broad satire on Socrates and his associates and a good example of the prejudice Socrates is dealing with, for it presents him propounding fantastic theories about matter and religion and teaching students how to avoid payment of debts. 6. He says this tongue in cheek, for he is actually paying no attention to legal propriety. This becomes clearer below, where he goes so far as to paraphrase the actual terms of the indictment and put into the mouths of his accusers the prejudice he claims is the basis of their action.

task is not an easy one; I quite understand the nature of it. And so leaving the event with God, in obedience to the law I will now make my defence.

I will begin at the beginning, and ask what is the accusation which has given rise to the slander of me, and in fact has encouraged Meletus to prefer this charge against me. Well, what do the slanderers say? They shall be my prosecutors, and I will sum up their words in an affidavit: 'Socrates is an evil-doer, and a curious person, who searches into things under the earth, and in heaven, and he makes the worse appear the better cause; and he teaches the aforesaid doctrines to others.' Such is the nature of the accusation: it is just what you have yourselves seen in the comedy of Aristophanes, who has introduced a man whom he calls Socrates, going about and saying that he walks in air, and talking a deal of nonsense concerning matters of which I do not pretend to know either much or little—not that I mean to speak disparagingly of any one who is a student of natural philosophy.[7] I should be very sorry if Meletus could bring so grave a charge against me. But the simple truth is, O Athenians, that I have nothing to do with physical speculations. Very many of those here present are witnesses to the truth of this, and to them I appeal. Speak then, you who have heard me, and tell your neighbors whether any of you have ever known me hold forth in few words or in many upon such matters. . . . You hear their answer. And from what they say of this part of the charge you will be able to judge of the truth of the rest.

As little foundation is there for the report that I am a teacher, and take money;[8] this accusation has no more truth in it than the other. Although, if a man were really able to instruct mankind, to receive money for giving instruction would, in my opinion, be an honor to him. There is Gorgias of Leontium, and Prodicus of Ceos, and Hippias of Elis,[9] who go the round of the cities, and are able to persuade the young men to leave their own citizens by whom they might be taught for nothing, and come to them whom they not only pay, but are thankful if they may be allowed to pay them. There is at this time a Parian[1] philosopher residing in Athens, of whom I have heard; and I came to hear of him in this way:—I came across a man who has spent a world of money on the Sophists, Callias, the son of Hipponicus, and knowing that he had sons, I asked him: 'Callias,' I said, 'if your two sons were foals or calves, there would be no difficulty in finding some one to put over them; we should hire a trainer of horses, or a farmer probably, who would improve and perfect them in their own proper virtue and excellence; but as they are human beings, whom are you thinking of placing over them? Is there any one who understands human and political virtue? You must have thought about the matter, for you have sons; is there any one?' 'There is,' he said. 'Who is he?' said I; 'and of what country? and what does he charge?' 'Evenus the Parian,' he replied; 'he is the man, and his charge is five minae.'[2] Happy is Evenus, I said to myself; if he really has this wisdom, and teaches at such

7. In Aristophanes' comedy Socrates first appears suspended in a basket; when asked what he is doing, he replies, "I walk in air and contemplate the sun." He explains that only by suspending his intelligence can he investigate celestial matters. 8. Unlike Socrates, who beggared himself in the quest for truth, the professional teachers made great fortunes. The wealth of Protagoras, the first of the Sophists who demanded fees, was proverbial. 9. In the Peloponnese. Hippias claimed to be able to teach any and all subjects, including handicrafts. Gorgias was famous as the originator of an antithetical, ornate prose style that had great influence. Leontium is in Sicily. Prodicus taught rhetoric and was well known for his pioneering grammatical studies. Ceos is an island in the Aegean. 1. From Paros, a small island in the Agean. 2. A relatively moderate sum; Protagoras is said to have charged one hundred minae for a course of instruction.

a moderate charge. Had I the same, I should have been very proud and conceited; but the truth is that I have no knowledge of the kind.

I dare say, Athenians, that some one among you will reply, 'Yes, Socrates, but what is the origin of these accusations which are brought against you; there must have been something strange which you have been doing? All these rumors and this talk about you would never have arisen if you had been like other men: tell us, then, what is the cause of them, for we should be sorry to judge hastily of you.' Now I regard this as a fair challenge, and I will endeavor to explain to you the reason why I am called wise and have such an evil fame. Please to attend then. And although some of you may think that I am joking, I declare that I will tell you the entire truth. Men of Athens, this reputation of mine has come of a certain sort of wisdom which I possess. If you ask me what kind of wisdom, I reply, wisdom such as may perhaps be attained by man, for to that extent I am inclined to believe that I am wise; whereas the persons of whom I was speaking have a superhuman wisdom, which I may fail to describe, because I have it not myself; and he who says that I have, speaks falsely, and is taking away my character. And here, O men of Athens, I must beg you not to interrupt me, even if I seem to say something extravagant. For the word which I will speak is not mine. I will refer you to a witness who is worthy of credit; that witness shall be the God of Delphi[3]—he will tell you about my wisdom, if I have any, and of what sort it is. You must have known Chaerephon;[4] he was early a friend of mine, and also a friend of yours, for he shared in the recent exile of the people,[5] and returned with you. Well, Chaerephon, as you know, was very impetuous in all his doings, and he went to Delphi and boldly asked the oracle to tell him whether—as I was saying, I must beg you not to interrupt—he asked the oracle to tell him whether any one was wiser than I was, and the Pythian prophetess answered, that there was no man wiser. Chaerephon is dead himself; but his brother, who is in court, will confirm the truth of what I am saying.

Why do I mention this? Because I am going to explain to you why I have such an evil name. When I heard the answer, I said to myself, What can the god mean? and what is the interpretation of his riddle? for I know that I have no wisdom, small or great. What then can he mean when he says that I am the wisest of men? And yet he is a god, and cannot lie; that would be against his nature. After long consideration, I thought of a method of trying the question. I reflected that if I could only find a man wiser than myself, then I might go to the god with a refutation in my hand. I should say to him, 'Here is a man who is wiser than I am; but you said that I was the wisest.' Accordingly I went to one who had the reputation of wisdom, and observed him—his name I need not mention; he was a politician whom I selected for examination—and the result was as follows: When I began to talk with him, I could not help thinking that he was not really wise, although he was thought wise by many, and still wiser by himself; and thereupon I tried to explain to him that he thought himself wise, but was not really wise; and the consequence was that he hated me, and his enmity was shared by several who

3. Apollo. 4. One of Socrates' closest associates (he appears in Aristophanes' comedy); he was an enthusiastic enough partisan of the democratic regime to have to go into exile in 404 B.C. when the Thirty Tyrants carried on an oligarchic reign of terror. 5. This refers to the exile into which all known champions of democracy were forced until the democracy was restored.

were present and heard me. So I left him, saying to myself, as I went away: Well, although I do not suppose that either of us knows anything really beautiful and good, I am better off than he is,—for he knows nothing, and thinks that he knows; I neither know nor think that I know. In this latter particular, then, I seem to have slightly the advantage of him. Then I went to another who had still higher pretensions to wisdom, and my conclusion was exactly the same. Whereupon I made another enemy of him, and of many others besides him.

Then I went to one man after another, being not unconscious of the enmity which I provoked, and I lamented and feared this: But necessity was laid upon me,—the word of God, I thought, ought to be considered first. And I said to myself, Go I must to all who appear to know, and find out the meaning of the oracle. And I swear to you, Athenians, by the dog I swear![6]—for I must tell you the truth—the result of my mission was just this: I found that the men most in repute were all but the most foolish; and that others less esteemed were really wiser and better. I will tell you the tale of my wanderings and of the 'Herculean' labors, as I may call them, which I endured only to find at last the oracle irrefutable. After the politicians, I went to the poets; tragic, dithyrambic,[7] and all sorts. And there, I said to myself, you will be instantly detected; now you will find out that you are more ignorant than they are. Accordingly, I took them some of the most elaborate passages in their own writings, and asked what was the meaning of them—thinking that they would teach me something. Will you believe me? I am almost ashamed to confess the truth, but I must say that there is hardly a person present who would not have talked better about their poetry than they did themselves. Then I knew that not by wisdom do poets write poetry, but by a sort of genius and inspiration; they are like diviners or soothsayers who also say many fine things, but do not understand the meaning of them.[8] The poets appeared to me to be much in the same case; and I further observed that upon the strength of their poetry they believed themselves to be the wisest of men in other things in which they were not wise. So I departed, conceiving myself to be superior to them for the same reason that I was superior to the politicians.

At last I went to the artisans, for I was conscious that I knew nothing at all, as I may say, and I was sure that they knew many fine things; and here I was not mistaken, for they did know many things of which I was ignorant, and in this they certainly were wiser than I was. But I observed that even the good artisans fell into the same error as the poets;—because they were good workmen they thought that they also knew all sorts of high matters, and this defect in them overshadowed their wisdom; and therefore I asked myself on behalf of the oracle, whether I would like to be as I was, neither having their knowledge nor their ignorance, or like them in both; and I made answer to myself and to the oracle that I was better off as I was.

This inquisition has led to my having many enemies of the worst and most dangerous kind, and has given occasion also to many calumnies. And I am called wise, for my hearers always imagine that I myself possess the wisdom which I find wanting in others: but the truth is, O men of Athens, that God

6. A euphemistic oath (compare "by George"). 7. The dithyramb was a short performance by a chorus, produced, like tragedy, at state expense and at a public festival. 8. For a fuller exposition of this famous theory of poetic inspiration see Plato's *Ion*.

only is wise; and by his answer he intends to show that the wisdom of men is worth little or nothing; he is not speaking of Socrates, he is only using my name by way of illustration, as if he said, He, O men, is the wisest, who, like Socrates, knows that his wisdom is in truth worth nothing. And so I go about the world, obedient to the god, and search and make enquiry into the wisdom of any one, whether citizen or stranger, who appears to be wise; and if he is not wise, then in vindication of the oracle I show him that he is not wise; and my occupation quite absorbs me, and I have no time to give either to any public matter of interest or to any concern of my own, but I am in utter poverty by reason of my devotion to the god.

There is another thing:—young men of the richer classes, who have not much to do, come about me of their own accord; they like to hear the pretenders examined, and they often imitate me, and proceed to examine others; there are plenty of persons, as they quickly discover, who think that they know something, but really know little or nothing; and then those who are examined by them instead of being angry with themselves are angry with me: This confounded Socrates, they say; this villainous misleader of youth!—and then if somebody asks them, Why, what evil does he practice or teach? they do not know, and cannot tell; but in order that they may not appear to be at a loss, they repeat the ready-made charges which are used against all philosophers about teaching things up in the clouds and under the earth, and having no gods, and making the worse appear the better cause; for they do not like to confess that their pretence of knowledge has been detected—which is the truth; and as they are numerous and ambitious and energetic, and are drawn up in battle array and have persuasive tongues, they have filled your ears with their loud and inveterate calumnies. And this is the reason why my three accusers, Meletus and Anytus and Lycon, have set upon me; Meletus, who has a quarrel with me on behalf of the poets; Anytus, on behalf of the craftsmen and politicians; Lycon, on behalf of the rhetoricians:[9] and as I said at the beginning, I cannot expect to get rid of such a mass of calumny all in a moment. And this, O men of Athens, is the truth and the whole truth; I have concealed nothing, I have dissembled nothing. And yet, I know that my plainness of speech makes them hate me, and what is their hatred but a proof that I am speaking the truth?—Hence has arisen the prejudice against me; and this is the reason of it, as you will find out either in this or in any future enquiry.

I have said enough in my defence against the first class of my accusers; I turn to the second class. They are headed by Meletus, that good man and true lover of his country, as he calls himself. Against these, too, I must try to make a defence:—Let their affidavit be read: it contains something of this kind: It says that Socrates is a doer of evil, who corrupts the youth; and who does not believe in the gods of the state, but has other new divinities of his own.[1] Such is the charge; and now let us examine the particular counts. He says that I am a doer of evil, and corrupt the youth; but I say, O men of

9. The connection of Meletus with poetry and of Lycon with rhetoric is known only from this passage.
1. The precise meaning of the charge is not clear. As this translation indicates, the Greek words may mean "new divinities," with a reference to Socrates' famous inner voice, which from time to time warned him against action on which he had decided. Or the words may mean "practicing strange rites," though this charge is difficult to understand. In any case, the importance of the phrase is that it implies religious belief of some sort and can later be used against Meletus when he loses his head and accuses Socrates of atheism.

Athens, that Meletus is a doer of evil, in that he pretends to be in earnest when he is only in jest, and is so eager to bring men to trial from a pretended zeal and interest about matters in which he really never had the smallest interest. And the truth of this I will endeavor to prove to you.

Come hither, Meletus, and let me ask a question of you.[2] You think a great deal about the improvement of youth?

Yes, I do.

Tell the judges, then, who is their improver; for you must know, as you have taken the pains to discover their corrupter, and are citing and accusing me before them. Speak, then, and tell the judges who their improver is.—Observe, Meletus, that you are silent, and have nothing to say. But is not this rather disgraceful, and a very considerable proof of what I was saying, that you have no interest in the matter? Speak up, friend, and tell us who their improver is.

The laws.

But that, my good sir, is not my meaning. I want to know who the person is, who, in the first place, knows the laws.

The judges,[3] Socrates, who are present in court.

What, do you mean to say, Meletus, that they are able to instruct and improve youth?

Certainly they are.

What, all of them, or some only and not others?

All of them.

By the goddess Here,[4] that is good news! There are plenty of improvers, then. And what do you say of the audience,—do they improve them?

Yes, they do.

And the senators?[5]

Yes, the senators improve them.

But perhaps the members of the assembly[6] corrupt them?—or do they too improve them?

They improve them.

Then every Athenian improves and elevates them; all with the exception of myself; and I alone am their corrupter? Is that what you affirm?

That is what I stoutly affirm.

I am very unfortunate if you are right. But suppose I ask you a question: How about horses?[7] Does one man do them harm and all the world good? Is not the exact opposite the truth? One man is able to do them good, or at least not many;—the trainer of horses, that is to say, does them good, and others who have to do with them rather injure them? Is not that true, Meletus, of horses, or any other animals? Most assuredly it is; whether you and

2. Socrates avails himself of his right to interrogate the accuser. He is, of course, a master in this type of examination, for he has spent his life in the practice of puncturing inflated pretensions and exposing logical contradictions in the arguments of his adversaries. He is here fulfilling his earlier promise to defend himself in the manner to which he has been accustomed and use the words that he has been in the habit of using in the agora (p. 781). 3. The jury; there was no judge in the Athenian law court. The Athenian jury was large; in this trial it probably consisted of five hundred citizens. In the following questions Socrates forces Meletus to extend the capacity to improve the youth to successively greater numbers, until it appears that the entire citizen body is a good influence and Socrates the only bad one. Meletus is caught in the trap of his own demagogic appeal. 4. Hera. 5. The five hundred members of the standing council of the assembly. 6. The sovereign body in the Athenian constitution, theoretically an assembly of the whole citizen body. 7. This simple analogy is typical of the Socratic method; he is still defending himself in his accustomed manner.

Anytus say yes or no. Happy indeed would be the condition of youth if they had one corrupter only, and all the rest of the world were their improvers. But you, Meletus, have sufficiently shown that you never had a thought about the young: your carelessness is seen in your not caring about the very things which you bring against me.

And now, Meletus, I will ask you another question—by Zeus I will: Which is better, to live among bad citizens, or among good ones? Answer, friend, I say; the question is one which may be easily answered. Do not the good do their neighbors good, and the bad do them evil?

Certainly.

And is there any one who would rather be injured than benefited by those who live with him? Answer, my good friend, the law requires you to answer—does any one like to be injured?

Certainly not.

And when you accuse me of corrupting and deteriorating the youth, do you allege that I corrupt them intentionally or unintentionally?

Intentionally, I say.

But you have just admitted that the good do their neighbors good, and evil do them evil. Now, is that a truth which your superior wisdom has recognized thus early in life, and am I, at my age, in such darkness and ignorance as not to know that if a man with whom I have to live is corrupted by me, I am very likely to be harmed by him; and yet I corrupt him, and intentionally, too—so you say, although neither I nor any other human being is ever likely to be convinced by you. But either I do not corrupt them, or I corrupt them unintentionally; and on either view of the case you lie. If my offence is unintentional, the law has no cognizance of unintentional offences: you ought to have taken me privately, and warned and admonished me; for if I had been better advised, I should have left off doing what I only did unintentionally—no doubt I should; but you would have nothing to say to me and refused to teach me. And now you bring me up in this court, which is not a place of instruction, but of punishment.

It will be very clear to you, Athenians, as I was saying, that Meletus has no care at all, great or small, about the matter. But still I should like to know, Meletus, in what I am affirmed to corrupt the young. I suppose you mean, as I infer from your indictment, that I teach them not to acknowledge the gods which the state acknowledges, but some other new divinities or spiritual agencies in their stead. These are the lessons by which I corrupt the youth, as you say.

Yes, that I say emphatically.

Then, by the gods, Meletus, of whom we are speaking, tell me and the court, in somewhat plainer terms, what you mean! for I do not as yet understand whether you affirm that I teach other men to acknowledge some gods, and therefore that I do believe in gods, and am not an entire atheist—this you do not lay to my charge,—but only you say that they are not the same gods which the city recognizes—the charge is that they are different gods. Or, do you mean that I am an atheist simply, and a teacher of atheism?

I mean the latter—that you are a complete atheist.[8]

8. Meletus jumps at the most damaging charge and falls into the trap (see n. 1, p. 785).

What an extraordinary statement! Why do you think so, Meletus? Do you mean that I do not believe in the godhead of the sun or moon, like other men?

I assure you, judges, that he does not: for he says that the sun is stone, and the moon earth.[9]

Friend Meletus, you think that you are accusing Anaxagoras: and you have but a bad opinion of the judges, if you fancy them illiterate to such a degree as not to know that these doctrines are found in the books of Anaxagoras the Clazomenian,[1] which are full of them. And so, forsooth, the youth are said to be taught them by Socrates, when [they can buy the book in the theater district for one drachma at most][2] and laugh at Socrates if he pretends to father these extraordinary views. And so, Meletus, you really think that I do not believe in any god?

I swear by Zeus that you believe absolutely in none at all.

Nobody will believe you, Meletus, and I am pretty sure that you do not believe yourself. I cannot help thinking, men of Athens, that Meletus is reckless and impudent, and that he has written this indictment in a spirit of mere wantonness and youthful bravado. Has he not compounded a riddle, thinking to try me? He said to himself:—I shall see whether the wise Socrates will discover my facetious contradiction, or whether I shall be able to deceive him and the rest of them. For he certainly does appear to me to contradict himself in the indictment as much as if he said that Socrates is guilty of not believing in the gods, and yet of believing in them—but this is not like a person who is in earnest.

I should like you, O men of Athens, to join me in examining what I conceive to be his inconsistency; and do you, Meletus, answer. And I must remind the audience of my request that they would not make a disturbance[3] if I speak in my accustomed manner:

Did ever man, Meletus, believe in the existence of human things, and not of human beings? . . . I wish, men of Athens, that he would answer, and not be always trying to get up an interruption. Did ever any man believe in horsemanship, and not in horses? or in flute-playing, and not in flute-players? No, my friend; I will answer to you and to the court, as you refuse to answer for yourself. There is no man who ever did. But now please to answer the next question: Can a man believe in spiritual and divine agencies, and not in spirits or demigods?

He cannot.

How lucky I am to have extracted that answer, by the assistance of the court! But then you swear in the indictment that I teach and believe in divine or spiritual agencies (new or old, no matter for that); at any rate, I believe in spiritual agencies,—so you say and swear in the affidavit; and yet if I believe in divine beings, how can I help believing in spirits or demigods;—

9. Meletus falls back on the old prejudices that Socrates claims are the real indictment against him.
1. Clazomenae is in Asia Minor. Anaxagoras was a fifth-century philosopher and an intimate friend of Pericles, but this did not save him from indictment for impiety. He was condemned and forced to leave Athens. He is famous for his doctrine that matter was set in motion and ordered by Intelligence *(Nous)*, which, however, did not create it. He also declared that the sun was a mass of red-hot metal larger than the Peloponnese and that there were hills and ravines on the moon.
2. The translator took this to mean that the doctrines of Anaxagoras were reflected in the works of the tragic poets; the bracketed passage reflects what is now the generally accepted interpretation.
3. Presumably due to the frustration of the enemies of Socrates, who see him assuming complete control of the proceedings and turning them into a street-corner argument of the type in which he is invincible.

must I not? To be sure I must; and therefore I may assume that your silence gives consent. Now what are spirits or demigods? are they not either gods or the sons of gods?

Certainly they are.

But this is what I call the facetious riddle invented by you: the demigods or spirits are gods, and you say first that I do not believe in gods, and then again that I do believe in gods; that is, if I believe in demigods. For if the demigods are the illegitimate sons of gods, whether by the nymphs or by any other mothers, of whom they are said to be the sons—what human being will ever believe that there are no gods if they are the sons of gods? You might as well affirm the existence of mules, and deny that of horses and asses. Such nonsense, Meletus, could only have been intended by you to make trial of me. You have put this into the indictment because you had nothing real of which to accuse me. But no one who has a particle of understanding will ever be convinced by you that the same men can believe in divine and superhuman things, and yet not believe that there are gods and demigods and heroes.

I have said enough in answer to the charge of Meletus: any elaborate defence is unnecessary; but I know only too well how many are the enmities which I have incurred, and this is what will be my destruction if I am destroyed;—not Meletus, nor yet Anytus, but the envy and detraction of the world, which has been the death of many good men, and will probably be the death of many more; there is no danger of my being the last of them.

Some one will say: And are you not ashamed, Socrates, of a course of life which is likely to bring you to an untimely end? To him I may fairly answer: There you are mistaken: a man who is good for anything ought not to calculate the chance of living or dying; he ought only to consider whether in doing anything he is doing right or wrong—acting the part of a good man or of a bad. Whereas, upon your view, the heroes who fell at Troy were not good for much, and the son of Thetis[4] above all, who altogether despised danger in comparison with disgrace; and when he was so eager to slay Hector, his goddess mother said to him, that if he avenged his companion Patroclus, and slew Hector, he would die himself—'Fate,' she said, in these or the like words, 'waits for you next after Hector'; he, receiving this warning, utterly despised danger and death, and instead of fearing them, feared rather to live in dishonor, and not to avenge his friend. 'Let me die forthwith,' he replies, 'and be avenged of my enemy, rather than abide here by the beaked ships, a laughing-stock and a burden of the earth.' Had Achilles any thought of death and danger? For wherever a man's place is, whether the place which he has chosen or that in which he has been placed by a commander, there he ought to remain in hour of danger; he should not think of death or of anything but of disgrace. And this, O men of Athens, is a true saying.

Strange, indeed, would be my conduct, O men of Athens, if I who, when I was ordered by the generals whom you chose to command me at Potidaea and Amphipolis and Delium,[5] remained where they placed me, like any other man, facing death—if now, when, as I conceive and imagine, God orders me

4. Achilles (see *Iliad* 18.110ff.). 5. Three battles of the Peloponnesian War in which Socrates had fought as an infantryman. The battle at Potidaea (in northern Greece) occurred in 432 B.C. (for a fuller account of Socrates' conduct there see Plato's *Symposium*). The date of the battle at Amphipolis (in northern Greece) is uncertain. The battle at Delium (in central Greece) took place in 424 B.C.

to fulfil the philosopher's mission of searching into myself and other men, I were to desert my post through fear of death, or any other fear; that would indeed be strange, and I might justly be arraigned in court for denying the existence of the gods, if I disobeyed the oracle because I was afraid of death, fancying that I was wise when I was not wise. For the fear of death is indeed the pretence of wisdom, and not real wisdom, being a pretence of knowing the unknown; and no one knows whether death, which men in their fear apprehend to be the greatest evil, may not be the greatest good. Is not this ignorance of a disgraceful sort, the ignorance which is the conceit that man knows what he does not know? And in this respect only I believe myself to differ from men in general, and may perhaps claim to be wiser than they are: —that whereas I know but little of the world below,[6] I do not suppose that I know: but I do know that injustice and disobedience to a better, whether God or man, is evil and dishonorable, and I will never fear or avoid a possible good rather than a certain evil. And therefore if you let me go now, and are not convinced by Anytus, who said that since I had been prosecuted I must be put to death (or if not that I ought never to have been prosecuted at all); and that if I escape now, your sons will all be utterly ruined by listening to my words—if you say to me, Socrates, this time we will not mind Anytus, and you shall be let off, but upon one condition, that you are not to enquire and speculate in this way any more, and that if you are caught doing so again you shall die:—if this was the condition on which you let me go, I should reply: Men of Athens, I honor and love you; but I shall obey God rather than you, and while I have life and strength I shall never cease from the practice and teaching of philosophy, exhorting any one whom I meet and saying to him after my manner: You, my friend,—a citizen of the great and mighty and wise city of Athens,—are you not ashamed of heaping up the greatest amount of money and honor and reputation, and caring so little about wisdom and truth and the greatest improvement of the soul, which you never regard or heed at all? And if the person with whom I am arguing, says: Yes, but I do care; then I do not leave him or let him go at once; but I proceed to interrogate and examine and cross-examine him, and if I think that he has no virtue in him, but only says that he has, I reproach him with undervaluing the greater, and overvaluing the less. And I shall repeat the same words to every one whom I meet, young and old, citizen and alien, but especially to the citizens, inasmuch as they are my brethren. For know that this is the command of God; and I believe that no greater good has ever happened in the state than my service to the God. For I do nothing but go about persuading you all, old and young alike, not to take thought for your persons or your properties, but first and chiefly to care about the greatest improvement of the soul. I tell you that virtue is not given by money, but that from virtue comes money and every other good of man, public as well as private. This is my teaching, and if this is the doctrine which corrupts the youth, I am a mischievous person. But if any one says that this is not my teaching, he is speaking an untruth. Wherefore, O men of Athens, I say to you, do as Anytus bids or not as Anytus bids, and either acquit me or not; but whichever you

6. The next world (that is, the underworld); the dead were supposed to carry on a sort of existence below the Earth.

do, understand that I shall never alter my ways, not even if I have to die many times.

Men of Athens, do not interrupt,[7] but hear me; there was an understanding between us that you should hear me to the end: I have something more to say, at which you may be inclined to cry out; but I believe that to hear me will be good for you, and therefore I beg that you will not cry out. I would have you know, that if you kill such an one as I am, you will injure yourselves more than you will injure me. Nothing will injure me, not Meletus nor yet Anytus—they cannot, for a bad man is not permitted to injure a better than himself. I do not deny that Anytus may, perhaps, kill him, or drive him into exile, or deprive him of civil rights; and he may imagine, and others may imagine, that he is inflicting a great injury upon him: but there I do not agree. For the evil of doing as he is doing—the evil of unjustly taking away the life of another—is greater far.

And now, Athenians, I am not going to argue for my own sake, as you may think, but for yours, that you may not sin against the God by condemning me, who am his gift to you. For if you kill me you will not easily find a successor to me, who, if I may use such a ludicrous figure of speech, am a sort of gadfly, given to the state by God; and the state is a great and noble steed who is tardy in his motions owing to his very size, and requires to be stirred into life. I am that gadfly which God has attached to the state, and all day long and in all places am always fastening upon you, arousing and persuading and reproaching you. You will not easily find another like me, and therefore I would advise you to spare me. I dare say that you may feel out of temper (like a person who is suddenly awakened from sleep), and you think that you might easily strike me dead as Anytus advises, and then you would sleep on for the remainder of your lives, unless God in his care of you sent you another gadfly. When I say that I am given to you by God, the proof of my mission is this:—if I had been like other men, I should not have neglected all my own concerns or patiently seen the neglect of them during all these years, and have been doing yours, coming to you individually like a father or elder brother, exhorting you to regard virtue; such conduct, I say, would be unlike human nature. If I had gained anything, or if my exhortations had been paid, there would have been some sense in my doing so; but now, as you will perceive, not even the impudence of my accusers dares to say that I have ever exacted or sought pay of any one; of that they have no witness. And I have a sufficient witness to the truth of what I say—my poverty.

Some one may wonder why I go about in private giving advice and busying myself with the concerns of others, but do not venture to come forward in public and advise the state. I will tell you why. You have heard me speak at sundry times and in divers places of an oracle or sign which comes to me, and is the divinity which Meletus ridicules in the indictment. This sign, which is a kind of voice, first began to come to me when I was a child; it always forbids but never commands me to do anything which I am going to do. This is what deters me from being a politician. And rightly, as I think. For I am certain, O men of Athens, that if I had engaged in politics, I should

7. The disturbance this time is presumably more general, for Socrates is defying the court and the people.

have perished long ago, and done no good either to you or to myself. And do not be offended at my telling you the truth: for the truth is, that no man who goes to war with you or any other multitude, honestly striving against the many lawless and unrighteous deeds which are done in a state, will save his life; he who will fight for the right, if he would live even for a brief space, must have a private station and not a public one.

I can give you convincing evidence of what I say, not words only, but what you value far more—actions. Let me relate to you a passage of my own life which will prove to you that I should never have yielded to injustice from any fear of death, and that 'as I should have refused to yield' I must have died at once. I will tell you a tale of the courts, not very interesting perhaps, but nevertheless true. The only office of state which I ever held, O men of Athens, was that of senator: the tribe Antiochis,[8] which is my tribe, had the presidency at the trial of the generals who had not taken up the bodies of the slain after the battle of Arginusae;[9] and you proposed to try them in a body, contrary to law, as you all thought afterwards; but at the time I was the only one of the Prytanes who was opposed to the illegality, and I gave my vote against you; and when the orators threatened to impeach and arrest me, and you called and shouted, I made up my mind that I would run the risk, having law and justice with me, rather than take part in your injustice because I feared imprisonment and death. This happened in the days of the democracy. But when the oligarchy of the Thirty was in power,[1] they sent for me and four others into the rotunda, and bade us bring Leon the Salaminian from Salamis,[2] as they wanted to put him to death. This was a specimen of the sort of commands which they were always giving with the view of implicating as many as possible in their crimes; and then I showed, not in word only but in deed, that, if I may be allowed to use such an expression, I cared not a straw for death, and that my great and only care was lest I should do an unrighteous or unholy thing. For the strong arm of that oppressive power did not frighten me into doing wrong; and when we came out of the rotunda the other four went to Salamis and fetched Leon, but I went quietly home. For which I might have lost my life, had not the power of the Thirty shortly afterwards come to an end. And many will witness to my words.

Now do you really imagine that I could have survived all these years, if I had led a public life, supposing that like a good man I had always maintained the right and had made justice, as I ought, the first thing? No indeed, men of Athens, neither I nor any other man. But I have been always the same in

8. The Council of the Five Hundred consisted of fifty members of each of the ten tribes into which the population was divided. Socrates' tribe, like the other nine, was named after a mythical hero, in this case Antiochus. Each tribal delegation acted as a standing committee of the whole body for a part of the year. The members of this standing committee were called Prytanes. In acting as a member of the council Socrates was not "engaging in politics" but simply fulfilling his duty as a citizen when called on.

9. An Athenian naval victory over Sparta, in 406 B.C. The Athenian commanders failed to pick up the bodies of a large number of Athenians whose ships had been destroyed. Whether they were prevented from doing so by the wind or simply neglected this duty in the excitement of victory is not known; in any case, the Athenian population suspected the worst and put all ten generals on trial, not in a court of law but before the assembly. The generals were tried not individually, but in a group, and condemned to death. The six who had returned to Athens were executed, among them a son of Pericles.

1. Socrates gives two instances of his political actions, one under the democracy and one under the Thirty Tyrants. In both cases, he was in opposition to the government. In 404 B.C., with Spartan backing, the Thirty Tyrants (as they were known to their enemies) ruled for eight months over a defeated Athens. Prominent among them was Critias, who had been one of the rich young men who listened eagerly to Socrates.

2. Athenian territory, an island off Piraeus, the port of Athens. *Rotunda:* the circular building in which the Prytanes held their meetings.

all my actions, public as well as private, and never have I yielded any base compliance to those who are slanderously termed my disciples, or to any other. Not that I have any regular disciples. But if any one likes to come and hear me while I am pursuing my mission, whether he be young or old, he is not excluded. Nor do I converse only with those who pay; but any one, whether he be rich or poor, may ask and answer me and listen to my words; and whether he turns out to be a bad man or a good one, neither result can be justly imputed to me; for I never taught or professed to teach him anything. And if any one says that he has ever learned or heard anything from me in private which all the world has not heard, let me tell you that he is lying.

But I shall be asked, Why do people delight in continually conversing with you? I have told you already, Athenians, the whole truth about this matter: they like to hear the cross-examination of the pretenders to wisdom; there is amusement in it. Now this duty of cross-examining other men has been imposed upon me by God; and has been signified to me by oracles, visions, and in every way in which the will of divine power was ever intimated to any one. This is true, O Athenians; or, if not true, would be soon refuted. If I am or have been corrupting the youth, those of them who are now grown up and become sensible that I gave them bad advice in the days of their youth should come forward as accusers, and take their revenge; or if they do not like to come themselves, some of their relatives, fathers, brothers, or other kinsmen, should say what evil their families have suffered at my hands. Now is their time. Many of them I see in the court. There is Crito, who is of the same age and of the same deme[3] with myself, and there is Critobulus his son, whom I also see. Then again there is Lysanias of Sphettus, who is the father of Aeschines—he is present; and also there is Antiphon of Cephisus, who is the father of Epigenes; and there are the brothers of several who have associated with me. There is Nicostratus the son of Theosdotides, and the brother of Theodotus (now Theodotus himself is dead, and therefore he, at any rate, will not seek to stop him); and there is Paralus the son of Demodocus, who had a brother Theages; and Adeimantus the son of Ariston, whose brother Plato[4] is present; and Aeantodorus, who is the brother of Apollodorus, whom I also see. I might mention a great many others, some of whom Meletus should have produced as witnesses in the course of his speech; and let him still produce them, if he has forgotten—I will make way for him. And let him say, if he has any testimony of the sort which he can produce. Nay, Athenians, the very opposite is the truth. For all these are ready to witness on behalf of the corrupter, of the injurer of their kindred, as Meletus and Anytus call me; not the corrupted youth only—there might have been a motive for that—but their uncorrupted elder relatives. Why should they too support me with their testimony? Why, indeed, except for the sake of truth and justice, and because they know that I am speaking the truth, and that Meletus is a liar.

Well, Athenians, this and the like of this is all the defence which I have to offer. Yet a word more. Perhaps there may be some one who is offended at me, when he calls to mind how he himself on a similar, or even a less

3. Precinct; the local unit of Athenian administration. Crito was a friend of Socrates who later tried to persuade him to escape from prison. 4. The writer of the *Apology*.

serious occasion, prayed and entreated the judges with many tears, and how he produced his children in court, which was a moving spectacle, together with a host of relations and friends; whereas I, who am probably in danger of my life, will do none of these things. The contrast may occur to his mind, and he may be set against me, and vote in anger because he is displeased at me on this account.[5] Now if there be such a person among you,—mind, I do not say that there is,—to him I may fairly reply: My friend, I am a man, and like other men, a creature of flesh and blood, and not 'of wood or stone,' as Homer says;[6] and I have a family, yes, and sons, O Athenians, three in number, one almost a man, and two others who are still young; and yet I will not bring any of them hither in order to petition you for an acquittal. And why not? Not from any self-assertion or want of respect for you. Whether I am or am not afraid of death is another question, of which I will not now speak. But, having regard to public opinion, I feel that such conduct would be discreditable to myself, and to you, and to the whole state. One who has reached my years, and who has a name for wisdom, ought not to demean himself. Whether this opinion of me be deserved or not, at any rate the world has decided that Socrates is in some way superior to other men. And if those among you who are said to be superior in wisdom and courage, and any other virtue, demean themselves in this way, how shameful is their conduct! I have seen men of reputation, when they have been condemned, behaving in the strangest manner: they seemed to fancy that they were going to suffer something dreadful if they died, and that they could be immortal if you only allowed them to live; and I think that such are a dishonor to the state, and that any stranger coming in would have said of them that the most eminent men of Athens, to whom the Athenians themselves give honor and command, are no better than women. And I say that these things ought not to be done by those of us who have a reputation; and if they are done, you ought not to permit them; you ought rather to show that you are far more disposed to condemn the man who gets up a doleful scene and makes the city ridiculous, than him who holds his peace.

But, setting aside the question of public opinion, there seems to be something wrong in asking a favor of a judge, and thus procuring an acquittal, instead of informing and convincing him. For his duty is, not to make a present of justice, but to give judgment; and he has sworn that he will judge according to the laws, and not according to his own good pleasure; and we ought not to encourage you, nor should you allow yourself to be encouraged, in this habit of perjury—there can be no piety in that. Do not then require me to do what I consider dishonorable and impious and wrong, especially now, when I am being tried for impiety on the indictment of Meletus. For if, O men of Athens, by force of persuasion and entreaty I could overpower your oaths, then I should be teaching you to believe that there are no gods, and in defending should simply convict myself of the charge of not believing in them. But that is not so—far otherwise. For I do believe that there are gods, and in a sense higher than that in which any of my accusers believe in

5. The accepted ending of the speech for the defense was an unrestrained appeal to the pity of the jury. Socrates' refusal to make it is another shock for the prejudices of the audience. 6. In the *Odyssey* (19.173–74) Penelope says to her husband, Odysseus (who is disguised as a beggar), "Tell me your ancestry. You were not born of mythic oak or stone."

them. And to you and to God I commit my cause, to be determined by you as is best for you and me.[7]

There are many reasons why I am not grieved, O men of Athens, at the vote of condemnation. I expected it, and am only surprised that the votes are so nearly equal; for I had thought that the majority against me would have been far larger; but now, had thirty votes gone over to the other side, I should have been acquitted. And I may say, I think, that I have escaped Meletus. I may say more; for without the assistance of Anytus and Lycon, any one may see that he would not have had a fifth part of the votes,[8] as the law requires, in which case he would have incurred a fine of a thousand drachmae.

And so he proposes death as the penalty. And what shall I propose on my part, O men of Athens? Clearly that which is my due. And what is my due? What return shall be made to the man who has never had the wit to be idle during his whole life; but has been careless of what the many care for—wealth, and family interests, and military offices, and speaking in the assembly, and magistracies, and plots, and parties. Reflecting that I was really too honest a man to be a politician and live, I did not go where I could do no good to you or to myself; but where I could do the greatest good privately to every one of you, thither I went, and sought to persuade every man among you that he must look to himself, and seek virtue and wisdom before he looks to his private interests, and look to the state before he looks to the interests of the state; and that this should be the order which he observes in all his actions. What shall be done to such an one? Doubtless some good thing, O men of Athens, if he has his reward; and the good should be of a kind suitable to him. What would be a reward suitable to a poor man who is your benefactor, and who desires leisure that he may instruct you? There can be no reward so fitting as maintenance in the Prytaneum,[9] O men of Athens, a reward which he deserves far more than the citizen who has won the prize at Olympia in the horse or chariot race, whether the chariots were drawn by two horses or by many. For I am in want, and he has enough; and he only gives you the appearance of happiness, and I give you the reality. And if I am to estimate the penalty fairly, I should say that maintenance in the Prytaneum is the just return.

Perhaps you think that I am braving you in what I am saying now, as in what I said before about the tears and prayers. But this is not so. I speak rather because I am convinced that I never intentionally wronged any one, although I cannot convince you—the time has been too short; if there were a law at Athens, as there is in other cities, that a capital cause should not be decided in one day,[1] then I believe that I should have convinced you. But I

7. The jury reaches a verdict of guilty. It appears from what Socrates says later that the jury was split: 280 for this verdict and 220 against it. The penalty is to be settled by the jury's choice between the penalty proposed by the prosecution and that offered by the defense. The jury itself cannot propose a penalty. Meletus demands death. Socrates must propose the lightest sentence he thinks he can get away with, but one heavy enough to satisfy the majority of the jury who voted him guilty. The prosecution probably expects him to propose exile from Athens, but Socrates surprises them.

8. Socrates jokingly divides the votes against him into three parts, one for each of his three accusers, and points out that Meletus's votes fall below the minimum necessary to justify the trial.

9. The place in which the Prytanes, as representatives of the city, entertained distinguished visitors and winners at the athletic contests at Olympia.

1. There was such a law in Sparta.

cannot in a moment refute great slander; and, as I am convinced that I never wronged another, I will assuredly not wrong myself. I will not say of myself that I deserve any evil, or propose any penalty. Why should I? Because I am afraid of the penalty of death which Meletus proposes? When I do not know whether death is a good or an evil, why should I propose a penalty which would certainly be an evil? Shall I say imprisonment? And why should I live in prison, and be the slave of the magistrates of the year—of the Eleven?[2] Or shall the penalty be a fine, and imprisonment until the fine is paid? There is the same objection. I should have to lie in prison, for money I have none, and cannot pay. And if I say exile (and this may possibly be the penalty which you will affix), I must indeed be blinded by the love of life, if I am so irrational as to expect that when you, who are my own citizens, cannot endure my discourses and words, and have found them so grievous and odious that you will have no more of them, others are likely to endure me. No indeed, men of Athens, that is not very likely. And what a life should I lead, at my age, wandering from city to city, ever changing my place of exile, and always being driven out! For I am quite sure that wherever I go, there, as here, the young men will flock to me; and if I drive them away, their elders will drive me out at their request; and if I let them come, their fathers and friends will drive me out for their sakes.

Some one will say: Yes, Socrates, but cannot you hold your tongue, and then you may go into a foreign city, and no one will interfere with you? Now I have great difficulty in making you understand my answer to this. For if I tell you that to do as you say would be a disobedience to the God, and therefore that I cannot hold my tongue, you will not believe that I am serious; and if I say again that daily to discourse about virtue, and of those other things about which you hear me examining myself and others, is the greatest good of man, and that the unexamined life is not worth living, you are still less likely to believe me. Yet I say what is true, although a thing of which it is hard for me to persuade you. Also, I have never been accustomed to think that I deserve to suffer any harm. Had I money I might have estimated the offence at what I was able to pay, and not have been much the worse. But I have none, and therefore I must ask you to proportion the fine to my means. Well, perhaps I could afford a mina,[3] and therefore I propose that penalty: Plato, Crito, Critobulus, and Apollodorus, my friends here, bid me say thirty minae, and they will be the sureties. Let thirty minae be the penalty; for which sum they will be ample security to you.[4]

Not much time will be gained, O Athenians, in return for the evil name which you will get from the detractors of the city, who will say that you killed Socrates, a wise man; for they will call me wise, even although I am not wise, when they want to reproach you. If you had waited a little while, your desire would have been fulfilled in the course of nature. For I am far advanced in years, as you may perceive, and not far from death. I am speaking now not

2. A committee that had charge of prisons and public executions. 3. It is almost impossible to express the value of ancient money in modern terms. A mina was a considerable sum; in Aristotle's time (fourth century B.C.) one mina was recognized as a fair ransom for a prisoner of war. 4. The jury decides for death (according to a much later source, the vote this time was three hundred to two hundred). The decision is not surprising in view of Socrates' intransigence. Socrates now makes a final statement to the court.

to all of you, but only to those who have condemned me to death. And I have another thing to say to them: You think that I was convicted because I had no words of the sort which would have procured my acquittal—I mean, if I had thought fit to leave nothing undone or unsaid. Not so; the deficiency which led to my conviction was not of words—certainly not. But I had not the boldness or impudence or inclination to address you as you would have liked me to do, weeping and wailing and lamenting, and saying and doing many things which you have been accustomed to hear from others, and which, as I maintain, are unworthy of me. I thought at the time that I ought not to do anything common or mean when in danger: nor do I now repent of the style of my defence; I would rather die having spoken after my manner, than speak in your manner and live. For neither in war nor yet at law ought I or any man to use every way of escaping death. Often in battle there can be no doubt that if a man will throw away his arms, and fall on his knees before his pursuers, he may escape death; and in other dangers there are other ways of escaping death, if a man is willing to say and do anything. The difficulty, my friends, is not to avoid death, but to avoid unrighteousness; for that runs faster than death. I am old and move slowly, and the slower runner has overtaken me, and my accusers are keen and quick, and the faster runner, who is unrighteousness, has overtaken them. And now I depart hence condemned by you to suffer the penalty of death,—they too go their ways condemned by the truth to suffer the penalty of villainy and wrong; and I must abide by my award—let them abide by theirs. I suppose that these things may be regarded as fated,—and I think that they are well.

And now, O men who have condemned me, I would fain prophesy to you; for I am about to die, and in the hour of death men are gifted with prophetic power.[5] And I prophesy to you who are my murderers, that immediately after my departure punishment far heavier than you have inflicted on me will surely await you. Me you have killed because you wanted to escape the accuser, and not to give an account of your lives. But that will not be as you suppose: far otherwise. For I say that there will be more accusers of you than there are now; accusers whom hitherto I have restrained:[6] and as they are younger they will be more inconsiderate with you, and you will be more offended at them. If you think that by killing men you can prevent some one from censuring your evil lives, you are mistaken; that is not a way of escape which is either possible or honorable; the easiest and the noblest way is not to be disabling others, but to be improving yourselves. This is the prophecy which I utter before my departure to the judges who have condemned me.

Friends, who would have acquitted me, I would like also to talk with you about the thing which has come to pass, while the magistrates are busy, and before I go to the place at which I must die. Stay then a little, for we may as well talk with one another while there is time. You are my friends, and I should like to show you the meaning of this event which has happened to me. O my judges—for you I may truly call judges—I should like to tell you

5. As the dying Hector foretells the death of Achilles (see *Iliad* 22.418–24). 6. Socrates' prophecy was fulfilled, for all of the many different philosophical schools of the early fourth century B.C. claimed descent from Socrates and developed one or another aspect of his teachings.

of a wonderful circumstance. Hitherto the divine faculty of which the internal oracle is the source has constantly been in the habit of opposing me even about trifles, if I was going to make a slip or error in any matter; and now as you see there has come upon me that which may be thought, and is generally believed to be, the last and worst evil. But the oracle made no sign of opposition, either when I was leaving my house in the morning, or when I was on my way to the court, or while I was speaking, at anything which I was going to say; and yet I have often been stopped in the middle of a speech, but now in nothing I either said or did touching the matter in hand has the oracle opposed me. What do I take to be the explanation of this silence? I will tell you. It is an intimation that what has happened to me is a good, and that those of us who think that death is an evil are in error. For the customary sign would surely have opposed me had I been going to evil and not to good.

Let us reflect in another way, and we shall see that there is great reason to hope that death is a good; for one of two things—either death is a state of nothingness and utter unconsciousness, or, as men say, there is a change and migration of the soul from this world to another. Now if you suppose that there is no consciousness, but a sleep like the sleep of him who is undisturbed even by dreams, death will be an unspeakable gain. For if a person were to select the night in which his sleep was undisturbed even by dreams, and were to compare with this the other days and nights of his life, and then were to tell us how many days and nights he had passed in the course of his life better and more pleasantly than this one, I think that any man, I will not say a private man, but even the great king will not find many such days or nights, when compared with the others. Now if death be of such a nature, I say that to die is gain; for eternity is then only a single night. But if death is the journey to another place, and there, as men say, all the dead abide, what good, O my friends and judges, can be greater than this? If indeed when the pilgrim arrives in the world below, he is delivered from the professors of justice in this world, and finds the true judges who are said to give judgment there, Minos and Rhadamanthus and Aeacus and Triptolemus,[7] and other sons of God who were righteous in their own life, that pilgrimage will be worth making. What would not a man give if he might converse with Orpheus and Musaeus and Hesiod[8] and Homer? Nay, if this be true, let me die again and again. I myself, too, shall have a wonderful interest in there meeting and conversing with Palamedes, and Ajax the son of Telamon,[9] and any other ancient hero who has suffered death through an unjust judgment; and there will be no small pleasure, as I think, in comparing my own sufferings with theirs. Above all, I shall then be able to continue my search into true and false knowledge; as in this world, so also in the next and I shall find out who is wise, and who pretends to be wise, and is not. What would not a man give, O judges, to be able to examine the leader of the great

7. The mythical inventor of agriculture, who is associated with judgment in the next world only in this passage. Minos appears as a judge of the dead in Homer's *Odyssey* 11; Rhadamanthus and Aeacus, like Minos, were models of just judges in life and after death. The first three named by Socrates are sons of Zeus. 8. Greek poet (eighth century B.C.?) who wrote *The Works and Days*, a didactic poem containing precepts for the farmer. Orpheus and Musaeus are legendary poets and religious teachers. 9. Both victims of unjust trials. Palamedes, one of the Greek chieftains at Troy, was unjustly executed for treason on the false evidence of Odysseus. Ajax committed suicide after the arms of the dead Achilles were adjudged to Odysseus as the bravest warrior on the Greek side.

Trojan expedition; or Odysseus or Sisyphus,[1] or numberless others, men and women too! What infinite delight would there be in conversing with them and asking them questions! In another world they do not put a man to death for asking questions: assuredly not. For besides being happier than we are, they will be immortal, if what is said is true.

Wherefore, O judges, be of good cheer about death, and know of a certainty, that no evil can happen to a good man, either in life or after death. He and his are not neglected by the gods; nor has my own approaching end happened by mere chance. But I see clearly that the time had arrived when it was better for me to die and be released from trouble; wherefore the oracle gave no sign. For which reason, also, I am not angry with my condemners, or with my accusers; they have done me no harm, although they did not mean to do me any good; and for this I may gently blame them.

Still I have a favor to ask of them. When my sons are grown up, I would ask you, O my friends, to punish them; and I would have you trouble them, as I have troubled you, if they seem to care about riches, or anything more than about virtue; or if they pretend to be something when they are really nothing,—then reprove them, as I have reproved you, for not caring about that for which they ought to care, and thinking that they are something when they are really nothing. And if you do this, both I and my sons will have received justice at your hands.

The hour of departure has arrived, and we go our ways—I to die, and you to live. Which is better God only knows.

1. Famous for his unscrupulousness and cunning. Odysseus was the most cunning of the Greek chieftains at Troy and the hero of Homer's *Odyssey*. Each is presumably an example of the man who "pretends to be wise and is not."

ARISTOTLE

384–322 B.C.

One member of Plato's Academy, Aristotle, was to become as celebrated and influential as his teacher. He was not, like Plato, a native Athenian; he was born in northern Greece, at Stagira, close to the kingdom of Macedonia, which was eventually to become the dominant power in the Greek world. Aristotle entered the Academy at the age of seventeen but left it when Plato died (347 B.C.). He carried on his researches (he was especially interested in zoology) at various places on the Aegean; served as tutor to the young Alexander, son of Philip II of Macedon; and returned to Athens in 335, to found his own philosophical school, the Lyceum, where he established the world's first research library. At the Lyceum he and his pupils carried on research in zoology, botany, biology, physics, political science, ethics, logic, music, and mathematics. He left Athens when Alexander died in Babylon (323 B.C.) and the Athenians, for a while, were able to demonstrate their hatred of Macedon and everything connected with it; he died a year later.

The scope of his written work, philosophical and scientific, is immense; he is represented here by some excerpts from the *Poetics*, the first systematic work of literary criticism in our tradition.

Aristotle's Poetics, translated by James Hutton (1982), is the best source for the student.

From Poetics[1]

* * * Thus, Tragedy is an imitation of an action that is serious, complete, and possessing magnitude; in embellished language, each kind of which is used separately in the different parts; in the mode of action and not narrated; and effecting through pity and fear [what we call] the *catharsis*[2] of such emotions. By "embellished language" I mean language having rhythm and melody, and by "separately in different parts" I mean that some parts of a play are carried on solely in metrical speech while others again are sung.

The constituent parts of tragedy. Since the imitation is carried out in the dramatic mode by the personages themselves, it necessarily follows, first, that the arrangement of Spectacle will be a part of tragedy, and next, that Melody and Language will be parts, since these are the media in which they effect the imitation. By "language" I mean precisely the composition of the verses, by "melody" only that which is perfectly obvious. And since tragedy is the imitation of an action and is enacted by men in action, these persons must necessarily possess certain qualities of Character and Thought, since these are the basis for our ascribing qualities to the actions themselves—character and thought are two natural causes of actions—and it is in their actions that men universally meet with success or failure. The imitation of the action is the Plot. By plot I here mean the combination of the events; Character is that in virtue of which we say that the personages are of such and such a quality; and Thought is present in everything in their utterances that aims to prove a point or that expresses an opinion. Necessarily, therefore, there are in tragedy as a whole, considered as a special form, six constituent elements, viz. Plot, Character, Language, Thought, Spectacle, and Melody. Of these elements, two [Language and Melody] are the *media* in which they effect the imitation, one [Spectacle] is the *manner*, and three [Plot, Character, Thought] are the *objects* they imitate; and besides these there are no other parts. So then they employ these six forms, not just some of them so to speak; for every drama has spectacle, character, plot, language, melody, and thought in the same sense, but the most important of them is the organization of the events [the plot].

Plot and character. For tragedy is not an imitation of men but of actions and of life. It is in action that happiness and unhappiness are found, and the end[3] we aim at is a kind of activity, not a quality; in accordance with their characters men are of such and such a quality, in accordance with their actions they are fortunate or the reverse. Consequently, it is not for the purpose of presenting their characters that the agents engage in action, but

1. Translated by James Hutton. Bracketed text has been added for clarity. 2. This is probably the most disputed passage in the Western critical tradition. There are two main schools of interpretation, which differ in their understanding of the metaphor implied in the word *catharsis*. Some critics take the word to mean "purification," implying a metaphor from the religious process of purification from guilt; the passions are "purified" by the tragic performance because the excitement of these passions by the performance weakens them and reduces them to just proportions in the individual. This theory was supported by the German critic Lessing. Others take the metaphor to be medical, reading the word as "purging" and interpreting the phrase to mean that the tragic performance excites the emotions only to allay them, thus ridding the spectator of the disquieting emotions from which he or she suffers in everyday life. Tragedy thus has a therapeutic effect. 3. Purpose.

rather it is for the sake of their actions that they take on the characters they have. Thus, what happens—that is, the plot—is the end for which a tragedy exists, and the end or purpose is the most important thing of all. What is more, without action there could not be a tragedy, but there could be without characterization. * * *

Now that the parts are established, let us next discuss what qualities the plot should have, since plot is the primary and most important part of tragedy. I have posited that tragedy is an imitation of an action that is a whole and complete in itself and of a certain magnitude—for a thing may be a whole, and yet have no magnitude to speak of. Now a thing is a whole if it has a beginning, a middle, and an end. A beginning is that which does not come necessarily after something else, but after which it is natural for another thing to exist or come to be. An end, on the contrary, is that which naturally comes after something else, either as its necessary sequel or as its usual [and hence probable] sequel, but itself has nothing after it. A middle is that which both comes after something else and has another thing following it. A well-constructed plot, therefore, will neither begin at some chance point nor end at some chance point, but will observe the principles here stated. * * *

Contrary to what some people think, a plot is not ipso facto a unity if it revolves about one man. Many things, indeed an endless number of things, happen to any one man some of which do not go together to form a unity, and similarly among the actions one man performs there are many that do not go together to produce a single unified action. Those poets seem all to have erred, therefore, who have composed a *Heracleid,* a *Theseid,* and other such poems, it being their idea evidently that since Heracles was one man, their plot was bound to be unified. * * *

From what has already been said, it will be evident that the poet's function is not to report things that have happened, but rather to tell of such things as might happen, things that are possibilities by virtue of being in themselves inevitable or probable. Thus the difference between the historian and the poet is not that the historian employs prose and the poet verse—the work of Herodotus[4] could be put into verse, and it would be no less a history with verses than without them; rather the difference is that the one tells of things that have been and the other of such things as might be. Poetry, therefore, is a more philosophical and a higher thing than history, in that poetry tends rather to express the universal, history rather the particular fact. A universal is: The sort of thing that (in the circumstances) a certain kind of person will say or do either probably or necessarily, which in fact is the universal that poetry aims for (with the addition of names for the persons); a particular, on the other hand is: What Alcibiades[5] did or had done to him. * * *

Among plots and actions of the simple type, the episodic form is the worst. I call episodic a plot in which the episodes follow one another in no probable or inevitable sequence. Plots of this kind are constructed by bad poets on their own account, and by good poets on account of the actors; since they are composing entries for a competitive exhibition, they stretch the plot beyond what it can bear and are often compelled, therefore, to dislocate the natural order. * * *

4. Historian of the Persian Wars, a contemporary of Sophocles. 5. A brilliant but unscrupulous Athenian statesman (fifth century B.C.).

Some plots are simple, others complex; indeed the actions of which the plots are imitation are at once so differentiated to begin with. Assuming the action to be continuous and unified, as already defined, I call that action simple in which the change of fortune takes place without a reversal or recognition, and that action complex in which the change of fortune involves a recognition or a reversal or both. These events [recognitions and reversals] ought to be so rooted in the very structure of the plot that they follow from the preceding events as their inevitable or probable outcome; for there is a vast difference between following from and merely following after. * * *

Reversal (Peripety) is, as aforesaid, a change from one state of affairs to its exact opposite, and this, too, as I say, should be in conformance with probability or necessity. For example, in *Oedipus,* the messenger[6] comes to cheer Oedipus by relieving him of fear with regard to his mother, but by revealing his true identity, does just the opposite of this. * * *

Recognition, as the word itself indicates, is a change from ignorance to knowledge, leading either to friendship or to hostility on the part of those persons who are marked for good fortune or bad. The best form of recognition is that which is accompanied by a reversal, as in the example from *Oedipus.* * * *

Next in order after the points I have just dealt with, it would seem necessary to specify what one should aim at and what avoid in the construction of plots, and what it is that will produce the effect proper to tragedy.

Now since in the finest kind of tragedy the structure should be complex and not simple, and since it should also be a representation of terrible and piteous events (that being the special mark of this type of imitation), in the first place, it is evident that good men ought not to be shown passing from prosperity to misfortune, for this does not inspire either pity or fear, but only revulsion; nor evil men rising from ill fortune to prosperity, for this is the most untragic plot of all—it lacks every requirement, in that it neither elicits human sympathy nor stirs pity or fear. And again, neither should an extremely wicked man be seen falling from prosperity into misfortune, for a plot so constructed might indeed call forth human sympathy, but would not excite pity or fear, since the first is felt for a person whose misfortune is undeserved and the second for someone like ourselves—pity for the man suffering undeservedly, fear for the man like ourselves—and hence neither pity nor fear would be aroused in this case. We are left with the man whose place is between these extremes. Such is the man who on the one hand is not pre-eminent in virtue and justice, and yet on the other hand does not fall into misfortune through vice or depravity, but falls because of some mistake;[7] one among the number of the highly renowned and prosperous, such as Oedipus and Thyestes and other famous men from families like theirs.

It follows that the plot which achieves excellence will necessarily be single in outcome and not, as some contend, double, and will consist in a change of fortune, not from misfortune to prosperity, but the opposite from prosperity to misfortune, occasioned not by depravity, but by some great mistake on the part of one who is either such as I have described or better than this

6. The Corinthian herdsman. 7. The Greek word is *hamartia.* It has sometimes been translated as "flaw" (hence the expression "tragic flaw") and thought of as a moral defect, but comparison with Aristotle's use of the word in other contexts suggests strongly that he means by it "mistake" or "error" (of judgment).

rather than worse. (What actually has taken place confirms this; for though at first the poets accepted whatever myths came to hand, today the finest tragedies are founded upon the stories of only a few houses, being concerned, for example, with Alcmeon, Oedipus, Orestes, Meleager, Thyestes, Telephus, and such others as have chanced to suffer terrible things or to do them.) So, then, tragedy having this construction is the finest kind of tragedy from an artistic point of view. And consequently, those persons fall into the same error who bring it as a charge against Euripides that this is what he does in his tragedies and that most of his plays have unhappy endings. For this is in fact the right procedure, as I have said; and the best proof is that on the stage and in the dramatic contests, plays of this kind seem the most tragic, provided they are successfully worked out, and Euripides, even if in everything else his management is faulty, seems at any rate the most tragic of the poets. * * *

In the characters and the plot construction alike, one must strive for that which is either necessary or probable, so that whatever a character of any kind says or does may be the sort of thing such a character will inevitably or probably say or do and the events of the plot may follow one after another either inevitably or with probability. (Obviously, then, the denouement of the plot should arise from the plot itself and not be brought about "from the machine,' as it is in *Medea* and in the embarkation scene in the *Iliad*.[8] The machine is to be used for matters lying outside the drama, either antecedents of the action which a human being cannot know, or things subsequent to the action that have to be prophesied and announced; for we accept it that the gods see everything. Within the events of the plot itself, however, there should be nothing unreasonable, or if there is, it should be kept outside the play proper, as is done in the *Oedipus* of Sophocles.) * * *

The chorus in tragedy. The chorus ought to be regarded as one of the actors, and as being part of the whole and integrated into performance, not in Euripides' way but in that of Sophocles. In the other poets, the choral songs have no more relevance to the plot than if they belonged to some other play. And so nowadays, following the practice introduced by Agathon,[9] the chorus merely sings interludes. But what difference is there between the singing of interludes and taking a speech or even an entire episode from one play and inserting it into another?

8. The reference is to an incident in the second book of the *Iliad:* an attempt of the Greek rank and file to return home and abandon the siege is arrested by the intervention of Athena. If it were a drama she would appear *on the machine,* literally the machine that was employed in the theater to show the gods flying in space. It has come to mean any implausible way of solving complications of the plot. Medea escapes from Corinth "on the machine" in her magic chariot. 9. A younger contemporary of Euripides; most of his plays were produced in the fourth century B.C.

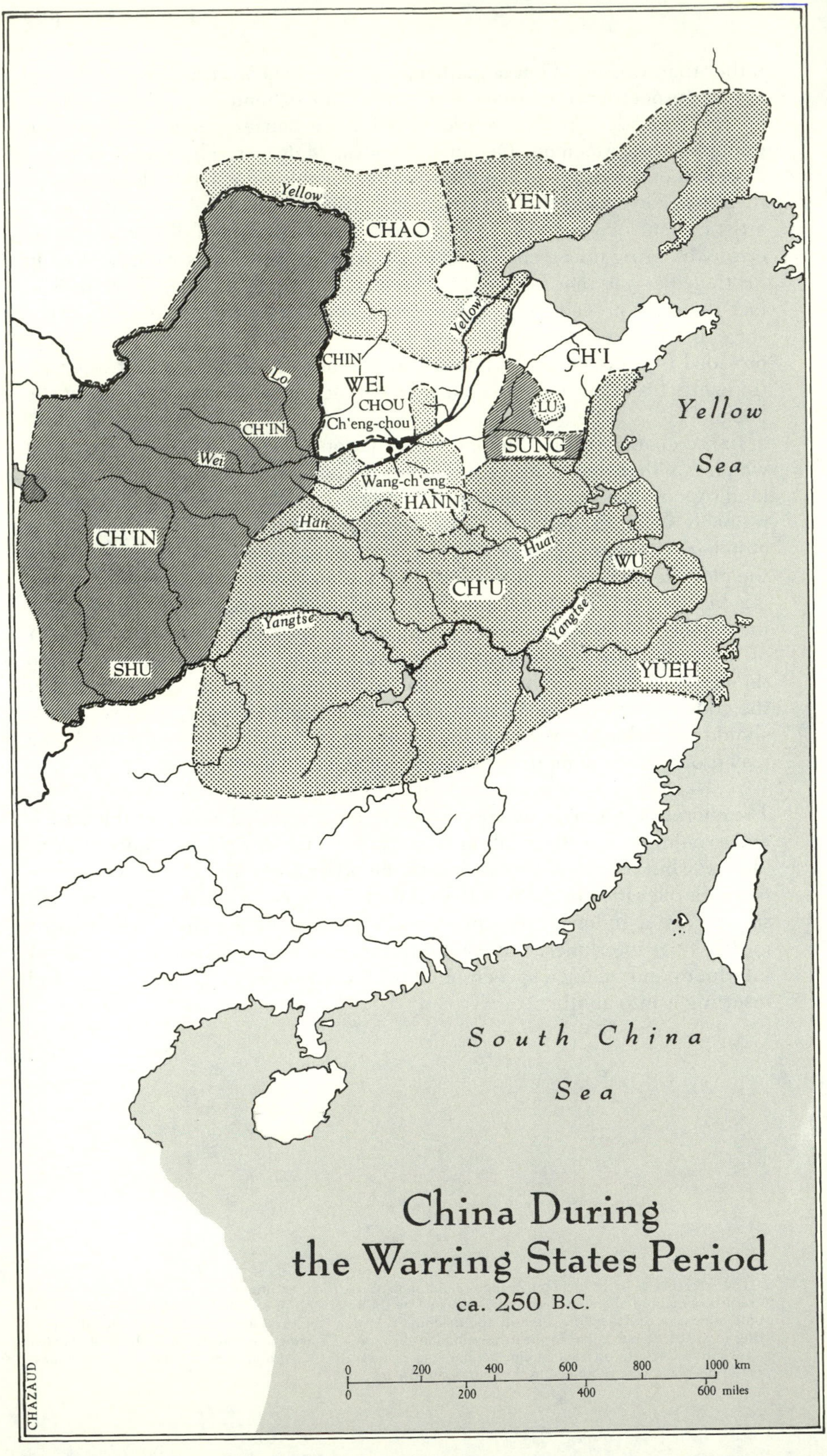

China During the Warring States Period

ca. 250 B.C.

Poetry and Thought in Early China

Many great civilizations have perished without consequence; they have left vast ruins in deserts and jungles. What we know of them comes from the imaginative reconstructions of scholars, from inscriptions, and from the accounts of early travelers. Other civilizations, like those of ancient Egypt and Mesopotamia, left extensive written records only to be at last swallowed up by other civilizations; the very names by which we refer to them—*Egypt* and *Mesopotamia*—are Greek.

Still other ancient civilizations began long histories that continue to the present; they set patterns and posed questions that shaped the actions and values of their descendants for thousands of years. The writings they produced—continuously read and reinterpreted—served as the binding that gave these civilizations a sense of their unity and continuity. Early in the third century A.D. Ts'ao P'i, the first emperor of the short Wei Dynasty, observed that literary works were "the greatest legacy in governing the kingdom." A writer himself, Ts'ao P'i understood the transience of power, even power well exercised, and he understood that the image of the period preserved in literary works would eventually become—far more than his substantial accomplishments—the "reality" of his age for the future.

In many ways, then, "China" is a literary fiction of cultural and historical unity that eventually became reality by being generally accepted as true. Ancient China covered a vast territory that was inhabited by a diverse people, who spoke a language divided by widely divergent dialects, as well as by many tribes, who spoke their own languages. It might easily have been fragmented, like Europe, by regional interests and linguistic differences. By accepting the writings of ancient China as their own, peoples on the expanding margins of the ancient heartland became "Chinese." Rome was truly an empire, a political center that ruled over many peoples, each with its own sense of distinct identity as a people. Although traditional China is called an empire, regional identity gave way to a belief in cultural unity, a cultural unity that has always sought expression in political unity.

ARCHAIC CHINA

Chinese civilization developed independently from that of the West in the Yellow River basin. Although scholars have noted the possibility of contact with central Asia in the development of its early civilization, China was geographically separated from the earlier Mesopotamian and Indus valley city civilizations and followed its own course. The first historical dynasty was the Shang (ca. 1750–1020 B.C.). Although traditional Chinese historians have treated it as a dynasty in the later sense, the Shang seems to have been a loose confederation of city-states ruled by princes who had (or claimed) a common ancestry, one of whom was acknowledged as king. It was during the Shang Dynasty that Chinese writing first developed, and from this period we have inscriptions on tortoiseshells that were used in divination. Throughout its history China retained the use of "characters," rather than changing to an alphabet or syllabary. Some written characters are pictograms (for example, *jih* 日, meaning "sun," from ⊙) and some are ideograms (for example, *shang* 上, signifying "above"), but most characters combine an element that indicates the sound and an element, called a "radical," that indicates a conceptual category (for example, *chao* 昭, "shining," consists of the sound element 召 and the radical 日, for "sun"). The fact that written characters remained the same, though they were pronounced differently at different times and in different regions, contributed significantly to the coherence of Chinese civilization.

The end of the second millennium B.C. saw the migration of the Chou peoples from the west into the Yellow River heartland and their conquest of the Shang. The Chou were an agrarian people, who traced their descent from Hou Chi, or Lord Millet. The Chou's justification of its conquest set the model for a Chinese polity that was to last for three thousand years. The last rulers of the Shang Dynasty were accused of misrule, of causing such hardship that Heaven grew angry and transferred its "mandate" to the Chou king Wen, whose son, King Wu, completed the overthrow. Such at least were the stories told in the courts of the Chou princes, who were given feudal domains throughout the territory that had once belonged to the Shang Dynasty. They ruled as stewards, responsible to the Chou king, who was in turn only a steward for Heaven.

The idea of Heaven changed through the centuries, and it was never a clearly defined deity: sometimes it was an anthropomorphic divinity, sometimes a natural and moral force, and in this early period, sometimes a collective of ancestral spirits. Power depended on virtuous rule, which in large measure meant holding to the statutes and models of the former kings. These models were preserved in a body of unwritten ritual practice and in a group of early texts: the *Book of Documents,* a collection of royal statements and proclamations from the early Chou; the *Book of Changes,* used for divination; and the *Classic of Poetry,* containing, among other things, hymns to the Chou ancestors and ballads recounting the history of the Chou people. These works, which became the core of the Confucian classics, were attributed to various ancient sages; most modern scholars take them as anonymous.

The belief that virtuous government would ensure continuous power proved tenacious even in the face of political realities that undermined it. After a few prosperous reigns, the Chou Dynasty grew increasingly weak. In 770 B.C., under pressure from new warlike tribes pressing in from the north and west, the capital was shifted east, marking the beginning of the period known as the Eastern Chou. A half century later saw the beginning of a court chronicle, called the *Spring and Autumn Annals,* from the feudal state of Lu in east China. The period it covers, from 722 to 466 B.C., is thus known as the Spring and Autumn Annals Period.

THE SPRING AND AUTUMN ANNALS AND WARRING STATES PERIODS

The Chou Dynasty proved far more influential in its dissolution than at the height of its dominion. Politically, it was reduced to a tiny sphere surrounded by vigorous states that were still, nominally, its feudal domains. The princes of these states plotted and warred with one another, struggling to reconcile political realities with a nostalgic sense of ceremony and custom. Meanwhile, on the southern and western borders of the old Chou domain, powerful new kingdoms were rising: Ch'u, Wu, and Yüeh in the south and Ch'in in the west. Although many of these new kingdoms developed from autonomous traditions, they gradually absorbed Chou culture, and their rulers often sought to trace their descent either from the Chou royal house or from more ancient north Chinese ancestors (much as European royal families in the Middle Ages and Renaissance often claimed Greek or Trojan ancestry).

The state that most saw itself as the preserver of Chou traditions was the eastern duchy of Lu, the home of Confucius (551–479 B.C.). In his collected sayings, the *Analects (Lun-yü),* Confucius created a remarkable fusion of ethics and idealized Chou traditions. Although later Confucians credited him with the editorship of the Confucian classics, modern scholars doubt this. Rather he was a teacher of traditional learning, around whom gathered a large group of disciples; the lineages of those disciples preserved through the difficult centuries that followed a version of Chou traditions that lasted until the Han Dynasty, when they were institutionalized.

Although the philosophers that followed Confucius offered compelling alternatives, his union of idealized history and social thought finally won out in the Chinese tradition. The small details of ceremony and decorum were accepted as outer forms of a social order in which respect for others came naturally. In the context of the times, it was a heroic position: it promised a dignity in one's actions that could stubbornly resist a world in which expediency increasingly ruled. One story tells of a disciple of Confucius who, about to be executed, asked the archers to wait a moment so that he could straighten his cap.

The early wars between the feudal domains were ceremonious affairs. The nobility rode in chariots and engaged in single combat. Battles seem to have involved more display than bloodshed, and often one side, recognizing the superior force of the enemy, would simply withdraw. As technology improved and allegiance to Chou traditions declined, wars among the domains became increasingly destructive. Early in the Spring and Autumn Annals Period small regions were ruled by aristocratic families, and their officers were chosen from lesser clans. By the fifth century B.C. these domains were evolving into centralized states, with bureaucracies whose primary loyalty was not to their families but to the prince. Chinese historians have called this period the Warring States.

Political upheaval precipitated intellectual upheaval. Various rival schools of thought appeared, most offering a political program meant to appeal to competing princes. The followers of the philosopher Mo-tzu (second half of the fifth century B.C.) preached an austere utilitarianism. Seeing that warfare, like Confucian ceremony, was wasteful, they became inventive technicians, developing means of defense against military aggression.

The overriding Confucian concern with government and social life inevitably produced extreme reactions. Some schools were interested more in the individual than in the polity. The most remarkable figure among such thinkers was Chuang Chou (fourth century B.C.), who was concerned almost exclusively with the life of the mind, and his writings return to the theme of the relativity of perception and value. Chuang Chou is often grouped with the shadowy figure Lao-tzu as an ancestor of Taoism. Lao-tzu's name is attached to a collection of poems from the late Warring States Period that advocate passivity and following the Way, the natural course of things.

In that same century the Confucian tradition was eloquently represented by Mencius. He held (like Rousseau and others later on) that the innate goodness of human nature was warped only by circumstance and that good government would permit the natural goodness of men and women to show itself once again. But the age clearly favored those who believed not in moral influence and self-cultivation but in increasing outward control. Arguing against Mencius, Hsün-tzu (third century B.C.) chose to view learning and Confucian ethics as a means to govern the human creature, otherwise driven by passions and appetites.

Hsün-tzu's vision of human nature and his fascination with control influenced the writings of Han Fei (died 233 B.C.). Han Fei, who belonged to a long Chinese tradition of writers on statecraft, composed treatises outlining a policy of rigid state control to strengthen his own tiny state of Han. The treatises did little for his own realm but found particular favor in the western kingdom of Ch'in, which already had a long tradition of authoritarian control. Those who followed the teachings of Han Fei's school came to be known as Legalists for their belief that the state depended on its subjects' absolute adherence to its laws and policies. Among the other states, Ch'in had a reputation for ruthlessness and untrustworthiness, but Ch'in's armies—well disciplined, well equipped, and well supplied—had steadily increased the size of the kingdom and, by the middle of the third century B.C., were driving west and south, overwhelming all rivals.

CH'IN AND HAN

As the ancient Mediterranean world is brought to a symbolic close by the fall of Rome, ancient China may be said to end in 221 B.C., with the establishment of a unified empire under Emperor Ch'in Shih-huang. Ch'in Shih-huang's draconian megalomania became legendary in later Chinese history, exerting as much fascination as horror. Though much of his statecraft was subtle, many of his most famous policies had a chilling simplicity. Some, such as unifying the currency and the script, deserve credit. But his solution to intellectual disagreement was to burn the books of all schools but those of the Legalists, whom he favored, and his solution to regional loyalties toward the old states was massive deportation. The final victory of Confucian traditionalism in the Han Dynasty was, in no small part, a reaction against Ch'in Shih-huang's disregard for all traditions and norms of humane behavior.

Ch'in's greatest enemy had been the large southern state of Ch'u. Like Ch'in, it had been steadily expanding at the expense of its neighbors and had spread along both sides of the Yangtse River. Though long within the north Chinese cultural sphere, Ch'u had rather different traditions from its neighbors, and it also had the strongest regional consciousness of any of the states. After its conquest by Ch'in, a folk rhyme circulated in Ch'u: "Though only three households be left in Ch'u, / The destroyer of Ch'in will surely be Ch'u." After Ch'in Shih-huang's death, rebellions broke out everywhere, and the Ch'u rebel Hsiang Yü defeated the major Ch'in armies. The last decade of the third century B.C. saw not only the destruction of Ch'in but also Hsiang Yü's struggle with a rival Ch'u army led by Liu Pang. Ultimately, Liu Pang was victorious and founded a new dynasty, the Han.

Ch'in survived less than twenty years; the Han Dynasty lasted more than four hundred. The imperial house of Liu (in Chinese the surname comes first), having inherited a unified empire and benefited from Ch'in's destruction of the old aristocracy, learned the lesson of flexibility. Some emperors tightened central control and others loosened it, but none attempted the absolute exercise of imperial will that Ch'in Shih-huang had assumed. The Liu patronized Taoism, shamanistic cults, and Confucianism, freely mixing adherence to traditions with policies that served state interest. With an eye to the reigning emperor and to the example of Ch'in, the Confucians liked to invoke the model of Chou, of rule that depends on the goodwill of those ruled. The Western term *China* names the civilization after Ch'in, but ever thereafter the Chinese have referred to themselves as the "people of Han."

FURTHER READING

A good general introduction to writing in this period can be found in Burton Watson, *Early Chinese Literature* (1962). Henri Maspero, *China in Antiquity* (first published 1927, English translation 1978), is an older, but still useful survey of early Chinese history and culture. Wang Ching-hsien, *From Ritual to Allegory: Seven Essays in Early Chinese Poetry* (1988), is a study of the *Book of Songs* (i.e., *Classic of Poetry*) and the *Chu-tz'u*. The best study of early Chinese philosophers is A. C. Graham, *Disputers of the Tao: Philosophical Argument in Ancient China* (1989). Early Chinese reflection on and interpretation of the ancient classics, using the case of the *Book of Songs*, are studied in Steven Van Zoeren, *Poetry and Personality* (1991).

PRONOUNCING GLOSSARY

The following list uses common English syllables to provide rough equivalents of selected words whose pronunciation may be unfamiliar to the general reader.

Ch'in: *chin*

Ch'in Shih-huang: *chin sherr–h-ang*

Chou: *joh*

Ch'u: *choo*

Chuang Chou: *jwahng joh*

Han Fei: *hahn fay*

Hou Chi: *hoh jee*

Hsiang Yü: *shyang yoo*

Hsün-tzu: *shyun–dzuh*

Lao-tzu: *lau–dzuh*

Liu Pang: *lyoo bahng*

Lun-yu: *lwun–yoo*

Mo-tzu: *mwo–dzuh*

Ts'ao P'i: *tsaw pee*

Wei: *way*

Wen: *wun*

Yüeh: *yoo-eh*

TIME LINE

TEXTS	CONTEXTS
ca. 1700–1020 B.C. Writing used on tortoise shells for divination and in inscriptions on bronze vessels	**ca. 1700–1020 B.C.** Shang Dynasty
	1020 Chou Dynasty overthrows the Shang Dynasty
ca. 1000 Earliest portions of ***The Classic of Poetry.*** • Earliest parts of the *Book of Changes,* the *Yi Ching*	
	ca. 820 Reign of King Hsüan and the expansion of the Chou kingdom south toward the Yangtse River
	770–256 Steady decline of the power of the Chou royal house and the rise of feudal states
	722 Beginning of the Spring and Autumn Annals period
ca. 600 ***The Classic of Poetry*** reaches its final form	
551–479 Confucius and the ***Analects***	
	403 "Warring States" period begins
	400–250 Period of the "hundred schools" of Chinese thought
	ca. 390–305 Confucian philosopher Mencius, who taught the inherent goodness of human nature
ca. 369–286 Taoist philosopher Chuang Chou and the early chapters of the ***Chuang Tzu***	
	350–221 Rise of the state of Ch'in in western China under the influence of a totalitarian political philosophy known as Legalism
340?–278 Ch'ü Yüan, poet of the southern state of Ch'u, to whom was attributed the composition of *The Nine Songs*	
	256 Ch'in dethrones the last Chou ruler

Boldface titles indicate works in the anthology.

TIME LINE

TEXTS	CONTEXTS
	221–206 Under influence of Ch'in Legalism, Confucianism and other schools of thought suppressed
	221 Ch'in Dynasty unifies China under Ch'in Shih-huang, the "First Emperor" • Great Wall extended
	206 Fall of Ch'in and the founding of the Han Dynasty; Han sponsors Confucianism
179–117 Ssu-ma Hsiang-ju, the greatest court poet of the Han and master of a form of long verse known as *fu* or "rhapsody"	
	140–86 Reign of Emperor Wu of the Han, with Chinese military conquests in Central Asia
	120 The Han court establishes a "Music Bureau," one of whose functions is to collect popular songs. Some of these lyrics survive
97 Ssu-ma Ch'ien completes the *Shih-chi,* the **Historical Records,** a comprehensive history of China up to the reign of Emperor Wu	
A.D. 32–92 Pan Ku, author of the *Han History* and of many rhapsodies	
	A.D. 57 Japan sends envoys to the Han court
100–200 The rise of anonymous poetry in the five-character line, which would be the most common poetic form for the rest of the premodern period	**ca. 100** Earliest introduction of Buddhism into China
	105 Earliest paper made
	196–220 The breakup of the Han into competing regions dominated by warlords • Ts'ao Ts'ao (155–220) is warlord of north China (200–220) and gathers the most eminent writers of the day to his court

CLASSIC OF POETRY

ca. 1000–600 B.C.

In contrast to other ancient literary cultures, which begin with epics, prose legends, or hymns to the gods, the Chinese tradition begins with lyric poetry. The *Classic of Poetry* (also known as *Book of Songs*) is a collection of 305 songs representing the heritage of the Chou people. The earliest in the collection are believed to date from around 1000 B.C. and the latest from around 600 B.C., at which time it seems to have reached something like its present form.

Although the collection circulated among the Chou aristocracy, it obviously drew from a wide variety of sources, and its diversity represents many levels of Chou society. There are temple hymns to the ancestors of the Chou ruling house, narrative ballads on the foundation and history of the dynasty, royal laments, songs of soldiers glorifying war and deploring war, love songs, marriage songs, hunting songs, songs of women whose husbands had deserted them, banquet songs, poems of mourning, and others. Many seem to have originated as folk songs, but these are mixed together with poems from the Chou aristocracy.

Down through the fifth century B.C. the *Classic of Poetry* served as the basic educational text of the Chou upper class. As the various Chou domains gradually evolved into independent states, the *Classic of Poetry* represented their common Chou heritage. The philosopher Confucius (551–479 B.C.) advised his disciples:

> By the *Poems* you can stir people and you can observe things through them; you can express your resentment in them and you can show sociable feelings. Close to home you can use them to serve your father, and on a larger scale you can use them to serve your ruler. Moreover, you can learn to recognize many names of birds, beasts, plants, and trees.*

By "observe" Confucius meant something like discovering universal precepts in the *Poems*. But that was not the only way in which the *Poems* were used. The power of the *Classic of Poetry* to "stir people" probably refers to their frequent use in conversation and diplomacy. Citation of one of the poems was often used to clinch a point in an argument or, more subtly, to express an opinion that one would rather not say openly. As with Homer's epics in early Greece, knowledge of the *Classic of Poetry* was considered an essential part of cultural education in early China.

Gradually, the transmission of the *Classic of Poetry* passed into the hands of the Confucian school, and by the fourth century B.C. it had become one of the texts in the canon of Confucian classics. Confucius was presumed to have been the editor of the collection, choosing and arranging these particular poems to show implicitly the glory and decline of Chou society. As a Confucian classic, the *Classic of Poetry* remained an essential part of Chinese education up to the twentieth century.

The great epics of early civilizations hold up an image of the values of those civilizations. The heroic values of the Homeric epics and their transformation in the *Aeneid* (p. 1055) tell us much about how those civilizations wished to see themselves. Ancient China produced no epic; it left instead the *Classic of Poetry*. In place of the relatively homogeneous point of view of the ancient epics, the *Classic of Poetry* is a collection of many voices; there are the voices of kings, aristocrats, peasants, soldiers, men, and women. The Chou Dynasty's sense of its own authority depended on Heaven's charge to rule, which was contingent on ruling well and receiving the support of the common people. As the ballad that tells of Chou's rise to power says, "Heaven cannot be trusted; / Kingship is easily lost." This same law, by which the Chou Dynasty destroyed the Shang Dynasty, applied no less to the Chou itself.

*Translated by Steven Owen.

Because the dynasty depended on the common people, their concerns were considered an essential part of the polity. Voices of protest are mingled with voices of celebration. And the great influence of the *Classic of Poetry* in later ages was as a continual reminder that society contains many legitimate voices.

Confucius is said to have once told his son that if he did not learn the *Classic of Poetry* he would have no way to speak. The *Poems* gave words to feelings that would otherwise be hard or uncomfortable to articulate. One famous story of a slightly later period tells of a ruler who, on discovering that his people were criticizing him, sent out spies to inform on anyone who spoke against him. His adviser was horrified and warned the ruler strongly against taking such an action, but the ruler ignored his advice. Eventually, the people became frightened and kept their silence, with the result that the ruler was finally overthrown. Traditional Chinese interpretations of the *Classic of Poetry* have always stressed the role of the *Poems* as vehicles for political and social protest. But in a broader sense, the diversity of the *Poems* acknowledged that the contrary forces in individual hearts could still, when given utterance, contribute to a society that would ultimately prove more durable than one dominated by social authority and ideology. The immense cultural authority of the *Classic of Poetry* made it a means to say what one truly thought, rather than silently submitting to social authority. This principle is often found as a theme within the *Poems* themselves, as in these lines of a young woman being pressed to marry against her will: "This heart of mine is no mirror / it cannot take in all."

Even the most pious Confucian moralists always stressed that the voices in the *Classic of Poetry* came naturally and spontaneously from human feeling. The way in which students were taught to read the *Classic of Poetry* had a profound influence on the future development of Chinese literature. It encouraged poets and readers alike to assume that a poem revealed the state of mind of the writer, the writer's nature, and the writer's circumstances. And this led to a notion of literature, particularly poetry, as a form of interior history, revealing in an intensely direct way both the person and the age.

However simple the poems of the *Classic of Poetry* may appear on the surface, they embody the central values (if not the realities) of early Chinese civilization. Again and again the poems return to a fascination with timely action, to the need to speak out, to balances and exchanges, and to acts of explanation. These are the values of an antiheroic world, in which domination and absolute superiority threaten the social fabric. Its gods, the collective ancestors or Heaven, function as numinous mechanisms, holy enforcers of the natural and moral order; unlike the Greek or Mesopotamian gods, they almost never have favorites or act on whim. These values of natural balance can appear in the humblest forms. A young woman tosses a man a piece of fruit as a love gift, and the young man answers with an exchange:

She cast a quince to me,
a costly garnet I returned;
it was no equal return,
but by this love will last.

The exchange is economically unequal, a jewel returned for fruit. But the young man acts at once to restore the exchange to balance, explaining that the jewel was not given as an object of value, but as a token and message, just as the fruit she threw had been a message.

The poem itself can be an exchange of sorts. In poem LXXVI, when the lover Chung-tzu shows his rashly masculine daring by breaking into the girl's homestead, the poem serves to block his advances; it is a force of words to counterbalance his physical force. Through the words she can tell him that she loves him but also remind him of her family and others in the village, whose opinions should be taken into consideration and weighed against his desires.

A basic introduction to the *Classic of Poetry* can be found in Wang Ching-hsien,

From Ritual to Allegory: Seven Essays in Early Chinese Poetry (1988). Pauline Yu, *The Reading of Imagery in the Chinese Tradition* (1987), has an excellent chapter on the traditional understanding of imagery in the *Classic of Poetry*.

PRONOUNCING GLOSSARY

The following list uses common English syllables to provide rough equivalents of selected words whose pronunciation may be unfamiliar to the general reader.

Chiang: *jyahng*

Chung-tzu: *joong–dzuh*

CLASSIC OF POETRY[1]

I. Fishhawk

The fishhawks sing *gwan gwan*
on sandbars of the stream.
Gentle maiden, pure and fair,
fit pair for a prince.

Watercress grows here and there,
right and left we gather it.
Gentle maiden, pure and fair,
wanted waking and asleep.

Wanting, sought her, had her not,
waking, sleeping, thought of her,
on and on he thought of her,
he tossed from one side to another.

Watercress grows here and there,
right and left we pull it.
Gentle maiden, pure and fair,
with harps we bring her company.

Watercress grows here and there,
right and left we pick it out.
Gentle maiden, pure and fair,
with bells and drums do her delight.

XX. Plums Are Falling

Plums are falling,
seven are the fruits;
many men want me,
let me have a fine one.

1. Translated by Stephen Owen.

Plums are falling,
three are the fruits;
many men want me,
let me have a steady one.

Plums are falling,
catch them in the basket;
many men want me,
let me be bride of one.

XXIII. Dead Roe Deer

A roe deer dead in the meadow,
all wrapped in white rushes.
The maiden's heart was filled with spring;
a gentleman led her astray.

Undergrowth in forest,
dead deer in the meadow,
all wound with white rushes,
a maiden white as marble.

Softly now, and gently, gently,
do not touch my apron, sir,
and don't set the cur to barking.

XXVI. Boat of Cypress

That boat of cypress drifts along,
it drifts upon the stream.
Restless am I, I cannot sleep,
as though in torment and troubled.
Nor am I lacking wine
to ease my mind and let me roam.

This heart of mine is no mirror,
it cannot take in all.
Yes, I do have brothers,
but brothers will not be my stay.
I went and told them of my grief
and met only with their rage.

This heart of mine is no stone;
you cannot turn it where you will.
This heart of mine is no mat;
I cannot roll it up within.
I have behaved with dignity,
in this no man can fault me.

My heart is uneasy and restless,
I am reproached by little men.
Many are the woes I've met,
and taken slights more than a few.
I think on it in the quiet,
and waking pound my breast.

Oh Sun! and you Moon!
Why do you each grow dim in turn?
These troubles of the heart
are like unwashed clothes.
I think on it in the quiet,
I cannot spread wings to fly away.

XLII. Gentle Girl

A gentle girl and fair
awaits by the crook of the wall;
in shadows I don't see her;
I pace and scratch my hair.

A gentle girl and comely
gave me a scarlet pipe;
scarlet pipe that gleams—
in your beauty I find delight.

Then she brought me a reed from the pastures,
it was truly beautiful and rare.
Reed—the beauty is not yours—
you are but beauty's gift.

LXIV. Quince

She cast a quince to me,
a costly garnet I returned;
it was no equal return,
but by this love will last.

She cast a peach to me,
costly opal I returned;
it was no equal return,
but by this love will last.

She cast a plum to me,
a costly ruby I returned;
it was no equal return,
but by this love will last.

LXXVI. Chung-tzu, Please

Chung-tzu, please
don't cross my village wall,
don't break the willows planted there.
It's not that I care so much for them,
but I dread my father and mother;
Chung-tzu may be in my thoughts,
but what my father and mother said—
that too may be held in dread.

Chung-tzu, please
don't cross my fence,
don't break the mulberries planted there.
It's not that I care so much for them,
but I dread my brothers;
Chung-tzu may be in my thoughts,
but what my brothers said—
that too may be held in dread.

Chung-tzu, please
don't cross into my garden,
don't break the sandalwood planted there.
It's not that I care so much for them,
but I dread others will talk much;
Chung-tzu may be in my thoughts,
but when people talk too much—
that too may be held in dread.

LXXXI. I Went Along the Broad Road

I went along the broad road
and took you by the sleeve—
do not hate me,
never spurn old friends.

I went along the broad road
and took you by the hand—
do not scorn me,
never spurn a love.

LXXXII. Rooster Crows

The woman said, "The rooster crows."
The man said, "Still the dark before dawn."

"Get you up, man—look at the night!—
the morning star is sparkling;
go roving and go roaming,
shoot the wild goose and the teal.

When your arrows hit them,
I will dress them just for you;
when they're dressed, we'll drink the wine,
and I will grow old with you.
There will be harps to attend us,
and all will be easy and good.

If I know that you will come,
I'll make a gift of many jewels;
if I know you will accept,
I'll show my care with many jewels;
if I know you will love me,
I'll answer you with many jewels."

CXL. Willows by the Eastern Gate

Willows by the Eastern Gate,
their leaves so thick and close.
Dusk had been the time set,
and now the morning star glows bright.

Willows by the Eastern Gate,
their leaves so dense and full.
Dusk had been the time set,
and now the morning star shines pale.

CCXLV. She Bore the Folk

She who first bore the folk—
Chiang it was, First Parent.
How was it she bore the folk?—
she knew the rite and sacrifice.
To rid herself of sonlessness
she trod the god's toeprint
  and she was glad.
She was made great, on her luck settled,
the seed stirred, it was quick.
She gave birth, she gave suck,
and this was Lord Millet.

When her months had come to term,
her firstborn sprang up.
Not splitting, not rending,

working no hurt, no harm.
He showed his godhead glorious,
the high god was greatly soothed.
He took great joy in those rites
and easily she bore her son.

She set him in a narrow lane,
but sheep and cattle warded him.
She set him in the wooded plain,
he met with those who logged the plain.
She set him on cold ice,
birds sheltered him with wings.
Then the birds left him
and Lord Millet wailed.
This was long and this was loud;
his voice was a mighty one.

And then he crept and crawled,
he stood upright, he stood straight.
He sought to feed his mouth,
and planted there the great beans.
The great beans' leaves were fluttering,
the rows of grain were bristling.
Hemp and barley dense and dark,
the melons, plump and round.

Lord Millet in his farming
had a way to help things grow:
He rid the land of thick grass,
he planted there a glorious growth.
It was in squares, it was leafy,
it was planted, it grew tall.
It came forth, it formed ears,
it was hard, it was good.
Its tassels bent, it was full,
he had his household there in Tai.

He passed us down these wondrous grains:
our black millets, of one and two kernels,
Millets whose leaves sprout red or white,
he spread the whole land with black millet,
And reaped it and counted the acres,
spread it with millet sprouting red or white,
hefted on shoulders, loaded on backs,
he took it home and began this rite.

And how goes this rite we have?—
at times we hull, at times we scoop,
at times we winnow, at times we stomp,
we hear it slosh as we wash it,
we hear it puff as we steam it.
Then we reckon, then we consider,

take artemisia, offer fat.
We take a ram for the flaying,
then we roast it, then we sear it,
to rouse up the following year.

We heap the wooden trenchers full,
wooden trenchers, earthenware platters.
And as the scent first rises
the high god is peaceful and glad.
This great odor is good indeed,
for Lord Millet began the rite,
and hopefully free from failing or fault,
it has lasted until now.

CONFUCIUS
551–479 B.C.

The *Analects* of Confucius (a title more lucidly translated as "Sayings") is the only work that we can confidently connect with the teacher Confucius, who gives his name to the secular social philosophy known as Confucianism. Confucius lived in a period when the unified Chou kingdom had split into a number of feudal states, most supposedly ruled by descendants of the Chou royal house. The period saw even that fragmented vestige of Chou legitimacy threatened by the rise of powerful families within the states.

Confucius himself was a native of Lu in eastern China, a state that prided itself on the preservation of Chou royal traditions but whose dukes were often at the mercy of the powerful Chi clan. Apparently because of a political conflict, Confucius left Lu in 497 B.C. and spent the next thirteen years wandering from regional court to regional court, gaining disciples and unsuccessfully seeking a prince who would try to implement his vision of traditional Chou values. At last he returned to Lu and lived out the rest of his life as a teacher, gathering a considerable following.

The *Analects* represents the memory of Confucius's teachings on the part of his disciples and was probably not written down until many centuries after his death. In its present form the *Analects* consists of twenty "books" or chapters, of which modern scholars consider the first fifteen to be authentic (we include passages from two of the last five books because they were considered just as authoritative as the first fifteen well into modern times). Although we can occasionally detect groupings of sayings, in general passages in the *Analects* are put together randomly.

To be a Confucian (the Chinese term is *Ju,* meaning roughly "traditionalist scholar") has meant many things during the nearly twenty-five hundred years since Confucius's death. These various meanings shifted and overlapped from age to age. For some scholars Confucianism was the study of ancient texts that embodied rituals and norms of behavior, for others it was a political philosophy, a social philosophy of the family, or the moral order of nature.

In the centuries that followed Confucius's death his teachings were absorbed into a growing interest in statecraft, and during the Han Dynasty, Confucian values became interwoven with the ideology of the imperial state. In later periods Chinese emperors may have supported Buddhism or religious Taoism out of personal devotion or political expediency, but Confucian learning and values were the very basis of the imperial state, by which the emperor held his office.

Confucius's reverence for antiquity centered on received texts and bodies of learning; these were the *Classic of Poetry,* the *Book of Documents* (*Shang shu*), the *Book of Changes* (*Yi ching*), the rituals (later written down in different texts), and a body of musical practice that accompanied the rituals and the *Classic of Poetry* (the music was lost after Confucius's time). In the third century B.C. these texts and traditions, along with a chronicle known as the *Ch'un-ch'iu,* became the core of what would be known as the Confucian classics. Other works came to be added to this core, including the *Analects* itself in the ninth century.

Before commenting on some of the central concerns of the *Analects,* we should consider its peculiar form and the significance of that form. In contrast to the imaginative sweep of works that founded other religious and philosophical traditions (and to the imaginative range of the *Chuang-Tzu* within the Chinese tradition), the *Analects* is a collection of terse and sometimes apparently innocuous sayings as well as a few longer anecdotes. The unity of the *Analects* resides not in an argument or a unified philosophy but rather in a person, Confucius. Instead of writing a treatise explaining his thoughts, the Confucius of the *Analects* responds to people and situations. The words are never thought of as the final and adequate statement of doctrine but as the circumstantial evidence of deeper wisdom. Confucianism is a philosophy of the relations between human beings, and its persuasive force rests not on a claim of transcendental truth but on the wisdom embodied in a person. Thus Confucius's terseness is read as a pregnant terseness, the utterances of someone who knew more and might have said more. The ideal here is captured in the disciple Tzu-kung's praise of Yen Hui, the most brilliant of Confucius's disciples: "When he is told one thing he understands ten." Throughout the *Analects* the reader is reminded that wisdom comes in fragments and fractions; the burden of full understanding is placed on the reader.

The moral philosophy of the *Analects* presupposes an idealized vision of the Chou past and its norms of behavior, which Confucius felt had been lost in his own age. The historically specific aspects of Confucius's values, such as his devotion to ancient rituals, make those values seem alien to a modern age; and indeed the modern reader may wonder why Confucianism remained so persuasive as a social philosophy, revived even in modern times.

The answer lies in looking beneath what is historically specific in the *Analects* to the hope of a perfect unity of social norm and natural behavior. This is succinctly expressed in Confucius's account of his spiritual development, culminating in the following: "At seventy I followed my heart's desire without overstepping the line." By study and self-cultivation, individuals can join their instinctive being and their social being. The hope is for a society whose members behave with a natural decency toward one another, respecting age and hierarchy and adapting to their changing roles. If the Confucianism of the *Analects* has a repugnance for anarchy and struggle, it has an equal repugnance for order achieved by coercion.

In one of the few extended passages in the *Analects,* Confucius asks a group of his disciples about their ambitions. Tzu-lu begins with a grand vision of restoring a state to power and morality. Sensing the master's disapproval, each of the subsequent disciples restricts his ambitions to an ever-narrower scope. At last the master comes to Tseng Hsi, who speaks of the joy in returning home from a festival with a group of friends. "The Master sighed and said, 'I am all in favour of Tien [Tseng Hsi].' " This is a touchstone text of Confucianism: what moves Confucius is the immediacy of Tseng Hsi's prospective joy in ritual and moral action. As Confucius says elsewhere, to delight in the Way is better than merely to understand it.

Confucius generally confined his interests to the human world and, as the *Analects* itself observes, did not speak about Heaven or the supernatural. This was not disbelief in transcendent being, but a remarkable desire to keep it out of human affairs, an ancient separation of church and state: "To keep one's distance from the gods and spirits while showing them reverence can be called wisdom."

The Confucian Way was one of social roles. These usually involved hierarchies of relations, but to Confucius social hierarchy was valid only if it came naturally and spontaneously. The only hierarchical relation that was above judgment was the relation between parent and child, and that natural relation of mutual but differing qualities of affection was the model to which all other social relations aspired.

No contemporary account of Confucianism can be complete without acknowledging the deep hostility it often inspires in modern China and Taiwan. Later, Confucianism became a tool of social coercion, and its demand that social norms of behavior be experienced as "natural" was an invitation to hypocrisy. But as with all religions and cultural philosophies, its historical failures do not entirely discredit the vision and hopes that first made it compelling.

Like other Chinese philosophers, Confucius speaks of the "Way." Each of the ancient Chinese philosophical schools used the term and interpreted the attributes of the Way differently. One should not grant too much value to the term itself; its importance lies in conceptualizing values and truth as process, a natural course of events and a natural course of action.

D. C. Lau's translation of the *Analects* (1979) has a long introduction that offers a lucid exposition of key concepts used in the work. The philosopher Herbert Fingarette, *Confucius—The Secular as Sacred* (1972), remains one of the most persuasive accounts of the appeal of the *Analects*.

PRONOUNCING GLOSSARY

The following list uses common English syllables to provide rough equivalents of selected words whose pronunciation may be unfamiliar to the general reader.

Ch'ang Chu: *jahng joo*
Chi: *jee*
Ch'i: *chee*
Chieh Ni: *jyeh nee*
Ch'ih: *cherr*
Chi K'ang Tzu: *jee kahng dzuh*
Chi-lu: *jee–loo*
Ching: *jing*
Ch'iu: *chyoh*
Chi Wen Tzu: *jee wun dzuh*
Ch'u: *choo*
Ch'un-ch'iu: *choo-en–chyoh*
Chung-kung: *jong–goong*
Ch'u Po-yu: *choo bwoh–yoo*
Fan Ch'ih: *fahn cherr*
Jan Ch'iu: *rahn chyoh*
Jan Yu: *rahn yoh*
K'uang: *kwahng*
K'ung: *koong*
Kung-hsi Hua: *goong–shee hwah*
Meng Ching Tzu: *mung jing dzuh*
Shang shu: *shahng shoo*
Shih Yu: *sherr yoo*
Shun: *shoo-un*
t'ai tsai: *tai dzai*
Tien: *dyen*
Tsai Yu: *dzai yoo*
Tseng Hsi: *dzung shee*
Tseng Tzu: *dzung dzuh*
Tzu-chang: *dzuh–jahng*
Tzu-hsia: *dzuh–shyah*
Tzu-kung: *dzuh–goong*
Tzu-lu: *dzuh–loo*
Wu Ch'eng: *woo chung*
Yen Hui: *yen hway*
Yen Yuan: *yen yoo-en*
Yi ching: *ee jing*
Yuan Jang: *yoo-en rahng*

From Analects[1]

BOOK I

1. The Master said, "Is it not a pleasure, having learned something, to try it out at due intervals? Is it not a joy to have friends come from afar? Is it not gentlemanly not to take offence when others fail to appreciate your abilities?"

11. The Master said, "Observe what a man has in mind to do when his father is living, and then observe what he does when his father is dead. If, for three years, he makes no changes to his father's ways, he can be said to be a good son."

BOOK II

1. The Master said, "The rule of virtue can be compared to the Pole Star which commands the homage of the multitude of stars without leaving its place."

2. The Master said, "The *Odes*[2] are three hundred in number. They can be summed up in one phrase,

Swerving not from the right path."

3. The Master said, "Guide them by edicts, keep them in line with punishments, and the common people will stay out of trouble but will have no sense of shame. Guide them by virtue, keep them in line with the rites, and they will, besides having a sense of shame, reform themselves."

4. The Master said, "At fifteen I set my heart on learning; at thirty I took my stand; at forty I came to be free from doubts; at fifty I understood the Decree of Heaven; at sixty my ear was atuned; at seventy I followed my heart's desire without overstepping the line."

7. The Master said, "There is no contention between gentlemen. The nearest to it is, perhaps, archery. In archery they bow and make way for one another as they go up and on coming down they drink together. Even the way they contend is gentlemanly."

19. Duke Ai asked "What must I do before the common people will look up to me?"

Confucius answered, "Raise the straight and set them over the crooked and the common people will look up to you. Raise the crooked and set them over the straight and the common people will not look up to you."

21. Duke Ai asked Tsai Wo about the altar to the god of earth. Tsai Wo replied, "The Hsia used the pine, the Yin used the cedar, and the men of Chou used the chestnut (*li*), saying that it made the common people tremble (*li*)."

1. Translated by D. C. Lau. 2. An alternative rendering of the poems of the *Classic of Poetry*.

The Master, on hearing of this reply, commented, "One does not explain away what is already done, one does not argue against what is already accomplished, and one does not condemn what has already gone by."

BOOK III

8. The Master said, "He has not lived in vain who dies the day he is told about the Way."

9. The Master said to Tzu-kung, "Who is the better man, you or Hui?"

"How dare I compare myself with Hui? When he is told one thing he understands ten. When I am told one thing I understand only two."

The Master said, "You are not as good as he is. Neither of us is as good as he is."

10. Tsai Yü was in bed in the daytime. The Master said, "A piece of rotten wood cannot be carved, nor can a wall of dried dung be trowelled. As far as Yü is concerned what is the use of condemning him?" The Master added, "I used to take on trust a man's deeds after having listened to his words. Now having listened to a man's words I go on to observe his deeds. It was on account of Yü that I have changed in this respect."

20. Chi Wen Tzu always thought three times before taking action. When the Master was told of this, he commented, "Twice is quite enough."

26. Yen Yüan and Chi-lu were in attendance. The Master said, "I suggest you each tell me what it is you have set your hearts on."

Tzu-lu said, "I should like to share my carriage and horses, clothes and furs with my friends, and to have no regrets even if they become worn."

Yen Yüan said, "I should like never to boast of my own goodness and never to impose onerous tasks upon others."

Tzu-lu said, "I should like to hear what you have set your heart on."

The Master said, "To bring peace to the old, to have trust in my friends, and to cherish the young."

BOOK VI

12. Jan Ch'iu said, "It is not that I am not pleased with your way, but rather that my strength gives out." The Master said, "A man whose strength gives out collapses along the course. In your case you set the limits beforehand."

13. The Master said to Tzu-hsia, "Be a gentleman *ju*,[3] not a petty *ju*."

20. The Master said, "To be fond of something is better than merely to know it, and to find joy in it is better than merely to be fond of it."

22. Fan Ch'ih asked about wisdom. The Master said, "To work for the things the common people have a right to and to keep one's distance

3. A traditionalist, one who follows received customs.

from the gods and spirits while showing them reverence can be called wisdom."

Fan Ch'ih asked about benevolence. The Master said, "The benevolent man reaps the benefit only after overcoming difficulties. That can be called benevolence."

23. The Master said, "The wise find joy in water; the benevolent find joy in mountains. The wise are active; the benevolent are still. The wise are joyful; the benevolent are long-lived."

BOOK VII

3. The Master said, "It is these things that cause me concern: failure to cultivate virtue, failure to go more deeply into what I have learned, inability, when I am told what is right, to move to where it is, and inability to reform myself when I have defects."

5. The Master said, "How I have gone downhill! It has been such a long time since I dreamt of the Duke of Chou."

16. The Master said, "In the eating of coarse rice and the drinking of water, the using of one's elbow for a pillow, joy is to be found. Wealth and rank attained through immoral means have as much to do with me as passing clouds."

27. The Master used a fishing line but not a cable; he used a corded arrow but not to shoot at roosting birds.

BOOK VIII

4. Tseng Tzu was seriously ill. When Meng Ching Tzu visited him, this was what Tseng Tzu said,

"Sad is the cry of a dying bird;
Good are the words of a dying man.

These are three things which the gentleman values most in the Way: to stay clear of violence by putting on a serious countenance, to come close to being trusted by setting a proper expression on his face, and to avoid being boorish and unreasonable by speaking in proper tones. As for the business of sacrificial vessels, there are officials responsible for that."

5. Tseng Tzu said, "To be able yet to ask the advice of those who are not able. To have many talents yet to ask the advice of those who have few. To have yet to appear to want. To be full yet to appear empty. To be transgressed against yet not to mind. It was towards this end that my friend used to direct his efforts."

8. The Master said, "Be stimulated by the *Odes,* take your stand on the rites and be perfected by music."

13. The Master said, "Have the firm faith to devote yourself to learning, and abide to the death in the good way. Enter not a state that is in peril; stay

not in a state that is in danger. Show yourself when the Way prevails in the Empire, but hide yourself when it does not. It is a shameful matter to be poor and humble when the Way prevails in the state. Equally, it is a shameful matter to be rich and noble when the Way falls into disuse in the state."

17. The Master said, "Even with a man who urges himself on in his studies as though he was losing ground, my fear is still that he may not make it in time."

BOOK IX

5. When under siege in K'uang, the Master said, "With King Wen[4] dead, is not culture *(wen)* invested here in me? If Heaven intends culture to be destroyed, those who come after me will not be able to have any part of it. If Heaven does not intend this culture to be destroyed, then what can the men of K'uang do to me?"

6. The *t'ai tsai*[5] asked Tzu-kung, "Surely the Master is a sage, is he not? Otherwise why should he be skilled in so many things?" Tzu-kung said, "It is true. Heaven set him on the path of sagehood. However, he is skilled in many things besides."

The Master, on hearing of this, said, "How well the *t'ai tsai* knows me! I was of humble station when young. That is why I am skilled in many menial things. Should a gentleman be skilled in many things? No, not at all."

12. The Master was seriously ill. Tzu-lu told his disciples to act as retainers. During a period when his condition had improved, the Master said, "Yu has long been practising deception. In pretending that I had retainers when I had none, who would we be deceiving? Would we be deceiving Heaven? Moreover, would I not rather die in your hands, my friends, than in the hands of retainers? And even if I were not given an elaborate funeral, it is not as if I was dying by the wayside."

13. Tzu-kung said, "If you had a piece of beautiful jade here, would you put it away safely in a box or would you try to sell it for a good price?" The Master said, "Of course I would sell it. Of course I would sell it. All I am waiting for is the right offer."

14. The Master wanted to settle amongst the Nine Barbarian Tribes of the east. Someone said, "But could you put up with their uncouth ways?" The Master said, "Once a gentleman settles amongst them, what uncouthness will there be?"

22. The Master said, "There are, are there not, young plants that fail to produce blossoms, and blossoms that fail to produce fruit?"

23. The Master said, "It is fitting that we should hold the young in awe. How do we know that the generations to come will not be the equal of the present? Only when a man reaches the age of forty or fifty without distin-

4. First ruler of the Chou Dynasty. 5. A title of high office. This person has not been identified.

guishing himself in any way can one say, I suppose, that he does not deserve to be held in awe."

28. The Master said, "Only when the cold season comes is the point brought home that the pine and the cypress are the last to lose their leaves."

BOOK XI

10. When Yen Yüan died, in weeping for him, the Master showed undue sorrow. His followers said, "You are showing undue sorrow." "Am I? Yet if not for him, for whom should I show undue sorrow?"

26. When Tzu-lu, Tseng Hsi, Jan Yu and Kung-hsi Hua were seated in attendance, the Master said, "Do not feel constrained simply because I am a little older than you are. Now you are in the habit of saying, 'My abilities are not appreciated,' but if someone did appreciate your abilities, do tell me how you would go about things."

Tzu-lu promptly answered, "If I were to administer a state of a thousand chariots, situated between powerful neighbours, troubled by armed invasions and by repeated famines, I could, within three years, give the people courage and a sense of direction."

The Master smiled at him.

"Ch'iu, what about you?"

"If I were to administer an area measuring sixty or seventy *li*[6] square, or even fifty or sixty *li* square, I could, within three years, bring the size of the population up to an adequate level. As to the rites and music, I would leave that to abler gentlemen."

"Ch'ih, how about you?"

"I do not say that I already have the ability, but I am ready to learn. On ceremonial occasions in the ancestral temple or in diplomatic gatherings, I should like to assist as a minor official in charge of protocol, properly dressed in my ceremonial cap and robes."

"Tien, how about you?"

After a few dying notes came the final chord, and then he stood up from his lute. "I differ from the other three in my choice."

The Master said, "What harm is there in that? After all each man is stating what he has set his heart upon."

"In late spring, after the spring clothes have been newly made, I should like, together with five or six adults and six or seven boys, to go bathing in the River Yi and enjoy the breeze on the Rain Altar, and then to go home chanting poetry."

The Master sighed and said, "I am all in favour of Tien."

When the three left, Tseng Hsi stayed behind. He said, "What do you think of what the other three said?"

"They were only stating what they had set their hearts upon."

"Why did you smile at Yu?"

"It is by the rites that a state is administered, but in the way he spoke Yu showed a lack of modesty. That is why I smiled at him."

"In the case of Ch'iu, was he not concerned with a state?"

6. A unit of distance, about one-quarter of a mile.

"What can justify one in saying that sixty or seventy *li* square or indeed fifty or sixty *li* square do not deserve the name of 'state'?"

"In the case of Ch'ih, was he not concerned with a state?"

"What are ceremonial occasions in the ancestral temple and diplomatic gatherings if not matters which concern rulers of feudal states? If Ch'iu plays only a minor part, who would be able to play a major role?"

BOOK XII

2. Chung-kung asked about benevolence. The Master said, "When abroad behave as though you were receiving an important guest. When employing the services of the common people behave as though you were officiating at an important sacrifice. Do not impose on others what you yourself do not desire. In this way you will be free from ill will whether in a state or in a noble family."

Chung-kung said, "Though I am not quick, I shall direct my efforts towards what you have said."

7. Tzu-kung asked about government. The Master said, "Give them enough food, give them enough arms, and the common people will have trust in you."

Tzu-kung said, "If one had to give up one of these three, which should one give up first?"

"Give up arms."

Tzu-kung said, "If one had to give up one of the remaining two, which should one give up first?"

"Give up food. Death has always been with us since the beginning of time, but when there is no trust, the common people will have nothing to stand on."

10. Tzu-chang asked about the exaltation of virtue and the recognition of misguided judgment. The Master said, "Make it your guiding principle to do your best for others and to be trustworthy in what you say, and move yourself to where rightness is, then you will be exalting virtue. When you love a man you want him to live and when you hate him you want him to die. If, having wanted him to live, you then want him to die, this is misguided judgement.

> If you did not do so for the sake of riches,
> You must have done so for the sake of novelty."[7]

11. Duke Ching of Ch'i asked Confucius about government. Confucius answered, "Let the ruler be a ruler, the subject a subject, the father a father, the son a son." The Duke said, "Splendid! Truly, if the ruler be not a ruler, the subject not a subject, the father not a father, the son not a son, then even if there be grain, would I get to eat it?"

18. The prevalence of thieves was a source of trouble to Chi K'ang Tzu who asked the advice of Confucius. Confucius answered, "If you yourself

7. The quotation seems to have no bearing on the subject under discussion and may not in fact belong here.

were not a man of desires,[8] no one would steal even if stealing carried a reward."

19. Chi K'ang Tzu asked Confucius about government, saying, "What would you think if, in order to move closer to those who possess the Way, I were to kill those who do not follow the Way?"

Confucius answered, "In administering your government, what need is there for you to kill? Just desire the good yourself and the common people will be good. The virtue of the gentleman is like in straitened circumstances for a long time, he may be said to be a complete man."

BOOK XIII

1. Tzu-lu asked about government. The Master said, "Encourage the people to work hard by setting an example yourself." Tzu-lu asked for more. The Master said, "Do not allow your efforts to slacken."

10. The Master said, "If anyone were to employ me, in a year's time I would have brought things to a satisfactory state, and after three years I should have results to show for it."

11. The Master said, "How true is the saying that after a state has been ruled for a hundred years by good men it is possible to get the better of cruelty and to do away with killing."

12. The Master said, "Even with a true king it is bound to take a generation for benevolence to become a reality."

20. Tzu-kung asked, "What must a man be like before he can be said truly to be a Gentleman?" The Master said, "A man who has a sense of shame in the way he conducts himself and, when sent abroad, does not disgrace the commission of his lord can be said to be a Gentleman."

"May I ask about the grade below?"

"Someone praised for being a good son in his clan and for being a respectful young man in the village."

"And the next?"

"A man who insists on keeping his word and seeing his actions through to the end can, perhaps, qualify to come next, even though he shows a stubborn petty-mindedness."

"What about men who are in public life in the present day?"

The Master said, "Oh, they are of such limited capacity that they hardly count."

24. Tzu-kung asked, " 'All in the village like him.' What do you think of that?"

The Master said, "That is not enough."

" 'All in the village dislike him.' What do you think of that?"

The Master said, "That is not enough either. 'Those in his village

8. That is, if you were not a thief yourself.

who are good like him and those who are bad dislike him.' That would be better."

BOOK XIV

35. The Master said, "There is no one who understands me." Tzu-kung said, "How is it that there is no one who understands you?" The Master said, "I do not complain against Heaven, nor do I blame Man. In my studies, I start from below and get through to what is up above. If I am understood at all, it is, perhaps, by Heaven."

38. Tzu-lu put up for the night at the Stone Gate. The gatekeeper said, "Where have you come from?" Tzu-lu said, "From the K'ung family." "Is that the K'ung who keeps working towards a goal the realization of which he knows to be hopeless?"

43. Yüan Jang sat waiting with his legs spread wide. The Master said, "To be neither modest nor deferential when young, to have passed on nothing worthwhile when grown up, and to refuse to die when old, that is what I call a pest." So saying, the Master tapped him on the shin with his stick.

BOOK XV

3. The Master said, "Ssu, do you think that I am the kind of man who learns widely and retains what he has learned in his mind?"

"Yes, I do. Is it not so?"

"No. I have a single thread binding it all together."

5. The Master said, "If there was a ruler who achieved order without taking any action, it was, perhaps, Shun. There was nothing for him to do but to hold himself in a respectful posture and to face due south."[9]

7. The Master said, "How straight Shih Yü is! When the Way prevails in the state he is as straight as an arrow, yet when the Way falls into disuse in the state he is still as straight as an arrow.

"How gentlemanly Ch'ü Po-yü is! When the Way prevails in the state he takes office, but when the Way falls into disuse in the state he allows himself to be furled and put away safely."

31. The Master said, "I once spent all day thinking without taking food and all night thinking without going to bed, but I found that I gained nothing from it. It would have been better for me to have spent the time in learning.

BOOK XVII

4. The Master went to Wu Ch'eng. There he heard the sound of stringed instruments and singing. The Master broke into a smile and said, "Surely you don't need to use an ox-knife to kill a chicken."

9. The direction the emperor's seat faces.

Tzu-yu answered, "Some time ago I heard it from you, Master, that the gentleman instructed in the Way loves his fellow men and that the small man instructed in the Way is easy to command."

The Master said, "My friends, what Yen says is right. My remark a moment ago was only made in jest."

9. The Master said, "Why is it none of you, my young friends, study the *Odes*? An apt quotation from the *Odes* may serve to stimulate the imagination, to show one's breeding, to smooth over difficulties in a group and to give expression to complaints.

"Inside the family there is the serving of one's father; outside, there is the serving of one's lord; there is also the acquiring of a wide knowledge of the names of birds and beasts, plants and trees."

BOOK XVIII

5. Chieh Yü, the Madman of Ch'u, went past Confucius, singing,

Phoenix, oh phoenix!
How thy virtue has declined!
What is past is beyond help,
What is to come is not yet lost.
Give up, give up!
Perilous is the lot of those in office today.

Confucius got down from his carriage with the intention of speaking with him, but the Madman avoided him by hurrying off, and in the end Confucius was unable to speak with him.

6. Ch'ang Chü and Chieh Ni were ploughing together yoked as a team. Confucius went past them and sent Tzu-lu to ask them where the ford was. Ch'ang Chü said, "Who is that taking charge of the carriage?" Tzu-lu said, "It is K'ung Ch'iu." "Then, he must be the K'ung Ch'iu of Lu." "He is." "Then, he doesn't have to ask where the ford is."

Tzu-lu asked Chieh Ni. Chieh Ni said, "Who are you?" "I am Chung Yu." "Then, you must be the disciple of K'ung Ch'iu of Lu?" Tzu-lu answered, "I am." "Throughout the Empire men are all the same. Who is there for you to change places with? Moreoever, for your own sake, would it not be better if, instead of following a Gentleman who keeps running away from men, you followed one who runs away from the world altogether?" All this while he carried on harrowing without interruption.

Tzu-lu went and reported what was said to Confucius.

The Master was lost in thought for a while and said, "One cannot associate with birds and beasts. Am I not a member of this human race? Who, then, is there for me to associate with? While the Way is to be found in the Empire, I will not change places with him."

CHUANG CHOU
ca. 369–286 B.C.

The period known as the Warring States, from 403 B.C. until the unification of China by the kingdom of Ch'in in 221 B.C., saw an intellectual diversity and vigor of philosophical debate unparalleled in later Chinese history. As the old Chou domains were gradually transforming themselves into contentious independent states, so the map of Chinese thought contained numerous schools and philosophical positions, and these also waged wars for hegemony. The relation between the political and philosophical maps was more than metaphorical; many of the philosophical schools dealt entirely or largely with political philosophy, and thinkers would travel from state to state, arguing with one another and competing for the patronage of princes.

There were, however, some philosophers who sought neither disciples nor patronage, who founded no school, and who were content to write. Such was the fourth-century philosopher Chuang Chou, to whom is attributed the first seven chapters of a work now called the *Chuang Tzu* (Master Chuang). Apart from the evidence of the *Chuang Tzu* itself, we know little about Chuang Chou as a historical person. Yet the first chapters of the *Chuang Tzu* show a remarkable mind at work.

The *Chuang Tzu* is often linked with the *Lao Tzu* as constituting the two primary texts of philosophical Taoism. The two works are quite different, both in style of writing and in style of thought. The *Lao Tzu* is largely in verse and repeats its pithy paradoxes over and over again. The *Chuang Tzu* is in a prose of constantly changing styles, with embedded verse passages. It moves from wise jokes and funny parables to moments of passionate seriousness, to tight philosophical arguments that turn imperceptibly into parodies of tight philosophical arguments. The structure of the first seven chapters is intricate: what seems at first to be a discontinuous series of parables gradually reveals itself as an echoing interplay of themes, sometimes taking the train of thought off in another direction, sometimes standing an earlier argument on its head.

Chuang Chou uses rapid shifts in scale and perspective to remind his readers that proportions, like values, are relative to a particular viewpoint. In Chapter 1, *Free and Easy Wandering,* he begins with a monstrous sea creature, whose name is K'un (Fish Eggs). The K'un is transformed into the P'eng bird, which is so large that its wings hang over the sky to both horizons. The P'eng flies so high that when it looks down all it sees is blue. All of a sudden the passage shifts to a hollow in a floor that, if filled with water, floats scraps. On a tiny scale this becomes the analogy of the huge P'eng requiring an amplitude of air to bear up its mighty wings. In dizzying sequence Chuang Chou constantly shifts scales, exercising the reader's imagination to break down his or her habitual perspective, which is based on human magnitude.

As he shifts physical perspective, Chuang Chou also shifts his own standpoint, undermining the authority of what he has previously written. Readers are often uncertain whether he is serious or putting them on, or serious in his putting them on. In Chapter 2 he moves into a logical argument on the relativity of the concepts "this" and "that" as well as "right" and "wrong." The argument is intricate and stylized, and at some point readers begin to suspect that they are reading the parody of an argument, a suspicion confirmed when Chuang Chou reaches his grand summation in a joke. But then readers realize that this was the only proper conclusion for an argument against the absolute validity of arguments.

In the present version of the *Chuang Tzu,* twenty-six additional chapters follow the first seven. These are a miscellaneous gathering of Taoist works and works from related schools. Although none can match the first seven chapters as unified wholes, they contain many smaller sections as good as anything found earlier. Here we find an endless parade of crazy sages, wise peasants, and craftsmen, with all the commonplaces of habitual authority and conventional morality held up for ridicule.

The *Chuang Tzu* is the most inventive and diverse writing in early China, yet throughout the book we find doubts about the capacity of language, and particularly of written language, to convey truth. We read of a duke reading; his wheelwright comes in and asks him what he is reading. When the duke says that he is reading the words of the sages, the wheelwright asks if they are dead. And when the duke says that they are indeed, the wheelwright tells him that he is reading only the "chaff and dregs," that what they really knew could not be passed on by words. Yet the *Chuang Tzu* rarely loses sight of the fact that it too is words, and it solves the problem by laughing at itself, stepping out from behind its own statements with a wink. This happens in the following famous passage from the later chapters, put in the mouth of Chuang Chou:

> The fish trap exists because of the fish; once you've gotten the fish, you can forget the trap. The rabbit snare exists because of the rabbit; once you've gotten the rabbit, you can forget the snare. Words exist because of the meaning; once you've gotten the meaning, you can forget the words. Where can I find a man who has forgotten the words so I can have a word with him?

The term *Tao* ("Way") was used by the Confucians and other thinkers as well as by the Taoists. The Way is simply the natural course of things. For the Confucians the Way is moral and potentially to be realized within society; in the *Chuang Tzu* the Way is amoral and escapes conventional human categories. Oppositions such as "up and down," "right and wrong," "this and that" all presume a limited perspective from which such distinctions can occur. The Way, in contrast, is everywhere and has no perspective whatsoever. Knowing that the words used to speak of such a Way are precisely the categories he is trying to get beyond, Chuang Chou can only use language against itself.

For another translation of the *Chuang Tzu* by one of the most distinguished scholars of Chinese philosophy, see A. C. Graham, *Chuang Tzu: The Inner Chapters* (1981). Graham also includes an excellent discussion of the *Chuang Tzu* in the context of other early thinkers in *Disputers of the Tao: Philosophical Argument in Ancient China* (1989).

PRONOUNCING GLOSSARY

The following list uses common English syllables to provide rough equivalents of selected words whose pronunciation may be unfamiliar to the general reader.

Chang Jo: *jahng roh*
Chang Wu-tzu: *jang woo–dzuh*
Ch'ang Yü: *chahng yoo*
Chao: *jow*
Ch'i: *chee*
Chieh Yü: *jyeh yoo*
Chien Wu: *jyen woo*
Ch'in Shih: *chin sherr*
Ching-shou: *jing–shoh*
Chuang Chou: *jwahng joh*
Chuang Tzu: *jwahng dzuh*
Chü Ch'üeh-tzu: *joo choo-eh–dzuh*
Hsiang-ch'eng: *shyahng–chuhng*
Hsi P'eng: *shee puhng*
Hsi-shih: *shee–sher*
Hsüan: *shwen*
Hsü Yu: *shoo yoh*
Huang-tzu Kao-ao: *hwahng–dzuh gow–ow*
Hui Tzu: *hway dzuh*
Kang-hsiang: *gahng–shyahng*
Kuan Chung: *gwan jong*
Kuei-lung: *gway–long*
K'ung Ch'iu: *kong chyoh*
Ku-she: *goo–shuh*
Lieh Tzu: *lyeh dzuh*

Lieh Yü-k'ou: *lyeh yoo–koh*
Mao-ch'iang: *mow–jyahng*
Meng-tzu Fan: *muhng–dzuh fahn*
Nieh Ch'üeh: *nyeh choo-eh*
P'ang-huang: *pahng–hwahng*
Pei-a: *bay–ah*
P'eng-tsu: *puhng–dzuh*
Sung Jung-tzu: *song rong–dzuh*
T'ang: *tahng*
Ting: *ding*
Tung-kuo: *dong–gwoh*
Tzu-ch'i: *dzuh–chee*
Tzu-kung: *dzuh–goong*
Wei-t'o: *way–twoh*
Wen-hui: *wen–hway*
Yang Tzu: *yahng dzuh*
Yüan-ch'u: *yoo-en–choo*

Chuang Tzu[1]

CHAPTER 1

Free and Easy Wandering

In the northern darkness there is a fish and his name is K'un.[2] The K'un is so huge I don't know how many thousand li[3] he measures. He changes and becomes a bird whose name is P'eng. The back of the P'eng measures I don't know how many thousand li across and, when he rises up and flies off, his wings are like clouds all over the sky. When the sea begins to move, this bird sets off for the southern darkness, which is the Lake of Heaven.

The *Universal Harmony*[4] records various wonders, and it says: "When the P'eng journeys to the southern darkness, the waters are roiled for three thousand li. He beats the whirlwind and rises ninety thousand li, setting off on the sixth-month gale." Wavering heat, bits of dust, living things blowing each other about—the sky looks very blue. Is that its real color, or is it because it is so far away and has no end? When the bird looks down, all he sees is blue too.

If water is not piled up deep enough, it won't have the strength to bear up a big boat. Pour a cup of water into a hollow in the floor and bits of trash will sail on it like boats. But set the cup there and it will stick fast, for the water is too shallow and the boat too large. If wind is not piled up deep enough, it won't have the strength to bear up great wings. Therefore when the P'eng rises ninety thousand li, he must have the wind under him like that. Only then can he mount on the back of the wind, shoulder the blue sky, and nothing can hinder or block him. Only then can he set his eyes to the south.

The cicada and the little dove laugh at this, saying, "When we make an effort and fly up, we can get as far as the elm or the sapanwood tree, but

1. Translated by Burton Watson. 2. *K'un* means fish roe. So Chuang Tzu begins with a paradox—the tiniest fish imaginable is also the largest fish imaginable [Translator's note]. 3. A unit of distance; in this period it was about 405 meters, or roughly a quarter of a mile. 4. Identified variously as the name of a man or the name of a book. Probably Chuang Tzu intended it as the latter, and is poking fun at the philosophers of other schools who cite ancient texts to prove their assertions [Translator's note].

sometimes we don't make it and just fall down on the ground. Now how is anyone going to go ninety thousand li to the south!"

If you go off to the green woods nearby, you can take along food for three meals and come back with your stomach as full as ever. If you are going a hundred li, you must grind your grain the night before; and if you are going a thousand li, you must start getting the provisions together three months in advance. What do these two creatures understand? Little understanding cannot come up to great understanding; the short-lived cannot come up to the long-lived.

How do I know this is so? The morning mushroom knows nothing of twilight and dawn; the summer cicada knows nothing of spring and autumn. They are the short-lived. South of Ch'u there is a caterpillar which counts five hundred years as one spring and five hundred years as one autumn. Long, long ago there was a great rose of Sharon that counted eight thousand years as one spring and eight thousand years as one autumn. They are the long-lived. Yet P'eng-tsu alone is famous today for having lived a long time, and everybody tries to ape him. Isn't it pitiful!

Among the questions of T'ang to Ch'i we find the same thing. In the bald and barren north, there is a dark sea, the Lake of Heaven. In it is a fish which is several thousand li across, and no one knows how long. His name is K'un. There is also a bird there, named P'eng, with a back like Mount T'ai and wings like clouds filling the sky. He beats the whirlwind, leaps into the air, and rises up ninety thousand li, cutting through the clouds and mist, shouldering the blue sky, and then he turns his eyes south and prepares to journey to the southern darkness.

The little quail laughs at him, saying, "Where does he think *he's* going? I give a great leap and fly up, but I never get more than ten or twelve yards before I come down fluttering among the weeds and brambles. And that's the best kind of flying anyway! Where does he think *he's* going?" Such is the difference between big and little.

Therefore a man who has wisdom enough to fill one office effectively, good conduct enough to impress one community, virtue enough to please one ruler, or talent enough to be called into service in one state, has the same kind of self-pride as these little creatures. Sung Jung-tzu[5] would certainly burst out laughing at such a man. The whole world could praise Sung Jung-tzu and it wouldn't make him exert himself; the whole world could condemn him and it wouldn't make him mope. He drew a clear line between the internal and the external, and recognized the boundaries of true glory and disgrace. But that was all. As far as the world went, he didn't fret and worry, but there was still ground he left unturned.

Lieh Tzu[6] could ride the wind and go soaring around with cool and breezy skill, but after fifteen days he came back to earth. As far as the search for good fortune went, he didn't fret and worry. He escaped the trouble of walking, but he still had to depend on something to get around. If he had only

5. Referred to elsewhere in the literature of the period as Sung Chien or Sung K'eng. . . . He taught a doctrine of social harmony, frugality, pacifism, and the rejection of conventional standards of honor and disgrace [Translator's note]. 6. A work attributed to Leih Yü-K'ou, a Taoist philosopher who appears frequently in the *Chuang Tzu*. It is of uncertain date and did not reach its present form until the 3rd or 4th century A.D. [adapted from Translator's note].

mounted on the truth of Heaven and Earth, ridden the changes of the six breaths, and thus wandered through the boundless, then what would he have had to depend on?

Therefore I say, the Perfect Man has no self; the Holy Man has no merit; the Sage has no fame.

Yao wanted to cede the empire to Hsü Yu.[7] "When the sun and moon have already come out," he said, "it's a waste of light to go on burning the torches, isn't it? When the seasonal rains are falling, it's a waste of water to go on irrigating the fields. If you took the throne, the world would be well ordered. I go on occupying it, but all I can see are my failings. I beg to turn over the world to you."

Hsü Yu said, "You govern the world and the world is already well governed. Now if I take your place, will I be doing it for a name? But name is only the guest of reality—will I be doing it so I can play the part of a guest? When the tailor-bird builds her nest in the deep wood, she uses no more than one branch. When the mole drinks at the river, he takes no more than a bellyful. Go home and forget the matter, my lord. I have no use for the rulership of the world! Though the cook may not run his kitchen properly, the priest and the impersonator of the dead at the sacrifice do not leap over the wine casks and sacrificial stands and go take his place."

Chien Wu said to Lien Shu, "I was listening to Chieh Yü's talk—big and nothing to back it up, going on and on without turning around. I was completely dumfounded at his words—no more end than the Milky Way, wild and wide of the mark, never coming near human affairs!"

"What were his words like?" asked Lien Shu.

"He said that there is a Holy Man living on faraway Ku-she Mountain, with skin like ice or snow, and gentle and shy like a young girl. He doesn't eat the five grains, but sucks the wind, drinks the dew, climbs up on the clouds and mist, rides a flying dragon, and wanders beyond the four seas. By concentrating his spirit, he can protect creatures from sickness and plague and make the harvest plentiful. I thought this was all insane and refused to believe it."

"You would!" said Lien Shu. "We can't expect a blind man to appreciate beautiful patterns or a deaf man to listen to bells and drums. And blindness and deafness are not confined to the body alone—the understanding has them too, as your words just now have shown. This man, with this virtue of his, is about to embrace the ten thousand things and roll them into one. Though the age calls for reform, why should he wear himself out over the affairs of the world? There is nothing that can harm this man. Though flood waters pile up to the sky, he will not drown. Though a great drought melts metal and stone and scorches the earth and hills, he will not be burned. From his dust and leavings alone you could mold a Yao or a Shun![8] Why should he consent to bother about mere things?"

A man of Sung who sold ceremonial hats made a trip to Yüeh, but the Yüeh people cut their hair short and tattoo their bodies and had no use for

7. A famous hermit. Yao was a legendary sage-king of great antiquity. 8. Another legendary sage-king of great antiquity.

such things. Yao brought order to the people of the world and directed the government of all within the seas. But he went to see the Four Masters of the faraway Ku-she Mountain, [and when he got home] north of the Fen River, he was dazed and had forgotten his kingdom there.

Hui Tzu[9] said to Chuang Tzu, "The king of Wei gave me some seeds of a huge gourd. I planted them, and when they grew up, the fruit was big enough to hold five piculs.[1] I tried using it for a water container, but it was so heavy I couldn't lift it. I split it in half to make dippers, but they were so large and unwieldly that I couldn't dip them into anything. It's not that the gourds weren't fantastically big—but I decided they were no use and so I smashed them to pieces."

Chuang Tzu said, "You certainly are dense when it comes to using big things! In Sung there was a man who was skilled at making a salve to prevent chapped hands, and generation after generation his family made a living by bleaching silk in water. A traveler heard about the salve and offered to buy the prescription for a hundred measures of gold. The man called everyone to a family council. 'For generations we've been bleaching silk and we've never made more than a few measures of gold,' he said. 'Now, if we sell our secret, we can make a hundred measures in one morning. Let's let him have it!' The traveler got the salve and introduced it to the king of Wu, who was having trouble with the state of Yüeh. The king put the man in charge of his troops, and that winter they fought a naval battle with the men of Yüeh and gave them a bad beating.[2] A portion of the conquered territory was awarded to the man as a fief. The salve had the power to prevent chapped hands in either case; but one man used it to get a fief, while the other one never got beyond silk bleaching—because they used it in different ways. Now you had a gourd big enough to hold five piculs. Why didn't you think of making it into a great tub so you could go floating around the rivers and lakes, instead of worrying because it was too big and unwieldly to dip into things! Obviously you still have a lot of underbrush in your head!"

Hui Tzu said to Chuang Tzu, "I have a big tree of the kind men call *shu*. Its trunk is too gnarled and bumpy to apply a measuring line to, its branches too bent and twisty to match up to a compass or square. You could stand it by the road and no carpenter would look at it twice. Your words, too, are big and useless, and so everyone alike spurns them!"

Chuang Tzu said, "Maybe you've never seen a wildcat or a weasel. It crouches down and hides, watching for something to come along. It leaps and races east and west, not hesitating to go high or low—until it falls into the trap and dies in the net. Then again there's the yak, big as a cloud covering the sky. It certainly knows how to be big, though it doesn't know how to catch rats. Now you have this big tree and you're distressed because it's useless. Why don't you plant it in Not-Even-Anything Village, or the field of Broad-and-Boundless, relax and do nothing by its side, or lie down for a free and easy sleep under it? Axes will never shorten its life, nothing can ever harm it. If there's no use for it, how can it come to grief or pain?"

9. A famous logician, who often appears as an interlocutor in dialogues with Chuang Chou. 1. A measure of volume. 2. Because the salve, by preventing the soldiers' hands from chapping, made it easier for them to handle their weapons [Translator's note].

CHAPTER 2

Discussion on Making All Things Equal

Tzu-ch'i of south wall sat leaning on his armrest, staring up at the sky and breathing—vacant and far away, as though he'd lost his companion.[3] Yen Ch'eng Tzu-yu, who was standing by his side in attendance, said, "What is this? Can you really make the body like a withered tree and the mind like dead ashes? The man leaning on the armrest now is not the one who leaned on it before!"

Tzu-ch'i said, "You do well to ask the question, Yen. Now I have lost myself. Do you understand that? You hear the piping of men, but you haven't heard the piping of earth. Or if you've heard the piping of earth, you haven't heard the piping of Heaven!"

Tzu-yu said, "May I venture to ask what this means?"

Tzu-ch'i said, "The Great Clod[4] belches out breath and its name is wind. So long as it doesn't come forth, nothing happens. But when it does, then ten thousand hollows begin crying wildly. Can't you hear them, long drawn out? In the mountain forests that lash and sway, there are huge trees a hundred spans around with hollows and openings like noses, like mouths, like ears, like jugs, like cups, like mortars, like rifts, like ruts. They roar like waves, whistle like arrows, screech, gasp, cry, wail, moan, and howl, those in the lead calling out *yeee!*, those behind calling out *yuuu!* In a gentle breeze they answer faintly, but in a full gale the chorus is gigantic. And when the fierce wind has passed on, then all the hollows are empty again. Have you never seen the tossing and trembling that goes on?"

Tzu-yu said, "By the piping of earth, then, you mean simply [the sound of] these hollows, and by the piping of man [the sound of] flutes and whistles. But may I ask about the piping of Heaven?"

Tzu-ch'i said, "Blowing on the ten thousand things in a different way, so that each can be itself—all take what they want for themselves, but who does the sounding?"

Great understanding is broad and unhurried; little understanding is cramped and busy. Great words are clear and limpid; little words are shrill and quarrelsome. In sleep, men's spirits go visiting; in waking hours, their bodies hustle. With everything they meet they become entangled. Day after day they use their minds in strife, sometimes grandiose, sometimes sly, sometimes petty. Their little fears are mean and trembly; their great fears are stunned and overwhelming. They bound off like an arrow or a crossbow pellet, certain that they are the arbiters of right and wrong. They cling to their position as though they had sworn before the gods, sure that they are holding on to victory. They fade like fall and winter—such is the way they dwindle day by day. They drown in what they do—you cannot make them turn back. They grow dark, as though sealed with seals—such are the excesses of their old age. And when their minds draw near to death, nothing can restore them to the light.

Joy, anger, grief, delight, worry, regret, fickleness, inflexibility, modesty, willfulness, candor, insolence—music from empty holes, mushrooms

3. The word "companion" is interpreted variously to mean his associates, his wife, or his own body [Translator's note]. 4. The earth

springing up in dampness, day and night replacing each other before us, and no one knows where they sprout from. Let it be! Let it be! [It is enough that] morning and evening we have them, and they are the means by which we live. Without them we would not exist; without us they would have nothing to take hold of. This comes close to the matter. But I do not know what makes them the way they are. It would seem as though they have some True Master, and yet I find no trace of him. He can act—that is certain. Yet I cannot see his form. He has identity but no form.

The hundred joints, the nine openings, the six organs, all come together and exist here [as my body]. But which part should I feel closest to? I should delight in all parts, you say? But there must be one I ought to favor more. If not, are they all of them mere servants? But if they are all servants, then how can they keep order among themselves? Or do they take turns being lord and servant? It would seem as though there must be some True Lord among them. But whether I succeed in discovering his identity or not, it neither adds to nor detracts from his Truth.

Once a man receives this fixed bodily form, he holds on to it, waiting for the end. Sometimes clashing with things, sometimes bending before them, he runs his course like a galloping steed, and nothing can stop him. Is he not pathetic? Sweating and laboring to the end of his days and never seeing his accomplishment, utterly exhausting himself and never knowing where to look for rest—can you help pitying him? I'm not dead yet! he says, but what good is that? His body decays, his mind follows it—can you deny that this is a great sorrow? Man's life has always been a muddle like this. How could I be the only muddled one, and other men not muddled?

If a man follows the mind given him and makes it his teacher, then who can be without a teacher? Why must you comprehend the process of change and form your mind on that basis before you can have a teacher? Even an idiot has his teacher. But to fail to abide by this mind and still insist upon your rights and wrongs—this is like saying that you set off for Yüeh today and got there yesterday.[5] This is to claim that what doesn't exist exists. If you claim that what doesn't exist exists, then even the holy sage Yü couldn't understand you, much less a person like me!

Words are not just wind. Words have something to say. But if what they have to say is not fixed, then do they really say something? Or do they say nothing? People suppose that words are different from the peeps of baby birds, but is there any difference, or isn't there? What does the Way rely upon, that we have true and false? What do words rely upon, that we have right and wrong? How can the Way go away and not exist? How can words exist and not be acceptable? When the Way relies on little accomplishments and words rely on vain show, then we have the rights and wrongs of the Confucians and the Mo-ists.[6] What one calls right the other calls wrong; what one calls wrong the other calls right. But if we want to right their wrongs and wrong their rights, then the best thing to use is clarity.

Everything has its "that," everything has its "this." From the point of view of "that" you cannot see it, but through understanding you can know it. So I say, "that" comes out of "this" and "this" depends on "that"—which is to

5. This was one of the paradoxes of the logician Hui Tzu [Translator's note]. 6. Followers of a utilitarian philosophical school who opposed the traditional ceremonies that the Confucians saw as essential to a good society.

say that "this" and "that" give birth to each other. But where there is birth there must be death; where there is death there must be birth. Where there is acceptability there must be unacceptability; where there is unacceptability there must be acceptability. Where there is recognition of right there must be recognition of wrong; where there is recognition of wrong there must be recognition of right. Therefore the sage does not proceed in such a way, but illuminates all in the light of Heaven.[7] He too recognizes a "this," but a "this" which is also "that," a "that" which is also "this." His "that" has both a right and a wrong in it; his "this" too has both a right and a wrong in it. So, in fact, does he still have a "this" and "that"? Or does he in fact no longer have a "this" and "that"? A state in which "this" and "that" no longer find their opposites is called the hinge of the Way. When the hinge is fitted into the socket, it can respond endlessly. Its right then is a single endlessness and its wrong too is a single endlessness. So, I say, the best thing to use is clarity.

To use an attribute to show that attributes are not attributes is not as good as using a nonattribute to show that attributes are not attributes. To use a horse to show that a horse is not a horse is not as good as using a non-horse to show that a horse is not a horse,[8] Heaven and earth are one attribute; the ten thousand things are one horse.

What is acceptable we call acceptable; what is unacceptable we call unacceptable. A road is made by people walking on it; things are so because they are called so. What makes them so? Making them so makes them so. What makes them not so? Making them not so makes them not so. Things all must have that which is so; things all must have that which is acceptable. There is nothing that is not so, nothing that is not acceptable.

For this reason, whether you point to a little stalk or a great pillar, a leper or the beautiful Hsi-shih, things ribald and shady or things grotesque and strange, the Way makes them all into one. Their dividedness is their completeness; their completeness is their impairment. No thing is either complete or impaired, but all are made into one again. Only the man of far-reaching vision knows how to make them into one. So he has no use [for categories], but relegates all to the constant. The constant is the useful; the useful is the passable; the passable is the successful; and with success, all is accomplished. He relies upon this alone, relies upon it and does not know he is doing so. This is called the Way.

But to wear out your brain trying to make things into one without realizing that they are all the same—this is called "three in the morning." What do I mean by "three in the morning"? When the monkey trainer was handing out acorns, he said, "You get three in the morning and four at night." This made all the monkeys furious. "Well, then," he said, "you get four in the morning and three at night." The monkeys were all delighted. There was no change in the reality behind the words, and yet the monkeys responded with joy and anger. Let them, if they want to. So the sage harmonizes with both right and wrong and rests in Heaven the Equalizer. This is called walking two roads.

The understanding of the men of ancient times went a long way. How far did it go? To the point where some of them believed that things have never existed—so far, to the end, where nothing can be added. Those at the next

7. Nature or the Way. 8. A reference to the statements of the logician Kung-sun Lung, "A white horse is not a horse" and "Attributes are not attributes in and of themselves" [Translator's note].

stage thought that things exist but recognized no boundaries among them. Those at the next stage thought there were boundaries but recognized no right and wrong. Because right and wrong appeared, the Way was injured, and because the Way was injured, love became complete. But do such things as completion and injury really exist, or do they not?

There is such a thing as completion and injury—Mr. Chao playing the lute is an example. There is such a thing as no completion and no injury—Mr. Chao not playing the lute is an example.[9] Chao Wen played the lute; Music Master K'uang waved his baton; Hui Tzu leaned on his desk. The knowledge of these three was close to perfection. All were masters, and therefore their names have been handed down to later ages. Only in their likes they were different from him [the true sage]. What they liked, they tried to make clear. What he is not clear about, they tried to make clear, and so they ended in the foolishness of "hard" and "white."[1] Their sons, too, devoted all their lives to their fathers' theories, but till their death never reached any completion. Can these men be said to have attained completion? If so, then so have all the rest of us. Or can they not be said to have attained completion? If so, then neither we nor anything else have ever attained it.

The torch of chaos and doubt—this is what the sage steers by. So he does not use things but relegates all to the constant. This is what it means to use clarity.

Now I am going to make a statement here. I don't know whether it fits into the category of other people's statements or not. But whether it fits into their category or whether it doesn't, it obviously fits into some category. So in that respect it is no different from their statements. However, let me try making my statement.

There is a beginning. There is not yet beginning to be a beginning. There is a not yet beginning to be a not yet beginning to be a beginning. There is being. There is nonbeing. There is a not yet beginning to be nonbeing. There is a not yet beginning to be a not yet beginning to be nonbeing. Suddenly there is nonbeing. But I do not know, when it comes to nonbeing, which is really being and which is nonbeing. Now I have just said something. But I don't know whether what I have said has really said something or whether it hasn't said something.

There is nothing in the world bigger than the tip of an autumn hair,[2] and Mount T'ai is tiny. No one has lived longer than a dead child, and P'eng-tsu died young. Heaven and earth were born at the same time I was, and the ten thousand things are one with me.

We have already become one, so how can I say anything? But I have just *said* that we are one, so how can I not be saying something? The one and what I said about it make two, and two and the original one make three. If we go on this way, then even the cleverest mathematician can't tell where

9. Chao Wen was a famous lute (*ch'in*) player. But the best music he could play (i.e., complete) was only a pale and partial reflection of the ideal music, which was thereby injured and impaired, just as the unity of the Way was injured by the appearance of love—i.e., man's likes and dislikes. Hence, when Mr. Chao refrained from playing the lute, there was neither completion nor injury [Translator's note]. 1. The logicians Hui Tzu and Kung-sun Lung spent much time discussing the relationship between attributes such as "hard" and "white" and the thing to which they pertain [Translator's note]. 2. The strands of animal fur were believed to grow particularly fine in autumn; hence "the tip of an autumn hair" is a cliché for something extremely tiny [Translator's note].

we'll end, much less an ordinary man. If by moving from nonbeing to being we get to three, how far will we get if we move from being to being? Better not to move, but to let things be!

The Way has never known boundaries; speech has no constancy. But because of [the recognition of a] "this," there came to be boundaries. Let me tell you what the boundaries are. There is left, there is right, there are theories, there are debates, there are divisions, there are discriminations, there are emulations, and there are contentions. These are called the Eight Virtues. As to what is beyond the Six Realms,[3] the sage admits its existence but does not theorize. As to what is within the Six Realms, he theorizes but does not debate. In the case of the *Spring and Autumn*,[4] the record of the former kings of past ages, the sage debates but does not discriminate. So [I say,] those who divide fail to divide; those who discriminate fail to discriminate. What does this mean, you ask? The sage embraces things. Ordinary men discriminate among them and parade their discriminations before others. So I say, those who discriminate fail to see.

The Great Way is not named; Great Discriminations are not spoken; Great Benevolence is not benevolent; Great Modesty is not humble; Great Daring does not attack. If the Way is made clear, it is not the Way. If discriminations are put into words, they do not suffice. If benevolence has a constant object, it cannot be universal. If modesty is fastidious, it cannot be trusted. If daring attacks, it cannot be complete. These five are all round, but they tend toward the square.[5]

Therefore understanding that rests in what it does not understand is the finest. Who can understand discriminations that are not spoken, the Way that is not a way? If he can understand this, he may be called the Reservoir of Heaven. Pour into it and it is never full, dip from it and it never runs dry, and yet it does not know where the supply comes from. This is called the Shaded Light.

So it is that long ago Yao said to Shun, "I want to attack the rulers of Tsung, K'uai, and Hsü-ao. Even as I sit on my throne, this thought nags at me. Why is this?"

Shun replied, "These three rulers are only little dwellers in the weeds and brush. Why this nagging desire? Long ago, ten suns came out all at once and the ten thousand things were all lighted up. And how much greater is virtue than these suns!"[6]

Nieh Ch'üeh asked Wang Ni, "Do you know what all things agree in calling right?"

"How would I know that?" said Wang Ni.

"Do you know that you don't know it?"

"How would I know that?"

"Then do things know nothing?"

"How would I know that? However, suppose I try saying something. What way do I have of knowing that if I say I know something I don't really not know it? Or what way do I have of knowing that if I say I don't know some-

3. Heaven, earth, and the four directions, i.e., the universe [Translator's note]. 4. Perhaps a reference to the *Spring and Autumn Annals*, a history of the state of Lu said to have been compiled by Confucius. But it may be a generic term referring to the chronicles of the various feudal states [Translator's note]. 5. All are originally perfect, but may become "squared," i.e., impaired by the misuses mentioned [Translator's note]. 6. Here virtue is to be understood in a good sense, as the power of the Way [Translator's note].

thing I don't really in fact know it? Now let me ask *you* some questions. If a man sleeps in a damp place, his back aches and he ends up half paralyzed, but is this true of a loach? If he lives in a tree, he is terrified and shakes with fright, but is this true of a monkey? Of these three creatures, then, which one knows the proper place to live? Men eat the flesh of grass-fed and grain-fed animals, deer eat grass, centipedes find snakes tasty, and hawks and falcons relish mice. Of these four, which knows how food ought to taste? Monkeys pair with monkeys, deer go out with deer, and fish play around with fish. Men claim that Mao-ch'iang and Lady Li were beautiful, but if fish saw them they would dive to the bottom of the stream, if birds saw them they would fly away, and if deer saw them they would break into a run. Of these four, which knows how to fix the standard of beauty for the world? The way I see it, the rules of benevolence and righteousness and the paths of right and wrong are all hopelessly snarled and jumbled. How could I know anything about such discriminations?"

Nieh Ch'üeh said, "If you don't know what is profitable or harmful, then does the Perfect Man likewise know nothing of such things?"

Wang Ni replied, "The Perfect Man is godlike. Though the great swamps blaze, they cannot burn him; though the great rivers freeze, they cannot chill him; though swift lightning splits the hills and howling gales shake the sea, they cannot frighten him. A man like this rides the clouds and mist, straddles the sun and moon, and wanders beyond the four seas. Even life and death have no effect on him, much less the rules of profit and loss!"

Chü Ch'üeh-tzu said to Chang Wu-tzu, "I have heard Confucius say that the sage does not work at anything, does not pursue profit, does not dodge harm, does not enjoy being sought after, does not follow the Way, says nothing yet says something, says something yet says nothing, and wanders beyond the dust and grime. Confucius himself regarded these as wild and flippant words, though I believe they describe the working of the mysterious Way. What do you think of them?"

Chang Wu-tzu said, "Even the Yellow Emperor would be confused if he heard such words, so how could you expect Confucius to understand them? What's more, you're too hasty in your own appraisal. You see an egg and demand a crowing cock, see a crossbow pellet and demand a roast dove. I'm going to try speaking some reckless words and I want you to listen to them recklessly. How will that be? The sage leans on the sun and moon, tucks the universe under his arm, merges himself with things, leaves the confusion and muddle as it is, and looks on slaves as exalted. Ordinary men strain and struggle; the sage is stupid and blockish. He takes part in ten thousand ages and achieves simplicity in oneness. For him, all the ten thousand things are what they are, and thus they enfold each other.

"How do I know that loving life is not a delusion? How do I know that in hating death I am not like a man who, having left home in his youth, has forgotten the way back?

"Lady Li was the daughter of the border guard of Ai.[7] When she was first taken captive and brought to the state of Chin, she wept until her tears

7. She was taken captive by Duke Hsien of Chin in 671 B.C., and later became his consort [Translator's note].

drenched the collar of her robe. But later, when she went to live in the palace of the ruler, shared his couch with him, and ate the delicious meats of his table, she wondered why she had ever wept. How do I know that the dead do not wonder why they ever longed for life?

"He who dreams of drinking wine may weep when morning comes; he who dreams of weeping may in the morning go off to hunt. While he is dreaming he does not know it is a dream, and in his dream he may even try to interpret a dream. Only after he wakes does he know it was a dream. And someday there will be a great awakening when we know that this is all a great dream. Yet the stupid believe they are awake, busily and brightly assuming they understand things, calling this man ruler, that one herdsman—how dense! Confucius and you are both dreaming! And when I say you are dreaming, I am dreaming, too. Words like these will be labeled the Supreme Swindle. Yet, after ten thousand generations, a great sage may appear who will know their meaning, and it will still be as though he appeared with astonishing speed.

"Suppose you and I have had an argument. If you have beaten me instead of my beating you, then are you necessarily right and am I necessarily wrong? If I have beaten you instead of your beating me, then am I necessarily right and are you necessarily wrong? Is one of us right and the other wrong? Are both of us right or are both of us wrong? If you and I don't know the answer, then other people are bound to be even more in the dark. Whom shall we get to decide what is right? Shall we get someone who agrees with you to decide? But if he already agrees with you, how can he decide fairly? Shall we get someone who agrees with me? But if he already agrees with me, how can he decide? Shall we get someone who disagrees with both of us? But if he already disagrees with both of us, how can he decide? Obviously, then, neither you nor I nor anyone else can decide for each other. Shall we wait for still another person?

"But waiting for one shifting voice [to pass judgment on] another is the same as waiting for none of them. Harmonize them all with the Heavenly Equality, leave them to their endless changes, and so live out your years. What do I mean by harmonizing them with the Heavenly Equality? Right is not right; so is not so. If right were really right, it would differ so clearly from not right that there would be no need for argument. If so were really so, it would differ so clearly from not so that there would be no need for argument. Forget the years; forget distinctions. Leap into the boundless and make it your home!"

Penumbra said to Shadow, "A little while ago you were walking and now you're standing still; a little while ago you were sitting and now you're standing up. Why this lack of independent action?"

Shadow said, "Do I have to wait for something before I can be like this? Does what I wait for also have to wait for something before it can be like this? Am I waiting for the scales of a snake or the wings of a cicada? How do I know why it is so? How do I know why it isn't so?"

Once Chuang Chou dreamt he was a butterfly, a butterfly flitting and fluttering around, happy with himself and doing as he pleased. He didn't know he was Chuang Chou. Suddenly he woke up and there he was, solid and unmistakable Chuang Chou. But he didn't know if he was Chuang Chou who had dreamt he was a butterfly, or a butterfly dreaming he was Chuang Chou. Between Chuang Chou and a butterfly there must be *some* distinction! This is called the Transformation of Things.

CHAPTER 3

The Secret of Caring for Life

Your life has a limit but knowledge has none. If you use what is limited to pursue what has no limit, you will be in danger. If you understand this and still strive for knowledge, you will be in danger for certain! If you do good, stay away from fame. If you do evil, stay away from punishments. Follow the middle; go by what is constant, and you can stay in one piece, keep yourself alive, look after your parents, and live out your years.

Cook Ting was cutting up an ox for Lord Wen-hui. At every touch of his hand, every heave of his shoulder, every move of his feet, every thrust of his knee—zip! zoop! He slithered the knife along with a zing, and all was in perfect rhythm, as though he were performing the dance of the Mulberry Grove or keeping time to the Ching-shou music.[8]

"Ah, this is marvelous!" said Lord Wen-hui. "Imagine skill reaching such heights!"

Cook Ting laid down his knife and replied, "What I care about is the Way, which goes beyond skill. When I first began cutting up oxen, all I could see was the ox itself. After three years I no longer saw the whole ox. And now—now I go at it by spirit and don't look with my eyes. Perception and understanding have come to a stop and spirit moves where it wants. I go along with the natural makeup, strike in the big hollows, guide the knife through the big openings, and follow things as they are. So I never touch the smallest ligament or tendon, much less a main joint.

"A good cook changes his knife once a year—because he cuts. A mediocre cook changes his knife once a month—because he hacks. I've had this knife of mine for nineteen years and I've cut up thousands of oxen with it, and yet the blade is as good as though it had just come from the grindstone. There are spaces between the joints, and the blade of the knife has really no thickness. If you insert what has no thickness into such spaces, then there's plenty of room—more than enough for the blade to play about it. That's why after nineteen years the blade of my knife is still as good as when it first came from the grindstone.

"However, whenever I come to a complicated place, I size up the difficulties, tell myself to watch out and be careful, keep my eyes on what I'm doing, work very slowly, and move the knife with the greatest subtlety, until—flop! the whole thing comes apart like a clod of earth crumbling to the ground. I stand there holding the knife and look all around me, completely satisfied and reluctant to move on, and then I wipe off the knife and put it away."

"Excellent!" said Lord Wen-hui. "I have heard the words of Cook Ting and learned how to care for life!"

8. The Mulberry Grove is identified as a rain dance from the time of King T'ang of the Shang dynasty, and the Ching-shou music as part of a longer composition from the time of Yao [Translator's note].

When Kung-wen Hsüan saw the Commander of the Right,[9] he was startled and said, "What kind of man is this? How did he come to be footless? Was it Heaven? Or was it man?"

"It was Heaven, not man," said the commander. "When Heaven gave me life, it saw to it that I would be one-footed. Men's looks are given to them. So I know this was the work of Heaven and not of man. The swamp pheasant has to walk ten paces for one peck and a hundred paces for one drink, but it doesn't want to be kept in a cage. Though you treat it like a king, its spirit won't be content."

When Lao Tan[1] died, Ch'in Shih went to mourn for him; but after giving three cries, he left the room.

"Weren't you a friend of the Master?" asked Lao Tzu's disciples.

"Yes."

"And you think it's all right to mourn him this way?"

"Yes," said Ch'in Shih. "At first I took him for a real man, but now I know he wasn't. A little while ago, when I went in to mourn, I found old men weeping for him as though they were weeping for a son, and young men weeping for him as though they were weeping for a mother. To have gathered a group like *that,* he must have done something to make them talk about him, though he didn't ask them to talk, or make them weep for him, though he didn't ask them to weep. This is to hide from Heaven, turn your back on the true state of affairs, and forget what you were born with. In the old days this was called the crime of hiding from Heaven. Your master happened to come because it was his time, and he happened to leave because things follow along. If you are content with the time and willing to follow along, then grief and joy have no way to enter in. In the old days, this was called being freed from the bonds of God.

"Though the grease burns out of the torch, the fire passes on, and no one knows where it ends."

FROM CHAPTER 4

In the World of Men

Carpenter Shih went to Ch'i and, when he got to Crooked Shaft, he saw a serrate oak standing by the village shrine. It was broad enough to shelter several thousand oxen and measured a hundred spans around, towering above the hills. The lowest branches were eighty feet from the ground, and a dozen or so of them could have been made into boats. There were so many sightseers that the place looked like a fair, but the carpenter didn't even glance around and went on his way without stopping. His apprentice stood staring for a long time and then ran after Carpenter Shih and said, "Since I first took up my ax and followed you, Master, I have never seen timber as beautiful as this. But you don't even bother to look, and go right on without stopping. Why is that?"

"Forget it—say no more!" said the carpenter. "It's a worthless tree! Make

9. Probably the ex-Commander of the Right, as he has been punished by having one foot amputated, a common penalty in ancient China. It's mutilating punishments such as these which Chuang Tzu has in mind when he talks about the need to "stay in one piece" [Translator's note]. 1. Or Lao Tzu, a contemporary of Confucius and reputed author of the *Tao-te-ching*.

boats out of it and they'd sink; make coffins and they'd rot in no time; make vessels and they'd break at once. Use it for doors and it would sweat sap like pine; use it for posts and the worms would eat them up. It's not a timber tree—there's nothing it can be used for. That's how it got to be that old!"

After Carpenter Shih had returned home, the oak tree appeared to him in a dream and said, "What are you comparing me with? Are you comparing me with those useful trees? The cherry apple, the pear, the orange, the citron, the rest of those fructiferous trees and shrubs—as soon as their fruit is ripe, they are torn apart and subjected to abuse. Their big limbs are broken off, their little limbs are yanked around. Their utility makes life miserable for them, and so they don't get to finish out the years Heaven gave them, but are cut off in mid-journey. They bring it on themselves—the pulling and tearing of the common mob. And it's the same way with all other things.

"As for me, I've been trying a long time to be of no use, and though I almost died, I've finally got it. This is of great use to me. If I had been of some use, would I ever have grown this large? Moreover you and I are both of us things. What's the point of this—things condemning things? You, a worthless man about to die—how do you know I'm a worthless tree?"

When Carpenter Shih woke up, he reported his dream. His apprentice said, "If it's so intent on being of no use, what's it doing there at the village shrine?"[2]

"Shhh! Say no more! It's only *resting* there. If we carp and criticize, it will merely conclude that we don't understand it. Even if it weren't at the shrine, do you suppose it would be cut down? It protects itself in a different way from ordinary people. If you try to judge it by conventional standards, you'll be way off!"

* * *

There's Crippled Shu—chin stuck down in his navel, shoulders up above his head, pigtail pointing at the sky, his five organs on the top, his two thighs pressing his ribs. By sewing and washing, he gets enough to fill his mouth; by handling a winnow and sifting out the good grain, he makes enough to feed ten people. When the authorities call out the troops, he stands in the crowd waving good-by; when they get up a big work party, they pass him over because he's a chronic invalid. And when they are doling out grain to the ailing, he gets three big measures and ten bundles of firewood. With a crippled body, he's still able to look after himself and finish out the years Heaven gave him. How much better, then, if he had crippled virtue!

When Confucius visited Ch'u, Chieh Yü, the madman of Ch'u, wandered by his gate crying, "Phoenix, phoenix, how his virtue failed! The future you cannot wait for; the past you cannot pursue. When the world has the Way, the sage succeeds; when the world is without the Way, the sage survives. In times like the present, we do well to escape penalty. Good fortune is light as a feather, but nobody knows how to hold it up. Misfortune is heavy as the earth, but nobody knows how to stay out of its way. Leave off, leave off—this teaching men virtue! Dangerous, dangerous—to mark off the ground

2. The shrine, or altar of the soil, was always situated in a grove of beautiful trees. So the oak was serving a purpose by lending an air of sanctity to the spot [Translator's note].

and run! Fool, fool—don't spoil my walking! I walk a crooked way—don't step on my feet. The mountain trees do themselves harm; the grease in the torch burns itself up. The cinnamon can be eaten and so it gets cut down; the lacquer tree can be used and so it gets hacked apart. All men know the use of the useful, but nobody knows the use of the useless!"

FROM CHAPTER 6

The Great and Venerable Teacher

Master Ssu, Master Yü, Master Li, and Master Lai were all four talking together. "Who can look upon nonbeing as his head, on life as his back, and on death as his rump?" they said. "Who knows that life and death, existence and annihilation, are all a single body? I will be his friend!"

The four men looked at each other and smiled. There was no disagreement in their hearts and so the four of them became friends.

All at once Master Yü fell ill. Master Ssu went to ask how he was. "Amazing!" said Master Yü. "The Creator is making me all crookedly like this! My back sticks up like a hunchback and my vital organs are on top of me. My chin is hidden in my navel, my shoulders are up above my head, and my pigtail points at the sky. It must be some dislocation of the yin and yang!"[3]

Yet he seemed calm at heart and unconcerned. Dragging himself haltingly to the well, he looked at his reflection and said, "My, my! So the Creator is making me all crookedy like this!"

"Do you resent it?" asked Master Ssu.

"Why no, what would I resent? If the process continues, perhaps in time he'll transform my left arm into a rooster. In that case I'll keep watch on the night. Or perhaps in time he'll transform my right arm into a crossbow pellet and I'll shoot down an owl for roasting. Or perhaps in time he'll transform my buttocks into cartwheels. Then, with my spirit for a horse, I'll climb up and go for a ride. What need will I ever have for a carriage again?

"I received life because the time had come; I will lose it because the order of things passes on. Be content with this time and dwell in this order and then neither sorrow nor joy can touch you. In ancient times this was called the 'freeing of the bound.' There are those who cannot free themselves, because they are bound by things. But nothing can ever win against Heaven—that's the way it's always been. What would I have to resent?"

Suddenly Master Lai grew ill. Gasping and wheezing, he lay at the point of death. His wife and children gathered round in a circle and began to cry. Master Li, who had come to ask how he was, said, "Shoo! Get back! Don't disturb the process of change!"

Then he leaned against the doorway and talked to Master Lai. "How marvelous the Creator is! What is he going to make of you next? Where is he going to send you? Will he make you into a rat's liver? Will he make you into a bug's arm?"

Master Lai said, "A child, obeying his father and mother, goes wherever he is told, east or west, south or north. And the yin and yang—how much more are they to a man than father or mother! Now that they have brought

3. The female and male principles, respectively; darkness and light, the duality by which all things function. Medical disorders were often described as imbalances of the yin and yang.

me to the verge of death, if I should refuse to obey them, how perverse I would be! What fault is it of theirs? The Great Clod burdens me with form, labors me with life, eases me in old age, and rests me in death. So if I think well of my life, for the same reason I must think well of my death. When a skilled smith is casting metal, if the metal should leap up and say, 'I insist upon being made into a Mo-yeh!'[4] he would surely regard it as very inauspicious metal indeed. Now, having had the audacity to take on human form once, if I should say, 'I don't want to be anything but a man! Nothing but a man!', the Creator would surely regard me as a most inauspicious sort of person. So now I think of heaven and earth as a great furnace, and the Creator as a skilled smith. Where could he send me that would not be all right? I will go off to sleep peacefully, and then with a start I will wake up."

Master Sang-hu, Meng-tzu Fan, and Master Ch'in-chang, three friends, said to each other, "Who can join with others without joining with others? Who can do with others without doing with others? Who can climb up to heaven and wander in the mists, roam the infinite, and forget life forever and forever?" The three men looked at each other and smiled. There was no disagreement in their hearts and so they became friends.

After some time had passed without event, Master Sang-hu died. He had not yet been buried when Confucius, hearing of his death, sent Tzu-kung[5] to assist at the funeral. When Tzu-kung arrived, he found one of the dead man's friends weaving frames for silkworms, while the other strummed a lute. Joining their voices, they sang this song:

Ah, Sang-hu!
Ah, Sang-hu!
You have gone back to your true form
While we remain as men, O!

Tzu-kung hastened forward and said, "May I be so bold as to ask what sort of ceremony this is—singing in the very presence of the corpse?"

The two men looked at each other and laughed. "What does this man know of the meaning of ceremony?" they said.

Tzu-kung returned and reported to Confucius what had happened. "What sort of men are they anyway?" he asked. "They pay no attention to proper behavior, disregard their personal appearance and, without so much as changing the expression on their faces, sing in the very presence of the corpse! I can think of no name for them! What sort of men are they?"

"Such men as they," said Confucius, "wander beyond the realm; men like me wander within it. Beyond and within can never meet. It was stupid of me to send you to offer condolences. Even now they have joined with the Creator as men to wander in the single breath of heaven and earth. They look upon life as a swelling tumor, a protruding wen, and upon death as the draining of a sore or the bursting of a boil. To men such as these, how could there be any question of putting life first or death last? They borrow the forms of different creatures and house them in the same body. They forget liver and gall, cast aside ears and eyes, turning and revolving, ending and beginning again, unaware of where they start or finish. Idly they roam beyond the dust

4. A famous sword of King Ho-lü (ruled 514–496 B.C.) of Wu [Translator's note]. 5. One of Confucius's disciples.

and dirt; they wander free and easy in the service of inaction. Why should they fret and fuss about the ceremonies of the vulgar world and make a display for the ears and eyes of the common herd?"

Tzu-kung said, "Well then, Master, what is this 'realm' that you stick to?"

Confucius said, "I am one of those men punished by Heaven. Nevertheless, I will share with you what I have."

"Then may I ask about the realm?"[6] said Tzu-kung.

Confucius said, "Fish thrive in water, man thrives in the Way. For those that thrive in water, dig a pond and they will find nourishment enough. For those that thrive in the Way, don't bother about them and their lives will be secure. So it is said, the fish forget each other in the rivers and lakes, and men forget each other in the arts of the Way."

Tzu-kung said, "May I ask about the singular man?"

"The singular man is singular in comparison to other men, but a companion of Heaven. So it is said, the petty man of Heaven is a gentleman among men; the gentleman among men is the petty man of Heaven."

Yen Hui said to Confucius, "When Meng-sun Ts'ai's mother died, he wailed without shedding any tears, he did not grieve in his heart, and he conducted the funeral without any look of sorrow. He fell down on these three counts, and yet he is known all over the state of Lu for the excellent way he managed the funeral. Is it really possible to gain such a reputation when there are no facts to support it? I find it very peculiar indeed!"

Confucius said, "Meng-sun did all there was to do. He was advanced beyond ordinary understanding and he would have simplified things even more, but that wasn't practical. However, there is still a lot that he simplified. Meng-sun doesn't know why he lives and doesn't know why he dies. He doesn't know why he should go ahead; he doesn't know why he should fall behind. In the process of change, he has become a thing [among other things], and he is merely waiting for some other change that he doesn't yet know about. Moreover, when he is changing, how does he know that he is really changing? And when he is not changing, how does he know that he hasn't already changed? You and I, now—we are dreaming and haven't waked up yet. But in his case, though something may startle his body, it won't injure his mind; though something may alarm the house [his spirit lives in], his emotions will suffer no death. Meng-sun alone has waked up. Men wail and so he wails, too—that's the reason he acts like this.

"What's more, we go around telling each other, I do this, I do that—but how do we know that this 'I' we talk about has any 'I' to it? You dream you're a bird and soar up into the sky; you dream you're a fish and dive down in the pool. But now when you tell me about it, I don't know whether you are awake or whether you are dreaming. Running around accusing others is not as good as laughing, and enjoying a good laugh is not as good as going along with things. Be content to go along and forget about change and then you can enter the mysterious oneness of Heaven."

6. The word *fang,* which I have translated as "realm," may also mean "method" or "procedure," and Confucius's answer seems to stress this latter meaning [Translator's note].

FROM CHAPTER 7

Fit for Emperors and Kings

The emperor of the South Sea was called Shu [Brief], the emperor of the North Sea was called Hu [Sudden], and the emperor of the central region was called Hun-tun [Chaos]. Shu and Hu from time to time came together for a meeting in the territory of Hun-tun, and Hun-tun treated them very generously. Shu and Hu discussed how they could repay his kindness. "All men," they said, "have seven openings so they can see, hear, eat, and breathe. But Hun-tun alone doesn't have any. Let's trying boring him some!"

Every day they bored another hole, and on the seventh day Hun-tun died.

FROM CHAPTER 12

Heaven and Earth

Tzu-kung traveled south to Ch'u, and on his way back through Chin, as he passed along the south bank of the Han, he saw an old man preparing his fields for planting. He had hollowed out an opening by which he entered the well and from which he emerged, lugging a pitcher, which he carried out to water the fields. Grunting and puffing, he used up a great deal of energy and produced very little result.

"There is a machine for this sort of thing," said Tzu-kung. "In one day it can water a hundred fields, demanding very little effort and producing excellent results. Wouldn't you like one?"

The gardener raised his head and looked at Tzu-kung. "How does it work?"

"It's a contraption made by shaping a piece of wood. The back end is heavy and the front end light and it raises the water as though it were pouring it out, so fast that it seems to boil right over! It's called a well sweep."

The gardener flushed with anger and then said with a laugh, "I've heard my teacher say, where there are machines, there are bound to be machine worries; where there are machine worries, there are bound to be machine hearts. With a machine heart in your breast, you've spoiled what was pure and simple; and without the pure and simple, the life of the spirit knows no rest. Where the life of the spirit knows no rest, the Way will cease to buoy you up. It's not that I don't know about your machine—I would be ashamed to use it!"

Tzu-kung blushed with chagrin, looked down, and made no reply. After a while, the gardener said, "Who are you, anyway?"

"A disciple of K'ung Ch'iu."[7]

"Oh—then you must be one of those who broaden their learning in order to ape the sages, heaping absurd nonsense on the crowd, plucking the strings and singing sad songs all by yourself in hopes of buying fame in the world! You would do best to forget your spirit and breath, break up your body and limbs—then you might be able to get somewhere. You don't even know how to look after your own body—how do you have any time to think about looking after the world! On your way now! Don't interfere with my work!"

7. That is, Confucius.

Tzu-kung frowned and the color drained from his face. Dazed and rattled, he couldn't seem to pull himself together, and it was only after he had walked on for some thirty li that he began to recover.

One of his disciples said, "Who was that man just now? Why did you change your expression and lose your color like that, Master, so that it took you all day to get back to normal?"

"I used to think there was only one real man in the world," said Tzu-kung. "I didn't know there was this other one. I have heard Confucius say that in affairs you aim for what is right, and in undertakings you aim for success. To spend little effort and achieve big results—that is the Way of the sage. Now it seems that this isn't so. He who holds fast to the Way is complete in Virtue; being complete in Virtue, he is complete in body; being complete in body, he is complete in spirit; and to be complete in spirit is the Way of the sage. He is content to live among the people, to walk by their side, and never know where he is going. Witless, his purity is complete. Achievement, profit, machines, skill—they have no place in this man's mind! A man like this will not go where he has no will to go, will not do what he has no mind to do. Though the world might praise him and say he had really found something, he would look unconcerned and never turn his head; though the world might condemn him and say he had lost something, he would look serene and pay no heed. The praise and blame of the world are no loss or gain to him. He may be called a man of Complete Virtue. I—I am a man of the wind-blown waves."

When Tzu-kung got back to Lu, he reported the incident to Confucius. Confucius said, "He is one of those bogus practitioners of the arts of Mr. Chaos. He knows the first thing but doesn't understand the second. He looks after what is on the inside but doesn't look after what is on the outside. A man of true brightness and purity who can enter into simplicity, who can return to the primitive through inaction, give body to his inborn nature, and embrace his spirit, and in this way wander through the everyday world—if you had met one like that, you would have had real cause for astonishment. As for the arts of Mr. Chaos, you and I need not bother to find out about them."

FROM CHAPTER 13

The Way of Heaven

Duke Huan was in his hall reading a book. The wheelwright P'ien, who was in the yard below chiseling a wheel, laid down his mallet and chisel, stepped up into the hall, and said to Duke Huan, "This book Your Grace is reading—may I venture to ask whose words are in it?"

"The words of the sages," said the duke.

"Are the sages still alive?"

"Dead long ago," said the duke.

"In that case, what you are reading there is nothing but the chaff and dregs of the men of old!"

"Since when does a wheelwright have permission to comment on the books I read?" said Duke Huan. "If you have some explanation, well and good. If not, it's your life!"

Wheelwright P'ien said, "I look at it from the point of view of my own work. When I chisel a wheel, if the blows of the mallet are too gentle, the chisel slides and won't take hold. But if they're too hard, it bites in and won't budge. Not too gentle, not too hard—you can get it in your hand and feel it in your mind. You can't put it into words, and yet there's a knack to it somehow. I can't teach it to my son, and he can't learn it from me. So I've gone along for seventy years and at my age I'm still chiseling wheels. When the men of old died, they took with them the things that couldn't be handed down. So what you are reading there must be nothing but the chaff and dregs of the men of old."

FROM CHAPTER 17

Autumn Floods

Once, when Chuang Tzu was fishing in the P'u River, the king of Ch'u sent two officials to go and announce to him: "I would like to trouble you with the administration of my realm."

Chuang Tzu held on to the fishing pole and, without turning his head, said, "I have heard that there is a sacred tortoise in Ch'u that has been dead for three thousand years. The king keeps it wrapped in cloth and boxed, and stores it in the ancestral temple. Now would this tortoise rather be dead and have its bones left behind and honored? Or would it rather be alive and dragging its tail in the mud?"

"It would rather be alive and dragging its tail in the mud," said the two officials.

Chuang Tzu said, "Go away! I'll drag my tail in the mud!"

When Hui Tzu was prime minister of Liang, Chuang Tzu set off to visit him. Someone said to Hui Tzu, "Chuang Tzu is coming because he wants to replace you as prime minister!" With this Hui Tzu was filled with alarm and searched all over the state for three days and three nights trying to find Chuang Tzu. Chuang Tzu then came to see him and said, "In the south there is a bird called the Yüan-ch'u—I wonder if you've ever heard of it? The Yüan-ch'u rises up from the South Sea and flies to the North Sea, and it will rest on nothing but the Wu-t'ung tree, eat nothing but the fruit of the Lien and drink only from springs of sweet water. Once there was an owl who had gotten hold of a half-rotten old rat, and as the Yüan-ch'u passed by, it raised its head, looked up at the Yüan-ch'u, and said, 'Shoo!' Now that you have this Liang state of yours, are you trying to shoo me?"

Chuang Tzu and Hui Tzu were strolling along the dam of the Hao River when Chuang Tzu said, "See how the minnows come out and dart around where they please! That's what fish really enjoy!"

Hui Tzu said, "You're not a fish—how do you know what fish enjoy?"

Chuang Tzu said, "You're not I, so how do you know I don't know what fish enjoy?"

Hui Tzu said, "I'm not you, so I certainly don't know what you know. On the other hand, you're certainly not a fish—so that still proves you don't know what fish enjoy!"

Chuang Tzu said, "Let's go back to your original question, please. You asked me *how* I know what fish enjoy—so you already knew I knew it when you asked the question. I know it by standing here beside the Hao."

FROM CHAPTER 18

Perfect Happiness

When Chuang Tzu went to Ch'u, he saw an old skull, all dry and parched. He poked it with his carriage whip and then asked, "Sir, were you greedy for life and forgetful of reason, and so came to this? Was your state overthrown and did you bow beneath the ax, and so came to this? Did you do some evil deed and were you ashamed to bring disgrace upon your parents and family, and so came to this? Was it through the pangs of cold and hunger that you came to this? Or did your springs and autumns pile up until they brought you to this?"

When he had finished speaking, he dragged the skull over and, using it for a pillow, lay down to sleep.

In the middle of the night, the skull came to him in a dream and said, "You chatter like a rhetorician and all your words betray the entanglements of a living man. The dead know nothing of these! Would you like to hear a lecture on the dead?"

"Indeed," said Chuang Tzu.

The skull said, "Among the dead there are no rulers above, no subjects below, and no chores of the four seasons. With nothing to do, our springs and autumns are as endless as heaven and earth. A king facing south on his throne could have no more happiness than this!"

Chuang Tzu couldn't believe this and said, "If I got the Arbiter of Fate to give you a body again, make you some bones and flesh, return you to your parents and family and your old home and friends, you would want that, wouldn't you?"

The skull frowned severely, wrinkling up its brow. "Why would I throw away more happiness than that of a king on a throne and take on the troubles of a human being again?" it said.

FROM CHAPTER 19

Mastering Life

The Invocator of the Ancestors, dressed in his black, square-cut robes, peered into the pigpen and said, "Why should you object to dying? I'm going to fatten you for three months, practice austerities for ten days, fast for three days, spread the white rushes, and lay your shoulders and rump on the carved sacrificial stand—you'll go along with that, won't you? True, if I were planning things from the point of view of a pig, I'd say it would be better to eat chaff and bran and stay right there in the pen. But if I were planning for myself, I'd say that if I could be honored as a high official while I lived, and get to ride in a fine hearse and lie among the feathers and trappings when I died, I'd go along with that. Speaking for the pig, I'd give such a life a flat refusal, but speaking for myself, I'd certainly accept. I wonder why I look at things differently from a pig?"

Duke Huan was hunting in a marsh, with Kuan Chung as his carriage driver, when he saw a ghost. The duke grasped Kuan Chung's hand and said, "Father Chung, what do you see?"[8]

"I don't see anything," replied Kuan Chung.

When the duke returned home, he fell into a stupor, grew ill, and for several days did not go out.

A gentleman of Ch'i named Huang-tzu Kao-ao said, "Your Grace, you are doing this injury to yourself! How could a ghost have the power to injure you! If the vital breath that is stored up in a man becomes dispersed and does not return, then he suffers a deficiency. If it ascends and fails to descend again, it causes him to be chronically irritable. If it descends and does not ascend again, it causes him to be chronically forgetful. And if it neither ascends nor descends, but gathers in the middle of the body in the region of the heart, then he becomes ill."

Duke Huan said, "But do ghosts really exist?"

"Indeed they do. There is the Li on the hearth and the Chi in the stove. The heap of clutter and trash just inside the gate is where the Lei-t'ing lives. In the northeast corner the Pei-a and Kuei-lung leap about, and the northwest corner is where the I-yang lives. In the water is the Kang-hsiang; on the hills, the Hsin; in the mountains, the K'uei; in the meadows, the P'ang-huang; and in the marshes, the Wei-t'o."

The duke said, "May I ask what a Wei-t'o looks like?"

Huang-tzu said, "The Wei-t'o is as big as a wheel hub, as tall as a carriage shaft, has a purple robe and a vermilion hat and, as creatures go, is very ugly. When it hears the sound of thunder or a carriage, it grabs its head and stands up. Anyone who sees it will soon become a dictator."

Duke Huan's face lit up and he said with a laugh, "*That* must have been what I saw!" Then he straightened his robe and hat and sat up on the mat with Huang-tzu, and before the day was over, though he didn't notice it, his illness went away.

FROM CHAPTER 20

The Mountain Tree

Chuang Chou was wandering in the park at Tiao-ling when he saw a peculiar kind of magpie that came flying along from the south. It had a wingspread of seven feet and its eyes were a good inch in diameter. It brushed against Chuang Chou's forehead and then settled down in a grove of chestnut trees. "What kind of bird is that!" exclaimed Chuang Chou. "Its wings are enormous but they get it nowhere; its eyes are huge but it can't even see where it's going!" Then he hitched up his robe, strode forward, cocked his crossbow and prepared to take aim. As he did so, he spied a cicada that had found a lovely spot of shade and had forgotten all about [the possibility of danger to] its body. Behind it, a praying mantis, stretching forth its claws, prepared to snatch the cicada, and it too had forgotten about its own form as it eyed its prize. The peculiar magpie was close behind, ready to make off with the praying mantis, forgetting its own true self as it fixed its eyes on the prospect

8. Duke Huan of Ch'i (ruled 685–643 B.C.) later became the first of the *pa*—dictators or hegemons who imposed their will upon the other feudal lords. Kuan Chung (died 645 B.C.) was his chief minister. As a special mark of esteem, the duke customarily addressed him as "Father Chung" [Translator's note].

of gain. Chuang Chou, shuddering at the sight, said, "Ah!—things do nothing but make trouble for each other—one creature calling down disaster on another!" He threw down his crossbow, turned about, and hurried from the park, but the park keeper [taking him for a poacher] raced after him with shouts of accusation.

Chuang Chou returned home and for three months looked unhappy. Lin Chü, in the course of tending to his master's needs, questioned him, saying, "Master, why is it that you are so unhappy these days?"

Chuang Chou said, "In clinging to outward form I have forgotten my own body. Staring at muddy water, I have been misled into taking it for a clear pool. Moreover, I have heard my Master say, 'When you go among the vulgar, follow their rules!' I went wandering at Tiao-ling and forgot my body. A peculiar magpie brushed against my forehead, wandered off to the chestnut grove, and there forgot its true self. And the keeper of the chestnut grove, to my great shame, took me for a trespasser! That is why I am unhappy."

Yang Tzu, on his way to Sung, stopped for the night at an inn. The innkeeper had two concubines, one beautiful, the other ugly. But the ugly one was treated as a lady of rank, while the beautiful one was treated as a menial. When Yang Tzu asked the reason, a young boy of the inn replied, "The beautiful one is only too aware of her beauty, and so we don't think of her as beautiful. The ugly one is only too aware of her ugliness, and so we don't think of her as ugly."

Yang Tzu said, "Remember that, my students! If you act worthily but rid yourself of the awareness that you are acting worthily, then where can you go that you will not be loved?"

FROM CHAPTER 21

T'ien Tzu-fang

Lord Yüan of Sung wanted to have some pictures painted. The crowd of court clerks all gathered in his presence, received their drawing panels, and took their places in line, licking their brushes, mixing their inks, so many of them that there were more outside the room than inside it. There was one clerk who arrived late, sauntering in without the slightest haste. When he received his drawing panel, he did not look for a place in line, but went straight to his own quarters. The ruler sent someone to see what he was doing, and it was found that he had taken off his robes, stretched out his legs, and was sitting there naked. "Very good," said the ruler. "This is a true artist!"

* * *

Lieh Yü-k'ou was demonstrating his archery to Po-hun Wu-jen. He drew the bow as far as it would go, placed a cup of water on his elbow, and let fly. One arrow had no sooner left his thumb ring than a second was resting in readiness beside his arm guard, and all the while he stood like a statue. Po-hun Wu-jen said, "This is the archery of an archer, not the archery of a nonarcher! Try climbing up a high mountain with me, scrambling over the steep rocks to the very brink of an eight-hundred-foot chasm—then we'll see what kind of shooting you can do!"

Accordingly they proceeded to climb a high mountain, scrambling over the steep rocks to the brink of an eight-hundred-foot chasm. There Po-hun Wu-jen, turning his back to the chasm, walked backwards until his feet projected half-way off the edge of the cliff, bowed to Lieh Yü-k'ou, and invited him to come forward and join him. But Lieh Yü-k'ou cowered on the ground, sweat pouring down all the way to his heels. Po-hun Wu-jen said, "The Perfect Man may stare at the blue heavens above, dive into the Yellow Springs below, ramble to the end of the eight directions, yet his spirit and bearing undergo no change. And here you are in this cringing, eye-batting state of mind—if you tried to take aim now, you would be in certain peril!"

FROM CHAPTER 22

Knowledge Wandered North

Master Tung-kuo asked Chuang Tzu, "This thing called the Way—where does it exist?"

Chuang Tzu said, "There's no place it doesn't exist."

"Come," said Master Tung-kuo, "you must be more specific!"

"It is in the ant."

"As low a thing as that?"

"It is in the panic grass."

"But that's lower still!"

"It is in the tiles and shards."

"How can it be so low?"

"It is in the piss and shit!"

Master Tung-kuo made no reply.

Chuang Tzu said, "Sir, your questions simply don't get at the substance of the matter. When Inspector Huo asked the superintendent of the market how to test the fatness of a pig by pressing it with the foot, he was told that the lower down on the pig you press, the nearer you come to the truth. But you must not expect to find the Way in any particular place—there is no thing that escapes its presence! Such is the Perfect Way, and so too are the truly great words. 'Complete,' 'universal,' 'all-inclusive'—these three are different words with the same meaning. All point to a single reality.

"Why don't you try wandering with me to the Palace of Not-Even-Anything—identity and concord will be the basis of our discussions and they will never come to an end, never reach exhaustion. Why not join with me in inaction, in tranquil quietude, in hushed purity, in harmony and leisure? Already my will is vacant and blank. I go nowhere and don't know how far I've gotten. I go and come and don't know where to stop. I've already been there and back, and I don't know when the journey is done. I ramble and relax in unbordered vastness; Great Knowledge enters in, and I don't know where it will ever end.

"That which treats things as things is not limited by things. Things have their limits—the so-called limits of things. The unlimited moves to the realm of limits; the limited moves to the unlimited realm. We speak of the filling and emptying, the withering and decay of things. [The Way] makes them full and empty without itself filling or emptying; it makes them wither and decay without itself withering or decaying. It establishes root and branch but knows no root and branch itself; it determines when to store up or scatter but knows no storing or scattering itself."

FROM CHAPTER 24

Hsü Wu-Kuei

The Yellow Emperor set out to visit Great Clod[9] at Chü-tz'u Mountain. Fang Ming was his carriage driver, while Ch'ang Yü rode at his right side; Chang Jo and Hsi P'eng led the horses and K'un Hun and Ku Chi followed behind the carriage. By the time they reached the wilds of Hsiang-ch'eng, all seven sages had lost their way and could find no one to ask directions from. Just then they happened upon a young boy herding horses, and asked him for directions. "Do you know the way to Chü-tz'u Mountain?" they inquired.

"Yes."

"And do you know where Great Clod is to be found?"

"Yes."

"What an astonishing young man!" said the Yellow Emperor. "You not only know the way to Chü-tz'u Mountain, but you even know where Great Clod is to be found! Do you mind if I ask you about how to govern the empire?"

"Governing the empire just means doing what I'm doing here, doesn't it?" said the young boy. "What is there special about it? When I was little, I used to go wandering within the Six Realms, but in time I contracted a disease that blurred my eyesight. An elderly gentleman advised me to mount on the chariot of the sun and go wandering in the wilds of Hsiang-ch'eng, and now my illness is getting a little better. Soon I can go wandering once more, this time beyond the Six Realms. Governing the empire just means doing what I'm doing—I don't see why it has to be anything special."

"It's true that the governing of the empire is not something that need concern you, Sir," said the Yellow Emperor. "Nevertheless, I would like to ask you how it should be done."

The young boy made excuses, but when the Yellow Emperor repeated his request, the boy said, "Governing the empire I suppose is not much different from herding horses. Get rid of whatever is harmful to the horses—that's all."

The Yellow Emperor, addressing the boy as "Heavenly Master," bowed twice, touching his head to the ground, and retired.

9. Here, the Way (see also n. 4, p. 838).

SSU-MA CH'IEN

(ca. 145–ca. 85 B.C.)

As the famous Greek and Latin historians were widely read throughout most of European history, Ssu-ma Ch'ien's *Historical Records* has always been popular in China as a source of pleasure and wisdom. Ssu-ma Ch'ien was completing a project begun by his father. Working under the powerful and centralizing Emperor Wu of the Han, Ssu-ma Ch'ien sought to draw together the diverse body of historical materials that were preserved in the imperial library and write an account of the past down to his own times. Legends that had once been located in some hazy and uncertain past were placed in historical time, defined by a single line of legitimate rulers.

Ssu-ma Ch'ien's form of writing history was very different from the narratives of Herodotus and Thucydides. He divided his work into several sections: there were chronicles of the rulers of dynasties and the ruling families of the great feudal domains; there were chronological tables; there were treatises on topics such as astronomy, the calendar, and music. The last half of the *Historical Records*, however, was devoted to biographies, frequently given in pairs, as Plutarch did.

Ssu-ma Ch'ien often became caught up in the stories of the lives he told, and he had good reason to do so. While Ssu-ma Ch'ien was an adviser in Emperor Wu's court, a minor frontier general, Li Ling, had surrendered to the Xiong-nu, a central Asian nation with whom China was often at war. Li Ling had led a relatively small army of infantry into Hsiung-nu territory, where he was supposed to meet up with other Chinese armies. Those armies failed to appear, and Li Ling was left to face an overwhelmingly superior force of Xiong-nu. He seems to have fought heroically until the few soldiers he had left were wounded, exhausted, and out of arrows. At this point he surrendered. Emperor Wu was enraged and had Li Ling's entire family executed. Admirably but unwisely, Ssu-ma Ch'ien argued on Li Ling's behalf to the emperor, who then turned his anger on Ssu-ma Ch'ien himself and sentenced him to castration. This sentence was a tacit command to commit suicide in order to escape the humiliation and suffering. Ssu-ma Ch'ien, however, had not completed his great project, the *Historical Records*, and he decided to undergo the punishment in order to finish his work. He was criticized for this by a man named Jen An—probably on the grounds that he was afraid to take the course of an honorable death. Later Jen An was himself sentenced to death, and Ssu-ma Ch'ien took that occasion to answer Jen An and to explain why he decided to act as he did.

Whenever Ssu-ma Ch'ien wrote of those who suffered injustice, he became deeply caught up in the question of why such injustice should occur. Nowhere is this more evident than in *The Biography of Po Yi and Shu Ch'i* two noble hermits who starved themselves to death for their principles. This biography, the first in the *Historical Records*, begins with the question of the historical reliability of received stories and ends questioning the justice of heaven.

Among the best-loved biographies of the *Historical Records* are those of the heroes of the Warring States, the period before Ch'in unified China. Confucian moralists often disapproved of these men (and of Ssu-ma Ch'ien's obvious interest in them). Here we see a code of heroism that is quite different from the Confucian and Taoist values that are conventionally associated with early China. These were men of extremes who made a promise or a vow and carried it through in spite of all. Perhaps the most famous of these heroes was Wu Tzu-hsü, who vowed revenge when the king of Ch'u killed his father. But the king died before Wu Tzu-hsü could complete his revenge; and after leading an army from a neighboring state to conquer Ch'u, he dug up the body of the dead king and gave it three hundred lashes. When a former friend wrote to say that this was too much, Wu Tzu-hsü made a famous reply: "The day draws toward nightfall; my road is long. I go against the tide, yet I will do this in spite of all."

In many cases a lord recognized talent in someone of lower status, and that act of recognition bound the man to the lord, whose gift of honor was often repaid by the sacrifice of the hero's life. In *The Prince of Wei* we see a wonderfully theatrical performance of deference on the part of the prince to Hou Ying, the gatekeeper; but by such honor paid to him, Hou Ying is bound. Nieh Cheng, a butcher, has to take care of his aged mother and his sister and tries desperately to avoid gifts from Yen Chung-tzu; but once his mother passes away, he feels he can repay the honor bestowed on him. The most remarkable of such heroes is perhaps Yü-jang, given below in a somewhat longer version than Ssu-ma Ch'ien's in the *Historical Records*. Honored by the Earl of Chih, Yü-jang decides to avenge the earl after he is killed by Lord Hsiang and others; Lord Hsiang, however, also "recognizes" Yü-jang—in the sense of recognizing his value and in the sense of recognizing Yü-jang's presence, despite Yü-jang's self-mutilating disguises. In Yü-jang's story we see clearly a "self" that transcends the physical body.

Ssu-ma Ch'ien's "self" was the historian, and he, too, endured mutilation of the body to be that self within, the person he wanted to be. Without male descendents in a patriarchal culture, the historian's hope for the future and for the memory of his family line was his book. While earlier writings were always thought of for current use, Ssu-ma Ch'ien wrote with the future in mind. He was successful: the *Historical Records* became the model of history writing in traditional China. For each dynasty there is a standard history, often published together as the *Twenty-four Histories*. The *Historical Records* is always the first work in that series, the "father" of a long line of children.

Stephen Durrant's *The Cloudy Mirror: Tension and Conflict in the Writings of Sima Qian* (1995) is a good overview of the issues in Ssu-ma Ch'ien's history. For extensive translations of the sections on the Han Dynasty, see Burton Watson's two-volume *Records of the Grand Historian of China* (1961); Watson's *Records of the Historian: Chapters from the Shi Chi of Ssu-ma Ch'ien* (1969) includes more selections from the pre-Han period.

PRONOUNCING GLOSSARY

The following list uses common English syllables to provide rough equivalents of selected words whose pronunciation may be unfamiliar to the general reader.

Chih: *jur*

Ch'in: *chin*

Ch'u: *choo*

Hou Ying: *hoh ving*

Hsiang: *syahng*

Hsiung-nu: *syoong-noo*

Jen An: *ruhn ahn*

Li Ling: *lee ling*

Nieh Cheng: *nyeh jehng*

Po Yi: *bwoh yee*

Shu Chi: *shoo chee*

Ssu-ma Ch'ien: *suh-mah chyen*

Wei: *way*

Wu: *woo*

Wu Tzu-hsü: *woo dzuh-syu*

Yen Chung-tzu: *yen juhng-dzuh*

Yü-jang: *yoo-rahng*

Letter in Reply to Jen An[1]

The Lord Historian, your obedient servant Ssu-ma Ch'ien to Jen An

Some time ago you were so kind as to grace me with a letter, instructing me to observe caution in my associations and to devote myself to recommending worthy gentlemen.[2] Your manner then was earnest and forthright, as if anticipating that I would not do as you directed, but would rather be swayed by what ordinary people said. I would never dare to act in such a way. I may be an old horse that has outlived its usefulness, but I always harkened to the influences from my seniors. When I consider how my body

1. Translated by Stephen Owen. 2. This is a polite way of saying that Ssu-ma Ch'ien should not have supported the cause of Li Ling.

has been mutilated, how fault has been found in whatever I have done, and how my desire to be of benefit has brought ruin to me instead, my heart bursts and I have no one to tell.

There is a saying: "For whom do you act, and who will pay attention to you?" When Chung-tzu Ch'i died, Po Ya never played his harp again.[3] Why was that? A man does something for the sake of someone who understands him, as a woman adorns herself for someone who is attracted to her. Some like me, whose flesh is now missing a part, can never be thought to flourish, even if I had qualities within me like Sui's pearl or Pien Ho's jade, or even if my actions were like those of Hsü Yu or Po Yi.[4] In fact, all they could do is win me ridicule and humiliation.

I should have answered your letter immediately, but at the time I was coming back from the east with His Majesty and I was also beset by minor problems. Few were the days when we could meet, and I was always in such a hurry that there was never even a moment when I could tell you everything that was on my mind.

Now you yourself stand accused of the gravest crimes. As the weeks and months pass, the last month of winter draws near;[5] and I am again constrained to accompany His Majesty to Yung. I fear that ultimately there will be no escaping your swift death. Were I never to have the opportunity to reveal all that torments me and make things clear to you, then in death your soul would harbor an unceasing resentment against me. Let me then tell you my thoughts, and please do not take it amiss that I have been negligent in replying.

I have learned that cultivating one's person is the treasurehouse of wisdom, that a love of offering things is the beginning of feeling for others, that taking and giving is the counterpart of a sense of right, that feeling shame determines courage, and that making one's name known is the ultimate end of action. Only after having all five of these may a man give himself to public life and be ranked among the best. There is no misfortune so miserable as desire for advantage, no grief so painful as a wound that festers within, no action more loathsome than one that brings dishonor upon one's ancestors, and no degradation greater than castration. Those who live on after castration are comparable to no one else. Nor is this true only of the present age—it has been this way from long ago in the past. In olden times when Duke Ling of Wei shared his carriage with the eunuch Yung-ch'ü, Confucius left for Ch'en; Shang Yang arranged an audience through Eunuch Ching, and Chao Lang's heart sank; when the eunuch Chao T'an joined the Emperor in his coach, Yuan Ssu turned pale. This has been considered shameful ever since antiquity. When a man of even middling qualities has business to conduct with a eunuch, he always feels ill at ease—not to mention a gentleman of strong spirit! The court may need capable men these days, but would you have a person who has been gelded recommend the outstanding gentlemen of the world for service!

It has been more than twenty years since I took over my father's profession, and though unworthy, I have had the opportunity to serve the throne. When

3. Po Ya was a famous harper; his close friend, Chung-tzu Ch'i, was the only person who truly understood what was in his heart when he played. Later, when Chung-tzu Ch'i died, Po Ya broke his harp and never played again. 4. Objects of great value and persons with a reputation for purity of behavior. 5. The last month of winter was the time for executions, including Jen An's.

I think it over, on the most important level I have not been able to contribute my loyalty or show my good faith, winning esteem for remarkable plans and the power of my talents, thus forming a natural bond with my wise lord. On the next level I have not been able to catch matters that have been overlooked, summoning worthy men to court and recommending those with abilities, bringing to the public eye those who live hidden in caves in the cliffs. On a still lower level I have not been able to take a place in the ranks and in assaults on cities or in battles in the open, to win glory by beheading generals and seizing the enemy's colors. Finally, on the lowest level, I have not been able to accumulate a stock of merit through continuous service, getting high office and a good salary, thus bringing honor and favor to family and friends. Having been successful in none of these, it is obvious that I have merely followed expedience and tried to please others, achieving nothing that deserves either praise or blame.

Previously, among the ranks of minor grandees, I took part in lesser deliberations of the outer court. On those occasions I brought in no grand plans, nor did I give matters their fullest consideration. Now, as a castrated servant who sweeps up, as the lowest of the low, if I were to try to lift my head, arch my brows, and hold forth with judgments, wouldn't that be showing contempt for the court and offering insult to those gentlemen now in power? What more is there for somebody like me to say!

It is not easy to explain the sequence of events clearly. When I was young I had an ungovernable disposition, and as I grew older I won no esteem from the people of my locale. I was fortunate that, on account of my father, His Majesty allowed me to offer him my meager skills and to frequent the royal apartments. I felt that I could never gaze on Heaven with a bowl covering my head, so I cut off contact with my friends and gave up all thought of the family property; day and night I tried to exercise my miserable talents to their utmost, striving single-mindedly to carry out my office and thus to please His Majesty and win his affection. Yet one thing happened that was a great mistake and had a very different effect.

Li Ling and I had both been in residence in the palace, but we were never good friends. Our interests led us in different directions, so we never even shared a cup of beer or had a direct and earnest relation. Nevertheless, I observed that he was a remarkable person, showing a son's proper devotion to his parents, true to his word with other gentlemen, scrupulous in matters of property, possessed of a sense of right in matters of giving and taking; in questions of status he would yield place, and he behaved deferentially, demonstrating respect and temperance. Always he longed to put his life on the line in responding to some crisis of the empire. He had always harbored these virtues, and to my mind he possessed the qualities of one of the great men of the state. When a subject would brave death thousands of times without thinking to save his own life, going forth to meet threats to the commonwealth, it is remarkable indeed. It truly pained me personally that those courtiers who keep themselves and their families out of harm's way plotted to do him mischief when one thing went wrong out of all that he had done.

The foot soldiers that Li Ling took with him were less than five thousand, and they marched deep into the lands of the nomads; on foot they crossed the khan's own preserve to dangle bait in the tiger's mouth; they brazenly flaunted a stronger force of barbarians and stood face to face against an army of millions. For more than ten days they did continuous battle with the khan and killed more than their own number. When the tribesmen tried to rescue the dead and carry back the wounded, they couldn't take care of themselves, and their chieftains, dressed in wool and furs, were all quaking in terror. Then the Good Princes of the Right and Left[6] were called up and anyone among the folk who could draw a bow; the whole nation surrounded them and attacked. They fought on the move across a thousand leagues, until their arrows were used up and they had nowhere to go. The relief column did not come; dead and wounded troops lay in heaps. Nevertheless, Li Ling gave a shout to cheer up his army, and not a soldier failed to rise; he was weeping, swallowing the tears running down his bloodied face. They drew their empty crossbows and faced down naked blades; facing north, they fought with the enemy to the death.

Before Li Ling was destroyed, a messenger brought word of him; and all the great lords, princes, and counts of Han lifted their goblets in a toast to his health. Several days afterward, the letter bearing news of Li Ling's defeat became known, and on this account His Majesty found no savor in his meals and took no pleasure in holding court. The great officers of the court were worried and fearful, not knowing what to do.

Without giving due consideration to my lowly position, I saw that His Majesty was despondent and distressed, and I truly wanted to offer him my sincere thoughts on the matter. I held that Li Ling always gave up fine food and shared meager fare with his attendant gentlemen, that he was able to get men to die for him to a degree that was unsurpassed even by the famous generals of antiquity. Though he was defeated, if one but considered his intentions, they should make up for it and repay what he owes the Han. Nothing could be done about what had happened, but those he had defeated were an accomplishment sufficient to make him famous in the empire. I had it in mind to make this case, but had not yet had the means. Then it happened that I was summoned and questioned; and I spoke highly of Li Ling's accomplishments in this way, wanting to set His Majesty's mind to rest and stop malicious comments.

I was not able to be entirely persuasive. Our wise ruler did not fully understand, thinking that I was trying to injure the Ni-shih general, Li Kuang-li,[7] and acting as a personal advocate of Li Ling. I was subsequently sent to prison. And never was I able to demonstrate the depth of my loyalty. In the end I was convicted of having tried to deceive the Emperor. My family was poor, and I didn't have the means to buy my way out. None of my friends came to my rescue. My colleagues, kin, and close friends did not say a single word on my behalf. The body is not a thing of wood or stone; and alone in the company of jailers, in the hidden depths of a dungeon, to whom could I complain? This you can see for yourself now, Jen An—was what happened to me any different? Since Li Ling surrendered alive, he ruined the good name of his family. Yet I too, in my turn, came to the silken chambers,[8] where the knife is used, and I am the laughingstock of the world. Oh, the misery of it!

6. The enemies were a people known as the Hsiung-nu. The "Good Princes" were secondary chieftains. 7. Li Kuang-li, entitled the "Ni-shih general," was the head of one of the larger armies that failed to meet up with Li Ling. 8. The "silken chambers" was where castrations were performed.

The matter is not easy to explain in a few words to ordinary people. My father's accomplishments were not such as would bring the imperial seal of investiture among the nobility; writers of history and astronomical calculations are close in status to diviners and soothsayers. His Majesty finds amusement in such, and we are kept by him on a par with singers and acrobats, thus held in contempt by the common opinion. Suppose that I had bowed to the law and accepted execution; it would have been like the loss of a single hair from a herd of cattle, a death no different from that of an ant or a cricket. And the world would never have granted that I might be compared to those who could die for principle. They would have considered it nothing more than a person finally accepting death because he could think of no way out of the gravity of his crime, someone with no other choice. Why is this? It would have been the consequence of the position in which I had so long established myself.

Human beings truly have but one death. There are deaths that seem heavier than Mount T'ai, but to some death seems lighter than a piece of swansdown. The difference lies in what is done by dying. Uppermost is not to bring dishonor upon one's forebears; next is not to bring dishonor upon oneself; next is not to dishonor the right or appearances; next is not to dishonor one's own words; next is to bear the dishonor of bending in submission; next is to bear the dishonor of changing into the uniform of a prisoner; next is to bear the dishonor of being flogged, tied with a rope to the pillory; next is to bear the dishonor of having one's head shaved and bound in metal chains; next is to bear the dishonor of having one's flesh cut and one's limbs amputated; but the worst of all is castration—that is the ultimate.

Tradition says: "Physical punishments are not applied to grandees." This means that a gentleman has no choice but to be severe in guarding his honor. The fierce tiger dwells in the depths of the mountains, and all creatures there quake in fear of him; but when he falls into a pit, he wags his tail for food—this follows gradually from constraining his fearsome power. Thus if you mark out the form of a prison cell on the ground, a gentleman will not enter it; and if you cut a piece of wood to represent the warden, he will not speak to it in his own defense; he has made of his mind to show who he is [by suicide]. But let him cross his hands and feet to receive the manacles and rope, let him expose his flesh to receive the blows of the rod, hide him away in an enclosed cell—and in a situation like this he will knock his head to the ground when he sees the warden and he will breathe hard in terror when he catches sight of the guards. Why is this? It is the natural outcome of constraining fearsome power. And brought to such a state, anyone who says that there is no dishonor is putting up a false front and deserves no esteem.

Yet King Wen, the Earl of the West,[9] may have been an earl, but he was held in the prison at Yu-li; Li Ssu was a minister, yet he endured each of the five punishments; Han Hsin of Huai-yin was a prince, yet he endured the stocks in Ch'en; of Peng Yüeh and Chang Ao, who sat on the throne and called themselves rulers, one went bound to prison, and the other, to death; Chiang-hou Chou-po executed all the members of the Lu clan and his power was greater than that of the five earls, yet he was imprisoned in a dungeon awaiting death; Wei Ch'i was a great general, yet he wore the prisoner's

9. The founder of the Chou Dynasty, first an earl and later King Wen.

uniform and was bound head, hands, and feet; Chi Pu became a slave of the Chu clan; Guan-fu bore dishonor in the guest chambers.

All these men had reached the positions of prince, count, general, or minister, and their fame was known far and wide; but when they were accused and brought before the law, they could not summon the resolution to kill themselves. When one is lying in the dirt, it is the same thing, both in ancient times and in the present—how could one think they were not dishonored! Judging from these examples, courage and fearfulness depend on the situation; resolution and weakness are circumstantial. Reflect on it—there's nothing strange about it! For if a man cannot commit suicide before he is brought to the law, he is already slowly slipping down to the whips and rods. And if he wants to assert his honor then, it is already far out of reach. Certainly this is the reason why the ancients thought it a grave matter to apply physical punishments to grandees.

By their very nature all human beings are greedy for life and hate death, care about their parents, are concerned for their wives and children. But it is otherwise for those who are stirred up by their sense of right, and in fact they cannot help themselves. I had the misfortune to lose both my parents early in life; and not having brothers to be my close family, I was all alone. And you can see how much I took wife and children into consideration! Yet a man of courage does not necessarily die for honor; and when fearful man aspires to the right, he will strive in any way he can. I may have been fearful and weak in choosing life at any cost, but I also recognize quite well the proper measure in how to act. How then could I come to the dishonor of letting myself sink into prison bonds? If even a captive slave girl can take her own life, certainly someone like me could do the same when all was lost. The reason I bore through it in silence and chose to live at any cost, the reason I did not refuse to be covered in muck was because I could not stand to leave something of personal importance to me unfinished, because I despised perishing without letting the glory of my writings be shown to posterity.

The number of rich and noble men in ancient times whose names have been utterly wiped away is beyond reckoning; the only ones who are known are the exceptional, those outside the norm. King Wen of Chou, when Earl of the West, was in captivity and elaborated the *Classic of Changes*; Confucius was in a desperate situation and wrote *The Springs and Autumns of Lu*; Ch'ü Yüan was banished, and only then composed the *Li Sao*; Tso Chiuming lost his sight, and he wrote *The Discourses of the Domains*; Sun-tzu had his feet amputated, and then his *Techniques of War* was drawn up; Lu Puwei was demoted to Shu, from which has been preserved the *Synopticon of Lu*; Han Fei was imprisoned by Ch'in and wrote "Troubles of Persuasion" and "Solitary Outrage." The three hundred *Poems*[1] were for the most part written as the expression of outrage by good men and sages. All of these men had something eating away at their hearts; they could not carry through their ideas of the Way, so they gave an account of what had happened before while thinking of those to come. In cases like Tso Ch'iu-ming's sightlessness or Sun-tzu's amputated feet, these men could never be employed; they withdrew and put their deliberations into writing in order to give full expression

1. The *Classic of Poetry*.

to their outrage, intending to reveal themselves purely through writing that would last into the future.

Being, perhaps, too bold, I have recently given myself over to writing that lacks ability. I have compiled neglected knowledge of former times from all over the world; I have examined these for veracity and have given an account of the principles behind success and defeat, rise and fall. In all there are one hundred and thirty chapters. In it I also wanted to fully explore the interaction between Heaven and Man, and to show the continuity of transformations of past and present. It will become an independent discourse that is entirely my own. The draft version was not yet completed when this misfortune happened to me; I could not bear that it not be completed, so I submitted to the most extreme punishment without showing my ire. When I have actually completed this book, I will have it stored away on some famous mountain, left for someone who will carry it through all the cities. Then I will have made up for the blame that I earlier incurred by submitting to dishonor. I could die thousands of deaths without feeling regret. This, however, may be said only to a wise man; you can't explain it to an ordinary person.

It is not easy to live enduring contempt, and the inferior sort of people usually put a malicious interpretation on things. It was by the spoken word that I met this misfortune; and if I am also exposed to the ridicule of the people of my native region, dishonoring my ancestors, how could I ever again face the tomb mound of my parents? The blot on our name would grow worse and worse, even after a hundred generations. Thus every day I feel a pang in the heart again and again. When I'm in the house, I am distracted, as though I am not there; when I'm outside, I don't know where I'm going. My thoughts keep returning to this shame, and I always break into a sweat that soaks my clothes. I am fit to serve only in the women's quarters, and I would rather take myself off to hide deep away in the caves of the cliffs. But I keep on following the ordinary world, rising and sinking, moving with the times, keeping in communication with fools.

Now you, Jen An, instructed me to recommend worthy men—would not that be the wrong thing to do, considering my private aims? Even if I wanted to give myself refinement and explain myself with gracious words, it would do no good, because ordinary people would not credit me and I would only earn more humiliation. Only when I am dead will the final judgment be made.

Writing cannot say all that is in a person's mind, thus I give you only the rough account of my thoughts.

Historical Records[1]

The Biography of Po Yi and Shu Ch'i

Texts by men of learning range most widely in what they include, yet we look into the Six Classics[2] for what is reliable. Although works were omitted from

1. Translated by Stephen Owen. 2. The Confucian Classics.

the *Poems* and *Documents*, still we can read writings from the times of Shun and Yü.[3]

Sage-King Yao planned to cede the throne and yielded his place to Shun. Between Shun's accession and that of Yü, governors and prefects all recommended men. Shun tested them in posts and let them perform their offices over several decades; only after there was ample evidence of merit and ability did he hand over the reins of government. This testifies to the fact that the empire is a weighty vessel, and the kingship is the supreme office. Thus it is no easy thing to pass the empire from one person to another.

And yet tellers of tales say that Yao offered up the empire to Hsü Yu, but Hsü Yu would not take it and fled out of shame into hiding. Pien Sui and Wu Kuang did the same in the time of Hsia. But how did these men become widely known?

This is my opinion as Lord Historian: I personally climbed Mount Chi, on whose summit was reputed to be the grave of Hsü Yu. When Confucius named the gentle, the good, and the sagely men of antiquity, he went into some detail in cases like Wu T'ai-po and Po Yi.[4] Now from what I have heard, Hsü Yu and Wu Kuang were supposed to have had the highest sense of right—why is it, then, that they are not even mentioned in passing in Confucius' writing?

Confucius said: "Po Yi and Shu Ch'i did not brood on old hatreds, and thus they felt little bitterness of spirit." He also said: "They sought feeling for their fellow man and achieved it—so how could they have known bitterness of spirit?" I myself am moved by Po Yi's sense of purpose, and when I look at his poem that has come down to us, I find it remarkable. This is the story about them.

> Po Yi and Shu Ch'i were two sons of the Lord of Ku-chu. Their father wanted Shu Ch'i to take his place, but when their father died, Shu Ch'i yielded to Po Yi. Po Yi said: "Those were our father's orders," and he fled into hiding. But Shu Ch'i also refused to become Lord of Ku-chu and fled into hiding. Then the people of the domain made the middle son lord.
>
> Then Po Yi and Shu Ch'i heard that the Earl of the West [King Wen of the Chou] took good care of the elderly, and they considered going to put themselves under his protection. But when they arrived, the Earl of the West had died; and King Wu had taken his father's Spirit Tablet, given his father the title "King Wen," and gone east to attack King Zhow of the Shang. Po Yi and Shu Ch'i stopped King Wu's horse and criticized him: "Can this be considered the right way for a son to behave, taking up arms even before your father's funeral rites have been completed? And can a subject murdering his ruler be considered feeling for one's fellow man?" The king's party wanted to put them to the sword, but his Counselor T'ai-kung said: "These men have a sense of right." And he helped them up and sent them away.
>
> When King Wu had settled the lawlessness of the Shang, all the world gave their allegiance to the Chou; yet Po Yi and Shu Ch'i thought that

3. Sage-kings of high antiquity. 4. Wu T'ai-po refused the right of the firstborn to inherit the rulership of Chou because his father wanted to give the throne to his younger brother. Po Yi did the same.

to be something shameful, and out of their sense of right they refused to eat the grain of Chou. They lived as hermits on Shou-yang Mountain and picked bracken ferns to eat. As they were dying of hunger, they composed a song, whose words go:

> We climbed West Hill,
> we picked its bracken.
> Brute force for brute force—
> he knew not it was wrong.
> Shen-nung, Yü, and Hsia[5]
> gone in a flash,
> where can we turn?
> Ah, let us depart now,
> our lifespans are done.

And then they died of hunger on Shou-yang Mountain.

Considered in this light, did they or did they not feel bitterness of spirit?

There are those who say: "The Way of Heaven shows no personal favorites and always provides for good men." Can we or can we not consider people like Po Yi and Shu Ch'i good men? To have such a history of kindness to one's fellow men and to be so pure in actions, yet to die from hunger! Of his seventy disciples, Confucius singled out Yen Hui for praise for his love of learning. Yet Yen Hui lived in dire poverty and never ate his fill even of grain mash or bran. And he died before his time. How is it then that Heaven repays good men with its gifts?

Chih the Outlaw killed innocent men every day and fed on their flesh. A brutal, savage man, he committed every kind of outrage and gathered a band of several thousand men who wreaked havoc all over the world. In the end he died at a ripe old age. From what virtue did this follow?

These are particularly clear and obvious cases. And if we come down to more recent times, conduct beyond the rules of morality and willful transgressions have brought lifetimes of carefree pleasures and great wealth passed on for endless generations. Others take care where they tread, speak up only when it is timely, take no dark byways, and are stirred only for justice and the common good; yet the number of such people who have met with disaster is beyond reckoning. I cannot understand this at all. Is this what is meant by the "Way of Heaven"?

Confucius said: "Men who follow different ways cannot make judgments for one another." Each person follows his own aims in life. He further said: "If wealth and noble station could be properly sought, I would seek them, even if it meant being the king's meanest servant; but since they cannot be sought, I will follow what I love." And: "Only in the cold of the year can you know that pine and cypress are the last to turn brown." When all the world is foul and corrupt, the pure man appears most clearly. Obviously what is considered so important by some is despised by others.

"The man of virtue is pained by the thought of dying without his name being known." [*Analects*]

Chia Yi[6] wrote:

5. Sage rulers of antiquity. 6. A Han writer.

Grasping men spend themselves for goods;
brash warriors spend themselves for glory.
The man overweening will die for power,
and the common man covets his life.

"Things of equal light reveal one another; things of the same kind seek one another." [*Classic of Changes*]

"Clouds follow the dragon; winds follow the tiger; the Sage arises and all things are perspicuous." [*Classic of Changes*]

Although Po Yi and Shu Ch'i were virtuous men, it was through Confucius that their names became more widely known. Though Yen Hui was devoted to learning, like the fly on the tail of a fine steed, his actions became more widely famed. It is most sad that men who live in caves in the cliffs may have an equal sense of appropriateness in their decisions, yet their good names are obliterated and never known. How can folk of the villages who wish to perfect their behavior and establish their names be known to later generations unless through some gentleman who rises high in the world?

In Ssu-ma Ch'ien's accounts of the Han, we see fine judgments of character within a complex political world. But in many of the narratives of the Warring States and the founding of the Han, we find something that might best be called historical romance. This is a world of stratagems, heroism, and sometimes betrayal; the currency of honor is, more often than not, death. The Prince of Wei is the perfect Warring States lord, using his wealth and the power of deference to gather loyal retainers to employ in his own commitments of honor. Hidden among the common folk everywhere are worthy men, capable of deeds of strength or sage advice. The discerning lord knows how to find them and win them over. Such barely visible heroes are necessary to counter a great danger. The Kingdom of Ch'in is the rising military power of the day, threatening the smaller states of North China, such as Wei and Chao.

The Prince of Wei

Wu-ch'i, the Prince of Wei, was the youngest son of King Chao of Wei and the half brother of King An-li [r. 278–243 B.C.]. When King Chao died, King An-li took the throne and enfeoffed the prince as Lord of Lin-ling.

That was the time when Fan Sui, out of his bitterness against Wei Ch'i, had fled Wei to become a royal adviser in Ch'in. Ch'in troops surrounded Ta-liang[1] and smashed Wei's army at the foot of Mount Hua-yang, sending Wei's general Mang Mao into flight. The King of Wei and the prince were deeply troubled because of this.

The prince was the sort of person who showed kindness to others and treated gentlemen with deference. No matter whether the person was virtuous or unworthy, he treated all with humility and received them with courtesy, taking care not to behave haughtily because of his wealth and noble rank. As a result gentlemen from several thousand leagues around flocked to his service, until he had three thousand retainers eating at his table. At this time, because of the prince's virtue and the number of his retainers, the high nobility of the domains did not dare use their troops in designs against Wei for more than ten years.

1. The capital of Wei.

Once the prince was playing chess with the King of Wei when beacon fires were lit from the northern reaches of the kingdom. They were told that raiders had come from Chao and crossed the border. The King of Wei quit the game and was going to summon his chief officers for consultation, but the prince stopped him, saying, "It's just the King of Chao out on a hunt; he's not raiding us." They returned to their game of chess, but the king was apprehensive and his mind wasn't on the game. After a short while word was again brought from the north: "The King of Chao is just hunting; he's not on a raid." The King of Wei was amazed and asked, "How did you know?" The prince replied, "One of my retainers has in-depth access to the King of Chao's secrets. Whatever the King of Chao does, my retainer reports it to me. This is how I knew." After that the King of Wei stood in awe of the prince's virtue and his abilities, and he dared not entrust the prince with political power in the kingdom.

In Wei there was a man named Hou Ying, who kept out of the public eye. Seventy years old, his household was poor, and he served as the gatekeeper of the Yi Gate in Ta-liang. The prince heard of him and went to visit him, with the intention of giving him a generous gift. Hou Ying refused to accept it, saying, "For several decades now I have cultivated my virtue and acted blamelessly; I could never accept a present from you simply because of the hardships of my life as a gatekeeper."

The prince then held a great party with beer for his guests and retainers. When everyone was seated, the prince set off with his chariots and riders, leaving the place of honor at his left empty. He personally made an invitation to Hou Ying at Yi Gate. Hou Ying straightened his tattered cap and robes, then got right up on the prince's chariot and took the position of the social superior. He didn't defer to the prince because he wanted to observe him. The prince took the reins in his own hand and became increasingly respectful. Then Hou Ying said to the prince, "I have a retainer in the butcher shops of the marketplace—I would like you and your entourage to make a detour to visit him." The prince then turned his chariot into the marketplace, where Hou Ying got down and met with his retainer Chu Hai. Watching out of the corner of his eye, he stood there a long time on purpose, talking to his retainer, and he secretly observed the prince. The prince's expression was even more calm. Meanwhile, Wei's generals, counselors, members of the royal family, and the prince's retainers filled his hall, waiting for the prince before beginning to drink. The people in the marketplace were all watching the prince holding the reins. And the attendant riders were all cursing Hou Ying under their breaths. Once Hou Ying saw that the prince's expression would never change, he took leave of his retainer and went back to the chariot.

When they reached his home, the prince led Hou Ying to the seat of honor, commending to him each of his guests in turn. The guests were all amazed. Then, growing merry from drink, the prince rose to offer a toast to Hou Ying. But then Hou Ying told the prince, "I've already done enough on your behalf today. I am but the person who bars Yi Gate, yet you came with chariots and horsemen to invite me personally into this great gathering of people. One should not overdo things, and today you have really overdone it. Nevertheless, I wanted to complete your reputation, so on purpose I made your chariots and riders stand there so long in the marketplace; I stopped by to visit my retainer in order to observe you, and you became even more respectful. The people of the marketplace all think of me as someone of no importance, and yet you found it within you to treat me with deference as an elder." At this the party ended, and thereafter Hou Ying became the most honored of the retainers.

Hou Ying told the prince, "The butcher I stopped by to visit is Chu Hai. He is a worthy man, but no one has been able to recognize his worth, so he lives out of the public eye among the butchers." The prince went to pay his respects a number of times, but Chu Hai purposefully did not return the greeting. And the prince thought it very strange.

In the twentieth year of King An-li's reign, King Zhaw of Ch'in had smashed the army of Chao at Ch'ang-ping and sent his troops on to surround the Chao capital at Han-tan. The prince's sister was the wife of the Lord of Ping-yüan, who was the younger brother of King Hui-wen of Chao. The Lord of Ping-yüan sent a number of letters to the King of Wei and the prince, asking that Wei save them. The King of Wei sent his general Chin Pi with a hundred thousand troops to save Chao; but the King of Ch'in sent an envoy to tell the King of Wei, "I am attacking Chao, and it will fall any day now; but if any of the great nobility dare to try to save it, I will move my troops to strike them first, once I have seized Chao." The King of Wei grew frightened and sent someone to stop Chin Pi and hold his army in a fortified camp at Yeh. He was to say publicly that he was going to save Chao, but in fact he was to keep his options open while observing the situation.

One after another the caps and carriages of envoys from the Lord of P'ing-yüan came through Wei and they reproved the prince: "The reason why I, Sheng, Lord of P'ing-yüan, allied myself with you through marriage was because of your noble sense of right, which makes you rush to someone in dire need. Han-tan may fall to Ch'in any day now and no rescue has come from Wei—where now is your willingness to rush to help someone in dire need! But even if you care nothing about me and would abandon me to Ch'in, have you no pity at all for your sister?"

The prince was very upset by this and often pleaded with the King of Wei; and the political strategists among his retainers plied the king with thousands of persuasive reasons. But the King of Wei stood in dread of Ch'in and he never heeded the prince.

Taking the measure of the situation, the prince realized that he would never win over the king; and he decided that he could not stay alive himself while letting Chao perish. He then called on his retainers, and gathered and mustered more than a hundred chariots and horsemen, intending to go against Ch'in's army with his retainers and to die together with Chao.

He went past Yi Gate and met with Hou Ying, explaining to him the entire situation that led him to plan to die before Ch'in's army. As he said his farewell and went on his way, Hou Ying said, "Do the best you can! I'm old and can't go with you." After going several leagues, the prince felt uneasy and said to himself, "I have treated Hou Ying perfectly in every way! Everyone in the world knows about it. Now I'm going off to die, yet Hou Ying never offered the least piece of advice to see me off. Could I have possibly failed him in some way?" He turned his chariot around and went back to ask Hou Ying, who laughed and said, "I knew quite well that you would be back." He continued, "You delight in gentlemen-retainers, and your reputation is known all over the world. Now there is a crisis, and having no other recourse, you plan to go against Ch'in's army. I would compare this to tossing meat to a ravenous tiger. What will you accomplish by that? How will you make use of your retainers? Still, you have treated me generously, so that when you left, I didn't see you off, knowing by this that you would feel wronged and come back."

The prince bowed to him several times and next asked him what to do. Hou Ying then made the others withdraw and spoke quietly to the prince: "I have heard that the tally authorizing Chin Pi to use his troops is always in the king's bedchamber. Lady Ju enjoys his favors most often; and since she passes in and out of the king's bedchamber, it is within her power to steal it. I have heard that Lady Ju's father was murdered, and this has occupied her thoughts for three years. She has sought to get revenge on her father's killer from the king on down, but she has never gotten satisfaction. When Lady Ju pleads weeping before you, send a retainer to cut off her enemy's head and respectfully present it to her. In her readiness to die for you Lady Ju would refuse you nothing, but she will not be able to think of any means. Indeed, all you have to do is open your mouth once and ask this of her, and Lady Ju will surely agree. Then you will get the tally to seize Chin Pi's army, go north to save Chao, and make Ch'in retreat back to the west. This will be a campaign worthy of the Five Overlords."

The prince followed his plan and made the request of Lady Ju. And the outcome was that Lady Ju stole the tally for Chin Pi's troops and gave it to the prince.

When the prince set out, Hou Ying said, "When a general is away from the capital, there are cases when he will not accept his ruler's orders if it seems in the best interest of the kingdom. Once you match the tallies, if Chin Pi does not give you the troops and makes further inquiries, you will be in a very dangerous situation.[2] My retainer, the butcher Chu Hai, should go together with you; he is a man of strength and force. If Chin Pi obeys, that would be best; but if he doesn't obey, have Chu Hai strike him.

At this the prince began to weep, and Hou Ying said, "Are you dreading death—why are you weeping?" The prince replied, "Chin Pi is a stout-hearted old general from way back. When I go there, I'm afraid he won't obey me and I'll have to kill him. That's the only reason I'm weeping. Of course I don't dread dying."

Next the prince went to make his request of Chu Hai. Chu Hai laughed and said, "I am just a butcher who wields a knife in the marketplace, yet you have personally paid your respects to me on a number of occasions. The reason why I didn't respond was that such a small courtesy would have been of no use. Now you are in a crisis, and this is the season for me to put my life at your disposal." He then went off together with the prince. The prince visited Hou Ying to take his leave, and Hou Ying said, "It would be right that I go with you, but I am too old. Reckon up the number of days you will be traveling, and on the day when you are to reach Chin Pi's army, I will face north and cut my throat as my farewell to you, my prince." Then the prince set off.

When he reached Yeh, he pretended that the King of Wei had ordered

2. Authority was delegated by means of a broken tally, of which the ruler kept half. By bringing the ruler's half of the tally and matching it up with the general's half, the bearer demonstrated that he was acting on the authority of the ruler.

him to take Chin Pi's place. Chin Pi's matched the tallies, but doubted him; raising his hand, he looked at the prince and said, "Here I am surrounded by a host of a hundred thousand, camped on the frontier, bearing a grave responsibility to the kingdom. How is it that you can come in a single chariot to take my place?" He was not going to obey. Chu Hai drew an iron club weighing twenty-five pounds out of his sleeve and bludgeoned Chin Pi to death. The prince then took command of Chin Pi's army. He had his officers convey these commands to the army: "If a father and son are both in the army, let the father go home; if brothers are both in the army, let the elder go home; if there is an only son with no brothers, let him go home to take care of his parents." From this he got eighty thousand select troops and advanced to strike the army of Ch'in. The Ch'in army broke its siege and left. Thus he rescued Han-tan and saved Chao.

The King of Chao and the Lord of P'ing-yüan personally welcomed the prince at the edge of the city. The Lord of P'ing-yüan carried a quiver of arrows as a sign of respect, and he led the way for the prince. The King of Chao bowed to him repeatedly, saying, "None of the virtuous and worthy men since ancient times is your equal." And at this time the Lord of Ping-yüan did not dare compare him with anyone.

The prince had said his farewell to Hou Ying; and when he had reached the army, Hou Ying at last faced north and cut his own throat.

The King of Wei was enraged that the prince had stolen his tally for the army, then bluffed Chin Pi and killed him. And for his own part the prince too knew this. Having forced Ch'in to withdraw and having saved Chao, he had the generals take the army back to Wei, while he and his retainers stayed in Chao.

King Hsiao-ch'eng of Chao was indebted to the prince for having seized Chin Pi's troops by a bluff and saved Chao, so he planned with the Lord of P'ing-yüan to give the prince five cities as a fief. When the prince heard of this, he felt very proud of himself and his face showed his sense of his own achievements. One of the prince's retainers counseled him, "There are some things that should not be forgotten and some things that you should always forget. If you are in debt to someone else, you should not forget it; but if someone else is in debt to you, I would encourage you to forget it. To have pretended to be acting under the King of Wei's order and seized Chin Pi's troops in order to save Chao was indeed a great achievement to Chao, but to Wei it was not being a loyal subject. You are in fact very proud of yourself and think it was a great achievement, but in my own opinion you shouldn't have taken this course."

At this the prince immediately rebuked himself, and it seemed as if he couldn't stand himself. The King of Chao had the stairs swept and welcomed him personally; and carrying out the ceremony of a host, he led the prince to the western stairs. But the prince backed away and declined the honor, going up by the eastern stairs. He spoke of his own transgressions, having been disloyal to Wei and having accomplished nothing important for Chao. The King of Chao accompanied him drinking until sundown, but he couldn't bring himself to present the five cities because of the prince's modesty. In the end the prince stayed in Chao. The King of Chao gave him Hao as a tributary city, and even the King of Wei restored to him his fief of Hsin-ling. But the prince stayed in Chao.

The prince heard that in Chao there was a recluse, one Master Mao, who hid himself among gamblers, and another, Master Hsüeh, who hid himself among tavern keepers. The prince wanted to meet both of them, but they both concealed themselves and were unwilling to meet him. When the prince found out where they were, he went secretly on foot to keep them company, and he enjoyed it greatly. The Lord of P'ing-yüan heard about this and told his wife, "I first heard of your brother the prince as someone without peer in all the world. Now I heard about him recklessly keeping company with gamblers and tavern keepers. The prince is a reckless man."

The lady informed the prince about this. The prince then took his leave of her, saying, "I first heard of the Lord of P'ing-yüan as a worthy man, and for that reason I betrayed the King of Wei to save Chao—to satisfy the Lord of P'ing-yüan. Those with whom the Lord of P'ing-yüan keeps company are only the arrogant and overbearing; he does not seek out gentlemen. When I, Wu-chi, was back in Ta-liang, I heard constantly of the worthiness of these two men; and when I came to Chao, I was afraid that I wouldn't get the chance to meet them. I was even afraid that they might not want me to keep them company. If now the Lord of P'ing-yüan considers this a cause for embarrassment, then *he* is not worth keeping company." At this he started packing to depart.

The lady repeated everything that he had said to the Lord of P'ing-yüan. And the Lord of P'ing-yüan removed his cap and apologized, insisting that the prince stay. When the Lord of P'ing-yüan's followers heard of this, half of them left the Lord of P'ing-yüan for the prince; and again gentlemen from all the world over flocked to the prince, until the prince had taken all the Lord of P'ing-yüan's retainers.

The prince stayed in Chao for ten years without returning. When the Ch'in ruler heard that the prince was in Chao, he constantly sent troops eastward to raid Wei. The King of Wei was deeply troubled by this and sent envoys to go ask help from the prince. But the prince was afraid that the king was angry with him, and he gave this warning to his followers: "Whoever dares come as an envoy of the king of Wei dies!" His retainers then all abandoned Wei and went to Chao, and none of them dared urge the prince to return. Then both Masters Mao and Hsüeh went to meet the prince and said, "The reason why you are treated with importance in Chao and your fame is known among the great nobility is due only to the existence of Wei. Ch'in now attacks Wei. If you do not take pity on Wei in its hour of dire distress and then Ch'in should smash Ta-liang and level the ancestral temples of its former kings, how will you have the face to stand up in the world?" Before they finished speaking, the expression on the prince's face suddenly changed; he told his drivers to prepare his train to go home and rescue Wei.

The King of Wei met the prince, and they came together in tears. And the king gave the prince the seal of the supreme general of his armies. The prince then took command. In the thirtieth year of King An-li of Wei, the prince sent envoys to all the high lords of the domains. When the high lords heard that the prince was the general, each sent generals with troops to rescue Wei. The prince led the troops of the Five Domains to crush the Ch'in army at Ho-wai, putting their general Meng Ao to flight and following up on their victory by pursuing the Ch'in army to Han-ku Pass, where they so subdued the troops of Ch'in that they did not dare come forth.

At this time the prince's power shook the whole world, and retainers of the high lords of the domains submitted their techniques of warfare to him. The prince put each down under its appropriate name, in what is commonly called today *The Military Techniques of the Prince of Wei*.

The King of Ch'in was greatly troubled by this and had ten thousand measures of silver transported to Wei to win over a retainer of Chin Pi. He ordered him to speak ill of the prince to the King of Wei, saying, "The prince fled the kingdom and lived for ten years in a foreign country. Now he is a general of Wei, and the generals of the high lords of the domains are all subordinate to him. The high lords have heard only of the Prince of Wei; they have not heard of the King of Wei. And if the prince should take advantage of the moment to establish himself as king and ruler, the high lords would stand in dread of the prince's power and would join to support his taking the throne."

On numerous occasions Ch'in made devious use of Wei's intelligence network by sending false congratulations to the prince regarding whether he had taken the throne as King of Wei. Hearing such slander every day, the King of Wei could not help believing it, and finally he sent someone to replace the prince as general.

Knowing that he had been removed from office because of repeated slander, the prince refused to go to court on the pretext of illness. He spent the whole night long drinking with his retainers, drinking strong brew, and consorting with many women. For four years he drank and made merry day and night, until at last he died of the effects of drinking. King An-li of Wei died that same year.

When Ch'in heard that the prince was dead, Meng Ao was sent to attack Wei. He took twenty cities and established them as the "Eastern Province." After that, Ch'in nibbled away at Wei, and eighteen years later took the King of Wei captive and sacked Ta-liang.

When Kao-tzu[3] the founder of our dynasty, first lived as a humble man, he frequently heard of the virtues of the prince. Later when he became Son of Heaven, he would always offer up prayers to the prince whenever he passed Ta-liang. In his twelfth year [195 B.C.], returning from attacking against Ching-pu, he established five families to take charge of maintaining the prince's tomb so that offerings would be made to the prince in every season forevermore.

The Lord Historian: I have passed by the ruins of Ta-liang and have looked for the place known as the Yi Gate. The Yi Gate was the eastern gate of the city. Among the princes of this world there were others who delighted in gentlemen-retainers. Still there was good reason why the Lord of Hsin-ling made contact with those who lived, removed from the public eye, in the caves of cliffs, and felt no shame in forming relationships with those socially beneath him. It was not for nothing that his fame crowned the high lords of the domains. Whenever our Founder passed by there, he ordered that offerings be made without end.

3. The first ruler of the Han.

From *The Schemes of the Warring States: Yü-jang*

Yü-jang, grandson of Pi Yang of Ch'in, first entered the service of the houses of the Fan and Chung-hang,[1] but he was unhappy there. He quit and went to the Earl of Chih of Ch'in, who treated him with great favor. When the three branches of Chin[2] divided up the realm of the house of the Earl of Chih, it was Lord Hsiang of Chao who felt the greatest ill will toward the Earl of Chih and took his skull as his drinking vessel. Yü-jang had fled into hiding in the hills and said, "A liegeman dies for the man who appreciates him; a woman makes herself beautiful for the man who is pleased with her. May I then take vengeance on this enemy of the house of the Earl of Chih!" He changed his name and made himself a branded criminal.[3] Thus he got into the palace as a plasterer of the latrines, with the purpose of assassinating Lord Hsiang.[4]

Lord Hsiang was on his way to the latrine and had a trembling of the heart. He had the plasterer seized and questioned, and it turned out to be Yü-jang, who had put a sharp edge on his trowel. Yü-jang said, "I wanted to take revenge on the enemy of the Earl of Chih." His entourage wanted to put Yü-jang to death, but Lord Hsiang of Chao said, "This is a liegeman of principle. I will merely keep him away from me. The Earl of Chih is dead and has no offspring, yet one who served him will go so far as to seek revenge on his enemies. This is one of the most worthy men in the world." And in the end he had Yü-jang set free.

Yü-jang next put lacquer on his body to cover it with sores; he got rid of his whiskers and eyebrows and mutilated himself to alter his appearance. He then went begging. Even his wife did not recognize him. But she said, "Since this man doesn't look at all like my husband, why does his voice sound so much like that of my husband?" After this he swallowed ashes to make himself hoarse and changed the sound of his voice.

A friend said to him, "The course you are following is one of great hardship, yet one that does not do the deed. If you would be spoken of as a man of powerful will, then it will be so; but you will not be spoken of as a resourceful man. If you used your talents in the skillful service of Lord Hsiang, he would certainly draw you close to him and make you his favorite. If you could get close to him, then you could do whatever you wanted. This would be very easy, and the deed could be done." Yü-jang then laughed and answered him, "This would be to take revenge on the second man who appreciated me for the sake of the first man who appreciated me. This would be to turn outlaw against a new lord for the sake of a former lord. Nothing could more violate the principle of the bond between a lord and one who serves him. What I intend in doing as I do is to make clear the bond between a lord and one who serves him—it is not to take the easy way. To give a pledge of fealty and serve a man while seeking to assassinate him is to serve one's lord with duplicity in the heart. This hard thing that I do now may even put to shame all those in the world who in later times serve their lords with duplicity in their hearts."

After some while, Lord Hsiang was to go forth, and Yü-jang hid under a

1. Noble houses of the kingdom of Ch'in. 2. In 403 B.C. the kingdom of Ch'in was divided into three smaller kingdoms. 3. Criminals were branded so they could be recognized. 4. It was the responsibility of a son to take revenge for the killing of his father.

bridge across which he would have to pass. But when Lord Hsiang reached the bridge, his horse reared, whereupon Lord Hsiang said, "Yü-jang must be here." He ordered someone to question the man, and it was indeed Yü-jang. Thereupon Lord Hsiang of Chao faced Yü-jang and said, "Did you not once serve the house of Fan and Chung-hang? Yet when the Earl of Chih destroyed those houses, you did not take revenge on him, but rather pledged him your fealty. The Earl of Chih is dead now, so why only in this case are you so deeply determined to take revenge on his enemy?" Yü-jang said, "I served the houses of Fan and Chung-hang, yet they treated me as an ordinary man. So in return I behave toward them like an ordinary man. The Earl of Chih treated me like one of the liegeman of the domain. So in return I behave like a liegeman of the domain."

Lord Hsiang gave a great sigh and shed tears, saying, "Oh, Yü-jang! You have already become famous for what you have done on the Earl of Chih's account. And I forgave you then—that too was enough. You make plans on your own behalf now, and I may not forgive you." And he ordered his men to form a ring around him.

Then Yü-jang said, "I have heard it said that a wise ruler does not force a man to conceal his principles and I have heard that one who serves with loyalty, to make his fame complete, does not cling to life. Before you were lenient and forgave me, and for this the whole world praises your virtue. I do indeed accept the punishment that must follow from what has happened today. Still, if I could ask for your coat and stab it, I would feel no resentment in my death. I cannot expect this, but I reveal what is within me."

Thereupon Lord Hsiang saw that Yü-jang did indeed have principles, and he ordered one who served him to take his coat and give it to Yü-jang. Yü-jang drew out his sword, leapt around several times, shouted to Heaven, and stabbed the coat, saying, "By this I take vengeance for the Earl of Chih." Then he fell on his sword and died. On the day he died the liegemen of Chao heard of it, and they all wept.

From *Biographies of the Assassins: Nieh Cheng*

Nieh Cheng came from the Deepwell section of the city of Chih. He killed someone, and to escape his enemies' revenge, he went to Ch'i with his mother and sister. There he worked as a butcher.

Some time later Yen Chung-tzu of P'u-yang was in the service of Count Ai of Han, and he had a quarrel with Hsia Lei, the Minister of Han. Fearing that he would be executed, Yen Chung-tzu fled and traveled about looking for someone who could get revenge on Hsia Lei. When he reached Ch'i, some of the local people said that Nieh Cheng was a man of courage and daring, who lived out of the public eye among butchers in order to escape his enemies.

Yen Chung-tzu went to his gate to pay his respects but was repeatedly turned away. After that he had beer prepared and went to offer a congratulatory toast to Nieh Cheng's mother. When everyone was feeling the effects of the beer, Yen Chung-tzu presented a hundredweight of gold to Nieh Cheng's mother to wish her a long life. Nieh Cheng was alarmed at such generosity and was determined to refuse it. Yen Chung-tzu pressed it on him with just as much determination, but Nieh Cheng refused, saying, "I am lucky to still have my aged mother. Our household may be poor, but I make my living here as a dog butcher so that I can provide her delicacies to eat every day. She is well provided for, and I dare not accept your gift."

Yen Chung-tzu had the others withdraw and then said to Nieh Cheng, "I have an enemy and have roamed through many of the great domains. When I came to Ch'i, however, I heard of your high sense of right, sir, and this is why I presented the hundredweight of gold—to use for ordinary expenses in taking care of your aged mother and in that way to get on good terms with you. I wouldn't dare expect anything from you for it." Nieh Cheng replied, "The only reason I have curtailed my ambitions and accepted the indignity of working as a butcher in the marketplace has been to take care of my aged mother. So long as my mother is alive, I do not dare commit myself to anyone." Yen Chung-tzu insisted that Nieh Cheng give way, but in the end Nieh Cheng refused to accept the gift. Nevertheless, Yen Chung-tzu played out his proper role as a guest and then left.

Some time later Nieh Cheng's mother died. After she was buried and the period of mourning completed, Nieh Cheng said, "To think that I am but a man of the marketplace, one who wields the knife as a butcher, while Yen Chung-tzu is an adviser of the high nobility, and yet he did not think it too much to turn his carriage and riders to meet me! The way I treated him was ungenerous in the extreme. I had done nothing important to deserve it, yet he offered a hundredweight in gold for my mother's sake. Even though I didn't accept it, in doing this he was simply showing how deeply he understood me. How can I just do nothing when a good and worthy man has been stirred to glaring rage and then personally shows his confidence in a poor, and humble man? When he pressed me earlier, I acted as I did only because of my mother. Now that my mother has lived out her natural span, I will be of use to this man who so well understands me."

He next went west to P'u-yang, and meeting Yen Chung-tzu said, "The only reason that I could not commit myself to you earlier was because my mother was still alive. Now unfortunately her years are over. Who is it that you want me to take revenge on? Please let me carry this matter through." Yen Chung-tzu told him the whole story: "My enemy is Hsia Lei, the Minister of Han. Hsia Lei is also the uncle of the ruler of Han. His kindred are very numerous, and whenever he stays outside his compound, he is extremely well guarded. I tried to get people to assassinate him, but none was ever successful. Now I am lucky that you have not rejected me, so let me increase the number of carriages, mounts, and strong warriors to assist you." Nieh Cheng replied, "The distance between Han and Wei is not very great. If you're going to kill a minister and that minister is also a relation of the ruler of a domain, the situation is such that you should not use many people. If you use many people, something will inevitably go wrong; if something goes wrong, word will inevitably leak out; and if word leaks out, the entire domain of Han will be your enemy. Then you really would be in danger!" Thus Nieh Cheng refused carriages, horses, and men. He then said farewell and set out alone.

Sword in hand, he came to Han. Hsia Lei, the Minister of Han, was seated in his office, and there was a great throng of men with weapons and pikes standing guard around him. Nieh Cheng went directly in, climbed the stairs, and stabbed Hsia Lei to death. His entourage was in great confusion. Nieh

Cheng gave a loud shout and killed several dozen men. Then he cut the skin off his face, gouged out his eyes, cut himself open and pulled out his entrails, and died.

The ruler of Han took Nieh Cheng's corpse and had it exposed in the marketplace, trying to find out who the man was—but no one knew. He then offered a reward of a thousand silver pieces to anyone who could tell him who killed the minister Hsia Lei. But after a long time no one came forward with this knowledge.

Nieh Cheng's sister Jung heard that someone had assassinated the Minister of Han, but that the criminal could not be ascertained because no one in the kingdom knew his name; thus they had exposed his corpse and offered a reward of a thousand pieces of silver. At this she let out a moan. "Could this be my younger brother? Alas, Yen Chung-tzu understood my brother all too well!" She went to the capital of Han and to its marketplace, and the dead man was indeed Nieh Cheng. She collapsed on the corpse, weeping with the utmost grief. And she said, "This man was known as Nieh Cheng, from the Deepwell quarter of the city of Chih." The crowds of people walking through the marketplace all said, "This man assaulted the minister of our domain, and the king has posted a reward of a thousand pieces of silver for his name—haven't you heard? How can you dare come here and recognize him?"

Jung answered them, "I have heard. Nevertheless, the reason why Nieh Cheng endured disgrace and abandoned himself to the commerce of the marketplace was so that our aged mother would come to no harm and because I was not yet married. Once our mother had passed away and I had married, Yen Chung-tzu selected my brother to be his friend, even in his degraded position. He was so kind and generous that my brother had no choice. A gentleman will indeed die for someone who understands him. And now, because I was still alive, he has gone further, mutilating himself so there will be no traces to follow. How could I stand in dread paying with my own life, and by doing so wipe away forever my worthy brother's name?" This amazed the people in the marketplace of Han. Then she called out to Heaven several times, until, with a piteous moan, she died at Nieh Cheng's side.

When this story was heard in Chih, Ch'u, Ch'i, and Wei, everyone said, "It is not just that Nieh Cheng showed ability—his sister too was a woman of fierce principles. Suppose that Nieh Cheng had truly known that his sister lacked the determination to simply endure the situation and that she would surely cross a thousand leagues of perils, unmindful of the troubles that would come from recognizing the exposed corpse, just to proclaim his name. Had he known that, he would not necessarily have committed himself to Yen Chung-tzu."

But Yen Chung-tzu may indeed also be known as someone capable of acquiring gentlemen by his ability to understand a person's worth.

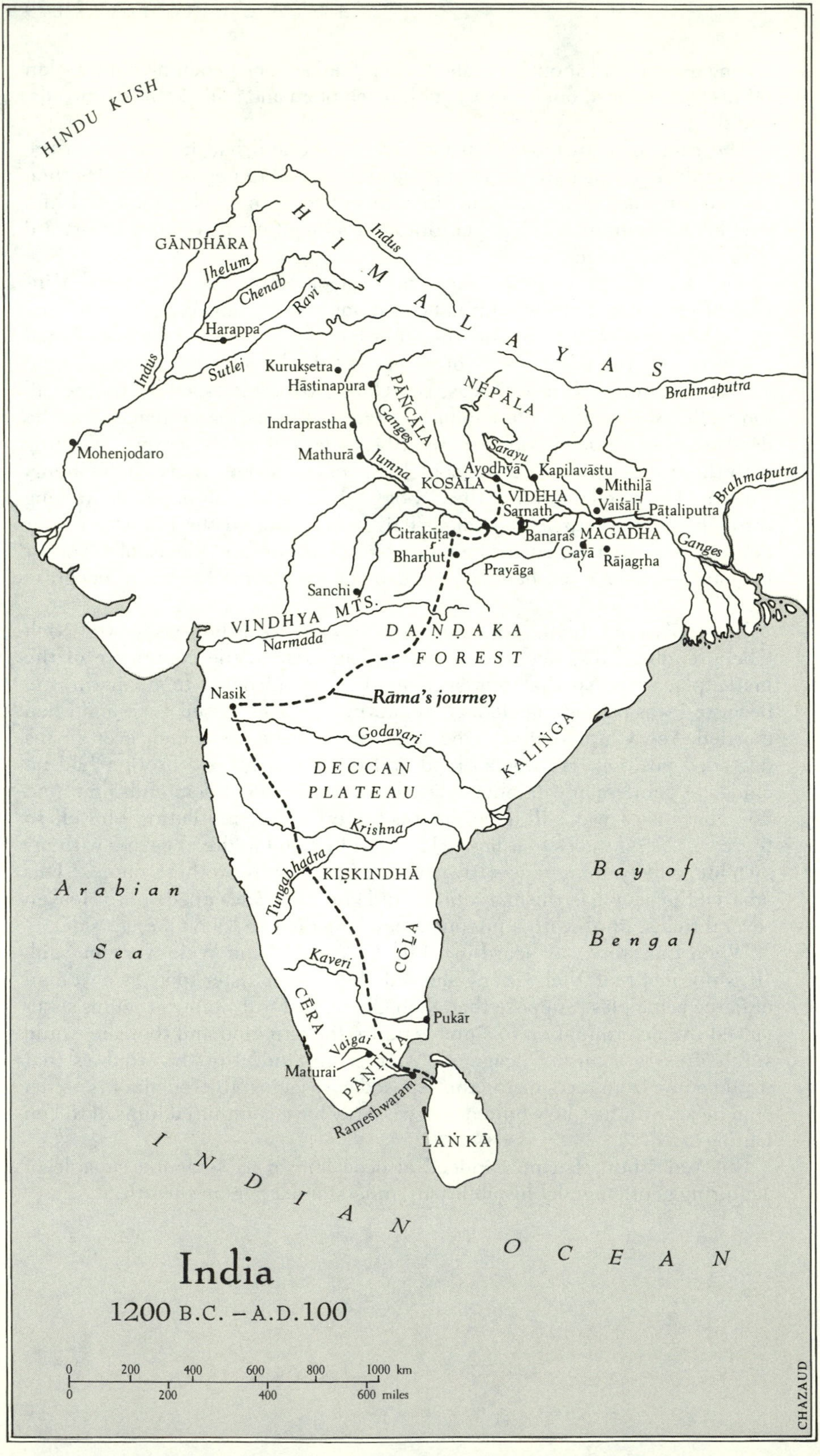

HINDU KUSH
H I M A L A Y A S
GĀNDHĀRA
Indus
Jhelum
Chenab
Ravi
Harappa
Sutlej
Indus
Kurukṣetra
Hāstinapura
Indraprastha
Mathurā
Mohenjodaro
PĀÑCĀLA
Ganges
Jumna
NEPĀLA
Sarayu
Ayodhyā
Kapilavāstu
KOSALA
VIDEHA
Mithilā
Vaiśālī
Pāṭaliputra
Sarnath
Brahmaputra
Brahmaputra
Citrakūṭa
Banaras
MAGADHA
Gayā
Rājagṛha
Ganges
Bharhut
Prayāga
Sanchi
VINDHYA MTS.
Narmada
D A Ṇ Ḍ A K A
F O R E S T
Nasik
Rāma's journey
Godavari
DECCAN
PLATEAU
KALIṄGA
Krishna
Tungabhadra
KIṢKINDHĀ
Arabian
Sea
Bay of
Bengal
CŌḺA
Kaveri
CĒRA
Pukār
Vaigai
Maturai
PĀṆṬIYA
Rameshwaram
LAṄKĀ
I N D I A N   O C E A N
India
1200 B.C. – A.D. 100
0 200 400 600 800 1000 km
0 200 400 600 miles
CHAZAUD

India's Heroic Age

Modern India, with a population of 800 million, has remained remarkably in touch with its ancient roots in the face of centuries of change. The dominant pattern of Indian cultural history is a many-layered pluralism in which numerous subcultures defined by ethnic, religious, and linguistic differences coexist and relate with each other in complex yet coherent ways. This pluralism pervades and colors the vast body of oral and written literature that India has produced over 3,500 years, in more than twenty languages and innumerable local dialects.

The Aryans, a group of nomadic tribes who apparently originated in central Asia and entered India around 1500 B.C., brought with them an early form of Sanskrit, a language that, along with nearly all the major languages of Europe and many in Asia, belongs to the Indo-European family. In India, Sanskrit became the principal language of classical literature, administration, and all forms of intellectual endeavor, maintaining this role almost up to the nineteenth century. Sanskrit's primary cultural association is with Hinduism, India's dominant religious tradition, a direct descendant of the Vedic religion of the Aryans. Gautama Buddha (563–483 B.C.) and Mahāvīra (died 468 B.C.), noblemen of Aryan clans who founded the Buddhist and Jain religious paths as radical alternatives to the Vedic religion, preached their messages in Pali and Prakrit, popular dialects related to Sanskrit. Hindi and the other modern languages of north India descended from the various Prakrit dialects. Sanskrit and its related languages and dialects are known as the Indo-Aryan languages.

Classical Tamil, the language of the ancient literature (first through third centuries A.D.) of south India, is the oldest example of Dravidian, a family of languages to which all the modern languages in south India belong. In later times, the literatures and cultures of both north and south India developed through continuous and fruitful interchange. From the twelfth century onward, various conquering Muslim dynasties—the Mughals (or Moguls) were the latest of these—brought to Indian literature and civilization not only the sensibility of Islam but also the heritage of the Arabic and Persian languages and literatures. Beginning in the seventeenth century, the activities of the British East India Company laid the foundation for British colonial rule and led to the establishment of Western-style education. Though British rule lasted only until India's independence in 1947, the English language and Western ideas have become a permanent piece of India's cultural mosaic.

THE LEGACY OF THE *VEDAS* AND *UPANIṢADS*

As in China, Egypt, and the Near East, civilization in India appears to have begun in a river valley. Of the Indus valley civilization that flourished in great cities such as Mohenjo Daro and Harappa (ca. 3000–1500 B.C.) in northwestern India (now largely in Pakistan) we have only archeological remains, which include writing in a script that has not yet been deciphered. Thus it is with the Aryans that the continuous history of Indian civilization and religion begins together with the history of Indian literature. Cattle breeders who eventually developed an agriculture, the Aryans settled in the Indus valley and left as their legacy the *Vedas,* four books of sacred hymns that accompanied the worship of gods who were personifications of nature and the powers of the cosmos. The following verses—from a hymn in the *Rig Veda* to Sūrya, the sun god—epitomize the spirit and imagery of Vedic myth and poetry:

> His brilliant banners draw upwards the god who knows all creatures, so that everyone may see the sun.
> The constellations, along with the nights, steal away like thieves, making way for the sun who gazes on everyone . . .
> He is the eye with which, O Purifying Varuṇa [god of law], you look upon the busy one among men.
> You cross heaven and the vast realm of space, O sun, measuring days by nights, looking upon the generations.
> Seven bay mares carry you in the chariot, O sun god with hair of flame, gazing from afar.
> We have come up out of darkness, seeing the higher light around us, going to the sun, the god among the gods, the highest light.*

Preserved in what appears to be an unbroken oral tradition of memorization and recitation, the *Vedas* are Hinduism's primary scripture. For thousands of years priests have chanted Vedic hymns at the major sacramental rites of naming, initiation, marriage, and death; and Hindu rituals are modeled on the Vedic fire sacrifice. Hindus regard the hymns as divine revelation: poet-seers called *ṛṣi* "saw" the verses in their mind's eye and spontaneously recited them in the form of sacred utterance (*mantra*). Tracing their ancestry to the ancient *ṛṣi,* the brahmans, priestly transmitters of the Vedic hymns and rites, have traditionally commanded the highest status in the Hindu class hierarchy.

The last hymns of the *Rig Veda* (ca. 1000 B.C.), reflect a change in the Aryan worldview. The concluding verses of the creation hymn called *Nāsadīya* (The Hymn of Nonexistence) capture the skeptical spirit that signaled the end of the Vedic age and the beginning of an age of spiritual quest and philosophical speculation:

> Who really knows? Who will here proclaim it? Whence was it produced? Whence is this creation? The gods came afterwards, with the creation of this universe. Who then knows whence it has arisen?
> Whence this creation has arisen—perhaps it formed itself, or perhaps it did not—the one who looks down on it, in the highest heaven, only he knows—or perhaps he does not know.†

The *Vedas* were followed by the *Upaniṣads* (Mystic Doctrines), a genre of philosophical texts containing the mystical and philosophical speculations of thinkers who rejected the ritualistic religion of the *Vedas* in favor of a quest for ultimate wisdom. The prose dialogues of the oldest of these works, the *Bṛhadāraṇyaka Upaniṣad* (The Great Mystic Doctrine of the Forest) and *Chāndogya Upaniṣad* (The Mystic Doctrine of the *Sāma Veda*), written around 900 to 800 B.C., take place between eager pupils—men and women from diverse social classes—and wise teachers, among whom are warriors and artisans as well as brahmans and hermits. The sages of the early *Upaniṣads* teach that a single divine essence (Brahman, different from brahman, the priestly class) pervades the universe, that the human soul is a manifestation of this divine essence, and that spiritual emancipation consists in mystically knowing the essential unity between self and universe. The teachings of the sages did not in effect undermine the authority of the *Vedas,* nor did they result in significant social upheaval. On the other hand, the concepts of the personal spiritual quest, the wise teacher (*guru*), and the transforming power of knowledge remain enduring motifs in Indian civilization.

*Translated by Wendy Doniger O'Flaherty. †Translated by Wendy Doniger O'Flaherty.

THOUGHT AND LITERATURE OF THE HEROIC AGE

The literature of India's heroic age, produced between 550 B.C. and A.D. 100, reflects the spread of Aryan civilization over much of north India. It records the development of the Buddhist and Hindu religions from the Vedic civilization and provides a window into the non-Aryan civilization of the Tamil-speaking peoples of south India. The Sanskrit poems *Rāmāyaṇa* (ca. 550 B.C.) and *Mahābhārata* (the main portions of which date back in their present form at least to the fourth century B.C.) are India's earliest epics and express seminal Hindu values in the making.

Composed and edited over a period of nine hundred years (roughly 550 B.C.–A.D. 400), the epics are heroic narratives of an earlier time, originally recited by bards on the battlefield and at royal rituals, preserved in a fluid oral tradition, and finally reworked (like much of the Old Testament of the Bible) by priestly elites. Although the poems contain much mythic and legendary material and each is attributed to a legendary author who, like the Vedic poets, is called a seer (*ṛṣi*), there is reason to believe that they are grounded in actual events that took place between the ninth and seventh centuries B.C., when carriers of the Vedic culture spread eastward in north India. The *Mahābhārata,* attributed to Vyāsa, tells the story of a great civil war among Aryan clans, while the *Rāmāyaṇa* of Vālmīki narrates the exile and adventures of Prince Rāma of Kosala. Together the two epics present a poetic history of the north Indian royal houses and the foundations of Aryan rule in the valley of the river Ganges. Hence their traditional Indian classification as *itihāsa* ("historical narrative," literally "thus it was").

Despite similarities with the *Iliad* and *Odyssey* (which suggest a kinship that might well go back to common Indo-European roots), the flavor of the *Rāmāyaṇa* and *Mahābhārata* is unmistakably Indian, and Hindus have valued the epics above all as sacred narratives that embody religious and ethical teachings. Included among the Hindu scriptures (in a class of texts known as "tradition"), the two epics have served, and continue to serve, as living cultural forces with deep personal meaning for Hindus from all walks of life. The Sanskrit versions of Vālmīki and Vyāsa have given rise to innumerable subsequent retellings in the major Indian languages, while the epic narratives have provided the themes for much of Indian art and literature over the last two thousand years. And their universal dimensions have allowed the Indianized cultures of Southeast Asia—Java, Thailand, and Malaysia, for instance—to "translate" them into their own cultural idioms and so to embrace them as beloved epics of their own.

Not only Hindus but most Indians grow up hearing the *Rāmāyaṇa* and *Mahābhārata,* as told by members of the family or professional storytellers, and seeing them enacted in diverse forms of theater and dance. And it is here that young Hindus first encounter *dharma,* held to be the guiding principle of proper human conduct, and the doctrine of *karma.* In traditional Hindu thought *dharma* (literally, "that which holds") is the force that supports the universe—that is, "holds" it together. It is the underlying principle of the social, moral, and cosmic orders, which are described and classified in hierarchically ordered, interlinked sets of four categories. There are four cyclic ages of the cosmos (*yuga*). There are four "classes" (*varṇa*) in society: the learned or priestly brahman, the *kṣatriya* (warrior and administrator), the *vaiśya* (merchant, farmer, or other member of the productive community), and the *śūdra* (laborer). Likewise, there are four stages of life: celibate student, householder, forest dweller, and wandering ascetic. Although the progression of *yugas* from one to four records a process of decay (somewhat analogous to the decline from golden to iron ages in traditional Western thought) and the four classes are organized from high to low, the stages of life reverse the progression, moving from lower to higher on the spiritual plane.

The dynamic center of all these schemes is the scheme of the four spheres, or goals, that should, ideally, govern life. This set of categories begins with *dharma* (here used in a second, somewhat narrower, sense to mean the sphere of sacred duty, righteousness, and moral law); followed by *artha,* the sphere of worldly profit, wealth, and political power; *kāma,* the sphere of pleasure and love; and *mokṣa,* the ultimate goal of life, the sphere in which one seeks liberation from the constraints of worldly existence. All men, including *śūdras,* are bound by a prescribed program of sacred duty (*dharma*) that is appropriate to their class (*varṇa*), but only men of the three upper classes, known as the "twice born" classes (initiation into the rites and texts of the *Veda* is considered to be a second birth), may work their way through the stages of life toward *mokṣa.* Women form a class in themselves, for a woman's *dharma* is defined as that of a wife, allowing women no identities or aspirations apart from their allegience to their husbands.

The four classes are concerned only with determining one's place in the cosmic scheme of things. The Hindu man's actual status is determined by his being born into one of the innumerable castes (*jāti,* literally, "birth"), which, defined by occupation, kinship, marriage practices, and other factors, make up a minutely stratified society with rigid divisions among groups and individuals. Although the epics and later Hindu texts reflect a constantly shifting balance of power among the brahman, warrior, and merchant classes, the religious basis of the caste system guarantees the subordination of a large number of "service" castes to a small number of elite groups. Furthermore, the idea of sacred duty combines with the doctrine of *karma* to form a powerful rationale for the perpetuation of social hierarchy.

Karma is the premise on which all three ancient religions of India build their doctrines of the ultimate goal of religion. According to the theory of *karma,* all creatures are ultimately responsible for their own existential conditions, and existence is invariably bound up with suffering. To exist is to be perpetually engaged in action (the basic meaning of the word *karma* is "a deed, that which is done"). All deeds, good and bad, have inevitable results, which must be borne by the doer in an existential state, so that the soul is trapped in an endless cycle of birth and death (known as *saṃsāra,* "going round and round").

The earliest descriptions of the theory of *karma,* implying the entire sequence described above, are found in the *Upaniṣads,* whose authors were engaged in contemplating ways to transcend the limitations of the human condition. The thinkers of the *Upaniṣads* put forward the theory that the soul or self is a pure and immutable entity, untouched by *karma,* and that liberation from the cycle of rebirth can be achieved by identifying oneself with this pure self. Gautama Buddha rejected the concept of an immortal soul, concentrating instead on the suffering that was thought to result from *karma* and on the urgent need of all creatures to be freed from this burden of suffering. In the form of animal fables and popular tales, the *Jātaka* stories illustrate the Buddha's teaching regarding the path to liberation from rebirth, a unique combination of radical detachment from desire, the root cause of *karma,* and an ethic of action directed only toward the welfare of one's fellow creatures. Every person, regardless of caste, gender, or social status, could follow the Buddha's path (the *Dharma*) with the ultimate aim of becoming liberated from *karma* rebirth by becoming a *buddha,* or "an enlightened one."

Buddhism arose from social and political contexts that were very different from those of the Hindu epics. Gautama Buddha was a prince of the Śākyas, an Aryan republican tribe on the Nepal border in the Himalayas. It was among the many tribal oligarchies and republics that flourished in northeastern India in the sixth century that he found his largest following, constituted especially of merchants, artisans, women, and others to whom the ritual religion and social hierarchies of early Hinduism had little to offer. Buddhist literature vividly reflects the cosmopolitan atmosphere and urban, mercantile civilization of the Mauryan empire (322–186 B.C.), India's first major empire, established by kings of an eastern Indian dynasty who, in the wake of Alexander of Macedon's invasion (326 B.C.), conquered most of India. A

Buddhist canonical text records the conversion of Menander, a Greek king of northwestern India; and under the enthusiastic patronage of Aśoka (269–232 B.C.)—the greatest of the Mauryan emperors—Buddhism spread as far south as the island of Sri Lanka and traveled, along with textiles and spices, to lands to the north and west of India.

The populist, egalitarian religions preached by Gautama Buddha and his near-contemporary Mahāvīra presented a formidable challenge to the elaborate socio-religious system engineered by the Hindu elites. The god Kṛṣṇa's teachings to the hero Arjuna in the *Bhagavad-Gītā* represent, among other things, a synthesis of the attempts of Hindu thinkers to come to grips with the need of all Hindus, men and women alike, for a nonhierarchical and more personal path to the distant goal of liberation from *karma* rebirth. The eventual triumph of the Hindu religion in India is based, however, not on the greater appeal of its philosophical tenets over those of the rival religions but on its ability to synthesize and absorb features from those very rivals and, above all, on its molding of the cults of charismatic popular gods such as Kṛṣṇa (or Krishna) into a religion of salvation and grace, which attracted even the Greco-Bactrians, Śakas, and others who ruled in north India from the dissolution of the Mauryan empire to the fourth century A.D.

For Hindus the terror of rebirth is mitigated by belief in a triad of great gods who are the highest manifestations of the divine principle underlying the universe. Brahmā, Viṣṇu, and Śiva respectively create, preserve, and destroy the universe and all creatures through the *yuga* cycles of cosmic time. Although there are many gods, Viṣṇu, the preserver, and Śiva, the destroyer, stand out as supreme deities, for Hindus worship one or the other as God, whose grace will help deliver them from the bonds of *karma* rebirth. Kṛṣṇa, the teacher of the *Bhagavad-Gītā*, is an incarnation of Viṣṇu, and his revelation of his divine identity to his devotee Arjuna constitutes the supreme mystery of this mystical text. For the heroes of the epics the belief in God and gods offers an alternative to the mechanistic view of *karma* and suffering. In explaining actions and events, they refer as often to the deeds of the gods and to fate (by which they mean the collective will of the gods as opposed to the will of the individual) as to *karma*.

Although the ancient Tamil poems included here reveal an intimate knowledge of Aryan civilization and religion, everything about them—from the society they portray to the metaphors they employ—is permeated with a Tamil warrior ethos that is completely different from the values embodied in the texts in the north Indian languages. These poems, which give supreme value to love and war and to the lives of men and women in this world, perhaps come closest to Western ideals of the literature of a "heroic age." For most Hindus, however, Rāma and Arjuna are heroes precisely because they are able to temper the inherent violence of the warrior's way of life with compassion and ascetic self-control, thereby lifting their acts to a higher moral plane. In the Buddhist tradition, Gautama Buddha is a superhuman hero-king, one who was destined to become a "world conqueror" (*cakravartin*) with his teaching of spiritual perfection, and a little more than two hundred years after the Buddha's death, Emperor Aśoka affirmed the power of this heroic ideal by laying down his weapons and proclaiming, by public edicts carved on rock, his preference for the "conquest of righteousness" to conquest by the sword.

FURTHER READING

Arthur Llewellyn Basham, *The Wonder That Was India* (1954), is the best general introduction to Indian civilization up to 1565. William Theodore De Bary, ed., *Sources of Indian Tradition* (1958), is a comprehensive volume of the textual sources of Indian thought from the beginnings to the present, with concise, accessible introductory notes. Thomas J. Hopkin, *The Hindu Religious Tradition* (1971), and R. C. Zaehner, *Hinduism* (1900), are more detailed introductions to Hinduism, while similar treatments of Buddhism may be found in Edward Conze, *Buddhism: Its Essence and Development* (1900), and Richard Robinson and Willard Johnson, *The Buddhist Religion* (1900). Edward C. Dimock et al., eds., *The Literatures of India: An Introduction* (1974), is an excellent introduction to Indian literature. For Indian mythology and the Hindu gods, consult Veronica Ions, *Indian Mythology* (1967), as well as A. K. Coomaraswamy and Sister Nivedita, *Myths of the Hindus and Buddhists* (1967).

PRONOUNCING GLOSSARY

The following list uses common English syllables and stress accents to provide rough equivalents of selected words whose pronunciation may be unfamiliar to the general reader.

Arjuna: *uhr'-joo-nuh*
artha: *uhr'-tuh*
Aśoka: *uh-shoh'-kuh*
Bhagavad-Gītā: *buh'-guh-vuhd–gee'-tah*
Bṛhadāraṇyaka Upaniṣad: *bree-huhd-ah'-ruhn-yuh-kuh oo-puh'-nee-shuhd*
cakravartin: *chuh'-kruh-vuhr-teen*
kāma: *kah'-muh*
Kṛṣṇa: *kreesh'-nuh*
kṣatriya: *kshuh-tree-yuh*
Mahābhārata: *muh-hah-bah'-ruh-tah*
mokṣa: *mohk'-shuh*
Rāmāyaṇa: *rah-mah'-yuh-nuh*
ṛṣi: *ree'-shee*
Śākya: *shahk'-yuh*
saṃsāra: *suhm-sah'-ruh*
Śiva: *shee'-vuh*
śūdra: *shoo'-druh*
Sūrya: *soor'-yuh*
Upaniṣad: *oo-puh'-nee-shuhd*
vaísya: *vai'-shyuh*
Viṣṇu: *veesh'-noo*
Vyāsa: *vee-yah'-suh*
yuga: *yoo'-guh*

TIME LINE

TEXTS	CONTEXTS
	ca. 3000–1500 B.C. Indus Valley civilization flourishes in urban centers • Writing in use
ca. 1500–1200 B.C. Composition of the *Rig Veda,* oldest of the four Vedas, texts of hymns and chants in an archaic form of the Sanskrit language, for the fire sacrifice of the Aryan Vedic religion	**ca. 1500** Aryan tribes speaking Sanskrit, an Indo-European language, enter India via the northwest and settle in the Indus Valley
ca. 900 The Sanskrit *Upaniṣads,* dialogues and meditations of philosophers on the nature of existence, the soul, and the universe	
ca. 700 Homer's ***Iliad*** and ***Odyssey***	**ca. 700** Emergence of kingdoms and republics in northern India
	563–483 Gautama Buddha, founder of Buddhism, preaches in Pāli, a dialect related to Sanskrit. He establishes an order of monks and nuns and spreads his new religion in the Ganges River Valley in north India • Mahāvīra, Buddha's contemporary, founds Jainism, a religion emphasizing nonviolence and asceticism
ca. 550 Vālmīki's Sanskrit poem ***The Rāmāyaṇa,*** a heroic epic recounting the deeds of the north Indian prince Rāma	
480–400 Aeschylus, Sophocles, and Euripides	
ca. 400 B.C.–400 A.D. The Sanskrit epic ***The Mahābhārata,*** the narrative of a great war among north Indian clansmen, takes shape	
ca. 400 B.C. Pāṇini writes the *Aṣṭādhyāyī* (Eight chapters), the authoritative grammar of the Sanskrit language and a model for modern linguistic science	

Boldface titles indicate works in the anthology.

TIME LINE

TEXTS	CONTEXTS
4th century B.C. Early version of ***The Jātaka,*** a collection of stories about the Buddha in the spoken dialect known as Pali	**ca. 326** Alexander of Macedon invades India
	269–232 Asóka Maurya, emperor of India, spreads Buddhism in Sri Lanka, patronizes Buddhist art, and issues royal edicts in praise of Buddhist ethics in Prakrit, spoken dialects related to Sanskrit
200–100 The Sanskrit text *Saddharmapuṇḍarīka* (The lotus of the good law), expounding the doctrines of Mahayana (later) Buddhism, is written	**ca. 200** Beginning of Buddhist cave sanctuaries and art at Ajanta in western India, and of the Hindu Bhagavata cult of devotion to a personal God
100 B.C.–A.D. 250 Under the patronage of south Indian kings, anthologies of lyric poems of love and war are produced in Tamil, a language unrelated to Sanskrit and the north Indian languages	
1st century B.C. ***The Bhagavad-Gītā,*** the mystical teaching of the god Kṛṣṇa to the hero Arjuna, is added to ***The Mahābhārata***	**ca. 90** The Śakas, a Scythian tribe from Bactria (to the northwest of modern Afghanistan), invade India
	50 B.C.–A.D. 250 The Sātavāhana kings of central India patronize lyric poetry and narrative literature in Prakrit dialects
ca. A.D. 100 Aśvaghoṣa writes *Buddhacarita* (Acts of the Buddha), a Sanskrit epic poem in the courtly style, on the life of the Buddha • The early Buddhist canonical texts in the Pali language, including the ***Jātaka*** stories, are written down in Sri Lanka	**1st–2nd centuries** Buddhism spreads to China
100–200 The *Dharma Śāstra* of Manu (The laws of Manu), the authoritative treatise on laws and codes of conduct according to the Hindu religion, is completed	

THE RĀMĀYAṆA OF VĀLMĪKI
ca. 550 B.C.

The Sanskrit epic poem *Rāmāyaṇa* (The Way of Rāma) by Vālmīki is the oldest literary version (ca. 550 B.C.) of the tale of the exile and adventures of Prince Rāma, a story that was known from Indian folk traditions as early as the seventh century B.C. Because ancient tradition the world over placed little value on the identity of authors or artists, all we know about Vālmīki is gleaned from legends about the circumstances that led him to compose the *Rāmāyaṇa*, work of 24,000 verses, divided into seven "books," called *kāṇḍa*. It is probable that, like Homer, he gathered and shaped the scattered material of many oral traditions into the poetic whole that we read today.

Vālmīki's *Rāmāyaṇa* became the source for a multitude of versions composed in all the major Indian languages over several centuries. The story has also been preserved in oral traditions by storytellers and continues to be enacted in countless regional folk theaters in India. It would be no exaggeration to say that the Rāma story is *the* great story of Indian civilization, the one narrative that all Indians have known and loved through the ages and whose popularity remains undiminished to this day.

In the Indian tradition, Vālmīki is celebrated as the "first poet," his *Rāmāyaṇa* the "original poem." The poem itself begins with the tale of the sage Vālmīki's invention of metrical verse. Responding to Vālmīki's question about who in the world is a perfect man, the sage Nārada outlines the story of the hero Rāma, whose wife was abducted by a demon-king. Brooding on the sad tale, Vālmīki goes for a walk along the banks of the Tamasā River, where he sees a pair of mating herons. Suddenly, a hunter shoots the male bird, and the female cries in anguish as she sees her mate's body writhing on the ground. Moved to intense compassion by her grief, Vālmīki utters inspired words in lyric verse in the form of a couplet. Thus was born, Vālmīki tells us, the *śloka,* the meter of the epics and of many other works in Sanskrit. The legend reflects the classical Indian ideal of the poet as one who transforms the raw emotion and chaos of real life into an ordered work of art. In point of fact, Vālmīki's style is only a crude forerunner of the later *kāvya* style of classical Sanskrit poetry, which abounds in complex meters, figures of speech, and descriptions. On the other hand, the epic retains many of the formulaic devices of oral poetry that we have already met in Homer, such as ready-made epithets that can slip easily into convenient slots in the metrical line—for instance, the formula "Rāma, devoted to righteousness" (*rāmo dharmabhṛtām varaḥ*), which occupies exactly one-quarter of the *śloka* verse.

The *Rāmāyaṇa* blends historical saga, nature myth, morality tale, and religious mythology. Rāma is associated with the line of Ikṣvāku kings who ruled the kingdom of Kosala in the Ganges valley of north India from their capital in Ayodhyā in the sixth and fifth centuries B.C. Legends surrounding the Ikṣvāku royal house and the adventures of Rāma form the core of the epic, Books 2 to 6. Books 1, *Bāla* (Childhood), and 7, *Uttara* (The Last Book), generally agreed to be additions to the original Vālmīki text, form a frame for the central narrative, introducing and completing the story of Rāma as a divine incarnation (*avatāra*).

In the core story, Rāvaṇa, a powerful king of the *rākṣasas*—evil demons who continually threaten social and moral order (*dharma*) in the world—has obtained a boon (gift) of invulnerability to gods and other superhuman beings who combat him. The gods persuade Viṣṇu, the great god whose function it is to preserve *dharma* in the universe, to incarnate himself as a man in order to destroy Rāvaṇa. Viṣṇu is thus born as Rāma, the son of Daśaratha, king of Kosala, by his senior queen, Kausalyā. Sons born at the same time to Daśaratha's two younger queens—Kaikeyī bore Bharata, and Sumitrā bore the twins Lakṣmaṇa and Śatrughna—share in Viṣṇu's divine essence. All four princes are noble heroes, but Rāma is a paragon of princely virtues. As youths, Rāma and Lakṣmaṇa go to the forest retreat of the hermit Viśvāmitra to guard his sacrificial rites from hostile demons. They then travel to Mithilā, the capital of Videha in eastern India, where Rāma wins the princess Sītā by besting other suitors in a contest to bend a magical bow, a motif we have already met in the *Odyssey*. Sītā, whose name means "furrow," is in reality the daughter of goddess Earth, but has been brought up by King Janaka.

Book 2, *Ayodhyā*, centers on prince Rāma's disinheritance. When King Daśaratha proclaims Rāma as his heir apparent, the whole capital city of Ayodhyā rejoices. Queen Kaikeyī, her jealousy roused by the counsel of a hunchback maidservant, decides to place her own son, Bharata, on the throne. She demands that Rāma be exiled to a life of hardship in the forest for fourteen years and that Bharata—who is absent from the court at this time—be made heir to the kingdom. She reminds the king that, according to a promise he had made her in the past, he owes her two favors of her choice. Bound by his word, Daśaratha has no alternative but to comply. Rāma accepts his exile, and Sītā and Lakṣmaṇa voluntarily join him. When the three have departed, Ayodhyā is left desolate, and the king dies of a broken heart. Upon his return, Bharata is horrified at the events that have taken place in his name. He chastises Kaikeyī and tries to hand over the kingdom to Rāma, but Rāma, wishing to honor his father's word, will serve out his exile, and Bharata agrees to rule as regent until his return.

A very different atmosphere dominates Books 3 to 6—*Āraṇya* (The Forest), *Kiṣkindhā* (The Kingdom of the Monkeys), *Sundara* (The Beautiful), and *Yuddha* (The War). Here, as in Odysseus's stories in Phaeacia, characters and events represent types traceable to older myths and folktales. "The Forest Book" narrates the adventures of Rāma, Sītā, and Lakṣmaṇa in the wildernesses of central and western India. Here the trio meets gentle hermits and ascetic sages, but also shape-shifting demons who attack the hermitages and devour their inhabitants. In several episodes Rāma puts to rout the *rākṣasas*, who infest the forest, and Rāvaṇa, the ten-headed king of demons, vows revenge. Using a magic deer to lure Rāma and Lakṣmaṇa away from their forest home, he kidnaps Sītā in his flying chariot. Rāma and Lakṣmaṇa set out in search of Sītā. Their southward journey brings them to Kiṣkindhā, kingdom of the monkeys (*vānaras*), and Rāma strikes up an alliance with the monkey chief Sugrīva. In return for Rāma's help in killing his powerful brother Vāli, who has unfairly seized his kingdom, Sugrīva sends out a horde of monkeys to locate Sītā.

"The Beautiful Book," Book 5, so called because of its fine descriptive passages, is devoted to the exploits of the powerful monkey Hanumān, who emerges as a hero in his own right. Searching in the southern direction, Hanumān, whose father is the wind god himself, leaps the ocean in a single bound and searches for Rāma's wife in the *rākṣasas'* fabulous island kingdom of Laṅkā (identified with modern Sri Lanka). He finds Sītā a prisoner in Rāvaṇa's pleasure grove, still rejecting his suit (like Penelope in the *Odyssey*) and despairing of Rāma's ever coming to rescue her. Hanumān consoles her, wreaks havoc in Laṅkā, and returns to report to Rāma. In the sixth book, the monkeys build a fabulous bridge and Rāma leads a monkey army to attack Rāvaṇa's rich city. The demons are routed; Rāma kills the *rākṣasa* king and liberates Sītā. After Sītā proves her chastity in an ordeal by fire, the hero returns with her and Lakṣmaṇa to Ayodhyā, where he is crowned.

Tragedy pervades Book 7, *Uttara*. Public scandal concerning Sītā's chastity during her captivity in Rāvaṇa's palace forces King Rāma to abandon her to life in the forest. She takes refuge in the hermitage of the poet-sage Vālmīki on a bank of the Ganges River and there gives birth to Rāma's twin sons. From Vālmīki the twins Lava and Kuśa learn the saga of Rāma, which they later sing in their father's court. On hearing the story, Rāma asks Sītā to come back to him, but Sītā declares that the purpose of her life has been fulfilled and cries out to her mother, the goddess Earth, who opens up to receive her. Rāma continues his rule until it is time for him to end his incarnation as a mortal.

The later literary versions of the *Rāmāyaṇa* have become classics in their own right. Kampaṉ's *Irāmāvatāram* (The Incarnation of Rāma, twelfth century) is celebrated as the greatest poem in the Tamil language. Tulsīdās's Hindi *Rāmcaritmānas* (Sacred Lake of the Acts of Rāma, sixteenth century), which celebrates Rāma's divinity, is a major work in the mystical literary tradition of *bhakti*. Most post-Vālmīki versions of the Rāmāyaṇa end with Rāma's return to Ayodhyā and his coronation, choosing the positive connotations and narrative closure of this ending over the troubling complexities of the events of Vālmīki's last Book.

As noted on page 883, Vālmīki's *Rāmāyaṇa* and its later adaptations have been enjoyed by Indian audiences in forms as vastly different as religious plays, bedtime stories, and, most recently, "classic" comics and a television serial. Every year, all over India, millions of readers, listeners, and viewers weep at Rāma's exile and the death of Daśaratha, cheer as the monkey Hanumān leaps the sea to Laṅkā, share in Sītā's anguish as she climbs the pyre for her trial by fire, and rejoice at the death of Rāvaṇa. For them, the poem's mythic, political, and social dimensions are of a piece, and the deeds of a warrior-prince of ancient Kosala seem as relevant today as in India's heroic age. Rāma and Sītā are worshiped as deities in temples all over India. Nevertheless, the Rāma story's enduring appeal for Indians, especially as Vālmīki presents it, lies in the affinities people continue to feel with its moral and psychological world.

Character and situation particularly occupy *Ayodhyā*, perhaps the most dramatic of the epic's books. Rāma's character remains the focal point throughout, as he responds to the arguments of various members of his family at a time of personal crisis. At stake are issues of political importance, like succession to the throne, but also significant are the complex relationships within a large patriarchal family. Through the drama of *Ayodhyā*, Rāma teaches the ways of right action according to *dharma*, or sacred duty, the principle on which the hierarchical relationships of the Indian family and society are based.

Faced with disinheritance, Rāma sees clearly that a son's highest duty is to honor his father's word, even if this means giving up the kingdom. His position does not go unchallenged: his mother protests against the exile; his brother is angered and recommends rising against the unjust king; the helpless Daśaratha himself begs Rāma to foil his wicked stepmother and take power. Rāma rejects all these arguments, considering them tainted by self-interest, whereas the actions of the ideal man and perfect king are governed by *dharma*, conceived to be the transcendent ethical basis of the entire social order. In accepting his exile, Rāma points out, he is not merely obeying his father's command, but upholding the integrity of the king's word. The prince's deference to father and king is not simple filial subservience, or "duty" in any narrow sense, but an act honoring *dharma* and, therefore, of cosmic significance, requiring the highest moral courage. It is precisely Rāma's act of renunciation that makes him fit for kingship. On the other hand, where injustice unambiguously demands aggressive action, as when Sītā is abducted, he acts in the manner of the conventional warrior-king, although even here he is guided by his sense of cosmic rather than merely personal responsibility.

For Indians, Rāma's heroism lies in his attitude as well as in his acts. He gives up the kingdom with a generous spirit, cheerfully undertakes the exile imposed on him, treats with kindness and courtesy even those who would harm him, and faces adversity with stoic courage. A slayer of demons, he is equally able to subordinate all personal interest to the universally applicable value of *dharma*. In this he differs from the heroes of Homeric epic and Greek tragedy, whose nobility centers in the passionate intensity with which they illuminate particular heroic virtues. Virgil's "virtuous Aeneas" perhaps comes closest to Vālmīki's Rāma in his dedication to founding Rome, a mandate for the sake of which he gives up his love for Dido; but Rāma embodies a unique blend of virtues, one not expressed even in the characters of the heroes of the *Mahābhārata*, the other Indian epic (pp. 953–1001). In the broader context of Indian civilization, only Rāma's heroism combines the strong sense of duty and dedication to social responsibility demanded of the ideal king and the ideal member of the structured Hindu social order with the ascetic qualities of such figures as the Buddha, who renounces the world in order to seek perfection on the spiritual plane. It was this combination of qualities that moved India's great leader of the twentieth century, Mahatma Gandhi, to admire Rāma as his personal hero and the personification of the ideal man.

In Vālmīki the portraits of Rāma and Sītā as models of behavior for Indian men and women take on depth and color through contrast with other figures who act in less than perfect ways. Rāma's brothers Bharata and Lakṣmaṇa are clearly idealized in their unswerving devotion to their elder brother; yet both are capable of rebelling at the unjust behavior of their elders. Daśaratha is portrayed as a venial old man; Rāvaṇa's intelligence is clouded by lust. If Rāma is both the ideal man and king, Sītā's role as the exemplar for women is focused solely on her conduct as a wife; not only does she voluntarily accompany her husband in exile, but obeys and honors him during the public trial that he makes her undergo, even though she knows that she does not deserve this humiliation. Measured against this paragon of wifely devotion, not only Kaikeyī, but Rāma's own mother, the benign Kausalyā, emerges as a flawed woman: if Kaikeyī's selfishness leads her to inflict great suffering upon her husband, Kausalyā needs to be reminded by Rāma that it is her duty to stand by her husband in adversity.

Not perfect conduct alone, but the capacity to suffer deeply endears Rāma and Sītā to traditional Indian audiences. Although he is an incarnation, throughout the epic Rāma is painfully aware of his own—and others'—suffering, and his awareness of the absolute, transcendent nature of *dharma* in no way prevents him from being compassionate to those who are less perfect than he. The hero's compassion, coupled with the solitude of his burden of duty and knowledge, renders him a lonely yet sympathetic figure. As the eternally self-sacrificing wife, Sītā, on the other hand, embodies the suffering of the Hindu Everywoman. These very qualities have been passionately criticized by some modern Indian readers, who see in the idealization of Rāma and Sītā the perpetuation of patriarchal and hierarchical values that go against the spirit of modern India's striving toward an egalitarian society.

But even critics of the epic's social teachings acknowledge the emotional power of Vālmīki's treatment of the story of Rāma. Despite its stress on absolute standards of morality, and despite the fairy-tale–like quality of the hero's conflict with demons, Vālmīki's *Rāmāyaṇa* is sensitive to the complexity of human character. Although the moral standards of Ayodhyā are superior to those of the monkey kingdom and Rāvaṇa's kingdom, even these lesser realms are redeemed by inhabitants who perform acts of goodness, piety, and love. The hunchback Mantharā and the weak-willed Kaikeyī are able to generate evil in Ayodhyā itself, while in Laṅkā Rāvaṇa's wife Maṇḍodarī is as devoted to him as Sītā is to Rāma. The greatest appeal of the ape Hanumān, perhaps the most beloved and popular character in the *Rāmāyaṇa*, is his childlike innocence and his supreme devotion to Rāma, which moves him to risk his life for his lord. Rāvaṇa himself exhibits humanity in his love for his sister, brothers, and sons, while his two *rākṣasa* brothers follow contrasting codes, both virtuous; Kumbhakarṇa remains loyal to his elder brother Rāvaṇa to the end, while the pious Vibhīṣaṇa, measuring *dharma* by a more abstract standard than simple loyalty, abandons the evil Rāvaṇa for Rāma. Much as it is a poem about *dharma,* Vālmīki's *Rāmāyaṇa* is also about human emotion and the redemptive power of love.

SANSKRIT METER AND *ŚLOKA*

Contrary to the Vālmīki legend, the *śloka* meter is one of the meters of the Vedic hymns. Like most Sanskrit meters, and unlike the stress-based meters of English, the *śloka* is a syllabic meter—i.e., it is scanned by the number of syllables per unit. Short syllables (⏑) are those that end in a short vowel, not followed by more than one consonant: for example, ***bha-ra-ta*** (buh-ruh-tuh). Long syllables (—) are syllables ending in long vowels or those ending in a short vowel with more than one consonant following: for example, ***rā-ma*** (rah-muh) and ***dhar-ma*** (dhuhr-muh). The thirty-two syllables of the *śloka* fall naturally into two "lines" of sixteen syllables each, but the structure of the entire couplet is based on a division into four quarters (*pāda*), the pattern of the beginning of each quarter being flexible (×):

×××× ⏑−−⏓ ×××× ⏑−⏑⏓
×××× ⏑−−⏓ ×××× ⏑−⏑⏓

Here is an example from the *Rāmāyaṇa:*

să dădārśāsănē rāmō *vĭṣāṇṇāṃ pĭtărāṃ śŭbhē*
kāikēyyā săhĭtāṃ dīnāṃ *mŭkhēnă părĭśūṣyătā*

Swami Venkatasananda's condensed prose translation in *The Concise Rāmāyaṇa* (1988) conveys the narrative power of Vālmīki's epic. Noteworthy among the many popular retellings of the main story of Vālmīki's *Rāmāyaṇa* are A. K. Coomaraswamy and Sister Nivedita's version in *Myths of the Hindus and Buddhists* (1967) and C. Rajagopalachari's in *Rāmāyaṇa* (1951). Older translations of the entire epic text, such as Hari Prasad Shastri's prose translation in three volumes (*The Rāmāyaṇa of Vālmīki*, 1957), and N. Raghunathan's *Śrīmad Vālmīki Rāmāyaṇa*, 3 vol. (1981–82), will soon be superseded by the excellent, readable, liberally annotated Princeton translation, with good introductory essays, by a number of scholars headed by Robert Goldman, *The Rāmāyaṇa of Vālmīki: An Epic of Ancient India* (1984), when all seven volumes are complete (five have appeared so far). In addition to the books and articles on the epic mentioned in the introduction, readers interested in the social background of Vālmīki's epic should refer to J. L. Brockington, *Righteous Rāma: The Evolution of an Epic* (1984). For later versions of the Rāma story in relation to Vālmīki, see Paula Richman, ed., *Many Rāmāyaṇas: The Diversity of a Narrative Tradition in South Asia* (1991).

PRONOUNCING GLOSSARY

The following list uses common English syllables and stress accents to provide rough equivalents of selected words whose pronunciation may be unfamiliar to the general reader.

Aditi: *uh'-dee-tee*

Agastya: *uh-guhs'-tya*

Aṅgada: *uhn'-guh-duh*

Āraṇya: *ah-ruhn'-yuh*

Aśoka: *uh-shoh'-kuh*

Ayodhyā: *uh-yoh'-dhyah*

Bāla: *bah'-luh*

Bharata: *bhuh'-ruh-ta*

Brahmā: *bruh'-mah*

Citrakūṭa: *chee-truh-koo'-tuh*

Daṇḍaka: *duhn'-duh-kuh*

Daśaratha: *duh'-shuh-ruh'-tha*

dharma: *dhuhr'-muh*

gandharva: *guhn-dhuhr'-vuh*

Godāvarī: *goh-dah'-vuh-ree*

Hanumān: *huh'-noo-mahn*

Ikṣvāku: *eeksh-vah'-koo*

Indra: *een'-dra*

Indrajit: *een'-druh-jeet*

Jāmbavān: *jahm'-buh-vahn*

Janaka: *juh'-nuh-ka*

Janasthāna: *juh-nuh-stah'-nuh*

Jaṭāyu: *juh-tah'-yoo*

Kaikeyī: *kai-kay'-yee*

Kailāsa: *kai-lah'-suh*

Kāṇḍa: *kahn'-da*

Kaśyapa: *kuhsh'-yuh-puh*

Kausalyā: *kow'-suhl-yah*

Khara: *khuh'-ruh*

Kiṣkindhā: *keesh'-keen-dah*

Kumbhakarṇa: *koom'-bhuh-kuhr-nuh*

Kuśa: *koo'shuh*

Lakṣmaṇa: *luhksh'-muh-nuh*
Lakṣmī: *luhksh'-mee*
Laṅkā: *luhn'-kah*
Lava: *luh'-vuh*
Maināka: *mai-nah'-kuh*
Mantharā: *muhn'-thuh-rah*
Mārīca: *mah-ree'-chuh*
Mātali: *mah'-tuh-lee*
Nāga: *nah'-guh*
Nahuṣa: *nuh'-hoo-shuh*
Nārāyaṇa: *nah-rah'-yuh-nuh*
Pañcavaṭī: *puhn'-chuh-vuh-tee*
Puṣpaka: *poosh'-puh-kuh*
rākṣasa: *rah'-kshuh-suh*
Rāma: *rah'-muh*
Rāmāyaṇa: *rah-mah'-yuh-nuh*
Rāvaṇa: *rah'-vuh-nuh*
Sagara: *suh'-guh-ruh*
Sāgara: *sah'-guh-ruh*
Sampāti: *suhm-pah'-tee*
Śatrughna: *shuh-troo'-gnuh*
Simhikā: *seeh'-mee-kah*
Simśapā: *sheem'-shuh-puh*
Sītā: *see'-tah*
Śiva: *shee'-vuh*
śloka: *shloh'-kuh*
Sugrīva: *soo-gree'-vuh*
Sumantra: *soo-muhn'-truh*
Sumitrā: *soo-mee'-trah*
Sundara: *soon'-duh-ruh*
Surasā: *soo'-ruh-sah*
Śūrpaṇakhā: *shoor'-puh-nuh-khah*
Trijaṭā: *tree'-juh-tah'*
Uttara: *oot'-tuh-ruh*
Vāli: *vah'-lee*
Vālmīki: *vahl-mee'-kee*
vānara: *vah'-nuh-ruh*
Vasiṣṭha: *vuh-see'-shta*
Veda: *vay'-duh*
Vibhīṣaṇa: *vee-bhee'-shuh-nuh*
Vinatā: *vee-nuh-tah'*
Viṣṇu: *vish'-noo*
Vṛtra: *vree'-truh*
Yuddha: *yood'-duh*
yuvarāja: *yoo'-vuh-rah'-juh*

The Rāmāyaṇa of Vālmīki[1]

From *Book 2*

Ayodhyā

AYODHYĀ 15–16

The brāhmaṇas[2] had got everything ready for the coronation ceremonies. Gold pots of holy water from all the sacred rivers, most of them gathered at their very source, were ready. All the paraphernalia like the umbrella, the chowries,[3] an elephant and a white horse, were ready, too.

But, the king did not emerge, though the sun had risen and the auspicious hour was fast approaching. The priests and the people wondered: "Who can awaken the king, and inform him that he had better hurry up!" At that moment, Sumantra[4] emerged from the palace. Seeing them, he told them:

1. Translated by Swami Venkatesananda. 2. Priests, members of the highest caste. 3. Yak-tail fans used to ward off flies; kings were attended by fan bearers. 4. King Daśaratha's charioteer and chief bard. The charioteer/bard (*sūta*) composed and narrated ancient epics and sagas.

"Under the king's orders I am going to fetch Rāma." But, on second thought, knowing that the preceptors and the priests commanded even the king's respect, he returned to the king's presence to announce that they were awaiting him. Standing near the king, Sumantra sang: "Arise, O king! Night has flown. Arise and do what should be done." The weary king asked: "I ordered you to fetch Rāma, and I am not asleep. Why do you not do as you are told to do?" This time, Sumantra hurried out of the palace and sped to Rāma's palace.

Entering the palace and proceeding unobstructed through the gates and entrances of the palace, Sumantra beheld the divine Rāma, and said to him: "Rāma, the king who is in the company of queen Kaikeyī desires to see you at once." Immediately, Rāma turned to Sītā and announced: "Surely, the king and mother Kaikeyī wish to discuss with me some important details in connection with the coronation ceremony. I shall go and return soon." Sītā, for her part, offered a heartfelt prayer to the gods: "May I have the blessing of humbly serving you during the auspicious coronation ceremony!"

As Rāma emerged from his palace there was great cheer among the people who hailed and applauded him. Ascending his swift chariot he proceeded to the king's palace, followed by the regalia. Women standing at the windows of their houses and richly adorned to express their joy, showered flowers on Rāma. They praised Kausalyā, the mother of Rāma; they praised Sītā, Rāma's consort: "Obviously she must have done great penance to get him as her husband." The people rejoiced as if they themselves were being installed on the throne. They said to one another: "Rāma's coronation is truly a blessing to all the people. While he rules, and he will rule for a long time, no one will even have an unpleasant experience, or ever suffer." Rāma too was happy to see the huge crowds of people, the elephants and the horses—indicating that people had come to Ayodhyā from afar to witness the coronation.

AYODHYĀ 17–18

As Rāma proceeded in his radiant chariot towards his father's palace, the people were saying to one another: "We shall be supremely happy hereafter, now that Rāma will be king. But, who cares for all this happiness? When we behold Rāma on the throne, we shall attain eternal beatitude!" Rāma heard all this praise and the people's worshipful homage to him, with utter indifference as he drove along the royal road.[5] The chariot entered the first gate to the palace. From there on Rāma went on foot and respectfully entered the king's apartments. The people who had accompanied him eagerly waited outside.

Rushing eagerly and respectfully to his father's presence, Rāma bowed to the feet of his father and then devoutly touched the feet of his mother Kaikeyī, too. "O Rāma!" said the king: he could not say anything more, because he was choked with tears and grief. He could neither see nor speak to Rāma. Rāma sensed great danger: as if he had trodden on a most poisonous serpent. Turning to Kaikeyī, Rāma asked her: "How is it that today the king does not speak kindly to me? Have I offended him in any way? Is he not well? Have I offended prince Bharata or any of my mothers? Oh, it is agonizing: and

5. Rāma is an equanimous hero, one who is not affected by praise or blame.

incurring his displeasure I cannot live even for an hour. Kindly reveal the truth to me."

In a calm, measured and harsh tone, Kaikeyī now said to Rāma: "The king is neither sick nor angry with you. What he must tell you he does not wish to, for fear of displeasing you. He granted me two boons. When I named them, he recoiled. How can a truthful man, a righteous king, go back on his own word? Yet that is his predicament at the moment. I shall reveal the truth to you if you assure me that you will honor your father's promise." For the first time Rāma was distressed: "Ah, shame! Please do not say such things to me! For the sake of my father I can jump into fire. And, I assure you, Rāma does not indulge in double talk. Hence, tell me what the king wants to be done."

Kaikeyī lost no time. She said: "Long ago I rendered him a great service, and he granted me two boons. I claimed them now: and he promised. I asked for these boons: that Bharata should be crowned, and that you should go away to Daṇḍaka forest now. If you wish to establish that both you and your father are devoted to truth, let Bharata be crowned with the same paraphernalia that have been got ready for you, and go away to the forest for fourteen years. Do this, O best of men, for that is the word of your father; and thus would you redeem the king."

AYODHYĀ 19–20

Promptly and without the least sign of the slightest displeasure, Rāma said: "So be it! I shall immediately proceed to the forest, to dwell there clad in bark and animal skin.[6] But why does not the king speak to me, nor feel happy in my presence? Please do not misunderstand me; I shall go, and I myself will gladly give away to my brother Bharata the kingdom, wealth, Sītā and even my own life, and it is easier when all this is done in obedience to my father's command. Let Bharata be immediately requested to come. But it breaks my heart to see that father does not say a word to me directly."

Kaikeyī said sternly: "I shall attend to all that, and send for Bharata. I think, however, that you should not delay your departure from Ayodhyā even for a moment. Even the consideration that the father does not say so himself, should not stop you. Till you leave this city, he will neither bathe nor eat." Hearing this, the king groaned, and wailed aloud: "Alas, alas!" and became unconscious again. Rāma decided to leave at once and he said to Kaikeyī: "I am not fond of wealth and pleasure: but even as the sages are, I am devoted to truth. Even if father had not commanded me, and you had asked me to go to the forest I would have done so! I shall presently let my mother and also Sītā know of the position and immediately leave for the forest."

Rāma was not affected at all by this sudden turn of events. As he emerged from the palace, with Lakṣmaṇa, the people tried to hold the royal umbrella over him: but he brushed them aside. Still talking pleasantly and sweetly with the people, he entered his mother's apartment. Delighted to see him, Kausalyā began to glorify and bless him and asked him to sit on a royal seat. Rāma did not, but calmly said to her: "Mother, the king has decided to crown Bharata as the yuvarājā[7] and I am to go to the forest and live there as a

6. Hermits and ascetics who lived in forests had to wear tree bark and animal skins. Queen Kaikeyī's demands included requiring Rāma to live the austere life of a hermit. 7. Crown prince.

hermit for fourteen years." When she heard this, the queen fell down unconscious and grief-stricken. In a voice choked with grief, she said: "If I had been barren, I would have been unhappy; but I would not have had to endure this terrible agony. I have not known a happy day throughout my life. I have had to endure the taunts and the insults of the other wives of the king. Nay, even he did not treat me with kindness or consideration: I have always been treated with less affection and respect than Kaikeyī's servants were treated. I thought that after your birth, and after your coronation my luck would change. My hopes have been shattered. Even death seems to spurn me. Surely, my heart is hard as it does not break into pieces at this moment of the greatest misfortune and sorrow. Life is not worth living without you; so if you have to go to the forest, I shall follow you."

AYODHYĀ 21

Lakṣmaṇa said: "I think Rāma should not go to the forest. The king has lost his mind, overpowered as he is by senility and lust. Rāma is innocent. And, no righteous man in his senses would forsake his innocent son. A prince with the least knowledge of statesmanship should ignore the childish command of a king who has lost his senses." Turning to Rāma, he said: "Rāma, here I stand, devoted to you, dedicated to your cause. I am ready to kill anyone who would interfere with your coronation—even if it is the king! Let the coronation proceed without delay."

Kausalyā said: "You have heard Lakṣmaṇa's view. You cannot go to the forest because Kaikeyī wants you to. If, as you say, you are devoted to dharma, then it is your duty to stay here and serve me, your mother. I, as your mother, am as much worthy of your devotion and service as your father is: and I do not give you permission to go to the forest. If you disobey me in this, terrible will be your suffering in hell. I cannot live here without you. If you leave, I shall fast unto death."

Rāma, devoted as he was to dharma, spoke: "Among our ancestors were renowned kings who earned fame and heaven by doing their father's bidding. Mother, I am but following their noble example." To Lakṣmaṇa he said: "Lakṣmaṇa, I know your devotion to me, love for me, your prowess and your strength. The universe rests on truth: and I am devoted to truth. Mother has not understood my view of truth, and hence suffers. But I am unable to give up my resolve. Abandon your resolve based on the principle of might; resort to dharma;[8] let not your intellect become aggressive. Dharma, prosperity and pleasure are the pursuit of mankind here;[9] and prosperity and pleasure surely follow dharma: even as pleasure and the birth of a son follow a dutiful wife's service of her husband. One should turn away from that action or mode of life which does not ensure the attainment of all the three goals of life, particularly of dharma; for hate springs from wealth and the pursuit of pleasure is not praiseworthy. The commands of the guru, the king, and one's aged father, whether uttered in anger, cheerfully, or out of lust, should be obeyed by one who is not of despicable behavior, with a view to the promotion of dharma. Hence, I cannot swerve from the path of dharma which demands

8. The religious and moral law, code of righteousness. 9. The phrase "*dharma*, prosperity and pleasure" refers to the first three goals of life for Hindu householders: "religious acts, wealth and public life, and sexual love and family life."

that I should implicitly obey our father. It is not right for you, mother, to abandon father and follow me to the forest, as if you are a widow. Therefore, bless me, mother, so that I may have a pleasant and successful term in the forest."

AYODHYĀ 22–23

Rāma addressed Lakṣmaṇa again: "Let there be no delay, Lakṣmaṇa. Get rid of these articles assembled for the coronation. And with equal expedition make preparations for my leaving the kingdom immediately. Only thus can we ensure that mother Kaikeyī attains peace of mind. Otherwise she might be worried that her wishes may not be fulfilled! Let father's promise be fulfilled. Yet, so long as the two objects of Kaikeyī's desire are not obtained, there is bound to be confusion in everyone's mind. I must immediately leave for the forest; then Kaikeyī will get Bharata here and have him installed on the throne. This is obviously the divine will and I must honor it without delay. My banishment from the kingdom as well as my return are all the fruits of my own doing (kṛtānta: end of action). Otherwise, how could such an unworthy thought enter the heart of noble Kaikeyī? I have never made any distinction between her and my mother; nor has she ever shown the least disaffection for me so far. The 'end' (reaction) of one's own action cannot be foreseen: and this which we call 'daiva' (providence or divine will) cannot be known and cannot be avoided by anyone. Pleasure, pain, fear, anger, gain, loss, life and death—all these are brought about by 'daiva.' Even sages and great ascetics are prompted by the divine will to give up their self-control and are subjected to lust and anger. It is unforeseen and inviolable. Hence, let there be no hostility towards Kaikeyī; she is not to blame. All this is not her doing, but the will of the divine."

Lakṣmaṇa listened to all this with mixed feelings: anger at the turn events had taken, and admiration for Rāma's attitude. Yet, he could not reconcile himself to the situation as Rāma had done. In great fury, he burst forth: "Your sense of duty is misdirected, O Rāma. Even so is your estimation of the divine will. How is it, Rāma, that being a shrewd statesman, you do not see that there are self-righteous people who merely pretend to be good for achieving their selfish and fraudulent ends? If all these boons and promises be true, they could have been asked for and given long ago! Why did they have to wait for the eve of coronation to enact this farce? You ignore this aspect and bring in your argument of the divine will! Only cowards and weak people believe in an unseen divine will: heroes and those who are endowed with a strong mind do not believe in the divine will. Ah, people will see today how my determination and strong action set aside any decrees of the divine will which may be involved in this unrighteous plot. Whoever planned your exile will go into exile! And you will be crowned today. These arms, Rāma, are not handsome limbs, nor are these weapons worn by me ornaments: they are for your service."

AYODHYĀ 24–25

Kausalyā said again: "How can Rāma born of me and the mighty emperor Daśaratha live on food obtained by picking up grains and vegetables and fruits that have been discarded? He whose servants eat dainties and delicacies—how will he subsist on roots and fruits? Without you, Rāma, the fire of separation from you will soon burn me to death. Nay, take me with you, too, if you must go."

Rāma replied: "Mother, that would be extreme cruelty towards father. So long as father lives, please serve him: this is the eternal religion. To a woman her husband is verily god himself. I have no doubt that the noble Bharata will be very kind to you and serve you as I serve you. I am anxious that when I am gone, you should console the king so that he does not feel my separation at all. Even a pious woman who is otherwise righteous, if she does not serve her husband, is deemed to be sinner. On the other hand, she who serves her husband attains blessedness even if she does not worship the gods, perform the rituals or honor the holy men."

Seeing that Rāma was inflexible in his resolve, Kausalyā regained her composure and blessed him. "I shall eagerly await your return to Ayodhyā, after your fourteen years in the forest," said Kausalyā.

Quickly gathering the articles necessary, she performed a sacred rite to propitiate the deities and thus to ensure the health, safety, happy sojourn and quick return of Rāma. "May dharma which you have protected so zealously protect you always," said Kausalyā to Rāma. "May those to whom you bow along the roads and the shrines protect you! Even so, let the missiles which the sage Viśvāmitra[1] gave you ensure your safety. May all the birds and beasts of the forest, celestial beings and gods, the mountains and the oceans, and the deities presiding over the lunar mansions, natural phenomena and the seasons be propitious to you. May the same blessedness be with you that Indra enjoyed on the destruction of his enemy Vṛtra, that Vinatā bestowed upon her son Garuḍa, that Aditi pronounced upon her son Indra when he was fighting the demons, and that Viṣṇu enjoyed while he measured the heaven and earth.[2] May the sages, the oceans, the continents, the Vedas and the heavens be propitious to you."[3]

As Rāma bent low to touch her feet, Kausalyā fondly embraced him and kissed his forehead, and then respectfully went round him before giving him leave to go.

AYODHYĀ 26–27

Taking leave of his mother, Rāma sought the presence of his beloved wife, Sītā. For her part, Sītā who had observed all the injunctions and prohibitions connected with the eve of the coronation and was getting ready to witness the auspicious event itself, perceived her divine spouse enter the palace and with a heart swelling with joy and pride, went forward to receive him. His demeanor, however, puzzled her: his countenance reflected sorrow and anxiety. Shrewd as she was she realized that something was amiss, and hence asked Rāma: "The auspicious hour is at hand; and yet what do I see! Lord,

1. "Missiles" (*astra*) are magical weapons bestowed on worthy heroes by gods and sages. The sage Viśvāmitra had presented the young Rāma and Lakṣmaṇa with such missiles when they protected his sacrificial rites in the forest from attacks by demons (Book 1, *Bāla*). 2. The narrative of the heroic god Indra's victory over the dragonlike demon Vṛtra is an important myth in the *Rig Veda*, the oldest of the Hindu scriptures. Aditi is the mother of the gods. The eagle Garuḍa is the mount of Viṣṇu, the god of preservation. In the fifth of his ten incarnations, Viṣṇu took the form of a dwarf (Vāmana), who subsequently grew into the gigantic figure Trivikrama ("the god of three strides"), spanned earth and sky with two strides, then crushed the demon Bali with his third step. 3. The four *Vedas* are the ancient scriptures of the Hindus. The oceans, continents, and heavens of the Hindu universe are held to have sacred powers.

why are you not accompanied by the regalia, by men holding the ceremonial umbrella, by the royal elephant and the horses, by priests chanting the Vedas, by bards singing your glories? How is it that your countenance is shadowed by sorrow?"

Without losing time and without mincing words, Rāma announced: "Sītā, the king has decided to install Bharata on the throne and to send me to the forest for fourteen years. I am actually on my way to the forest and have come to say good-bye to you. Now that Bharata is the yuvarājā, nay king, please behave appropriately towards him. Remember: people who are in power do not put up with those who sing others' glories in their presence: hence do not glorify me in the presence of Bharata. It is better not to sing my praises even in the presence of your companions. Be devoted to your religious observances and serve my father, my three mothers and my brothers. Bharata and Śatrughna should be treated as your own brothers or sons. Take great care to see that you do not give the least offense to Bharata, the king. Kings reject even their own sons if they are hostile, and are favorable to even strangers who may be friendly. This is my counsel."

Sītā feigned anger, though in fact she was amused. She replied to Rāma: "Your advice that I should stay here in the palace while you go to live in the forest is unworthy of a heroic prince like you, Lord. Whereas one's father, mother, brother, son and daughter-in-law enjoy their own good or misfortune, the wife alone shares the life of her husband. To a woman, neither father nor son nor mother nor friends but the husband alone is her sole refuge here in this world and in the other world, too. Hence I shall accompany you to the forest. I shall go ahead of you, clearing a path for you in the forest. Life with the husband is incomparably superior to life in a palace, or an aerial mansion, or a trip to heaven! I have had detailed instructions from my parents on how to conduct myself in Ayodhyā! But I shall not stay here. I assure you, I shall not be a burden, an impediment, to you in the forest. Nor will I regard life in the forest as exile or as suffering. With you it will be more than heaven to me. It will not be the least hardship to me; without you, even heaven is hell."

AYODHYĀ 28–29

Thinking of the great hardships they would have to endure in the forest, however, Rāma tried to dissuade Sītā in the following words: "Sītā, you come of a very wealthy family dedicated to righteousness. It is therefore proper that you should stay behind and serve my people here. Thus, by avoiding the hardships of the forest and by lovingly serving my people here, would you gladden my heart. The forest is not a place for a princess like you. It is full of great dangers. Lions dwell in the caves; and it is frightening to hear their roar. These wild beasts are not used to seeing human beings; the way they attack human beings is horrifying even to think about. Even the paths are thorny and it is hard to walk on them. The food is a few fruits which might have fallen on their own accord from the trees: living on them, one has to be contented all day. Our garments will be bark and animal skins: and the hair will have to be matted and gathered on the top of the head. Anger and greed have to be given up, the mind must be directed towards austerity and one should overcome fear even where it is natural. Totally exposed to the inclemencies of nature, surrounded by wild animals, serpents and so on, the forest is full of untold hardships. It is not a place for you, my dear."

This reiteration on the part of Rāma moved Sītā to tears. "Your gracious solicitude for my happiness only makes my love for you more ardent, and my determination to follow you more firm. You mentioned animals: they will never come anywhere near me while you are there. You mentioned the righteousness of serving your people: but, your father's command that you should go to the forest demands I should go, too; I am your half: and because of this, again I cannot live without you. In fact you have often declared that a righteous wife will not be able to live separated from her husband. And listen! This is not new to me: for even when I was in my father's house, long before we were married, wise astrologers had rightly predicted that I would live in a forest for some time. If you remember, I have been longing to spend some time in the forest, for I have trained myself for that eventuality. Lord, I feel actually delighted at the very thought that I shall at last go to the forest, to serve you constantly. Serving you, I shall not incur the sin of leaving your parents: thus have I heard from those who are well-versed in the Vedas and other scriptures, that a devoted wife remains united with her husband even after they leave this earth-plane. There is therefore no valid reason why you should wish to leave me here and go. If you still refuse to take me with you, I have no alternative but to lay down my life."

AYODHYĀ 30–31

To the further persuasive talk of Rāma, Sītā responded with a show of annoyance, courage and firmness. She even taunted Rāma in the following words: "While choosing you as his son-in-law, did my father Janaka realize that you were a woman at heart with a male body? Why, then are you, full of valor and courage, afraid even on my account? If you do not take me with you I shall surely die; but instead of waiting for such an event, I prefer to die in your presence. If you do not change your mind now, I shall take poison and die." In sheer anguish, the pitch of her voice rose higher and higher, and her eyes released a torrent of hot tears.

Rāma folded her in his arms and spoke to her lovingly, with great delight: "Sītā, I could not fathom your mind and therefore I tried to dissuade you from coming with me. Come, follow me. Of course I cannot drop the idea of going to the forest, even for your sake. I cannot live having disregarded the command of my parents. Indeed, I wonder how one could adore the unmanifest god, if one were unwilling to obey the commands of his parents and his guru whom he can see here. No religious activity nor even moral excellence can equal service of one's parents in bestowing supreme felicity on one. Whatever one desires, and whatever region one desires to ascend to after leaving this earth-plane, all this is secured by the service of parents. Hence I shall do as commanded by father; and this is the eternal dharma. And you have rightly resolved, to follow me to the forest. Come, and get ready soon. Give away generous gifts to the brāhmaṇas and distribute the rest of your possessions to the servants and others."

Lakṣmaṇa now spoke to Rāma: "If you are determined to go, then I shall go ahead of you." Rāma, however, tried to dissuade him: "Indeed, I know that you are my precious and best companion. Yet, I am anxious that you should stay behind and look after our mothers. Kaikeyī may not treat them well. By thus serving our mothers, you will prove your devotion to me." But Lakṣmaṇa replied quickly: "I am confident, Rāma, that Bharata will look after all the mothers, inspired by your spirit of renunciation and your adherence to dharma. If this does not prove to be the case, I can exterminate all of them in no time. Indeed, Kausalyā is great and powerful enough to look after herself: she gave birth to you! My place is near you; my duty to serve you."

Delighted to hear this, Rāma said: "Then let us all go. Before leaving I wish to give away in charity all that I possess to the holy brāhmaṇas. Please get them all together. Take leave of your friends and get our weapons ready, too."

* * *

From *Book 3*

Āraṇya

ĀRAṆYA 14–15

Rāma, Lakṣmaṇa and Sītā were proceeding towards Pañcavaṭī.[4] On the way they saw a huge vulture. Rāma's first thought was that it was a demon in disguise. The vulture said: "I am your father's friend!" Trusting the vulture's words, Rāma asked for details of its birth and ancestry.

The vulture said: "You know that Dakṣa Prajāpati[5] had sixty daughters and the sage Kaśyapa married eight of them. One day Kaśyapa said to his wives: 'You will give birth to offspring who will be foremost in the three worlds.' Aditi, Diti, Danu and Kālaka listened attentively; the others were indifferent. As a result, the former four gave birth to powerful offspring who were superhuman. Aditi gave birth to thirty-three gods. Diti gave birth to demons. Danu gave birth to Aśvagrīva. And, Kālaka had Naraka and Kālikā. Of the others, men were born of Manu, and the sub-human species from the other wives of Kaśyapa. Tāmra's daughter was Sukī whose granddaughter was Vinatā who had two sons, Garuḍa and Aruṇa. My brother Sampāti and I are the sons of Aruṇa. I offer my services to you, O Rāma. If you will be pleased to accept them, I shall guard Sītā when you and Lakṣmaṇa may be away from your hermitage. As you have seen, this formidable forest is full of wild animals and demons, too."

Rāma accepted this new friendship. All of them now proceeded towards Pañcavaṭī in search of a suitable place for building a hermitage. Having arrived at Pañcavaṭī, identified by Rāma by the description which the sage Agastya had given, Rāma said to Lakṣmaṇa: "Pray, select a suitable place here for building the hermitage. It should have a charming forest, good water, firewood, flowers and holy grass." Lakṣmaṇa submitted: "Even if we live together for a hundred years, I shall continue to be your servant. Hence, Lord, you select the place and I shall do the needful." Rejoicing at Lakṣmaṇa's attitude, Rāma pointed to a suitable place, which satisfied all the requisites of a hermitage. Rāma said: "This is holy ground; this is charming; it is frequented by beasts and birds. We shall dwell here." Immediately Lakṣmaṇa set about building a hermitage for all of them to live in.

4. "Five banyan trees," a grove in western India, toward which Rāma has been directed by the sage Agastya.
5. A progenitor god in ancient Hindu mythology.

Rāma warmly embraced Lakṣmaṇa and said: "I am delighted by your good work and devoted service: and I embrace you in token of such admiration. Brother, you divine the wish of my heart, you are full of gratitude, you know dharma; with such a man as his son, father is not dead but is eternally alive."

Entering that hermitage, Rāma, Lakṣmaṇa and Sītā dwelt in it with great joy and happiness.

ĀRAṆYA 16

Time rolled on. One day Lakṣmaṇa sought the presence of Rāma early in the morning and described what he had seen outside the hermitage. He said: "Winter, the season which you love most, has arrived, O Rāma. There is dry cold everywhere; the earth is covered with foodgrains. Water is uninviting; and fire is pleasant. The first fruits of the harvest have been brought in; and the agriculturists have duly offered some of it to the gods and the manes, and thus reaffirmed their indebtedness to them. The farmer who thus offers the first fruits to gods and manes is freed from sin.

"The sun moves in the southern hemisphere; and the north looks lusterless. Himālaya, the abode of snow, looks even more so! It is pleasant to take a walk even at noon. The shade of a tree which we loved in summer is unpleasant now. Early in the morning the earth, with its rich wheat and barley fields, is enveloped by mist. Even so, the rice crop. The sun, even when it rises, looks soft and cool like the moon. Even the elephants which approach the water, touch it with their trunk but pull the trunk quickly away on account of the coldness of the water.

"Rāma, my mind naturally thinks of our beloved brother Bharata. Even in this cold winter, he who could command the luxury of a king, prefers to sleep on the floor and live an ascetic life. Surely, he, too, would have got up early in the morning and has perhaps had a cold bath in the river Sarayū. What a noble man! I can even now picture him in front of me: with eyes like the petals of a lotus, dark brown in color, slim and without an abdomen, as it were. He knows what dharma is. He speaks the truth. He is modest and self-controlled, always speaks pleasantly, is sweet-natured, with long arms and with all his enemies fully subdued.[6] That noble Bharata has given up all his pleasures and is devoted to you. He has already won his place in heaven, Rāma. Though he lives in the city; yet, he has adopted the ascetic mode of life and follows you in spirit.

"We have heard it said that a son takes after his mother in nature: but in the case of Bharata this has proved false. I wonder how Kaikeyī, in spite of having our father as her husband, and Bharata as her son, has turned out to be so cruel."

When Lakṣmaṇa said this, Rāma stopped him, saying: "Do not speak ill of our mother Kaikeyī, Lakṣmaṇa. Talk only of our beloved Bharata. Even though I try not to think of Ayodhyā and our people there, when I think of Bharata, I wish to see him."

6. A list of the conventional attributes of a handsome, brave, and virtuous warrior.

Āraṇya 17–18

After their bath and morning prayers, Rāma, Lakṣmaṇa and Sītā returned to their hermitage. As they were seated in their hut, there arrived upon the scene a dreadful demoness. She looked at Rāma and immediately fell in love with him! He had a handsome face; she had an ugly face. He had a slender waist; she had a huge abdomen. He had lovely large eyes; she had hideous eyes. He had lovely soft hair; she had red hair. He had a lovable form; she had a terrible form. He had a sweet voice; hers resembled the barking of a dog. He was young; she was haughty. He was able; her speech was crooked. He was of noble conduct; she was of evil conduct. He was beloved; she had a forbidding appearance. Such a demoness spoke to Rāma: "Who are you, young men; and what are both of you doing in this forest, with this lady?"

Rāma told her the whole truth about himself, Lakṣmaṇa and Sītā, about his banishment from the kingdom, etc. Then Rāma asked her: "O charming lady,[7] now tell me who you are." At once the demoness replied: "Ah, Rāma! I shall tell you all about myself immediately. I am Śūrpaṇakhā, the sister of Rāvaṇa. I am sure you have heard of him. He has two other brothers, Kumbhakarṇa and Vibhīṣaṇa.[8] Two other brothers Khara and Dūṣaṇa live in the neighborhood here. The moment I saw you, I fell in love with you. What have you to do with this ugly, emaciated Sītā? Marry me. Both of us shall roam about this forest. Do not worry about Sītā or Lakṣmaṇa: I shall swallow them in a moment." But, Rāma smilingly said to her: "You see I have my wife with me here. Why do you not propose to my brother Lakṣmaṇa who has no wife here?" Śūrpaṇakhā did not mind that suggestion. She turned to Lakṣmaṇa and said: "It is all right. You please marry me and we shall roam about happily." She was tormented by passion.

Lakṣmaṇa said in a teasing mood: "O lady, you see that I am only the slave of Rāma and Sītā. Why do you choose to be the wife of a slave? You will only become a servant-maid. Persuade Rāma to send away that ugly wife of his and marry you." Śūrpaṇakhā turned to Rāma again. She said: "Unable to give up this wife of yours, Sītā, you turn down my offer. See, I shall at once swallow her. When she is gone you will marry me; and we shall roam about in this forest happily." So saying, she actually rushed towards Sītā. Rāma stopped her in time, and said to Lakṣmaṇa: "What are you doing, Lakṣmaṇa? It is not right to jest with cruel and unworthy people. Look at the plight of Sītā. She barely escaped with her life. Come, quickly deform this demoness and send her away."

Lakṣmaṇa drew his sword and quickly cut off the nose and the ears of Śūrpaṇakhā. Weeping and bleeding she ran away. She went to her brother Khara and fell down in front of him.

* * *

Summary Distraught and furious, Śūrpaṇakhā asks her brothers Khara and Dūṣaṇa, who live in nearby Janasthāna, to avenge her insult by killing Rāma and Lakṣmaṇa. However, Rāma and Lakṣmaṇa kill the brothers and all their troops.

7. This formulaic phrase used in addressing a lady is meant ironically here. 8. The names of the demons are suggestive: Śūrpaṇakhā ("woman with nails as large as winnowing baskets") and Kumbhakarṇa ("pot ear").

ĀRAṆYA 32–33

Śūrpaṇakhā witnessed the wholesale destruction of the demons of Janasthāna,[9] including their supreme leader Khara. Stricken with terror, she ran to Laṅkā. There she saw her brother Rāvaṇa, the ruler of Laṅkā, seated with his ministers in a palace whose roof scraped the sky.[1] Rāvaṇa had twenty arms, ten heads, was broad chested and endowed with all the physical qualifications of a monarch. He had previously fought with the gods, even with their chief Indra. He was well versed in the science of warfare and knew the use of the celestial missiles in battle. He had been hit by the gods, even by the discus[2] of lord Viṣṇu, but he did not die. For, he had performed breathtaking austerities for a period of ten thousand years, and offered his own heads in worship to Brahmā the creator and earned from him the boon that he would not be killed by any superhuman or subhuman agency (except by man). Emboldened by this boon, the demon had tormented the gods and particularly the sages.

Śūrpaṇakhā entered Rāvaṇa's presence, clearly displaying the physical deformity which Lakṣmaṇa had caused to her. She shouted at Rāvaṇa in open assembly: "Brother, you have become so thoroughly infatuated and addicted to sense-pleasure that you are unfit to be a king any longer. The people lose all respect for the king who is only interested in his own pleasure and neglects his royal duties. People turn away from the king who has no spies, who has lost touch with the people and whom they cannot see, and who is unable to do what is good for them. It is the employment of spies that makes the king 'far-sighted' for through these spies he sees quite far. You have failed to appoint proper spies to collect intelligence for you. Therefore, you do not know that fourteen thousand of your people have been slaughtered by a human being. Even Khara and Dūṣaṇa have been killed by Rāma. And, Rāma has assured the ascetics of Janasthāna which is your territory, that the demons shall not do them any harm. They are now protected by him. Yet, here you are; reveling in little pleasures!

"O brother, even a piece of wood, a clod of earth or just dust, has some use; but when a king falls from his position he is utterly useless. But that monarch who is vigilant, who has knowledge of everything, through his spies, who is self-controlled, who is full of gratitude and whose conduct is righteous—he rules for a long time. Wake up and act before you lose your sovereignty."

This made Rāvaṇa reflect.

ĀRAṆYA 34–35

And, Rāvaṇa's anger was roused. He asked Śūrpaṇakhā: "Tell me, who is it that disfigured you thus? What do you think of Rāma? Why has he come to Daṇḍaka forest?"

Śūrpaṇakhā gave an exact and colorful description of the physical appearance of Rāma. She said: "Rāma is equal in charm to Cupid himself. At the same time, he is a formidable warrior. When he was fighting the demons of Janasthāna, I could not see what he was doing; I only saw the demons falling

9. A region near Pañcavaṭī. 1. A conventional description of a palace or mansion. 2. A wheel with sharp points, Viṣṇu's weapon.

dead on the field. You can easily understand when I tell you that within an hour and a half he had killed fourteen thousand demons. He spared me, perhaps because he did not want to kill a woman. He has a brother called Lakṣmaṇa who is equally powerful. He is Rāma's right hand man and alter ego; Rāma's own life-force moving outside his body. Oh, you must see Sītā, Rāma's wife. I have not seen even a celestial nymph who could match her in beauty. He who has her for his wife, whom she fondly embraces, he shall indeed be the ruler of gods. She is a fit bride for you; and you are indeed the most suitable suitor for her. In fact, I wanted to bring that beautiful Sītā here so that you could marry her: but Lakṣmaṇa intervened and cruelly mutilated my body. If you could only look at her for a moment, you would immediately fall in love with her. If this proposal appeals to you, take some action quickly and get her here."

Rāvaṇa was instantly tempted. Immediately he ordered his flying chariot to be got ready. This vehicle which was richly adorned with gold, could move freely wherever its owner willed. Its front part resembled mules with fiendish heads. Rāvaṇa took his seat in this vehicle and moved towards the seacoast. The coastline of Laṅkā was dotted with hermitages inhabited by sages and also celestial and semi-divine beings. It was also the pleasure resort of celestials and nymphs who went there to sport and to enjoy themselves. Driving at great speed through them, Rāvaṇa passed through caravan parks scattered with the chariots of the celestials. He also drove through dense forests of sandal trees, banana plantations and cocoanut palm groves. In those forests there were also spices and aromatic plants. Along the coast lay pearls and precious stones. He passed through cities which had an air of opulence.

Rāvaṇa crossed the ocean in his flying chariot and reached the hermitage where Mārīca[3] was living in ascetic garb, subsisting on a disciplined diet. Mārīca welcomed Rāvaṇa and questioned him about the purpose of his visit.

Āraṇya 36–37

Rāvaṇa said to Mārīca: "Listen, Mārīca. You know that fourteen thousand demons, including my brother Khara and the great warrior Triśira have been mercilessly killed by Rāma and Lakṣmaṇa who have now promised their protection to the ascetics of Daṇḍaka forest, thus flouting our authority. Driven out of his country by his angry father, obviously for a disgraceful action, this unrighteous and hard-hearted prince Rāma has killed the demons without any justification. And, they have even dared to disfigure my beloved sister Śūrpaṇakhā. I must immediately take some action to avenge the death of my brother and to restore our prestige and our authority. I need your help; kindly do not refuse this time.

"Disguising yourself as a golden deer of great beauty, roam near the hermitage of Rāma. Sītā would surely be attracted, and she would ask Rāma and Lakṣmaṇa to capture you. When they go after you, leaving Sītā alone in the hermitage, I shall easily abduct Sītā." Even as Rāvaṇa was unfolding this plot, Mārīca's mouth became dry and parched with fear. Trembling with fear, Mārīca said to Rāvaṇa:

3. An uncle of Rāvaṇa, expert in sorcery.

"O king, one can easily get in this world a counselor who tells you what is pleasing to you; but hard it is to find a wise counselor who tells you the unpleasant truth which is good for you—and harder it is to find one who heeds such advice. Surely, your intelligence machine is faulty and therefore you have no idea of the prowess of Rāma. Else, you would not talk of abducting Sītā. I wonder: perhaps Sītā has come into this world to end your life, or perhaps there is to be great sorrow on account of Sītā, or perhaps maddened by lust, you are going to destroy yourself and the demons and Laṅkā itself. Oh, no, you were wrong in your estimation of Rāma. He is not wicked; he is righteousness incarnate. He is not cruel hearted; he is generous to a fault. He has not been disgraced and exiled from the kingdom. He is here to honor the promise his father had given his mother Kaikeyī, after joyously renouncing his kingdom.

"O king, when you entertain ideas of abducting Sītā you are surely playing with fire. Please remember: when you stand facing Rāma, you are standing face to face with your own death. Sītā is the beloved wife of Rāma, who is extremely powerful. Nay, give up this foolish idea. What will you gain by thus gambling with your sovereignty over the demons, and with your life itself? Please consult the noble Vibhīṣaṇa and your virtuous ministers before embarking upon such unwise projects. They will surely advise you against them."

* * *

Āraṇya 42

Rāvaṇa was determined, and Mārīca knew that there was no use arguing with him. Hence, after the last-minute attempt to avert the catastrophe, Mārīca said to Rāvaṇa: "What can I do when you are so wicked? I am ready to go to Rāma's āśrama.[4] God help you!" Not minding the taunt, Rāvaṇa expressed his unabashed delight at Mārīca's consent. He applauded Mārīca and said: "That is the spirit, my friend: you are now the same old Mārīca that I knew. I guess you had been possessed by some evil spirit a few minutes ago, on account of which you had begun to preach a different gospel. Let us swiftly get into this vehicle and proceed to our destination. As soon as you have accomplished the purpose, you are free to go and to do what you please!"

Both of them got into the flying chariot and quickly left the hermitage of Mārīca. Once again they passed forests, hills, rivers and cities: and soon they reached the neighborhood of the hermitage of Rāma. They got down from that chariot which had been embellished with gold. Holding Mārīca by the hand, Rāvaṇa said to him: "Over there is the hermitage of Rāma, surrounded by banana plantations. Well, now, get going with the work for which we have come here." Immediately Mārīca transformed himself into an attractive deer. It was extraordinary, totally unlike any deer that inhabited the forest. It was unique. It dazzled like a huge gem stone. Each part of its body had a different

4. Hermitage.

color. The colors had an unearthly brilliance and charm. Thus embellished by the colors of all the precious stones, the deer which was the demon Mārīca in disguise, roamed about near the hermitage of Rāma, nibbling at the grass now and then. At one time it came close to Sītā; then it ran away and joined the other deer grazing at a distance. It was very playful, jumping about and chasing its tail and spinning around. Sītā went out to gather flowers. She cast a glance at that extraordinary and unusual deer. As she did so, the deer too, sensing the accomplishment of the mission, came closer to her. Then it ran away, pretending to be afraid. Sītā marveled at the very appearance of this unusual deer the like of which she had not seen before and which had the hue of jewels.

ĀRAṆYA 43

From where she was gathering flowers, Sītā, filled with wonder to see that unusual deer, called out to Rāma: "Come quick and see, O Lord; come with your brother. Look at this extraordinary creature. I have never seen such a beautiful deer before." Rāma and Lakṣmaṇa looked at the deer, and Lakṣmaṇa's suspicions were aroused: "I am suspicious; I think it is the same demon Mārīca in disguise. I have heard that Mārīca could assume any form at will, and through such tricks he had brought death and destruction to many ascetics in this forest. Surely, this deer is not real: no one has heard of a deer with rainbow colors, each one of its limbs shining resplendent with the color of a different gem! That itself should enable us to understand that it is a demon, not an animal."

Sītā interrupted Lakṣmaṇa's talk, and said: "Never mind, one thing is certain; this deer has captivated my mind. It is such a dear. I have not seen such an animal near our hermitage! There are many types of deer which roam about near the hermitage; this is just an extraordinary and unusual deer. It is superlative in all respects: its color is lovely, its texture is lovely, and even its voice sounds delightful. It would be a wonderful feat if it could be caught alive. We could use it as a pet, to divert our minds. Later we could take it to Ayodhyā: and I am sure all your brothers and mothers would just adore it. If it is not possible to capture it alive, O Lord, then it can be killed, and I would love to have its skin. I know I am not behaving myself towards both of you: but I am helpless; I have lost my heart to that deer. I am terribly curious."

In fact, Rāma was curious, too! And so, he took Sītā's side and said to Lakṣmaṇa: "It is beautiful, Lakṣmaṇa. It is unusual. I have never seen a creature like this. And, princes do hunt animals and cherish their skins.[5] By sporting and hunting kings acquire great wealth! People say that that is real wealth which one pursues without premeditation. So, let us try to get the deer or its skin. If, as you say, it is a demon in disguise, then surely it ought to be killed by me, just as Vātāpi who was tormenting and destroying sages and ascetics was justly killed by the sage Agastya.[6] Vātāpi fooled the ascetics till he met the sage Agastya. This Mārīca, too, has fooled the ascetics so far:

5. Hermits are required to take a vow of nonviolence, but Rāma, a warrior prince, is allowed to carry arms and to hunt. 6. The demon Vātāpi killed ascetics by tricking them. Disguising himself, he would invite innocent wayfarers to a meal. He would magically conceal himself in the food, thus entering his guests' bellies; he would then kill the men by splitting open their stomachs. The sage Agastya outwitted and killed Vātāpi by digesting his meal, and with it, the demon himself, before he could tear the sage's stomach open.

till coming to me today! The very beauty of his hide is his doom. And, you, Lakṣmaṇa, please guard Sītā with great vigilance, till I kill this deer with just one shot and bring the hide along with me."

ĀRAṆYA 44–45

Rāma took his weapons and went after the strange deer. As soon as the deer saw him pursuing it, it started to run away. Now it disappeared, now it appeared to be very near, now it ran fast, now it seemed confused—thus it led Rāma far away from his hermitage. Rāma was fatigued, and needed to rest. As he was standing under a tree, intrigued by the actions of the mysterious deer, it came along with other deer and began to graze not far from him. When Rāma once again went for it, it ran away. Not wishing to go farther nor to waste more time, Rāma took his weapon and fitted the missile of Brahmā[7] to it and fired. This missile pierced the illusory deer-mask and into the very heart of the demon. Mārīca uttered a loud cry, leapt high into the sky and then dropped dead onto the ground. As he fell, however, he remembered Rāvaṇa's instructions and assuming the voice of Rāma cried aloud: "Hey Sītā; Hey Lakṣmaṇa."

Rāma saw the dreadful body of the demon. He knew now that Lakṣmaṇa was right. And, he was even more puzzled by the way in which the demon wailed aloud before dying. He was full of apprehension. He hastened towards the hermitage.

In the hermitage, both Sītā and Lakṣmaṇa heard the cry. Sītā believed it was Rāma's voice. She was panic-stricken. She said to Lakṣmaṇa: "Go, go quickly: your brother is in danger. And, I cannot live without him. My breath and my heart are both violently disturbed." Lakṣmaṇa remembered Rāma's admonition that he should stay with Sītā and not leave her alone. He said to her: "Pray, be not worried." Sītā grew suspicious and furious. She said to him: "Ah, I see the plot now! You have a wicked eye on me and so have been waiting for this to happen. What a terrible enemy of Rāma you are, pretending to be his brother!" Distressed to hear these words, Lakṣmaṇa replied: "No one in the three worlds can overpower Rāma, blessed lady! It was not his voice at all. These demons in the forest are capable of simulating the voice of anyone. Having killed that demon disguised as a deer, Rāma will soon be here. Fear not." His calmness even more annoyed Sītā, who literally flew into a rage. She said again: "Surely, you are the worst enemy that Rāma could have had. I know now that you have been following us, cleverly pretending to be Rāma's brother and friend. I know now that your real motive for doing so is either to get me or you are Bharata's accomplice. Ah, but you will not succeed. Presently, I shall give up my life. For I cannot live without Rāma." Cut to the quick by these terrible words, Lakṣmaṇa said: "You are worshipful to me: hence I cannot answer back. It is not surprising that women should behave in this manner: for they are easily led away from dharma; they are fickle and sharp-tongued. I cannot endure what you said just now. I shall go. The gods are witness to what took place here. May those gods protect you. But I doubt if when Rāma and I return, we shall find you." Bowing to her, Lakṣmaṇa left.

7. The creator god in the triad of Hindu great gods.

ĀRAṆYA 46

Rāvaṇa was looking for this golden opportunity. He disguised himself as an ascetic, clad in ocher robes, carrying a shell water-pot, a staff and an umbrella, and approached Sītā who was still standing outside the cottage eagerly looking for Rāma's return. His very presence in that forest was inauspicious: and even the trees and the waters of the rivers were frightened of him, as it were. In a holy disguise, Rāvaṇa stood before Sītā: a deep well covered with grass; a death-trap.

Gazing at the noble Sītā, who had now withdrawn into the cottage and whose eyes were raining tears, Rāvaṇa came near her, and though his heart was filled with lust, he was chanting Vedic hymns. He said to Sītā in a soft, tender and affectionate tone: "O young lady! Pray, tell me, are you the goddess of fortune or the goddess of modesty, or the consort of Cupid himself?" Then Rāvaṇa described her incomparable beauty in utterly immodest terms, unworthy of an anchorite whose form he had assumed. He continued: "O charming lady! You have robbed me of my heart. I have not seen such a beautiful lady, neither a divine or a semi-divine being. Your extraordinary form and your youthfulness, and your living in this forest, all these together agitate my mind. It is not right that you should live in this forest. You should stay in palaces. In the forest monkeys, lions, tigers and other wild animals live. The forest is the natural habitat of demons who roam freely. You are living alone in this dreadful forest: are you not afraid, O fair lady? Pray, tell me, why are you living in this forest?"

Rāvaṇa was in the disguise of a brāhmaṇa. Therefore, Sītā offered him the worship and the hospitality that it was her duty to offer a brāhmaṇa. She made him sit down; she gave him water to wash his feet and his hands. Then she placed food in front of him.

Whatever she did only aggravated his lust and his desire to abduct her and take her away to Laṅkā.

ĀRAṆYA 47–48

Sītā, then, proceeded to answer his enquiry concerning herself. He appeared to be a brāhmaṇa; and if his enquiry was not answered, he might get angry and curse her.[8] Sītā said: "I am a daughter of the noble king Janaka; Sītā is my name. I am the beloved consort of Rāma. After our marriage, Rāma and I lived in the palace of Ayodhyā for twelve years." She then truthfully narrated all that took place just prior to Rāma's exile to the forest. She continued: "And so, when Rāma was twenty-five and I was eighteen, we left the palace and sought the forest-life.[9] And so the three of us dwell in this forest. My husband, Rāma, will soon return to the hermitage gathering various animals and also wild fruits. Pray, tell me who you are, O brāhmaṇa, and what you are doing in this forest roaming all alone."

Rāvaṇa lost no time in revealing his true identity. He said: "I am not a brāhmaṇa, O Sītā: I am the lord of demons, Rāvaṇa. My very name strikes terror in the hearts of gods and men. The moment I saw you, I lost my heart

8. Priestly *brāhmaṇas* (brahmins) and sages have the power to curse people as well as to bestow boons. 9. Rāma must have been thirteen and Sītā six years old when they were married. The practice of "child marriage" continued in India until very recently.

to you; and I derive no pleasure from the company of my wives. Come with me, and be my queen, O Sītā. You will love Laṅkā. Laṅkā is my capital, it is surrounded by the ocean and it is situated on the top of a hill. There we shall live together, and you will enjoy your life, and never even once think of this wretched forest-life."

Sītā was furious to hear this. She said: "O demon-king! I have firmly resolved to follow Rāma who is equal to the god of gods, who is mighty and charming, and who is devoted to righteousness.[1] If you entertain a desire for me, his wife, it is like tying yourself with a big stone and trying to swim across the ocean: you are doomed. Where are you and where is he: there is no comparison. You are like a jackal; he the lion.[2] You are like base metal; he gold."

But Rāvaṇa would not give up his desire. He repeated: "Even the gods dare not stand before me, O Sītā! For fear of me even Kubera the god of wealth abandoned his chariot and ran away to Kailāsa. If the gods, headed by Indra, even sense I am angry, they flee. Even the forces of nature obey me. Laṅkā is enclosed by a strong wall; the houses are built of gold with gates of precious stones. Forget this Rāma, who lives like an ascetic, and come with me. He is not as strong as my little finger!" Sītā was terribly angered: "Surely you seek the destruction of all the demons, by behaving like this, O Rāvaṇa. It cannot be otherwise since they have such an unworthy king with no self-control. You may live after abducting Indra's wife, but not after abducting me, Rāma's wife."

ĀRAṆYA 49–50

Rāvaṇa made his body enormously big and said to Sītā: "You do not realize what a mighty person I am. I can step out into space, and lift up the earth with my arms; I can drink up the waters of the oceans; and I can kill death itself. I can shoot a missile and bring the sun down. Look at the size of my body." As he expanded his form, Sītā turned her face away from him. He resumed his original form with ten heads and twenty arms. Again he spoke to Sītā: "Would you not like to be renowned in the three worlds? Then marry me. And, I promise I shall do nothing to displease you. Give up all thoughts of that mortal and unsuccessful Rāma."

Rāvaṇa did not wait for an answer. Seizing Sītā by her hair and lifting her up with his arm, he left the hermitage. Instantly the golden chariot appeared in front of him. He ascended it, along with Sītā. Sītā cried aloud: "O Rāma." As she was being carried away, she wailed aloud: "O Lakṣmaṇa, who is ever devoted to the elder brother, do you not know that I am being carried away by Rāvaṇa?" To Rāvaṇa, she said: "O vile demon, surely you will reap the fruits of your evil action: but they do not manifest immediately." She said as if to herself: "Surely, Kaikeyī would be happy today." She said to the trees, to the river Godāvarī, to the deities dwelling in the forest, to the animals and birds: "Pray, tell Rāma that I have been carried away by the wicked Rāvaṇa." She saw Jaṭāyu and cried aloud: "O Jaṭāyu! See, Rāvaṇa is carrying me away."

Hearing that cry, Jaṭāyu woke up. Jaṭāyu introduced himself to Rāvaṇa:

1. A special epithet of Rāma. "God of gods": an epithet used for warriors, kings, and heroes. It is a reference to Indra, king of heaven and all the gods. 2. King of animals, the lion represents regal majesty and courage, while the jackal is the embodiment of cunning and deceit.

"O Rāvaṇa, I am the king of vultures, Jaṭāyu. Pray, desist from this action unworthy of a king. Rāma, too, is a king; and his consort is worthy of our protection. A wise man should not indulge in such action as would disgrace him in the eyes of others. And, another's wife is as worthy of protection as one's own. The cultured and the common people often copy the behavior of the king. If the king himself is guilty of unworthy behavior what becomes of the people? If you persist in your wickedness, even the prosperity you enjoy will leave you soon.

"Therefore, let Sītā go. One should not get hold of a greater load than one can carry; one should not eat what he cannot digest. Who will indulge in an action which is painful and which does not promote righteousness, fame or permanent glory? I am sixty thousand years old and you are young. I warn you. If you do not give up Sītā, you will not be able to carry her away while I am alive and able to restrain you! I shall dash you down along with that chariot."

ĀRAṆYA 51

Rāvaṇa could not brook this insult: he turned towards Jaṭāyu in great anger. Jaṭāyu hit the chariot and Rāvaṇa; Rāvaṇa hit Jaṭāyu back with terrible ferocity. This aerial combat between Rāvaṇa and Jaṭāyu looked like the collision of two mountains endowed with wings. Rāvaṇa used all the conventional missiles, the Nālikas, the Nārācas and the Vikarṇis. The powerful eagle shrugged them off. Jaṭāyu tore open the canopy of the chariot and inflicted wounds on Rāvaṇa himself.

In great anger, Jaṭāyu grabbed Rāvaṇa's weapon (a cannon) and broke it with his claws. Rāvaṇa took up a more formidable weapon which literally sent a shower of missiles. Against these Jaṭāyu used his own wings as an effective shield. Pouncing upon this weapon, too, Jaṭāyu destroyed it with his claws. Jaṭāyu also tore open Rāvaṇa's armor. Nay, Jaṭāyu even damaged the gold-plated propellers of Rāvaṇa's flying chariot, which had the appearance of demons, and thus crippled the craft which would take its occupant wherever he desired and which emitted fire. With his powerful beak, Jaṭāyu broke the neck of Rāvaṇa's pilot.

With the chariot thus rendered temporarily useless, Rāvaṇa jumped out of it, still holding Sītā with his powerful arm. While Rāvaṇa was still above the ground, Jaṭāyu again challenged him: "O wicked one, even now you are unwilling to turn away from evil. Surely, you have resolved to bring about the destruction of the entire race of demons. Unknowingly or wantonly, you are swallowing poison which would certainly kill you and your relations. Rāma and Lakṣmaṇa will not tolerate this sinful act of yours: and you cannot stand before them on the battlefield. The manner in which you are doing this unworthy act is despicable: you are behaving like a thief not like a hero." Jaṭāyu swooped on Rāvaṇa and violently tore at his body.

Then there ensued a hand-to-hand fight between the two. Rāvaṇa hit Jaṭāyu with his fist; but Jaṭāyu tore Rāvaṇa's arms away. However, new ones sprang up instantly. Rāvaṇa hit Jaṭāyu and kicked him. After some time, Rāvaṇa drew his sword and cut off the wings of Jaṭāyu. When the wings were thus cut, Jaṭāyu fell, dying. Looking at the fallen Jaṭāyu, Sītā ran towards him in great anguish, as she would to the side of a fallen relation. In inconsolable grief, Sītā began to wail aloud.

ĀRAṆYA 52–53

As Sītā was thus wailing near the body of Jaṭāyu, Rāvaṇa came towards her. Looking at him with utter contempt, Sītā said: "I see dreadful omens, O Rāvaṇa. Dreams as also the sight and the cries of birds and beasts are clear indicators of the shape of things to come.[3] But you do not notice them! Alas, here is Jaṭāyu, my father-in-law's friend who is dying on my account. O Rāma, O Lakṣmaṇa, save me, protect me!"

Once again Rāvaṇa grabbed her and got into the chariot which had been made airworthy again. The Creator, the gods and the celestials who witnessed this, exclaimed: "Bravo, our purpose is surely accomplished."[4] Even the sages of the Daṇḍaka forest inwardly felt happy at the thought, "Now that Sītā has been touched by this wicked demon, the end of Rāvaṇa and all the demons is near." As she was carried away by Rāvaṇa, Sītā was wailing aloud: "O Rāma, O Lakṣmaṇa."

Placed on the lap of Rāvaṇa, Sītā was utterly miserable. Her countenance was full of sorrow and anguish. The petals of the flowers that dropped from her head fell and covered the body of Rāvaṇa for a while. She was of beautiful golden complexion; and he was of dark color. Her being seated on his lap looked like an elephant wearing a golden sash, or the moon shining in the midst of a dark cloud, or a streak of lightning seen in a dense dark cloud.

The chariot streaked through the sky as fast as a meteor would. On the earth below, trees shook as if to reassure Sītā: "Do not be afraid," the waterfalls looked as if mountains were shedding tears, and people said to one another, "Surely, dharma has come to an end, as Rāvaṇa is carrying Sītā away."

Once again Sītā rebuked Rāvaṇa: "You ought to feel ashamed of yourself, O Rāvaṇa. You boast of your prowess; but you are stealing me away! You have not won me in a duel, which would be considered heroic. Alas, for a long, long time to come, people will recount your ignominy, and this unworthy and unrighteous act of yours will be remembered by the people. You are taking me and flying at such speed: hence no one can do anything to stop you. If only you had the courage to stop for a few moments, you would find yourself dead. My lord Rāma and his brother Lakṣmaṇa will not spare you. Leave me alone, O demon! But, you are in no mood to listen to what is good for your own welfare. Even as, one who has reached death's door loves only harmful objects. Rāma will soon find out where I am and ere long you will be transported to the world of the dead."

Rāvaṇa flew along, though now and then he trembled in fear.

ĀRAṆYA 54–55

The chariot was flying over hills and forests and was approaching the ocean. At that time, Sītā beheld on the ground below, five strong vānaras[5]

3. See the description of Trijaṭā's dream, below (pp. 940–41). Dreams and omens play a comparable role in the culture of the Greeks and Romans as well. 4. We are reminded here that Viṣṇu incarnated himself as Rāma at the request of the gods, who wished Rāvaṇa to be killed. 5. Some scholars have suggested that *vānaras*, usually translated as "monkeys" or "apes," refers to tribal people or apelike human beings. This translator has left the word untranslated.

seated and watching the craft with curiosity. Quickly, Sītā took off the stole she had around her shoulders and, removing all her jewels and putting them in that stole, bundled them all up and threw the bundle into the midst of the vānaras, in the hope that should Rāma chance to come there they would give him a clue to her whereabouts.

Rāvaṇa did not notice this but flew on. And now the craft, which shot through space at great speed, was over the ocean; a little while after that, Rāvaṇa entered Laṅkā along with his captive Sītā. Entering his own apartments, Rāvaṇa placed Sītā in them, entrusting her care to some of his chief female attendants. He said to them: "Take great care of Sītā. Let no male approach these apartments without my express permission. And, take great care to let Sītā have whatever she wants and asks for. Any neglect on your part means instant death."

Rāvaṇa was returning to his own apartments: on the way he was still considering what more could be done to ensure the fulfilment of his ambition. He sent for eight of the most ferocious demons and instructed them thus: "Proceed at once to Janasthāna. It was ruled by my brother Khara; but it has now been devastated by Rāma. I am filled with rage to think that a mere human being could thus kill Khara, Dūṣaṇa and all their forces. Never mind: I shall put an end to Rāma soon. Keep an eye on him and keep me informed of his movements. You are free to bring about the destruction of Rāma." And, the demons immediately left.

Rāvaṇa returned to where Sītā was and compelled her to inspect the apartments. The palace stood on pillars of ivory, gold, crystal and silver and was studded with diamonds. The floor, the walls, the stairways—everything was made of gold and diamonds. Then again he said to Sītā: "Here at this place there are over a thousand demons ever ready to do my bidding. Their services and the entire Laṅkā I place at your feet. My life I offer to you; you are to me more valuable than my life. You will have under your command even the many good women whom I have married. Be my wife. Laṅkā is surrounded by the ocean, eight hundred miles on all sides. It is unapproachable to anybody; least of all to Rāma. Forget the weakling Rāma. Do not worry about the scriptural definitions of righteousness: we shall also get married in accordance with demoniacal wedding procedure. Youth is fleeting. Let us get married soon and enjoy life."

Āraṇya 56

Placing a blade of grass between Rāvaṇa and herself,[6] Sītā said: "O demon! Rāma, the son of king Daśaratha, is my lord, the only one I adore. He and his brother Lakṣmaṇa will surely put an end to your life. If they had seen you lay your hands on me, they would have killed you on the spot, even as they laid Khara to eternal rest. It may be that you cannot be killed by demons and gods; but you cannot escape being killed at the hands of Rāma and Lakṣmaṇa. Rāvaṇa, you are doomed, beyond doubt. You have already lost your life, your good fortune, your very soul and your senses, and on account of your evil deeds Laṅkā has attained widowhood.[7] Though

6. The magical power of Sītā's virtue allows her to use even a blade of grass as an effective barrier between herself and her abductor. 7. The ancient Indian king was considered to be the husband of the land he ruled, and kingdoms were often personified as a goddess (e.g., Laṅkā, p. 931).

you do not perceive this, death is knocking at your door, O Rāvaṇa. O sinner, you cannot under any circumstances lay your hands on me. You may bind this body, or you may destroy it: it is after all insentient matter, and I do not consider it worth preserving, nor even life worth living—not in order to live a life which will earn disrepute for me."

Rāvaṇa found himself helpless. Hence, he resorted to threat. He said: "I warn you, Sītā. I give you twelve months in which to make up your mind to accept me as your husband. If within that time you do not so decide, my cooks will cut you up easily for my breakfast." He had nothing more to say to her. He turned to the female attendants surrounding her and ordered them: "Take this Sītā away to the Aśoka grove. Keep her there. Use every method of persuasion that you know of to make her yield to my desire. Guard her vigilantly. Take her and break her will as you would tame a wild elephant."

The demonesses thereupon took Sītā away and confined her to the Aśoka grove, over which they themselves mounted guard day and night. Sītā did not find any peace of mind there, and stricken with fear and grief, she constantly thought of Rāma and Lakṣmaṇa.

It is said that at the same time, the creator Brahmā felt perturbed at the plight of Sītā. He spoke to Indra, the chief of gods: "Sītā is in the Aśoka grove. Pining for her husband, she may kill herself. Hence, go reassure her, and give her the celestial food to sustain herself till Rāma arrives in Laṅkā." Indra, thereupon, appeared before Sītā. In order to assure her of his identity he showed that his feet did not touch the ground and his eyes did not wink.[8] He gave her the celestial food, saying: "Eat this, and you will never feel hunger or thirst, nor will fatigue overpower you." While Indra was thus talking to Sītā, the goddess of sleep (Nidrā) had overpowered the demonesses.

Āraṇya 57–58

Mārīca, the demon who had disguised himself as a unique deer, had been slain. But Rāma was intrigued and puzzled by the way in which Mārīca died, after crying: "O Sītā, O Lakṣmaṇa." Rāma sensed a deep and vicious plot. Hence he made haste to return to his hermitage. At the same time, he saw many evil omens. This aggravated his anxiety. He thought: "If Lakṣmaṇa heard that voice, he might rush to my aid, leaving Sītā alone. The demons surely wish to harm Sītā; and this might well have been a plot to achieve that purpose."

As he was thus brooding and proceeding towards his hermitage, he saw Lakṣmaṇa coming towards him. The distressed Rāma met the distressed Lakṣmaṇa; the sorrowing Rāma saw the sorrowful Lakṣmaṇa. Rāma caught hold of Lakṣmaṇa's arm and asked him, in an urgent tone: "O Lakṣmaṇa, why have you left Sītā alone and come? My mind is full of anxiety and terrible apprehension. When I see all these evil omens around us, I fear that something terrible has happened to Sītā. Surely Sītā has been stolen, killed or abducted."

Lakṣmaṇa's silence and grief-stricken countenance added fuel to the

8. Attributes of the immortals.

fire of anxiety in Rāma's heart. He asked again: "Is all well with Sītā? Where is my Sītā, the life of my life, without whom I cannot live even for an hour? Oh, what has happened to her? Alas, Kaikeyī's desire has been fulfilled today. If I am deprived of Sītā, I shall surely die. What more could Kaikeyī wish for? If, when I enter my hermitage, I do not find Sītā alive, how shall I live? Tell me, Lakṣmaṇa; speak. Surely, when that demon cried: 'O Lakṣmaṇa' in my voice, you were afraid that something had happened to me. Surely, Sītā also heard that cry and in a state of terrible mental agony, sent you to me. It is a painful thing that thus Sītā has been left alone; the demons who were waiting for an opportunity to hit back have been given that opportunity. The demons were sore distressed by my killing of the demon Khara. I am sure that they have done some great harm to Sītā, in the absence of both of us. What can I do now? How can I face this terrible calamity?"

Still, Lakṣmaṇa could not utter a word concerning what had happened. Both of them arrived near their hermitage. Everything that they saw reminded them of Sītā.

ĀRAṆYA 59–60

And, once again before actually reaching the hermitage, and full of apprehension on account of Sītā, Rāma said to Lakṣmaṇa: "Lakṣmaṇa, you should not have come away like this, leaving Sītā alone in the hermitage. I had entrusted her to your care." When Rāma said this again and again, Lakṣmaṇa replied: "I have not come to you, leaving Sītā alone, just because I heard the demon Mārīca cry: 'O Lakṣmaṇa, O Sītā' in your voice. I did so only upon being literally driven by Sītā to do so. When she heard the cry, she immediately felt distressed and asked me to go to your help. I tried to calm her saying: 'It is not Rāma's voice; it is unthinkable that Rāma, who is capable of protecting even the gods, would utter the words, 'save me.' She, however, misunderstood my attitude. She said something very harsh, something very strange, something which I hate even to repeat. She said: 'Either you are an agent of Bharata or you have unworthy intentions towards me and therefore you are happy that Rāma is in distress and do not rush to his help.' It is only then that I had to leave."

In his anxiety for Sītā, Rāma was unimpressed by this argument. He said to Lakṣmaṇa: "Swayed by an angry woman's words, you failed to carry out my words; I am not highly pleased with what you have done, O Lakṣmaṇa."

Rāma rushed into their hermitage. But he could find no trace of Sītā in it. Confused and distressed beyond measure, Rāma said to himself, as he continued to search for Sītā: "Where is Sītā? Alas, she could have been eaten by the demons. Or, taken away by someone. Or, she is hidden somewhere. Or, she has gone to the forest." The search was fruitless. His anguish broke its bounds. Not finding her, he was completely overcome by grief and he began to behave as if he were mad.[9]

Unable to restrain himself, he asked the trees and the birds and the ani-

9. The description of the lover maddened by grief, searching for his beloved, is a theme in many literary traditions; examples include the Greek myth of Orpheus's search for Eurydice and the Persian story of Majnun ("the mad lover"), who wanders in the wilderness looking for Laila.

mals of the forest; "Where is my beloved Sītā?" The eyes of the deer, the trunk of the elephant, the boughs of trees, the flowers—all these reminded Rāma of Sītā. "Surely, you know where my beloved Sītā is. Surely, you have a message from her. Won't you tell me? Won't you assuage the pain in my heart?" Thus Rāma wailed. He thought he saw Sītā at a distance and going up to 'her,' he said: "My beloved, do not run away. Why are you hiding yourself behind those trees? Will you not speak to me?" Then he said to himself: "Surely it was not Sītā. Ah, she has been eaten by the demons. Did I leave her alone in the hermitage only to be eaten by the demons?" Thus lamenting, Rāma roamed awhile and ran around awhile.

ĀRAṆYA 61–62

Again Rāma returned to the hermitage, and, seeing it empty, gave way to grief again. He asked Lakṣmaṇa: "Where has my beloved Sītā gone, O Lakṣmaṇa? Or, has she actually been carried away by someone?" Again, imagining that it was all fun and a big joke which Sītā was playing, he said: "Enough of this fun, Sītā; come out. See, even the deer are stricken with grief because they do not see you." Turning to Lakṣmaṇa again, he said: "Lakṣmaṇa, I cannot live without my Sītā. I shall soon join my father in the other world. But, he may be annoyed with me and say: 'I told you to live in the forest for fourteen years; how have you come here before that period?' Ah Sītā, do not forsake me."

Lakṣmaṇa tried to console him: "Grieve not, O Rāma. Surely, you know that Sītā is fond of the forest and the caves on the mountainside. She must have gone to these caves. Let us look for her in the forest. That is the proper thing to do; not to grieve."

These brave words took Rāma's grief away. Filled with zeal and eagerness, Rāma along with Lakṣmaṇa, began to comb the forest. Rāma was distressed: "Lakṣmaṇa, this is strange; I do not find Sītā anywhere." But Lakṣmaṇa continued to console Rāma: "Fear not, brother; you will surely recover the noble Sītā soon."

But this time, these words were less meaningful to Rāma. He was overcome by grief, and he lamented: "Where shall we find Sītā, O Lakṣmaṇa, and when? We have looked for her everywhere in the forest and on the hills, but we do not find her." Lamenting thus, stricken with grief, with his intelligence and his heart robbed by the loss of Sītā, Rāma frequently sighed in anguish, muttering: "Ah my beloved."

Suddenly, he thought he saw her, hiding herself behind the banana trees, and now behind the karnikara trees. And, he said to 'her': "My beloved, I see you behind the banana trees! Ah, now I see you behind the karnikara tree: my dear, enough, enough of this play: for your fun aggravates my anguish. I know you are fond of such play; but pray, stop this and come to me now."

When Rāma realized that it was only his hallucination, he turned to Lakṣmaṇa once more and lamented: "I am certain now that some demon has killed my beloved Sītā. How can I return to Ayodhyā without Sītā? How can I face Janaka, her father? Oh, no: Lakṣmaṇa, even heaven is useless without Sītā; I shall continue to stay in the forest; you can return to Ayodhyā. And you can tell Bharata that he should continue to rule the country."

ĀRAṆYA 63–64

Rāma was inconsolable and even infected the brave Lakṣmaṇa. Shedding tears profusely, Rāma continued to speak to Lakṣmaṇa who had also fallen a prey to grief by this time: "No one in this whole world is guilty of as many misdeeds as I am, O Lakṣmaṇa: and that is why I am being visited by sorrow upon sorrow, grief upon grief, breaking my heart and dementing me. I lost my kingdom, and I was torn away from my relations and friends. I got reconciled to this misfortune. But then I lost my father. I was separated from my mother. Coming to this hermitage, I was getting reconciled to that misfortune. But I could not remain at peace with myself for long. Now this terrible misfortune, the worst of all, has visited me.

"Alas, how bitterly Sītā would have cried while she was carried away by some demon. May be she was injured; may be her lovely body was covered with blood. Why is it that when she was subjected to such suffering, my body did not split into pieces? I fear that the demon must have cut open Sītā's neck and drunk her blood. How terribly she must have suffered when she was dragged by the demons.

"Lakṣmaṇa, this river Godāvarī was her favorite resort. Do you remember how she used to come and sitting on this slab of stone talk to us and laugh? Probably she came to the river Godāvarī in order to gather lotuses? But, no: she would never go alone to these places.

"O sun! You know what people do and what people do not do. You know what is true and what is false. You are a witness to all these. Pray, tell me, where has my beloved Sītā gone. For, I have been robbed of everything by this grief. O wind! You know everything in this world, for you are everywhere. Pray, tell me, in which direction did Sītā go?"

Rāma said: "See, Lakṣmaṇa, if Sītā is somewhere near the river Godāvarī." Lakṣmaṇa came back and reported that he could not find her. Rāma himself went to the river and asked the river: "O Godāvarī, pray tell me, where has my beloved Sītā gone?" But the river did not reply. It was as if, afraid of the anger of Rāvaṇa, Godāvarī kept silent.

Rāma was disappointed. He asked the deer and the other animals of the forest: "Where is Sītā? Pray, tell me in which direction has Sītā been taken away." He then observed the deer and the animals; all of them turned southwards and some of them even moved southwards. Rāma then said to Lakṣmaṇa: "O Lakṣmaṇa, see, they are all indicating that Sītā has been taken in a southerly direction."

ĀRAṆYA 64

Lakṣmaṇa, too, saw the animals' behavior as sure signs indicating that Sītā had been borne away in a southerly direction, and suggested to Rāma that they should also proceed in that direction. As they were thus proceeding, they saw petals of flowers fallen on the ground. Rāma recognized them and said to Lakṣmaṇa: "Look here, Lakṣmaṇa, these are petals from the flowers that I had given to Sītā. Surely, in their eagerness to please me, the sun, the wind and the earth, have contrived to keep these flowers fresh."

They walked further on. Rāma saw footprints on the ground. Two of them he immediately recognized as those of Sītā. The other two were big—obviously the footprints of a demon. Bits and pieces of gold were strewn on the ground. Lo and behold, Rāma also saw blood which he concluded was Sītā's blood: he wailed again: "Alas, at this spot, the demon killed Sītā to eat her flesh." He also saw evidence of a fight: and he said: "Perhaps there were two demons fighting for the flesh of Sītā."

Rāma saw on the ground pieces of a broken weapon, an armor of gold, a broken canopy, and the propellers and other parts of a flying chariot. He also saw lying dead, one who had the appearance of the pilot of the craft. From these he concluded that two demons had fought for the flesh of Sītā, before one carried her away. He said to Lakṣmaṇa: "The demons have earned my unquenchable hate and wrath. I shall destroy all of them. Nay, I shall destroy all the powers that be who refuse to return Sītā to me. Look at the irony of fate, Lakṣmaṇa: we adhere to dharma, but dharma could not protect Sītā who has been abducted in this forest! When these powers that govern the universe witness Sītā being eaten by the demons, without doing anything to stop it, who is there to do what is pleasing to us? I think our meekness is misunderstood to be weakness. We are full of self-control, compassion and devoted to the welfare of all beings: and yet these virtues have become as good as vices in us now. I shall set aside all these virtues and the universe shall witness my supreme glory which will bring about the destruction of all creatures, including the demons. If Sītā is not immediately brought back to me, I shall destroy the three worlds—the gods, the demons and other creatures will perish, becoming targets of my most powerful missiles. When I take up my weapon in anger, O Lakṣmaṇa, no one can confront me, even as no one can evade old age and death."

Āraṇya 65–66

Seeing the world-destroying mood of Rāma, Lakṣmaṇa endeavored to console him. He said to Rāma:

"Rāma, pray, do not go against your nature. Charm in the moon, brilliance in the sun, motion in the air, and endurance in the earth—these are their essential nature: in you all these are found and in addition, eternal glory. Your nature cannot desert you; even the sun, the moon and the earth cannot abandon their nature! Moreover, being king, you cannot punish all the created beings for the sin of one person. Gentle and peaceful monarchs match punishment to crime: and, over and above this, you are the refuge of all beings and their goal. I shall without fail find out the real criminal who has abducted Sītā; I shall find out whose armor and weapons these are. And you shall mete out just punishment to the sinner. Oh, no, no god will seek to displease you, O Rāma: Nor these trees, mountains and rivers. I am sure they will all eagerly aid us in our search for Sītā. Of course, if Sītā cannot be recovered through peaceful means, we shall consider other means.

"Whom does not misfortune visit in this world, O Rāma? And, misfortune departs from man as quickly as it visits him. Hence, pray, regain your composure. If you who are endowed with divine intelligence betray lack of endurance in the face of this misfortune, what will others do in similar circumstances?

"King Nahuṣa, who was as powerful as Indra, was beset with misfortune.[1]

1. King Nahuṣa, an ancestor of Rāma, became so powerful that he claimed the throne of Indra, king of gods, but an arrogant act soon effected his fall from his exalted position.

The sage Vasiṣṭha, our family preceptor, had a hundred sons and lost all of them on one day! Earth is tormented by volcanic eruptions, and earthquakes. The sun and the moon are afflicted by eclipses. Misfortune strikes the great ones and even the gods.

"For, in this world people perform actions whose results are not obvious; and these actions which may be good or evil, bear their own fruits. Of course, these fruits are evanescent. People who are endowed with enlightened intelligence know what is good and what is not good. People like you do not grieve over misfortunes and do not get deluded by them.

"Why am I telling you all this, O Rāma? Who in this world is wiser than you? However, since, as is natural, grief seems to veil wisdom, I am saying all this. All this I learnt only from you: I am only repeating what you yourself taught me earlier. Therefore, O Rāma, know your enemy and fight him."

ĀRAṆYA 67–68

Rāma then asked Lakṣmaṇa: "O Lakṣmaṇa, tell me, what should we do now?" Lakṣmaṇa replied: "Surely, we should search this forest for Sītā."

This advice appealed to Rāma. Immediately he fixed the bayonet to his weapon and with a look of anger on his face, set out to search for Sītā. Within a very short time and distance, both Rāma and Lakṣmaṇa chanced upon Jaṭāyu, seriously and mortally wounded and heavily bleeding. Seeing that enormous vulture lying on the ground, Rāma's first thought was: "Surely, this is the one that has swallowed Sītā." He rushed forward with fixed bayonet.

Looking at Rāma thus rushing towards him, and rightly inferring Rāma's mood, Jaṭāyu said in a feeble voice: "Sītā has been taken away by Rāvaṇa. I tried to intervene. I battled with the mighty Rāvaṇa. I broke his armor, his canopy, the propellers and some parts of his chariot. I killed his pilot. I even inflicted injuries on his person. But he cut off my wings and thus grounded me." When Rāma heard that the vulture had news of Sītā, he threw his weapon away and kneeling down near the vulture embraced it.

Rāma said to Lakṣmaṇa: "An additional calamity to endure, O Lakṣmaṇa. Is there really no end to my misfortune? My misfortune plagues even this noble creature, a friend of my father's." Rāma requested more information from Jaṭāyu concerning Sītā, and also concerning Rāvaṇa. Jaṭāyu replied: "Taking Sītā with him, the demon flew away in his craft, leaving a mysterious storm and cloud behind him. I was mortally wounded by him. Ah, my senses are growing dim. I feel life ebbing away, Rāma. Yet, I assure you, you will recover Sītā." Soon Jaṭāyu lay lifeless. Nay, it was his body, for he himself ascended to heaven. Grief-stricken afresh, Rāma said to Lakṣmaṇa: "Jaṭāyu lived a very long life; and yet has had to lay down his life today. Death, no one in this world can escape. And what a noble end! What a great service this noble vulture has rendered to me! Pious and noble souls are found even amongst subhuman creatures, O Lakṣmaṇa. Today I have forgotten all my previous misfortunes: I am extremely tormented by the loss of this dear friend who has sacrificed his life for my sake. I shall myself cremate it, so that it may reach the highest realms."

Rāma himself performed the funeral rites, reciting those Vedic mantras[2]

2. Sacred chants, usually from the scriptures.

which one recites during the cremation of one's own close relations. After this, Rāma and Lakṣmaṇa proceeded on their journey in search of Sītā.

* * *

Summary The monkey hordes sent to search for Sītā in the southern direction by Sugrīva, king of the monkeys, are disheartened and take refuge in a cave near the southern ocean to discuss their course of action.

From *Book 4*

Kiṣkindhā

KIṢKINDHĀ 56, 57, 58

The sound, the gust of wind and dust preceded the arrival near the cave of a huge vulture. The vānaras who were seated on a flat surface outside the cave saw the vulture perched on a big rock. The vulture was known as Sampāti and was the brother of Jaṭāyu. It said to itself: "Surely, unseen providence is in control of the whole world. By that benign providence it has been decreed that my food should thus arrive at my very door, as it were. As and when each one of these vānaras dies I shall eat the flesh." The vānaras, however, heard this and were greatly disturbed.

With a mind agitated by intense fear, Aṅgada[3] said to Hanumān: "Death has come to us, disguised as a vulture. But, then, did not the noble Jaṭāyu give up his life in the service of Rāma. Even so we shall die in his service. Jaṭāyu suffered martyrdom while actually trying to help Sītā; but we, unfortunately, have not been able to find where she is."

Sampāti heard this. His mind was now disturbed. He asked: "Who is there who mentioned the name of my dearly beloved brother Jaṭāyu? I have not heard from him or of him for a very long time. Hearing of his murder my whole being is shaken. How did it happen?"

Even after this, the vānaras were skeptical: however, they helped Sampāti get down from the rock. Aṅgada then related the whole story of Rāma, including his friendship with Sugrīva and the killing of Vāli. He concluded: "We were sent in search of Sītā. We cannot find her. And the time-limit set by Sugrīva has expired. Afraid to face him, we have decided to fast unto death, lying here."

Sampāti said: "Jaṭāyu was my brother. Both of us flew to the abode of Indra when the latter had killed the demon Vṛtra. Jaṭāyu was about to faint, while we were near the sun. And I shielded him. By the heat of the sun my wings were burnt and I fell down here.[4] Though wingless and powerless, I shall help you in my own way, O vānaras, for the sake of Rāma. Some time ago, I saw a beautiful lady being carried away by Rāvaṇa: she was crying: 'O Rāma, O Lakṣmaṇa.' He dwells in Laṅkā, an island eight hundred miles from here. There, I can actually see Rāvaṇa and also Sītā living in Laṅkā, on

3. Son of Vāli, brother of Sugrīva, king of the monkeys. 4. This narrative is similar to the Greek myth of Icarus. Endowed with wings made by his father, Daedulus, Icarus flew too close to the sun, his wings melted, and he plunged to his death.

account of the strength of my vision. I can also see through intuition that you will find Sītā before returning to Kiṣkindhā. Now, take me to the seaside so that I can offer libations for the peace of my brother's soul." The vānaras gladly obliged Sampāti.

KIṢKINDHĀ 59–60

Jāmbavān who heard Sampāti mention that he had seen Sītā, approached Sampāti and asked: "Pray, tell me in detail where Sītā is and who has seen her?" Sampāti replied:

"Indeed, my son Supārśva had an even more direct encounter with Rāvaṇa and Sītā than I had. I shall narrate the story to you in detail. Please listen.

"I told you that in a foolhardy attempt to fly to the sun, my wings got burnt. I fell down wingless on this mountain. Just as the celestials are excessively lustful, snakes possess terrible anger, deer are easily frightened, and we vultures are voracious eaters. How could I appease insatiable hunger when I had no wings? My son Supārśva volunteered to supply me with food regularly. One day, recently, he failed to appear at the usual time, and I was tormented by hunger. When I took him to task for that lapse, he narrated what had happened that day. He said: 'I was looking for some meat to bring to you for your meal. At that time I saw a big demon flying away with a lady in his arms. I stopped him wishing to bring both of them for your meal today. But he begged of me to let him go: who could deny such a request? So I let him go. Later, some of the sages in the region exclaimed: "By sheer luck has Sītā escaped alive today." After they had flown away, I went on looking in that direction for a considerable time, and I saw that lady dropping ornaments on the hills. I was delayed by all this, O father!' It was from my son Supārśva that I heard about the abduction of Sītā in the first place. I could not challenge and kill Rāvaṇa, because I had neither wings nor the strength for it. But I shall render service to Rāma in my own way.

There lived on this mountain a great sage named Niśākara. On the day that Jaṭāyu and I flew towards the sun and on which my wings had been completely burnt, I fell down here. I remained unconscious for some time. Later I regained consciousness. With great difficulty I reached the hermitage of the sage, as I was eager to see him. After some time I saw him coming to the hermitage, surrounded by bears, deer, tigers, lions and snakes! When he entered the hermitage, they returned to the forest. He merely greeted me and went in. But soon he came back to where I was and said: 'Are you not Sampāti? Was not Jaṭāyu your brother? Both of you used to come here in human forms, to salute me. Ah, I recognize you. But tell me: who has burnt your wings and why have they been burnt?' "

KIṢKINDHĀ 61, 62, 63

Sampāti continued: "My physical condition and the loss of wings and vitality prevented me from giving a complete account of our misadventure. However, I said to the sage: 'Determined to pursue the sun, we flew towards it. We soared high into the sky. From there we looked at the earth: the cities looked like cart-wheels! We heard strange noises in the space. The mountains on earth looked like pebbles; the rivers looked like strings which bound the earth! The Himālaya and the Vindhya[5] appeared to be elephants bathing in a pond. And our sense of sight was playing tricks with us. It looked as if the earth were on fire. We then concentrated on the sun to get our bearings right. It looked as big as the earth. Jaṭāyu decided to return. I followed him. I tried to shield him against the fierce rays of the sun; and my wings were burnt. Jaṭāyu fell in Janasthāna, I think. I am here on the Vindhya.[6] What shall I do now? I have lost everything. My heart seeks death which I shall meet by jumping off a peak.'

"The sage, however, contemplated for a while and said: 'Do not despair. You will get back your wings, sight, life force and strength. A prediction have I heard: soon the earth will be ruled by king Daśaratha whose son Rāma will go to the forest in obedience to his father's will, and there Rāma will lose his wife Sītā in search of whom he will send vānaras. When you inform the vānaras where Sītā is kept in captivity, you will gain new wings. In fact, I can make your wings grow now: but it is better you get them after rendering a great service to Rāma.' Soon afterwards, the sage left this world.

"I have impatiently been waiting for you all, all these hundreds of years. I have often thought of committing suicide; but I have abandoned the idea every time, knowing that I have an important mission in life. I even scolded my son the other day for his having let Rāvaṇa get away with Sītā; but I myself could not pursue Rāvaṇa."

As Sampāti was speaking thus, new wings sprouted from his sides, even as the vānaras were looking on. The vānaras were delighted. Sampāti continued: "It is by the grace of the sage Niśākara that I have regained these wings, O vānaras. And, the sprouting of these wings is positive proof that you will be successful in finding Sītā."

Sampāti flew away, in an attempt to see if he could still fly! The vānaras had abandoned the idea of fasting unto death. They had regained their enthusiasm and their morale. They set out once again in search of Sītā.

KIṢKINDHĀ 64–65

Sampāti's words inspired confidence in the vānaras, but that enthusiasm lasted only till they actually faced the ocean itself. They reached the northern shore of the southern ocean, and stopped there. When they saw the extent of the ocean, their hearts sank. All of them wailed with one voice: "How can we get beyond this and search for Sītā?"

Aṅgada said to them: "Do not despair, O vānaras! He who yields to despondency is robbed of his strength and valor, and he does not reach his goal." Upon hearing this, all the vānaras surrounded Aṅgada, awaiting his plan. He continued: "Who can cross this ocean? Who will fulfill the wish of Sugrīva? Surely, it is by the grace of that vānara who is able to cross this ocean that we shall all be able to return home and behold our wives and children: it is by his grace that Rāma and Lakṣmaṇa can experience great joy." No one answered. Aṅgada said again: "Surely, you know that you have immeasurable

5. The Himalaya mountain range spans the northern and northeastern borders of the Indian subcontinent. The Vindhya Mountains are located in the northern part of central India. 6. The location of Sampāti's cave in the "Vindhya" is problematic since soon after the monkeys meet the old vulture, they reach the shore of the southern ocean, across which Hanumān leaps to the island of Laṅkā.

strength. No one can obstruct your path. Come on, speak up. Let me hear how far each one of you can go."

One by one the mightiest amongst the vānaras answered: "I can go eighty miles." "I can go double that distance." "I can cover treble that distance." And so on till Jāmbavān's turn[7] came. He said: "In days of yore I had great strength and I could easily have gone across and returned. But on account of my great age I have grown weak. Once upon a time when lord Viṣṇu assumed the gigantic form (to measure the whole earth with one foot, and the sky with the other) I went round him. But now, alas, I am incapable of crossing this little ocean."

Aṅgada himself declared: "I can surely cross this ocean and go to Laṅkā. But I am not sure if I can make the return journey. And, if I do not return, my going to Laṅkā would have been in vain." But Jambavān intervened and said: "Oh, no: you should not undertake this task. When an expedition is organized the commander himself should not participate in it. You are the very root of this whole expedition. And, the wise say that one should always protect the root; for so long as the root is preserved one can always expect to reap the harvest. You are our respected leader, and you should therefore not risk your own life in this venture."

Aṅgada said: "If no one else can cross the ocean and I should not, then we are all doomed to die here. What shall we do?" Jambavān, however, had other ideas: he said: "O prince, there is someone amongst us who can do this."

KIṢKINDHĀ 66–67

Jāmbavān said to Hanumān: "What about you, O mighty hero? Why don't you speak up? Your might is equal to that of Sugrīva, nay even to that of Rāma and Lakṣmaṇa; and yet you are quiet.

"I shall remind you of your birth and your ancestry. There once was a nymph called Puñjikasthalā. She was once cursed by a sage as a result of which she was reborn as Añjanā, the daughter of a vānara chief called Kuñjara. Añjanā married Kesari. This nymph who had the body of a human woman was once resting on the top of a hill. It is said that the wind-god, by whom her clothes had been blown up revealing her attractive legs, fell in love with her. Her body was, as it were, embraced by the wind-god. But she was furious and exclaimed: 'Who dares to violate my chastity?' The wind-god replied: 'Nay, I shall not violate you, O vānara lady! However, since as wind I have entered your body, you will bear a child who will vie with me in power.'

"Añjanā gave birth to you, O Hanumān! When you were a baby, you once saw the sun in the sky. You thought it was a fruit, and jumped up to pluck it from the sky. But, Indra struck you down with his thunderbolt and you fell down.[8] Your left chin was broken; and hence you came to be known as hanu-man. It is said that when you were thus injured, the wind-god was angered; there was no movement of wind in the world. The frightened gods propitiated the wind-god; and Brahmā the creator then gave you the boon of invincibility in battle. When Indra come to know that you did not die on

7. Jāmbavān is a *ṛkṣa,* a word usually translated as "bear." 8. A thunderbolt-wielding king of the gods, Indra is the Indian counterpart of the Greek god Zeus.

being hit by the thunderbolt, he conferred a boon on you, that you will die only when you wish to.

"There is no one equal to you in strength or in the ability to cross this ocean, nay, an ocean far wider than this. All others are despondent; the mission surely depends upon you."

When his glory was thus sung and he was reminded of his own power, Hanumān grew in stature, as it were. Seeing him thus filled with enthusiasm, the other vānaras jumped for joy. Hanumān grew in size; and shook his tail in great delight. He said: "Of course I can cross this ocean! With the strength of my arms I can push this ocean away. Stirred by my legs, the ocean will overflow its bounds. I can break up mountains. I can leap into the sky and sail along. I am equal to the wind-god in strength and valor. No one is equal to me other than Garuḍa of divine origin. I can even lift up the island of Laṅkā and carry it away."

Greatly inspired by Hanumān's words, the vānaras exclaimed with one voice: "Bravo, O Hanumān. You have saved us all. We shall pray for the success of your mission, standing on one leg till you return." Hanumān ascended the mountain, ready to leap.

From *Book 5*

Sundara

Hanumān was preparing to jump across the ocean and to cross the ocean to go to Laṅkā. Before undertaking this momentous and vital adventure, he offered prayers to the sun-god, to Indra, to the wind-god, to the Creator and to the elements. He turned to the east and offered his salutations to the wind-god, his own divine parent. He turned his face now to the south, in order to proceed on his great mission.

As he stood there, with his whole being swelling with enthusiasm, fervor and determination, and as he pressed his foot on the mountain before taking off from there, the whole mountain shook. And the shock caused the trees to shed their flowers, birds and beasts to leave their sheltered abodes, subterranean water to gush forth, and even the pleasure-loving celestials and the peace-loving ascetics to leave the mountain resorts, to fly into the sky and watch Hanumān's adventure from there. Giving proof of their scientific skill and knowledge, these celestials and sages remained hovering over the hill, eager to witness Hanumān's departure to Laṅkā. They said to one another: "This mighty Hanumān who is the god-child of the wind-god himself, will swiftly cross this ocean; for he desires to cross the ocean in order to achieve the mission of Rāma and the mission of the vānaras."

Hanumān crouched on the mountain, ready to go. He tensed his body in an effort to muster all the energy that he had. He held his breath in his heart and thus charged himself with even more energy.

He said to the vānaras who surrounded him: "I shall proceed to Laṅkā with the speed of the missile discharged by Rāma. If I do not find Sītā there, I shall with the same speed go to the heaven to search for her. And, if I do not see her even there, I shall get hold of Rāvaṇa, bind him and bring him over to the presence of Rāma. I shall definitely return with success. If it is difficult to bind Rāvaṇa and bring him, I shall uproot Laṅkā itself and bring it to Rāma."

After thus reassuring the vānaras, Hanumān took to the sky. The big trees that stood on the mountain were violently drawn into the slip-stream. Some of these trees flew behind Hanumān; others fell into the ocean; and yet others shed their blossoms on the hill tops, where they lay as a colorful carpet, and on the surface of the ocean where they looked like stars in the blue sky.

SUNDARA 1

The mighty Hanumān was on his way to Laṅkā. He flew in the southerly direction, with his arms outstretched. One moment it looked as if he would soon drink the ocean; at another as if he desired to drink the blue sky itself. He followed the course of wind, his eyes blazing like fire, like lightning.

Hanumān flying in the air with his tail coiled up behind looked like a meteor with its tail flying from north to the south. His shadow was cast on the surface of the ocean: this made it appear as if there were a big ship on the ocean. As he flew over the surface of the ocean, the wind generated by his motion greatly agitated the ocean. He actually dashed the surface of the ocean with his powerful chest. Thus the sea was churned by him as he flew over it. Huge waves arose in his wake with water billowing high into fine spray which looked like clouds. Flying thus in the sky, without any visible support, Hanumān appeared to be a winged mountain.

Hanumān was engaged in the mission of Rāma: hence the sun did not scorch him. Rāma was a descendant of the solar dynasty. The sages who were present there in their ethereal forms showered their blessings upon him.

Sāgara, the deity presiding over the ocean, bethought to himself: "In days of yore, Rāma's ancestors the sons of king Sagara, rendered an invaluable service to me.[9] And it therefore behoves me to render some service to this messenger of Rāma who is engaged in the service of Rāma. I should see that Hanumān does not tire himself and thus fail in his mission. I should arrange for him to have some rest before he proceeds further."

Thus resolved, Sāgara summoned the deity presiding over the mountain named Maināka which had been submerged in the ocean, and said to Maināka: "O Maināka, Indra the chief of gods has established you here in order to prevent the denizens from the subterranean regions from coming up. You have the power to extend yourself on all sides. Pray, rise up and offer a seat to Hanumān who is engaged on an important mission on behalf of Rāma, so that he can refresh himself before proceeding further."

SUNDARA 1

Readily agreeing to this request, the mountain Maināka rose from the bed of the ocean. As Hanumān flew towards Laṅkā he saw this mountain actually emerge from the ocean and come into his view. However, he considered that it was an obstacle to his progress towards Laṅkā, an obstruction on his path,

9. Looking for the horse that was stolen from their father's royal sacrifice, the 60,000 sons of Rāma's ancestor Sagara dug up the entire earth and its surrounding continents and seas, thus expanding the ocean's domain.

to be quickly overcome. Hanumān actually flew almost touching the peak of the mountain and by the force of the motion, the peak was actually broken.

Assuming a human-form the deity presiding over the Maināka mountain addressed Hanumān who was still flying: "O Hanumān, pray accept my hospitality. Rest a while on my peak. Refresh yourself. The ocean was extended by the sons of king Sagara, an ancestor of Rāma. Hence the deity presiding over the ocean wishes to return the service as a token of gratitude: thus to show one's gratitude is the eternal dharma. With this end in view, the ocean-god has commanded me to rise to the surface and offer you a resting place. It is our tradition to welcome and to honor guests, even if they are ordinary men: how much more important it is that we should thus honor men like you! There is yet another reason why I plead that you should accept my hospitality! In ancient times, all the mountains were endowed with wings. They used to fly around and land where they liked; thus, they terrorized sages and other beings. In answer to their prayer, Indra the chief of gods, wielded his thunderbolt and clipped off the wings of the mountains. As Indra was about to strike me, the wind-god bore me violently away and hid me in the ocean—so that I escaped Indra's wrath. I owe a debt of gratitude to the wind-god who is your god-father. Pray, allow me to discharge that debt by entertaining you."

Hanumān replied politely: "Indeed, I accept your hospitality, in spirit. Time is passing; and I am on an urgent mission. Moreover, I have promised not to rest till my task is accomplished. Hence, forgive my rudeness and discourtesy: I have to be on my way." As a token acceptance of Maināka's hospitality, Hanumān touched the mountain with his hand and was soon on his way. The gods and the sages who witnessed this scene were greatly impressed with Maināka's gesture of goodwill and Hanumān's unflagging zeal and determination. Indra, highly pleased with the Maināka mountain, conferred upon it the boon of fearlessness.

SUNDARA 1

The gods and the sages overseeing Hanumān's flight to Laṅkā had witnessed his first feat of strength when he took off from the Mahendra mountain, and his second feat of strength and enthusiasm when he declined even to rest and insisted on the accomplishment of the mission. They were eager to assure themselves still more conclusively of his ability to fulfill the task he had undertaken.

The gods and the sages now approached Surasā (mother of the Nāgas)[1] and said to her: "Here is Hanumān, the god-child of the wind-god, who is flying across the ocean. Pray, obstruct his path just a short while. Assume a terrible demoniacal form, with the body as big as a mountain, with terrible looking teeth and eyes, and mouth as wide as space. We wish to ascertain Hanumān's strength. And we therefore wish to see whether when he is confronted by you, he triumphs over you or becomes despondent."

In obedience to their command, Surasā assumed a terrible form and confronted Hanumān with her mouth wide open. She said to him, as he

1. A class of serpents or demigods.

approached her mouth while flying in the air: "Ah, fate has decreed that you should serve as my food today! Enter my mouth and I shall eat you up."

Hanumān replied: "O lady, I am on an important mission. Rāma, the son of king Daśaratha, came to the forest to honor his father's promise. While he was in the forest with his wife, Sītā, and his brother, Sītā was abducted by Rāvaṇa, the ruler of Laṅkā. I am going to Laṅkā to find her whereabouts. Do not obstruct my path now. Let me go. If the gods have ordained that I should enter your mouth, I promise that as soon as I discover Sītā and inform Rāma of her whereabouts, I shall come back and enter your mouth."

But, Surasā could not be put off. She repeated: "No one can escape me; and it has been decreed that you shall enter my mouth." She opened her mouth wide. Hanumān, by his yogic power, made himself minute, quickly entered her mouth and as quickly got out! He then said to her: "O lady, let me now proceed. I have fulfilled your wish and honored the gods' decree: I have entered your mouth! Salutations to you! I shall go to where Sitā is kept in captivity."

Surasā abandoned her demoniacal form and resumed her own form which was pleasant to look at. She blessed Hanumān: "Go! You will surely find Sītā and re-unite her with Rāma." The gods and the sages were thrilled to witness this third triumph of Hanumān.

SUNDARA 1

Hanumān continued to fly towards Laṅkā, along the aerial route which contains rain-bearing clouds, along which birds course, where the masters of music[2] move about, and along which aerial cars which resemble lions, elephants, tigers, birds and snakes, fly—the sky which is also the abode of holy men and women with an abundant store of meritorious deeds, which serves as a canopy created by the creator Brahmā to protect living beings on earth, and which is adorned with planets, the moon, the sun and the stars.

As he flew onwards, he left behind him a black trail which resembled black clouds, and also trails which were red, yellow and white. He often flew through cloud-formations.

A demoness called Simhikā saw Hanumān flying fearlessly in the sky and made up her mind to attack him. She said to herself: "I am hungry. Today I shall swallow this big creature and shall appease my hunger for some time." She caught hold of the shadow cast by Hanumān on the surface of the ocean. Immediately, Hanumān's progress was arrested and he was violently pulled down. He wondered: "How is it that suddenly I am dragged down helplessly?" He looked around and saw the ugly demoness Simhikā. He remembered the description which Sugrīva had given of her and knew it was Simhikā without doubt.

Hanumān stretched his body and the demoness opened her mouth wide. He saw her mouth and her inner vital organs through it. In the twinkling of an eye, he reduced himself to a minute size and dropped into her mouth. He disappeared into that wide mouth. The gods and the sages witnessing this were horrified. But with his adamantine nails he tore open the vital parts of

2. Gandharvas, a class of demigods.

the demoness and quickly emerged from her body. Thus, with the help of good luck, firmness and dexterity Hanumān triumphed over this demoness. The gods applauded this feat and said: "He in whom are found (as in you) these four virtues (firmness, vision, wisdom and dexterity) does not despair in any undertaking."

Hanumān had nearly covered the eight hundred miles, to his destination. At a short distance he saw the shore of Laṅkā. He saw thick forests. He saw the mountains known as Lamba. And he saw the capital city Laṅkā built on the mountains. Not wishing to arouse suspicion, he softly landed on the Lamba mountains which were rich in groves of Ketaka, Uddalaka and cocoanut trees.

SUNDARA 2

Though Hanumān had crossed the sea, covering a distance of eight hundred miles, he felt not the least fatigue nor exhaustion. Having landed on the mountain range close to the shore of the ocean, Hanumān roamed the forests for some time. In them he saw trees of various kinds, bearing flowers and fruits. He saw the city of Laṅkā situated on the top of a hill, surrounded by wide moats and guarded by security forces of demons. He approached the northern gate to the city and quietly surveyed it. That gate was guarded by the most ferocious looking demons armed to the teeth with the most powerful weapons. Standing there, he thought of Rāvaṇa, the abductor of Sītā.

Hanumān thought: "Even if the vānara forces do come here, of what use would that be? For Rāvaṇa's Laṅkā cannot be conquered even by the gods. Only four of us can cross the ocean and come here—Aṅgada, Nīla, Sugrīva and myself. And that is totally useless. One cannot negotiate with these demons and win them over by peaceful means. Anyhow, I shall first find out if Sītā is alive or not, and only then consider the next step."

In order to find out where Sītā was kept in captivity, he had to enter Laṅkā. The wise Hanumān considered that aspect of his mission. He thought: "Surely, I must be very careful, cautious and vigilant. If I am not, I might ruin the whole mission. An undertaking even after it has been carefully deliberated and decided upon will fail if it is mishandled by an ignorant or inefficient messenger. Therefore I should consider well what should be done and with due regard to all the pros and cons, I should vigilantly ensure that I do nothing which ought not to be done. I should enter the city in such a way that my presence and my movements are not detected; and I see that Rāvaṇa's security forces are so very efficient that it will not be easy to escape detection."

Thus resolved, Hanumān reduced himself to a small size, to the size of a cat as it were, and when darkness had fallen, proceeded towards the city. Even from a distance he could see the affluence that the city enjoyed. It had buildings of many stories. It had archways made of gold. It was brilliantly lit and tastefully decorated. The city was of unimaginable beauty and glory. When Hanumān saw it, he was filled with a mixture of feelings, feelings of despondence, and joy—joy at the prospect of seeing Sītā, and despondency at the thought of the difficulty involved in it.

Unnoticed by the guards, Hanumān entered the gateway.

SUNDARA 3

Hanumān was still contemplating the difficulties of the imminent campaign for the recovery of Sītā. Conquering Laṅkā by force seemed to him to be out of the question. He thought: "Possibly only Kumuda, Aṅgada, Suṣena, Mainda, Dvivida, Sugrīva, Kuśaparva, Jāmbavān and myself may be in a position to cross the ocean and come here. However, in spite of the heavy odds against such a campaign, there is the immeasurable prowess of Rāma and Lakṣmaṇa: surely they can destroy the demons without any difficulty whatsoever."

As he was entering the city, he was intercepted by Laṅkā, the guardian of the city. She questioned him: "Who are you, O vānara? This city of Laṅkā cannot be entered by you!" Hanumān was in no mood to reveal his identity: and he questioned her, in his turn: "Who are you, O lady? And why do you obstruct my path?" Laṅkā replied: "At the command of the mighty Rāvaṇa, I guard this city. No one can ignore me and enter this city: and you, O vānara, will soon enter into eternal sleep, slain at my hands!"

Hanumān said to her: "I have come as a visitor to this city, to see what is to be seen here. When I have seen what I wish to see, I shall duly return to where I have come from. Pray, let me proceed." But Laṅkā continued to say: "You cannot enter without overpowering me or winning my permission," and actually hit Hanumān on his chest with her hand.

Hanumān's anger was aroused. Yet, he controlled himself: for he did not consider it right to kill a woman! He clenched his fist and struck Laṅkā. She fell down, and then revealed: "Compose yourself, O vānara! Do not kill me. The truly strong ones do not violate the code of chivalry, and they do not kill a woman. I am Laṅkā, and he who has conquered me has conquered Laṅkā. That was what Brahmā the creator once said: 'When a vānara overpowers you, know that then the demons have cause for great fear.' I am sure that this prophecy refers to you, O vānara! I realize now that the inevitable destruction of the demons of Laṅkā has entered the territory in the form of Sītā who has been forcibly brought here by Rāvaṇa. Go, enter the city: and surely you will find Sītā and accomplish all that you desire to accomplish."

SUNDARA 4–5

Hanumān did not enter the city through the heavily guarded main gate, but climbed over the wall. Then he came to the main road and proceeded towards his destination—the abode of Rāvaṇa. On the way Hanumān saw the beautiful mansions from which issued the sound of music, and the sound of the citizens' rejoicing. He saw, too, prosperous looking mansions of different designs calculated to bring happiness and greater prosperity to the owners of the mansions. He heard the shouts of wrestling champions. Here and there he heard bards and others singing the glories of Rāvaṇa, and he noticed that these bards were surrounded by citizens in large numbers, blocking the road.

Right in the heart of the city, Hanumān saw in the main square numerous spies of Rāvaṇa: and these spies looked like holy men, with matted hair, or with shaven heads, clad in the hides of cows or in nothing at all. In their hands they carried all sorts of weapons, right from a few blades of grass to maces and sticks. They were of different shapes and sizes and of different appearance and complexions. Hanumān also saw the garrison with a hundred thousand soldiers right in front of the inner apartments of Rāvaṇa.

Hanumān approached the palace of Rāvaṇa himself. This was a truly heavenly abode. Within the compound of the palace and around the building there were numerous horses, chariots, and also flying chariots. The palace was built of solid and pure gold and the inside was decorated with many precious stones, fragrant with incense and sandalwood which had been sprinkled everywhere: Hanumān entered the palace.

It was nearly midnight. The moon shone brilliantly overhead. From the palace wafted the strains of stringed musical instruments; good-natured women were asleep with their husbands; the violent night-stalkers[3] also emerged from their dwellings to amuse themselves. In some quarters, Hanumān noticed wrestlers training themselves. In some others, women were applying various cosmetic articles to themselves. Some other women were sporting with their husbands. Others whose husbands were away looked unhappy and pale, though they were still beautiful. Hanumān saw all these: but he did not see Sītā anywhere.

Not seeing Sītā, the beloved wife of Rāma, Hanumān felt greatly distressed and unhappy and he became moody and dejected.

SUNDARA 6, 7, 8

Hanumān was greatly impressed by the beauty and the grandeur of Rāvaṇa's palace which he considered to be the crowning glory of Laṅkā itself. He did not all at once enter Rāvaṇa's inner apartments. First he surveyed the palaces of the other members of the royal family and the leaders of the demons, like Prahasta. He surveyed the palaces of Rāvaṇa's brothers Kumbhakarṇa and Vibhīṣaṇa, as also that of Rāvaṇa's son Indrajit. He was greatly impressed by the unmistakable signs of prosperity that greeted him everywhere. After thus looking at the palaces of all these heroes, Hanumān reached the abode of Rāvaṇa himself.

Rāvaṇa's own inner apartments were guarded by terrible looking demons, holding the most powerful weapons in their hands. Rāvaṇa's own private palace was surrounded by more armed forces; and even these garrisons were embellished by gold and diamonds. Hanumān entered the palace and saw within it palanquins, couches, gardens and art galleries, special chambers for enjoying sexual pleasures and others for indulging in other pastimes during the day. There were also special altars for the performance of sacred rituals. The whole palace was resplendent on account of the light emitted by precious stones which were found everywhere. Everywhere the couches, the seats and the dining vessels were of gold; and the floor of the whole palace was fragrant with the smell of wine and liquor. In fact Hanumān thought that the palace looked like heaven on earth, resplendent with the wealth of precious gems, and fragrant with the scent of a variety of flowers which covered its dome making it look like a flower-covered hill.

There were swimming pools with lotuses and lilies. In one of them there was the carved figure of a lordly elephant offering worship to Lakṣmī, the goddess of wealth.

3. A class of demons. The word is also used more generally for "demons."

Right in the center of the palace stood the best of all flying chariots, known as Puṣpaka. It had been painted with many colors and provided with numerous precious gems. It was decorated with lovely figures of snakes, birds, and horses fashioned of gems, silver and coral. Every part of that flying chariot had been carefully engineered, only the very best materials had been used, and it had special features which even the vehicles of the gods did not have—in fact, in it had been brought together only special features! Rāvaṇa had acquired it after great austerities and effort.

Hanumān saw all this. But, he did not see Sītā anywhere!

SUNDARA 9

Hanumān ascended the chariot Puṣpaka from which he could easily look into the inner apartments of Rāvaṇa! As he stood on the chariot, he smelled the extraordinary odor emanating from Rāvaṇa's dining room—the odor of wines and liquors, the smell of excellent food. The smell was appetizing and Hanumān thought the food should be nourishing. And, he saw at the same time the beautiful hall of Rāvaṇa which had crystal floors, with inlaid figures made of ivory, pearls, diamonds, corals, silver and gold. The hall was resplendent with pillars of gems. There was on the floor, a carpet of extraordinary beauty and design. On the walls were murals of several countries' landscapes. This hall thus provided all the five senses with the objects for their utmost gratification! A soft light illumined this hall.

On the carpet beautiful women lay asleep. With their mouths and their eyes closed, they had fallen asleep, after drinking and dancing, and from their bodies issued the sweet fragrance of lotuses. Rāvaṇa, sleeping there surrounded by these beautiful women, looked like the moon surrounded by the stars in the night sky. They were all asleep in beautiful disorder. Some were using their own arms as the pillow, others used the different parts of yet others' bodies as their pillow. Their hair was in disarray. Their dress was in disarray, too. But none of these conditions diminished the beauty of their forms. From the breath of all the women there issued the smell of liquor.

These women had come from different grades of society. Some of them were the daughters of royal sages, others those of brāhmaṇas, yet others were the daughters of gandharvas (celestial artists), and, of course, some were the daughters of demons: and all of them had voluntarily sought Rāvaṇa, for they loved him. Some he had won by his valor; others had become infatuated with him. None of these women had been carried away by Rāvaṇa against their wish. None of them had been married before. None of them had desire for another man. Rāvaṇa had never before abducted any woman, except Sītā.

Hanumān thought for a moment: Rāvaṇa would indeed have been a good man if he had thus got Sītā too, to be his wife: that is, before she had married Rāma and if he had been able to win her by his valor or by his charm. But, Hanumān contemplated further: by abducting the wife of Rāma, Rāvaṇa had certainly committed a highly unworthy action.

SUNDARA 10–11

In the center of that hall, Hanumān saw the most beautiful and the most luxurious bed: it was celestial in its appearance, built entirely of crystal and decked with gems. The lord of the demons, Rāvaṇa himself was asleep on it. The sight of this demon was at first revolting to Hanumān; so he turned his face away from Rāvaṇa. But then he turned his gaze again to Rāvaṇa. He saw that the two arms of Rāvaṇa were strong and powerful, and they were adorned with resplendent jewelry. His face, his chest, in fact his whole body was strong and radiant. His limbs shone like the lightning.

Around this bed were others on which the consorts of Rāvaṇa were asleep. Many of them had obviously been entertaining the demon with their music; and they had fallen asleep with the musical instruments in their arms. On yet another bed was asleep the most charming of all the women in that hall: she surpassed all the others in beauty, in youth and in adornment. For a moment Hanumān thought it was Sītā: and the very thought that he had seen Sītā delighted him.

But that thought did not last long. Hanumān realized: "It cannot be. For, separated from Rāma, Sītā will not sleep, nor will she enjoy herself, adorn herself or drink anything. Nor will Sītā ever dwell with another man, even if he be a celestial: for truly there is none equal to Rāma." He turned away from the hall, since he did not see Sītā there.

Next, Hanumān searched the dining hall and the kitchen: there he saw varieties of meats and other delicacies, condiments and a variety of drinks. The dining hall floor had been strewn with drinking vessels, fruits and even anklets and armlets which had obviously fallen from their wearers as they were drinking and getting intoxicated.

While he was thus inspecting the palace and searching for Sītā, a thought flashed in Hanumān's mind: was he guilty of transgressing the bounds of morality, in as much as he was gazing at the wives of others, while they were asleep with their ornaments and clothes in disarray? But, he consoled himself with the thought: "True, I have seen all these women in Rāvaṇa's apartment. But, no lustful thought has entered my mind! The mind alone is the cause of good and evil actions performed by the senses; but my mind is devoted to and established in righteousness. Where else can I look for Sītā, except among the womenfolk in Rāvaṇa's palace: shall I look for a lost woman among a herd of deer? I have looked for Sītā in this place with a pure mind; but she is not to be seen."

SUNDARA 12–13

Hanumān had searched the whole palace of Rāvaṇa. But he could not find Sītā. He reflected: "I shall not yield to despair. For, it has been well said that perseverance alone is the secret of prosperity and great happiness; perseverance alone keeps all things going, and crowns all activities with success. I shall search those places which I have not yet searched." He then began to search for Sītā in other parts of the palace. He saw many, many other women, but not Sītā.

Hanumān then searched for Sītā outside the palace. Yet, he could not find her. Once again dejection gripped him. He thought: "Sītā is to be found nowhere; yet Sampāti did say that he saw Rāvaṇa and he saw Sītā, too. Perhaps it was mistaken identity. It may be that slipping from the control of Rāvaṇa, Sītā dropped her body into the sea. Or, it may be she died of shock. Or, perhaps when she did not yield to him, Rāvaṇa killed her and ate her flesh. But it is impossible that she had consented to be Rāvaṇa's consort. Whether she is lost, or she has perished or has died, how can I inform Rāma about it? On the other hand, to inform Rāma and not to inform Rāma—both these appear to be objectionable. What shall I do now?" He also reflected on the consequence of his returning to Kiṣkindhā with no news of Sītā. He felt certain that: "When Rāma hears the bad news from me, he will give up his life. So will Lakṣmaṇa. And then their brothers and mothers in Ayodhyā. Nor could Sugrīva live after Rāma departs from this world. He will be followed to the other world by all the vānaras of Kiṣkindhā. What a terrible calamity will strike Ayodhyā and Kiṣkindhā if I return without news of Sītā's safety!" He resolved: "It is good that I should not return to Kiṣkindhā. Like an ascetic I shall live under a tree here. Or, I can commit suicide by jumping into the sea. However, the wise ones say that suicide is the root of many evils, and that if one lives one is sure to find what one seeks."

The consciousness of his extraordinary strength suddenly seized Hanumān! He sprang up and said to himself: "I shall at once kill this demon Rāvaṇa. Even if I cannot find Sītā, I shall have avenged her abduction by killing her abductor. Or, I shall kidnap him and take him to Rāma." Then he thought of a few places in Laṅkā he had not yet searched: one of them was Aśoka-grove. He resolved to go there. Before doing so, he offered a prayer: "Salutations to Rāma and Lakṣmaṇa; salutations to Sītā, the daughter of Janaka. Salutations to Rudra, Indra, Yama, the wind-god, to the moon, fire, and the Maruts." He turned round in all directions and invoked the blessings of all. He knew he needed them for he felt that demons of superhuman strength were guarding the Aśoka-grove.

SUNDARA 14–15

Hanumān then climbed the palace wall and jumped into the Aśoka-grove. It was most beautiful and enchanting, with trees and creepers of innumerable types.

In that grove, Hanumān also saw the bird sanctuary, the ponds and artificial swimming pools hemmed by flights of steps which had been paved with expensive precious and semi-precious stones. He also saw a hill with a waterfall flowing from its side. Not far from there, he saw a unique Aśoka or Simśapā tree which was golden in its appearance. The area around this tree was covered with trees which had golden leaves and blossoms, giving the appearance that they were ablaze.

Climbing up that unique Simśapā tree, Hanumān felt certain that he would soon see Sītā. He reasoned: "Sītā was fond of the forests and groves, according to Rāma. Hence, she will doubtless come to this yonder lotus-pond. Rāma did say that she was fond of roaming the forest: surely, then, she would wish to roam this grove, too. It is almost certain that the grief-stricken Sītā would come here to offer her evening prayers. If she is still alive, I shall surely see her today."

Seated on that Aśoka or Simśapā tree, Hanumān surveyed the whole of the grove. He was enthralled by the beauty of the grove, of the trees, and of the blossoms which were so colorful that it appeared as if the whole place were afire. There were numerous other trees, too, all of which were delightful to look at. While he was thus surveying the scene, he saw a magnificent temple, not far from him. This temple had a hall of a thousand pillars, and looked like the Kailāsa.[4] The temple had been painted white. It had steps carved out of coral. And its platforms were all made of pure gold.

4. The Himalayan peak on which the god Śiva dwells.

And, then, Hanumān saw a radiant woman with an ascetic appearance. She was surrounded by demonesses who were apparently guarding her. She was radiant though her garments were soiled. She was beautiful in form, though emaciated through sorrow, hunger and austerity. Hanumān felt certain that it was Sītā, and that it was the same lady whom he had momentarily seen over the Ṛṣymūka hill. She was seated on the ground. And, she was frequently sighing, surely on account of her separation from Rāma. With great difficulty, Hanumān recognized her as Sītā: and in this he was helped only by the graphic and vivid description that Rāma had given him.

Looking at her, thus pining for Rāma, and recollecting Rāma's love for her, Hanumān marveled at the patience of Rāma in that he could live without Sītā even for a short while.

SUNDARA 16–17

Hanumān contemplated the divine form of Sītā for a few minutes; and he once again gave way to dejection. He reflected: "If even Sītā who is highly esteemed by the noble and humble Lakṣmaṇa, and who is the beloved of Rāma himself, could be subjected to such sorrow, indeed one should conclude that Time is all-powerful. Surely, Sītā is utterly confident in the ability of Rāma and Lakṣmaṇa to rescue her; and hence she is tranquil even in this misfortune. Only Rāma deserves to be her husband, and she to be Rāma's consort." How great was Rāma's love for Sītā! And, what an extraordinary person Sītā was! Hanumān continued to "weigh" her in his own mind's balance: "It was for the sake of Sītā that thousands of demons in the Daṇḍaka forest were killed by Rāma. It was for her sake alone that Rāma killed Vāli and Kabandha. Khara, Dūṣaṇa, Triśira—so many of these demons met their end because of her. And, why not: she is such a special person that if, for her sake, Rāma turned the whole world upside down it would be proper. For, she was of extraordinary birth, she is of extraordinary beauty and she is of extraordinary character. She is unexcelled in every way. And, what an extraordinary love she has for Rāma, in that she patiently endures all sorts of hardships living, as she does, as a captive in Laṅkā. Again, Rāma pines for her and is eagerly waiting to see her, to regain her. Here she is, constantly thinking of Rāma: she does not see either these demonesses guarding her, nor the trees, flowers or fruits, but with her heart centered in Rāma, she sees him alone constantly." He was now certain that that lady was in fact Sītā.

The moon had risen. The sky was clear and the moonlight enabled Hanumān to see Sītā clearly. He saw the demonesses guarding Sītā. They were hideous-looking and deformed in various parts of their bodies. Their lips, breasts and bellies were disproportionately large and hanging. Some were very tall; others were very short. They were mostly dark-complexioned. Some of them had ears, etc., that made them look like animals. They were querulous, noisy, and fond of flesh and liquor. They had smeared their bodies with meat and blood; and they ate meat and blood. Their very sight was revolting and frightening. There in their midst was Sītā.

Sītā's dress and her appearance reflected her grief. At the foot of the tree whose name, Aśoka, meant free of sorrow, was seated Sītā immersed in an ocean of sorrow, surrounded by these terrible demonesses! It was only her confidence in the prowess and the valor of her lord Rāma that sustained her life. Hanumān mentally prostrated to Rāma, to Lakṣmaṇa and to Sītā and hid himself among the branches of the tree.

SUNDARA 18, 19, 20

Night was drawing to a close. In his palace, Rāvaṇa was being awakened by the Vedic recitation of brāhmaṇa-demons who were well versed in the Vedas and other scriptural texts, and also by musicians and bards who sang his praises. Even before he had time to adorn himself properly, Rāvaṇa thought of Sītā and longed intensely to see her. Quickly adorning himself with the best of ornaments and clad in splendid garments, he entered the Aśoka-grove, accompanied by a hundred chosen women who carried golden torches, fans, cushions and other articles. They were still under the influence of alcohol: and Rāvaṇa, though mighty and powerful, was under the influence of passion for Sītā.

Hanumān recognized the person he had seen asleep in the palace the previous night.

Seeing him coming in her direction, the frightened Sītā shielded her torso with her legs and hands, and began to weep bitterly. Pining for Rāma, distressed on account of her separation from him and stricken with grief, the most beautiful and radiant Sītā resembled eclipsed fame, neglected faith, enfeebled understanding, forlorn hope, ruined prospect, disregarded command, and obstructed worship; eclipsed moon, decimated army, fuelless flame, river in drought. She was constantly engaged in the prayer that Rāma might soon triumph over Rāvaṇa and rescue her.

Rāvaṇa appeared to be chivalrous in his approach to Sītā, and his words were meaningful and sweet: he said to Sītā, "Pray, do not be afraid of me, O charming lady! It is natural for a demon to enjoy others' wives and abduct them forcibly; it is the demon's own dharma. But, I shall not violate you against your wishes. For, I want to win your love; I want to win your esteem. I have enough strength to restrain myself. Yet, it breaks my heart to see you suffer like this; to see you, a princess, dressed like this in tattered and dirty garments. You are born to apply the most delightful cosmetic articles, to wear royal attire, and to adorn yourself with the most expensive jewels. You are young, youthful: this is the time to enjoy yourself, for youth is passing. There is none in the three worlds who is as beautiful as you are, O princess: for, having fashioned you, the Creator has retired. You are so beautiful that no one in the three worlds—not even Brahamā the creator—could but be overcome by passion. When you accept me, all that I have will become yours. Even my chief wives will become your servants. Let me warn you: no one in the three worlds is my match in strength and valor. Rāma, even if he is alive, does not even know where you are: he has no hope of regaining you. Give up this foolish idea of yours. Let me behold you appropriately dressed and adorned. And, let us enjoy life to your heart's content."

SUNDARA 21–22

Rāvaṇa's words were extremely painful to the grief-stricken Sītā. She placed a blade of grass in front of her, unwilling even to speak to Rāvaṇa directly, and said: "You cannot aspire for me any more than a sinful man can aspire for perfection! I will not do what is unworthy in the eyes of a chaste wife. Surely, you do not know dharma, nor do you obviously listen to the advice of wise counselors. Set an example to your subjects, O demon: and consort with your own wives; desire for others' wives will lead to infamy. The world rejoices at the death of a wicked man: even so it will, soon, on your death. But do not desire for me. You cannot win me by offering me power or wealth: for I am inseparable from Rāma even as light from the sun. He is the abode of righteousness, of dharma; take me back to him and beg his pardon. He loves those who seek his refuge. If you do not, you will surely come to grief: for no power on earth can save you from Rāma's weapon. His missiles will surely destroy the entire Laṅkā. In fact, if you had not stolen me in the absence of Rāma and Lakṣmaṇa, you would not be alive today: you could not face them, you coward!"

Rāvaṇa's anger was roused, and he replied: "Normally, women respond to a pleasant approach by a man. But you seem to be different, O Sītā. You rouse my anger; but my desire for you subdues that anger. My love for you prevents me from killing you straight away; though you deserve to be executed, for all the insulting and impudent words you utter. Well, I had fixed one year as the time-limit for you to make up your mind. Ten months have elapsed since then. You have two more months in which to decide to accede to my wish. If you fail to do so, my cooks will prepare a nice meal of your flesh for me to eat."

But, Sītā remained unmoved. She said to Rāvaṇa: "You are prattling, O wicked demon: I can by my own spiritual energy reduce you to ashes: but I do not do so on account of the fact that I have not been so ordered by Rāma and I do not want to waste my own spiritual powers."

The terrible demon was greatly enraged by these words of Sītā. He threatened her: "Wait, I shall destroy you just now." But he did not do so. However, he said to the demonesses guarding Sītā: "Use all your powers to persuade Sītā to consent to my proposal." Immediately, Rāvaṇa's consorts embraced him and pleaded: "Why don't you enjoy our company, giving up your desire for Sītā? For, a man who seeks the company of one who has no love for him comes to grief, and he who seeks the company of one who loves him enjoys life." Hearing this and laughing aloud, Rāvaṇa walked away.

SUNDARA 23–24

After Rāvaṇa had left the grove, the demonesses said: "How is it that you do not value Rāvaṇa's hand? Perhaps you do not know who he is. Of the six Prajāpatis who were the sons of the creator himself, Pulastya is the fourth; of Pulastya was the sage Viśrava born, and he was equal to Pulastya himself in glory. And this Rāvaṇa is the son of Viśrava. He is know as Rāvaṇa because he makes his enemies cry.[5] It is a great honor to accept his proposal. Moreover, this Rāvaṇa worsted in battle the thirty-three deities presiding over the universe. Hence he is superior even to the gods. And, what is most important: he surely loves you so much that he is prepared to abandon his own favorite wives and give you all his love."

Sītā was deeply pained by these words uttered by the demonesses. She said: "Enough of this vulgar and sinful advice. A human being should not

5. *Rāvaṇa,* from the verb *ru,* "to roar," "to cry."

become the wife of a demon. But, even that is irrelevant. I shall not under any circumstance abandon my husband and seek another." The demonesses were enraged and began to threaten Sītā. And, Hanumān was witnessing all this.

The demonesses said again: "You have shown enough affection to the unworthy Rāma. Excess of anything is undesirable and leads to undesirable result. You have so far conformed to the human rules of conduct. It is high time that you abandoned that code, abandoned the human Rāma and consented to be Rāvaṇa's wife. We have so far put up with the rude and harsh words you have uttered; and we have so far offered you loving and wholesome advice, intent as we are on your welfare. But you seem to be too stupid to see the truth. You have been brought here by Rāvaṇa; you have crossed the ocean. Others cannot cross the ocean and come to your rescue. We tell you this, O Sītā: even Indra cannot rescue you from here. Therefore, please do as we tell you, in your interest. Enough of your weeping. Give up this sorrow which is destructive. Abandon this wretched life. Attain love and pleasure. Make haste, O Sītā: for youth, especially of women, is but momentary and passes quickly. Make up your mind to become Rāvaṇa's wife. If, however, you are obstinate, we shall ourselves tear your body and eat your heart."

Other demonesses took up the cue and began to threaten Sītā. They said: "When I first saw this lovely woman brought into Laṅkā by Rāvaṇa the desire arose in me that I should eat her liver and spleen, her breasts and her heart. I am waiting for that day. . . . What is the delay? Let us report to the king that she died and he will surely ask us to eat her flesh! . . . . We should divide her flesh equally and eat it, there should be no quarrel amongst us. . . . After the meal, we shall dance in front of the goddess Bhadrakāli."

SUNDARA 25–26

In utter despair, Sītā gave vent to her grief by thinking aloud: "The wise ones have rightly said that untimely death is not attained here either by man or a woman. Hence though I am suffering intolerable anguish on account of my separation from my beloved husband, I am unable to give up my life. This grief is slowly eating me. I can neither live nor can I die. Surely, this is the bitter fruit of some dreadful sin committed in a past birth. I am surrounded by these demonesses: and how can Rāma reach me here? Fie upon human birth, and fie upon the state of dependence upon others, as a result of which I cannot even give up my life.

"What a terrible misfortune it was that even though I was living under the protection of Rāma and Lakṣmaṇa, I was abducted by Rāvaṇa, in their absence. Even more terrible it is that having been separated from my beloved husband I am confined here surrounded by these terrible demonesses. And, the worst part of it is: in spite of all these misfortunes, my heart does not burst with anguish thus letting me die. Of course, I shall never allow Rāvaṇa to touch me, so long as I am alive.

"I wonder why Rāma has not taken steps to come to my aid. For my sake he killed thousands of demons while we were in the forest. True I am on an island; but Rāma's missiles have no difficulty crossing oceans and finding their target. Surely, he does not know where I am. Alas, even Jaṭāyu who could have informed Rāma of what had happened was killed by Rāvaṇa. If only he knew I was here, Rāma would have destroyed Laṅkā and dried up the ocean with his missiles. All the demonesses of Laṅkā would weep then, as I am weeping now; all the demons would be killed by Rāma. Laṅkā would be one huge crematorium.

"I see all sorts of evil portents. I shall be re-united with Rāma. He will come. He will destroy all these demons. If only Rāma comes to know where I am, Laṅkā will be turned desolate by him, burnt by his terrible missiles. On the other hand, the time is fast running out: the time limit that Rāvaṇa had fixed for me to decide. Two more months: and I shall be cut into pieces for Rāvaṇa's meal. May it be that Rāma himself is no more, having succumbed to grief on account of my separation? Or, may it be that he has turned an ascetic? Usually, people who love each other forget each other when they are separated: but not so Rāma whose love is eternal. Blessed indeed are the holy sages who have reached enlightenment and to whom the pleasant and the unpleasant are non-different. I salute the holy ones. And, fallen into this terrible misfortune, I shall presently give up my life."

SUNDARA 27

Hearing the words of Sītā, some of the demonesses grew terribly angry. They threatened: "We shall go and report all this to Rāvaṇa; and then we shall be able to eat you at once." Another demoness named Trijaṭā just then woke up from her slumber and announced: "Forget all this talk about eating Sītā, O foolish ones! I have just now dreamt a dream which forewarns that a terrible calamity awaits all of you." The demonesses asked: "Tell us what the dream was."

Trijaṭā narrated her dream in great detail: "I saw in my dream Rāma and Lakṣmaṇa, riding a white chariot. Sītā was sitting on a white mountain, clad in shining white robes. Rāma and Sītā were re-united. Rāma and Lakṣmaṇa then got on a huge elephant which Sītā, too, mounted. Sītā held out her arms and her hands touched the sun and the moon. Rāma, Lakṣmaṇa and Sītā later mounted the Puṣpaka chariot and flew away in a northerly direction. From all these I conclude that Rāma is divine and invincible.

"Listen to me further. In another dream I saw Rāvaṇa. His head had been shaven. He was covered with oil. He wore crimson clothes. He was drunk. He had fallen from the Puṣpaka chariot. Later, I saw him dressed in black but smeared in a red pigment and dragged by a woman riding a vehicle drawn by donkeys. He fell down from the donkey. He was prattling like a mad man. Then he entered a place which was terribly dark and foul-smelling. Later a dark woman with body covered in mud, bound Rāvaṇa's neck and dragged him away in a southerly direction.[6] I saw Kumbhakarṇa as also the sons of Rāvaṇa in that dream; all of them undergoing the same or similar treatment. Only Vibhīṣaṇa's luck was different. He was clad in a white garment, with white garlands, and had a royal white umbrella held over his head.[7]

"I also saw in that dream that the whole of Laṅkā had been pushed into the sea, utterly destroyed and ruined. I also saw a rather strange dream. I saw Laṅkā burning furiously: though Laṅkā is protected by Rāvaṇa who is

6. The south is the direction of misfortune, the ancestors, and death. 7. In this context, the color white symbolizes virtue, purity, and sovereignty.

mighty and powerful, a vānara was able to set Laṅkā ablaze, because the vānara was a servant of Rāma.

"I see a clear warning in these dreams, O foolish women! Enough of your cruelty to Sītā; I think it is better to please her and win her favor. I am convinced that Sītā will surely achieve her purpose and her desire to be reunited with Rāma."

Hearing this, Sītā felt happy and said: "If this comes true, I shall certainly protect all of you."

SUNDARA 28, 29, 30

But, the demonesses did not pay heed to Trijaṭā. And, Sītā thought:

"Truly have the wise ones declared that death never comes to a person before the appointed time. My time has come. Rāvaṇa has said definitely that if I do not agree to him I will be put to death. Since I can never, never love him, it is certain that I shall be executed. Hence, I am condemned already. I shall, therefore, incur no blame if I voluntarily end my life today. O Rāma! O Lakṣmaṇa! O Sumitrā! O Kausalyā! O Mother! Caught helplessly and brought to this dreadful place, I am about to perish. Surely it was my own 'bad-time' that approached me in the form of that golden deer, and I, a foolish woman sent the two princes in search of it. Maybe, they were killed by some demon. Or, maybe they are alive and do not know where I am.

"Alas, whatever virtue I practiced and the devotion with which I served my own lord and husband, all these have come to naught; I shall presently abandon this ill-fated life of mine. O Rāma, after you complete the fourteen-year term of exile, you will return to Ayodhyā and enjoy life with the queens you might marry. But, I who loved you and whose heart is forever fastened to you, shall soon be no more.

"How shall I end this life? I have no weapon; nor will anyone here give me a weapon or poison to end my life. Ah, I shall use this string with which my hair has been tied and hang myself from this tree."

Thinking aloud in this manner, Sītā contemplated the feet of Rāma and got ready to execute herself. At the same time, however, she noticed many auspicious omens which dissuaded her from her wish to end her life. Her left eye, left arm and left thigh throbbed.[8] Her heart was gladdened, her sorrow left her for the moment, her despair abated, and she became calm and radiant once again.

Hanumān, sitting on the tree, watched all this. He thought: "If I meet Sītā in the midst of these demonesses, it would be disastrous. In fact, she might get frightened and cry and before I could make the announcement concerning Rāma, I might be caught. I can fight all the demons here; but then I might be too weak to fly back. I could speak to her in the dialect of the brāhmaṇa; but she might suspect a vānara speaking Sanskrit to be Rāvaṇa himself![9] To speak to Sītā now seems to be risky; yet, if I do not, she might commit suicide. If one does not act with due regard to place and time, the contrary results ensue. I shall sing the glories of Rāma softly and thus win

8. In the case of men, the throbbing of the right eye, arm, or thigh signifies good fortune. 9. Women and those lower in the caste system than the brahmans or the three highest castes apparently spoke in different dialects. Sītā can speak Sanskrit because she is a lady of high status.

Sītā's confidence. Then I shall deliver Rāma's message to her in a manner which will evoke her confidence."

SUNDARA 31, 32, 33

After deep deliberation, Hanumān decided upon the safest and the wisest course! Softly, sweetly, clearly and in cultured accents, he narrated the story of Rāma. He said: "A descendant of the noble Ikṣvāku was the emperor Daśaratha, who was a royal sage in as much as he was devoted to asceticism and righteousness, while yet ruling his kingdom. His eldest son Rāma was equally powerful, glorious and righteous. To honor his father's promise to his step-mother, Rāma went to the Daṇḍaka forest along with his brother Lakṣmaṇa, and his wife Sītā. There, Rāma killed thousands of demons. A demon disguised as a deer tricked Rāma and Lakṣmaṇa away, and at that time, the wicked Rāvaṇa abducted Sītā. Rāma went searching for her; and while so wandering the forest cultivated the friendship of the vānara Sugrīva. Sugrīva commissioned millions of vānaras to search for Sītā. Endowed with extraordinary energy, I crossed the ocean; and blessed I am that I am able to behold that Sītā."

Sītā was supremely delighted to hear that speech. She looked up and down, around and everywhere, and saw the vānara Hanumān. But, seeing the vānara seated on the tree, Sītā was frightened and suspicious. She cried aloud. "O Rāma, O Lakṣmaṇa." She was terror-stricken as the vānara approached her; but she was pleasantly surprised to see that he came humbly and worshipfully. She thought: "Am I dreaming? I hope not; it forebodes ill to dream of a vānara. Nay, I am not dreaming. Maybe, this is hallucination. I have constantly been thinking of Rāma. I have constantly uttered his name, and talked about him. Since my whole being is absorbed in him, I am imagining all this. But, I have reasoned out all this carefully within myself; yet, this being here is not only clearly seen by me, but it talks to me, too! I pray to the gods, may what I have just heard be true."

With his palms joined together in salutation over his head, Hanumān humbly approached Sītā and asked: "Who are you, O lady? Are you indeed the wife of that blessed Rāma?"

Highly pleased with this question, Sītā thereupon related her whole story: "I am the daughter-in-law of king Daśaratha, and the daughter of king Janaka. I am the wife of Rāma. We lived happily in Ayodhyā for twelve years. But when Rāma was about to be crowned, his step-mother Kaikeyī demanded the boon from her husband that Rāma should be banished to the forest. The king swooned on hearing this; but Rāma took it upon himself to fulfill that promise. I followed him; and Lakṣmaṇa, too, came with us. One day when they were away, Rāvaṇa forcibly carried me and brought me here. He has given me two more months to live; after which I shall meet my end."

SUNDARA 34–35

Once again bowing down to Sītā, Hanumān said to her: "O divine lady, I am a messenger sent by Rāma. He, as also his brother Lakṣmaṇa, send their greetings and hope that you are alive and well." Sītā rejoiced and thought to herself: "Surely, there is a lot of truth in the old adage: 'Happiness is bound to come to the man who lives, even though after a long time.' " But, as

Hanumān came near her, she grew suspicious and would not even look at him: she thought, and said to him: "O Rāvaṇa! Previously you assumed the disguise of a mendicant and abducted me. Now, you have come to torment me in the guise of a vānara! Pray, leave me alone." But, on the other hand, she reasoned to herself: "No this cannot be; for on seeing this vānara, my heart rejoices."

Hanumān, however, reassured her: "O blessed Sītā, I am a messenger sent by Rāma who will very soon kill these demons and rescue you from their captivity. Rāma and Lakṣmaṇa constantly think of you. So does king Sugrīva whose minister Hanumān, I am. Endowed with extraordinary energy I crossed the sea. I am not what you suspect me to be!"

At her request, Hanumān recounted the glories of Rāma:[1] "Rāma is equal to the gods in beauty, charm and wisdom. He is the protector of all living beings, of his own people, of his work and of his dharma; he is the protector of people of different occupations, of good conduct, and he himself adheres to good conduct and makes others do so, too. He is mighty, friendly, well-versed in scriptures and devoted to the holy ones. He is endowed with all the characteristics of the best among men, which are: broad shoulders, strong arms, powerful neck, lovely face, reddish eyes, deep voice, dark-brown colored skin; he has firm chest, wrist and fist; he has long eyebrows, arms and scrotum; he has symmetrical locks, testicles and knees; he has strong bulging chest, abdomen and rim of the navel; reddish in the corner of his eyes, nails, palms and soles; he is soft in his glans, the lines of his feet and hair; he has deep voice, gait and navel; three folds adorn the skin of his neck and his abdomen; the arch of his feet, the lines on his soles, and the nipples are deep; he has short generative organ, neck, back and shanks; three spirals adorn the hair on his head; there are four lines at the root of his thumb; and four lines on his forehead; he is four cubits tall; the four pairs of his limbs (cheeks, arms, shanks and knees) are symmetrical; even so the other fourteen pairs of limbs; his limbs are long. He is excellent in every way. Lakṣmaṇa, Rāma's brother, is also full of charm and excellences."

SUNDARA 35–36

Hanumān then narrated in great detail all that had happened. He mentioned in particular how Rāma was moved to tears when Hanumān showed him the pieces of jewelry that Sītā had dropped on the hill. He concluded that narrative by affirming: "I shall certainly attain the glory of having seen you first; and Rāma too will soon come here to take you back." He also revealed to Sītā his own identity: "Kesari, my father, lived on the mountain known as Malayavān. Once he went to the Gokarṇa mountain at the command of the sages to fight and to kill a demon named Sāmbasadana who tormented the people. I was born of the wind-god and my mother Añjanā. I tell you again, O divine lady, that I am a vānara, and I am a messenger sent by Rāma; here, behold the ring which has been inscribed with the name of Rāma. Whatever might have been the cause of your suffering captivity, it has almost come to an end."

1. In the description that follows, Hanumān reiterates many of the qualities and attributes ascribed to Rāma throughout the epic. This conventional portrait of the ideal man blends physical characteristics and character traits.

When she saw the signet ring, Sītā felt the presence of Rāma himself; she was filled with joy. Her attitude to Hanumān, too, immediately and dramatically changed. She exclaimed: "You are heroic, capable, and wise, too, O best among vānaras. What a remarkable feat you have accomplished by crossing this vast ocean, a distance of eight hundred miles.[2] Surely, you are not an ordinary vānara in that you are not afraid of even Rāvaṇa. I am delighted to hear that Rāma and Lakṣmaṇa are well. But why has he not rescued me yet: he could dry up the ocean, in fact he could even destroy the whole earth with his missiles if he wanted to. Perhaps, they had to wait for the propitious moment, and that moment which would mean the end of my suffering has not yet arrived.

"O Hanumān, tell me more about Rāma. Does he continue to rely on both self-effort and divine agency in all that he undertakes? Tell me, O Hanumān, does he still love me as before? And, I also hope that, pining for me, he does not waste away. And also tell me: how will Rāma rescue me from here. Will Bharata send an army? When he renounced the throne and when he took me to the forest, he displayed extraordinary firmness: is he still as firm in his resolves? Oh, I know that he loves me more than anyone else in this world."

Hanumān replied: "You will soon behold Rāma, O Sītā! Stricken with grief on account of his separation from you, Rāma does not eat meat, nor drink wine; he does not even wish to ward off flies and mosquitoes that assail him. He thinks of you constantly. He hardly sleeps; and if he does, he wakes up calling out 'Ah Sītā.' When he sees a fruit or flower, he thinks of you." Hearing the glories of Rāma, Sītā was rid of sorrow; hearing of his grief, Sītā grew equally sorrowful.

SUNDARA 37

Sītā replied to Hanumān: "Your description of Rāma's love for me comes to me like nectar mixed with poison. In whatever condition one may be, whether one is enjoying unlimited power and prosperity or one is in dreadful misery, the end of one's action drags a man as if he were tied with a rope. Look at the way in which Rāma, Lakṣmaṇa and I have been subjected to sorrow: surely, no one can overcome destiny. I wonder when the time will come when I shall be united with Rāma once again. Rāvaṇa gave me one year, of which ten months have passed and only two are left. At the end of those two months, Rāvaṇa will surely kill me. There is no alternative. For, he does not fancy the thought of taking me back to Rāma. In fact, such a course was suggested by Rāvaṇa's own brother Vibhīṣaṇa: so his own daughter Kalā told me. But Rāvaṇa turns a deaf ear upon such wise counsel."

Hanumān said to Sītā: "I am sure that Rāma will soon arrive here, with an army of forest-dwellers and other tribes, as soon as I inform him of your whereabouts. But, O divine lady, I have another idea. You can rejoin your husband this very day. I can enable you to end this sorrow instantly. Pray, do not hesitate; get on my back, and seek union (yogam) with Rāma now. I have the power to carry you, or even Laṅkā, Rāvaṇa and everything in it! No one will be able to pursue me or to overcome me. What a great triumph it will be if I return to Kiṣkindhā with you on my back!"

2. Not a realistic estimate of the distance between Laṅkā and the southern tip of India.

For a moment Sītā was thrilled at this prospect. But she remarked almost in jest: "You are speaking truly like a vānara, an ignorant tribesman. You are so small: and you think you can carry me over the ocean!" Hanumān, thereupon, showed Sītā his real form. Seeing him stand like a mountain in front of her, Sītā felt sure that his confidence was justified, but said to him: "O mighty Hanumān, I am convinced that you can do as you say. But I do not think it is proper for me to go with you. You may proceed at great speed; but I may slip and fall into the ocean. If I go with you, the demons will suspect our relationship and give it an immoral twist. Moreover, many demons will pursue you: how will you, unarmed as you are, deal with them and at the same time protect me? I might once again fall into their hands. I agree you have the power to fight them: but if you kill them all, it will rob Rāma of the glory of killing them and rescuing me. Surely, when Rāma and Lakṣmaṇa come here with you, they will destroy the demons and liberate me. I am devoted to Rāma; and I will not of my own accord touch the body of another man. Therefore, O Hanumān, enable Rāma and Lakṣmaṇa to come here with greatest expedition."

SUNDARA 38

Hanumān, the wise vānara, was highly impressed and thoroughly convinced of the propriety of Sītā's arguments. He applauded them, and prayed: "If you feel you should not come, pray, give me a token which I might take back with me and which Rāma might recognize."

This suggestion revived old memories and moved Sītā to tears. She said to Hanumān: "I shall give you the best token. Please remind my glorious husband of a delightful episode in our forest-life which only he and I know. This happened when we were living near Citrakooṭa hill. We had finished our bath; and we had had a lot of fun playing in water, Rāma was sitting on my lap. A crow began to worry me. I kept it away threatening it with stones. It hid itself. When I was getting dressed and when my skirt slipped a little, the crow attacked me again: but I defended myself angrily. Looking at this Rāma laughed, while sweetly pacifying me.

"Both of us were tired. I slept on Rāma's lap for sometime. Later Rāma slept with his head resting on my lap. The crow (who was Indra's son in disguise) attacked me again and began to inflict wounds on my body. A few drops of blood trickled from my chest and fell on Rāma who awoke. Seeing the vicious crow perched on a nearby tree, Rāma picked up the missile named after the creator and hurled it at the crow. That crow flew round to the three worlds but found no asylum anywhere else.

"Eventually it sought refuge with Rāma himself. Rāma was instantly pacified. Yet, the missile could not be neutralized. The crow sacrificed its right eye and saved its life." As she was narrating the story, Sītā felt the presence of Rāma and addressed him: "O Rāma, you were ready to use the Brahmā-missile towards a mere crow for my sake; why do you suffer my abduction with patience? Though I have you as my lord and master, yet I live here like a destitute! Have you no compassion for me: it was from you I learnt that compassion is the greatest virtue!" She said to Hanumān again: "No power on earth can confront Rāma. It is only my ill-luck that prevents them from coming to my rescue."

Hanumān explained: "It was only ignorance of your whereabouts that has caused this delay, O divine lady. Now that we know where you are, the destruction of the demons is at hand." Sītā said: "The fulfillment of this mission depends upon you; with your aid, Rāma will surely succeed in his mission. But, please tell Rāma that I shall be alive only for a month more." Then as a further token, Sītā took off a precious jewel from her person and gave it to Hanumān. Receiving that jewel, and with Sītā's blessings Hanumān was ready to depart.

* * *

From *Book 6*

Yuddha

YUDDHA 109, 110, 111

When Rāma and Rāvaṇa began to fight, their armies stood stupefied, watching them! Rāma was determined to win; Rāvaṇa was sure he would die: knowing this, they fought with all their might. Rāvaṇa attacked the standard on Rāma's car; and Rāma similarly shot the standard on Rāvaṇa's car. While Rāvaṇa's standard fell; Rāma's did not. Rāvaṇa next aimed at the "horses" of Rāma's car: even though he attacked them with all his might, they remained unaffected.

Both of them discharged thousands of missiles: these illumined the skies and created a new heaven, as it were! They were accurate in their aim and their missiles unfailingly hit the target. With unflagging zeal they fought each other, without the least trace of fatigue. What one did the other did in retaliation.

Rāvaṇa shot at Mātali[3] who remained unaffected by it. Then Rāvaṇa sent a shower of maces and mallets at Rāma. Their very sound agitated the oceans and tormented the aquatic creatures. The celestials and the holy brāhmaṇas witnessing the scene prayed: "May auspiciousness attend to all the living beings, and may the worlds endure forever. May Rāma conquer Rāvaṇa." Astounded at the way in which Rāma and Rāvaṇa fought with each other, the sages said to one another: "Sky is like sky, ocean is like ocean; the fight between Rāma and Rāvaṇa is like Rāma and Rāvaṇa—incomparable."

Taking up a powerful missile, Rāma correctly aimed at the head of Rāvaṇa; it fell. But another head appeared in its place. Every time Rāma cut off Rāvaṇa's head, another appeared! Rāma was puzzled. Mātali, Rāma's driver, said to Rāma: "Why do you fight like an ordinary warrior, O Rāma? Use the Brahmā-missile; the hour of the demon's death is at hand."

Rāma remembered the Brahmā-missile which the sage Agastya had given him. It had the power of the wind-god for its "feathers"; the power of fire and sun at its head; the whole space was its body; and it had the weight of a mountain. It shone like the sun or the fire of nemesis. As Rāma took it in his hands, the earth shook and all living beings were terrified. Infallible in its destructive power, this ultimate weapon of destruction shattered the chest of Rāvaṇa, and entered deep into the earth.

Rāvaṇa fell dead. And the surviving demons fled, pursued by the vānaras.

3. Indra, king of the gods, has sent his own charioteer, Mātali, to drive Rāma's chariot in battle.

The vānaras shouted in great jubilation. The air resounded with the drums of the celestials. The gods praised Rāma. The earth became steady, the wind blew softly and the sun was resplendent as before. Rāma was surrounded by mighty heroes and gods who were all joyously felicitating him on the victory.

YUDDHA 112, 113

Seeing Rāvaṇa lying dead on the battlefield, Vibhīṣaṇa burst into tears. Overcome by brotherly affection, he lamented thus: "Alas, what I had predicted has come true: and my advice was not relished by you, overcome as you were by lust and delusion. Now that you have departed, the glory of Laṅkā has departed. You were like a tree firmly established in heroism with asceticism for its strength, spreading out firmness in all aspects of your life: yet you have been cut down. You were like an elephant with splendor, noble ancestry, indignation, and pleasant nature for parts: yet you have been killed. You, who were like blazing fire have been extinguished by Rāma."

Rāma approached the grief-stricken Vibhīṣaṇa and gently and lovingly said to him: "It is not right that you should thus grieve, O Vibhīṣaṇa, for a mighty warrior fallen on the battlefield. Victory is the monopoly of none: a hero is either slain in battle or he kills his opponent. Hence our ancients decreed that the warrior who is killed in combat should not be mourned. Get up and consider what should be done next."

Vibhīṣaṇa regained his composure and said to Rāma: "This Rāvaṇa used to give a lot in charity to ascetics; he enjoyed life; he maintained his servants well; he shared his wealth with his friends, and he destroyed his enemies. He was regular in his religious observances; learned he was in the scriptures. By your grace, O Rāma, I wish to perform his funeral in accordance with the scriptures, for his welfare in the other world." Rāma was delighted and said to Vibhīṣaṇa: "Hostility ends at death. Take steps for the due performance of the funeral rites. He is your brother as he is mine, too."

The womenfolk of Rāvaṇa's court, and his wives, hearing of his end, rushed out of the palace, and, arriving at the battlefield, rolled on the ground in sheer anguish. Overcome by grief they gave vent to their feelings in diverse heart-rending ways. They wailed: "Alas, he who could not be killed by the gods and demons, has been killed in battle by a man standing on earth. Our beloved lord! Surely when you abducted Sītā and brought her to Laṅkā, you invited your own death! Surely it was because death was close at hand that you did not listen to the wise counsel of your own brother Vibhīṣaṇa, and you ill-treated him and exiled him. Even later if you had restored Sītā to Rāma, this evil fate would not have overtaken you. However, it is surely not because you did what you liked, because you were driven by lust, that you lie dead now: God's will makes people do diverse deeds. He who is killed by the divine will dies. No one can flout the divine will, and no one can buy the divine will nor bribe it."

* * *

YUDDHA 115, 116

Rāma returned to the camp where the vānara troops had been stationed. He turned to Lakṣmaṇa and said: "O Lakṣmaṇa, install Vibhīṣaṇa on the throne of Laṅkā and consecrate him as the king of Laṅkā. He has rendered invaluable service to me and I wish to behold him on the throne of Laṅkā at once."

Without the least loss of time, Lakṣmaṇa made the necessary preparations and with the waters of the ocean consecrated Vibhīṣaṇa as king of Laṅkā, in strict accordance with scriptural ordinance. Rāma, Lakṣmaṇa and the others were delighted. The demon-leaders brought their tributes and offered them to Vibhīṣaṇa who in turn placed them all at Rāma's feet.

Rāma said to Hanumān: "Please go, with the permission of king Vibhīṣaṇa, to Sītā and inform her of the death of Rāvaṇa and the welfare of both myself and Lakṣmaṇa." Immediately Hanumān left for the Aśoka-grove. The grief-stricken Sītā was happy to behold him. With joined palms Hanumān submitted Rāma's message and added: "Rāma desires me to inform you that you can shed fear, for you are in your own home as it were, now that Vibhīṣaṇa is king of Laṅkā." Sītā was speechless for a moment and then said: "I am delighted by the message you have brought, O Hanumān; and I am rendered speechless by it. I only regret that I have nothing now with which to reward you; nor is any gift equal in value to the most joyous tidings you have brought me." Hanumān submitted: "O lady, the very words you have uttered are more precious than all the jewels of the world! I consider myself supremely blessed to have witnessed Rāma's victory and Rāvaṇa's destruction." Sītā was even more delighted: she said, "Only you can utter such sweet words, O Hanumān, endowed as you are with manifold excellences. Truly you are an abode of virtues."

Hanumān said: "Pray, give me leave to kill all these demonesses who have been tormenting you so long." Sītā replied: "Nay, Hanumān, they are not responsible for their actions, for they were but obeying their master's commands. And, surely, it was my own evil destiny that made me suffer at their hands. Hence, I forgive them. A noble man does not recognize the harm done to him by others: and he never retaliates, for he is the embodiment of goodness. One should be compassionate towards all, the good and the wicked, nay even towards those who are fit to be killed: who is free from sin?" Hanumān was thrilled to hear these words of Sītā, and said: "Indeed you are the noble consort of Rāma and his peer in virtue and nobility. Pray, give me a message to take back to Rāma." Sītā replied: "Please tell him that I am eager to behold his face." Assuring Sītā that she would see Rāma that very day, Hanumān returned to Rāma.

YUDDHA 117, 118, 119

Hanumān conveyed Sītā's message to Rāma who turned to king Vibhīṣaṇa and said: "Please bring Sītā to me soon, after she has had a bath and has adorned herself." Immediately Vibhīṣaṇa went to Sītā and compelled her to proceed seated in a palanquin, to where Rāma was. Vānaras and demons had gathered around her, eager to look at Sītā. And Vibhīṣaṇa, in accordance with the tradition, wished to ensure that Sītā was not seen by these and rebuked them to go away. Restraining him, Rāma said: "Why do you rebuke them, O Vibhīṣaṇa? Neither houses nor clothes nor walls constitute a veil for a woman; her character alone is her veil. Let her descend from the palanquin and walk up to me." So she did.

Rāma said sternly: "My purpose has been accomplished, O Sītā. My prowess has been witnessed by all. I have fulfilled my pledge. Rāvaṇa's wickedness has been punished. The extraordinary feat performed by Hanumān in crossing the ocean and burning Laṅkā[4] has borne fruit. Vibhīṣaṇa's devotion has been rewarded." Rāma's heart was in a state of conflict, afraid as he was of public ridicule. Hence, he continued: "I wish to let you know that all this was done not for your sake, but for the sake of preserving my honor. Your conduct is open to suspicion, hence even your sight is displeasing to me. Your body was touched by Rāvaṇa: how then can I, claiming to belong to a noble family, accept you? Hence I permit you to go where you like and live with whom you like—either Lakṣmaṇa, Bharata, Śatrughna, Sugrīva or even Vibhīṣaṇa. It is difficult for me to believe that Rāvaṇa, who was so fond of you, would have been able to keep away from you for such a long time."

Sītā was shocked. Rāma's words wounded her heart. Tears streamed down her face. Wiping them, she replied: "O Rāma, you are speaking to me in the language of a common and vulgar man speaking to a common woman. That which was under my control, my heart, has always been yours; how could I prevent my body from being touched when I was helpless and under another person's control? Ah, if only you had conveyed your suspicion through Hanumān when he came to meet me, I would have killed myself then and saved you all this trouble and the risk involved in the war." Turning to Lakṣmaṇa, she said: "Kindle the fire, O Lakṣmaṇa: that is the only remedy. I shall not live to endure this false calumny." Lakṣmaṇa looked at Rāma and with his approval kindled the fire. Sītā prayed: "Even as my heart is ever devoted to Rāma, may the fire protect me. If I have been faithful to Rāma in thought, word or deed, may the fire protect me. The sun, the moon, the wind, earth and others are witness to my purity; may the fire protect me." Then she entered into the fire, even as an oblation poured into the fire would. Gods and sages witnessed this. The women who saw this screamed.

YUDDHA 120, 121

Rāma was moved to tears by the heart-rending cries of all those women who witnessed the self-immolation of Sītā. At the same time, all the gods, including the trinity—the Creator, the Preserver, and the Redeemer (or Transformer)[5]—arrived upon the scene in their personal forms. Saluting Rāma, they said: "You are the foremost among the gods, and yet you treat Sītā as if you were a common human being!"

Rāma replied to these divinities: "I consider myself a human being, Rāma the son of Daśaratha. Who I am, and whence I am, may you tell me!"

Brahmā the creator said: "You are verily lord Nārāyaṇa.[6] You are the imperishable cosmic being. You are the truth. You are eternal. You are the supreme dharma of the worlds. You are the father even of the chief of the gods, Indra. You are the sole refuge of perfected beings and holy men. You are the Om, and you are the spirit of sacrifice.[7] You are that cosmic being with infinite

4. When Hanumān destroys the groves of Laṅkā, Rāvaṇa's henchmen capture him and set his tail on fire. Hanumān sets fire to Laṅkā's mansions with his fiery tail and himself escapes unhurt. 5. The triad of the three great gods, Brahmā (Creator), Viṣṇu (Preserver), and Śiva (Destroyer or Transformer). 6. Viṣṇu in his primeval cosmic form. 7. The sacred chant (mantra) and the sacrificial rite of the *Vedas*.

heads, hands and eyes.[8] You are the support of the whole universe. The whole universe is your body. Sītā is Lakṣmī[9] and you are lord Viṣṇu, who is of a dark hue, and who is the creator of all beings. For the sake of the destruction of Rāvaṇa you entered into a human body. This mission of ours has been fully accomplished by you. Blessed it is to be in your presence; blessed it is to sing your glories; they are truly blessed who are devoted to you, for their life will be attended with success."

As soon as Brahmā finished saying this, the god of fire emerged from the fire in his personal form, holding up Sītā in his hands. Sītā shone in all her radiance. The god of fire who is the witness of everything that takes place in the world, said to Rāma: "Here is your Sītā, Rāma. I find no fault in her. She has not erred in thought, word or deed. Even during the long period of her detention in the abode of Rāvaṇa, she did not even think of him, as her heart was set on you. Accept her: and I command you not to treat her harshly."

Rāma was highly pleased at this turn of events. He said: "Indeed, I was fully aware of Sītā's purity. Even the mighty and wicked Rāvaṇa could not lay his hands upon her with evil intention. Yet, this baptism by fire was necessary, to avoid public calumny and ridicule, for though she was pure, she lived in Laṅkā for a long time. I knew, too, that Sītā would never be unfaithful to me: for we are non-different from each other even as the sun and its rays are. It is therefore impossible for me to renounce her."

After saying so, Rāma was joyously reunited with Sītā.

YUDDHA 122, 123

Lord Śiva then said to Rāma: "You have fulfilled a most difficult task. Now behold your father, the illustrious king Daśaratha who appears in the firmament to bless you and to greet you."

Rāma along with Lakṣmaṇa saw that great monarch, their father clad in a raiment of purity and shining by his own luster. Still seated in his celestial vehicle, Daśaratha lifted up Rāma and placing him on his lap, warmly embraced him and said: "Neither heaven nor even the homage of the gods is as pleasing to me as to behold you, Rāma. I am delighted to see that you have successfully completed the period of your exile and that you have destroyed all your enemies. Even now the cruel words of Kaikeyī haunt my heart; but seeing you and embracing you, I am rid of that sorrow, O Rāma. You have redeemed my word and thus I have been saved by you. It is only now that I recognize you to be the supreme person incarnated as a human being in this world in order to kill Rāvaṇa."

Rāma said: "You remember that you said to Kaikeyī, 'I renounce you and your son'? Pray, take back that curse and may it not afflict Kaikeyī and Bharata." Daśaratha agreed to it and then said to Lakṣmaṇa: "I am pleased with you, my son, and you have earned great merit by the faithful service you have rendered to Rāma."

Lastly, king Daśaratha said to Sītā: "My dear daughter, do not take to heart the fire ordeal that Rāma forced you to undergo: it was necessary to reveal to the world your absolute purity. By your conduct you have exalted yourself

8. The cosmic being described here is Puruṣa, or "Man," a primeval being with innumerable heads, arms, and eyes who was offered as the sacrificial victim by the gods and sages in the first sacrifice, described in a hymn of the *Rig Veda*. 9. Goddess-consort of Viṣṇu.

above all women." Having thus spoken to them, Daśaratha ascended to heaven.

Before taking leave of Rāma, Indra prayed: "Our visit to you should not be fruitless, O Rāma. Command me, what may I do for you?" Rāma replied: "If you are really pleased with me, then I pray that all those vānaras who laid down their lives for my sake may come back to life. I wish to see them hale and hearty as before. I also wish to see the whole world fruitful and prosperous." Indra replied: "This indeed is an extremely difficult task. Yet, I do not go back on my word, hence I grant it. All the vānaras will come back to life and be restored to their original form, with all their wounds healed. Even as you had asked, the world will be fruitful and prosperous."

Instantly, all the vānaras arose from the dead and bowed to Rāma. The others who witnessed this marveled and the gods beheld Rāma who had all his wishes fulfilled. The gods returned to their abodes.

* * *

Summary After crowning Vibhīṣaṇa king of Laṅkā, Rāma, Lakṣmaṇa and Sītā fly to Ayodhyā in Rāvaṇa's flying chariot, accompanied by Vibhīṣaṇa, Sugrīva, Hanumān, and the monkey hordes.

YUDDHA 130

Bharata immediately made the reception arrangements. He instructed Śatrughna: "Let prayers be offered to the gods in all temples and houses of worship with fragrant flowers and musical instruments."

Śatrughna immediately gave orders that the roads along which the royal procession would wend its way to the palace should be leveled and sprinkled with water, and kept clear by hundreds of policemen cordoning them. Soon all the ministers, and thousands of elephants and men on horse-back and in cars went out to greet Rāma. The royal reception party, seated in palanquins,[1] was led by the queen-mother Kausalyā herself; Kaikeyī and the other members of the royal household followed—and all of them reached Nandigrāma.[2]

From there Bharata headed the procession with the sandals of Rāma placed on his head, with the white royal umbrella and the other regalia.[3] Bharata was the very picture of an ascetic though he radiated the joy that filled his heart at the very thought of Rāma's return to the kingdom.

Bharata anxiously looked around but saw no signs of Rāma's return! But, Hanumān reassured him: "Listen, O Bharata, you can see the cloud of dust raised by the vānaras rushing towards Ayodhyā. You can now hear the roar of the Puṣpaka flying chariot."

"Rāma has come!"—these words were uttered by thousands of people at the same time. Even before the Puṣpaka landed, Bharata humbly saluted Rāma who was standing on the front side of the chariot. The Puṣpaka landed. As Bharata approached it, Rāma lifted him up and placed him on his lap. Bharata bowed down to Rāma and also to Sītā and greeted Lakṣmaṇa. And he embraced Sugrīva, Jāmbavān, Aṅgada, Vibhīṣaṇa and others. He said to Sugrīva: "We are four brothers, and with you we are five. Good deeds promote friendship, and evil is a sign of enmity."

1. Litters in which people were carried by bearers. 2. The village outside the city of Ayodhyā, from which Bharata ruled the kingdom on behalf of Rāma. 3. By carrying Rāma's sandals on his head, Bharata indicates his subservience to and reverence for Rāma as his sovereign, elder brother, and teacher.

Rāma bowed to his mother who had become emaciated through sorrow, and brought great joy to her heart. Then he also bowed to Sumitrā and Kaikeyī. All the people thereupon said to Rāma: "Welcome, welcome back, O Lord."

Bharata placed the sandals in front of Rāma, and said: "Rāma here is your kingdom which I held in trust for you during your absence. I consider myself supremely blessed in being able to behold your return to Ayodhyā. By your grace, the treasury has been enriched tenfold by me, as also the storehouses and the strength of the nation." Rāma felt delighted. When the entire party had disembarked, he instructed that the Puṣpaka be returned to its original owner, Kubera.[4]

YUDDHA 131

The coronation proceedings were immediately initiated by Bharata. Skilled barbers removed the matted locks of Rāma. He had a ceremonial bath and he was dressed in magnificent robes and royal jewels. Kausalyā herself helped the vānara ladies to dress themselves in royal robes; all the queens dressed Sītā appropriately for the occasion. The royal chariot was brought; duly ascending it, Rāma, Lakṣmaṇa and Sītā, went in a procession to Ayodhyā, Bharata himself driving the chariot. When he had reached the court, Rāma gave his ministers and counselors a brief account of the events during his exile, particularly the alliance with the vānara chief Sugrīva, and the exploits of Hanumān. He also informed them of his alliance with Vibhīṣaṇa.

At Bharata's request, Sugrīva despatched the best of the vānaras to fetch water from the four oceans, and all the sacred rivers of the world. The aged sage Vasiṣṭha thereupon commenced the ceremony in connection with the coronation of Rāma. Rāma and Sītā were seated on a seat made entirely of precious stones. The foremost among the sages thereupon consecrated Rāma with the appropriate Vedic chants. First the brāhmaṇas, then the virgins, then the ministers and warriors, and later the businessmen poured the holy waters on Rāma.[5] After that the sage Vasiṣṭha placed Rāma on the throne made of gold and studded with precious stones, and placed on his head the dazzling crown which had been made by Brahmā the creator himself. The gods and others paid their homage to Rāma by bestowing gifts upon him. Rāma also gave away rich presents to the brāhmaṇas and others, including the vānara chiefs like Sugrīva. Rāma then gave to Sītā a necklace of pearls and said: "You may give it to whom you like, Sītā." And, immediately Sītā bestowed that gift upon Hanumān.

After witnessing the coronation of Rāma, the vānaras returned to Kiṣkindhā. So did Vibhīṣaṇa return to Laṅkā. Rāma looked fondly at Lakṣmaṇa and expressed the wish that he should reign as the prince regent. Lakṣmaṇa did not reply: he did not want it. Rāma appointed Bharata as prince regent. Rāma thereafter ruled the earth for a very long time.

During the period of Rāma's reign, there was no poverty, no crime, no fear, and no unrighteousness in the kingdom. All the people constantly spoke of Rāma; the whole world had been transformed into Rāma. Everyone was devoted to dharma. And Rāma was highly devoted to dharma, too. He ruled for eleven thousand years.

4. God of wealth. 5. The brāhmaṇas, ministers and warriors, and businessmen represent the three high castes in Hindu society.

YUDDHA 131

Rāma's rule of the kingdom was characterized by the effortless and spontaneous prevalence of dharma. People were free from fear of any sort. There were no widows in the land: people were not molested by beasts and snakes, nor did they suffer from diseases. There was no theft, no robbery nor any violence. Young people did not die making older people perform funeral services for them. Everyone was happy and everyone was devoted to dharma; beholding Rāma alone, no one harmed another. People lived long and had many children. They were healthy and they were free from sorrow. Everywhere people were speaking all the time about Rāma; the entire world appeared to be the form of Rāma. The trees were endowed with undying roots, and they were in fruition all the time and they flowered throughout the year. Rain fell whenever it was needed. There was a pleasant breeze always. The brāhmaṇas (priests), the warriors, the farmers and businessmen, as also the members of the servant class, were entirely free from greed, and were joyously devoted to their own dharma and functions in society. There was no falsehood in the life of the people who were all righteous. People were endowed with all auspicious characteristics and all of them had dharma as their guiding light. Thus did Rāma rule the world for eleven thousand years, surrounded by his brothers.

This holy epic Rāmāyaṇa composed by the sage Vālmīki, promotes dharma, fame, long life and in the case of a king, victory. He who listens to it always is freed from all sins. He who desires sons gets them, and he who desires wealth becomes wealthy, by listening to the story of the coronation of Rāma. The king conquers the whole world, after overcoming his enemies. Women who listen to this story will be blessed with children like Rāma and his brothers. And they, too, will be blessed with long life, after listening to the Rāmāyaṇa. He who listens to or reads this Rāmāyaṇa propitiates Rāma by this; Rāma is pleased with him; and he indeed is the eternal lord Viṣṇu.

LAVA AND KUŚA said: Such is the glorious epic, Rāmāyaṇa. May all recite it and thus augment the glory of dharma, of lord Viṣṇu. Righteous men should regularly listen to this story of Rāma, which increases health, long-life, love, wisdom and vitality.

THE MAHĀBHĀRATA

ca. 400 B.C.–A.D. 400

The *Mahābhārata* (Great Epic of the Bhārata War) tells the story of a war fought by the Kauravas and Pāṇḍavas (two branches of the Kuru, or Bhārata, clan) over succession to the kingdom of Kurukṣetra (Land of the Kurus) with its capital Hāstinapura in the Ganges River valley in north India. It is probable that, like the *Iliad*, the *Mahābhārata* is based on the memory of a historical event, but its real importance for the Indian people has been as an ancestral narrative. In Indian tradition, India is called *bhārata-varṣa* ("the continent, or land, of the Bhāratas"), after Bharata, a founding member of the Kuru lineage. *Bharat* is also the name (in Sanskrit and the modern Indian languages) chosen by the Indian government for the nation created in 1947.

The *Mahābhārata* is attributed to Kṛṣṇa Dvaipāyana Vyāsa. *Vyāsa* means "compiler" or "arranger," indicating that he was probably no more than an esteemed editor of the vast poem of 100,000 verses arranged in 18 books, which appears to have grown to its present epic size over a period of 700 years. Like Vālmīki, Vyāsa appears as an important character in his own poem. Unlike the *Rāmāyaṇa*, however, Vyāsa's sprawling epic, which is eight times as long as the *Iliad* and *Odyssey* put together, has no pretensions to an aesthetically unified structure. Its core narrative is intertwined with philosophical and didactic passages and a large number of secondary tales, many of them well known in their own right. Also, in spite of its later date, the *Mahābhārata* is closer to the rough-hewn style of the oral poets than to Vālmīki's polished verse. But these differences have in no way detracted from the epic's popularity, and both the chief episodes and the subsidiary narratives have been a fertile source of themes for generations of poets and artists.

The narrative technique of the *Mahābhārata* matches the complexity of its story, and offers the earliest example of a style that is characteristic of Indian story literature. In the epic's own telling, the tale does not come to us directly from Vyāsa, but as it is retold by several generations of narrators. A group of forest sages hear the epic saga from Sūta, also known as Ugraśravas (He of the Awesome Voice), in a period of rest during a long Vedic sacrificial session. Sūta has himself memorized the story as told by the bard Vaiśaṃpāyana to King Janamejaya (the only surviving descendant of the epic's protagonists) at an expiatory sacrifice. Vaiśaṃpāyana's voice soon takes over the telling, to be superseded in turn by that of his teacher Vyāsa, the epic's putative author and witness to the Mahābhārata War. The voices of still other narrators emerge periodically in the many "branch" stories embedded in the text. These multiple narrative frames tell us something about the evolution of the epic, its social contexts, and its transmission in oral tradition.

It would appear that *sūtas*, bards who were also charioteers, recited genealogies and epic tales in assemblies of *kṣatriya* clans and on the battlefield. Brahman priests, who conducted sacrificial rites for kings, and sages who guided them in mystical knowledge, learned the hero stories from the *sūtas*, molding them to their own purposes. While the *śloka* couplet (illustrated on pp. 893–94) is the basic meter of the *Mahābhārata*, large portions of the core narrative are framed in stanzas in a longer meter called *triṣṭubh* (see pp. 957–58), the mix of meters being perhaps yet another indication that diverse oral traditions have come together in the final version of the poem.

The first five of the eighteen books (*parva*) of the *Mahābhārata* are concerned with the events that lead up to the war. Books 6 through 9 cover the war itself, and the nine remaining books treat the aftermath of the war and the events and rites that bring to an end the heroic age, the epic narrative, and the *dvāpara yuga*, the third of the four eras in a cycle of cosmic time.

Book 1, *Ādi* (Origins), traces the complicated genealogy of the Kurus and the rise of enmity between the five Pāṇḍavas (sons of Pāṇḍu), the protagonists of the epic, and their evil cousins, the one hundred Kauravas (sons of Dhṛtarāṣṭra). (It is also explained how the poet Vyāsa is actually the father of King Pāṇḍu and is doubly the "father" of the epic, both as its putative author and as ancestor of its chief characters.) A curse that forbids Pāṇḍu sexual intercourse forces him to engineer heirs for himself with the help of his senior wife Kuṅtī's magical ability to produce offspring by invoking gods. Kuṅtī herself bears Yudhiṣṭhira, Bhīma, and Arjuna as the gifts of Dharma (god of law), Vāyu (the wind god), and Indra (king of the gods), respectively. And the junior wife Mādrī gives birth to the twins Nakula and Sahadeva by invoking the Aśvins, twin gods known as "the twin horsemen." Thus are born the five Pāṇḍavas, the epics's protagonists. Meanwhile, Dhṛtarāṣṭra's queen Gāṅdhārī miraculously gives birth to a daughter and one hundred evil sons, the Kauravas. The eldest son is Duryodhana, villain of the epic story.

Uncertain paternity and clouded claims to royal inheritance end in an explosive situation. Pāṇḍu rules the kingdom in place of his elder half brother Dhṛtarāṣṭra, who is disqualified because of his blindness. But then Pāṇḍu dies when the Pāṇḍavas and Kauravas are still boys, and Dhṛtarāṣṭra assumes the regency of the kingdom until the princes come of age. Nominally, he is regent for Pāṇḍu's son Yudhiṣṭhira, who, as the eldest among all the Pāṇḍavas and Kauravas, is the rightful heir to the throne. But the weak-willed old man allows his crooked sons to bid for the kingdom through treacherous means, paving the way for the great war, which all but annihilates the clans of north India.

As the princes grow up together, the Pāṇḍavas excel in princely virtues and achievements, arousing the jealousy of the less talented Kauravas, especially Duryodhana, who eventually makes an abortive attempt to kill his cousins. Later, when the young Arjuna wins the hand of Princess Draupadī, daughter of King Drupada of Pāñcāla, in an archery contest, the princess becomes the wife of all five brothers. Arjuna also marries Subhadrā, sealing the Pāṇḍavas' friendship with Kṛṣṇa Vāsudeva, her brother and incarnation of the preserver god Viṣṇu (see p. 1010); Kṛṣṇa is himself a brother of Kuntī. The multiple marriage of Draupadī is an anomalous situation in a society in which, though kings and noblemen could have many wives, women could marry only one man. Scholars have pointed out that the marriage can be explained at two levels. Historically, the multiple marriage of the princess may indicate the epic's acknowledgment of the practice of polyandry among some ancient Indian tribes and clans (some Himalayan tribes still practice polyandry). At the level of mythology, just as the five Pāṇḍava brothers together represent the warrior and royal attributes of their divine fathers, Draupadī represents the goddess Śrī, royal fortune, as an attribute shared by the brothers. Another explanation, given in the epic itself, is accepted by most readers. When the five brothers brought Draupadī back with them, their mother Kuntī, not realizing that the "prize" her sons had won was a princess, told them to share it equally among themselves; the obedient princes honored their mother's word.

Book 2, *Sabhā* (The Assembly Hall), a substantial portion of which is presented here, begins with a temporary peace between the rival princes. Dhṛtarāṣṭra divides up the Kuru kingdom, the Kauravas ruling in Hāstinapura and the Pāṇḍavas in the new city called Indraprastha ("Indra's Land"), which they build in the forest tract allotted to them. Following an ancient tradition, Yudhiṣṭhira sends his brothers to "conquer the world" symbolically (that is, to extract recognition of Yudhiṣṭhira's overlordship from kings in all of north India and parts of Afghanistan) and declares himself universal monarch. The magician-architect Maya builds a magnificent assembly hall (*sabhā*), in which Yudhiṣṭhira celebrates the "royal consecration" (*rājasūya*), the Vedic sacrifice establishing universal sovereignty. Although Duryodhana knows that, as the chief of the Kuru princes, Yudhiṣṭhira is acting within his rights, he is driven mad by jealousy, especially when he witnesses the opulent assembly hall and the consecration of Yudhiṣṭhira. Seeking once more to reverse the good fortune of the Pāṇḍavas, Duryodhana draws on the tradition of a ritual dice game played at the end of royal consecration and challenges Yudhiṣṭhira to a dice match at his own capital, Hāstinapura. Bound by ancient ritual tradition, Yudhiṣṭhira is forced to accept the challenge, despite his aversion to gambling.

For the success of his plan, Duryodhana relies on the skill of his maternal uncle, Śakuni Saubala, who is both an expert at dice and an unscrupulous player who cheats at the game. Tricked by Śakuni at each throw of the dice, Yudhiṣṭhira is forced to stake all his possessions, including himself and his family, and loses everything. Now slaves of the Kauravas, the Pāṇḍavas watch helplessly as the sons of Dhṛtarāṣṭra drag Draupadī to the assembly hall and insult her. Dominated by Duryodhana, the Kaurava nobles hesitate to speak up against this injustice, but Draupadī challenges the propriety of the outcome of the dice game. Aware of Śakuni's treachery and afraid to endorse what Draupadī has exposed as being manifestly unjust, King Dhṛtarāṣṭra sets the Pāṇḍavas free. However, Duryodhana persuades his father that, owing to the contested nature of the previous round of dice, Yudhiṣṭhira is obliged to play the dice one last time, risking all in a single, decisive play. Yudhiṣṭhira loses, and the Pāṇḍavas and Draupadī are forced to accept exile in the forest for thirteen years, the last of these in hiding, before they can regain their kingdom.

The forest exile is described in Book 3, *Āraṇyaka* or *Vana* (The Forest), full of adventures and stories portraying the forest as a mysterious realm of encounter with the sacred and the supernatural. The heroes and their wife hear morally elevating tales from hermits, combat demons, and win celestial weapons from the gods. Book 4, *Virāṭa*, describes the final year of exile, spent in hiding in the court of King Virāṭa. The incidents surrounding the clever and ironic disguises of the Pāṇḍavas in this book resonate with the narrative of Odysseus's return to Ithaca in disguise. At the end of the thirteen years, the Kauravas do not keep their word, all attempts at maintaining the peace fail, and war is declared (Book 5, *Udyoga*, The Preparation for War), with every clansman in north India allying himself with the one or the other party.

As noblemen of the Hāstinapura court, Bhīṣma, the princes' granduncle, and the other Kuru elder statesmen have no alternative but to fight on the Kaurava side. Kṛṣṇa, the incarnation come to help restore *dharma*, counsels and helps the Pāṇḍavas throughout the preparation for battle and the war itself. In Book 6, in the celebrated discourse known as the *Bhagavad-Gītā* (The Song of God, p. 1010), Kṛṣṇa explains to the deeply troubled Arjuna why Arjuna is morally obliged to engage in war with his kinsmen and elders. The war rages for eighteen days, with spectacular heroic deeds, single combat among champions, and tragic deaths (Books 6–9). It ends in the annihilation of the Kauravas but for three warriors, who take revenge by massacring the Pāṇḍava camp in a night raid (Book 10, *Sauptika*, The Slaughter of the Sleeping Camp). Only the five Pāṇḍava heroes and the women of the contending families survive. An atmosphere of tragic resignation and piety pervades the eight final books of the epic, whose topics include advice on *dharma*, funeral rites for the dead heroes, the lament of the women, Yudhiṣṭhira's coronation, the last days of Kṛṣṇa, the birth of Arjuna's grandson, and the ascent of the Pāṇḍavas to heaven.

The *Mahābhārata* contrasts strikingly with the *Rāmāyaṇa*. Where the hero Rāma combines seemingly paradoxical virtues in a single persona, in the *Mahābhārata* there are five heros, each exhibiting in an exaggerated way very different qualities. It is likely that the Pāṇḍavas collectively represent sovereignty, martial ability, and fertility—the three essential functions attributed to ancient Indo-European gods and heroes. Certainly, each of the heroes closely resembles his divine father. Thus in his love of *dharma* (sacred law) Yudhiṣṭhira, son of Dharma (the personification of law), is the ideal king but not an effective warrior. Bhīma, son of the wind god (and thus half brother to the *Rāmāyaṇa's* Hanumān), is aptly distinguished by his enormous girth, strength, appetite, impetuosity, and love of brute force. As the son of the warrior god Indra, Arjuna, the third Pāṇḍava, mediates between the qualities of his elder brothers, playing the shining prince (*arjuna* means "white, shining"), the great archer, the courageous but disciplined warrior, the romantic lover. Masters of horses and cattle, the twins Nakula and Sahadeva command the Aśvins' gifts of beauty, fecundity, and healing.

A further distinction between the Pāṇḍavas and Rāma is that none of the *Mahābhārata* heroes is a paragon of virtue. Each is continually engaged in a struggle to act honorably in a morally ambiguous world. And in the many impassioned arguments that take place among the brothers and their common wife, the epic illuminates the ambiguities of the heroic character itself, presenting the heroes' dominant character traits as flaws as much as virtues. To be sure, there is a certain degree of allegorization in the opposition of the five good brothers and the hundred bad brothers. But evil shows a very human face in the personality of the archvillain Duryodhana, and the struggle between him and the Pāṇḍavas has none of the mythical quality of the confrontation between the supremely virtuous Rāma and the grotesque ten-headed demon Rāvaṇa.

Likewise, it is hard to imagine a sharper contrast to Rāma's wife, Sītā, than the Pāṇḍavas' wife, Draupadī, who in Book 2 challenges and questions the Kuru warriors and elders, reproaches her husbands for their passivity, and swears vengeance upon being insulted. True, despite being married to five men, she rivals Sītā in her chastity and loyalty, yet her presence throughout the epic is that of a strong, intelligent warrior princess who speaks her mind. The minor stories in the *Mahābhārata*, too, offer many examples of intelligent, independent, eloquent women. Modern Indian feminists are turning to Draupadī and her sisters, who have rarely been held up as behavioral models for women in India, as powerful paradigms for overturning what some have termed the "Sītā syndrome."

The *Mahābhārata* is hailed a poem that teaches a universal *dharma*. However, the epic's persistent focus, in peace as in war, is the public life of a clan society in which, as in the *Iliad*, warrior values and rituals dominate. The conspicuous exchange of gifts at Yudhiṣṭhira's royal consecration resembles a tribal rite distributing plunder among warriors and their allies. Duryodhana's envy of Yudhiṣṭhira has a Greek analogue in the quarrel between Achilles and Agamemnon over warriors' prizes at the beginning of the *Iliad*: at stake is not so much wealth as a warrior's pride. The dice game, too, belongs to heroic rituals in which wealth is staked in a gamble of great risk; it is Yudhiṣṭhira's duty as newly established king to oblige any nobleman who challenges him to a game of dice.

The assembly of the Kurus more nearly resembles the Danish court in *Beowulf* than the court of Ayodhyā in the *Rāmāyaṇa*. When a question of law is raised, the old king confers with the members of the assembly, and low-caste bards play more important roles than brahmans or sages. When the Kauravas insult Draupadī with obscene language and gestures, Bhīma swears that he will break Duryodhana's thigh and drink Duḥśāsana's blood. The same ethos of honor and violent action dominate the war books, where enmities born of wounded pride and nursed over long periods of time come to fruition in gruesome deaths. Bhīma does indeed fulfill his terrible vows.

Nowhere is the ambiguity of the *Mahābhārata's* heroic code more poignantly illustrated than in the life and death of Karṇa, a half brother of the Pāṇḍavas. Karṇa is a premarital son of Kuntī, born when she tests her magical gift by invoking Sūrya, the sun god. The frightened princess sets the baby adrift in the Ganges River, from which he is rescued by a charioteer and his wife who brought him up as their own son. Karṇa hates his Pāṇḍava half brothers from the time when, as young men, they refuse to compete with him in an archery contest because of his low birth. When Kuntī reveals his true birth to him and begs him to fight on the Pāṇḍava side, he chooses to remain loyal to Duryodhana, who has befriended him. At the end of the Book of Karṇa, with the incarnate Kṛṣṇa urging him on in the name of *dharma*—the triumph of the wronged Pāṇḍavas over the evil Kauravas—Arjuna kills the noble Karṇa with an arrow, not in fair fight, but as he struggles to extricate his chariot wheel from the mud.

At war's end, Hāstinapura lies in ruins, the Kuru line is all but wiped out, and the heroic age is crawling to its inglorious end. If Hindus find the perfection of *dharma* in the behavior of the chief characters in the *Rāmāyaṇa*, they confront in the apocalyptic vision of the *Mahābhārata* its complexity, as they respond to a powerful story of human frailty and fortitude in the face of events of cosmic proportions.

Two translations have been used in this selection. C. V. Narasimhan's prose translation of select verses conveys the sweep and flow of the core narrative. The long excerpt from J. A. B. van Buitenen's complete translation of the dice-game episode in Book 2 evokes the dramatic and poetic qualities of the epic's central episodes and of the many voices of the epic's narrators.

THE *TRIṢṬUBH* METER

Adapted from a Vedic meter, the epic *triṣṭubh* is a stanzaic meter of four "quarters" (*pāda*) with eleven syllables per quarter (on the principles of Sanskrit syllabic meter, see p. 893). Short (⏑) and long (—) syllables form the following pattern in each quarter:

⏓–⏓–   ⏑⏑–   –⏑––
–⏑⏑
–⏑–

Here's an example from the *Mahābhārata:*

tatas sūtas tasya vaśānugāmī
bhītaś ca kopād drupadātmajāyāḥ
vihāya mānam punar eva sabhyān
uvāca kṛṣṇām kim aham bravīmi

So the *sūta* [bard] who was in Duryodhana's service,
But afraid of the wrath of the Drupada Princess,
Shed all his pride and asked the assembled,
"Who am I to speak to a Draupadī?

The *śloka*, the principal meter of the epic, is explained on pages 893–94.

Readers who wish to follow the central narrative of the *Mahābhārata* but are (understandably) daunted by the epic's bulk will enjoy C. V. Narasimhan's lucid, accurate translation of selections treating the main story in the *Mahābhārata: An English Version Based on Selected Verses* (1965). Narasimhan's book is also a handy tool for locating specific incidents or subplots, which may be pursued in greater detail in Manmatha Nath Dutt's six-volume translation of the entire work: *A Prose English Translation of the Mahābhārata* (1895–1905). A complete translation of the first five books of the epic by J. A. B. van Buitenen (*The Mahābhārata*, 1973) is available, and the remaining books are being translated by other scholars. In his *Mahābhārata: Attributed to Kṛṣṇa Dvaipāyana Vyāsa* (1971), in addition to a good introduction to literary and cultural aspects of the epic and to its career in India and Southeast Asia, Barend A. van Nooten offers a summary of the contents of the eighteen books and a useful bibliography. For two twentieth-century Indian interpretations of the epic, see *The Meaning of the Mahābhārata* (1957) by V. S. Sukthankar, the chief editor of the critical edition of the text, and *Yugānta: The End of an Epoch* (1971), by Irawati Karve, an eminent anthropologist.

PRONOUNCING GLOSSARY

The following list uses common English syllables and stress accents to provide rough equivalents of selected words whose pronunciation may be unfamiliar to the general reader.

Abhimanyu: *uhb-bee-muhn'-yoo*
agnihotra: *uh'-gnee-hoh-truh*
Arjuna: *uhr-joo'-nuh*
Aśvin: *uhsh'-veen*
Bharata: *buhh'-ruh-tuh*
Bhārata: *bah'-ṛuh-tuh*
Bhīma: *bhee'-muh*
Bhīmasena: *bee-muh-say'-nuh*
Bhīṣma: *beesh'-muh*
Brahmā: *bruh'-mah*
brāhmaṇa: *brah'-muh-nuh*
Dhanaṃjaya: *duh-nuhm'-juh-yuh*
Dharma: *duhr'-muh*
Dhārtarāṣṭra: *dahr-tuh-rah'-shtra*
Dhṛtarāṣṭra: *dhree'-tuh-rahsh-truh*
Draupadī: *drow'-puh-dee*
Droṇa: *droh'-nuh*
Drupada: *droo'-puh-duh*
Duḥśāsana: *duh-shah'-suh-nuh*
Duryodhana: *door-yoh'-duh-nuh*
Gaṅdhāra: *gahnd-hah'-ruh*
Gāṅdhārī: *gahn-dhah'-ree*

Hāstinapura: *hahs-tee'-nuh-poo-ruh*
Iṅdra: *een'-druh*
Indraprastha: *eend-ruh-pruhs'-tuh*
Karṇa: *kuhr'-nuh*
Kaunteya: *kaun-tay'-yuh*
Kaurava: *kow'-ruh-vuh*
Kṛṣṇā: *kreesh-nah'*
Kṛṣṇa: *kreesh'-nuh*
Kṛṣṇa Vāsudeva: *kreesh'-nuh vah-soo-day'-yuh*
kṣatriya: *kshuh'-tree-yuh*
Kuṅtī: *koon'-tee*
Kuru: *koo'-roo*
Kurukṣetra: *koo-roo-kshay'-truh*
Mādrī: *mah'-dree*
Nakula: *nuh'-koo-luh*
Pāñcālī: *pahn'-chah-lee*
Pāṇḍava: *pahn'-duh-vuh*
Pāṇḍu: *pahn'-doo*
Pārtha: *pahrt'-huh*
Sahadeva: *suh-huh-day'-vuh*
Śakuni Saubala: *shuh'-koo-nee sow'-buh-luh*
Śalya: *shuhl'-yuh*
Sūta: *soo'-tuh*
svayaṃvara: *svuh-yuhm'-vuh-ruh*
Vaiśampāyana: *vye-shum-pah'-yuh-nuh*
Varuṇa: *vuh'-roo-nuh*
Vidura: *vee'-doo-ruh*
Vikarṇa: *vee-kuhr'-nuh*
Vyāsa: *vee-yah'-suh*
Yājñasenī: *yah-gyuh-say'-nee*
Yudhiṣṭhira: *yoo-dee'-shthee-ruh*

The Mahābhārata

From *Book 1*[1]

Ādi [*Origins*]

7

From their birth, Bhīṣma brought up Dhṛtarāṣṭra and Pāṇḍu and the wise Vidura as if they were his own sons. In accordance with the usual rites of their order, they engaged themselves in study and the observance of vows; by the time they had grown to young manhood, they were expert in athletic feats, adept in archery, learned in the scriptures, and skilfull in fighting with club, sword, and shield. They were skilled in horsemanship and in the management of elephants; they were learned in the science of morality. They shone equally in history, mythology, and many other branches of learning, and mastered the inner meaning of the scriptures. In all these activities they became proficient with practice. Pāṇḍu excelled all men in the science of archery, and Dhṛtarāṣṭra in personal strength. There was none in the three worlds to equal Vidura in his devotion to religion and virtue, and in his knowledge of the science of morality.

Bhīṣma heard from the Brāhmaṇas[2] that Gāṅdhārī, daughter of Subala, had been worshiping the bountiful deity Śiva, and obtained the boon that she would bear one hundred sons. He then sent emissaries to the king of

1. Translated by C. V. Narasimhan. 2. Priests, members of the highest caste.

Gāṅdhāra, seeking her hand on behalf of Dhṛtarāṣṭra. Subala hesitated on account of the blindness of the bridegroom. But taking into consideration his noble blood and the fame of the Kurus, he bestowed the virtuous Gāṅdhārī on Dhṛtarāṣṭra.

Gāṅdhārī was informed of the blindness of Dhṛtarāṣṭra, and of her parents' wish notwithstanding to bestow her upon him. Devoted to her husband, Gāṅdhārī bandaged her own eyes with a cloth, gathered into many folds, out of her desire not to excel her husband in any way. In due course Śakuni, the son of the king of Gāṅdhāra, brought his sister, endowed with great wealth, to the Kurus, and gave her away in the proper manner to Dhṛtarāṣṭra. He then returned to his own capital. The beautiful Gāṅdhārī pleased all the Kurus by her exemplary conduct and respectful attentions.

One day Gāṅdhārī pleased Vyāsa, who had arrived at the palace hungry and fatigued. He granted her a boon, and she expressed her desire to have one hundred sons like her husband. Some time afterwards, she became pregnant, but bore the burden in her womb for two years without being delivered, and was therefore much afflicted with grief.

Meanwhile she heard that Pāṇḍu's queen Kuṅtī had borne a son, bright as the morning sun. She could not help feeling that in her case the time of bearing the child in the womb was too long. Deprived of reason by her grief, she struck her womb with force, without the knowledge of Dhṛtarāṣṭra. Thereupon she brought forth a hard mass of flesh like an iron ball which had been in her womb for two years. On learning this, Vyāsa, best of ascetics, soon came to her and saw that mass of flesh. He asked Gāṅdhārī, "What have you done?" She revealed the truth to him, saying "Having heard that Kuṅtī had first given birth to a prince, bright as the sun, I struck at my womb in grief. You gave me the boon that I should bear one hundred sons. But only this ball of flesh has emerged instead."

Vyāsa said, "O Gāṅdhārī, it shall be as I said. I have never uttered a lie even in jest. Let one hundred jars, filled with ghee, be brought quickly and let cool water be sprinkled on this ball of flesh." The ball of flesh, being thus cooled with water, split into parts, each about the size of a thumb. These were then placed in the jars, which were stationed in a concealed spot and carefully watched. The holy one bade Gāṅdhārī open the lids of the jars only after two years. Having given these instructions and made these arrangements, the holy and wise Vyāsa went to the Himālaya mountains to perform penance.

It was thus that Prince Duryodhana was born. According to the order of birth, however, Yudhiṣṭhira, the eldest son of Pāṇḍu, was senior to him. As soon as a son had been born to him, Dhṛtarāṣṭra said: "Summon the Brāhmaṇas, as well as Bhīṣma and Vidura. The prince Yudhiṣṭhira is the eldest of our line. There is no doubt that he should succeed to the kingdom in his own right."

At that time beasts of prey, jackals, and crows[3] made ominous noises everywhere. Seeing these frightful portents, the assembled Brāhmaṇas and the wise Vidura said to Dhṛtarāṣṭra, "It is clear that your son will be the exterminator of your race. The peace of the family depends upon his being aban-

3. The howling of jackals is inauspicious; these animals are associated with cunning, cowardice, and treachery.

doned. There will be great calamity in keeping him." Though he was thus adjured by Vidura and by all those learned Brāhmaṇas, the king did not heed their advice, because of his natural love for his son. There were born within a month one hundred sons to Dhṛtarāṣṭra, and also a daughter, Duḥśalā.

8

The chief of the Yadus, named Śūra, had a son, Vasudeva, and a daughter, Pṛthā, whose beauty was matchless on earth. As had been promised, Śūra gave Pṛthā in adoption to his childless cousin and close friend, the high-souled Kuṅtibhoja. Hence she also came to be known as Kuṅtī. In her adopted father's house Kuṅtī's duties were to worship the family deities and look after the guests.

One day, by her solicitude, she pleased the terrible and notoriously short-tempered sage Durvāsa, who was learned in the mysteries. Through his foresight, Durvāsa could see that Kuṅtī would have difficulty in conceiving sons. He therefore taught her an invocatory spell, saying to her, "Through the radiance of those celestials whom you invoke by this spell, you will obtain progeny."

After a while the virtuous Kuṅtī out of curiosity tried the spell and invoked the sun god. That brilliant deity the Sun, who sees everything in the world, immediately appeared before her, and the beautiful Kuṅtī was overcome by astonishment at this wondrous sight. The light of the universe, the Sun, got her with child. Thus was born the hero of divine ancestry, known all over the world by the name of Karṇa, the foremost of warriors. He was born wearing armor and earrings.[4] Thereafter the Sun restored Kuṅtī's maidenhood and returned to heaven.

Afraid of her friends and relatives, Kuṅtī resolved to hide her transgression. She accordingly threw her handsome son into the river, from which he was rescued by a charioteer. He and his wife Rādhā brought up the infant as their own son, giving him the name of Vasuṣeṇa,[5] because he was endowed with wealth even at birth, namely armor and earrings. Vasuṣeṇa grew up to be very strong and energetic, and adept in the use of all weapons. He used to worship the Sun until the afternoon sun scorched his back. When he was thus engaged in worship, the heroic, truthful, and high-souled Vasuṣeṇa would give away to the Brāhmaṇas anything on earth which they requested of him.

Once Iṇdra,[6] the protector of all living things, came to him for alms, adopting the guise of a Brāhmaṇa, and asked him for his armor and the earrings. Perplexed though he was at Iṇdra's request, he cut off the armor from his body, and also his earrings from his ears, and gave them, dripping with blood, to Iṅdra with joined hands. Greatly surprised at his generosity, Iṇdra gave him the Śakti weapon, saying, "Be your foe a celestial, asura, human being, Gaṅdharva, Nāga, or Rākṣasa, if you hurl this missile at him, it will certainly kill him."[7] The son of Sūrya, who till then was known by the name of Vasuṣeṇa, came to be called Karṇa [the cutter] after this act of unequaled generosity.

4. As we shall learn from the incidents narrated below, Karṇa was born with armor and earrings bonded to his body. 5. "Endowed with wealth." 6. King of the gods. 7. Asuras, Gaṅdharvas, Nāgas and Rākṣasas are various classes of supernatural beings.

9

Kuṅtibhoja held a svayaṁvara[8] for his beautiful and virtuous daughter. There she saw that tamer of lions and elephants,[9] the mighty Pāṇḍu, in the midst of all the kings present. She chose him for her husband, even as Paulomī chose Iṅdra.

Bhīṣma also obtained for Pāṇḍu, in exchange for much wealth, the daughter of the king of Madra, Mādrī, who was famous for her beauty in all the three worlds, after which he solemnized the marriage of the high-souled[1] Pāṇḍu.

One day, while roaming in the forest, Pāṇḍu saw two deer in the act of mating, and hit both of them with five sharp and swift arrows, embellished with golden feathers. They were an ascetic, the son of a sage, and his wife, with whom he was thus disporting in the form of a deer. "I am the sage Kiṅdama, without equal in austerity," said the deer. "You have killed me in the act of mating in the form of a deer, a form I have assumed out of modesty. Though you will not be visited with the sin of killing a Brāhmaṇa, since you did not know who I was, you shall however be punished similarly: when you are overcome by desire in the company of your wife, you shall also die!"

Thus cursed, Pāṇḍu returned to his capital, and explained his predicament to his queens, after which he said to Kuṅtī: "At my request, you should have children endowed with all good qualities by the grace of a Brāhmaṇa who is a great sage; if you do so, I shall go the same way as those with sons." To this request, Kuṅtī, ever interested in her husband's welfare, replied to Pāṇḍu, "O king, since you so desire, I shall invoke a god as taught me by Durvāsa, so that we may have issue." Pāṇḍu said: "Among the gods Dharma is the one who bestows spiritual merit. Hence I request you to invoke the god Dharma this very day."

Gāṅdhārī had been pregnant for a year when Kuṅtī invoked the eternal Dharma[2] for progeny, worshiping him and repeating in the proper form the invocation which Durvāsa had taught her. She was then united with Dharma in his spiritual form and, in time, gave birth to a fine boy. As soon as the child was born, a voice with no visible source said: "This child will certainly be virtuous. He will be known as Yudhiṣṭhira; he will be famous over the three worlds.[3] He will be splendid, determined, and renowned."

Having been blessed with this virtuous son, Pāṇḍu bade Kuṅtī ask for a son of great physical strength, since the Kṣatriyas were the foremost in strength. In response to her husband's request, Kuṅtī invoked Vāyu,[4] who begot the mighty Bhīma, of great strength. On his birth, the supernatural voice said: "This child will be the greatest of all strong men." Duryodhana was born on the very day on which Bhīma was born.

Thereafter the illustrious Pāṇḍu consulted with the great sages and asked Kuṅtī to observe certain vows for one full year. At the end of the period Pāṇḍu said, "O beautiful one, Iṅdra the king of the celestials is pleased. Invoke him and conceive a son." In response, the illustrious Kuṅtī invoked Iṅdra, the lord of the celestials, who came to her and begot Arjuna. As soon as the prince was born, a supernatural voice boomed over the whole sky with

8. The assembly or contest in which a princess or other high-born lady chose a bridegroom for herself.
9. Epic epithet for a brave warrior. 1. Noble, virtuous (*mahātmā*). 2. God personifying the cosmic and moral law. 3. Heaven, earth, and the underworld. 4. The wind god.

a loud and deep roar, saying: "O Kuṅtī, this child will be as strong as Kārtavīrya and Śibi,[5] invincible in battle as Iṅdra himself. He will spread your fame everywhere, and will acquire many celestial weapons."

After the birth of Kuṅtī's sons, and those of Dhṛtarāṣṭra, Mādrī privately spoke to Pāṇḍu thus, "It is my great grief that, though we are of equal rank, my husband should have sons by Kuṅtī alone. If the princess Kuṅtī will arrange that I may have sons, she will do me a great kindness, and it will also be of benefit to you."

Thereupon Pāṇḍu again spoke to Kuṅtī privately. He said, "O blessed lady, give me some more sons, and ensure the funeral oblations for myself and my ancestors. O blameless one, aid Mādrī, as though with a raft across the river, by helping her to obtain progeny. Thus you will obtain great renown."

Kuṅtī then said to Mādrī, "Think of some celestial by whose grace you may obtain worthy offspring." Thereupon Mādrī reflected a little and invoked the twin Aśvins.[6] Both of them came to her and sired twin sons, namely Nakula and Sahadeva, unmatched for beauty on earth. On their birth, the supernatural voice said: "The twins will be handsome and good, and will excel all men in beauty, energy, and wealth. They will glow with splendor."

The sages living in Śataśṛṅga invoked blessings on the princes and performed their birth rites with devotion. They named the eldest of Kuṅtī sons Yudhiṣṭhira, the second Bhīmasena, and the third Arjuna. Mādrī's twin sons they named Nakula and Sahadeva. The five sons of Pāṇḍu and the hundred sons of Dhṛtarāṣṭra, the ornaments of the Kuru race, bloomed like lotuses in a lake.

One day Pāṇḍu saw Mādrī adorned with jewels, and his desire was aroused. But as soon as he touched her, he died. Thereupon Mādrī ascended Pāṇḍu's funeral pyre, asking Kuṅtī to bring up her children with kindness and love. Then Vidura, King Dhṛtarāṣṭra, Bhīṣma, and other relatives performed the last rites of Pāṇḍu and Mādrī and offered the funeral oblations.

Thereafter the sons of Pāṇḍu were brought by the citizens to Hāstinapura. There the Pāṇḍavas performed all the purifying rites prescribed in the scriptures. They grew up in royal style in their father's house, sporting with the sons of Dhṛtarāṣṭra, whom they excelled in all the boyish games. Bhīma vanquished all the sons of Dhṛtarāṣṭra in various feats. Seeing his extraordinary strength, Duryodhana, the mighty son of Dhṛtarāṣṭra, conceived a lasting enmity towards him.

10

Once the great sage Bharadvāja happened to see the beautiful nymph Dhṛtācī in the sacrificial place, when her dress was accidentally blown aside by the wind. Aroused by this sight, the sage dropped his seed in a vessel [droṇa], in which the wise Droṇa was born. He read all the Scriptures.

Bharadvāja had a royal friend, named Pṛṣata, who had a son named Drupada. Prince Drupada went every day to Bharadvāja's hermitage, where he played and studied with Droṇa. When Pṛṣata died, the mighty Drupada succeeded to the kingdom of the Northern Pāñcālas.

At about the same time the illustrious Bharadvāja also passed away;

5. Legendary heroes. 6. The gods known as the "twin horsemen."

thereupon, in accordance with his late father's wishes, and being desirous of offspring, Droṇa married Kṛpī, the daughter of Śaradvata. Ever engaged in sacrifices and penance, the pious Kṛpī bore Droṇa a son, named Aśvatthāmā. As soon as he was born, he neighed like a horse. Thereupon a voice from the skies said, "As this child neighed like a horse and could be heard over a great distance, he will be known by the name of Aśvatthāmā [the horse-voiced]."

Droṇa, who was extremely pleased at having a son, then became deeply interested in the study of archery. He heard that the great-souled Paraśurāma was giving away all his wealth to Brāhmaṇas.[7] Seeing Paraśurāma as he was leaving for the forest, Droṇa said, "Know me to be Droṇa, best of Brāhmaṇas, who has come to you seeking wealth."

Paraśurāma said, "O treasury of penance! I have already given away to the Brāhmaṇas my gold and whatever wealth I had." "O Paraśurāma," said Droṇa, "give me then all your arms and weapons, and teach me the secrets of launching and withdrawing them." Paraśurāma said: "So be it!" He gave away all his weapons to Droṇa and taught him the science of arms and all its secrets. Droṇa, considering himself amply rewarded and feeling well pleased, went to see his dear friend Drupada.

In due course approaching Drupada, the son of Pṛṣata, Droṇa said, "Know me as your friend." Drupada said: "Our former friendship was based on the bonds of skill; but time, that erodes everything, wears out friendship too." Thus rebuffed by Drupada, the mighty Droṇa was filled with wrath. He reflected for a moment, while he made up his mind as to his course of action, and then went to Hāstinapura, the city of the foremost of the Kurus.

11

Anxious to give his grandsons a superior education, Bhīṣma inquired about tutors who were brave and well skilled in the science of arms. He decided that the preceptor of the Kurus should be strong, intelligent, and illustrious, and complete master of the science of arms.

When he heard that a stranger had arrived [in Hāstinapura], Bhīṣma knew that this must be Droṇa and decided that he was the right tutor for his grandsons. Welcoming Droṇa, he asked him why he had come to Hāstinapura. Droṇa told him everything. Bhīṣma then appointed Droṇa as the preceptor and gave him various gifts. He presented his grandsons, including the sons of Pāṇḍu, according to custom, and handed them over to Droṇa, who accepted them all as his pupils.

Droṇa called them aside when they saluted him, and said privately to them: "O princes, in my heart I have one special yearning; promise me that you will fulfill it when you have become proficient in arms." To these words the Kuru princes made no reply. Arjuna, however, gave his promise.

Thereupon Droṇa taught Arjuna how to fight from the back of a horse, on an elephant, on a chariot or on the ground, in single combat or in a crowd. He taught him how to fight with the club, the sword, the spear, and the dart. Two of Droṇa's pupils, Duryodhana and Bhīma, became highly proficient in

7. The brahmin Paraśurāma had vowed to exterminate the *kṣatriya* class.

club fighting; Aśvatthāmā surpassed the others in the mysteries of the science of arms; the twins Nakula and Sahadeva outshone everybody in swordsmanship; Yudhiṣṭhira was first among car[8]-warriors.

Arjuna reigned supreme in every field; he excelled all in intelligence, in concentration, in strength, and in zest, and was famous unto the limits of the ocean as the foremost of car-warriors. He was unequaled not only in the use of arms but also in his love and regard for his preceptor. Though all the royal pupils received the same instruction, yet the mighty Arjuna by his excellence became the only Atiratha[9] among all the princes. The wicked sons of Dhṛtarāṣṭra became jealous of Bhīma's strength and Arjuna's many accomplishments.

When the sons of Dhṛtarāṣṭra and Pāṇḍu had thus become proficient in arms, Droṇa said to King Dhṛtarāṣṭra, "O king, your sons have completed their studies. Permit them to display their skill." The king replied, with joy in his heart: "O Droṇa, O best of Brāhmaṇas, great is your achievement!" By order of the king, the masons built a huge arena according to the rules, with a grandstand for the king and the royal ladies. Then, with Yudhiṣṭhira at their head, the heroic princes followed each other in the order of their age and began to display their wonderful skill in arms.

At the command of the preceptor, the youthful Arjuna, equipped with leather protector for the finger, his quiver full of arrows, bow in hand, and wearing golden armor, performed the initial rites of propitiation and entered the arena like the evening cloud reflecting the rays of the setting sun. His very entrance caused a stir among the spectators. When they had calmed down a little, Arjuna displayed before his preceptor his easy mastery of arms and his great skill in the use of the sword, the bow, and the club.

While the spectators were watching Arjuna's feats in wide-eyed wonder, that conqueror of hostile cities, Karṇa, entered the spacious arena. The entire assembly of people remained motionless staring at the newcomer. Curious to know his name, they asked one another in agitation, "Who is he?" Then, in a voice deep as thunder, Karṇa, foremost of eloquent men, said to Arjuna, whom he did not know to be his brother: "O Arjuna, I shall repeat before these spectators all that you have just done. Do not be surprised." Thus challenged, Arjuna was abashed and angry, but Duryodhana was touched with affection for the challenger. With the permission of Droṇa, the powerful Karṇa, ever fond of battle, duplicated all the feats that Arjuna had displayed a little earlier.

Thereupon Duryodhana with his brothers embraced Karṇa with joy and spoke to him thus: "O mighty hero, welcome to you! Your arrival is our good fortune. The entire Kuru kingdom and I myself are at your service." Karṇa replied, "I desire only your friendship."

Karṇa then challenged Arjuna to a duel. When the two heroes were ready with their great bows, Kṛpa, the son of Śaradvata, who knew all the rules governing such duels, said: "O mighty hero, tell us of your father and mother, of your family, and of the royal line which you adorn. It is only after knowing your lineage that Arjuna can decide whether or not to fight with you." Duryodhana announced, "O preceptor, it is said that royalty may

8. Car = chariot. 9. A champion at chariot fighting.

be claimed by three classes of men, namely, by a person of noble birth, by a hero, and by a leader of soldiers. If Arjuna is unwilling to engage in a duel with one who is not a king, I shall install Karṇa at once as the king of Aṅga."

Without delay the mighty car-warrior Karṇa was seated on a golden seat, and crowned as the king of Aṅga by those learned in the rites, with unhusked rice, flowers, waterpots, gold, and much wealth. When the cheers subsided, Karṇa said to the Kaurava king, Duryodhana, "What can I give you compared with your gift of a kingdom? O great king, I shall do your bidding." Duryodhana replied, "I seek only your friendship." Then Karṇa said, "So be it!" They thereupon joyfully embraced each other and felt very happy.

Having obtained Karṇa, Duryodhana forgot his fears aroused by Arjuna's skill in arms. The heroic Karṇa, accomplished in arms, spoke words of comfort to Duryodhana. Yudhiṣṭhira too was impressed with the conviction that there was no bowman on earth like Karṇa.

12

One day the preceptor Droṇa called his pupils together and asked for his dakṣiṇā[1] from them all. He said, "I want you to capture the king of Pāñcāla, Drupada, in battle and bring him securely to me. That will be the most precious dakṣiṇā you can give me." Saying "So be it!" and armed with quivers of arrows, the princes mounted their cars and went with Droṇa to win wealth for their preceptor. They attacked the Pāñcālas and killed them, and then besieged the capital of the famous Drupada. Successful in capturing Drupada, along with his ministers, they brought him to Droṇa.

Droṇa, remembering his former enmity towards Drupada, now humiliated, bereft of wealth, and completely subdued, spoke thus to him, "I have quickly laid waste your kingdom and your capital. Do you wish to renew our old friendship and to receive your life at my hands?" Smiling, he added, "O king, be not afraid for your life. We Brāhmaṇas are lenient. I seek your friendship again. I shall grant you one half of your kingdom. You may rule the territory lying to the south of the Gāṅgā, and I shall rule the northern part. O king of Pāñcāla, if it pleases you, know that I am your friend from now on." Drupada said, "O Brāhman, such generosity is not surprising in men of noble soul and great strength. I am pleased to accept your friendly offer and I desire your eternal friendship."

Then Droṇa released Drupada, and with a pleased heart he bestowed upon him half the kingdom. Drupada, however, was unable to recover his peace of mind, being obsessed by his hatred of Droṇa. He knew he could not hope to avenge his defeat by superior force, nor by spiritual power, in which too he was aware of being weak. Hence King Drupada desired the birth of a son, who would be the instrument of his revenge.[2]

1. The fee given by students to their preceptors (*guru*) at the completion of their studies. 2. King Drupada performs a special fire sacrifice to the gods, seeking the birth of a son who would be an invincible warrior. Born out of Drupada's sacrificial fire, Prince Dhṛṣṭadyumna, fighting on the Pāṇḍava side during the great war between the Pāṇḍavas and their cousins, does kill Droṇa. Drupada's daughter Draupadī is also born from his sacrificial fire.

From *Book 2*[3]

Sabhā [The Assembly Hall]

58

ŚAKUNI[4] SAID:

You have lost vast wealth of the Pāṇḍavas, Yudhiṣṭhira. Tell me what wealth you have left, Kaunteya,[5] what you have not yet lost!

YUDHIṢṬHIRA SAID:

I know of untold riches that I possess, Saubala. But, Śakuni, pray, why do you ask about my wealth? Myriad, ton, million, crore,[6] a hundred million, a billion, a hundred thousand crores, an ocean count of drops I can stake! That is my stake, king, play me for it!

VAIŚAṂPĀYANA[7] SAID:

At these words Śakuni decided, tricked, and cried "Won!" at Yudhiṣṭhira.[8]

YUDHIṢṬHIRA SAID:

I have countless cattle and horses and milch cows and sheep and goats, whatever belongs to our color of people east of the Indus, Saubala.[9] That is my stake, king, I play you for it!

VAIŚAṂPĀYANA SAID:

At these words Śakuni decided, tricked, and cried "Won!" at Yudhiṣṭhira.

YUDHIṢṬHIRA SAID:

My city, my country, the wealth of all my people, excepting brahmins, all my people themselves, excepting brahmins, are the wealth I have left, king. That is my stake, king, I play you for it!

VAIŚAṂPĀYANA SAID:

At these words Śakuni decided, tricked, and cried "Won!" at Yudhiṣṭhira.

YUDHIṢṬHIRA SAID:

Here are the ornaments with which the princes glitter, the earrings and breastplates and all the adornment of their bodies. That is my stake, king, I play you for it!

VAIŚAṂPĀYANA SAID:

At these words Śakuni decided, tricked, and cried "Won!" at Yudhiṣṭhira.

YUDHIṢṬHIRA SAID:

---

3. Translated by J. A. B. van Buitenen. Forced to accept Duryodhana's challenge to a dice match, which is properly a part of the rite of the consecration of the ancient "universal monarch," Yudhiṣṭhira arrives at Hāstinapura, accompanied by his brothers and Draupadī. The Kuru nobles have assembled at the Hāstinapura court to watch the dice match. Duryodhana's uncle Śakuni, trickster and expert at dice, plays the game on Duryodhana's behalf. At each play of the dice, Yudhiṣṭhira stakes his valuable possessions, including gold, precious jewels, elephants and chariots, a splendid horse, and many male and female servants. Each time, Śakuni plays deceitfully, winning the stake on Duryodhana's behalf.   4. Śakuni Saubala, son of the king of Gandhāra, brother of Queen Gāndhārī, and maternal uncle to the Kauravas.   5. Son of Kuntī.   6. Ten million.   7. The bard who recounts the story of the Mahābhārata war to King Janamejaya, descendant of the Pāṇḍavas.   8. This refrain is spoken by the bard-narrator. We do not know how the *Mahābhārata's* game of dice was actually played, but it may have been a game in which a number of dice (*akṣa*) were placed in a dicing cup or stock of dice, and the players drew (grasped, grabbed) from this stock. The epic does not describe the rules of the game, but the following things are suggested: the dice were rearranged, and one of the players had to make a guess (as to the number? odds and evens?); if the drawer won, he continued to lead the play.   9. The Indus River flows in the northwest region of the Indian subcontinent, in modern Pakistan. "Color": Although the basic meaning of the word *varṇa* is "color," here, as elsewhere, it does not denote skin color, but indicates one of the four major social classes (*varṇa*) of ancient Indian society (brahmin, warrior, merchant, servant). Here the warrior class is meant.

This dark youth with the bloodshot eyes and the lion shoulders and the large arms,[1] this Nakula and all he owns shall be one throw.

ŚAKUNI SAID:

But Prince Nakula is dear to you, King Yudhiṣṭhira! If we win this stake, what more do you have to gamble?

VAIŚAṂPĀYANA SAID:

Having said this, Śakuni addressed those dice and cried "Won!" at Yudhiṣṭhira.

YUDHIṢṬHIRA SAID:

This Sahadeva preaches the Laws,[2]
And has in the world earned the name of a scholar:
For this loving prince who does not deserve it,
I play with you like an enemy!

VAIŚAṂPĀYANA SAID:

At these words Śakuni decided, tricked, and cried "Won!" at Yudhiṣṭhira.

ŚAKUNI SAID:

I have now won, king, these two dear sons of Mādrī. Yet methinks Bhīmasena and Arjuna are dearer to you.

YUDHIṢṬHIRA SAID:

Surely this is an Unlaw[3] that you are perpetrating, without looking to propriety! You want to pluck us like flowers!

ŚAKUNI SAID:

A drunk falls into a hole, a distracted man walks into a tree trunk, you are our elder and better, king—farewell to you, bull of the Bharatas![4] When gamblers play, Yudhiṣṭhira, they prattle like madmen of things they have not seen asleep or awake!

YUDHIṢṬHIRA SAID:

Like a ferry he carried us over in battle,
Defeater of foes, a prince of vigor;
For this world hero who does not deserve it,
For Phalguna[5] I play you, Śakuni!

VAIŚAṂPĀYANA SAID:

At these words Śakuni decided, tricked, and cried "Won!" at Yudhiṣṭhira.

ŚAKUNI SAID:

Here I have won the Pāṇḍavas' bowman,
The left-handed archer,[6] of Pāṇḍu the son!
Now gamble, O king, your beloved Bhīma,
If that's what you, Pāṇḍava, have left to throw!

YUDHIṢṬHIRA SAID:

Who led us, who guided us to the battle, 5
Like the Thunderbolt-wielder[7] the Dānavas' foe,
Looking down, great-spirited, knitting his brow,
With a lion's shoulders and lasting wrath,

1. Characteristics of an ideal warrior. 2. *Dharma*. Stanzas in the *triṣṭubh* meter, such as this one, have been translated in a four-line verse format. 3. The opposite of *dharma*. 4. "Superior (mighty as a bull) warrior in the family of Bharata" (a formulaic phrase). The bull represents might and virility. 5. Arjuna. 6. Arjuna, who could shoot with both hands. 7. The Vedic hero-god Indra wields the thunderbolt and leads the gods in battle against the Dānavas (demons).

Whose equal in might is nowhere to be found,
The first of club warriors, enemy-killer—
For this good prince who does not deserve it
I play you, king, for Bhīmasena!

VAIŚAMPĀYANA SAID:
At these words Śakuni decided, tricked, and cried "Won!" at Yudhiṣṭhira.

ŚAKUNI SAID:
You have lost great wealth, you have lost your brothers, your horses and elephants. Now tell me, Kaunteya, if you have anything left to stake!

YUDHIṢṬHIRA SAID:
I myself am left, dearly loved by all my brothers. When won, we shall slave for you to our perdition.

VAIŚAMPĀYANA SAID:
At these words Śakuni decided, tricked, and cried "Won!" at Yudhiṣṭhira.

ŚAKUNI SAID:
This is the worst you could have done, losing yourself! If there is something left to stake, it is evil to stake oneself!

VAIŚAMPĀYANA SAID:
Thus spoke the man so dexterous at dicing, who had won in the gaming all those brothers arrayed there, the champions of the world, each with one throw.

ŚAKUNI SAID:
Yet there is your precious queen, and one throw is yet unwon. Stake Kṛṣṇā of Pāñcāla,[8] and win yourself back with her!

YUDHIṢṬHIRA SAID:
She is not too short or too tall, not too black or too red, and her eyes are red with love[9]—I play you for her! Eyes like the petals of autumn lotuses, and fragrance as of autumn lotuses, a beauty that waits on autumn lotuses—the peer of the Goddess of Fortune![1] Yes, for her lack of cruelty, for the fullness of her body, for the straightness of her character does a man desire a woman. Last she lies down who was the first to wake up, who knows what was done or left undone, down to the cowherds and goatherds. Her sweaty lotuslike face shines like a lotus. Her waist shaped like an altar,[2] hair long, eyes the color of copper, not too much body hair . . . such is the woman, king, such is the slender-waisted Pāñcālī, for whom I now throw, the beautiful Draupadī! Come on, Saubala!

VAIŚAMPĀYANA SAID:
When the King Dharma had spoken this word, Bhārata,[3] the voices that were raised by the elders spelled of "Woe! Woe!" The hall itself shook, king, and talk started among the kings. Bhīṣma, Droṇa, Kṛpa, and others broke out in sweat.[4] Vidura buried his face in his hands and looked as though he had fainted; he sat, head down, brooding, wheezing like a snake.[5] But Dhṛtarāṣṭra, exhilarated, kept asking, "Has he won, has he won?" for he did not

8. Kṛṣṇā ("dark lady," from *kṛṣṇa*, "dark" or "black") is a name of Draupadī, princess of Pāñcāla. 9. Bloodshot eyes, suggesting passion and intoxication, are a sign of beauty in women. 1. Goddess of Fortune and consort of the god Viṣṇu and of kings, Śrī is associated with the red lotus. 2. The altar of the Vedic sacrifice is narrow at the middle. 3. Descendant of Bharata. 4. Son of King Śantanu and the river goddess Gaṅgā (Ganges), Bhīṣma is the granduncle of the Pāṇḍavas and Kauravas. Droṇa is their *guru* (teacher) in the martial arts. 5. Born to Vyāsa and a maidservant at the Hāstinapura court, Vidura the Steward is a half brother of Dhṛtarāṣṭra and Pāṇḍu.

keep his composure. Karṇa, Duḥśāsana,[6] and their cronies were mightily pleased, but of others in the hall the tears flowed freely. But Saubala, without hesitation, with the glow of the winner and high with passion, again addressed the dice and cried, "We have won!"

59

DURYODHANA SAID:

All right, you Steward,[7] bring Draupadī,
The beloved wife whom the Pāṇḍavas honor,
Let her sweep the house and run on our errands—
What a joy to watch!—with the serving wenches!

VIDURA SAID:

The incredible happens through people like you,
You don't know it, nitwit, you are tied in a noose!
You hang over a chasm and do not grasp it,
You dumb deer to anger tigers!

You are carrying poisonous snakes on your head, their pouches full of venom! Don't infuriate them, fool, lest you go to Yama![8] Kṛṣṇā is not a slave yet, Bhārata! I think she was staked when the king was no longer his own master.

Dhṛtarāṣṭra's son the prince bears fruit,
Like the bamboo, only to kill himself:[9]
He is ripe for death, but he fails to see
That dicing leads to a dangerous feud.

Be never hurtful or speak cruelly,
Nor extort the last from a penniless man,
Nor speak the wounding, hell-earning words
That when voiced hurt another man.

Those words beyond need fly from the mouth,
And the one they hurt grieves day and night:
Those words that strike where the other hurts
No wise man will loose on another man.

For this goat, they say, dug up a knife,
When a knife was missing, by pawing the ground.
It became a means to cut its own throat:
So dig up no feud with Pāṇḍu's sons!

They don't speak either good or ill
Of the forest-dweller or householder,
But of the ascetic of mature wisdom,
The same people bark like the curs they are.

This dreadful crooked door tilts toward hell—
You know it not, Dhṛtarāṣṭra's son;
There are many will follow you down that road,
Now the game has been won, with Duḥśasana!

6. Younger brother of Duryodhana. 7. Vidura. 8. God of death. 9. Bamboo bears fruit only after many years and then dies.

The gourds will sink and the rocks will float,
And the ships will forever be lost on the seas.
Before the fool prince, Dhṛtarāṣṭra's son,
Will lend his ear to my apt words!

For this to be sure spells the end of the Kurus,
A grisly end, the perdition of all.
The words of the sage, so apt, and his friends
Are no longer heard, and greed just grows!

60

VAIŚAṂPĀYANA SAID:

"A plague on the Steward," he said and rose,
Maddened with pride, Dhṛtarāṣṭra's son,
And he looked at his usher in the hall
And to him he spoke amidst those grandees,

"Go, usher, and bring me Draupadī here!
You have nothing to fear from the Pāṇḍavas.
The Steward is timid and speaks against it,
But never did he wish that *we* should prosper!"

The usher, a bard, at his master's word
Went quickly out upon hearing the king,
And he entered, a dog in a lion's den,
Crawling up to the Queen of the Pāṇḍavas.

THE USHER SAID:

Yudhiṣṭhira, crazed by the dicing game,
Has lost you to Duryodhana, Draupadī.
Come enter the house of Dhṛtarāṣṭra,
To your chores I must lead you, Yājñasenī!

DRAUPADĪ SAID:

How dare you speak so, an usher, to me?
What son of a king would hazard his wife?
The king is befooled and crazed by the game—
Was there nothing left for him to stake?

THE USHER SAID:

When nothing was left for him to stake,
Ajātaśatru[1] wagered you.
Already the king had thrown for his brothers,
And then for himself—then, Princess, for you.

DRAUPADĪ SAID:

Then go to the game and, son of a bard, ask in the assembly, "Bhārata, whom did you lose first, yourself or me?" When you have found out, come and take me, son of a bard!

VAIŚAṂPĀYANA SAID:

He went to the hall and asked Draupadī's question. "As the owner of whom did you lose us?" so queries Draupadī. "Whom did you lose first, yourself or

1. "Invincible," an epithet of Yudhiṣṭhira.

me?" But Yudhiṣṭhira did not stir, as though he had lost consciousness, and made no reply to the bard, whether good or ill.

DURYODHANA SAID:

Let Kṛṣṇā of the Pāñcālas come here and ask the question herself. All the people here shall hear what she or he has to say.

VAIŚAṂPĀYANA SAID:

As he was in Duryodhana's service; the usher, who was the son of a bard, went to the king's lodgings and, as though shuddering, said to Draupadī.

The men in the hall are summoning, Princess!
Methinks that the fall of the Kurus has come.
That fool will not protect our fortunes
If *you* have to come to the hall, O Princess.

DRAUPADĪ SAID:

That is how he disposes, the All-Disposer,[2]
Both touches touch the sage and the fool:
He said, "In this world only Law is supreme":
He shall bring us peace when the Law is obeyed!

VAIŚAṂPĀYANA SAID:

But Yudhiṣṭhira, on hearing what Duryodhana wanted to do, sent an acceptable messenger to Draupadī, O bull of the Bhāratas. In her one garment, knotted below, weeping and in her courses,[3] she went to the hall, the Pāñcāla princess, and stood before her father-in-law.

Watching the courtiers' faces, the Prince
Duryodhana said gleefully to the bard,
"Bring her here, good usher, right here on this spot,
So the Kauravas may speak up to her face!"

So the *sūta* who was in Duryodhana's service,
But afraid of the wrath of the Drupada Princess,
Shed all his pride and asked the assembled,
"Who am I to speak to a Draupadī?"

DURYODHANA SAID:

Duḥśāsana, he is a fool, this bard's son,
He is terrified of the Wolf-Belly![4]
Fetch and bring yourself Yajñasena's daughter,
How can our powerless rivals prevent you?

VAIŚAṂPĀYANA SAID:

Thereupon the son of the king rose up,
On hearing his brother, eyes reddened with wrath,
And entered the dwelling of those great warriors,
And he said to Draupadī, daughter of kings,

"All right now, come, Pāñcālī, you're won!
Look upon Duryodhana, without shame!
You shall now love the Kurus, long-lotus-eyed one,[5]
You've been won under Law, come along to the hall!"

2. God. 3. She is menstruating. In observing the menstrual taboos of women of her class, she has been secluded, her hair is not dressed, and she wears only one garment (the lower?) instead of the customary two cloths (an upper and a lower one). 4. Bhīma's enormous appetite earns him this epithet. 5. Woman with elongated eyes shaped like a lotus petal, a mark of beauty.

In bleak spirits did she rise,
And wiped with her hand her pallid face.
In despair she ran where the women sat
Of the aged king, the bull of the Kurus.

And quickly the angry Duḥśāsana
Came rushing to her with a thunderous roar;
By the long-tressed black and flowing hair
Duḥśāsana grabbed the wife of a king.

The hair that at the concluding bath
Of the king's consecration had been sprinkled
With pure-spelled water, Dhṛtarāṣṭra's son
Now caressed with force, unmanning the Pāṇḍus.[6]

Duḥśāsana, stroking her, led her and brought her,
That Kṛṣṇā of deep black hair, to the hall,
As though unprotected amidst her protectors,
And tossed her as wind tosses a plantain tree.

And as she was dragged, she bent her body
And whispered softly, "It is now my month!
This is my sole garment, man of slow wit,
You cannot take me to the hall, you churl!"

But using his strength and holding her down,
By her deep black locks, he said to Kṛṣṇā,
"To Kṛṣṇa and Jiṣṇu, to Hari and Nara,[7]
Cry out for help! I shall take you yet!

"Sure, you be in your month, Yajñasena's daughter,
Or wear a lone cloth, or go without one!
You've been won at the game and been made a slave,
And one lechers with slaves as the fancy befalls!"

Her hair disheveled, her half skirt drooping,
Shaken about by Duhśāsana,
Ashamed and burning with indignation,
She whispered again, and Kṛṣṇā said,

"In the hall are men who have studied the books,
All follow the rites and are like unto Iṅdras.
They are all my *gurus*[8] or act for them:
Before their eyes I cannot stand thus!

"You ignoble fool of cruel feats,
Don't render me nude, do not debase me!
These sons of kings will not condone you,
Were Iṅdra and Gods to be your helpmates!

"The king, son of Dharma,[9] abides by the Law,
And the Law is subtle, for the wise to find out:

6. As an important part of the royal consecration of Yudhiṣṭhira, the queen's hair had been anointed with sacred waters to the accompaniment of sacred chants ("pure spells"). By laying hands on the Pāṇḍavas' wife and desecrating Yudhiṣṭhira's sovereignty, Duḥśāsana is doubly *unmanning* them. 7. Both pairs refer to Arjuna and Kṛṣṇa, who rescue Draupadī whenever she is in trouble. 8. Teachers, elders. 9. Yudhiṣṭhira.

But even at his behest I would not
Give the least offense and abandon my virtue.

"It is *base* that amidst the Kaurava heroes
You drag me inside while I am in my month;
There is no one here to honor you for it,
Though surely they do not mind your plan.

"Damnation! Lost to the Bhāratas
Is their Law and the ways of sagacious barons,
When all these Kauravas in their hall
Watch the Kuru Law's limits overstridden!

"There is no mettle in Droṇa and Bhīṣma,
Nor to be sure in this good man;
The chiefs of the elders amongst the Kurus
Ignore this dread Unlaw of this king."

As she piteously spoke the slim-waisted queen
Threw a scornful glance at her furious husbands
And inflamed with the fall of her sidelong glances,
The Pāṇḍavas, wrapped with wrath in their limbs.

Not the kingdom lost, nor the riches looted,
Nor the precious jewels plundered did hurt
As hurt that sidelong glance of Kṛṣṇā,
That glance of Kṛṣṇā sent in fury.

Duḥśāsana, though, watched only Kṛṣṇā
Who was looking down on her wretched lords,
And shaking her wildly—she was close to fainting—
Cried cruelly "Slave!" and laughed aloud.

And Karṇa applauded his word to the full
And heartily laughing acknowledged it,
And Subala's son, king of Gāndhāra,
Likewise cheered on Duḥśāsana.

Apart from these two and Duryodhana,
All other men who sat in the hall,
On seeing Kṛṣṇā dragged into the hall,
Were filled with misery beyond measure.

BHĪṢMA SAID:

As the Law is subtle, my dear, I fail
To resolve your riddle the proper way:
A man without property cannot stake another's—
But given that wives are the husband's chattels?

Yudhiṣṭhira may give up all earth
With her riches, before he'd give up the truth.
The Pāṇḍava said, "I have been won,"
Therefore I cannot resolve this doubt.

No man is Śakuni's peer at the dice,
And he left Yudhiṣṭhira his own choice.
The great-spirited man does not think he was cheating,
Therefore I cannot speak to the riddle.

DRAUPADĪ SAID:

In the meeting hall he was challenged, the king,
By cunning, ignoble, and evil tricksters
Who love to game; he had never much tried it.
Why then do you say he was left a choice?

Pure, the best of Kurus and Pāṇḍavas,
He did not wake up to the playing of tricks,
He attended the session and when he'd lost all,
Only then he agreed to hazard me.

They stand here, the Kurus, they stand in their hall,
Proud owners of sons and daughters-in-law:
Examine ye all this word of mine,
And resolve my riddle the proper way!

VAIŚAMPĀYANA SAID:

So she piteously spoke and flowing with tears
Kept looking at those who were her husbands;
Meanwhile Duḥśāsana said many words
That were bitter and mean and none that were gentle.

The Wolf-Belly looked and watched how she
Was dragged, in her courses, with upper cloth drooping,[1]
Who so little deserved it, in desperate pain;
He looked at his brother and gave voice to his rage.

61

BHĪMA SAID:

There are a lot of whores in the country of gamblers, Yudhiṣṭhira, but they never throw for them, for they have pity even for women of that stripe. The tribute that the king of the Kāśīs[2] brought and all our vast wealth, the gems that the other kings of the earth brought in, the mounts and prizes, the armor and weaponry, the kingdom, yourself and we have all been staked and lost to others. This I didn't mind much, for you are the master of all we possess. But you went too far, I think, when you staked Draupadī. She did not deserve this! After she had won Pāṇḍavas as a girl, she is now because of you plagued by Kauravas, mean and cruel tricksters! It is because of her that I hurl my fury at you! I shall burn off your arms! Sahadeva![3] Bring the fire!

ARJUNA SAID:

Never before have you said words like these, Bhīmasena! Surely your respect for the Law has been destroyed by our harsh enemies! Don't fall in with the enemy's plans, obey your highest Law: no one may overreach his eldest brother by Law. The king was challenged by his foes, and, remembering the baronial Law,[4] he played at the enemy's wish. *That* is our great glory!

BHĪMASENA SAID:

If I'd thought he'd done it for his own glorification, I'd have forced his arms together and burned them in the blazing fire, Dhanaṃjaya![5]

1. The mention of the upper cloth suggests that this verse might belong to a different version of the narrative than the one we have been following. The other verses indicate that Draupadī is wearing a single (lower) cloth. 2. The ruler of Benares (Kāśī) and surrounding kingdoms, one of many kings who brought tribute to Yudhiṣṭhira at his royal consecration. 3. Sahadeva is the keeper of the Pāṇḍavas' ritual fires. 4. The code of the *kṣatriya* or warrior class. 5. "Winner of wealth," an epithet of Arjuna.

VAIŚAṂPĀYANA SAID:

Hereupon, seeing the grief of the Pāṇḍavas and the torment of Pāñcālī, Vikarṇa, a son of Dhṛtarāṣṭra's,[6] spoke out: "Ye kings! Answer the question that Yajñasena's daughter has asked! We must decide or we shall go to hell! Bhīṣma and Dhṛtarāṣṭra are the eldest of the Kurus; they are here but say nought, nor does the sagacious Vidura. Droṇa Bhāradvāja is here, the teacher of us all, and so is Kṛpa, yet even they, most eminent of brahmins, do not speak to the question! All the other kings, assembled here from every horizon, should shed all partisan feelings and speak up as they think. Consider the question that the beautiful Draupadī has raised repeatedly, kings, and whatever your side, make your answer!"

Thus did he speak many times to all the men who were sitting in the hall, but none of the kings said aught, whether good or bad. Vikarṇa spoke again and again to all those kings, and sighing, kneading his hands, he finally said, "Make your answer, kings, or do not. But I shall tell you, Kaurava, what I think is right in this matter. Ye best of men, they recount four vices that are the curse of a king: hunting, drinking, dicing, and fornicating. A man with those addictions abandons the Law, and the world does not condone his immoderate deeds. The Pāṇḍava was under the sway of his vice when the gamblers challenged him and he staked Draupadī. The innocent woman is held in common by all the Pāṇḍavas, and the Pāṇḍava staked her when he already had gambled away his own freedom. It was Saubala who mentioned Kṛṣṇā when he wanted a stake. Considering all this I do not think she has been won."

When they heard this, there was a loud outcry from the men in the hall as they praised Vikarṇa and condemned Saubala. When the noise died down, the son of Rādhā,[7] fairly fainting with fury, grasped his shining arm and said, "Are there not many mockeries of the truth found in Vikarṇa? As the fire burns the block from which it was drilled, so the fire he generates will lead to his perdition! All these men here have failed to reply despite Kṛṣṇā's urging. I hold that Draupadī has been won, and so do they hold. You are torn to pieces by your own folly, Dhārtarāṣṭra,[8] for, still a child, you announce in the assembly what should be said by your elders. A younger brother of Duryodhana's, you do not know the true facts of the Law, if you stupidly maintain that Kṛṣṇā, who has been won, has not in fact been won. How, son of Dhṛtarāṣṭra, can you hold that Kṛṣṇā has not been won when the eldest Pāṇḍava staked all he owned in the assembly hall? Draupadī is part of all he owns, bull of the Bharatas, then how can you hold that Kṛṣṇā, won by Law, has not been won? Draupadī was mentioned by name and the Pāṇḍavas allowed her to be staked—then by what reasoning do you hold that she has not been won?

"Or if you think that it was against the Law to bring her into the hall clad in one piece of clothing, listen to what I have to say in reply to that. The Gods have laid down that a woman shall have one husband, scion of Kuru. She admits to many men and assuredly is a whore![9] Thus there is, I think,

6. Thus, Duryodhana's brother. 7. Karṇa, half brother of the Pāṇḍavas, abandoned by his mother Kuntī at birth, and brought up by the charioteer Adhiratha and his wife Rādhā. 8. Son of Dhṛtarāṣṭra. 9. Karṇa's hatred of the Pāṇḍavas comes across very clearly in this speech. This is one of the very few places in the epic in which Draupadī's marriage to five men is condemned as being immoral.

nothing strange about taking her into the hall, or to have her in one piece of clothing, or for that matter naked! She, the Pāṇḍava's wealth, and the Pāṇḍavas themselves have all been won by Saubala here according to the Law.

"Duḥśāsana, this Vikarṇa is only a child, blabbing of wisdom! Strip the clothes from the Pāṇḍavas and Draupadī!"

Hearing this, all the Pāṇḍavas shed their upper clothes[1] and sat down in the assembly hall. Then Duḥśāsana forcibly laid hold of Draupadī's robe, O king, and in the midst of the assembly began to undress her. But when her skirt was being stripped off, lord of the people, another similar skirt appeared every time. A terrible roar went up from all the kings, a shout of approval, as they watched that greatest wonder on earth. And in the midst of the kings Bhīma, lips trembling with rage, kneading hand in hand, pronounced a curse in a mighty voice: "Take to heart this word of mine, ye barons that live on this earth, a word such as never has been spoken before nor any one shall ever speak hereafter! May I forfeit my journey to all my ancestors, if I do not carry out what I say, if I not tear open in battle the chest of this misbegotten fiend, this outcaste of the Bharatas, and drink his blood!"

When they heard this curse, which exhilarated all the world, they offered him much homage and reviled Dhṛtarāṣṭra's son. A pile of clothes was heaped up in the middle of the hall, when Duḥśāsana, tired and ashamed, at last desisted and sat down. The gods among men[2] in the hall raised the hair-raising cry of "Fie!" as they watched the sons of Kuntī. The people shouted, "The Kauravyas[3] refuse to answer the question," and condemned the Dhṛtarāṣṭra.

Thereupon, raising his arms and stopping the crowd in the hall, Vidura, who knew all the Laws, made his speech.[4]

VIDURA SAID:

Draupadī, having raised the question, now weeps piteously as though she has none left to protect her. If you do not resolve it, men in this hall, the Law will be offended. The man who comes to the hall with a grievance is like a blazing fire: the men in the hall must appease him with true Law. If a man comes with a grievance and raises a question of Law with the men in the hall, they must resolve the question and shed all partiality. Vikarṇa has answered the question according to his lights, kings of men; you too must speak to the question according to yours. If a person sits in the hall and fails to answer a question, although he sees the Law, he incurs half the guilt that accrues if the answer is false. And he who has gone to the hall, knows the Law, yet resolves it falsely, certainly incurs the full guilt of the falsehood.

Summary Vidura recounts a lengthy story portraying the fall of those who fail to answer a question of dharma in a public assembly. Draupadī and Bhīṣma urge the assembled noblemen to answer Draupadī's challenge.

1. A gesture of subordination, here equivalent to stripping. The Pāṇḍavas are wearing two loose cloths, one tied around the waist and the other draped over the shoulders. 2. Kings, chiefs. 3. Kauravas. 4. Despite his partially low birth (his mother was a maidservant), Vidura is respected for his knowledge of the law.

62

VAIŚAṂPĀYANA SAID:

Upon witnessing all those many events
And Draupadī screeching, a winged osprey,
The kings said nought, neither good nor bad,
For they feared for Dhṛtarāṣṭra's son.

And seeing the sons and grandsons of kings
Keep silent, the son of Dhṛtarāṣṭra
Began to smile and said this word
To the daughter of the Pāñcāla king:

"Let the question now rest with the mettlesome Bhīma,
With Arjuna and with Sahadeva,
And your husband Nakula, Draupadī:
Let them speak the word that you have begotten.

"In the midst of these nobles they must declare
For thy sake that Yudhiṣṭhira's not thy master,
And thus they must make King Dharma a liar.
Pāñcalī, so you escape servitude!

"King Dharma, great-spirited, firm in the Law,
The peer of Indra, himself must declare
Whether he owns you or does not own you;
At his word you must choose, the one or the other.

"For all the Kauravas in the assembly
Are caught inside your misery:
They cannot resolve it, the noble-hearted,
And they look to your unfortunate masters."

The men in the hall all loudly approved
The word that the king of the Kurus had spoken;
There were those who cheeringly waved their clothes,
But also cries of "Woe!" were heard.
And all the kings in cheerful spirits
Applauded the Law of the first of the Kurus.

All the kings looked at Yudhiṣṭhira, their faces turned sideways: "What will the law-wise prince say? What will the Terrifier[5] say, the Pāṇḍava undefeated in battle? And Bhīmasena and the twins?" thus they wondered, greatly curious. When the noise had died down, Bhīmasena spoke, grasping his broad, sandal-scented[6] arm.

"Had Yudhiṣṭhira the King Dharma not been our own guru and lord of our family we should never have suffered this! He owns our merit and our austerities, he commands our lives. If he holds himself defeated, so are we defeated. No mortal who walks the earth would have escaped me with his life, for touching the hair of Pāñcālī! Look at my arms, long and round like iron-studded bludgeons: once caught in them not the God of the Hundred

5. Arjuna. 6. Scented with a fragrant paste made from sandalwood.

Sacrifices[7] could escape from them! But now, like this, tied by the noose of the Law, constrained by his gravity and held back by Arjuna, I wreak no havoc! But if the King Dharma unleashes me, I shall crush the evil band of Dhṛtarāṣṭra with the swordlike flats of my hands, as a lion flattens small game!" And at once Bhīṣma and Droṇa and Vidura spoke: "Bear with it! With you anything is possible!"

63

KARṆA SAID:

There are three who own no property,
A student, a slave, a dependent woman:
The wife of a slave, you are his now, my dear;
A masterless slave wench, you are now slave wealth!

Come in and serve us with your attentions:
That is the chore you have left in this house.
Dhṛtarāṣṭra's men, and not the Pārthas,[8]
Are now your masters, child of a king!

Now quickly choose you another husband
Who will not gamble your freedom away:
For license with masters is never censured:
That is the slave's rule, remember it!

Won have been Nakula, Bhīmasena,
Yudhiṣṭhira, Sahadeva, Arjuna!
Become a slave, come inside, Yājñasenī!
The ones who are won are no longer your men.

What use are now to the Pārtha[9] himself,
His gallantry and his manliness?
In the midst of the hall he has gambled away
The daughter of Drupada, king of Pāñcāla!

VAIŚAṂPĀYANA SAID:

Hearing this, Bhīma bore it no longer;
A man tormented, he panted hard;
But avowed to the king and trapped by the Law,
Burning him down with wrath-shot eye,

BHĪMA SAID:

I do not anger at a sūta's son,[1]
For the Law of serfdom is surely upon us:
But could our enemies now have held me,
If you had not thrown for her, my liege?

VAIŚAṂPĀYANA SAID:

When he had heard the words of Rādheya,[2] Prince Duryodhana said to

7. Iṅdra. Vedic Aryans gave him one hundred sacrificial offerings. Compare Homer, who refers to the Greek practice of offering hecatombs (sacrifices of a hundred cattle) to the gods. 8. Sons of Pṛthā (Kuṅtī). 9. Son of Pṛthā (Kuṅtī), here an epithet of Yudhiṣṭhira. 1. Karṇa is the adopted son of a charioteer-bard, and his real birth (as Kuṅtī's son and thus half brother of the Pāṇḍavas) is unknown even to him. 2. Karṇa, son of Rādhā (the charioteer's wife).

Yudhiṣṭhira, who was sitting silent and mindless, "Bhīma and Arjuna and the twins follow your orders, king. Answer the question, whether you think she has been won!" This he said to the Kaunteya,[3] and crazed by his ascendancy, he took his cloth[4] and looked invitingly at Pāñcālī. Then, smiling up at Rādheya, and taunting Bhīma, he exposed to Draupadī who was watching him his left thigh, soft like a banana tree and auspiciously marked—an elephant trunk and a thunderbolt in one.[5] The Wolf-Belly saw it and, widening his bloodshot eyes, spoke up in the midst of the kings, willing the assembly to listen: "May the Wolf-Belly never share the world of his fathers, if I fail to break that thigh with my club in a great battle!" And as he raged, flames of the fire burst forth from all the orifices of his body, as from the hollows of a tree that is on fire.

VIDURA SAID:

Kings! Watch for the ultimate danger from Bhīma!
Kings! Watch it as if it were Varuṇa's noose![6]
For surely the hostile fate has emerged
That the Gods set of old for the Bhāratas.

This has been an overplay, Dhārtarāṣṭras.
Who fight over a woman in this hall!
Your security now seems much imperiled,
For evil counsels the Kurus now spell.

Kurus, quickly decide on the Law of the case.
If it's wrongly perceived the assembly will suffer.
If this gamester here had staked her before,
He'd have been undefeated and still been her master.

Like a stake that is won in a dream is the stake,
If the stake is put up by one who does not own it!
You have listened to Gāndhārī's son,[7]
Now Kurus, don't run from the Law of the case!

DURYODHANA SAID:

I stay with the word of Bhīmasena
And Arjuna's word and the word of the twins:
If they say Yudhiṣṭhira wasn't their master,
Then Yājñasenī, you won't be a slave!

ARJUNA SAID:

The king was our master when first he played us,
Great-spirited Dharma, the son of Kuntī:
But whose master is he who has lost himself?
That you should decide, ye Kurus assembled!

VAIŚAMPĀYANA SAID:

And there in the house of the King Dhṛtarāṣṭra
At the agnihotra[8] a jackal barked,

3. Yudhiṣṭhira, son of Kuntī. 4. He either waves his upper cloth or picks up an end of the cloth at his waist. 5. A sexual suggestion need not be ruled out; however, Duryodhana is inviting Draupadī to become *his* queen. In sculpture and painting, the queen consort is portrayed as sitting on the king's left thigh. 6. As the Vedic god of law, Varuṇa binds people with his noose. 7. Duryodhana. 8. A Vedic rite in which an offering of milk is made to the sun god at dawn and dusk.

The donkeys, they brayed in response, O king,
And so on all sides the grisly birds.[9]

And Vidura, sage of all portents, listened
To the horrible sound, so did Saubala;
And Bhīṣma and Droṇa and wise Gautama
Made loud declarations of "Peace!" and "Peace!"

Thereupon Gāndhārī and Vidura the wise,
Who both had observed that ghastly omen,
At once unhappily told the king;
Whereupon the king gave voice to his word:

"You're lost, Duryodhana, shallow-brain,
Who in this hall of the bulls of the Kurus
Berated a woman most uncouthly,
And her a Draupadī, married by Law!"

Having spoken the wise Dhṛtarāṣṭra withdrew,
For he wished for the weal of his allies-in-law;
Kṛṣṇā Pāñcālī he pacified,
And thinking with insight, informed of the facts,

DHṚTARĀṢṬRA SAID:

Choose a boon for me, Pāñcālī, whatever you wish;[1] for you are to me the most distinguished of my daughters-in-law, bent as you are on the Law!

DRAUPADĪ SAID:

If you give me a boon, bull of the Bharatas, I choose this: the illustrious Yudhiṣṭhira, observer of every Law, shall be no slave! Do not let these little boys, who do not know my determined son, say of Prativindhya[2] when he happens to come in, "Here comes the son of a slave!" He has been a *king's* son, as no man has been anywhere. Spoiled as he is, he shall die, Bhārata, when he finds out that he has been a slave's son!

DHṚTARĀṢṬRA SAID:

I give you a second boon, good woman, ask me! My heart has convinced me that you do not deserve only a single boon.

DRAUPADĪ SAID:

With their chariots and bows I choose Bhīmasena and Dhanaṃjaya, Nakula and Sahadeva, as my second boon!

DHṚTARĀṢṬRA SAID:

Choose a third boon from us; two boons do not honor you enough. For of all of my daughters-in-law you are the best, for you walk in the Law.

DRAUPADĪ SAID:

Greed kills Law, Sir, I cannot make another wish. I am not worthy to take a third boon from you, best of kings. As they say, the commoner has one boon, the baron and his lady two, but three are the king's, great king, and a hundred the brahmin's. They were laid low, my husbands, but they have been saved: and they will find the good things, king, with their own good acts!

9. Evil omens. 1. Frightened by the evil omens, Dhṛtarāṣṭra tries to compensate for his sons' treachery by granting a wish (boon) to the aggrieved Draupadī. Compare King Daśaratha in the *Rāmāyaṇa* (p. 897), who is also bound by his word to fulfill his queen's wishes. 2. His father is Yudhiṣṭhira.

64

KARṆA SAID:

Of all the women of mankind, famous for their beauty, of whom we have heard, no one have we heard accomplished such a deed! While the Pārthas and the Dhārtarāṣṭras are raging beyond measure, Kṛṣṇā Draupadī has become the salvation of the Pāṇḍavas! When they were sinking, boatless and drowning, in the plumbless ocean, the Pāñcālī became the Pāṇḍavas' boat, to set them ashore!

VAIŚAṂPĀYANA SAID:

Hearing this amidst the Kurus, that a woman had become the refuge of the sons of Pāṇḍu, resentful Bhīmasena said glumly, "Devala has declared that there are three stars in man—offspring, deeds, and knowledge; for creatures live on through them. When the body has become impure, void of life, emptied, and cast off by the kinsmen, it is these three that survive of a man. Our light has been darkened, for our wife has been defiled, Dhanaṃjaya: how can offspring be born from one defiled?"

ARJUNA SAID:

Bhāratas never babble of the insults, spoken or unspoken, from a lower man. The best people always remember only the good acts, not the hostilities they have been shown, acknowledging them because they have confidence in themselves.

BHĪMA SAID:

I shall here and now kill all the enemies that have assembled! Or you go outside, Bhārata, lord among the kings, and cut them to their roots! What is the use for us to argue here, why suffer, Bhārata? I am going to kill them here and now, and you sway this world!

VAIŚAṂPĀYANA SAID:

When Bhīmasena had spoken, surrounded by his younger brothers like a lion amidst deer, he kept glancing at his club. While the Pārtha of unsullied deeds sought to appease and cool him off, the powerful strong-armed Bhīma began to sweat with his inner heat. From the ears and the other orifices of the raging man fire issued forth, smoking and sparking. His face became fierce to behold, with its folds of knitted brows, as the face of Yama himself when the end of the Eon has come. Yudhiṣṭhira restrained the strong-armed Bhīma with his arm, O Bhārata. "Don't!" he said. "Stay quiet!" And when he had restrained the strong-armed man, whose eyes were bloodshot with rage, Yudhiṣṭhira went up to his father Dhṛtarāṣṭra and folded his hands.

65

YUDHIṢṬHIRA SAID:

King, what should we do? Command us, you are our master. For we always wish to obey your behest, Bhārata.

DHṚTARĀṢṬRA SAID:

Ajātaśatru, good luck to you! Go ye in peace and comfort. I give you my leave: rule your own kingdom with your own treasures. But keep in mind this admonition that I, an old man, utter; I have thought it through with my mind, as it is proper and beneficent above all.

Yudhiṣṭhira, my wise son, you know the subtle course of the Laws, you are courteous and you attend to your elders. Where there is wisdom there is serenity: become serene, Bhārata. An ax does not sink in if it is not on wood, but on wood it cuts. The best among men do not remember hostilities; they see the virtues, not the faults, and they do not stoop to enmity. It is the lowliest that hurl insults in a quarrel, Yudhiṣṭhira; the middling ones return the insults, but the best and the steady ones never babble about hostile insults, spoken or unspoken. The good only remember the good that was done, not the hostile deeds, acknowledging it because they have confidence in themselves.

You have behaved nobly in this meeting of good people, therefore, my son, do not brood in your heart on Duryodhana's offensiveness. Look at your mother Gāndhārī, and at me, your old blind father before you, who longs for your virtues. It was from affection that I allowed this dicing game, as I wished to see my friends and find out the strengths and weaknesses of my sons. King, the Kurus whose ruler you are and whose councillor is the sagacious Vidura, expert in all the fields of knowledge, are they to be pitied? In you there is Law, in Arjuna prowess, in Bhīmasena might, in the twins, foremost among men, there is faith and obedience to their elders.

Ajātaśatru, good luck to you! Return to the Khāṇḍava Tract. May you have brotherly bonds with your brethren, and may your mind abide by the Law!

VAIŚAMPĀYANA SAID:

At his words Yudhiṣṭhira the King Dharma, first of the Bharatas, having fulfilled the full covenant of the nobles, departed with his brothers. Riding their cloudlike chariots they started with Kṛṣṇā, and in cheerful spirits, for their good city Indraprastha.[3]

Summary At the end of the Pāṇḍava exile, the Kauravas refuse to hand over the kingdom to Yudhiṣṭhira as promised. Kṛṣṇa, the divine incarnation, approaches the Kauravas on Yudhiṣṭhira's behalf with a proposal for a peaceful settlement between the feuding cousins. Duryodhana rejects the proposal and opts for all-out war.

From *Book* 5[4]

Udyoga [*The Preparation for War*]

42

Dhṛtarāṣṭra said to Kṛṣṇa, "O Kṛṣṇa, I agree with what you have said to me. It will lead to the attainment of heaven, besides being beneficial to the world, as well as virtuous and just. But I am not my own master and I cannot do what I would like to do. O Kṛṣṇa, try and persuade my wicked son Duryodhana, who disregards the injunctions of the scriptures. Then you will have discharged a great duty as a friend."

So Kṛṣṇa addressed himself to the wrathful Duryodhana, in sweet words pregnant with virtue and worldly profit, "O Duryodhana, listen to these words of mine, which are meant for your benefit and that of your followers. Born

3. Duryodhana succeeds in arranging a replay of the dice game, with the outcome to be decided by a single throw of the dice. Yudhiṣṭhira loses, and the Pāṇḍavas are exiled for thirteen years. 4. Books 5, 8, 9, 11, and 12 translated by C. V. Narasimhan.

as you are in a family of very wise men, and endowed as you are with learning and good conduct and with all good qualities, it is right and proper that you should behave honorably. In this case your obstinacy is perverse and unrighteous, and it will result in great and terrible loss of life. O tiger among men, be reconciled with the Pāṇḍavas, who are wise, heroic, energetic, self-restrained, and greatly learned. It is beneficial to you, and will be appreciated by the wise Dhṛtarāṣṭra, as well as by the grandfather Bhīṣma, Droṇa, and the intelligent Vidura. Let there be some survivors of the Kuru race and let not the whole race be destroyed, and do not let yourself, O king, become notorious as the exterminator of the race."

Duryodhana became enraged on hearing the words of Kṛṣṇa. Bhīṣma said to him, "Kṛṣṇa has spoken as a friend wishing peace; listen to his words, my dear son, and do not follow the lead of anger." But Duryodhana did not heed Bhīṣma's advice. He remained under the influence of wrath, breathing hard. Then Droṇa told him, "Kṛṣṇa said words to you which are filled with virtue and profit, my dear son; so did Bhīṣma, the son of Śaṅtanu; heed them, O ruler of men." At the end of Droṇa's speech, Vidura spoke in similar terms to Duryodhana, the irate son of Dhṛtarāṣṭra. "Duryodhana," he said, "I do not grieve for you, but for these two old people, your father and Gāṅdhārī your mother." Dhṛtarāṣṭra then said to Duryodhana, who was seated along with his brothers and surrounded by other kings, "O Duryodhana, listen to this advice given by the great-souled Kṛṣṇa; accept his words which are beneficial, of eternal validity and conducive to our salvation."

So, among the assembled Kurus, Duryodhana had to listen to this counsel which he little liked. Finally he said in reply to Kṛṣṇa, "No doubt, as is proper, you have spoken to me after due consideration; but you find fault only with me. I have not committed the slightest fault, nor do I see even the smallest misconduct on my side after a searching examination. I may recall that the Pāṇḍavas were defeated at a game of dice in which they engaged of their own free will and in the course of which their kingdom was won by Śakuni; what misconduct was there on my part? Indeed, you will remember that I ordered at the time the return of the wealth which the Pāṇḍavas had lost. It is not our fault that the Pāṇḍavas were defeated at another game of dice and were then banished to the forest. The principal duty of a Kṣatriya is that he should lie down on a bed of arrows in the battlefield. I am ready to do so. I shall not, during my lifetime, allow the Pāṇḍavas to regain the share of the kingdom that was given them by our ancestors in early days."

After reflecting on Duryodhana's speech, Kṛṣṇa, his eyes red with anger, spoke these words to Duryodhana in that assembly of the Kurus: "It is your desire to get the bed of a hero, and it will be fulfilled; you and your advisers will not have to wait long. Soon there will be a great massacre. O fool, you think that there is nothing blameworthy in your conduct towards the Pāṇḍavas. All the kings here know the truth of what I am now going to say. Being jealous of the prosperity of the great Pāṇḍavas, you arranged for a game of dice in evil cabal with Śakuni. Who save yourself could have treated the wife of your brothers in the way you did? After dragging Draupadī to the council hall, who else could have spoken to her as you did? You went to great trouble to burn the Pāṇḍavas alive when they were mere boys, and were staying with their mother at Vāraṇāvata, but that attempt of yours did not succeed. By poison, by snake, and by rope, in fact by every means, you have attempted the destruction of the sons of Pāṇḍu, but you have not been successful. You have been urged again and again, by your mother and by your father and also by Bhīṣma, Droṇa, and Vidura, to make peace but you do not wish to do so."

When Kṛṣṇa had thus charged the wrathful Duryodhana, Duḥśāsana said these words in the assembly of the Kurus, "If you do not make peace of your own free will with the Pāṇḍavas, it looks as if the Kauravas will make you over to Yudhiṣṭhira bound hand and foot." Hearing these words of his brother, Duryodhana could no longer restrain himself. He got up from his seat hissing like a huge serpent. Disregarding all those present—Vidura, King Dhṛtarāṣṭra, Bāhlika, Kṛpa, Somadatta, Bhīṣma, Droṇa, and Kṛṣṇa—that shameless and wicked prince walked out of the court.

43

Dhṛtarāṣṭra then said to Vidura, "Go, my friends, to the wise Gāndhārī; get her here; along with her I shall try to persuade our son." In response to the request of Dhṛtarāṣṭra, Vidura brought the farsighted Gāndhārī. By command of Dhṛtarāṣṭra and also at the request of Gāndhārī, Vidura had the wrathful Duryodhana brought back. Seeing her son, who was following the wrong course, Gāndhārī spoke these significant words, "O Duryodhana, my dear son, listen to these words of mine which will be to your benefit and that of your followers, and which will bring you all happiness. It is my fond and earnest wish, as well as that of Bhīṣma, your father, and other well-wishers, the chief of whom is Droṇa, that you should make peace."

Disregarding those sensible words spoken by his mother, the obstinate Duryodhana again went to his own palace burning with rage. Then he consulted King Śakuni, the expert in the game of dice, as well as Karṇa and Duḥśāsana. The four, namely, Duryodhana, Karṇa, Śakuni, and Duḥśāsana, reached the following conclusion: "Kṛṣṇa means to waste no time, and wants to capture us first in concert with Dhṛtarāṣṭra and Bhīṣma. We shall, however, capture Kṛṣṇa by force, before he can carry out his plan."

Coming to know of this plan through Sātyaki, Vidura said to Dhṛtarāṣṭra, "O king, your sons are approaching the hour of doom, because they are ready to perpetrate an infamous act, even though they are incapable of doing it." He then informed the king of Duryodhana's nefarious plot. On hearing this, Dhṛtarāṣṭra said to Vidura, "Bring here again the sinful Duryodhana, who covets the kingdom." Therefore Vidura made the reluctant Duryodhana return once more to the council chamber, along with his brothers.

King Dhṛtarāṣṭra addressed Duryodhana, Karṇa, Duḥśāsana, and the kings who surrounded them, "O you of inhuman conduct, of exceeding sinfulness, having for your supporters only petty men, I know of your secret desire to commit a wicked deed. Kṛṣṇa cannot be captured by force, even as air cannot be held by the hand, as the moon cannot be touched, and as the earth cannot be supported on the head." Vidura's warning was: "If you try to use force on the mighty Kṛṣṇa, you, along with your advisers, will perish like an insect falling into the flame."

When Vidura had finished speaking, Kṛṣṇa said to Duryodhana, "O Duryodhana! since, out of your folly, you suppose me to be alone, you think you can effect my capture by overpowering me." So saying, he laughed aloud.

And at his laughter the body of the great-souled one became like lightning. From his body issued forth gods only as big as the thumb but bright as rays of fire. Brahmā was found to be on his brow and Rudra on his breast. On his arms appeared the regents of the earth and from his mouth issued forth the god of fire. When Kṛṣṇa thus showed himself on the floor of the assembly hall, celestial drums were sounded and there was a shower of flowers. After a moment he discarded that celestial and wonderful form. Taking Sātyaki by the hand, Kṛṣṇa went out, with the permission of the sages present in the court.

As he was about to depart on the chariot which was ready for him, the great king Dhṛtarāṣṭra again said to Kṛṣṇa, "You have seen, O Kṛṣṇa, what little influence I wield over my sons; you have been a witness to that; nothing has happened behind your back." Then Kṛṣṇa said to Dhṛtarāṣṭra, and to Droṇa and the grandfather Bhīṣma, and to Vidura, and to Bāhlika and Kṛpa, "Your exalted selves are witnesses to what went on in the assembly of the Kurus; how today that fool, like an uneducated and unmannerly fellow, walked out. Now you have heard the ruler of the earth Dhṛtarāṣṭra say that he is powerless in the matter. With the permission of all of you I shall go to Yudhiṣṭhira."

Then in that large, white chariot, furnished with tinkling bells, Kṛṣṇa went first to see his aunt Kuṅtī. Entering her abode, he bowed at her feet, after which he briefly described to her what had happened in the assembly of the Kurus. Having completed his report he respectfully circumambulated her, and took leave of her.

When Kṛṣṇa had left, Bhīṣma and Droṇa said to Duryodhana, "The sons of Kuṅtī will do what Kṛṣṇa advises, and they will not be pacified without the restoration of the kingdom. The Pāṇḍavas and Draupadī too were persecuted by you in the assembly hall, but they were bound by the ties of virtue at that time. Now they have in Arjuna a master of all weapons and in Bhīma a giant of firm determination. They have the Gāṇḍīva bow and the two quivers and the chariot and the flag, and they have Kṛṣṇa as their ally. The Pāṇḍavas will not forgive the past."

44

Before leaving Hāstinapura, Kṛṣṇa met Karṇa and said to him: "O Karṇa, you know the eternal instruction of the holy books and are fully conversant with all their subtleties. The two classes of sons called Kānīna and Sahoḍha who are borne by a girl before her marriage have for their father the man who marries their mother subsequently—so it is said by people conversant with the holy books. You were born in that way and you are therefore morally the son of Pāṇḍu; so come with me and be a king in your own right. Let us go together to the Pāṇḍava camp, and let the sons of Pāṇḍu know you to be the son of Kuṅtī born before Yudhiṣṭhira. The five Pāṇḍava brothers will clasp your feet, as will the five sons of Draupadī, and the invincible son of Subhadrā.[5] Enjoy the kingdom in company with your brothers, the sons of Pāṇḍu, who are ever engaged in prayer and sacrifice and other auspicious ceremonies. Let your friends rejoice and in the same

5. Abhimanyu, son of Arjuna and Subhadrā.

way let your enemies suffer; be reconciled today with your brothers, the sons of Pāṇḍu."

Karṇa replied: "I have no doubt, O Kṛṣṇa, that you have spoken these words out of good will, love, and friendship, and also out of the desire to do me good. Before her wedding with Pāṇḍu, Kuṅtī conceived me by the Sun-god, and at his command she abandoned me as soon as I was born. I know I was born in this way and I am therefore morally the son of Pāṇḍu. I was however left destitute at birth by Kuṅtī, who had no thought of my welfare. On the other hand, I have been practically a member of the family of Dhṛtarāṣṭra and, under the protection of Duryodhana, I have enjoyed sovereignty for thirteen years without let or hindrance. Relying on me, Duryodhana has made preparations for war with the Pāṇḍavas. At this stage, I cannot behave treacherously towards Duryodhana out of fear of being slain or captured, or from covetousness."

Kṛṣṇa said, "I fear that this world will surely come to an end, O Karṇa, since my advice does not seem acceptable to you." "O Kṛṣṇa," replied Karṇa, "I shall see you again if I survive this great battle which has come upon us. Otherwise we shall surely meet in heaven. I now feel that I shall meet you only there, O sinless one."

Having learnt of the failure of Kṛṣṇa's mission, Kuṅtī decided to make a personal appeal to Karṇa. Thus resolved, she went towards the river Gaṅgā for the attainment of her object. On the banks of the river she heard the sound of the chanting of hymns by her son, the kind and truthful Karṇa. That austere lady waited behind Karṇa, whose arms were raised and whose face was turned to the east, till the end of his devotions, which continued till his back had been scorched by the rays of the sun. Karṇa then turned and, seeing Kuṅtī, did her honor by saluting her and folding his hands before her, according to proper form.

Karṇa first introduced himself, by saying, "I am Karṇa, the son of Rādhā and of Adhiratha, and I salute you. Why are you come here? Tell me what I may do for you." Kuṅtī replied, "You are the son of Kuṅtī and not the son of Rādhā; nor is Adhiratha your father. O Karṇa, you are not born in the race of Sūta;[6] know this word of mine to be true. I conceived you illegitimately when I was an unmarried girl and you were the first in my womb; you were born in the palace of Kuṅtibhoja, my dear son. The maker of brightness, the Sun-god, begot you on me, O Karṇa. O my son, you were born in my father's palace, wearing earrings, clad in a coat of mail, like a divine being. But, owing to ignorance of your true birth, you are now serving the sons of Dhṛtarāṣṭra, without recognizing your brothers. That is not proper, my son. Let the Kurus witness today the union between Karṇa and Arjuna; and seeing that true reconciliation among brothers let dishonest men bow down!"

Then Karṇa heard an affectionate voice issue from the solar disc from afar. It was Sūrya himself, speaking with the affection of a father. The voice said, "O Karṇa, Kuṅtī has spoken the truth. Act according to the advice of your mother; by doing so, you will benefit greatly." But in spite of this entreaty both by his mother and by his father, Karṇa's attitude did not waver.

"O Kṣatriya[7] lady," he said, "I cannot heed the words you have spoken and I do not feel that the way to virtue lies in my doing as you urge me to do.

6. Charioteer. 7. The class of warriors.

What you did to me was sinful, and I have thereby suffered what is tantamount to the destruction of my fame. Though I was born as a Kṣatriya I did not get the baptismal rites of a Kṣatriya; it was all your sinful doing; what enemy can possibly do me a greater injury? Without having shown me any mercy at that time, you come today to urge me, who was deprived of the rites of my order as a Kṣatriya at birth, to be reconciled to my brothers. You did not think as a mother of my good and you have now come to me purely out of desire for your own good. Unknown as a brother before, and recognized as such now, by whom shall I be called a Kṣatriya if I go over to the side of the Pāṇḍavas on the eve of battle?

"This is the time for those who have obtained their living from Duryodhana to show their fidelity," Karṇa continued, "and I shall do so even at the risk of my life. I shall stay on the side of the sons of Dhṛtarāṣṭra, and I shall fight your sons with all my might and prowess; I do not speak falsely to you. I promise you this: it is with Arjuna alone, among all the forces of Yudhiṣṭhira, that I shall fight. Killing Arjuna in battle, I shall obtain great merit. Slain by him, I shall obtain great glory. O illustrious lady, you will thus always be left with five sons; with Arjuna dead and me alive, or with me slain and Arjuna alive."

When she heard Karṇa's words, Kuṅtī trembled with grief. Embracing her son, who was unmoved in his fortitude, she said, "Indeed, what you say is possible. As you say, fate is all-powerful." Before leaving him, Kuṅtī said to Karṇa, "May you be blessed and may all be well with you." Karṇa also saluted her, and the two went their own ways.

45

Kṛṣṇa returned to Yudhiṣṭhira and reported the failure of his mission. The virtuous and just Yudhiṣṭhira, after hearing Kṛṣṇa's account, said to his brothers, "You have heard what happened in that assemblage of the Kurus and you have no doubt understood what Kṛṣṇa has said. Therefore let us make a division of our army; here are the seven Akṣauhiṇis[8] which are gathered for our victory. Listen to the names of those famous men who are to be their respective commanders. Drupada, Virāṭa, Dhṛṣṭadyamma and Śikhaṇḍī, Sātyaki, Cekitāna, and Bhīma endued with strength, these heroes, who are prepared to sacrifice their lives if necessary, will be the commanders of my army."

There was a speedy gathering of the soldiers and there was everywhere the trumpeting of elephants, the neighing of horses, and the clatter of chariot wheels, which mingled with the noise caused by the blare of the conch and the sound of the drum. The mobilization of that army caused a roar like that of the sea at high tide. Indeed, the tumult of those happy warriors seemed to reach the very heavens.

Forty thousand chariots, five times that number of horses, ten times that number of foot soldiers, and sixty thousand elephants were gathered there. Anādhṛṣṭi and Cekitāna, the king of Cedi, and Sātyaki surrounded Yudhiṣṭhira along with Kṛṣṇa and Arjuna. Finally, they reached Kurukshetra with

8. Battalions.

their army ready for action and they then blew their conches. All the soldiers of the army became cheerful on hearing the thunderous sound of Kṛṣṇa's conch, the Pāñcajanya.

The next morning, King Duryodhana surveyed his forces, which consisted of eleven Akṣauhiṇis. Dividing his men, elephants, chariots, and horses into superior, inferior, and indifferent, he distributed them among his forces. He selected men who were wise and also heroic to be the leaders of his army. They were Kṛpa, Droṇa, Śalya, Jayadratha the king of the Siṅdhus, Sudakṣiṇa the king of the Kāṁbojas, Kṛtavarmā, Aśvatthāmā the son of Droṇa, Karṇa, Bhūriśravas, Śakuni the son of Subala, and Bāhlika the great car-warrior.

Then, with clasped hands, Duryodhana went to Bhīṣma along with the other kings, and said to him, "Without a commander in chief even a large army is broken up like a swarm of ants when engaged in battle. You are like the sun among the luminous bodies, the moon among deciduous herbs,[9] Kubera among the Yakṣas,[1] Iṅdra among the gods. If you lead and protect us, we shall be like the gods protected by Iṅdra, and we shall surely be invincible even if faced by the denizens of heaven."

Bhīṣma replied, "I am at your disposal, O Duryodhana; but as you are dear to me, so are the Pāṇḍavas. It is my duty to look after their welfare too, but I shall fight on your side since I have promised to do so. In a moment I can make this world destitute of men, gods, asuras, and rākṣasas by the strength of my weapons. But I cannot kill these sons of Pāṇḍu. Instead, I shall slay ten thousand of the opposing warriors every day. In this way, I shall try to bring about their defeat, if indeed they do not kill me before I have time to carry out my plans in the battle."

"There is another condition," Bhīṣma continued, "on which I shall be commander in chief of your army; it is only fair that I should tell you about it now. Either let Karṇa fight first or I myself, but not both, since Karṇa always compares his prowess in battle with mine." Karṇa replied, "O king, I shall not fight as long as Bhīṣma the son of Gaṅgā[2] lives. Should Bhīṣma be slain, I shall fight with Arjuna, the wielder of the Gāṇḍīva bow."

Meanwhile, in the Pāṇḍava camp, Yudhiṣṭhira summoned before him Drupada, Virāṭa, Sātyaki, Dhṛṣṭadyumna, Dhṛṣṭaketu, Śikhaṇḍī, and the king of Magadha, and made these heroes, who were eager for battle, the leaders of his army. Finally he installed Dhṛṣṭdyumna, who had emerged from the sacrificial fire for causing the death of Droṇa, as commander in chief.[3] The curly-haired Arjuna was made supreme commander over all those great men, while Kṛṣṇa was chosen as the guide of Arjuna and the driver of his horses.

Seeing that a very destructive battle was about to take place, Balarāma, elder brother of Kṛṣṇa, entered the encampment of the royal Pāṇḍavas. He said, "There will be a very fierce massacre; it is surely ordained by fate and cannot be averted. Both these heroes, Bhīma and Duryodhana, well skilled in fighting with the mace, are my pupils and I bear the same affection for both of them. I shall now go on a pilgrimage to the sacred waters of the Sarasvatī for ablutions, for I cannot stay and look on with indifference while this destruction of the Kurus takes place."

9. The moon is the "lord of plants." 1. The Yakṣa is a type of demigod; Kubera is the guardian of wealth. 2. The river goddess Ganges. 3. The son won through a sacrifice to the gods by King Drupada, Droṇa's sworn enemy, in order to avenge the insult he had suffered at Droṇa's hands.

From *Book 8*

Karṇa [*The Book of Karṇa*]

47

When the mighty bowman Droṇa was slain, the Kaurava host became pale-faced and gloomy. Seeing his own forces standing as if paralyzed and lifeless, King Duryodhana said to them, "Relying on the strength of your arms, I have challenged the Pāṇḍavas to this battle. Victory or death is the lot of all warriors. Why wonder then at the fall of Droṇa? Let us resume the fighting in all directions, encouraged by the sight of the lofty-minded Karṇa, the son of Vikartana, mighty bowman and wielder of celestial weapons, who is roving about in the field of battle. Permit me to remind you that it was he who slew Ghaṭotkaca, that creator of illusions, with the indomitable Śakti weapon." Then all those kings, headed by Duryodhana, quickly installed Karṇa as commander in chief, and bathed him according to rites with golden and earthen pitchers of holy water.

As the sixteenth day dawned, Karṇa summoned the Kaurava forces to battle with loud blasts on his conch. He arranged his army in the form of a makara,[4] and proceeded to attack the Pāṇḍavas, desirous of victory. On the Pāṇḍava side, Arjuna, whose car was drawn by white horses, formed a counter-array in the shape of a half-moon.

The day's fighting was marked by many duels, between Bhīma and Aśvatthāmā, Sahadeva and Duḥśāsana, Nakula and Karṇa, Ulūka and Yuyutsu, Kṛpa and Dhṛṣṭadyumna, and Śikhaṇḍī and Kṛtavarmā. While they were thus engaged, the sun disappeared behind the western mountains. Then both sides retired from the field and proceeded to their own encampments.

Before the fighting began on the seventeenth day, Karṇa said to Duryodhana, "Today, O king, I will go forth and battle with the famous Pāṇḍava, Arjuna. Either I shall slay that hero, or he shall slay me. You are aware of his energy, weapons, and resources. My bow, known by the name of Vijaya,[5] is the greatest of all weapons. It was made by Viśvakarmā[6] in accordance with Iṅdra's wishes, and is a celestial and excellent weapon. On this count I believe I am superior to Arjuna."

"Now you must know," continued Karṇa, "in what respect Arjuna is superior to me. Kṛṣṇa, born of the Dāśārha race, who is revered by all people, is the holder of the reins of his horses. He who is verily the creator of the universe thus guards Arjuna's car. On our side Śalya, who is the ornament of all assemblies, is of equal heroism. Should he take over the duties of my charioteer, then victory will surely be yours. Let the irresistible Śalya, therefore, act as my charioteer."

Duryodhana thereupon went to see Śalya. Humbly approaching the Madra prince, he affectionately spoke these words to him: "You have heard what Karṇa has said, namely that he chooses you, foremost of princes, as his charioteer. Therefore, for the destruction of the Pāṇḍavas, and for my own good, be pleased to become Karṇa's charioteer. As that foremost of chario-

4. A crocodile or other aquatic animal. 5. "Victor." 6. The smith of the gods.

teers, Kṛṣṇa, counsels and protects Arjuna, so should you support Karṇa at all times."

Śalya replied, "You are insulting me, O Duryodhana, or surely you must doubt my loyalty, since you so readily request me to do the work of a charioteer. You praise Karṇa and consider that he is superior to us. But I do not consider him to be my equal in the field of battle. Knowing that I can strike down the enemy, why do you wish to employ me in the office of charioteer to the lowborn Karṇa?"

Duryodhana replied to Śalya with great affection and high respect. Desirous of achieving his main objective, he addressed him in a friendly manner, saying sweetly, "O Śalya, what you say is doubtless true. However, in making this request I have a certain purpose. Even as Karṇa is reckoned to be superior to Arjuna in many ways so are you, in the opinion of the whole world, superior to Kṛṣṇa. As the high-souled Kṛṣṇa is expert in the handling of horses, even so, O Śalya, are you doubly skilled. There is no doubt about it."

Thus flattered, Śalya said, "O Duryodhana! As you tell me that amongst all these troops there is none but myself who is more accomplished than Kṛṣṇa, I am pleased with you. I therefore agree to act as the charioteer of the famous Karṇa while he is engaged in battle with Arjuna, foremost of the Pāṇḍavas. But there is one condition on which I accept your proposal: that I shall give vent in Karṇa's presence to such expressions as I may wish."[7] Duryodhana, who was accompanied by Karṇa, readily accepted this condition, saying, "So be it."

48

After Śalya had taken over as his charioteer, Karṇa said to him, "Today I shall fearlessly fight Kṛṣṇa and Arjuna, foremost among all wielders of weapons. My mind is, however, troubled by the curse of Paraśurāma, the best of Brāhmaṇas. In my early days, desirous of obtaining a celestial weapon, I lived with him in the disguise of a Brāhmaṇa.[8] But, O Śalya, in order to benefit Arjuna, Iṅdra,[9] the king of the gods, took on the horrible form of an insect and stung my thigh. Even so, I remained motionless for fear of disturbing my preceptor. When he woke up, he saw what had happened. He subsequently learnt the deception I had practiced on him, and cursed me, that the invocation for the weapon I had obtained by such trickery would not come to my memory at the time of dire need."

"Once while wandering in the forest," Karṇa continued, "I accidentally killed the sacrificial cow of a Brāhmaṇa.[1] Although I offered him seven hundred elephants with large tusks, and many hundreds of male and female slaves, the best of Brāhmaṇas was still not pleased, and although I begged for forgiveness, he said: 'O sūta, what I have prophesied will happen. It cannot be otherwise.' He had said, 'Your wheel[2] shall fall into a hole.' In this battle, while I am fighting, that will be my only fear."

During the fighting on that day there was a dreadful and thrilling battle between Karṇa and the Pāṇḍavas which increased the domain of the god of

7. That is, to address him in an insulting manner. 8. The brahmin Paraśurāma had vowed to exterminate the *kṣatriyas* and had mastered the science of magical weapons, which could be discharged and retracted with the help of incantations. 9. Iṅdra is Arjuna's father. 1. Cows are sacred animals, and the low-born Karṇa's offense is doubly serious since the sacred cow belonged to a brahmin. 2. Chariot wheel.

Death. After that terrible and gory combat only a few of the brave Samśaptakas survived. Then Dhṛṣṭadyumna and the rest of the Pāṇḍavas rushed towards Karṇa and attacked him. As a mountain receives heavy rainfall, so Karṇa received those warriors in battle. Elsewhere on the battlefield Duḥśāsana boldly went up to Bhīma and shot many arrows at him. Bhīma leapt like a lion attacking a deer, and hurried towards him. The struggle that took place between those two, incensed against each other and careless of life, was truly superhuman.

Fighting fiercely, Prince Duḥśāsana achieved many difficult feats in that duel. With a single shaft he cut off Bhīma's bow; with six shafts he pierced Bhīma's driver. Then, without losing a moment, he pierced Bhīma himself with many shafts discharged with great speed and power, while Bhīma hurled his mace at the prince. With that weapon, from a distance of ten bow-lengths, Bhīma forcibly dislodged Duḥśāsana from his car. Struck by the mace, and thrown to the ground, Duḥśāsana began to tremble. His charioteer and all his steeds were slain, and his car too was smashed to pieces by Bhīma's weapon.

Then Bhīma remembered all the hostile acts of Duḥśāsana towards the Pāṇḍavas. Jumping down from his car, he stood on the ground, looking steadily on his fallen foe. Drawing his keen-edged sword, and trembling with rage, he placed his foot upon the throat of Duḥśāsana and, ripping open the breast of his enemy, drank his warm lifeblood, little by little. Then, looking at him with wrathful eyes, he said, "I consider the taste of this blood superior to that of my mother's milk, or honey, or ghee, or wine, or excellent water, or milk, or curds, or buttermilk."

All those who stood around Bhīma and saw him drink the blood of Duḥśāsana fled in terror, saying to each other, "This one is no human being!" Bhīma then said, in the hearing of all those heroes, "O wretch among men, here I drink your lifeblood. Abuse us once more now, 'Beast, beast,' as you did before!"

Having spoken these words, the victorious Bhīma turned to Kṛṣṇa and Arjuna, and said, "O you heroes, I have accomplished today what I had vowed in respect of Duḥśāsana! I will soon fulfill my other vow by slaying that second sacrificial beast,[3] Duryodhana! I shall kick the head of that evil one with my foot in the presence of the Kauravas, and I shall then obtain peace!" After this speech, Bhīma, drenched with blood, uttered loud shouts and roared with joy, even as the mighty Iṅdra of a thousand eyes after slaying Vṛtra.[4]

49

Fleeing in the face of Arjuna's onslaught, the broken divisions of the Kauravas saw Arjuna's weapon swelling with energy and careering like lightning. But Karṇa destroyed that fiery weapon of Arjuna with his own weapon of great power[5] which he had obtained from Paraśurāma. The encounter between Arjuna and Karṇa became very fierce. They attacked each other with arrows like two fierce elephants attacking each other with their tusks.

Karṇa then fixed on his bowstring the keen, blazing, and fierce shaft which he had long polished and preserved with the object of destroying Arjuna.

3. The animal offered as a victim in a sacrifice. 4. In an important Vedic myth the god Iṅdra slays the dragonlike demon Vṛtra. 5. A magical weapon.

Placing in position that shaft of fierce energy and blazing splendor, that venomous weapon which had its origin in the family of Airāvata[6] and which lay within a golden quiver covered by sandal dust,[7] Karṇa aimed it at Arjuna's head. When he saw Karṇa aim that arrow, Śalya said, "O Karṇa, this arrow will not succeed in hitting Arjuna's neck! Aim carefully, and discharge another arrow that may succeed in striking the head of your enemy!" His eyes burning in wrath, Karṇa replied, "O Śalya, Karṇa never aims an arrow twice!"

Thereupon Karṇa carefully let loose that mighty snake in the form of an arrow, which he had worshiped for many long years, saying, "You are slain, O Arjuna!" Seeing the snake aimed by Karṇa, Kṛṣṇa, strongest among the mighty, exerted his whole strength and pressed down Arjuna's chariot with his feet into the earth. When the car itself had sunk into the ground the steeds, too, bent their knees and laid themselves down upon the earth. The arrow then struck and dislodged Arjuna's diadem, that excellent ornament celebrated throughout the earth and the heavens.

The snake said, "O Kṛṣṇa! Know me as one who has been wronged by Arjuna. My enmity towards him stems from his having slain my mother!"

Then Kṛṣṇa said to Arjuna, "Slay that great snake which is your enemy." Thus urged by Kṛṣṇa, Arjuna asked, "Who is this snake that advances of his own accord against me, as if right against the mouth of Garuḍa?"[8] Kṛṣṇa replied, "While you were worshiping the fire-god at the Khāndava forest, this snake was ensconced within his mother's body, which was shattered by your arrows." As the snake took a slanting course across the sky, Arjuna cut it to pieces with six keen shafts, so that it fell down on the earth.

Then, because of the curse of the Brāhmaṇa, Karṇa's chariot wheel fell off, and his car began to reel. At the same time, he forgot the invocation for the weapon he had obtained from Paraśurāma. Unable to endure these calamities, Karṇa waved his arms and began to rail at righteousness, saying, "They that are conversant with virtue say that righteousness protects the righteous! But today righteousness does not save me."

Speaking thus, he shed tears of wrath, and said to Arjuna, "O Pāṇḍava! Spare me for a moment while I extricate my wheel from the earth! You are on your car while I am standing weak and languid on the ground. It is not fair that you should slay me now! You are born in the Kṣatriya order. You are the scion of a high race. Recollect the teachings of righteousness, and give me a moment's time!"

Then, from Arjuna's chariot, Kṛṣṇa said, "It is fortunate, O Karṇa, that you now remember virtue. It is generally true that those who are mean rail at Providence when they are afflicted by distress, but forget their own misdeeds. You and Duryodhana and Duḥśāsana and Śakuni caused Draupadī, clad in a single garment, to be brought into the midst of the assembly. On that occasion, O Karṇa, this virtue of yours was not in evidence! When Śakuni, skilled in dicing, vanquished Yudhiṣṭhira who was unacquainted with it, where was this virtue of yours? Out of covetousness, and relying on Śakuni, you again summoned the Pāṇḍavas to a game of dice. Whither then had this virtue of yours gone?"

When Kṛṣṇa thus taunted Karṇa, Arjuna became filled with rage. Remem-

6. Celestial white elephant, mount of Indra, king of gods. 7. Fragrant sandalwood powder.
8. Garuḍa, the celestial eagle, is the enemy of snakes.

bering the incidents to which Kṛṣṇa alluded, he blazed with fury and, bent upon Karṇa's speedy destruction, took out of his quiver an excellent weapon. He then fixed on his bow that unrivaled arrow, and charged it with mantras. Drawing his bow Gāṇḍīva, he quickly said, "Let this shaft of mine be a mighty weapon capable of speedily destroying the body and heart of my enemy. If I have ever practiced ascetic austerities, gratified my preceptors, and listened to the counsels of well-wishers, let this sharp shaft, so long worshiped by me, slay my enemy Karṇa by that Truth!"

Having uttered these words, Arjuna discharged for the destruction of Karṇa, that terrible shaft, that blazing arrow fierce and efficacious as a rite prescribed in the Atharva of Aṅgiras,[9] and invincible against the god of Death himself in battle. Thus sped by that mighty warrior, the shaft endowed with the energy of the Sun caused all the points of the compass to blaze with light. The head of the commander of the Kaurava army, splendid as the Sun, fell like the Sun disappearing in the blood-red sunset behind the western hills. Cut off by Arjuna's arrow and deprived of life, the tall trunk of Karṇa, with blood gushing from every wound, fell down like the thunder-riven summit of a mountain of red chalk with crimson streams running down its sides after a shower of rain.

Then from the body of the fallen Karṇa a light, passing through the atmosphere, illumined the sky. This wonderful sight was seen by all the warriors on the battlefield. After the heroic Karṇa was thus thrown down and stretched on the earth, pierced with arrows and bathed in blood, Śalya, the king of the Madras, withdrew with Karṇa's car. The Kauravas, afflicted with fear, fled from the field, frequently looking back on Arjuna's lofty standard which blazed in splendor.

Summary Śalya is appointed Marshal of the Kaurava army on the eighteenth and last day of the war.

From *Book 9*

Śalya [*The Book of Śalya*]

71

After the fall of Ulūka and Śakuni, their followers were enraged. Prepared to sacrifice their lives in that fierce encounter, they began to oppose the Pāṇḍavas. Duryodhana too was filled with rage. Collecting his remaining chariots, still many hundreds in number, as well as his elephants, horses, and foot soldiers, he said these words to those warriors: "Kill the Pāṇḍavas with their friends and allies in this battle, and also the Pāñcāla prince with his own army. Then you may turn back from the field."

Respectfully obeying that mandate, the invincible warriors proceeded once more against the Pāṇḍavas. But because it had no leader, that army was destroyed in an instant by those great warriors the Pāṇḍavas. Thus all the eleven akṣauhiṇis[1] of troops which had been collected by Duryodhana were killed by the Pāṇḍavas and the Sṛñjayas.

9. The *Atharva Veda*, the fourth Veda, consisting mainly of magical spells, composed by the sage Aṅgiras.
1. Battalions.

Looking on all sides, Duryodhana saw the field empty, and himself deprived of all his troops. Meanwhile the Pāṇḍavas, greatly pleased at having attained all their objects, were roaring aloud in joy. Overcome by despair, and bereft of troops and animals, Duryodhana decided to flee from the field. Taking up his mace, he fled on foot towards a lake.

In Duryodhana's army, which had consisted of many hundreds of thousands of warriors, not one single car-warrior was alive, save Aśvatthāmā the heroic son of Droṇa, Kṛtavarmā, Kṛpa, and Duryodhana himself. Duryodhana said to Sañjaya, "Tell the blind king that his son Duryodhana has entered into the lake." He then entered the waters of the lake, which he charmed by his power of wizardry.

Then the old men, who had been engaged to look after the ladies of the royal household, started for the city, followed by the princesses, who wept aloud when they heard of the destruction of the whole army. After the flight of the royal ladies the Kaurava camp was entirely empty, except for the three car-warriors. Filled with anxiety, and hoping to rescue Duryodhana, they too proceeded towards the lake.

Meanwhile Yudhiṣṭhira and his brothers felt happy, and ranged over the field with the desire to kill Duryodhana. Though they searched carefully for him everywhere, they could not discover the Kuru king who, mace in hand, had fled quickly from the field of battle, entered the lake, and solidified the water by his magic.

Not seeing Duryodhana who had thus concealed himself, and wishing to put an end to that sinful man's evil courses, the Pāṇḍavas sent spies in all directions on the field of battle. Some hunters brought news of Duryodhana's whereabouts to Bhīma. Rewarding them with immense wealth, Bhīma disclosed this news to the righteous King Yudhiṣṭhira, saying, "Duryodhana, O king, has been found by the hunters who supply me with meat. He for whom you feel sorry now lies within a lake whose waters have been turned solid by him."

Thereupon, with Kṛṣṇa in the lead, Yudhiṣṭhira proceeded toward that lake, accompanied by Arjuna, the twins, Dhṛṣṭadyumna, the invincible Śikhaṇḍī, Uttamaujus, Yudhāmanyu, the great car-warrior Sātyaki, the five sons of Draupadī, and those amongst the Pāñcālas who had survived, with all their elephants, and infantry by the hundreds.

72

Having arrived at the banks of the Dvaipāyana lake, they saw the reservoir enchanted by Duryodhana. Then Yudhiṣṭhira said to Kṛṣṇa, "Behold, the son of Dhṛtarāṣṭra has charmed these waters by his power of wizardry, and lives within them, without fear of injury." Kṛṣṇa replied, "With your own power of wizardry, O Bhārata, destroy this illusion of Duryodhana."

Then Yudhiṣṭhira derisively said to Duryodhana, who was still within the waters of the lake, "Why, O Duryodhana, have you charmed these waters, after having caused the death of all the Kṣatriyas, as well as your own family? Why have you entered this lake today, in order to save your own life? Arise and fight us, O Suyodhana!"

From the depths of the lake, Duryodhana replied, "It was not for the sake of saving my life, nor from fear, nor from grief, that I entered this lake. It was only out of fatigue that I did so. The Kurus for whose sake I desired sovereignty, those brothers of mine, all lie dead on the battlefield. This empty earth is now yours. Who could wish to rule a kingdom bereft of allies? As for myself, clad in deerskins I shall retire to the forest. Friendless as I am, I have no desire to live."

"You may now be willing, O Suyodhana," said Yudhiṣṭhira, "to make a gift of the earth to me. However, I do not wish to rule the earth as a gift from you. Before this, you would not agree to give me even so much of the earth as could be covered by the point of a needle. Either rule the earth after having defeated us, or go to the celestial regions after being slain by us."

Duryodhana said, "You Pāṇḍavas have friends, cars, and animals. I, however, am alone now, without a car or a mount. Alone as I am, and devoid of weapons, how can I venture to fight on foot against countless foes, all well armed and having cars? O Yudhiṣṭhira, fight one at a time with me. It is not fair that one should be called upon to fight with many, especially when that one is without armor, tired and wounded, and devoid of both animals and troops."

Thus challenged, Yudhiṣṭhira replied, "Fight any one of us, choosing whatever weapon you like. The rest of us will remain spectators. I grant you also this other wish of yours, that if you kill any one of us, you shall then become king. Otherwise, you shall be killed, and go to heaven."

"Brave as you are," answered Duryodhana, "if you allow me the option of fighting only one of you, I choose to fight with this mace that I have in my hand. Let any of you who thinks that he is a match for me come forward and fight me on foot, armed with mace." So saying, Duryodhana emerged from the water and stood there, mace in hand, his limbs covered with blood.

At the conclusion of this parley Kṛṣṇa, worked up with wrath, said to Yudhiṣṭhira, "Planning to kill Bhīma, O king, Duryodhana has practiced with the mace upon a statue of iron for thirteen years. Except for Bhīma, I do not at this moment see any match for Duryodhana. However, Bhīma has not practiced as hard as Duryodhana. I do not see any man in the world today, nor even a god, who can defeat the mace-armed Duryodhana in battle. In a fair fight between Duryodhana and Bhīma, our victory will be in doubt because Duryodhana is powerful, practiced, and skillful."

Bhīma was, however, more confident. He said, "I shall surely kill Duryodhana in battle. I feel that the victory of the righteous Yudhiṣṭhira is certain. This mace of mine is one and a half times as heavy as Duryodhana's. Do not give way to anxiety. I dare to fight him, selecting the mace as the weapon. All of you, O Kṛṣṇa, witness this encounter!"

After Bhīma had said these words, Kṛṣṇa joyfully applauded him and said, "Thanks to you, O mighty Bhīma, the righteous King Yudhiṣṭhira will regain prosperity after achieving the destruction of all his foes. You should, however, always fight with care against Duryodhana. He is endowed with skill and strength and loves to fight."

When the fierce duel was about to start, and when all the great Pāṇḍavas had taken their seats, Balarāma[2] came there, having heard that a battle between those two heroes, both of whom were his disciples, was about to start. Seeing him, the Pāṇḍavas and Kṛṣṇa were filled with joy. They greeted him and saluted him with due rites. They then said to him, "Witness, O Rāma, the skill in battle of your two disciples."

2. Kṛṣṇa's brother, an expert mace fighter.

73

The duel then began. Duryodhana and Bhīma fought like two bulls attacking each other with their horns. The clash of their maces produced loud peals like those of thunderbolts. After the fierce and terrible battle had lasted for some time, both contenders were exhausted. They rested for some time and then, taking up their maces, they once again began to ward off each other's attacks.

While the fight was thus raging between those two heroes, Arjuna said to Kṛṣṇa, "Who, in your opinion, is the better of these two? What is their respective merit? Tell me this, O Kṛṣṇa!"

Kṛṣṇa replied, "They are equally well instructed. Bhīma is possessed of greater strength while Duryodhana has greater skill and has practiced harder. If he fights fairly, Bhīma will never succeed in gaining victory. If, however, he fights unfairly, he will surely be able to kill Duryodhana. At the time of the gambling Bhīma promised to break the thighs of Duryodhana with his mace in battle. Let him now fulfill his vow. Let him, by deception, kill the Kuru king who is the master of deception! If Bhīma does not kill him by unfair means, the son of Dhṛtarāṣṭra will surely retain the kingdom!"

Thereupon Arjuna, before Bhīma's sight, struck his own left thigh. Understanding that sign, Bhīma began to move about with his mace raised, making many kinds of maneuvers. Seeing the energetic and angry Bhīma rushing towards him and desiring to thwart his blow, Duryodhana thought of the maneuver called avasthāna, and prepared to jump upwards.

Bhīma fully understood the object of his opponent. Rushing at him, with a loud roar, he fiercely hurled his mace at Duryodhana's thighs, as the latter jumped into the air. The mace, hurled by Bhīma, broke the thighs of Duryodhana, and he fell down, so that the earth resounded.

Having struck Duryodhana down, Bhīma approached the Kuru chief and said, "O wretch, formerly you laughed at Draupadī who had only one bit of cloth in the midst of the assembly, and you called us cows. Bear now the consequences of that insult." Saying this, he kicked the head of his fallen foe with his left foot.[3]

Balarāma became highly incensed when he saw Duryodhana thus brought down by a blow aimed at his thighs. Raising his arms, he sorrowfully said in the midst of those kings, "Oh, fie on Bhīma, that in such a fair fight a blow should have been inflicted below the navel! Never before has such a foul blow been seen in an encounter with the mace!

"Having unfairly killed the righteous King Duryodhana," Balarāma continued, "Bhīma shall be known in the world as an unfair fighter! The righteous Duryodhana, on the other hand, shall acquire eternal blessedness!"

Kṛṣṇa then said to Yudhiṣṭhira, "O king of virtue, why do you permit such a wrong act? Why do you suffer the head of the insensible and fallen Duryodhana to be thus kicked by Bhīma with his foot? Conversant as you are with the rules of morality, why do you look on this deed with indifference?"

Yudhiṣṭhira said, "O Kṛṣṇa, Bhīma's action in angrily touching the head of the fallen king with his foot does not please me, nor am I glad at this extermination of my race! But remember how we were cheated by the sons of Dhṛtarāṣṭra! Remember too the many harsh words they addressed to us,

3. The left foot and hand have sinister associations.

and how they sent us in exile into the forest. On account of all those things Bhīma has been nursing a great grief in his heart! Bearing all this in mind, O Kṛṣṇa, I looked on his actions with indifference!"

* * *

From *Book 11*

Strī [*The Book of the Women*]

81

Having lost all his sons, King Dhṛtarāṣṭra was grief-stricken. Looking like a tree shorn of its branches, he was overcome by depression and lost his power of speech. The wise Sañjaya approached the king and said to him, "Why do you grieve, O monarch? Forget your sorrow, and arrange for the due performance of the obsequial rites of your fathers, sons, grandsons, kinsmen, preceptors, and friends."

Dhṛtarāṣṭra lamented, "Deprived as I am of sons and counselors and all my friends, I shall have to wander in sorrow over the earth. In the midst of the assembly, Kṛṣṇa told me what was for my good. He said, 'Let us end hostilities, O king! Let your son take the entire kingdom, except for five villages.' Foolishly I disregarded that advice, and I am now forced to repent. I must have committed great sins in my previous births, and hence the Creator has made me suffer such grief in this life. Ask the Pāṇḍavas to come and see me this very day, determined as I am upon following the long way that leads to the regions of Brahmā."

Though he too was grief-stricken because of the death of his own sons, Yudhiṣṭhira, accompanied by his brothers, set out to see Dhṛtarāṣṭra. He was followed by Kṛṣṇa and Sātyaki, and by Yuyutsu. The grieving princess Draupadī too, accompanied by the Pāñcāla ladies, sorrowfully followed.

Having duly saluted their sire, the Pāṇḍavas announced themselves to him, each uttering his own name. Dhṛtarāṣṭra first greeted the eldest son of Pāṇḍu, Yudhiṣṭhira, who was the cause of the slaughter of all his sons. Having embraced Yudhiṣṭhira, and spoken a few comforting words to him, the wicked Dhṛtarāṣṭra sought Bhīma, like a fire ready to burn everything that would approach it. Understanding his wicked intentions towards Bhīma, Kṛṣṇa dragged away the real Bhīma, and presented an iron statue of the second son of Pāṇḍu to the old king. Grasping with his two arms that iron statue, the powerful king broke it into pieces, taking it for the real Bhīma.

His passion gone, the king then cast off his anger and became normal. Overcome by grief, he began to weep aloud, "Alas, O Bhīma! Alas!" Knowing that he was no longer under the influence of anger, and that he was truly sorry for having, as he believed, slain Bhīma, Kṛṣṇa said, "Do not grieve, O Dhṛtarāṣṭra, for you have not killed Bhīma. What you broke was only an iron statue."

82

Then, at the request of Dhṛtarāṣṭra, the Pāṇḍava brothers, accompanied by Kṛṣṇa, went to see Gāndhārī. The innocent Gāndhārī was grief-stricken at the death of her hundred sons. Recalling that Yudhiṣṭhira had killed all his enemies, she wished to curse him. Knowing her evil intentions, Vyāsa prepared to keep them from being fulfilled.

He said to her, "Do not be angry with the Pāṇḍavas, O Gāndhārī! May you have peace! Control the words you are about to say! Listen to my counsel." Gāndhārī said, "Thanks to the folly of Duryodhana and Śakuni, of Karṇa and Duḥśāsana, this extinction of the Kurus has taken place. But in the very presence of Kṛṣṇa, Bhīma did something that excites my anger. Having challenged Duryodhana to a deadly duel with the mace, and knowing that my son was superior to him in skill, he struck him below the navel. It is this that provokes my wrath. Why should heroes forget their duties to save their lives?"

Hearing these words of Gāndhārī, Bhīma was afraid, and tried to soothe her. He said, "Whether the deed was fair or unfair, I did it through fear and to protect my own self! Please forgive me now! Your son was incapable of being killed by anybody in a fair fight. And therefore I did what was unfair."

Gāndhārī then said, "When Vṛṣasena had deprived Nakula of his horses, you drank Duḥśāsana's blood in battle. That was an act of cruelty which is censured by the good, becoming only to an unworthy person. It was an evil act, O Bhīma!"

"It is wrong to drink the blood of even a stranger," Bhīma replied. "One's brother is like one's own self, and there is no difference between them. The blood, however, did not pass my lips and teeth, as Karṇa knew well. Only my hands were covered with Duḥśāsana's blood. When Draupadī was seized by the hair after the gambling match, in my anger I gave vent to certain words which I still remember. For all the years to come I would have been deemed to have neglected the duties of a Kṣatriya if I had left that promise unfulfilled. It was for this reason, O queen, that I committed that act." Gāndhārī wailed, "You have killed a hundred sons of this old man [Dhṛtarāṣṭra]! Why did you not spare even one son of this old couple, deprived of their kingdom, who had committed only a minor offense?"

83

Filled with anger at the slaughter of all her sons and grandsons, Gāndhārī then inquired after Yudhiṣṭhira, saying, "Where is the king?" After she had asked for him, Yudhiṣṭhira approached her, trembling and with joined hands, and said these soft words, "Here is Yudhiṣṭhira, O queen, that cruel destroyer of your sons! I deserve your curses, for I am the real cause of this universal destruction! Curse me! I do not care for life, for kingdom, or for wealth, having killed such friends."

Sighing heavily, Gāndhārī could say nothing to Yudhiṣṭhira as, overcome with fear, he stood in her presence. When Yudhiṣṭhira, with body bent, was about to prostrate himself at her feet, the far-sighted Kuru queen, conversant as she was with righteousness, directed her eyes from within the folds of the cloth that covered them to the tip of Yudhiṣṭhira's toe. Thereupon, the king whose nails had till then been perfect came to have a scorched nail on his toe.[4]

Seeing this, Arjuna moved behind Kṛṣṇa, and the other Pāṇḍavas too became restless. Meanwhile Gāndhārī shook off her anger, and comforted

4. The queen's righteous anger has the power to reduce her sons' killer to ashes.

the Pāṇḍavas as a mother should. With her permission those heroes then proceeded to see their mother.

Seeing her sons after a long time, Kuntī, who had been filled with anxiety for them, covered her face with a fold of her garment and shed copious tears. She then repeatedly embraced and patted each of her sons. Next she consoled Draupadī who had lost all her children and who was lying on the bare earth, wailing piteously. Raising the grief-stricken princess of Pāñcāla who was weeping thus, Kuntī began to comfort her.

Accompanied by Draupadī, and followed by her sons, Kuntī then proceeded towards the sorrowful Gāndhārī, though she herself was in greater sorrow. Seeing that illustrious lady with her daughter-in-law, Gāndhārī said, "Do not grieve thus, O daughter. I too am much afflicted with grief. I think this universal destruction has been caused by the irresistible course of Time. Since it was not brought about by human agency, this dreadful slaughter was inevitable. What the wise Vidura foretold, after Kṛṣṇa's supplication for peace had failed, has now come to pass!"

Gāndhārī then said to Kṛṣṇa, "The Pāṇḍavas and the sons of Dhṛtarāṣṭra have destroyed each other. Why did you look on while they were thus exterminating each other? Because you were deliberately indifferent to their destruction, you shall obtain the fruit of this act. O Kṛṣṇa, by constant service to my husband I have acquired a little merit. By that merit, which was so difficult to obtain, I now curse you. Since you remained indifferent while the Kauravas and Pāṇḍavas slew each other, O Kṛṣṇa, you shall be the slayer of your own kinsmen. Thirty-six years hence you shall, after causing the death of your kinsmen, friends, and son, perish by ignoble means in the wilderness."[5]

From *Book 12*

Śānti [*The Book of Peace*]

84

Along with Vidura, Dhṛtarāṣṭra, and all the Bhārata ladies, the Pāṇḍavas offered oblations of water to all their departed kinsmen and friends. The noble descendants of the Kurus then passed a month of purification outside the city. Many famous sages came there to see the virtuous King Yudhiṣṭhira. Among them were Vyāsa, Nārada, the great sage Devala, Devasthāna, and Kaṇva, and their worthy disciples.

Yudhiṣṭhira said, "I am haunted by grief because of the death in battle of young Abhimanyu, the sons of Draupadī, Dhṛṣṭadyumna, Virāṭa, King Drupada, Vasuṣeṇa, King Dhṛṣṭaketu, and other kings coming from various countries. I feel that, through my desire to recover my kingdom, I caused the destruction of my kinsmen and the extermination of my own race. I am an evil-doer and a sinner and the cause of the destruction of the earth. Seated as I am now, I shall starve myself to death."

5. Gāndhārī's curse comes true, becoming the means by which the divine Kṛṣṇa ends his incarnation.

Vyāsa consoled Yudhiṣṭhira, saying, "You should not, O king, grieve so. I shall repeat what I have once said. All this is Destiny. Do what you have been created to do by your Maker. That is your fulfillment. Remember, O king, you are not your own master.

"O king, do not indulge in grief!" Vyāsa continued. "Remember the duties of a Kṣatriya. All those fighters were killed while performing their legitimate duties. You too have performed the duties of a Kṣatriya and obtained the kingdom blamelessly. Do your duty now, O son of Kuṅtī, and you shall obtain happiness in the next world." Thus was Yudhiṣṭhira comforted, and persuaded to return to his kingdom.

When the Pāṇḍavas reentered the city, many thousands of citizens came out to greet them. Entering the interior of the palace, the illustrious Yudhiṣṭhira approached the deities and worshiped them with offerings of gems and incense and garlands of all kinds.

Freed of his grief and his sickness of heart, Yudhiṣṭhira cheerfully sat facing eastward on an excellent seat made of gold. Those two heroes, Sātyaki and Kṛṣṇa, sat facing him on a seat covered by a rich carpet. On either side of the king sat the great-minded Bhīma and Arjuna upon two soft seats set with gems. Upon a white ivory couch, decked with gold, sat Kuṅtī with Sahadeva and Nakula.

Then by Kṛṣṇa's leave the priest Dhaumya consecrated, according to rule, an altar facing the east and the north. He next seated the great Yudhiṣṭhira and Draupadī upon a soft seat covered with a tiger-skin, called Sarvatobhadra. Thereafter he began to pour libations of clarified butter upon the sacrificial fire while chanting the prescribed incantations. King Dhṛtarāṣṭra was first to anoint Yudhiṣṭhira and all the others followed him. Thus worshiped by those pious men, Yudhiṣṭhira the king of virtue, with his friends, was restored to his kingdom.

Accepting the greetings of his subjects, King Yudhiṣṭhira answered them, saying: "Blessed are the sons of Pāṇḍu, whose merits, deservedly or otherwise, are thus recited in this world by the foremost of Brāhmaṇas assembled together. King Dhṛtarāṣṭra, however, is our father and supreme deity. Those who wish to please me should obey his commands and respect his every wish. The whole world is his, as are the Pāṇḍavas, and everybody else. These words of mine should be borne in mind by all of you."

Having given the citizens and the villagers leave to depart, the Kuru king appointed his brother Bhīma as yuvarāja.[6] He gladly appointed the highly intelligent Vidura to help him with advice and to look after the sixfold requirements[7] of the state. The venerable Sañjaya, wise and thoughtful and endued with every accomplishment, was designated as the superintendent of finances.

Nakula was placed in charge of the forces, to give them food and pay and to look after the other affairs of the army. Yudhiṣṭhira made Arjuna responsible for resisting hostile forces and punishing the wicked. Dhaumya, the foremost of priests, was asked to attend to the Brāhmaṇas and to perform all Vedic rites and all other rites. Sahadeva was always to remain by Yudhiṣṭhira's side, as his protector.

6. Crown prince. 7. Peace, war, military expeditions, cease-fire, instigating strife among enemies, and the defense of the kingdom.

THE JĀTAKA
fourth century B.C.

The *Jātaka* is a collection of 547 stories, the second part of the three-part *Tripiṭaka,* or (Three Baskets [of texts]), the primary canon of Buddhism. Like the rest of the *Tripiṭaka,* the *Jātaka* is in Pali, a north Indian dialect related to Sanskrit, which appears to have been the literary language of early Buddhism. *Jātaka* means "the story of a birth," and the *Jātakas* are stories, in a mixture of prose and verse, of the 550 lives through which Gautama Buddha is said to have passed before his birth as Prince Siddhārtha of the Śākya clan in northern India in 563 B.C. In his earlier births Gautama is said to have been a Bodhisattva, who in each life—born as animal, person, or god—moves a step closer to perfect wisdom, to becoming a Buddha (an "enlightened being"). *Bodhisattva* (from the Pali word *Bodhisatta*) is "a being destined to achieve enlightenment." For Buddhists the life of Gautama Buddha, like that of Jesus for Christians, is both extraordinary and exemplary, but in a religion whose goal is to overcome *karma* and rebirth through knowledge, that life is viewed as the culmination of exemplary acts performed and remembered throughout hundreds of births. The perennial appeal of the *Jātakas,* however, derives not only from their doctrinal importance, but from their being in reality popular folktales and fables adapted to a religious context.

The arrangement of the *Jātaka* as we have it today may have been made as late as the fourth century A.D., based on the text preserved by Sri Lankan Buddhist monks. Many *Jātakas,* however, are sculpted on the north Indian relic shrines (*stūpa*) of the Buddha at Bharhut and Sanchi (second century B.C. to first century A.D.), the earliest surviving Buddhist monuments in India, thus confirming the antiquity and importance of these tales in the tradition. From the very outset, Buddhism was a popular and a proselytizing religion, and both the Buddha and his disciples freely used familiar stories to attract the masses to whom they preached the new doctrine. Storytelling was also an integral part of ancient Indian culture in general, which placed great value on the spoken word as a medium for teaching.

To be sure, there is nothing intrinsically Buddhist about many of the tales, which appear in Hindu and Jain collections as well, all later than the *Jātaka.* These include the *Pañcatantra,* the most famous of them all. The stories *The Talkative Tortoise, The Ass in the Lion's Skin,* and *The Jackal and the Crow* are familiar to Western readers from beast fable collections in their own traditions, apparently acquired from Indian sources through early contacts among Indians, Greeks, Persians, Jews, and Arabs. Similarly, taken out of its religious context, the *Jātaka* of *The Cheating Merchant* is no more than a tale of a clever man who outwits a crook. Other *Jātaka* tales, however, have a uniquely Buddhist flavor. In the *Jātakas* about the hare and about the king of the monkeys the principal actors are animals, but heroic and magnanimous animals who abundantly display the characteristic virtues of a Buddha-to-be. So does the self-sacrificing hero of the very popular Vessantara *Jātaka,* which in 785 verses alternating with prose treats the Bodhisattva's career as the good prince Vessantara. Both types of story retain elements of their folkloric origins; the hare *Jātaka* is obviously a Buddhist adaptation of the Indian folktale of how the moon got its pattern of markings, which Indians believe to be the figure of a hare.

The figure of the Buddha links these tales that were originally so disparate in milieu and intent. Each tale opens with the Buddha in conversation with his monks or lay followers. A question from one of them brings to the teacher's mind a story of the past (that is, of one of his past lives as a Bodhisattva), which he then relates to illustrate a point of conduct. This is the main narrative, with its most dramatic moments highlighted by one or more verses (*gāthā*), spoken by a character or characters within it. At the end, the Buddha comments on his role as the Bodhisattva hero of the tale. This rebirth theme, together with the specifically Buddhist ideals of conduct expounded, mark the story as a *jātaka.*

It is not clear that each of the 547 stories was originally tied to particular virtues, but from early on the *Jātakas* became associated with the "six perfections" (*pāramitā*) of the Bodhisattva—generosity, rectitude, patience, vigorous effort, meditation, and wisdom—and it is as illustrations of these perfections that they have been interpreted. Perhaps the best of these interpretations is Āryaśūra's *Jātakamālā* (ca. fourth century A.D.), a classical Sanskrit poem that recounts 35 *Jātaka* stories, which became an authoritative source for Chinese, Japanese, and Tibetan Buddhists.

Comparing *Jātaka* tales featuring animals with their counterparts in the *Pañcatantra* reveals how different the *Jātakas* are from Hindu tales in their preoccupation with *karma* and how differently the two traditions use animals as symbols of human character traits. The *Jātakas* of the hare and the monkey king show the Bodhisattva as idealized animal. The Buddhist learns the perfection of giving by studying the heroic and utterly selfless acts of the monkey king and hare, who give up their own lives for others. Not all the characters in the stories are thus idealized. Shades of "human" weakness and villainy loom large in the greed and deception of the hare's animal friends, in the human king's gluttony, and in the jealousy of the monkey who breaks the monkey king's back (identified as Gautama Buddha's evil cousin Devadatta, in a previous birth). The ultimate lesson, however, is clear: the only virtuous action is that which is free of violence and is motivated by an ardent desire for the welfare of others, even if it causes great suffering to oneself. In the Buddhist doctrine utterly selfless acts and attitudes are a crucial component of the path to enlightenment and thus to liberation from the cycle of birth and death.

The moral emphasis of the *Jātakas* is balanced throughout by their lively spirit and their loving attention to the detail of everyday life, social customs, and human and animal traits—qualities that almost overshadow the "moral" in such tales as *The Cheating Merchant.* Audience interest is enhanced by vivid descriptions of the lives of animals of forest and field and encounters with men and women of all social classes and occupations: queens, merchants, goldsmiths, weavers. Typical touches of realism enliven the description of the field guard's evening meal in *The Hare's Self-Sacrifice:* "A lizard and a jar of curds, . . . two spits of roasted flesh," and likewise the monkey king's failure to reach the tree because he forgets to factor in the bamboo shoot tied around his waist. We also learn much about the hospitality to older beliefs that made Buddhism attractive to the common people. The role of the tree sprite in the story of the merchant and the worship of the deceased monkey king corroborate what we know from Buddhist art, that nature cults played an important part in popular Buddhism, as did the worship of Vedic gods such as Sakka (another name for Iṅdra, king of the gods), who appear in the stories. The *Jātaka* of the monkey king also strikes a populist note as an exemplum for Buddhist rulers.

As Buddhism spread, the *Jātakas* spread with it to become a part of the literature, art, and culture of Sri Lanka, Burma, Tibet, China, Japan, Java, and other countries in east and Southeast Asia. Many of the fables in Aesop (of which the version we now have dates to no earlier than the fourteenth century) and some of the tales in the *Arabian Nights,* La Fontaine, Boccaccio, and Chaucer appear to be based on earlier Indian models, passed on to west Asia and Europe through translations into many languages, including Hebrew, Arabic, and Greek. Because versions of *Jātaka* stories also appear in Hindu and Jain collections, it is not always possible to trace a tale back to a particular Indian source. It is certain, however, that the popular medieval religious romance *Barlaam and Joasaph* (or *Josaphat*)—which exists in many European languages and derives from a Greek work of the same name by St. John of Damascus, a Christian monk of the eighth century—is a story of the Bodhisattva, that name transformed into "Joasaph" and "Josaphat" in transcription from one language to another. Fascinating windows into Buddhist thought and ancient Indian society, the *Jātakas* have also contributed greatly to India's rich legacy of stories to world literature.

A complete translation of the *Jātaka* is available in six volumes edited by E. B. Cowell, *The Jātaka: Or Stories of the Buddha's Former Births* (1981). H. T. Francis and E. J. Thomas offer a selection in *Jātaka Tales* (1956). M. Cummings, *The Lives of the Buddha in the Art and Literature of Asia* (1982), is an excellent introduction to the best-known *Jātakas* in the art and literature of Asia, from Afghanistan to China. For accounts of the fascinating tale of the transmission of the *Jātakas* to Europe readers may turn to T. W. Rhys Davids's introduction to *Buddhist Birth Stories, the Story of the Lineage (Nidāna-kathā)* (1880). The Sanskrit *Jātakamālā* has been beautifully rendered by Peter Khoroche in *Once the Buddha Was a Monkey: Āryaśūra's Jātakamālā* (1989).

PRONOUNCING GLOSSARY

The following list uses common English syllables and stress accents to provide rough equivalents of selected words whose pronunciation may be unfamiliar to the general reader.

Bodhisatta: *boh-dee-suht'-tuh*

Bodhisattva: *boh-dee-sut'-tvuh*

Devadatta: *day'-vuh-duht-tuh*

Jātaka: *jah'-tuh-kuh*

Pañcatantra: *puhn'-chuh-tuhn'-truh*

Śākya: *shah'-kee-yuh*

The Jātaka

The Cheating Merchant[1]

Once on a time when Brahmadatta was reigning in Benares,[2] the Bodhisatta[3] was born into a merchant's family and on name-day was named "Wise." When he grew up he entered into partnership with another merchant named "Wisest," and traded with him. And these two took five hundred waggons of merchandise from Benares to the country-districts, where they disposed of their wares, returning afterwards with the proceeds to the city. When the time for dividing came, Wisest said, "I must have a double share." "Why so?" asked Wise. "Because while you are only Wise, I am Wisest. And Wise ought to have only one share to Wisest's two." "But we both had an equal interest in the stock-in-trade and in the oxen and waggons. Why should you have two shares?" "Because I am Wisest." And so they talked away till they fell to quarrelling.

"Ah!" thought Wisest, "I have a plan." And he made his father hide in a hollow tree, enjoining the old man to say, when the two came, "Wisest should have a double portion." This arranged, he went to the Bodhisatta and proposed to him to refer the claim for a double share to the competent decision of the Tree-Sprite.[4] Then he made his appeal in these words: "Lord

1. Translated by E. B. Cowell. 2. Many *Jātaka* tales begin with this phrase. We do not know of any historical king by the name Brahmadatta. Because Benares is the place where Gautama Buddha preached his first sermon (the "Deer-Park Sermon") and as it is situated on the sacred river Ganges, it is the great holy city of the Hindus. 3. "A being on the path to enlightenment," or a Buddha-to-be; more commonly known by the Sanskrit equivalent Bodhisattva. In the *Jātaka* the term always connotes Gautama Buddha in one of his previous incarnations. 4. One of the many demigods whose worship was absorbed into early Buddhism from popular cults of tree worship (male and female tree deities are abundantly represented in early Buddhist art).

Tree-Sprite, decide our cause!" Hereupon the father, who was hidden in the tree, in a changed voice asked them to state the case. The cheat addressed the tree as follows: "Lord, here stands Wise, and here stand I Wisest. We have been partners in trade. Declare what share each should receive."

"Wise should receive one share, and Wisest two," was the response.

Hearing this decision, the Bodhisatta resolved to find out whether it was indeed a Tree-Sprite or not. So he filled the hollow trunk with straw and set it on fire. And Wisest's father was half roasted by the rising flames and clambered up by clutching hold of a bough. Falling to the ground, he uttered this stanza:—

> Wise rightly, Wisest wrongly got his name;
> Through Wisest, I'm nigh roasted in the flame.

Then the two merchants made an equal division and each took half, and at their deaths passed away to fare according to their deserts.

"Thus you see," said the Master, "that your partner was as great a cheat in past times as now." Having ended his story, he identified the Birth by saying, "The cheating merchant of to-day was the cheating merchant in the story, and I the honest merchant named Wise."

The Hare's Self-Sacrifice[1]

Once upon a time when Brahmadatta was reigning in Benares, the Bodhisatta came to life as a young hare and lived in a wood. On one side of this wood was the foot of a mountain, on another side a river, and on the third side a border-village. The hare had three friends—a monkey, a jackal and an otter. These four wise creatures lived together and each of them got his food on his own hunting-ground, and in the evening they again came together. The hare in his wisdom by way of admonition preached the Truth[2] to his three companions, teaching that alms are to be given, the moral law to be observed, and holy days to be kept. They accepted his admonition and went each to his own part of the jungle and dwelt there.

And so in the course of time the Bodhisatta one day observing the sky, and looking at the moon knew that the next day would be a fast-day,[3] and addressing his three companions he said, "To-morrow is a fast-day. Let all three of you take upon you the moral precepts, and observe the holy day. To one that stands fast in moral practice, almsgiving brings a great reward. Therefore feed any beggars[4] that come to you by giving them food from your own table." They readily assented, and abode each in his own place of dwelling.

On the morrow quite early in the morning, the otter sallied forth to seek

1. Translated by H. T. Francis and E. J. Thomas. 2. Most likely an early version of the moral law that the Buddha systematized in his doctrine of Four Noble Truths. 3. In the lunisolar calendar followed by Buddhism, Hinduism, and Jainism, some days, corresponding to particular phases of the moon, are set aside for keeping fasts. 4. Begging is part of the vow of poverty observed by Buddhist monks and many Hindu ascetics.

his prey and went down to the bank of the Ganges. Now it came to pass that a fisherman had landed seven red fish, and stringing them together on a withe, he had taken and buried them in the sand on the river's bank. And then he dropped down the stream, catching more fish. The otter, scenting the buried fish, dug up the sand till he came upon them, and pulling them out cried thrice, "Does anyone own these fish?" And not seeing any owner he took hold of the withe with his teeth and laid the fish in the jungle where he dwelt, intending to eat them at a fitting time. And then he lay down, thinking how virtuous he was! The jackal too sallied forth in quest of food and found in the hut of a field-watcher two spits, a lizard and a pot of milk-curd. And after thrice crying aloud, "To whom do these belong?" and not finding an owner, he put on his neck the rope for lifting the pot, and grasping the spits and the lizard with his teeth, he brought and laid them in his own lair, thinking, "In due season I will devour them," and so lay down, reflecting how virtuous he had been.

The monkey also entered the clump of trees, and gathering a bunch of mangoes laid them up in his part of the jungle, meaning to eat them in due season, and then lay down, thinking how virtuous he was. But the Bodhisatta in due time came out, intending to browse on the kusa-grass,[5] and as he lay in the jungle, the thought occurred to him, "It is impossible for me to offer grass to any beggars that may chance to appear, and I have no sesame, rice, and such like. If any beggar shall appeal to me, I shall have to give him my own flesh to eat." At this splendid display of virtue, Sakka's[6] white marble throne manifested signs of heat. Sakka on reflection discovered the cause and resolved to put this royal hare to the test. First of all he went and stood by the otter's dwelling-place, disguised as a brahmin, and being asked why he stood there, he replied, "Wise Sir, if I could get something to eat, after keeping the fast, I would perform all my ascetic duties." The otter replied, "Very well, I will give you some food," and as he conversed with him he repeated the first stanza:[7]

Seven red fish I safely brought to land from Ganges flood,
O brahmin, eat thy fill, I pray, and stay within this wood.

The brahmin said, "Let be till to-morrow. I will see to it by and by." Next he went to the jackal, and when asked by him why he stood there, he made the same answer. The jackal, too, readily promised him some food, and in talking with him repeated the second stanza:

A lizard and a jar of curds, the keeper's evening meal,
Two spits of roasted flesh withal I wrongfully did steal:
Such as I have I give to thee: O brahmin, eat, I pray,
If thou shouldst deign within this wood a while with us to stay.

5. Used in Hindu rituals. 6. Indra, king of gods, who rewards those who display extraordinary virtue. 7. The traditional stanza known as *gāthā*. The formula by which the stanzas are introduced shows that they were meant to be memorized. The Pali stanzas in the *Jātaka* tales are very old, stylistically more archaic than the stanzas of the Hindu epics, and seem to have been used by monks as keys to memorize and summarize the tales.

Said the brahmin, "Let be till to-morrow. I will see to it by and by." Then he went to the monkey, and when asked what he meant by standing there, he answered just as before. The monkey readily offered him some food, and in conversing with him gave utterance to the third stanza:

An icy stream, a mango ripe, and pleasant greenwood shade,
'Tis thine to enjoy, if thou canst dwell content in forest glade.

Said the brahmin, "Let be till to-morrow. I will see it by and by." And he went to the wise hare, and on being asked by him why he stood there, he made the same reply. The Bodhisatta on hearing what he wanted was highly delighted, and said, "Brahmin, you have done well in coming to me for food. This day will I grant you a boon that I have never granted before, but you shall not break the moral law by taking animal life.[8] Go, friend, and when you have piled together logs of wood, and kindled a fire, come and let me know, and I will sacrifice myself by falling into the midst of the flames, and when my body is roasted, you shall eat my flesh and fulfil all your ascetic duties." And in thus addressing him the hare uttered the fourth stanza:

Nor sesame, nor beans, nor rice have I as food to give,
But roast with fire my flesh I yield, if thou with us wouldst live.

Sakka, on hearing what he said, by his miraculous power caused a heap of burning coals to appear, and came and told the Bodhisatta. Rising from his bed of kusa-grass and coming to the place, he thrice shook himself that if there were any insects within his coat, they might escape death. Then offering his whole body as a free gift he sprang up, and like a royal swan, alighting on a cluster of lotuses, in an ecstasy of joy he fell on the heap of live coals. But the flame failed even to heat the pores of the hair on the body of the Bodhisatta, and it was as if he had entered a region of frost. Then he addressed Sakka in these words: "Brahmin, the fire you have kindled is icy-cold: it fails to heat even the pores of the hair on my body. What is the meaning of this?" "Wise Sir," he replied, "I am no brahmin. I am Sakka, and I have come to put your virtue to the test." The Bodhisatta said, "If not only thou, Sakka, but all the inhabitants of the world were to try me in this matter of almsgiving, they would not find in me any unwillingness to give," and with this the Bodhisatta uttered a cry of exultation like a lion roaring. Then said Sakka to the Bodhisatta, "O wise hare, be thy virtue known throughout a whole aeon."[9] And squeezing the mountain, with the essence thus extracted, he daubed the sign of a hare on the orb of the moon.[1] And after depositing the hare on a bed of young kusa-grass, in the same wooded part of the jungle, Sakka returned to his own place in heaven. And these four wise creatures dwelt happily and harmoniously together, fulfilling the moral law and observing holy days, till they departed to fare according to their deeds.

8. According to the Buddha, the taking of life results in evil *karma;* therefore, he stressed extreme nonviolence. 9. A unit of cosmic time, consisting of a thousand cycles of four ages. 1. Throughout India the markings on the moon are recognized as being in the shape of a hare, and this *Jātaka* is one of the tales that explains its origin. Folklorists have discovered legends about a hare on the moon among other peoples, including the Kalmuks, the Hottentots, and some native American groups.

The Monkey's Heroic Self-Sacrifice[1]

Once upon a time when Brahmadatta was reigning in Benares, the Bodhisatta was born as a monkey.[2] When he grew up and attained stature and stoutness, he was strong and vigorous, and lived in the Himalaya with a retinue of eighty thousand[3] monkeys. Near the Ganges bank there was a mango tree (others say it was a banyan), with branches and forks, having a deep shade and thick leaves, like a mountain-top.[4] Its sweet fruits, of divine fragrance and flavour, were as large as water-pots: from one branch the fruits fell on the ground, from one into the Ganges water, from two into the main trunk of the tree. The Bodhisatta, while eating the fruit with a troop of monkeys, thought, "Someday danger will come upon us owing to the fruit of this tree falling on the water"; and so, not to leave one fruit on the branch which grew over the water, he made them eat or throw down the flowers at their season from the time they were of the size of a chick-pea. But notwithstanding, one ripe fruit, unseen by the eighty thousand monkeys, hidden by an ant's nest, fell into the river, and stuck in the net above the king of Benares who was bathing for amusement with a net above him and another below. When the king had amused himself all day and was going away in the evening, the fishermen, who were drawing the net, saw the fruit and not knowing what it was, shewed it to the king. The king asked, "What is this fruit?" "We do not know, sire." "Who will know?" "The foresters, sire." He had the foresters called, and learning from them that it was a mango, he cut it with a knife, and first making the foresters eat of it, he ate of it himself and had some of it given to his seraglio and his ministers. The flavour of the ripe mango remained, pervading the king's whole body. Possessed by desire[5] of the flavour, he asked the foresters where that tree stood, and hearing that it was on a river bank in the Himalaya quarter, he had many rafts joined together and sailed upstream by the route shewn by the foresters. The exact account of days is not given. In due course they came to the place, and the foresters said to the king, "Sire, there is the tree." The king stopped the rafts and went on foot with a great retinue, and having a bed prepared at the foot of the tree, he lay down after eating the mango fruit and enjoying the various excellent flavours. At every side they set a guard and made a fire. When the men had fallen asleep, the Bodhisatta came at midnight with his retinue. Eighty thousand monkeys moving from branch to branch ate the mangoes. The king, waking and seeing the herd of monkeys, roused his men and calling his archers said, "Surround these monkeys that eat the mangoes so that they may not escape, and shoot them: to-morrow we will eat mangoes with monkey's flesh." The archers obeyed, saying, "Very well," and surrounding the tree stood with arrows ready. The monkeys seeing them and fearing death, as they could not escape, came to the Bodhisatta and said, "Sire, the archers stand round the tree, saying, 'We will shoot those vagrant monkeys': what

1. Translated by H. T. Francis and E. J. Thomas. 2. As demonstrated by the role of Hanumān, Rāma's monkey helper in the *Rāmāyaṇa*, monkeys are beloved characters in Indian folklore; there are several *Jātaka*s about the Bodhisattva's births as a monkey. 3. A large number or a multitude. 4. The tree is gigantic. A banyan tree (a kind of fig tree with spreading aerial roots) of that size would have made a suitable home for a large monkey troop, but its fruit hardly compares with the sweet mango, the allure of which is a crucial point in this tale. 5. Identified as the root cause of existential suffering.

are we to do?" and so stood shivering. The Bodhisatta said, "Do not fear, I will give you life"; and so comforting the herd of monkeys, he ascended a branch that rose up straight, went along another branch that stretched towards the Ganges, and springing from the end of it, he passed a hundred bow-lengths and lighted on a bush on the bank. Coming down, he marked the distance, saying, "That will be the distance I have come": and cutting a bamboo shoot at the root and stripping it, he said, "So much will be fastened to the tree, and so much will stay in the air," and so reckoned the two lengths, forgetting the part fastened on his own waist. Taking the shoot he fastened one end of it to the tree on the Ganges bank and the other to his own waist, and then cleared the space of a hundred bow-lengths with a speed of a cloud torn by the wind. From not reckoning the part fastened to his waist, he failed to reach the tree: so seizing a branch firmly with both hands he gave signal to the troop of monkeys, "Go quickly with good luck, treading on my back along the bamboo shoot." The eighty thousand monkeys escaped thus, after saluting the Bodhisatta and getting his leave. Devadatta[6] was then a monkey and among that herd: he said, "This is a chance for me to see the last of my enemy," so climbing up a branch he made a spring and fell on the Bodhisatta's back. The Bodhisatta's back broke and great pain came on him. Devadatta having caused that maddening pain went away: and the Bodhisatta was alone. The king being awake saw all that was done by the monkeys and the Bodhisatta: and he lay down thinking, "This animal, not reckoning his own life, has caused the safety of his troop." When day broke, being pleased with the Bodhisatta, he thought, "It is not right to destroy this king of the monkeys: I will bring him down by some means and take care of him": So turning the raft down the Ganges and building a platform there, he made the Bodhisatta come down gently, and had him clothed with a yellow robe on his back and washed in Ganges water, made him drink sugared water, and had his body cleansed and anointed with oil refined a thousand times; then he put an oiled skin on a bed and making him lie there, he set himself, on a low seat, and spoke the first stanza:

You made yourself a bridge for them to pass in safety through:
What are you then to them, monkey, and what are they to you?

Hearing him, the Bodhisatta instructing the king spoke the other stanzas:

Victorious king, I guard the herd, I am their lord and chief,
When they were filled with fear of thee and stricken sore with grief.

I leapt a hundred times the length of bow outstretched that lies,
When I had bound a bamboo-shoot firmly around my thighs:

I reached the tree like thunder-cloud sped by the tempest's blast;
I lost my strength, but reached a bough: with hands I held it fast.

And as I hung extended there held fast by shoot and bough,
My monkeys passed across my back and are in safety now.

Therefore I fear no pain of death, bonds do not give me pain,
The happiness of those was won o'er whom I used to reign.

6. Gautama Buddha's evil cousin, who appears in many *Jātakas*.

A parable for thee, O king, if thou the truth would'st read:
The happiness of kingdom and of army and of steed
And city must be dear to thee, if thou would'st rule indeed.

The Bodhisatta, thus instructing and teaching the king, died. The king, calling his ministers, gave orders that the monkey-king should have obsequies like a king, and he sent to the seraglio, saying, "Come to the cemetery, as retinue for the monkey-king, with red garments, and dishevelled hair, and torches in your hands." The ministers made a funeral pile with a hundred waggon loads of timber. Having prepared the Bodhisatta's obsequies in a royal manner, they took his skull, and came to the king. The king caused a shrine to be built at the Bodhisatta's burial-place, torches to be burnt there and offerings of incense and flowers to be made; he had the skull inlaid with gold, and put in front raised on a spearpoint: honouring it with incense and flowers, he put it at the king's gate when he came to Benares, and having the whole city decked out he paid honour to it for seven days. Then taking it as a relic and raising a shrine, he honoured it with incense and garlands all his life; and established in the Bodhisatta's teaching he did alms and other good deeds, and ruling his kingdom righteously became destined for heaven.

THE BHAGAVAD-GĪTĀ
first century B.C.

The Sanskrit poem *Bhagavad-Gītā* (Song of the Lord) has been for centuries the great scripture of the Hindus and the Indian text most familiar to the West. The American writer Henry David Thoreau (1817–1862) took the *Gītā* with him to his retreat on Walden Pond, and the *Gītā* was the inspiring force in the life and thought of the eminent modern Indian leader Mahatma Gandhi (1869–1948). The enduring and seemingly universal appeal of this philosophical poem written in India two thousand years ago derives from the powerful, immediate way in which it addresses fundamental human concerns.

The *Bhagavad-Gītā* is a poem in eighteen chapters (and seven hundred verses), forming part of the sixth book of the Sanskrit epic the *Mahābhārata* (p. 953), which narrates the story of a great war between the virtuous Pāṇḍavas and their evil cousins, the Kauravas, sons of King Dhṛtarāṣṭra of Hāstinapura. The *Gītā* opens at a dramatic moment in the epic narrative, with the blind Kaurava king asking the bard Sanjaya to describe to him what his sons and their enemies did after gathering at the battlefield of Kurukṣetra. The bard reports the reactions of Arjuna, champion among the Pāṇḍava heroes, and the ensuing dialogue between him and his charioteer Krishna (or Kṛṣṇa). Arriving at the battlefield, Arjuna sees cousins, teachers, uncles, and kinsmen standing ready to fight against each other. Horrified at the prospect of killing his kin and overcome by dejection, he lays down his weapons and refuses to fight. But Krishna, who is in reality an incarnation of Viṣṇu (the preserver god), tells Arjuna that his sacred duty (*dharma*) requires him to fight and explains to him how, far from miring him in the dreaded cycle of *karma* and rebirth, action performed in the spirit of sacred duty will advance him on the path to emancipation of the spirit, the Hindu's ultimate religious goal. Krishna's discourse, punctuated by Arjuna's questions, becomes *The Song of the Lord* (*Bhagavad-Gītā*).

There is reason to believe that the *Gītā,* originally an independent philosophical dialogue similar to earlier and contemporary texts such as the *Upaniṣads* and the Buddhist scriptures, was deliberately placed in the popular *Mahābhārata* epic at the beginning of the tale of the great war to give dramatic force to its teachings and underscore its relevance to the lives of common people. Although also an exalted hero, at this point in the narrative Arjuna is a vulnerable human being caught in a very human dilemma. Krishna, on the other hand, is no ordinary teacher, but God, come to instruct his human friend. This new configuration of elements fortified a view that was at once revolutionary for its time (ca. first century A.D.) and designed to preserve the Hindu social hierarchy.

By the end of the first century B.C. the Buddhist and Jain religions had gained a considerable following among the Indian masses and among kings and merchants as well. Focusing on the problem of *karma*—the belief that all actions involve inevitable consequences that must be suffered through many lives—Buddhism in particular offered men and women from all walks of life a religious path on which ethical action could be combined with contemplative spiritual practices, eventually leading to liberation from the burden of *karma*. In the Hindu social order, on the other hand, rigid and hierarchical correlations between birth and occupation locked people into existential situations that held no such prospect of ultimate freedom.

Arjuna's dilemma is a dramatic illustration of the problem: how can a Hindu warrior (*kṣatriya*), whose sacred duty *(dharma)* involves the taking of life (which, by an absolute standard, would entail evil *karma*), ever be liberated from rebirth, which is the ultimate goal of the religious person? The *Gītā* appears to have been the response of brahman thinkers who stood to lose the most from the potential disintegration of the Hindu social system. Through Krishna's teachings, the anonymous author of the *Gītā* articulates a new doctrine that will justify the hierarchies of class and social duty (he uses the word *lokasaṃgraha,* "social solidarity") at the same time that it offers universal access to the ultimate goal of the emancipation of the soul from suffering and rebirth, thus answering the personal spiritual needs of Hindus from resistant and disenfranchised groups.

The *Gītā* owes its success to the attractive and ingenious way in which it harmonizes widely differing strands of ancient Indian religious thought and practice. The text synthesizes the contemplative vision of the Buddhists and the sages of the *Upaniṣads* with a philosophy of active engagement in worldly life. Krishna's teachings allow each Hindu to venture on a personal spiritual quest without abandoning social responsibility and its attendant security. Drawing on all of the older religious sects and schools of philosophy, the *Gītā* has accommodated radically different interpretations through the centuries. But the author's stroke of genius is without question his integration of a new teaching of salvation through divine grace, linked to the cult of a popular god, with the older theory of *karma.*

The *Gītā* is a complex text, weaving together as it does ancient, often contradictory ideas regarding existential questions that have preoccupied Indians for centuries. The poet uses the rhetorical device of Arjuna's doubts to repeat and consolidate previous arguments or to reject them as no longer useful, in what is essentially a technique of progressive illumination. In response to Arjuna's anguish at being unable to reconcile the conflict between sacred duty and the personal desire for liberation, Krishna explains to him the real nature of the soul and of action in the universe. He tells the hero that the soul (*ātman,* "the individual self") is not simply the ego but is in reality identical with Brahman, the immortal spirit underlying the entire universe. The knowledge of the soul's immortality, says Krishna, will dispel Arjuna's fear that he is personally responsible for particular actions. For the philosopher-teachers of the *Upaniṣads,* who propounded the theory of an immortal soul, this knowledge (*jñāna*) is the highest end of religious life, but for Krishna it is only a discipline (*yoga*), the first step toward liberation from birth and death.

If the soul is immortal, then Arjuna wants to know why it is involved in action, which inevitably causes rebirth. Adapting aspects of the doctrine of the Sāṃkhya philosophy, Krishna explains the riddle of an immortal soul's engagement in worldly action and a material universe. The perpetual action of all things with and on each other that constitutes the world process is an aspect of the union between God, who is the supreme embodiment of the immortal soul, and material nature, which is the substance of the universe. Action or change is an inescapable reality of living in the world; although the soul is immortal, in its embodied condition it is inevitably involved in deeds. God is himself engaged in the perpetual process of the world on which depend the cosmic, moral, and social orders, constituting *dharma* in its broadest sense. To withdraw from action, says Krishna, is thus an act of self-delusion and the abdication of moral and social responsibility.

This explanation only increases Arjuna's perplexity. If action is inevitable, how can the soul ever cease to be embodied (reborn)? Here Krishna turns to the Yoga philosophy, which propounds the doctrine of *yoga* ("a yoking"), the disciplining of the senses and the mind as the soul's path to transcendence over matter. Moving beyond the thought of traditional Yoga philosophers, he offers the new teaching of *karma yoga* (the "discipline of action") as the solution to Arjuna's problem. It is not action itself but desire for the fruit (profit or reward) of action that results in rebirth. If a person were to discipline his (the *Gītā*'s descriptions are all in the masculine gender) senses and mind to act with no desire whatsoever for the gains that will result, *karma* would not affect his soul. A person who acts in this disciplined way is the perfected *yogi* ("man of discipline"), and his soul is certain to be liberated from birth and death.

But how, then, does one know right action from wrong? The Hindu social order of *dharma,* based on cosmic and moral principles, relieves individuals of the responsibility of determining the content of action: right, or good, action is simply the sacred duty that has been prescribed for one's class, caste, and stage of life. In short, social and moral law takes care of the content of action, but the individual has control over the spirit in which he performs action and, therefore, over how his deeds will affect his soul. When acting in the world is transformed into *yoga,* a key concept in the *Gītā,* it becomes the very means for the soul's liberation from worldly existence.

Intriguing as Krishna's teachings are, they are still philosophical discourses whose greatest appeal is to the intellect. What drives the doctrine home for the majority of Hindus is the emotional power of Arjuna's vision of Krishna's omnipotent form as God, the theophany with which the teaching is clinched. At Arjuna's request, Krishna reveals to him his infinite form, showing himself as the source and refuge of all creatures and the entire universe and, as "time grown old," their destroyer as well. Profoundly moved, Arjuna sings a hymn to Krishna, but he is eventually overcome by terror and awe and begs Krishna to resume his familiar, gentle form once more.

In Chapter 11 and elsewhere, the *Gītā* draws on the theology of the Bhagavatas—a group who worshiped Krishna as God and an incarnation of Viṣṇu—and develops the doctrine of *bhakti yoga,* the discipline of devotion. Recognizing God's grace and love in Krishna's earlier discourse as much as in the cosmic vision, Arjuna is at last ready to accept this final teaching, according to which the best way to overcome worldly desire is to make of all one's deeds a loving sacrifice to God. Krishna asserts that love of God will annul the power of desire and, therefore, of *karma,* but what is equally important is that the discipline of sacred duty will become a joyous, transfiguring experience. In his revelation of himself as God, Krishna declares, "If they rely on me, Arjuna, / women, commoners, men of low rank, / even men born in the womb of evil, / reach the highest way." And as if to illustrate this transition from duty to joy, the author of the *Bhagavad-Gītā* gives his auditors and readers not a dry philosophical tract but a poem in which the simple epic stanzas—in the *śloka* (pp. 893–94) and *triṣṭubh* (pp. 957–58) meters—acquire an elegant, epigrammatic quality rendered memorable by vivid metaphors such as the one of the yogi who "does not waver, / like a lamp sheltered from the wind" and the likening of the brilliance of Krishna's divine epiphany to "the light of a thousand suns" rising in the sky at once.

Thoreau is only one among many Western thinkers who have found the *Gītā* ideal of the man of spiritual discipline (*yogi*) attractive. For Indian intellectuals in the late nineteenth century the work had an additional dimension. It was in response to Western education and Western critiques of Hinduism and Indian civilization under British colonial rule that Indian leaders from a very wide range of philosophies—from Swami Vivekananda (1863–1902) to Mahatma Gandhi—found the ideal text for India and the twentieth century in the *Bhagavad-Gītā*.

Much Western writing of the nineteenth century depicts Indians as a passive people with no social consciousness, attributing these shortcomings in part to the lack of a universal scripture and ethical code in Hinduism. Modern Indian leaders have found in the moral teaching of the *Gītā* and its spirit of pluralism and synthesis their greatest inspiration for political and social activism, for service to the Indian people, and for the creation of a modern democratic nation. Most have interpreted the text's spiritual egalitarianism in social terms, arguing that the *Gītā* teachings support, indeed demand, the abolition of traditional social hierarchies such as caste. For Swami Vivekananda, the twentieth-century Indian philosopher Sarvepalli Radhakrishnan (1888–1975), and others, the *Gītā* represents not a scripture for Hindus alone but a universal ethic for the modern world. In our own time, its vision of Krishna as God has flowered anew in the International Krishna Consciousness movement initiated by Swami A. C. Bhaktivedanta (1896–1977). The most remarkable reading of the *Gītā*'s teachings, however, is the one offered by Mahatma Gandhi, who argued that absolute nonviolence is the only logical culmination of Krishna's doctrine of "desireless action." That this ancient text continues to capture the imagination of so many modern thinkers is eloquent testimony to its vitality.

Among the scriptures of the world, the *Bhagavad-Gītā* is second only to the Bible in the number of times it has been translated. Barbara Stoler Miller, *The Bhagavad-Gītā: Krishna's Counsel in Time of War* (1986), is the most accessible modern translation of the work, enhanced by a lucid introductory essay and a glossary of key words. Among older translations and interpretations, readers might find it useful to consult Eliot Deutsch for a good explanation of key philosophical ideas, and S. Radhakrishnan for the parallel Sanskrit text (in transliteration), accompanied by a commentary from the point of view of an eminent modern Indian philosopher. On Indian interpreters of the *Gītā*, see Robert Minor, *Modern Interpreters of the Bhagavadgītā* (1986). For the *Gītā*'s career in the West, consult Eric Sharpe, *The Universal Gītā: Western Images of the Bhagavad Gītā, A Bicentennial Survey* (1985).

PRONOUNCING GLOSSARY

The following list uses common English syllables and stress accents to provide rough equivalents of selected words whose pronunciation may be unfamiliar to the general reader.

Bhagavad-Gītā: *buh'-guh-vuhd–gee'-tah*

Bhagavān: *buh'-guh-vahn*

Dhṛtarāṣṭra: *dree'-tuh-rahsh-truh*

Jñāna: *gyah'-nuh*

Krishna (Kṛṣṇa): *kreesh'-nuh*

kṣatriya: *kshuh'-tree-yuh*

Kurukṣetra: *koo-roo-kshay'-truh*

lokasaṃgraha: *loh'-kuh-suhn'-gruh-huh*

Mahābhārata: *muh-hah-bah'-ruh-tuh*

Sāṃkhya: *sahn'-kyuh*

śloka: *shloh'-kuh*

triṣṭubh: *tree'-shtoobh*

Upaniṣad: *oo-puh'-nee-shuhd*

The Bhagavad-Gītā[1]

From *The First Teaching*

[ARJUNA'S[2] DEJECTION]

20 Arjuna, his war flag a rampant monkey,
saw Dhritarashtra's[3] sons assembled
as weapons were ready to clash,
and he lifted his bow.

21 He told his charioteer:
"Krishna,[4]
halt my chariot
between the armies!

22 Far enough for me to see
these men who lust for war,
ready to fight with me
in the strain of battle.

23 I see men gathered here,
eager to fight,
bent on serving the folly
of Dhritarashtra's son."[5]

24 When Arjuna had spoken,
Krishna halted
their splendid chariot
between the armies.

25 Facing Bhishma and Drona[6]
and all the great kings,
he said, "Arjuna, see
the Kuru men[7] assembled here!"

26 Arjuna saw them standing there:
fathers, grandfathers, teachers,
uncles, brothers, sons,
grandsons, and friends.

27 He surveyed his elders
and companions in both armies,
all his kinsmen
assembled together.

28 Dejected, filled with strange pity,
he said this:
"Krishna, I see my kinsmen
gathered here, wanting war.

1. Translated by Barbara Stoler Miller. Verse numbers run to the left of the text. 2. The third of the five Pāṇḍava brothers. 3. The blind king of the Hāstinapura and father of the Kauravas. 4. Incarnation of Viṣṇu, the preserver god. 5. Here Duryodhana. 6. Preceptor of the Kauravas and the Pāṇḍavas. Bhishma is their granduncle. 7. The Kauravas.

29 My limbs sink,
my mouth is parched,
my body trembles,
the hair bristles on my flesh.

30 The magic bow[8] slips
from my hand, my skin burns,
I cannot stand still,
my mind reels.

31 I see omens of chaos,
Krishna; I see no good
in killing my kinsmen
in battle.

32 Krishna, I see no victory,
or kingship or pleasures.
What use to us are kingship,
delights, or life itself?

33 We sought kingship, delights,
and pleasures for the sake of those
assembled to abandon their lives
and fortunes in battle.

34 They are teachers, fathers, sons,
and grandfathers, uncles, grandsons,
fathers and brothers of wives,
and other men of our family.

35 I do not want to kill them
even if I am killed, Krishna;
not for kingship of all three worlds,
much less for the earth!

36 What joy is there for us, Krishna,
in killing Dhritarashtra's sons?
Evil will haunt us if we kill them,
though their bows are drawn to kill.

37 Honor forbids us to kill
our cousins, Dhritarashtra's sons;
how can we know happiness
if we kill our own kinsmen?

38 The greed that distorts their reason
blinds them to the sin they commit
in ruining the family, blinds them
to the crime of betraying friends.

39 How can we ignore the wisdom
of turning from this evil
when we see the sin
of family destruction, Krishna?

8. Gāṇḍīva, which he won from the fire god.

40 When the family is ruined,
the timeless laws of family duty
perish; and when duty is lost,
chaos overwhelms the family.

41 In overwhelming chaos, Krishna,
women of the family are corrupted;
and when women are corrupted,
disorder[9] is born in society.

42 This discord drags the violators
and the family itself to hell;
for ancestors fall when rites
of offering rice and water lapse.[1]

43 The sins of men who violate
the family create disorder in society
that undermines the constant laws
of caste and family duty.

44 Krishna, we have heard
that a place in hell
is reserved for men
who undermine family duties.

45 I lament the great sin
we commit when our greed
for kingship and pleasures
drives us to kill our kinsmen.

46 If Dhritarashtra's armed sons
kill me in battle when I am unarmed
and offer no resistance,
it will be my reward."

47 Saying this in the time of war,
Arjuna slumped into the chariot
and laid down his bow and arrows,
his mind tormented by grief.

From *The Second Teaching*

[PHILOSOPHY AND SPIRITUAL DISCIPLINE]

LORD KRISHNA:

11 You grieve for those beyond grief,
and you speak words of insight;
but learned men do not grieve
for the dead or the living.

12 Never have I not existed,
nor you, nor these kings;
and never in the future
shall we cease to exist.

9. Specifically, disruption of the proper ordering of the four principal social classes: brahman, warrior, merchant, and laborer. 1. Hindus are required to make these ritual offerings to their ancestors.

13 Just as the embodied self
enters childhood, youth, and old age,
so does it enter another body;
this does not confound a steadfast man.[2]

14 Contacts with matter make us feel
heat and cold, pleasure and pain.
Arjuna, you must learn to endure
fleeting things—they come and go!

15 When these cannot torment a man,
when suffering and joy are equal
for him and he has courage,
he is fit for immortality.

16 Nothing of nonbeing comes to be,
nor does being cease to exist;
the boundary between these two
is seen by men who see reality.

17 Indestructible is the presence
that pervades all this;
no one can destroy
this unchanging reality.

18 Our bodies are known to end,
but the embodied self is enduring,
indestructible, and immeasurable;
therefore, Arjuna, fight the battle!

19 He who thinks this self a killer
and he who thinks it killed,
both fail to understand;
it does not kill, nor is it killed.

20 It is not born,
it does not die;
having been,
it will never not be;
unborn, enduring,
constant, and primordial,
it is not killed
when the body is killed.

21 Arjuna, when a man knows the self
to be indestructible, enduring, unborn,
unchanging, how does he kill
or cause anyone to kill?

22 As a man discards
worn-out clothes
to put on new
and different ones,
so the embodied self

2. Here Krishna begins to explain the implications of reincarnation, emphasizing the identity of the seemingly finite embodied soul with the infinite and imperishable universal spirit (Brahman).

discards
its worn-out bodies
to take on other new ones.

23 Weapons do not cut it,
fire does not burn it,
waters do not wet it,
wind does not wither it.

24 It cannot be cut or burned;
it cannot be wet or withered;
it is enduring, all-pervasive,
fixed, immovable, and timeless.

25 It is called unmanifest,
inconceivable, and immutable;
since you know that to be so,
you should not grieve!

26 If you think of its birth
and death as ever-recurring,
then too, Great Warrior,
you have no cause to grieve!

27 Death is certain for anyone born,
and birth is certain for the dead;
since the cycle is inevitable,
you have no cause to grieve!

28 Creatures are unmanifest in origin,
manifest in the midst of life,
and unmanifest again in the end.
Since this is so, why do you lament?

29 Rarely someone
sees it,
rarely another
speaks it,
rarely anyone
hears it—
even hearing it,
no one really knows it.

30 The self embodied in the body
of every being is indestructible;
you have no cause to grieve
for all these creatures, Arjuna!

31 Look to your own duty;[3]
do not tremble before it;
nothing is better for a warrior
than a battle of sacred duty.

32 The doors of heaven open
for warriors who rejoice

3. *Dharma,* which for Arjuna is that of his class (warrior) and stage of life (householder).

to have a battle like this
thrust on them by chance.

33 If you fail to wage this war
of sacred duty,
you will abandon your own duty
and fame only to gain evil.

34 People will tell
of your undying shame,
and for a man of honor
shame is worse than death.

* * *

47 Be intent on action,
not on the fruits of action;
avoid attraction to the fruits
and attachment to inaction!

48 Perform actions, firm in discipline,
relinquishing attachment;
be impartial to failure and success—
this equanimity is called discipline.

49 Arjuna, action is far inferior
to the discipline of understanding;[4]
so seek refuge in understanding—pitiful
are men drawn by fruits of action.

50 Disciplined by understanding,
one abandons both good and evil deeds;
so arm yourself for discipline—
discipline is skill in actions.

51 Wise men disciplined by understanding
relinquish the fruit born of action;
freed from these bonds of rebirth,
they reach a place beyond decay.

52 When your understanding passes beyond
the swamp of delusion,
you will be indifferent to all
that is heard in sacred lore.[5]

53 When your understanding turns
from sacred lore to stand fixed,
immovable in contemplation,
then you will reach discipline.[6]

54 ARJUNA:
Krishna, what defines a man
deep in contemplation whose insight
and thought are sure? How would he speak?

4. The rational facilities, including intuitive intelligence, in contrast to the mind, or discursive intellect. **5.** The *Vedas* and their ritualistic doctrine. Krishna says that the older ritualistic learning is useless for the emancipation of the soul from *karma*. **6.** Used in its broadest sense.

How would he sit? How would he move?

55 LORD KRISHNA:
When he gives up desires in his mind,
is content with the self within himself,[7]
then he is said to be a man
whose insight is sure, Arjuna.

56 When suffering does not disturb his mind,
when his craving for pleasures has vanished,
when attraction, fear, and anger are gone,
he is called a sage whose thought is sure.

57 When he shows no preference
in fortune or misfortune
and neither exults nor hates,
his insight is sure.

58 When, like a tortoise retracting
its limbs, he withdraws his senses
completely from sensuous objects,
his insight is sure.

From *The Third Teaching*

[DISCIPLINE OF ACTION]

ARJUNA:
1 If you think understanding
is more powerful than action,
why, Krishna, do you urge me
to this horrific act?

2 You confuse my understanding
with a maze of words;
speak one certain truth
so I may achieve what is good.

LORD KRISHNA:
3 Earlier I taught the twofold
basis of good in this world—
for philosophers, disciplined knowledge;
for men of discipline, action.

4 A man cannot escape the force
of action by abstaining from actions;
he does not attain success
just by renunciation.

5 No one exists for even an instant
without performing action;
however unwilling, every being is forced
to act by the qualities of nature.[8]

7. A play on the word *ātman,* which means both "the self" (soul) and "oneself." Only one who has realized the true (immutable) nature of the self can be *content with the self within himself.* Krishna now begins to describe the techniques and effects of withdrawing one's senses from the outside and focusing them on the interior self, the infinite soul. 8. That is, sublimity, dynamism (passion), and inertia.

6 When his senses are controlled
but he keeps recalling
sense objects with his mind,
he is a self-deluded hypocrite.

7 When he controls his senses
with his mind and engages in the discipline
of action with his faculties of action,
detachment sets him apart.

8 Perform necessary action;
it is more powerful than inaction;
without action you even fail
to sustain your own body.

9 Action imprisons the world
unless it is done as sacrifice;
freed from attachment, Arjuna,
perform action as sacrifice!

10 When creating living beings and sacrifice,
Prajapati, the primordial creator, said:
"By sacrifice will you procreate!
Let it be your wish-granting cow![9]

11 Foster the gods with this,
and may they foster you;
by enriching one another,
you will achieve a higher good.

12 Enriched by sacrifice, the gods
will give you the delights you desire;
he is a thief who enjoys their gifts
without giving to them in return."

13 Good men eating the remnants
of sacrifice are free of any guilt,
but evil men who cook for themselves
eat the food of sin.

14 Creatures depend on food,
food comes from rain,
rain depends on sacrifice,
and sacrifice comes from action.

15 Action comes from the spirit of prayer,
whose source is OM,[1] sound of the imperishable;
so the pervading infinite spirit
is ever present in rites of sacrifice.

16 He who fails to keep turning
the wheel here set in motion
wastes his life in sin,

9. This image derives from the importance of cattle in Vedic society and religion. Prajapati is a god of the *Vedas.* In the Vedic worldview the preservation of the universe depended on sacrifices made to the gods, and such ritual was at the center of the religion. 1. Beginning with the *Upaniṣads,* the primeval sound, representing the infinite spirit that underlies the universe.

addicted to the senses, Arjuna.

17 But when a man finds delight
within himself and feels inner joy
and pure contentment in himself,
there is nothing more to be done.

18 He has no stake here
in deeds done or undone,
nor does his purpose
depend on other creatures.

19 Always perform with detachment
any action you must do;
performing action with detachment,
one achieves supreme good.

20 Janaka[2] and other ancient kings
attained perfection by action alone;
seeing the way to preserve
the world, you should act.

21 Whatever a leader does,
the ordinary people also do.
He sets the standard
for the world to follow.

22 In the three worlds,[3]
there is nothing I must do,
nothing unattained to be attained,
yet I engage in action.

23 What if I did not engage
relentlessly in action?
Men retrace my path
at every turn, Arjuna.

24 These worlds would collapse
if I did not perform action;
I would create disorder in society,
living beings would be destroyed.

25 As the ignorant act with attachment
to actions, Arjuna,
so wise men should act with detachment
to preserve the world.

* * *

ARJUNA:

36 Krishna, what makes a person
commit evil
against his own will,
as if compelled by force?

2. Celebrated character in the dialogues of the *Bṛhadāraṇyaka Upaniṣad*; an exemplar of the warrior-king who is also a man of discipline (a *yogi*). **3.** Heaven, earth, and the underworld.

LORD KRISHNA:
37 It is desire and anger, arising
from nature's quality of passion;
know it here as the enemy,
voracious and very evil!

38 As fire is obscured by smoke
and a mirror by dirt,
as an embryo is veiled by its caul,
so is knowledge obscured by this.

39 Knowledge is obscured
by the wise man's eternal enemy,
which takes form as desire,
an insatiable fire, Arjuna.

40 The senses, mind, and understanding
are said to harbor desire;
with these desire obscures knowledge
and confounds the embodied self.

41 Therefore, first restrain
your senses, Arjuna,
then kill this evil
that ruins knowledge and judgment.

42 Men say that the senses are superior
to their objects, the mind superior to the senses,
understanding superior to the mind;
higher than understanding is the self.

43 Knowing the self beyond understanding,
sustain the self with the self.
Great Warrior, kill the enemy
menacing you in the form of desire!

From *The Sixth Teaching*

[THE MAN OF DISCIPLINE][4]

10 A man of discipline should always
discipline himself, remain in seclusion,
isolated, his thought and self well controlled,
without possessions or hope.

11 He should fix for himself
a firm seat in a pure place,
neither too high nor too low,
covered in cloth, deerskin, or grass.

12 He should focus his mind and restrain
the activity of his thought and senses;
sitting on that seat, he should practice
discipline for the purification of the self.

4. The *yogi*. This teaching has much in common with the descriptions of the psychological and physical techniques of *yoga* presented by Yoga philosophers.

13 He should keep his body, head,
and neck aligned, immobile, steady;
he should gaze at the tip of his nose
and not let his glance wander.

14 The self tranquil, his fear dispelled,
firm in his vow of celibacy, his mind restrained,
let him sit with discipline,
his thought fixed on me, intent on me.

15 Disciplining himself,
his mind controlled,
a man of discipline finds peace,
the pure calm that exists in me.

16 Gluttons have no discipline,
nor the man who starves himself,
nor he who sleeps excessively
or suffers wakefulness.

17 When a man disciplines his diet
and diversions, his physical actions,
his sleeping and waking,
discipline destroys his sorrow.

18 When his controlled thought
rests within the self alone,
without craving objects of desire,
he is said to be disciplined.

19 "He does not waver, like a lamp sheltered
from the wind" is the simile recalled
for a man of discipline, restrained in thought
and practicing self-discipline.

20 When his thought ceases,
checked by the exercise of discipline,
he is content within the self,
seeing the self through himself.

21 Absolute joy beyond the senses
can only be grasped by understanding;
when one knows it, he abides there
and never wanders from this reality.

22 Obtaining it, he thinks
there is no greater gain;
abiding there, he is unmoved,
even by deep suffering.

23 Since he knows that discipline
means unbinding the bonds of suffering,
he should practice discipline resolutely,
without despair dulling his reason.

24 He should entirely relinquish
desires aroused by willful intent;

he should entirely control
his senses with his mind.

25 He should gradually become tranquil,
firmly controlling his understanding;
focusing his mind on the self,
he should think nothing.

26 Wherever his faltering mind
unsteadily wanders,
he should restrain it
and bring it under self-control.

27 When his mind is tranquil, perfect joy
comes to the man of discipline;
his passion is calmed, he is without sin,
being one with the infinite spirit.

28 Constantly disciplining himself,
free from sin, the man of discipline
easily achieves perfect joy
in harmony with the infinite spirit.

29 Arming himself with discipline,
seeing everything with an equal eye,
he sees the self in all creatures
and all creatures in the self.

30 He who sees me everywhere
and sees everything in me
will not be lost to me,
and I will not be lost to him.

31 I exist in all creatures,
so the disciplined man devoted to me
grasps the oneness of life;
wherever he is, he is in me.

32 When he sees identity in everything,
whether joy or suffering,
through analogy with the self,
he is deemed a man of pure discipline.

Summary In the Seventh to Tenth Teachings Krishna explains diverse aspects of the nature of the infinite spirit, gradually unveiling the mystery of his own identity as the highest manifestation of that universal spirit and thus leading up to the revelation of his cosmic form in the Eleventh Teaching.

From *The Eleventh Teaching*

[THE VISION OF KRISHNA'S TOTALITY]

ARJUNA:

1 To favor me you revealed
the deepest mystery of the self,

and by your words
my delusion is dispelled.

2 I heard from you in detail
how creatures come to be and die,
Krishna, and about the self
in its immutable greatness.

3 Just as you have described
yourself, I wish to see your form
in all its majesty,
Krishna, Supreme among Men.

4 If you think I can see it,
reveal to me
your immutable self.
Krishna, Lord of Discipline.

LORD KRISHNA:

5 Arjuna, see my forms
in hundreds and thousands;
diverse, divine,
of many colors and shapes.

6 See the sun gods, gods of light,
howling storm gods, twin gods of dawn,
and gods of wind, Arjuna,
wondrous forms not seen before.

7 Arjuna, see all the universe,
animate and inanimate,
and whatever else you wish to see;
all stands here as one in my body.

8 But you cannot see me
with your own eye;
I will give you a divine eye to see
the majesty of my discipline.

SANJAYA:[5]

9 O King, saying this, Krishna,
the great lord of discipline,
revealed to Arjuna
the true majesty of his form.

10 It was a multiform, wondrous vision,
with countless mouths and eyes[6]
and celestial ornaments,
brandishing many divine weapons.

11 Everywhere was boundless divinity
containing all astonishing things,
wearing divine garlands and garments,
anointed with divine perfume.

5. The bard who is retelling the events of the battle to King Dhṛtarāṣṭra. 6. Standard elements of icons of the Hindu gods, which are worshiped as manifestations of the gods themselves. In most icons, the Hindu gods have four or more arms.

12 If the light of a thousand suns
were to rise in the sky at once,
it would be like the light
of that great spirit.

13 Arjuna saw all the universe
in its many ways and parts,
standing as one in the body
of the god of gods.

* * *

44 I bow to you,
I prostrate my body,
I beg you to be gracious,
Worshipful Lord—
as a father to a son,
a friend to a friend,
a lover to a beloved,
O God, bear with me.[7]

45 I am thrilled,
and yet my mind
trembles with fear
at seeing
what has not been seen before.
Show me, God, the form I know—
be gracious, Lord of Gods,
Shelter of the World.

46 I want to see you
as before,
with your crown and mace,
and the discus in your hand.
O Thousand-Armed God,[8]
assume the four-armed form
embodied
in your totality.

LORD KRISHNA:

47 To grace you, Arjuna,
I revealed
through self-discipline
my higher form,
which no one but you
has ever beheld—
brilliant, total,
boundless, primal.

48 Not through sacred lore
or sacrificial ritual

7. The tradition of worshiping God in the intimate relational modes described here became the staple of a popular Hindu religious practice called *bhakti* ("loving devotion to God"). 8. In this form Viṣṇu-Krishna represents Puruṣa, the cosmic man of the *Rig Veda*. The mace and discus are emblems of Viṣṇu's four-armed form.

or study or charity,
not by rites
or by terrible penances
can I be seen in this form
in the world of men
by anyone but you, Great Hero.

49 Do not tremble
or suffer confusion
from seeing
my horrific form;
your fear dispelled,
your mind full of love,
see my form again
as it was.

SANJAYA:
50 Saying this to Arjuna,
Krishna once more
revealed
his intimate form;
resuming his gentle body,
the great spirit
let the terrified hero
regain his breath.

ARJUNA:
51 Seeing your gentle human form,
Krishna, I recover
my own nature,
and my reason is restored.

LORD KRISHNA:
52 This form you have seen
is rarely revealed;
the gods are constantly craving
for a vision of this form.

53 Not through sacred lore,
penances, charity, or sacrificial rites
can I be seen in the form
that you saw me.

54 By devotion alone
can I, as I really am,
be known and seen
and entered into, Arjuna.

55 Acting only for me, intent on me,
free from attachment,
hostile to no creature, Arjuna,
a man of devotion comes to me.

THE TAMIL ANTHOLOGIES
ca. 100–250

The poems of the *Eight Anthologies* and the *Ten Songs* are the earliest literary works extant in classical Tamil. While most of the poems in the *Eight Anthologies* range in length from four to forty lines, the poems of the *Ten Songs* run to hundreds of lines. Of the 2,381 poems, 102 are by anonymous authors, and the 473 named poets include 12 women (3 of whom are represented here). The ancient Tamil poets called themselves *pulavaṉs* ("scholars, learned persons"), in contrast to the many kinds of anonymous bards and other professional performers they mention in their poems. Later legends speak of the *pulavaṉs* as members of an academy of scholars (*caṅkam*); the poetry is itself styled *caṅkam* poetry. Whatever we may make of this claim, the poems are manifestly complex, classical literary works that are unrelated to poetic traditions in Sanskrit and that make selective use of stylistic elements (such as formulaic phrases) from earlier Tamil oral poetry. The sophisticated poetics of *caṅkam* literature are explained in a text on grammar and rhetoric called *Tolkāppiyam* (Old Composition; ca. fourth century A.D.), which inaugurates a long tradition of scholarly commentary.

For the *caṅkam* poets, the two great themes of poetry are love and war, expressions of the "inner" and "outer" lives of the kings and local chiefs who are the patrons and heroes of the poems. The multiple connotations of *akam* and *puṟam*, the ancient Tamil words used to identify love and war poetry, respectively, suggest that they are fundamental conceptual categories that apply not just to poetry but to life itself. *Akam* means, among other things, "inner part," "inside," "home," "heart," and "love," while *puṟam* connotes the opposite values: "outer part," "outside," "public life," and "war." And the two words have retained some of these meanings in modern Tamil as well. Some poets specialized in one or the other genre, and a focus on *akam* or *puṟam* themes is one of the principles around which the Tamil poems are organized.

In *puṟam* poems the poet sings the praise of his or her patron, glorifying his exploits in war, and his generosity to poets and suppliants in peace. The best poems, like Kapilar's poem on Pāri (included here), manage to capture both sides of the hero in a single description. Many *puṟam* poems are in praise of the kings of the Cōḻa, Pāṇṭiya, and Cēra dynasties. The poems dedicated to these kings paint vivid pictures of sieges and of a prosperous, cosmopolitan urban civilization, especially in Pandyan Maturai and seaports such as the Cōḻa city of Pukār or Kāvirip paṭṭiṉam (Ptolemy's Khaberis) on the east coast. But like Pāri, whose rule extended over nothing greater than a few villages and a hill called Paṟampu, many of the patrons of the Tamil poets were minor chiefs who ruled over small tracts of land and perpetually engaged in skirmishes with their neighbors and with the three great kings. In the stirring poems of the *pulavaṉs*, however, these petty chieftains emerge as heroes of epic stature.

Adopting the voices of a nameless hero (*talaivaṉ*), heroine (*talaivi*), and the heroine's girlfriend (*tōḻi*)—who acts as her confidante and go-between—*akam* poems focus on particular moments in an intimate relationship, exploring the emotional and psychological nuances of love. Whereas *puṟam* poems celebrate individual heroes, the anonymity of the characters in the love poems preserves the privacy of the inner world while evoking its universality. Just as men and public affairs dominate *puṟam* poems, women's points of view are primary to poetry of the inner part; the majority of the poems in the *akam* collection *Anthology of Short Poems* are spoken by the heroine and her girlfriend. Interestingly, there is no systematic correlation between the author's gender and the gender of the speaker in the poems. The celebrated male poet Kapilar wrote some of the finest love poems in female voices in the anthologies, and the female poet Auvaiyār is renowned for her *puṟam* poems (both poets are represented here).

Unlike the early Sanskrit poets, the *caṅkam* poets are not interested in philosophical abstractions, moral lessons, or mythology. Theirs is a profoundly anthropocentric poetry, a passionate celebration of life in this world and of human emotions and acts. The aesthetic of *caṅkam* poetry is founded on deeply felt resonances between the human and natural worlds; yet even here the poets are not interested in the natural world for its own sake but rather for what it can reveal about human experience.

At the center of classical Tamil poetics is a scheme of five conventional "landscapes." In this scheme each of the actual landscape types of the Tamil countryside connotes both a natural phenomenon and, in precise correlation with it, an aspect of love between a man and a woman. Each landscape is named after a flower or plant characteristic of it. Thus the hill landscape is called *kuṟiñci,* for the *kuṟiñci* (mountain conehead) flower; the pasture is named *mullai* for jasmine; the field is *marutam,* for the queen's flower; the seashore is *neytal,* for the blue water lily; and the wasteland is *pālai,* for the ivorywood, an evergreen tree that grows in the desert.

Poems that are set in a hill landscape (or allude to some of its features) immediately signal lovers' meetings. Pastoral poems are about domestic happiness or marriage. Field poems speak of the married hero's infidelity (usually with courtesans) and lover's quarrels. Seashore poems evoke separation and anxious waiting; and the wasteland landscape suggests elopement, hardship, or the hero's journey across the desert or drought-parched wilderness in search of wealth. Though each element of a particular landscape—bird or animal, tribe or occupation (all of these elements are codified)—is by itself capable of evoking the specific phase of love that is correlated with that landscape, the skillful poet will bring together elements from different landscapes to effect tension and contrast. The *caṅkam* poets use the schematic landscapes as a language of symbols to create intricately designed, richly suggestive poems. Some poets of the anthologies, like the Poet of the Long White Moonlight, are known simply by an arresting nature image in their poems.

Despite differences in technique and mood, the five landscapes, both real and conventional, bind the love and war poems together in a single universe of discourse. Kapilar's keenly observed, sensuous description of the landscape of Pāri's hill in *His Hill* (a *puṟam* poem, included here) is by implication a description of the chieftain himself, a hero ferocious in combat but also generous to a fault. The sensitive lover of the *akam* poems is identical to the brave warrior whose mother proudly declares, in a typical *puṟam* poem: "This womb was once / a lair / for that tiger. / You can see him now / only on battlefields." The categories *akam* and *puṟam* are the two faces of the Tamil warrior-hero, the two halves of the idealized ancient Tamil heroic world evoked in *caṅkam* poetry. Much in that world is alien to modern sensibilities. Yet in their powerful concrete images and spare design the love poems in particular are remarkably close to modern poetry, and like Sappho's voice, the voices of the anonymous lovers in these ancient poems speak to us with an astonishing immediacy.

THE *AKAVAL* METER

Classical Tamil meter recognizes two kinds of metrical units: *nēr* (here represented by *N*), a single syllable that can be long (have a long vowel) (–) or short (⏑); and *nirai* (here represented by *nn*), two syllables in the sequence short-short (⏑ ⏑) or short-long (⏑ –). Two metrical units make a basic foot. Thus the standard four-foot line of the *akaval* meter contains eight metrical units. In *What She Said [1]* the line scans as follows:

<table>
<tr><td>N N |</td><td>N N</td><td>| nn nn |</td><td>N N</td></tr>
<tr><td>kuṉ-ṟak |</td><td>kū-kai</td><td>| kuḻa-ṟiṉu</td><td>| muṉ-ṟiṟ</td></tr>
<tr><td>(koon′-ruhk)</td><td>(koo′-hye)</td><td>(koo′-zhuh
ree′-noo) |</td><td>(moon′-reer)</td></tr>
</table>

Varying combinations of *nēr* and *nirai* result in lines of varying rhythm.

A. K. Ramanujan's luminous translations and eminently accessible introductions in *The Interior Landscape: Love Poems from a Classical Tamil Anthology* (1967) and *Poems of Love and War: From the Eight Anthologies and the Ten Long Poems of Classical Tamil* (1985) are the best introduction to classical Tamil poetry and poetics. The fine translations in George L. Hart III, *Poets of the Tamil Anthologies: Ancient Poems of Love and War* (1979), include several selections and themes not available in the Ramanujan volumes. Hart's *The Poems of Ancient Tamil: Their Milieu and Their Sanskrit Counterparts* (1975) is an outstanding study of *caṅkam* poetry from literary, social historical, and comparative perspectives. In *Tamil Heroic Poetry* (1969) K. Kailasapathy compares Tamil poetry with other traditions of heroic poetry, including Homer.

PRONOUNCING GLOSSARY

The following list uses common English syllables and stress accents to provide rough equivalents of selected words whose pronunciation may be unfamiliar to the general reader.

akam: *uh'-huhm*

Atiyamāṉ Neṭumāṉ Añci: *uh'-dee-yuh-mahn neh'-doo-mahn uhn'-jee*

Auvaiyār: *au'-vai-yahr*

caṅkam: *suhn'-guhm*

Cēra: *say'-ruh*

Cōḻa: *soh'-luh*

Kapilar: *kuh'-bee-luhr*

kuṟiñci: *koo-reen'-jee*

Kuṟuntokai: *koo-roon'-do-hai*

marutam: *muh'-roo-duhm*

mullai: *mool'-lai*

Pāṇṭiya: *pahn'-dee-yuh*

Paṟampu: *puh-ruhm'-boo*

Pāri: *pah'-ree*

Pukār: *poo-hahr'*

pulavaṉ: *poo'-luh-vuhn*

Puṟanāṉūṟu: *poo'-ruh-nah-noo'-roo*

talaivaṉ: *tuhl-ai'-vuhn*

Tolkāppiyam: *tol-hahp'-pee-yuhm*

THE TAMIL ANTHOLOGIES[1]

What She Said [1]

Once: if an owl hooted on the hill,
if a male ape leaped and loped
out there on the jackfruit bough in our yard
my poor heart would melt for fear. But now
in the difficult dark of night
nothing can stay its wandering
on the long sloping mountain-ways
of his coming.

Kapilar
Kuṟuntokai 153[2]

1. Translated by A. K. Ramanujan. 2. Poem 153 from the *Kuṟuntokai* collection. Kapilar was the most famous of the *caṅkam* poets, was a friend of several kings, and wrote many fine *akam* and *puṟam* poems.

What She Said [2]

Only the thief[3] was there, no one else.
And if he should lie, what can I do?

There was only
a thin-legged heron standing
on legs yellow as millet stems
and looking
for lampreys
in the running water
when he took me.

Kapilar
Kuruntokai 25

What She Said [3]

When my lover is by my side
I am happy
as a city
in the rapture of a carnival,

and when he is gone
I grieve like a deserted house
in a little hamlet
of the wastelands

where the squirrel[4] plays
in the front yard.

Aṉilāṭu Muṉṟilār[5]
Kuruntokai 41

What She Said [4]

Don't they really have
in the land where he has gone
such things
as house sparrows

dense-feathered, the color of fading water lilies,
pecking at grain drying on yards,

3. Suggests the clandestine nature of the affair and the heroine's fear that her lover is not trustworthy; however, the word was also used as a term of endearment. 4. We infer the "landscape" from component elements such as the "deserted house" and "the squirrel." 5. The Poet of the Squirrel Playing in the Front Yard; nothing else is known of this poet.

playing with the scatter of the fine dust
of the streets' manure
and living with their nestlings
in the angles of the penthouse

and miserable evenings,

and loneliness?

Māmalāṭaṉ
Kuṟuntokai 46

What She Said [5]

I am here. My virtue
lies in grief
in the groves near the sea.
My lover
is back in his hometown. And our secret
is with the gossips
in public places.

Veṇpūti
Kuṟuntokai 97

What Her Girl-Friend Said

In the seaside grove
where he drove back in his chariot
the *neytal*[6] flowers are on the ground,
some of their thick petals plowed in
and their stalks broken

by the knife-edge of his wheels' golden rims
furrowing the earth.

Ōta Ñāni
Kuṟuntokai 227

What the Concubine Said

You know he comes from
where the fresh-water shark in the pools
catch with their mouths

6. Water lily. The seashore landscape is the setting for separation and grief.

the mangoes as they fall, ripe
from the trees on the edge of the field.[7]

At our place
he talked big.

Now, back in his own,
when others raise their hands
and feet,
he will raise his too:

like a doll
in a mirror
he will shadow
every last wish
of his son's dear mother.

Ālaṅkuṭi Vaṅkaṉār
Kuṟuntokai 8

What She Said [6]

Bless you, my heart.
The shell bangles slip
from my wasting hands.
My eyes, sleepless for days,
are muddied.
Get up, let's go, let's get out
of this loneliness here.

Let's go
where the tribes wear
the narcotic wreaths of *cannabis*
beyond the land of Kaṭṭi,
the chieftain with many spears,
let's go, I say,
to where my man is,

enduring even
alien languages.[8]

Māmūlaṉār
Kuṟuntokai 11

What He Said [1]

The heart, knowing
no fear,

7. The field landscape is the setting of infidelity and lover's quarrels.
8. Exotic tribes and alien languages suggest perilous journeys through barren lands. *Cannabis:* marijuana.

has left me
to go and hold my love
but my arms,
left behind,
cannot take hold.

So what's the use?

In the space between us,
murderous tigers
roar like dark ocean waves,
circling
in O how many woods
between us
and our arms' embrace?

Aḷḷūr Naṉmullai[9]
Kuṟuntokai 237

What He Said [2]

My love is a two-faced thief.
In the dead of night
she comes like the fragrance
of the Red-Speared Chieftain's[1] forest hills,
to be one with me.

And then, she sheds the petals
of night's several flowers,
and does her hair again
with new perfumes and oils,
to be one with her family at dawn

with a stranger's different face.

Kapilar
Kuṟuntokai 312

A Chariot Wheel

Enemies,
take care
when you enter
the field of battle
and face
our warrior

9. A female poet. 1. Murukaṉ, Tamil god of the hills.

who is like a chariot wheel
made thoughtfully over a month
by a carpenter
who tosses off eight chariots
in a day.

Auvaiyār
on Atiyamāṉ Neṭumāṉ Añci
Puṟanāṉūṟu 87[2]

His Hill

Pāri's Paṟampu hill[3]
is quite a place.

Even if all three of you kings
should surround it[4]
with your great drums of war,
remember
it has four things
not grown under the plows
of plowmen:

one, wild rice
grows in the tiny-leaved bamboos;
two, ripening jackfruit,
crammed with segments
of sweet flesh;
three, down below
grow sweet potatoes
under fat creepers;
four,
beehives break
as their colors ripen
to a purple,
and the rich tall hill
drips with honey.

The hill is wide as the sky,
the pools flash like stars.
Even if you have
elephants
tied to every tree there,
and chariots
standing in every field,
you will never take the hill.
He will not give in
to the sword.

2. That is, poem 87 of the *Puṟanāṉūṟu* collection of four hundred *puṟam* poems; this poem belongs to the subgenre "pitched battle." Auvaiyār was a famous female poet, whose friendship with the Cēra king Añci is the subject of many legends. 3. The site of a fort from which the chieftain Pāri ruled his three hundred villages. 4. The kings of the Cēra, Pāṇṭiya, and Cōḻa dynasties have besieged the hill.

But I know a way
to take it:

pick carefully
your lute-strings, string little lutes,
and with your dancing women
with dense fragrant hair
behind you,

go singing and dancing
to Pāri,

and he'll give you
both hill and country.

Kapilar
on Pāri
Puṟanāṉūṟu 109

Mothers[5]

You stand against the pillar
of my hut and ask:
Where is your son?

I don't really know.
This womb was once
a lair
for that tiger.

You can see him now
only on battlefields.

Kāvaṟpeṇṭu[6]
Puṟanāṉūṟu 86

Earth's Bounty

Bless you, earth:

field,
forest,
valley,
or hill,

5. The warrior-hero's mother is conventionally portrayed as rejoicing in her son's valor. 6. A female poet.

you are only
as good
as the good young men
in each place.

Auvaiyār
Pu̱ṟanāṉūṟu 187

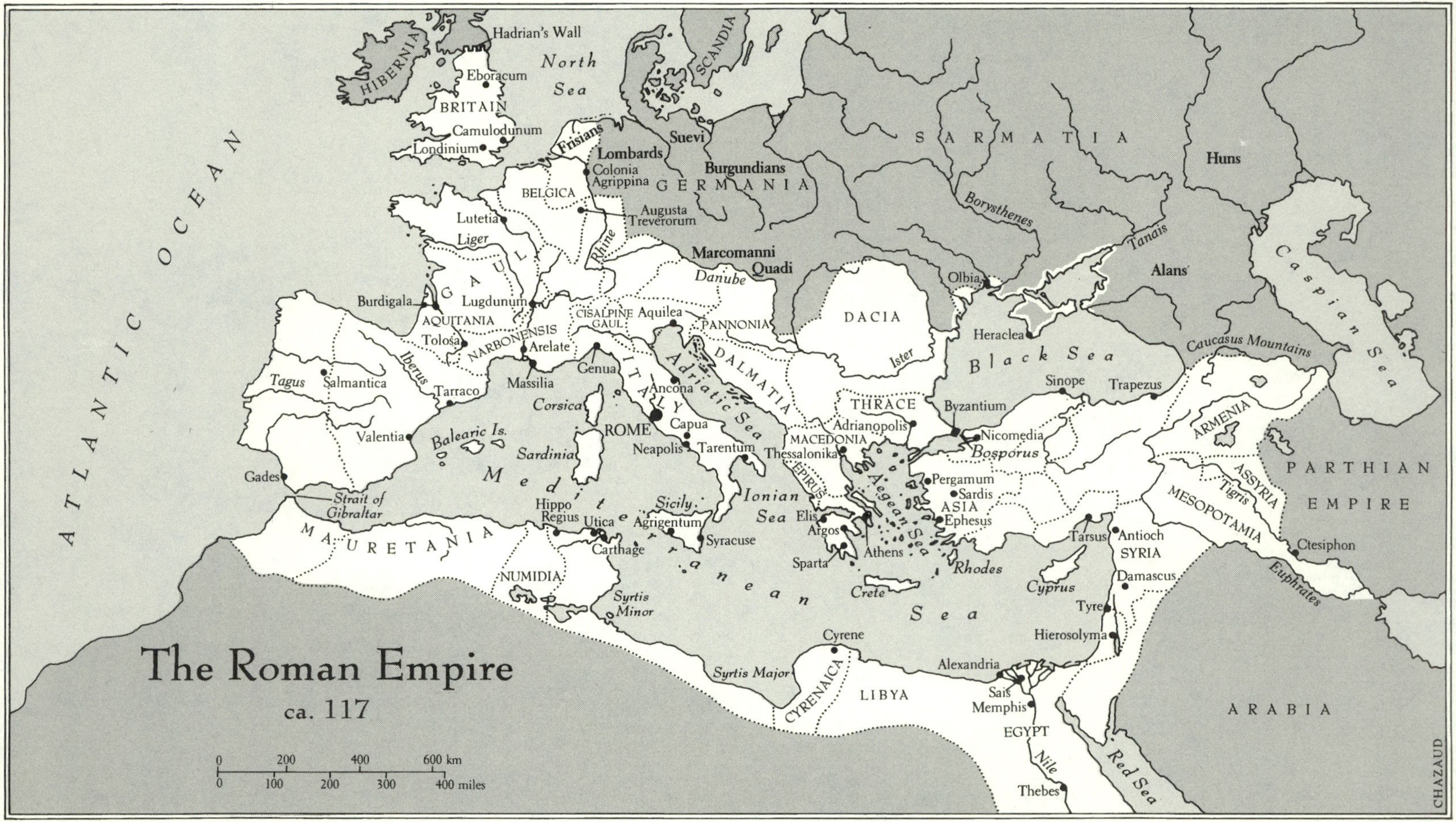
The Roman Empire
ca. 117
ATLANTIC OCEAN
HIBERNIA
Hadrian's Wall
North Sea
Eboracum
BRITAIN
Camulodunum
Londinium
Frisians
Lombards
Suevi
SCANDIA
Colonia Agrippina
Burgundians
GERMANIA
BELGICA
Augusta Treverorum
Lutetia
Liger
GAUL
Rhine
Marcomanni
Quadi
Danube
SARMATIA
Huns
Borysthenes
Tanais
Alans
Caspian Sea
Olbia
DACIA
Ister
Heraclea
Black Sea
Caucasus Mountains
Burdigala
AQUITANIA
Lugdunum
Tolosa
NARBONENSIS
Arelate
Massilia
CISALPINE GAUL
Aquilea
PANNONIA
DALMATIA
Genua
ITALY
Ancona
Adriatic Sea
ROME
Capua
Neapolis
Tarentum
Tagus
Salmantica
Iberus
Tarraco
Valentia
Balearic Is.
Corsica
Sardinia
Gades
Strait of Gibraltar
MAURETANIA
Hippo Regius
Utica
Carthage
Sicily
Agrigentum
Syracuse
NUMIDIA
Syrtis Minor
Mediterranean Sea
Ionian Sea
THRACE
Adrianopolis
MACEDONIA
Thessalonika
EPIRUS
Elis
Argos
Athens
Sparta
Aegean Sea
Crete
Byzantium
Nicomedia
Bosporus
Pergamum
Sardis
ASIA
Ephesus
Rhodes
Sinope
Trapezus
ARMENIA
ASSYRIA
Tigris
MESOPOTAMIA
PARTHIAN EMPIRE
Ctesiphon
Euphrates
Tarsus
Antioch
SYRIA
Damascus
Cyprus
Tyre
Hierosolyma
Cyrene
CYRENAICA
Syrtis Major
LIBYA
Alexandria
Sais
Memphis
EGYPT
Nile
Thebes
Red Sea
ARABIA
0 200 400 600 km
0 100 200 300 400 miles
CHAZAUD

The Roman Empire

When Alexander died in 323 B.C., the city of Rome, situated on the Tiber in the western coastal plain of Italy, was engaged in a struggle for the control of the surrounding areas. By the middle of the third century B.C., it dominated most of the Italian peninsula. Expansion southward brought Rome into collision with Carthage, a city in North Africa that was then the greatest power in the western Mediterranean. Two protracted wars resulted (264–241 and 218–201 B.C.), and it was only at the end of a third, shorter war (149–146 B.C.) that the Romans destroyed their great rival. The second Carthaginian (or Punic) War was particularly hard-fought, both in Spain and in Italy itself, where the Carthaginian general Hannibal, having made a spectacular crossing of the Alps, operated for years, and where Rome's southern Italian allies defected to Carthage and had to be slowly rewon. Rome, however, emerged from this war in 201 B.C. not merely victorious but a world power. The next two decades saw frequent wars—in Spain, in Greece, and in Asia Minor—that laid the foundations of the Roman empire. These successes changed Roman social, cultural, and economic life profoundly.

From early on, the Romans had come into contact with Greek culture through the sophisticated Greek cities of southern Italy and Sicily; now, with their involvement in affairs in mainland Greece, this contact intensified. Greek culture began to permeate Roman; the comedies of Plautus and his younger contemporary Terence are just one manifestation of this influence (and of the Roman transformation of Greek tradition). Economic changes were just as far-reaching. The military victories brought in huge numbers of enslaved war captives, and in parts of the Italian countryside wealthy men, mainly aristocrats, accumulated large landholdings that were systematically worked by slaves. With the waning in number of small farmers came an increase in the urban-poor population. Trade and crafts were on the rise, and newly wealthy businessmen were in a position to challenge the power of the senatorial class, whose wealth was based in land and who had long exerted de facto control over the government. These developments laid the groundwork for the sharp conflicts that plagued Rome later in the second century B.C. and that led in the next century to civil war and eventually the demise of the Republic and its replacement by imperial rule. For now, general prosperity masked these potential conflicts, especially the growing gulf between the wealthy classes and the poor, but the new wealth itself strained the traditional fabric of Roman society.

These were the changes and the tensions that accompanied the transformation of Rome from city-state on the traditional model to world imperial power. By the end of the first century B.C., Rome was the capital of an empire that stretched from the Straits of Gibraltar to the frontiers of Palestine. This empire gave peace and orderly government to the Mediterranean area for the next two centuries, and for two centuries after that it maintained a desperate but losing battle against the invading tribes moving in from the north and east. When it finally went down, the empire left behind it the ideal of the world-state, an ideal that was to be taken over by the medieval Church, which ruled from the same center, Rome, and which claimed a spiritual authority as great as the secular authority it replaced.

The achievements of the Romans, not only their conquests but also their success in consolidating the conquests and organizing the conquered, were due in large part to their talent for practical affairs. They might have had no aptitude for pure mathematics, but they could build an aqueduct to last two thousand years. Though they were not notable as political theorists, they organized a complicated yet stable federation that held Italy loyal to them in the presence of invading armies. Romans were conservative to the core; their strongest authority was *mos maiorum*, the custom of predecessors. A monument of this conservatism, the great body of Roman law, is one of their greatest contributions to Western civilization. The quality Romans most admired was *gravitas,* seriousness of attitude and purpose, and their highest words of commendation were "manliness," "industry," "discipline." Pericles, in his funeral speech, praised Athenian adaptability, versatility, and grace. This would have seemed strange praise to a Roman, whose idea of personal and civic virtue was different. "By her ancient customs and her men the Roman state stands," says Ennius the Roman poet, in a line that by its metrical heaviness emphasizes the stability implied in the key word "stands": *moribus antiquis res* stat *Romana virisque*.

Greek history begins not with a king, a battle, or the founding of a city, but with an epic poem. The Romans, on the other hand, had conquered half the world before they began to write. The stimulus to the creation of Latin literature was the Greek literature that the Romans discovered when, in the second century B.C., they assumed political responsibility for Greece and the Near East. Latin literature began with a translation of the *Odyssey,* made by a Greek prisoner of war, and with the exception of satire, until Latin literature became Christian, the model was always Greek. The Latin writer (especially the poet) borrowed wholesale from his Greek original, not furtively, but openly and proudly, as a tribute to the master from whom he had learned. But this frank acknowledgment of indebtedness should not blind us to the fact that Latin literature is original, and sometimes profoundly so. This is true above all of Virgil, who based his epic on Homer but chose as his theme the coming of the Trojan prince Aeneas to Italy, where he was to found a city from which, in the fullness of time, would come "the Latin race . . . and the high walls of Rome."

When Virgil was born in 70 B.C. the Roman Republic, which had conquered and now governed the Mediterranean world, had barely recovered from one civil war and was drifting inexorably toward another. The institutions of the city-state proved inadequate for world government. The civil conflict that had disrupted the Republic for more than a hundred years ended finally in the establishment of a powerful executive. Although the Senate, which had been the controlling body of the Republic, retained an impressive share of the power, the new arrangement developed inevitably toward autocracy, the rule of the executive, the emperor, as he was called once the system was stabilized. The first of the long line of Roman emperors who gave stable government to the Roman world during the first two centuries A.D. was Octavius, known generally by his title, Augustus. He had made his way cautiously through the intrigues and bloodshed that followed the murder of his uncle Julius Caesar in 44 B.C. until by 31 B.C. he controlled the western half of the empire. In that year he fought a decisive battle with the ruler of the eastern half of the empire, Mark Antony, who was supported by Cleopatra, queen of Egypt. Octavius's victory at Actium united the empire under one authority and ushered in an age of peace and reconstruction.

For the next two hundred years the successors of Augustus, the Roman emperors, ruled the ancient world with only occasional disturbances, most of them confined to Rome, where emperors who flagrantly abused their immense power—Nero, for example—were overthrown by force. The second half of this period was described by Gibbon, the great historian of imperial Rome, as the period "in the history of the world during which the condition of the human race was most happy and prosperous." The years A.D. 96–180, those of the "five good emperors," were in fact remarkable: this was the longest period of peace that has ever been enjoyed by the inhabitants of an area that included Britain, France, all southern Europe, the Middle East, and the whole of North Africa. Trade and agriculture flourished, and the cities with their public baths, theaters, and libraries offered all the amenities of civilized life. Yet there was apparent, especially in the literature of the second century, a spiritual emptiness. Petronius's *Satyricon* paints a sardonic portrait of the vulgar display and intellectual poverty of the newly rich who can think only in terms of money and possessions. The old religion offered no comfort to those who looked beyond mere material ends; it had been too closely knit into the fabric of the independent city-state and was inadequate for a time in which men were citizens of the world. New religions arose or were imported from the East, universal religions that made their appeal to all nations and classes: the worship of the Egyptian goddess Isis, of the Persian god Mithras, who offered bliss in the life to come, and of the Hebrew prophet Jesus, crucified in Jerusalem and believed risen from the dead. This was the religion that, working underground and often suppressed (there was a persecution of the Christians under Nero in the first century, another under the last of the "good emperors" Marcus Aurelius in the second), finally triumphed and became the official and later the exclusive religion of the Roman world. As the empire in the third and fourth centuries disintegrated under the never-ending invasions by peoples from the north, the Church, with its center and spiritual head in Rome, converted the new inhabitants and so made possible the preservation of much of that Latin and Greek literature that was to serve the European Middle Ages and, later, the Renaissance, as a model and a basis for their own great achievements in the arts and letters.

FURTHER READING

John Boardman, Jasper Griffin, and Oswyn Murray, eds., *The Oxford History of the Classical World* (1986), is a handsomely illustrated survey, by many different specialists, of the whole sweep of classical culture—social, political, literary, artistic, and religious. Michael Grant, *History of Rome* (1978), presents a well-illustrated, eminently readable survey. For a survey of Roman civilization organized according to different types of people and their social experiences, see Andrea Giardina, ed., *The Romans* (1993). For a detailed survey of Roman literature, see E. J. Kenney and W. V. Clausen, eds., *The Cambridge History of Classical Literature*, vol. 2: *Latin Literature* (1982). A rich and beautifully illustrated survey of women in Greece and Rome is Elaine Fantham, Helene Foley, Natalie Kampen, Sarah Pomeroy, and Alan Shapiro, eds., *Women in the Classical World* (1994).

TIME LINE

TEXTS	CONTEXTS
	753 B.C. Traditional date of the foundation of Rome
	ca. 750 Foundation of Carthage (North Africa)
	735 Greek colony at Syracuse (Sicily)
	7th century Greek colonies at Marseilles (France) and Cyrene (North Africa)
	509 Expulsion of the king; Rome becomes a republic
	451 Roman law codified—the Twelve Tablets
	264 Rome controls Italy south of the river Po; defeats Carthage at sea
	227 Sicily becomes the first Roman province
	218–202 Hannibal of Carthage invades Italy, fails to capture Rome, defeated at Zama near Carthage in 202
	197 Spain becomes a Roman province
	91–89 Social war in Italy; Italians gain Roman citizenship
	87–81 Civil war ending in dictatorship of Sulla
ca. 84?–54? B.C. Catullus	
	74 Cyrene becomes a Roman province
70–19 Virgil, author of ***The Aeneid***	
	58–50 Julius Caesar conquers Gaul
	47 Julius Caesar dictator; murdered in 44
43–A.D. 17 Ovid, author of ***Metamorphoses***	

Boldface titles indicate works in the anthology.

TIME LINE

TEXTS	CONTEXTS
	27–23 Octavian (now Augustus) establishes imperial regime
	ca. 6 Birth of Jesus
ca. A.D. 10–66 Petronius, author of ***The Satyricon***	
	A.D. 14–37 Tiberius emperor
	37–41 Caligula emperor
	41–54 Claudius emperor
	54–68 Nero emperor
	64 Persecution of Christians under Nero

CATULLUS
84?–54? B.C.

Gaius Valerius Catullus, born in the northern Italian city of Verona, lived out his short life in the last violent century of the Roman republic, but his poetry gives little hint that it was produced amid political upheaval. The 116 poems by him that have come down to us present a rich variety: imitations of Greek poets, long poems on Greek mythological themes, scurrilous personal attacks on contemporary politicians and private individuals, lighthearted verses designed to amuse his friends, and a magnificent marriage hymn. He also wrote a series of poems about his love affair with a Roman woman he calls Lesbia but who may have been Clodia, the enchanting but complex sister of one of Rome's most violent aristocrats turned political gangster. These poems, from which our selection is taken, present all the phases of the liaison, from the unalloyed happiness of the first encounters through doubt and hesitation to despair and virulent accusation, ending in heartbroken resignation to the bitter fact of Lesbia's betrayal.

Their tone ranges from the heights of joy at passionate love requited through the torments of simultaneous love and hate to the depths of morbid self-pity. Their direct and simple language seems to give readers immediate access to the experience of desire and betrayal and the feelings it arouses. In one sense, this impression is surely correct. But the poems are exceedingly complex. The passion is joined with considerable learning, and it is one of the remarkable characteristics of Catullus's poetry that strong emotion and sophistication are not at odds with each other but complementary. Poem 51, for example, powerfully describes the physical symptoms of love in the speaker; it is a translation into Latin of one of Sappho's most passionate Greek lyrics. Or consider poem 2, on Lesbia's pet sparrow: scholars have long suspected, probably correctly, an obscene double meaning in this pet.

There are further complexities. Many of the poems are addressed to someone—Lesbia, Catullus himself, or some third party—and the reader is a privileged audience to this communication. Who the addressee is and the relation between that person and the poet subtly shape the reader's view of the situation described in each poem. In poem 83, for example, when Lesbia seems to abuse "Catullus" in the presence of her husband, the speaker interprets this as a sign of love to which the husband is obtusely oblivious. Perhaps. Or is this a wishful interpretation? Who really is the dupe? Does the reader ever get access to Lesbia's feelings? Catullus's poetry is not simply a spontaneous outpouring of emotion, but a carefully meditated portrayal of a love affair in which the poet's persona as well as his mistress is a character; and that gives depth and range to its passion.

The best general introduction to Catullus, with essential background and perceptive discussion of the poetry, is Charles Martin, *Catullus* (1992). For more detailed but highly readable discussions of contemporary culture and society, Clodia and her circle, and the poems' relation to this context, T. P. Wiseman, *Catullus and His World: A Reappraisal* (1985), is excellent. Two older books are still valuable: A. L. Wheeler, *Catullus and the Traditions of Ancient Poetry* (1934), and E. A. Havelock, *The Lyric Genius of Catullus* (1964). The first puts Catullus in his cultural and literary context; the second translates selected poems and offers a sensitive appreciation of them. Kenneth Quinn, *Catullus: An Interpretation* (1973), gives an interesting if idiosyncratic view of the poetry. For a depiction of Catullus as well as Lesbia/Clodia and her circle in a carefully researched historical detective novel, see Steven Saylor, *The Venus Throw* (1995).

PRONOUNCING GLOSSARY

The following list uses common English syllables and stress accents to provide rough equivalents of selected words whose pronunciation may be unfamiliar to the general reader.

Aurelius: *ow-ree'-lee-us*
Catullus: *kah-tul'-lus*
Hyrcani: *heer-kah'-nee*
Sagae: *sah'-gai*

[LYRICS]

5[1]

Lesbia, let us live only for loving,
and let us value at a single penny
all the loose flap of senile busybodies!
Suns when they set are capable of rising,
but at the setting of our own brief light
night is one sleep from which we never waken.
Give me a thousand kisses, then a hundred,
another thousand next, another hundred,
a thousand without pause & then a hundred,
until when we have run up our thousands
we will cry bankrupt, hiding our assets
from ourselves & any who would harm us,
knowing the volume of our trade in kisses.

2

Sparrow, you darling pet of my beloved,
which she caresses, presses to her body
or teases with the tip of one sly finger
until you peck at it in tiny outrage!
—for there are times when my desired, shining
lady is moved to turn to you for comfort,
to find (as I imagine) ease for ardor,
solace, a little respite from her sorrow—
if I could only play with you as she does,
and be relieved of my tormenting passion!

51[2]

To me that man seems like a god in heaven,
seems—may I say it?—greater than all gods are,
who sits by you & without interruption
watches you, listens

1. All selections translated by Charles Martin. The order of the poems in this anthology is the logical one determined by the progress of Catullus's love affair with Lesbia. The numbers, however, refer to the order of the poems in the manuscripts. 2. A translation into Latin of Sappho's Greek poem *Like the very gods in my sight is he* (see above, p. 532), that reproduces Sappho's metrical scheme (imitated in the English translation).

to your light laughter, which casts such confusion
onto my senses, Lesbia, that when I
gaze at you merely, all of my well-chosen
words are forgotten[3]

as my tongue thickens & a subtle fire
runs through my body while my ears are deafened
by their own ringing & at once my eyes are
covered in darkness!

Leisure, Catullus. More than just a nuisance,
leisure: you riot, overmuch enthusing.
Fabulous cities & their sometime kings have
died of such leisure.[4]

86

Many find Quintia stunning. I find her attractive:
tall, "regal," fair in complexion—these points are granted.
But stunning? No, I deny it: the woman is scarcely venerious,
there's no spice at all in all the length of her body!
Now Lesbia is stunning, for Lesbia's beauty is total:
and by that sum all other women are diminished.

87

No other woman can truthfully say she was cherished
as much as Lesbia was when I was her lover.
Never, in any such bond, was fidelity greater
than mine, in my love for you, ever discovered.

109

Darling, we'll both have equal shares in the sweet love you offer,
and it will endure forever—you assure me.
O heaven, see to it that she can truly keep this promise,
that it came from her heart & was sincerely given,
so that we may spend the rest of our days in this lifelong
union, this undying compact of holy friendship.

3. *All . . . forgotten* is a guess at the sense of a line missing in the original. 4. The final stanza may not belong to this poem; if it does, it is Catullus's addition to his Sapphic original.

83

Lesbia hurls abuse at me in front of her husband:
that fatuous person finds it highly amusing!
Nothing gets through to you, jackass—for silence would signal
that she'd been cured of me, but her barking & bitching
show that not only [have][5] I not been forgotten,
—but that this burns her: and so she rants & rages.

70

My woman says there is no one whom she'd rather marry
than me, not even Jupiter,[6] if he came courting.
That's what she says—but what a woman says to a passionate lover
ought to be scribbled on wind, on running water.

72

You used to say that you wished to know only Catullus,
Lesbia, and wouldn't take even Jove before me!
I didn't regard you just as my mistress then: I cherished you
as a father does his sons or his daughters' husbands.
Now that I know you, I burn for you even more fiercely,
though I regard you as almost utterly worthless.
How can that be, you ask? It's because such cruelty forces
lust to assume the shrunken place of affection.

85

I hate & love. And if you should ask how I can do both,
I couldn't say; but I feel it, and it shivers me.

75

To such a state have I been brought by your mischief, my Lesbia,
and so completely ruined by my devotion,
that I couldn't think kindly of you if you did the best only,
nor cease to love, even if you should do—everything.

5. Editorial substitution for the translator's *haven't*.
6. Jupiter (or Jove) was the supreme god of the Roman pantheon, corresponding to the Greek Zeus.

8

Wretched Catullus! You have to stop this nonsense,
admit that what you see has ended is over!
Once there were days which shone for you with rare brightness,
when you would follow wherever your lady led you,
the one we once loved as we will love no other;
there was no end in those days to our pleasures,
when what you wished for was what she also wanted.
Yes, there were days which shone for you with rare brightness.
Now she no longer wishes; you mustn't want it,
you've got to stop chasing her now—cut your losses,
harden your heart & hold out firmly against her.
Goodbye now, lady. Catullus' heart is hardened,
he will not look to you nor call against your wishes—
how you'll regret it when nobody comes calling!
So much for you, bitch—your life is all behind you!
Now who will come to see you, thinking you lovely?
Whom will you love now, and whom will you belong to?
Whom will you kiss? And whose lips will you nibble?
But *you,* Catullus! *You* must hold out now, firmly!

58

Lesbia, Caelius[7]—yes, our darling,
yes, *Lesbia,* the Lesbia Catullus
once loved uniquely, more than any other!
—now on streetcorners & in wretched alleys
she shucks the offspring of greathearted Remus.[8]

11[9]

Aurelius & Furius, true comrades,
whether Catullus penetrates to where in
outermost India booms the eastern ocean's
   wonderful thunder;

whether he stops with Arabs or Hyrcani,
Parthian bowmen or nomadic Sagae;[1]
or goes to Egypt, which the Nile so richly
   dyes, overflowing;

even if he should scale the lofty Alps, or
summon to mind the mightiness of Caesar

7. Perhaps the Marcus Caelius Rufus who was one of Clodia's lovers and whom the statesman and orator Cicero defended when she sued him for trying to poison her. 8. Brother of Romulus, founder of Rome; symbol of Rome's greatness. 9. Like poem 51, also in Sapphic meter. 1. These are all peoples on the fringes of the Roman empire (and so in Roman eyes exotic and menacing).

viewing the Gallic Rhine, the dreadful Britons[2]
at the world's far end—

you're both prepared to share in my adventures,
and any others which the gods may send me.
Back to my girl then, carry her this bitter
message, these spare words:

May she have joy & profit from her cocksmen,
go down embracing hundreds all together,
never with love, but without interruption
wringing their balls dry;

nor look to my affection as she used to,
for she has left it broken, like a flower
at the edge of a field after the plowshare
brushes it, passing.

76

If any pleasure can come to a man through recalling
decent behavior in his relations with others,
not breaking his word, and never, in any agreement,
deceiving men by abusing vows sworn to heaven,
then countless joys will await you in old age, Catullus,
as a reward for this unrequited passion!
For all of those things which a man could possibly say or
do have all been said & done by you already,
and none of them counted for anything, thanks to her vileness!
Then why endure your self-torment any longer?
Why not abandon this wretched affair altogether,
spare yourself pain the gods don't intend you to suffer!
It's hard to break off with someone you've loved such a long time:
it's hard, but you have to do it, somehow or other.
Your only chance is to get out from under this sickness,
no matter whether or not you think you're able.
O gods, if pity is yours, or if ever to any
who lay near death you offered the gift of your mercy,
look on my suffering: if my life seems to you decent,
then tear from within me this devouring cancer,
this heavy dullness wasting the joints of my body,
completely driving every joy from my spirit!
Now I no longer ask that she love me as I love her,
or—even less likely—that she give up the others:
all that I ask for is health, an end to this foul sickness!
O gods, grant me this in exchange for my worship.

2. Julius Caesar (100–44 B.C.) began the conquest of Gaul in 58 B.C. and in 55 B.C. made an expedition to Britain.

VIRGIL
70–19 B.C.

Publius Virgilius Maro was born in northern Italy, and very little is known about his life. The earliest work that is certainly his is the *Bucolics,* a collection of poems in the pastoral genre that have had enormous influence. These were followed by the *Georgics,* a didactic poem on farming, in four books, which many critics consider his finest work. The *Aeneid,* the Roman epic, was left unfinished at his death.

Like all the Latin poets, Virgil built on the solid foundations of his Greek predecessors. The story of Aeneas, the Trojan prince who came to Italy and whose descendants founded Rome, combines the themes of the *Odyssey* (the wanderer in search of home) and the *Iliad* (the hero in battle). Virgil borrows Homeric turns of phrase, similes, sentiments, and whole incidents; his Aeneas, like Achilles, sacrifices prisoners to the shade of a friend and, like Odysseus, descends alive to the world of the dead. But unlike Achilles, Aeneas does not satisfy the great passion of his life, nor, like Odysseus, does he find a home and peace. The personal objectives of both of Homer's heroes are sacrificed by Aeneas for a greater objective. His mission, imposed on him by the gods, is to found a city, from which, in the fullness of time, will spring the Roman state.

Homer presents us in the *Iliad* with the tragic pattern of the individual will, Achilles' wrath. But Aeneas is more than an individual. He is the prototype of the ideal Roman ruler; his qualities are the devotion to duty and the seriousness of purpose that were to give the Mediterranean world two centuries of ordered government after Augustus. Aeneas's mission begins in disorder in the burning city of Troy, but he leaves it, carrying his father on his shoulders and leading his little son by the hand. This famous picture emphasizes the fact that, unlike Achilles, he is securely set in a continuity of generations, the immortality of the family group, just as his mission to found a city, a home for the gods of Troy whose statues he carries with him, places him in a political and religious continuity. Achilles has no future. When he mentions his father and son, neither of whom he will see again, he emphasizes for us the loneliness of his short career. Odysseus has a father, wife, and son, and his heroic efforts are directed toward reestablishing himself in his proper context, that home in which he will be no longer a man in a world of magic and terror but a man in an organized and continuous community. But he fights for himself. Aeneas, on the other hand, suffers and fights, not for himself, but for the future; his own life is unhappy, and his death miserable. Yet he can console himself with the glory of his sons to come, the pageant of Roman achievement that he is shown by his father in the world below and that he carries on his shield. Aeneas's future is Virgil's present; the consolidation of the Roman peace under Augustus is the reward of Aeneas's unhappy life of effort and suffering.

Summarized like this, the *Aeneid* sounds like propaganda, which, in one sense of the word, it is. What saves it from the besetting fault of even the best propaganda—the partial concealment of the truth—is the fact that Virgil maintains an independence of the power that he is celebrating and sees his hero in the round. He knows that the Roman ideal of devotion to duty has another side, the suppression of many aspects of the personality, and that the man who wins and uses power must sacrifice much of himself, must live a life that, compared with that of Achilles or Odysseus, is constricted. In Virgil's poem Aeneas betrays the great passion of his life, his love for Dido, queen of Carthage. He does it reluctantly, but nevertheless he leaves her, and the full realization of what he has lost comes to him only when he meets her ghost in the world below. He weeps (as he did not at Carthage) and he pleads, in stronger terms than he did then, the overriding power that forced him to depart: "I left your land against my will, my queen." She leaves him without a word, her silence as impervious to pleas and tears as his was once at Carthage, and she goes back to join her first love, her husband, Sychaeus. Aeneas has sacrificed his love to something greater, but this does not insulate him from unhappiness. The limitations on the dedicated individual are emphasized by the contrasting figure of Dido, who follows her own impulse always, even in death. By her death, Virgil tells us expressly, she forestalls fate, breaks loose from the pattern in which Aeneas remains to the bitter end.

The angry reactions that this part of the poem has produced in many critics are the true measure of Virgil's success. Aeneas does act in such a way that he forfeits much of our sympathy, but this is surely exactly what Virgil intended. The Dido episode is not, as many critics have supposed, a flaw in the great design, a case of Virgil's sympathy outrunning his admiration for Aeneas; it is Virgil's emphatic statement of the sacrifice that the Roman ideal of duty demands. Aeneas's sacrifice is so great that few of us could make it ourselves, and none of us can contemplate it in another without a feeling of loss. It is an expression of the famous Virgilian sadness that informs every line of the *Aeneid* and that makes a poem that was in its historical context a command performance into the great epic that has dominated Western literature ever since.

VIRGIL IN LATIN

Conticuere omnes intentique ora tenebant;
inde toro pater Aeneas sic orsus ab alto:
  Infandum, regina, iubes renovare dolorem,
Troianas ut opes et lamentabile regnum
eruerint Danai, quaeque ipse miserrima uidi
et quorum pars magna fui. quis talia fando
Myrmidonum Dolopomue aut duri miles Ulixi
temperet a lacrimis? et iam nox umida caelo
praecipitat suadentque cadentia sidera somnos.
sed si tantus amor casus cognoscere nostros
et breviter Troiae supremum audire laborem,
quamquam animus meminisse horret luctuque refugit,
incipiam.

This is the beginning of book 2 of the *Aeneid;* Aeneas, at the banquet in Carthage, tells the story of the fall of Troy. The long lines do not employ rhyme but they have a regular rhythmic pattern based not on stress, as in English verse, but on length of syllable—that is, the time taken to pronounce it. Some vowels are naturally long, and others naturally short, but a short vowel may be made long by position (if it is followed by two consonants, it takes just as much time to pronounce as if it were naturally long). The line consists of six feet, either dactyl (– ◡ ◡) or spondee (– –). In the first four feet various combinations are employed, but the last two feet, except in cases where a special effect is sought, are always dactyl plus spondee.

This hexameter (six-foot) line is capable of great variety, contained always in the formal pattern. Unfortunately, attempts to reproduce its disciplined variety in English stressed verse (Longfellow's "This is the forest primeval," for example) have not proved successful, and the translator has used a modern adaptation of the basic English line, the iambic pentameter of Shakespeare and Milton.

The subtle variation of the rhythm is not the only problem faced by translators; they must also try to compensate for the loss of effects that depend on the flexibility of Latin word order. In English, syntactical relationship is determined by that order: "man bites dog" means the opposite of "dog bites man." In Latin, because the terminations of the nouns show who does what to whom, "man bites dog" is *vir mordet canem,* and "dog bites man" *canis mordet virum.* Consequently, the words can be arranged in any order with no change of meaning. *Virum canis mordet, canis virum mordet,* and any other combination of these three elements all mean the same thing: "dog bites man." But the word order is not without its force; it can indicate emphasis. Normal order—subject, object, verb (for the Latin verb tends toward the end of the sentence)—would be *canis virum mordet*. But putting *virum*, the object, first—*virum canis mordet*—would draw attention to that word: "it was a *man* the dog bit."

This is a simple example; much more complicated effects are available to a poet in extended sentences. Line 3 of the passage quoted above, for example, uses the flexibility of word order not only for emphasis but also for exploring the possibilities of ambiguity and surprise offered by a highly inflected language. *Infandum* ("unspeakable, something that cannot be said") is the first word, and we do not know from its termination whether it is subject or object or whether it is to be understood as a noun ("an unspeakable thing") or an adjective for which a noun will be supplied later. *Regina* ("queen") could, according to its termination, be the subject of the sentence, but the context, Aeneas's reply to the queen's request for his story, suggests strongly that it is a form of address: "Unspeakable, oh Queen." The subject comes with the next word, the verb *iubes;* its termination shows that this is the second person, the "you" form—"you command." She has commanded something unspeakable. Is the reader being prepared for a refusal on the part of Aeneas to tell his story? *Renovare* defines the queen's order—"to renew"—and *dolorem* tells us what he is to renew—"sorrow." And the termination of this word suggests that the first word of the line, *infandum,* is in fact an adjective defining *dolorem.* The line, when one reaches this last word, re-forms itself into an unexpected pattern: "Unspeakable, oh Queen, is the sorrow you command me to renew." The line is enclosed between the two most important words in Aeneas's statement, *infandum* and *dolorem;* its last word imposes on us a slight change in our understanding of its first and so redirects attention to that solemn opening word of Aeneas's evocation of the fall of Troy, three long syllables heavy with grief for the lost splendor of a city that is now ash and rubble.

Useful and accessible discussions of basic aspects of the *Aeneid* and of its historical and literary context are W. A. Camps, *An Introduction to Virgil's Aeneid* (1969); Jasper Griffin, *Virgil* (1986); and K. W. Gransden, *Virgil, the Aeneid* (1990). R. D. Williams, *The Aeneid of Virgil: A Companion to the Translation of C. Day Lewis* (1985), gives a summary and outline of the poem, with brief notes on specific passages. W. S. Anderson, *The Art of the Aeneid* (1969), is a sensible book-by-book reading of the poem. Brooks Otis, *Virgil: A Study in Civilized Poetry* (1963, 1985), and R. O. A. M. Lyne, *Further Voices in Virgil's Aeneid* (1987), are more detailed but readable and influential works of criticism. Valuable collections of essays by various authors are Steele Commager, ed., *Virgil: A Collection of Critical Essays* (1966); Harold Bloom, ed., *Virgil* (1986); and Harold Bloom, ed., *Virgil's Aeneid* (1987). Useful commentary on the *Aeneid* and on various aspects of Virgil's work may be found in Nicholas Horsfall, ed., *A Companion to the Study of Virgil* (2000).

PRONOUNCING GLOSSARY

The following list uses common English syllables and stress accents to provide rough equivalents of selected words whose pronunciation may be unfamiliar to the general reader.

Aeneas: *i-nee'-uhs*

Aeneid: *i-nee'-id*

Anchisës: *an-kai'-seez*

Andromachë: *an-dro'-ma-kee*

Aurora: *aw-roh'-rah*

Automedon: *aw-to'-me-don*

Charon: *kah'-ron*

Chimaera: *kai-meer'-uh*

Cyllenë: *si-lee'-nee*

Cytherëa: *si-the-ree'-uh*

Danaans: *da'-nay-unz*

Deiphobus: *day-i'-fo-bus*

Dido: *dai'-doh*

Dionysus: *dai-oh-nai'-sus*

Eumenidës: *yoo-me'-ni-deez*

Hecate: *he'-kat-ee*

Lethe: *lee'-thee*

Musaeus: *moo-see'-us*

Peneleus: *pee-ne'-lyoos*

Phrygian: *fri'-jun*

Pirithoüs: *pi-ri'-thoh-us*
Scaean: *see'-an*
Teucer: *tyoo'-ser*
Thymoetes: *thee-moy'-teez*
Tisiphone: *ti-si'-fo-nee*
Xanthus: *zan'-thus*

The Aeneid[1]

FROM BOOK I

[*Prologue*]

I sing of warfare and a man at war.[2]
From the sea-coast of Troy in early days
He came to Italy by destiny,
To our Lavinian[3] western shore,
A fugitive, this captain, buffeted
Cruelly on land as on the sea
By blows from powers of the air—behind them
Baleful Juno[4] in her sleepless rage.
And cruel losses were his lot in war,
Till he could found a city and bring home
His gods to Latium, land of the Latin race,
The Alban[5] lords, and the high walls of Rome.
Tell me the causes now, O Muse, how galled
In her divine pride, and how sore at heart
From her old wound, the queen of gods compelled him—
A man apart, devoted to his mission—
To undergo so many perilous days
And enter on so many trials. Can anger
Black as this prey on the minds of heaven?
Tyrian[6] settlers in that ancient time
Held Carthage,[7] on the far shore of the sea,
Set against Italy and Tiber's[8] mouth,
A rich new town, warlike and trained for war.
And Juno, we are told, cared more for Carthage
Than for any walled city of the earth,
More than for Samos,[9] even. There her armor
And chariot were kept, and, fate permitting,
Carthage would be the ruler of the world.
So she intended, and so nursed that power.
But she had heard long since
That generations born of Trojan blood
Would one day overthrow her Tyrian walls,

1. Translated by Robert Fitzgerald. 2. Aeneas, a Trojan champion in the fight for Troy, son of Venus (or Aphrodite, the goddess of love) and Anchisës, and a member of the royal house of Troy. 3. Near Rome, named after the city of Lavinium. After the fall of Troy, Aeneas went in search of a new home, eventually settling here. 4. Wife of the ruler of the gods (Hera in Greek). As in the *Iliad,* she is a bitter enemy of the Trojans. 5. The city of Alba Longa was founded by Aeneas's son Ascanius. Romulus and Remus, the builders of Rome, were also from Alba. Latium is the coastal plain on which Rome is situated. 6. From Tyre, on the coast of Palestine, the principal city of the Phoenicians, a seafaring people. 7. On the coast of North Africa, opposite Sicily. Originally a Tyrian colony, it became a rich commercial center, controlling traffic in the western Mediterranean. 8. The river that flows through Rome. 9. A large island off the coast of Asia Minor, famous for its cult of Hera (Juno).

And from that blood a race would come in time
With ample kingdoms, arrogant in war,
For Libya's ruin: so the Parcae[1] spun.
In fear of this, and holding in memory
The old war she had carried on at Troy
For Argos'[2] sake (the origins of that anger,
That suffering, still rankled: deep within her,
Hidden away, the judgment Paris[3] gave,
Snubbing her loveliness; the race she hated;
The honors given ravished Ganymede),
Saturnian Juno,[4] burning for it all,
Buffeted on the waste of sea those Trojans
Left by the Greeks and pitiless Achilles,
Keeping them far from Latium. For years
They wandered as their destiny drove them on
From one sea to the next: so hard and huge
A task it was to found the Roman people.

[*Aeneas Arrives in Carthage*]

Summary The story opens with a storm, provoked by Juno's agency, which scatters Aeneas's fleet off Sicily and separates him from his companions. He lands on the African coast near Carthage. Setting out with his friend Achatës to explore the country, he meets his mother, Venus (Aphrodite), who tells him that the rest of his ships are safe and directs him to the city just founded by Dido, the queen of Carthage. Venus surrounds Aeneas and Achatës with a cloud so that they can see without being seen.

Meanwhile
The two men pressed on where the pathway led,
Soon climbing a long ridge that gave a view
Down over the city and facing towers.
Aeneas found, where lately huts had been,
Marvelous buildings, gateways, cobbled ways,
And din of wagons. There the Tyrians[5]
Were hard at work: laying courses for walls,
Rolling up stones to build the citadel,
While others picked out building sites and plowed
A boundary furrow. Laws were being enacted,
Magistrates and a sacred senate chosen.
Here men were dredging harbors, there they laid
The deep foundation of a theater,
And quarried massive pillars to enhance
The future stage—as bees in early summer
In sunlight in the flowering fields

1. The Fates, who were imagined as female divinities who spun human destinies. Rome captured and destroyed Carthage in 146 B.C. Libya is used as an inclusive name for the North African coast. 2. Home city of the Achaean (Greek) kings Agamemnon and Menelaus. Juno was on their side when they went to Troy to retrieve Helen, Menelaus's wife. 3. Son of King Priam of Troy. He was asked to judge which goddess—Venus, Juno, or Minerva (Athena)—was most beautiful. All three offered bribes, but Venus's promise (of Helen's love) prevailed, and Paris awarded her the prize. 4. Her father was Saturn, a Titan. Ganymede was a Trojan boy of extreme beauty who was taken up into heaven by Jupiter (Zeus), ruler of the gods. 5. See p. 1055, n. 6.

Hum at their work, and bring along the young
Full-grown to beehood; as they cram their combs
With honey, brimming all the cells with nectar,
Or take newcomers' plunder, or like troops
Alerted, drive away the lazy drones,
And labor thrives and sweet thyme scents the honey.
Aeneas said: "How fortunate these are
Whose city walls are rising here and now!"

He looked up at the roofs, for he had entered,
Swathed in cloud—strange to relate—among them,
Mingling with men, yet visible to none.
In mid-town stood a grove that cast sweet shade
Where the Phoenicians, shaken by wind and sea,
Had first dug up that symbol Juno showed them,
A proud warhorse's head: this meant for Carthage
Prowess in war and ease of life[6] through ages.
Here being built by the Sidonian[7] queen
Was a great temple planned in Juno's honor,
Rich in offerings and the godhead there.
Steps led up to a sill of bronze, with brazen
Lintel, and bronze doors on groaning pins.
Here in this grove new things that met his eyes
Calmed Aeneas' fear for the first time.
Here for the first time he took heart to hope
For safety, and to trust his destiny more
Even in affliction. It was while he walked
From one to another wall of the great temple
And waited for the queen, staring amazed
At Carthaginian promise, at the handiwork
Of artificers and the toil they spent upon it:
He found before his eyes the Trojan battles
In the old war, now known throughout the world—
The great Atridae, Priam, and Achilles,
Fierce in his rage at both sides.[8] Here Aeneas
Halted, and tears came.
"What spot on earth,"
He said, "what region of the earth, Achatës,
Is not full of the story of our sorrow?
Look, here is Priam. Even so far away
Great valor has due honor; they weep here
For how the world goes, and our life that passes
Touches their hearts. Throw off your fear. This fame
Insures some kind of refuge."
He broke off
To feast his eyes and mind on a mere image,

6. Because they would have a land fertile enough to support horses. 7. From Sidon, a Phoenician city.
8. Because Achilles, the greatest warrior on the Achaean side, quarreled with Agamemnon. *Atridae:* sons of Atreus—Agamemnon and Menelaus.

Sighing often, cheeks grown wet with tears,
To see again how, fighting around Troy,
The Greeks broke here, and ran before the Trojans,
And there the Phrygians[9] ran, as plumed Achilles
Harried them in his warcar. Nearby, then,
He recognized the snowy canvas tents
Of Rhesus,[1] and more tears came: these, betrayed
In first sleep, Diomedes devastated,
Swording many, till he reeked with blood,
Then turned the mettlesome horses toward the beachhead
Before they tasted Trojan grass or drank
At Xanthus ford.[2]
And on another panel
Troilus,[3] without his armor, luckless boy,
No match for his antagonist, Achilles,
Appeared pulled onward by his team: he clung
To his warcar, though fallen backward, hanging
On to the reins still, head dragged on the ground,
His javelin scribbling S's in the dust.
Meanwhile to hostile Pallas'[4] shrine
The Trojan women walked with hair unbound,
Bearing the robe of offering, in sorrow,
Entreating her, beating their breasts. But she,
Her face averted, would not raise her eyes.
And there was Hector, dragged around Troy walls
Three times, and there for gold Achilles sold him,
Bloodless and lifeless. Now indeed Aeneas
Heaved a mighty sigh from deep within him,
Seeing the spoils, the chariot, and the corpse
Of his great friend, and Priam, all unarmed,
Stretching his hands out.
He himself he saw
In combat with the first of the Achaeans,
And saw the ranks of Dawn, black Memnon's[5] arms;
Then, leading the battalion of Amazons
With half-moon shields, he saw Penthesilëa[6]
Fiery amid her host, buckling a golden
Girdle beneath her bare and arrogant breast,
A girl who dared fight men, a warrior queen.
Now, while these wonders were being surveyed
By Aeneas of Dardania,[7] while he stood
Enthralled, devouring all in one long gaze,
The queen paced toward the temple in her beauty,
Dido, with a throng of men behind.

9. Trojans. 1. King of Thrace, who came to the aid of Troy just before the end of the war. 2. An oracle proclaimed that if Rhesus's horses ate Trojan grass and drank the water of the river Xanthus, Troy would not fall. Odysseus and Diomedes went into the Trojan lines at night, killed the king, and stole the horses. 3. A young son of Priam. 4. Athena (see *Iliad* 6.218ff.). 5. King of the Ethiopians, who fought on the Trojan side. 6. Queen of the Amazons, killed by Achilles. 7. The kingdom of Troy.

As on Eurotas bank or Cynthus ridge
Diana[8] trains her dancers, and behind her
On every hand the mountain nymphs appear,
A myriad converging; with her quiver
Slung on her shoulders, in her stride she seems
The tallest, taller by a head than any,
And joy pervades Latona's[9] quiet heart:
So Dido seemed, in such delight she moved
Amid her people, cheering on the toil
Of a kingdom in the making. At the door
Of the goddess' shrine, under the temple dome,
All hedged about with guards on her high throne,
She took her seat. Then she began to give them
Judgments and rulings, to apportion work
With fairness, or assign some tasks by lot,
When suddenly Aeneas saw approaching,
Accompanied by a crowd, Antheus and Sergestus
And brave Cloanthus,[1] with a few companions,
Whom the black hurricane had driven far
Over the sea and brought to other coasts.
He was astounded, and Achatës too
Felt thrilled by joy and fear: both of them longed
To take their friends' hands, but uncertainty
Hampered them. So, in their cloudy mantle,
They hid their eagerness, waiting to learn
What luck these men had had, where on the coast
They left their ships, and why they came. It seemed
Spokesmen for all the ships were now arriving,
Entering the hall, calling for leave to speak.
When all were in, and full permission given
To make their plea before the queen, their eldest,
Ilioneus, with composure said:

"Your majesty,
Granted by great Jupiter freedom to found
Your new town here and govern fighting tribes
With justice—we poor Trojans, worn by winds
On every sea, entreat you: keep away
Calamity of fire from our ships!
Let a godfearing people live, and look
More closely at our troubles. Not to ravage
Libyan hearths or turn with plunder seaward
Have we come; that force and that audacity
Are not for beaten men.

There is a country
Called by the Greeks Hesperia, very old,
Potent in warfare and in wealth of earth;

8. Virgin goddess of the hunt (Artemis in Greek). Eurotas is a river near Sparta where Diana was worshiped. Cynthus is a mountain on the island of Delos, Diana's birthplace. 9. Diana's mother (Leto in Greek).
1. Ship captains of Aeneas's fleet from whom he had been separated in the storm.

Oenotrians farmed it; younger settlers now,
The tale goes, call it by their chief's[2] name, Italy.
We laid our course for this.
But stormy Orion[3] and a high sea rising
Deflected us on shoals and drove us far,
With winds against us, into whelming waters,
Unchanneled reefs. We kept afloat, we few,
To reach your coast. What race of men is this?
What primitive state could sanction this behavior?
Even on beaches we are denied a landing,
Harried by outcry and attack, forbidden
To set foot on the outskirts of your country.
If you care nothing for humanity
And merely mortal arms, respect the gods
Who are mindful of good actions and of evil!

We had a king, Aeneas—none more just,
More zealous, greater in warfare and in arms.
If fate preserves him, if he does not yet
Lie spent amid the insensible shades but still
Takes nourishment of air, we need fear nothing;
Neither need you repent of being first
In courtesy, to outdo us. Sicily too
Has towns and plowlands and a famous king
Of Trojan blood, Acestës.[4] May we be
Permitted here to beach our damaged ships,
Hew timbers in your forest, cut new oars,
And either sail again for Latium, happily,
If we recover shipmates and our king,
Or else, if that security is lost,
If Libyan waters hold you, Lord Aeneas,
Best of Trojans, hope of Iulus[5] gone,
We may at least cross over to Sicily
From which we came, to homesteads ready there,
And take Acestës for our king."
Ilioneus
Finished, and all the sons of Dardanus[6]
Murmured assent. Dido with eyes downcast
Replied in a brief speech:
"Cast off your fear,
You Teucrians, put anxiety aside.
Severe conditions and the kingdom's youth
Constrain me to these measures, to protect
Our long frontiers with guards.
Who has not heard
Of the people of Aeneas, of Troy city,

2. Italus. *Hesperia:* the western country. The Oenotrians were the original inhabitants of Italy. 3. The setting of this constellation in November signaled the onset of stormy weather at sea. 4. His mother was Trojan; he had offered Aeneas and his people a home in his dominions. 5. Ascanius, Aeneas's son. 6. Ancestor of the Trojans.

Her valors and her heroes, and the fires
Of the great war? We are not so oblivious,
We Phoenicians. The sun yokes his team
Within our range[7] at Carthage. Whether you choose
Hesperia Magna and the land of Saturn
Or Eryx[8] in the west and King Acestës,
I shall dispatch you safely with an escort,
Provisioned from my stores. Or would you care
To join us in this realm on equal terms?
The city I build is yours; haul up your ships;
Trojan and Tyrian will be all one to me.
If only he were here, your king himself,
Caught by the same easterly, Aeneas!
Indeed, let me send out trustworthy men
Along the coast, with orders to comb it all
From one end of Libya to the other,
In case the sea cast the man up and now
He wanders lost, in town or wilderness."

Elated at Dido's words, both staunch Achatës
And father Aeneas had by this time longed
To break out of the cloud. Achatës spoke
With urgency:
"My lord, born to the goddess,
What do you feel, what is your judgment now?
You see all safe, our ships and friends recovered.
One is lost;[9] we saw that one go down
Ourselves, amid the waves. Everything else
Bears out your mother's own account of it."

He barely finished when the cloud around them
Parted suddenly and thinned away
Into transparent air. Princely Aeneas
Stood and shone in the bright light, head and shoulders
Noble as a god's. For she who bore him[1]
Breathed upon him beauty of hair and bloom
Of youth and kindled brilliance in his eyes,
As an artist's hand gives style to ivory,
Or sets pure silver, or white stone of Paros,[2]
In framing yellow gold. Then to the queen
He spoke as suddenly as, to them all,
He had just appeared:
"Before your eyes I stand,
Aeneas the Trojan, that same one you look for,
Saved from the sea off Libya.
You alone,

7. I.e., we are not outside the circuit of the sun; we are part of the civilized world and hear the news. 8. On the west coast of Sicily. *Land of Saturn*: an old legend connected Italy with Saturn, the father of Jupiter. 9. One ship, captained by Orontes, sank in the storm. 1. Venus. 2. The marble of the island of Paros was famous.

Moved by the untold ordeals of old Troy,
Seeing us few whom the Greeks left alive,
Worn out by faring ill on land and sea,
Needy of everything—you'd give these few
A home and city, allied with yourselves.
Fit thanks for this are not within our power,
Not to be had from Trojans anywhere
Dispersed in the great world.
May the gods—
And surely there are powers that care for goodness,
Surely somewhere justice counts—may they
And your own consciousness of acting well
Reward you as they should. What age so happy
Brought you to birth? How splendid were your parents
To have conceived a being like yourself!
So long as brooks flow seaward, and the shadows
Play over mountain slopes, and highest heaven
Feeds the stars, your name and your distinction
Go with me, whatever lands may call me."

With this he gave his right hand to his friend
Ilioneus, greeting Serestus with his left,
Then took the hands of those brave men, Cloanthus,
Gyas, and the rest.
Sidonian Dido
Stood in astonishment, first at the sight
Of such a captain, then at his misfortune,
Presently saying:
"Born of an immortal
Mother though you are, what adverse destiny
Dogs you through these many kinds of danger?
What rough power brings you from sea to land
In savage places? Are you truly he,
Aeneas, whom kind Venus bore
To the Dardanian, the young Anchisës,
Near to the stream of Phrygian Simoïs?
I remember the Greek, Teucer,[3] came to Sidon,
Exiled, and in search of a new kingdom.
Belus, my father, helped him. In those days
Belus campaigned with fire and sword on Cyprus
And won that island's wealth. Since then, the fall
Of Troy, your name, and the Pelasgian kings
Have been familiar to me. Teucer, your enemy,
Spoke often with admiration of the Teucrians
And traced his own descent from Teucrian stock.
Come, then, soldiers, be our guests. My life
Was one of hardship and forced wandering
Like your own, till in this land at length

3. A warrior who fought at Troy and was later exiled from his home. He founded a city on the island of Cyprus. He is not the Trojan king Teucer.

Fortune would have me rest. Through pain I've learned
To comfort suffering men."
She led Aeneas
Into the royal house, but not before
Declaring a festal day in the gods' temples.
As for the ships' companies, she sent
Twenty bulls to the shore, a hundred swine,
Huge ones, with bristling backs, and fatted lambs,
A hundred of them, and their mother ewes—
All gifts for happy feasting on that day.

Now the queen's household made her great hall glow
As they prepared a banquet in the kitchens.
Embroidered table cloths, proud crimson-dyed,
Were spread, and set with massive silver plate,
Or gold, engraved with brave deeds of her fathers,
A sequence carried down through many captains
In a long line from the founding of the race.

BOOK II

[How They Took the City][4]

The room fell silent, and all eyes were on him,
As Father Aeneas from his high couch began:

"Sorrow too deep to tell, your majesty,
You order me to feel and tell once more:
How the Danaans[5] leveled in the dust
The splendor of our mourned-forever kingdom—
Heartbreaking things I saw with my own eyes
And was myself a part of. Who could tell them,
Even a Myrmidon or Dolopian
Or ruffian of Ulysses,[6] without tears?
Now, too, the night is well along, with dewfall
Out of heaven, and setting stars weigh down
Our heads toward sleep. But if so great desire
Moves you to hear the tale of our disasters,
Briefly recalled, the final throes of Troy,
However I may shudder at the memory
And shrink again in grief, let me begin.

Knowing their strength broken in warfare, turned
Back by the fates, and years—so many years—
Already slipped away, the Danaan captains
By the divine handicraft of Pallas built
A horse of timber, tall as a hill,
And sheathed its ribs with planking of cut pine.
This they gave out to be an offering
For a safe return by sea, and the word went round.

4. At the banquet that Dido gives for Aeneas, he relates, at her request, the story of the fall of Troy.
5. The Greeks.
6. Odysseus in Greek. Myrmidons and Dolopians were Achilles' soldiers.

But on the sly they shut inside a company
Chosen from their picked soldiery by lot,
Crowding the vaulted caverns in the dark—
The horse's belly—with men fully armed.

Offshore there's a long island, Tenedos,
Famous and rich while Priam's kingdom lasted,
A treacherous anchorage now, and nothing more.
They crossed to this and hid their ships behind it
On the bare shore beyond. We thought they'd gone,
Sailing home to Mycenae before the wind,
So Teucer's town is freed of her long anguish,
Gates thrown wide! And out we go in joy
To see the Dorian[7] campsites, all deserted,
The beach they left behind. Here the Dolopians
Pitched their tents, here cruel Achilles lodged,
There lay the ships, and there, formed up in ranks,
They came inland to fight us. Of our men
One group stood marveling, gaping up to see
The dire gift of the cold unbedded goddess,[8]
The sheer mass of the horse.
Thymoetes shouts
It should be hauled inside the walls and moored
High on the citadel—whether by treason
Or just because Troy's fate went that way now.
Capys opposed him; so did the wiser heads:
'Into the sea with it,' they said, 'or burn it,
Build up a bonfire under it,
This trick of the Greeks, a gift no one can trust,
Or cut it open, search the hollow belly!'

Contrary notions pulled the crowd apart.
Next thing we knew, in front of everyone,
Laocoön with a great company
Came furiously running from the Height,[9]
And still far off cried out: 'O my poor people,
Men of Troy, what madness has come over you?
Can you believe the enemy truly gone?
A gift from the Danaans, and no ruse?
Is that Ulysses' way, as you have known him?
Achaeans must be hiding in this timber,
Or it was built to butt against our walls,
Peer over them into our houses, pelt
The city from the sky. Some crookedness
Is in this thing. Have no faith in the horse!
Whatever it is, even when Greeks bring gifts
I fear them, gifts and all.'
He broke off then
And rifled his big spear with all his might
Against the horse's flank, the curve of belly.

7. Greek. 8. Athena. 9. The citadel, the acropolis.

It stuck there trembling, and the rounded hull
Reverberated groaning at the blow.
If the gods' will had not been sinister,
If our own minds had not been crazed,
He would have made us foul that Argive den
With bloody steel, and Troy would stand today—
O citadel of Priam, towering still!

But now look: hillmen, shepherds of Dardania,
Raising a shout, dragged in before the king
An unknown fellow with hands tied behind—
This all as he himself had planned,
Volunteering, letting them come across him,
So he could open Troy to the Achaeans.
Sure of himself this man was, braced for it
Either way, to work his trick or die.
From every quarter Trojans run to see him,
Ring the prisoner round, and make a game
Of jeering at him. Be instructed now
In Greek deceptive arts: one barefaced deed
Can tell you of them all.
As the man stood there, shaken and defenceless,
Looking around at ranks of Phrygians,
'Oh god,' he said, 'what land on earth, what seas
Can take me in? What's left me in the end,
Outcast that I am from the Danaans,
Now the Dardanians will have my blood?'

The whimpering speech brought us up short; we felt
A twinge for him. Let him speak up, we said,
Tell us where he was born, what news he brought,
What he could hope for as a prisoner.
Taking his time, slow to discard his fright,
He said:
'I'll tell you the whole truth, my lord,
No matter what may come of it. Argive
I am by birth, and will not say I'm not.
That first of all: Fortune has made a derelict
Of Sinon, but the bitch
Won't make an empty liar of him, too.
Report of Palamedes[1] may have reached you,
Scion of Belus' line, a famous man
Who gave commands against the war. For this,
On a trumped-up charge, on perjured testimony,
The Greeks put him to death—but now they mourn him,
Now he has lost the light. Being kin to him,
In my first years I joined him as companion,
Sent by my poor old father on this campaign,
And while he held high rank and influence

1. A Greek warrior who advised Agamemnon to abandon the war against Troy; his downfall was engineered by Ulysses, who planted forged proofs of dealings with the enemy in his tent.

In royal councils, we did well, with honor.
Then by the guile and envy of Ulysses—
Nothing unheard of there!—he left this world,
And I lived on, but under a cloud, in sorrow,
Raging for my blameless friend's downfall.
Demented, too, I could not hold my peace
But said if I had luck, if I won through
Again to Argos, I'd avenge him there.
And I roused hatred with my talk; I fell
Afoul now of that man. From that time on,
Day in, day out, Ulysses
Found new ways to bait and terrify me,
Putting out shady rumors among the troops,
Looking for weapons he could use against me.
He could not rest till Calchas[2] served his turn—
But why go on? The tale's unwelcome, useless,
If Achaeans are all one,
And it's enough I'm called Achaean, then
Exact the punishment, long overdue;
The Ithacan[3] desires it; the Atridae
Would pay well for it.'
Burning with curiosity,
We questioned him, called on him to explain—
Unable to conceive such a performance,
The art of the Pelasgian. He went on,
Atremble, as though he feared us:
'Many times
The Danaans wished to organize retreat,
To leave Troy and the long war, tired out.
If only they had done it! Heavy weather
At sea closed down on them, or a fresh gale
From the Southwest would keep them from embarking,
Most of all after this figure here,
This horse they put together with maple beams,
Reached its full height. Then wind and thunderstorms
Rumbled in heaven. So in our quandary
We sent Eurypylus to Phoebus'[4] oracle,
And he brought back this grim reply:

'Blood and a virgin slain[5]
You gave to appease the winds, for your first voyage
Troyward, O Danaans. Blood again
And Argive blood, one life, wins your return.'

When this got round among the soldiers, gloom
Came over them, and a cold chill that ran
To the very marrow. Who had death in store?
Whom did Apollo call for? Now the man
Of Ithaca haled Calchas out among us

2. The prophet of the Greek army. 3. Ulysses. 4. Apollo. Eurypylus was a minor Greek chieftain.
5. Iphigenia, Agamemnon's daughter.

In tumult, calling on the seer to tell
The true will of the gods. Ah, there were many
Able to divine the crookedness
And cruelty afoot for me, but they
Looked on in silence. For ten days the seer
Kept still, kept under cover, would not speak
Of anyone, or name a man for death,
Till driven to it at last by Ulysses' cries—
By prearrangement—he broke silence, barely
Enough to designate me for the altar.[6]
Every last man agreed. The torments each
Had feared for himself, now shifted to another,
All could endure. And the infamous day came,
The ritual, the salted meal, the fillets[7] . . .
I broke free, I confess it, broke my chains,
Hid myself all night in a muddy marsh,
Concealed by reeds, waiting for them to sail
If they were going to.
Now no hope is left me
Of seeing my home country ever again,
My sweet children, my father, missed for years.
Perhaps the army will demand they pay
For my escape, my crime here, and their death,
Poor things, will be my punishment. Ah, sir,
I beg you by the gods above, the powers
In whom truth lives, and by what faith remains
Uncontaminated to men, take pity
On pain so great and so unmerited!'

For tears we gave him life, and pity, too.
Priam himself ordered the gyves removed
And the tight chain between. In kindness then
He said to him:
'Whoever you may be,
The Greeks are gone; forget them from now on;
You shall be ours. And answer me these questions:
Who put this huge thing up, this horse?
Who designed it? What do they want with it?
Is it religious or a means of war?'

These were his questions. Then the captive, trained
In trickery, in the stagecraft of Achaea,
Lifted his hands unfettered to the stars.
'Eternal fires of heaven,' he began,
'Powers inviolable, I swear by thee,
As by the altars and blaspheming swords
I got away from, and the gods' white bands[8]
I wore as one chosen for sacrifice,
This is justice, I am justified
In dropping all allegiance to the Greeks—

6. The altar of sacrifice. 7. Tufts of wool attached to the victim. 8. The fillets.

As I had cause to hate them; I may bring
Into the open what they would keep dark.
No laws of my own country bind me now.
Only be sure you keep your promises
And keep faith, Troy, as you are kept from harm
If what I say proves true, if what I give
Is great and valuable.
The whole hope
Of the Danaans, and their confidence
In the war they started, rested all along
In help from Pallas. Then the night came
When Diomedes and that criminal,
Ulysses, dared to raid her holy shrine.
They killed the guards on the high citadel
And ripped away the statue, the Palladium,[9]
Desecrating with bloody hands the virginal
Chaplets of the goddess. After that,
Danaan hopes waned and were undermined,
Ebbing away, their strength in battle broken,
The goddess now against them. This she made
Evident to them all with signs and portents.
Just as they set her statue up in camp,
The eyes, cast upward, glowed with crackling flames,
And salty sweat ran down the body. Then—
I say it in awe—three times, up from the ground,
The apparition of the goddess rose
In a lightning flash, with shield and spear atremble.
Calchas divined at once that the sea crossing
Must be attempted in retreat—that Pergamum[1]
Cannot be torn apart by Argive swords
Unless at Argos first they beg new omens,
Carrying homeward the divine power
Brought overseas in ships. Now they are gone
Before the wind to the fatherland, Mycenae,
Gone to enlist new troops and gods. They'll cross
The water again and be here, unforeseen.
So Calchas read the portents. Warned by him,
They set this figure up in reparation
For the Palladium stolen, to appease
The offended power and expiate the crime.
Enormous, though, he made them build the thing
With timber braces, towering to the sky,
Too big for the gates, not to be hauled inside
And give the people back their ancient guardian.
If any hand here violates this gift
To great Minerva,[2] then extinction waits,
Not for one only—would god it were so—
But for the realm of Priam and all Phrygians.

9. The statue of Pallas Athena. An oracle stated that Troy could not be captured as long as the Palladium remained in place in the shrine. 1. The citadel of Troy. 2. Athena.

If this proud offering, drawn by your hands,
Should mount into your city, then so far
As the walls of Pelops' town[3] the tide of Asia
Surges in war: that doom awaits our children.'

This fraud of Sinon, his accomplished lying,
Won us over; a tall tale and fake tears
Had captured us, whom neither Diomedes
Nor Larisaean[4] Achilles overpowered,
Nor ten long years, nor all their thousand ships.

And now another sign, more fearful still,
Broke on our blind miserable people,
Filling us all with dread. Laocoön,
Acting as Neptune's[5] priest that day by lot,
Was on the point of putting to the knife
A massive bull before the appointed altar,
When ah—look there!
From Tenedos, on the calm sea, twin snakes—
I shiver to recall it—endlessly
Coiling, uncoiling, swam abreast for shore,
Their underbellies showing as their crests
Reared red as blood above the swell; behind
They glided with great undulating backs.
Now came the sound of thrashed seawater foaming;
Now they were on dry land, and we could see
Their burning eyes, fiery and suffused with blood,
Their tongues a-flicker out of hissing maws.
We scattered, pale with fright. But straight ahead
They slid until they reached Laocoön.
Each snake enveloped one of his two boys,
Twining about and feeding on the body.
Next they ensnared the man as he ran up
With weapons: coils like cables looped and bound him
Twice round the middle; twice about his throat
They whipped their back-scales, and their heads towered,
While with both hands he fought to break the knots,
Drenched in slime, his head-bands black with venom,
Sending to heaven his appalling cries
Like a slashed bull escaping from an altar,
The fumbled axe shrugged off. The pair of snakes
Now flowed away and made for the highest shrines,
The citadel of pitiless Minerva,
Where coiling they took cover at her feet
Under the rondure of her shield. New terrors
Ran in the shaken crowd: the word went round
Laocoön had paid, and rightfully,
For profanation of the sacred hulk
With his offending spear hurled at its flank.

3. Argos. Pelops was Atreus's father. 4. After Larissa, a town in Achilles' homeland of Thessaly.
5. Poseidon in Greek.

'The offering must be hauled to its true home,'
They clamored. 'Votive prayers to the goddess
Must be said there!'
So we breached the walls
And laid the city open. Everyone
Pitched in to get the figure underpinned
With rollers, hempen lines around the neck.
Deadly, pregnant with enemies, the horse
Crawled upward to the breach. And boys and girls
Sang hymns around the towrope as for joy
They touched it. Rolling on, it cast a shadow
Over the city's heart. O Fatherland,
O Ilium, home of gods! Defensive wall
Renowned in war for Dardanus's people!
There on the very threshold of the breach
It jarred to a halt four times, four times the arms
In the belly thrown together made a sound—
Yet on we strove unmindful, deaf and blind,
To place the monster on our blessed height.
Then, even then, Cassandra's[6] lips unsealed
The doom to come: lips by a god's command
Never believed or heeded by the Trojans.
So pitiably we, for whom that day
Would be the last, made all our temples green
With leafy festal boughs throughout the city.

As heaven turned, Night from the Ocean stream
Came on, profound in gloom on earth and sky
And Myrmidons in hiding. In their homes
The Teucrians lay silent, wearied out,
And sleep enfolded them. The Argive fleet,
Drawn up in line abreast, left Tenedos
Through the aloof moon's friendly stillnesses
And made for the familiar shore. Flame signals
Shone from the command ship. Sinon, favored
By what the gods unjustly had decreed,
Stole out to tap the pine walls and set free
The Danaans in the belly. Opened wide,
The horse emitted men; gladly they dropped
Out of the cavern, captains first, Thessandrus,
Sthenelus and the man of iron, Ulysses;
Hand over hand upon the rope, Acamas, Thoas,
Neoptolemus[7] and Prince Machaon,
Menelaus and then the master builder,
Epeos, who designed the horse decoy.
Into the darkened city, buried deep
In sleep and wine, they made their way,
Cut the few sentries down,

6. Daughter of King Priam of Troy. She was able to foretell the future correctly, but because of a curse, no one believed her prophecies (see Aeschylus's *Agamemnon* 1202ff.). 7. Son of Achilles.

Let in their fellow soldiers at the gate,
And joined their combat companies as planned.

That time of night it was when the first sleep,
Gift of the gods, begins for all mankind,
Arriving gradually, delicious rest.
In sleep, in dream, Hector appeared to me,
Gaunt with sorrow, streaming tears, all torn—
As by the violent car on his death day—
And black with bloody dust,
His puffed-out feet cut by the rawhide thongs.
Ah god, the look of him! How changed
From that proud Hector who returned to Troy
Wearing Achilles' armor,[8] or that one
Who pitched the torches on Danaan ships;
His beard all filth, his hair matted with blood,
Showing the wounds, the many wounds, received
Outside his father's city walls. I seemed
Myself to weep and call upon the man
In grieving speech, brought from the depth of me:

'Light of Dardania, best hope of Troy,
What kept you from us for so long, and where?
From what far place, O Hector, have you come,
Long, long awaited? After so many deaths
Of friends and brothers, after a world of pain
For all our folk and all our town, at last,
Boneweary, we behold you! What has happened
To ravage your serene face? Why these wounds?'

He wasted no reply on my poor questions
But heaved a great sigh from his chest and said:
'Ai! Give up and go, child of the goddess,
Save yourself, out of these flames. The enemy
Holds the city walls, and from her height
Troy falls in ruin. Fatherland and Priam
Have their due; if by one hand our towers
Could be defended, by this hand, my own,
They would have been. Her holy things, her gods
Of hearth and household[9] Troy commends to you.
Accept them as companions of your days;
Go find for them the great walls that one day
You'll dedicate, when you have roamed the sea.'

As he said this, he brought out from the sanctuary
Chaplets and Vesta,[1] Lady of the Hearth,

8. Hector stripped it from the corpse of Patroclus, Achilles' close friend, whom Hector killed in battle. Achilles avenged Patroclus by killing Hector. 9. The Romans kept images of household gods, the Penatës, in a shrine in their homes; the custom is here transferred, unhistorically, to Troy. 1. The goddess of the hearth and fire, which, in the temple, was never allowed to go out.

With her eternal fire.
While I dreamed,
The turmoil rose, with anguish, in the city.
More and more, although Anchises' house
Lay in seclusion, muffled among trees,
The din at the grim onset grew; and now
I shook off sleep, I climbed to the roof top
To cup my ears and listen. And the sound
Was like the sound a grassfire makes in grain,
Whipped by a Southwind, or a torrent foaming
Out of a mountainside to strew in ruin
Fields, happy crops, the yield of plowing teams,
Or woodlands borne off in the flood; in wonder
The shepherd listens on a rocky peak.
I knew then what our trust had won for us,
Knew the Danaan fraud: Deïphobus'[2]
Great house in flames, already caving in
Under the overpowering god of fire;
Ucalegon's already caught nearby;
The glare lighting the straits beyond Sigeum;[3]
The cries of men, the wild calls of the trumpets.

To arm was my first maddened impulse—not
That anyone had a fighting chance in arms;
Only I burned to gather up some force
For combat, and to man some high redoubt.
So fury drove me, and it came to me
That meeting death was beautiful in arms.
Then here, eluding the Achaean spears,
Came Panthus, Orthrys' son, priest of Apollo,
Carrying holy things, our conquered gods,
And pulling a small grandchild along: he ran
Despairing to my doorway.
'Where's the crux,
Panthus,' I said. 'What strongpoint shall we hold?'

Before I could say more, he groaned and answered:
'The last day for Dardania has come,
The hour not to be fought off any longer.
Trojans we have been; Ilium has been;
The glory of the Teucrians is no more;
Black Jupiter has passed it on to Argos.
Greeks are the masters in our burning city.
Tall as a cliff, set in the heart of town,
Their horse pours out armed men. The conqueror,
Gloating Sinon, brews new conflagrations.
Troops hold the gates—as many thousand men
As ever came from great Mycenae; others
Block the lanes with crossed spears; glittering

2. A son of Priam. 3. A promontory overlooking the strait that connects the Aegean with the Black Sea.

In a combat line, swordblades are drawn for slaughter.
Even the first guards at the gates can barely
Offer battle, or blindly make a stand.'

Impelled by these words, by the powers of heaven,
Into the flames I go, into the fight,
Where the harsh Fury, and the din and shouting,
Skyward rising, calls. Crossing my path
In moonlight, five fell in with me, companions:
Ripheus, and Epytus, a great soldier,
Hypanis, Dymas, cleaving to my side
With young Coroebus, Mygdon's son. It happened
That in those very days this man had come
To Troy, aflame with passion for Cassandra,
Bringing to Priam and the Phrygians
A son-in-law's right hand. Unlucky one,
To have been deaf to what his bride foretold!
Now when I saw them grouped, on edge for battle,
I took it all in and said briefly,
'Soldiers,
Brave as you are to no end, if you crave
To face the last fight with me, and no doubt of it,
How matters stand for us each one can see.
The gods by whom this kingdom stood are gone,
Gone from the shrines and altars. You defend
A city lost in flames. Come, let us die,
We'll make a rush into the thick of it.
The conquered have one safety: hope for none.'

The desperate odds doubled their fighting spirit:
From that time on, like predatory wolves
In fog and darkness, when a savage hunger
Drives them blindly on, and cubs in lairs
Lie waiting with dry famished jaws—just so
Through arrow flights and enemies we ran
Toward our sure death, straight for the city's heart,
Cavernous black night over and around us.
Who can describe the havoc of that night
Or tell the deaths, or tally wounds with tears?
The ancient city falls, after dominion
Many long years. In windows, on the streets,
In homes, on solemn porches of the gods,
Dead bodies lie. And not alone the Trojans
Pay the price with their heart's blood; at times
Manhood returns to fire even the conquered
And Danaan conquerors fall. Grief everywhere,
Everywhere terror, and all shapes of death.

Androgeos was the first to cross our path
Leading a crowd of Greeks; he took for granted
That we were friends, and hailed us cheerfully:

'Men, get a move on! Are you made of lead
To be so late and slow? The rest are busy
Carrying plunder from the fires and towers.
Are you just landed from the ships?'
                                        His words
Were barely out, and no reply forthcoming
Credible to him, when he knew himself
Fallen among enemies. Thunderstruck,
He halted, foot and voice, and then recoiled
Like one who steps down on a lurking snake
In a briar patch and jerks back, terrified,
As the angry thing rears up, all puffed and blue.
So backward went Androgeos in panic.
We were all over them in a moment, cut
And thrust, and as they fought on unknown ground,
Startled, unnerved, we killed them everywhere.
So Fortune filled our sails at first. Coroebus,
Elated at our feat and his own courage,
Said:
        'Friends, come follow Fortune. She has shown
The way to safety, shown she's on our side.
We'll take their shields and put on their insignia!
Trickery, bravery: who asks, in war?
The enemy will arm us.'
                                He put on
The plumed helm of Androgeos, took the shield
With blazon and the Greek sword to his side.
Ripheus, Dymas—all were pleased to do it,
Making the still fresh trophies our equipment.
Then we went on, passing among the Greeks,
Protected by our own gods now no longer;
Many a combat, hand to hand, we fought
In the black night, and many a Greek we sent
To Orcus.[4] There were some who turned and ran
Back to the ships and shore; some shamefully
Clambered again into the horse, to hide
In the familiar paunch.
                                When gods are contrary
They stand by no one. Here before us came
Cassandra, Priam's virgin daughter, dragged
By her long hair out of Minerva's shrine,
Lifting her brilliant eyes in vain to heaven—
Her eyes alone, as her white hands were bound.
Coroebus, infuriated, could not bear it,
But plunged into the midst to find his death.
We all went after him, our swords at play,
But here, here first, from the temple gable's height,
We met a hail of missiles from our friends,
Pitiful execution, by their error,
Who thought us Greek from our Greek plumes and shields.

4. The abode of the dead.

Then with a groan of anger, seeing the virgin
Wrested from them, Danaans from all sides
Rallied and attacked us: fiery Ajax,[5]
Atreus' sons, Dolopians in a mass—
As, when a cyclone breaks, conflicting winds
Will come together, Westwind, Southwind, Eastwind
Riding high out of the Dawnland; forests
Bend and roar, and raging all in spume
Nereus[6] with his trident churns the deep.
Then some whom we had taken by surprise
Under cover of night throughout the city
And driven off, came back again: they knew
Our shields and arms for liars now, our speech
Alien to their own. They overwhelmed us.
Coroebus fell at the warrior goddess' altar,
Killed by Peneleus; and Ripheus fell,
A man uniquely just among the Trojans,
The soul of equity; but the gods would have it
Differently. Hypanis, Dymas died,
Shot down by friends; nor did your piety,
Panthus, nor Apollo's fillets shield you
As you went down.
Ashes of Ilium!
Flames that consumed my people! Here I swear
That in your downfall I did not avoid
One weapon, one exchange with the Danaans,
And if it had been fated, my own hand
Had earned my death. But we were torn away
From that place—Iphitus and Pelias too,
One slow with age, one wounded by Ulysses,
Called by a clamor at the hall of Priam.
Truly we found here a prodigious fight,
As though there were none elsewhere, not a death
In the whole city: Mars[7] gone berserk, Danaans
In a rush to scale the roof; the gate besieged
By a tortoise shell of overlapping shields.[8]
Ladders clung to the wall, and men strove upward
Before the very doorposts, on the rungs,
Left hand putting the shield up, and the right
Reaching for the cornice. The defenders
Wrenched out upperworks and rooftiles: these
For missiles, as they saw the end, preparing
To fight back even on the edge of death.
And gilded beams, ancestral ornaments,
They rolled down on the heads below. In hall
Others with swords drawn held the entrance way,
Packed there, waiting. Now we plucked up heart

5. The lesser Ajax, son of Oileus, who raped Cassandra after dragging her away from the shrine; as punishment, he was drowned on his way back to Greece. This is not the great Greek warrior Ajax; he had committed suicide before Troy fell (see *Odyssey* 11). 6. An old sea god and father of the Nereids, the sea nymphs. 7. The war god (Ares in Greek). 8. When attacking a walled position, Roman soldiers protected themselves from overhead missiles by holding their shields above their heads, forming a "roof," which looked like the plates of a tortoiseshell.

To help the royal house, to give our men
A respite, and to add our strength to theirs,
Though all were beaten. And we had for entrance
A rear door, secret, giving on a passage
Between the palace halls; in other days
Andromachë, poor lady, often used it,
Going alone to see her husband's parents
Or taking Astyanax[9] to his grandfather.
I climbed high on the roof, where hopeless men
Were picking up and throwing futile missiles.
Here was a tower like a promontory
Rising toward the stars above the roof:
All Troy, the Danaan ships, the Achaean camp,
Were visible from this. Now close beside it
With crowbars, where the flooring made loose joints,
We pried it from its bed and pushed it over.
Down with a rending crash in sudden ruin
Wide over the Danaan lines it fell;
But fresh troops moved up, and the rain of stones
With every kind of missile never ceased.

Just at the outer doors of the vestibule
Sprang Pyrrhus,[1] all in bronze and glittering,
As a serpent, hidden swollen underground
By a cold winter, writhes into the light,
On vile grass fed, his old skin cast away,
Renewed and glossy, rolling slippery coils,
With lifted underbelly rearing sunward
And triple tongue a-flicker. Close beside him
Giant Periphas and Automedon,
His armor-bearer, once Achilles' driver,
Besieged the place with all the young of Scyros,[2]
Hurling their torches at the palace roof.
Pyrrhus shouldering forward with an axe
Broke down the stony threshold, forced apart
Hinges and brazen door-jambs, and chopped through
One panel of the door, splitting the oak,
To make a window, a great breach. And there
Before their eyes the inner halls lay open,
The courts of Priam and the ancient kings,
With men-at-arms ranked in the vestibule.
From the interior came sounds of weeping,
Pitiful commotion, wails of women
High-pitched, rising in the formal chambers
To ring against the silent golden stars;
And, through the palace, mothers wild with fright
Ran to and fro or clung to doors and kissed them.
Pyrrhus with his father's brawn stormed on,
No bolts or bars or men availed to stop him:

9. Son of Andromachë and Hector. 1. Neoptolemus. 2. Island in the north Aegean where Neoptolemus grew up.

Under his battering the double doors
Were torn out of their sockets and fell inward.
Sheer force cleared the way: the Greeks broke through
Into the vestibule, cut down the guards,
And made the wide hall seethe with men-at-arms—
A tumult greater than when dykes are burst
And a foaming river, swirling out in flood,
Whelms every parapet and races on
Through fields and over all the lowland plains,
Bearing off pens and cattle. I myself
Saw Neoptolemus furious with blood
In the entrance way, and saw the two Atridae;
Hecuba[3] I saw, and her hundred daughters,
Priam before the altars, with his blood
Drenching the fires that he himself had blessed.
Those fifty bridal chambers, hope of a line
So flourishing; those doorways high and proud,
Adorned with takings of barbaric gold,
Were all brought low: fire had them, or the Greeks.

What was the fate of Priam, you may ask.
Seeing his city captive, seeing his own
Royal portals rent apart, his enemies
In the inner rooms, the old man uselessly
Put on his shoulders, shaking with old age,
Armor unused for years, belted a sword on,
And made for the massed enemy to die.
Under the open sky in a central court
Stood a big altar; near it, a laurel tree
Of great age, leaning over, in deep shade
Embowered the Penatës. At this altar
Hecuba and her daughters, like white doves
Blown down in a black storm, clung together,
Enfolding holy images in their arms.
Now, seeing Priam in a young man's gear,
She called out:
'My poor husband, what mad thought
Drove you to buckle on these weapons?
Where are you trying to go? The time is past
For help like this, for this kind of defending,
Even if my own Hector could be here.
Come to me now: the altar will protect us,
Or else you'll die with us.'
She drew him close,
Heavy with years, and made a place for him
To rest on the consecrated stone.
Now see
Politës, one of Priam's sons, escaped
From Pyrrhus' butchery and on the run
Through enemies and spears, down colonnades,

3. Wife of Priam and mother of Hector.

Through empty courtyards, wounded. Close behind
Comes Pyrrhus burning for the death-stroke: has him,
Catches him now, and lunges with the spear.
The boy has reached his parents, and before them
Goes down, pouring out his life with blood.
Now Priam, in the very midst of death,
Would neither hold his peace nor spare his anger.

'For what you've done, for what you've dared,' he said,
'If there is care in heaven for atrocity,
May the gods render fitting thanks, reward you
As you deserve. You forced me to look on
At the destruction of my son: defiled
A father's eyes with death. That great Achilles
You claim to be the son of—and you lie—
Was not like you to Priam, his enemy;
To me who threw myself upon his mercy
He showed compunction, gave me back for burial
The bloodless corpse of Hector, and returned me
To my own realm.'
The old man threw his spear
With feeble impact; blocked by the ringing bronze,
It hung there harmless from the jutting boss.
Then Pyrrhus answered:
'You'll report the news
To Pelidēs,[4] my father; don't forget
My sad behavior, the degeneracy
Of Neoptolemus. Now die.'
With this,
To the altar step itself he dragged him trembling,
Slipping in the pooled blood of his son,
And took him by the hair with his left hand.
The sword flashed in his right; up to the hilt
He thrust it in his body.
That was the end
Of Priam's age, the doom that took him off,
With Troy in flames before his eyes, his towers
Headlong fallen—he that in other days
Had ruled in pride so many lands and peoples,
The power of Asia.
On the distant shore
The vast trunk headless lies without a name.

For the first time that night, inhuman shuddering
Took me, head to foot. I stood unmanned,
And my dear father's image came to mind
As our king, just his age, mortally wounded,
Gasped his life away before my eyes.
Creusa[5] came to mind, too, left alone;
The house plundered; danger to little Iulus.

4. Achilles, son of Peleus. 5. Aeneas's wife.

I looked around to take stock of my men,
But all had left me, utterly played out,
Giving their beaten bodies to the fire
Or plunging from the roof.
It came to this,
That I stood there alone. And then I saw
Lurking beyond the doorsill of the Vesta,
In hiding, silent, in that place reserved,
The daughter of Tyndareus.[6] Glare of fires
Lighted my steps this way and that, my eyes
Glancing over the whole scene, everywhere.
That woman, terrified of the Trojans' hate
For the city overthrown, terrified too
Of Danaan vengeance, her abandoned husband's
Anger after years—Helen, that Fury
Both to her own homeland and Troy, had gone
To earth, a hated thing, before the altars.
Now fires blazed up in my own spirit—
A passion to avenge my fallen town
And punish Helen's whorishness.
'Shall this one
Look untouched on Sparta and Mycenae
After her triumph, going like a queen,
And see her home and husband, kin and children,
With Trojan girls for escort, Phrygian slaves?
Must Priam perish by the sword for this?
Troy burn, for this? Dardania's littoral
Be soaked in blood, so many times, for this?
Not by my leave. I know
No glory comes of punishing a woman,
The feat can bring no honor. Still, I'll be
Approved for snuffing out a monstrous life,
For a just sentence carried out. My heart
Will teem with joy in this avenging fire,
And the ashes of my kin will be appeased.'

So ran my thoughts. I turned wildly upon her,
But at that moment, clear, before my eyes—
Never before so clear—in a pure light
Stepping before me, radiant through the night,
My loving mother came: immortal, tall,
And lovely as the lords of heaven know her.
Catching me by the hand, she held me back,
Then with her rose-red mouth reproved me:
'Son,
Why let such suffering goad you on to fury
Past control? Where is your thoughtfulness
For me, for us? Will you not first revisit
The place you left your father, worn and old,
Or find out if your wife, Creusa, lives,

6. Helen.

And the young boy, Ascanius—all these
Cut off by Greek troops foraging everywhere?
Had I not cared for them, fire would by now
Have taken them, their blood glutted the sword.
You must not hold the woman of Laconia,[7]
That hated face, the cause of this, nor Paris.
The harsh will of the gods it is, the gods,
That overthrows the splendor of this place
And brings Troy from her height into the dust.
Look over there: I'll tear away the cloud
That curtains you, and films your mortal sight,
The fog around you.—Have no fear of doing
Your mother's will, or balk at obeying her.—
Look: where you see high masonry thrown down,
Stone torn from stone, with billowing smoke and dust,
Neptune is shaking from their beds the walls
That his great trident pried up, undermining,
Toppling the whole city down. And look:
Juno in all her savagery holds
The Scaean Gates,[8] and raging in steel armor
Calls her allied army from the ships.
Up on the citadel—turn, look—Pallas Tritonia[9]
Couched in a stormcloud, lightening, with her Gorgon![1]
The Father himself empowers the Danaans,
Urges assaulting gods on the defenders.
Away, child; put an end to toiling so.
I shall be near, to see you safely home.'

She hid herself in the deep gloom of night,
And now the dire forms appeared to me
Of great immortals, enemies of Troy.
I knew the end then: Ilium was going down
In fire, the Troy of Neptune[2] going down,
As in high mountains when the countrymen
Have notched an ancient ash, then make their axes
Ring with might and main, chopping away
To fell the tree—ever on the point of falling,
Shaken through all its foliage, and the treetop
Nodding; bit by bit the strokes prevail
Until it gives a final groan at last
And crashes down in ruin from the height.

Now I descended where the goddess guided,
Clear of the flames, and clear of enemies,
For both retired; so gained my father's door,
My ancient home. I looked for him at once,
My first wish being to help him to the mountains;

7. Helen. 8. One of the principal entrances to Troy. 9. The significance of this adjective is not known; perhaps a reference to her birthplace, Lake Tritonis, in North Africa. But the birthplace legend may have been invented to explain the title. 1. Monster whose appearance turned people to stone; Athena had a Gorgon face on her shield. 2. Neptune was hostile to Troy, although he had helped build the city.

But with Troy gone he set his face against it,
Not to prolong his life, or suffer exile.

'The rest of you, all in your prime,' he said,
'Make your escape; you are still hale and strong.
If heaven's lords had wished me a longer span
They would have saved this home for me. I call it
More than enough that once before I saw
My city taken and wrecked,[3] and went on living.
Here is my death bed, here. Take leave of me.
Depart now. I'll find death with my sword arm.
The enemy will oblige; they'll come for spoils.
Burial can be dispensed with. All these years
I've lingered in my impotence, at odds
With heaven, since the Father of gods and men
Breathed high winds of thunderbolt upon me
And touched me with his fire.'[4]
He spoke on
In the same vein, inflexible. The rest of us,
Creusa and Ascanius and the servants,
Begged him in tears not to pull down with him
Our lives as well, adding his own dead weight
To the fates' pressure. But he would not budge,
He held to his resolve and to his chair.
I felt swept off again to fight, in misery
Longing for death. What choices now were open,
What chance had I?
'Did you suppose, my father,
That I could tear myself away and leave you?
Unthinkable; how could a father say it?
Now if it please the powers above that nothing
Stand of this great city; if your heart
Is set on adding your own death and ours
To that of Troy, the door's wide open for it:
Pyrrhus will be here, splashed with Priam's blood;
He kills the son before his father's eyes,
The father at the altars.
My dear mother,
Was it for this, through spears and fire, you brought me,
To see the enemy deep in my house,
To see my son, Ascanius, my father,
And near them both, Creusa,
Butchered in one another's blood? My gear,
Men, bring my gear. The last light calls the conquered.
Give me back to the Greeks. Let me take up
The combat once again. We shall not all
Die this day unavenged.'
I buckled on
Swordbelt and blade and slid my left forearm

3. By the hero Heracles. 4. Anchisēs was struck by a thunderbolt and crippled as punishment by Jupiter for being the lover of Venus.

Into the shield-strap, turning to go out,
But at the door Creusa hugged my knees,
Then held up little Iulus to his father.

'If you are going out to die, take us
To face the whole thing with you. If experience
Leads you to put some hope in weaponry
Such as you now take, guard your own house here.
When you have gone, to whom is Iulus left?
Your father? Wife?—one called that long ago.'

She went on, and her wailing filled the house,
But then a sudden portent came, a marvel:
Amid his parents' hands and their sad faces
A point on Iulus' head seemed to cast light,
A tongue of flame that touched but did not burn him,
Licking his fine hair, playing round his temples.
We, in panic, beat at the flaming hair
And put the sacred fire out with water;
Father Anchises lifted his eyes to heaven
And lifted up his hands, his voice, in joy:

'Omnipotent Jupiter, if prayers affect you,
Look down upon us, that is all I ask,
If by devotion to the gods we earn it,
Grant us a new sign, and confirm this portent!'
The old man barely finished when it thundered
A loud crack on the left. Out of the sky
Through depths of night a star fell trailing flame
And glided on, turning the night to day.
We watched it pass above the roof and go
To hide its glare, its trace, in Ida's[5] wood;
But still, behind, the luminous furrow shone
And wide zones fumed with sulphur.
Now indeed
My father, overcome, addressed the gods,
And rose in worship of the blessed star.

'Now, now, no more delay. I'll follow you.
Where you conduct me, there I'll be.
Gods of my fathers,
Preserve this house, preserve my grandson. Yours
This portent was. Troy's life is in your power.
I yield. I go as your companion, son.'
Then he was still. We heard the blazing town
Crackle more loudly, felt the scorching heat.

'Then come, dear father. Arms around my neck:
I'll take you on my shoulders, no great weight.
Whatever happens, both will face one danger,

5. The mountain range near Troy.

Find one safety. Iulus will come with me,
My wife at a good interval behind.
Servants, give your attention to what I say.
At the gate inland there's a funeral mound
And an old shrine of Ceres the Bereft;[6]
Near it an ancient cypress, kept alive
For many years by our fathers' piety.
By various routes we'll come to that one place.
Father, carry our hearthgods, our Penatës.
It would be wrong for me to handle them—
Just come from such hard fighting, bloody work—
Until I wash myself in running water.'

When I had said this, over my breadth of shoulder
And bent neck, I spread out a lion skin
For tawny cloak and stooped to take his weight.
Then little Iulus put his hand in mine
And came with shorter steps beside his father.
My wife fell in behind. Through shadowed places
On we went, and I, lately unmoved
By any spears thrown, any squads of Greeks,
Felt terror now at every eddy of wind,
Alarm at every sound, alert and worried
Alike for my companion and my burden.
I had got near the gate, and now I thought
We had made it all the way, when suddenly
A noise of running feet came near at hand,
And peering through the gloom ahead, my father
Cried out:
'Run, boy; here they come; I see
Flame light on shields, bronze shining.'
I took fright,
And some unfriendly power, I know not what,
Stole all my addled wits—for as I turned
Aside from the known way, entering a maze
Of pathless places on the run—
Alas,
Creusa, taken from us by grim fate, did she
Linger, or stray, or sink in weariness?
There is no telling. Never would she be
Restored to us. Never did I look back
Or think to look for her, lost as she was,
Until we reached the funeral mound and shrine
Of venerable Ceres. Here at last
All came together, but she was not there;
She alone failed[7] her friends, her child, her husband.
Out of my mind, whom did I not accuse,
What man or god? What crueller loss had I
Beheld, that night the city fell? Ascanius,

6. So called because she mourns the loss of her daughter, Proserpina (Persephone in Greek). Her Greek name is Demeter. 7. The original Latin does not imply fault and is better read "was not to be found" (literally, "was lacking to").

My father, and the Teucrian Penatës,
I left in my friends' charge, and hid them well
In a hollow valley.
I turned back alone
Into the city, cinching my bright harness.
Nothing for it but to run the risks
Again, go back again, comb all of Troy,
And put my life in danger as before:
First by the town wall, then the gate, all gloom,
Through which I had come out—and so on backward,
Tracing my own footsteps through the night;
And everywhere my heart misgave me: even
Stillness had its terror. Then to our house,
Thinking she might, just might, have wandered there.
Danaans had got in and filled the place,
And at that instant fire they had set,
Consuming it, went roofward in a blast;
Flames leaped and seethed in heat to the night sky.
I pressed on, to see Priam's hall and tower.
In the bare colonnades of Juno's shrine
Two chosen guards, Phoenix and hard Ulysses,
Kept watch over the plunder. Piled up here
Were treasures of old Troy from every quarter,
Torn out of burning temples: altar tables,
Robes, and golden bowls. Drawn up around them,
Boys and frightened mothers stood in line.
I even dared to call out in the night;
I filled the streets with calling; in my grief
Time after time I groaned and called Creusa,
Frantic, in endless quest from door to door.
Then to my vision her sad wraith appeared—
Creusa's ghost, larger than life, before me.
Chilled to the marrow, I could feel the hair
On my head rise, the voice clot in my throat;
But she spoke out to ease me of my fear:

'What's to be gained by giving way to grief
So madly, my sweet husband? Nothing here
Has come to pass except as heaven willed.
You may not take Creusa with you now;
It was not so ordained, nor does the lord
Of high Olympus give you leave. For you
Long exile waits, and long sea miles to plough.
You shall make landfall on Hesperia
Where Lydian Tiber[8] flows, with gentle pace,
Between rich farmlands, and the years will bear
Glad peace, a kingdom, and a queen for you.
Dismiss these tears for your beloved Creusa.
I shall not see the proud homelands of Myrmidons

8. The river was the center of many settlements of Etruscans, who were supposed to be immigrants from Lydia, in Asia Minor.

Or of Dolopians, or go to serve
Greek ladies, Dardan lady that I am
And daughter-in-law of Venus the divine.
No: the great mother of the gods[9] detains me
Here on these shores. Farewell now; cherish still
Your son and mine.'
With this she left me weeping,
Wishing that I could say so many things,
And faded on the tenuous air. Three times
I tried to put my arms around her neck,
Three times enfolded nothing, as the wraith
Slipped through my fingers, bodiless as wind,
Or like a flitting dream.
So in the end
As night waned I rejoined my company.
And there to my astonishment I found
New refugees in a great crowd: men and women
Gathered for exile, young—pitiful people
Coming from every quarter, minds made up,
With their belongings, for whatever lands
I'd lead them to by sea.
The morning star
Now rose on Ida's ridges, bringing day.
Greeks had secured the city gates. No help
Or hope of help existed.
So I resigned myself, picked up my father,
And turned my face toward the mountain range."

Summary Aeneas goes on to tell the story of his wanderings in search of a new home. By the end of the evening, Dido, who began to fall in love with him before the banquet (through the intervention of Venus and Juno, who both promote the affair, each for different reasons), now feels the full force of her passion for Aeneas.

BOOK IV

[*The Passion of the Queen*]

The queen, for her part, all that evening ached
With longing that her heart's blood fed, a wound
Or inward fire eating her away.
The manhood of the man, his pride of birth,
Came home to her time and again; his looks,
His words remained with her to haunt her mind,
And desire for him gave her no rest.
When Dawn
Swept earth with Phoebus' torch and burned away
Night-gloom and damp, this queen, far gone and ill,
Confided to the sister of her heart:
"My sister Anna, quandaries and dreams
Have come to frighten me—such dreams!
Think what a stranger

9. Cybele, an Asiatic mother goddess worshiped (according to Virgil) at Troy.

Yesterday found lodging in our house:
How princely, how courageous, what a soldier.
I can believe him in the line of gods,
And this is no delusion. Tell-tale fear
Betrays inferior souls. What scenes of war
Fought to the bitter end he pictured for us!
What buffetings awaited him at sea!
Had I not set my face against remarriage
After my first love died and failed me, left me
Barren and bereaved—and sick to death
At the mere thought of torch and bridal bed—
I could perhaps give way in this one case
To frailty. I shall say it: since that time
Sychaeus, my poor husband, met his fate,
And blood my brother[1] shed stained our hearth gods,
This man alone has wrought upon me so
And moved my soul to yield. I recognize
The signs of the old flame, of old desire.
But O chaste life, before I break your laws,
I pray that Earth may open, gape for me
Down to its depth, or the omnipotent
With one stroke blast me to the shades, pale shades
Of Erebus[2] and the deep world of night!
That man who took me to himself in youth
Has taken all my love; may that man keep it,
Hold it forever with him in the tomb."

At this she wept and wet her breast with tears.
But Anna answered:
"Dearer to your sister
Than daylight is, will you wear out your life,
Young as you are, in solitary mourning,
Never to know sweet children, or the crown
Of joy that Venus brings? Do you believe
This matters to the dust, to ghosts in tombs?
Granted no suitors up to now have moved you,
Neither in Libya nor before, in Tyre—
Iarbas[3] you rejected, and the others,
Chieftains bred by the land of Africa
Their triumphs have enriched—will you contend
Even against a welcome love? Have you
Considered in whose lands you settled here?
On one frontier the Gaetulans, their cities,
People invincible in war—with wild
Numidian horsemen, and the offshore banks,
The Syrtës; on the other, desert sands,
Bone-dry, where fierce Barcaean[4] nomads range.

1. Pygmalion, king of Tyre who killed Sychaeus, Dido's *first love* (line 21). Sychaeus's ghost warned her in a dream to leave Tyre and seek a new home. 2. The lower depths of Hades, the underworld. 3. The most prominent of Dido's African suitors. 4. African groups that lived near Carthage. The Gaetulans, a savage people, lived to the southwest. The Numidians were the most powerful group. The Barcaeans lived to the east.

Or need I speak of future wars brought on
From Tyre, and the menace of your brother?
Surely by dispensation of the gods
And backed by Juno's will, the ships from Ilium
Held their course this way on the wind.
Sister,
What a great city you'll see rising here,
And what a kingdom, from this royal match!
With Trojan soldiers as companions in arms
By what exploits will Punic[5] glory grow!
Only ask the indulgence of the gods,
Win them with offerings, give your guests ease,
And contrive reasons for delay, while winter
Gales rage, drenched Orion storms at sea,
And their ships, damaged still, face iron skies."

This counsel fanned the flame, already kindled,
Giving her hesitant sister hope, and set her
Free of scruple. Visiting the shrines
They begged for grace at every altar first,
Then put choice rams and ewes to ritual death
For Ceres Giver of Laws, Father Lyaeus,
Phoebus, and for Juno most of all
Who has the bonds of marriage in her keeping.[6]
Dido herself, splendidly beautiful,
Holding a shallow cup, tips out the wine
On a white shining heifer, between the horns,
Or gravely in the shadow of the gods
Approaches opulent altars. Through the day
She brings new gifts, and when the breasts are opened
Pores over organs, living still, for signs.[7]
Alas, what darkened minds have soothsayers!
What good are shrines and vows to maddened lovers?
The inward fire eats the soft marrow away,
And the internal wound bleeds on in silence.

Unlucky Dido, burning, in her madness
Roamed through all the city, like a doe
Hit by an arrow shot from far away
By a shepherd hunting in the Cretan woods—
Hit by surprise, nor could the hunter see
His flying steel had fixed itself in her;
But though she runs for life through copse and glade
The fatal shaft clings to her side.
Now Dido

5. Carthaginian. 6. Ceres, the goddess who guarantees the growth of crops; Lyaeus (Dionysus or Bacchus), the wine god; and Phoebus (Apollo) are selected as deities especially connected with the founding of cities. One of Apollo's titles is "founder," and Ceres and Lyaeus control the essential crops that will enable the colonists to live. Dido prays to these gods at the moment when she is about to abandon her responsibilities as founder of a city. A similar irony is present in her prayer to Juno, who oversees the marriage bond, at the moment when she is about to break her long fidelity to the memory of Sychaeus. 7. An Etruscan and Roman practice was to inspect the entrails of the sacrificial victim and interpret irregular or unusual features as signs of the future.

Took Aeneas with her among her buildings,
Showed her Sidonian wealth, her walls prepared,
And tried to speak, but in mid-speech grew still.
When the day waned she wanted to repeat
The banquet as before, to hear once more
In her wild need the throes of Ilium,
And once more hung on the narrator's words.
Afterward, when all the guests were gone,
And the dim moon in turn had quenched her light,
And setting stars weighed weariness to sleep,
Alone she mourned in the great empty hall
And pressed her body on the couch he left:
She heard him still, though absent—heard and saw him.
Or she would hold Ascanius in her lap,
Enthralled by him, the image of his father,
As though by this ruse to appease a love
Beyond all telling.
Towers, half-built, rose
No farther; men no longer trained in arms
Or toiled to make harbors and battlements
Impregnable. Projects were broken off,
Laid over, and the menacing huge walls
With cranes unmoving stood against the sky.

As soon as Jove's[8] dear consort saw the lady
Prey to such illness, and her reputation
Standing no longer in the way of passion,
Saturn's daughter said to Venus:
"Wondrous!
Covered yourself with glory, have you not,
You and your boy, and won such prizes, too.
Divine power is something to remember
If by collusion of two gods one mortal
Woman is brought low.
I am not blind.
Your fear of our new walls has not escaped me,
Fear and mistrust of Carthage at her height.
But how far will it go? What do you hope for,
Being so contentious? Why do we not
Arrange eternal peace and formal marriage?
You have your heart's desire: Dido in love,
Dido consumed with passion to her core.
Why not, then, rule this people side by side
With equal authority? And let the queen
Wait on her Phrygian lord, let her consign
Into your hand her Tyrians as a dowry."

Now Venus knew this talk was all pretence,
All to divert the future power from Italy

8. Jupiter's.

To Libya; and she answered:
"Who would be
So mad, so foolish as to shun that prospect
Or prefer war with you? That is, provided
Fortune is on the side of your proposal.
The fates here are perplexing: would one city
Satisfy Jupiter's will for Tyrians
And Trojan exiles? Does he approve
A union and a mingling of these races?
You are his consort: you have every right
To sound him out. Go on, and I'll come, too."

But regal Juno pointedly replied:
"That task will rest with me. Just now, as to
The need of the moment and the way to meet it,
Listen, and I'll explain in a few words.
Aeneas and Dido in her misery
Plan hunting in the forest, when the Titan
Sun comes up with rays to light the world.
While beaters in excitement ring the glens
My gift will be a black raincloud, and hail,
A downpour, and I'll shake heaven with thunder.
The company will scatter, lost in gloom,
As Dido and the Trojan captain come
To one same cavern. I shall be on hand,
And if I can be certain you are willing,
There I shall marry them and call her his.
A wedding, this will be."
Then Cytherëa,[9]
Not disinclined, nodded to Juno's plea,
And smiled at the stratagem now given away.

Dawn came up meanwhile from the Ocean stream,
And in the early sunshine from the gates
Picked huntsmen issued: wide-meshed nets and snares,
Broad spearheads for big game, Massylian[1] horsemen
Trooping with hounds in packs keen on the scent.
But Dido lingered in her hall, as Punic
Nobles waited, and her mettlesome hunter
Stood nearby, cavorting in gold and scarlet,
Champing his foam-flecked bridle. At long last
The queen appeared with courtiers in a crowd,
A short Sidonian cloak edged in embroidery
Caught about her, at her back a quiver
Sheathed in gold, her hair tied up in gold,
And a brooch of gold pinning her scarlet dress.
Phrygians came in her company as well,
And Iulus, joyous at the scene. Resplendent
Above the rest, Aeneas walked to meet her,
To join his retinue with hers. He seemed—

9. Venus. 1. After Massilia (Marseilles), in southern France.

Think of the lord Apollo in the spring
When he leaves wintering in Lycia
By Xanthus torrent, for his mother's isle
Of Delos, to renew the festival;
Around his altars Cretans, Dryopës,
And painted Agathyrsans[2] raise a shout,
But the god walks the Cynthian ridge alone
And smooths his hair, binds it in fronded laurel,
Braids it in gold; and shafts ring on his shoulders.
So elated and swift, Aeneas walked
With sunlit grace upon him.
                                        Soon the hunters,
Riding in company to high pathless hills,
Saw mountain goats shoot down from a rocky peak
And scamper on the ridges; toward the plain
Deer left the slopes, herding in clouds of dust
In flight across the open lands. Alone,
The boy Ascanius, delightedly riding
His eager horse amid the lowland vales,
Outran both goats and deer. Could he only meet
Amid the harmless game some foaming boar,
Or a tawny lion down from the mountainside!

Meanwhile in heaven began a rolling thunder,
And soon the storm broke, pouring rain and hail.
Then Tyrians and Trojans in alarm—
With Venus' Dardan grandson[3]—ran for cover
Here and there in the wilderness, as freshets
Coursed from the high hills.
                                        Now to the self-same cave
Came Dido and the captain of the Trojans.
Primal Earth herself and Nuptial Juno
Opened the ritual, torches of lightning blazed,
High Heaven became witness to the marriage,
And nymphs cried out wild hymns from a mountain top.
        That day was the first cause of death, and first
Of sorrow. Dido had no further qualms
As to impressions given and set abroad;
She thought no longer of a secret love
But called it marriage. Thus, under that name,
She hid her fault.
                            Now in no time at all
Through all the African cities Rumor goes—
Nimble as quicksilver among evils. Rumor
Thrives on motion, stronger for the running,
Lowly at first through fear, then rearing high,
She treads the land and hides her head in cloud.
As people fable it, the Earth, her mother,
Furious against the gods, bore a late sister
To the giants Coeus and Enceladus,

2. Pilgrims from various regions. 3. Ascanius.

Giving her speed on foot and on the wing:
Monstrous, deformed, titanic. Pinioned, with
An eye beneath for every body feather,
And, strange to say, as many tongues and buzzing
Mouths as eyes, as many pricked-up ears,
By night she flies between the earth and heaven
Shrieking through darkness, and she never turns
Her eye-lids down to sleep. By day she broods,
On the alert, on rooftops or on towers,
Bringing great cities fear, harping on lies
And slander evenhandedly with truth.
In those days Rumor took an evil joy
At filling countrysides with whispers, whispers,
Gossip of what was done, and never done:
How this Aeneas landed, Trojan born,
How Dido in her beauty graced his company,
Then how they reveled all the winter long
Unmindful of the realm, prisoners of lust.

These tales the scabrous goddess put about
On men's lips everywhere. Her twisting course
Took her to King Iarbas, whom she set
Ablaze with anger piled on top of anger.
Son of Jupiter Hammon by a nymph,
A ravished Garamantean, this prince
Had built the god a hundred giant shrines,
A hundred altars, each with holy fires.
Alight by night and day, sentries on watch,
The ground enriched by victims' blood, the doors
Festooned with flowering wreaths. Before his altars
King Iarbas, crazed by the raw story,
Stood, they say, amid the Presences,
With supplicating hands, pouring out prayer:

"All powerful Jove, to whom the feasting Moors
At ease on colored couches tip their wine,
Do you see this? Are we then fools to fear you
Throwing down your bolts? Those dazzling fires
Of lightning, are they aimless in the clouds
And rumbling thunder meaningless? This woman
Who turned up in our country and laid down
A tiny city at a price, to whom
I gave a beach to plow—and on my terms—
After refusing to marry me has taken
Aeneas to be master in her realm.
And now Sir Paris with his men, half-men,
His chin and perfumed hair tied up
In a Maeonian bonnet, takes possession.
As for ourselves, here we are bringing gifts
Into these shrines—supposedly your shrines—
Hugging that empty fable."
Pleas like this

From the man clinging to his altars reached
The ears of the Almighty. Now he turned
His eyes upon the queen's town and the lovers
Careless of their good name; then spoke to Mercury,[4]
Assigning him a mission:
"Son, bestir yourself,
Call up the Zephyrs,[5] take to your wings and glide.
Approach the Dardan captain where he tarries
Rapt in Tyrian Carthage, losing sight
Of future towns the fates ordain. Correct him,
Carry my speech to him on the running winds:
No son like this did his enchanting mother
Promise to us, nor such did she deliver
Twice from peril at the hands of Greeks.
He was to be the ruler of Italy,
Potential empire, armorer of war;
To father men from Teucer's[6] noble blood
And bring the whole world under law's dominion.
If glories to be won by deeds like these
Cannot arouse him, if he will not strive
For his own honor, does he begrudge his son,
Ascanius, the high strongholds of Rome?
What has he in mind? What hope, to make him stay
Amid a hostile race, and lose from view
Ausonian progeny, Lavinian lands?[7]
The man should sail: that is the whole point.
Let this be what you tell him, as from me."

He finished and fell silent. Mercury
Made ready to obey the great command
Of his great father, and he first tied on
The golden sandals, winged, that high in air
Transport him over seas or over land
Abreast of gale winds; then he took the wand
With which he summons pale souls out of Orcus
And ushers others to the undergloom,
Lulls men to slumber or awakens them,
And opens dead men's eyes. This wand in hand,
He can drive winds before him, swimming down
Along the stormcloud. Now aloft, he saw
The craggy flanks and crown of patient Atlas,
Giant Atlas, balancing the sky
Upon his peak[8]—his pine-forested head
In vapor cowled, beaten by wind and rain.
Snow lay upon his shoulders, rills cascaded
Down his ancient chin and beard a-bristle,
Caked with ice. Here Mercury of Cyllenë[9]
Hovered first on even wings, then down

4. The messenger god; Hermes in Greek. 5. The west winds. 6. The first Trojan king. 7. The dowry of Lavinia, daughter of Latinus, whom Aeneas marries. *Ausonian:* Italian. 8. The Atlas Mountains are in western North Africa; the reference here is also to the Titan Atlas, who, as punishment for his part in the revolt against Jupiter, must hold up the heavens on his shoulders. 9. A mountain in Arcadia and Mercury's birthplace.

He plummeted to sea-level and flew on
Like a low-flying gull that skims the shallows
And rocky coasts where fish ply close inshore.
So, like a gull between the earth and sky,
The progeny of Cyllenë, on the wing
From his maternal grandsire, split the winds
To the sand bars of Libya.
Alighting tiptoe
On the first hutments, there he found Aeneas
Laying foundations for new towers and homes.
He noted well the swordhilt the man wore,
Adorned with yellow jasper; and the cloak
Aglow with Tyrian dye upon his shoulders—
Gifts of the wealthy queen, who had inwoven
Gold thread in the fabric. Mercury
Took him to task at once:
"Is it for you
To lay the stones for Carthage's high walls,
Tame husband that you are, and build their city?
Oblivious of your own world, your own kingdom!
From bright Olympus he that rules the gods
And turns the earth and heaven by his power—
He and no other sent me to you, told me
To bring this message on the running winds:
What have you in mind? What hope, wasting your days
In Libya? If future history's glories
Do not affect you, if you will not strive
For your own honor, think of Ascanius,
Think of the expectations of your heir,
Iulus, to whom the Italian realm, the land
Of Rome, are due."
And Mercury, as he spoke,
Departed from the visual field of mortals
To a great distance, ebbed in subtle air.
Amazed, and shocked to the bottom of his soul
By what his eyes had seen, Aeneas felt
His hackles rise, his voice choke in his throat.
As the sharp admonition and command
From heaven had shaken him awake, he now
Burned only to be gone, to leave that land
Of the sweet life behind. What can he do? How tell
The impassioned queen and hope to win her over?
What opening shall he choose? This way and that
He let his mind dart, testing alternatives,
Running through every one. And as he pondered
This seemed the better tactic: he called in
Mnestheus, Sergestus and stalwart Serestus,
Telling them:
"Get the fleet ready for sea,
But quietly, and collect the men on shore.
Lay in ship stores and gear."
As to the cause

For a change of plan, they were to keep it secret,
Seeing the excellent Dido had no notion,
No warning that such love could be cut short;
He would himself look for the right occasion,
The easiest time to speak, the way to do it.
The Trojans to a man gladly obeyed.

The queen, for her part, felt some plot afoot
Quite soon—for who deceives a woman in love?
She caught wind of a change, being in fear
Of what had seemed her safety. Evil Rumor,
Shameless as before,[1] brought word to her
In her distracted state of ships being rigged
In trim for sailing. Furious, at her wits' end,
She traversed the whole city, all aflame
With rage, like a Bacchantë[2] driven wild
By emblems shaken, when the mountain revels
Of the odd year possess her, when the cry
Of Bacchus rises and Cithaeron[3] calls
All through the shouting night. Thus it turned out
She was the first to speak and charge Aeneas:

"You even hoped to keep me in the dark
As to this outrage, did you, two-faced man,
And slip away in silence? Can our love
Not hold you, can the pledge we gave not hold you,
Can Dido not, now sure to die in pain?
Even in winter weather must you toil
With ships, and fret to launch against high winds
For the open sea? Oh, heartless!
Tell me now,
If you were not in search of alien lands
And new strange homes, if ancient Troy remained,
Would ships put out for Troy on these big seas?
Do you go to get away from me? I beg you,
By these tears, by your own right hand,[4] since I
Have left my wretched self nothing but that—
Yes, by the marriage that we entered on,
If ever I did well and you were grateful
Or found some sweetness in a gift from me,
Have pity now on a declining house!
Put this plan by, I beg you, if a prayer
Is not yet out of place.
Because of you, Libyans and nomad kings
Detest me, my own Tyrians are hostile;
Because of you, I lost my integrity
And that admired name by which alone

1. Earlier, Rumor (a semidivine being) had spread the report of Dido's "marriage," which had incited Iarbas to make his indignant prayer to Jupiter. 2. A female devotee of the god Bacchus, in an ecstatic trance at the festival held every other year in the god's honor. 3. Mountain near Thebes, sacred to Bacchus. 4. The handclasp with which he pledged his love and that Dido took as an earnest of marriage.

I made my way once toward the stars.
To whom
Do you abandon me, a dying woman,
Guest that you are—the only name now left
From that of husband? Why do I live on?
Shall I, until my brother Pygmalion comes
To pull my walls down? Or the Gaetulan
Iarbas leads me captive? If at least
There were a child by you for me to care for,
A little one to play in my courtyard
And give me back Aeneas, in spite of all,
I should not feel so utterly defeated,
Utterly bereft."
She ended there.
The man by Jove's command held fast his eyes
And fought down the emotion in his heart.
At length he answered:
"As for myself, be sure
I never shall deny all you can say,
Your majesty, of what you meant to me.
Never will the memory of Elissa[5]
Stale for me, while I can still remember
My own life, and the spirit rules my body.
As to the event, a few words. Do not think
I meant to be deceitful and slip away.
I never held the torches of a bridegroom,
Never entered upon the pact of marriage.
If Fate permitted me to spend my days
By my own lights, and make the best of things
According to my wishes, first of all
I should look after Troy and the loved relics
Left me of my people. Priam's great hall
Should stand again; I should have restored the tower
Of Pergamum for Trojans in defeat.
But now it is the rich Italian land
Apollo tells me I must make for: Italy,
Named by his oracles. There is my love;
There is my country. If, as a Phoenician,
You are so given to the charms of Carthage,
Libyan city that it is, then tell me,
Why begrudge the Teucrian new lands
For homesteads in Ausonia? Are we not
Entitled, too, to look for realms abroad?
Night never veils the earth in damp and darkness,
Fiery stars never ascend the east,
But in my dreams my father's troubled ghost[6]
Admonishes and frightens me. Then, too,
Each night thoughts come of young Ascanius,
My dear boy wronged, defrauded of his kingdom,

5. Dido. 6. Anchisës had died in Sicily just before Aeneas, leaving for Italy, was blown by the storm winds to Carthage.

Hesperian lands of destiny. And now
The gods' interpreter, sent by Jove himself—
I swear it by your head and mine—has brought
Commands down through the racing winds! I say
With my own eyes in full daylight I saw him
Entering the building! With my very ears
I drank his message in! So please, no more
Of these appeals that set us both afire.
I sail for Italy not of my own free will."

During all this she had been watching him
With face averted, looking him up and down
In silence, and she burst out raging now:

"No goddess was your mother. Dardanus
Was not the founder of your family.
Liar and cheat! Some rough Caucasian cliff
Begot you on flint. Hyrcanian[7] tigresses
Tendered their teats to you. Why should I palter?
Why still hold back for more indignity?
Sigh, did he, while I wept? Or look at me?
Or yield a tear, or pity her who loved him?
What shall I say first, with so much to say?
The time is past when either supreme Juno
Or the Saturnian father[8] viewed these things
With justice. Faith can never be secure.
I took the man in, thrown up on this coast
In dire need, and in my madness then
Contrived a place for him in my domain,
Rescued his lost fleet, saved his shipmates' lives.
Oh, I am swept away burning by furies!
Now the prophet Apollo, now his oracles,
Now the gods' interpreter, if you please,
Sent down by Jove himself, brings through the air
His formidable commands! What fit employment
For heaven's high powers! What anxieties
To plague serene immortals![9] I shall not
Detain you or dispute your story. Go,
Go after Italy on the sailing winds,
Look for your kingdom, cross the deepsea swell!
If divine justice counts for anything,
I hope and pray that on some grinding reef
Midway at sea you'll drink your punishment
And call and call on Dido's name!
From far away I shall come after you
With my black fires, and when cold death has parted
Body from soul I shall be everywhere
A shade to haunt you! You will pay for this,

7. Near the Caspian Sea. *Caucasian:* after Caucasus Mountains, also near the Caspian Sea. The adjective connoted outlandishness and cruelty. 8. Jupiter. 9. A reference to the Epicurean idea that the gods are unaffected by human events.

Unconscionable! I shall hear! The news will reach me
Even among the lowest of the dead!"

At this abruptly she broke off and ran
In sickness from his sight and the light of day,
Leaving him at a loss, alarmed, and mute
With all he meant to say. The maids in waiting
Caught her as she swooned and carried her
To bed in her marble chamber.
Duty-bound,
Aeneas, though he struggled with desire
To calm and comfort her in all her pain,
To speak to her and turn her mind from grief,
And though he sighed his heart out, shaken still
With love of her, yet took the course heaven gave him
And went back to the fleet. Then with a will
The Teucrians fell to work and launched ships
Along the whole shore: slick with tar each hull
Took to the water. Eager to get away,
The sailors brought oar-boughs out of the woods
With leaves still on, and oaken logs unhewn.
Now you could see them issuing from the town
To the water's edge in streams, as when, aware
Of winter, ants will pillage a mound of spelt
To store it in their granary; over fields
The black battalion moves, and through the grass
On a narrow trail they carry off the spoil;
Some put their shoulders to the enormous weight
Of a trundled grain, while some pull stragglers in
And castigate delay; their to-and-fro
Of labor makes the whole track come alive.
At that sight, what were your emotions, Dido?
Sighing how deeply, looking out and down
From your high tower on the seething shore
Where all the harbor filled before your eyes
With bustle and shouts! Unconscionable Love,
To what extremes will you not drive our hearts!
She now felt driven to weep again, again
To move him, if she could, by supplication,
Humbling her pride before her love—to leave
Nothing untried, not to die needlessly.

"Anna, you see the arc of waterfront
All in commotion: they come crowding in
From everywhere. Spread canvas calls for wind,
The happy crews have garlanded the sterns.
If I could brace myself for this great sorrow,
Sister, I can endure it, too. One favor,
Even so, you may perform for me.
Since that deserter chose you for his friend
And trusted you, even with private thoughts,
Since you alone know when he may be reached,

Go, intercede with our proud enemy.
Remind him that I took no oath at Aulis[1]
With Danaans to destroy the Trojan race;
I sent no ship to Pergamum. Never did I
Profane his father Anchisës' dust and shade.
Why will he not allow my prayers to fall
On his unpitying ears? Where is he racing?
Let him bestow one last gift on his mistress:
This, to await fair winds and easier flight.
Now I no longer plead the bond he broke
Of our old marriage, nor do I ask that he
Should live without his dear love, Latium,
Or yield his kingdom. Time is all I beg,
Mere time, a respite and a breathing space
For madness to subside in, while my fortune
Teaches me how to take defeat and grieve.
Pity your sister. This is the end, this favor—
To be repaid with interest when I die."

She pleaded in such terms, and such, in tears,
Her sorrowing sister brought him, time and again.
But no tears moved him, no one's voice would he
Attend to tractably. The fates opposed it;
God's will blocked the man's once kindly ears.
And just as when the north winds from the Alps
This way and that contend among themselves
To tear away an oaktree hale with age,
The wind and tree cry, and the buffeted trunk
Showers high foliage to earth, but holds
On bedrock, for the roots go down as far
Into the underworld as cresting boughs
Go up in heaven's air: just so this captain,
Buffeted by a gale of pleas
This way and that way, dinned all the day long,
Felt their moving power in his great heart,
And yet his will stood fast; tears fell in vain.

On Dido in her desolation now
Terror grew at her fate. She prayed for death,
Being heartsick at the mere sight of heaven.
That she more surely would perform the act
And leave the daylight, now she saw before her
A thing one shudders to recall: on altars
Fuming with incense where she placed her gifts,
The holy water blackened, the spilt wine
Turned into blood and mire. Of this she spoke
To no one, not to her sister even. Then, too,
Within the palace was a marble shrine
Devoted to her onetime lord, a place
She held in wondrous honor, all festooned

1. Alluding to the Greek alliance's oath when departing from Aulis for Troy.

With snowy fleeces and green festive boughs.
From this she now thought voices could be heard
And words could be made out, her husband's words,
Calling her, when midnight hushed the earth;
And lonely on the rooftops the night owl
Seemed to lament, in melancholy notes,
Prolonged to a doleful cry. And then, besides,
The riddling words of seers in ancient days,
Foreboding sayings, made her thrill with fear.
In nightmare, fevered, she was hunted down
By pitiless Aeneas, and she seemed
Deserted always, uncompanioned always,
On a long journey, looking for her Tyrians
In desolate landscapes—
as Pentheus gone mad
Sees the oncoming Eumenidës[2] and sees
A double sun and double Thebes appear,
Or as when, hounded on the stage, Orestës[3]
Runs from a mother armed with burning brands,
With serpents hellish black,
And in the doorway squat the Avenging Ones.

So broken in mind by suffering, Dido caught
Her fatal madness and resolved to die.
She pondered time and means, then visiting
Her mournful sister, covered up her plan
With a calm look, a clear and hopeful brow.

"Sister, be glad for me! I've found a way
To bring him back or free me of desire.
Near to the Ocean boundary, near sundown,
The Aethiops' farthest territory lies,
Where giant Atlas turns the sphere of heaven
Studded with burning stars. From there
A priestess of Massylian[4] stock has come;
She had been pointed out to me: custodian
Of that shrine named for daughters of the west,
Hesperidës;[5] and it is she who fed
The dragon, guarding well the holy boughs
With honey dripping slow and drowsy poppy.
Chanting her spells she undertakes to free
What hearts she wills, but to inflict on others
Duress of sad desires; to arrest
The flow of rivers, make the stars move backward,
Call up the spirits of deep Night. You'll see

2. Pentheus, king of Thebes, persecuted the worshipers of Bacchus and imprisoned the god himself. He was later mocked by the god, who inspired him with the Dionysiac spirit (and perhaps with wine) so that he saw double. In this state he was led off to his death on Cithaeron. These events are dramatized in Euripides' play *The Bacchanals* (*Bacchae*) but the Eumenidës (Furies) are not mentioned there. Perhaps Virgil is using them simply as a symbol for madness. 3. Another reference to Greek tragedy; in Aeschylus's *Choephoroe* (*The Libation Bearers*), Orestës kills his mother, Clytaemnestra, and is pursued by the Furies. In other tragic contexts he is represented as pursued by the ghost of his mother. 4. From the African tribe. 5. The daughters of Hesperus, who lived in a garden that contained golden apples and was guarded by a dragon.

Earth shift and rumble underfoot and ash trees
Walk down mountainsides. Dearest, I swear
Before the gods and by your own sweet self,
It is against my will that I resort
For weaponry to magic powers. In secret
Build up a pyre in the inner court
Under the open sky, and place upon it
The arms that faithless man left in my chamber,
All his clothing, and the marriage bed
On which I came to grief—solace for me
To annihilate all vestige of the man,
Vile as he is: my priestess shows me this."

While she was speaking, cheek and brow grew pale.
But Anna could not think her sister cloaked
A suicide in these unheard-of rites;
She failed to see how great her madness was
And feared no consequence more grave
Than at Sychaeus' death. So, as commanded,
She made the preparations. For her part,
The queen, seeing the pyre in her inmost court
Erected huge with pitch-pine and sawn ilex,
Hung all the place under the sky with wreaths
And crowned it with funereal cypress boughs.
On the pyre's top she put a sword he left
With clothing, and an effigy on a couch,
Her mind fixed now ahead on what would come.
Around the pyre stood altars, and the priestess,
Hair unbound, called in a voice of thunder
Upon three hundred gods, on Erebus,
On Chaos, and on triple Hecatë,[6]
Three-faced Diana. Then she sprinkled drops
Purportedly from the fountain of Avernus.[7]
Rare herbs were brought out, reaped at the new moon
By scythes of bronze, and juicy with a milk
Of dusky venom; then the rare love-charm
Or caul torn from the brow of a birthing foal
And snatched away before the mother found it.
Dido herself with consecrated grain
In her pure hands, as she went near the altars,
Freed one foot from sandal straps, let fall
Her dress ungirdled, and, now sworn to death,
Called on the gods and stars that knew her fate.
She prayed then to whatever power may care
In comprehending justice for the grief
Of lovers bound unequally by love.

The night had come, and weary in every land
Men's bodies took the boon of peaceful sleep.

6. Diana as goddess of sorcery and the moon. *Erebus:* the lowest depth of the underworld. *Chaos:* the void or chasm; according to the Greek poet Hesiod, the first god to come into being and father of Night and Erebus. In Hesiod he is the empty space between earth and the underworld. 7. A lake in southern Italy that was supposed to be the entrance to the lower world.

The woods and the wild seas had quieted
At that hour when the stars are in mid-course
And every field is still; cattle and birds
With vivid wings that haunt the limpid lakes
Or nest in thickets in the country places
All were asleep under the silent night.
Not, though, the agonized Phoenician queen:
She never slackened into sleep and never
Allowed the tranquil night to rest
Upon her eyelids or within her heart.
Her pain redoubled; love came on again,
Devouring her, and on her bed she tossed
In a great surge of anger.
So awake,
She pressed these questions, musing to herself:

"Look now, what can I do? Turn once again
To the old suitors, only to be laughed at—
Begging a marriage with Numidians
Whom I disdained so often? Then what? Trail
The Ilian ships and follow like a slave
Commands of Trojans? Seeing them so agreeable,
In view of past assistance and relief,
So thoughtful their unshaken gratitude?
Suppose I wished it, who permits or takes
Aboard their proud ships one they so dislike?
Poor lost soul, do you not yet grasp or feel
The treachery of the line of Laömedon?[8]
What then? Am I to go alone, companion
Of the exultant sailors in their flight?
Or shall I set out in their wake, with Tyrians,
With all my crew close at my side, and send
The men I barely tore away from Tyre
To sea again, making them hoist their sails
To more sea-winds? No: die as you deserve,
Give pain quietus with a steel blade.
Sister,
You are the one who gave way to my tears
In the beginning, burdened a mad queen
With sufferings, and thrust me on my enemy.
It was not given me to lead my life
Without new passion, innocently, the way
Wild creatures live, and not to touch these depths.
The vow I took to the ashes of Sychaeus
Was not kept."
So she broke out afresh
In bitter mourning. On his high stern deck
Aeneas, now quite certain of departure,
Everything ready, took the boon of sleep.
In dream the figure of the god returned

8. A king of Troy who twice broke his promise, once to Heracles and once to Apollo and Poseidon.

With looks reproachful as before: he seemed
Again to warn him, being like Mercury
In every way, in voice, in golden hair,
And in the bloom of youth.
"Son of the goddess,
Sleep away this crisis, can you still?
Do you not see the dangers growing round you,
Madman, from now on? Can you not hear
The offshore westwind blow? The woman hatches
Plots and drastic actions in her heart,
Resolved on death now, whipping herself on
To heights of anger. Will you not be gone
In flight, while flight is still within your power?
Soon you will see the offing boil with ships
And glare with torches; soon again
The waterfront will be alive with fires,
If Dawn comes while you linger in this country.
Ha! Come, break the spell! Woman's a thing
Forever fitful and forever changing."

At this he merged into the darkness. Then
As the abrupt phantom filled him with fear,
Aeneas broke from sleep and roused his crewmen:
"Up, turn out now! Oarsmen, take your thwarts!
Shake out sail! Look here, for the second time
A god from heaven's high air is goading me
To hasten our break away, to cut the cables.
Holy one, whatever god you are,
We go with you, we act on your command
Most happily! Be near, graciously help us,
Make the stars in heaven propitious ones!"

He pulled his sword aflash out of its sheath
And struck at the stern hawser. All the men
Were gripped by his excitement to be gone,
And hauled and hustled. Ships cast off their moorings,
And an array of hulls hid inshore water
As oarsmen churned up foam and swept to sea.

Soon early Dawn, quitting the saffron bed
Of old Tithonus,[9] cast new light on earth,
And as air grew transparent, from her tower
The queen caught sight of ships on the seaward reach
With sails full and the wind astern. She knew
The waterfront now empty, bare of oarsmen.
Beating her lovely breast three times, four times,
And tearing her golden hair,
"O Jupiter,"
She said, "will this man go, will he have mocked

9. Human consort of Aurora (Eos in Greek), the dawn goddess. He is old because, although she made him immortal when she took him to her bed, she forgot to obtain for him the gift of eternal youth.

My kingdom, stranger that he was and is?
Will they not snatch up arms and follow him
From every quarter of the town? and dockhands
Tear our ships from moorings? On! Be quick
With torches! Give out arms! Unship the oars!
What am I saying? Where am I? What madness
Takes me out of myself? Dido, poor soul,
Your evil doing has come home to you.
Then was the right time, when you offered him
A royal scepter. See the good faith and honor
Of one they say bears with him everywhere
The hearthgods of his country! One who bore
His father, spent with age, upon his shoulders!
Could I not then have torn him limb from limb
And flung the pieces on the sea? His company,
Even Ascanius could I not have minced
And served up to his father at a feast?
The luck of battle might have been in doubt—
So let it have been! Whom had I to fear,
Being sure to die? I could have carried torches
Into his camp, filled passage ways with flame,
Annihilated father and son and followers
And given my own life on top of all!
O Sun, scanning with flame all works of earth,
And thou, O Juno, witness and go-between
Of my long miseries; and Hecatë,
Screeched for at night at crossroads in the cities;
And thou, avenging Furies, and all gods
On whom Elissa dying may call: take notice,
Overshadow this hell with your high power,
As I deserve, and hear my prayer!
If by necessity that impious wretch
Must find his haven and come safe to land,
If so Jove's destinies require, and this,
His end in view, must stand, yet all the same
When hard beset in war by a brave people,
Forced to go outside his boundaries
And torn from Iulus, let him beg assistance,
Let him see the unmerited deaths of those
Around and with him, and accepting peace
On unjust terms, let him not, even so,
Enjoy his kingdom or the life he longs for,
But fall in battle before his time and lie
Unburied on the sand![1] This I implore,
This is my last cry, as my last blood flows.
Then, O my Tyrians, besiege with hate
His progeny and all his race to come:
Make this your offering to my dust. No love,

1. Dido's prophecy-wish does come true. Aeneas meets resistance in Italy, and at one point in the war he must leave Ascanius behind and beg aid from King Evander. One of the conditions of peace is that his people call themselves Latins (not Trojans). He is eventually drowned in an Italian river, never to see the glory of his descendants.

No pact must be between our peoples; No,
But rise up from my bones, avenging spirit!
Harry with fire and sword the Dardan countrymen
Now, or hereafter, at whatever time
The strength will be afforded. Coast with coast
In conflict, I implore, and sea with sea,
And arms with arms: may they contend in war,
Themselves and all the children of their children!"[2]

Now she took thought of one way or another,
At the first chance, to end her hated life,
And briefly spoke to Barcë, who had been
Sychaeus' nurse; her own an urn of ash
Long held in her ancient fatherland.
"Dear nurse,
Tell Sister Anna to come here, and have her
Quickly bedew herself with running water
Before she brings out victims for atonement.
Let her come that way. And you, too, put on
Pure wool around your brows. I have a mind
To carry out that rite to Stygian[3] Jove
That I have readied here, and put an end
To my distress, committing to the flames
The pyre of that miserable Dardan."

At this with an old woman's eagerness
Barcë hurried away. And Dido's heart
Beat wildly at the enormous thing afoot.
She rolled her bloodshot eyes, her quivering cheeks
Were flecked with red as her sick pallor grew
Before her coming death. Into the court
She burst her way, then at her passion's height
She climbed the pyre and bared the Dardan sword—
A gift desired once, for no such need.
Her eyes now on the Trojan clothing there
And the familiar bed, she paused a little,
Weeping a little, mindful, then lay down
And spoke her last words:
"Remnants dear to me
While god and fate allowed it, take this breath
And give me respite from these agonies.
I lived my life out to the very end
And passed the stages Fortune had appointed.
Now my tall shade goes to the under world.
I built a famous town, saw my great walls,
Avenged my husband, made my hostile brother
Pay for his crime. Happy, alas, too happy,
If only the Dardanian keels had never

2. These prophecies also come true. The Romans and Carthaginians fought three wars (the Punic Wars); Rome won them all, razing Carthage after the third. In the third century B.C. Hannibal invaded Italy, winning many battles, although he failed to take Rome. 3. After the river Styx, which flowed in the underworld.

Beached on our coast." And here she kissed the bed.
"I die unavenged," she said, "but let me die.
This way, this way,[4] a blessed relief to go
Into the undergloom. Let the cold Trojan,
Far at sea, drink in this conflagration
And take with him the omen of my death!"

Amid these words her household people saw her
Crumpled over the steel blade, and the blade
Aflush with red blood, drenched her hands. A scream
Pierced the high chambers. Now through the shocked city
Rumor went rioting, as wails and sobs
With women's outcry echoed in the palace
And heaven's high air gave back the beating din,
As though all Carthage or old Tyre fell
To storming enemies, and, out of hand,
Flames billowed on the roofs of men and gods.
Her sister heard the trembling, faint with terror,
Lacerating her face, beating her breast,
Ran through the crowd to call the dying queen:

"It came to this, then, sister? You deceived me?
The pyre meant this, altars and fires meant this?
What shall I mourn first, being abandoned? Did you
Scorn your sister's company in death?
You should have called me out to the same fate!
The same blade's edge and hurt, at the same hour,
Should have taken us off. With my own hands
Had I to build this pyre, and had I to call
Upon our country's gods, that in the end
With you placed on it there, O heartless one,
I should be absent? You have put to death
Yourself and me, the people and the fathers
Bred in Sidon, and your own new city.
Give me fresh water, let me bathe her wound
And catch upon my lips any last breath
Hovering over hers."
Now she had climbed
The topmost steps and took her dying sister
Into her arms to cherish, with a sob,
Using her dress to stanch the dark blood flow.
But Dido trying to lift her heavy eyes
Fainted again. Her chest-wound whistled air.
Three times she struggled up on one elbow
And each time fell back on the bed. Her gaze
Went wavering as she looked for heaven's light
And groaned at finding it. Almighty Juno,
Filled with pity for this long ordeal
And difficult passage, now sent Iris[5] down

4. In Latin *sic, sic;* the repetition represents two thrusts of the sword. 5. As in Homer, a divine messenger; sometimes identified with the rainbow.

Out of Olympus to set free
The wrestling spirit from the body's hold.
For since she died, not at her fated span
Nor as she merited, but before her time
Enflamed and driven mad, Proserpina
Had not yet plucked from her the golden hair,[6]
Delivering her to Orcus of the Styx.
So humid Iris through bright heaven flew
On saffron-yellow wings, and in her train
A thousand hues shimmered before the sun.
At Dido's head she came to rest.
"This token
Sacred to Dis[7] I bear away as bidden
And free you from your body."
Saying this,
She cut a lock of hair. Along with it
Her body's warmth fell into dissolution,
And out into the winds her life withdrew.

Summary After his hurried departure from Carthage, Aeneas goes to Sicily, to the kingdom of his friend Acestēs. There he organizes funeral games in honor of his father, Anchisēs (who had died in Sicily on their first visit there), and leaves behind those of his following who are unwilling to go on to the uncertainty of a settlement in Italy. Once on Italian soil, Aeneas, obeying instructions from his dead father, who had appeared to him in a dream, consults the Sibyl, who guides him down to the world of the dead. There he is to see his father and the vision of his race, which is to be his only reward, for he will die before his people are settled in their new home.

FROM BOOK VI

[*Aeneas in the Underworld*]

Gods who rule the ghosts; all silent shades;
And Chaos and infernal Fiery Stream,[8]
And regions of wide night without a sound,
May it be right to tell what I have heard,
May it be right, and fitting, by your will,
That I describe the deep world sunk in darkness
Under the earth.
Now dim to one another
In desolate night they[9] walked on through the gloom,
Through Dis's homes all void, and empty realms,
As one goes through a wood by a faint moon's
Treacherous light, when Jupiter veils the sky
And black night blots the colors of the world.
Before the entrance, in the jaws of Orcus,
Grief and avenging Cares have made their beds,
And pale Diseases and sad Age are there,
And Dread, and Hunger that sways men to crime,

6. Queen of the underworld. Before a human died she was thought to cut a lock of his or her hair as an offering to Dis, god of the underworld. Dido (by suicide) dies unexpectedly; thus Juno sends Iris to cut the lock. 7. Hades in Greek. 8. A translation of *Phlegethon*, the name of one of the underworld rivers. 9. Aeneas and the Sibyl.

And sordid Want—in shapes to affright the eyes—
And Death and Toil and Death's own brother, Sleep,
And the mind's evil joys; on the door sill
Death-bringing War, and iron cubicles
Of the Eumenidës, and raving Discord,
Viperish hair bound up in gory bands.
In the courtyard a shadowy giant elm
Spreads ancient boughs, her ancient arms where dreams,
False dreams, the old tale goes, beneath each leaf
Cling and are numberless. There, too,
About the doorway forms of monsters crowd—
Centaurs, twiformed Scyllas, hundred-armed
Briareus, and the Lernaean hydra
Hissing horribly, and the Chimaera
Breathing dangerous flames, and Gorgons, Harpies,[1]
Huge Geryon, triple-bodied ghost.
Here, swept by sudden fear, drawing his sword,
Aeneas stood on guard with naked edge
Against them as they came. If his companion,
Knowing the truth, had not admonished him
How faint these lives were—empty images
Hovering bodiless—he had attacked
And cut his way through phantoms, empty air.

The path goes on from that place to the waves
Of Tartarus's Acheron. Thick with mud,
A whirlpool out of a vast abyss
Boils up and belches all the silt it carries
Into Cocytus.[2] Here the ferryman,
A figure of fright, keeper of waters and streams,
Is Charon, foul and terrible, his beard
Grown wild and hoar, his staring eyes all flame,
His sordid cloak hung from a shoulder knot.
Alone he poles his craft and trims the sails
And in his rusty hull ferries the dead,
Old now—but old age in the gods is green.[3]

Here a whole crowd came streaming to the banks,
Mothers and men, the forms with all life spent
Of heroes great in valor, boys and girls
Unmarried, and young sons laid on the pyre
Before their parents' eyes—as many souls
As leaves that yield their hold on boughs and fall
Through forests in the early frost of autumn,
Or as migrating birds from the open sea

1. All mythical creatures. Centaurs were half human and half horse. Scyllas have many heads. Briareus had fifty heads. The Hydra had nine heads; but if one were cut off, two would grow in its place. The Chimaera was one-third lion, one-third goat, and one-third snake. Here the Harpies are spirits of the storm wind that carry souls to Hades. 2. A river of the underworld; the name suggests "mourning" or "lamentation." Tartarus is in the lower depths of the underworld. Acheron is another river. 3. I.e., age in gods does not affect their vitality or strength. Thus Charon, although old, is still able to ferry the souls of the dead over the river Styx.

That darken heaven when the cold season comes
And drives them overseas to sunlit lands.
There all stood begging to be first across
And reached out longing hands to the far shore.

But the grim boatman now took these aboard,
Now those, waving the rest back from the strand.
In wonder at this and touched by the commotion,
Aeneas said:
"Tell me, Sister, what this means,
The crowd at the stream. Where are the souls bound?
How are they tested, so that these turn back,
While those take oars to cross the dead-black water?"

Briefly the ancient priestess answered him:

"Cocytus is the deep pool that you see,
The swamp of Styx beyond, infernal power
By which the gods take oath and fear to break it.
All in the nearby crowd you notice here
Are pauper souls, the souls of the unburied.
Charon's the boatman. Those the water bears
Are souls of buried men. He may not take them
Shore to dread shore on the hoarse currents there
Until their bones rest in the grave, or till
They flutter and roam this side a hundred years;
They may have passage then, and may return
To cross the deeps they long for."
Anchisës' son
Had halted, pondering on so much, and stood
In pity for the souls' hard lot. Among them
He saw two sad ones of unhonored death,
Leucaspis and the Lycian fleet's commander,
Orontës,[4] who had sailed the windy sea
From Troy together, till the Southern gale
Had swamped and whirled them down, both ship and men.
Of a sudden he saw his helmsman, Palinurus,
Going by, who but a few nights before
On course from Libya, as he watched the stars,
Had been pitched overboard astern. As soon
As he made sure of the disconsolate one
In all the gloom, Aeneas called:
"Which god
Took you away from us and put you under,
Palinurus? Tell me. In this one prophecy
Apollo, who had never played me false,
Falsely foretold you'd be unharmed at sea
And would arrive at the Ausonian coast.

4. Trojans lost at sea in the storm that took Aeneas to Carthage.

Is the promise kept?"
But the shade said:
"Phoebus' caldron[5]
Told you no lie, my captain, and no god
Drowned me at sea. The helm that I hung on to,
Duty bound to keep our ship on course,
By some great shock chanced to be torn away,
And I went with it overboard. I swear
By the rough sea, I feared less for myself
Than for your ship: with rudder gone and steersman
Knocked overboard, it might well come to grief
In big seas running. Three nights, heavy weather
Out of the South on the vast water tossed me.
On the fourth dawn, I sighted Italy
Dimly ahead, as a wave-crest lifted me.
By turns I swam and rested, swam again
And got my footing on the beach, but savages
Attacked me as I clutched at a cliff-top,
Weighted down by my wet clothes. Poor fools,
They took me for a prize and ran me through.
Surf has me now, and sea winds, washing me
Close inshore.
By heaven's happy light
And the sweet air, I beg you, by your father,
And by your hopes of Iulus' rising star,
Deliver me from this captivity,
Unconquered friend! Throw earth on me—you can—
Put in to Velia[6] port! Or if there be
Some way to do it, if your goddess mother
Shows a way—and I feel sure you pass
These streams and Stygian marsh by heaven's will—
Give this poor soul your hand, take me across,
Let me at least in death find quiet haven."
When he had made his plea, the Sibyl said:
"From what source comes this craving, Palinurus?
Would you though still unburied see the Styx
And the grim river of the Eumenidës,
Or even the river bank, without a summons?
Abandon hope by prayer to make the gods
Change their decrees. Hold fast to what I say
To comfort your hard lot: neighboring folk
In cities up and down the coast will be
Induced by portents to appease your bones,
Building a tomb and making offerings there
On a cape forever named for Palinurus."

The Sibyl's words relieved him, and the pain
Was for a while dispelled from his sad heart,

5. The Pythia, priestess of Apollo at Delphi, delivered the god's prophecies seated on a tripod, a three-legged shallow caldron. 6. South of the Bay of Naples, near Cape Palinuro (named after Aeneas's pilot).

Pleased at the place-name. So the two walked on
Down to the stream. Now from the Stygian water
The boatman, seeing them in the silent wood
And headed for the bank, cried out to them
A rough uncalled-for challenge:
"Who are you
In armor, visiting our rivers? Speak
From where you are, stop there, say why you come.
This is the region of the Shades, and Sleep,
And drowsy Night. It breaks eternal law
For the Stygian craft to carry living bodies.
Never did I rejoice, I tell you, letting
Alcidës cross, or Theseus and Pirithous,[7]
Demigods by paternity though they were,
Invincible in power. One forced in chains
From the king's own seat the watchdog of the dead
And dragged him away trembling. The other two
Were bent on carrying our lady off
From Dis's chamber."
This the prophetess
And servant of Amphrysian Apollo[8]
Briefly answered:
"Here are no such plots,
So fret no more. These weapons threaten nothing.
Let the great watchdog at the door howl on
Forever terrifying the bloodless shades.
Let chaste Proserpina remain at home
In her uncle's house. The man of Troy, Aeneas,
Remarkable for loyalty, great in arms,
Goes through the deepest shades of Erebus
To see his father.
If the very image
Of so much goodness moves you not at all,
Here is a bough"[9]—at this she showed the bough
That had been hidden, held beneath her dress—
"You'll recognize it."
Then his heart, puffed up
With rage, subsided. They had no more words.
His eyes fixed on the ancient gift, the bough,
The destined gift, so long unseen, now seen,
He turned his dusky craft and made for shore.
There from the long thwarts where they sat he cleared
The other souls and made the gangway wide,
Letting the massive man step in the bilge.
The leaky coracle groaned at the weight
And took a flood of swampy water in.
At length, on the other side, he put ashore
The prophetess and hero in the mire,

7. They came to kidnap Proserpina, failed, and were imprisoned. *Alcidës:* Heracles, who, as one of his labors, was to bring Cerberus, the watchdog of Hades, up from the lower world. He also managed to rescue Theseus. 8. An elaborate learned allusion; Apollo had once served as herdsman to King Admetus on the banks of the river Amphrysus in Thessaly. 9. The golden bough that Aeneas had been ordered to take as tribute to Proserpina.

A formless ooze amid the grey-green sedge.
Great Cerberus barking with his triple throat
Makes all that shoreline ring, as he lies huge
In a facing cave. Seeing his neck begin
To come alive with snakes, the prophetess
Tossed him a lump of honey and drugged meal
To make him drowse. Three ravenous gullets gaped
And he snapped up the sop. Then his great bulk
Subsided and lay down through all the cave.
Now seeing the watchdog deep in sleep, Aeneas
Took the opening: swiftly he turned away
From the river over which no soul returns.

Now voices crying loud were heard at once—
The souls of infants wailing. At the door
Of the sweet life they were to have no part in,
Torn from the breast, a black day took them off
And drowned them all in bitter death. Near these
Were souls falsely accused, condemned to die.
But not without a judge, or jurymen,
Had these souls got their places: Minos reigned
As the presiding judge, moving the urn,
And called a jury of the silent ones[1]
To learn of lives and accusations. Next
Were those sad souls, benighted, who contrived
Their own destruction, and as they hated daylight,
Cast their lives away. How they would wish
In the upper air now to endure the pain
Of poverty and toil! But iron law
Stands in the way, since the drear hateful swamp
Has pinned them down here, and the Styx that winds
Nine times around exerts imprisoning power.
Not far away, spreading on every side,
The Fields of Mourning came in view, so called
Since here are those whom pitiless love consumed
With cruel wasting, hidden on paths apart
By myrtle woodland growing overhead.
In death itself, pain will not let them be.
He saw here Phaedra, Procris, Eriphylë
Sadly showing the wounds her hard son gave;
Evadnë and Pasiphaë, at whose side
Laodamia walked, and Caeneus,[2]

1. The dead. Minos, once king of Crete, is now judge of the dead. The magistrate of a Roman court decided the order in which cases were heard by drawing lots from an urn. 2. Virgil's words in the original are ambiguous (perhaps to reflect the ambiguity of the sex of Caeneus). The usual explanation of the passage is that Caenis (a woman) was changed by Neptune into a man (Caeneus) but returned to her original sex after death. Because the name occurs here in a list of women, this seems the most likely explanation. Phaedra was the wife of Theseus, king of Athens, who fell in love with Hippolytus, her husband's son by another woman; the result was her death by suicide and Hippolytus's death through his father's curse. Procris was killed by her husband in an accident that was brought about by her own jealousy. Eriphylë betrayed her husband for gold and was killed by her own son. Evadnë threw herself on the pyre of her husband, who was killed by Jupiter for impiety. Pasiphaë was the wife of Minos; she was made to fall in love with a bull, and their union produced the Minotaur. Laodamia begged to be allowed to talk with her dead husband; the request was granted by the gods, and when his time came to return she went with him to the underworld.

A young man once, a woman now, and turned
Again by fate into the older form.
Among them, with her fatal wound still fresh,
Phoenician Dido wandered the deep wood.
The Trojan captain paused nearby and knew
Her dim form in the dark, as one who sees,
Early in the month, or thinks to have seen, the moon
Rising through cloud, all dim. He wept and spoke
Tenderly to her:
"Dido, so forlorn,
The story then that came to me was true,
That you were out of life, had met your end
By your own hand. Was I, was I the cause?
I swear by heaven's stars, by the high gods,
By any certainty below the earth,
I left your land against my will, my queen.
The gods' commands drove me to do their will,
As now they drive me through this world of shades,
These mouldy waste lands and these depths of night.
And I could not believe that I would hurt you
So terribly by going. Wait a little.
Do not leave my sight.
Am I someone to flee from? The last word
Destiny lets me say to you is this."

Aeneas with such pleas tried to placate
The burning soul, savagely glaring back,
And tears came to his eyes. But she had turned
With gaze fixed on the ground as he spoke on,
Her face no more affected than if she were
Immobile granite or Marpesian[3] stone.
At length she flung away from him and fled,
His enemy still, into the shadowy grove
Where he whose bride she once had been, Sychaeus,
Joined in her sorrows and returned her love.
Aeneas still gazed after her in tears,
Shaken by her ill fate and pitying her.

With effort then he took the given way,
And they went on, reaching the farthest lands
Where men famous in war gather apart.
Here Tydeus came to meet him, and then came
Parthenopaeus, glorious in arms,
Adrastus[4] then, a pallid shade. Here too
Were Dardans long bewept in the upper air,
Men who died in the great war. And he groaned
To pick these figures out, in a long file,
Glaucus, Medon, Thersilochus, besides
Antenor's three sons, then the priest of Ceres

3. From the island of Paros. 4. Three of the seven Argive attackers of Thebes in the generation before the Trojan War. Tydeus was father of Diomedes.

Polyboetës, then Idaeus, holding
Still to his warcar, holding his old gear.
To right and left they crowd the path and stay
And will not have enough of seeing him,
But love to hold him back, to walk beside him,
And hear the story of why he came.
Not so
Agamemnon's phalanx, chiefs of the Danaans:
Seeing the living man in bronze that glowed
Through the dark air, they shrank in fear. Some turned
And ran, as once, when routed, to the ships,
While others raised a battle shout, or tried to,
Mouths agape, mocked by the whispering cry.
Here next he saw Deïphobus, Priam's son,
Mutilated from head to foot, his face
And both hands cruelly torn, ears shorn away,
Nose to the noseholes lopped by a shameful stroke.
Barely knowing the shade who quailed before him
Covering up his tortured face, Aeneas
Spoke out to him in his known voice:
"Deïphobus,
Gallant officer in high Teucer's line,
Who chose this brutal punishment, who had
So much the upper hand of you? I heard
On that last night that you had fallen, spent
After a slaughter of Pelasgians—
Fallen on piled-up carnage. It was I
Who built on Rhoeteum Point an empty tomb
And sent a high call to your soul three times.
Your name, your armor, marks the place. I could not
Find you, friend, to put your bones in earth
In the old country as I came away."

And Priam's son replied:
"You left undone
Nothing, my friend, but gave all ritual due
Deïphobus, due a dead man's shade. My lot
And the Laconian woman's[5] ghastly doing
Sank me in this hell. These are the marks
She left me as her memorial. You know
How between one false gladness and another
We spent that last night—no need to remind you.
When the tall deadly horse came at one bound,
With troops crammed in its paunch, above our towers,
She made a show of choral dance and led
Our Phrygian women crying out on Bacchus
Here and there—but held a torch amid them,
Signalling to Danaans from the Height.
Worn by the long day, heavily asleep,
I lay in my unlucky bridal chamber,

5. Helen's.

And rest, profound and sweet, most like the rest
Of death, weighed on me as I lay. Meanwhile
She, my distinguished wife,[6] moved all my arms
Out of the house—as she had slipped my sword,
My faithful sword, out from beneath my pillow—
Opened the door and called in Menelaus,
Hoping no doubt by this great gift to him,
Her lover, to blot old infamy out. Why hold back
From telling it? The two burst in the bedroom,
Joined by that ringleader of atrocity,
Ulysses, of the windking's[7] line. O gods,
If with pure lips I pray, requite the Greeks
With equal suffering! But you, now tell me
What in the world has brought you here alive:
Have you come from your sea wandering, and did heaven
Direct you? How could harrying fortune send you
To these sad sunless homes, disordered places?"

At this point in their talk Aurora,[8] borne
Through high air on her glowing rosy car
Had crossed the meridian: should they linger now
With stories they might spend the allotted time.
But at Aeneas' side the Sibyl spoke,
Warning him briefly:
"Night comes on, Aeneas,
We use up hours grieving. Here is the place
Where the road forks: on the right hand it goes
Past mighty Dis's walls, Elysium way,
Our way; but the leftward road will punish
Malefactors, taking them to Tartarus."
Deïphobus answered her:
"No need for anger,
Reverend lady. I'll depart and make
The tally in the darkness full again.
Go on, sir, glory of us all! Go on,
Enjoy a better destiny."
He spoke,
And even as he spoke he turned away.
Now of a sudden Aeneas looked and saw
To the left, under a cliff, wide buildings girt
By a triple wall round which a torrent rushed
With scorching flames and boulders tossed in thunder,
The abyss's Fiery River. A massive gate
With adamantine pillars faced the stream,
So strong no force of men or gods in war
May ever avail to crack and bring it down,
And high in air an iron tower stands
On which Tisiphonë,[9] her bloody robe
Pulled up about her, has her seat and keeps

6. Deïphobus had married Helen after the death of Paris. 7. Aeolus's. His son was Sisyphus, one of the great tricksters of Greek legend, who was reputed to be Ulysses' actual father, rather than Laertes. 8. Dawn goddess. 9. One of the Furies.

Unsleeping watch over the entrance way
By day and night. From the interior, groans
Are heard, and thud of lashes, clanking iron,
Dragging chains. Arrested in his tracks,
Appalled by what he heard, Aeneas stood.

"What are the forms of evil here? O Sister,
Tell me. And the punishments dealt out:
Why such a lamentation?"
Said the Sibyl:
"Light of the Teucrians, it is decreed
That no pure soul may cross the sill of evil.
When, however, Hecatë[1] appointed me
Caretaker of Avernus wood, she led me
Through heaven's punishments and taught me all.
This realm is under Cretan Rhadamanthus'[2]
Iron rule. He sentences. He listens
And makes the souls confess their crooked ways,
How they put off atonements in the world
With foolish satisfaction, thieves of time,
Until too late, until the hour of death.
At once the avenger girdled with her whip,
Tisiphonë, leaps down to lash the guilty,
Vile writhing snakes held out on her left hand,
And calls her savage sisterhood. The awaited
Time has come, hell gates will shudder wide
On shrieking hinges. Can you see her now,
Her shape, as doorkeeper, upon the sill?
More bestial, just inside, the giant Hydra
Lurks with fifty black and yawning throats.
Then Tartarus itself goes plunging down
In darkness twice as deep as heaven is high
For eyes fixed on etherial Olympus.
Here is Earth's ancient race, the brood of Titans,[3]
Hurled by the lightning down to roll forever
In the abyss. Here, too, I saw those giant
Twins of Aloeus[4] who laid their hands
Upon great heaven to rend it and to topple
Jove from his high seat, and I saw, too,
Salmoneus paying dearly for the jape
Of mimicking Jove's fire, Olympus' thunder:
Shaking a bright torch from a four-horse car
He rode through Greece and his home town in Elis,
Glorying, claiming honor as a god—
Out of his mind, to feign with horses' hoofs
On bronze the blast and inimitable bolt.
The father almighty amid heavy cloud
Let fly his missile—no firebrand for him

1. Goddess of witchcraft, often identified with Diana by the Romans. 2. Brother of Minos, king of Crete, and like him a judge of the dead. 3. The second generation of gods, offspring of Earth and Sky, overthrown by the Olympians under Jupiter (Zeus). 4. Otus and Ephialtes, who piled Mt. Pelion on top of Mt. Ossa in order to scale heaven and attack Jupiter.

Nor smoky pitchpine light—and spun the man
Headlong in a huge whirlwind.
One had sight
Of Tityos,[5] too, child of all-mothering Earth,
His body stretched out over nine whole acres
While an enormous vulture with hooked beak
Forages forever in his liver,
His vitals rife with agonies. The bird,
Lodged in the chest cavity, tears at his feast,
And tissues growing again get no relief.
As for the Lapiths, need I tell: Ixion,
Pirithoüs,[6] and the black crag overhead
So sure to fall it seems already falling.
Golden legs gleam on the feasters' couches,
Dishes in royal luxury prepared
Are laid before them—but the oldest Fury
Crouches near and springs out with her torch.
Her outcry, if they try to touch the meal.
Here come those who as long as life remained
Held brothers hateful, beat their parents, cheated
Poor men dependent on them; also those
Who hugged their newfound riches to themselves
And put nothing aside for relatives—
A great crowd, this—then men killed for adultery,
Men who took arms in war against the right,
Not scrupling to betray their lords. All these
Are hemmed in here, awaiting punishment.
Best not inquire what punishment, what form
Of suffering at their last end overwhelms them.
Some heave at a great boulder, or revolve,
Spreadeagled, hung on wheel-spokes. Theseus
Cleaves to his chair and cleaves to it forever.
Phlegyas in his misery teaches all souls
His lesson, thundering out amid the gloom:
'Be warned and study justice, not to scorn
The immortal gods.' Here's one who sold his country,
Foisted a tyrant on her, set up laws
Or nullified them for a price; another
Entered his daughter's room to take a bride
Forbidden him. All these dared monstrous wrong
And took what they dared try for. If I had
A hundred tongues, a hundred mouths, a voice
Of iron, I could not tell of all the shapes
Their crimes had taken, or their punishments."

All this he heard from her who for long years
Had served Apollo. Then she said:
"Come now,

5. Punished for trying to rape Leto (Latona). Odysseus sees him in the land of the dead also (*Odyssey* 11.646–54). 6. Ixion tried to rape Juno, and Pirithoüs aided Theseus in his unsuccessful attempt to carry off Proserpina from the underworld. The punishment described here, however, was traditionally assigned to Tantalus, another of the great sinners.

Be on your way, and carry out your mission.
Let us go faster. I can see the walls
The Cyclops' forges built and, facing us,
The portico and gate[7] where they command us
To leave the gifts required."
On this the two
In haste strode on abreast down the dark paths
Over the space between, and neared the doors.
Aeneas gained the entrance, halted there,
Asperged his body with fresh water drops,
And on the sill before him fixed the bough.

Now that at last this ritual was performed,
His duty to the goddess done, they came
To places of delight, to green park land,
Where souls take ease amid the Blessed Groves.
Wider expanses of high air endow
Each vista with a wealth of light. Souls here
Possess their own familiar sun and stars.
Some train on grassy rings, others compete
In field games, others grapple on the sand.
Feet moving to a rhythmic beat, the dancers
Group in a choral pattern as they sing.
Orpheus, the priest of Thrace, in his long robe
Accompanies, plucking his seven notes
Now with his fingers, now with his ivory quill.
Here is the ancient dynasty of Teucer,
Heroes high of heart, beautiful scions,
Born in greater days: Ilus, Assaracus,
And Dardanus,[8] who founded Troy. Aeneas
Marvels to see their chariots and gear
Far off, all phantom: lances fixed in earth,
And teams unyoked, at graze on the wide plain.
All joy they took, alive, in cars and weapons,
As in the care and pasturing of horses,
Remained with them when they were laid in earth.
He saw, how vividly! along the grass
To right and left, others who feasted there
And chorused out a hymn praising Apollo,
Within a fragrant laurel grove, where Po[9]
Sprang up and took his course to the world above,
The broad stream flowing on amid the forest.
This was the company of those who suffered
Wounds in battle for their country; those
Who in their lives were holy men and chaste
Or worthy of Phoebus in prophetic song;
Or those who bettered life, by finding out
New truths and skills; or those who to some folk
By benefactions made themselves remembered.

7. The entrance to Elysium, the paradise of the souls of the blessed. This gate can be passed only with the token of the golden bough. 8. Trojan ancestors. 9. An Italian river.

They all wore snowy chaplets on their brows.
To these souls, mingling on all sides, the Sibyl
Spoke now, and especially to Musaeus,[1]
The central figure, toward whose towering shoulders
All the crowd gazed:
"Tell us, happy souls,
And you, great seer, what region holds Anchises,
Where is his resting place? For him we came
By ferry across the rivers of Erebus."
And the great soul answered briefly:
"None of us
Has one fixed home. We walk in shady groves
And bed on riverbanks and occupy
Green meadows fresh with streams. But if your hearts
Are set on it, first cross this ridge; and soon
I shall point out an easy path."
So saying,
He walked ahead and showed them from the height
The sweep of shining plain. Then down they went
And left the hilltops.
Now Aeneas' father
Anchises, deep in the lush green of a valley,
Had given all his mind to a survey
Of souls, till then confined there, who were bound
For daylight in the upper world.[2] By chance
His own were those he scanned now, all his own
Descendants, with their futures and their fates,
Their characters and acts. But when he saw
Aeneas advancing toward him on the grass,
He stretched out both his hands in eagerness
As tears wetted his cheeks. He said in welcome:

"Have you at last come, has that loyalty
Your father counted on conquered the journey?
Am I to see your face, my son, and hear
Our voices in communion as before?
I thought so, surely; counting the months I thought
The time would come. My longing has not tricked me.
I greet you now, how many lands behind you,
How many seas, what blows and dangers, son!
How much I feared the land of Libya
Might do you harm."
Aeneas said:
"Your ghost,
Your sad ghost, father, often before my mind,
Impelled me to the threshold of this place.
My ships ride anchored in the Tuscan sea.
But let me have your hand, let me embrace you,

1. A legendary singer, like Orpheus. 2. I.e., destined to be reincarnated, as Anchisës will explain.

Do not draw back."
At this his tears brimmed over
And down his cheeks. And there he tried three times
To throw his arms around his father's neck,
Three times the shade untouched slipped through his hands,
Weightless as wind and fugitive as dream.
Aeneas now saw at the valley's end
A grove standing apart, with stems and boughs
Of woodland rustling, and the stream of Lethe[3]
Running past those peaceful glades. Around it
Souls of a thousand nations filled the air,
As bees in meadows at the height of summer
Hover and home on flowers and thickly swarm
On snow-white lilies, and the countryside
Is loud with humming. At the sudden vision
Shivering, at a loss, Aeneas asked
What river flowed there and what men were those
In such a throng along the riverside.
His father Anchises told him:
"Souls for whom
A second body is in store: their drink
Is water of Lethe, and it frees from care
In long forgetfulness. For all this time
I have so much desired to show you these
And tell you of them face to face—to take
The roster of my children's children here,
So you may feel with me more happiness
At finding Italy."
"Must we imagine,
Father, there are souls that go from here
Aloft to upper heaven, and once more
Return to bodies' dead weight? The poor souls,
How can they crave our daylight so?"
"My son,
I'll tell you, not to leave you mystified,"
Anchisës said, and took each point in order:

First, then, the sky and lands and sheets of water,
The bright moon's globe, the Titan sun and stars,
Are fed within by Spirit, and a Mind
Infused through all the members of the world
Makes one great living body of the mass.
From Spirit come the races of man and beast,
The life of birds, odd creatures the deep sea
Contains beneath her sparkling surfaces,
And fiery energy from a heavenly source
Belongs to the generative seeds of these,
So far as they are not poisoned or clogged
By mortal bodies, their free essence dimmed

3. River of forgetfulness.

By earthiness and deathliness of flesh.
This makes them fear and crave, rejoice and grieve.
Imprisoned in the darkness of the body
They cannot clearly see heaven's air;[4] in fact
Even when life departs on the last day
Not all the scourges of the body pass
From the poor souls, not all distress of life.
Inevitably, many malformations,
Growing together in mysterious ways,
Become inveterate. Therefore they undergo
The discipline of punishments and pay
In penance for old sins: some hang full length
To the empty winds, for some the stain of wrong
Is washed by floods or burned away by fire.
We suffer each his own shade. We are sent
Through wide Elysium, where a few abide
In happy lands, till the long day, the round
Of Time fulfilled, has worn our stains away,
Leaving the soul's heaven-sent perception clear,
The fire from heaven pure.[5] These other souls,
When they have turned Time's wheel a thousand years,
The god calls in a crowd to Lethe stream,
That there unmemoried they may see again
The heavens and wish re-entry into bodies."
Anchises paused. He drew both son and Sibyl
Into the middle of the murmuring throng,
Then picked out a green mound from which to view
The souls as they came forward, one by one,
And to take note of faces.
"Come," he said,
"What glories follow Dardan generations
In after years, and from Italian blood
What famous children in your line will come,
Souls of the future, living in our name,
I shall tell clearly now, and in the telling
Teach you your destiny. That one you see,
The young man leaning on a spear unarmed,
Has his allotted place nearest the light.
He will be first to take the upper air,
Silvius, a child with half Italian blood
And an Alban name, your last born, whom your wife,
Lavinia,[6] late in your great age will rear
In forests to be king and father of kings.
Through him our race will rule in Alba Longa.
Next him is Procas, pride of the Trojan line,
And Capys, too, then Numitor, then one

4. The idea that the body is the tomb of the soul is found also in Plato. Like a number of other ideas in Anchisës' speech (such as reincarnation), it was characteristic of Orphism, a set of beliefs that underlay various mystery rituals outside the state religions of Greece and Rome. 5. These souls, having successfully purged the impurities of the body, are now ready to return to the company of the gods. The other souls whom Anchisës goes on to mention must undergo further rebirths before they are purified. They include the souls of the future Romans, whom Aeneas now surveys. 6. The bride Aeneas will win by war in the second half of the poem.

Whose name restores you: Silvius Aeneas,[7]
Both in arms and piety your peer,
If ever he shall come to reign in Alba.
What men they are! And see their rugged forms
With oakleaf crowns shadowing their brows. I tell you,
These are to found Nomentum, Gabii,
Fidenae town, Collatia's hilltop towers,
Pometii, Fort Inuus, Bola, Cora[8]—
Names to be heard for places nameless now.
Then Romulus, fathered by Mars, will come
To make himself his grandfather's companion,
Romulus, reared by his mother, Ilia,
In the blood-line of Assaracus. Do you see
The double plume of Mars fixed on his crest,
See how the father of the gods himself
Now marks him out with his own sign of honor?
Look now, my son: under his auspices
Illustrious Rome will bound her power with earth,
Her spirit with Olympus. She'll enclose
Her seven hills with one great city wall,
Fortunate in the men she breeds. Just so
Cybelë Mother,[9] honored on Berecynthus,
Wearing her crown of towers, onward rides
By chariot through the towns of Phrygia,
In joy at having given birth to gods,
And cherishing a hundred grandsons, heaven
Dwellers with homes on high.
                                        Turn your two eyes
This way and see this people, your own Romans.
Here is Caesar, and all the line of Iulus,
All who shall one day pass under the dome
Of the great sky: this is the man, this one,
Of whom so often you have heard the promise,
Caesar Augustus, son of the deified,
Who shall bring once again an Age of Gold
To Latium, to the land where Saturn reigned
In early times. He will extend his power
Beyond the Garamants[1] and Indians,
Over far territories north and south
Of the zodiacal stars, the solar way,
Where Atlas, heaven-bearing, on his shoulder
Turns the night-sphere, studded with burning stars.
At that man's coming even now the realms
Of Caspia and Maeotia tremble, warned
By oracles, and the seven mouths of Nile
Go dark with fear. The truth is, even Alcidës[2]

7. Kings of Alba Longa, the city (Rome's forerunner) founded in Italy by Ascanius. Silvius Aeneas was son of the Silvius mentioned in line 628 and grandson of Aeneas. Numitor was father of Ilia (or Rhea Silvia), the mother by Mars of Romulus and Remus (see lines 644–50). 8. Towns near Rome. 9. The great mother goddess of Asia Minor, whose cult was important in Rome from an early period. Mt. Berecynthus, near Troy, was a center of her Asian cult. One of her attributes was a crown that resembled a city wall with turrets. 1. A people of Africa. 2. Hercules.

Never traversed so much of earth—I grant
That he could shoot the hind with brazen hoofs
Or bring peace to the groves of Erymanthus,
Or leave Lerna affrighted by his bow.[3]
Neither did he who guides his triumphal car
With reins of vine-shoots twisted, Bacchus, driving
Down from Nysa's height his tiger team.
Do we lag still at carrying our valor
Into action? Can our fear prevent
Our settling in Ausonia?
Who is he
So set apart there, olive-crowned, who holds
The sacred vessels in his hands? I know
That snowy mane and beard: Numa,[4] the king,
Who will build early Rome on a base of laws,
A man sent from the small-town poverty
Of Curës to high sovereignty. After him
Comes Tullus, breaker of his country's peace,
Arousing men who have lost victorious ways,
Malingering men, to war. Near him is Ancus,
Given to boasting, even now too pleased
With veering popularity's heady air.
Do you care to see now, too, the Tarquin kings
And the proud soul of the avenger, Brutus,[5]
By whom the bundled *fasces* are regained?
Consular power will first be his, and his
The pitiless axes.[6] When his own two sons
Plot war against the city, he will call
For the death penalty in freedom's name—
Unhappy man, no matter how posterity
May see these matters. Love of the fatherland
Will sway him—and unmeasured lust for fame.
Now see the Decii and the Drusi there,
And stern Torquatus, with his axe, and see
Camillus[7] bringing the lost standards home.
That pair,[8] however, matched in brilliant armor,
Matched in their hearts' desire now, while night
Still holds them fast, once they attain life's light
What war, what grief, will they provoke between them—
Battle-lines and bloodshed—as the father
Marches from the Alpine ramparts, down
From Monaco's walled height, and the son-in-law,
Drawn up with armies of the East, awaits him.
Sons, refrain! You must not blind your hearts

3. Three of Hercules' labors: killing the Cerynaian hind, the Erymanthian boar, and the hydra of Lerna. 4. The second king of Rome. His successors are mentioned in the next ten lines. 5. Avenger of the rape of Lucretia by Sextus, son of Tarquin the Proud; after Tarquin was expelled from Rome, the kingship was abolished. This Brutus (claimed as ancestor by the assassin of Julius Caesar) was the first consul, chief magistrate of the republic that succeeded the monarchy at Rome. 6. Rods (*fasces*) wrapped around an axe were the symbol of the consul's power. 7. All heroic figures from Rome's past. 8. Julius Caesar and his opponent in the Civil War, Pompey. The war was provoked when Caesar crossed the Alps from Gaul and entered Italy with an army. Pompey had married Caesar's daughter, Julia.

To that enormity of civil war,
Turning against your country's very heart
Her own vigor of manhood. You above all
Who trace your line from the immortals, you
Be first to spare us. Child of my own blood,[9]
Throw away your sword!
Mummius[1] there,
When Corinth is brought low, will drive his car
As victor and as killer of Achaeans
To our high Capitol. Paulus will conquer
Argos and Agamemnon's old Mycenae,
Defeating Perseus,[2] the Aeacid,
Heir to the master of war, Achilles—thus
Avenging his own Trojan ancestors
And the defilement of Minerva's shrine.
Great Cato![3] Who would leave you unremarked,
Or, Cossus, you, or the family of Gracchi,
Or the twin Scipios, bright bolts of war,
The bane of Libya, or you, Fabricius,
In poverty yet powerful, or you,
Serranus, at the furrow, casting seed?
Where, though I weary, do you hurry me,
You Fabii? Fabius Maximus,
You are the only soul who shall restore
Our wounded state by waiting out the enemy.
Others will cast more tenderly in bronze
Their breathing figures, I can well believe,
And bring more lifelike portraits out of marble;
Argue more eloquently, use the pointer
To trace the paths of heaven accurately
And accurately foretell the rising stars.
Roman, remember by your strength to rule
Earth's peoples—for your arts are to be these:
To pacify, to impose the rule of law,
To spare the conquered, battle down the proud."
Anchises paused here as they gazed in awe,
Then added:
"See there, how Marcellus[4] comes
With spoils of the commander that he killed:
How the man towers over everyone.
Cavalry leader, he'll sustain the realm
Of Rome in hours of tumult, bringing to heel
The Carthaginians and rebellious Gaul,
And for the third time in our history

9. Caesar's family, the Julii, traced their ancestry back through Ascanius (Iulus) to Aeneas and Anchisës.
1. Roman general, one of the conquerors of Greece, who sacked the city of Corinth in 167 B.C. 2. Macedonian king defeated by the Roman general Aemilius Paulus in 168 B.C. He claimed descent from Achilles. 3. Statesman and orator of the early second century B.C., known for his sternness and rigid morals (and so an embodiment of Romanness). He begins a list of illustrious figures out of Rome's past, almost all of them famous generals. 4. A Roman general famous for killing the leader of Gauls from northern Italy in 222 B.C. in single combat and for leading the fight against Hannibal in the Second Punic War.

He'll dedicate an enemy general's arms
To Father Romulus."
But here Aeneas
Broke in, seeing at Marcellus' side
A young man[5] beautifully formed and tall
In shining armor, but with clouded brow
And downcast eyes:
"And who is that one, Father
Walking beside the captain as he comes:
A son, or grandchild from the same great stock?
The others murmur, all astir. How strong
His presence is! But night like a black cloud
About his head whirls down in awful gloom."

His father Anchisës answered, and the tears
Welled up as he began:
"Oh, do not ask
About this huge grief of your people, son.
Fate will give earth only a glimpse of him,
Not let the boy live on. Lords of the sky,
You thought the majesty of Rome too great
If it had kept these gifts. How many groans
Will be sent up from that great Field of Mars
To Mars' proud city, and what sad rites you'll see,
Tiber, as you flow past the new-built tomb.
Never will any boy of Ilian race
Exalt his Latin forefathers with promise
Equal to his; never will Romulus' land
Take pride like this in any of her sons.
Weep for his faithful heart, his old-world honor,
His sword arm never beaten down! No enemy
Could have come through a clash with him unhurt,
Whether this soldier went on foot or rode,
Digging his spurs into a lathered mount.
Child of our mourning, if only in some way
You could break through your bitter fate. For you
Will be Marcellus. Let me scatter lilies,
All I can hold, and scarlet flowers as well,
To heap these for my grandson's shade at least,
Frail gifts and ritual of no avail."

So raptly, everywhere, father and son
Wandered the airy plain and viewed it all.
After Anchises had conducted him
To every region and had fired his love
Of glory in the years to come, he spoke
Of wars that he must fight, of Laurentines,
And of Latinus' city, then of how
He might avoid or bear each toil to come.

5. Another Marcellus, Augustus's nephew and presumptive heir, who died in 23 B.C. at the age of nineteen.

There are two gates of Sleep, one said to be
Of horn, whereby the true shades pass with ease,
The other all white ivory agleam
Without a flaw, and yet false dreams are sent
Through this one by the ghosts to the upper world.
Anchises now, his last instructions given,
Took son and Sibyl there and let them go
By the Ivory Gate.
Aeneas made his way
Straight to the ships to see his crews again,
Then sailed directly to Caieta's port.
Bow anchors out, the sterns rest on the beach.

Summary After returning from the underworld to the upper air, Aeneas begins his settlement in Italy. He is offered the hand of the princess Lavinia by her father Latinus, but this provokes a war against the Trojans, led by King Turnus of Laurentum. While Aeneas is on an embassy to seek help from the Etruscans, his mother, Venus, comes to him at night with the armor made for him by Vulcan (Hephaestus in Greek), her husband and guardian of fire. On the shield is carved a representation of the future glories of Rome.

FROM BOOK VIII

[*The Shield of Aeneas*]

Venus the gleaming goddess,
Bearing her gifts, came down amid high clouds
And far away still, in a vale apart,
Sighted her son beside the ice-cold stream.
Then making her appearance as she willed
She said to him:
"Here are the gifts I promised,
Forged to perfection by my husband's craft,
So that you need not hesitate to challenge
Arrogant Laurentines or savage Turnus,
However soon, in battle."
As she spoke
Cytherëa[6] swept to her son's embrace
And placed the shining arms before his eyes
Under an oak tree. Now the man in joy
At a goddess' gifts, at being so greatly honored,
Could not be satisfied, but scanned each piece
In wonder and turned over in his hands
The helmet with its terrifying plumes
And gushing flames, the sword-blade edged with fate,
The cuirass of hard bronze, blood-red and huge—
Like a dark cloud burning with sunset light
That sends a glow for miles—the polished greaves[7]
Of gold and silver alloy, the great spear,
And finally the fabric of the shield

6. So called because she was born from the sea foam off the Greek island Cythera. 7. Leg pieces.

Beyond description.
There the Lord of Fire,
Knowing the prophets, knowing the age to come,
Had wrought the future story of Italy,
The triumphs of the Romans: there one found
The generations of Ascanius' heirs,
The wars they fought, each one. Vulcan had made
The mother wolf, lying in Mars' green grotto;
Made the twin boys at play about her teats,[8]
Nursing the mother without fear, while she
Bent round her smooth neck fondling them in turn
And shaped their bodies with her tongue.[9]
Nearby,
Rome had been added by the artisan,
And Sabine women roughly carried off
Out of the audience at the Circus games;
Then suddenly a new war coming on
To pit the sons of Romulus against
Old Tatius[1] and his austere town of Curës.
Later the same kings, warfare laid aside,
In arms before Jove's altar stood and held
Libation dishes as they made a pact
With offering of wine. Not far from this
Two four-horse war-cars, whipped on, back to back,
Had torn Mettus apart (still, man of Alba,
You should have kept your word) and Roman Tullus[2]
Dragged the liar's rags of flesh away
Through woods where brambles dripped a bloody dew.
There, too, Porsenna stood, ordering Rome
To take the exiled Tarquin back,[3] then bringing
The whole city under massive siege.
There for their liberty Aeneas' sons
Threw themselves forward on the enemy spears.
You might have seen Porsenna imaged there
To the life, a menacing man, a man in anger
At Roman daring: Cocles who downed the bridge,
Cloelia[4] who broke her bonds and swam the river.

On the shield's upper quarter Manlius,
guard of the Tarpeian Rock, stood fast
Before the temple and held the Capitol,[5]

8. The twins who were to build Rome, Romulus and Remus, sons of Mars the war god, were cast out into the woods and there suckled by a she-wolf. 9. See Ovid's *Metamorphoses* 15.330–33. 1. A Sabine king. Because the new city of Rome consisted mostly of men, the Romans decided to steal women from the Sabines. The Romans invited them to an athletic festival, and at a given signal every Roman carried off a Sabine bride. The war that followed ended in the amalgamation of the Roman and Sabine peoples. 2. The king who punished Mettus for breaking an agreement made during the early wars of Rome. Mettus was torn apart by two chariots moving in opposite directions. 3. The Etruscan king Porsenna attempted to restore Tarquin, the last of the Roman kings, to the throne from which he had been expelled. 4. A Roman hostage held by Porsenna. Horatius Cocles, with two companions, defended the bridge across the Tiber to give the Romans time to destroy it. 5. In 392 B.C. Manlius was in charge of the citadel (*Tarpeian Rock*) at a time when the Gauls from the north held all the rest of the city. They made a night attack on the citadel, but Manlius, awakened by the cackling of the sacred geese, beat it off, and saved Rome.

Where Romulus' house[6] was newly thatched and rough.
Here fluttering through gilded porticos
At night, the silvery goose warned of the Gauls
Approaching: under cover of the darkness
Gauls amid the bushes had crept near
And now lay hold upon the citadel.
Golden locks they had and golden dress,
Glimmering with striped cloaks, their milky necks
Entwined with gold. They hefted Alpine spears,
Two each, and had long body shields for cover.
Vulcan had fashioned naked Luperci
And Salii[7] leaping there with woolen caps
And fallen-from-heaven shields, and put chaste ladies
Riding in cushioned carriages through Rome
With sacred images. At a distance then
He pictured the deep hell of Tartarus,
Dis's high gate, crime's punishments, and, yes,
You, Catiline,[8] on a precarious cliff
Hanging and trembling at the Furies' glare.
Then, far away from this, were virtuous souls
And Cato[9] giving laws to them. Mid-shield,
The pictured sea flowed surging, all of gold,
As whitecaps foamed on the blue waves, and dolphins
Shining in silver round and round the scene
Propelled themselves with flukes and cut through billows.
Vivid in the center were the bronze-beaked
Ships and the fight at sea off Actium.
Here you could see Leucata[1] all alive
With ships maneuvering, sea glowing gold,
Augustus Caesar leading into battle
Italians, with both senators and people,
Household gods and great gods: there he stood
High on the stern, and from his blessed brow
Twin flames gushed upward, while his crest revealed
His father's star. Apart from him, Agrippa,[2]
Favored by winds and gods, led ships in column,
A towering figure, wearing on his brows
The coronet adorned with warships' beaks,
Highest distinction for command at sea.
Then came Antonius with barbaric wealth
And a diversity of arms, victorious
From races of the Dawnlands and Red Sea,

6. In Virgil's time there was still preserved at Rome a rustic building that was supposed to have been the dwelling place of Romulus. 7. The twelve priests of Mars, who danced in his honor carrying shields that had fallen from heaven. *Luperci:* priests celebrating the Lupercalia, a festival promoting fertility. 8. Leader of a conspiracy to overthrow the Republic; it was halted mainly through the efforts of Cicero, consul in 63 B.C. Catiline connotes the type of discord, represented by the civil war that almost destroyed the Roman state, to which Augustus later put an end. 9. The noblest of the republicans who had fought Julius Caesar; he stood for honesty and the seriousness that the Romans most admired. He committed suicide in 47 B.C. after Caesar's victory in Africa. Before taking his life he read through Plato's *Phaedo,* a dialogue concerned with the immortality of the soul, which ends with an account of the death of Socrates. 1. A promontory near Actium, on the west coast of Greece, which had a temple of Apollo on it. The naval battle fought here in 31 B.C. was the decisive engagement of the civil war. Augustus, the master of the western half of the empire, defeated Antony, who held the eastern half and was supported by Cleopatra, queen of Egypt. 2. Augustus's admiral at Actium.

Leading the power of the East, of Egypt,
Even of distant Bactra[3] of the steppes
And in his wake the Egyptian consort came
So shamefully. The ships all kept together
Racing ahead, the water torn by oar-strokes,
Torn by the triple beaks, in spume and foam.
All made for the open sea. You might believe
The Cyclades[4] uprooted were afloat
Or mountains running against mountain heights
When seamen in those hulks pressed the attack
Upon the other turreted ships. They hurled
Broadsides of burning flax on flying steel,
And fresh blood reddened Neptune's fields. The queen
Amidst the battle called her flotilla on
With a sistrum's[5] beat, a frenzy out of Egypt,
Never turning her head as yet to see
Twin snakes of death behind, while monster forms
Of gods of every race, and the dog-god
Anubis[6] barking, held their weapons up
Against our Neptune, Venus, and Minerva.
Mars, engraved in steel, raged in the fight
As from high air the dire Furies came
With Discord, taking joy in a torn robe,
And on her heels, with bloody scourge, Bellona.[7]

Overlooking it all, Actian[8] Apollo
Began to pull his bow. Wild at this sight,
All Egypt, Indians, Arabians, all
Sabaeans[9] put about in flight, and she,
The queen, appeared crying for winds to shift
Just as she hauled up sail and slackened sheets.
The Lord of Fire had portrayed her there,
Amid the slaughter, pallid with death to come,
Then borne by waves and wind from the northwest,
While the great length of mourning Nile awaited her
With open bays, calling the conquered home
To his blue bosom and his hidden streams.
But Caesar then in triple triumph[1] rode
Within the walls of Rome, making immortal
Offerings to the gods of Italy—
Three hundred princely shrines throughout the city.
There were the streets, humming with festal joy
And games and cheers, an altar to every shrine,
To every one a mothers' choir, and bullocks
Knifed before the altars strewed the ground.
The man himself, enthroned before the snow-white
Threshold of sunny Phoebus, viewed the gifts
The nations of the earth made, and he fitted them

3. On the borders of India. 4. A chain of islands in the Aegean Sea. 5. An Oriental rattle, used in the worship of Isis. 6. The Egyptian death god, depicted with the head of a jackal. 7. A Roman war goddess. 8. So called because of his temple at Actium; the temple (and its cult statue) overlooked the sea battle. 9. Arabs from the Yemen. 1. For victories in Dalmatia and at Actium and Alexandria.

To the tall portals. Conquered races passed
In long procession, varied in languages
As in their dress and arms. Here Mulciber,[2]
Divine smith, had portrayed the Nomad tribes
And Afri with ungirdled flowing robes,
Here Leleges and Carians, and here
Gelonians[3] with quivers. Here Euphrates,
Milder in his floods now, there Morini,[4]
Northernmost of men; here bull-horned Rhine,
And there the still unconquered Scythian Dahae;
Here, vexed at being bridged, the rough Araxes.[5]
All these images on Vulcan's shield,
His mother's gift, were wonders to Aeneas.
Knowing nothing of the events themselves,
He felt joy in their pictures, taking up
Upon his shoulder all the destined acts
And fame of his descendants.

Summary In the course of the desperate battles that follow, the young Pallas, entrusted to Aeneas's care by his father, is killed by the Italian champion Turnus, who takes and wears the belt of Pallas as the spoil of victory. The fortunes of the war later change in favor of the Trojans, and Aeneas kills the Etruscan king Mezentius, Turnus's ally. Eventually, as the Italians prepare to accept the generous peace terms offered by Aeneas, Turnus forestalls them by accepting Aeneas's challenge to single combat to decide the issue. But this solution is frustrated by the intervention of Juno, who foresees Aeneas's victory. She prompts Turnus's sister, the river nymph Juturna, to intervene in an attempt to save Turnus's life. Juturna stirs up the Italians, who are watching the champions prepare for the duel; the truce is broken, and in the subsequent fighting Aeneas is wounded by an arrow. Healed by Venus, he returns to the fight, and the Italians are driven back. Turnus finally faces his adversary. His sword breaks on the armor forged by Vulcan, and he runs from Aeneas. He is saved by Juturna, who, assuming the shape of his charioteer, hands him a fresh sword. At this point Jupiter intervenes to stop the vain attempts of Juno and Juturna to save Turnus.

FROM BOOK XII

[*The Death of Turnus*]

Omnipotent Olympus' king meanwhile
Had words for Juno, as she watched the combat
Out of a golden cloud. He said:
"My consort,
What will the end be? What is left for you?
You yourself know, and say you know, Aeneas
Born for heaven, tutelary of this land,
By fate to be translated to the stars.[6]
What do you plan? What are you hoping for,
Keeping your seat apart in the cold clouds?
Fitting, was it, that a mortal archer
Wound an immortal? That a blade let slip

2. Vulcan. 3. Peoples from Scythia (in the Balkans). The Leleges and Carians were from Asia Minor. 4. A Belgian tribe. 5. A turbulent river in Armenia. Augustus built a new bridge over it. 6. Aeneas is destined for immortality, because after his death he will be worshiped as a local god.

Should be restored to Turnus, and new force
Accrue to a beaten man? Without your help
What could Juturna do? Come now, at last
Have done, and heed our pleading, and give way.
Let yourself no longer be consumed
Without relief by all that inward burning;
Let care and trouble not forever come to me
From your sweet lips. The finish is at hand.
You had the power to harry men of Troy
By land and sea, to light the fires of war
Beyond belief, to scar a family
With mourning before marriage.[7] I forbid
Your going further."
So spoke Jupiter,
And with a downcast look Juno replied:

"Because I know that is your will indeed,
Great Jupiter, I left the earth below,
Though sore at heart, and left the side of Turnus.
Were it not so, you would not see me here
Suffering all that passes, here alone,
Resting on air. I should be armed in flames
At the very battle-line, dragging the Trojans
Into a deadly action. I persuaded
Juturna—I confess—to help her brother
In his hard lot, and I approved her daring
Greater difficulties to save his life,
But not that she should fight with bow and arrow.
This I swear by Styx' great fountainhead
Inexorable, which high gods hold in awe.
I yield now and for all my hatred leave
This battlefield. But one thing not retained
By fate I beg for Latium, for the future
Greatness of your kin: when presently
They crown peace with a happy wedding day—
So let it be—and merge their laws and treaties,
Never command the land's own Latin folk
To change their old name, to become new Trojans,
Known as Teucrians; never make them alter
Dialect or dress. Let Latium be.
Let there be Alban kings for generations,
And let Italian valor be the strength
Of Rome in after times. Once and for all
Troy fell, and with her name let her lie fallen."

The author of men and of the world replied
With a half-smile:
"Sister of Jupiter[8]
Indeed you are, and Saturn's other child,

7. A reference not only to the Italian losses but also to the suicide of Amata, wife of King Latinus, who hanged herself when the Trojans assaulted the city just before the duel between Aeneas and Turnus began.
8. Jupiter and Juno (like the Greek Zeus and Hera) are brother and sister as well as husband and wife.

To feel such anger, stormy in your breast.
But come, no need; put down this fit of rage.
I grant your wish. I yield, I am won over
Willingly. Ausonian folk will keep
Their fathers' language and their way of life,
And, that being so, their name. The Teucrians
Will mingle and be submerged, incorporated.
Rituals and observances of theirs
I'll add, but make them Latin, one in speech.
The race to come, mixed with Ausonian blood,
Will outdo men and gods in its devotion,
You shall see—and no nation on earth
Will honor and worship you so faithfully."

To all this Juno nodded in assent
And, gladdened by his promise, changed her mind.
Then she withdrew from sky and cloud.
That done,
The Father set about a second plan—
To take Juturna from her warring brother.
Stories are told of twin fiends, called the Dirae,
Whom, with Hell's Megaera,[9] deep Night bore
In one birth. She entwined their heads with coils
Of snakes and gave them wings to race the wind.
Before Jove's throne, a step from the cruel king,
These twins attend him and give piercing fear
To ill mankind, when he who rules the gods
Deals out appalling death and pestilence,
Or war to terrify our wicked cities.
Jove now dispatched one of these, swift from heaven,
Bidding her be an omen to Juturna.
Down she flew, in a whirlwind borne to earth,
Just like an arrow driven through a cloud
From a taut string, an arrow armed with gall
Of deadly poison, shot by a Parthian[1]—
A Parthian or a Cretan[2]—for a wound
Immedicable; whizzing unforeseen
It goes through racing shadows: so the spawn
Of Night went diving downward to the earth.

On seeing Trojan troops drawn up in face
Of Turnus' army, she took on at once
The shape of that small bird[3] that perches late
At night on tombs or desolate roof-tops
And troubles darkness with a gruesome song.
Shrunk to that form, the fiend in Turnus' face
Went screeching, flitting, flitting to and fro
And beating with her wings against his shield.
Unstrung by numbness, faint and strange, he felt
His hackles rise, his voice choke in his throat.

9. One of the Dirae, literally "dreadful ones." 1. Parthia was the most dangerous neighbor of the Roman Empire in the east. 2. Parthian mounted archers were famous, as were Cretan archers. 3. The owl.

As for Juturna, when she knew the wings,
The shriek to be the fiend's, she tore her hair,
Despairing, then she fell upon her cheeks
With nails, upon her breast with clenched hands.

"Turnus, how can your sister help you now?
What action is still open to me, soldierly
Though I have been? Can I by any skill
Hold daylight for you? Can I meet and turn
This deathliness away? Now I withdraw,
Now leave this war. Indecent birds, I fear you;
Spare me your terror. Whip-lash of your wings
I recognize, that ghastly sound, and guess
Great-hearted Jupiter's high cruel commands.
Returns for my virginity, are they?
He gave me life eternal[4]—to what end?
Why has mortality been taken from me?
Now beyond question I could put a term
To all my pain, and go with my poor brother
Into the darkness, his companion there.
Never to die? Will any brook of mine
Without you, brother, still be sweet to me?
If only earth's abyss were wide enough
To take me downward, goddess though I am,
To join the shades below!"
So she lamented,
Then with a long sigh, covering up her head
In her grey mantle, sank to the river's depth.

Aeneas moved against his enemy
And shook his heavy pine-tree spear. He called
From his hot heart:
"Rearmed now, why so slow?
Why, even now, fall back? The contest here
Is not a race, but fighting to the death
With spear and sword. Take on all shapes there are,
Summon up all your nerve and skill, choose any
Footing, fly among the stars, or hide
In caverned earth—"
The other shook his head,
Saying:
"I do not fear your taunting fury,
Arrogant prince. It is the gods I fear
And Jove my enemy."
He said no more,
But looked around him. Then he saw a stone,
Enormous, ancient, set up there to prevent
Landowners' quarrels. Even a dozen picked men
Such as the earth produces in our day
Could barely lift and shoulder it. He swooped

4. Jupiter had been the lover of Juturna and had rewarded her with immortality.

And wrenched it free, in one hand, then rose up
To his heroic height, ran a few steps,
And tried to hurl the stone against his foe—
But as he bent and as he ran
And as he hefted and propelled the weight
He did not know himself. His knees gave way,
His blood ran cold and froze. The stone itself,
Tumbling through space, fell short and had no impact.

Just as in dreams when the night-swoon of sleep
Weighs on our eyes, it seems we try in vain
To keep on running, try with all our might,
But in the midst of effort faint and fail;
Our tongue is powerless, familiar strength
Will not hold up our body, not a sound
Or word will come: just so with Turnus now:
However bravely he made shift to fight
The immortal fiend blocked and frustrated him.
Flurrying images passed through his mind.
He gazed at the Rutulians,[5] and beyond them,
Gazed at the city, hesitant, in dread.
He trembled now before the poised spear-shaft
And saw no way to escape; he had no force
With which to close, or reach his foe, no chariot
And no sign of the charioteer, his sister.
At a dead loss he stood. Aeneas made
His deadly spear flash in the sun and aimed it,
Narrowing his eyes for a lucky hit.
Then, distant still, he put his body's might
Into the cast. Never a stone that soared
From a wall-battering catapult went humming
Loud as this, nor with so great a crack
Burst ever a bolt of lightning. It flew on
Like a black whirlwind bringing devastation,
Pierced with a crash the rim of sevenfold shield,
Cleared the cuirass' edge, and passed clean through
The middle of Turnus' thigh. Force of the blow
Brought the huge man to earth, his knees buckling,
And a groan swept the Rutulians as they rose,
A groan heard echoing on all sides from all
The mountain range, and echoed by the forests.
The man brought down, brought low, lifted his eyes
And held his right hand out to make his plea:

"Clearly I earned this, and I ask no quarter.
Make the most of your good fortune here.
If you can feel a father's grief—and you, too,
Had such a father in Anchisës—then
Let me bespeak your mercy for old age
In Daunus,[6] and return me, or my body,

5. The Italian troops watching the combat between Turnus and Aeneas. 6. Father of Turnus.

Stripped, if you will, of life, to my own kin.
You have defeated me. The Ausonians
Have seen me in defeat, spreading my hands.
Lavinia is your bride. But go no further
Out of hatred."
Fierce under arms, Aeneas
Looked to and fro, and towered, and stayed his hand
Upon the sword-hilt. Moment by moment now
What Turnus said began to bring him round
From indecision. Then to his glance appeared
The accurst swordbelt surmounting Turnus' shoulder,
Shining with its familiar studs—the strap
Young Pallas wore when Turnus wounded him
And left him dead upon the field; now Turnus
Bore that enemy token on his shoulder—
Enemy still. For when the sight came home to, him,
Aeneas raged at the relic of his anguish
Worn by this man as trophy. Blazing up
And terrible in his anger, he called out:

"You in your plunder, torn from one of mine,
Shall I be robbed of you? This wound will come
From Pallas: Pallas makes this offering
And from your criminal blood exacts his due."

He sank his blade in fury in Turnus' chest.
Then all the body slackened in death's chill,
And with a groan for that indignity
His spirit fled into the gloom below.

OVID

43 B.C.–A.D. 17

Born in the year after Julius Caesar's assassination, Ovid did not know the time of civil war, when no one's property, or life, was safe. He was twenty-four when Virgil died, and he turned to different themes: the sophisticated and somewhat racy life of the urban elite in Rome, love in its manifold social and psychological guises, Greco-Roman myth and local Italian legend. Like Catullus and Virgil, he was profoundly influenced by the learned and polished works of the Greek Alexandrian period, but like his predecessors he translated their example into his personal idiom and used it for his own purposes. He was a versifier of genius. "Whatever I tried to say," he wrote, "came out in verse," and Alexander Pope adapted the line for his own case: "I lisped in numbers for the numbers came." Elegance, wit, and precision remained the hallmarks of Ovid's poetry throughout his long and productive career, and his way of telling stories was extraordinary for its subtlety and its depth of psychological understanding. His influence on the poets and artists of the Middle Ages, the Renaissance, and beyond was massive, second only, if at all, to Virgil's.

The early years of Ovid's manhood were marked by rapid literary and social success in the brilliant society of a capital intent on enjoying the peace and prosperity inaugurated by Augustus. The *Amores*, or "Love Affairs," unabashed chronicles of a Roman Don Juan, was his first publication. It was soon followed by the *Art of Love*, a handbook of seduction (originally circulated as books 1 and 2, for men; book 3, for women, was added by popular request). Not content with teaching his readers how to start a love affair, Ovid then advised them how to end it, in the *Remedies of Love*. At some point he wrote a poem on women's cosmetics; another, the *Fasti* (never finished), on the Roman calendar; and a collection of poetic letters, the *Heroides*, purporting to have been written by heroines of legend, such as Helen, to their lovers. In A.D. 8 Ovid was banished by imperial decree to the town of Tomi, in what is now Romania. It was on the fringe of the empire, and to a devotee of Roman high life it was a grim place indeed. He remained there until his death, sending back to Rome poetic epistles, collected as the *Sorrows* and the *Letters from Pontus*, that asked for pardon—to no effect. The reason for his banishment is not known. Involvement in some scandal concerning Augustus's daughter Julia is a possibility, but the ultimate cause was probably the love poetry, which ran afoul of Augustus's political and social program. Augustus was trying hard, by propaganda and legislation, to revive old Roman standards of morality and cannot have found Ovid's *Art of Love*, with its suggestion that Rome was a prime location for seduction, amusing. He correctly read the poem as political critique, a mode of resistance to the authoritarian imposition of moral reform. Ovid's greatest work, the *Metamorphoses*, suggests a similar critique. It was still unfinished at the time of his exile.

METAMORPHOSES

Virgil had written what Augustus wanted to be the "official" epic of the new order, which was to be seen as the fulfillment of a history that began with Aeneas's journey from Troy to Italy. The *Aeneid*, for all its innovations, was an epic in the traditional style: it focused on the deeds of a single hero, and it exemplified and transmitted its culture's dominant values. The *Metamorphoses* is recognizably epic; it is the only poem Ovid wrote in the epic meter, dactylic hexameter. But it can be seen as a critical response to Virgil, even an anti-*Aeneid*. Ovid produced a series of stories using the Alexandrian form of the *epyllion*, or "miniature epic," and he strung these together into a long narrative of fifteen books. The transitions between them, and the connections drawn by the narrator, are often transparently contrived—perhaps in mockery of the idea of narrative unity. There is no single hero, and one would have to seek hard for representative national values presented without irony. There is, however, a common element to these stories: all in one way or another involve changes of shape. And despite its leisurely and roundabout course, the narrative has a discernible direction—as Ovid says in his introduction, "from the world's beginning to our day." Starting with the creation of the world, the transformation of matter into living bodies (the first great metamorphosis), Ovid regales his readers with tales of human beings changed into animals, flowers, and trees. He proceeds through Greek myth to stories of early Rome and so to his own time, including, as the final metamorphosis, the ascension of the murdered Julius Caesar to the heavens in the form of a star and the divine promise that Augustus too, far in the future, will become a god.

Fluidity, then, is a key concept of the *Metamorphoses*. It underlies both the narrative style and the vision of the world the poem projects. Virgil also told of a transformation, the new (Roman) order arising from the ruins of the old (Troy). But once the transformation was completed by the Augustan order, there was to be stability, permanence. Ovid tells of a world ceaselessly coming to be in a process that never ends. To Virgil's story of national origins he opposes creation itself, which sets the pattern of instability, the fleetingness of form, and constant transformation. Ambivalence and ambiguity there may be in the *Aeneid*—but within a single set of Roman values summed up in Aeneas himself. Ovid's epic without a hero presents shifting perspectives and offers the reader no single point of view or end point from which to judge his very complex narratives. Virgil responded to the chaos of civil war with a vision of political stability; Ovid responds in turn to the new order. To the forced imposition of political and moral unity he opposes fluidity itself.

The political implications do not exhaust the richness of the *Metamorphoses,* though they are never far to seek. Within the poem's large-scale framework, each story in turn engages and delights the reader with its verbal wit, the cunningly calculated emphasis on this or that telling detail, the shifts between pathos and ironic distance, and the brilliant psychological insights suggested by the narrative or the characters' words and actions. Ovid constantly plays with narrative technique. A story will be told partly from one character's perspective, and then, with a sudden shift, partly from another's. One story will be embedded in another, with a consequent imposition of one narrative voice on top of another, as when, in the excerpt from book 10 printed below, Venus tells Adonis the story of Atalanta. This story is set within the tale of the goddess's love for Adonis and of his death, which is one of a series of stories sung by Orpheus within the poem's main narrative. In such cases, both the immediate and the larger contexts give the same story different shades of meaning. And there are thematic connections between stories. Daphne and Syrinx are turned into plants (the laurel and the reed) that are henceforth attributes of the gods who tried to rape them: a form of appropriation that substitutes for sexual violence. Just as Jupiter turns Io, the girl *he* has raped, into a cow, so he tricks Europa, in order to possess her, by becoming a seductively handsome bull. Europa offers the god-bull flowers; the terrified Proserpina, victim of a far more direct and brutal rape, drops the flowers she has been collecting when the god of Death carries her on his chariot beneath the Earth.

As these examples indicate, a common element of many stories in books 1 and 2 is the portrayal of important male gods as both destructive and ridiculous in their lust. "Slow your pace," Apollo calls to the fleeing Daphne in fear that she will fall and disfigure herself, "I pray you, stay your flight. I'll slow down, too." Or, as the narrator comments on Jupiter-as-bull, "Majesty and love do not go hand in glove." As the examples also show, the poem contains a number of stories of rape. Ovid gives different perspectives on what is essentially the same situation in order to emphasize the variety of possible responses to it by different readers, and he leaves it to those readers to evaluate their own responses. That is, fluidity not only is a theme of the poem but also characterizes the multiple positions open to the reader. In addition, one of the possible implications of these stories of rape is, again, political, for rape is the ultimate imposition of control. When powerful gods, however ridiculous they may appear, force themselves on defenseless women, imposed authority is held up to questioning. After all, as Ovid points out gleefully in the *Art of Love,* a rape was at the heart of Rome's foundation legend: it was through the rape of the Sabine women that the male inhabitants of the new city acquired wives and were able to supply Rome with future citizens.

The stories selected here from later in the *Metamorphoses* bring out other aspects of gender and sexuality. From the story of Iphis and Ianthe we learn that the instability of gender is not a modern discovery; nor is the recognition that the roles it determines for women and men in society are more or less arbitrary. That episode, the last in book 9, ends with the triumph of heterosexual love. The tales from book 10 all have to do, in one way or another, with the psychopathology of love. The case of Pygmalion may seem an exception, but we should remember that it begins with his hatred of women for their loose morals, and that the story as a whole, whatever it may say about the power of art, can also be read as a fable of the male fabrication of woman—her person and her functions—according to his desires. In the same way, Atalanta's conquest by Hippomenes represents, in the Greek and Roman cultural code, the "taming" of the "wild" virgin into marriage; but the story ends as a tale of divine wrath against this couple, and it is told by Venus to a lover whom she is about to lose to death. These stories, and others, including Myrrha's consummated love for her own father, are narrated by Orpheus, the archetypal poet, after his failure to bring Eurydice back from the underworld. Ovid tells us—and it seems to be his invention—that in reaction to his loss Orpheus had turned to pederasty, and that he was torn to pieces in his native Thrace by Maenads, female worshipers of Dionysus.

The Italian Baroque sculptor Giovanni Bernini carved statue groups of Apollo and Daphne and of Hades and Proserpina—stunning translations of Ovid's poetry into marble. Among their many allusions to the *Metamorphoses,* Milton and Dante both used Ovid's version of the Proserpina story: the former in book 9 of *Paradise Lost* as an image of the entry of death into the world, the latter in the *Purgatorio* to emphasize redemption from death. It was surely not only the fact that the *Metamorphoses* draws into itself most of the major classical myths (and a number of lesser-known stories as well) that has made the poem a source of subjects for artists and poets ever since but also the memorable ways these stories are told and their rich potential for meaning. The poem has many themes, but it also tells about itself: the irresistible power of a well-told narrative to hold the attention and shape the imagination of those who read or listen to it.

Sara Mack, *Ovid* (1988), provides an excellent introduction to all of Ovid's poems for the general reader, with a long chapter on the *Metamorphoses*. A classic treatment of this poem is Brooks Otis, *Ovid as an Epic Poet* (1966, 1970). G. K. Galinsky, *Ovid's Metamorphoses: An Introduction to the Basic Aspects*, is also a useful guide. L. P. Wilkinson, *Ovid Recalled* (1955), abridged as *Ovid Surveyed* (1962), gives a comprehensive overview of various aspects of Ovid's poetry. For later poets' and artists' uses of Ovid, see the essays collected in Charles Martindale, *Ovid Renewed: Ovidian Influences on Literature and Art from the Middle Ages to the Twentieth Century* (1988).

PRONOUNCING GLOSSARY

The following list uses common English syllables and stress accents to provide rough equivalents of selected words whose pronunciation may be unfamiliar to the general reader.

Achelous: *a-kel-oh'-us*

Alpheus: *al'-fyoos*

Anapos: *a-nap'-os*

Arethusa: *a-reth-oos'-a*

Calliope: *kal-lai'-o-pee*

Cenchreis: *ken-kray'-is*

Ceres: *see'-reez*

Cinyras: *kin-ee'-ras*

Cyane: *see-ah'-nee*

Daedalus: *dee'-dal-us/dai'-dal-us*

Epaphus: *e-paf'-us*

Erigone: *e-rig'-o-nee*

Europa: *yoo-roh'-pa*

Hippomenes: *hip-po'-men-eez*

Icarus: *i'-kar-us*

Inachus: *i'-na-kus*

Iphis: *i'-fis*

Isis: *ai'-sis*

Naiads: *nai'-adz*

Osiris: *oh-sai'-ris*

Pasiphae: *pa-sif'-ay-ee*

Peneus: *pen'-yoos/pen-ay'-us*

Phoebus: *fee'-bus*

Proserpina: *pros-ehr'-pi-na*

Pygmalion: *pig-may'-lyon*

Satyr: *say'-ter*

Telethusa: *tel-e-thoo'-sa*

Typhoeus: *ti-foy'-oos*

Tenedos: *ten'-e-dos*

Metamorphoses[1]

FROM BOOK I

[*Prologue*]

My soul would sing of metamorphoses.
But since, o gods, you were the source of these
bodies becoming other bodies, breathe
your breath into my book of changes: may
the song I sing be seamless as its way
weaves from the world's beginning to our day.

* * *

[*Apollo and Daphne*]

Now Daphne[2]—daughter of the river-god,
Peneus—was the first of Phoebus'[3] loves.
This love was not the fruit of random chance:
what fostered it was Cupid's cruel wrath.
For now, while Phoebus still was taking pride
in his defeat of Python,[4] he caught sight
of Cupid as he bent his bow to tie
the string at the two ends. He said: "Lewd boy,
what are you doing with that heavy bow?[5]
My shoulders surely are more fit for it;
for I can strike wild beasts—I never miss.
I can fell enemies; just recently
I even hit—my shafts were infinite—
that swollen serpent, Python, sprawled across
whole acres with his pestilential paunch.
Be glad your torch can spark a bit of love:
don't try to vie with me for praise and wreaths!"
And Venus' son replied: "Your shafts may pierce
all things, o Phoebus, but you'll be transfixed
by mine; and even as all earthly things
can never equal any deity,
so shall your glory be no match for mine."

That said, he hurried off; he beat his wings
until he reached Parnassus' shady peak;
there, from his quiver, Cupid drew two shafts
of opposite effect: the first rejects,
the second kindles love. This last is golden,
its tip is sharp and glittering; the first
is blunt, its tip is leaden—and with this
blunt shaft the god pierced Daphne. With the tip
of gold he hit Apollo; and the arrow

1. All selections translated by Allen Mandelbaum. 2. The name *Daphne* means "laurel" in Greek. 3. Apollo's. 4. The enormous snake that Apollo had to kill in order to found his oracle at Delphi. 5. The bow was one of Apollo's attributes.

pierced to the bones and marrow.
And at once
the god of Delos[6] is aflame with love;
but Daphne hates its very name; she wants
deep woods and spoils of animals she hunts;
it is Diana, Phoebus' virgin sister,
whom she would emulate. Around her hair—
in disarray—she wears a simple band.
Though many suitors seek her, she spurns all;
she wants to roam uncurbed; she needs no man;
she pays no heed to marriage, love, or husbands.
Her father often said: "You're in my debt:
a son-in-law is owed me." And he said:
"You owe me grandsons." But his daughter scorns,
as things quite criminal, the marriage torch
and matrimony; with a modest blush
on her fair face, she twines her arms around
her father's neck: "Allow me to enjoy
perpetual virginity," she pleads;
"o dear, dear father, surely you'll concede
to me the gift Diana has received
from her dear father."[7] And in fact, Peneus
would have agreed. O Daphne, it's your beauty
that will prevent your getting that dear gift.
Your fair form contradicts your deepest wish.

Phoebus is lovestruck; having seen the girl,
he longs to wed her and, in longing, hopes;
but though he is the god of oracles,
he reads the future wrongly. Even as,
when grain is harvested, the stubble left
will burn, or as the hedges burn when chance
has led some traveler to bring his torch
too close, or to forget it on the road
when he went off at dawn, so Phoebus burns,
so is his heart aflame; with hope he feeds
a fruitless love. He looks at Daphne's hair
as, unadorned, it hangs down her fair neck,
and says: "Just think, if she should comb her locks!"
He sees her lips and never tries of them;
her fingers, hands, and wrists are unsurpassed;
her arms—more than half-bare—cannot be matched;
whatever he can't see he can imagine;
he conjures it as even more inviting.
But swifter than the lightest breeze, she flees
and does not halt—not even when he pleads:
"O, daughter of Peneus, stay! Dear Daphne,
I don't pursue you as an enemy!
Wait, nymph! You flee as would the lamb before
the wolf, the deer before the lion, or

6. Island in the Aegean Sea where Apollo was born. 7. Jove.

the trembling dove before the eagle; thus
all flee from hostile things, but it is love
for which I seek you now! What misery!
I fear you'll stumble, fall, be scratched by brambles
and harm your faultless legs—and I'm to blame.
You're crossing trackless places. Slow your pace;
I pray you, stay your flight. I'll slow down, too.
But do consider who your lover is.
I'm not a mountain dweller, not a shepherd,
no scraggly guardian of flocks and herds.
Too rash, you don't know whom you're fleeing from;
in fact, that's why you run. I am the lord
of Delphi's land, and Claros, Tenedos,
and regal Patara.[8] Jove is my father.
Through me, all is revealed: what's yet to be,
what was, and what now is. The harmony
of song and lyre is achieved through me.
My shaft is sure in flight; but then there's he
whose arrow aimed still more infallibly,
the one who wounded me when I was free
of any love within my heart. I am
the one who has invented medicine,[9]
but now there is no herb to cure my passion;
my art, which helps all men, can't heal its master."

He'd have said more, but Daphne did not halt;
afraid, she left him there, with half-done words.
But even then, the sight of her was striking.
The wind laid bare her limbs; against the nymph
it blew; her dress was fluttering; her hair
streamed in the breeze; in flight she was more fair.

But now the young god can't waste time: he's lost
his patience; his beguiling words are done;
and so—with love as spur—he races on;
he closes in. Just as a Gallic hound[1]
surveys the open field and sights a hare,
and both the hunter and the hunted race
more swiftly—one to catch, one to escape
(he seems about to leap on his prey's back;
he's almost sure he's won; his muzzle now
is at her heels; the other, still in doubt—
not sure if she is caught—slips from his mouth;
at the last instant, she escapes his jaws):
such were the god and girl; while he is swift
because of hope, what urges her is fear.
But love has given wings to the pursuer;
he's faster—and his pace will not relent.
He's at her shoulders now; she feels his breath

8. All centers of Apollo's cult. 9. Apollo was, among other functions, god of healing. 1. A hunting breed famous for speed.

upon the hair that streams down to her neck.
Exhausted, wayworn, pale, and terrified,
she sees Peneus' stream nearby; she cries:
"Help me, dear father; if the river-gods
have any power, then transform, dissolve
my gracious shape, the form that pleased too well!"
As soon as she is finished with her prayer,
a heavy numbness grips her limbs; thin bark
begins to gird her tender frame, her hair
is changed to leaves, her arms to boughs; her feet—
so keen to race before—are now held fast
by sluggish roots; the girl's head vanishes,
becoming a treetop. All that is left
of Daphne is her radiance.
And yet
Apollo loves her still; he leans against
the trunk; he feels the heart that beats beneath
the new-made bark; within his arms he clasps
the branches as if they were human limbs;
and his lips kiss the wood, but still it shrinks
from his embrace, at which he cries: "But since
you cannot be my wife, you'll be my tree.
O laurel, I shall always wear your leaves
to wreathe my hair, my lyre, and my quiver.
When Roman chieftains crown their heads with garlands
as chants of gladness greet their victory,
you will be there. And you will also be
the faithful guardian who stands beside
the portals of Augustus' house and keeps
a close watch on the Roman crown of oak leaves.[2]
And even as my head is ever young,
and my hair ever long, may you, unshorn,
wear your leaves, too, forever: never lose
that loveliness, o laurel, which is yours!"

Apollo's words were done. With new-made boughs
the laurel nodded; and she shook her crown,
as if her head had meant to show consent.

[*Io and Jove*]

In Thessaly[3] there is a deep-set valley
surrounded on all sides by wooded slopes
that tower high. They call that valley Tempe.
And the Peneus River, as it flows
down from Mount Pindus' base—waves flecked with foam—
runs through that valley. In its steep descent,
a heavy fall, the stream gives rise to clouds
and slender threads of mist—like curling smoke;

2. The laurel tree, sacred to Apollo, was the symbol of victory in athletic contests or in war. The oak was sacred to Jupiter. 3. A region of central Greece.

and from on high, the river sprays treetops;
its roar resounds through places near and far.
This is the home, the seat, the sanctuary
of that great stream. And here, within a cave
carved out of rock, sat Daphne's father, god
and ruler of these waters and of all
the nymphs who made their home within his waves.
And it was here that—though they were unsure
if they should compliment or comfort him—
first came the river-gods of his own region:
Enipeus, restless river; poplar-rich
Sperchios; veteran Apidanus
and gentle Aeas and Amphrysus; then
the other, distant rivers came—all those
who, on whatever course their currents flow,
lead down their wayworn waters to the sea.

The only missing god was Inachus.[4]
He had retreated to his deepest cave,
and as he wept, his tears increased his waves;
the disappearance of his daughter, Io,
had left him desperate. He did not know
if she was still alive or with the Shades;
he could not find her anywhere, and so
he thought that she was nowhere; in his heart
his fears foresaw things devious and dark.

Now it was Jove who had caught sight of Io;
she was returning from her father's stream,
and Jove had said: "O virgin, you indeed
would merit Jove and will make any man
you wed—whoever he may be—most glad.
But now it's time for you to seek the shade
of those deep woods" (and here he pointed toward
a nearby forest); "for the sun is high—
at its midcourse; such heat can't be defied.
And do not be afraid to find yourself
alone among the haunts of savage beasts:
within the forest depths you can be sure
of safety, for your guardian is a god—
and I am not a common deity:
for I am he who holds within his hand
the heavens' scepter: I am he who hurls
the roaming thunderbolts. So do not flee!"
But even as he spoke, she'd left behind
the pasturelands of Lerna, and the plains
around Lyrceus' peak,[5] fields thick with trees.
Then with a veil of heavy fog, the god

4. A river near Argos. 5. *Lyrceus:* a mountain on the border between Argos and Arcadia to the west. *Lerna:* a marsh in the territory of Argos, near the coast.

concealed a vast expanse of land; Jove stopped
her flight; he raped chaste Io.

Meanwhile Juno,
from heaven's height, had chanced to cast her eyes
on Argus' center; she was stupefied
to see that hovering clouds, in full daylight,
had brought about a darkness deep as night;
she knew that this could not be river mist
or fog that rises up from the damp soil.
So Saturn's daughter[6] looked around to see
just where her Jove might be—so frequently
she'd caught him sneaking or, more flagrantly,
at play. And since he wasn't in the sky,
she said: "I am mistaken or betrayed";
and then, descending from the heavens' height,
she stood upon the ground and told the clouds
that they must now recede.
Jove had foreseen
his wife's arrival; he had changed the daughter
of Inachus: she now was a white heifer.
And even as a heifer she was lovely.
Great Juno—grudgingly—praised the cow's beauty,
then asked who was her owner, where did she
come from, what herd did she belong to—all
as if she were aware of nothing. Jove,
contriving, said the earth had given birth
to this fine heifer—hoping that would stop
his wife's barrage. And Juno asked to have
the heifer as a gift. What should he do?
It would be cruel to consign his love;
but if he kept her, he would just raise doubts.
On one side, shame keeps urging: Give her up.
Love, on the other side, insists: Do not.

Love could have overcome his shame, but if
he should refuse so slight, so poor a gift
to one who was his sister and his wife,
he'd have to run a disconcerting risk,
since Juno could conclude that, after all,
this heifer was no cow. So, in the end,
the goddess got her rival as a present.
Yet Juno still suspected treachery;
to ward off any wiles, she now entrusted
the heifer to Arestor's son; for Argus
was gifted with a hundred eyes, and he
would sleep with only two of these eyes shut
at any time, in turn—the rest he left
awake and watchful. He was Io's guardian;

6. Juno.

no matter where he turned, he always kept
some eyes on her; though he might turn his back,
he still had her in view. By day he let
the heifer graze; but when the sun had set,
he locked her in and tied, around her neck,
a shameful halter. She was always fed
on leaves from trees and bitter herbs, and slept
upon the ground—and it was often bare
of grass; poor Io drank from muddy streams
and, when she tried to lift her arms to plead
with Argus, found she had no arms to stretch;
and when she tried to utter some lament,
nothing but lowings issued from her lips,
a sound that she was frightened to emit—
her own voice frightened her.
And Io reached
the shores on which she had so often played,
the river banks of Inachus; she stared
at her strange horns reflected in the waves,
and at her muzzle; and she fled, dismayed
and terrified. Not even Inachus
and all his Naiads knew just who she was;
but she would trail her father and her sisters
and let them touch her as she sidled up
to be admired. Once, old Inachus
had plucked some grass and held it out to her:
she licked her father's hands, and tried to kiss
his palms, and then began to weep; and if
she could have uttered words, she would have told
her name and wretched fate and begged for aid.
Instead of words, it's letters that she traced
in sand—she used her hoof: so she revealed
her transformation—all of her sad tale.
"What misery!" cried Inachus; he clasped
her horns and neck; and snow-white Io moaned.
"What misery!" he wailed. "Are you my daughter,
the one whom I have sought through all the world?
My sorrow at the loss of you was less
than in my finding you; and now there's silence;
my words receive no answer, only sighs
and lowing—these must serve as your reply.
To think that—unaware, oblivious—
I was intent on all your wedding rites,
your marriage torch, and I was hoping for
a son-in-law and then grandsons. But now
it is a bull whom you must wed; you'll bear
a bull as son. And I can't kill myself,
however deep my grief: sad fate indeed
to be a god: the gate of death is closed
against me; I am doomed to bear this sorrow
eternally."
And while her father mourned,

Argus, the many-eyed, came up, and drove
old Inachus away; her guardian grabbed
poor Io; and to other pasturelands,
he thrust her. Then he sat upon a peak
and, from that height, kept all the fields in sight.

But now the ruler of the gods cannot
endure his Io's suffering so much;
he summons Mercury, the son that Jove
had by the shining Pleiad;[7] he instructs
his son to murder Argus. And at once,
with his winged sandals, Mercury flies off;
within his hand, he grasps the potent wand
that can bring sleep; his cap is on his head.
And so arrayed, the son of Jove descends—
down from his father's fortress high in heaven
to earth. He sets aside his cap, his wings;
the wand is all he keeps but makes it seem
a shepherd's crook; and then, in rural guise,
along stray paths, the son of Maia drives
some goats he'd rustled from the countryside;
and as he goes, upon the reeds he'd tied
together—rustic pipes—he plays a song.

And Argus is entranced by those strange sounds:
"Whoever you may be," he says, "sit down
beside me on this rock; no other spot
can offer richer grass to all your flock;
and there is perfect shade for shepherds here."

So Mercury joins Argus on the rock
and whiles away the time with varied talk;
he plays upon the reeds—with that he hopes
that Argus' watchful eyes will drop their guard.
But Argus tries to ward off languid sleep;
and though some of his eyes have shut, he keeps
the rest awake and watchful. And indeed,
since pipes had been invented recently,
he asks how that invention came about.

The god replied: "On the cool mountainside
of Arcady, among the woodland nymphs
whose home was in the forest of Nonacris,
one was most famous—she whom they called Syrinx.[8]
And more than once that nymph had been pursued
but had eluded all the guile and wiles
of Satyrs[9] and the many gods who dwell
in shaded woods or on the fertile fields.
For like Diana, goddess of Ortygia,[1]

7. Maia. 8. The name means "shepherd's pipe," which is a musical instrument made of reeds.
9. Woodland creatures, half man, bald, bearded, and highly sexed. 1. An old name of Delos.

she was a devotee of chastity;
and she dressed like Diana, so that one
might well have thought she was Latona's daughter[2]—
except for this: Diana bore a bow
of gold, while Syrinx' was of cornel wood.
Despite that difference, she was often taken
to be Diana. And one day, as she
was coming back from Mount Lycaeus, Pan[3]
caught sight of Syrinx. He—whose head was wreathed
with sharp pine needles—said . . ."
And much was left
to tell: how Syrinx, scorning all his pleas,
fled through the barren waste until she reached
the placid, sandy stream of Ladon: here
the river blocked her flight, and so she begged
her sister water nymphs to change her shape.
And Pan, who thought that he had caught the nymph,
did not clutch her fair body but marsh reeds;
and he began to sigh; and then the air,
vibrating in the reeds, produced a sound
most delicate, like a lament. And Pan,
enchanted by the sweetness of a sound
that none had ever heard before, cried out:
"And this is how I shall converse with you!"
He took unequal lengths of reeds, and these
Pan joined with wax: this instrument still keeps
the name Pan gave it then, the nymph's name—Syrinx.

When Mercury was just about to tell
these things, he saw that Argus' hundred eyes
had given in to sleep; they all were closed.
At once he checks his talk; and to abet
the power of sleep, with his enchanted wand
he touches lightly Argus' drowsing eyes;
and then, unhesitatingly, he strikes
the watchman with a sword curved like a scythe;
he strikes the nodding head just where the neck
and body join; he knocks it off the rock
and sends it tumbling, bleeding, down the steep
descent, and stains the cliffside with that blood.

O Argus, you lie low; the light that glowed
in many pupils now is spent; one night
alone now holds in sway your hundred eyes.

And Juno took the hundred eyes of Argus
and set them on her sacred bird: she filled
the feathers of the peacock's tail with jewels
that glittered like the stars. And then the goddess

2. Diana (her mother was Leto or Latona). 3. A god of the wild mountain pastures and woods, with goat's feet and horns. *Mount Lycaeus:* high mountain in Arcadia.

unleashed her rage; she struck her Grecian rival
at once: she sent a Fury to harass
poor Io's eyes and mind; she pierced her breast
with an invisible, relentless goad;
she drove the frightened girl across the world—
a fugitive.
And nothing else was left
for way-worn Io on her endless path
but to seek refuge on your banks, o Nile.
And there she knelt and, drawing back her head,
lifted her eyes—she had no other way
to plead or pray—up to the stars, with moans
and tears and wretched lowings, as if she,
beseeching Jove, asked him to end her grief.
At that, Jove threw his arms round Juno's neck;
he begged his wife to end this punishment.
"You need not fear the future," so he pledged;
"she'll never cause you harm or grief again—"
and as his witness for the oath he'd sworn,
it was the Stygian marsh he called upon.[4]
Now Io, with the goddess' rage appeased,
regains the form she had before: she sheds
the rough hairs on her body, and her horns
recede; her round eyes shrink, her mouth retracts,
her arms and hands appear again; and each
of Io's hoofs is changed into five nails.
There's no trace of the heifer that is left,
except the lovely whiteness of her flesh.
Content that just two feet now meet her needs,
the nymph stands up but hesitates to speak
for fear that, like a heifer, she will low;
then, timidly, she once again employs
the power of speech she had—for so long—lost.
And now she is a celebrated goddess,
revered by crowds clothed in white linen: Isis.

Her son was Epaphus, and it's believed
that she gave birth to him from great Jove's seed;
he shares his mother's shrines in many cities.

* * *

FROM BOOK II

[*Europa and Jove*]

And when he[5] was in heaven once again,
his father, Jove, draws him apart and says
(though not revealing to his son the cause
for all of this—that is, the call of love):

4. Gods swore solemn oaths by the Styx, one of the rivers of the underworld. 5. Mercury, son of Jove and messenger of the gods. He has been in Athens, where he tried to have a love affair with Herse, daughter of King Cecrops, was promised help and then foiled by her sister Aglauros, and took his revenge on Aglauros by turning her into a statue.

"My son, who always faithfully fulfill
whatever I may ask, do not waste time;
glide down to earth—be swift as usual—
and find the land from which your mother's star[6]
is seen on high along the left-hand skies
(the men who live there call that country Sidon).[7]
You'll see a herd (the king's own cattle) grazing
far off, on a green hillside; drive that herd
down to the shore."
He spoke—at once his words
were acted on: the herd was headed shoreward.
That beach was where the daughter of the king,
Europa, always played with her companions.

Now, majesty and love do not go hand
in glove—they don't mix well. And so, great Jove
renounced his solemn sceptre: he—the lord
and father of the gods—whose right hand holds
his massive weapons, three-pronged lightning bolts,
the king whose simple nod can shake the world—
takes on the semblance of a bull; among
the herd he lows; he mingles with the heifers;
he roams the tender grass—a handsome presence.
He's white—precisely like untrodden snow,
like snow intact, untouched by rainy Auster.[8]
His neck has robust muscles; from his shoulders,
his dewlap[9] hangs. His horns, it's true, are small,
but so well wrought, one would have thought a craftsman
had made them; they were more translucent than
pure gems. His brow has nothing menacing;
his gaze inspires no fear. He seems so calm.

Agenor's daughter[1] stares at him in wonder:
he is so shapely, so unthreatening.
At first, however, though he is not fierce,
she is afraid to touch him. Then she nears,
draws closer, and her hand holds flowers out
to his white face. Delighted, as he waits—
a lover—for still other, greater joys,
he kisses her fair hands—no easy test
to check his eagerness, delay the rest.
And now the great bull sports along the grass,
and now he stretches snow-white flanks along
the golden sands. Her fear has disappeared,
and now he offers to the girl his chest,
that she might stroke him with her virgin hand;
and now his horns, that she might twine them round
with garlands. At a certain point, Europa
dares to sit down upon his back: the girl

6. Maia, Mercury's mother, had been transformed into a star in the constellation Pleiades. 7. One of the principal cities of Phoenicia (the modern Lebanon). 8. The south wind, bringer of rain. 9. A fold of loose skin hanging from the neck. 1. Europa. Agenor was the Phoenician king.

is not aware of what he is in truth.
And then, as casually as he can,
the god moves off, away from the dry sands;
with his feigned hooves, he probes the shallows, then
advances even farther; soon he bears
his prey out to the waves, the open sea.

Europa now is terrified; she clasps
one horn with her right hand; meanwhile the left
rests on the bull's great croup.[2] She turns to glance
back at the shore, so distant now. Her robes
are fluttering—they swell in the sea breeze.

FROM BOOK V

[*Ceres and Proserpina*]

The Muse
was still not finished with her words,[3] when through
the air, there came the sound of whirring wings
and, from the high boughs, voices offered greetings.
Minerva looked on high: she tried to find
what tongues had voiced those sounds, which seemed so like
the speech of humans—but it was magpies
she saw upon those branches. There were nine
who, all aligned, lamented their sad fate;
whatever sounds they like, they imitate.
And as Minerva wondered, even as
a goddess speaks to goddess, one Muse said:

"Those whom you see have only recently
been added to the many families
of birds; they faced a contest, and they lost.
Their father was rich Pierus, the lord
of Pella; and they had Paeonian[4]
Evippe as their mother. Nine times she
had called upon the powerful Lucina[5]
for help, and nine times she had given birth.
Those stupid sisters—proud that they were nine
in number—traveled through Haemonia
and through Achaia,[6] touching every town,
until at last they came to Helicon
and challenged us to match their art of song:
'O goddesses of Thespia,[7] it's time
you stop beguiling the untutored mob
with counterfeited songs; for you are frauds.
If you are confident, compete with us!

2. Rump. 3. Minerva (equivalent of the Greek Athena) has come to Mount Helicon in central Greece, the home of the nine Muses (daughters of Zeus and Memory, patronesses of poetry and the other arts). One of the Muses has told her of an attempt recently made to trap and rape them by the wicked Pyreneus.
4. *Pella:* city of Macedonia, in northern Greece. The Paeonians were a tribe living north of Macedonia.
5. Goddess of childbirth. 6. Regions of central Greece. The sisters are traveling south toward Helicon.
7. Largest city near Mount Helicon.

Neither your voice nor art can match our own,
and we can match your numbers. If you lose,
then yield to us the spring of Pegasus[8]
and Aganippe, too, your other fount;
and if you win, we will concede to you
the plains of all our broad Emathia[9]
as far as our snow-clad Paeonia.
And let the nymphs be judges of this test!'

"Though it was shameful to contend with them,
there was more shame—we thought—in turning down
their challenge. So the Nymphs were called to judge:
they swore upon their streams and then sat down
on benches that were formed of porous stone.

"Now all was ready; without drawing lots,
the one who'd been the first to challenge us
began. She sang the battle of the gods
and Giants; she—unjustly—glorified
the Giants and belittled the great gods.
She said that, when Typhoeus[1] bounded up
from Earth's abyss, the gods on high were so
afraid that they ran off and did not stop
until, exhausted, they were taken in
by Egypt, at the point where seven mouths
divide the flow of Nile. And then she dared
to tell us that Typhoeus, son of Earth,
had reached their refuge; and to hide, the gods
took on deceitful shapes as camouflage:[2]
'So Jove became a ram, the lord of flocks;
that's why the Libyan Ammon[3] still is shown
with curving horns. The god of Delos hid
within a crow's shape, Bacchus in a kid,
and Phoebus' sister in a cat; the daughter
of Saturn took the form of a white heifer;
and just as Venus hid herself as fish,
Cyllene's god[4] became a winged ibis.'

"With that, her song was done; her voice had been
accompanied by chords upon the strings.

"Now we—the Muses of Aonia—
were challenged to reply. But if your time
is short, and other cares call you away,
you may not want to hear the song we sang."
"No, no; you can be sure," Minerva said;
"I'll listen from the start until you end."

8. Hippocrene ("horse fountain"), said to have been created on Mount Helicon by a blow of the winged horse Pegasus's hoof. 9. A region of Macedonia. 1. Monstrous son of Earth. Like the Earth-born Giants, he challenged Jove and the Olympian gods and was defeated—a detail omitted in this song, which ridicules the gods. 2. An "explanation" of the Egyptian gods' animal forms. 3. Chief Egyptian god, identified by the Greeks and Romans with Zeus/Jove, who had an important oracular cult in the Libyan desert (west of the Nile Valley and part of Egypt under Roman rule). 4. Mercury, born on Mount Cyllene in the Greek Peloponnesus.

She sat down in the woodland's pleasant shade.
The Muse replied: "We chose Calliope;[5]
for all of us, she would—as one—compete.
Our sister rose; her flowing tresses wreathed
with ivy, she began to pluck the strings;
and their vibrations joined her mournful chant:

" 'The first to furrow earth with the curved plow,
the first to harvest wheat, the first to feed
the world with food men cultivate in peace,
the first to bless the earth with laws—was Ceres;[6]
all things are gifts she gave. I want to sing
of Ceres: may my offering be worthy—
this goddess surely merits poetry.

" 'The island mass of Sicily is heaped
upon a giant's body: underneath
its soil and stones Typhoeus lies—the one
who dared to hope for heaven as his kingdom.
He writhes; he often tries to rise again.
But Mount Pelorus (closest to the land
of the Italians) crushes his right hand;
his left is in Pachynus' grip, just as
his legs are in Mount Lilybaeum's grasp;[7]
his head is pressed—vast Etna[8] holds it fast.
Beneath this mountain, on his back, in rage,
Typhoeus' mouth spits ashes, vomits flames.
He often strives to heave aside the ground—
the towns and heavy peaks that pin him down.
Then earth quakes. As it trembles, even he
who rules the kingdom of the silent dead
is anxious, for the crust of Sicily
may split and a wide crack reveal things secret:
daylight might penetrate so deep that it
would terrify the trembling Shades. His fear
of such disaster led that lord of darkness
to leave his sunless kingdom. Mounted on
his chariot—it was drawn by two black stallions—
he carefully assessed the island mass.
When he was sure that there were no vast cracks.
that Sicily was everywhere intact,
his fears were ended. Then, as Pluto rode
from site to site, down from her mountain slopes
of Eryx,[9] Venus saw him. As she clasped
her winged son, Cupid, this is what she asked:

" ' "O you, my son, my weapon and my armor,
dear Cupid—you, my power—take those shafts
to which both gods and mortals must submit;

5. "Lovely Voice": Muse of epic poetry. 6. The Greek Demeter, goddess of grain. 7. Mountains on the northeast, southeast, and western promontories of Sicily, respectively. 8. The great (and still active) volcano approximately in the center of the east coast of Sicily. 9. Mountain in western Sicily with an important cult of Venus.

with one of your swift arrows pierce the chest
of Pluto—god who, when the lots were cast,
assigning the three realms, received the last.
You conquer and command sky-deities—
not even Jove is free from your decrees;
sea-gods are governed by your rule—and he
who is the god of gods who rule the sea.
And why should Tartarus[1] elude our laws?
Why not extend your mother's power—and yours?
One-third of all the world is still not ours.
We have been slow to act, but indecision
has earned us nothing more than scorn in heaven.
And—son—if my authority should weaken,
then yours would suffer, too. Do you not see
how both Athena and the hunting goddess,
Diana, would defy me? And the daughter
of Ceres, if we let her choose, will be
like them: she is so bent on chastity.
But for the sake of all I share with you,
please join that goddess-girl, Proserpina,
to her great uncle, Pluto." This, she asked.
Love, opening his quiver—he respects
his mother—from his thousand shafts selects
the sharpest, surest shaft—the arrow most
responsive to the pressure of his bow.
Across his knee, the pliant bow is bent;
Love's hooked barb pierces Pluto through the chest.

" 'Not far from Enna's[2] walls there are deep waters.
That lake—called Pergus—hears a music richer,
more songs of swans, than even the Cayster[3]
hears as its current courses. Tall hills circle
that lake. Woods crown the slopes—and like a veil,
the forest boughs abate the flames of Phoebus.
Beneath those leaves, the air is cool, the soil
is damp—with many flowers, many colors.
There spring is never-ending. In that grove
Proserpina was playing, gathering
violets and white lilies. She had filled
her basket and, within her tunic's folds,
had tucked fresh flowers, vying with her friends
to see which girl could gather more of them.
There Pluto—almost in one instant—saw,
was struck with longing, carried that girl off—
so quick—unhesitating—was his love.

" 'The goddess-girl was terrified. She called—
in grief—upon her mother and companions,
but more upon her mother. She had ripped

1. The underworld. 2. A city in central Sicily. 3. River in Lydia in Asia Minor, proverbial for its many swans.

her tunic at its upper edge, and since
the folds were loosened now, the flowers fell.
So simple is the heart of a young girl
that, at that loss, new grief is what she felt.
Her captor urged his chariot, incited
his horses, calling each by name and shaking
the dark-rust reins upon their necks and manes.
He galloped over the deep lake and through
the pools of the Palici, where the soil
spews fumes of sulfur and the waters boil.
He reached that place where the Bacchiadae—
a race that came from Corinth, which is bathed
by seas upon two sides—had built their city[4]
between two harbors of unequal size.

" 'Between the spring of Cyane and the spring
of Arethusa (which had flowed from Greece),
there is a stretch of sea that is hemmed in,
confined between two narrow horns of land.
Among those waves lived Cyane, Sicily's
most celebrated nymph, and she had given
her name to that lagoon. Above the eddies,
just at the center, Cyane rose, waist-high.
She recognized Proserpina and cried:
"Pluto, you cannot pass. You cannot be
the son-in-law of Ceres unless she
gives her consent. To ask is not to rape.
And if I may compare small things to great,
I, too, was wooed—by Anapis[5]—but I
wed him in answer to his prayers and pleas—
he never used the terror you abuse."
That said, she stretched her arms upon both sides
to block his chariot. But Saturn's son
could not contain his anger any longer:
he spurred his terrifying stallions, whirled
his royal scepter with his sturdy arm.
He struck the very depths of Cyane's pool.
The blow was such that, down to Tartarus,
earth opened up a crater: on that path
he plunged to darkness in his chariot.

" 'But Cyane nursed an inconsolable—
a silent—wound that was incurable:
a sadness for the rape of Ceres' daughter
and for the violation of the waters
of her own pool—for Pluto's scorn and anger.
She gave herself to tears and then dissolved
into the very pool of which she had—
till now—been the presiding deity.
You could have seen the softening of her limbs,

4. Syracuse, on the southeastern coast of Sicily. 5. River that empties into the sea near Syracuse.

the bones and nails that lost solidity.
Her slender hairs, her fingers, legs, and feet—
these were the first to join the waves. In fact,
the slenderest parts can sooner turn into
cool waters. Shoulders, back, and sides, and breasts
were next to vanish in thin streams. At last,
clear water flows through Cyane's weakened veins,
and there is nothing left that one can grasp.

" 'Meanwhile, the heartsick Ceres seeks her daughter:
she searches every land, all waves and waters.
No one—not Dawn with her dew-laden hair,
nor Hesperus[6]—saw Ceres pause. She kindled
two pinewood torches in the flames of Etna.
Through nights of frost, a torch in either hand,
she wandered. Ceres never rested. When
the gracious day had dimmed the stars, again
the goddess searched from west to east, from where
the sun would set to where the sun ascends.

" 'Worn out and racked by thirst—she had not wet
her lips at any spring along her path—
she chanced to see a hut whose roof was thatched
with straw. And Ceres knocked at that poor door,
which an old woman opened. When she saw
the goddess there and heard her ask for water,
she gave her a sweet drink in which she'd soaked
roast barley. While the goddess drank this brew,
a boy came up to her; and scornful, rude,
he laughed and said she drank too greedily.
Offended, Ceres stopped her sipping, threw
the brew and all of its pearl-barley grains
full in his face. So—soaked—his face soon showed
those grains as spots; his arms were changed to claws;
a tail was added to his altered limbs.
And that his form might not inflict much harm,
the goddess shrank him, left him small—much like
a lizard, and yet tinier in size.
This wondrous change was watched by the old woman,
who wept to see it, even as she tried
to touch the transformed shape: he scurried off
to find a place to hide. The name he got
is suited to his skin: the starry newt—
a beast that glitters with his starlike spots.

" 'To tell the lands and seas that Ceres crossed
would take too long: the world was not enough
to satisfy the searching mother. She
returned to Sicily, explored again
each part. She reached the pool of Cyane.

6. The evening star.

If Cyane had not been changed, she now
would have told Ceres all she knew; but while
she longs to speak, she lacks a tongue to tell.

" 'Yet Cyane transmitted one sure clue:
upon the surface of her waters floats
the girdle that Proserpina had worn;
that girdle—one that Ceres knew so well—
had chanced to fall into the sacred pool.
No sooner had she recognized that sign,
than Ceres—as if now, for the first time,
she knew her daughter had been stolen—tore
her unkempt hair; her hands beat at her breast
again, again. She did not know as yet
just where her daughter was, but she condemned
all lands. She said they were ungrateful and
unworthy of the gift of harvests she
had given them—above all, Sicily,
the place that showed the trace of the misdeed.
And there, in Sicily, she—without pity—
shattered the plows that turned the soil; her fury
brought death to both the farmers and their cattle.
She spoiled the seeds; she ordered the plowed fields
to fail; she foiled the hope and trust of mortals.
Now Sicily's fertility—renowned
throughout the world—appears to be a lie:
as soon as grass is in the blade, it dies,
undone by too much rain or too much sun.
The stars and winds bring blight; the greedy birds
devour the seed as soon as it is sown;
the crop is blocked by chokeweeds, tares, and thorns.
Then Arethusa, whom Alpheus[7] loved,
lifted her head above her waters—these
had flowed to Sicily from Grecian Elis.
She brushed her dripping hair back from her brow
and said: "O Ceres, mother of the girl
you seek throughout the world, you, mother of
earth's fruits and grain, forgo your fury, end
your devastating violence. This land
does not deserve your scourging: it was forced
to yield before the bandit's brutal course.
And I do not beseech you on behalf
of my own homeland. I was not born here:
I come from Pisa,[8] in the land of Elis.
My origins were there—yet Sicily
is dearer to me than all other countries.
I, Arethusa, have a newfound home:
sweet Sicily is now my country—and,
kind Ceres, may your mercy save this island.

7. River that flows past Olympia in Elis, a region of the western Peloponnesus in mainland Greece.
8. The Greek district in which Olympia is located.

" ' "Why I have left my homeland, why I crossed
so vast a stretch of sea until I touched
Ortygia[9]—there will yet be time enough
to speak of that, a time when you are free
of cares, a moment of tranquillity.
But I can tell you now my journey's path:
earth, opening a chasm, let me pass.
I flowed through caverns deep below the surface,
then—here—I lifted up my head again,
again I saw the stars I had forgotten.
But in my passage underneath the earth
among the eddies of the Styx, I saw
Proserpina with my own eyes: she was
downcast, still somewhat touched by fear—and yet
she was a queen within that world of darkness,
the powerful companion—mighty mistress—
of Pluto, tyrant of the underworld."

" 'Hearing these things, the mother, Ceres, stood
as motionless as stone. Long moments passed:
her mind seemed lost. When that paralysis
of fear had given way to grief no less
oppressive, Ceres, on her chariot,
rode toward the upper air. With shadowed eyes,
her hair disheveled, hate-inflamed, she cried:
"For one who is of both your blood and mine,
o Jupiter, I come to plead with you.
Though I, her mother, do not matter, you
at least can care to save your daughter—I
should hope your care will not be any less
because she owes her birth to me. Our daughter,
after so long a search, is found—if one
can speak of finding when it just confirms
the loss more certainly, when finding means
no more than merely knowing where she is.
As for his theft of her—that I can bear—
he only has to give her back! My daughter
is mine no longer, but you cannot let
a robber win her as his wife—through theft."

" 'Then Jupiter replied: "We share the care
and tenderness we owe to our dear daughter.
But if we would have things named properly,
then we must speak of love, not injury
or robbery. We should not be ashamed
of Pluto as a son-in-law—if only
you, goddess, would consent to that. Were he
to lack all else, it is no meager thing
to be the brother of a Jupiter!
But he, in fact, has many other splendors:

9. The island on which Syracuse was founded.

the portion of the world assigned to him
is, after all, a kingdom, only less
than what my portion is—and only chance
assigned this part to me and that to him.
In any case, if you are so intent
on separating them, Proserpina
can see the sky again—on one condition:
that in the world below, she has not taken
food to her lips. This is the Fates' edict."

" 'These were his words. And yet, though Ceres wanted
to bring her daughter back, the Fates prevented
Proserpina's return, for she had broken
her fast: the girl, in all her innocence,
while she was wandering through a well-kept garden
within the underworld, from a bent branch
had plucked a pomegranate. She had taken—
peeling away its pale rind—seven seeds
and pressed them to her lips. No one had seen
that act of hers—except Ascalaphus
(the son, they say, that Orphne—not the least
famous among Avernus' nymphs—conceived
out of her love for Acheron,[1] and bore
within the dark groves of the underworld).
He saw her taste those seeds: denouncing her,
he thwarted her return to earth. She moaned—
the queen of Erebus.[2] Then, in revenge,
she changed that witness. He was made a bird
of evil omen: on his head she poured
waters of Phlegethon.[3] Enormous eyes
and beak and feathers now are his. Deprived
of what he was, he now wears tawny wings;
his head is swollen, and his nails grow long
and hook back, forming claws; and it is hard
for him to move the feathers that now sprout
upon his sluggish arms. He has become
the bird that men detest—that would announce
calamities. He is the lazy screech-owl,
bringer of bitter auguries to mortals.

" 'Ascalaphus indeed seems to have earned
his punishment—his tongue was indiscreet.
But, Achelous'[4] daughters, why do you,
as Sirens, have birds' feathers and birds' feet—
and features like a girl's? Is it because
you, Sirens skilled in song, had been among
the band of friends who joined Proserpina
when she was gathering spring flowers near Enna?
For after you—in vain—had searched all lands

1. Acheron ("Woe") is one of the rivers, and Avernus a lake, in the underworld. *Orphne:* the name means "darkness" in Greek. 2. The underworld. 3. Fiery river of the underworld. 4. Large river in northwest Greece.

for her, so that the waves might also witness
that search for one you loved, you voiced a plea
to be allowed to glide above the sea,
using your arms as oars to beat the air.
You found the gods were well disposed to answer:
your limbs were wrapped—at once—in golden feathers.
But you were mesmerizing, suasive singers,
born to entrance the ears; and that your lips
not lose that gift, each one of you was left
with young girl's features and a human voice.

" 'And what did Jupiter do then? Between
his brother Pluto and his grieving sister,
he has to strike a balance: he divides
the turning year into two equal portions.
Proserpina is shared by the two kingdoms:
the goddess is to spend six months beside
her husband, and six months beside her mother.
At once, the goddess' face and spirit alter:
her brow, which until then seemed overcast
even to somber Pluto, now is glad,
just as, when it defeats the dark rainclouds,
the sun appears—victorious and proud.

" 'Generous Ceres, now at peace—at last
she has her daughter back—returns to ask
you, Arethusa, why you fled from Greece
and why you have become a sacred spring.
The waves fall still. Their tutelary goddess
raises her head above the depths; and after
her hands have twisted dry her damp green tresses,
she tells the tale of how—long since—Alpheus,
the river-god of Elis, longed for her.

" ' "I was," she says, "one of the nymphs who live
in the Achaean woods. I was intent
on tracks and trails and setting hunting nets—
no nymph had greater passion for such tasks.
I never wanted to be known for beauty—
I thought my courage was conspicuous,
but all my fame was for mere loveliness.
One day—no day that I forget—I made
my way back from the forest of Stymphalus.
That day was hot—but twice as hot for me:
the hunting had been hard, and I was weary.
I came upon a stream. Unmurmuring
and unperturbed it glided, crystalline—
so clear down to the riverbed that one
could count each pebble there. That stream was so
transparent that it did not seem to flow.
Along the riverbanks the slopes received
the shadows cast by gray-white willow trees

and poplars nourished by those waters—shade
that was the gift of nature. I drew near
And first I bathed my feet, then I went in
up to my knees. But now I wanted more
cool water: I undid my dress. I left
my soft gown draped on a bent willow branch;
naked, I plunged into the stream; and while
I strike those waters in a thousand ways,
dividing, joining, splashing as I play,
my arms withdrawing, plunging in—I hear
the strangest murmur rising from the depths.
I seek the nearest riverbank—in fear.
'Where do you flee so quickly, Arethusa?'
Alpheus, from his waters, called to me.
'Where do you flee so quickly?'—so did he
again speak hoarsely. I could only flee
without my dress—left on the other shore.
My nakedness only inflames him more.
He hurries after me; naked, I seem
to him that much more ready for the taking.
I race; he—fiercely—presses after me:
even as doves with trembling wings will flee
the hawk, and hawk pursue the frightened doves.

" ' "I passed Orchomenus, Psophis, Cyllene,
the vales of Maenalus, chill Erymanthus,[5]
and Elis; I sustained my pace; Alpheus
did not outrace me. But I could not match
his strength: my speed was spent—it could not last
as long as his. Yet, over level fields
and wooded hills, across the spurs and rocks
no path had ever marked, I did not stop.
The sun was at my back, and I could see
a giant shadow stretch ahead of me—
perhaps a phantom fashioned by my fear;
but I could surely hear his dread footsteps,
and I could feel his massive panting breath
upon the band that clasped my hair. As I
collapsed, exhausted by that course, I cried:
'Diana, save me! He is at my side!
I was your weapons' faithful guardian,
the huntress whom you chose to bear your bow,
the keeper of your quiver and your arrows.'

" ' "The goddess had been touched. And she detached
one cloud from a thick cloudbank, and she cast
that cloud around me.[6] And when I was wrapped
in darkness, then Alpheus, ignorant
of where I was, searched in the mist—vainly.

5. Cities and mountains of Arcadia, the region of the central Peloponnesus.

6. Conventional means in ancient epic of making someone invisible.

Around the spot where she had hidden me,
he circled twice, and twice—unknowing—cried:
'O Arethusa, Arethusa!' I
was in the grip of what great misery!
Was I not like the lamb when it can hear
wolves howl around the fold? Or like the hare
that, hidden by a hedge, can see the dread
muzzles of the dogs and dares not stir?

" ' "And yet Alpheus does not leave; aware
that I have stopped—no footprints trail beyond—
Alpheus probes the cloud that cloaks the ground.
I am beset. Cold sweat runs down my flesh;
My body rains dark drops, my hair drips dew,
and where I move my feet a pool is born.
In less time than it takes to tell you now
all that was happening, I am a spring.

" ' "But in those waters, he, the river-god
Alpheus, recognizes me, his love;
leaving the human likeness he had worn,
he once again takes on his river form,
that he might mingle with me. And the goddess
of Delos[7] cracked a chasm through earth's crust:
I plunged into deep caverns, then was brought
here to Ortygia, dear to me because
its name is like the other name of Delos,[8]
the island of Diana—and because
Ortygia is the place where, from below
the earth, up toward the air and sky, I flowed."

" 'When Arethusa's tale had reached its end,
the goddess of fertility prepared
her chariot; she yoked her sacred pair
of dragons. With their bits held tight, she rides
upon the air, between the earth and sky.
Once at Athena's town,[9] on touching ground,
she gives her chariot as well as seeds
of grain to young Triptolemus,[1] and these
she'd have him scatter wide in many lands.
The youth flies over Europe and the breadth
of Asia; reaching Scythia, he descends.
The ruler of that land is Lyncus, and
he enters the king's palace. When he's asked
to tell how he had come, and what and why
might be his name and country, he replies:
"My home is famous Athens; and my name,
Triptolemus. No ship has brought me here
across the waves; my feet did not cross land:
the air disclosed its roads to me; I bring

7. Diana. 8. Also called Ortygia. 9. Athens. 1. Son of the king of Eleusis, Demeter's great cult center near Athens.

the gifts of Ceres; if you scatter these
across your spacious fields, they're sure to yield
rich harvests—cultivated, peaceful food."
And Lyncus, that barbarian, was struck
by envy; but that he might come to be
far-famed as a great benefactor, he
received his guest with hospitality.

" 'Yet when his guest was fast asleep, the king
attacked; his blade was just about to pierce
the chest of the Athenian when Ceres
transformed the Scythian king into a lynx,
then had Triptolemus ride off; across
the air, he drove her sacred dragon pair.'

"Calliope was done: her learned song,
sung with such skill, stopped here. The Nymphs, as one,
agreed: we goddesses of Helicon
had won. The losers could not stand their loss.
They shouted insults at us. As they scoffed,
Calliope replied: 'You challenged us:
for that alone, you merit punishment.
But now you dare to add your rude abuse.
Our patience is not endless: you would test
our anger, and our wrath will rage—unchecked.'
The sisters jeer and fleer; they scorn our threats;
but even as we warned them, when they lift
their hands to mock us, they now notice this:
the feathers sprouting from their fingers and
the plumage covering their arms. And each
can see a sister's face with rigid beak
protruding now, and see new birds retreat
into the trees. And when they try to beat
their breasts, they all are borne by flapping wings;
they fly into the air as insolent
magpies, the mocking dwellers in the woods.
Yet, though they now are winged, their endless need
for sharp, impulsive, harsh, derisive speech
remains: their old loquacity—they keep."

FROM BOOK IX

[*Iphis and Ianthe*]

Word of this prodigy[2] might well have stirred
all Crete—its hundred towns—if Crete itself
had not—so recently—produced its own
great miracle: when Iphis changed her form.

In Phaestus, close to Gnossus' royal city,
there lived a man called Ligdus. Though the son
of humble parents, Ligdus was freeborn.

2. The transformation of Byblis, who loved her brother Caunus, into a fountain.

And like his lineage, his property
was modest; but he'd lived most honestly—
he bore no stain, no blame. And when his wife
was just about to have their child, he turned
to her with these admonitory words:
"There are two things for which I pray: the first,
that you may suffer little in childbirth;
the second, that your child may be a boy.
Our means are meager—girls require more.[3]
So, if by chance (I pray it not be so)
you bear a female, I would have you know
that (hateful as it is—and may the gods
forgive me) I shall have her put to death."
Such were his words. They both were bathed in tears:
he who had ordered this, and she who must
obey. Though Telethusa, his dear wife,
entreated Ligdus not to set such limits
upon the birth they both had longed for so,
she prayed in vain. He would not change his course.

And now the hour of birth drew close; her womb
was full—a burden she could hardly bear—
when at midnight she saw—or thought she saw—
an image in her dreams: before her bed
stood Isis[4] and her train of deities.
Upon her forehead she bore lunar horns
and, round her head, a yellow garland—stalks
of wheat that had been wrought in gleaming gold;
and she had other signs of royalty.
Beside her stood the barking god, Anubis;
sacred Bubastis; Apis, in his cloak
of many colors; and Osiris' son,[5]
who checks his voice and, with his finger on
his lips, urges our silence. There were sistrums;[6]
and there, at Isis' side, Osiris,[7] he
who always is longed for; and the Egyptian
snake swollen with his soporific venom.[8]
And Telethusa, who saw all of this
as if she were awake, heard Isis say:
"O Telethusa, you, who worship me
so faithfully, can set aside despair:
there is no need to heed your husband's order.
And once Lucina has delivered you,
don't hesitate to let your newborn live.
I am the goddess who, when called upon
for help and hope, bring comfort: I respond.
No, I am not a thankless deity."
Her counsel ended here. The goddess left.

3. They had to be provided with a dowry when they reached marriageable age. 4. Egyptian goddess of fertility, marriage, and maternity, whose cult was widespread in the Roman world. 5. Horus, or Harpocrates. 6. Sacred rattles used in Isis's cult. 7. Husband of Isis, killed by his brother Set and restored to life by Isis, and so a figure of rebirth. 8. Set, whom the Greeks identified with the snaky Typhoeus.

The Cretan woman rose up from her bed,
rejoicing; stretching out her blameless hands
unto the stars, she prayed—a suppliant—
that what she'd seen in dreams would be confirmed.
Her labor pains grew more intense, and soon
she'd given easy birth: a girl was born.
Now, to deceive her husband, Telethusa
gave orders to the nurse (for she alone
knew of this guile) to feed the newborn child
and to tell everyone it was a son.
And Ligdus thanked the gods, and to the child
he gave the name of Ligdus' father: Iphis.
And Telethusa was most pleased with this:
it was a name that suited male or female—
a neutral name, whose use involved no tricks.
No one unmasked the pious lie. She dressed
her Iphis as a boy—and whether one
assigned them to a daughter or a son,
the features of the child were surely handsome.

Some thirteen years had come; thirteen had gone.
O Iphis, now, for you, your father found
a bride, the blond Ianthe—there was none
among the girls of Phaestus who had won
more praise for the perfection of her form.
Her father was a man of Crete, Telestes.

Iphis and she were equal in their age,
their beauty; and the two of them were trained
by the same tutors; they had learned—together—
the basic rudiments of arts and letters.
In sum, they had shared much; and so when love
had struck their unsuspecting hearts, they both
shared one same wound—but not with equal hopes.
Ianthe waits impatiently to wed;
she longs for what was promised and accepted,
her wedding one she takes to be a man;
while Iphis is in love with one she knows
is never to be hers; and just for this,
the flame is still more fierce; and now she burns—
a virgin for a virgin. It is hard
to check her tears.
"What end awaits me now?"
she says. "I am possessed by love so strange
that none has ever known its monstrous pangs.
If heaven meant to spare me, then the gods
should have done so; and if the gods' intent
was to destroy me, then the means they chose
could have been natural—a normal woe.
Cows don't love cows, and mares do not love mares;
but sheep desire rams, and does are drawn
by stags. And birds, too, follow that same norm;

among the animals, no female wants
a female! Would I could annul myself!
Yes, it is true that all monstrosities
occur in Crete; and here Pasiphae[9]
has loved a bull. But even that is less
insane than what I feel; for, after all,
she was a female longing for a male.
Yet she was able to attain her goal:
when she appeared in heifer's guise, then he—
deceived—appeased her with adultery.
But how can I be helped? For even if
the world's most cunning minds were gathered here,
if Daedalus[1] himself flew back to Crete
on waxen wings, what could he do? Nothing—
no learned art—can ever make of me
a boy. And it cannot change you, Ianthe.

"Why then not summon all your mettle, Iphis?
Return to your own self; extinguish this
flame that is hopeless, heedless, surely foolish.
For you were born a girl; and now, unless
you would deceive yourself, acknowledge that:
accept it; long for what is lawful; love
as should a woman love! What gives most life
to love is hope; it's hope that lets love thrive—
but it is hope of which you are deprived.
No guardian keeps you from her loving touch;
no jealous husband keeps a sleepless watch,
and no harsh father; nor would she herself
deny you what you seek; yet you cannot
possess her. Though all things may favor you,
though men and gods may help in your pursuit,
you can't be happy. Even now there's no
desire of mine that's been denied; the gods
have been benevolent—they've given me
as much as they could give; and what I want
is what my father and Ianthe want,
and what my future father-in-law wants.
It's nature, with more power than all of these,
that does not want it: my sole enemy
is nature! Now the longed-for moment nears,
my wedding day is close at hand: Ianthe
will soon be mine—but won't belong to me.
With all that water, we shall thirst indeed.
Why do you, Juno, guardian of brides,
and you, too, Hymen,[2] come to grace these rites
at which there is no husband—just two brides?"

9. Wife of King Minos of Crete, and mother by the bull of the Minotaur. 1. Fabled craftsman, who devised the heifer disguise for Pasiphae and, later, the labyrinth for the Minotaur. Forced to flee Crete, he made waxen wings for himself and his son Icarus. 2. God of marriage, whose presence was invoked at weddings.

Her words were done. Meanwhile the other virgin,
whose passion matches Iphis', prays, o Hymen,
that you be quick to come. But Telethusa,
who fears the very thing Ianthe seeks,
delays the date; at times she feigns some illness
and often uses omens seen in dreams
as an excuse. But no pretext is left,
and now the wedding day is imminent—
indeed it looms tomorrow. She removes
the bands that circle her and Iphis' heads;
with hair unbound, she holds the altar fast
and pleads: "O Isis, you who make your home
in Mareota's fields and Paraetonium
and Pharos and the Nile, whose waters flow
to seven mouths, I pray you, help us now
and heal the fear we feel. O goddess, I
have seen you: yes, I saw and recognized
you and your regal signs—your mighty band
of gods, the torches, and the sistrums' sounds—
and I can still remember your commands.
If my dear daughter is alive, if I
have not been punished, we owe all of this
to your advice, your gift. Take pity, Isis:
we two indeed have need of you." Her words
were followed by her tears.
The goddess seemed
to shake her altar (and Osiris had
in fact done that): her temple doors had trembled;
one saw the glitter of her crescent horns;
one heard the clash and clatter of her sistrums.
Still not completely sure, yet glad to have
such hopeful auguries, the mother left
the temple. Iphis walked behind her, but
her stride was longer than it was before,
and her complexion darker; she was more
robust; her features had grown sharper, and
her hair was shorter, without ornaments.
You are more vigorous than you had been,
o Iphis, when you still were feminine—
for you who were a girl so recently
are now a boy! So, bring your offerings
unto the shrines; set fear aside—rejoice!

They bring their offerings, and then they add
a votive tablet, one on which they had
inscribed these words: "These gifts, which Iphis pledged
as girl, are paid by him as man." And when
the first rays of the next day's sun again
revealed the wide world, Venus, Juno, and
Hymen assembled: marriage flames were lit,
and the boy Iphis made Ianthe his.

FROM BOOK X[3]

[*Pygmalion*]

"Pygmalion had seen the shameless lives
of Cyprus' women;[4] and disgusted by
the many sins to which the female mind
had been inclined by nature, he resigned
himself: for years he lived alone, without
a spouse: he chose no wife to share his couch.

"Meanwhile, Pygmalion began to carve
in snow-white ivory, with wondrous art,
a female figure more exquisite than
a woman who was born could ever match.
That done, he falls in love with his own work.
The image seems, in truth, to be a girl;
one could have thought she was alive and keen
to stir, to move her limbs, had she not been
too timid: with his art, he's hidden art.
He is enchanted and, within his heart,
the likeness of a body now ignites
a flame. He often lifts his hand to try
his work, to see if it indeed is flesh
or ivory; he still will not admit
it is but ivory. He kisses it:
it seems to him that, in return, he's kissed.
He speaks to it, embraces it; at each
caress, the image seems to yield beneath
his fingers: and he is afraid he'll leave
some sign, some bruise. And now he murmurs words
of love, and now he offers gifts that girls
find pleasing: shells, smooth pebbles, little birds,
and many-colored flowers, painted balls,
and amber tears that the Heliades[5]
let drop from trees. He—after draping it
with robes—adorns its fingers with fine gems,
its neck with a long necklace; light beads hang
down from its ears, and ribbons grace its breast.
All this is fair enough, but it's not less
appealing in its nakedness. He rests
the statue on the covers of his bed,
on fabric dyed with hues of Sidon's shells;[6]
he calls that form the maid that shares his couch
and sets its head on cushions—downy, soft—
delicately, as if it could respond.

3. This selection of stories is part of the song sung by Orpheus after he has failed to redeem his wife, Eurydice, from the underworld. His theme, announced in the prologue of his song, is "boys the gods have loved, and girls / incited by unlawful lust and passions, / who paid the penalty for their transgressions."
4. Orpheus has just told of the Propoetides of Cyprus, who became the first women to prostitute themselves as punishment for having denied Venus's divinity.
5. Daughters of the Sun, turned to pine trees in mourning for their brother Phaethon. Their tears were the source of amber (actually fossilized pine resin).
6. Purple or red, a costly dye from shellfish found off the coast of Phoenicia.

"The day of Venus' festival had come—
the day when, from all Cyprus, people thronged;
and now—their curving horns are sheathed with gold—
the heifers fall beneath the fatal blows
that strike their snow-white necks; the incense smokes.
Pygmalion, having paid the honors owed
to Venus, stopped before the altar: there
the sculptor offered—timidly—this prayer:
'O gods, if you indeed can grant all things,
then let me have the wife I want'—and here
he did not dare to say 'my ivory girl'
but said instead, 'one like my ivory girl.'
And golden Venus (she indeed was there
at her own feast-day) understood his prayer:
three times the flame upon her altar flared
more brightly, darting high into the air—
an omen of the goddess' kindly care.
At once, Pygmalion, at home again,
seeks out the image of the girl; he bends
over his couch; he kisses her. And when
it seems her lips are warm, he leans again
to kiss her; and he reaches with his hands
to touch her breasts. The ivory had lost
its hardness; now his fingers probe; grown soft,
the statue yields beneath the sculptor's touch,
just as Hymettian[7] wax beneath the sun
grows soft and, molded by the thumb, takes on
so many varied shapes—in fact, becomes
more pliant as one plies it. Stupefied,
delighted yet in doubt, afraid that he
may be deceived, the lover tests his dream:
it is a body! Now the veins—beneath
his anxious fingers—pulse. Pygmalion
pours out rich thanks to Venus; finally,
his lips press lips that are not forgeries.
The young girl feels these kisses; blushing, she
lifts up her timid eyes; she seeks the light;
and even as she sees the sky, she sees
her lover. Venus graces with her presence
the wedding she has brought about. And when
the moon shows not as crescent but as orb
for the ninth time, Pygmalion's wife gives birth
to Paphos—and in honor of that child,
Cyprus has since been called the Paphian isle.

[*Myrrha and Cinyras*]

"And Paphos' son was Cinyras, a man
who, if he'd not had children, might have found
some happiness. The tale I now would sing

7. Of Hymettos, a mountain near Athens famous for its honey.

is dread indeed: o daughters, fathers, leave;
or if your minds delight in listening,
do not put trust in me, do not believe
the truth that I will tell; or if you must
believe it, then believe the penalty
that punishes such acts. In any case,
if nature can permit so foul a sin
to see the light, I do congratulate
this region of the world, my Thracian race;[8]
I'm grateful that we are so far away
from lands where such obscenities take place.

"Panchaea's land[9] is rich in balsam and
in cinnamon and unguents; and its trees
drip incense, and its soil has many flowers.
What need had it for myrrh? Did it deserve
so sad a plant? O Myrrha, Cupid had
no part in your undoing—for he says
his arrow did not strike you; he declares
his torches innocent. The firebrand
and venom-swollen snakes were brought from Styx
by one of the three Sisters:[1] she did this
to crush you. Yes, to hate a father is
a crime, but love like yours is worse than hate.

"Young lords from every land, the noblest men
from all the Orient, have sought your hand;
among all these, choose one as your dear husband.
But, Myrrha, there is one who can't belong
to those from whom you choose.
"And she, in truth,
knows that; she strives; she tries; she would subdue
her obscene love: 'Where has my mind led me?
What am I plotting? Gods, I do beseech,
and, too, I call upon the piety
I owe my parents: check my sacrilege,
prevent my sinning—if it is a sin.
Parental piety does not exclude
such love: the other animals pursue
delight and mate without such niceties.
There's nothing execrable when a heifer
is mounted by her father; stallions, too,
mate with their daughters; and a goat can choose
to couple with his child; the female bird
conceives from that same seed which fathered her.
Blessed are those who have that privilege.
It's human scruples that have stifled us
with jealous edicts; law is envious—

8. A reminder that these stories form Orpheus's song in Thrace. 9. An imaginary island near Arabia, rich in spices. 1. The Furies.

what nature would permit, the law forbids.
And yet they say that there are tribes in which
the mother mates with her own son, the daughter
with her own father, and the loving bonds,
so reinforced, make families more fond.
But I—to my misfortune—was not born
among those tribes; instead I am—forlorn—
denied the very man for whom I long.
But why do I keep coming back again,
again, to this? I must dismiss such thoughts:
blot out my lust. Yes, Cinyras deserves
much love—but as a father. Were I not
his daughter, I could lie with him; but since
I'm his, he can't be mine; and that close link
dictates my loss. If I were but a stranger,
I would have had some chance. But now I want
to leave my native land: nothing but flight
can save me from so foul a flaw. And yet
I stay: this evil ardor holds me here,
that I may gaze at Cinyras, and touch
and speak to him, and give him kisses if
I cannot hope for more. Would you transgress
beyond that? Can you let such sacrilege
incite you? Do you know what holy ties
and names would be confronted by your crimes?
Would you be your own mother's rival and
your father's mistress? Would you want to be
a sister to your son? Your brother's mother?
And those three Sisters, don't they make you fear?
Their hair is wreathed with serpents, and they bear
barbaric brands when they appear before
the eyes and faces of unholy souls.
Come now, your body's still unstained: do not
debauch your soul with lust, defile the code
of nature with a lawless mating. Though
you will it, nature will not have it so;
for Cinyras is pious in his ways,
a man of virtue. Would that he were prey
to my same frenzy, to that passion's sway!'

"These were her words. Now Cinyras, confused,
does not know what to do: the suitors crowd—
so many worthy men. He calls upon
his daughter to select the one she wants,
and he lists all their names. At first, the girl
is silent: staring at him, she's in doubt;
and warm tears veil her eyes. Her father thinks
these tears are simply signs of modesty,
forbids her weeping, dries her cheeks; and then
he kisses her. She takes too much delight
in this; and when he asks what kind of man

she'll have her husband be, she answers: 'One
like you.' Not understanding what is hid
beneath her words, he praises her for this:
'And may you always be so filial.'
When she hears him say 'filial,' the girl
lowers her eyes: she knows she's criminal.

"Midnight: now sleep sets cares and flesh to rest.
But Myrrha does not sleep: she cannot check
the fire that feeds on her; she is held fast—
her madness does not slack; first she despairs
and then is set to try; she is ashamed;
but though she longs, she cannot find a plan.
As, when the axes strike the massive trunk,
the tree will waver at the moment just
before the final blow: one does not know
which way it is to fall; upon all sides
men now rush off—so, too, enfeebled by
so many blows from many sides, the mind
of Myrrha leans this way, then that. At last
it seems no thing can check her love, bring rest,
except for death. On death she now is set.
She rises from her bed: she ties her belt
around a ceiling beam—to hang herself.

" 'Dear Cinyras, farewell,' his daughter moans,
'I hope you come to know why I would die.'
Then she begins to run the cord around
her pallid neck. They say her murmurs reached
the ears of her old nurse, who faithfully
stood watch before the door of her dear charge.
The nurse leaps up at once; on opening
the door, she sees her Myrrha readying
the tools of death; in one same moment, she
cries out and beats her breast and tears her dress
and snatches off the rope from Myrrha's neck.
And only after that, the nurse takes time
to weep, to clasp her Myrrha, and to ask
why she was driven to the noose. The girl
is silent, speechless; staring at the ground,
she's sorry her attempt at death was foiled—
she was too slow. But her old nurse insists:
she bares her white hairs and her withered breasts;
she calls on all the days and nights she'd spend
on Myrrha in the cradle, and she begs:
what grief had brought her Myrrha to this pass?
But Myrrha turns aside those pleas; she groans.
The nurse is set on finding out, and so
she promises not only to hold close
the secret but to help her: 'I am old,
but I'm not useless. If it is a stroke

of madness that afflicts you, my dear girl,
I know a woman who has charms and herbs
to heal you; and if anyone has cast
an evil spell upon you, magic rites
can purify you; and to cure your plight,
you can bring offerings, a sacrifice
unto the gods, and so appease their wrath
if they, in anger, led you to this pass.
I've thought of all that could have brought distress.
This house can only bring you happiness:
yes, all things here go well; your mother and
your father are alive and prosperous.'
As soon as she has heard those words, 'your father,'
the girl sighs deeply; but the nurse—although
she has begun to sense that Myrrha's soul
is sick with love—does not as yet suspect
a passion so profane. And stubbornly,
she probes: she wants to hear in full the cause
of Myrrha's pain—whatever it might be.
She hugs the tearful girl to her old breast
and, holding Myrrha in her frail arms, says:
'I know, I know: you are in love. But set
your fears aside; you'll find that I can help;
and I shall keep your secret; Cinyras
won't hear a word of this. But, come, confess.'
The frenzied girl breaks loose and, on her bed,
collapses, helpless; as she sinks her head
into the cushions, Myrrha cries: 'Don't seek
the source of this! Stop probing, I beseech!
The thing you want to find is my foul crime!'

"At that, the girl's old nurse is horrified.
And as she stretches out her hands that shake
with years and fears, the old nurse falls; prostrate
before the feet of her dear girl, she pleads
and menaces: she threatens to reveal
the noose, the try at suicide—but then
she promises to help if Myrrha will
just tell the truth about her secret love.
The young girl lifts her head; against the breast
of her old nurse, it's many tears she sheds.
Again, again, she tries—she would confess—
but checks her voice; ashamed, she hides her face
within her robes and sighs: 'How happy you,
my mother, are beside the mate you chose.'
And Myrrha says no more; she only moans.
Then through the nurse's body, to the bone,
a shudder lances, sharp and cold (she knows,
she knows); her white hair stiffens on her head;
she tries with warning word on word to rid
the girl from that dread love; and Myrrha knows

the nurse's pleas are just; but she is set
on death if what she wants cannot be had.
At this, the nurse says: 'Live, for you will have
your . . . ' Daring not to utter 'father,' she
falls still; but then—before the gods on high—
she vows to keep the promise she had made.

"And now, their bodies clothed in snow-white robes,
all pious wives were honoring the feast
of Ceres; her first fruits, the ears of wheat,
were bound in garlands as an offering
on these, the days they celebrate each year.
This was the time when women, for nine nights,
shun union with their husbands; any touch
of man is banned. Cenchreis, the king's wife,
has joined the throng; she shares these secret rites.
When, in her wretched zeal, the old nurse finds
that Cinyras is drunk with wine, deprived,
without his lawful wife, she tells the king
that a young girl is now in love with him;
but she does not reveal the girl's true name—
the girl whose beauty she is quick to praise.
And when he wants to know the young girl's age,
she says, 'the same as Myrrha's.' When he tells
the nurse to fetch that girl, she runs to find
her Myrrha and, 'My dear, we've won,' she cries;
'you can rejoice!' The wretched girl is stirred,
and yet her joy is not complete; a sad
foreboding grips her heart, but she is glad:
the virgin's mind is torn by such discord.

"The hour when all is silent now is here.
And, seen between the stars of the two Bears,
Boötes,[2] veering downward with his wain,
inclines his guide-pole. Myrrha makes her way
to her misdeed. The golden moon now flees
the sky; black clouds conceal the stars; the night
has lost its flaring lights. The first to hide
their faces at the shameless sight were you,
o Icarus,[3] and dear Erigone,
your daughter, she whose holy love for you
won her a starry place—her sacred due.
Three times young Myrrha stumbles on her path,
an omen telling her she should turn back;
three times the screech-owl, with his eerie chant,
warns her. But still the longing daughter moves
ahead; her shame is muted by the black

2. The Ox-herder, a constellation, thought to drive Ursa Major, the Great Bear (also called the Wagon [*Wain*]). 3. More properly Ikarios, a mythic Athenian. He received Dionysus into the city, and the god rewarded him with wine, which he shared with his countrymen. Feeling its effect, they thought they had been poisoned and killed him. His daughter Erigone hanged herself in grief, and both were changed into constellations.

of night. Her left hand grips her nurse hard fast,
and with her right she gropes and probes. At last
she's at the threshold, opening the door;
and now she is inside the room. Her knees
are trembling; and as blood and color flee,
her face is pale; her courage leaves; as she
draws closer to her crime, her fears increase;
the girl repents of her audacity:
she would turn back if she could go unseen.
As Myrrha hesitates, her old nurse takes
her hand; she draws her toward the high bed's side—
consigns her to the king and says: 'Take her,
o Cinyras; she's yours.' And she unites
those two in dark damnation. Cinyras
obscenely welcomes to his bed the flesh
of his own flesh; he helps her to defeat
her virgin's shame; he sets her fears at ease.
Perhaps because she is so young, the king
calls timid Myrrha 'daughter,' even as
she calls him 'father'; so do they complete
their sacrilege; they name their guilt in speech.

"Filled with her father, Myrrha leaves that room;
she bears his impious seed within her womb.
And on the second night, again they lie
together; so it went, time after time,
until the father, keen to recognize
the girl he'd held so often, carried in
a lamp—and saw his daughter and his sin.
Struck dumb by grief, he pulls his gleaming sword
out from its sheath, which hung along the wall.

"And Myrrha fled. The night was kind; the shades
and darkness favored her; the girl escaped
her death; she crossed the open fields; she left
palm-rich Arabia and Panchaea's lands.
Nine times the moon had shown its crescent horns,
and still she wandered on. At last she stayed
her weary steps in the Sabaeans' land.[4]
Her womb was heavy now—so hard to carry.
Not knowing what to hope for—torn between
her fear of death and the fatigue of living—
she gathered up her wishes and beseeched:
'Oh, if there is some god to hear the plea
of one who knows that she is guilty, I
accept the death that I deserve. But lest
I, in my life, profane the living and,
in death, profane the dead, do banish me
from both these realms; transform me, and deny

4. Arabia Felix, the southern tip of the Arabian peninsula.

both life and death to me.'
"And some god heard
the girl confess her guilt: her final plea
was answered. As she spoke, the earth enclosed
her legs; roots slanted outward from her toes;
supported by those roots, a tall trunk rose.
Her bones became tough wood (although her marrow
remained unchanged); her blood was turned to sap;
her arms became long boughs; her fingers, twigs;
her skin was now dark bark. And as it grew,
the tree had soon enveloped her full womb;
then it submerged her breasts and was about
to wrap itself around her neck; but she—
impatient—met the rising bark: she sank
down, down, until her face was also bark.
Her flesh had lost the senses it once had,
but she still wept—and, trickling down the tree,
tears fell. But even tears can gain long fame:
myrrh, dripping from that trunk, preserves the name
of Myrrha, mistress of that tree; and she
will be remembered through the centuries.

[*Venus and Adonis*]

"But when the misbegotten child had grown
inside the wood, it wanted to come forth
to leave its mother. Halfway up the trunk,
the pregnant tree was swollen; all the bark
was taut with that full burden. But the pain
and pangs could not find words; though this is birth,
there is no speech that can beseech Lucina.
And yet the tree trunk bends and moans in labor;
the bark is wet with fallen tears. Lucina
takes pity: standing near the groaning boughs
she lays her hands upon them, even as
she speaks that spell which shepherds safe childbirth.
At that, the tree trunk cracked, the bark was torn;
the tree delivered what had weighed it down;
a living thing, a wailing boy was born:
Adonis. And the Naiads[5] set him on
the tender meadow and anointed him
with myrrh, his mother's tears. And even Envy
would praise his beauty, for indeed his body
is like the naked Cupid artists paint.
And to remove the only difference,
just add a quiver to Adonis or
remove the quiver from the Cupid's form.

"The flight of time eludes our eyes, it glides
unseen; no thing is swifter than the years.

5. Water nymphs.

Yes, he who is the son of his own sister
and his grandfather, was but recently
enclosed within a tree. But recently
a newborn, then a handsome baby boy,
Adonis has become a youth, a man;
his beauty now surpasses what he was,
inflaming even Venus' love, and thus
avenging that dread fire—incestuous—
which Venus made his mother, Myrrha, suffer.
And this is how that vengeance came about.

"One day, as Cupid, son of Venus, kissed
his mother, unaware, he scratched her breast:
an arrow jutting from his quiver chanced
to graze her. Though the goddess felt the prick
and pushed her son aside, the wound was far
more deep than it had seemed to her at first.

"And Venus now is taken by the mortal
Adonis' beauty: she no longer cares
for her Cythera's[6] shores; she cannot spare
the time to visit sea-encircled Paphos
and Cnidos, rich with fish; and she neglects
her Amathus,[7] the city rich with ores.
She even finds the skies too tedious:
she much prefers Adonis. She stays close
to him; it is with him she always goes;
and she, who always used to seek the shade—
there she could rest at ease and cultivate
her beauty—now frequents the mountain slopes,
the woods, the rocks beset by spiny thorns;
as if she were Diana,[8] Venus keeps
her tunic tied above her knees. She spurs
the hounds and chases after game: that is,
those beasts whom it is safe to hunt—the hares
that leap headlong, the stags with branching horns,
or does. But she is careful to avoid
stout boars, rapacious wolves, bears armed with claws,
and lions stained with blood of slaughtered herds.
Adonis, she would warn you, too, to stay
away from those fierce beasts: 'Be bold,' she says,
'when you approach the timid animals,
those who are quick to flee: but do not be
audacious when you face courageous beasts.
Dear boy, do not be reckless when the risk
involves me, too; don't let me lose you just
because you wanted glory; don't provoke
those animals whom nature has armed well.
Your youth, your loveliness—the many things

6. Island south of the Peloponnesus and, like Cyprus, sacred to Venus. 7. Cities on Cyprus and (Cnidos) in Asia Minor, important centers of Venus's cult. 8. Virgin and huntress, the antithesis of Venus.

with which you have enchanted even me—
don't move the lion or the bristling boar,
don't touch the eyes and hearts of those fierce beasts.
Those boars have lightning in their curving claws;
the tawny lion's wrath is wild and raw—
I do indeed detest that race.' At this,
he asked her why, and she replied: 'Adonis,
you'll hear the answer now: an ancient crime—
which had a monstrous outcome. But since I
am weary now—you see, I'm not quite used
to such hard labors—let us profit by
the poplar, here at hand; its shade invites,
and here, along the grass, we can recline.
I want to rest beside you.' She stretched out
along the ground and held him close—for he
had stretched out, too. And pillowing her head
upon his chest, the goddess—even as
she mingled kisses with her words—began:

" 'You may have heard of Atalanta: one
who, when she ran, would beat the fastest men.
That was no idle rumor, for she won
in truth. And, too, you would have found it hard
to say if she was worthier of praise
for her amazing speed or splendid grace.

" 'Now she had gone to ask the oracle
about a husband: "No, you have no need
of any husband"—so the god replied—
"you must shun any marriage. This advice
will not be taken; though you stay alive,
you will have lost yourself." Then, terrified
by what the god had said, she lived unwed
within the shadowed forests; to hold off
the crowd of her insistent suitors, she
set harsh conditions for her matrimony:
"Whoever hopes to have me," so she said,
"must first defeat me in a footrace; bed
and wife are what await the man who wins;
for all of those who are too slow, it's death
they'll get. These are the terms of this contest."
Yes, she showed little pity; but her beauty
was so entrancing that, despite the terms
that Atalanta set, a reckless crowd
of suitors came to race that fateful course.

" 'Of those who took their seats to watch the race,
one was Hippomenes. He had exclaimed:
"Can anyone be fool enough to risk
his life to gain a wife?" So he condemned
those young fanatics' love. But when she sheds
her clothes and shows her splendid form (much like
my own, or what your beauty, too, would be

were you a woman), then Hippomenes,
astonished, lifts his hands and cries: "Forgive me,
you whom I just rebuked! I did not know
the value of the prize you wanted so."
And even as he praises her, love grows:
his hope, that none would outrace Atalanta;
his fear, that some young suitor now may win—
and this spurs jealousy in him. "But why
don't I risk, too? Why not compete?" he cries;
"the god helps those who dare." Hippomenes
is pondering this course, when she flies by
as if her feet were wings. She seems to speed
as swiftly as a Scythian arrow, but
the young Aonian[9] is even more
astonished by the splendor of her form—
a grace that is enhanced as she competes.
She wears gold sandals on her rapid feet;
her hair is fluttering over her white shoulders
as, at her knees, the ribbons with white borders
are fluttering; and all her young, fair body
is flushed with rose, just as a purple awning
within a marble hall will lend white walls
a darker hint, a veil, a shadowed tint.
The stranger notices all this; and now
they cross the finish line; and she has won;
a victor, she receives the festal crown
of garlands. The defeated suitors go
with heavy groans, to pay the deaths they owe.

" 'And yet Hippomenes is not dismayed
and not delayed by their sad fate. He makes
his way to her; eyes fixed upon her face;
"Why seek such easy glory, why outrace
such sluggish men?" he says. "Contend with me,
for then, if fortune gives me victory,
your losing to so grand an enemy
would not bring shame to you. For I can claim
Megareus of Onchestus as my father,
and he had Neptune as grandfather: thus,
I am the great-grandson of one who rules
the waters; and my worth does not belie
my lineage. And if I meet defeat,
for having outraced me, Hippomenes,
you'll gain unending fame." And as he speaks,
the eyes of Atalanta take him in
most tenderly. Oh, does she want to win
or does the virgin long to lose to him?

" 'So Atalanta wonders, inwardly:
"Is there some god who, wishing to destroy
fair youths, has willed the ruin of this boy

9. From Boeotia, a region in central Greece.

and prods him now to seek me out as wife
and risk his own dear life? Were I to judge,
I'd hardly say that I was worth that much.
It's not his self that stirs me—it's his years:
he's young—and yet he's bold, a fearless soul!
He's young, yet he can claim that he is fourth
within the line of sons descended from
the monarch of the seas! And he loves me
and wants so much to marry me that if
an evil fate should foil him, he will live
no more! No, stranger, leave while you still can;
forget this savage marriage; wedding me
means sure fatality. No woman would
refuse to marry you; you'll surely find
a wiser girl to welcome you. But why
must I, who've sent so many to their deaths,
feel such distress for you? He can take care
of his own self. Then let him perish, too,
since, after all, the death of those who wooed
was not enough to warn him off; he must
be weary of this life. But that would mean
he died because he wished to live with me;
is that a just, a seemly penalty
to pay for having loved? My victory—
if I should win—is not a thing to envy.
Yet that is not my fault. Can't you renounce?
But if you're mad enough to try, I would
that you might be more swift than me. Yes, yes,
his gaze, his face have charm and tenderness.
Ah, poor Hippomenes, I would that you
had not set eyes on me. You were so worthy
of life. If I were just more fortunate,
if wretched fate had not forbidden me
to marry, you would be the only one
with whom I'd ever want to share my couch."
Such were her troubled words; a neophyte
whom Cupid now has touched for the first time,
indeed she loves—but knows not that she does.

" 'But now the people and her father—all
call for another trial—as usual.
Hippomenes, a son of Neptune's race,
prays urgently to me: "O Venus, may
I count upon your favor as I dare
to face this test; and may you treat with care
the love that she has stirred in me." His plea
was gentle, and it was a gentle breeze
that bore that prayer to me. And I confess,
it moved me—but so little time was left.

" 'There is a field the Cypriots have called
the field of Tamasus; within that isle

there is no place more fair. In ancient times
that field was set aside as sacred site:
a holy place they added to my shrines.
Within that field there grows a tree with leaves
of gold; its crackling branches also gleam
with tawny gold. And when his gentle plea
reached me, I was, by chance, returning from
that sacred site—my hands were carrying
three golden apples gathered from that tree.
Invisible to all but him, I drew
close to Hippomenes; I taught him how
to use the apples. Blaring trumpets now
announce the race's start: and from their crouch,
those two flash out; they skim the sandy course
with flying feet. Indeed, one might have thought
that she and he could even graze the sea
yet leave their feet still dry; or speed across
a field of standing grain and leave the stalks
untouched. Applause and shouts are loud; the crowd
cheers on Hippomenes, and some cry out:
"Go, go; this is the time to take the lead,
to give it all you have, Hippomenes!
Don't spare your speed! Don't slack—and you will win!"
It's hard to say if this applause brought more
delight to Megareus' heroic son
or Scheneus' virgin daughter. As they sped,
how many times did she, about to pass
Hippomenes, relent and gaze at length
upon his face until, at last, she raced
ahead—reluctantly? And now his throat
is weary: he is parched; he pants, and yet
the run is long, the goal is still far off.
And finally, he drops the first of those
three golden apples. Even as it rolls,
she is enchanted by the gleaming gold;
she veers off course to pick it up. The crowd
applauds Hippomenes, who takes the lead.
But she recoups her loss; a surge of speed—
once more the girl has gained the lead. And when
he throws the second apple, she retrieves
that apple, too, but passes him again.
The final stretch is all that's left. He pleads:
"O goddess, giver of this gift to me,
do stand beside me now." With all the force
of youth he throws the gleaming golden fruit—
obliquely, distantly—off course. The girl
seemed hesitant—uncertain of her choice:
to let it lie or pick it up. But I
compelled her: she went off; she picked it up.
So she lost time—and, too, the weight of three
gold apples hampered her. So that my story
not take much longer than that race, I say

she was outstripped; the winner led away
his prize, his wife.
" 'But now, Adonis, I
must ask you this: did I not merit thanks
for all I did? Did I not earn sweet incense
to honor me? But he forgot completely:
I had no incense and no thanks from him.
At that offense, my wrath was spurred; and lest
in time to come I ever suffer such
a slight again, I saw that I would have
to make them serve as an example: I
incited my own self against that pair.
One day, they chanced to pass before the shrine
that, to fulfill a vow that he had pledged,
Echion built: a temple for Cybele,
the Mother of the gods, a shrine that stood
concealed within the shadows of deep woods.
The pair had journeyed long; they needed rest;
and I ignited him: Hippomenes—
such is my power as a deity—
was struck with an indecent, sudden need
for Atalanta's body. Near that shrine,
there was a cavelike cell where little light
could filter; it was vaulted by soft rock,
the pumice of that place—a sacred cave,
where men had venerated deities
for age on age, beyond all memory:
indeed a priest had set within that cell
the wooden statues of the ancient gods.
Hippomenes, on entering that cave,
was quick to desecrate the sacred place
with lust. The hallowed statues turned away
their eyes; the Mother goddess,[1] turret-crowned,
was set to plunge the obscene lovers down
into the waves of Styx. But then that seemed
too slight a penalty: instead, she wraps
their necks in tawny manes; their fingers take
the shape of cunning claws; their arms are changed
to legs; their weight moves forward to their chests;
and they grow tails that sweep along the ground;
their faces harden now; they speak in growls,
not words; the wild woods are their mating place.
As lions, they strike terror into all;
but they indeed are tame when, yoked, they draw
Cybele's chariot: they champ tight bits.

" 'Avoid those beasts, dear boy, and any sort
of animal that will not turn its back
and flee from you but, ready to attack,

1. Cybele, a fertility goddess of Asia Minor known as the Great Mother. She was often pictured wearing a crown that resembled a city wall with towers, and flanked by lions or riding in a cart drawn by them.

stands firm, chest forward; no, I would not have
your daring damage you and ruin me.'

"So did the goddess warn Adonis; then
she yoked her swans, rode off across the air.
But daring is not keen to heed such warnings.
By chance, Adonis' hounds had caught a scent
that led them to a wild boar's hidden den;
the trail was sure. The boar was roused
out of the woods: Adonis' spearhead caught
the boar—a slanting thrust. With his curved snout,
the savage beast worked free—he had torn out
the spearhead stained with his own blood. The chase
is on: he charges at Adonis now.
The youth, in fear of his own life, runs hard,
but he is caught: the boar sinks his long tusks
into Adonis' groin; he fells him—and
the boy lies prone along the yellow sands.

"On her light chariot, Venus, who was drawn
across the middle air by her winged swans,
had not reached Cyprus yet; she heard, far off,
the dying boy—his moans. She turned around
her white swans and rode back. When, from the heights,
she saw him lifeless there, a bleeding corpse,
she leaped down to the ground. And Venus tore
her hair, and—much unlike a goddess[2]—beat
her hands against her breast. She challenged fate:
'But destiny does not rule all. Adonis,
your memory will live eternally:
each year they will repeat this final scene—
your day of death, my day of grief, will be
enacted in a feast that bears your name.

" 'I shall transform your blood into a flower.
If you, Proserpina, were once allowed
the metamorphosis of Mentha,[3] when
you changed that nymph into a fragrant plant—
the mint—can anyone begrudge me if
I change the form of Cinyras' dear son?'
That said, she sprinkled scented nectar on
his blood, which then fermented, even as
bright bubbles form when raindrops fall on mud.
One hour had yet to pass when, from that gore,
a bloodred flower sprang, the very color
of pomegranates when that fruit is ripe
and hides sweet seeds beneath its pliant rind.
And yet Adonis' blossoms have brief life:

2. Because these gestures are typical of women mourning the dead, as goddesses usually do not have to do. 3. Hades' mistress, trampled by the jealous Proserpina and transformed into the mint (the meaning of her name).

his flower is light and delicate; it clings
too loosely to the stem and thus is called
Anemone—'born of the wind'—because
winds shake its fragile petals, and they fall."

PETRONIUS
died A.D. 66

It is not certain that Titus Petronius (Arbiter) was the author of the *Satyricon*, but he is the best candidate. A friend of Nero's, he committed suicide at the imperial order after becoming involved in the Pisonian conspiracy against the emperor in A.D. 65. A brilliant account of Petronius's character and death is given by Tacitus in the *Annals* (book 16, chapters 18 and 19).

It is in the satiric masterpiece of this Roman aristocrat that the pragmatic, materialistic attitude Christianity was to supplant is most clearly displayed. It was probably written during the principate of Nero (A.D. 54–68), a period in which the material benefits and the spiritual weakness of the new order had already become apparent. The *Satyricon* itself has survived only in fragments; we know nothing certain about the scope of the work as a whole, but from the fragments it is clear that this book is the work of a satiric genius, perhaps the most original genius of Latin literature.

Dinner with Trimalchio, one of the longer fragments (printed here), shows us a tradesman's world. The narrator, a student of literature, and his cronies may have an aristocratic disdain for the businessmen at whose tables they eat, but they know that Trimalchio and his kind have inherited the Earth. Trimalchio began life as a foreign slave, but he is now a multimillionaire. The representative of culture, Agamemnon the teacher, drinks his wine and praises his fatuous remarks; he is content to be the court jester, the butt of Trimalchio's witticisms. Trimalchio knows no god but Mercury, the patron of business operations, but the gold bracelet, which represents a percentage of his income that he has dedicated to Mercury, he wears on his own arm rather than depositing it in a shrine of the god. He identifies himself with the god, and worships himself, the living embodiment of the power of money. The conversation at his table is a sardonic revelation of the temper of a whole civilization. Written in brilliantly humorous and colloquial style, it exposes mercilessly a blindness to spiritual values of any kind, a distrust of the intellect, and a ferocious preoccupation with the art of cheating one's neighbor. The point is made more effective by the conscious evocation of the epic tradition throughout the work: the names alone of the teacher, Agamemnon, and his assistant in instruction, Menelaus; the wall paintings that show "the *Iliad,* and *Odyssey,* and the gladiatorial show given by Laenas"; Trimalchio's exhibition of monstrous ignorance of Homer (which nobody dares to correct); the Nestorian tone of Ganymedes, who regrets the old days when men were men (he is talking of the time when Safinius forced the bakers to lower the price of bread)—one touch after another reminds us that these figures are the final product of a tradition that began with Achilles and Odysseus.

The satire is witty, but it is nonetheless profound. Trimalchio and his friends all live for the moment, in material enjoyment, but they know that it cannot last. "Let's think of the living" is their watchword, but they cannot forget the dead. And as the banquet goes on, the thought of death, suppressed beneath the debased Epicureanism of Trimalchio and his associates, emerges slowly to the surface of their consciousness and comes to dominate it completely. The last arrival at the banquet is Habinnas the undertaker, and his coming coincides with the last stage of Trimalchio's drunkenness, the maudlin exhibition of his funeral clothes and the description of his tomb. "I want to die," says the Sibyl in the story Trimalchio tells early in the evening; at its end Trimalchio himself acts out his own funeral, complete with ointment, robes, wine, and trumpet players. The fact of death, the one fact that the practical materialism of Trimalchio and his circle can neither deny nor assimilate, asserts itself triumphantly as the supreme fact in the emptiness of Trimalchio's mind.

The introduction to *Petronius: The Satyricon* (1977), translated by J. P. Sullivan, will be helpful to the student, as will William Arrowsmith's introduction to his *The Satyricon of Petronius* (1959) and the introduction and notes to *Satyrica* (1996), translated by Bracht Branham and Daniel Kinney. J. P. Sullivan, *The 'Satyricon' of Petronius: A Literary Study* (1969), and Niall Slater, *Reading Petronius* (1990), are full-length critical discussions of the work.

PRONOUNCING GLOSSARY

The following list uses common English syllables and stress accents to provide rough equivalents of selected words whose pronunciation may be unfamiliar to the general reader.

Encolpius: *en-kol'-pi-us*

Gaius: *gai'-us*

Scintilla: *sin-til'-lah*

Trimalchio: *tri-mal'-ki-oh*

The Satyricon

[*Dinner with Trimalchio*[1]]

Summary The narrator, Encolpius, is a penniless vagabond who is a student of rhetoric under a master named Agamemnon. His close associates are Ascyltus, a fellow student, and Giton, a handsome boy who has no particular occupation. After some disreputable and very tiring adventures they are invited, as pupils of Agamemnon, to a banquet. The scene of the story is an unidentified city in southern Italy, the time probably about A.D. 50.

The next day but one finally arrived. But we were so knocked about that we wanted to run rather than rest. We were mournfully discussing how to avoid the approaching storm,[2] when one of Agamemnon's slaves broke in on our frantic debate.

"Here," said he, "don't you know who's your host today? It's Trimalchio—he's terribly elegant. . . . He has a clock in the dining-room and a trumpeter[3] all dressed up to tell him how much longer he's got to live."

This made us forget all our troubles. We dressed carefully and told Giton, who was very kindly acting as our servant, to attend us at the baths.[4]

We did not take our clothes off but began wandering around, or rather exchanging jokes while circulating among the little groups. Suddenly we saw a bald old man in a reddish shirt, playing ball with some long-haired boys. It was not so much the boys that made us watch, although they alone were worth the trouble, but the old gentleman himself. He was taking his exercise in slippers and throwing a green ball around. But he didn't pick it up if it

1. Translated by J. P. Sullivan. 2. A repetition of the unsavory incidents they have just experienced. 3. To sound off every hour on the hour. A clock was a rare and expensive item. The name Trimalchio suggests "triply blessed" or "triply powerful." 4. A public institution; they were magnificent buildings, containing not only baths of many types and temperatures but places for conversation and games and even libraries.

touched the ground; instead there was a slave holding a bagful, and he supplied them to the players. We noticed other novelties. Two eunuchs stood around at different points: one of them carried a silver chamber pot, the other counted the balls, not those flying from hand to hand according to the rules, but those that fell to the ground. We were still admiring these elegant arrangements when Menelaus[5] hurried up to us.

"This is the man you'll be dining with," he said. "In fact, you are now watching the beginning of the dinner."

No sooner had Menelaus spoken than Trimalchio snapped his fingers. At the signal the eunuch brought up the chamber pot for him, while he went on playing. With the weight off his bladder, he demanded water for his hands, splashed a few drops on his fingers and wiped them on a boy's head.

It would take too long to pick out isolated incidents. Anyway, we entered the baths where we began sweating at once and we went immediately into the cold water. Trimalchio had been smothered in perfume and was already being rubbed down, not with linen towels, but with bath-robes of the finest wool. As this was going on, three masseurs sat drinking Falernian[6] in front of him. Through quarreling they spilled most of it and Trimalchio said they were drinking his health.[7] Wrapped in thick scarlet felt he was put into a litter. Four couriers with lots of medals went in front, as well as a go-cart in which his favourite boy was riding—a wizened, bleary-eyed youngster, uglier than his master. As he was carried off, a musician with a tiny set of pipes took his place by Trimalchio's head and whispered a tune in his ear the whole way.

We followed on, choking with amazement by now, and arrived at the door with Agamemnon at our side. On the doorpost a notice was fastened which read:

ANY SLAVE LEAVING THE HOUSE WITHOUT HIS MASTER'S
PERMISSION WILL RECEIVE ONE HUNDRED LASHES

Just at the entrance stood the hall-porter, dressed in a green uniform with a belt of cherry red. He was shelling peas into a silver basin. Over the doorway hung—of all things—a golden cage from which a spotted magpie greeted visitors.

As I was gaping at all this, I almost fell over backwards and broke a leg. There on the left as one entered, not far from the porter's cubbyhole, was a huge dog with a chain round its neck. It was painted on the wall and over it, in big capitals, was written:

BEWARE OF THE DOG

My colleagues laughed at me, but when I got my breath back I went to examine the whole wall. There was a mural of a slave market, price tags and all. Then Trimalchio himself, holding a wand of Mercury and being led into Rome by Minerva.[8] After this a picture of how he learned accounting and, finally how he became a steward. The painstaking artist had drawn it all in great detail with descriptions underneath. Just where the colonnade ended Mercury hauled him up by the chin and rushed him to a high platform. . . .

I began asking the porter what were the pictures they had in the middle.

5. Appropriately enough, Agamemnon's assistant in instruction. 6. A famous wine from Campania, south of Rome. 7. He claims they are pouring a libation. 8. Patron goddess of arts and skills (Athena in Greek). Mercury (Hermes in Greek), as a trickster, is the patron god of thieves and business.

"The *Iliad,* and *Odyssey,* and the gladiatorial show given by Laenas," he told me.

Time did not allow us to look at many things there . . . by now we had reached the dining-room. . . .

Finally we took our places. Boys from Alexandria poured iced water over our hands. Others followed them and attended to our feet, removing any hangnails with great skill. But they were not quiet even during this troublesome operation: they sang away at their work. I wanted to find out if the whole staff were singers, so I asked for a drink. In a flash a boy was there, singing in a shrill voice while he attended to me—and anyone else who was asked to bring something did the same. It was more like a musical comedy than a respectable dinner party.

Some extremely elegant hors d'oeuvre were served at this point—by now everyone had taken his place with the exception of Trimalchio, for whom, strangely enough, the place at the top was reserved. The dishes for the first course included an ass of Corinthian bronze with two panniers, white olives on one side and black on the other. Over the ass were two pieces of plate, with Trimalchio's name and the weight of the silver inscribed on the rims. There were some small iron frames shaped like bridges supporting dormice sprinkled with honey and poppy seed. There were steaming hot sausages too, on a silver gridiron with damsons and pomegranate seeds underneath.

We were in the middle of these elegant dishes when Trimalchio himself was carried in to the sound of music and set down on a pile of tightly stuffed cushions. The sight of him drew an astonished laugh from the guests. His cropped head stuck out from a scarlet coat; his neck was well muffled up and he had put round it a napkin with a broad purple stripe and tassels dangling here and there. On the little finger of his left hand he wore a heavy gilt ring and a smaller one on the last joint of the next finger. This I thought was solid gold, but actually it was studded with little iron stars. And to show off even more of his jewellery, he had his right arm bare and set off by a gold armlet and an ivory circlet fastened with a gleaming metal plate.

After picking his teeth with a silver toothpick, he began: "My friends, I wasn't keen to come into the dining room yet. But if I stayed away any more, I would have kept you back, so I've deprived myself of all my little pleasures for you. However, you'll allow me to finish my game."

A boy was at his heels with a board of terebinth wood[9] with glass squares, and I noticed the very last word in luxury—instead of white and black pieces he had gold and silver coins. While he was swearing away like a trooper over his game and we were still on the hors d'oeuvre, a tray was brought in with a basket on it. There sat a wooden hen, its wings spread round it the way hens are when they are broody. Two slaves hurried up and as the orchestra played a tune they began searching through the straw and dug out peahens' eggs, which they distributed to the guests.

Trimalchio turned to look at this little scene and said: "My friends, I gave orders for that bird to sit on some peahens' eggs. I hope to goodness they are not starting to hatch. However, let's try them and see if they are still soft."

We took up our spoons (weighing at least half a pound each) and cracked

9. A very hard wood that takes a high polish and is very expensive (like everything Trimalchio has).

the eggs, which were made of rich pastry. To tell the truth, I nearly threw away my share, as the chicken seemed already formed. But I heard a guest who was an old hand say: "There should be something good here." So I searched the shell with my fingers and found the plumpest little figpecker, all covered with yolk and seasoned with pepper.

At this point Trimalchio became tired of his game and demanded that all the previous dishes be brought to him. He gave permission in a loud voice for any of us to have another glass of mead if we wanted it. Suddenly there was a crash from the orchestra and a troop of waiters—still singing—snatched away the hors d'oeuvre. However in the confusion one of the side-dishes happened to fall and a slave picked it up from the floor. Trimalchio noticed this, had the boy's ears boxed and told him to throw it down again. A cleaner came in with a broom and began to sweep up the silver plate along with the rest of the rubbish. Two long-haired Ethiopians followed him, carrying small skin bottles like those they use for scattering sand in the circus, and they poured wine over our hands—no one ever offered us water.

Our host was complimented on these elegant arrangements. "You've got to fight fair," he replied. "That is why I gave orders for each guest to have his own table. At the same time these smelly slaves won't crowd so."

Carefully sealed wine bottles were immediately brought, their necks labelled:

FALERNIAN
CONSUL OPIMIUS[1]
ONE HUNDRED YEARS OLD

While we were examining the labels, Trimalchio clapped his hands and said with a sigh:

"Wine has a longer life than us poor folks. So let's wet our whistles. Wine is life. I'm giving you real Opimian. I didn't put out such good stuff yesterday, though the company was much better class."

Naturally we drank and missed no opportunity of admiring his elegant hospitality. In the middle of this a slave brought in a silver skeleton, put together in such a way that its joints and backbone could be pulled out and twisted in all directions. After he had flung it about on the table once or twice, its flexible joints falling into various postures, Trimalchio recited:

"Man's life alas! is but a span,
So let us live it while we can,
We'll be like this when dead."

After our applause the next course was brought in. Actually it was not as grand as we expected, but it was so novel that everyone stared. It was a deep circular tray with the twelve signs of the Zodiac arranged round the edge. . . .

After this course Trimalchio got up and went to the toilet. Free of his domineering presence, we began to strike up a general conversation. Dama[2] started off by calling for bigger glasses.

1. The wine was labeled with the name of the man who was consul in the year it was bottled. Opimius was consul in 121 B.C.; because it was in this year that the custom of dating the wine by the consul's name began, Trimalchio's wine was the oldest possible. If genuine, it would have been undrinkable. 2. One of Trimalchio's friends. Like those of Seleucus and Phileros, who join the conversation later, his name is Greek.

"The day's nothin'," he said, "It's night 'fore y'can turn around. So the best thing's get out of bed and go straight to dinner. Lovely cold weather we've had too. M'bath hardly thawed me out. Still, a hot drink's as good as an overcoat. I've been throwin' it back neat, and I'm pretty tight—the wine's gone to m'head."

This started Seleucus off.

"Me now," he said, "I don't have a bath every day. It's like gettin' rubbed with fuller's earth,[3] havin' a bath. The water bites into you, and as the days go by, your heart turns to water. But when I've knocked back a hot glass of wine and honey, kiss-my-arse I say to the cold weather. Mind you, I couldn't have a bath—I was at a funeral today. Poor old Chrysanthus has just given up the ghost—nice man he was! It was only the other day he stopped me in the street. I still seem to hear his voice. Dear, dear! We're just so many walking bags of wind. We're worse than flies—at least flies have got some strength in them, but we're no more than empty bubbles.

"And what would he have been like if he hadn't been on a diet? For five days he didn't take a drop of water or a crumb of bread into his mouth. But he's gone to join the majority. The doctors finished him—well, hard luck, more like. After all, a doctor is just to put your mind at rest. Still, he got a good sendoff—he had a bier and all beautifully draped. His mourners—several of his slaves were left their freedom—did him proud, even though his widow was a bit mean with her tears. Suppose now he hadn't been so good to her! But women as a sex are real vultures. It's no good doing them a favour, you might as well throw it down a well. An old passion is just an ulcer."

He was being a bore and Phileros said loudly:

"Let's think of the living. He's got what he deserved. He lived an honest life and he died an honest death. What has he got to complain about? He started out in life with just a penny and he was ready to pick up less than that from a muck-heap, if he had to use his teeth. He went up in the world. He got bigger and bigger till he got where you see, like a honeycomb. I honestly think he left a solid hundred thousand and he had the lot in hard cash. But I'll be honest about it—seeing I'm a bit of a cynic—he had a foul mouth and too much lip. He wasn't a man, he was just murder.

"Now his brother was a fine man, a real friend to his friends, always ready with a helping hand or a decent meal.

"Chrysanthus had bad luck at first, but the first vintage set him on his feet. He fixed his own price when he sold the wine. And what properly kept his head above water was a legacy he came in for, when he pocketed more than was left to him. And the blockhead, when he had a quarrel with his brother, cut him out of his will in favour of some sod we've never heard of. You're leaving a lot behind when you leave your own flesh and blood. But he took advice from his slaves and they really fixed him. It's never right to believe all you're told, especially for a business man. But it's true he enjoyed himself while he lived. You got it, you keep it. He was certainly Fortune's favourite—lead turned to gold in his hand. Mind you, it's easy when everything runs smoothly.

"And how old do you think he was? Seventy or more! But he was hard as

3. A strong solvent used by cleaners.

nails and carried his age well. His hair was black as a raven's wing. I knew the man for ages and ages and he was still an old lecher. I honestly don't think he left the dog alone. What's more, he liked little boys—he could turn his hand to anything. Well, I don't blame him—after all, he couldn't take anything else with him."

This was Phileros, then Ganymedes said:

"You're all talking about things that don't concern heaven or earth. Meanwhile, no one gives a damn the way we're hit by the corn situation. Honest to God, I couldn't get hold of a mouthful of bread today. And look how there's still no rain. It's been absolute starvation for a whole year now. To hell with the food officers! They're in with the bakers—'You be nice to me and I'll be nice to you.' So the little man suffers, while those grinders of the poor never stop celebrating. Oh, if only we still had the sort of men I found here when I first arrived from Asia. Like lions they were. That was the life! Come one, come all! If white flour was inferior to the very finest, they'd thrash those bogeymen till they thought God Almighty was after them.

"I remember Safinius—he used to live by the old arch then; I was a boy at the time. He wasn't a man, he was all pepper. He used to scorch the ground wherever he went. But he was dead straight—don't let him down and he wouldn't let you down. You'd be ready to play *morra*[4] with him in the dark. But on the city council, how he used to wade into some of them—no beating about the bush, straight from the shoulder! And when he was in court, his voice got louder and louder like a trumpet. He never sweated or spat—I think there was a touch of the old acid about him. And very affable he was when you met him, calling everyone by name just like one of us. Naturally at the time corn was dirt cheap. You could buy a penny loaf that two of you couldn't get through. Today—I've seen bigger bull's-eyes.

"Ah me! It's getting worse every day. This place is going down like a calf's tail. But why do we have a third-rate food officer who wouldn't lose a penny to save our lives? He sits at home laughing and rakes in more money a day than anyone else's whole fortune. I happen to know he's just made a thousand in gold. But if we had any balls at all, he wouldn't be feeling so pleased with himself. People today are lions at home and foxes outside.

"Take me, I've already sold the rags off my back for food and if this shortage continues, I'll be selling my bit of a house. What's going to happen to this place if neither god nor man will help us? As I hope to go home tonight, I'm sure all this is heaven's doing.

"Nobody believes in heaven, see, nobody fasts, nobody gives a damn for the Almighty. No, people only bow their heads to count their money. In the old days high-class ladies used to climb up the hill barefoot, their hair loose and their hearts pure, and ask God for rain. And he'd send it down in bucketfuls right away—it was then or never—and everyone went home like drowned rats. Since we've given up religion the gods nowadays keep their feet well wrapped up. The fields just lie . . ."

"Please, please," broke in Echion the rag merchant, "be a bit more cheerful. 'First it's one thing, then another,' as the yokel said when he lost his spotted pig. What we haven't got today, we'll have tomorrow. That's the way life goes. Believe me, you couldn't name a better country, if it had the people.

4. A game (still played in southern Italy) that requires the players to match the number of fingers held out by the opponent.

As things are, I admit, it's having a hard time, but it isn't the only place. We mustn't be soft. The sky don't get no nearer wherever you are. If you were somewhere else, you'd be talking about the pigs walking round ready roasted back here.

"And another thing, we'll be having a holiday with a three-day show that's the best ever—and not just a hack troupe of gladiators but freedmen for the most part. My old friend Titus has a big heart and a hot head. Maybe this, maybe that, but something at all events. I'm a close friend of his and he does nothing by halves. He'll give us cold steel, no quarter and the slaughterhouse right in the middle where all the stands can see it. And he's got the wherewithal—he was left thirty million when his poor father died. Even if he spent four hundred thousand, his pocket won't feel it and he'll go down in history. He's got some big brutes already, and a woman who fights in a chariot and Glyco's steward, who was caught having fun with his mistress. You'll see quite a quarrel in the crowd between jealous husbands and romantic lovers. But that half-pint Glyco threw his steward to the lions,[5] which is just giving himself away. How is it the servant's fault when he's forced into it? It's that old pisspot who really deserves to be tossed by a bull. But if you can't beat the ass you beat the saddle. But how did Glyco imagine the poisonous daughter of Hermogenes[6] would ever turn out well? The old man could cut the claws off a flying kite, and a snake don't hatch old rope. Glyco—well, Glyco's got his. He's branded for as long as he lives and only the grave will get rid ot it. But everyone pays for their mistakes.

"But I can almost smell the dinner Mammaea is going to give us[7]—two denarii apiece for me and the family. If he really does it, he'll make off with all Norbanus's votes, I tell you he'll win at a canter. After all, what good has Nobanus done us? He put on some half-pint gladiators, so done in already that they'd have dropped if you blew at them. I've seen animal-killers[8] fight better. As for the horsemen killed, he got them off a lamp[9]—they ran round like cocks in a backyard. One was just a carthorse, the other couldn't stand up, and the reserve was just one corpse instead of another—he was practically hamstrung. One boy did have a bit of spirit—he was in Thracian armour,[1] and even he didn't show any initiative. In fact, they were all flogged afterwards, there were so many shouts of 'Give 'em what for!' from the crowd. Pure yellow, that's all. 'Well, I've put on a show for you,' he says. 'And I'm clapping you,' says I. 'Reckon it up—I'm giving more than I got. So we're quits.'

"Hey, Agamemnon! I suppose you're saying 'What is that bore going on and on about?' It's because a good talker like you don't talk. You're a cut above us, and so you laugh at what us poor people say. We all know you're off your head with all that reading. But never mind! Some day I'll get you to come down to my place in the country and have a look at our little cottage. We'll find something to eat—a chicken, some eggs. It'll be nice, even though the unreliable weather this year has made off with everything. Anyway, we'll find enough to fill our bellies.

"And my kid is growing up to be a pupil of yours. He can divide by four

5. Glyco was permitted by law to punish his slave by forcing him to fight wild beasts in the arena. 6. Presumably Glyco's father-in-law. 7. A public banquet given by Mammaea as part of his electoral campaign. His rival, Norbanus, has been giving gladiatorial shows. 8. Professional fighters of wild animals, considered inferior to gladiators. 9. I.e., they were as small as the horsemen depicted on a lamp. 1. Light armor, such as that worn by soldiers from Thrace, a savage country northeast of Greece.

already. If God spares him, you'll have him ready to do anything for you. In his spare time, he won't take his head out of his exercise book. He's clever and there's good stuff in him, even if he is crazy about birds. Only yesterday I killed his three goldfinches and told him a weasel ate them. But he's found some other silly hobbies, and he's having a fine time painting. Still, he's already well ahead with his Greek, and he's starting to take to his Latin, though his tutor is too pleased with himself and unreliable—he just comes and goes. He knows his stuff but doesn't want to work. There is another one as well, not so clever but he is conscientious—he teaches the boy more than he knows himself. In fact, he makes a habit of coming around on holidays, and whatever you give him, he's happy.

"Anyway, I've just bought the boy some law books, as I want him to pick up some legal training for home use. There's a living in that sort of thing. He's done enough dabbling in poetry and such like. If he objects, I've decided he'll learn a trade—barber, auctioneer, or at least a barrister—something he can't lose till he dies. Well, yesterday I gave it to him straight: 'Believe me, my lad, any studying you do will be for your own good. You see Phileros the solicitor—if he hadn't studied, he'd be starving today. It's not so long since he was humping round loads on his back. Now he can even look Norbanus in the face. An education is an investment, and a proper profession never goes dead on you.' "

This was the sort of conversation flying round when Trimalchio came in, dabbed his forehead and washed his hands in perfume. There was a short pause, then he said:

"Excuse me, dear people, my inside has not been answering the call for several days now. The doctors are puzzled. But some pomegranate rind and resin in vinegar has done me good. But I hope now it will be back on its good behaviour. Otherwise my stomach rumbles like a bull. So if any of you wants to go out, there's no need for him to be embarrassed. None of us was born solid. I think there's nothing so tormenting as holding yourself in. This is the one thing even God Almighty can't object to. Yes, laugh, Fortunata,[2] but you generally keep me up all night with this sort of thing.

"Anyway, I don't object to people doing what suits them even in the middle of dinner—and the doctors forbid you to hold yourself in. Even if it's a longer business, everything is there just outside—water, bowls, and all the other little comforts. Believe me, if the wind goes to your brain it starts flooding your whole body too. I've known a lot of people die from this because they wouldn't be honest with themselves."

We thanked him for being so generous and considerate and promptly proceeded to bury our amusement in our glasses. Up to this point we'd not realized we were only in mid-stream, as you might say.

The orchestra played, the tables were cleared, and then three white pigs were brought into the dining-room, all decked out in muzzles and bells. The first, the master of ceremonies announced, was two years old, the second three, and the third six. I was under the impression that some acrobats were on their way in and the pigs were going to do some tricks, the way they do in street shows. But Trimalchio dispelled this impression by asking:

"Which of these would you like for the next course? Any clodhopper can

2. Trimalchio's wife.

do you a barnyard cock or a stew and trifles like that, but my cooks are used to boiling whole calves."

He immediately sent for the chef and without waiting for us to choose he told him to kill the oldest pig.

He then said to the man in a loud voice:

"Which division are you from?"

When he replied he was from number forty, Trimalchio asked:

"Were you bought or were you born here?"

"Neither," said the chef, "I was left to you in Pansa's will."

"Well, then," said Trimalchio, "see you serve it up carefully—otherwise I'll have you thrown into the messenger's division."

So the chef, duly reminded of his master's magnificence, went back to his kitchen, the next course leading the way.

Trimalchio looked around at us with a gentle smile: "If you don't like the wine, I'll have it changed. It is up to you to do it justice. I don't buy it, thank heaven. In fact, whatever wine really tickles your palate this evening, it comes from an estate of mine which as yet I haven't seen. It's said to join my estates at Tarracina and Tarentum. What I'd like to do now is add Sicily to my little bit of land, so that when I want to go to Africa, I could sail there without leaving my own property.

"But tell me, Agamemnon, what was your debate about today? Even though I don't go in for the law, still I've picked up enough education for home consumption. And don't you think I turn my nose up at studying, because I have two libraries, one Greek, one Latin. So tell us, just as a favour, what was the topic of your debate?"

Agamemnon was just beginning, "A poor man and a rich man were enemies . . ." when Trimalchio said: "What's a poor man?" "Oh, witty!" said Agamemnon, and then told us about some fictitious case or other. Like lightning Trimalchio said: "If this happened, it's not a fictitious case—if it didn't happen, then it's nothing at all."

We greeted this witticism and several more like it with the greatest enthusiasm.

"Tell me, my dear Agamemnon," continued Trimalchio, "do you remember the twelve labours of Hercules and the story of Ulysses—how the Cyclops tore out his thumb with a pair of pincers.[3] I used to read about them in Homer, when I was a boy. In fact, I actually saw the Sibyl at Cumae with my own eyes dangling in a bottle, and when the children asked her in Greek: 'What do you want, Sybil?' she used to answer: 'I want to die.' "

Summary Presents for the guests are distributed, with a slave announcing the nature of each gift and making in each case an atrocious pun on the name of the guest.

We laughed for ages. There were hundreds of things like this but they've slipped my mind now.

Ascyltus, with his usual lack of restraint, found everything extremely funny, lifting up his hands and laughing till the tears came. Eventually one

3. Trimalchio refers to Ulysses' (Odysseus's) adventures in the cave of the Cyclops (*Odyssey* 9); despite what he goes on to say, he has obviously not read Homer.

of Trimalchio's freedman[4] friends flared up at him—the one sitting above me, in fact.

"You with the sheep's eyes," he said, "what's so funny? Isn't our host elegant enough for you? You're better off, I suppose, and used to a bigger dinner. Holy guardian here preserve me! If I was sitting by him, I'd make him bleat! A fine pippin he is to be laughing at other people! Some fly-by-night from god knows where—not worth his own piss. In fact, if I pissed round him, he wouldn't know where to turn.

"By god, it takes a lot to make me boil, but if you're too soft, worms like this only come to the top. Look at him laughing! What's he got to laugh at? Did his father pay cash for him? You're a Roman knight,[5] are you? Well, my father was a king.

" *'Why are you only a freedman?'* did you say? Because I went into service voluntarily. I wanted to be a Roman citizen, not a subject with taxes to pay. And today, I hope no one can laugh at the way I live. I'm a man among men, and I walk with my head up. I don't owe anybody a penny—there's never been a court-order out for me. No one's said *'Pay up!'* to me in the street.

"I've bought a bit of land and some tiny pieces of plate. I've twenty bellies to feed, as well as a dog. I bought my old woman's freedom so nobody could wipe his dirty hands on *her* hair. Four thousand I paid for myself. I was elected to the Augustan College[6] and it cost me nothing. I hope when I die I won't have to blush in my coffin.

"But you now, you're such a busybody you don't look behind you. You see a louse on somebody else, but not the fleas on your own back. You're the only one who finds us funny. Look at the professor now—he's an older man than you and we get along with him. But you're still wet from your mother's milk and not up to your ABC yet. Just a crackpot—you're like a piece of wash-leather in soak, softer but no better! You're grander than us—well, have two dinners and two suppers! I'd rather have my good name than any amount of money. When all's said and done, who's ever asked me for money twice? For forty years I slaved but nobody ever knew if I was a slave or a free man. I came to this colony when I was a lad with long hair—the town-hall hadn't been built then. But I worked hard to please my master—there was a real gentleman, with more in his little finger-nail than there is in your whole body. And I had people in the house who tried to trip me up one way or another, but still—thanks be to his guardian spirit!—I kept my head above water. That's real success: being born free is as easy as all get-out. Now what are you gawping at, like a goat in a vetch field?"

At this remark, Giton, who was waiting on me, could not suppress his laughter and let out a filthy guffaw, which did not pass unnoticed by Ascyltus's opponent. He turned his abuse on the boy.

"So!" he said, "you're amused too, are you, you curly-headed onion? A merry Saturnalia[7] to you! Is it December, I'd like to know? When did *you* pay your liberation tax?[8] Look, he doesn't know what to do, the gallow's bird, the crow's meat.

4. A former slave who had bought his freedom. 5. A Roman class including all who had property above a certain amount. 6. The state religion was the worship of Augustus, the emperor; the office of priest might be sold or conferred. 7. A December festival in honor of an ancient Italian deity at which the normal order of everyday life was reversed and the slaves and children made fun of their masters. 8. As a freed slave he had to pay 5 percent of his value to the treasury.

"God's curse on you, and your master too, for not keeping you under control! As sure as I get my bellyful, it's only because of Trimalchio that I don't take it out of you here and now. He's a freedman like myself. We're doing all right, but those good-for-nothings, well—. It's easy to see, like master, like man. I can hardly hold myself back, and I'm not naturally hot-headed—but once I start, I don't give a penny for my own mother.

"All right! I'll see you when we get outside, you rat, you excrescence. I'll knock your master in the dirt before I'm an inch taller or shorter. And I won't let you off either, by heaven, even if you scream down God Almighty. Your cheap curls and your no-good master won't be much use to you then—I'll see to that. I'll get my teeth into you, all right. Either I'm much mistaken about myself or you won't be laughing at us behind your golden beard. Athena's curse on you and the man who first made you such a forward brat.

"I didn't learn no geometry or criticism and such silly rubbish, but I can read the letters on a notice board and I can do my percentages in metal, weights, and money. In fact, if you like, we'll have a bet. Come on, here's my cash. Now you'll see how your father wasted his money, even though you do know how to make a speech.

"Try this:

> Something we all have.
> Long I come, broad I come. What am I?

"I'll give you it: something we all have that runs and doesn't move from its place: something we all have that grows and gets smaller.[9]

"You're running round in circles, you've had enough, like the mouse in the pisspot. So either keep quiet or keep out of the way of your betters, they don't even know you're alive—unless you think I care about your box-wood rings that you swiped from your girl friend! Lord make me lucky! Let's go into town and borrow some money. You'll soon see they trust this iron one.

"Pah! a drownded fox makes a nice sight, I must say. As I hope to make my pile and die so famous that people swear by my dead body, I'll hound you to death. And he's a nice thing too—the one who taught you all these tricks—a muttonhead, not a master. We learned different. Our teacher used to say: 'Are your things in order? Go straight home. No looking around. And be polite to your elders.' Nowadays it's all an absolute muck-heap. They turn out nobody worth a penny. I'm like you see me and I thank God for the way I was learnt." . . .

In the middle of all this, a lictor[1] knocked at the double doors and a drunken guest entered wearing white, followed by a large crowd of people. I was terrified by this lordly apparition and thought it was the chief magistrate arriving. So I tried to rise and get my bare feet on the floor. Agamemnon laughed at this panic and said:

"Get hold of yourself, you silly fool. This is Habinnas—Augustan College and monumental mason."

Relieved by this information I resumed my position and watched Habinnas' entry with huge admiration. Being already drunk, he had his hands on

9. There is no agreement about the correct answer to these riddles. Suggested answers are, to the first, the foot; the second, the eye; the third, hair. 1. A magistrate's attendant.

his wife's shoulders; loaded with several garlands, oil pouring down his forehead and into his eyes, he settled himself into the place of honour and immediately demanded some wine and hot water. Trimalchio, delighted by these high spirits, demanded a larger cup for himself and asked how he had enjoyed it all.

"The only thing we missed," replied Habinnas, "was yourself—the apple of my eye was here. Still, it was damn good. Scissa was giving a ninth-day dinner[2] in honour of a poor slave of hers she'd freed on his death-bed. And I think she'll have a pretty penny to pay in liberation tax because they reckon he was worth fifty thousand. Still, it was pleasant enough, even if we did have to pour half our drinks over his wretched bones."

"Well," said Trimalchio, "what did you have for dinner?"

"I'll tell you if I can—I've such a good memory that I often forget my own name. For the first course we had a pig crowned with sausages and served with blood-puddings and very nicely done giblets, and of course beetroot and pure wholemeal bread—which I prefer to white myself: it's very strengthening and I don't regret it when I do my business. The next course was cold tart and a concoction of first-class Spanish wine poured over hot honey. I didn't eat anything at all of the actual tart, but I dived right into the honey. Scattered round were chickpeas, lupines, a choice of nuts and an apple apiece—though I took two. And look, I've got them tied up in a napkin, because if I don't take something in the way of a present to my youngster, I'll have a row on my hands.

"Oh, yes, my good lady reminds me. We had a hunk of bearmeat set before us, which Scintilla was foolish enough to try, and she practically spewed up her guts; but I ate more than a pound of it, as it tasted like real wild-boar. And I say if bears can eat us poor people, it's all the more reason why us poor people should eat bears.

"To finish up with, we had some cheese basted with new wine, snails all round, chitterlings, plates of liver, eggs in pastry hoods, turnips, mustard, and some filthy concoction—good riddance to that. There were pickled cumin seeds too, passed round in a bowl and some people were that bad-mannered they took three handfuls. You see, we sent the ham away.

"But tell me something, Gaius, now I ask—why isn't Fortunata at the table?"

"You know her," replied Trimalchio, "unless she's put the silver away and shared out the left-overs among the slaves, she won't put a drop of water to her mouth."

"All the same," retorted Habinnas, "unless she sits down, I'm shagging off."

And he was starting to get up, when at a given signal all the servants shouted *"Fortunata"* four or five times. So in she came with her skirt tucked up under a yellow sash to show her cerise petticoat underneath, as well as her twisted anklets and gold-embroidered slippers. Wiping her hands on a handkerchief which she carried round her neck, she took her place on the couch where Habbinas' wife was reclining. She kissed her. "Is it really you?" she said, clapping her hands together.

It soon got to the point where Fortunata took the bracelets from her great

2. On the last day of the mourning period.

fat arms and showed them to the admiring Scintilla. In the end she even undid her anklets and her gold hair net, which she said was pure gold. Trimalchio noticed this and had it all brought to him and commented:

"A woman's chains, you see. This is the way us poor fools get robbed. She must have six and a half pounds on her. Still, I've got a bracelet myself, made up from one-tenth per cent to Mercury[3]—and it weighs not an ounce less than ten pounds."

Finally, for fear he looked like a liar, he even had some scales brought in and had them passed round to test the weight.

Scintilla was no better. From round her neck she took a little gold locket, which she called her "lucky box." From it she extracted two earrings and in her turn gave them to Fortunata to look at.

"A present from my good husband," she said, "and no one has a finer set."

"Hey!" said Habinnas, "you cleaned me out to buy you a glass bean. Honestly, if I had a daughter, I'd cut her little ears off. If there weren't any women, everything would be dirt cheap. As it is, we've got to drink cold water and piss it out hot."

Meanwhile, the women giggled tipsily between themselves and kissed each other drunkenly, one crying up her merits as a housewife, the other crying about her husband's demerits and boy friends. While they had their heads together like this, Habinnas rose stealthily and taking Fortunata's feet, flung them up over the couch.

"Oh, oh!" she shrieked, as her underskirt wandered up over her knees. So she settled herself in Scintilla's lap and hid her disgusting red face in her handkerchief.

Then came an interval, after which Trimalchio called for dessert. . . .

Fortunata was now wanting to dance, and Scintilla was doing more clapping than talking, when Trimalchio said:

"Philargyrus—even though you are such a terrible fan of the Greens[4]—you have my permission to join us. And tell your dear Menophila to sit down as well."

Need I say more? We were almost thrown out of our places, so completely did the household fill the dining-room. I even noticed that the chef was actually given a place above me, and he was reeking of pickles and sauce. And he wasn't satisfied with just having a place, but he had to start straight off on an imitation of the tragedian Ephesus, and then challenge his master to bet against the Greens winning at the next races.

Trimalchio became expansive after this argument.

"My dear people," he said, "slaves are human beings too. They drink the same milk as anybody else, even though luck's been agin 'em. Still, if nothing happens to me, they'll have their taste of freedom soon. In fact, I'm setting them all free in my will. I'm giving Philargyrus a farm, what's more, and the woman he lives with. As for Cario, I'm leaving him a block of flats, his five per cent manumission tax, and a bed with all the trimmings. I'm making Fortunata my heir, and I want all my friends to look after her.

"The reason I'm telling everyone all this is so my household will love me now as much as if I was dead."

3. Trimalchio sets aside a percentage of his profits to offer to his patron deity. 4. One of the teams in the chariot races.

Everyone began thanking his lordship for his kindness, when he became very serious and had a copy of his will brought in. Amid the sobs of his household he read out the whole thing from beginning to end.

Then looking at Habinnas, he said:

"What have you to say, my dear old friend? Are you building my monument the way I told you? I particularly want you to keep a place at the foot of my statue and put a picture of my pup there, as well as paintings of wreaths, scent-bottles, and all the contests of Petraites,[5] and thanks to you I'll be able to live on after I'm dead. And another thing! See that it's a hundred feet facing the road and two hundred back into the field. I want all the various sorts of fruit round my ashes and lots and lots of vines. After all, it's a big mistake to have nice houses just for when you're alive and not worry about the one we have to live in for much longer. And that's why I want this written up before anything else:

THIS MONUMENT DOES NOT GO TO THE HEIR

"But I'll make sure in my will that I don't get done down once I'm dead. I'll put one of my freedmen in charge of my tomb to look after it and not let people run up and shit on my monument. I'd like you to put some ships there too, sailing under full canvas, and me sitting on a high platform in my robes of office, wearing five gold rings and pouring out a bagful of money for the people. You know I gave them all a dinner and two denarii apiece. Let's have in a banqueting hall as well, if you think it's a good idea, and show the whole town having a good time. Put up a statue of Fortunata on my right, holding a dove, and have her leading her little dog tied to her belt—and this dear little chap as well, and great big wine jars sealed up so the wine won't spill. And perhaps you could carve me a broken wine jar and boy crying over it. A clock in the middle, so that anybody who looks at the time, like it or not, has got to read my name. As for the inscription now, take a good look and see if this seems suitable enough:

HERE SLEEPS
GAIUS POMPEIUS TRIMALCHIO
MAECENATIANUS
ELECTED TO THE AUGUSTAN COLLEGE IN HIS ABSENCE
HE COULD HAVE BEEN ON EVERY BOARD IN ROME
BUT HE REFUSED
GOD-FEARING BRAVE AND TRUE
A SELF-MADE MAN
HE LEFT AN ESTATE OF 30,000,000
AND HE NEVER HEARD A PHILOSOPHER
FAREWELL
AND YOU FARE WELL, TRIMALCHIO."

Summary After a visit to the baths, where Encolpius and his friends make an unsuccessful attempt to escape, the dinner is resumed.

After this dish Trimalchio looked at the servants and said:

"Why haven't you had dinner yet? Off you go and let some others come on duty."

5. A popular gladiator.

Up came another squad and as the first set called out: "Good night, Gaius!" the new arrivals shouted: "Good evening, Gaius!"

This led to the first incident that damped the general high spirits. Not a bad-looking boy entered with the newcomers and Trimalchio jumped at him and began kissing him at some length. Fortunata, asserting her just and legal rights, began hurling insults at Trimalchio, calling him a low scum and a disgrace, who couldn't control his beastly desires. "You dirty dog!" she finally added.

Trimalchio took offence at this abuse and flung his glass into Fortunata's face. She screamed as though she'd lost an eye and put her trembling hands across her face. Scintilla was terrified too and hugged the quaking woman to her breast. An obliging slave pressed a little jug of cold water to her cheek, while Fortunata rested her head on it and began weeping. Trimalchio just said:

"Well, well, forgotten her chorus days, has she? She doesn't remember, but she was bought and sold, and I took her away from it all and made her as good as the next. Yet she puffs herself up like a frog and doesn't even spit for luck. Just a great hunk, not a woman. But those as are born over a shop don't dream of a house. May I never have a day's good luck again, if I don't teach that Cassandra in clogs some manners!

"There was I, not worth twopence, and I could have had ten million. And you know I'm not lying about it. Agatho, who ran a perfume shop for the lady next door, he took me on one side and said: 'You don't want to let your family die out, you know!' But me, trying to do the right thing and not wanting to look changeable, I cut my own throat.

"All right! I'll make you want to dig me up with your bare nails. Just so you'll know on the spot what you've done for yourself—Habinnas! I don't want you to put her statue on my tomb, so at least when I'm dead I won't have any more squabbles. And another thing! just to show I can get my own back—when I'm dead I don't want her to kiss me."

After this thunderbolt, Habinnas began asking him to calm down: "None of us are without faults," he said, "we're not gods, we're human!" Scintilla said the same, calling him Gaius, and she began asking him, in the name of his guardian spirit, to give in.

Trimalchio held back his tears no longer. "I ask you, Habinnas," he said, "as you hope to enjoy your bit of savings—if I did anything wrong, spit in my face. I kissed this very careful little fellow, not for his pretty face, but because he's careful with money—he says his ten times table, he reads a book at sight, he's got himself some Thracian kit out of his daily allowance, and he's bought himself an easy chair and two cups out of his own pocket. Doesn't he deserve to be the apple of my eye? But Fortunata won't have it.

"Is that the way you feel, high heels? I'll give you a piece of advice: don't let your good luck turn your head, you kite, and don't make me show my teeth, my little darling—otherwise you'll feel my temper. You know me: once I've decided on something, it's fixed with a twelve-inch nail.

"But to come back to earth—I want you to enjoy yourselves, my dear people. After all, I was once like you are, but being the right sort, I got where I am. It's the old headpiece that makes a man, the rest is all rubbish. 'Buy right—sell right!'—that's me! Different people will give you a different line. I'm just on top of the world, I'm that lucky.

"But you, you snoring thing, are you still moaning? I'll give you something to moan about in a minute.

"However, as I'd started to say, it was my shrewd way with money that got me to my present position. I came from Asia as big as this candlestick. In fact, every day I used to measure myself against it, and to get some whiskers round my beak quicker, I used to oil my lips from the lamp. Still, for fourteen years I was the old boy's fancy. And there's nothing wrong if the boss wants it. But I did all right by the old girl too. You know what I mean—I don't say anything because I'm not the boasting sort.

"Well, as heaven will have it, I became boss in the house, and the old boy, you see, couldn't think of anything but me. That's about it—he made me co-heir with the Emperor[6] and I got a senator's fortune. But nobody gets enough, never. I wanted to go into business. Not to make a long story of it, I built five ships, I loaded them with wine—it was absolute gold at the time—and I sent them to Rome. You'd have thought I ordered it—every single ship was wrecked. That's fact, not fable! In one single day Neptune swallowed up thirty million. Do you think I gave up? This loss honestly wasn't more than a flea-bite to me—it was as if nothing had happened. I built more boats, bigger and better and luckier, so nobody could say I wasn't a man of courage. You know, the greater the ship, the greater the confidence. I loaded them again—with wine, bacon, beans, perfumes and slaves. At this point Fortunata did the decent thing, because she sold off all her gold trinkets, all her clothes, and put ten thousand in gold pieces in my hand. This was the yeast my fortune needed to rise. What heaven wants, soon happens. In one voyage I carved out a round ten million. I immediately bought back all my old master's estates. I built a house, I invested in slaves, and I bought up the horse trade. Whatever I touched grew like a honeycomb. Once I had more than the whole country, then down tools! I retired from business and began advancing loans through freedmen.

"Actually I was tired of trading on my own account, but it was an astrologer who convinced me. He happened to come to our colony, a sort of Greek, Serapa by name, and he could have told heaven itself what to do. He even told me things I'd forgotten. He went through everything for me from A to Z. He knew me inside out—the only thing he didn't tell me was what I ate for dinner the day before. You'd have thought he'd never left my side.

"Wasn't there that thing, Habinnas?—I think you were there: 'You got your lady wife out of those *certain circumstances*. You are not lucky in your friends. Nobody thanks you enough for your trouble. You have large estates. You are nursing a viper in your bosom.'

"And he said—though I shouldn't tell you—I have thirty years, four months, two days to live. What's more, I shall soon receive a legacy. My horoscope tells me this. If I'm allowed to join my estates to Apulia,[7] I'll have lived enough.

"Meantime, under the protection of Mercury, I built this house. As you know, it was still a shack, now it's a shrine. It has four dining-rooms, twenty bedrooms, two marble colonnades, a row of boxrooms up above, a bedroom where I sleep myself, a nest for this viper, and a really good lodge for the

6. An honor that Trimalchio shared with many others, for it was customary (as a prudent measure, to avoid confiscation on some pretext or other) to include a bequest to the emperor in one's will. 7. The south-eastern extremity of Italy.

porter. The guest apartment takes a hundred guests. In fact, when Scaurus[8] came here, he didn't want to stay anywhere else, even though he's got his father's guest house down by the sea. And there are a lot of other things I'll show you in a second.

"Believe me: have a penny, and you're worth a penny. You got something, you'll be thought something. Like your old friend—first a frog, now a king.

"Meantime, Stichus, bring out the shroud and the things I want to be buried in. Bring some cosmetic cream too, and a sample from that jar of wine I want my bones washed in."

Stichus did not delay over it, but brought his white shroud and his formal dress into the dining-room. . . . Trimalchio told us to examine them and see if they were made of good wool. Then he said with a smile:

"Now you, Stichus, see no mice or moths get at those—otherwise I'll burn you alive. I want to be buried in style, so the whole town will pray for my rest."

He opened a bottle of nard on the spot, rubbed some on all of us and said:

"I hope this'll be as nice when I'm dead as when I'm alive." The wine he had poured into a big decanter and he said:

"I want you to think you've been invited to my wake."

The thing was becoming absolutely sickening, when Trimalchio, showing the effects of his disgusting drunkenness, had a fresh entertainment brought into the dining-room, some cornet players. Propped up on a lot of cushions, he stretched out along the edge of the couch and said: "Pretend I'm dead and say something nice."

The cornet players struck up a dead march. One man in particular, the slave of his undertaker (who was the most respectable person present) blew so loudly that he roused the neighbourhood. As a result, the fire brigade, thinking Trimalchio's house was on fire, suddenly broke down the front door and began kicking up their own sort of din with their water and axes.

Seizing this perfect chance, we gave Agamemnon the slip and escaped as rapidly as if there really were a fire.

8. Unidentified. The name is aristocratic, but it may be a reference to a well-known manufacturer of fish sauce from Pompeii.

A Note on Translation

Reading literature in translation is a pleasure on which it is fruitless to frown. The purist may insist that we ought always read in the original languages, and we know ideally that this is true. But it is a counsel of perfection, quite impractical even for the purist, since no one in a lifetime can master all the languages whose literatures it would be a joy to explore. Master languages as fast as we may, we shall always have to read to some extent in translation, and this means we must be alert to what we are about: if in reading a work of literature in translation we are not reading the "original," what precisely are we reading? This is a question of great complexity, to which justice cannot be done in a brief note, but the following sketch of some of the considerations may be helpful.

One of the memorable scenes of ancient literature is the meeting of Hector and Andromache in Book VI of Homer's *Iliad*. Hector, leader and mainstay of the armies defending Troy, is implored by his wife Andromache to withdraw within the city walls and carry on the defense from there, where his life will not be con stantly at hazard. In Homer's text her opening words to him are these: *δαιμόνιε, φθίσει σε τὸ σὸν μένος* (daimonie, phthisei se to son menos). How should they be translated into English?

Here is how they have actually been translated into English by capable translators, at various periods, in verse and prose:

1. George Chapman, 1598:

> O noblest in desire,
> Thy mind, inflamed with others' good, will set thy self on fire.

2. John Dryden, 1693:

> Thy dauntless heart (which I foresee too late),
> Too daring man, will urge thee to thy fate.

3. Alexander Pope, 1715:

> Too daring Prince! . . .
> For sure such courage length of life denies,
> And thou must fall, thy virtue's sacrifice.

4. William Cowper, 1791:

> Thy own great courage will cut short thy days,
> My noble Hector. . .

5. Lang, Leaf, and Myers, 1883 (prose):

> Dear my lord, this thy hardihood will undo thee. . . .

6. A. T. Murray, 1924 (prose):

> Ah, my husband, this prowess of thine will be thy doom. . . .

7. E. V. Rieu, 1950 (prose):

"Hector," she said, "you are possessed. This bravery of yours will be your end."

8. I. A. Richards, 1950 (prose):

"Strange man," she said, "your courage will be your destruction."

9. Richmond Lattimore, 1951:

Dearest,
Your own great strength will be your death. . . .

10. Robert Fitzgerald, 1979:

O my wild one, your bravery will be
Your own undoing!

11. Robert Fagles, 1990:

reckless one,
Your own fiery courage will destroy you!

From these strikingly different renderings of the same six words, certain facts about the nature of translation begin to emerge. We notice, for one thing, that Homer's word *μένος* (menos) is diversified by the translators into "mind," "dauntless heart," "such courage," "great courage," "hardihood," "prowess," "bravery," "courage," "great strength," "bravery," and "fiery courage." The word has in fact all these possibilities. Used of things, it normally means "force"; of animals, "fierceness" or "brute strength" or (in the case of horses) "mettle"; of men and women, "passion" or "spirit" or even "purpose." Homer's application of it in the present case points our attention equally—whatever particular sense we may imagine Andromache to have uppermost—to Hector's force, strength, fierceness in battle, spirited heart and mind. But since English has no matching term of like inclusiveness, the passage as the translators give it to us reflects this lack and we find one attribute singled out to the exclusion of the rest.

Here then is the first and most crucial fact about any work of literature read in translation. It cannot escape the linguistic characteristics of the language into which it is turned: the grammatical, syntactical, lexical, and phonetic boundaries that constitute collectively the individuality or "genius" of that language. A Greek play or a Russian novel in English will be governed first of all by the resources of the English language, resources that are certain to be in every instance very different, as the efforts with *μένος* show, from those of the original.

Turning from *μένος* to *δαιμόνιε* (daimonie) in Homer's clause, we encounter a second crucial fact about translations. Nobody knows exactly what shade of meaning *δαιμόνιε* had for Homer. In later writers the word normally suggests divinity, something miraculous, wondrous; but in Homer it appears as a vocative of address for both chieftain and commoner, man and wife. The coloring one gives it must therefore be determined either by the way one thinks a Greek wife of Homer's era might actually address her husband (a subject on which we have no information whatever) or in the way one thinks it suitable for a hero's wife to address her husband in an epic poem, that is to say, a highly stylized and formal work. In general, the translators of our century will be seen to have abandoned formality to stress the intimacy; the wifeliness; and, especially in Lattimore's case, a certain chiding tenderness, in Andromache's appeal: (6) "Ah, my husband," (7) "Hector" (with perhaps a hint, in "you are possessed," of the alarmed distaste with which wives have so often viewed their husbands' bellicose moods), (8) "Strange man," (9) "Dearest," (10) "O my wild one" (mixing an almost motherly admiration with reproach and concern), and (11) "reckless one." On the other hand, the older translators have obviously removed Andromache to an epic or heroic distance from her beloved, whence she sees and kindles to his selfless courage, acknowledging, even in the moment of pleading with him to be otherwise, his moral grandeur and the tragic destiny this too certainly implies: (1) "O noblest in desire, . . . inflamed by others' good"; (2) "Thy dauntless heart (which I foresee too late), / Too daring man"; (3) "Too daring Prince! . . . / And thou must fall, thy virtue's sacrifice"; (4) "My noble Hector." Even the less specific "Dear my lord" of Lang, Leaf, and Myers looks in the same direction because of its echo of the speech of countless Shakespearean men and women who have shared this powerful moral sense: "Dear my lord, make me acquainted with your cause of grief"; "Perseverance, dear my lord, keeps honor bright"; etc.

The fact about translation that emerges from all this is that just as the translated work reflects the individuality of the language it is turned into, so it reflects the individuality of the age in which it is made, and the age will permeate it everywhere like yeast in dough. We think of one kind of permeation when we think of the governing verse forms and attitudes toward verse at a given epoch. In Chapman's time, experiments seeking an "heroic" verse form for English were widespread, and accordingly he tries a "fourteener" couplet (two rhymed lines of seven stresses each) in his *Iliad* and a pentameter couplet in his *Odyssey*. When Dryden and Pope wrote, a closed pentameter couplet had become established as the heroic form par excellence. By Cowper's day, thanks largely to the prestige of *Paradise Lost,* the couplet had gone out of fashion for narrative poetry in favor of blank verse. Our age, inclining to prose and in verse to proselike informalities and relaxations, has, predictably, produced half a dozen excellent prose translations of the *Iliad* but only three in verse (by Fagles, Lattimore, and Fitzgerald), all relying on rhythms that are much of the time closer to the verse of William Carlos Williams and some of the prose of novelists like Faulkner than to the swift firm tread of Homer's Greek. For if it is true that what we translate from a given work is what, wearing the spectacles of our time, we see in it, it is also true that we see in it what we have the power to translate.

Of course, there are other effects of the translator's epoch on a translation besides those exercised by contemporary taste in verse and verse forms. Chapman writes in a great age of poetic metaphor and, therefore, almost instinctively translates his understanding of Homer's verb *φθίσει* (phthisei, "to cause to wane, consume, waste, pine") into metaphorical terms of flame, presenting his Hector to us as a man of burning generosity who will be consumed by his very ardor. This is a conception rooted in large part in the psychology of the Elizabethans, who had the habit of speaking of the soul as "fire," of one of the four temperaments as "fiery," of even the more material bodily processes, like digestion, as if they were carried on by the heat of fire ("concoction," "decoction"). It is rooted too in that characteristic Renaissance élan so unforgettably expressed in characters such as Tamburlaine and Dr. Faustus, the former of whom exclaims to the stars above:

> . . . I, the chiefest lamp of all the earth,
> First rising in the East with mild aspect,
> But fixèd now in the meridian line,
> Will send up fire to your turning spheres,
> And cause the sun to borrow light of you. . . .

Pope and Dryden, by contrast, write to audiences for whom strong metaphor has become suspect. They therefore reject the fire image (which we must recall is not present in the Greek) in favor of a form of speech more congenial to their age, the *sententia* or aphorism, and give it extra vitality by making it the scene of a miniature drama: in Dryden's case, the hero's dauntless heart "urges" him (in the double sense of physical as well as moral pressure) to his fate; in Pope's, the hero's courage, like a judge, "denies" continuance of life, with the consequence that he "falls"—and here Pope's second line suggests analogy to the sacrificial animal—the victim of his own essential nature, of what he is.

To pose even more graphically the pressures that a translator's period brings, consider the following lines from Hector's reply to Andromache's appeal that he withdraw, first in Chapman's Elizabethan version, then in Lattimore's twentieth-century one:

Chapman, 1598:

> The spirit I did first breathe
> Did never teach me that—much less since the contempt of death
> Was settled in me, and my mind knew what a Worthy was,
> Whose office is to lead in fight and give no danger pass
> Without improvement. In this fire must Hector's trial shine.
> Here must his country, father, friends be in him made divine.

Lattimore, 1951:

> and the spirit will not let me, since I have learned to be valiant
> and to fight always among the foremost ranks of the Trojans,
> winning for my own self great glory, and for my father.

If one may exaggerate to make a necessary point, the world of Henry V and Othello suddenly gives way here to our own, a world whose discomfort with any form of heroic self-assertion is remarkably mirrored in the burial of Homer's key terms (*spirit, valiant, fight, foremost, glory*)—five out of twenty-two words in the original, five out of thirty-six in the translation—in a cushioning huddle of harmless sounds.

Besides the two factors so far mentioned (language and period) as affecting the character of a translation, there is inevitably a third—the translator, with a particular degree of talent; a personal way of regarding the work to be translated; a special hierarchy of values, moral, aesthetic, metaphysical (which may or may not be summed up in a "worldview"); and a unique style or lack of it. But this influence all readers are likely to bear in mind, and it needs no laboring here. That, for example, two translators of Hamlet, one a Freudian, the other a Jungian, will produce impressively different translations is obvious from the fact that when Freudian and Jungian argue about the play in English they often seem to have different plays in mind.

We can now return to the question from which we started. After all allowances have been made for language, age, and individual translator, is anything of the original left? What, in short, does the reader of translations read? Let it be said at once that in utility prose—prose whose function is mainly referential—the reader who reads a translation reads everything that matters. "Nicht Rauchen," "Défense de Fumer," and "No Smoking," posted in a railway car, make their point, and the differences between them in sound and form have no significance for us in that context. Since the prose of a treatise and of most fiction is preponderantly referential, we rightly feel, when we have paid close attention to Cervantes or Montaigne or Machiavelli or Tolstoy in a good English translation, that we have had roughly the same experience as a native Spaniard, Frenchman, Italian, or Russian. But *roughly* is the correct word; for good prose points iconically *to* itself as well as referentially beyond itself, and everything that it points to in itself in the original (rhythms, sounds, idioms, wordplay, etc.) must alter radically in being translated. The best analogy is to imagine a Van Gogh painting reproduced in the medium of tempera, etching, or engraving: the "picture" remains, but the intricate interanimation of volumes with colorings with brushstrokes has disappeared.

When we move on to poetry, even in its longer narrative and dramatic forms—plays like *Oedipus,* poems like the *Iliad* or the *Divine Comedy*—our situation as English readers worsens appreciably, as the many unlike versions of Andromache's appeal to Hector make very clear. But, again, only appreciably. True, this is the point at which the fact that a translation is *always* an interpretation explodes irresistibly on our attention; but if it is the best translation of its time, like John Ciardi's translation of the *Divine Comedy* for our time, the result will be not only a sensitive interpretation but also a work with intrinsic interest in its own right—at very best, a true work of art, a new poem. In these longer works, moreover, even if the translation is uninspired, many distinctive structural features—plot, setting, characters, meetings, partings, confrontations, and specific episodes generally—survive virtually unchanged. Hence even in translation it remains both possible and instructive to compare, say, concepts of the heroic or attitudes toward women or uses of religious ritual among civilizations as various as those reflected in the *Iliad,* the *Mahābhārata, Beowulf,* and the epic of *Son-Jara.* It is only when the shorter, primarily lyrical forms of poetry are presented that the reader of translations faces insuperable disadvantage. In these forms, the referential aspect of language has a tendency to disappear into, or, more often, draw its real meaning and accreditation from, the iconic aspect. Let us look for just a moment at a brief poem by Federico García Lorca and its English translation (by Stephen Spender and J. L. Gili):

¡Alto pinar!
Cuatro palomas por el aire van.

Cuatro palomas
vuelan y tornan.
Llevan heridas
sus cuatro sombras.

¡Bajo pinar!
Cuatro palomas en la tierra están.

Above the pine trees:
Four pigeons go through the air.

Four pigeons
fly and turn round.
They carry wounded
their four shadows.

Below the pine trees:
Four pigeons lie on the earth.

In this translation the referential sense of the English words follows with remarkable exactness the referential sense of the Spanish words they replace. But the life of Lorca's poem does not lie in that sense. It lies in such matters as the abruptness, like an intake of breath at a sudden revelation, of the two exclamatory lines (1 and 7), which then exhale musically in images of flight and death; or as the echoings of *palomas* in *heridas* and *sombras,* bringing together (as in fact the hunter's gun has done) these unrelated nouns and the unrelated experiences they stand for in a sequence that seems, momentarily, to have all the logic of a tragic action, in which *doves* become *wounds* become *shadows,* or as the external and internal rhyming among the five verbs, as though all motion must (as in fact it must) end with *están.*

Since none of this can be brought over into another tongue (least of all Lorca's rhythms), the translator must decide between leaving a reader to wonder why Lorca is a poet to be bothered about at all and making a new but true poem, whose merit will almost certainly be in inverse ratio to its likeness to the original. Samuel Johnson made such a poem in translating Horace's famous *Diffugere nives,* and so did A. E. Housman. If we juxtapose the last two stanzas of each translation, and the corresponding Latin, we can see at a glance that each has the consistency and inner life of a genuine poem and that neither of them (even if we consider only what is obvious to the eye, the line-lengths) is very close to Horace:

Cum semel occideris, et de te splendida Minos
fecerit arbitria,

non, Torquate, genus, non te facundia, non te
restituet pietas.

Infernis neque enim tenebris Diana pudicum
liberat Hippolytum
nec Lethaea valet Theseus abrumpere caro
vincula Pirithoo.

Johnson:

Not you, Torquatus, boast of Rome,
When Minos once has fixed your doom,
Or eloquence, or splendid birth,
Or virtue, shall restore to earth.
Hippolytus, unjustly slain,
Diana calls to life in vain;
Nor can the might of Theseus rend
The chains of hell that hold his friend.

Housman:

When thou descendest once the shades among,
The stern assize and equal judgment o'er,
Not thy long lineage nor thy golden tongue,
No, nor thy righteousness, shall friend thee more.

Night holds Hippolytus the pure of stain,
Diana steads him nothing, he must stay;
And Theseus leaves Pirithous in the chain
The love of comrades cannot take away.

The truth of the matter is that when the translator of short poems chooses to be literal, most or all of the poetry is lost; and when the translator succeeds in forging a new poetry, most or all of the original author is lost. Since there is no way out of this dilemma, we have always been sparing, in this anthology, in our use of short poems in translation.

In this Expanded Edition, we have adjusted our policy to take account of the two great non-Western literatures in which the short lyric or "song" has been the principal and by far most cherished expression of the national genius. During much of its history from earliest times, the Japanese imagination has cheerfully exercised itself, with all the delicacy and grace of an Olympic figure skater, inside a rigorous verse pattern of five lines and thirty-one syllables: the *tanka.* Chinese poetry, while somewhat more liberal to itself in line length, has been equally fertile in the fine art of compression and has only occasionally, even in its earliest, most experimental phase, indulged in verse lines of more than seven characters, often just four, or in poems of more than fifty lines, usually fewer than twenty. What makes the Chinese and Japanese lyric more difficult than most other lyrics to translate satisfactorily into English is that these compressions combine with a flexibility of syntax (Japanese) or a degree of freedom from it (Chinese) not available in our language. They also combine with a poetic sensibility that shrinks from exposition in favor of sequences and juxtapositions of images: images grasped and recorded in, or *as if in,* a moment of pure perception unencumbered by the explanatory linkages, background scenarios, and other forms of contextualization that the Western mind is instinctively driven to establish.

Whole books, almost whole libraries, have been written recently on the contrast of East and West in worldviews and value systems as well as on the need of each for the other if there is ever to be a community of understanding adequate to the realities both face. Put baldly, much too simply, and without the many exceptions and qualifications that rightly spring to mind, it may be said that a central and characteristic Western impulse, from the Greeks on down, has been to see the world around us as something to be *acted on:* weighed, measured, managed, used, even (when economic interests prevail over all others) fouled. Likewise, put oversimply, it may be said that a central and characteristic Eastern counterpart to this over many centuries (witness Taoism, Buddhism, and Hinduism, among others) has been to see that same world as something to be *received*: contemplated, touched, tasted, smelled, heard, and most especially, immersed in until observer and observed are one. To paint a bamboo, a stone, a butterfly, a person—so runs a classical Chinese admonition for painters—you must *become* that bamboo, that stone, that butterfly, that person, then paint from the inside. No one need be ashamed of being poor, says Confucius, putting a similar emphasis on *receiving* experience, "only of not being cultivated in the perception of beauty."

The problem that these differences in linguistic freedom and philosophical outlook pose for the English translator of classical Chinese and Japanese poetry may be glimpsed, even if not fully grasped, by considering for a moment in some detail a typical Japanese *tanka* (*Kokinshu,* 9) and a typical Chinese "song" (*Book of Songs,* 23). In its own language but transliterated in the Latin alphabet of the West, the *tanka* looks like this:

kasumi tachi
ko no me mo haru no
yuki fureba
hana naki sato mo
hana zo chirikeru

In a literal word-by-word translation (so far as this is possible in Japanese, since the language uses many particles without English equivalents and without dictionary meaning in modifying and qualifying functions—for example, *no, mo,* and *no* in line 2), the poem looks like this:

haze rises
tree-buds swell
when snow falls
village(s) without flower(s)
flower(s) fall(s)

The three best-known English renderings of this *tanka* look like this:

1. Helen Craig McCullough:

When snow comes in spring—
fair season of layered haze
and burgeoning buds—
flowers fall in villages
where flowers have yet to bloom.

2. Laurel Rasplica Rodd and Mary Catherine Henkenius:

When the warm mists veil
all the buds swell while yet the
spring snows drift downward
even in the hibernal
village crystal blossoms fall.

3. Robert H. Brower and Earl Miner:

With the spreading mists
The tree buds swell in early spring
And wet snow petals fall—

So even my flowerless country village
Already lies beneath its fallen flowers.

The reader will notice at once how much the three translators have felt it desirable or necessary to add, alter, rearrange, and explain. In McCullough's version the time of year is affirmed twice, both as "spring" and as "fair season of . . . haze"; the haze is now "layered"; the five coordinate perceptions of the original (haze, swelling buds, a snowfall, villages without flowers, flowers drifting down) have been structured into a single sentence with one main verb and two subordinate clauses spelling out "when" and "where"; and the original poem's climax, in a scene of drifting petallike snowflakes, has been shifted to a bleak scenery of absence: "flowers have yet to bloom." The final stress, in other words, is not on the fulfilled moment in which snow flowers replace the cherry blossoms, but on the cherry blossoms not yet arrived.

Similar additions and explanations occur in Rodd and Henkenius's version. This time the mist is "warm" and "veil[s] all" to clarify its connection with "buds." Though implicit already in "warm" and "burgeoning," spring is invoked again in "spring snows," and the snows are given confirmation in the following line by the insistently Latinate "hibernal," chosen, we may reasonably guess, along with "veil," "all," "swell," "while," "crystal," and "fall" to replace some of the chiming internal rhyme in the Japanese: *ko, no, mo, no, sato, mo, zo.* To leave no *i* undotted, "crystal" is imported to assure us that the falling "blossoms" of line 5 are really snowflakes, and the scene of flowerlessness that in the original (line 4) accounts for a special joy in the "flowering" of the snowflakes (line 5) vanishes without trace.

Brower and Miner's also fills in the causative links between "spreading mists" and swelling buds; makes sure that we do not fail to see the falling snow in flower terms ("wet snow petals"), thus losing, alas, the element of surprise, even magic, in the transformation of snowflakes into flowers that the original poem holds in store in its last two lines; and tells us (somewhat redundantly) that villages are a "country" phenomenon and (somewhat surprisingly) that this one is the speaker's home. In this version, as in the original and Rodd and Henkenius's, the poem closes with the snow scene, but here it is a one-time affair and "already" complete (lines 4 and 5), not a recurrent phenomenon that may appear under certain conditions anywhere at any time.

Some of the differences in these translations arise inevitably from different tradeoffs, as in the first version, where the final vision of falling snow blossoms is let go presumably to achieve the lovely lilting echo and rhetorical turn of "flowers fall in villages / where flowers have yet to bloom." Or as in Rodd and Henkenius's version, where preoccupations with internal rhyme have obviously influenced word choices, not always for the better. Or as in all three versions, where different efforts to remind the reader of the wordplay on *haru* (in the Japanese poem both a noun meaning "spring" and a verb meaning "swell") have had dissimilar but perhaps equally indifferent results. Meantime, the immense force compacted into that small word in the original as both noun and verb, season of springtime and principal of growth, cause and effect (and thus in a sense the whole mighty process of earth's renewal, in which an interruption by snow only foretells a greater loveliness to come) fizzles away unfelt. A few differences do seem to arise from insufficient command of the nerves and sinews of English poetry, but most spring from the staggering difficulties of responding in any uniform way to the minimal clues proffered by the original text. The five perceptions—haze, buds, snowfall, flowerless villages, flowers falling—do not as they stand in the Japanese or any literal translation quite compose for readers accustomed to Western poetic traditions an adequate poetic whole. This is plainly seen in the irresistible urge each of the translators has felt to catch up the individual perceptions, as English tends to require, in a tighter overall grammatical and syntactical structure than the original insists on. In this way they provide a clarifying network of principal and subordinate, time when, place where, and cause why. Yet the inevitable result is a disassembling, a spinning out, spelling out, thinning out of what in the Japanese is an as yet unraveled imagistic excitement, creating (or memorializing) in the poet's mind, and then in the mind of the Japanese readers, the original thrill of consciousness when these images, complete with the magical transformation of snow into the longed-for cherry blossoms, first flashed on the inward eye.

What is comforting for us who must read this and other Japanese poems in translation is that each of the versions given here retains in some form or other all or most of the five images intact. What is less comforting is that the simplicity and suddenness, the explosion in the mind, have been diffused and defused.

When we turn to the Chinese song, we find similarly contesting forces at work. In one respect, the Chinese language comes over into English more readily than Japanese, being like English comparatively uninflected and heavily dependent on word order for its meanings. But in other respects, since Chinese like Japanese lacks distinctions of gender, of singular and plural, of *a* and *the,* and in the classical mode in which the poems in this anthology are composed, also of tenses, the pressure of the English translator to rearrange, straighten out, and fill in to "make sense" for his or her readers remains strong.

Let us examine song no. 23 of the *Shijing*. In its own Chinese characters, it looks like this:

野有死麕

野有死麕。白茅
包之。有女懷春。
吉士誘之。
林有樸樕。野有
死鹿。白茅純束。
有女如玉。
舒而脫脫兮。無
感我帨兮。無使
尨也吠。

Eleven lines in all, each line having four characters as its norm, the poem seemingly takes shape around an implicit parallel between a doe in the forest, possibly killed by stealth and hidden under long grass or rushes (though on this point as on all others the poem refuses to take us wholly into confidence), and a young girl possibly "ruined" (as she certainly would have been in the post-Confucian society in which the *Shijing* was prized and circulated, though here again the poem keeps its own counsel) by loss of her virginity before marriage.

In its bare bones, with each character given an approximate English equivalent, a translation might look like this:

wild(s)	is	dead	deer
white	grass(es)	wrap/cover	(it).
is	girl	feel	spring.
fine	man	tempt	(her).
woods	is(are)	bush(es),	underbrush.
wild(s)	is	dead	deer.
white	grass(es)	bind	bundle.
is	girl	like	jade.
slow	——	slow	slow.
not	move	my	sash.
not	cause	dog	bark.

Lines 1 to 4, it seems plain, propose the parallel of slain doe and girl, whatever that parallel may be intended to mean. Lines 5 to 8 restate the parallel, adding that the girl is as beautiful as jade and (apparently) that the doe lies where the "wild" gives way to smaller growth. If we allow ourselves to account for the repetition (here again is a Western mind-set in search of explanatory clues) by supposing that lines 1 to 4 signal at some subliminal level the initiation of the seduction and lines 5 to 8, again subliminally, its progress or possibly its completion, lines 9 to 11 fall easily into place as a miniature drama enacting in direct speech the man's advances and the girl's gradually crumbling resistance. They also imply, it seems, that the seduction takes place not in the forest, as we might have been led to suppose by lines 1 to 8, but in a dwelling with a vigilant guard dog.

Interpreted just far enough to accommodate English syntax, the poem reads as follows:

1. Wai-lim Yip:

> In the wilds, a dead doe.
> White reeds to wrap it.
> A girl, spring-touched.
> A fine man to seduce her.
> In the woods, bushes.
> In the wilds, a dead deer.
> White reeds in bundles.
> A girl like jade.
> Slowly. Take it easy.
> Don't feel my sash!
> Don't make the dog bark!

Interpreted a stage further in a format some have thought better suited to English poetic traditions, the poem reads:

2. Arthur Waley:

> In the wilds there is a dead doe,
> With white rushes we cover her.
> There was a lady longing for spring,
> A fair knight seduced her.
>
> In the woods there is a clump of oaks,
> And in the wilds a dead deer
> With white rushes well bound.
> There was a lady fair as jade.
>
> "Heigh, not so hasty, not so rough.
> "Heigh, do not touch my handkerchief.
> "Take care or the dog will bark."

Like the original and the literal translation, this version leaves the relationship between the doe's death and the girl's seduction unspecified and problematic. It holds the doe story in present tenses, assigning the girl story to the past. Still, much has been changed to give the English poem an explanatory scenario. The particular past assigned to the girl story, indeterminate in the Chinese original, is here fixed as the age of knights and ladies; and the seduction itself, which in the Chinese hovers as an eternal possibility within the timeless situation of man and maid ("A fine man *to* seduce her"), is established as completed long ago: "A fair knight seduced her." A teasing oddity in this version is the mysterious "we" who "cover" the slain doe, never to be heard from again.

Take interpretation toward its outer limits and we reach what is perhaps best called a "variation" on this theme:

3. Ezra Pound:

> Lies a dead doe on yonder plain
> whom white grass covers,
> A melancholy maid in spring

is luck
for
lovers
Where the scrub elm skirts the wood
be it not in white mat bound,
As a jewel flawless found
dead as a doe is maidenhood.
Hark!
Unhand my girdle knot.
Stay, stay, stay
or the dog
may
bark.

Here too the present is pushed back to a past by the language the translator uses: not a specific past, as with the era of knights and ladies, but any past in which contemporary speech still features such (to us) archaic formalisms as "Unhand" or "Hark," and in which the term "maid" still signifies a virgin and in which virginity is prized to an extent that equates its loss with the doe's loss of life. But these evocations of time past are so effectively countered by the obtrusively present tense throughout (lines 1, 2, 4, 7, 8, 10, 11, 12, 13, and 15) that the freewheeling "variation" remains in this important respect closer to the spirit of the original than Waley's translation. On the other hand, it departs from the original and the two other versions by brushing aside the reticence that they carefully preserve as to the precise implications of the girl-deer parallel, choosing instead to place the seduction in the explanatory framework of the oldest story in the world: the way of a man with a maid in the springtime of life.

What both these examples make plain is that the Chinese and Japanese lyric, however contrasting in some ways, have in common at their center a complex of highly charged images generating something very like a magnetic field of potential meanings that cannot be got at in English without bleeding away much of the voltage. In view of this, the best practical advice for those of us who must read these marvelous poems in English translations is to focus intently on these images and ask ourselves what there is in them or in their effect on each other that produces the electricity. To that extent, we can compensate for a part of our losses, learn something positive about the immense explosive powers of imagery, and rest easy in the secure knowledge that translation even in the mode of the short poem brings us (despite losses) closer to the work itself than not reading it at all. "To a thousand cavils," said Samuel Johnson, "one answer is sufficient; the purpose of a writer is to be read, and the criticism which would destroy the power of pleasing must be blown aside." Johnson was defending Pope's Homer for those marks of its own time and place that make it the great interpretation it is, but Johnson's exhilarating common sense applies equally to the problem we are considering here. Literature is to be read, and the criticism that would destroy the reader's power to make some form of contact with much of the world's great writing must indeed be blown aside.

Maynard Mack

Sources

Brower, Robert H., and Earl Miner. *Japanese Court Poetry.* Stanford: Stanford University Press, 1961.

The Classic Anthology Defined by Confucius. Tr. Ezra Pound. New Directions, 1954.

Kokinshū: A Collection of Poems Ancient and Modern. Tr. Laurel Rasplica Rodd and Mary Catherine Henkenius. Princeton: Princeton University Press, 1984.
Kokin Wakashū: The First Imperial Anthology of Japanese Poetry. Tr. and ed. Helen Craig McCullough. Stanford: Stanford University Press, 1985.
Legge, James. *The Chinese Classics.* Hong Kong: Hong Kong University Press, 1960.
Waley, Arthur. *170 Chinese Poems.* New York, 1919.

Aeschylus: *Agamemnon* and *Eumenides* from THE ORESTEIA, by Aeschylus, translated by Robert Fagles. Copyright © 1966, 1967, 1975 by Robert Fagles. Used by permission of Viking Penguin, a division of Penguin Putnam Inc.

Akhenaten: *Hymn to the Sun* from ANCIENT EGYPTIAN LITERATURE: AN ANTHOLOGY, translated by John L. Foster. Copyright © 2001. By permission of the University of Texas Press. Selections from LOVE SONGS OF THE NEW KINGDOM, translated from the Ancient Egyptian by John L. Foster. Copyright © 1969, 1970, 1971, 1972, 1973, 1974. By permission of the author and the University of Texas Press. Selections from ANCIENT EGYPTIAN LITERATURE: AN ANTHOLOGY translated by John L. Foster. Copyright © 2001. By permission of the University of Texas Press.

Aristophanes: *Lysistrata* from ARISTOPHANES: FOUR COMEDIES, edited by William Arrowsmith and translated by Douglass Parker. Copyright © 1969. Reprinted by permission of the publisher, The University of Michigan Press.

Aristotle: Selections from POETICS, translated by James Hutton. Copyright © 1982 by W. W. Norton & Company. Used by permission of W. W. Norton & Company, Inc.

The Bhagavad-Gītā: Selections from THE BHAGAVAD-GĪTĀ, translated by Barbara Stoler Miller, copyright © 1986 by Barbara Stoler Miller. Used by permission of Bantam Books, a division of Random House, Inc.

Catullus: Selections from POEMS OF CATULLUS, translated by Charles Martin (pp. 4, 7, 10, 14, 51, 59, 107, 109, 112–113, 120–124, & 146). Copyright © 1989. Reprinted by permission of The Johns Hopkins University Press.

Chuang Chou: Excerpts from THE COMPLETE WORKS OF CHUANG TZU, translated by Burton Watson. © 1968 Columbia University Press. Reprinted by permission of the publisher.

Classic of Poetry: Selections from AN ANTHOLOGY OF CHINESE LITERATURE: BEGINNING TO 1911 by Stephen Owen, Editor & Translator. Copyright © 1996 by Stephen Owen and The Council for Cultural Planning and Development of the Executive Yuan of the Republic of China. Used by permission of W. W. Norton & Company, Inc.

Confucius: Selections from THE ANALECTS, translated by D. C. Lau. Copyright © 1979 by D. C. Lau. Reprinted by permission of Penguin Books Ltd.

Euripides: *Medea* from THE GREAT PLAYS OF EURIPIDES by Euripides, translated by Rex Warner, copyright © 1958, renewed 1986 by Rex Warner. Used by permission of Dutton Signet, a division of Penguin Putnam Inc. MEDEA by Euripides translated by Rex Warner published by Bodley Head. Used by permission of The Random House Group Limited.

Gilgamesh: THE EPIC OF GILGAMESH: AN ENGLISH VERSION by N. K. Sandars (Penguin Classics 1960, second revised edition 1972) copyright © N. K. Sandars, 1960, 1964, 1972. Reprinted by permission of Penguin Books Ltd.

Homer: Selections from THE ILIAD by Homer, translated by Robert Fagles, copyright © 1990 by Robert Fagles. Introduction and notes copyright © 1990 by Bernard Knox. Reprinted by permission of Viking Penguin, a division of Penguin Putnam Inc.

Homer: THE ODYSSEY, translated by Robert Fitzgerald. Copyright © 1961, 1963 by Robert Fitzgerald. Copyright renewed © 1989, 1991 by Benedict R. C. Fitzgerald on behalf of the Fitzgerald children. Reprinted by permission of Farrar, Straus & Giroux, Inc.

The Interior Landscape: Selections by A. K. Ramanujan from THE INTERIOR LANDSCAPE: LOVE POEMS FROM A CLASSICAL TAMIL ANTHOLOGY, Indiana University Press, 1967. Reprinted by permission of Molly A. Daniels Ramanujan.

The Jātaka: *The Hare's Self-Sacrifice* and *The Monkey's Heroic Self-Sacrifice* from JĀTAKA TALES, translated by H. T. Francis and E. J. Thompson. Copyright © 1957 by Jaico Publishing House. Reprinted by permission of Cambridge University Press. *The Cheating Merchant* from THE JĀTAKA OR STORIES OF THE BUDDHA'S FORMER BIRTHS, translated by E. B. Cowell. Reprinted by permission of North Point Press.

The Mahābhārata: Excerpts from THE MAHĀBHĀRATA, translated by Chakravari Narasimhan. © 1965 Columbia University Press. Reprinted by permission of the publisher. *The Assembly Hall* from THE MAHĀBHĀRATA, edited and translated by J. A. B. van Buitenen. Copyright © by the University of Chicago. Reprinted by University of Chicago Press.

Ovid: Excerpts from THE METAMORPHOSES OF OVID: A NEW VERSE TRANSLATION, English translation copyright © 1993 by Allen Mandelbaum. Reprinted by permission of Harcourt, Inc.

Petronius: *Dinner with Trimalchio* from THE SATYRICON, translated by J. P. Sullivan. Copyright © by J. P. Sullivan. Reprinted by permission of David Higham Associates Limited.

Ssu-ma Ch'ien: From *Historical Records: Biography of Bo Yi and Shu Ch'i,* translated by Stephen Owen; from *Historical Records: Letter in Reply to Jen An,* translated by Stephen Owen; from *Historical Records: The Prince of Wei,* translated by Stephen Owen; and from *Biographies of the Assassins: Nieh Cheng,* translated by Stephen Owen from AN ANTHOLOGY OF CHINESE LITERATURE: BEGINNINGS TO 1911 by Stephen Owen, Editor & Translator. Copyright © 1996 by Stephen Owen and The Council for Cultural Planning and Development of the Executive Yuan of the Republic of China. Used by permission of W. W. Norton & Company, Inc.

The Rāmāyaṇa of Vālmīki: Excerpts from CONCISE RĀMĀYAṆA OF VĀLMĪKI by Swami Venkatesananda. Reprinted by permission of the State University of New York Press © 1988, State University of New York. All rights reserved.

Sappho: Selections from GREEK LYRICS, edited and translated by Richmond Lattimore. Reprinted by permission of the University of Chicago Press.

Index